D1254468

Pathways to Psychology

Pathways to Psychology

ROBERT J. STERNBERG
Yale University

HARCOURT BRACE COLLEGE PUBLISHERS

FORT WORTH PHILADELPHIA SAN DIEGO NEW YORK ORLANDO AUSTIN SAN ANTONIO

TORONTO MONTREAL LONDON SYDNEY TOKYO

Publisher	CHRISTOPHER P. KLEIN
Acquisitions editor	EARL MCPEEK
Developmental editor	MEERA DASH/SUSAN PETTY
Senior product manager	SUSAN KINDEL
Project editor	STEVE NORDER/LOUISE SLOMINSKY
Production manager	JANE TYNDALL PONCETI
Art director	BURL DEAN SLOAN
Cover/part opener illustrator	TERRY HOFF
Editorial associate	SHARI HATCH
Photo researcher	SUE C. HOWARD
Literary permissions editor	CRISTI GRIDER

Literary and illustration credits begin on p. 517 and constitute a continuation of the copyright page.

Library of Congress Catalog Card Number: 96-78389

Copyright © 1997 by Harcourt Brace & Company

All rights reserved. No part of this publication may be reproduced or transmitted in any form or by any means, electronic or mechanical, including photocopy, recording, or any information storage and retrieval system, without permission in writing from the publisher.

Requests for permission to make copies of any part of the work should be mailed to: Permissions Department, Harcourt Brace & Company, 6277 Sea Harbor Drive, Orlando, Florida 32887-6777.

Address for Editorial Correspondence:
Harcourt Brace College Publishers, 301 Commerce Street, Suite 3700, Fort Worth, TX 76102.

Address for Orders:
Harcourt Brace & Company,
6277 Sea Harbor Drive, Orlando, FL 32887-6777. 1-800-782-4479, or 1-800-433-0001 (in Florida).

ISBN: 0-15-501047-6 (softcover)
ISBN: 0-15-505331-0 (hardcover)

Printed in the United States of America

6 7 8 9 0 1 2 3 4 5   032   10 9 8 7 6 5 4 3 2 1

To Alejandra

To the Instructor

As a child, I bombed on IQ tests. By the time I reached college, I was determined to understand why. I decided to major in psychology. However, I received a grade of C in the introductory psychology course. It was looking like the IQ tests might have been right—I did not seem to have the ability to study psychology. Fortunately, I switched to math, did worse in math than I had in psychology, and switched back to psychology, where I have been ever since. I have come to realize that the way my introductory psychology course was taught did not match the way I best learn.

These experiences have helped me to shape this book. In the introductory psychology course, students think to learn, in order to learn to think. I am committed to the view that students learn and think in different ways, and that teaching and testing need to take into account these diverse styles of learning and thinking if they are to recognize and reward students' many different kinds of talents.

PATHWAYS TO LEARNING AND THINKING

The unifying vision underlying this book is one of multiple pathways to psychology. These pathways include the diverse routes by which students can successfully learn and understand psychology. In this book, three icons are used to represent three kinds of thinking. Analytical thinking is represented by a person reflecting, creative thinking by a paintbrush, and practical thinking by a wheel. My own Triarchic Theory of Intelligence identifies three ways of thinking: analytically— by analyzing, comparing and contrasting, evaluating, and critiquing; creatively— by discovering, exploring, inventing, and imagining; and practically —by using, applying, and implementing. These three processes complement memory learning as students build up a rich and well-organized knowledge base.

The book also recognizes the diverse pathways of input as well as output that appeal to different learners. Students are given opportunities to learn both visually and verbally, and to learn by doing, as well as by reading and listening. Thus, this is a book for *all* students, including but, in no way limited to, those who learn best in traditional ways.

PATHWAYS TO VIEWING PSYCHOLOGY

Just as there are different pathways to learning and thinking about psychology, so are there different pathways to the field of psychology itself. These pathways lead us through different terrains. They emphasize different questions, theories, and methods, and often apply to different areas of psychology. Ultimately, however, just as all roads once led to Rome, so do all the pathways presented here lead to psychology. By following and exploring these various pathways, students learn about the different fields of psychology, and from different points of view. The fundamental idea of these pathways is expressed through the discussions, questions, activities, and artwork throughout the book.

The book equally balances the diverse pathways to psychology, with regard not only to approach, but also to content. Such balance is especially important today, when traditional boundaries within the field are breaking down. For example, biological methods are used in the study of learning and emotion, and cognitive methods are used in the study of attribution and depression. These integrations are illustrated throughout the text.

PATHWAYS TO HUMAN DIVERSITY

Just as there are different pathways to thinking about psychology, so are there different pathways of thinking in the populations studied by psychologists. This book explores multicultural pathways to psychological diversity not because multiculturalism is "in," but because there is no other way to understand psychology fully. I have lived with the richness of multiculturalism in my own experience, and I have embraced it with enthusiasm in research with my colleagues.

For example, Lynn Okagaki and I have found that parents of children of diverse ethnic groups have different conceptions of what it means for their children to be intelligent. In raising their children, parents try to develop the skills that will help the children show the behavior that their groups consider to be adaptively intelligent. How intelligent the children are perceived to be in the school, however, depends largely on the extent to which the parents' beliefs about intelligence match those of the children's teachers. Without understanding the children's strengths, the teachers cannot possibly appreciate the children's full complement of abilities.

Psychology represents one pathway to human understanding, but it does not provide the only pathway. While studying psychology, students are also studying other courses. Students learn better when they see the links between what they are learning not only across areas within a given discipline, but also across different disciplines. For this reason, *Pathways to Psychology* makes extensive use of art and quotations from diverse sources. Students can see how methods for studying human nature may vary, but how the principles of human nature remain the same. This book will take students along the diverse pathways to learning and thinking about those principles.

Distinctive pedagogical features in every chapter encourage students to develop and apply their own pathways. The following features appear in every chapter.

- A chapter outline in question format provides a preview framework for organizing the material.
- **Pathways to Understanding** thinking questions in the margins and at the ends of chapters test creative, practical, and analytical skills.
- **Practical Psychology** boxes show how psychology can be used outside of the classroom.
- **Branching Out** applications sections, appearing in most chapters, show how to extend what is learned in new and interesting directions.
- **Finding Your Way** demonstrations involve students in the topics.
- A running glossary includes definitions and a pronunciation guide (where needed).

- Literary quotes in the margins help students to put the material in a multi-disciplinary context.

- CD-ROM icons show where topics are covered in minilectures in *Psychology: The Core on CD-ROM.*

- **Big Picture** sections summarize the key point of each major section.

- A page-referenced chapter summary appears at the end of each chapter.

- **Pathways to Knowledge** questions test factual comprehension of topics.

THE ANCILLARY PROGRAM: PATHWAYS TO TEACHING

The *Pathways to Psychology* ancillary program was developed with the help of a faculty panel from diverse colleges and universities. After this feedback was gathered, the ancillary authors, the Harcourt Brace team, and I met to develop the program at the Southeast Teaching of Psychology conference in 1996. As a result of highly effective teamwork, you will find a complete program reinforcing the *Pathways* themes and information covered in the textbook.

The Study Guide, by Ellen Pastorino and Susann Doyle (Gainesville College), opens with a description of effective ways of studying, different thinking and learning styles, and test-taking strategies. Each chapter has a variety of types of exercises to help students master the material. The practice tests include a self-assessment scale. An extensive front section of the study guide provides studying and test-taking strategies.

Drs. Pastorino and Doyle have taught introductory psychology for more than 10 years at diverse two-year and four-year institutions. They have collaborated on several articles, and on a daily basis, they conquer the challenge of meeting various students' needs when tackling the learning process. They have brought their collective expertise to producing a truly outstanding study guide.

The Test Bank, also by Drs. Doyle and Pastorino, is coordinated and consistent with the study guide. Each chapter has approximately 125 multiple-choice and essay items, classified by the ways of thinking described and used in the textbook. Each item is also identified by level of difficulty, learning objective, textbook features, and page number. Prior to generation of the final draft, I reviewed each item to verify quality and consistency with the textbook. The test items also were reviewed by a panel of experts and instructors including Jorge Conesa (Everett Community College), William Price (North Country Community College), Nancy Simpson (Trident Technical College), and Jim Turcott (Kalamazoo Valley Community College). The test bank is available in printed and computerized versions.

EXAMaster+™ Computerized Test Banks (IBM, MAC, and WINDOWS versions) offer easy-to-use options for text creation.

- *EasyTest* creates a test from a single screen in just a few easy steps. Instructors choose parameters, then select questions from the database or let *EasyTest* randomly select them.

- *FullTest* offers a range of options that includes selecting, editing, adding, or linking questions or graphics; random selection of questions from a wide range of criteria; creating criteria; blocking questions; and printing up to 99 different versions of the same test and answer sheet.

- **On-Line Testing** allows instructors to create a test in *EXAMaster+*™, save it to the OLT subdirectory or diskette, and administer the test on-line. The results of the test can then be imported to *ESAGrade*.

- **ESAGrade** can be used to set up new classes, to record grades from tests or assignments utilizing scantron, and to analyze grades and produce class and individual statistics. *ESAGrade* comes packaged with *EXAMaster+*™.

- **RequesTest** is a service for instructors without access to a computer. A software specialist will compile questions according to the instructor's criteria and mail or fax the test master within 48 hours!

- **The Software Support Hotline** is available to answer questions 24 hours a day, 7 days a week.

(1-800 telephone numbers for these services are provided in the preface to the printed test bank.)

The Instructor's Manual, by Stephen Chew (Samford University), provides easy-to-find information to help instructors minimize their time and maximize their effectiveness in preparing for lectures. The manual is designed to help instructors develop class presentations consistent with the textbook and to facilitate use and integration of the other ancillary items available to users of *Pathways to Psychology*. An introductory section includes teaching tips and a sample syllabus. Each chapter includes teaching objectives, extensive lecture outlines, handouts, suggestions for incorporating the other items in the package, and forms that assist in coordination of the course. The final section includes a video instructor's manual.

Dr. Chew is an experienced introductory psychology instructor who has led seminars on college teaching. He has given guest lectures at a number of community colleges and state universities, maintaining an emphasis on making students lifelong learners. His experience and dedication to teaching have resulted in a manual that helps instructors to locate and use the information that they need.

Additional ancillaries available to qualified adopters include:

- **Psychology MediaActive**™—A CD-ROM psychology image bank to be used with commercially available presentation packages like Power-Point™ and Astound™, as well as Harcourt Brace's *LectureActive*™ 2.0 for IBM and Macintosh.

- **LectureActive™ Presentation Software, Version 2.0**—This updated version of *LectureActive*™ allows instructors to create presentations that include imagery from Harcourt Brace's *Dynamic Concepts in Psychology II* videodisc, *Psychology MediaActive*™, and materials the instructor has prepared, such as text screens or scanned images.

- **The Harcourt Brace Psychology and Human Development Multimedia Library**™—Consisting of a variety of videos and videodiscs for classroom presentation, this library's selections include materials exclusively created for Harcourt Brace as well as videos from *Films for the Humanities and Sciences, Pyramid Films, PBS Video*, and other sources. Please contact your sales representative for adoption requirements and other details.

- **Introductory Psychology Overhead Transparencies**—This set of more than 130 acetates covers the full range of topics typical to an introductory psychology course.

- **The Whole Psychology Catalog: Instructional Resources to Enhance Student Learning, 1997,** by Michael B. Reiner (Kennesaw

State College)—Instructors can easily supplement course work and assignments with this manual of perforated pages containing experimental exercises, questionnaires, lecture outlines, visual aids, and Internet and World Wide Web guides.

■ **Harcourt Brace Psychology Instructor's Resources on the Web**— Come visit us at www.hbcollege.com

Harcourt Brace College Publishers may provide complimentary instructional aids and ancillaries or ancillary packages to those adopters qualified under our adoption policy. Please contact your sales representative for more information. If, as an adopter or potential user, you receive ancillaries that you do not need, please return them to your sales representative or send them to:

Attn: Returns Department
Troy Warehouse
465 South Lincoln Drive
Troy, MO 63379

ACKNOWLEDGMENTS

A host of instructors and colleagues reviewed portions of the manuscript in various drafts. I am indebted to Lou Banderet (Quinsigamond Community College), Don Devers (Northern Virginia Community College), Charles Early (Roanoke College), John Foust (Parkland College), Richard Gist (Johnson Community College), Kathryn Jennings (Salt Lake City Community College), Jane Kelly (Hinds Community College), D. Brett King (University of Colorado), Mike Knight (University of Central Oklahoma), Kris Kumar (Westchester University of Pennsylvania), Kevin Larkin (West Virginia University), Paul Levy (University of Akron), Dan Lipscomb (Collin County Community College), Joan Piroch (Coastal Carolina University), Cary Schawel (Oakton Community College), Peggy Skinner (South Plains Junior College), Lori Temple (University of Nevada at Las Vegas), Harry Tiemann (Mesa State College), Tim Tomczak (Genesee Community College), Jim Turcott (Kalamazoo Valley Community College), and Frank Vattano (Colorado State University).

I am also grateful to colleagues who contributed valuable information concerning multicultural diversity to the following chapters: Toy Caldwell-Colbert (University of Illinois) in "Abnormal Psychology," Janet Fritz (Colorado State University) in "Thought and Language," Jules Harell (Howard University) in "Health Psychology," Yvette Harris (Miami [Ohio] University) in "What Is Psychology?," Fred Leong (Ohio State University) in "Personality," Chieh Li (Northeastern University) in "Intelligence and Creativity," David McPhee (Colorado State University) in "Development," Joan Miller (Yale University) in "Social Psychology" and "Motivation and Emotion," and Kumea Shorter-Gooden (California School of Professional Psychology) in "Psychotherapy."

My thanks also go out to the following instructors who helped to review the ancillary program: Bill Bachofner (Victor Valley Community College), Eugene Butler (Quinsigamond Community College), Minor Chamblin (University of North Florida), Dennis Cogan (Texas Tech University), Jorge Conesa (Everett Community College), Linda Noble (Kennesaw State College), William Price (North Country Community College), Nancy Simpson (Trident Technical College), Peggy Skinner (South Plains Junior College), Jim Turcott (Kalamazoo Valley Community College), and Diana Younger (University of Texas-Permian Basin).

I am also grateful to Tina Oldham, Chris Klein, and Earl McPeek, all of whom served as acquisitions editors at various stages, for their support and encouragement of this project; to Meera Dash and Susan Petty, for their superb work in managing the development of this book; to Shari Hatch, for her excellent suggestions and developmental assistance; to steve Norder and Louise Slominsky, for their responsibility and exacting standards in seeing the book through the production process; to Jane Ponceti, for ensuring that production deadlines were met; to Burl Sloan, for his creative oversight and development of the art program; to Sue Howard, for securing an outstanding set of photos; to Ted Buchholz, president of Harcourt Brace College Publishers, for his support and encouragement of my work on this and other projects; to Sai Durvaula, my administrative assistant, for helping at all stages in the coordination with everyone involved in the project; to Susan Kindel, senior marketing manager, for her sensitivity to market demands at all phases of the project; to the Harcourt Brace sales representatives all over the world who have made a concerted effort to make potential adopters aware of what the book has to offer; and most of all, to my wife, Alejandra Campos, and my children, Seth and Sara Sternberg, all of whom have contributed to my ideas about psychology and put up with me while I worked on this book.

Robert J. Sternberg

To the Student

HOW TO USE THIS TEXTBOOK

When I received a grade of C in my introductory psychology course, I thought I did not have the ability to study psychology. I switched my major to math, but I did even worse in math, and switched back to psychology, where I stayed. Now, after 29 years, I realize that students in introductory courses think and learn in different ways.

I wrote *Pathways to Psychology* to help you succeed in your introductory psychology class. Use this textbook to help you strengthen and improve your learning and thinking skills, as well as to understand the multiple perspectives in psychology.

Please spend a few minutes looking over the following pages. This section will help you take full advantage of some of the unique features of this book.

Bob Sternberg

The theme of this book is "pathways to psychology." The chapters use "pathways" in a variety of ways, to show there are many ways to learn, understand, think about, and use psychology.

A **chapter outline** opens the chapter. Each major section heading poses a question, which alerts you to the key issue that the section will explore.

CHAPTER OUTLINE

What Developmental Trends
Have Psychologists Observed?

What Are the Roles of
Maturation and Learning?
   The Nature–Nurture Controversy:
     Maturation Versus Learning
   The Roles of Maturation and
     Learning: The Developmental
     Theories of Piaget and Vygotsky

What Happens During Prenatal
Development?

How Do Infants and Young
Toddlers Develop?
   What Can Newborns Do?
   Physical Development During
     Infancy
   Cognitive Development in Infancy
   Socioemotional Development During
     Infancy
   What Is Your Temperament?

How Do Children Develop?
   Cognitive Development During
     Childhood
   Socioemotional Development
   What Should Parents Look for in
     High-Quality Child Care?

What Develops During Puberty
and Adolescence?
   Physical Development During
     Adolescence
   Cognitive Development During
     Adolescence
   Socioemotional Development

How Do Adults Develop
and Age?

68

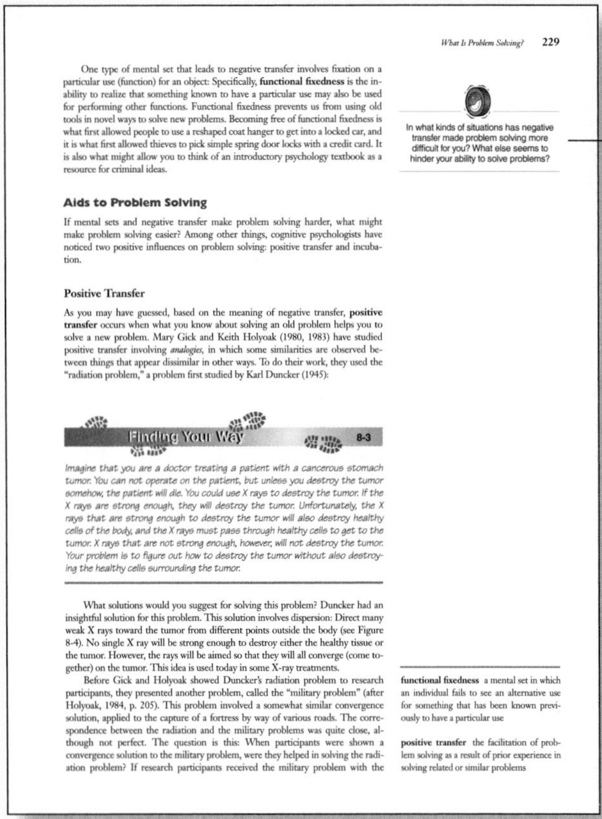

Three kinds of **thinking questions** appear in the margins of each chapter. These questions will help you build and practice your creative, practical, and analytical thinking skills so that you truly understand the material presented. You can always identify the skill by the icon:

  (1) a paintbrush signifies **creative** thinking;

 (2) an automobile wheel represents **practical** thinking; and

(3) a person reflecting indicates **analytical** thinking.

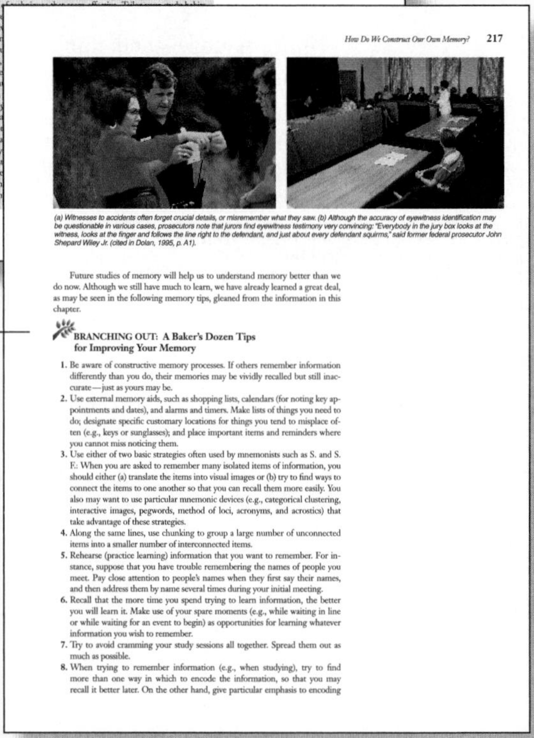

Two features provide how-to applications to guide you in using psychological principles in your life.

Practical Psychology boxes show examples of how psychology can be used outside of the classroom.

Branching Out sections within the text weave applications of psychology into the main narrative.

Reproduced sample page (left):

One type of mental set that leads to negative transfer involves fixation on a particular use (function) of an object: Specifically, **functional fixedness** is the inability to realize that something known to have a particular use may also be used for performing other functions. Functional fixedness prevents us from using old tools in novel ways to solve new problems. Becoming free of functional fixedness is what first allowed people to use a reshaped coat hanger to get into a locked car, and it is what first allowed thieves to pick simple spring door locks with a credit card. It is also what might allow you to think of an introductory psychology textbook as a resource for criminal ideas.

Aids to Problem Solving

If mental sets and negative transfer make problem solving harder, what might make problem solving easier? Among other things, cognitive psychologists have noticed two positive influences on problem solving: positive transfer and incubation.

Positive Transfer

As you may have guessed, based on the meaning of negative transfer, **positive transfer** occurs when what you know about solving an old problem helps you to solve a new problem. Mary Gick and Keith Holyoak (1980, 1983) have studied positive transfer involving *analogies*, in which some similarities are observed between things that appear dissimilar in other ways. To do their work, they used the "radiation problem," a problem first studied by Karl Duncker (1945):

Finding Your Way 8-3

Imagine that you are a doctor treating a patient with a cancerous stomach tumor. You can not operate on the patient, but unless you destroy the tumor somehow, the patient will die. You could use X rays to destroy the tumor. If the X rays are strong enough, they will destroy the tumor. Unfortunately, the X rays that are strong enough to destroy the tumor will also destroy healthy cells of the body, and the X rays must pass through healthy cells to get to the tumor. X rays that are not strong enough, however, will not destroy the tumor. Your problem is to figure out how to destroy the tumor without also destroying the healthy cells surrounding the tumor.

What solutions would you suggest for solving this problem? Duncker had an insightful solution for this problem. This solution involves dispersion: Direct many weak X rays toward the tumor from different points outside the body (see Figure 8-4). No single X ray will be strong enough to destroy either the healthy tissue or the tumor. However, the rays will be aimed so that they will all converge (come together) on the tumor. This idea is used today in some X-ray treatments.

Before Gick and Holyoak showed Duncker's radiation problem to research participants, they presented another problem, called the "military problem" (after Holyoak, 1984, p. 205). This problem involved a somewhat similar convergence solution, applied to the capture of a fortress by way of various roads. The correspondence between the radiation and the military problems was quite close, although not perfect. The question is this: When participants were shown a convergence solution to the military problem, were they helped in solving the radiation problem? If research participants received the military problem with the

In what kinds of situations has negative transfer made problem solving more difficult for you? What else seems to hinder your ability to solve problems?

functional fixedness a mental set in which an individual fails to see an alternative use for something that has been known previously to have a particular use

positive transfer the facilitation of problem solving as a result of prior experience in solving related or similar problems

---

Reproduced sample page (Practical Psychology):

PRACTICAL PSYCHOLOGY 2-1

How to Master Difficult Material and How to Prepare for a Test

1. Make sure that you understand the key terms in the material you are learning. Look up any important words you do not know. In the margins of this textbook are definitions of many of the key terms in each chapter; also, a glossary of terms appears at the end of the book. In addition, you may want to keep a dictionary handy to look up unfamiliar words that may not be defined in the margins or in the glossary.
2. Make a study guide for yourself. Include in your guide some lists of key points, terms, and ideas, as well as any other important information you find difficult to remember. When you rehearse (practice learning) the material, review your own notes, as well as the summaries provided in your textbook.
3. Try to learn the information in a form that matches the form in which you will want to remember the information later. For instance, if your instructor likes to give quizzes that match each structure of the brain or nervous system with the function of each structure, practice matching the structures and their functions while you are studying for the quiz.
4. Make up your own cues for retrieving information. Often, the most effective cues relate the new information to what you already know. Some students make drawings or charts that make it easier for them to remember material. Other students make up little songs or rhymes (e.g., "receptors get clues from the eyes and the nose; effectors cause wiggles in lips and in toes"). Another technique is to make up word games for steps in a process or for parts that make up a whole. (For instance, a word game for linking the lobes in the brain to their functions might be to think of action words that have the same initial letters as the names of the lobes: "forethought [frontal lobe—planning], prickling [parietal lobe—skin sensations], twanging [temporal lobe—hearing], and observing [occipital lobe—vision].")
5. Until you know your own stylistic preferences for studying, use a variety of techniques (e.g., talking with others, writing down, drawing pictures or charts, making and using flash cards). Once you have tried various techniques, drop the use of techniques that do not work well for you, and increase your use of techniques that do. For example, if you form a habit to your own pr...
6. Overlearn the ...ing the material, experiencing the ...tremely well ou... perform well on ...
7. If you feel overly... yourself. For ex... continuing to b... each of your ma... your way up to y...
8. Your efforts to ...grades you hope... hard. You are m... and effort are in...

Reproduced sample page (Branching Out):

(a) Witnesses to accidents often forget crucial details, or misremember what they saw. (b) Although the accuracy of eyewitness identification may be questionable in various cases, prosecutors note that jurors find eyewitness testimony very convincing: "Everybody in the jury box looks at the witness, looks at the finger and follows the line right to the defendant, and just about every defendant squirms," said former federal prosecutor John Shepard Wiley Jr. (cited in Dolan, 1995, p. A1).

Future studies of memory will help us to understand memory better than we do now. Although we still have much to learn, we have already learned a great deal, as may be seen in the following memory tips, gleaned from the information in this chapter.

BRANCHING OUT: A Baker's Dozen Tips for Improving Your Memory

1. Be aware of constructive memory processes. If others remember information differently than you do, their memories may be vividly recalled but still inaccurate—just as yours may be.
2. Use external memory aids, such as shopping lists, calendars (for noting key appointments and dates), and alarms and timers. Make lists of things you need to do; designate specific customary locations for things you tend to misplace often (e.g., keys or sunglasses); and place important items and reminders where you cannot miss noticing them.
3. Use either of two basic strategies often used by mnemonists such as S. and S. F.: When you are asked to remember many isolated items of information, you should either (a) translate the items into visual images or (b) try to find ways to connect the items to one another so that you can recall them more easily. You also may want to use particular mnemonic devices (e.g., categorical clustering, interactive images, pegwords, method of loci, acronyms, and acrostics) that take advantage of these strategies.
4. Along the same lines, use chunking to group a large number of unconnected items into a smaller number of interconnected items.
5. Rehearse (practice learning) information that you want to remember. For instance, suppose that you have trouble remembering the names of people you meet. Pay close attention to people's names when they first say their names, and then address them by name several times during your initial meeting.
6. Recall that the more time you spend trying to learn information, the better you will learn it. Make use of your spare moments (e.g., while waiting in line or while waiting for an event to begin) as opportunities for learning whatever information you wish to remember.
7. Try to avoid cramming your study sessions all together. Spread them out as much as possible.
8. When trying to remember information (e.g., when studying), try to find more than one way in which to encode the information, so that you may recall it better later. On the other hand, give particular emphasis to encoding

CD-ROM Multimedia Interfaces let you know that more information about a particular topic is available in *Psychology: The Core on CD-ROM.* The CD-ROM minilectures enable you to develop different ways of understanding these topics.

MINILECTURE
Why We Dream (Ch 6)

Behold! at once the little people [who create dreams] begin to bestir themselves in the same quest, and labour all night long, . . . and at last a jubilant leap to wakefulness, with the cry, "I have it, that'll do!" upon [the dreamer's] lips.

Robert Louis Stevenson

command the movements of our skeletal muscles is blocked. According to the activation–synthesis hypothesis, our brains may interpret this inability to move as a dream of being unable to escape from some danger.

Yet another theory of dreaming is nearly the opposite of Freud's. According to this theory (Crick & Mitchison, 1983), dreaming is the mind's attempt to get rid of mental garbage. Thus, whereas Freud suggested that we should examine our dreams closely, Francis Crick and G. Mitchison suggested that we should ignore the mental garbage being tossed out by our brains.

Scientists may never be able to come up with a theory of dream interpretation that applies to all people in all situations. Dreams are highly personal, so many people can and do freely interpret their own dreams as they choose to do so. Within the context of their current lives and past memories, they draw whatever conclusions seem appropriate to them.

 **Finding Your Way**   5-3

This is probably the first time you have seen this instruction in a textbook: Stop reading your textbook, and take a few minutes to daydream. When you return to studying, think about both the content and the process of your daydreaming. How does daydreaming seem to differ from what you know about the content and the process of dreams that come to you during your sleep?

What happens when we sleep and dream? The normal circadian rhythms of adults include about 8 (give or take 4) hours of sleep, but sleep disorders can disturb this normal pattern. Sleep occurs in a series of four N-REM stages, as well as in a REM stage during which we dream. Various theories of dreaming have been suggested, but none has yet been confirmed by research.

IS HYPNOSIS AN ALTERED STATE?

The Phenomenon of Hypnosis: Real or Fake?

hypnosis an altered state of consciousness that usually involves deep relaxation and extreme sensitivity to suggestion and appears to bear some resemblance to sleep

posthypnotic suggestion an instruction received during hypnosis, which the individual is to implement after having wakened, often despite having no recollection of having received the instruction

An altered state of consciousness that somewhat resembles sleep is **hypnosis.** A person undergoing hypnosis is usually deeply relaxed and extremely sensitive to suggestion. For example, hypnotized people may imagine that they see or hear things when they are prompted to do so (Bowers, 1976). Hypnotized people may also receive a posthypnotic suggestion. In a **posthypnotic suggestion,** participants are given instructions during hypnosis to carry out after they wake from the hypnotic state. Participants often do not remember receiving the instructions, and many do not even recall having been hypnotized (Ruch, 1975).

Hypnotized research participants also may not sense things that they otherwise would sense. For example, a hypnotized person may not feel pain when dipping an arm into icy cold water. Hypnosis has been particularly effective in

---

Finding Your Way demonstrations ask you to participate in an exercise that will help you remember the key points you are learning. Active learning is one of the best ways to remember something.

A summary, called **The Big Picture,** ends each major section. Try to answer the question before reading the summary answer. These summaries highlight and reinforce the key points made in that section.

A **Running Glossary** allows you to learn and review terms at your own pace. It includes a pronunciation guide for difficult terms.

Informative Illustrations showing parts and functions enable you to master anatomical material visually and verbally.

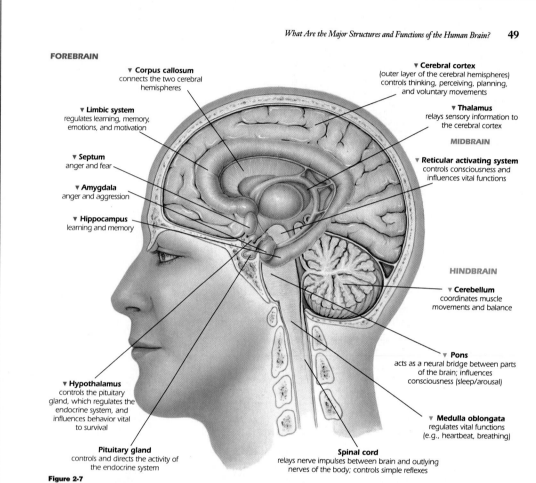

FOREBRAIN

▼ **Corpus callosum**
connects the two cerebral hemispheres

▼ **Cerebral cortex**
(outer layer of the cerebral hemispheres) controls thinking, perceiving, planning, and voluntary movements

▼ **Limbic system**
regulates learning, memory, emotions, and motivation

▼ **Thalamus**
relays sensory information to the cerebral cortex

MIDBRAIN

▼ **Septum**
anger and fear

▼ **Reticular activating system**
controls consciousness and influences vital functions

▼ **Amygdala**
anger and aggression

▼ **Hippocampus**
learning and memory

HINDBRAIN

▼ **Cerebellum**
coordinates muscle movements and balance

▼ **Pons**
acts as a neural bridge between parts of the brain; influences consciousness (sleep/arousal)

▼ **Hypothalamus**
controls the pituitary gland, which regulates the endocrine system, and influences behavior vital to survival

▼ **Medulla oblongata**
regulates vital functions (e.g., heartbeat, breathing)

Pituitary gland
controls and directs the activity of the endocrine system

Spinal cord
relays nerve impulses between brain and outlying nerves of the body; controls simple reflexes

Figure 2-7
Major Structures of the Forebrain, the Midbrain, and the Hindbrain
The structures of the forebrain (identified with blue labels), the midbrain (identified with red labels), and the hindbrain (identified with green labels) perform essential functions for survival, as well as for high-level thinking and feeling.

volved in vital physiological functions), the **pons** (a neural bridge from one part of the brain to another and one of several structures influencing consciousness), and the **cerebellum** (which governs many aspects of producing appropriate muscle movements). Although each of these subcortical (*sub-*, below; *cortical*, related to the cerebral cortex) structures is important to the human mind and behavior, the cortex deserves special attention.

The Cerebral Hemispheres and the Cerebral Cortex

The **cerebral cortex** (plural: cortices) is a thin layer (about 2 millimeters thick) wrapped around the outward surface of the brain. In human beings, the cerebral cortex contains many folds. These folds greatly increase the area covered by the cerebral cortex: If the wrinkly human cerebral cortex were smoothed out, it would cover about 2 square feet. About 80% of the human brain is cerebral cortex (Kolb & Whishaw, 1990). The cerebral cortex is responsible for our being able to

MINILECTURE
Structure of the Brain (Cb 3)

pons a brain structure containing nerve cells that pass signals from one part of the brain to another, thereby serving as a kind of bridge

cerebellum a brain structure that controls bodily coordination, balance, and muscle tone

cerebral cortex a thin layer of tissue on the surface of the brain, which is responsible for most high-level cognitive processes

A **page-referenced summary** at the end of the chapter reviews point by point the key topics in the chapter.

SUMMARY

Summary **131**

1. A *sensation* is a message that the brain receives from a sense. A *sense* is a physical system that collects information for the brain and transduces it from one form of energy into electrochemical energy, which the brain can use for making sense of the sensation.

How Do Psychologists Study the Senses? 104

2. *Psychophysics* is the study of the relationship between physical stimulation of a sense organ and its psychological effects.
3. *Detection* refers to the ability to sense a stimulus. The smallest amount of physical energy of a given kind that can be sensed (detected) 50% of the time is operationally defined as the *absolute threshold* for that kind of stimulus.
4. *Signal-detection theory* (SDT) is used for analyzing responses in terms of *hits* (true positive responses), *false alarms* (false positives), *correct rejections* (true negatives), and *misses* (false negatives).
5. *Discrimination* involves distinguishing between one stimulus and another. The *just-noticeable difference* (*jnd*) (also termed the *difference threshold*) is the minimum amount of difference that can be detected between two stimuli at least 50% of the time.
6. As the intensity of a stimulus increases, larger and larger differences between stimuli are needed to generate a jnd.

What Are Some Biological Properties Common to All Senses? 106

7. All of the senses share particular biological properties, such as psychophysical *thresholds*, *transduction*, *sensory coding*, and *adaptation*.
8. Each sense has specialized sensory *receptor cells*. These cells take in a particular form of energy and transduce it into an electrochemical form that sensory neurons can transmit to the brain.
9. Through sensory coding, sensory receptors convey a range of information, such as the *intensity (amplitude)* and the *quality* (e.g., *wavelength*) of a stimulus.
10. When our senses detect changes in energy, receptor cells send an alert to the brain. *Adaptation* is the temporary physiological response to a change in the environment; it varies according to the intensity of the change stimulus.

How Do We See? 108

11. We can see because the receptors of our eyes receive and transduce energy from a portion of the electromagnetic spectrum of light.
12. The cornea and the *lens* of the eye bend light and focus it on the retina. *Accommodation* is the process by which the focusing of the lens enables us to see objects clearly at varying distances from us.

13. The *retina* is the structure in which photoreceptors transduce the electromagnetic energy in light into the electrochemical energy of neural impulses.
14. There are two separate visual systems of photoreceptors. The *rod* system is used primarily for vision in dim light, and the *cone* system is used primarily for vision in bright light.
15. Three properties of color are *hue*, which matches the psychological sensation of color; *saturation*, which is the psychological sensation of the richness of a color; and *brightness*, which is our psychological impression of physical light intensity. Color, saturation, and brightness are psychological, rather than physical, phenomena.
16. The *trichromatic theory* of color vision posits that we see color through the actions and interactions of cone receptors for three primary colors—red, green, and blue.
17. The *opponent-process theory* of color vision states that we see color through the opposing actions of paired cone receptors for red versus green and blue versus yellow, as well as black versus white.

How Do We Hear? 112

18. In the inner ear is a *basilar membrane*. On the surface of this membrane are *hair cells*, which transduce the mechanical energy of sound waves into electrochemical energy that can be processed by the brain.
19. According to *place theory*, we hear differing pitches based on the differing locations of the hair cells that are stimulated on the basilar membrane.
20. According to *frequency theory*, the vibrations of the basilar membrane reproduce the vibrations of the sounds that enter the ear.
21. The two methods for locating the source of a sound both depend on the different locations of each ear on the head: The *time-difference method* works best for low-frequency sounds, and the *intensity-difference method* works best for high-frequency sounds.

How Do We Sense Taste, Smell, Touch, Movement, and Other Sensations? 116

22. We are able to taste because of interactions between chemical substances and *taste buds*, which are sensory receptors on the bumps on our tongues. According to a widely accepted theory of taste, the various sensory receptors in the tongue are particularly sensitive to various combinations of the four primary tastes: *sweet*, *sour*, *bitter*, and *salty*.
23. We are able to smell because of interactions between chemical substances and sensory receptors in our nasal cavities. According to *lock-and-key theory*, we smell something when there is a special fit between the shape of a molecule that enters our noses and the olfactory receptors there. According to *vibration theory*, we smell something when a molecule which has entered our nasal cavity creates a unique vibratory pattern that is picked up by receptor cells.

Pathways to Knowledge questions test your factual comprehension of those topics.

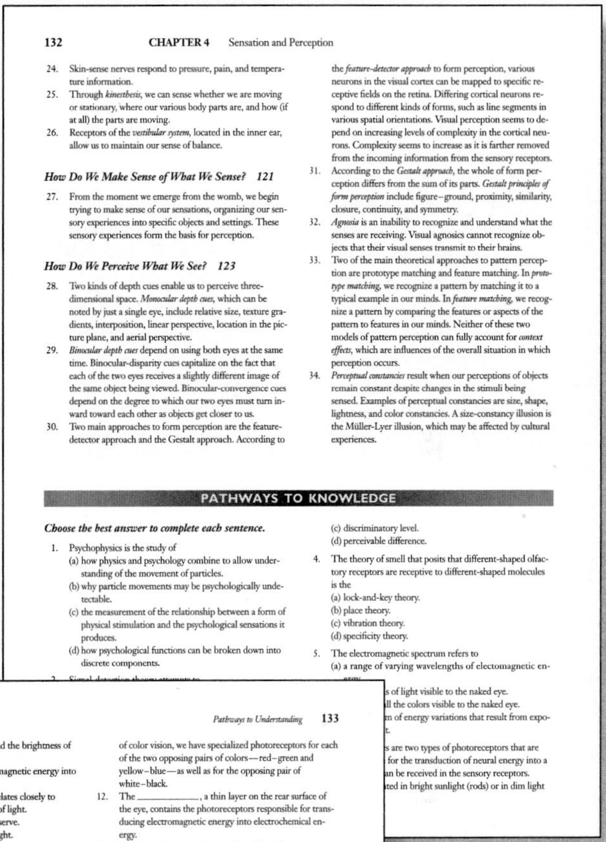

132 **CHAPTER 4** Sensation and Perception

24. Skin-sense nerves respond to pressure, pain, and temperature information.
25. Through *kinesthesis*, we can sense whether we are moving or stationary, where our various body parts are, and how (if at all) the parts are moving.
26. Receptors of the *vestibular system*, located in the inner ear, allow us to maintain our sense of balance.

How Do We Make Sense of What We Sense? 121

27. From the moment we emerge from the womb, we begin trying to make sense of our sensations, organizing our sensory experiences into specific objects and settings. These sensory experiences form the basis for perception.

How Do We Perceive What We See? 123

28. Two kinds of depth cues enable us to perceive three-dimensional space. *Monocular depth cues*, which can be noted by just a single eye, include relative size, texture gradients, interposition, linear perspective, location in the picture plane, and aerial perspective.
29. *Binocular depth cues* depend on using both eyes at the same time. Binocular-disparity cues capitalize on the fact that each of the two eyes receives a slightly different image of the same object being viewed. Binocular-convergence cues depend on the degree to which our two eyes must turn inward toward each other as objects get closer to us.
30. Two main approaches to form perception are the feature-detector approach and the Gestalt approach. According to

the *feature-detector approach* to form perception, various neurons in the visual cortex can be mapped to specific receptive fields on the retina. Differing cortical neurons respond to different kinds of forms, such as line segments in various spatial orientations. Visual perception seems to depend on increasing levels of complexity in the cortical neurons. Complexity seems to increase as it is farther removed from the incoming information from the sensory receptors.
31. According to the *Gestalt approach*, the whole of form perception differs from the sum of its parts. *Gestalt principles of form perception* include figure–ground, proximity, similarity, closure, continuity, and symmetry.
32. *Agnosia* is an inability to recognize and understand what the senses are receiving. Visual agnosias cannot recognize objects that their visual senses transmit to their brains.
33. Two of the main theoretical approaches to pattern perception are prototype matching and feature matching. In *prototype matching*, we recognize a pattern by matching it to a typical example in our minds. In *feature matching*, we recognize a pattern by comparing the features or aspects of the pattern to features in our minds. Neither of these two models of pattern perception can fully account for *context effects*, which are influences of the overall situation in which perception occurs.
34. *Perceptual constancies* result when our perceptions of objects remain constant despite changes in the stimuli being sensed. Examples of perceptual constancies are size, shape, lightness, and color constancies. A size-constancy illusion is the Müller-Lyer illusion, which may be affected by cultural experiences.

PATHWAYS TO KNOWLEDGE

Choose the best answer to complete each sentence.

1. Psychophysics is the study of
   (a) how physics and psychology combine to allow understanding of the movement of particles.
   (b) why particle movements may be psychologically undetectable.
   (c) the measurement of the relationship between a form of physical stimulation and the psychological sensations it produces.
   (d) how psychological functions can be broken down into discrete components.

2. Signal-detection theory attempts to

   (c) discriminatory level.
   (d) perceivable difference.

4. The theory of smell that posits that different-shaped olfactory receptors are receptive to different-shaped molecules is the
   (a) lock-and-key theory.
   (b) place theory.
   (c) vibration theory.
   (d) specificity theory.

5. The electromagnetic spectrum refers to
   (a) a range of varying wavelengths of electromagnetic en-

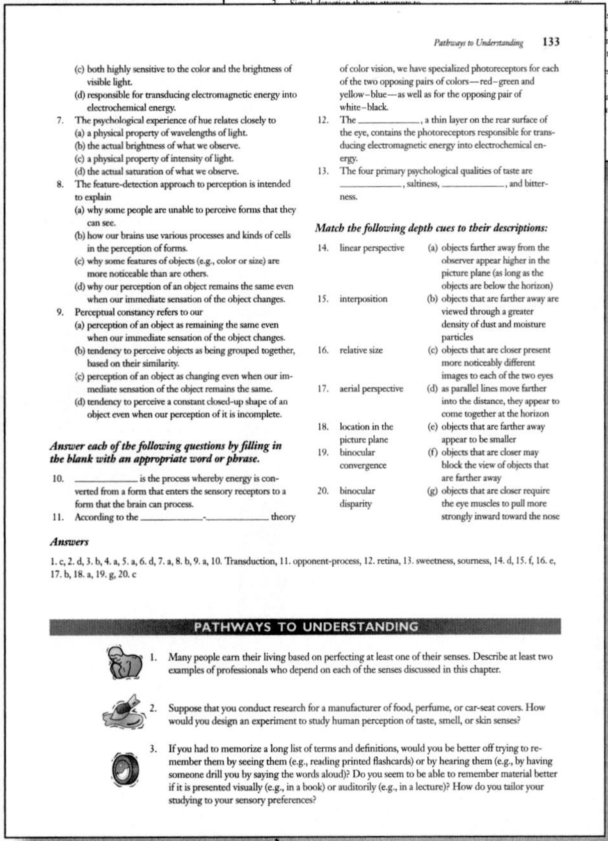

Pathways to Understanding **133**

(c) both highly sensitive to the color and the brightness of visible light.
(d) responsible for transducing electromagnetic energy into electrochemical energy.

7. The psychological experience of hue relates closely to
   (a) a physical property of wavelengths of light.
   (b) the actual brightness of what we observe.
   (c) a physical property of intensity of light.
   (d) the actual saturation of what we observe.
8. The feature-detection approach to perception is intended to explain
   (a) why some people are unable to perceive forms that they can see.
   (b) how our brains use various processes and kinds of cells in the perception of forms.
   (c) why some features of objects (e.g., color or size) are more noticeable than others.
   (d) why our perception of an object remains the same even when our immediate sensation of the object changes.
9. Perceptual constancy refers to our
   (a) perception of an object as remaining the same even when our immediate sensation of the object changes.
   (b) tendency to perceive objects as being grouped together, based on their similarity.
   (c) perception of an object as changing even when our immediate sensation of the object remains the same.
   (d) tendency to perceive a constant closed-up shape of an object even when our perception of it is incomplete.

Answer each of the following questions by filling in the blank with an appropriate word or phrase.

10. _____ is the process whereby energy is converted from a form that enters the sensory receptors to a form that the brain can process.
11. According to the _____-_____ theory

of color vision, we have specialized photoreceptors for each of the two opposing pairs of colors—red–green and yellow–blue—as well as for the opposing pair of white–black.
12. The _____, a thin layer on the rear surface of the eye, contains the photoreceptors responsible for transducing electromagnetic energy into electrochemical energy.
13. The four primary psychological qualities of taste are _____, saltiness, _____, and bitterness.

Match the following depth cues to their descriptions:

14. linear perspective   (a) objects farther away from the observer appear higher in the picture plane (as long as the objects are below the horizon)
15. interposition   (b) objects that are farther away are viewed through a greater density of dust and moisture particles
16. relative size   (c) objects that are closer present more noticeably different images to each of the two eyes
17. aerial perspective   (d) as parallel lines move farther into the distance, they appear to come together at the horizon
18. location in the picture plane   (e) objects that are farther away appear to be smaller
19. binocular convergence (f) objects that are closer may block the view of objects that are farther away
20. binocular disparity   (g) objects that are closer require the eye muscles to pull more strongly inward toward the nose

Answers

1. c, 2. d, 3. b, 4. a, 5. a, 6. d, 7. a, 8. b, 9. a, 10. Transduction, 11. opponent-process, 12. retina, 13. sweetness, sourness, 14. d, 15. f, 16. e, 17. b, 18. a, 19. g, 20. c

PATHWAYS TO UNDERSTANDING

1. Many people earn their living based on perfecting at least one of their senses. Describe at least two examples of professionals who depend on each of the senses discussed in this chapter.

2. Suppose that you conduct research for a manufacturer of food, perfume, or car-seat covers. How would you design an experiment to study human perception of taste, smell, or skin senses?

3. If you had to memorize a long list of terms and definitions, would you be better off trying to remember them by seeing them (e.g., reading printed flashcards) or by hearing them (e.g., by having someone drill you by saying the words aloud)? Do you seem to be able to remember material better if it is presented visually (e.g., in a book) or auditorily (e.g., in a lecture)? How do you tailor your studying to your sensory preferences?

Pathways to Understanding questions at the end of the chapter, like questions in the margins, enable you to exercise your creative, practical, and analytical thinking skills in mastering the material.

STUDY GUIDE TO ACCOMPANY

Pathways to Psychology

ELLEN E. PASTORINO
SUSANN M. DOYLE
ROBERT J. STERNBERG

ADDITIONAL STUDY AIDS

The following are available for student purchase. Ask your college bookstore manager for ordering information.

The Study Guide reflects the theme of the textbook and provides study tips, practice exams, and "answer guides" to the "Pathways to Understanding" questions.

ISBN: 0-15-504068-5

Psychology: The Core on CD-ROM lets you explore psychology through dozens of interactive, multimedia minilectures. Multiple choice questions let you test your mastery of the material.

ISBN: 0-15-502591-0 (Macintosh)
ISBN: 0-15-502959-2 (Windows)

HARCOURT INTERACTIVE

PSYCHOLOGY

THE CORE   CD-ROM

Contents in Brief

PART I   **Introducing Psychology** 1

      Chapter 1   What Is Psychology? 3
      Chapter 2   Biological Psychology 35
      Chapter 3   Development 69

PART II   **Cognitive Processes** 101

      Chapter 4   Sensation and Perception 103
      Chapter 5   Consciousness 135
      Chapter 6   Learning 163
      Chapter 7   Memory 191
      Chapter 8   Thought and Language. 223
      Chapter 9   Intelligence and Creativity 253

PART III   **Social Processes** 281

      Chapter 10   Social Psychology 283
      Chapter 11   Motivation and Emotion. 317
      Chapter 12   Personality 351

PART IV   **Clinical and Health Psychology** 383

      Chapter 13   Abnormal Psychology 385
      Chapter 14   Psychotherapy 415
      Chapter 15   Health Psychology. 447

Statistical Appendix 477

Glossary 485

References 497

Acknowledgments 517

Photo Credits 519

Author Index 521

Subject Index 529

Contents

PART I   Introducing Psychology 1

Chapter 1   What Is Psychology? 3

What Is Psychology? 4

Why Do Psychologists Do What They Do? 7

How Do Psychologists Conduct Research? 11

    Tests and Surveys 11

    Case Studies 11

    Naturalistic Observation 12

    Experiments 13

How Do Psychologists Determine
Cause and Effect? 16

    Controlled Experimental Designs 16

    Correlational Designs 20

What Ethical Issues Do Psychologists Face? 22

How Did Psychology Emerge as a Science? 24

    Early Roots of Psychology 25

    Emergence of Psychology: Diverse Perspectives 27

What Are the Main 20th-Century
Perspectives on Psychology? 28

Chapter 2   Biological Psychology 35

What Is Our Biological History? 36

    Evolutionary Theory 36

    Genetics 37

How Is the Nervous System Organized? 40

    The Central Nervous System 40

    The Peripheral Nervous System 44

What Are the Major Structures and Functions
of the Human Brain? 45

    Viewing the Brain 45

    Structures and Functions of the Brain 47

    The Cerebral Hemispheres and the
    Cerebral Cortex 49

How Is Information Processed in the
Nervous System? 55

    Neurons 55

    Conduction of Information Within Neurons 58

    Communication Between Neurons 60

How Does the Endocrine System Work? 62

Chapter 3   Development 69

What Developmental Trends Have
Psychologists Observed? 71

What Are the Roles of Maturation and Learning? 71

    The Nature–Nurture Controversy:
    Maturation Versus Learning 71

The Roles of Maturation and Learning: The
Developmental Theories of Piaget and Vygotsky 72
What Happens During Prenatal Development? 74
How Do Infants and Young Toddlers Develop? 76
What Can Newborns Do? 76
Physical Development During Infancy 77
Cognitive Development in Infancy 77
Socioemotional Development During Infancy 78
How Do Children Develop? 82
Cognitive Development During Childhood 82
Socioemotional Development 86
What Develops During Puberty and Adolescence? . . . 90
Physical Development During Adolescence 90
Cognitive Development During Adolescence 90
Socioemotional Development 91
How Do Adults Develop and Age? 95

PART II   Cognitive Processes 101

Chapter 4   Sensation and Perception 103
How Do Psychologists Study the Senses? 104
Detection 105
Discrimination: The Just-Noticeable Difference 106
What Are Some Biological Properties Common
to All Senses? 106
Receptor Cells and Transduction 106
Sensory Coding 107
Detection of Changes in Stimuli 107
How Do We See? 108
The Nature of Light 108
Anatomy of the Eye 108
How We See 109
Color 109
How Do We Hear? 112
The Nature of Sound 112
How We Hear 113
Locating Sounds 114
How Do We Sense Taste, Smell, Touch,
Movement, and Other Sensations? 116
Taste 116
Smell 118
Skin Senses 120
Body Senses 120
How Do We Make Sense of What We Sense? 121
How Do We Perceive What We See? 123
Space Perception 123
Form Perception 124
Perceptual Constancies 128

Chapter 5 **Consciousness** 135
How Does Attention Work? 137
What Levels of Consciousness Do We Experience? . . 139
The Preconscious Level 139
The Subconscious Level. 141
What Happens During Altered States
of Consciousness? 142
What Happens When We Sleep and Dream? 143
Stages of Sleep 143
Sleep Deprivation 144
Circadian Rhythms. 145
Sleep Disorders 146
Dreams 147
Is Hypnosis an Altered State? 148
The Phenomenon of Hypnosis: Real or Fake? 148
Theories of Hypnosis 150
What Happens When We Meditate? 151
How Do Drugs Induce Alterations
in Consciousness? 151
Pattern of Drug Use 151
Narcotics 153
Central Nervous System Depressants. 154
Central Nervous System Stimulants 156
Hallucinogenics 156
Treatment of Drug Abuse 157

Chapter 6 **Learning** 163
What Are Some Preprogrammed Responses? 164
What Is Classical Conditioning? 166
Pavlov's Discovery of Classical Conditioning. 167
The Basics of Classical Conditioning 168
Why Does Classical Conditioning Occur?. 169
Phases and Features of Classical Conditioning 170
Surprising Relationships Between the Stimulus
and the Response. 172
What Is Operant Conditioning? 174
Thorndike's Law of Effect 175
Reinforcement 176
Punishment. 177
How Is Operant Conditioning Implemented? 179
Skinner and the Experimental Analysis of Behavior. . . 182
What Is Social Learning? 184

Chapter 7 **Memory** 191
How Do Psychologists Study Memory? 192
Case Studies of Memory Deficiencies: Amnesia 192
Case Studies of Outstanding Memory:
Mnemonists 193
Experimental Study of Memory 193

How Have Psychologists Traditionally
Viewed Memory? 197
    Sensory Memory 198
    Short-Term Memory 198
    Long-Term Memory. 199
What Are Some Alternative Ways to
View Memory? 201
    Alternative Views of Memory Processes 201
    A Neuropsychological View of Memory 203
How Is Information Encoded, Stored,
and Retrieved? 205
    Encoding of Information 205
    Storage and Forgetting 208
    Retrieval 210
How Do We Construct Our Own Memory? 212

Chapter 8   **Thought and Language** 223
What Is Problem Solving? 225
    Well-Structured Problems: Heuristics
    and Algorithms 225
    Ill-Structured Problems: Insight 227
    Hindrances to Problem Solving 228
    Aids to Problem Solving 229
    Expertise: Knowledge and Problem Solving. 231
What Are Judgment and Decision Making? 232
    Decision-Making Strategies 232
    Heuristics and Biases of Judgment 234
What Is Reasoning? 236
    Deductive Reasoning 237
    Inductive Reasoning 237
What Is Language? 238
How Do We Acquire Language? 241
How Do We Understand and Arrange Words? 243
    Semantics: The Study of Meaning 243
    Syntax: The Study of Structure 243
How Do We Use Language in a Social Context? 245
    Linguistic Relativity and Linguistic Universals. 246
    Bilingualism 247

Chapter 9   **Intelligence and Creativity** 253
What Are Two Traditional Approaches to
Studying Intelligence? 254
How Do Psychologists Assess Intelligence? 256
    Mental Age and the Intelligence Quotient 256
    Deviation IQ Scores. 256
    The Stanford–Binet Intelligence Scales. 257
    The Wechsler Scales 257
    Additional Tests Related to Intelligence Testing 259
    Characteristics of Intelligence Tests 260

How Should We Try to Understand the
Nature of Intelligence?..........................261
   Structures and Processes of Intelligence 261
   Context of Intelligence 262
   Intelligence as a System 266
What Have We Learned About Extremes
of Intelligence? 269
   Intellectual Giftedness 269
   Mental Retardation 270
Is Intelligence Inherited? 272
Can We Improve Intelligence? 273
What Is Creativity, and How Does It Emerge?......275

PART III Social Processes 281

  Chapter 10 **Social Psychology**..........................283
How Is Social Cognition?......................285
   Cognitive-Consistency Theory 285
   Attribution Theory...........................287
How Do We Form and Change Our Attitudes? 288
Why Are We Attracted to the People We
Like or Love? 291
   Theories of Liking and Interpersonal Attraction 291
   Theories of Love 292
   Attraction...................................292
How Do We Communicate in Our
Personal Relationships? 294
What Happens When We Interact in Groups?......295
   Social Facilitation and Social Interference 295
   Social Loafing 296
   Group Polarization...........................297
   Groupthink..................................297
When and How Do We Conform, Comply,
and Obey? 299
   Conformity..................................299
   Compliance..................................301
   Obedience 301
What Leads Us to Show Prosocial Behavior? 304
What Leads Us to Show Antisocial Behavior?......307
   Prejudice....................................307
   Aggression 310

  Chapter 11 **Motivation and Emotion** 317
How Did Early Psychologists Explain Motivation? ..318
How Does Human Physiology Influence
Human Motivation?...........................319
   Homeostatic-Regulation Theory..................319
   Opponent-Process Theory 324
   Arousal Theory...............................326

How Do Psychological and Other Needs
Influence Motivation? 327
  Murray's Theory of Needs. 327
  McClelland's Need for Achievement 327
  Maslow's Need Hierarchy 328
How Does Cognition Influence Motivation? 330
  Intrinsic and Extrinsic Motivators. 330
  Curiosity, Self-determination, and Self-efficacy. 331
What Emotions Do People Feel? 335
How Do Psychologists Approach Trying to
Understand Emotions? 338
  Emotions in an Evolutionary Perspective. 338
  Psychophysiological Approaches to Emotion. 339
  Cognitive Approaches to Emotion 342
  Cross-cultural Approaches to Emotion 344
How Do People Express Emotions? 346
  Culture and Emotional Expression. 346
  Social Functions of Emotional Expression 347

Chapter 12   **Personality** 351
How Do Psychodynamic Psychologists
View Personality? 352
  The Nature of Psychodynamic Theories 352
  Psychoanalysis: The Theory of Sigmund Freud 354
  The Neo-Freudians 358
How Do Humanistic Psychologists
View Personality? 362
How Do Cognitive–Behavioral Psychologists
View Personality? 364
  Early Behavioristic Approaches 364
  The Social-Learning Theory of Julian Rotter 365
  The Social-Cognitive Theory of Albert Bandura 366
How Do Trait Theorists View Personality? 367
  Theories Based on Individual Variations of
  Universal Personality Traits 369
  Theories Based on Individual Sets of Distinctive
  Personality Traits. 371
How Do Interactionist Psychologists
View Personality? 372
How Do Psychologists Assess Personality? 374
  Assessments Based on Psychodynamic Theories:
  Projective Personality Tests 374
  Assessments Based on Trait Theories:
  Objective Tests 376
  Evaluation of Personality Tests. 377

PART IV Clinical and Health Psychology 383

Chapter 13   **Abnormal Psychology** 385
What Is Abnormal Behavior? 386

How Have People Explained Abnormal Behavior?. . . 388
    Demonological Explanations. 388
    Clinical Explanations 388
How Do Clinicians Diagnose Abnormal Behavior? . . 391
What Are Anxiety Disorders? 392
What Are Mood Disorders? 395
    Depressive Disorders 395
    Bipolar Disorders. 396
What Are Dissociative Disorders? 398
What Is Schizophrenia? 399
    Types of Schizophrenia 401
    Demographic Issues in Schizophrenia 401
What Are Impulse-Control Disorders? 403
What Are Personality Disorders? 404
What Disorders Are Usually First Diagnosed
in Infancy, Childhood, or Adolescence? 404
What Are Some Additional
Psychological Disorders? 405
How Do Psychologists View Suicide? 406
What Legal Issues Do Clinicians Face? 409
    Criminal Law. 409
    Civil Law 410

Chapter 14 **Psychotherapy** 415
How Have Some Early Methods of
Psychotherapeutic Intervention? 416
How and Why Do Clinicians Diagnose
Abnormal Behavior? 417
How Do Different Psychologists
Approach Psychotherapy? 418
    Psychodynamic Therapy. 419
    Humanistic Therapies. 420
    Behavior Therapies. 422
    Cognitive Approaches to Therapy. 423
    Biological Therapies 425
    Multicultural Approaches to Psychotherapy 429
What Are Some Alternatives to
Individual Psychotherapy? 431
    Group Therapy. 431
    Couples and Family Therapy 431
    Self-Help 433
Is There an Optimal Approach to Psychotherapy? . . . 435
How Effective Is Psychotherapy? 437
What Are Some Key Ethical Issues
in Psychotherapy? 440

Chapter 15 **Health Psychology** 447
What Do Health Psychologists Study? 448
How Can People Enhance Their Health Through
Lifestyle Choices? 450

How Do Personality and Stress Influence Health? . . . 452
    Stressors 453
    Stress Responses 457
    Personality and Perceived Stress 459
How Do Personality Patterns Relate to Illness? 463
    Type-A Versus Type-B Behavior Patterns 463
    Hardiness and Stress Resistance 464
How Do Our Minds Experience Pain? 465
    Kinds of Pain 466
    Personality and Pain 467
How Do People Live with Serious, Chronic
Health Problems? 468
    AIDS: Incidence and Prevention 469
    Psychological Models for Coping with
    Chronic Illness 470

Statistical Appendix 477
    Descriptive Statistics 477
    Measures of Central Tendency 478
    Measures of Variability 480
    The Normal Distribution 481
    Types of Scores 481
    Correlation and Regression 482
    Inferential Statistics 484

Glossary 485

References 497

Acknowledgments 517

Photo Credits 519

Author Index 521

Subject Index 529

Pathways to Psychology

PART
I

Introducing Psychology

CHAPTER 1
What Is Psychology?

CHAPTER 2
Biological Psychology

CHAPTER 3
Development

CHAPTER OUTLINE

What Is Psychology?

Why Do Psychologists Do What They Do?
What Have Psychologists Learned About When, Where, and How to Study?

How Do Psychologists Conduct Research?
Tests and Surveys
Case Studies
Naturalistic Observation
Experiments
What Else Have Psychologists Learned About How to Study?

How Do Psychologists Determine Cause and Effect?
Controlled Experimental Designs
Correlational Designs

What Ethical Issues Do Psychologists Face?

How Did Psychology Emerge as a Science?
Early Roots of Psychology
Emergence of Psychology: Diverse Perspectives

What Are the Main 20th-Century Perspectives on Psychology?

What Is Psychology?

What is your Psy-Q? Test your psychological intuition—do you already know the answers to questions psychologists have studied? (1) If you need help in an emergency situation, are you more likely to be helped if there are fewer people available to help you, or more likely to be helped if there are more people available to help? (2) Do significant creative insights usually evolve over many years, or do they appear all of a sudden? (3) What kinds of persons are most likely to cope effectively with long-term or terminal illness—persons who are unrealistically optimistic about their own ability to cope with the problems of having the illness, or persons who realistically evaluate themselves and their situation? (To find the answers, read this chapter.)

WHAT IS PSYCHOLOGY?

What questions interest you about how or why people think, feel, or act as they do?

Do you ever wonder about what it means to be smart, to love someone, to be attractive to someone? Do you want to know how salespeople persuade you to buy things you do not want? Do you sometimes wish you could better understand how to get along with other people or how to study and learn more effectively? These kinds of questions are answered by studying **psychology,** the study of *mind* (the means by which people perceive, think, and feel) and *behavior* (what people do).

To study psychology is to try to understand how we think, feel, learn, perceive, act, interact with others, and even understand ourselves. As a student of introductory psychology, you are now a *psychologist*—you study the mind and behavior. You and your fellow psychologists (both amateurs and professionals) study various *phenomena* (processes or events that can be observed, e.g., the process of decision making, the expression of emotions, or the response to a personal crisis). (Table 1-1 shows some of the questions asked by psychologists when studying phenomena related to diverse fields of psychology.)

Psychology is a social science; stated simply, psychologists and other *social scientists* study people. Actually, some psychologists and other social scientists also

psychology the study of the mind and of the behavior of people and other organisms

TABLE 1-1

What Do Psychologists Do?

Field of psychology	Sample problems and questions
Psychobiology—The biological structures and processes underlying thought, feeling, motivation, and behavior (see Chapter 2)	■ What portion of the brain is active when a person learns the meaning of a new word? ■ How do various kinds of drugs affect the brain and behavior?
Developmental psychology—How people develop over time (see Chapter 3)	■ How do children form attachments to their parents? ■ How do people acquire an understanding of what others expect of them in social interactions?
Cognitive psychology—How people perceive, learn, remember, and think about information (see Chapters 4, 5, 6, 7, 8, and 9)	■ Why do people remember some facts but forget others? ■ How do people think when they play chess or solve everyday problems?
Social psychology—How people interact with each other, both as individuals and in groups (see Chapter 10)	■ Why are people attracted to one another, and why do people like and even love one another? ■ Why are people sometimes generous and helpful, and why are they sometimes not?
Personality psychology—Personal dispositions that lead people to behave as they do (see Chapters 11 and 12)	■ Why are some people highly sociable, whereas others seem to prefer just the company of very few other people? ■ What makes some people highly conscientious and others less so?
Clinical psychology—Understanding and treatment of abnormal behavior (see Chapters 13 and 14)	■ What behavior is just a little out of the ordinary, and what behavior is truly abnormal? ■ What causes people to do things that they themselves consider inappropriate and even abnormal and would like to stop if they could?
Health psychology—The dynamic interaction between the mind and the physical health of the body (see Chapter 15)	■ How does terminal illness (e.g., AIDS) affect how people think or feel about themselves and other people? ■ How do personality factors contribute to the likelihood that people will become ill with particular diseases (e.g., heart disease or cancer)?

Note: Some other specialties exist, as well. For example:
   Educational psychology uses psychology to improve and develop methods of teaching and learning.
   Industrial/organizational psychology applies psychology to decision making about employees and hiring in institutional settings, such as workplaces and businesses.
   Engineering psychology deals with human–machine systems and how instruments such as computers and automobile dashboards can be made more user-friendly.
   Psycholinguistics investigates the ways in which humans learn and use language.

Psychobiologists probe the relationship of the brain and the mind, using both case studies and experimental methods, often employing sophisticated technological equipment.

In exploring how people think, cognitive psychologists use various methods, such as controlled experiments, tests, computer simulations, and naturalistic observation.

For investigating how people interact, social psychologists use diverse methods ranging from experiments to surveys to naturalistic observations.

To study how people change across the life span, developmental psychologists use various methods, including elaborately controlled experiments involving sophisticated equipment, intensive case studies, naturalistic observations, and surveys.

study the minds and behavior of other animals, but generally, they do so in order to gain insights into human beings. Different kinds of social scientists have slightly different perspectives and emphases in their study of people.

- *Psychologists* generally focus on the individual person alone or in interaction with others and the environment.

- *Political scientists* study systems and structures of human power relationships.

- *Economists* study the various ways in which resources are traded, produced, and used.

- *Sociologists* study groups of individuals, such as groups of people in various kinds of work or having different incomes.

- *Physical anthropologists* study human evolution from simpler animals and even from one-celled creatures.

- *Cultural anthropologists* seek insight into various cultures.

In addition to social scientists, various other scientists also study the human mind and behavior: For example, *geneticists* study the influence of heredity on the mind and behavior, and *physiologists* study how the processes of the body influence the mind and behavior. Psychologists also learn from artists, computer scientists, novelists, and many other persons who try to understand the human mind and behavior.

Personality psychologists use various methods to investigate personality, such as tests.

Clinical psychologists (who have doctorates in psychology) and psychiatrists (who have medical degrees) frequently use case studies, tests, and various other methods for conducting research, as well as for diagnosing and treating patients.

By learning from diverse sources, psychologists may avoid some of the pitfalls of studying the human mind and behavior from only one point of view. Consider the following story (Hunt, 1959, p. 10):

> Once upon a time, an anthropologist was telling an English folk-fable to a gathering of the Bemba of Rhodesia. She glowingly described "a young prince who climbed glass mountains, crossed chasms, and fought dragons, all to obtain the hand of a maiden he loved." The Bemba were plainly bewildered, but remained silent. Finally an old chief spoke up, voicing the feelings of all present in the simplest of questions: "Why not take another girl?" he asked.

The chief's question illustrates not only that various cultures may view romantic love in different ways, but also that psychologists must ask various kinds of questions when studying how people find and pursue someone to love. By considering multiple points of view (e.g., anthropological studies, as well as European literature), we can avoid making false assumptions about how people think, feel, and act.

Most of us can guess quite a bit about the human mind and behavior just through our own experiences. Why do psychologists go to the trouble of using

Health psychologists use diverse methods (e.g., surveys, case studies, experiments, naturalistic observation) for studying how the mind interacts with our physical health.

In addition to the main kinds of psychologists described in Table 1-1, there are many other kinds of psychologists. For instance, engineering psychologists deal with how to enable humans (e.g., data analysts) and machines (e.g., computers) to work well together.

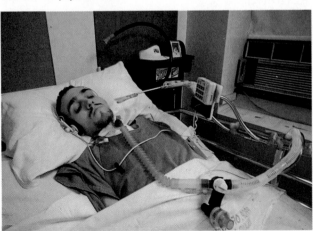

Would you climb glass mountains and fight dragons to gain the love of someone you find attractive? How do most people find and attract someone to love?

scientific methods to study human behavior and the human mind? For one thing, psychologists often find out things that surprise them. For example, Bibb Latané and John Darley (1968, 1970) surprised their colleagues when they found that if you need help in an emergency situation, you are more likely to be helped if there are fewer, rather than more, people available to help you (see Chapter 10).

The object of all psychology is to give us a totally different idea of the things we know best.

Paul Valéry

What is psychology? Psychology is the study of the mind and of behavior.

WHY DO PSYCHOLOGISTS DO WHAT THEY DO?

Does all psychological research lead to surprising discoveries? No, but it does help us to learn more about the human mind and behavior—even when what we discover does not astonish us. We generally distinguish among four main goals for psychological research: description, explanation, prediction, and control. (See Table 1-2 for a summary of these goals.)

Description involves observing and noting what, when, and how people think, feel, or act in various kinds of situations. To create accurate descriptions, psychologists must make observations and gather **data** (observable facts). Take, for example, the observation that about half of all people who get married end up divorcing their spouses. Before trying to understand why people do or do not stay married, psychologists may describe how people feel, think, and act when they have stayed married up to a certain point, and compare those data to parallel descriptions of people whose marriages have ended in divorce. Once psychologists have fully and

data facts, numbers, and other information

TABLE 1-2
Four Primary Goals of Psychological Research

Goal—How psychologists try to achieve it	Questions in trying to reach this goal
Description—Try to characterize how people (and other living beings) think, feel, or act in various kinds of situations	What happens? When does it happen? How does it happen?
Explanation—Try to understand why people think, feel, or act as they do	Why does it happen?
Prediction—Attempt to anticipate how people will think, feel, or act, based on available information about past performance	What will happen next?
Control—Seek to influence how people think, feel, or act	How can we influence people's thoughts, feelings, or actions?

accurately described what, when, and how something happens, they can try to explain why it happens.

Explanation addresses why people think, feel, or act as they do. To explain various data, psychologists propose tentative **hypotheses,** which are preliminary guesses about how to interpret and explain what is observed. Psychologists and other scientists use various formal methods for gathering data as the basis for their hypotheses. Informally, we all constantly gather data about what we observe, and we frequently form tentative hypotheses regarding what we have observed. For instance, based on your observations of married people, why do you believe some people stay married, whereas others end up being divorced?

You, as a budding psychologist, may very well come up with some accurate hypotheses to explain why some people stay married and others divorce. How do you know which of your hypotheses—or those of anyone else—are correct? As a psychologist, you might conduct research that tests the various hypotheses; based on your findings, you could then see which hypothesis does a better job of explaining the phenomenon in question. Often, when psychologists conduct research, they find out some information that supports their own hypotheses and other information that does not support their initial beliefs. As psychologists conduct more research and learn more about the phenomena of interest, they modify their hypotheses or perhaps replace their old hypotheses with new ones that better explain the new information.

For example, suppose that psychologist Kim Yee initially proposed this hypothesis: People who stay married are better listeners and communicators than people who divorce. She might then conduct research to assess the two-way communication skills of people who are about to marry. She could then trace the progress of their marriages and observe any changes in their communication skills. Chances are, some information she gathered would confirm her hypothesis and other information would not. (Even superior communication skills are no guarantee of a long-lasting marriage. For instance, a highly communicative pair of jealous and adultering axe murderers might have other problems.) Given this new information, Kim would revise her hypothesis, allowing for other factors that may influence whether people stay married.

Psychologists, like other people, sometimes make mistakes. Often, their own beliefs (e.g., Kim's belief in the importance of communication skills) bias their interpretation of data. Hypotheses based on personal beliefs may lead to the trap of *confirmation bias,* the tendency to confirm what is already believed to be true.

How do psychologists and other scientists avoid the trap of confirmation bias? For one thing, they base their research on what others before them have discovered and what others around them are discovering. That is, science is *cumulative,* building up over time. In order to accumulate knowledge, scientists agree to share

hypothesis   tentative statement of belief regarding expected outcomes

NASA scientists failed to take steps to avoid confirmation bias, and the crew aboard the shuttle Challenger *suffered the tragic consequences of that error.*

information—to make it *public.* The key way they do so is by publishing their findings in scientific journals.

By reading how various findings were obtained, other scientists can see whether they agree with the original interpretations. The other scientists may then come up with their own interpretations. If they are surprised by the findings, and they doubt the results, they can even *replicate* the work (i.e., repeat the research procedures that were described in the published report). In that way, scientists can *verify* (confirm the accuracy of) the data.

Often, the beliefs that lead to various research hypotheses come from a **theory,** an organized set of general principles that explain a phenomenon or a set of phenomena. Theories allow us to make predictions, based on those general principles. Informative theory and research enable us not only to describe and explain how people think, feel, and act as they do, but also to *predict* how people will think, feel, and so on. *Prediction* can be very important in practice, as well as in theory.

For example, according to one theory in psychology, people tend to engage in behavior that is rewarded and to avoid behavior that is punished (e.g., described in Skinner, 1974). According to this theory, the rewards and punishments people receive affect whether they will continue or will stop behaving in particular ways. A prediction based on this theory may be that people will tend to stay in marriages they find rewarding and will tend to leave marriages they find to be unpleasant. It turns out that this prediction is partly true. Psychologists have observed that many people who have been unhappily married or who have divorced have reported that their marriages—or their spouses—were not rewarding (Notarius & Markman, 1993; Weiss, 1975). On the other hand, other factors (e.g., communication patterns) seem to influence marital happiness and the likelihood of either long-lasting marriage or speedy divorce (Gottman, 1994; Notarius & Markman, 1993). For some psychological phenomena, once we can predict outcomes (e.g., marital happiness or unhappiness), we can start looking for ways to try to influence or control them.

In psychology, one method of *control* is **psychotherapy,** the use of psychological means to help people to control mental disorders and their related bodily problems, as well as to improve or enhance people's adjustment to their life circumstances. Psychotherapy often involves *therapeutic interventions*—active attempts to change thoughts, attitudes, or actions that cause problems for the

Science may be described as the art of systematic over-simplification.

Karl Popper

theory a statement of general principles explaining one or more phenomena (events or processes)

psychotherapy a use of psychological principles to treat mental disorders or otherwise to improve psychological adjustment and well-being

PRACTICAL PSYCHOLOGY   1-1

What Have Psychologists Learned About When, Where, and How to Study?

Here are a few tips for productive studying.

1. Do not try to skimp on the time you spend studying. How much you learn is a function of how much time you devote to learning.
2. Spread out your study sessions. Study a little at a time, rather than bunching your study sessions together or spending long hours studying at one stretch. To avoid having to cram for tests, set small, realistic study goals for yourself, which you can accomplish each day or each week.
3. Do not try to study when you are tired, hungry, or otherwise unable to concentrate on understanding what you are studying. Study when you feel refreshed and ready to learn the material.
4. You should study material in a context that is as close as possible to that in which you will be tested on the material (i.e., in the same type of setting). Ask yourself the characteristics of the setting in which you will be tested (e.g., type of room, noise level, lighting), and try to study in such a setting. In addition, it may help you to study in a variety of contexts with features similar to the testing environment (e.g., a study hall, a library reading room, a dorm study lounge).

What behavior of the people in your environment do you wish you could predict? What behavior of the people with whom you interact do you wish you could control?

person. Many married people who are experiencing difficulties in their marriage seek help from psychotherapists to address and possibly to resolve the problems in their marriage.

Although this textbook does not provide psychotherapy—or anything resembling psychotherapy—it may be able to help you with a difficult task you are now facing: studying. The information in Practical Psychology 1-1 describes what psychologists have learned about when, where, and how to study. It will help you to put their knowledge to work in your own life.

In sum, psychologists try to describe, explain, predict, or control the processes and products of the human mind. Often, they can try to meet more than one goal

Although most people who marry expect to have a lasting marriage, about half of all marriages end in divorce. Why do some couples stay married longer than do others?

during their work. The goals also often interact, so that achieving one goal helps in achieving another. In order to achieve these goals, psychologists use particular methods of conducting research.

Why do psychologists do what they do? Psychologists seek to find ways to describe, explain, predict, and sometimes control how people think, feel, and act.

HOW DO PSYCHOLOGISTS CONDUCT RESEARCH?

Psychologists can use various methods to study problems that interest them: (a) tests and surveys, (b) case studies, (c) naturalistic observation, and (d) experiments. These research methods are summarized in Table 1-3, which highlights some of the advantages and disadvantages of each method.

Research is formalized curiosity. It is poking and prying with a purpose.

Zora Neale Hurston

Tests and Surveys

One way to study human behavior is to use tests. **Tests** are procedures for measuring a characteristic or an ability at a particular time and in a particular place. In tests, the responses are scored as being either right or wrong, or at least as being stronger (more accurate, more appropriate, more creative, etc.) or weaker. Test scores vary not only across people, but also for a given person, due to various factors such as ill health or noise in the environment, that can affect performance at the time of testing.

Unlike tests, **questionnaires,** used in conducting **surveys,** almost never have right or wrong answers. They typically measure beliefs and opinions rather than abilities or knowledge. For example, you might use a questionnaire for a survey to determine the attitudes or opinions of students regarding the use of alcohol or the usefulness of survey data. Surveys can easily be interpreted in many ways. During political campaigns, you probably have heard the exact same survey data interpreted entirely differently by opposing candidates. Nonetheless, surveys are handy research tools.

If you were to conduct a survey of students at your school, what topic would you study? What are three questions you might include in your questionnaire?

Case Studies

Surveys and tests can be used to gather some information about a lot of people. In **case studies,** psychologists gather a lot of information about only a few people. That is, psychologists investigate a few individuals intensively in order to draw general conclusions about how those individuals think or feel, or about how or why they do what they do. The psychologists may then apply these conclusions to the studied individuals and perhaps to others as well.

Psychologists use case studies in various ways. For one thing, many psychologists use case studies when they treat clients in *clinical* work. *Clinical* refers to the observation and treatment of patients with physical or psychological problems, as might be done in a medical clinic. *Clinicians* are psychologists, who usually have PhD (doctor of philosophy) or PsyD (doctor of psychology) degrees; psychiatrists, who typically have MD (doctor of medicine) degrees; and other professionals who provide treatment to clients. For clinicians, case studies are essential for

test a method for measuring a given ability or attribute in particular individuals at a particular time and in a particular place

survey a method of observing various people's responses to questions regarding their beliefs and opinions

questionnaire a set of questions used for conducting a survey

case study intensive investigation of a single individual or set of individuals

TABLE 1-3
Research Methods

Method	Advantages	Disadvantages
Tests and surveys—Tools for obtaining samples of behavior, beliefs, and abilities at a particular time and place	1. Ease of administration 2. Ease of scoring and statistical analysis	1. May not be able to generalize results beyond a specific place, time, and test content 2. May be discrepancies between real-life behavior and test behavior
Case studies—Intensive studies of single individuals, which draw general conclusions about behavior	Highly detailed information, including the context surrounding the person being studied	1. Small samples of people, which reduce the researcher's ability to generalize conclusions 2. Limitations on the reliability of the data
Naturalistic observations—Observations of real-life situations, as in classrooms, work settings, or homes	1. Wide applicability of results 2. Understanding of behavior in natural contexts	1. Loss of experimental control 2. Possibility that the observer's presence may influence the observed behavior
Experiments—Controlled investigations that study cause-and-effect relationships through the manipulation of variables	1. Precise control of independent variables 2. Usually, large numbers of subjects that allow results to be generalized	1. Usually, less intensive study of individual subjects 2. Limitations on the ability to generalize to real-life behavior

Think about your own experiences with insight. Have your own most worthwhile insights tended to involve a series of small insights that built up over time, or one sudden flash of profound realization?

understanding the problems of individual clients, as well as for deepening their insights into psychological problems in general.

Researchers also use case studies to gain insight into the human mind and behavior. Some psychologists study many individuals. For example, Robert Weiss drew on many case studies to find some common reasons why marriages fail (Weiss, 1975). Other investigators study just one person in great depth: Howard Gruber (1981) studied Charles Darwin (famous for his theory of evolution; see Chapter 2). To Gruber, the case-study method offered details he needed in order to understand how creativity changes over a lifetime (described in Gruber, 1995). Gruber concluded that creative insights evolve over many years, rather than appearing all of a sudden, and that most major creative insights are a combination of many minor insights.

Naturalistic Observation

In **naturalistic observation,** also known as *field study*, the researcher leaves the laboratory or the clinic. Out in the community ("the field"), the naturalistic observer listens, watches, and records what people do and say during their normal activities. For example, Shirley Heath (1983), an anthropologist, found dramatic differences in how parents and children defined intelligence across three different U.S. communities. These differences included differing emphases given to nonverbal communication skills, verbal skills, memory skills, and academic skills. Parents in one community (Trackton) more strongly emphasized nonverbal communication skills, whereas parents in the other two communities (Roadville and Gateway) more strongly emphasized verbal skills. When the children went to school, verbal skills were emphasized more than were nonverbal ones, giving children from Roadville and Gateway a competitive edge in the school setting.

What is the value of Heath's naturalistic observations? For one thing, we learn from her studies that different kinds of parenting styles may lead to differences in

naturalistic observation a research method in which the researcher observes people engaged in the normal activities of their daily lives

Psychologists often use naturalistic observation to study children at home, in school, at a park, or in other natural settings.

how well children are prepared for the school environment. For another thing, we learn that intelligence is multifaceted, involving far more than the intellectual skills that are used in school. A child from Roadville or Gateway placed in Trackton might appear relatively unintelligent by Trackton standards, due to the child's relatively weaker background in developing nonverbal skills. Unfortunately for the children from Trackton, the intellectual abilities valued at home did not closely match what the school valued. However, if schools had valued the nonverbal skills emphasized in Trackton homes, the children from Roadville and Gateway might have had more difficulty performing well in school.

Experiments

In the strictest scientific sense, an **experiment** is an investigation that studies cause–effect relationships. It does so by controlling variables. *Variables* are characteristics or quantities that vary. In general, experimenters carefully manipulate one or more particular variables to note their effects on other variables.

A given experiment has two main kinds of variables: independent and dependent. **Independent variables** are carefully controlled by the experimenter, so that some aspects of the investigation are varied, but other aspects are not allowed to vary. The values of **dependent variables** depend on how one or more independent variables affect the phenomenon being studied in the experiment.

You probably do not conduct rigorously controlled scientific experiments every day, but you often do manipulate independent variables to observe their effects on dependent variables. For example, in trying to find out why your car will not start, you manipulate various independent variables (e.g., the battery, the fuel supply, the ignition) and observe the effects of your manipulations on the dependent variable (whether the car starts). In trying to find the best recipe for your favorite dish, you manipulate various independent variables (e.g., the ingredients, the sequence of steps, the cooking time or temperature), and you observe their effects on the dependent variable (i.e., how delicious the resulting dish tastes). In a wide variety of situations, you manipulate one or more independent variables and observe their effects on the dependent variables.

Of course, in your everyday experiences, you probably do not exert rigorous control of every variable or conduct sophisticated analyses of your data. In scientific research, the method of experimentation is much more tightly controlled. For example, suppose that Juana Perez wants to know whether the use of word

How have the skills emphasized in your home and your community aided you in preparing for the tasks you face in college? What skills do you believe you need to develop more fully in order to succeed in college?

experiment an investigation of cause–effect relationships done by controlling or carefully manipulating particular variables to note their effects on other variables

independent variable an attribute that is manipulated by the experimenter, while other attributes are held constant (not varied)

dependent variable an outcome characteristic that varies as a consequence of variation in one or more independent variabls

TABLE 1-4
Summary of Key Terms in the Experimental Method

Term and definition	Example (in Juana's study)
Independent variable—Aspects of the experiment that are controlled directly by the experimenter	The means of writing a paper (here, pen vs. word processor
Dependent variable—Outcomes, events, or characteristics that are influenced or affected by the experimental control of the independent variables	The quality of the writing in the paper
Experimental condition (also called *treatment condition*)—The condition in which subjects are exposed to a particular treatment	The condition in which the subjects have access to the use of word processors in writing the paper
Control condition—The condition in which subjects are not exposed to the experimental treatment; they may be exposed to an alternative treatment or to no treatment at all	The condition in which the subjects do not have access to word processors

processors affects the quality of writing. Juana has half of her participants (sometimes called subjects) use word processors to write a brief report. She has the rest of the participants use pen and paper to write the report. Juana then has all the reports typed so that they look similar, and a panel of experts rates the quality of the writing. In this case, the independent variable is the means of writing the paper, and the dependent variable is the quality of the writing.

Experiments involve at least two different types of conditions. In the first type of condition, the **experimental condition,** participants are exposed to an experimental treatment. The experimental condition is also described as the *treatment condition.* In Juana's experiment, the treatment is the use of word processors. In the second type of condition, the **control condition,** the participants do not receive the experimental treatment. In the control condition, the participants do not have access to word processors. Juana's goal is to see whether the participants who use word processors perform the writing task differently than do the participants who do not use word processors.

Usually, two different groups of participants are used for the experimental condition and the control condition. When two or more groups of participants are used, the participants who receive the experimental treatment are the *experimental group.* The participants who are used as a comparison group are the *control group.* The control group may receive some alternative treatment or no treatment at all. Psychologists compare the outcomes for the control group with the outcomes for the experimental group. The use of control groups also allows psychologists to minimize the influence of *confounding variables* (situational or personal characteristics that would make it hard to draw conclusions without being confused). Without a control group, it is usually hard to draw any conclusions at all. In Juana's experiment, the experimental group works with word processors, and the control group works with pen and paper. If Juana had all of her participants use word processors, the lack of a comparison group would leave Juana unsure of whether the quality of work in the writing task was higher (or lower) than otherwise as a function of the use of word processors. If the essays were all quite good (or bad), it might be because of the choice of topic, the abilities of the participants, or whatever. (See Table 1-4 for a summary of the key terms in this section.)

Thus far, we have defined *experiment* in the strictest sense. In addition, however, people sometimes broaden the use of the term *experiment.* More loosely speaking, an experiment studies the effect(s) of some variables on other variables. The key benefit of using experiments is the ability to draw conclusions regarding causality.

experimental condition a situation in which some experimental participants are exposed to a specific set of circumstances, involving a treatment linked to an independent variable

control condition a situation in which some experimental participants are subjected to a carefully prescribed set of circumstances, which are like those of the experimental condition but do not involve the introduction of the independent variable

PRACTICAL PSYCHOLOGY   1-2

What Else Have Psychologists Learned About How to Study?

Psychologists have learned a great deal about how people can learn material in ways that help them to remember it. Following are a few more tips on how you can put psychological findings to work when you study:

5. Check your understanding. Use the "Pathways to Knowledge" and "Pathways to Understanding" sections at the end of each chapter in this textbook, to check that you understand and remember the key information in this chapter. In addition, look for opportunities to discuss what you are learning with other students, either in class or after class.

6. Periodically review your lecture notes, and review the key points in what you are reading. Take advantage of various opportunities for reviewing key information in this textbook (e.g., "The Big Picture" and the end-of-chapter "Summary"). In addition, create other ways to review what you have read. After you have read a paragraph or two, go back and highlight key terms, concepts, and statements. Make notes in the margins of the book or on separate sheets of paper regarding the key information from each section of each chapter.

7. Make use of various *advance organizers*, which give you a hint about what information to expect, so that you can better organize the information. In this textbook, advance organizers include chapter outlines, section headings, and introductions to chapter sections. (*Note:* If you are reading a book that does not have advance organizers, you can create your own by quickly scanning each chapter or section before you actually read it, noting especially information printed in different typefaces.)

8. Think critically about the information you hear (in lectures and discussions) and read (in textbooks). In the margins of this textbook are various questions intended to help you to think critically about what you are reading. Take advantage of these questions, and think of other questions that you might ask yourself about the information you are reading or hearing.

9. Whenever possible, try to relate what you are reading or hearing (e.g., in a lecture or a discussion) to your own experiences. When reading this textbook, take advantage of the various experiences (called "Finding Your Way") and questions (e.g., in the margins and at the end of each chapter) designed to help you relate what you are reading to your own experiences. In your notes, include comments that help you to relate the new information to what you already know. When you are reviewing your notes (or the chapter summaries), try to think of new ways to relate what you have learned to what you already know, and add those ideas to your notes.

10. Use visual learning techniques. Use the various figures, photos, and tables in this textbook to form mental pictures of key ideas, so that you will be better able to remember them.

11. Monitor your own learning to find out which styles you prefer. For instance, two friends of mine have differing styles of learning. Sally cannot listen to and understand a lecture unless she is taking notes, and she cannot read a book without a pen in her hand for scribbling in the margin (or at least making notes on paper if she is reading a borrowed book). Bernie, on the other hand, is distracted by note-taking and remembers what he hears better if he focuses on listening. When he reads, he sometimes draws pictures in the margins of the book. These pictures capture the key concepts being described. Bernie also finds that he remembers information better if he has a chance to discuss it with other people.

12. If you expect to do well in school, and you try hard to succeed, the chances are that you will succeed!

Readers are plentiful; thinkers are rare.

Harriet Martineau

Whoever does not try, does not learn.

Iraqi Jewish saying

By using a variety of research methods, psychologists have been able to study many aspects of how people think, feel, and act. Much of the work of psychologists is intended as **basic research,** which involves a search for fundamental relationships and principles of the human mind and behavior. In addition to basic research, psychologists often conduct **applied research,** which is a search for ways in which to put psychological discoveries to practical use. Among the many outcomes of applied research is information that directly relates to your own experiences: how to study so that you remember the information you are learning. See Practical Psychology 1-2, and put psychology to work for you.

How do psychologists conduct research? Psychologists conduct research by using tests and surveys, case studies, naturalistic observation, and experiments.

HOW DO PSYCHOLOGISTS DETERMINE CAUSE AND EFFECT?

The preceding section described four different kinds of research methods that psychologists can use. How do researchers choose which method to use? For one thing, the problem being studied may affect the choice of method. Howard Gruber (1981) particularly wanted to find out what makes someone a brilliantly creative and revolutionary scientist. It seems doubtful that he could have used surveys or experiments to find all that he wanted to know.

Another important issue also influences the choice of research method: *causality,* which is the link between a particular cause and a particular effect. A major goal of psychological research is to investigate cause-and-effect relationships. What do researchers need to do to be able to infer that "so-and-so" causes "such-and-such"? They design experiments that allow them to draw *causal inferences,* tentative conclusions about the likelihood that particular events or characteristics of a situation cause other events or characteristics. For example, they might ask whether a particular independent variable (e.g., use of word processors) was responsible for variation in the value of a given dependent variable (e.g., quality of writing). Based on their findings, they might try to infer the likelihood (probability) that the independent variable caused the change observed in the dependent variable.

For various reasons, however, it is not always possible to detect a clear causal relationship between independent and dependent variables. For one thing, the ability to draw causal inferences depends on how the research is designed. **Research design** affects two key aspects of the experiment: (1) How are variables chosen, and how do they relate to each other? (2) How are participants assigned to the experimental and the control groups?

Next, we consider three basic kinds of designs in psychological research: controlled experimental, quasi-experimental, and correlational designs. In particular, we emphasize the kinds and degrees of causal inference that can be drawn from each. (See Table 1-5 for a summary of the similarities and differences among these three designs, including the advantages and disadvantages of each.)

Controlled Experimental Designs

In a **controlled experimental design,** the experimenter manipulates (controls) one or more independent variables in order to see the effect on one or more dependent variables. In any experiment, variables other than the independent

It is often interesting, in retrospect, to consider the trifling causes that lead to great events.

Patricia Moyes

basic research investigations devoted to the study of fundamental underlying relationships and principles, which may not offer any immediate, obvious, or practical value

applied research investigations that are intended to lead to clear, immediate, obvious, and practical uses, which may not lead to fundamental understandings of the human mind and behavior

research design a way of choosing and interrelating a set of experimental variables, and of selecting and assigning subjects to experimental and control conditions

controlled experimental design a plan for conducting research in which the experimenter carefully manipulates or controls independent variables in order to see their effects on dependent variables

TABLE 1-5
Research Designs

Type of design	Advantages	Disadvantages
Controlled experimental design—Experimenter manipulates or controls one or more independent variables and observes the effects on the dependent variable or variables; subjects are randomly assigned to control or treatment conditions	Permits conclusions regarding the causal outcomes of the treatment variable(s)	May not apply to settings outside the laboratory; depends on the use of a sample that truly represents the entire population of interest; may involve ethical concerns
Quasi-experimental design—Has many of the features of an experimental design, but subjects are not randomly assigned to control versus treatment conditions; in some cases, there is no control group at all **Correlational design**—Researchers observe the degree of association between two or more attributes that occur naturally. Researchers do not directly manipulate the variables themselves, and they do not randomly assign subjects to groups.	May be more convenient in some situations; may be used when random assignment of participants is difficult or unethical; may be easier to study larger numbers of participants	Do not typically permit conclusions regarding causal relationships between variable(s)

variable—including even random variations—may affect the dependent variables. The experimenter must find a way to tell the effects of these other variables apart from the effects of the independent variables. To do so, the experimenter also includes in his or her design one or more control groups of participants who are not in the experimental group. If the experiment involves a particular treatment condition, the participants in the control group do not receive the experimental treatment: They may receive no treatment, or they may receive an alternative treatment.

In a controlled experimental design, participants must be randomly assigned to the experimental and the control groups. This random assignment is important. It ensures that later differences in the results for each group are not due to preexisting differences in the participants. Suppose that John Banks and Jane Barker designed an experiment in which they assigned men to the treatment group (using word processors) and women to the control group (using pens and paper). No matter what findings resulted, they could not be sure whether the results were due to the intended treatment (word processors vs. pens and paper) or to the sex differences between the members of the two groups.

Recall that Juana conducted a similar experiment assessing whether the use of word processors affects the quality of writing. In contrast to John and Jane, Juana randomly assigned participants to treatment and control conditions. Because Juana randomly assigned participants to each condition, she was able to determine that differences between the treatment group and the control group were due to the treatment variable, not to prior differences between the two groups.

Even very minor differences between groups may affect the outcomes. For instance, suppose that we gave a test of learning early in the day. Suppose also that we assigned the first 20 participants who arrived to the treatment group, and we assigned the second 20 participants to the control group. In this case, we might suspect that differences between the two groups could be associated with promptness (early arrivers might be more hard working), with tiredness (early arrivers might still be tired), or with some other factor associated with whether the participants arrived earlier or later.

MINILECTURE
The Experimental Method (Ch 1)

What are some ways you can think of to ensure that participants will be randomly assigned to either a treatment or a control condition?

Alcohol is a good preservative for everything but brains.

Mary Pettibone Poole

What are some psychological phenomena that cannot appropriately or feasibly be studied using controlled experimental designs?

quasi-experimental design a plan for conducting research that resembles a controlled experimental design but that does not ensure the random assignment of subjects to the treatment and the control groups

representative sample a subset of a population, carefully chosen to represent the proportionate diversity of the population

Figure 1-1

Choosing a Representative Sample
How representative is this sample of people? Psychologists try to obtain representative samples of a population. They statistically analyze data based on samples, to get some idea about the population of interest.

In some situations, it is not possible to assign persons randomly to a treatment group and a control group. Suppose that Ima Brewer wishes to study the effects of long-term alcohol abuse on psychological health. Ethically, she must accept for the alcoholic group those persons who already are alcoholics, and she must accept for the control group those who are not. She cannot randomly assign people to one group or the other and then insist that those assigned to the drinking group become alcoholics. When it is either unethical or impractical to ensure random assignment of participants to the treatment and the control groups, researchers can use quasi-experimental research designs. In **quasi-experimental designs,** researchers do whatever they can to provide experimental control, but they recognize that they cannot provide full experimental control. When using quasi-experimental designs, researchers are less able to infer the causes of psychological phenomena.

In contrast to quasi-experimental designs, controlled experimental designs allow researchers to draw causal inferences. Causal inferences are not final conclusions, however. In experimental research, we can never be sure that the findings we obtain with a group of participants are not due to chance—purely a random accident of the data—because even very remote possibilities sometimes occur. For example, although your chances of winning a major state lottery by purchasing one ticket are about 1 in 5,200,000 (Siskin, Staller, & Rorvik, 1989), you cannot rule out altogether the possibility of winning. You may still win. It is just unlikely.

The only way for psychologists to be 100% sure that particular findings apply to all people is to conduct experiments on an entire *population* (every single person of interest). Unfortunately, it is rarely practical or even possible to study everyone in a population. Therefore, we have to settle for studying what we believe to be a **representative sample,** a subset of individuals from a population, carefully chosen to represent the population as a whole.

As you may imagine, some portions of a total population are easier to study than are other portions. Therefore, some people are under- or overrepresented in research samples. For example, women and persons of color are often underrepresented (too rarely studied), and men, whites, and college students are often overrepresented (commonly studied) in research, relative to their representation in, say, the world population. Samples drawn largely from easily accessible members of a population are termed *samples of convenience* (Lonner & Berry, 1986).

One way to increase the accuracy of causal inferences about a population, based on a particular sample, is to use statistical analysis. Statistical analysis helps researchers to minimize errors in two ways: First, it offers an accurate and consistent means of describing a sample from a population (e.g., the average annual salaries reported by 30-year-olds in the sample). Second, it provides a consistent

These graduates have good reasons to smile: First, they have achieved a very difficult task, and second, their financial prospects are now much brighter as a result of their hard work. According to the U.S. Department of Commerce, in 1992, women college graduates earned an average of almost twice as much as women high school graduates who did not enter college; men college graduates earned an average of more than 1½ times as much as men high school graduates who did not go on to college.

basis for inference about the characteristics of an entire population, based on the characteristics of only a sample.

Descriptive statistics (which describe the particular sample of interest) are usually less difficult to determine than are *inferential statistics* (which suggest conclusions about the sample, relative to the population from which it is drawn). For example, to describe the annual salaries of college graduates versus nongraduates, we would add up all the annual salaries of each group, divide each total by the number of people in each group, and find the average annual salary for each group. Now, suppose that the average annual salaries of college graduates in our sample were far greater than the annual salaries of nongraduates. Based on the salary differences we found, we might infer that, in general, graduates from college on average are later earning larger annual salaries.

To increase the accuracy of our inferences, we use inferential statistics. Inferential statistics allow us to draw reasoned conclusions about the population based on the descriptive sample data. Such statistics can help us to evaluate the difference between a treatment group and a control group (or even another treatment group). In particular, we can assess how likely it is that the obtained difference is not caused merely by chance variations in the data.

Researchers use the concept of **statistical significance** to show the likelihood that a result is not caused by chance fluctuations. If the statistical probability reaches a particular preset point (usually 95% or 99%), we consider the result statistically significant. Why is this finding statistically significant? Think about it. If there were a 95% or a 99% chance that the results were not due to chance fluctuations, then there would be only a 5% or a 1% chance that the results were a fluke of random variations.

For example, psychologist Shelley Taylor (1983) was studying how people cope with the stress of having a life-threatening or long-term illness. She hoped to find out what enables some people to cope with stress more effectively than do others. She noticed that more adaptive persons seem to have "overly positive views of the self, an exaggerated sense of personal control, and unrealistic optimism about the future." That is, people who have an unrealistically positive outlook actually cope better with the stress of having a serious illness than do people who more realistically appraise themselves and their situation.

Taylor then used inferential statistics to determine whether (a) the positive illusions she observed just happened, by chance, to be related to better adaptability, or (b) the relationship between positive illusions and greater ability to cope was likely to be real—that is, statistically significant. She found that the relationship was statistically significant at the 0.05 ("point oh five") level of probability (p). That level of significance means that there is a chance of only 5% or less that her results

statistical significance characterization of a result as most likely due to systematic rather than chance factors

were a fluke due to random variation. Had her results been statistically significant at the 0.01 level of probability, there would have been only a chance of 1% or less that her findings were due to random variation. The smaller the probability of obtaining a result due to random variations, the greater is the statistical significance of the result. In other words, the results are more likely to apply not only in the particular sample that was selected, but in the entire population as well. In addition to their statistical significance, Taylor's findings have *practical significance*, in that they have led to various applications in the treatment of persons facing serious illness and other sources of stress.

Two important limitations affect the interpretation of statistical inferences: First, we can never be absolutely certain that a difference is not due to chance. We can be 99% confident (with a 0.01 level of significance) or even more confident, but we can never be 100% confident (with a 0.00 level). Second, we can never prove the null hypothesis. The **null hypothesis** is the tentative prediction that there is no difference between groups of participants. That is, we cannot prove that a particular variable has no effect or that there is no difference in the population between groups exposed to two or more different conditions. We can only say that we have not yet found any effect or any difference.

The way to do research is to attack the facts at the point of greatest astonishment.

Celia Green

Suppose that you heard that a particular kind of food might cause a serious illness. What level of statistical significance would prompt you to avoid the particular kind of food?

Finding Your Way   1-1

Watch commercial television, or listen to commercial radio, and choose an advertising claim that you can study (e.g., "New Head-Ex relieves painful headaches faster than the leading brand of pain reliever"). Think about how to design an experiment to test this claim. Fill in the missing information in Table 1-6, describing your experiment.

Correlational Designs

When researchers use correlational research designs, they cannot draw any conclusions regarding causation. In general, a *correlation* means that two or more things are related to each other in some way. In a pure **correlational design,** researchers try to see how strongly two (or more) existing attributes are associated with each other. *Attributes* are characteristics of the participants, of the setting, or of the situation being studied. In correlational designs, researchers do not directly control the variables themselves, and they do not randomly assign participants to groups. Instead, researchers usually observe participants in naturally preexisting groups. For example, they may study the relationship between the characteristics of individual participants (e.g., age or sex) and particular behavior (e.g., performance on certain tasks). Researchers often study how the speed and accuracy of performing various tasks differs for males versus females or for adults versus children. They may also study the relationship between behavior and particular situations or settings, such as the performance of particular students in two or more classrooms, or of particular employees in two or more work settings.

When two attributes show some degree of statistical relationship to one another, they are *correlated.* **Correlation** is expressed as a number on a scale that ranges from −1 to 0 to 1, as follows (see Figure 1-2):

> +1 indicates a perfect *positive correlation* (as A increases, so does B, and vice versa). Example—the amount of air blown into a balloon in relation to the volume (size) of the balloon (until it pops)

> 0 indicates no correlation at all. Example—the colorfulness of a balloon in relation to the volume of the balloon

null hypothesis a proposed expectation of *no* difference or relation

correlational design a plan for conducting research by assessing the degree of association between two (or more) attributes (characteristics of subjects or of a setting or situation)

correlation the statistical relationship between two attributes, expressed as a number ranging from −1 (a negative correlation) to 0 (no correlation) to +1 (a positive correlation)

TABLE 1-6

Hypothetical Experiment Testing an Advertising Claim

How would you devise an experiment to test an advertising claim?

Elements of an experiment	Your experiment to test an advertising claim	An example of an experiment to test an advertising claim
Hypothesis		Participants who have headaches and who use Head-Ex will show more rapid relief from headaches than will participants who have headaches and who use Brand Y or participants who have headaches and who use a sugar-pill (called a "placebo") having no active ingredients.
Independent variable		The use of Head-Ex, Brand Y, or a placebo
Dependent variable		Speed of headache relief
Experimental treatment condition #1		Participants who have headaches will be given Head-Ex pills
Experimental treatment condition #2		Participants who have headaches will be given Brand Y pills
Control condition		Participants who have headaches will be given placebos
Null hypothesis		There are no differences among the three groups (the two treatment groups and the control group) that will influence the outcome of the experiment.
Method of measuring outcomes		All participants will be asked to rate (on a scale from 1 to 9) the painfulness of their headaches, at 1-minute intervals, for up to 2 hours
Means of drawing a representative sample		Recruit volunteers from among patients in a pain-relief clinic; sampling bias may arise because not all persons who have headaches are likely to show up at a pain-relief clinic, and not all patients at such a clinic will volunteer for the study

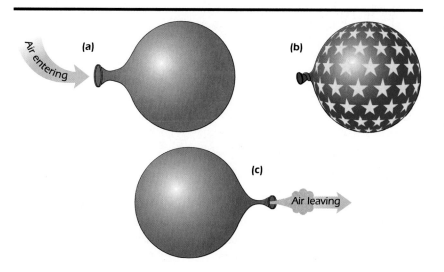

Figure 1-2

Correlation: Positive Versus None Versus Negative

(a) Positive correlation: the amount of air going into a balloon, in relation to the volume (size) of the balloon; (b) no correlation: the colorfulness of a balloon, in relation to the volume of the balloon; (c) negative correlation: the amount of air seeping out of a balloon, in relation to the volume of the balloon.

Psychology which explains everything / explains nothing.

Marianne Moore

MINILECTURE

Correlations (Ch 1)

Figure 1-3

Graphic Representations of Correlations

These graphs (called "scatterplots") show that a given pair of variables may have (a) a positive correlation (i.e., when one variable increases or decreases in value, the value of the other does likewise); (b) no correlation (i.e., the increase or decrease in the value of one variable has no relationship whatsoever to variation in the value of the other variable); or (c) a negative correlation (i.e., when the value of one variable increases, the value of the other decreases, and vice versa).

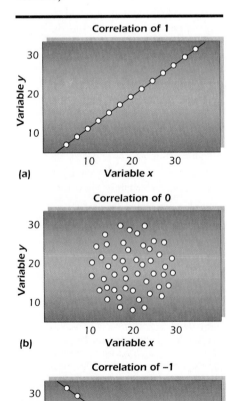

−1 indicates a perfect *negative correlation* (as A increases, B decreases, and vice versa). Example—the amount of air that seeps out of a balloon in relation to the volume of the balloon

Numbers between 0 and +1 indicate some degree of positive correlation (e.g., 0.7, 0.23, 0.01). Numbers between 0 and −1 indicate some degree of negative correlation (e.g., −0.03, −0.2, −0.75). Perfect correlations of −1 and 1 are extremely rare. Figure 1-3 shows how correlations appear in graphic form.

For both positive and negative correlations, it is usually difficult to figure out which of two related attributes was the causal attribute. In fact, it may be that neither attribute caused the other one. Instead, perhaps an entirely different attribute caused the relationship. For example, we might gather data about participants' school grades and then give the participants a test of *self-efficacy* (belief in one's own competence) in order to determine whether there is a connection between school grades and self-efficacy. Both variables were having effects before the experiment started, and the experimenters did not (and could not) exercise control over either one. Suppose that we find a correlation between self-efficacy and school grades. We might expect it to be positive in some degree, and it is: Persons with high self-efficacy tend to have better grades in school, and persons with low self-efficacy tend to have poorer grades (Bandura, 1977a). Does this correlation mean that low self-efficacy causes poor grades, that poor grades cause low self-efficacy, or that both poor grades and low self-efficacy depend on some third variable, which we have not yet identified (such as feelings of rejection in childhood)?

Correlational designs are useful in spotting whether relationships exist and in estimating how strong the relationships are. However, they do not specify exactly what might cause the relationship. Because researchers typically cannot infer causality when they use correlational studies, they generally prefer to use controlled experimental designs whenever possible. Frequently, however, correlational designs are unavoidable. For instance, it would be impossible to design a controlled experiment to study the influence of age on memory. We cannot randomly assign a set of participants to have particular ages. Similarly, ethical considerations would prevent you from randomly assigning participants to engage in dangerous or unhealthful behavior. Several other ethical issues also arise in considering how psychologists conduct research.

How do psychologists figure out what causes what? Psychologists are able to infer causality by conducting experiments in which they control or manipulate independent variables and observe their effects on dependent variables. Sometimes, psychologists conduct correlational research, which does not allow them to infer causality unless additional information permits such inferences.

WHAT ETHICAL ISSUES DO PSYCHOLOGISTS FACE?

Psychological researchers constantly must face ethical questions that arise in their research. Almost all research institutions (such as universities) require that researchers get advance approval for their experiments, and special review boards generally check over the plans for research, as well as the final outcomes. These boards protect the rights of persons who participate in psychological experiments. Some of the main ethical research issues are deception, confidentiality, and physical or psychological pain.

Sometimes, psychological researchers *deceive* their participants. Usually, when psychologists deceive their participants, they do so by not telling the participants the true purpose of an experiment until after the experiment is over. Why would psychologists try to deceive their own research participants? Generally, when experimenters hide the purpose of an experiment, they do so in order to get the participants to behave as normally, naturally, and realistically as possible. For some experiments, if participants knew the purpose of the experiment, that knowledge might affect their behavior.

For example, suppose that you want to study the personality characteristics of people who are helpful. First, you tell your participants the purpose of your experiment, next you give them a personality test, and then you put them in a situation in which they see someone who needs help. Just how normally, naturally, and realistically do you think they will respond?

If, occasionally, psychologists must deceive their participants in order to find out what the psychologists want to know, they must also take two key steps for the benefit of their participants. First, participants in a study are required to give **informed consent** before participating in the research. When participants are asked to give informed consent, they are told (a) what kinds of tasks they may be expected to perform, and (b) what kinds of situations they may expect to face. Participants must also be told that they are free to leave the experiment at any time, without fear of any negative consequences.

Second, after the research is completed, the participants must be fully debriefed about the research. During *debriefing*, participants are told the true purpose of the experiment, told about any deception that may have been involved, and given the reason for the deception. Most review boards will allow minor deceptions if the research meets three criteria: (1) The proposed research is valuable enough to justify the deception; (2) deception is necessary to fulfill the purpose of the experiment; and (3) the deception is fully explained after the experiment ends.

A second major issue in research is **confidentiality**—the assurance that information about individual participants will be kept private. The large majority of experiments in psychology are conducted anonymously—participants' names are not associated with their data. Occasionally, however, researchers must keep track of the names attached to the data. For example, research cannot be anonymous when researchers plan to conduct *follow-up work* (in which earlier behavior is linked to later behavior, e.g., when correlating earlier test scores to later grade-point averages). If the research participants are not anonymous, however, experimenters go to great lengths to ensure that names of participants and their individual data are known only to those persons involved in the investigation who must know the names.

In the past, it was up to individual psychologists to ensure that experimental participants were not exposed to undue physical or psychological discomfort or distress. Nowadays, researchers continue to try to predict whether an experiment might possibly cause any distress, and then they try to reduce that possibility (unless distress itself is the topic being studied). In addition, however, contemporary research psychologists must obtain the approval of institutional review boards prior to conducting experiments. These institutional review boards generally do not permit studies that may cause any long-lasting pain or harm. Further, if participating in a study might cause short-term pain or distress, participants must be fully informed in advance regarding these possible events.

Animal subjects (participants), of course, cannot give informed consent, and they cannot leave whenever they wish. Nonetheless, most institutions try hard to protect the health and well-being of animals. The animals must be given all they need in terms of food, shelter, and freedom from harm or discomfort. At the same time, some of our most important discoveries in both medicine and psychology

Those who trust us, educate us.

George Eliot

---

informed consent an experimental procedure in which prospective participants are fully informed regarding the general nature of the anticipated treatment procedure and any possible harmful consequences of the treatment

confidentiality an ethical practice in which researchers ensure the privacy of personal information regarding individual research participants

Many animal-rights activists feel strongly that animals should never be the subject of scientific experimentation, under any circumstances. In contrast, most scientists believe that as long as animals are provided with the basic resources of food and shelter, and the animals are not subjected to harsh or painful treatment, animal experimentation is justified by the gains in knowledge that result. Do you believe animals should be the subjects of experimentation? Why or why not?

Since we humans have the better brain, isn't it our responsibility to protect our fellow creatures from, oddly enough, ourselves?

Joy Adamson

Those who cannot remember the past are condemned to repeat it.

George Santayana

have come from research in which animals were subjected to disease, untested treatments, and the like. The ethical decisions involved in animal research are not easy to make. Review boards and policymakers try to weigh the costs and benefits involved in all research, whether it involves human or animal participants.

Only since the late 1960s and early 1970s have special review boards become a standard means of evaluating proposed research. In fact, if some of the psychological studies conducted prior to that time were proposed today (see the discussions of studies by Stanley Milgram and by Philip Zimbardo in Chapter 10), they might not pass the scrutiny of contemporary review boards. Given the benefit of hindsight, it is now easy to see how researchers should have been more careful to protect the psychological well-being of participants. Although each of us would prefer to base our knowledge on foresight, we must often rely on what we learn from hindsight. By studying our past, we can more effectively shape our future.

What ethical issues do psychologists face? Psychologists address ethical issues related to deception, confidentiality, and physical or psychological discomfort or distress.

HOW DID PSYCHOLOGY EMERGE AS A SCIENCE?

How do we determine our ethical views and interpret contemporary ideas? In part, what seems reasonable today is shaped by the ideas of both the people around us now and the people who came before us. Most of the ideas discussed in this book came from psychologists who are alive now (or who were alive recently). However, to understand what researchers have discovered recently, it will help you to know about the ideas that led up to this point.

Early Roots of Psychology

Where and when did the study of psychology begin? Our existing historical records do not trace the earliest human efforts to understand the ways in which we humans think, feel, and act. In fact, historians now recognize that much of what we know—or think we know—about history reflects the points of view of those who have written the accounts of history. Historians—like the rest of us—are influenced by the society in which they are writing their historical records. In the field of psychology, the historical records that have reached us have been written primarily by Europeans. Therefore, these records have tended to highlight the contributions of Europeans and to downplay the contributions of non-Western cultures.

In this chapter, we trace the roots of psychology only as far back as ancient Greece. Actually, however, there were many highly sophisticated civilizations in Asia (e.g., ancient China) and Africa (e.g., ancient Egypt) for centuries before Europeans developed their civilization. Also, many technological advances occurred outside of Europe thousands of years before Europeans either imported them or invented them independently. Africans and Asians produced many developments in technology (e.g., agricultural methods and simple machines), medicine (e.g., herbal medications), literature (e.g., legends and a written alphabet), art (e.g., paintings and metalwork), and politics (e.g., hierarchical government and division of labor), among other fields.

At last, centuries later, the seeds of civilization reached the northern shores of the Mediterranean. There, the seeds took root and grew. The ancient Greeks recorded some early ideas about human psychology in their literature. Psychology even takes its name from the ancient Greek myth of *Psyche*.

Although we can learn much about psychology from literature, we usually trace the earliest roots of psychology to two different approaches to human behavior: philosophy and physiology. Persons who study *philosophy* try to understand the general nature of many aspects of the world. They do so mostly through **introspection** (*intro-*, inward, within; *-spect*, look; self-examination of inner ideas and experiences). In particular, the philosopher Plato (ca. 428–348 B.C.) urged his followers to use a **rationalist** (from *ratio*, meaning reason or thought) approach to understanding the world. Rationalists use philosophical analysis (reasoning) in order to understand human behavior, as well as other aspects of the world and people's interactions in the world.

You probably use rationalist approaches to handling many of the everyday situations you face. For instance, when you and a friend disagree regarding where to eat or what to do, you each offer supporting reasons for your choices, and you evaluate each other's arguments according to how well reasoned they seem to be. You are more likely to go along with your friend's ideas if your friend shows you good reasons for doing so.

An alternative tradition approaches psychology by studying *physiology* (the observation and study of functional processes in living beings). Aristotle (ca. 384–322 B.C.) (a biologist, as well as a philosopher) disagreed with Plato's rationalist, introspective approach. He preferred to use **empiricism.** That is, he believed that we learn what we want to know by gathering *empirical* evidence, which we can gain through experience and observation. The Aristotelian view is associated with empirical methods for conducting research. We use these methods in laboratories or in the field to observe how people think and behave. Empiricists tend to *induce* general principles or tendencies, based on observations of many specific instances of a phenomenon.

For example, empiricists might study why people sleep by observing humans and other animals before, while, and after they sleep. From their observations, they might come up with a few ideas about why sleep occurs. They would then devise some experiments to test their ideas. If the tests did not support their ideas, they would reject the ideas—no matter how clever or well reasoned the

How should historians address their natural tendency to view historical events in terms of their own society? How can historians gather information without relying only on the written records of people (usually men) who had the time, the education, and the knowledge to write such records?

introspection self-examination of inner ideas and experiences

rationalist person who believes that knowledge is most effectively acquired through reasoning

empiricism approach asserting that knowledge is most effectively acquired through observation

Rationalist Plato (ca. 428–348 B.C.) disagreed with empiricist Aristotle (ca. 384–322 B.C.) regarding the best path to knowledge.

ideas seemed to be. A rationalist, in contrast, might either reject the observations, if the ideas seemed well reasoned, or never make the observations in the first place.

You probably use empirical strategies in solving many of the problems you face. For example, when deciding to buy a car, you probably gather data (e.g., prices and features) about many cars. You may even read consumer reports about the fuel economy, maintenance and repair costs, and safety records of the cars that interest you. When you finally choose a car, your use of empirical data will increase the likelihood that you will be satisfied with your choice.

Scientific understanding relies on combining both empirical and rational approaches to studying human behavior. We must base our understanding on empirical studies of what is actually happening in the world. However, observations alone are not enough. We must also interpret what we observe in order to understand some of the general principles that govern the observed phenomena. By using rational methods, we can formulate theories and hypotheses that explain what we have observed.

In your everyday experiences as an amateur psychologist, you use both empiricism and rationalism. By observing (empirically) your own actions and those of the people around you, you notice patterns regarding how people think, feel, and act. You have probably noticed that many couples on a first date seem to feel nervous, acting clumsily and speaking awkwardly. You probably also have used reasoning to form your own informal theories regarding why people feel and act as they do on first dates. Both empiricism and rationalism aid you in your study of how people think, feel, and act.

Psychology has a long past, but only a short history.

Hermann Ebbinghaus

Emergence of Psychology: Diverse Perspectives

From its earliest beginnings, the field of psychology has used both rationalist and empiricist methods in trying to understand the human mind and behavior. The two main early psychological perspectives were structuralism and functionalism. The goal of **structuralism** was to understand the structure of the mind by studying the mind's parts and contents. Structuralists tried to analyze the contents of the mind into their basic elements. For example, a structuralist analysis of how people perceive a blade of grass might consider the shape, color, texture, and size of each blade. In contrast, **functionalism** focused on the processes of the human mind and behavior. Whereas structuralists asked, "What are the basic contents [structures] of the human mind?" functionalists asked, "What do people do, and how and why do they do it?"

A perspective closely tied to functionalism was **pragmatism,** which focused on finding practical uses for the study of the mind and behavior. Thus, pragmatists asked, "What can you do with your knowledge of psychology?" For example, pragmatists might be particularly interested in understanding how to use what we know about perception to help people to perceive situations accurately (e.g., in an air-traffic control tower), rather than in understanding the basic elements people perceive at a given time.

Associationism followed the early approaches of structuralism, functionalism, and pragmatism. It emphasized studying how events or ideas can become associated with one another in the mind, to result in a form of learning. For example, associationists might seek to discover links between perceptions regarding dangerous situations and particular outcomes of those situations. Some of the main theorists, methods of study, and criticisms of structuralism, functionalism (and pragmatism), and associationism are listed in Table 1-7.

MINILECTURE

Psychology in the 1800's and Beyond (Ch 2)

The fact that an opinion has been widely held is no evidence whatever that it is not utterly absurd.

Bertrand Russell

structuralism the first major school of thought in psychology, which focuses on analyzing the components of the mind, such as particular sensations

functionalism a school of psychology that focuses on active psychological processes, rather than on passive psychological structures or elements

pragmatism a school of psychology that focuses on the usefulness of knowledge

associationism a school of psychology that examines how events or ideas can become associated with one another in the mind

TABLE 1-7

Major Early Psychological Perspectives

Perspective	Key methods	Key thinkers	Key criticisms
Structuralism—The nature of consciousness; analysis of consciousness into its constituent components (elementary sensations)	Introspection (self-observation)	Wilhelm Wundt (1832–1920) Edward Titchener (1867–1927)	No means for understanding the processes of thought Lack of application to the world outside the structuralist's laboratory Rigid use of introspective techniques
Functionalism and pragmatism—Mental operations; practical uses of consciousness; the total relationship of the organism to its environment	Whatever works best	William James (1842–1910) John Dewey (1859–1952)	Too vague Too many different techniques Too much emphasis on applications of psychology; not enough study of fundamental issues
Associationism—Mental connections between two events or between two ideas, which lead to forms of learning	Empirical strategies, applied to self-observation and to animal studies	Hermann Ebbinghaus (1850–1909) Edward Lee Thorndike (1874–1949) Ivan Pavlov (1849–1936)	Overly simplistic Doesn't well explain cognition, emotion, or many other psychological processes

To get an idea of how psychologists from each of these early perspectives might approach a problem differently, suppose that you wanted to understand how you recognize the face of a friend. If you were a structuralist, you might analyze all the elements of your friend's face, including its size, shape, features, colors, and so on. If you were a functionalist or a pragmatist, you might focus on how the process of recognizing a friend's face serves useful purposes for you. If you were an associationist, you might study all the things and events you have associated with the face of your friend, which influence your recognition of your friend's face.

How did psychology emerge as a science? Psychology's roots stem from the rationalist traditions of philosophy and the empiricist traditions of physiology. Early psychological perspectives include structuralism, functionalism, pragmatism, and associationism.

WHAT ARE THE MAIN 20TH-CENTURY PERSPECTIVES ON PSYCHOLOGY?

MINILECTURE

Modern Psychology (Ch 2)

behaviorism a school of psychology that focuses entirely on the association between the environment and emitted behavior

Gestalt psychology a school of psychology holding that psychological phenomena are best understood when viewed as organized, structured wholes, rather than when analyzed into numerous components (pronounced "gess-TAHLT")

cognitivism a school of psychology that underscores the importance of perception, learning, and thought as bases for understanding much of human behavior

psychobiology a branch of psychology that seeks to understand behavior through studying anatomy and physiology, especially of the brain

During the 20th century, associationism became much more highly specialized in studying various types of learning through association (e.g., learning as a result of an association between a particular behavior and a particular reward; see Chapter 6). An outgrowth of associationism is the 20th-century psychological school of **behaviorism,** which emphasizes the study of observable behavior. Behaviorists have been especially interested in studying how an event in the environment may be linked to a particular observable behavior. They focus on trying to find ways to study extremely simple events and behaviors, which are much easier to control and to observe than are more complex ones.

Whereas behaviorism takes the whole of human experience and separates it into distinct behaviors, linked to particular events, **Gestalt psychology** emphasizes the importance of seeing certain psychological phenomena (such as anxiety or depression) as wholes, which Gestalt psychologists believe should not and cannot fruitfully be taken apart. To Gestaltists, "the whole [of a psychological phenomenon] differs from the sum of its parts." That is, behaviorists approached psychology *analytically* (breaking a whole psychological phenomenon into various elements), whereas Gestaltists approached it *holistically* (as a whole, without breaking it into parts).

Another school of psychology, **cognitivism,** uses both analytic and holistic approaches to understanding how people think. To cognitivists, even psychological phenomena such as depression and anxiety may be better understood by considering people's thoughts and their thought processes. For instance, cognitivistic treatments for anxiety and depression focus on changing maladaptive thought patterns to more adaptive ones. Cognitivists primarily use experimental methods, but they also use various other methods, such as case studies and tests in their efforts to understand how and why people think as they do.

Whereas cognitivists may use almost any approach to study the phenomena of human thinking, researchers in the field of **psychobiology** (also termed *biological psychology* or *physiological psychology*) may examine almost any psychological phenomenon by focusing on the physiological foundations underlying human thoughts, feelings, and actions. Psychobiologists interested in anxiety or depression would look for biological changes in the brain that might underlie these psychological states.

One of the best-known approaches to psychology has biological origins. Early in the 20th century, a *neurologist* (medical doctor who treats ailments of the brain and nervous system) came up with a very complex and wide-reaching theory based on his study of patients in his medical practice. The neurologist was Sigmund Freud, and his theory of human motivation, personality, and behavior is **psychodynamic psychology.** The clinical practice of Freud's psychodynamic theory is *psychoanalysis,* which is still being practiced by many psychiatrists and other psychotherapists today. Freudian theory and therapy emphasize the importance of unconscious forces that influence human motivation and behavior.

In contrast, **humanistic psychology** emphasizes conscious rather than unconscious experiences and psychological processes. Humanistic psychology also emphasizes that humans have free will and the ability to fulfill their great human potential. Whereas psychodynamic psychologists might treat anxiety and depression by focusing on unconscious forces underlying these psychological states, humanistic psychologists would focus on helping the individual to tap her or his own inner potentials for change, for self-healing, and for creating a sense of well-being.

Yet another perspective emphasizes an appreciation of how humans fulfill their great potential in a variety of ways, depending on the context in which they find themselves: According to **cultural psychology,** human thoughts, feelings, and actions depend largely on the cultural context in which people find themselves, particularly their culture (e.g., their social patterns and beliefs) and their gender (the social roles they assume, based on whether they are male or female). Cultural psychologists observe that the way in which people express depression and anxiety depends on the social context in which people live and on the social roles they assume. Similarly, the causes of people's feelings of anxiety and depression vary, depending on their social contexts and their social roles.

Table 1-8 summarizes some of the main theorists, methods of study, and criticisms of the 20th-century psychological perspectives. In the following chapter, we explore the basics of the psychobiological perspective.

What are the main 20th-century perspectives on psychology? The main 20th-century psychological perspectives include behaviorism, Gestalt psychology, cognitivism, psychodynamic psychology, psychobiology, humanistic psychology, and cultural psychology.

1-2

What was your Psy-Q? As you found in reading this chapter, (1) if you need help in an emergency situation, you are more likely to be helped if there are fewer people available to help you than if there are more people available to help. (2) Significant creative insights typically evolve over many years. (3) The persons most likely to cope effectively with long-term or terminal illness are

psychodynamic psychology a school of psychology that emphasizes the importance of (a) conflicting unconscious mental processes and (b) early childhood experiences

humanistic psychology a school of psychology that emphasizes human potential, as guided by holistic approaches to conscious experiences, rather than analytic approaches to unconscious experience

cultural psychology a school of psychology that emphasizes the importance of cultural context in the study of the human mind and behavior

TABLE 1-8
Major 20th-Century Psychological Perspectives

Perspective	Key methods	Key developers	Key criticisms
Behaviorism—Analysis of observable behavior without inferences about mental events	Experiments; often focus on animal subjects	John Watson B. F. Skinner	Doesn't address internal causes of behavior; often slights thoughts and emotions Doesn't explain many aspects of human behavior
Gestalt psychology—Holistic study of behavior; behavior not merely an additive sum of parts	Experiments and observation (focus on whole context, not on controlling separate variables)	Max Wertheimer Kurt Koffka Wolfgang Köhler	Lack of evidence to support theories Lack of experimental control Lack of precise definitions
Cognitivism—Perspective describing how people acquire, store, and use knowledge	Experiments and naturalistic observation	Herbert Simon Ulric Neisser	Many aspects of human behavior (e.g., social and cultural contexts) tend to be neglected
Psychobiology—Biological bases of learning, thought, and emotion; particular emphasis on the workings of the brain and nervous system	Experiments and case studies; examination of brains experiencing mental disorders	Roger Sperry and his students	Not all aspects of human behavior are now subject to investigation via biopsychological study; many aspects ethically may not be studied now in humans, and animal investigations sometimes may not generalize to humans
Psychodynamic psychology—Theory of personality development and psychotherapy; focus on unconscious experience in personal development	Psychoanalysis, based on clinical case studies	Sigmund Freud Neo-Freudians (e.g., Carl Jung, Erik Erikson)	Overreliance on case-study research; too little supporting evidence; cannot be disconfirmed Overly comprehensive
Humanistic psychology—Focus on free will and self-actualization of human potential, and on conscious rather than unconscious experience	Clinical practice and case-study observations; holistic rather than analytic approach	Abraham Maslow Carl Rogers	Theories not particularly comprehensive Limited research base
Cultural psychology—Study of how people think, feel, and act in the cultural context in which they find themselves	Naturalistic observations and surveys of people within various cultural and social contexts	Patricia Greenfield Michael Cole	Not enough emphasis on experimentation Not enough emphasis on the role of biological influences on the human mind and behavior Not enough emphasis on individuals and on individual differences

unrealistically optimistic about their own ability to cope with the problems of having the illness.

If you did not predict these answers accurately, congratulations! You found out why psychologists have to do research to find answers to questions about how people think, feel, and act—we cannot know the answers to such questions without conducting scientific research. If you did predict these answers accurately, congratulations! Although you probably will not pass the final for this course without doing any reading or attending any lectures, you probably will be able to come up with some insightful hypotheses to test when conducting psychological research.

What Is Psychology? **4**

1. *Psychology,* the study of the human mind and behavior, is a *social science.* Psychologists try to understand how people think, learn, perceive, feel, interact with others, and understand themselves.

Why Do Psychologists Do What They Do? **7**

2. Psychologists seek to describe, explain, predict, and perhaps even sometimes control the human mind and behavior. Often, particular research, however, addresses only one or two of these goals. Scientific research is cumulative, with new studies building on old ones.

How Do Psychologists Conduct Research? **11**

3. Psychologists use various research methods, such as (a) *tests and surveys;* (b) *case studies;* (c) *naturalistic observation;* and (d) *experiments.*

4. In an *experiment,* a researcher studies *cause-and-effect relations* by controlling one or more *independent variables* in order to observe the effects on one or more *dependent variables.* Ideally, an experiment should include a *control group* to ensure that differences in results are due to the experimental treatment and not to irrelevant group differences.

How Do Psychologists Determine Cause and Effect? **16**

5. Because we generally cannot conduct studies on whole populations, we use *sample statistics* (numbers that characterize the sample we have assessed), generally based on the assumption that the researcher has found a *random sample* of the population under study.

6. We are never able to prove the *null hypothesis* (which states that there is no difference between two or more groups under study). Even so, we can demonstrate that a particular difference has reached a given level of *statistical significance*—that is, the difference is unlikely to have occurred due to random fluctuations of the data.

7. Psychological researchers try to draw causal inferences (conclusions about cause-and-effect relationships). *Controlled experimental designs* are better suited to drawing such inferences than are *quasi-experimental designs,* which lack at least one experimental characteristic, or than are *correlational studies,* which show associations between variables.

What Ethical Issues Do Psychologists Face? **22**

8. Scientists, including psychologists, must address questions of ethical research procedures. Most questions center on whether human participants or animal subjects are treated fairly. Research institutions today have standard policies that require both *informed consent* and *debriefing.* Most institutions have also set up boards of review to study and approve proposed research; some government agencies also monitor research practices, especially as they pertain to animals.

How Did Psychology Emerge as a Science? **24**

9. By studying the historical development in issues of *philosophy* and *physiology,* we can trace the history of the foundations of psychology. Some of the most important questions in the history of psychology are whether *rationalist* or *empiricist* methods are the better way to gain knowledge. In fact, a combination of both methods typically works best.

10. Psychology traces its roots back to archaic Greece. In fact, the word *psychology* (the study of the mind and behavior) is derived from the Greek word *psyche.*

11. The ancient Greek philosophers Plato and Aristotle raised issues that continue to be discussed today. Plato was a *rationalist,* emphasizing the use of reasoning as a way to find knowledge. Aristotle emphasized the world we can see and touch as the route to reality and truth, which made him an *empiricist.* In contrast to Plato, Aristotle believed that knowledge is learned through interactions with and direct observation of the environment.

12. Over time, psychologists have approached the study of the mind and behavior from different perspectives. At first, *structuralists* tried to analyze consciousness into its constituent components in terms of elementary sensations.

13. *Functionalists* tried to understand what people do and why. A similar outlook was adopted by *pragmatists,* who focused on how to apply knowledge to practice.

14. *Associationism* examines how events or ideas can become associated with one another in the mind, to result in a form of learning.

What Are the Main 20th-Century Perspectives on Psychology? **28**

15. An offshoot of associationism, *behaviorism,* is based on the belief that the science of psychology should deal only with observable behavior.

16. *Gestalt psychology* is based on the notion that the whole differs from the sum of its parts.

17. *Cognitivism* emphasizes the importance of understanding how people think.

18. The basis of *psychodynamic psychology* is that many of the thoughts and feelings that motivate behavior are unconscious.

19. *Psychobiology* studies how human physiology interacts with human behavior.

20. *Humanistic psychology* studies how people consciously fulfill their inner potential.

21. *Cultural psychology* studies how people think, feel, and act in relation to the social context in which they find themselves.

PATHWAYS TO KNOWLEDGE

Choose the best answer to complete each sentence.

1. Many psychologists study the behavior of college students
   (a) simply because it is relatively easy to do so.
   (b) because the behavior of college students is typical of that of most intelligent people.
   (c) because the behavior of college students offers a good role model of how people should behave.
   (d) because college students are much more cooperative with experimenters than are other research participants.

2. The four main goals of psychological research are
   (a) description, explanation, control, and verifiability.
   (b) description, assessment, explanation, and manipulation.
   (c) description, assessment, prediction, and manipulation.
   (d) description, explanation, control, and prediction.

3. When psychologists say that a particular research finding is statistically significant, they mean that the finding is
   (a) going to be very important in the field of interest.
   (b) unlikely to have occurred by chance.
   (c) going to lead to important psychological treatments.
   (d) going to have many widespread applications outside of the psychological laboratory.

4. An independent variable is
   (a) the only variable of interest.
   (b) a variable that is independently verified.
   (c) a variable with a value that depends on the value of the dependent variable.
   (d) a variable that is manipulated by the experimenter.

5. When psychologists notice that two characteristics always seem to go together, they
   (a) are usually able to say which characteristic caused the other one to occur.
   (b) cannot come to any conclusions regarding causality unless they get more information.
   (c) determine that the characteristics are multiplicatively correlated.
   (d) determine that the characteristics are inversely correlated.

6. An experimental condition differs from a control condition, in that
   (a) participants in the control condition stay the same while participants in the experimental condition vary.
   (b) the experimental treatment is applied in the experimental condition but not in the control condition.
   (c) the experimenter controls the control condition but does not control the experimental condition.
   (d) the treatment varies in the control condition while the treatment stays constant in the experimental condition.

7. Scientists are better able to draw conclusions about the effectiveness of a particular treatment when they
   (a) study people who are not exposed to the experimental treatment, as well as people who are exposed to it.

(b) expose a group of people to the treatment and then carefully study all of the effects of the treatment on those people.
(c) study female volunteers who receive the treatment and compare them with male volunteers who do not receive the treatment.
(d) give the treatment to people who ask for the treatment and to people who do not ask for it, and then they compare the treatment results for the two groups.

Answer each of the following questions by filling in the blank with an appropriate word or phrase.

8. _____ is a research method in which a participant's behavior is observed in its natural environment.

9. Scientists generate _____, which are predictions or tentative proposals regarding expectations for research outcomes.

10. An _____ is a controlled investigation in which a researcher studies the effects of one or more variables on one or more other variables.

11. An example of a _____ design would be a study examining whether certain personality variables are correlated with criminal behavior.

Match the following theories to their main emphases:

12. Structuralism
13. Functionalism

14. Pragmatism

15. Associationism

16. Behaviorism

17. Gestalt psychology

18. Cognitivism

(a) Functions of thought
(b) Mental connections between two events or between two ideas, which lead to forms of learning
(c) Analysis of conscious experience into its constituent components (elementary sensations)
(d) The workings of the brain and nervous system, as they affect thoughts, emotions, and actions
(e) Theory of personality development and psychotherapy focusing on unconscious experiences in personal development
(f) Practical uses of psychological research
(g) Analysis of observable behavior without considering inferences about mental events

19. Psychobiology

    (h) Self-actualization of human potential, based primarily on conscious rather than unconscious experience

20. Psychodynamic psychology

    (i) Understanding how people think in order to understand human behavior

21. Humanistic psychology

    (j) Holistic study of behavior, rather than analysis of an additive sum of parts

22. Cultural psychology

    (k) The cultural contexts in which people think, feel, and act

Answers

1. a, 2. d, 3. b, 4. d, 5. b, 6. b, 7. a, 8. Naturalistic observation, 9. hypotheses, 10. experiment, 11. correlational, 12. c, 13. a, 14. f, 15. b, 16. g, 17. j, 18. i, 19. d, 20. e, 21. h, 22. k

PATHWAYS TO UNDERSTANDING

1. If you could naturalistically observe a psychological phenomenon that differs across cultures, what would you study, and in what cultures would you study it? Why would this phenomenon interest you?

2. If you were in charge of an ethics committee charged with deciding which experiments should be permitted, what questions about the experiments would you want to have answered?

3. How did early psychological perspectives pave the way for 20th-century perspectives?

CHAPTER OUTLINE

What Is Our Biological History?
Evolutionary Theory
Genetics

How Is the Nervous System Organized?
The Central Nervous System
 How to Master Difficult Material and
How to Prepare for a Test
The Peripheral Nervous System

What Are the Major Structures and Functions of the Human Brain?
Viewing the Brain
Structures and Functions of the Brain
The Cerebral Hemispheres and the
Cerebral Cortex

How Is Information Processed in the Nervous System?
Neurons
Conduction of Information Within
Neurons
Communication Between Neurons

How Does the Endocrine System Work?

Biological Psychology

Grace, who had been a very loving and patient mother to Mercedes and Roxanne when they were little girls, was now an emotional terrorist, ready to explode at any time. One Thanksgiving, Mercedes had finished making the gravy and started calling the guests to the table to eat. Their family tradition was that as soon as everyone was seated at the table, and before anyone began to eat, each person took a turn acknowledging something for which she or he felt grateful. Before anyone else was seated, however, Grace sat down and immediately started serving herself and eating. Mercedes—surprised—teased her mother, "Hey, let's wait until everyone else sits down before we start eating." Grace jumped up, screaming, "You don't want to give me any food. You just want me to starve to death! I'm going somewhere I can get something to eat!" That instant, Grace grabbed her purse, ran to her car, and drove off, while everyone else stood around the front door, stunned.

In retrospect, Mercedes and Roxanne recalled this incident as an early sign of the trouble that lay ahead. As the years passed, more and more aspects of Grace's life became unmanageable. Her relationships with family and friends were volatile, and many of Grace's friends stopped seeing her altogether. Even her job performance suffered. Accustomed to receiving honors and praise for her academic and educational achievements early in her life, Grace ended up being forced to retire early because her job performance was grossly inadequate. At last, at age 60, Grace was diagnosed as having *Alzheimer's disease,* a brain disorder that starts by attacking the person's thought processes, continues by destroying the individual's personality and emotions, and ends by destroying the person's ability to control the physiological functions that sustain life.

For Grace, the link between her brain and her thinking seemed evident as the devastating disorder that attacked her brain increasingly impaired her ability to think, as well as to feel and eventually even to function at all. For most of us, however, this link is not quite so obvious. For thousands of years, philosophers and scientists have tried to understand the relationship between the body (the brain) and the mind (how we think, feel, etc.). How do the mind and body interact? Can they even be separated? What happens to our bodies when we "lose our minds"? How do our brains enable us to think, speak, plan, reason, learn, remember, and feel emotion?

Psychobiologists want to know about both human anatomy and human physiology. *Anatomy* is the study of structures of the body and of the interrelationships among these structures; *structures* are the organized physical parts of the body. *Physiology* is the study of the functions and processes of the body; *functions* are processes that serve useful purposes. Psychobiologists study anatomy and physiology in order to discover the biological bases for how we think, feel, and act.

WHAT IS OUR BIOLOGICAL HISTORY?

One way of studying the biological bases of the mind and of behavior is to investigate heredity and evolution: How do your distinctive inherited characteristics affect what you do, think, and feel, and how does our shared human inheritance affect our common human actions, thoughts, and feelings?

Evolutionary Theory

Evolutionary theory describes changes in physiology and behavior across many generations of individuals. In 1859, Charles Darwin (1809–1882) proposed that species have developed and changed over time. These changes occur through **natural selection,** known commonly as "survival of the fittest." At any given time, some members of some species may be able to cope with the conditions in the environment better than do others. The individuals who can cope most effectively are most likely to survive and to reproduce most often, as compared with individuals who are less fit. In contrast, the individuals who are not as fit may die sooner and may produce fewer offspring. In fact, if all members of a particular species are unsuited to the environment, the entire species may become extinct. Ultimately, more fit individuals are selected by nature for survival—hence, the term *natural selection.*

The key to natural selection is the relationship between individuals and the environment in which they are trying to survive (and to produce offspring). For example, an individual who was a relatively slow runner but who had terrific rock-climbing skill would be unlikely to survive in an environment with large, open plains, in which the ability to run from predators was crucial. On the other hand, that same individual would probably survive quite well in a very mountainous environment, in which a less skilled individual might be more likely to fall while trying to climb away from predators on rocky cliffs. Thus, natural selection might lead to the survival of some individuals with particular characteristics in one kind of environment but different individuals, with different characteristics, in another kind of environment. Natural selection affects only those characteristics that help or hinder the individual in surviving until adulthood, finding a mate, and ultimately producing offspring.

If environments—and all the living creatures in the environments—never changed, there would be no evolution. However, environments are constantly changing. Volcanoes build new land areas, weather changes cause droughts and floods, and so on. These changes lead to changes in the natural selection of plants and animals that will survive in the environment. If a given animal's food source dies away, and the animal cannot find a new food source, that animal will not survive. These constant changes in environment lead to changes in the natural selection of which individuals will survive. According to Darwin, the changing natural selection of individuals explains evolutionary changes in species, which are now well documented through fossils.

How have Darwin's ideas about natural selection come to influence psychology? For one thing, the study of evolution has made us more aware of how the human brain affects human behavior. Throughout human evolution, our brains have provided us with greater ability to control what we do voluntarily. Over time, our actions have become more voluntary and less instinctual than the actions of other animals.

Humans can learn to like anything, that's why we are such a successful species. . . . You can drop humans anywhere and they'll thrive—only the rat does as well.

Jeanette Desor

Adapt or perish, now as ever, is Nature's inexorable imperative.

H. G. Wells

What aspects of your own behavior—and the behavior of those you observe—seem to you to originate in our evolutionary adaptation to early human environments?

natural selection evolutionary mechanism by which organisms have developed and changed, based on what is commonly called the "survival of the fittest"

In the late nineteenth-century, a dark and a light variety of moths living in the forests of England illustrated the principle of natural selection. When industrial pollution blackened the forests, the darker moths were less visible to the birds that ate them, so they increased in number. The lighter moths became fewer in number because they were so easily seen against the sooty trees. Recently, however, air-pollution controls have reduced the amount of soot on the trees, and the light moth is making a comeback.

Genetics

A key mechanism by which natural selection may occur relates to *genetics*, the study of inherited variations among individuals. Natural selection can occur as a result of genetic *mutation*, a sudden permanent change in an inherited characteristic. Genetic mutation permits brand-new characteristics to appear between one generation and the next. Mutations may arise as a result of exposure to radiation, infectious agents (e.g., bacteria or viruses), harmful chemicals, or various other environmental influences. Most mutations are harmful and lead to reduced adaptability to the environment. Occasionally, though, a mutation helps an individual adapt, in which case it favors that individual over others in the struggle for survival.

Genetic mutations occur in the **genes,** the physiological building blocks through which we inherit particular characteristics. Genes are parts of chromosomes, rod-shaped bodies containing many genes. Humans have 23 pairs of **chromosomes,** for a total of 46 (23 x 2). Almost all of the cells of your body have each of these 23 pairs of chromosomes. The genetic material contained in chromosomes is deoxyribonucleic acid (DNA).

Our genes determine our *genetic traits*, distinctive inherited characteristics that govern everything from our eye color to our blood type. We receive our genes, and therefore our traits, when we are conceived by our parents. The genetic makeup of a specific pair of genes an individual receives for a given trait forms that individual's **genotype** for that trait.

Some genes dominate other genes. Thus, when two different genes are paired, the dominant (stronger) genes appear in an individual's **phenotype,** which is the observable outcome of heredity. Whenever a gene for a **dominant trait** (a strong attribute—e.g., brown eyes) is paired with a gene for a **recessive trait** (a weaker, dominated characteristic—e.g., blue eyes), the dominant trait shows up in the phenotype, but the recessive trait does not. That is, when both a dominant gene and a recessive gene are present, the phenotype shows only the dominant trait.

Figure 2-1 illustrates how dominant and recessive traits may be expressed. The first chart (a) shows the possible outcomes when a parent with brown eyes (a phenotype of brown eyes and a genotype with two dominant genes for brown eyes—BB) produces children with a parent who has blue eyes (a phenotype of blue eyes and a genotype with two recessive genes for blue eyes—bb). As the chart shows, all the potential offspring appear to have brown eyes, but all of them have a *mixed genotype* (containing both a dominant and a recessive gene for a given trait)

gene a basic physiological building block for the hereditary transmission of genetic traits in all life forms

chromosomes rod-shaped bodies that contain innumerable genes; occur in pairs

genotype the genetic makeup for inherited traits, which is *not* subject to environmental influence (except in cases of genetic mutation)

phenotype expression of an inherited trait, based on the dominant expression of the trait in the genotype and also subject to environmental influence

dominant trait the stronger expression of a genetic trait, which appears in the phenotype of an organism when the genotype comprises two dominant expressions of a trait or a dominant and a recessive expression of a trait

recessive trait the weaker expression of a genetic trait in a pair of traits, which appears in the phenotype when the genotype comprises two recessive expressions of the trait

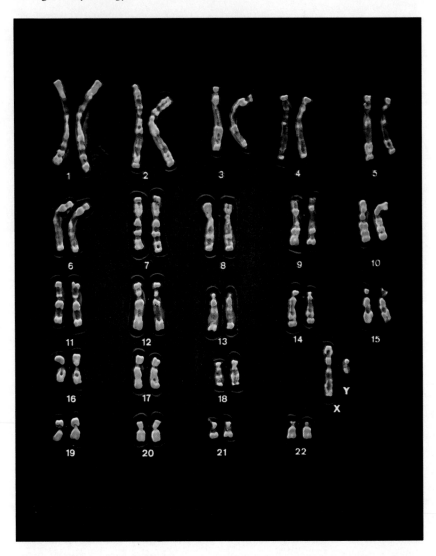

Humans have 23 pairs of chromosomes, including the pair that determines each person's sex.

The natural world is dynamic. From the expanding universe to the hair on a baby's head, nothing is the same from now to the next moment.

Helen Hoover

for eye color (Bb). As Figure 2-1(b) shows, when two parents with a mixed genotype (a phenotype for brown eyes) produce children, any of three outcomes are possible for each of their children: a phenotype for brown eyes with a BB genotype (1 chance in 4), a phenotype for blue eyes with a bb genotype (1 chance in 4), or a phenotype for brown eyes with a mixed genotype (Bb or bB; 2 chances in 4, or 1 chance in 2).

In fact, the expression of hereditary characteristics is more complicated than this description might lead you to believe. (For instance, more than one gene may be involved in the expression of a given trait.) Moreover, a single genotype can be expressed as a range of phenotypes. For example, a person's height is highly heritable, but particular individuals may show a range of heights, depending on other factors such as nutrition. Genes help to determine phenotypes, but the environment also influences the expression of our inherited traits.

Human heredity is highly complex, and many variables influence how heredity is expressed. Therefore, researchers have trouble controlling all the variables necessary to study it effectively in humans. Genetically identical twins provide an effective way to study genetic influences on our biological and psychological makeup. Because twins have an identical genetic inheritance, any differences between them can be attributed to environmental influences. Based on twin studies and other evidence, scientists have concluded that both our heredity and our environment are important, and both work together to influence the human mind and behavior.

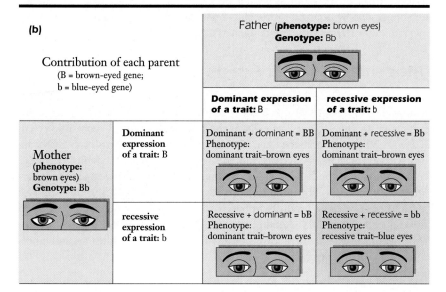

Figure 2-1

**Inherited Characteristics—
Eye Color**
*(a) What are the possible outcomes when a
brown-eyed parent (genotype BB) and a blue-
eyed parent (genotype bb) produce children?
(b) What are the possible outcomes when two
brown-eyed parents with mixed genotypes (Bb)
produce children? What are the possible genotypes and phenotypes of the children of these
couples?*

Finding Your Way   **2-1**

*Make a list of 10 of your physical characteristics that are due, at least in
part, to inheritance (e.g., eye color, height, ease of developing muscle strength,
keen vision, tendency to develop ailments such as diabetes, sickle-cell anemia,
or arthritis). Make three columns next to your list: (1) "Adaptive advantage";
(2) "Adaptive disadvantage"; and (3) "No adaptive effects." For each item in
your list, indicate the adaptive advantages and disadvantages, or indicate "no
effects." To what kinds of environments are you well suited?*

MINILECTURE

Traits (Ch 3)

The preceding section sketched how our genetic inheritance affects our biological makeup. We also hinted that our inherited anatomy and physiology, our biological makeup, affect many aspects of our mind—how we think, feel, and act.
Two physiological systems powerfully affect our mind and behavior: the nervous
system and the endocrine (hormonal) system. To psychologists, the nervous system, discussed next, is the primary one of these two systems. The endocrine system
is discussed at the conclusion of this chapter.

What is our biological history? Our biological history has been shaped by the processes of evolution (involving natural selection); organisms that survive to reproductive age are able to pass on their traits through the mechanisms of genetic transmission.

HOW IS THE NERVOUS SYSTEM ORGANIZED?

The *nervous system* is a physiological network that enables us to interact with the environment. Through it, we receive, process, and respond to information about the environment and about ourselves. In this section, we describe the major subdivisions and specialized structures of the human nervous system. Following this section, we describe the brain in greater detail. We conclude our discussion of the nervous system by noting how information moves through it. (Figure 2-2 shows a diagram of the overall structure of the nervous system.)

The Central Nervous System

The softest, freest, most pliable and changeful living substance . . . the hardest and most iron-bound as well.

Charlotte Perkins Gilman

The nervous system is divided into two main parts: the central nervous system (comprising the brain and spinal cord) and the peripheral nervous system (comprising all the other nerves throughout the body). The **central nervous system** (CNS) also has two parts: the brain and the spinal cord. Both parts of the CNS are protected by an outer bony covering and by an inner liquid cushion. The clear, colorless liquid that moves around throughout the brain and the spinal cord is *cerebrospinal fluid* (CSF). The brain is constantly producing fresh CSF. The CSF also helps to remove waste products from the CNS, as does the rich supply of blood that nourishes the CNS. Another physiological protection for the brain is the *blood–brain barrier*, a dense network of tiny blood vessels that filter the substances that enter or leave the brain.

central nervous system the part of the nervous system comprising the brain and the spinal cord, including all of the neurons therein

The Brain and the Spinal Cord

The **brain** is the organ in our bodies that is most directly responsible for our thoughts, emotions, and motivations. The importance of the brain's activity is shown by the fact that it uses up considerably more of the body's resources than would seem to be justified by its size: It accounts for only 2.5% (one fortieth) of the weight of an adult human body, but it uses about 20% (one fifth) of the circulating blood, of the available *glucose* (the blood sugar that supplies the body with energy), and of the available oxygen (the gas we pull in from the air through breathing).

brain the organ of the body that most directly controls thoughts, emotions, motivations, and actions, and that responds to information received from elsewhere in the body, such as through sensory receptors

In your brain is a huge number of **neurons** (nerve cells). Individual neurons work together to form nerves. **Nerves** are organized strings of neurons that extend from your brain down through the center of your back to the rest of your body, by way of your spinal cord. Your **spinal cord** is a complex tangle of nerves that stretch from your brain to your tailbone. Your skull encloses and protects your brain, and your spinal column protects your spinal cord. Your *spinal column* consists of a series of interconnected *vertebrae*, your backbone. One function of the spinal cord is to collect information from the outlying nerves (in the peripheral nervous system) and to *transmit* (send) this information to the brain. A complementary function is to relay information back from the brain to the outlying nerves.

neuron nerve cell, involved in neural communication within the nervous system

nerve bundle of neurons that can be observed as a fiber extending from the central nervous system out to various parts of the body

spinal cord a slender, roughly cylindrical bundle of interconnected neural fibers, which is enclosed within the spinal column and which extends through the center of the back, starting at the brain and ending at the base of the spine

The two-directional communication of the nervous system involves two different kinds of nerves and neurons: receptors and effectors. In general, a **receptor**

receptor a physiological structure designed to receive something (e.g., a given substance or a particular kind of information), such as sensory information from the sense organs

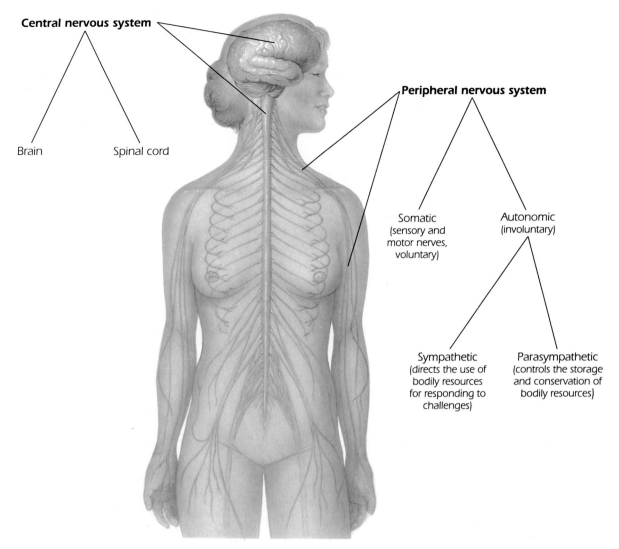

Figure 2-2
Divisions of the Nervous System
The main divisions of the nervous system are the central nervous system (which comprises the brain and the spinal cord) and the peripheral nervous system (which comprises the somatic nervous system and the autonomic nervous system).

Right now, what sensory information is your brain receiving from your receptor nerves and neurons? What kinds of movements (e.g., of your eyes, hands, and so on) are you making now, as a result of effector nerves and neurons that are transmitting information from your brain and spinal cord?

is something (such as a structure of the body) that receives something else (such as a message or a substance). In particular, receptor nerves and neurons receive *sensory information* (e.g., sights, sounds, smells) from the outlying nerves of the body. The receptors then transmit that information back up through the spinal cord to the brain. In the opposite direction, **effectors** transmit information from the CNS to the outlying nerves of the body. For voluntary movements, our brains transmit *motor information* (e.g., regarding movements of the muscles) telling our bodies what to do. Sometimes, however, our bodies make involuntary movements.

Spinal Reflexes

The involuntary, automatic reactions of our bodies are termed **reflexes.** During reflexive reactions, the spinal cord transmits a message directly from receptor nerves to effector nerves. On these occasions, the message does not pass through the brain until after the body has responded to the sensory information (see Figure 2-3).

effectors the neurons and nerves that transmit motor information from the brain through the spinal cord (voluntary movements) or directly from the spinal cord (reflexes), thus controlling bodily responses

reflex an automatic physiological response to an external stimulus, which occurs directly through the spinal cord

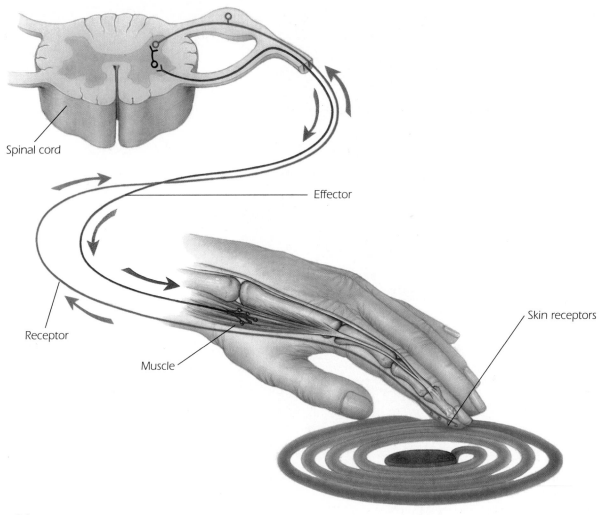

Figure 2-3
Spinal Reflex
Sometimes, the spinal cord transforms incoming information from receptor nerves directly into outgoing information that is then sent to effector nerves. These direct-connection responses, termed reflexes, *allow for speedy protective reactions.*

Our body is a machine for living. It is organized for that, it is its nature.

Leo Tolstoy

What kinds of outcomes might occur if humans had no spinal reflexes?

Reflexes offer much faster responses than do voluntary responses. For example, it takes only about 50 *milliseconds* (thousandths of a second) from the time a particular place in your knee is tapped until your calf and foot jerk forward. In comparison, it takes many hundreds of milliseconds for you to move your knee in response to your voluntary decision to move it.

Quick reflexes allow the body to respond immediately to particular sensory information, bypassing the route through the brain. For example, when you touch a very hot oven, you immediately withdraw your hand. You do not pause to think, "Gosh, that hurts. I should probably move away from that." Reflexes do more than just help us to avoid pain. They also help us to minimize any damage that might result from whatever is causing the pain (e.g., fires or cuts). Thus, our reflexes better enable us to survive.

Through the reflex response, the spinal cord can act alone. However, the spinal cord has no conscious awareness of pain or of any other sensations. For conscious awareness to occur, the sensation must reach the brain.

In sum, the body is an exceptionally well-organized system. Lower levels in the command system can respond without going through the brain when an immediate need arises. However, higher levels in the system are needed for us to understand and to interact meaningfully with the world around us.

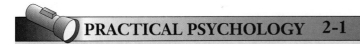

PRACTICAL PSYCHOLOGY 2-1

How to Master Difficult Material and How to Prepare for a Test

1. Make sure that you understand the key terms in the material you are learning. Look up any important words you do not know. In the margins of this textbook are definitions of many of the key terms in each chapter; also, a glossary of terms appears at the end of the book. In addition, you may want to keep a dictionary handy to look up unfamiliar words that may not be defined in the margins or in the glossary.

2. Make a study guide for yourself. Include in your guide some lists of key points, terms, and ideas, as well as any other important information you find difficult to remember. When you rehearse (practice learning) the material, review your own notes, as well as the summaries provided in your textbook.

3. Try to learn the information in a form that matches the form in which you will want to remember the information later. For instance, if your instructor likes to give quizzes that match each structure of the brain or nervous system with the function of each structure, practice matching the structures and their functions while you are studying for the quiz.

4. Make up your own cues for retrieving information. Often, the most effective cues relate the new information to what you already know. Some students make drawings or charts that make it easier for them to remember material. Other students make up little songs or rhymes (e.g., "receptors get clues from the eyes and the nose; effectors cause wiggles in lips and in toes"). Another technique is to make up word games for steps in a process or for parts that make up a whole. (For instance, a word game for linking the lobes in the brain to their functions might be to think of function words that have the same initial letters as the names of the lobes: "forethought [frontal lobe—planning], prickling [parietal lobe—skin sensations], twanging [temporal lobe—hearing], and observing [occipital lobe—vision].")

5. Until you know your own stylistic preferences for studying, use a variety of techniques (e.g., talking with others, writing notes, drawing pictures or charts, making and using flash cards). Once you have tried various techniques, drop the use of techniques that do not work well for you, and increase your use of techniques that seem effective. Tailor your study habits to your own preferred style of learning. Review information in a format that most effectively helps you to recall the information.

6. Overlearn the information that you will want to recall at the time of the test. If you can just barely remember the information when you are reviewing the material, it will probably be difficult to recall it easily when you are experiencing the stress of a testing situation. If you know the material extremely well outside of the testing situation, however, you will probably perform well on the test.

7. If you feel overly anxious as you get ready to take a test, take steps to relax yourself. For example, concentrate on breathing slowly and deeply. While continuing to breathe slowly and deeply, alternately tense and then relax each of your major muscles, starting at the tips of your toes and working your way up to your face muscles.

8. Your efforts to study hard will be rewarded. Even if you do not achieve the grades you hope for, you will come much closer to doing so if you work hard. You are more likely to do well when you recognize that motivation and effort are important to your success (Noel, Forsyth, & Kelley, 1987).

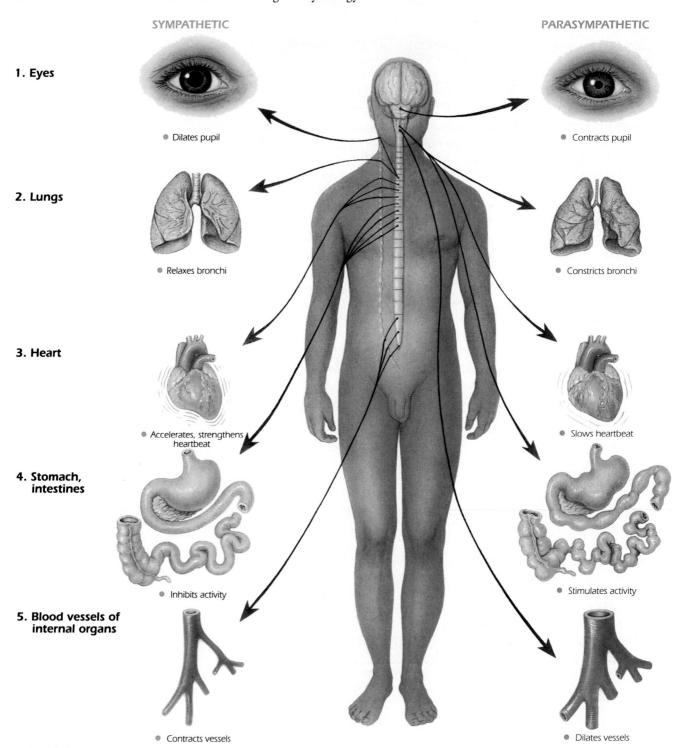

SYMPATHETIC

PARASYMPATHETIC

1. Eyes

● Dilates pupil

● Contracts pupil

2. Lungs

● Relaxes bronchi

● Constricts bronchi

3. Heart

● Accelerates, strengthens heartbeat

● Slows heartbeat

4. Stomach, intestines

● Inhibits activity

● Stimulates activity

5. Blood vessels of internal organs

● Contracts vessels

● Dilates vessels

Figure 2-4

The Autonomic Nervous System

The two parts of the autonomic nervous system are the sympathetic nervous system (identified with red labels) and the parasympathetic nervous system (identified with blue labels), both of which are involved in metabolism and other self-regulating physiological processes.

The human body, including the brain, may be exceptionally well organized, but the human ability to absorb a lot of new information has its limits. Before you read about any more new terms or about any more details of the body and the brain, you may want to take a moment to read the information in Practical Psychology 2-1, which offers some suggestions for how to master difficult and complex material and how to prepare for taking a test.

The Peripheral Nervous System

MINILECTURE
*Organization of the
Nervous System (Cb 3)*

The CNS includes the brain and spinal cord; the **peripheral nervous system** (PNS) includes all the other nerve cells, which lie outside of the brain and spinal cord. The PNS even includes the nerves of the face and head that are not part of the brain. Essentially, the PNS helps to get information back and forth between the CNS and the rest of the body. The PNS connects with receptors that receive information from our external sensory organs (e.g., skin and eyes) and from our internal body organs (e.g., stomach and heart). It also connects with effectors in parts of the body that let you wink, wiggle your toes (or your nose), and so on. Most of the PNS nerves lack the surrounding protective bone that encases the brain and spinal cord.

The PNS has two main parts: (1) the *somatic nervous system*, which controls relatively quick, voluntary movements of the muscles attached to our skeleton; and (2) the *autonomic nervous system*, which controls movement of our nonskeletal muscles. Our *nonskeletal muscles* include the heart muscles, the blood vessels, and the muscles of the internal body organs (e.g., the muscles of the digestive tract). We have little or no voluntary control over the muscles of the autonomic (*auto-*, self; *-nomic*, governing or regulating) nervous system. We are usually not even aware of their functioning. In general, the autonomic nervous system responds more slowly and for longer periods of time than does the somatic nervous system.

The autonomic nervous system itself is divided into two parts: the sympathetic nervous system and the parasympathetic nervous system (see Figure 2-4). Both systems are involved with your metabolism. Through *metabolism*, your body captures, stores, and uses energy and material resources from food, and it gets rid of whatever your body does not use. In general, your sympathetic nervous system uses up your bodily resources to help you do whatever you need to do, such as when you confront challenging situations; your parasympathetic nervous system, on the other hand, helps you to store and to conserve your bodily resources so that you will have them when you need them.

How is the nervous system organized? The nervous system is organized into two main parts: the central nervous system (which comprises the brain and the spinal cord) and the peripheral nervous system (which comprises all the nerves in our body that are outside of the brain and the spinal cord).

WHAT ARE THE MAJOR STRUCTURES AND FUNCTIONS OF THE HUMAN BRAIN?

Psychobiologists are particularly interested in the human brain. Before we explore *what* scientists have learned about the brain, it may be helpful to find out *how* scientists have learned what they know.

Viewing the Brain

Scientists can use many methods for studying the human brain. For centuries, investigators have been able to *dissect* (separate into parts for examination) a brain after a person has died. Even today, this method is often used for studying the brain. In particular, researchers look carefully at people whose behavior shows signs of brain damage while they are alive. The researchers document these case studies of patients as thoroughly as possible. Later, after the patients die, the researchers examine the patients' brains for *lesions* (areas where body tissue has been damaged).

The brain is the last and greatest biological frontier . . . the most complex thing we have yet discovered in the universe.

James Watson

peripheral nervous system one of the two main parts of the nervous system, comprising the nerve cells that lie outside of the brain and the spinal cord, including the nerves of the face and head

TABLE 2-1

Techniques for Viewing the Brain

Technique	What questions can be answered by using these techniques?
Techniques performed on a nonliving brain	
Dissection—Separating and observing the structures of the brain with the naked eye, with microscopes, and with various special techniques for studying details about the brain's chemistry and biology	How do the various structures of the brain normally look, and how are they organized in the brain? How do case records of a person's unusual behavior relate to abnormalities in the person's brain?
Techniques performed on living animals	
Surgical procedures—(a) Create specific injuries in particular locations in the animal's brain, then carefully observe how those injuries affect the animal's ability to function. (b) Implant tiny devices that conduct electrical activity to or from body tissues, electrically stimulate particular locations in the brain, and observe the animal's behavior.	What kinds of functions and behaviors are affected by lesions or by electrical stimulation in particular locations in the brain?
Techniques that investigate the living human brain	
Electroencephalograms (EEGs) and *event-related potentials* (ERPs) record changes in electrical activity across large areas of the brain.	How does the brain behave differently when a person is dreaming? Does brain activity appear odd in a person who behaves abnormally?
X-ray photos and *angiograms* use X rays to show the bones or the blood vessels in the head. In *computerized axial tomograms* (CAT scans), a computer analyzes a rotating series of X rays and produces images showing detailed cross-sectional slices of the brain.	Is there any damage to the skull that might affect the brain? Are there any abnormalities of the blood flow to the brain? Do the major structures in the brain appear normal?
In *magnetic resonance imaging* (MRI), a computer analyzes the information from a rotating scanner that detects magnetic changes in the molecules of the brain. The computer then generates a picture of the brain, which is much more precise than CAT-scan images.	What are some detailed features of the structures of this brain? How do unusual characteristics of a person's behavior relate to unusual features of the person's brain?
Positron emission tomography (PET scan) is based on the notion that areas of the brain that are working the hardest are also using the most glucose. PET scans show much more clearly the active workings of the brain than do studies that measure electrical activity.	Which parts of the brain are working hardest during various kinds of mental and physical activities?

One must always tell what one sees. Above all, which is more difficult, one must always see what one sees.

Charles Péguy

Then the researchers infer that the lesioned locations may be related to the behavior that was affected. In this way, they trace an observed type of behavior to a particular location in the brain. (Table 2-1 shows some of the techniques that can be used for studying human brains after death.)

Scientists also want to understand the physiological processes and functions of the living brain. To study the changing activity of the living brain, scientists must use *in vivo* (within living organisms) research. Many in vivo techniques are performed on animals. Because the monkey brain is so similar to the human brain, monkeys are often the subjects in such experiments. (Table 2-1 shows some of the in vivo techniques performed on animals, as well as on humans.)

Some in vivo techniques are used with humans, too. For example, psychologists (and physicians—medical doctors) sometimes record electrical activity in the brain, which appears as waves of various widths (frequencies) and heights (intensities) (see Figure 2-5). Psychologists also use various methods of producing a still

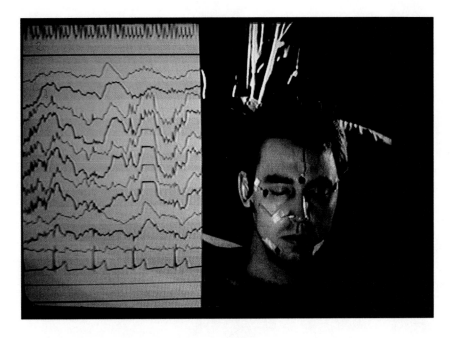

Figure 2-5

Electroencephalograms (EEGs)

Psychologists use EEGs to record electrical activity in the brain and translate the data into wave patterns, which can be analyzed.

image of the structures of the brain. Many of these methods are based on the use of X rays (see Figures 2-6a and 2-6b), but more recently, some methods use magnetism (see Figure 2-6c). In addition, psychologists are able to study the behavior of the living brain by examining how the brain uses up a form of radioactive glucose during various activities (see Figure 2-6d). What are the various regions of the brain that may be using up this glucose?

Structures and Functions of the Brain

The brain can be divided into three major regions: forebrain, midbrain, and hindbrain. These labels describe the front-to-back physical arrangement of the three regions during *prenatal* (before birth) development. However, the physical arrangement of these regions changes so much that by the time of birth, the *forebrain* is above the *midbrain* and the *hindbrain*. Figure 2-7 shows the locations of many of the important structures in these regions.

The forebrain comprises the brain structures that most intrigue psychobiologists: the *basal ganglia* (essential to motor function), the **thalamus** (acting as a relay station for transmitting sensory information that enters the brain, projecting the information to the correct regions of the cerebral cortex), the **hypothalamus** (responsible for controlling the endocrine [hormonal] system and for influencing behavior related to survival, consciousness, and emotional reactions), and both the cortex and the limbic system. The *cortex* (responsible for most of our thinking and perceiving) is of such great psychological importance that it is discussed at length in a subsequent section. The **limbic system** is also crucial to many aspects of psychological function, such as learning (see Chapter 6), memory (see Chapter 7), and emotions and motivation (see Chapter 11). Within the limbic system, the *amygdala* plays a key role in anger and aggression, and the *septum* influences anger and fear. A related structure that particularly interests cognitive psychologists and neurologists is the **hippocampus,** which influences learning and memory, and which may be implicated in neurological disorders such as Alzheimer's disease. The hypothalamus is also sometimes classified as being part of the limbic system.

The midbrain contains several structures, including most of the **reticular activating system,** which is essential to life, as it controls heartbeat, breathing, consciousness (sleep, arousal), attention, and movement. The hindbrain contains the rest of the reticular activating system, as well as the *medulla oblongata* (in which many nerves cross from one side of the body to the opposite side of the brain; in-

Any sufficiently advanced technology is indistinguishable from magic.

Arthur C. Clarke

He had decided to live forever or die in the attempt, and his only mission each time he went up was to come down alive.

Joseph Heller

thalamus a brain structure that primarily serves as a relay station for sensory information

hypothalamus a brain structure that plays a key role in regulating behavior related to species survival (fighting, feeding, fleeing, and mating)

limbic system a system of brain structures involved in emotion, motivation, and learning

hippocampus a portion of the **limbic system;** plays an essential role in the formation of new memories (*hippocampus*, "seahorse," its approximate shape [Greek])

reticular activating system a complex network of neurons essential to the regulation of consciousness and to such vital functions as heartbeat and breathing

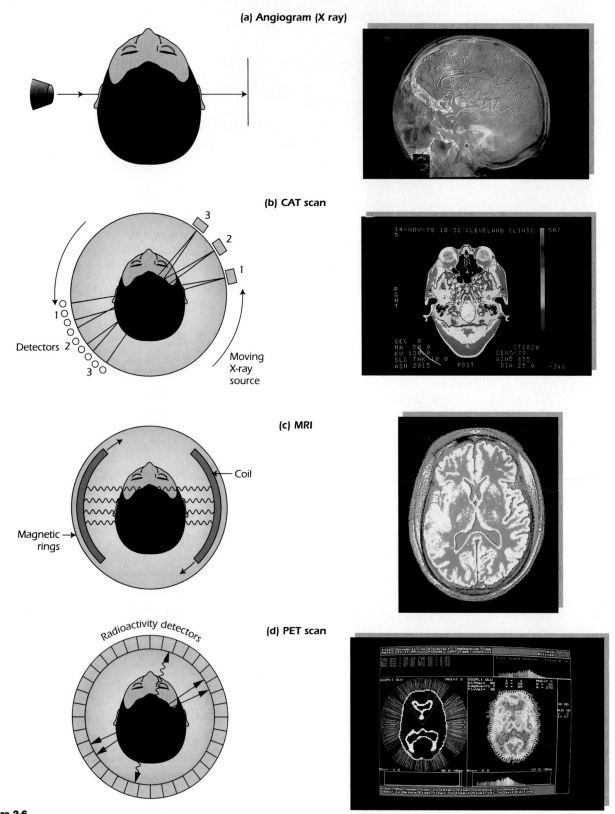

Figure 2-6
Images of the Brain
Various techniques have been developed to picture the structures—and sometimes the processes—of the brain. (a) A brain angiogram highlights the blood vessels of the brain. (b) A CAT-scan image of a brain uses a series of rotating scans (one of which is pictured here) to produce a 3-D view of brain structures. (c) A rotating series of MRI scans (one of which is pictured here) shows a clearer 3-D picture of brain structures than CAT scans show. (d) These still photographs of PET scans of a brain show different metabolic processes during different activities. PET scans permit the study of brain physiology.

FOREBRAIN

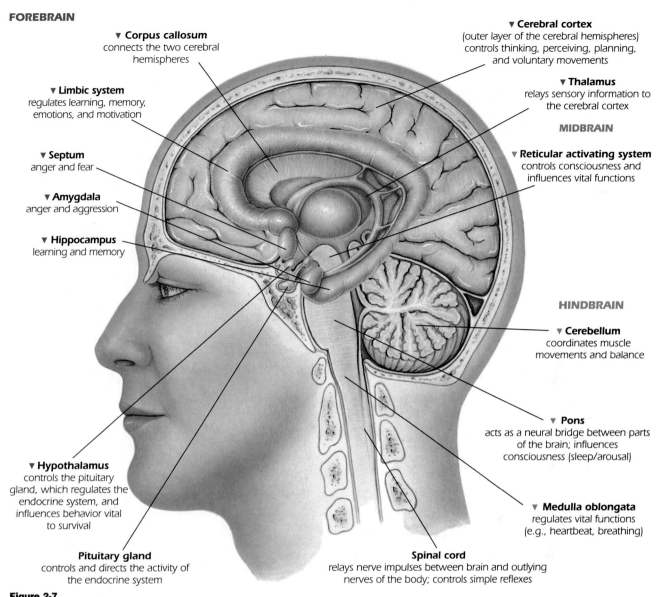

▼ **Corpus callosum**
connects the two cerebral
hemispheres

▼ **Cerebral cortex**
(outer layer of the cerebral hemispheres)
controls thinking, perceiving, planning,
and voluntary movements

▼ **Limbic system**
regulates learning, memory,
emotions, and motivation

▼ **Thalamus**
relays sensory information to
the cerebral cortex

MIDBRAIN

▼ **Septum**
anger and fear

▼ **Reticular activating system**
controls consciousness and
influences vital functions

▼ **Amygdala**
anger and aggression

▼ **Hippocampus**
learning and memory

HINDBRAIN

▼ **Cerebellum**
coordinates muscle
movements and balance

▼ **Pons**
acts as a neural bridge between parts
of the brain; influences
consciousness (sleep/arousal)

▼ **Hypothalamus**
controls the pituitary
gland, which regulates the
endocrine system, and
influences behavior vital
to survival

▼ **Medulla oblongata**
regulates vital functions
(e.g., heartbeat, breathing)

Pituitary gland
controls and directs the activity of
the endocrine system

Spinal cord
relays nerve impulses between brain and outlying
nerves of the body; controls simple reflexes

Figure 2-7
Major Structures of the Forebrain, the Midbrain, and the Hindbrain
*The structures of the forebrain (identified with blue labels), the midbrain (identified with red labels), and the hindbrain (identified with green labels)
perform essential functions for survival, as well as for high-level thinking and feeling.*

volved in vital physiological functions), the **pons** (a neural bridge from one part of the brain to another and one of several structures influencing consciousness), and the **cerebellum** (which governs many aspects of producing appropriate muscle movements). Although each of these subcortical (*sub-*, below; *cortical*, related to the cerebral cortex) structures is important to the human mind and behavior, the cortex deserves special attention.

The Cerebral Hemispheres and the Cerebral Cortex

The **cerebral cortex** (plural: cortices) is a thin layer (about 2 millimeters thick) wrapped around the outward surface of the brain. In human beings, the cerebral cortex contains many folds. These folds greatly increase the area covered by the cerebral cortex: If the wrinkly human cerebral cortex were smoothed out, it would cover about 2 square feet. About 80% of the human brain is cerebral cortex (Kolb & Whishaw, 1990). The cerebral cortex is responsible for our being able to

MINILECTURE

Structure of the Brain (Ch 3)

pons a brain structure containing nerve cells that pass signals from one part of the brain to another, thereby serving as a kind of bridge

cerebellum a brain structure that controls bodily coordination, balance, and muscle tone

cerebral cortex a thin layer of tissue on the surface of the brain, which is responsible for most high-level cognitive processes

When you read about the various structures and functions of the brain, which do you believe are the most important in distinguishing humans from other animals? Which functions are the most important for survival?

THE FAR SIDE   By GARY LARSON

"Whoa! *That* was a good one! Try it, Hobbs — just poke his brain right where my finger is."

The Far Side © 1986 FarWorks, Inc./ Distributed by Universal Press Syndicate. Reprinted with permission. All rights reserved.

A minor operation: one performed on somebody else.

Anonymous

corpus callosum a dense body of nerve fibers that connect the two cerebral hemispheres

think—to plan, to coordinate thoughts and actions, to perceive visual and sound patterns, to use language, and so on. Without it, we would not be human.

The grayish surface of the cerebral cortex, sometimes termed *gray matter*, contains gray nerve cells that process information. Underneath the gray matter is the *white matter*. White matter includes mostly white-colored nerve fibers that conduct information throughout the cerebral cortex. Both the white and the gray matter are essential to human intelligence.

The crumpled-looking cerebral cortex forms into the left and right *cerebral hemispheres* (*hemi-*, half; *spheres*, 3-D round shapes). Although the two hemispheres look similar, they function differently. The left hemisphere is specialized for some kinds of activities, the right for other kinds. For one thing, most sensory information crosses from one side of the body to the opposite hemisphere of the brain: Sensory receptors in the right foot, right ear, and right nostril send information to the left hemisphere. Receptors on the left side generally send information to the right hemisphere. The same crossing occurs when the hemispheres of the brain send motor information to the rest of the body. The left hemisphere directs the motor responses on the right side of the body, and the right hemisphere directs the left side of the body. This crossed pattern is termed *contralateral* (*contra-*, opposite; *lateral*, side) transmission. Some *ipsilateral* (same side) transmission occurs as well: Visual information from each eye goes to *both* hemispheres.

Despite this general tendency for the hemispheres to be specialized (have special functions) contralaterally, the hemispheres do communicate with one another. The **corpus callosum** (dense body [Latin]) is a dense collection of nerve fibers that connects the two cerebral hemispheres. This connection permits transmission of information back and forth (see Figure 2-7). After information reaches one hemisphere, the information can travel quickly and easily through the corpus callosum to the other hemisphere.

Hemispheric Specialization

In 1861, Paul Broca (1824–1880) noted that he had found a lesion in a particular area in the left cerebral hemisphere of a former patient of his. Before Broca's patient died, the patient had suffered from *aphasia* (impaired or lost ability to speak, due to brain damage). Broca suggested that the left-hemisphere lesion may have caused the aphasia. Since then, research has shown that "Broca's area" (the region of the brain where Broca observed the lesion) does contribute to speech (see Figure 2-8). Curiously, although people with lesions in Broca's area cannot speak fluently, they can use their voices to sing or to shout.

Another important early researcher, Carl Wernicke (1848–1905), studied language-deficient patients who could speak, but whose speech made no sense. He also traced language ability to the left hemisphere, though to a different precise location, now known as Wernicke's area (see Figure 2-8). More recently, other researchers have found other areas of the brain to be involved in the comprehension and expression of language, but Broca's area and Wernicke's area are still recognized as key to normal language function.

The early discoveries about the link between the brain and the mind, such as those by Broca and his predecessors, were initially rejected or ignored by the scientific community. Subsequent discoveries have been more readily accepted, and in 1981, Roger Sperry (1920–1994), David Hubel (1926–), and Torsten Wiesel (1924–) were awarded a Nobel Prize for their work on the physiology of the brain. (The work by Hubel and Wiesel is discussed in Chapter 4; in this chapter, we focus on Sperry's work on hemispheric specialization.)

Sperry argued (1964) that each hemisphere behaves in many respects like a separate brain. Sperry and his colleagues developed a technique for studying the brain—a total severing of the corpus callosum. This technique effectively cut the connection between the two hemispheres. Thus, this procedure essentially created two separate specialized brains, which processed different information and performed separate functions.

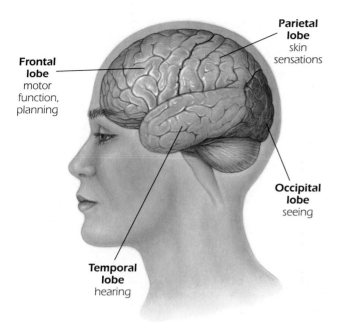

Frontal lobe
motor function, planning

Parietal lobe
skin sensations

Occipital lobe
seeing

Temporal lobe
hearing

(a) Anatomical areas (left lateral view)

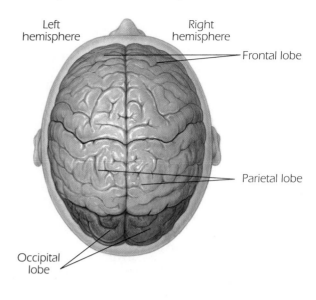

Left hemisphere

Right hemisphere

Frontal lobe

Parietal lobe

Occipital lobe

(b) Anatomical areas (top view)

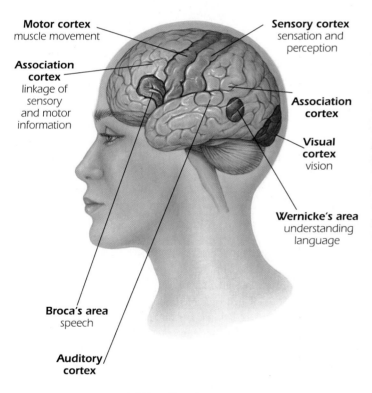

Motor cortex
muscle movement

Association cortex
linkage of sensory and motor information

Broca's area
speech

Auditory cortex

Sensory cortex
sensation and perception

Association cortex

Visual cortex
vision

Wernicke's area
understanding language

(c) Functional areas

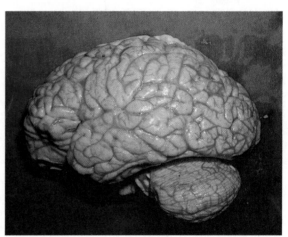

Figure 2-8
Lobes of the Cerebral Cortex
The cortical lobes are named for the bones of the skull overlying these regions: the frontal lobe, the parietal lobe, the temporal lobe, and the occipital lobe. Broca's area, in the frontal lobe, and Wernicke's area, in the temporal lobe, play important roles in expressing language.

Epileptic patients who have undergone operations that cut through the corpus callosum are termed *split-brain* patients. Split-brain research reveals fascinating possibilities regarding the ways we think. Many researchers in this field (Farah, 1988; Gazzaniga, 1985; Zaidel, 1983) have argued that each of the two hemispheres is specialized for distinct kinds of functions. In particular, some researchers

MINILECTURE

Split-Brain Procedure (Ch 3)

Ursula Bellugi and her colleagues have had key insights regarding language and the brain by studying persons like this mother and son, whose native language is American Sign Language.

The left hemisphere became the one to have if you were having only one.

Howard Gardner

Think about your own behavior. What are three things that you could do now that would involve activity in the left hemisphere of your brain? What are three other things you could do that would involve the right hemisphere of your brain? (*Hint:* Remember about contralateral and sensory processing.)

have suggested that the left hemisphere specializes in language functions. In contrast, the right hemisphere specializes in *spatial* (involving spatial orientation and perception) functions.

At present, other researchers have suggested alternative explanations for many of the findings regarding hemispheric specialization. We cannot now confidently say exactly what each hemisphere does or can do. As always, alternative scientific interpretations of the same data make science both frustrating and exciting. One way to strengthen particular interpretations is to use the method of *converging operations.* In this method, researchers use multiple kinds of procedures for studying a research question. They then look to see whether the various procedures *converge* (come together) on a single answer or set of answers to the question. In the case of hemispheric specialization, EEG studies have provided converging evidence. These studies show more electrical activity occurs in the left hemisphere during a verbal task, but more occurs in the right hemisphere during a spatial task (Kosslyn, 1988; Springer & Deutsch, 1985).

Another way to approach the hemispheric specialization of language functions is to study the brains and the thinking of persons who learn to use languages other than spoken English. Ursula Bellugi and her colleagues have studied individuals whose native language is American Sign Language (ASL). For native signers, the use of ASL is localized in the left hemisphere (Bellugi, Poizner, & Klima, 1989; Corina et al., 1992a; Corina, Vaid, & Bellugi, 1992b; Haglund et al., 1993; Poizner, Bellugi, & Klima, 1990). On the other hand (so to speak), gestures that are not specific ASL signs are localized in the right hemispheres of native signers, just as they are in native speakers of English. Similarly, spatial information seems to be localized in the right hemisphere of native ASL signers (Poizner et al., 1984). These findings support the view that language, not just speech, is localized in the left hemisphere.

Lobes of the Cerebral Hemispheres and Cerebral Cortex

Hemispheric specialization is only one way through which to view the various parts of the cerebral cortex. Another way is to divide the cortex into four **lobes** (rounded sections): frontal, parietal, temporal, and occipital (see Figure 2-8). The *frontal lobe* handles planning, reasoning, and other high-level thought processes, as well as motor processing (see Figure 2-9); the *parietal lobe* governs *somatosensory* processing (sensations of feeling in the skin and in the muscles of the body) (see Figure 2-10); the *temporal lobe* handles auditory processing (hearing); and the *occipi-*

lobes each of the four major regions of the cerebral cortex, comprising the frontal lobe (motor, planning), occipital lobe (visual), parietal lobe (somatosensory), and temporal lobe (auditory)

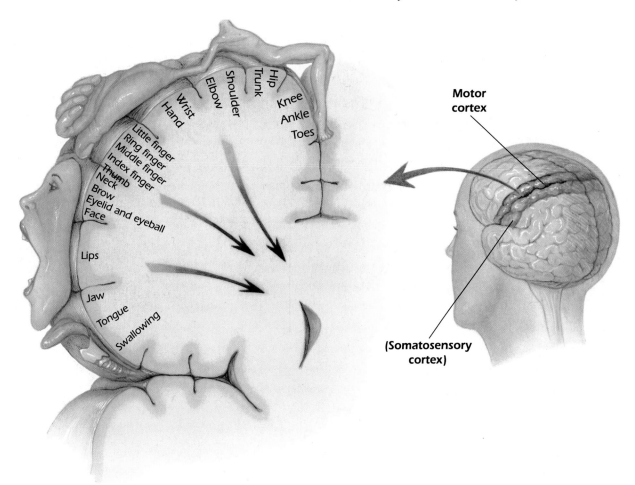

Figure 2-9
Homunculus of the Motor Cortex
A homunculus *(little person)* resembles a little person; in this case, a map is drawn as a cross-section of the cerebral cortex surrounded by the figure of a small upside-down person, whose body parts map out the parts of the primary motor cortex in the frontal lobe. Note that parts of the body that involve more control of muscle movements (e.g., your hands) take up larger proportions of the areas of the motor cortex.

tal lobe oversees visual processing (seeing). In addition to these localized functions, the lobes also interact constantly, and many functions overlap among the lobes.

Also in the cerebral hemispheres are projection areas. *Projection areas* are specialized regions of the cortex involved in relaying sensory and motor information within the brain. Receptor nerves transmit sensory information that arrives in the brain from various sensory receptors to the thalamus (in the forebrain; see Figure 2-7). There, the thalamus projects the information to the appropriate areas in the lobes. Similarly, motor information from the cortex goes to the projection areas, which then send that information downward through the spinal cord. From the spinal cord, motor information travels through the PNS to reach and direct the movement of the appropriate muscles.

The areas of the lobes that are not just sending or receiving somatosensory, motor, auditory, or visual information are association areas. **Association areas** link sensory and motor information. For instance, when we use language, which requires complex links among pieces of information, the association areas of our brains are active. In fact, Broca's area and Wernicke's area, discussed earlier, are both in association areas of the cortex.

The association areas of other animals are relatively small. These animals think very little about the sensations they receive before deciding what actions to take. In humans, association areas make up roughly 75% of the cerebral cortex. We humans do a lot of thinking about our sensations and our actions.

His mind was an intricate, multigeared machine, or perhaps some little animal with skittery paws.

Anne Tyler

association areas regions of the cerebral lobes that are not part of the sensory or motor cortices but that are believed to connect (associate) the activity of the sensory and motor cortices

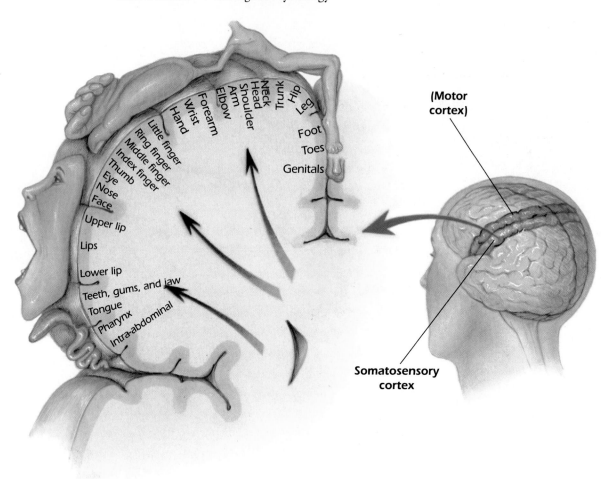

Figure 2-10

Homunculus of the Somatosensory Cortex

This homunculus maps the somatosensory cortex in the parietal lobe, identifying the parts of the body from which it receives sensory information. Note that parts of the body that are more highly sensitive (e.g., your mouth and tongue) take up proportionately larger areas of the somatosensory cortex.

Thus far, we have discussed the nervous system in terms of the parts that can be seen without using a microscope. We have also discussed briefly what kinds of information are processed in the brain, as well as how and where the brain processes the information it receives. We now turn to the tiny parts of the nervous system, which can be seen only by using microscopes or other specialized equipment.

Finding Your Way   **2-2**

Think about your own activities and experiences within the past 24 hours. How have your recent experiences stimulated each lobe of your cortex? How have your experiences stimulated your association areas to link your sensations and actions? What have you done recently that shows off the remarkable mental processing that goes on in your brain?

What are the major structures and functions of the human brain?
Various technologies permit us to view both the structures and some of the
functions of the brain. The major structures of the human brain include the
thalamus, the hypothalamus, the limbic system (which is sometimes viewed
as including the hypothalamus), the reticular activating system, the pons, and
the cerebellum, as well as a structure of particular interest to psychologists:
the cerebral cortex. The major functions of the human brain include thinking, feeling, and generating action, all of which are based on processing
incoming sensory information and carried out by sending outgoing instructions that control motor responses.

HOW IS INFORMATION PROCESSED IN THE NERVOUS SYSTEM?

Neurons

To understand how the nervous system processes information, we need to know
about the major structures and functions of the neurons that form the nervous system (see Figure 2-11). First, we examine the structure of the neuron. Later, we discuss the key function of all neurons, which is to allow for communication within
the nervous system.

Three Types of Neurons

There are three types of neurons: sensory neurons, motor neurons, and interneurons. Each type of neuron serves a different function. **Sensory neurons** receive
information about the internal and external environment. They connect with
sensory *receptor cells*, which are specially designed to *receive* a particular kind of

sensory neuron nerve cell that receives information from the environment through
sensory receptors and then carries that
information toward the central nervous
system

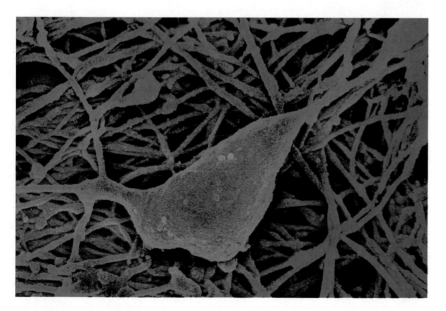

Figure 2-11
Neurons
*Most humans have more than 100 billion
(100,000,000,000) neurons in their nervous
system. (If a team of scientists were to count 3
neurons per second, the team would take more
than 1,000 years to finish counting.) For the
most part, these neurons cannot be replaced,
at least in adults: Once a neuron dies, it is gone
forever.*

information. The receptor cells detect distinctive changes in the sensory organs, such as the skin, ears, tongue, eyes, nose, muscles, joints, and internal organs (see Chapter 4). Sensory neurons carry information away from the sensory receptor cells and *toward* the spinal cord or the brain.

Motor neurons carry information *away from* the spinal cord and the brain and toward the various other parts of the body (e.g., arms and legs). When the body parts receive the information, the information tells the parts to respond in some way. Both motor neurons and sensory neurons are part of the peripheral nervous system. For example, your sensory and motor neurons may send information to and from your stomach (through your autonomic nervous system) or to and from your toe muscles (through your somatic nervous system).

Interneurons (*inter-*, between) work between the sensory neurons and the motor neurons. They receive signals from either sensory neurons or other interneurons. Then, they send signals either to other interneurons or to motor neurons. In complex organisms such as humans, most neurons are interneurons.

The spinal reflex (see Figure 2-12) illustrates how the neurons interact: (1) *Sensory neurons* receive a message from specialized sensory-receptor cells; the message arrives in a biological code that can be translated roughly into English as, "Yikes! Hot! Hand hurts!" (2) *Interneurons* receive the message from the sensory neurons. (3) The interneurons translate the sensory message into a motor message. (4) The interneurons send the biologically coded motor message to the motor neurons; the biological code can be translated roughly into English as, "Move that hand!" (5) The *motor neurons* send the message to the muscles responsible for moving the hand. Meanwhile, other interneurons send the incoming message through the spinal cord to the brain. The brain then interprets the incoming message as pain and more deliberately figures out what to do about the situation.

motor neuron nerve cell that carries information *away from* the spinal cord and the brain and toward the body parts that are supposed to respond to the information in some way

interneuron a type of nerve cell, which transmits information between sensory and motor neurons

Figure 2-12

The Spinal Reflex Revisited: Three Types of Neurons

In the spinal reflex, sensory neurons receive a message (a sensory stimulus, i.e., a sensation) and then transmit the message to interneurons, which transmit the message through the spinal cord to motor neurons. The motor neurons then send the message to muscles that respond reflexively to the message.

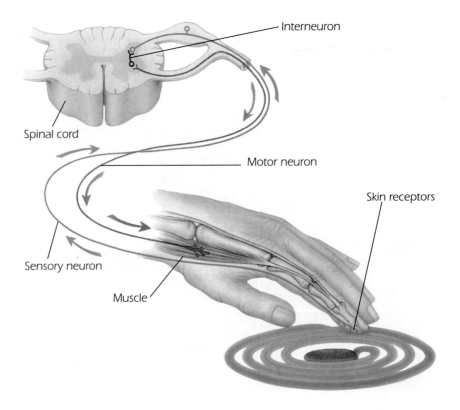

Interneuron

Spinal cord

Motor neuron

Skin receptors

Sensory neuron

Muscle

Parts of the Neuron

Not all neurons are alike in their structure, but almost all neurons have four basic parts: a soma, dendrites, an axon, and terminal buttons (see Figure 2-13). We discuss each part in turn, as well as the important junction between neurons—the synapse.

The **soma** (body—the body of the cell) sustains the life of the neuron. It contains the cell *nucleus*, which performs metabolic and reproductive functions for the cell. At one end of the neuron, the edges of the soma branch out to the **dendrites** (meaning "trees"; the branching dendrites look like trees). On the external *membranes* (thin surface layers) of the soma and the dendrites are distinctive receptors for chemical messengers. These receptors receive chemical messages from other neurons.

When the soma or dendrites receive a message, they pass the message to the **axon.** The axon (a long, thin tube) responds in one of two ways to the messages received by the dendrites and soma. Usually, the axon seems to ignore the information, but sometimes, it sends the information through the length of the neuron. At the opposite end of the neuron from the soma and dendrites is the axon *terminus* (end). At its terminus, the axon can send the message to other neurons.

There are two basic kinds of axons. Both kinds occur in about equal proportions in the human nervous system. What distinguishes the two kinds of axons? One kind of axon is coated with *myelin*, a white fatty substance, and the other is not. *Myelinated* axons are surrounded by a **myelin sheath,** which insulates and protects the axon from being disturbed by the *electrochemical* (involving chemicals with electrical charges) activity of nearby neurons. The myelin sheath also speeds up the process of sending information through the axon. Myelinated axons can send messages at 100 meters per second (equal to about 224 miles per hour), or even faster.

soma the part of the neuron that performs vital functions for the life of the cell

dendrites the primary parts of the neuron involved in receiving communications from other cells via distinctive receptors on their external membranes

axon the long, thin, tubular part of the neuron, which responds to information received by the dendrites and soma of the neuron by either ignoring or transmitting the information through the neuron to the axon's terminal buttons

myelin sheath a protective, insulating layer of myelin, which coats the axons of some neurons

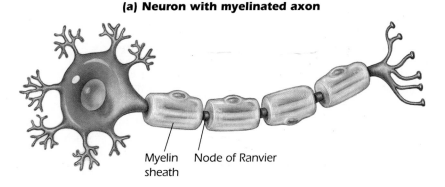

(a) Neuron with myelinated axon

Myelin sheath   Node of Ranvier

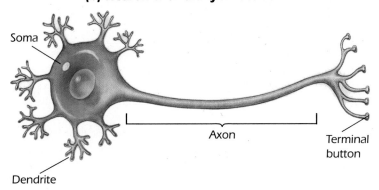

(b) Neuron with unmyelinated axon

Soma

Axon

Terminal button

Dendrite

Figure 2-13

Parts of a Neuron

Each neuron comprises four basic parts: a soma, dendrites, an axon, and terminal buttons, although the size and shape of these parts may differ, depending on the location and function of the neuron. As these schematics illustrate, the axon may be myelinated (a) or unmyelinated (b).

Myelin is not spread evenly around the length of the axon. Instead, there are small gaps in the myelin coating along the axon. These gaps in the myelin are termed *nodes of Ranvier*. Somewhat surprisingly, these gaps in the myelin sheath help to speed up *neural transmission* (*neural* means that it has to do with the nervous system, and *transmission* is the process of sending information; in this case, the information travels through the nervous system). It seems that neural impulses save time by leaping from node to node across the myelin sheath.

The second kind of axon has no myelin sheath. Typically, these axons are narrower and shorter than the myelinated ones. The narrowness of these axons also slows the rate at which they send neural impulses. Because the narrow, unmyelinated axons are also usually shorter, they generally have less distance to travel. Therefore, they do not need to send impulses as quickly as do the long, thick, myelinated axons. In unmyelinated axons, the speed of sending impulses is sometimes as relatively slow as 5 meters (a little more than 5 yards) per second. (On the other hand, most of us would be lucky to be able to run that fast!)

The terminus of each axon branches into various *terminal buttons*. The small knobby terminal buttons do not directly touch the dendrites of the next neuron. Even so, they play a key role in sending information within the nervous system. Specifically, they release a chemical messenger into the **synapse**, a tiny gap between neurons (see Figure 2-14). The synapse is the gap between the terminal buttons of one neuron and the dendrites (or sometimes the soma) of the next neuron.

The width of neuronal somas ranges from about 5 to about 100 *microns* (thousandths of a millimeter, millionths of a meter). Dendrites, too, are tiny, generally a few hundred microns in length. Axons, however, can vary considerably in length. Some axons are as short as a few hundred microns. In fact, some axons are so short that they are almost impossible to find as a separate part of the neuron. However, the axons of some of the longer motor neurons can reach from the spinal cord to the fingers and the toes. To picture the relative size of the parts of a neuron, imagine enlarging a long spinal neuron. You could make the soma the size of an orange. In relative terms, the axon would stretch the length of 240 football fields (roughly 14 miles).

Conduction of Information Within Neurons

For neuronal communication to occur, two interactive processes are needed. First, each neuron must be able to send information from the dendrites and the soma at one end, through the axon, to the terminal buttons at the other end. When information travels through the neuron, it is termed *conduction*, much like the conduction of electricity through the wires in your home. Because this conduction occurs within one neuron, it is *intraneuronal*, which means "within the neuron."

In the second process, information must get from one neuron to another, so that information can travel throughout the nervous system. When information is sent from one neuron to another, it is termed *transmission*, just as radio waves are transmitted from a radio station to the radio receiver in your car or home. Because transmission occurs between two or more neurons, it is *interneuronal*, which means "between the neurons."

In the nervous system, the body does not use electrical wires or radio waves. Instead, it sends the information in the form of electrochemical messages. The electrochemical information takes the form of *ions*—chemical particles that have positive or negative electrical charges, which are both inside and outside of the neurons. We consider intraneuronal conduction first.

Sometimes, the electrochemical activity surrounding the neuron generates an **action potential** (neural "firing" as a result of a change in the electrochemical balance inside and outside a neuron) along the membrane of the neuron. During an action potential, ions quickly flood in and out of the neuron, across the neuronal

MINILECTURE
Neurons (Ch 3)

---

synapse the area comprising the interneuronal gap, the terminal buttons of one neuron's axon, and the dendrites (or sometimes the soma) of the next neuron

action potential a change in the electrochemical balance inside and outside a neuron; occurs when electrochemical stimulation of the neuron reaches or exceeds the neuron's threshold of excitation

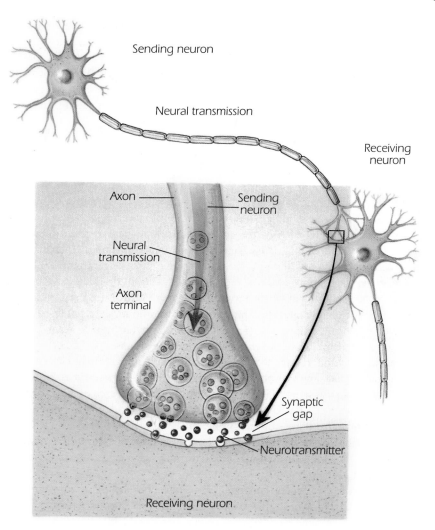

Sending neuron

Neural transmission

Receiving neuron

Axon

Sending neuron

Neural transmission

Axon terminal

Synaptic gap

Neurotransmitter

Receiving neuron

Figure 2-14
The Synapse
This simplified drawing shows the neuron-to-neuron transfer of messages in the synapse.

membrane. This rapid transfer of ions changes the electrochemical balance inside and outside the neuron.

Although change is essential to neural communication (and to life itself), too much change can be overwhelming. Our neurons are constantly surrounded by the electrochemical activity of our bodies. If our neurons generated action potentials in response to every slight electrochemical charge, chaos would result. Therefore, our neurons are somewhat choosy in reacting to electrochemical activity. Neurons do *not* respond to electrochemical charges of *most* levels of intensity and frequency. However, once a charge reaches or surpasses a certain level, the neuron generates an action potential. The required level of electrochemical charge for a neuron is its **threshold of excitation.** At or above a neuron's threshold, an action potential is generated. Below that threshold, no action potential occurs. Different neurons require different thresholds of excitation for generating action potentials. For all neurons, however, when an action potential occurs, the neuron fires.

The action potential carries impulses through the axon, from one end to the other. Action potentials are *all-or-none* reactions. Either the electrical charge is strong enough to generate an action potential, or it is not. Once the threshold is reached, the charge travels all the way down the axon without losing strength.

You might compare the firing of a neuron to a sneeze. To generate a sneeze, a substance must irritate the membranes of your nose beyond a certain point. Once

threshold of excitation the level of electrochemical stimulation, at or above which an action potential may be generated, but below which an action potential cannot be generated

What all-or-none reactions have you observed in your own experiences?

the irritating substance crosses that threshold, you will definitely sneeze. Similarly, a neuron will definitely fire once its threshold level has been reached.

To summarize, intraneuronal conduction occurs when a neuron generates an action potential along its axon. Action potentials are set off by an electrical charge at or beyond the neuron's threshold of excitation. This process starts a complex reaction that conducts the electrochemical message through the neuron. Impulses travel especially fast in myelinated axons.

Communication Between Neurons

The conduction of information within each neuron is essential. However, the work of each individual neuron would be useless if there were no way for neurons to communicate with one another.

We already know *where* (in the synapse) and *when* (whenever an action potential triggers release of a chemical messenger) neurons communicate. The *what* of interneuronal communication is a variety of chemical messengers, termed **neurotransmitters** and *neuromodulators*. (See Table 2-2, later in this section, for a brief description of both types of chemical messengers.) We still need to explain *how* neurons communicate. Stated simply, this is how they do so (see also Figure 2-14): (1) One neuron ("Neuron A") releases a neurotransmitter from its terminal buttons. (2) The neurotransmitter enters and crosses the synapse. (3) The neurotransmitter reaches the receptors in the dendrites (or soma) of another neuron ("Neuron B"). (4) The neurotransmitters from Neuron A keep stimulating Neuron B until Neuron B reaches its distinctive threshold of excitation. (5) Within Neuron B, when the neuron reaches its threshold of excitation, it generates an action potential that travels down its axon. (6) Within fractions of a second, the action potential of Neuron B reaches the terminal buttons of Neuron B. Neuron B then releases its own neurotransmitter into the next synapse (perhaps with Neuron C); and so on.

In practice, the process is not really that simple. For one thing, large numbers (often hundreds) of neurons meet at any given synapse. Also, various presynaptic neurons release various kinds of neurotransmitters (see Table 2-2). Carefully review the neurotransmitters and neuromodulators, described in Table 2-2, to see the wide range of mental processes they influence.

Just as various neurons produce various kinds of neurotransmitters and neuromodulators, different postsynaptic neurons have different kinds of receptor sites for neurotransmitters. Each kind of neurotransmitter has a distinctive shape, based on its chemical structure. Each kind of receptor site also has a distinctive shape, based on its physiological structure. *Neuroscientists* (psychologists and other scientists interested in studying the nervous system) have come up with a useful metaphor for picturing the interaction of neurotransmitters and receptors: Imagine that the characteristic shape of a given receptor is a keyhole, and the peculiar shape of a given neurotransmitter is a key (Restak, 1984). When the shape of the key matches the shape of the keyhole, the receptor responds. (In Chapter 5, Figure 5-5 illustrates this key-and-keyhole mechanism.)

So far, we know that at any given synapse, countless neurons are sending and receiving neurochemical messages. Neurons are spurting various kinds of neurotransmitters and neuromodulators into the synapse. In response, some neurons are receiving the different kinds of neurotransmitters and neuromodulators. When a particular neurotransmitter matches a particular receptor site, the receptor may respond in either of two ways. The receptor may become either excited or inhibited.

Receptors may be *excited* by some of the neurotransmitters that fit them. The more excited the receptors become, the more likely that the neurons will reach their threshold of excitation and will fire. Other receptors, however, are actually *inhibited* (held back from acting; restrained) by certain neurotransmitters they receive. When postsynaptic receptors are inhibited, neurons are *less* likely to reach their threshold of excitation. Furthermore, the degree of excitation or inhibition is

neurotransmitter chemical messenger, released by the terminal buttons on the axon of a presynaptic neuron, that carries the chemical messages across the synapse to receptor sites on the receiving dendrites or soma of the postsynaptic neuron

TABLE 2-2

Common Neurotransmitters and Neuromodulators

Acetylcholine (ACh)	■ *Action in the CNS:* Excites neuronal receptor sites ■ *Action in the CNS:* May be involved in memory (inferred from its concentration in the hippocampus); deficits of acetylcholine may be implicated in some memory disorders (e.g., Alzheimer's disease) ■ *Action in the PNS:* Can cause contraction of the skeletal muscles, leading to movement ■ *Action in the PNS:* Can inhibit the neurons in the muscles of the heart
Dopamine	■ Influences several important activities, including movement, attention, and learning ■ Most receptors are inhibitory, but some receptors are excitatory ■ Deficits (too little) are associated with symptoms of *Parkinson's disease,* such as tremors, rigidity of limbs, and difficulty in balance ■ Excesses (too much) may be associated symptoms of schizophrenia (see Chapter 13)
Norepinephrine and epinephrine	■ Involved in the regulation of alertness and wakefulness (see Chapter 5)
Serotonin	■ Involved in arousal, sleep, and dreaming ■ Affects the regulation of mood, appetite, and sensitivity to pain
Amino-acid neurotransmitters such as glutamate (glutamic acid), aspartate, glycine, and GABA (gamma-aminobutyric acid)	■ About 1,000 times more prevalent in the brain than are acetylcholine, dopamine, norepinephrine, epinephrine, and serotonin ■ Can act as neurotransmitters or as neuromodulators ■ Imbalances have been linked to seizures, Huntington's chorea (a neurological disorder), and the fatal effects of tetanus
Neuropeptides	■ Perhaps the best known are *endorphins* (meaning *endoge-*nous m*orphine*s) and other neuropeptides linked to pain relief and to stress reactions (see Chapter 15) ■ Some serve as specific neurotransmitters such as those involved in hunger, thirst, and reproductive processes (see Chapter 11) ■ Others serve as neuromodulators, enhancing or diminishing the responsivity of the excitatory or inhibitory receptors for particular neurotransmitters

influenced by the actions of the neuromodulators. These neuromodulators either increase or decrease the responsiveness of the neurons.

A very rough metaphor for how this process might work is to imagine that you are trying to decide whether to transfer to a particular school. You do not have time to visit the school yourself, but someone you know is visiting the school and keeps sending you messages about the school. For you, some of these messages excite your desire to attend the school, and other messages inhibit your desire to attend the school. If you do not become excited enough about the school, you will not take any action to transfer, but the more the messages you hear about the

MINILECTURE
*Neurotransmitters and the
Synapse (Ch 3)*

school excite you, the more likely you are to transfer. On the other hand, the more the messages you hear inhibit you, the less likely you are to go to the school.

To summarize, countless presynaptic neurons are squirting neurotransmitters and neuromodulators into the synapse. Some receptors match particular neurotransmitters, and others do not. When a match occurs, some receptors of an affected postsynaptic neuron are excited, and others are inhibited. In addition, neuromodulators strengthen or weaken the responsivity of the receiving neurons. In order for a neuron to fire, the total exciting effects (minus any inhibiting effects) on a neuron must reach the neuron's threshold of excitation.

When you think about all that is involved in getting one neuron to fire, it seems a miracle that any of us can think or act at all. In fact, however, it does not take long for a message to cross the synapse. Sometimes it takes as little as half a millisecond, and it rarely takes longer than a second.

Before we conclude this section, we consider one more process that affects neural communication. Think about all the neurotransmitters and neuromodulators constantly spilling into each synapse. Even when neurons receive these substances, they do not absorb all of the neurochemicals, so what happens to the unused substances? If the extra neurochemicals stayed in the synapse, they would overstimulate the postsynaptic neurons. Fortunately, through the process of *reuptake*, neurons *reabsorb* (take up again) some of the leftover transmitter chemicals that they have released into the synapse.

Under most circumstances, the human nervous system superbly communicates specific sensory and motor information. It quickly sends sensory information from our sense organs to our brains, it processes that information, and then it sends motor information from our brains to our muscles. The speedy communication of specific information enables us to respond immediately to our environments. Sometimes, however, our bodies use a different means of communication. This other communication network is the endocrine system.

How is information processed in the nervous system? Within the nervous system, individual neurons transmit information electrochemically through the release of neurotransmitters into synapses; at each synapse, each of the receiving neurons may be stimulated until it reaches its distinctive threshold of excitation and generates an action potential causing the information to be passed on to the next neuron.

HOW DOES THE ENDOCRINE SYSTEM WORK?

endocrine system a physiological communication network that operates via glands that secrete hormones directly into the bloodstream

gland group of cells that secretes chemical substances

hormone chemical substance secreted by one or more glands; regulates many physiological processes through specific actions on cells and may affect the way a receptive cell goes about its activities

The **endocrine system** (*endo-*, inside; *-crine*, referring to secretion; secreting or releasing inside) operates by means of glands. A **gland** is a group of cells that produces and secretes a chemical substance. In particular, endocrine glands release their chemical products directly into the bloodstream. The blood then carries the secreted substances to *target cells*, which respond to the substances. The target cells of various organs usually respond distinctively. (For example, target cells in the heart may react differently than do target cells in the stomach.) Figure 2-15 illustrates the locations of the main endocrine glands and their key functions.

The chemical substances secreted by endocrine-system glands are **hormones,** which specifically affect the activities of target cells. Hormones work in either of two ways: (1) They can interact with receptors on the surfaces of target cells; or

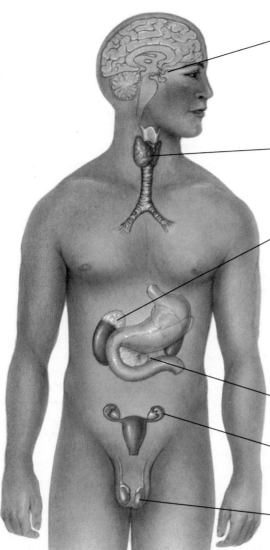

Pituitary gland
Links the endocrine system and the nervous system (via the hypothalamus); controls and directs the activity of the endocrine system, releasing hormones that both directly and indirectly affect other physiological functions

Thyroid gland
Secretes the hormone that increases body metabolism, thereby affecting growth and affecting every process and structure of the body

Adrenal glands
Influence mood, energy level, and reaction to stress

Adrenal medulla
Secretes hormones that govern sudden arousal in response to challenging situations; also governs recovery from sudden arousal

Adrenal cortex
Produces more than 50 different hormones that perform various functions, many of which are vital to physiological survival

Pancreas
Regulates levels of glucose in the blood

Ovaries (in females)
Regulate reproductive system, secondary sex characteristics, and sexual behavior

Testes (in males)
Regulate reproductive system, secondary sex characteristics, and sexual behavior

Figure 2-15

Major Endocrine Glands of the Body

The adrenal glands, thyroid gland, and pituitary gland are among the most important of the endocrine glands, but other glands carry out other important physiological functions as well.

(2) they can enter target cells directly and interact with specialized receptor molecules inside the cells. There are several parallels between neurotransmitters and hormones, as shown in Table 2-3: Both hormones and neurotransmitters (a) are chemical messengers, (b) function within complex communications networks, (c) are secreted by a specific set of cells, (d) communicate information to another set of cells, and (e) affect the receiving cells in different ways, largely depending on the nature of the receptors that receive the chemicals. For instance, as Table 2-3 shows, some substances (e.g., epinephrine and norepinephrine) function as neurotransmitters in the brain and as hormones in the bloodstream. As hormones, however, the chemicals travel a much longer and less direct route to the target cells than they travel as neurotransmitters.

The endocrine system operates largely without our conscious control, and hormones are released reflexively. The glands generally release hormones in response to a stimulus from either inside or outside the body. A *stimulus* is anything that prompts (stimulates) a reaction. Inside the body, the stimulus that prompts the secretion of hormones is often a process by which the body monitors its own activity.

The body monitors the endocrine system in two ways: (1) It checks the levels of each hormone in the bloodstream; and (2) it checks the effects of hormones on

What hormones can you name? What have you heard about their effect on how you think, feel, or act?

TABLE 2-3

Parallels Between Hormones and Neurotransmitters

What are some parallels between these chemical messengers?	Hormones	Neurotransmitters
What are some examples of these chemical substances?	Androgen, epinephrine, estrogen, norepinephrine, thyroxine	Acetylcholine, dopamine, epinephrine, norepinephrine, serotonin
What is the communications network within which the substances operate?	Endocrine system	Nervous system
What is the set of cells that secrete the substance, sending the chemical message?	Glands	Presynaptic neurons
Where are the receptors on the cells that receive the chemical message?	Receptors in or on the target cells	Receptors on the dendrites or somas of postsynaptic neurons
What is an example of how the same chemical messages can lead to different specific actions, depending on the receptors that receive the messages?	Receptors in the digestive system respond to hormones differently than receptors in the heart	Inhibitory receptors respond to neurotransmitters by inhibiting the neuron, but excitatory receptors respond by exciting the neuron

particular bodily processes. Using the first method, the body answers the following question about each hormone: Have the amounts of this hormone in the bloodstream reached a desirable level? The second method seeks answers to this question: Has each hormone completely finished the set of tasks that the hormone was supposed to perform? The answers are then fed back to the glands. If the answer to either question is "yes," the gland stops secreting the hormone. If both answers are "no," the secretion continues. This self-monitoring process is termed a *negative-feedback loop* (see Figure 2-16).

To summarize, the endocrine system secretes hormones into the bloodstream to stimulate various responses in the body. In some ways, the endocrine system is self-regulating. However, it is also subject to control by the nervous system by way of the hypothalamus (see Figure 2-7). Both the endocrine system and the nervous system are essential parts of human physiology. In the next chapter, we discuss how human physiology and its psychological counterparts develop across the life span.

Figure 2-16

Negative-Feedback Loop

Through a negative-feedback loop, the body finds out whether the hormones in the bloodstream have reached a desirable level, and it checks to see whether the hormones have accomplished their tasks. If the monitoring processes feed back "yes" responses, the hormone secretion stops.

Negative feedback loop

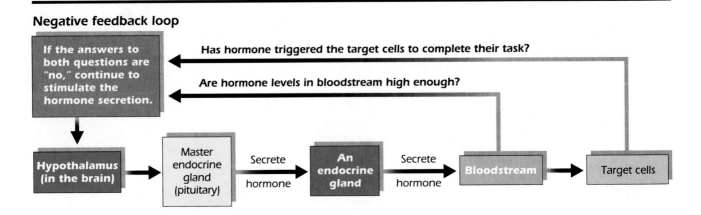

How does the endocrine system work? The endocrine system comprises glands that secrete hormones into the bloodstream; each target organ responds distinctively to the hormones that reach it through the bloodstream.

SUMMARY

1. *Biological psychology* is the study of how biology affects behavior. By studying the nervous and endocrine systems, psychologists are beginning to answer many questions about how the mind and the body interact.

What Is Our Biological History? 36

2. According to Darwin's notion of *natural selection*, less adaptable organisms tend to become less numerous than organisms that are better able to adapt to the existing and changing environment.

3. A *mutation* occurs when a genetic message is changed.

4. *Genes* are the biological units that contribute to the hereditary transmission of traits. Genetic *traits* are characteristics or patterns of behavior that may be inherited. Genes are located on *chromosomes*, which come in pairs. Humans have 23 pairs of chromosomes in almost every cell of the body.

5. A *genotype* is the genetic code for a trait, and a *phenotype* is the actual visible expression of the trait in the organism. A given genotype may produce a range of phenotypes, depending on the environment in which the organism develops.

How Is the Nervous System Organized? 40

6. The nervous system is divided into two main parts: the *central nervous system (CNS)*, consisting of the brain and the spinal cord, and the *peripheral nervous system (PNS)*, consisting of the rest of the nervous system (e.g., the nerves in the face, legs, and arms).

7. The *blood–brain barrier* restricts the substances that may enter or leave the brain.

8. *Receptors* are structures that receive something. In particular, receptor neurons receive *sensory information* (e.g., sensations in the eyes, ears, and skin) from the outlying nerves of the body. The sensory neurons then transmit that information back up through the spinal cord to the brain. *Effectors* transmit *motor information* (e.g., movements of the muscles) from the CNS, controlling how the body acts in response to the information it receives.

9. A *reflex* is an automatic, involuntary response to stimulation. In many situations, reflexes can pass directly through the spinal cord, bypassing the brain. The brain is required, however, to assign conscious meaning to stimuli.

10. The peripheral nervous system has two parts: the somatic nervous system and the autonomic nervous system. The *somatic nervous system* controls voluntary movement of skeletal muscles, whereas the *autonomic nervous system* controls the involuntary muscles, such as those of the internal body organs.

What Are the Major Structures and Functions of the Human Brain? 45

11. A fundamental way to view the human brain is to *dissect* it (i.e., to separate its tissues for examination).

12. Some psychologists study animal nervous systems.

13. *Electroencephalograms (EEG)* measure and record electrical activity in the brain.

14. Although X-ray technology allows for X-ray photos and angiograms, a more psychologically revealing use of this technology is the creation of a *computerized axial tomogram (CAT scan)*, in which a computer analyzes a series of X-ray pictures and then constructs an image of the brain.

15. *Magnetic resonance imaging (MRI)* provides relatively detailed pictures of the brain based on computer analysis of magnetic changes in the molecules of the brain.

16. *Positron emission tomography (PET scan)* shows the brain in action by tracing the brain's consumption of glucose (a simple sugar).

17. There are three main parts of the brain: the *forebrain*, which includes both the cortex and the limbic system, which are important to intelligent human thinking, feeling, and behaving; the *midbrain*, which includes most of the *reticular activating system* controlling heartbeat, breathing, consciousness, attention, and movement; and the *hindbrain*, which controls many vital functions of the body.

18. The highly convoluted *cerebral cortex* is the source of human abilities to reason, think abstractly, plan, and perceive and analyze sensory patterns.

19. The cerebral cortex covers the left and right hemispheres of the brain. The two hemispheres are connected by the *corpus callosum*. In general, each hemisphere contralaterally controls the opposite side of the body.

20. Based on extensive *split-brain* research, many investigators believe that the two hemispheres of the brain have specialized functions.

21. Sometimes, psychologists view the cortex as comprising four separate lobes. Roughly speaking, higher thought and motor processing occur in the *frontal lobe*, somatosensory (skin sensations) processing occurs in the *parietal lobe*, auditory processing in the *temporal lobe*, and visual processing in the *occipital lobe*.

22. Association areas are also located in the lobes and appear to link motor and sensory information.

How Is Information Processed in the Nervous System?   55

23. A *neuron* is an individual nerve cell. *Nerves* are bunches of neurons.

24. There are three functional types of neurons: (1) *sensory neurons*, through which the CNS receives information from the environment; (2) *motor neurons*, which carry information away from the CNS toward the outlying nerves of the PNS; and (3) *interneurons*, which transmit information between sensory and motor neurons.

25. The *soma* (cell body) of a neuron is responsible for the life of the nerve cell.

26. The branchlike *dendrites* are the structures through which neurons receive chemical messages.

27. *Axons* are the stuctures through which neurons conduct an action potential, which leads to the transmission of electrochemical messages. Some axons (usually relatively long ones) are covered by segments of *myelin*, a white, fatty substance. Myelin increases the speed and accuracy of conducting information through the neuron.

28. At the end of each axon are branches with knobs termed *terminal buttons*. Each terminal button releases a chemical *neurotransmitter*.

29. Between the terminal buttons of one neuron and the dendrites of the next neuron is a *synapse*, a tiny gap.

30. When a neuron reaches its particular *threshold of excitation*, the neuron generates an *all-or-none* action potential. During an *action potential*, ions quickly flood both ways across the neuronal membrane. This rapid transfer of ions changes the electrochemical balance inside and outside the neuron. Intraneuronal communication (the "firing" of a neuron) depends on generating an action potential.

31. The receptors on postsynaptic neurons can respond to a neurotransmitter in one of two ways: They can become either *excited* (more likely to fire) or *inhibited* (less likely to fire) by the neurotransmitter. In addition, *neuromodulators* may weaken or strengthen the likelihood that a receiving neuron will respond.

32. To avoid having too many neurotransmitters in the synapse, the terminal buttons can reabsorb the excess through *reuptake*.

33. Neurotransmitters include *acetylcholine*, *dopamine*, and *serotonin*, as well as *glutamate* and *GABA*. Neuropeptides include *endorphins* and many other chemicals involved in physiological regulation.

How Does the Endocrine System Work?   62

34. In the *endocrine system*, glands (organs that secrete a substance into the body) can secrete their products directly into the bloodstream. These endocrine secretions are *hormones*. The release of hormones is regulated by a *negative feedback loop* (which monitors the levels of hormone in the bloodstream and monitors the effects of the hormones).

35. The nervous and endocrine systems are somewhat parallel: Both are communication systems, and both use chemical substances as messengers: neurotransmitters and hormones, respectively. The brain has some control over the endocrine system, just as hormones can influence the brain.

PATHWAYS TO KNOWLEDGE

Choose the best answer to complete each sentence.

1. Unlike the other two types of neurons, sensory neurons
   (a) carry electrochemical messages from the brain and spinal cord to parts of the body that may respond to the messages.
   (b) receive information from receptor cells and send this information to the brain or spinal cord.
   (c) may be found exclusively in the central nervous system.
   (d) have two functions: to send signals from motor neurons, and to receive signals from neurosensory receptors.

2. The four basic parts of a neuron are
   (a) axon, soma, myelin sheath, and dendrites
   (b) axon, soma, myelin sheath, and nodes of Ranvier
   (c) axon, soma, dendrites, and terminal buttons
   (d) axon, soma, myelin sheath, and terminal buttons

3. A synapse is
   (a) a gap between regions of myelin on an axon.
   (b) a gap between the terminal buttons of some neurons and the dendrites of other neurons.
   (c) a part of the axon, which may or may not be composed of myelin.
   (d) a part of the dendrite, which has terminal buttons for receiving neurotransmitters from other neurons.

4. The reuptake of neurotransmitters allows
   (a) neurotransmitters to be absorbed by the dendrites and soma of a receiving neuron.

(b) neurotransmitters to be reabsorbed by the terminal buttons of a neuron that previously released the neurochemicals.

(c) dendrites of receiving neurons to re-release neurotransmitters back into the synapse.

(d) dendrites that release one type of neurotransmitter to take up leftover transmitter substances released by neurons that release different types of neurotransmitters.

5. Effector nerves and neurons differ from receptor nerves and neurons, in that

(a) effectors send information quickly to the central nervous system, whereas receptors send information rather slowly to the central nervous system.

(b) effectors send information to the brain and spinal cord, but receptors send information to the outlying areas of the body.

(c) effectors receive motor information from the brain and spinal cord and send it to the outlying areas of the body, but receptors send information from the sense organs and the outlying areas of the body to the brain and spinal cord.

(d) effectors transmit sensory and motor information to the brain, but receptors receive sensory and motor information from the brain.

Answer each of the following questions by filling in the blank with an appropriate word or phrase.

6. A _____ is a structural change in a gene, which affects a hereditary characteristic.

7. Genes are located on _____.

8. A _____ for a genetic trait is the observable expression of the trait, whereas the _____ is the actual genetic makeup that an individual has for a particular genetic trait.

9. A _____ expression of a genetic trait appears in the phenotype of any individual who has at least one gene for the trait; in contrast, a _____ expression of a genetic trait appears only when a given individual has both genes for that expression of the trait.

10. The _____ of the endocrine system secrete _____ directly into the bloodstream.

11. When a neuron has been stimulated sufficiently to reach its _____ _____ _____, it generates an _____ _____ (and is said to "fire").

12. The two parts of the nervous system are the _____ _____ _____, which comprises the brain and the spinal cord, and the _____ _____ _____, which comprises all the other neurons of the areas lying outside of the brain and spinal cord.

Match the following parts of the brain to their main functions:

13. hippocampus
14. cerebellum
15. cerebral cortex
16. temporal lobe of the cortex
17. hypothalamus
18. corpus callosum
19. occipital lobe of the cortex
20. thalamus
21. parietal lobe

(a) higher order thinking
(b) connects two cerebral hemispheres
(c) bodily coordination
(d) species survival-fighting, fleeing, feeding, and mating
(e) learning
(f) somatosensory processing
(g) main relay station projecting sensory information to the appropriate areas of the cerebral cortex
(h) visual processing
(i) auditory processing

Answers

1. b, 2. c, 3. b, 4. b, 5. c, 6. mutation, 7. chromosomes, 8. phenotype, genotype, 9. dominant, recessive, 10. glands, hormones, 11. threshold of excitation, action potential, 12. central nervous system, peripheral nervous system, 13. e, 14. c, 15. a, 16. i, 17. d, 18. b, 19. h, 20. g, 21. f

PATHWAYS TO UNDERSTANDING

1. Suppose that you were a master bioengineer who could create a genetic breakthrough to enhance the adaptability of humans. What change (or changes) would you make?

2. Suppose that it were possible to make the change (or changes) you suggested in response to the preceding question. What ethical issues would be involved in making that change (or those changes)?

3. Karl Lashley, a pioneering neuropsychologist in the study of brain localization, suffered from migraine headaches. Many scientists have personal reasons for being intensely curious about the phenomena they study. What aspects of human behavior particularly puzzle you? Which areas and structures of the brain might you wish to study to find out about those aspects of behavior? Why?

CHAPTER OUTLINE

What Developmental Trends Have Psychologists Observed?

What Are the Roles of Maturation and Learning?
>The Nature–Nurture Controversy: Maturation Versus Learning
>The Roles of Maturation and Learning: The Developmental Theories of Piaget and Vygotsky

What Happens During Prenatal Development?

How Do Infants and Young Toddlers Develop?
>What Can Newborns Do?
>Physical Development During Infancy
>Cognitive Development in Infancy
>Socioemotional Development During Infancy
>What Is Your Temperament?

How Do Children Develop?
>Cognitive Development During Childhood
>Socioemotional Development
>What Should Parents Look for in High-Quality Child Care?

What Develops During Puberty and Adolescence?
>Physical Development During Adolescence
>Cognitive Development During Adolescence
>Socioemotional Development

How Do Adults Develop and Age?

CHAPTER
3

Development

"Like it? Well, I don't see why I oughtn't like it. Does a boy get a chance to white-wash a fence every day?"

That put the thing in a new light. Ben stopped nibbling his apple. Tom swept his brush daintily back and forth—stepped back to note the effect—added a touch here and there—criticized the effect again—Ben watching every move and getting more and more interested, more and more absorbed. Presently he said:

"Say, Tom, let *me* whitewash a little."

Tom considered, was about to consent; but he altered his mind:

"No—no—I reckon it wouldn't hardly do, Ben. You see, Aunt Polly's awful par-ticular about this fence—right here on the street, you know—but if it was the back fence I wouldn't mind and *she* wouldn't. Yes, she's awful particular about this fence; it's got to be done very careful; I reckon there ain't one boy in a thousand, maybe two thousand, that can do it the way it's got to be done."

"No—is that so? Oh come, now—lemme just try. Only just a little—I'd let *you,* if you was me, Tom." . . .

Tom gave up the brush with reluctance in his face, but alacrity in his heart. . . . By the time Ben was fagged out, Tom had traded the next chance to Billy Fisher for a kite, in good repair; and when *he* played out, Johnny Miller bought in for a dead rat and a string to swing it with—and so on, and so on, hour after hour. . . .

If he hadn't run out of whitewash, he would have bankrupted every boy in the village.

—*Mark Twain*

development changes that are associated with increasing physiological maturity, experience, or an interaction of physiological changes and experiences with the environment

cognitive development the process by which people's thinking changes across the life span

socioemotional development the process by which people learn about themselves as human beings, as well as by which they learn to interact with each other, across the life span; may be viewed as including emotional, personality, interpersonal, and moral development

Although Tom Sawyer never received particularly good grades in school, we cannot fail to notice that Tom is a pretty smart fellow. Tom's poor performance in the classroom, in light of his demonstrated competence elsewhere, may have been puzzling to his teachers and frustrating to his Aunt Polly. Tom's behavior shows how difficult it can be to determine a person's *competence* (what the person is capable of doing), based on the person's *performance* (what the person actually does). Mark Twain's story about Tom Sawyer also shows some of the excitement of studying how people develop: By definition, developmental psychologists look for changes in how people think, feel, and act as a result of their increasing maturity and their accumulating experiences.

Development involves both quantitative and qualitative changes associated with increasing physiological maturity and experience. Quantitative changes in the individual include increases in size (e.g., height or weight) and in amount (e.g., number of brain cells). Qualitative changes usually involve increasing complexity, organization, and sophistication.

Psychological development includes both cognitive development and socioemotional development. **Cognitive development** is the process by which people think differently at different times in their lives. **Socioemotional development** is the process of change in a person's emotions, personality, interpersonal (social)

Socioemotional development involves emotional, personality, interpersonal (social), and moral development.

relationships, and moral beliefs and actions. This chapter deals with both of these kinds of development, as well as with physical development, for each major period of the life span: infancy, childhood, adolescence, and adulthood.

WHAT DEVELOPMENTAL TRENDS HAVE PSYCHOLOGISTS OBSERVED?

Psychologists have noticed several trends that characterize development across the life span. Some of these trends are obvious: For example, humans grow taller and heavier between infancy and adulthood. Other trends are more subtle, such as the trend toward **differentiation,** in which

the *few* become *many* (e.g., a few neural connections in the brain develop into many connections),

the *simple* becomes more *complex* (e.g., one-word expressions become grammatical speech),

the *general* becomes more highly *specialized* (e.g., walking becomes running, climbing, and skipping),

and the *homogeneous* (having a uniform makeup of identical elements) becomes more *diverse* (e.g., identical newly conceived cells become various kinds of cells for making bones, nerves, or muscles).

Researchers use two main methods for detecting developmental trends. The first is to observe individuals *longitudinally* (noting the characteristics of particular persons as they change over time); the second is to observe individuals *cross-sectionally* (noting the characteristics of various people of different ages). Sometimes, researchers also combine the two methods. Psychologists seek not only to *describe* various developmental trends, but also to *understand* these trends by asking how and why particular changes occur.

What developmental trends have psychologists observed? Developmental trends involve qualitative changes, such as increasing differentiation, as well as quantitative changes, such as growth, which characterize development across the life span.

WHAT ARE THE ROLES OF MATURATION AND LEARNING?

The Nature–Nurture Controversy: Maturation Versus Learning

How and why do developmental changes occur? Developmental psychologists often disagree about exactly how to answer this question. A main point of disagreement centers on the **nature–nurture controversy.** This controversy concerns why we develop as we do. Do we develop in particular ways because of our inherited characteristics (our *nature*) or because of our interactions with the environment (our *nurture*)? It seems that as soon as some psychologists find data to support the importance of nature, other psychologists find new information emphasizing the importance of nurture. Many developmental psychologists have

differentiate become more highly specialized into distinct parts or types

nature–nurture controversy a debate regarding whether our psychological makeup arises from our inherited characteristics (our nature) or from our interactions with the environment (our nurture)

The advancement of learning is the highest commandment.

Maimonides

In your opinion, which of your skills are more dependent on your experiences (nurture), and which are more dependent on your innate ability to develop those skills (nature)?

This child's innate musical talent (his nature) might never have been discovered if he had been raised in a home in which music was not an important part of his environment (his nurture).

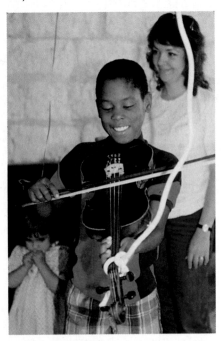

maturation   any relatively permanent change in an individual that occurs strictly as a result of the biological processes of getting older

learning   any relatively permanent change in an individual that occurs strictly as a result of that individual's experiences in interacting with the environment

schema   mental framework for organizing what is known about a particular concept

assimilation   the process of trying to restore cognitive equilibrium by incorporating new information into existing schemas

concluded that there is really no conflict at all—that in fact most of development can be viewed in terms of the interaction between the two.

How are nature and nurture expressed in development? Development can occur in two different ways: by maturation (developmental processes linked to nature) and by learning (developmental processes linked to nurture). **Maturation** is any relatively permanent change in an individual that occurs as a result of internally (biologically) prompted processes of development, without regard to personal experiences or any other environmental considerations. Physical growth in height, for example, occurs as a result of maturational processes (although some environmental influences, e.g., diet, may influence these processes). **Learning** is any relatively permanent change that occurs because of interactions with the environment (see Chapter 6). If you learn how to swim or to ride a bicycle, you will do so chiefly as a result of learning—assuming, of course, that you are mature enough to learn these skills (e.g., 1-year-olds do not learn to ride bicycles regardless of how skillfully they are taught).

Maturation is preprogrammed; it will happen for the most part regardless of the environment. In contrast, learning will take place only if the individual has particular experiences. Almost all psychologists recognize that both maturation and learning interactively influence our development, but some psychologists may more strongly emphasize one process or the other.

The Roles of Maturation and Learning: The Developmental Theories of Piaget and Vygotsky

The theories of Jean Piaget (1896–1980) and of Lev Vygotsky (1896–1934) illustrate how two different theorists give different emphasis to maturation versus learning in explaining the processes of cognitive development. Piaget suggested that cognitive development occurs largely as a result of internal processes of maturation. Piaget's theory does not discount environmental influences, but it emphasizes internal developmental processes that gradually unfold—from the inside out. To Piaget, development is chiefly a biological process by which the individual adapts to the environment.

Piaget believed that cognitive development occurs in stages that evolve as children develop increasingly complex **schemas** (also called *schemata*)—mental frameworks for what the children know about the world. In many situations, the child's existing way of thinking and the child's existing schemas are well suited for adapting to the challenges of the environment; the child is thus in a state of cognitive equilibrium (balance). For example, suppose that 2-year-old Howie uses the word *doggie* to embrace all the four-legged furry creatures that he believes are like his own dog. As long as all the four-legged creatures that Howie sees are like the dogs he has already seen, Howie remains in a state of cognitive equilibrium.

At other times, however, the child is presented with information that does not fit with the child's existing schemas, so cognitive disequilibrium arises. The imbalance comes from shortcomings in thinking as the child faces new challenges. When imbalances occur, the child tries to restore equilibrium through one of two equilibrative processes: assimilation and accommodation. In **assimilation,** the child incorporates the new information into her or his existing schemas. For example, suppose that Howie's dog is a Great Dane, and Howie goes to the park and sees a poodle, a cocker spaniel, and a Siberian husky. Howie must assimilate the new information into his existing schema for *doggies*—not a big deal.

Suppose, however, that Howie also visits a small zoo and sees a wolf, a rhinoceros, a bear, a lion, a zebra, and a camel. Howie cannot assimilate these diverse creatures into his existing schema for *doggies*. Instead, he must somehow modify his existing schemas to allow for the new information. Piaget would suggest that

Jean Piaget (left) learned a great deal about how children think by observing children (including his own) and paying a great deal of attention to what appeared to be errors in their reasoning. Lev Vygotsky (right, with his daughter) also observed children closely, but paid attention especially to the role of society in molding their behavior.

Howie modifies existing schemas through **accommodation**—changing the existing schemas to fit the relevant new information about the environment. Together, the processes of assimilation and accommodation result in a more sophisticated level of thought than was previously possible. As children become more adept thinkers, they become less **egocentric**—that is, they become increasingly able to see how others may view a situation.

Unlike Piaget, Vygotsky strongly emphasized the role of learning in his theory of cognitive development. In Vygotsky's theory, social influences are more important to cognitive development than are biological influences. To Vygotsky (1962, 1978), development proceeds from the outside in, rather than from the inside out. Specifically, cognitive development occurs through **internalization,** whereby individuals absorb knowledge from their social context. When children interact with the people in their environment, they re-create within themselves the interactions they observe. Thus, in Vygotsky's view, the people in a child's world can help or hinder the child's development of thought and knowledge.

Although Vygotsky emphasized the role of the environment, he also appreciated the importance of what each child brought to interactions with the environment. According to Vygotsky, children develop their intellect within a **zone of proximal development (ZPD)**. The ZPD is the range of ability between a child's developed, observable level of ability and the child's full, potentially hidden, capacity for developing further at a given time.

accommodation the process of trying to restore cognitive equilibrium by modifying existing schemas or even creating new ones to fit new information

egocentric focused on one's own views, without being able to see how others may view a situation

internalization the process of absorbing knowledge from a given social environmental context

zone of proximal development (ZPD) a range between the developed abilities that a child clearly shows and the latent capacities that the child might be able to show, given the appropriate environment in which to do so

No person is too old to learn.

French saying

To summarize, whereas Piaget emphasized maturation (nature), Vygotsky emphasized learning (nurture). Nonetheless, both theorists recognized that development involves an interaction of nature and nurture.

What are the roles of maturation and learning? Both maturation and learning are important processes of development, but some psychologists, such as Piaget, have emphasized maturation, and other psychologists, such as Vygotsky, have emphasized learning.

WHAT HAPPENS DURING PRENATAL DEVELOPMENT?

The influence of nature begins at the moment of conception, when the father's sperm fertilizes the mother's *ovum* (human egg). Once the one-celled ovum is fertilized, it is termed a **zygote,** the name for the first of three stages of prenatal development. The single-celled zygote immediately begins dividing into hundreds of virtually identical cells. While the zygote divides, it travels downward to the uterus (about a 3- to 7-day trip to travel several inches). The zygote takes about another week to become firmly *implanted* (deeply embedded) in the internal wall of the uterus. During implantation, cell division continues, but some of the cells begin to differentiate into specialized types of cells with distinctive functions. For example, some cells of the zygote begin to form a placenta. The **placenta** lines the wall of the uterus and provides nourishment through the umbilical cord, which attaches the placenta to the developing individual.

Once implanted (at about 2 weeks after conception), the individual is considered an **embryo,** the second of the three stages of prenatal development. The embryo stage lasts from about the end of the second week until about the beginning of the ninth week. During the development of the embryo, the cells further differentiate: One type of cell becomes the nervous system, sense organs, and skin; another type becomes the internal organs (e.g., intestines); and a third type becomes the muscles, skeleton, and blood vessels. By the end of this stage (at about 8 weeks after conception), the cells of the inch-long embryo have differentiated in many ways, including formation of a distinct heart (which begins beating at about 1 month after conception), a primitive brain and intestinal tract, a face, eyes, ears, fingers, toes, and even male or female genitals. Early development proceeds from head to tail and from the center of the body to the outer extremities. Thus, legs and arms, as well as feet and hands, develop later than internal structures do. For many systems of the body, the embryo stage is a **critical period** of rapid growth and development. For instance, the systems governing blood circulation and the function of the brain develop rapidly in the embryo. During critical periods of embryonic development, essential changes occur, and after critical periods, such changes are less likely to occur easily, fully, or adequately, if they can occur at all.

Nurture—through the maternal environment—can most dramatically affect the course of embryonic development during critical periods. If the mother smokes (Frazier et al., 1961; Golbus, 1980), drinks alcohol (Abel, 1984; Barr et al., 1990), or consumes any other toxic drugs or other substances (Adler, 1989; Chasnoff et al., 1989; Finnegan, 1982), the embryo she carries may not develop properly

zygote an individual in the first of three stages of prenatal development (from the time of conception to implantation and cell differentiation)

placenta a protective membrane containing a dense network of blood vessels through which the mother's body supplies needed resources (e.g., oxygen, sources of energy, and material resources such as protein and minerals) and removes waste products

embryo an individual in the second of the three stages of prenatal development (from about 2 weeks after conception until about the end of the 8th week); the individual undergoes tremendous differentiation and rapid growth and is easily influenced by the maternal environment

critical period a time of rapid growth and development, during which particular changes typically occur if they are ever to occur; that is, such changes typically do not occur after the critical period

(Bornstein & Bruner, 1989; Bornstein & Krasgenor, 1989). For instance, the brain and other parts of the nervous system may fail to develop properly if the mother consumes too much alcohol during her pregnancy. Unfortunately, many women are not even fully aware of their pregnancy during this time, and they may unwittingly harm their unborn children. In addition, a pregnant woman may be exposed to harmful influences against her will. For example, she may be unable to avoid breathing polluted air, or she may become infected with a virus such as rubella (German measles).

The final period of prenatal development is the stage of the **fetus,** which lasts from about the ninth week after conception until the time of birth. During this stage, the fetus continues to grow larger and heavier (to about 7–7½ pounds, 20 inches at birth), and the systems of the body grow more complex. For instance, the brain develops many neural connections, and many of the cells in the nervous system develop myelin sheaths (see Chapter 2). Throughout the entire prenatal period, the mother's attention to her own health and nutrition strongly affects the health and development of her unborn child.

After 9 or so months of enjoying the most intimate of human relationships, mother and fetus work together to deliver the infant out of the womb and into the less protected—and far more interesting—world outside. In this world, the infant must breathe, maintain a stable body temperature, obtain and digest food, eliminate waste, and perform many other independent activities for the rest of its natural life. Fortunately, most newborns arrive well equipped to do so.

Like the mother, so is the daughter.

Ezekiel

MINILECTURE

Prenatal Development (Ch 12)

---

fetus an individual in the third of the three stages of prenatal development (from about the 9th week until birth); a time during which the individual develops enough sophistication to be able to survive outside the mother's uterus

During prenatal development, the internal organ systems develop before the outer parts of the body develop, and development generally proceeds from the head downward.

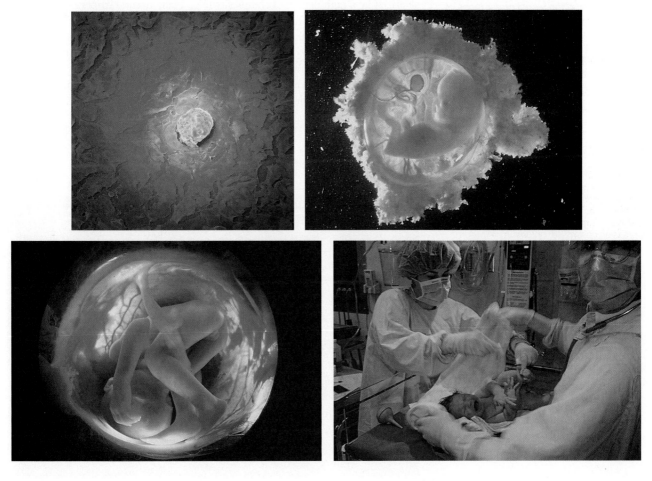

What happens during prenatal development? Throughout three stages of prenatal development—zygote, embryo, and fetus—increasing differentiation occurs largely from head to tail and from the center of the body to the outer extremities. During critical periods of development, environmental influences may have the most profound effects on how development proceeds.

HOW DO INFANTS AND YOUNG TODDLERS DEVELOP?

What Can Newborns Do?

In recent decades, psychologists have recognized the remarkable capabilities of the **neonate** (newborn). Just what can newborns do? To start with, although newborns are very near-sighted, they seem to have a set of inborn rules that guides how they scan the environment (Haith, 1979). For example, infants seem to have a general rule to scan the environment broadly, but to stop scanning and explore in depth if they see an edge. Quite conveniently, edges are more likely to contain interesting information than are uninterrupted surfaces.

Infants also prefer to look at particular kinds of objects; these objects are characterized by a high degree of complexity (e.g., many narrow stripes vs. a few wide ones), many visual contours (e.g., edges and patterns vs. solid regions of color), curved rather than straight contours, high contrast between light and dark (e.g., black and white vs. gray), and frequent movements (described in Banks & Salapatek, 1983). Quite conveniently, every parent has available a highly stimulating object that perfectly matches these criteria: a human face. In fact, infants as young as 4 days of age prefer looking at a human face to looking at other visual patterns (Fantz, 1958, 1961).

Within just a few days after birth, infants can hear voices clearly, and they seem to prefer listening to the human voice. They particularly notice the child-

Bearing in mind the visual preferences of infants, draw or describe some toys that would be appropriate for young infants. For example, design a mobile with particularly interesting objects for young infants lying on their backs.

neonate newborn (*neo-*, new; *-nate*, born)

Newborns seem to have an inborn knack for imitating some of the facial expressions of their caregivers (e.g., a smile, pout, open-mouthed expression of surprise, or tongue protrusion).

directed speech (formerly called "motherese") that characterizes the way in which adults communicate with infants. Some psychologists suggest that newborns seem custom-designed to gain the attention—and perhaps even the love—of their caregivers. Infants can also detect smells; breast-fed 6-day-olds seem to prefer the smell of their own mothers' milk to that of other breast-feeding women, and breast-fed 3-month-olds seem to prefer the body smells of their own mothers over those of other mothers (MacFarlane, 1975; Russell, 1976).

In comparison with the senses of vision, hearing, and smell, the sensory system that appears most fully developed at birth is that of touch. For instance, Jean Mandler (1990) found that 1-month-old infants can link some visual and tactile (touch) sensations. When infants were given a chance to suck on either a bumpy or a smooth pacifier (see Figure 3-1), the infants seemed to recognize which type of pacifier they had been sucking. Recall that early development proceeds from the head downward (and from the center of the body to the outer extremities), so infants' sensory and motor skills are highly developed in the sensory receptors and muscles of their mouths before they develop in regions of the body farther from the head and from the center of the body (e.g., in the hands or feet).

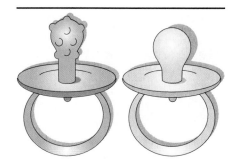

Figure 3-1
Familiar Versus Unfamiliar
Even 1-month-old infants can readily integrate their senses of touch and of vision when given the chance to use the well-developed sensory and motor skills of their mouths. For example, after sucking on one of the two types of pacifiers shown here, 1-month-olds looked longer at the kind of pacifier on which they had sucked (Mandler, 1990).

Physical Development During Infancy

Maturational changes in physical abilities were among the first aspects of development to be studied extensively. For example, Nancy Bayley's (1968) *Bayley Scales of Infant Development* specify the ages at which infants normally begin performing various kinds of physical **motor** tasks (involving movements of the muscles) (see Figure 3-2). Usually, the ages at which children develop particular motor skills (or particular reflexes) bear little direct relationship to the children's cognitive or socioemotional development or to their future intelligence or adult personality (Bloom, 1964). The exception to this rule occurs when the development of these skills falls far below the normal age range.

Cognitive Development in Infancy

During infancy, physical development provides the foundation and framework for all other aspects of development. In fact, according to developmental psychologist Jean Piaget (1969, 1972), infant cognitive development is characterized by *sensory* (involving the senses) and *motor* (involving muscle movements and coordination) development. Piaget even identified the period of infant cognitive development as the **sensorimotor stage.**

According to Piaget, during the sensorimotor stage of cognitive development, infants gradually adapt their reflexive actions (e.g., random kicking or arm movements) to bring those actions under conscious control. For example, if a young infant accidentally kicks a mobile and makes it move in an interesting way, the infant will purposely try to control the muscles that kicked the mobile, to make the interesting movements of the mobile continue or occur again. Hence, as infants gain mastery over their motor system, they gain increasing control over (a) their interactions with their environment, and (b) the sensations they will experience because of these interactions.

Just what kinds of sensations do infants consider interesting? They tend to be most interested in stimuli that are moderately unfamiliar. That is, they are more interested in stimuli that are somewhat unusual than in stimuli that are either highly familiar or highly unusual (and perhaps therefore overwhelming).

If infants can distinguish unfamiliar from familiar stimuli in their environments, they must be able to remember something about their environments, at least for short periods of time. On the other hand, throughout infancy and even the first few years after birth, children's long-term memories (which last a long period of time) are highly unstable. Researchers have found little evidence that

Imagine yourself as an infant or young child, and describe your view of and experiences in the world before and after learning to crawl, to sit, or to walk. How would your opportunities for thinking about and interacting with your environment change?

motor related to moving the muscles

sensorimotor stage Piaget's first stage of development (about the first 2 years after birth), during which the child builds on reflexes and develops the first mental representations of things that are not being sensed at the moment

1 MONTH	2 MONTHS	3 MONTHS	4 MONTHS	5 MONTHS	6 MONTHS
   • Prefers to lie on back • Cannot hold head erect; head sags forward • Hands usually tightly fisted	• When lying on stomach, can lift head 45° and extend legs • Head-bobbing gradually disappears; may hold head erect		• Can roll from back to side • When lying on stomach, can lift head 90°, arms and legs lift and extend • Can sit propped up for 10-15 minutes	• Can roll from back to stomach • May "bounce" when held standing	

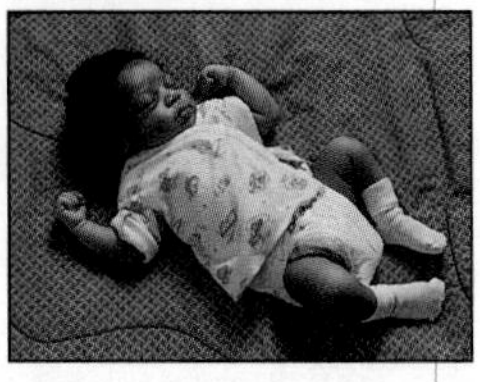

Figure 3-2
Bayley's "Landmarks of Motor Development and Ages of Occurrence"
These landmarks served as the basis for the Bayley Scales of Infant Development. *Particular motor accomplishments do not directly correlate with particular cognitive changes. However, these accomplishments do alter how the child can interact with the environment. Also, the child's interactions may facilitate cognitive development.*

MINILECTURE
Object Permanence (Ch 12)

You go through so many changes as a child, then you grow up and discover that none of that stuff mattered, except for the impression it made on your mind.

Joan Walton Collaso

How have some aspects of your own cognitive development affected your socioemotional development?

object permanence the cognitive realization that objects may continue to exist even when they are not currently being sensed

anyone can remember large numbers of specific experiences from their first few years of life.

Despite young children's apparent inability to form lasting memories of specific experiences, young children do learn a great deal. In fact, much of what people learn during those early years continues to serve as a solid foundation for subsequent learning. For example, through their experiences and interactions with objects and people in their environment, infants achieve a major cognitive milestone: They develop a sense of object permanence. **Object permanence** is the ability to form mental representations of objects (and people) that can continue to be held in mind even when those objects cannot be seen, heard, or otherwise sensed (see Figure 3-3). Basically, what infants 4 months old or younger see is what they get—what they know to exist. These infants have not developed a way of mentally representing anything they do not sense at the moment. Anything that young infants cannot sense directly simply ceases to exist for them. Over the following months, infants begin to form stable, permanent mental representations of objects and people, which the infants can continue to hold in mind even when those objects and people are not immediately perceptible to them. By age 9 months, infants have developed a sense of object permanence.

The development of object permanence means that when young infants can neither see nor hear their parents, they have no mental representation of their parents to carry in their minds until their parents reappear. Hence, they may need more frequent assurance of their parents' presence, at least until they develop a sense of object permanence. In addition to influencing children's interactions with their parents, congnitive development influences socioemotional development in other ways. Recall, for example, that newborns seem to be mentally tuned in to human faces and voices. This innate interest in people seems to continue throughout infancy.

Socioemotional Development During Infancy

The socioemotional development of infants centers on emotional development, interpersonal (social) development, and personality development.

7 MONTHS	8 MONTHS	9 MONTHS	10 MONTHS	11 MONTHS	12 MONTHS
▪ When lying on back, can lift feet to mouth ▪ Can sit erect for a few minutes ▪ May crawl ▪ Can stand supporting full body weight on feet–if held up		▪ Creeps on hands and knees ▪ Can sit indefinitely ▪ Can pull self to standing position and may "cruise" by moving feet ▪ By 10 months may be able to sit down from standing position		▪ Pulls self actively to feet and "cruises" along table or crib ▪ May stand momentarily without support ▪ Can walk if one hand is held; may take a few steps alone	▪ Can get up without help and may take several steps alone ▪ Can creep upstairs on hands and knees ▪ May squat or stoop without losing balance ▪ Can throw ball

Emotional Development

We start our discussion of infant socioemotional development by considering the development of emotions. Infants show increasing emotional differentiation (Brazelton, 1983; Izard, Kagan, & Zajonc, 1984; Sroufe, 1979), as well as increasing cognitive control over their emotions. For example, young infants show a generalized response (a startle reflex) to such stimuli as loud noises. Older infants, however, show more specific emotional responses, which tend to involve more cognitive processing, such as when the infants show a fear of strangers.

Figure 3-3

Object Permanence

As this sequence of pictures shows, younger infants (at about 4 months of age) and older infants (by about 9 months of age) react quite differently to tasks requiring a sense of object permanence. In the object-permanence demonstration, an object is hidden under a blanket or behind a screen. An older infant realizes that the object continues to exist even when it is out of sight, and the infant pursues the hidden object. In contrast, as shown here, the younger one looks away as soon as the object disappears from sight. Once the young infant cannot sense the object's presence, the object no longer exists in the mind of the infant.

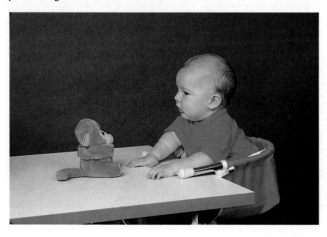 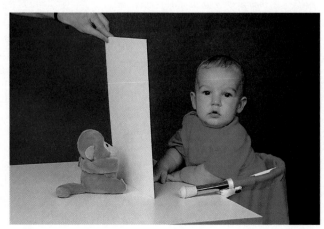

Emotional development also involves increasing awareness of, sensitivity to, and interaction with other persons. For one thing, infants form an **attachment**—a strong and relatively long-lasting emotional tie—to their parents and to other significant persons in their lives. Attachment is a mutual process of emotional bonding; parents help to cement this bonding by providing emotional and physical nurture to their infants. Infants encourage their parents' attachment through social smiles and through social referencing. *Social smiles* are the toothless grins that infants start flashing a few weeks after birth. Through *social referencing*, infants observe how their parents and other trusted adults react to new or ambiguous situations; then the infants figure out how they themselves should respond emotionally to these situations. For instance, if infants observe that their parents feel emotionally distressed when leaving the infants with a caregiver, the infants are also more likely to feel emotionally distressed.

At about the same time that infants are beginning to develop a sense of object permanence, the infants start to show separation anxiety. In **separation anxiety,** infants show varying degrees of fearfulness when briefly separated from their parents (or other primary caregivers). Infants also start showing *stranger anxiety*, a wariness of strangers. The ways in which infants show social and emotional developments (e.g., separation anxiety and stranger anxiety) depend partly on their personalities and partly on their relationships with significant persons (e.g., their parents).

Infant Personality Development

Temperament.   When psychologists study social and emotional development, they often emphasize likenesses in development across all or most individuals (e.g., the emergence of attachment, of separation anxiety, and even of social smiles). In contrast, when psychologists study personality development, they often emphasize individual differences in development. For example, some researchers have studied **temperament,** differences in an individual's characteristic mood and typical intensity and duration of emotions and motivations. Temperament influences the development of personality and of relationships with other people.

Alexander Thomas and Stella Chess conducted a well-regarded longitudinal study of temperament in children—birth through adolescence (e.g., Thomas &

Your children need your presence more than your presents.

Jesse Jackson

How and why do we develop emotions? Other than enriching our lives, what additional important purposes do they serve?

---

attachment   a strong and relatively long-lasting emotional tie between people

separation anxiety   fear of being separated from a primary caregiver, such as a parent

temperament   a person's distinctive tendency to show a particular mood and a particular intensity and duration of emotions

---

At about 8 months age (give or take a month or 2), infants start to show separation anxiety— *a fear of being separated from their mothers or other familiar adults. It may not be coincidental that when infants later acquire a concept of object permanence, they seem to be able to cope better with their anxiety about being separated from their primary caregivers.*

PRACTICAL PSYCHOLOGY   3-1

What Is Your Temperament?

According to Thomas and Chess, individual differences in nine distinctive characteristics of temperament have been observed to begin in infancy and to remain relatively stable at least through adolescence (Thomas & Chess, 1977; Thomas, Chess, & Birch, 1970). In the following chart, ask yourself the questions in the left-hand column (a possible range of answers is given in the right-hand column). At your next opportunity, ask someone who knew you as an infant (e.g., a parent or grandparent or older sibling) to describe your temperament during infancy. (You may have to rephrase the questions. For instance, instead of "How active are you?" you might ask this person, "How active was I when I was an infant?") How stable do your temperament characteristics appear to be?

What temperament characteristics do you observe in yourself?*	Characteristic (range of responses)
How active are you?	**Activity level** (very active to very inactive)
How predictable are your patterns of eating, sleeping, and so on?	**Rhythmicity** or regularity of biological cycles (very predictable to very unpredictable)
How outgoing are you?	**Approach/withdrawal** (very outgoing to very shy)
How ably do you adapt your responses to new situations?	**Adaptability** (very adaptable to very unadaptable)
How high a level of stimulation is needed to prompt you to respond?	**Threshold of reactivity** (very high to very low threshold)
How strongly and energetically do you respond to stimuli?	**Intensity and energy of reaction** (very strongly and energetically to very mildly and calmly)
In what kind of mood are you most of the time?	**Quality of dominant mood** (very happy and pleasant to very sad and unpleasant)
How easily are you distracted from pursuing activities in which you were already interested?	**Distractibility** (highly distractible to highly engaged)
How willing are you to continue to attempt activities or to solve problems in the face of obstacles?	**Attention span and persistence** despite obstacles (highly persistent to lacking in persistence)

* Can someone you know help you to answer these questions about yourself when you were an infant?

Chess, 1977; Thomas, Chess, & Birch, 1970). They found that infants showed individual differences in the nine distinctive temperamental characteristics shown in Practical Psychology 3-1 (characteristics such as activity level and adaptability). In addition, these investigators noted the importance of the **person–environment interaction**—the distinctive match between an individual's temperament and the treatment of the individual by other persons in the environment. For example, a highly active child might be well suited to a rowdy family environment with many siblings, but such a child might not be as well suited to a quiet family environment in which children are expected to engage only in restful activities.

Erikson's Psychosocial Theory of Personality Development.   Whereas Thomas and Chess focused on stable characteristics of temperament, Erik Erikson focused on changes in personality development across the life span. For Erikson, infant personality development centers on the establishment of a fundamental sense of trust—or of mistrust. In Erikson's view, infants come to establish a basic sense of trust through their relationship with their primary caregiver, who continually meets their basic physical and emotional needs for loving nurturance (e.g., food and drink), for physical and emotional comfort, and so on. Hence, infants learn either to *trust* or to *mistrust* that their needs will be met. They come to view the world as basically either friendly or hostile. Successful passage through this stage leads to the development of a hopeful attitude toward life.

How do infants and young toddlers develop? Infants and toddlers develop fundamental sensory and motor skills, which they use quite ably to begin to form mental representations of their environment, as illustrated by the development of object permanence. Infants and toddlers also form attachments to parents and other caregivers, and they develop a basic sense of trust.

You can do anything with children if only you play with them.

German proverb

HOW DO CHILDREN DEVELOP?

Cognitive Development During Childhood

Preoperational Thinking

According to Piagetian theory, young children (of ages 1½ or 2 to 6 or 7 years) are in the **preoperational stage** of cognitive development. During this stage, the young child becomes increasingly able to manipulate mental representations of familiar objects and events. *Representations* are things or ideas that stand for other things or ideas. The earliest mental representations are highly concrete (e.g., mental representations of parents who are out of sight). Eventually, however, these mental representations include *signs* (e.g., the familiar signs for men's and women's restrooms), which somewhat resemble what they represent, and *symbols*, which do not resemble what they represent and are chosen arbitrarily. For example, the words on this page are very abstract symbols, in which particular letters (symbols) are associated with particular sounds (more symbols), to be linked into words, phrases, and sentences (still more symbols), which have arbitrary meanings. (For example, there is only an arbitrary relationship between the words "rat," "cat," and "bat" and the particular kinds of mammals that those words represent.)

person–environment interaction   the distinctive fit between a given person and his or her environment

preoperational stage   Piaget's second stage of development (about age 2 years until the age of starting elementary school), during which the child develops language and concepts about physical objects

The original meaning of *infant* is "incapable of speech" (*Merriam-Webster's Collegiate Dictionary*, 1993). By definition, therefore, the emergence of language—and linguistic communication—signals the end of infancy. With the development of language comes the increasing development of concepts. According to Piaget, children develop conceptual schemas through the processes of assimilation and accommodation. Over time, young children use increasingly complex **representational thought** as they acquire more sophisticated concepts and language. Such thought enables them to characterize objects as well as concepts mentally. Early and highly concrete representations pave the way for later, less concrete ones. Additional characteristics of preoperational thinking include the following:

1. Initially, preoperational children tend to focus on only one aspect of a situation at a given time; they cannot *decenter* (consider more than one aspect of the situation at a time). For example, they cannot focus simultaneously on both the width and the height of a glass of milk; if they see a glass of milk poured from a short, wide glass into a tall, thin glass, they do not consider both the width and the height of the glass in thinking about the quantity of milk in each glass. Typically, they focus on the height of the glass. They believe that the *tall*, thin glass contains more milk than did the *short*, wide glass.
2. They also focus on *static* (unchanging) conditions rather than on *dynamic* (changing) processes. For example, in observing someone pour milk from a short, wide glass into a tall, thin glass, they give less thought to the process of pouring than to the states before and after the milk was poured.
3. Preoperational children find it difficult or impossible mentally to *reverse* (imagine undoing) a process. For example, after observing someone pour milk from a short, wide glass into a tall, thin glass, these children do not seem able to consider what would happen if the milk in the tall, thin glass were poured back into the short, wide glass, reversing the process.

To summarize, preoperational children show the developmental characteristics of *centration* (inability to focus on more than one aspect of a situation), an *emphasis on states* rather than on processes, and *irreversibility* of thought (inability mentally to reverse a process). These characteristics combine to make it virtually impossible for preoperational children to comprehend conservation of quantity. **Conservation of quantity** is the ability to recognize that the quantity (amount) of something remains the same, despite changes in appearance, as long as no amount of the substance was added or taken away. Figure 3-4 shows several examples of how preoperational children respond to tasks involving conservation of quantity.

Preoperational children also have difficulty with their understandings of causal relationships. On the one hand, when observing events with which they are highly familiar, young children demonstrate a pretty clear understanding of causal relationships (Gelman, Bullock, & Meck, 1980; Mandler, 1990). For example, if you were to ask 3-year-olds, "Why is the sidewalk wet?" most 3-year-olds (who have had experience with wet sidewalks) would probably suggest plausible causes (e.g., rain, sprinklers, water being poured or spilled). On the other hand, young children do not consistently reason *deductively* (from general principles to particular instances) or *inductively* (from many specific instances to some general principles). Instead, they frequently reason *transductively:* They reason based on associations due to coincidence (things happening to occur at about the same time) or due to functional relationships (things that are part of the same process, thing, or event; e.g., cats both have fur and drink milk, but neither of these functional cat-related features causes the occurrence of the other). As an example of transductive thinking, young children may observe that in American culture, carrying a purse and wearing facial makeup are associated with being a woman. Hence, they may reason transductively that carrying a purse and wearing facial makeup cause a person to be a woman.

We cannot learn everything from "general principles"—there may be exceptions.

Talmud

representational thought thinking involving mental images, such as images of tangible objects

conservation of quantity the principle that the quantity of something remains the same as long as nothing is removed or added, even if the appearance of the substance changes in form

Type	The child is shown:	The experimenter:	The child responds:
Liquid	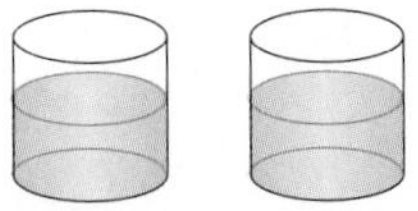 two equal short, wide glasses of water and agrees that they hold the same amount.	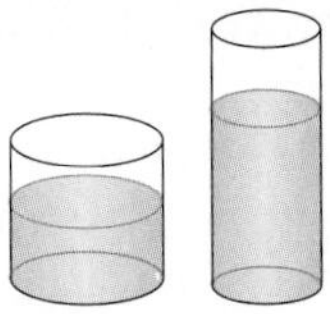 pours water from the short, wide glass into the tall, thin one and asks if one glass holds more water than the other or if both are the same.	**Preoperational child:** The tall glass has more. **Concrete operational child:** They hold the same amount.
Matter	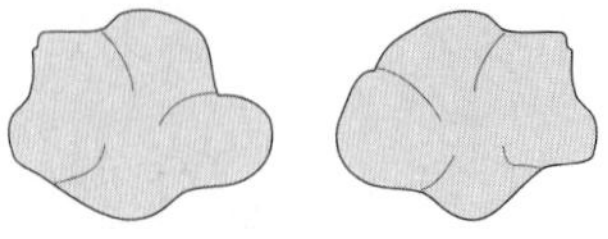 two equal ball of clay and agrees they are the same.	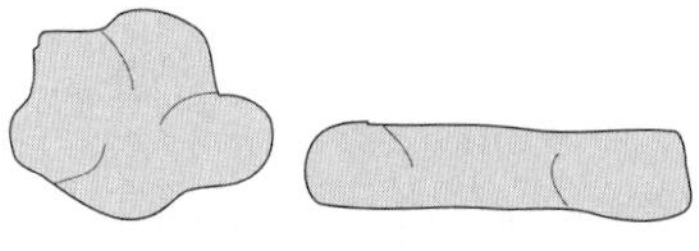 rolls one ball of clay into a sausage and asks if one has more clay or if both are the same.	**Preoperational child:** The long one has more clay. **Concrete operational child:** They both have the same amount.
Number	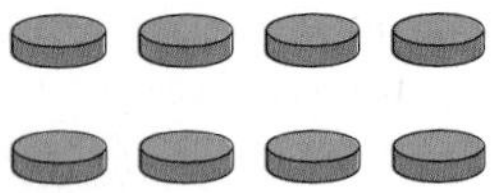 two rows of checkers and agrees that both rows have the same number.	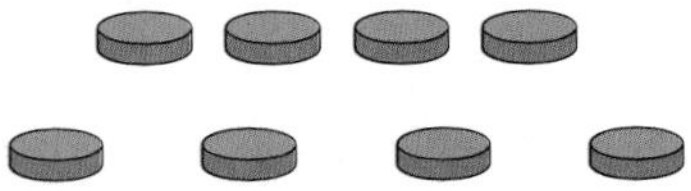 spreads out the second row and asks if one row has more checkers than the other or if both are the same.	**Preoperational child:** The longer row has more checkers. **Concrete operational child:** The number of checkers in each row has not changed.
Length	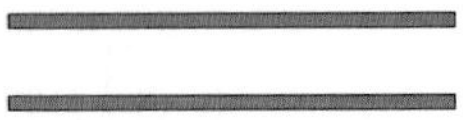 two sticks and agrees that they are the same length.	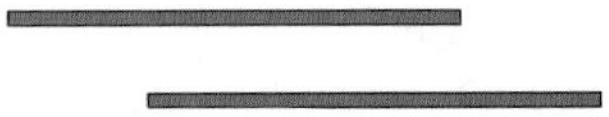 moves the bottom stick and asks if they are still the same length.	**Preoperational child:** The bottom stick is longer. **Concrete operational child:** They're the same length.
Volume	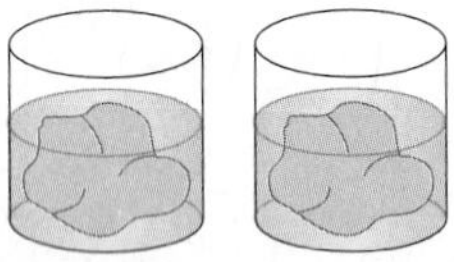 two balls of clay put in two glasses equally full of water and says the level is the same in both.	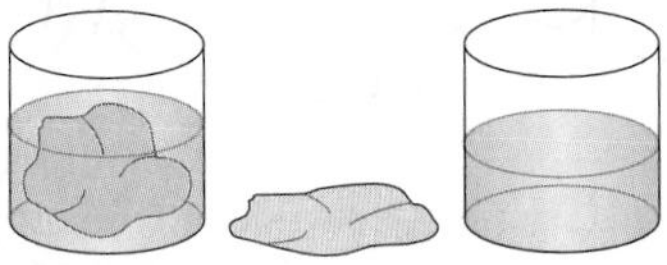 flattens one ball of clay and asks if the water level will be the same in both glasses.	**Preoperational child:** The water in the glass with the flat piece won't be as high as the water in the other glass. **Concrete operational child:** Nothing has changed; the levels will be the same in each glass.

Figure 3-4
Conservation of Quantity
During the preoperational stage, children have difficulty conserving quantity when perceptible changes occur. When viewing an experimenter transform the shape of a ball of clay, preoperational children tend to assert that there is more clay when the amount of matter of the clay appears to be greater (e.g., in a long sausage shape, as opposed to a ball of clay). When viewing an experimenter change the arrangement of checkers from a more dense pattern to a more scattered pattern, preoperational children tend to assert that there are more checkers in a dispersed arrangement than in the dense arrangement. When viewing an experimenter change the relative positions of sticks, preoperational children tend to assert that the moved stick is longer when it protrudes beyond the end of the other stick.

Concrete-Operational Thinking

After many experiences interacting with and observing their environment, children enter the **concrete-operational stage** (Piaget, 1972). In this stage, children begin to form mental rules about what they experience. We may characterize the shift from preoperational to concrete-operational thinking in terms of the following trends:

1. Through experiences with realistic events, children gradually differentiate reality from fantasy.
2. Through experiences with cause–effect relationships, children gradually come to infer principles regarding what cause will lead to a particular effect.
3. Through experiences with physically manipulating various numbers of concrete objects, children gradually can manipulate concepts about numbers (e.g., adding or subtracting).
4. Through their experiences in manipulating various kinds of quantities of substances, children can eventually *conserve quantity*, recognizing that the quantity of a substance stays the same despite changes in the appearance of the substance.

In Piaget's classic experiment on the conservation of quantity, the experimenter shows the child two short, stout beakers with liquid in them (see Figure 3-5). The experimenter has the child confirm that the two beakers contain the same amounts of liquid. Then, as the child watches, the experimenter pours the liquid from one beaker into a third beaker, which is taller and thinner than the other two. In the new beaker, the liquid in the narrower tube rises to a higher level

"How come PJ got 4 sandwiches and I only got 2?"

© 1995 by Bil Keane, Inc. Distributed by King Features Syndicate, Inc. All rights reserved. Reprinted with special permission of King Features Syndicate.

concrete-operational stage Piaget's third stage of development (about the period of elementary school), during which the child can mentally manipulate images of concrete objects

Figure 3-5
Conservation of Liquid Quantity
Can this child conserve matter, recognizing that the quantity is conserved (stays the same) despite superficial changes in the liquid's appearance?

MINILECTURE
Conservation (Ch 12)

than in the other, still-full, shorter beaker. When asked whether the amounts of liquid in the two full beakers are the same or different, the preoperational child says that there is now more liquid in the taller, thinner beaker because the liquid in that beaker reaches a perceptibly higher point. The child does not conceive that the amount is conserved despite the change in appearance. The concrete-operational child, on the other hand, says that the beakers contain the same amount of liquid, based on the child's internal schemas regarding the conservation of liquid.

During the concrete-operational stage, most children have entered school, and they spend large portions of their days engaged in learning to read and write, to understand various concepts, and to solve an array of problems involving the mental manipulation of concrete objects and ideas. In recent years, in addition to "reading, 'riting, and 'rithmetic," "reasoning" has become a fourth "R" of formal education. Children in the concrete-operational stage are developmentally ready to explore how reasoning may aid them in their thinking processes. In fact, a key characteristic of concrete-operational children, as opposed to preoperational children, is their readiness to engage in *metacognition* (thinking about their own thought processes). Their increasing ability to think about their own thought processes accompanies an increasing ability to think about how other people think and feel. This ability to consider the perspectives of other persons influences the children's social interactions, as well as their emotional and personality development.

Socioemotional Development

Emergence of Personality and Identity During Childhood

The personality and identity development of children centers on their development of independence, mastery, and a sense of personal competence; on the development of self-understanding and self-esteem; and on the development of gender identity.

Erikson's Theory of Personality and Identity Development.   According to Erikson, during early childhood (about ages 1–3 years), the main crisis young children face centers on the issue of *autonomy* versus *shame* and *doubt*. Children who do not master this stage doubt themselves and feel shame about themselves and their abilities in general. Children who master the challenge become autonomous—self-sufficient in walking, talking, eating, using the toilet, and so on.

A little later in childhood (at about ages 3–6 years), children face the difficult challenge of learning how to take *initiative*, to avoid *guilt*, and to assert themselves in socially acceptable ways. Somewhat older children (about ages 6–12 years) must face a crisis centered on the issue of *industry* versus *inferiority*. At this time, children learn a sense of capability and of industriousness in their work. Those who do not develop this sense develop instead feelings of incompetence, inferiority, and low self-worth.

When I discover who I am, I'll be free.

Ralph Ellison

Self-concept.   The development of feelings of self-worth is one aspect of the emergence of the self-concept. A broad, general definition of **self-concept** is that it is the way we view ourselves. Cross-cultural developmental psychologists such as Patricia Greenfield (1994) have suggested that our self-concept often depends on our sense of *independence* (i.e., our autonomy and individuality) and of *interdependence* (i.e., our sense of belongingness and collectivity) (e.g., described in Greenfield & Cocking, 1994; Markus & Kitayama, 1991). Although both of these aspects of self are important to all persons, the influence of culture determines how the two combine to characterize a specific individual. For example, some Asian and Latin American societies (such as in China, Japan, and Mexico) tend to emphasize the so-

self-concept an individual's beliefs, understandings, and judgments about her- or himself

cialization of individuals to be interdependent and collectivistic, whereas most Western societies tend to emphasize the fostering of independence and individualism. According to Greenfield, the orientation toward interdependence versus independence profoundly influences socioemotional and intellectual development at home, in the community, and at school.

Home, community, and school contexts also seem to influence two distinctive aspects of self-concept: self-understanding and self-esteem. Self-understanding is mainly cognitive, whereas self-esteem is mainly emotional. In particular, *self-understanding* refers to how we comprehend ourselves—as good students, as fair athletes, as thoughtful friends, and so on (Damon & Hart, 1982). *Self-esteem* refers to how much a person values him- or herself. According to research by Susan Harter (1990), our self-concepts become increasingly differentiated over the course of development. As we explore our abilities and learn more skills, we also have more arenas in which to gauge our self-worth. For example, during the elementary-school years, children's self-concept increasingly focuses on what children can *do*—dance, play soccer, achieve high grades.

In addition, the influence of other persons in the development of self-concept changes across the course of development. During early childhood, children's self-concept often reflects children's views of how their parents perceive them. Once children start school, the perceived opinions of their peers increasingly influence children's self-concepts.

Many observable characteristics of an individual can affect the development of self-esteem. The characteristics may include racial differences, regional or cultural accents, physical differences (e.g., weight, height, unusual features, or physical handicap), and the distinction of being male or female. (*Sex* is a person's biological distinction as being male or female, and *gender* is the social and psychological distinction as being male or female.) For example, self-esteem has been linked to gender differences. A report by the American Association of University Women (AAUW) Education Foundation has found that girls, who enter school roughly equal to boys in their abilities and self-esteem, leave school relatively deficient in mathematical ability and in self-esteem (AAUW, 1992). Why does this change occur? Among other things, research has shown that girls receive less attention from teachers and that curricula in schools heavily emphasize male achievements (Nelson, 1990; Sadker & Sadker, 1984). The differences in self-esteem become greatest during adolescence, when issues of sexuality and gender identity are highlighted.

At an early age, children believe that particular hair styles and clothing determine gender instead of merely signaling gender according to a particular society. If young children were to see this photo of Ernest Hemingway and were told that he grew up to be a man and a father, they might still believe that in this photo, he was a girl, but that he may have changed later to become a man.

Development of Gender Identity. Although most of us think of sexual-identity development as beginning some time in adolescence, children actually start to form their gender identifications by the age of 2 or 3 years (Thompson, 1975). **Gender typing,** the acquisition of gender-related roles, begins early, too. From ages 2 to 7 years, children seem to have rather rigid sex-role stereotypes. They use rigid stereotypes because they see gender identity as being determined by superficial characteristics, which can be changed, rather than as being characterized by biological distinctions, which cannot be changed. By the end of childhood, young people develop a sense that a person's sex cannot be changed just by changing superficial characteristics (e.g., hair length) or behaviors (e.g., carrying a purse).

There are many theories of gender typing (described in Beall & Sternberg, 1993; e.g., Bandura, 1977b; Bem, 1981; Benbow & Stanley, 1980; Huston, 1983, 1985; Kenrick & Trost, 1993). Some theorists more strongly emphasize the role of nature (physiological differences between the sexes), and others more strongly emphasize the role of nurture (differences due to socialization). Some theorists have also suggested the concept of *androgyny,* in which a person shows about equal degrees of feminine and masculine characteristics and behavior. Such a person acts in ways that seem appropriate to the situation, regardless of society's gender

gender typing process of acquiring gender-related roles for a given society

TABLE 3-1

Selman's Stages of Friendship
(After Selman, 1981; Berndt & Perry, 1986)

Stage	Example
Playmateship (preschool) Based on physical availability, convenience, and fleeting emotional state	María's best friend is Tanya because Tanya lives near María, so it is easy for them to play together. Their relationship is very volatile, however. They frequently have brief angry outbursts over toys, choice of activities, and who will do what during a particular activity.
One-way assistance (primary grades) Based on fulfillment of needs, such as companionship or desired toys or other materials	Cheng's best friend is Tom because Tom is willing to play with Cheng whenever Cheng wants to play, and Tom has lots of terrific toys.
Fair-weather cooperation (later elementary grades) Based on some mutuality and reciprocity, but poor conflict-management skills often disrupt the relationship	Isaac and Kareem are best friends because both of them cooperate with one another, share important decisions in a way that considers the needs of both boys, take turns doing fun activities, and share toys. Still, from time to time, they run into conflicts that their current social skills cannot help them resolve.
Intimate and mutually shared relationships (late childhood and early adolescence) Based on much more mutuality and reciprocity of emotional and other support	Susie and Joan have developed a strong friendship based on mutual cooperation. When they do disagree, they can usually find means to resolve their conflicts in ways that meet the needs of both girls.

How could you create an environment for children that would minimize sex-role stereotypes?

Tell me your friends, and I'll tell you who you are.

Assyrian proverb

stereotypes as to how people of a particular sex should react. A key aspect of gender identity is the way in which people form and develop interpersonal relationships.

Development of Interpersonal Relationships

Interpersonal development encompasses qualitative changes in how people relate to other people. For one thing, although parents continue to be important to people throughout the life span, particularly during childhood, friendships and other interactions with peers become increasingly important. Relationships with peers during childhood are important not only for the child's well-being, but eventually, for the well-being of the adult whom the child will become. During this time, children develop increasing awareness of others and increasingly consider the perspectives of other persons. These changes influence and are influenced by children's relationships with friends. Robert Selman (1981) has identified four stages of friendship during childhood. As Table 3-1 shows, these stages indicate increasing ability to consider the views of another person and increasing willingness to give, as well as to take.

Early in this century, families tended to include more children, so children spent a lot of time in the company of other children. During the 1950s, however, when families tended to be smaller and many mothers worked mostly at home, children spent a lot of time with one or two parents and one or two siblings. Nowadays, the trend seems to be for children to spend more time with other children once again. By the time this book reaches your hands, an estimated three fourths of the mothers with school-age children will be working outside the home (U.S. Bureau of Labor Statistics, 1994). At present, an extensive body of research (Andersson, 1989; Belsky, 1990; Clarke-Stewart, 1989; Field, 1990; Gottfried & Gottfried, 1988; Hoffman, 1989) has not led to definite conclusions regarding the effects of child care on preschoolers and school-aged children. Clearly, the quality of the child-care program influences the outcomes. What seems to matter most is not *whether* children are in a child-care program, but *which* child-care program they are in (see Practical Psychology 3-2).

interpersonal development process by which people change across the life span in the way they relate to other people

PRACTICAL PSYCHOLOGY   3-2

What Should Parents Look for in High-Quality Child Care?

The National Association for the Education of Young Children has suggested a long list of appropriate versus inappropriate child-care practices, from which we can summarize the following key features of high-quality child care:

1. Staff members try to facilitate both intellectual and socioemotional development of children.
2. Children are valued as individuals whose distinctive abilities and preferences for activities are recognized and appreciated.
3. Children are offered a wide variety of hands-on explorations of materials and diverse kinds of activities from which they may choose to work individually or in small groups.
4. Children are given meaningful experiences with language, both spoken and written. Literacy-related activities are naturally incorporated into the whole curriculum.
5. Teachers work with small numbers of children, with whom they frequently interact to facilitate, extend, and explore each child's interests.
6. Teachers set clear but reasonable age-appropriate limits and help children to regulate their own behavior. Teachers encourage and support children's social interactions, suggesting alternatives for conflict resolution when children cannot satisfactorily resolve conflicts unaided.

In addition to these practices, two factors also strongly influence the quality of the care given to children: *low staff:student ratios* (i.e., each adult caregiver is responsible for only a small number of children) and low *turnover of staff* (i.e., most staff persons continue working in the same site, with the same children, over an extended period of time). When each staff person has fewer children to supervise, each child receives better social and educational stimulation, as well as fundamental assurance of safety. When there is low turnover of staff, children can establish secure relationships with the persons who provide care to them. In addition, low staff turnover generally indicates that the care facility provides a pleasant work environment and that the staff members enjoy their work.

What is a particular characteristic of child care that you believe is important to the well-being of children? How might you test to see whether particular child-care settings provide this characteristic?

the BIG picture

How do children develop? Children become increasingly adept at thinking in terms of general principles and rules. This increasing facility allows them to be less dependent on what they observe directly, and enables them to conserve quantity, as well as to use inductive and deductive reasoning. Children also develop autonomy, initiative, and industry, as well as increasingly sophisticated self-concepts and gender identities. As the childhood years progress, children are increasingly able to form more mutually beneficial friendships.

WHAT DEVELOPS DURING PUBERTY AND ADOLESCENCE?

Physical Development During Adolescence

Adolescence need not be the time of stress and strain which Western society made it.

Margaret Mead

The end of childhood is signaled by the onset of puberty. During **puberty,** males and females reach sexual maturity, their reproductive systems begin to function (*primary sex characteristics*), and they develop *secondary sex characteristics* (e.g., male voice, female breasts and hips, and pubic and underarm hair). **Adolescence** is the period of time between the onset of puberty and the time the individual accepts the full responsibilities of being an adult.

During adolescence, people change from being seen as children to being seen as adults—both by themselves and by other persons. Although the change from childhood to adulthood occurs in all cultures, the form and the timing of the change vary cross-culturally (Berry et al., 1992). Thus, whereas puberty involves physiological changes largely affected by nature (e.g., development of secondary sex characteristics), adolescence often also involves psychological changes largely affected by nurture (e.g., social attitudes toward the appearance of secondary sex characteristics at particular ages).

Cognitive Development During Adolescence

We become adolescents when the words that adults exchange with one another become intelligible to us.

Natalia Ginzburg

The obvious changes in physical development that occur during adolescence are accompanied by striking changes in cognitive development. Clearly, adolescents know a lot more than younger children know, so they have a larger knowledge base—their thinking differs *quantitatively* from the thinking of younger children. In addition, many researchers agree that adolescent thinking differs *qualitatively* from earlier kinds of thinking (Andrich & Styles, 1994; Byrnes, 1988; Inhelder & Piaget, 1958; Kitchener & Brenner, 1990; Overton, 1990; Siegler, 1991). A major change centers on their ability to reason both *inductively* (formulating and testing hypotheses about what causes what, based on observing specific instances of a phenomenon) and *deductively* (applying known general principles to specific instances). According to Piaget's theory, these and other qualitative changes in thinking indicate that adolescents have reached the highest level of cognitive development—the **formal-operational stage**—in which they are able to manipulate abstract symbols mentally (Inhelder & Piaget, 1958).

An exciting aspect of adolescent thinking is the adolescent's ability to move beyond concrete, practical considerations. Unlike younger children—who chiefly conceive of only what they have previously seen, heard, or otherwise sensed—adolescents can conceive of what they have *never* seen, heard, or experienced. A whole world of possibilities opens up to them as they consider options that they have never observed before.

In addition to being able to explore possible options, adolescents can reasonably evaluate the options, thereby differentiating the possible from the impossible. Although adolescents can conceive of pixies, fairies, witches, and dragons, they can also realistically evaluate the improbability of the existence of such creatures, based on their own reasoning. Furthermore, they can consider logical reasons for beliefs that differ from their own. If asked to offer convincing evidence of Santa Claus's existence (e.g., to a young child), adolescents can do so, despite their own beliefs to the contrary. Adolescents' ability to consider viewpoints other than their own also enhances the flexibility and complexity of their thought processes. This is not to say that adolescents never use flawed reasoning, such as circular thinking (e.g., "We know that poor people are lazy because they don't have any money") or overgeneralization ("I know that smoking isn't really bad for your health because my Uncle Mort lived to be 100, and he smoked like a chimney from the age of 8"). (As Chapter 8 shows, adults often show similar weaknesses in their reasoning.)

puberty the period of physiological development during which males and females develop primary (i.e., functioning sex organs) and secondary sex characteristics (e.g., body hair and distinctive shape), thereby reaching sexual maturity

adolescence stage of psychological development between the start of puberty and the time the individual accepts the full responsibilities of being an adult in a given society

formal-operational stage Piaget's fourth stage of development (about the time of adolescence), during which the child becomes able to manipulate abstract ideas and formal relationships

Although adolescents are more able to consider the feelings and thoughts of other persons than are younger children, the adolescents continue to engage in some fallacies related to egocentrism (Elkind, 1967, 1985). A common fallacy of adolescent thinking centers on the *personal fable*, in which adolescents believe that they—as opposed to other persons—are somehow unique, destined for fame, fortune, or perhaps even heroism. Unfortunately, the personal fable usually accompanies an *invincibility fallacy*, in which the adolescent believes that he or she is not vulnerable to the same risks of tragic outcomes that affect other people. Hence, adolescents may continue to engage in unprotected sexual activity, unsafe driving, or using alcohol, cigarettes, or other drugs because they unreasonably believe that the undesirable outcomes that affect others will not affect them.

Socioemotional Development

Personal Identity

Many aspects of identity development (e.g., the development of gender identity) precede adolescence. Still, according to Erik Erikson (1968) and many other developmental psychologists, adolescence is typically characterized by a profound search for identity and by huge leaps in the development of the individual's awareness of her or his own personal identity. In Erikson's theory, adolescents face a crisis of *identity* versus *role confusion*. Adolescents try to figure out who they are, what they value, and who they will grow up to become. They try to integrate intellectual, social, sexual, ethical, and other aspects of themselves into a unified self-identity. Because of the tremendous importance of identity, other theorists have focused their attention specifically on the development of identity.

Erikson's theory highlights adolescence as a time when individuals face a *crisis* (turning point) in developing a sense of personal identity. James Marcia builds on the concept of personal identity and indicates in more detail the specific kinds of coping patterns that an adolescent can utilize on the way to adulthood. Specifically, Marcia (1966, 1980) has proposed that four patterns of coping can emerge as a result of internal conflicts and decision making. These patterns add another dimension to Erikson's stage of identity development, not a separate series of stages or substages. These four patterns are *identity achievement*, in which the person has searched for an identity and found it; *foreclosure*, in which the person has settled on an identity without having earnestly searched for it; *identity diffusion*, in which the person has no identity and has no interest in searching for one; and *moratorium*, in which the person is currently involved in searching for an identity. Table 3-2 summarizes the four coping patterns and the criteria for each patten. Persons who have reached identity achievement would move beyond Erikson's stage of development for identity, but persons with any of the other coping patterns would be blocked from progressing beyond that stage.

Peer Relationships

As the theories of Erikson and Marcia show, by late adolescence, young persons have turned their attention to understanding who they are as persons. They consider their beliefs, values, thoughts, and attitudes important to who they are. At the same time, adolescents also become keenly aware of how others view them. Their friendships and their relationships with their peers become central to how they spend their time and how they view themselves.

In fact, adolescents so greatly exaggerate the importance of how their peers view them that they come to develop a form of egocentrism in which they create within themselves an **imaginary audience** (Elkind, 1967, 1981, 1985): For a time, they feel themselves to be the constant object of the thoughts, judgments, and observations of other persons. When adolescents believe that these other persons judge their appearance or behavior harshly, their self-esteem suffers.

MINILECTURE
Formal Operations (Ch 12)

In no order of things is adolescence the time of the simple life.

Janet Erskine Stuart

How I wish I could pigeon-hole myself / and neatly fix a label on! / But self-knowledge comes too late / and by the time I've known myself / I am no longer what I was.

Mabel Segun

To what extent and in what areas have you achieved identity? In what ways do you see your identity as continuing to evolve and develop?

Show Miss Manners a grown-up who has happy memories of teenage years, with their endless round of merry-making and dancing the night away, and Miss Manners will show you a person who has either no heart or no memory.

Judith Martin

imaginary audience an adolescent's unfounded belief that other persons are constantly observing, paying attention to, and judging the adolescent

TABLE 3-2
Marcia's Coping Patterns for Achievement of Personal Identity

		Do you make commitments (e.g., to a career, to a mate, to your values)?	
		Yes	*No*
Have you engaged in a period of active search for identity?	*Yes*	Marcia would describe you as having reached *identity-achievement*, having a firm and relatively secure sense of who you are. You have made conscious and purposeful commitments to your occupation, religion, beliefs about sex roles, and the like. You have considered the views, beliefs, and values held by others in achieving this identity, but you have branched out to achieve your own resolution.	Your identity is in *moratorium*, and you are currently having an *identity crisis* (i.e., turning point). You do not yet have clear commitments to society or a clear sense of who you are, but you are actively trying to reach that point.
	No	Your identity is in *foreclosure*, in which case you have committed yourself to an occupation and various ideological positions, but you show little evidence of having followed a process of self-construction. You have simply adopted the attitudes of others, without serious searching and questioning. In essence, you have foreclosed on the possibility of arriving at your own unique identity.	You are experiencing *identity diffusion*, and you lack direction. Moreover, you do not seem to care that you have no strong identity. You are unconcerned about political, religious, moral, or even occupational issues. You go your own way, not worrying about why you are doing what you are doing.

Figure 3-6

Development of Moral Reasoning: Ages and Stages

The percentages of individuals (ages 10 through 36 years) who responded in terms of Lawrence Kohlberg's preconventional, conventional, and postconventional moral reasoning are summarized graphically here. Clearly, preconventional reasoning declines, conventional reasoning sharply increases, and postconventional reasoning increases slightly across the span of middle childhood through early adulthood. Note absence of individuals in Stage 6.

A more positive outcome of adolescents' awareness of what other persons think and feel is their increasing ability to view situations from the perspective of another person. Although none of us can always see how others view a situation, adolescents become increasingly able to do so, far more than they could have just a few years earlier. According to Piaget, this ability is related to decreasing egocentrism and increasing ability to decenter from just their own points of view. Lawrence Kohlberg built on Piaget's ideas to propose his own theory of moral development, which made use of moral dilemmas.

Kohlberg's Model of Moral Reasoning

Scenarios such as the following one form the basis for measuring the development of moral reasoning in Kohlberg's influential theory (1963, 1983, 1984). According to Kohlberg, your answers to the dilemma will depend on your level of moral reasoning, which progresses through six specific stages, embedded within three general levels. Your solutions do not determine your stage of moral reasoning; rather, the kinds of reasons you give to justify your solutions determine your moral stage (see Table 3-3 and Figure 3-6).

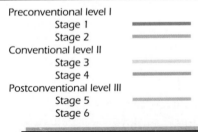

Preconventional level I
　　Stage 1
　　Stage 2
Conventional level II
　　Stage 3
　　Stage 4
Postconventional level III
　　Stage 5
　　Stage 6

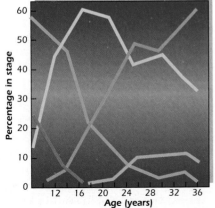

Finding Your Way　　3-1

In Europe, a woman was near death from a rare form of cancer. The doctors thought that one drug might save her: a form of radium a druggist had recently discovered. The drug was expensive to make, but the druggist was also charging ten times the cost of the drug; having paid $400 for the radium, the druggist charged $4,000 for a small dose. The sick woman's husband, Heinz, went to everyone he knew to borrow the money, but he could gather only $2,000. He begged the druggist to sell it more cheaply or to let him pay the rest later, but the druggist refused. So, having tried every legal means, Heinz desperately considered breaking into the drugstore to steal the drug for his wife (adapted from Kohlberg, 1963, 1983, 1984).

Suppose that you are Heinz. Should you steal the drug? Why or why not?

In your opinion, are there absolute, correct rules of right and wrong moral behavior? Why or why not?

Other psychologists have also found that the complexity of moral reasoning increases with age, roughly along the lines Kohlberg suggested (e.g., Rest, 1983). Moreover, even research in other cultures has been rather supportive of Kohlberg's theory in places such as Turkey (Nisan & Kohlberg, 1982), Israel (Snarey, Reimer, & Kohlberg, 1985a, 1985b), South Africa (Maqsud & Rouhani, 1990), Iceland (Keller, Eckensberger, & von Rosen, 1989), and Poland (Niemczynski et al., 1988), although some of the stages of morality do not apply without modification across cultures (e.g., studies in China; described in Ma, 1988). Not everyone agrees with Kohlberg's theory, however. One of the most striking criticisms of his theory comes from a former student of Kohlberg's—Carol Gilligan.

MINILECTURE
Kohlberg: Moral Development (Ch 13)

Gilligan's Model

According to Gilligan (1982), although women *can* conceive morality as men do, women tend *not* to do so. Whereas men focus on abstract, rational principles, such as justice and respect for the rights of others, women see morality more as a matter of caring and compassion. Gilligan has proposed that women pass though three basic levels of morality, although not all women reach Gilligan's third level. The first level involves the individual's concern only for herself; the second level involves self-sacrifice, in which concern for others predominates; and the third level involves integrating the responsibilities to both self and others.

Other psychologists (e.g., Baumrind, 1986; Gibbs et al., 1984; as well as Gilligan & Attanucci, 1988) have found similar sex differences in responses to moral dilemmas. At the same time, Lawrence Walker (1989), using a relatively large sample, found that most men and women, as well as girls and boys, used considerations of both caring and justice in their responses to moral dilemmas. However, although women were more likely to express a caring orientation than were men, girls were not more likely to do so than were boys.

How might you account for gender-related changes in moral development that occur between childhood and adulthood: Do you believe that they result more from nature (physiological maturation) or more from nurture (socialized learning)?

Psychologist Carol Gilligan has suggested that women, more than men, focus on the special obligations of their close relationships, and that they resolve moral issues with sensitivity to the social context, more than in regard to abstract principles. Also, whereas men are more likely to be competitive, women are more likely to be cooperative.

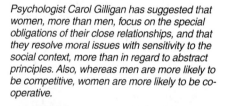

What develops during puberty and adolescence? Adolescence is the period of time between the onset of puberty (sexual maturation) and the assumption of the full responsibilities of adulthood. Adolescents can increasingly manipulate abstract symbols and concepts and can consider hypothetical situations. They confront many aspects of their personal identity, including their gender identity, their beliefs about how others view them, and their moral values.

TABLE 3-3
Kohlberg's Theory of the Development of Moral Reasoning

How did you respond to Heinz's dilemma, and on what basis did you reason your answer?

Level/stage	Basis for reasoning
Level I: Preconventional morality	The reasons to behave in ways that please other people or that avoid displeasing them are to avoid punishment or to obtain rewards. (Often characteristic of children's behavior between ages 7 and 10 years; 95% of 7-year-olds show judgments at this level)
Stage 1: Heteronomous morality (i.e., Don't get caught)	Egocentric consideration of whether the behavior leads to punishment or to reward for self, not considering the outcomes, interests, or well-being of others. That is, reasoning is based on the principle that might makes right, so people should obey authority.
Stage 2: Individualistic, instrumental morality (i.e., What's in it for me?)	Give-and-take exchanges guide behavior. In recognition that others, too, have their own interests and considerations, the reasoner in this stage tries to strike deals that serve the reasoner's interests and also the other party's interests.
Level II: Conventional morality	Social and societal rules have become internalized, and the individual conforms to those rules and expectations because it is right to do so. (Often characteristic of children's behavior between ages 10 and 16 years, and usually even beyond that age; moral judgments at this level were shown in no 7-year-olds, 20% of 10-year-olds, and most 13- and 16-year-olds)
Stage 3: Interpersonally normative morality (i.e., I'm being good/nice)	Mutual interpersonal expectations and interpersonal conformity guide reasoning. Rules of behavior become internalized, so that individuals seek to perceive themselves as behaving in ways that other people consider to be good, appropriate, or nice. These individuals conform to particular behaviors to please others.
Stage 4: Social-system morality (i.e., Preserve the social order)	Societal rules form the basis of moral reasoning, and the development of an internal conscience and a recognition of the importance of the social system guides moral reasoning. You have entered into social contracts, which you are morally obligated to fulfill.
Level III: Postconventional morality	The person accepts society's rules as a basis for most behavior, but the person has also formulated an internal set of moral principles; when there is a conflict between the internal rules and society's rules, the person will follow the internal moral principles. (Stage 5 is rare before age 16, apparent in about 20% of 16-year-olds, and still not common after that age. Stage 6 is almost never evident in people under age 20 years, and still is unusual even in adults.)
Stage 5: Human-rights and social-welfare morality (i.e., What ensures the rights and well-being of each person?)	Social contracts and individual rights form the basis of moral reasoning in this stage.
Stage 6: Morality of universal, reversible, and prescriptive general ethical principles (i.e., What's best from the point of view of each person involved, including the broadest ramifications of individual actions?)	An orientation toward universal principles of justice guides moral reasoning in this stage.

Thus far, this chapter has focused primarily on development in persons who have not yet reached adulthood. The field of psychological development, however, does not stop at adolescence. Many psychologists study **life-span development**— the changes in a person that occur over a lifetime.

HOW DO ADULTS DEVELOP AND AGE?

Cognitive development during adulthood involves a continuing increase in knowledge and skill, but after middle adulthood, people's speed of performing various mental operations (e.g., mental arithmetic) seems to decline somewhat (Bashore, Osman, & Hefley, 1989; Cerella, 1985; Denny, 1980; Poon, 1987; Schaie, 1989). Many other aspects of cognitive development in adults are discussed in other chapters of this textbook (e.g., see Chapters 7, 8, and 9). Here, the discussion centers on the development of personality and identity that occur during adulthood. In young and middle-aged adults, identity development centers mainly on family and work. Within the family, adults usually form intimate relationships with a partner (or a series of partners), and they come to identify themselves as part of this partnership. (Patterns of adult love and intimate relationships are discussed in Chapter 10.)

According to Erikson, during early adulthood, adults must resolve a crisis of *intimacy* versus *isolation*. The emerging adult tries to commit him- or herself to a loving intimate relationship. The adult who succeeds will learn how to love in a giving and nonselfish way. The adult who fails will develop a sense of isolation and may fail to connect with the significant others in his or her life. Most adults also eventually become parents, and for many years, their identity is at least partly shaped by their roles as parents.

In addition, adult identity usually relates to adults' roles as workers in particular careers. Patterns of career choice and development have been described as having an *exploration phase*, in which individuals search for a career that is compatible with their interests, values, and abilities; an *establishment phase*, in which individuals begin to be identified with a particular career; a *midcareer phase*, in which individuals have established and seek to maintain their chosen careers; and a *late-career phase*, in which individuals are fully established and may even be viewed as leaders or mentors to others in their chosen career.

According to Erikson, during middle adulthood, adults face a crisis of *generativity* versus *stagnation*. Adults try to be productive in their work and to contribute to the next generation. They may do so by formulating ideas, creating products, or raising children. People face seven major developmental tasks during middle adulthood (Havighurst, 1967): (1) reaching and then maintaining satisfactory performance in a career; (2) accepting and adjusting to the physical changes of the middle years; (3) adjusting to parents who are aging and sometimes needing increasing care and supervision; (4) assisting adolescent children in their transition to adulthood; (5) achieving adult social responsibilities (e.g., with family and friends); (6) relating to a spouse; and (7) developing leisure-time activities.

During later adulthood, most people retire or otherwise reduce their involvement in their careers, and they watch their own children become adults. They must again think about who they are now that their identities are not centered on raising children or on succeeding at work. According to Erikson, during late adulthood, adults confront a crisis of *integrity* versus *despair*. As they come to terms with their own mortality, people try to make sense of the lives they have led, and in particular, of the choices they have made. They may not feel as though every decision was right, in which case they must come to terms with their mistakes. Adults who succeed in this stage gain the wisdom and integrity of older age. Adults who fail may approach death with a sense of despair over mistakes or lost opportunities.

MINILECTURE

Adult Psychosocial Development (Ch 13)

The first half of life is spent in longing for the second—the second half in regretting the first.

French proverb

life-span development the changes that occur within a person over the life span

TABLE 3-4
Summary of Cognitive and Socioemotional Development

Period of development	Aspect of development: Theorist			
	Cognitive: Piaget	*Personality: Erikson*	*Friendship: Selman*	*Moral: Kohlberg*
Infancy	Sensorimotor	Trust versus mistrust		
Toddler period	Preoperational	Autonomy versus shame and doubt		Preconventional morality
Preschool years		Initiative versus guilt	Playmateship	
Middle childhood	Concrete operations	Industry versus inferiority	One-way assistance	Preconventional and conventional morality
			Fair-weather cooperation	
			Intimate and mutually shared relationships	
Adolescence	Formal operations	Identity versus role confusion		Conventional morality
Early adulthood		Intimacy versus isolation		Conventional morality (and in rare cases, post-conventional morality)
Middle adulthood		Generativity versus stagnation		
Late adulthood		Integrity versus despair		

How do adults develop and age? The major crises of adulthood center on issues of intimacy, generativity, and integrity, particularly as those issues relate to work and family.

In humans, the process of development continues throughout life. Table 3-4 summarizes some of the developmental changes that occur across the life span, according to four developmental theorists. Although each theorist focuses on just one aspect of development (i.e., cognition, personality, friendship, or moral reasoning), each aspect of development influences and is influenced by the others. At each phase of life, we view the world differently, based on both our maturational processes and our experiences. However, despite differences in development that influence how we perceive the world, we all must rely on similar fundamental processes of sensation and perception, the topic of the next chapter.

SUMMARY

What Developmental Trends Have Psychologists Observed? 71

1. Trends in *development* include qualitative changes, such as differentiation, and quantitative changes, such as growth. *Cognitive development* involves changes in thinking across the life span, and *socioemotional development* involves changes in people's emotions, personality, interpersonal interactions, moral beliefs, and behavior.

What Are the Roles of Maturation and Learning? 71

2. *Learning* refers to any relatively permanent change in thought or behavior, as a result of experience. *Maturation* refers to any relatively permanent change in thought or behavior that occurs simply as a result of aging, without regard to particular experiences. Today, almost all psychologists believe that both maturation and learning interact in influencing the course of development.

3. Jean Piaget proposed that cognitive development occurs largely through two processes of *equilibration:* (1) *assimilation,* whereby the child incorporates new information into the child's existing cognitive *schemas;* and (2) *accommodation,* whereby the child attempts to change his or her cognitive schemas to fit relevant aspects of the new environment.

4. As children grow older, they become less *egocentric*—that is, less focused on themselves and more able to see things from the perspectives of others.

5. Lev Vygotsky's theory of cognitive development stresses the importance of (a) *internalization,* whereby we incorporate into ourselves the knowledge we gain from social contexts; and (b) the *zone of proximal development,* which is the range between a child's existing undeveloped potential capacity and the child's developed ability.

What Happens During Prenatal Development? 74

6. Prenatal development is characterized by increasing differentiation during the stages of the *zygote,* the *embryo,* and the *fetus.* During the stage of the embryo, the maternal environment strongly influences the course of development because that stage is a time during which many systems of the body undergo *critical periods* of development.

How Do Infants and Young Toddlers Develop? 76

7. We know that infants possess many more abilities than we recognized previously. As we become smarter observers of infants, infants appear smarter to us.

8. Piaget's *sensorimotor stage* centers on the development of sensory and motor skills during the first 2 years after birth. At the end of the sensorimotor stage, children start to develop *internal representations*—thoughts about people and objects that the children cannot see, hear, or otherwise per-

ceive. The schema for *object permanence* develops during this stage.

9. Emotional development involves increasing specialization and sensitivity to the feelings of others.

10. *Temperament* refers to individual differences in the characteristic mood and in the typical intensity and duration of emotions. Temperament must be taken into account in observing the fit between a person and his or her environment.

11. According to Erikson, a crisis of trust versus mistrust occurs during infancy.

12. *Attachment* is a long-lasting emotional tie between two individuals, such as parent and child.

How Do Children Develop? 82

13. According to Piaget, young children (ages 1½–2 through 6 or 7 years) are in a *preoperational stage* of cognitive development. During this stage, they demonstrate *centration,* the tendency to center all thoughts on just one aspect of an object or concept. Somewhat older children (ages 6 or 7 to about 12 years) enter the *concrete-operational stage* of cognitive development and start to show *conservation of quantity*—they can recognize that two quantities remain the same, despite transformations on them that may change their appearance. They also begin to show inductive and deductive reasoning, although they still continue to show transductive reasoning.

14. According to Erikson, crises that occur during childhood include autonomy versus shame or doubt, initiative versus guilt, and industry versus inferiority.

15. *Self-concept* consists of *self-understanding,* which is an individual's definition of self, and *self-esteem,* which is the person's sense of self-worth. Self-understanding often depends on different aspects of the self, such as physical attributes, behavior, and social relationships. Self-esteem is based on self-judgments about personal worth in various realms.

16. Development of gender identity involves the growth of self-perceptions about sexuality and gender identifications. *Gender typing* is the acquisition of specific gender-related roles.

17. Research results on the effects of *child care* are somewhat contradictory, but most studies show that high-quality child care does children little harm and may offer some benefits.

18. Learning how to make friends is important to a child's development. Developmental patterns of friendship show children's increasing ability to look for more than immediate material rewards from friends and to see the perspective of other persons across the course of development.

What Develops During Puberty and Adolescence? 90

19. Puberty is the onset of developing sexual maturity. *Adolescence* is the period from the onset of puberty until the time

the individual is recognized as an adult, assuming the full adult responsibilities of the given society.

20. According to Piaget, adolescents are in the *formal-operational stage* of cognitive development, which is characterized by an increasing ability to manipulate abstract symbols, to carry out formal reasoning, and to consider hypothetical situations.

21. Adolescents commonly believe in the personal fable and the invincibility fallacy.

22. According to Erikson, adolescents confront the psychosocial crisis of identity versus role confusion.

23. According to Marcia, people's sense of *identity* can be categorized as being in a state of (a) *identity achievement*, if they have made their own decisions and have a firm sense of who they are; (b) *foreclosure*, if they have chosen their path with little thought; (c) *moratorium*, if they are still seeking an identity; or (d) *identity diffusion*, if they lack direction or commitment.

24. *Kohlberg's stage theory of moral development and reasoning* is the most widely accepted of such theories, although it has

been criticized for several reasons. In the *preconventional* stage, people reason to avoid punishment and to seek self-interest; in the *conventional* stage, they reason according to family and social rules; and in the *postconventional* stage, they reason according to universal ethical requirements.

25. Carol Gilligan has suggested an alternative series of moral-developmental stages for women, involving an orientation toward caring relationships more than toward an abstract notion of justice.

How Do Adults Develop and Age?   95

26. According to Erikson, adults face the psychosocial crises of intimacy versus isolation, generativity versus stagnation, and integrity versus despair.

27. Adult identity more strongly centers on family and career than on sexuality. Thus, the assumption of roles as a partner and as a parent is important to adult identity, as is the development of a career.

PATHWAYS TO KNOWLEDGE

Choose the best answer to complete each sentence.

1. Maturation refers to
   (a) the attainment of successive stages of cognitive development.
   (b) changes in an individual's thoughts or behavior as a result of biological processes of aging.
   (c) changes in an individual's thoughts or behavior as a result of accumulating experience.
   (d) the development of an individual's thoughts and behavior due to the interactions of biological and environmental factors.

2. Learning refers to
   (a) the attainment of successive stages of cognitive development.
   (b) relatively stable changes in an individual's thoughts or behavior as a result of biological processes of aging.
   (c) relatively stable changes in an individual's thoughts or behavior as a result of accumulating experience.
   (d) the development of an individual's thoughts and behavior due to the interactions of biological and environmental factors.

3. Piaget described *accommodation* as a process whereby
   (a) individuals modify their existing schemas to incorporate new information from the environment.
   (b) individuals add new information from the environment to their existing schemas, without modifying their schemas.

   (c) infants eventually realize that objects not immediately available to their senses still continue to exist.
   (d) infants maintain abstract, complex cognitive representations of events.

4. According to Erik Erikson, individuals confront the following crises during personality development:
   (a) trust versus mistrust, autonomy versus shame and doubt, identity versus role confusion.
   (b) initiative versus guilt, industry versus inferiority, intimacy versus isolation.
   (c) trust versus mistrust, optimism versus pessimism, extroversion versus introversion.
   (d) a and b.
   (e) b and c.

5. James Marcia has addressed the notion of identity development by suggesting four specific kinds of coping patterns:
   (a) diffusion, moratorium, internal, external
   (b) achievement, foreclosure, delayed, advanced
   (c) internal, external, delayed, advanced
   (d) diffusion, moratorium, achievement, foreclosure

6. Temperament is best described as an individual's
   (a) moods that are dependent on situational factors.
   (b) disposition and characteristic level of emotional reactivity.
   (c) stable personality characteristics in a given culture.
   (d) generalized mood state during a particular stage of development.

Answer each of the following questions by filling in the blank with an appropriate word or phrase.

7. According to Vygotsky, in the process of _____, people absorb knowledge from their surrounding social contexts.

8. Piaget's stages of cognitive development included the _____ stage (infancy and a little beyond), the preoperational stage (early childhood), the _____-_____ stage (middle childhood), and the formal-operations stage (adolescence and beyond).

9. According to Vygotsky, children can learn best when given opportunities for learning within their zone of _____ _____.

10. Lawrence Kohlberg's stages of moral reasoning are the _____ stage, the _____ stage, and the _____ stage.

11. According to Erik Erikson, the psychosocial crises people face in middle and late adulthood are the crises of _____ versus stagnation and _____ versus despair.

12. Self-concept comprises two aspects: _____ and _____.

Match the following developmental achievements or characteristics to the period of development with which they are most strongly associated:

13. conservation of quantity
14. object permanence
15. crisis of intimacy vs. isolation
16. invincibility fallacy
17. sensorimotor stage
18. generativity
19. formal-operations stage
20. concrete-operations stage

(a) infancy
(b) childhood
(c) adolescence
(d) adulthood

Answers

1. b, 2. c, 3. a, 4. d, 5. d, 6. b, 7. internalization, 8. sensorimotor, concrete-operations, 9. proximal development, 10. preconventional, conventional, postconventional, 11. generativity, integrity, 12. self-esteem, self-understanding, 13. b, 14. a, 15. d, 16. c, 17. a, 18. d, 19. c, 20. b

PATHWAYS TO UNDERSTANDING

1. What are some of the ways in which our limitations as researchers (i.e., limited tools, imaginations, resources, methods, etc.) limit our ability to identify some of the cognitive abilities of children? What steps should researchers take to avoid interpreting our own limitations as investigators as being limitations in the cognitive abilities of children?

2. Choose one of the ages or stages of development that differs from your own, and imagine being at that age or in that stage of development. Describe how you view the world, as well as how you think, feel, and act.

3. Give examples of your own gender-role development. In what ways do you conform to traditional gender roles, and in what ways have you departed from traditional gender roles?

PART II

Cognitive Processes

CHAPTER 4
Sensation and Perception

CHAPTER 5
Consciousness

CHAPTER 6
Learning

CHAPTER 7
Memory

CHAPTER 8
Thought and Language

CHAPTER 9
Intelligence and Creativity

CHAPTER OUTLINE

How Do Psychologists Study the Senses?
    Detection
    Discrimination: The Just-Noticeable
       Difference

What Are Some Biological Properties Common to All Senses?
    Receptor Cells and Transduction
    Sensory Coding
    Detection of Changes in Stimuli

How Do We See?
    The Nature of Light
    Anatomy of the Eye
    How We See
    Designs in Light and Dark
    Color

How Do We Hear?
    The Nature of Sound
    How We Hear
    Locating Sounds
    Adapting to a Sightless or Soundless
       Environment

How Do We Sense Taste, Smell, Touch, Movement, and Other Sensations?
    Taste
    Smell
    Skin Senses
    Body Senses

How Do We Make Sense of What We Sense?

How Do We Perceive What We See?
    Space Perception
    Form Perception
    Perceptual Constancies

Sensation and Perception

When I was quite a little girl, I learned to row and to swim, . . . Sometimes, . . . I go rowing without the rudder. It is fun to try to steer by the scent of watergrasses and lilies, and of bushes that grow on the shore. I use oars with leather bands, which keep them in position in the oarlocks, and I know by the resistance of the water when the oars are evenly poised. In the same manner I can also tell when I am pulling against the current. I like to contend with wind and wave. What is more exhilarating than to make your staunch little boat, obedient to your will and muscle, go skimming lightly over glistening, tilting waves, and to feel the steady imperious surge of the water!

I also enjoy canoeing, and . . . I especially like it on moonlight nights. I cannot . . . see the moon climb up the sky behind the pines . . . but I know she is there.

—*Helen Keller, 1902/1988*

Suppose that you were suddenly thrust into pitch darkness and absolute silence (because of an injury, an environmental disaster, or whatever). How would you use your other senses to get yourself something to eat?

We see things not as they are, but as we are. *Our perception is shaped by our previous experiences.*

Dennis Kimbro

Francis Galton (Charles Darwin's cousin) believed that he could assess people's intelligence by measuring their sensory, memory, and physical abilities. Do you think your own sensory, memory, and physical abilities accurately reflect your intelligence? Why or why not?

sense a physical system for receiving a particular kind of physical stimulation and translating that stimulation into an electro-chemical message

sensation a message regarding physical stimulation of a sensory receptor

perception the mental processes that organize and interpret sensory information that has been transmitted to the brain

psychophysics the systematic study of the relationship between the physical stimulation of a sense organ and the psychological sensations produced by that stimulation

In the preceding passage, Helen Keller, who was both blind and deaf from early childhood, shows how much we can learn about the world and how well we can use what we know to adapt to the world through the use of our senses. A **sense** is a physical system that collects information and then translates the information into a meaningful form that the brain can understand. A **sensation** is a message that the brain receives from the senses.

Sensory information may come from the external world or from the internal world of the body. As Chapter 2 showed, the sensory system communicates information in an electrochemical form. For example, you might use your eyes and nose to collect sensory information about a steaming, circular, flat, red and white object. Your eyes then somehow translate this information and send it to your brain through your sensory neurons.

When your brain receives these various sensations, it organizes, interprets, and makes sense of this sensory information. At last, your brain announces, "Pizza for dinner!" The high-level processing of information in your brain is **perception,** which takes up roughly where sensation leaves off. Perception usually refers to the cognitive (thinking) processes through which we interpret sensory messages. During perception, we *synthesize* (selectively combine and integrate) and assign meaning to our sensations. We do so by taking into account our expectations, our prior experiences, and perhaps even our culture.

Clearly, sensation and perception are highly interrelated. Even so, psychologists separate the two processes in order to study each more closely. In this chapter, we examine sensation before we study perception. Hence, the first part of this chapter describes how our senses provide us with the sensations of light, color, sound, taste, scent, pressure, temperature, pain, balance, and movement. The second part of this chapter describes how we meaningfully synthesize our sensations.

Even before we examine each sense individually, however, we discuss some phenomena that apply to all our senses. First, we explore how to study and measure the functioning of the senses. Second, we probe some biological properties common to all our senses.

HOW DO PSYCHOLOGISTS STUDY THE SENSES?

Psychophysics is the study and measurement of the functioning of the senses. Specifically, psychophysicists first observe particular forms of *physical stimulation* of the senses (e.g., light going to the eye or sound going to the ear). Then they observe what people seem to experience in their minds as *psychological sensations* (e.g., reporting what they see or hear). Finally—and most importantly—psychophysicists try to measure the relationship between a particular form of physical stimulation and the psychological sensations it produces. For example, a psychophysical experiment might measure the relationship between how quickly a light is flashed on and off and how easily you can detect separate flashes. Another experiment might measure the relationship between the physical *intensity* of a sound (the actual amount of stimulation that reaches your ears) and how loud you hear that sound to be.

Psychophysical measurements can be used in many practical ways. A common use involves testing whether people's senses are functioning normally. For example, the eye doctor who checks your vision determines how large the letters must be for you to see them clearly (see Figure 4-1).

Psychophysics is also useful in engineering psychology, such as in the design of instrument panels. How brightly should a car's dashboard gauges glow in order to be visible but not distracting at night? For that matter, in the development of almost any products, psychologists may be asked to provide psychophysical information regarding both the usefulness and the appeal of the products. For example, consumer psychologists tackle questions such as, "How strong can a perfume be without seeming to be overpowering?" Fundamentally, the key question asked by psychophysicists is, "How easily can people detect particular sensory stimuli?"

Detection

Absolute Threshold

Detection is the active psychophysical sensing of a stimulus. In sensory-detection studies, researchers ask how much light, sound, taste, or other sensory stimulation is needed in order for the human senses to detect it. For each kind of sensory stimulation, there is a minimum amount of physical energy that your senses can detect. This minimum detectable amount is your **absolute threshold** for that kind of sensory stimulation. In theory, you would never sense the stimulus below your absolute-threshold level, and you would always sense the stimulus above that level.

In reality, however, our sensations do not detect particular sensory stimuli at exactly the same levels all of the time. Thus, an absolute threshold cannot really be measured directly. To come up with a way to describe phenomena that cannot be measured directly, psychologists use **operational definitions,** which specify how to figure out a best guess about these phenomena. In psychophysics, psychologists operationally define the *absolute threshold* as the level of stimulation at which a stimulus is first detected 50% of the time during many attempts to detect the stimulus (see Figure 4-2).

Signal-Detection Theory

Often, people's expectations regarding a sensation affect the likelihood that they will detect it. For example, are you more likely to notice someone approaching your door when you expect a guest or when you do not expect one? **Signal-detection theory (SDT)** is a systematic method of measuring detection, which considers expectations and other thought-related influences on the detection of sensations.

According to SDT, there are four possible combinations of stimulus and response (Green & Swets, 1966; Swets, Tanner, & Birdsall, 1961). Suppose you are a spy, waiting to get a signal from your confederate, letting you know when it is safe to deliver your coded message (or your microfilm). The signal for safe delivery is the flicker of a light. One possibility is that the *signal* (the stimulus; in this case, the flicker of the light) is present, and you detect it (your response); this pairing is a *hit.* You correctly deliver the message. Another possibility is a *miss:* The light flickers, but you do not detect it. You should deliver the message, but you fail to do so, thereby endangering the well-being of your fellow agents and perhaps imperiling your country. A third possibility is a *false alarm:* The light does not flicker, but you think you see it flicker. You deliver the message when you should not—once again, your country is endangered. The fourth possibility is a *correct rejection:* The light does not flicker, and you do not think it does. You wait longer for an opportunity to deliver your message safely into the right hands. These combinations of stimuli and responses are summarized in Table 4-1.

TABLE 4-1
Signal Detection Matrix

Signal-detection theory	Detect a signal	Do not detect a signal
Signal present	Hit	Miss
Signal absent	False alarm	Correct rejection

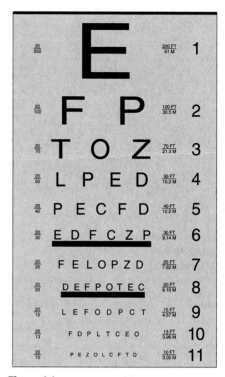

Figure 4-1
The Snellen Vision Chart
This familiar chart shows a psychophysical test used in measuring one aspect of visual sensation.

We live on the leash of our senses.

Diane Ackerman

MINILECTURE
Detection (Ch 4)

detect   notice the presence of a sensory stimulus

absolute threshold   a hypothetical minimum amount of physical energy that an individual can detect for each kind of sensory stimulation; operationally defined as the level at which a stimulus is first detected 50% of the time during many attempts to detect the stimulus

operational definition   a means for researchers to specify exactly how to test or to measure particular phenomena being studied

signal-detection theory (SDT)   a method of measuring the detection of a sensation, which takes into account the influence of expectations and decision making on detection

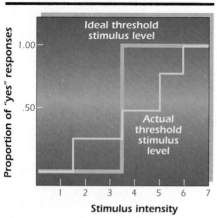

Figure 4-2

Sample Ideal and Real Absolute Thresholds

Because it is impossible to determine an ideal absolute threshold, psychologists define an absolute threshold as the level of stimulation that an individual can detect 50% of the time.

MINILECTURE
Discrimination (Ch 4)

difference threshold a hypothetical minimum amount of difference that can be detected between two stimuli (see also *jnd*)

just noticeable difference (jnd) a term operationally defined as the point at which an individual can detect the difference between two stimuli at least 50% of the time, over a series of attempts to detect the difference

receptor cell body cell that is especially suited to detecting and transforming a particular kind of energy that reaches the cell

Discrimination: The Just-Noticeable Difference

Being able to detect a single stimulus is certainly crucial in many circumstances. Often, however, the problem is not how strong or intense a stimulus must be in order for a person to detect it. Rather, the problem involves *discrimination:* the ability to detect the difference between one stimulus and another. For example, suppose that you were looking quickly at a digital timepiece. Were you seeing 1:11 or 1:17? Were the last two numerals alike (11) or different (17)?

The minimum amount of difference that can be detected between two stimuli is the difference threshold. A more common term for the **difference threshold** is the **just noticeable difference (jnd).** Just as our ability to detect sensory stimuli varies, so does our ability to detect differences between stimuli. For this reason, psychologists try to measure a jnd many times for a given kind of stimulus (e.g., different musical tones or different color chips), and then they average the data from all of their attempts. In practical terms, psychologists operationally define the *jnd* as the difference between two stimuli that can be detected at least 50% of the time.

Sensory-difference thresholds are important in everyday life and even in some professions. A coffee taster must be able to taste and smell the differences among various blends, grinds, and roasts of bean. Musicians must be able to hear whether their instruments are just a fraction of a note off-key. Engineering psychologists use jnds to help determine various aspects of product design. For example, each notch on a sound-volume dial of a stereo system must represent at least some jnd in loudness, or the dial is not effective.

An interesting phenomenon affects our sensation of the jnd. Physiologist Ernst Weber (1795–1878) noticed that the change needed to cause a jnd increases proportionally with increases in the intensity of a stimulus. That is, you may be able to detect a small difference in a low-intensity stimulus, but a much larger difference is needed for you to detect a difference in a high-intensity stimulus. For example, with your eyes closed, you could probably sense the difference in weight between a 5-ounce (0.14 kilogram) bag of cherries and a 6-ounce (0.17 kilogram) bag of cherries. However, you would probably find it almost impossible to detect the difference between a 10-pound (4.54 kilogram) bag of potatoes and a bag of potatoes weighing 10 pounds and 1 ounce (4.57 kilogram). Why would you sense the extra ounce (28 gram) the first time but not the second? As the stimulus intensity (here, the weight of the bag) increases, the amount of change needed to produce a jnd also increases. Therefore, the difference in weight would have to be much greater for you to sense the difference in the 10-pound bags.

So far, we have explored how psychologists measure sensory functioning. Next, we study what psychologists have discovered, based on those measurements.

How do psychologists study the senses? When studying psychophysics, psychologists try to relate measurements of physical stimulation to measurements of psychological experiences of sensations.

WHAT ARE SOME BIOLOGICAL PROPERTIES COMMON TO ALL SENSES?

Receptor Cells and Transduction

Various forms of physical energy stimulate our sense organs. **Receptor cells** are the structures of our sense organs that receive these various forms of energy.

Receptor cells are specialized to detect particular kinds of energy within the receptive fields of the cells. A *receptive field* is the area of the external world from which each receptor cell receives messages.

Different kinds of receptor cells are sensitive to different forms of energy. Our visual system has receptors sensitive to light waves (visible electromagnetic radiation). Our *gustatory* (taste) and *olfactory* (smell) systems have receptors for chemicals from foods and other substances. Our other senses (e.g., hearing, touch, and balance) have specialized receptors for mechanical energy from the air, from other objects, or even from within our own bodies.

Each of our sensory receptors **transduces** (converts) an incoming form of energy (mechanical, chemical, electromagnetic, etc.) into the electrochemical form of energy that is used by our nervous system. In general, for each sense, the set of specialized receptor cells transduces only the particular kind of stimulus energy the sense is designed to receive. For example, our *auditory* (hearing), *tactile* (touch), *kinesthetic* (motion), and *vestibular* (balance) systems transduce mechanical energy into electrochemical energy. The sensory neurons then carry those electrochemical messages to our brains for information processing.

Sensory Coding

How do our brains distinguish among assorted stimuli? The trill of a flute does not sound like the wail of an electric guitar. An onion's strong odor is noticeably distinct from a violet's mild scent. Each set of receptors must somehow be able to convey to the brain a range of information about individual stimuli. Otherwise, we would not know a loving caress from a hostile punch; we would only know that we felt—something. **Sensory coding** is the means by which sensory receptors convey this range of information about stimuli. Receptors and neurons use electrochemical codes to express shades of meaning in their messages.

For a given stimulus, sensory coding must convey a range of physical properties that affect our psychological perception of the stimulus. In particular, each sensory stimulus has at least two main features: (1) *intensity*, the amount of energy sensed (e.g., the strength of an odor), and (2) *quality*, the nature of the stimulus (e.g., the particular kind of smell, such as a skunk vs. a rose). For seeing and hearing, we can measure the physical intensity of the stimulus in terms of *amplitude*. For light waves, the psychological experience of greater amplitude is increased brightness; for sound waves, it is increased loudness. For seeing and hearing, we also measure *wavelength*, the distance from the peak of one sound wave or light wave to the peak of the next wave. For light waves, the physical wavelength is associated with the psychological experience of color. For sound waves, the physical wavelength is associated with pitch—how high or low we sense the tone to be. (Actually, sound waves are usually described in terms of the frequency of the waves, rather than in terms of the length of the waves.)

For all of the senses, intensity is usually coded in the form of how many neurons fire or how frequently they fire in response to a transduced sensory stimulus. The coding of sensory quality (e.g., color [vision], pitch [hearing], or saltiness [taste]) is more complex, and psychologists are continually making new discoveries regarding how we can sense various qualities of a stimulus. We more fully explore how our senses code the qualities of stimuli in the discussion of each sensory system.

Detection of Changes in Stimuli

In addition to energy transduction and sensory coding, another process is common to all the senses: how we detect changes in stimuli. Our senses readily detect changes in stimulus energy. When the stimulus energy changes, the sensory neurons alert the brain to the change. The sensory system also makes physiological adjustments to the change in the sensed stimulus. These adjustments occur through the process of adaptation.

There is no way in which to understand the world without first detecting it through the radar-net of our senses.

Diane Ackerman

transduce convert incoming energy from one form (e.g., mechanical, chemical, electromagnetic) into an electrochemical form of energy for use within the nervous system

sensory coding the physiological form of communication through which sensory receptors convey a range of information about stimuli within the nervous system

How do environmental polluters take advantage of people's ability to adapt to stimuli in their environment?

A small coin before one's eyes hides everything from sight.

Israel Salanter

How might you describe the experience of sight to someone who has never seen? In particular, how might you describe the cover of this book to someone who has never seen?

Sensory **adaptation** is a temporary physiological response to a sensed change in the environment. For example, your eyes automatically and unconsciously adapt to changes in light intensity (increases or decreases in brightness). Similarly, your sense of smell adapts to having a particular odor in the environment. A smell that you can hardly stand in the first minute may be barely detectable after a while. You need no training or previous experience to make these adaptations, and you will adapt just about exactly the same way the first time and every time thereafter. The degree to which your senses adapt relates directly to the intensity of the stimulus in the environment. It does not matter how many times you were previously exposed to the stimulus or how long it was between your last exposure and your present one. Furthermore, when the stimulus in the environment changes back again, your physiological mechanisms for adaptation change back again, too.

What are some biological properties common to all senses? For all of the senses, we have specialized receptor cells that transduce particular forms of energy (e.g., chemical or mechanical energy) into the electrochemical energy of the nervous system. The intensity of a sensation is usually coded as varying numbers of neurons firing at varying rates; the coding of sensory qualities is more complex than the coding of intensity. We seem to be particularly sensitive to changes in stimuli and to adapt to stimuli that are present for prolonged periods of time.

HOW DO WE SEE?

Have you ever wakened to total darkness? If you get out of bed, you stumble into and over things you did not remember noticing before you went to bed. In the dark, you appreciate your vision in a way that you do not when you see well. In order to understand vision, we need to know something about light, about the structure of the eye, and about how the eye interacts with light to enable us to see.

The Nature of Light

The receptors of our eyes seem well designed for receiving *light*, a form of electromagnetic energy. The qualities of light energy take the form of varying wavelengths, which together make up the *electromagnetic spectrum* (see Figure 4-3). Human eyes sense only a very narrow range of wavelengths within this broad spectrum. For example, humans cannot see wavelengths in the infrared or ultraviolet bands of the electromagnetic spectrum, although some other animals can do so.

Anatomy of the Eye

Light beams enter the eye through the **cornea,** a curved, clear outer surface that gathers the entering light and bends it toward the center of the eye. Next, the light passes through the **pupil,** a hole in the center of a circular muscle, of the **iris.** The light bends further as it passes through the eye's curved inner **lens.** The curved surfaces of the cornea and the lens work together: The curvature of the cornea increases or decreases to make big changes in the direction of the light rays, bending the rays toward the general direction of the rear surface of the eye. Then, the curvature of the lens increases or decreases, to make small changes in the bending of

adaptation a temporary physiological response to a sensed change in the environment, which is neither learned nor consciously controlled; the degree of adaptation depends directly on the degree of change in the stimulus, with greater changes producing greater adaptation

cornea the clear dome-shaped window through which light passes and which serves primarily as a curved exterior surface of the eye that gathers and focuses the entering light

pupil the hole in the iris (roughly in its center) through which light gains access to the interior of the eye, particularly the retina

iris a circular membrane that reflects light beams outward and away from the eye; surrounds the pupil, which is essentially a hole in the center of the iris

lens a curved interior structure of the eye, which bends light slightly, to focus light on the center of the rear surface of the eye

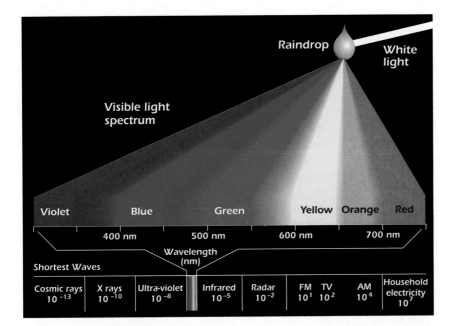

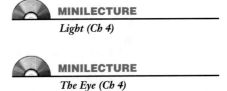

Figure 4-3
The Electromagnetic Spectrum
Within the wide range of the electromagnetic spectrum, humans are able to detect only a narrow band of wavelengths of light.

MINILECTURE
Light (Ch 4)

MINILECTURE
The Eye (Ch 4)

the rays, guiding the light more precisely from particular objects to focus on the center of the rear surface of the eye. Through the process of **accommodation,** the lens changes its curvature to focus on objects at different distances (see Figure 4-4).

The lens and cornea focus the entering light on the **retina,** a network of neurons on the back surface of the eye. Even though the retina is only about as thick as a single page in this book, it includes three main layers. The most important of the three layers is a layer of photoreceptors. **Photoreceptors** transduce light energy into electrochemical energy.

There are two kinds of photoreceptors: rods and cones. The **rods** are long, thin, and very numerous; the **cones** are relatively short, thick, and less numerous. Rods and cones also differ in their locations in the retina. Cones are more densely concentrated in the center of the retina, and rods are more densely concentrated in the outer region of the retina.

How We See

It appears that rods and cones also differ in their responses to light. This observation led biologist Max Schultze (1825–1874) to propose that there are two separate visual systems. One system, responsible for vision in dim light, depends on the rods. The other system depends on the cones. The cones, which are responsible for vision in brighter light and for the ability to see colors, provide much sharper and clearer vision than the rods offer. One reason for the greater clarity of cone vision over rod vision is that each cone gets more direct representation in the visual cortex than does each rod. Thus, although there are fewer cones than rods, the cones are relatively better represented in the brain.

Cones are more involved when you undergo **light adaptation**—adjustment to increases in light intensity, such as when you walk from a dark room into bright sunlight. In contrast, when you go from the bright outdoors into a dim or dark room, you undergo **dark adaptation,** in which your rods must become active enough to permit you to see relatively well in dim light. The phenomena of light and dark adaptation have important practical applications, as shown in Practical Psychology 4-1.

Color

Characteristics of Color Vision

We have a pretty clear view of how we sense differing intensities of light. However, there is considerable controversy regarding how we sense the qualities of light

accommodation the process by which the lens of the eye changes its curvature to focus on objects at different distances

retina a network of neurons covering most of the rear surface inside the eye; contains the photoreceptors that transduce light energy into electrochemical energy

photoreceptor receptor cell that receives and transduces light (*photo-*, light) energy into electrochemical energy

rod long, thin, and abundant type of photoreceptor, responsible mostly for vision in dim lighting

cone relatively short, thick, and less abundant type of photoreceptor, responsible mostly for very clear color vision in bright lighting

light adaptation the physiological adjustment to increases in light intensity, during which the cones become more active

dark adaptation the physiological adjustment to decreases in light intensity, during which the rods become more active

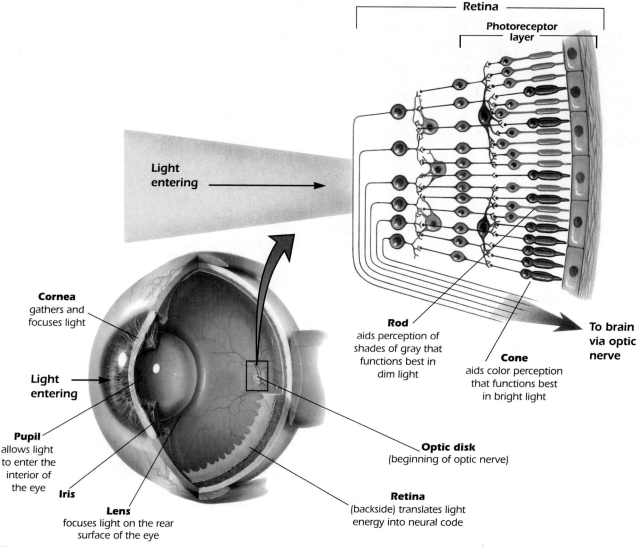

Figure 4-4
Anatomy of the Eye: How the Eye Adjusts to Focus Visual Images
The cornea of the eye makes gross adjustments of its curvature when light enters, and the lens makes finer adjustments of its curvature, to provide the best angle of focus for the entering light. Flatter lenses and corneas bend the light less and focus on more distant objects, whereas more curved lenses and corneas more clearly focus on closer objects. The various structures and processes of the human eye focus entering light on the retina, located on the rear surface of the eye.

PRACTICAL PSYCHOLOGY   4-1

Designs in Light and Dark

Engineering psychologists consider light and dark adaptation in the design of products and settings in which people work, play, and reside. When people go to and from extreme brightness or darkness, they cannot see as well. Hence, exit signs in darkened movie theaters must be easy to observe even before dark adaptation takes place. Stairs in the paths leading into or out of darkness or glaring light should have handrails, special illumination, or some other means of alerting people to their presence until adaptation takes place. Although adaptation occurs in almost the same way from our first entrance into bright light until our final exit into darkness, we lose some of our ability to adapt to darkness as we age. Hence, buildings designed particularly for use by older persons should allow for slower adaptation to changes in lighting.

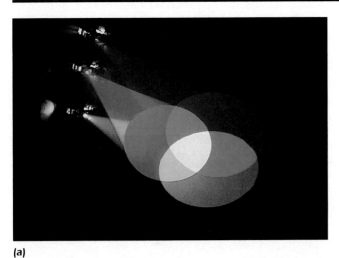
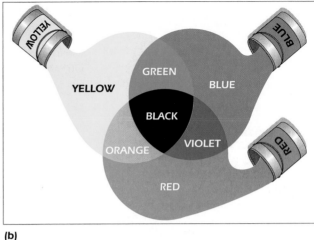

(a)   **(b)**

Figure 4-5
Color Mixtures
(a) In additive color mixtures, each light adds its wavelength to the color mixture, and the resulting sum of the wavelengths is what we see. When red light, blue light, and green light are mixed in different combinations, different colors appear. The additive mixture of all three colors of light produces white light. (b) Subtractive color mixtures may be obtained with various mixtures of pigments or filters. Most colored objects do not generate light; they reflect it. That is, the sky appears blue to us because it reflects blue light and absorbs all wavelengths other than blue, subtracting those colors from our sight. In subtractive mixtures, colors may be combined to subtract (absorb) more colors, reflecting fewer colors when more pigments are mixed.

related to color. Some of light's physical properties make colors psychologically appear the way they do to us. Wavelength produces the most basic quality for us: hue. The physical property of *hue* corresponds to the psychological property we call "color." We sense colors based on how our nervous systems react to particular wavelengths of the visible spectrum.

A second physical property of color is *purity*, which is the mixture of wavelengths of light that reaches the senses. The psychological property of *saturation* corresponds to purity. Highly saturated colors look rich and lively, with no hint of dull gray or flat brown. The third physical property of color is *intensity* (amplitude), which corresponds to the psychological property of *brightness*.

Colors can be mixed either additively or subtractively; the two processes work quite differently and result in different colors. When light waves of varying wavelengths are mixed, as when aiming spotlights of different colors (e.g., red, green, and blue) toward one point, we obtain an **additive mixture** (see Figure 4-5a). You are probably more familiar with **subtractive mixture.** When paints or other light-reflecting colors are mixed, they *absorb* (*subtract* from our vision) more wavelengths of light than each one absorbs individually. The more wavelengths of light that are subtracted, the darker the result looks. Figure 4-5(b) shows what happens when subtractively mixing together pigments of yellow, *cyan* (greenish blue as a pigment, but deep blue when used as an additive color), and *magenta* (purplish red).

Theories of Color Vision

The two main theories of color vision, the trichromatic theory and the opponent-process theory, try to explain how we can see so many different colors. The **trichromatic theory of color vision,** first proposed by Thomas Young (1773–1829) and later revived (1909/1962) by Hermann von Helmholtz (1821–1894), is based on the notion of primary colors. *Primary colors* (red, green, and blue) can combine additively to form all other colors. That is, perhaps we have three different types of cones, one type for each of the three primary colors. We

The eye is complicated. It mixes the colors [it sees] for you. . . . The painter must unmix them and lay them on again shade by shade, and then the eye of the beholder takes over and mixes them again.

Elizabeth Borton De Trevino

MINILECTURE

Dark Adaptation (Ch 4)

additive mixture the mixture of light waves of varying wavelengths, in which each wavelength of light adds to the other wavelengths

subtractive mixture the remaining combined wavelengths of light that are reflected from an object after other wavelengths of light have been absorbed (*subtracted* from the reflected light) by the object

trichromatic theory of color vision a theory that color vision depends on the responses of three different types of cones (for detecting red, green, and blue), in which the combined responses of these cones permits sensation of additive mixtures of the primary colors

Light of 450 nm

Hue: Blue + Red = Violet

Figure 4-6

Opponent-Process Theory

An alternative to trichromatic theory is opponent-process theory. Opponent-process theory suggests that there are two sets of opposing colors (blue versus yellow and red versus green), as well as the opposing sensations of black and white. According to this theory, the combinations of these opposing sensations explain color vision.

MINILECTURE

Color Vision (Ch 4)

opponent-process theory a theory of color vision based on opposing pairs (red–green, yellow–blue, and black–white) of receptors, in which the activity of the pairs either increases or decreases, depending on which member of the pair is being stimulated by a given sensation

see the full range of colors through the combined responses of each of the three kinds of cones.

The other major theory of color vision is **opponent-process theory.** The opponent-process theory of color vision was proposed originally (1878/1964) by Ewald Hering (1834–1918) and later formalized (1957) by Leo Hurvich and Dorothea Jameson. This theory is based on the notion of opposing pairs of photoreceptors. The theory specifies two pairs of two opposing colors—a blue–yellow pair and a red–green pair. Hurvich and Jameson also count black and white as a third, colorless, opposing pair. This colorless pair is perceived in much the same way as are the other two opposing pairs. Theoretically, each opponent pair works as a single unit. The activity of these units either increases or decreases, depending on which color in the pair is sensed (see Figure 4-6). People who are either partially or fully color blind appear to experience some kind of malfunctioning of these units—for example, the inability to distinguish red from green. Overall, there is both psychological and physiological evidence to support both the trichromatic theory and the opponent-process theory of color vision.

Up to this point, visual sensations have dominated our discussion of sensation. Through visual sensations, we can gain information from places far removed from the grasp of our hands—from mountains at the edge of the horizon and even from the moon, the sun, and the stars. Through auditory sensations, we can gain information from behind our backs, from around corners, and sometimes even through doors and walls. Our sense of hearing readily complements our sense of sight; the two together provide far more information than either alone can offer.

the **BIG picture**

How do we see? We can see because the photoreceptors in our retinas transduce the physical properties of electromagnetic light energy into electrochemical energy, which we sense as having the psychological properties of brightness, color, and saturation.

HOW DO WE HEAR?

To understand hearing, you need to know about the structures (anatomy) and processes (physiology) that permit us to hear: the interaction between sound and the ear.

The Nature of Sound

Physical Properties of Sound

Sound results from mechanical pressure on the air. To get a feel for the physical force of sound, place your hand gently over your throat, in the front of your neck, and speak aloud. The sound you produce will vibrate your hand. Similarly, when you pluck the string of a guitar, or clap your hands together, you are pushing on air molecules.

When sounds push on air molecules, the pushed molecules briefly crash into other air molecules, which then crash into still other air molecules. The result is a three-dimensional wave of mechanical energy. The air particles themselves do not move much—it is the wave of pressure that covers the distance. Compare this effect to a line of cars waiting at a stoplight. Along comes a speeder who fails to stop in time, rear-ending the last car in line. That car then hits the car in front of it, and

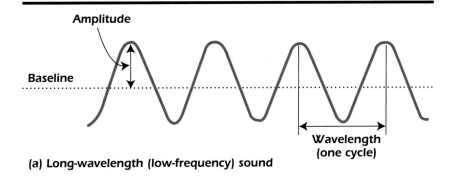

(a) Long-wavelength (low-frequency) sound

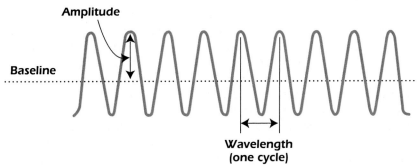

(b) Short-wavelength (high-frequency) sound

Figure 4-7
Properties of Sound Waves
Sound waves are generally measured in terms of amplitude *(which corresponds to the psychological sensation of loudness) and* frequency *(which corresponds to the psychological sensation of pitch). A third psychological dimension of sound is* timbre *(not shown here).*

so on. The mechanical pressure spreads in a wave forward through the line of cars. However, the car that started the wave does not move much at all.

Corresponding Physical and Psychological Properties of Sound Waves

The physical properties of sound waves affect how we sense and process these waves psychologically. The first two properties are familiar: the amplitude and the frequency (shorter wavelength); (see Figure 4-7). Sound amplitude (intensity) corresponds to our sensation of loudness: the higher the amplitude, the louder the sound. The usual unit of measurement for the intensity of sound is the *decibel (dB)*. Zero decibels is the absolute threshold for normal human hearing, at which most people can detect a sound at least 50% of the time. Table 4-2 shows the decibel levels of various common sounds.

The frequency (Figure 4-7) of sound corresponds to our psychological sensation of *pitch*—how high or low a tone sounds. A frequency of one cycle per second is 1 *hertz (Hz)*. The third psychological dimension of sound is timbre. *Timbre* is the quality of sound that allows us to tell the difference between a note played on a piano and the same note played on a harmonica.

How We Hear

The key mechanism for hearing the properties of sound lies deep inside the ear, in a set of fluid-filled canals. One of the membranes separating two of these canals is the **basilar membrane** (see Figure 4-8). On the basilar membrane are thousands of **hair cells,** which are our auditory (hearing) receptors. When sound vibrations reach the hair cells, the sound waves move parts of the hair cells. The hair cells then transduce the mechanical energy of the sound waves into electrochemical energy. The electrochemical energy is transmitted through the neurons to the brain.

Humans can generally hear sound waves in the range from about 20 to 20,000 Hz. Within this broad range, we are most sensitive to sounds in the middle of the range, roughly corresponding to the range of human voices. We are especially

Silence is another form of sound.

Jane Hollister Wheelwright

How does your ability to hear affect the way you interact with people in your environment? How does your hearing affect the tasks you need to perform?

basilar membrane one of the membranes separating two of the fluid-filled canals of the inner ear; on this membrane are the hair cells that transduce sound waves

hair cell auditory receptor that transduces sound waves into electrochemical energy

TABLE 4-2
Decibel Table

Decibel level	Example	Dangerous time exposure
0	Lowest sound audible to human ear (threshold)	
30	Quiet library, soft whisper	
40	Quiet office, living room, bedroom away from traffic	
50	Light traffic at a distance, refrigerator, gentle breeze	
60	Air conditioner at 20 feet, conversation	
70	Busy traffic, noisy restaurant (constant exposure)	Critical level begins
80	Subway, heavy city traffic, alarm clock at 2 feet, factory noise	More than 8 hours
90	Truck traffic, noisy appliances, shop tools, lawnmower	Less than 8 hours
100	Chain saw, boiler shop, pneumatic drill	2 hours
120	Rock concert in front of speakers, sandblasting, thunderclap	Immediate danger
140	Gunshot blast, jet plane	Any exposure is dangerous
180	Spacecraft launch	Hearing loss inevitable

Deafness has left me acutely aware of both the duplicity that language is capable of and the many expressions the body cannot hide.

Terry Galloway

MINILECTURE

Sound and the Ear (Ch 4)

place theory a theory that sensed variations in pitch arise from variations in the locations of the hair cells that are stimulated by particular sounds

frequency theory a theory that sensed variations in pitch arise from variations in the frequencies of the sound waves, which cause the hair cells to transmit neural impulses at the same rate as the frequency of the original sound wave

sensitive to changes in sounds, such as changes in pitch. Two major theories of how we sense pitch have been proposed: place theory and frequency theory.

Helmholtz (1863/1930) observed that the basilar membrane in the inner ear is wider at one end than at the other. According to Helmholtz's **place theory,** we hear variations in pitch based on variations in where the basilar membrane is stimulated. Hair cells located at the wider end respond to lower pitches, and hair cells located at the narrower end respond to higher pitches. Different hair cells also excite different neurons. Each neuron is sensitive to the specific frequencies that originally stimulated the basilar membrane. Some support for this theory has been found: Prolonged exposure to a very loud sound of a particular frequency damages the hair cells at a specific spot on the basilar membrane, causing hearing loss for sounds of that pitch.

Frequency theory does not rely on location to explain pitch. Instead, frequency theory suggests that the basilar membrane triggers neural impulses at the same rate as the frequency of the original sound wave. Pitch is determined by the frequency of the impulses that pass through the auditory nerve to reach the brain. A tone of 500 Hz produces 500 neural impulses per second, and so on. For very high frequencies, sets of neurons may cooperate to fire at rapid rates. For example, 40 neurons might cooperatively fire at a rate of 500 bursts per second for each, producing a total rate of 20,000—the upper limit of human hearing. Place theory and frequency theory each explain some, but not all, of what researchers have learned about how people hear pitch.

Locating Sounds

How do we figure out where sounds are coming from? The way we locate sounds is based on a very simple physiological fact: Our two ears are located about 6 inches apart on opposite sides of our heads. When a sound comes from our right, it has less distance to travel to reach the right ear than the left ear, so it reaches the right ear a little sooner than the left ear. We can detect differences in arrival times as brief as 10 microseconds (Durlach & Colburn, 1978). Another way we process sound location is by comparing the differences in the intensities of the sounds

Figure 4-8
Anatomy of the Ear
Shown here are (a) the various physical structures of the ear; and (b) a close-up view of the cochlea.

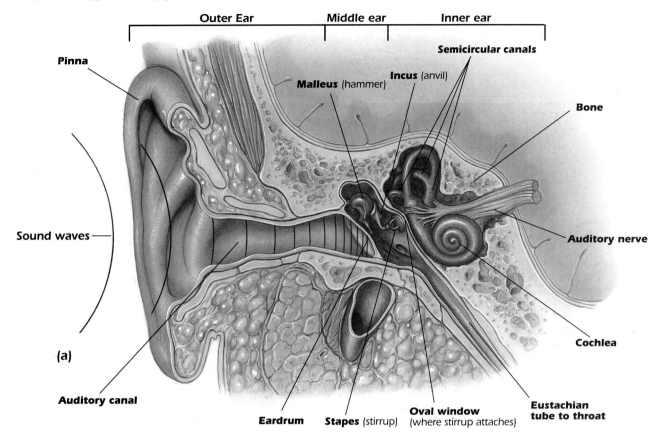

Outer Ear   Middle ear   Inner ear

Pinna

Semicircular canals

Malleus (hammer)   Incus (anvil)

Bone

Sound waves

Auditory nerve

(a)

Cochlea

Auditory canal

Eardrum   Stapes (stirrup)   Oval window (where stirrup attaches)   Eustachian tube to throat

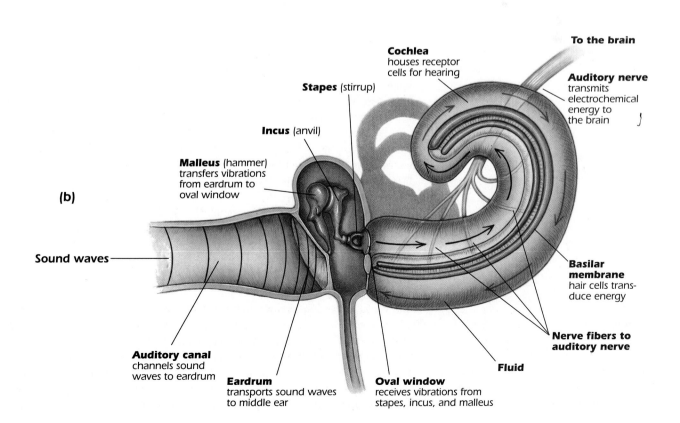

To the brain

Cochlea
houses receptor cells for hearing

Stapes (stirrup)

Auditory nerve
transmits electrochemical energy to the brain

Incus (anvil)

Malleus (hammer)
transfers vibrations from eardrum to oval window

(b)

Sound waves

Basilar membrane
hair cells transduce energy

Nerve fibers to auditory nerve

Auditory canal
channels sound waves to eardrum

Eardrum
transports sound waves to middle ear

Oval window
receives vibrations from stapes, incus, and malleus

Fluid

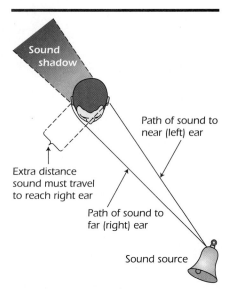

Figure 4-9
Locating Sounds
We locate the sources of sounds by using two methods: (a) In the time-difference method, *we note the time that a given sound arrives at each ear, and we figure out that the sound comes from somewhere nearer to the ear that heard the sound first. (b) In the* intensity-difference method, *we note the loudness of a given sound in each ear, and we conclude that the sound comes from somewhere nearer to the ear that heard the sound more loudly.*

Some prefer vinegar, and some prefer wine.

Talmud

taste bud clusters of taste receptor cells located on the tongue

reaching our ears. The farther ear receives a lower-intensity sound than the closer ear because the head absorbs some of the sound going to the farther ear. Apparently, the *time-difference method* works best for locating the source of low-frequency sounds, and the *intensity-difference method* works best for locating high-frequency sounds (see Figure 4-9).

How do we hear? We can hear because hair cells on the basilar membrane transduce the physical properties of mechanical energy from air waves into electrochemical energy having the psychological properties of loudness, pitch, and timbre.

Most of us rely on our sensations of sights and sounds to comprehend our environment and to monitor the events taking place around us. It is largely through hearing and seeing that we adapt to and shape our environment. Because of the power of these sensory systems, we sometimes fail to appreciate all we learn from our other senses. However, as the passage that opened this chapter illustrated, Helen Keller—like other persons who cannot see or hear—was able to adapt quite well to her surroundings by making the most of the other senses she had available. To find out more about how people adapt to a world without sights or sounds, see Practical Psychology 4-2.

HOW DO WE SENSE TASTE, SMELL, TOUCH, MOVEMENT, AND OTHER SENSATIONS?

Taste

We can see objects and hear events that occur at some distance from our bodies. In contrast, to use our sense of taste, we must come into physical contact with the things we taste. Just how does this intimate sensory system work?

There are two main requirements for being able to taste a stimulus: (1) The stimulus must contain chemical molecules that can dissolve in saliva, and (2) we must have enough saliva in our mouths to dissolve those chemicals. From these dissolved chemicals, we detect the four primary psychological qualities of saltiness, bitterness, sweetness, and sourness. Other tastes are produced by combinations of the four primary tastes, much as colors can be produced by a combination of the three primary colors.

As tasty substances enter the mouth, they land on the tongue, where they are detected by 1 or more taste buds. **Taste buds** are clusters of taste receptor cells located on the small visible bumps, or *papillae*, on the tongue (see Figure 4-10). Although there may be an average of about 10,000 taste buds on each person's tongue, according to Linda Bartoshuk and her colleagues (Bartoshuk, Duffy, & Miller, 1994), the actual number of taste buds on the tongue varies widely across individuals, so that some people are much more sensitive to tastes than others. The taste receptors seem specially tailored to receive particular kinds of chemicals (e.g., salts or acids). Contact with these tasty chemicals activates the taste buds, thereby beginning the transduction process. According to a widely accepted theory of taste (Pfaffman, 1974), different receptors more easily transduce each of the four different taste sensations from chemical energy into electrochemical energy. The transduced electrochemical messages travel through the sensory neurons to the brain.

PRACTICAL PSYCHOLOGY 4-2

Adapting to a Sightless or Soundless Environment

All of us rely on our senses for adapting to the world around us. When we lack information from one or more of our senses, we rely even more heavily on the remaining senses. We also depend on help from other people, from various kinds of technologies, and from learning various techniques to make the most of the sensory information we have. For instance, Helen Keller's relationship with Anne Sullivan made it possible for Keller to become a world-renowned lecturer and author. She was also able to benefit from the technological aids that were available around the turn of the century: She learned to read both raised letters and braille letters, and she learned to write, using a braille type-writer. (Keller could also lip-read pretty well by placing her hand on the mouth and neck of the speaker.) Through reading, Keller explored a vast world of experience extending far beyond the limitations of her sensory world.

Almost a century after Keller wrote the story of her life, many more op-tions have become available to extend the experiences of deaf and blind indi-viduals. Well-trained hearing-ear and seeing-eye dogs and other animal assistants can ably provide needed sensory information for independent living. In addition, technological aids can translate information from one sensory modality to another. Sounds can be translated into other sensations, such as sights or vibrations, enabling deaf persons to see "doorbells," feel the vibra-tions of an "alarm clock," and read the "voices" of a telephone caller or a tele-vision show. Similarly, sights can be translated into sounds: Speech-synthesis technologies can transform printed material into spoken words. Many blind students can now have access to almost any reading material of interest to them, through various reading services and technologies. Technological assis-tance for enhancing and supporting independent living are increasing almost daily: Voice-recognition systems can implement voiced commands, motion-detection systems can signal the presence of other persons, and so on.

Cultural changes, too, have widened the perceptible world of persons who cannot sense sights or sounds. Less than a century ago, most deaf chil-dren had little or no formal education. Many such children were not identi-fied as being deaf or were not given adequate opportunities to learn language until it was too late for them to acquire a native or nativelike mastery of lan-guage. Through the early detection of deafness and the increasingly wide-spread use of natural languages such as American Sign Language (ASL), children who might otherwise be deprived of language and of rich educational opportunities have been able to acquire language early enough to become flu-ent users (Sacks, 1990). Although it may be surprising to hearing persons, many persons who are deaf from birth are quite content with their soundless world and do not seek to hear. Even persons who become deaf later in life may come to feel that their soundless world is complete (Sacks, 1990), so that when asked whether they would chose to restore their hearing, they say they would not.

This wariness of restored hearing (or vision) may not be unfounded. For persons who have been blind or deaf from birth, the introduction of sight or of sound in adulthood may be more confusing than it is rewarding (Gregory, 1987; Sacks, 1995). To make sense of their sensations, they rely on the senses they have fine tuned over a lifetime for constructing a coherent and compre-hensible perceptual world. Only through tremendous effort and persistent practice can they adjust to regaining their vision or their hearing.

Deafness . . . means the loss of the most vital stimulus—the sound of the voice that brings language, sets thoughts astir and keeps us in the intellectual company of man.

Helen Keller

Why has there been less study of taste, smell, and the other body senses than of vision and hearing?

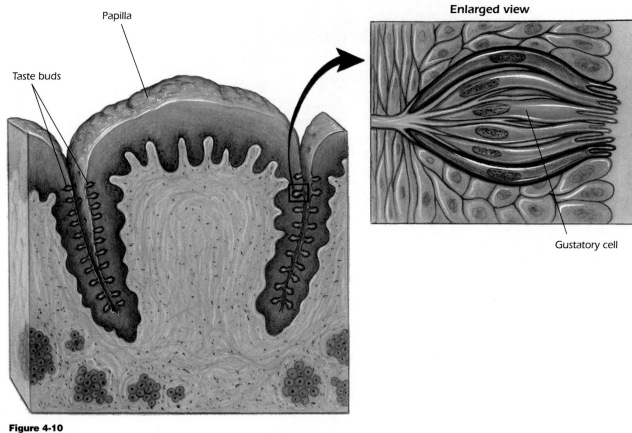

Figure 4-10
Taste Buds
This enlarged view shows just one taste bud, of the thousands of taste buds on a person's tongue.

Smell

For the sense of smell, almost more than any other, has the power to recall memories and it is a pity that we use it so little.

Rachel Carson

olfaction the sense of smell

The sense of smell, **olfaction,** enhances our ability to enjoy food (see Figure 4-11). In addition, it works independently of taste. Like taste, smell is chemically activated. When molecules in the air can dissolve in either water or fat, they can be sensed by our olfactory system.

Once our olfactory system detects scent-bearing molecules, we sense the odor. It is hard to specify absolute thresholds for smell, and we have different thresholds for detecting different substances. Also, the smell receptors of different people

Figure 4-11
The Importance of Smell to Perceived Taste
Many foods are much less easy to identify when they cannot be smelled.

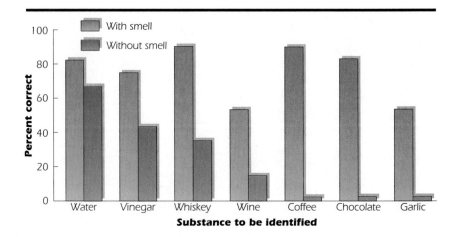

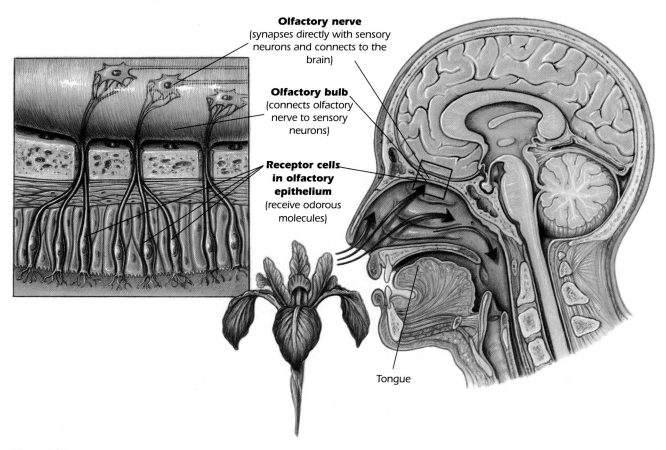

Olfactory nerve
(synapses directly with sensory neurons and connects to the brain)

Olfactory bulb
(connects olfactory nerve to sensory neurons)

Receptor cells in olfactory epithelium
(receive odorous molecules)

Tongue

Figure 4-12
The Nasal Cavity
Airborne molecules are drawn into the nasal cavity when we breathe. The sensitive skin in the nasal cavity houses the receptor cells that transduce the chemical energy of smell into the electrochemical energy understood by the nervous system.

have differing thresholds, and the sense of smell generally decreases with age. These differences have practical implications. Persons who have limited sensations of smell cannot rely on their ability to detect odors such as smoke, leaking gas, or contaminated food, so they must find other means of protecting themselves from such dangers (e.g., using smoke detectors, replacing gas heaters and stoves with electric ones, and discarding even remotely questionable foods).

For smell to occur, odorous molecules must be carried through the air into the nasal cavity, either through the nostrils or through air passages leading from the mouth. There, the molecules reach the olfactory receptors in the skin of the nasal cavity (see Figure 4-12). This skin is referred to as the *olfactory epithelium*. An electrochemical signal is produced, which travels along fibers of the *olfactory nerve* to the *olfactory bulb*, which is analogous in function to the retina of the eye. It processes the signals and carries the processed signals to the brain.

How, exactly, do the receptors for odor work? One idea is the **lock-and-key theory** (Amoore, 1970), which states that both odorous molecules and olfactory receptors have distinctive shapes. We smell something when there is a special fit between the shape of moleculers that enter our noses and the shape of specific olfactory receptors inside our noses (see Figure 4-13). Thus, different olfactory receptors are receptive to different-shaped molecules. When a given molecule fits a receptor, it is transduced into an electrochemical impulse.

A second theory is **vibration theory** (Wright, 1977, 1982), which states that the molecules of each distinctively smelled substance generate a specific vibration frequency. The distinctive pattern of vibrations is transduced into a characteristic

According to Linda Bartoshuk (1991), it appears that our taste preferences are largely inherited, but our smell preferences depend largely on our personal experiences. How have your experiences with smells shaped your preferences for particular foods? What smells appeal to you, and what smells sicken you?

lock-and-key theory a theory of how we smell, based on the matching of particular odorous molecules and particular smell receptors

vibration theory a theory that we smell because particular molecules generate particular frequencies of vibrations, which smell receptors transduce into electrochemical messages about particular smells

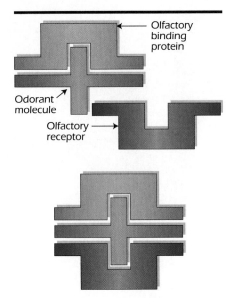

Figure 4-13
Lock-and-Key Theory
According to lock-and-key theory, the characteristic molecular shapes of various odorous chemicals match to the distinctive physiological shapes of the receptor cells. When the two shapes match, the mated receptor cell transduces the chemical into an electrochemical message about smell.

pattern of electrochemical energy of neural impulses. The brain interprets these characteristic patterns as specific odors. We sense smells through receptors in the skin inside our noses. The skin elsewhere on our bodies contains many other kinds of receptor cells.

Skin Senses

We often think of the **skin senses** as simply the sense of touch. The term *touch*, however, does not adequately describe the various sensations of pressure, temperature, and pain that we feel through our skin. We can feel various sensations through our skin because its many layers contain various kinds of sensory receptors.

Each different kind of sensory receptor in our skin can respond to a different kind of physical stimulus. When we sense these differing physical stimuli, our brains interpret these stimuli as psychological sensations of pain, warmth, vibration, pressure, and so on. Objects pressed against the skin change the skin's shape, causing the sensation of pressure. When even a single tiny hair on our skin is moved, we feel pressure from its movement. The temperature of whatever touches our skin leads to a sensation of warmth or cold. Slight electrical stimulation of our skin usually results in a sensation of pressure and perhaps of temperature. Too much of any kind of stimulation generally causes pain sensations. Pain serves an important role in alerting us that tissue damage has occurred for some reason (see Chapter 15). Even damage to internal tissues may lead to sensations of pain, particularly if the damage is severe and is located where there are pain receptors. (Ironically, there are *no* pain receptors located in the brain itself.)

Body Senses

Pain is not the only sensation that can be created by stimulation from inside our bodies. Your ability to walk or to make almost any intentional movements depends on your sense of kinesthesis and your vestibular sense (sense of balance). **Kinesthesis** is the sense that helps you to be aware of your skeletal muscle movements. Kinesthetic receptors are in the muscles and other tissues connecting your muscles and your bones. When these receptors detect changes in positions, they transduce this mechanical energy into electrochemical energy. This information is sent up the spinal cord and eventually reaches the brain.

Finding Your Way   **4-1**

Not seeing is believing: Close your eyes, and move your arms and your legs, changing their positions. Stop moving, but keep your eyes closed. Where are the various parts of your body in respect to one another? Open your eyes, and check to see whether you answered the question correctly. How did you do that?

skin senses the means by which we become sensitive to pressure, temperature, and pain stimulation directly on the skin

kinesthesis the sense through which receptors within our muscles and connective tissues inform us about the positions and movements of our skeletal muscles

vestibular system sense of balance, governed by receptors in the inner ear, which detect the position and movement of the head, relative to a source of gravity

The *vestibular* sense is, roughly speaking, the sense of balance. The vestibular sense is determined by the position and movement of the head relative to the source of gravity. The vestibular receptors for balance are located in the inner ear, in the **vestibular system.** The vestibular system tells the visual system how to control eye positions to adjust for head movements. This system also uses information from our eyes to help us sense motion and balance. In fact, input from the kinesthetic, vestibular, and visual systems comes together in the cerebral cortex.

Our senses are our gateways to thoughts, feelings, and ideas—our bridges from the external world, through our bodies, to our minds. Once we have gathered sensations into our minds, we must assign meaning to them—which calls for perception, the following topic.

How do we sense taste, smell, touch, movement, and other sensations? We sense taste and smell through receptors located on our tongues (taste) and in our nasal cavities (smell), which are sensitive to particular chemicals. We sense temperature, pressure, and pain through receptors in our skin; we sense kinesthesis through receptors in tissues connecting our bones and muscles; we detect vestibular sensations through receptors deep inside our inner ears.

HOW DO WE MAKE SENSE OF WHAT WE SENSE?

As the following passage shows, *perception*—the set of processes by which we recognize, organize, and make sense of our sensations—is no easy task. The passage describes the experiences of Virgil, a 50-year-old man whose sight was newly restored after a lifetime of blindness. Because he lacked the extensive visual experiences that usually pave the way for normal visual perception, Virgil had great difficulty in making sense of what he was newly able to see.

> In general, . . . if Virgil could identify an animal, it would be either by its motion or by virtue of a single feature—thus, he might identify a kangaroo because it leapt, a giraffe by its height. . . . [Virgil] thought that [the gorilla] looked just like a man. Fortunately, there was a life-size bronze statue of a gorilla in the enclosure. . . . Exploring it swiftly and minutely with his hands, [Virgil] had an air of assurance that he had never shown when examining anything by sight. It [became apparent] how skillful and self-sufficient he had been as a blind man, how naturally and easily he had experienced his world with his hands, . . .
>
> His face seemed to light up with comprehension as he felt the statue. "It's not like a man at all," he murmured. The statue examined, he opened his eyes, and turned around to the real gorilla standing before him in the enclosure. And now, in a way that would have been impossible before, he described [observable details of] the ape's [appearance].
>
> —Oliver Sacks

In middle adulthood, Virgil readily recognized, organized, and made sense of his auditory, tactile, and other sensations, but he could not do so with his new visual sensations. When surgeons restored Virgil's sight, they could not give him a lifetime of visual experience. Instead, Virgil had to gradually construct visual perceptions by translating information from the tactile and auditory world of his experience to apply it to the new visual sensations assaulting him from all directions.

Most of us begin to organize our sensory experiences from the moment we emerge from the womb. Over time, we mentally construct objects (e.g., the talking face and warm, soft skin of a parent) and settings (e.g., the sensations that characterize the crib, the kitchen, or the living area). Gradually, we build a perceptual world in which we can make sense of our sensations.

Because the scope of this chapter prohibits exploration of all aspects of perception, in the following section, we focus on how we use our knowledge and understanding of the world to give meaning to our visual sensations, in particular. Vision is the sense system on which we rely the most, and it is usually more easily controlled experimentally, so there has been more research on visual perception than on other aspects of perception. Even within the field of visual perception, the possibilities for exploration are vast. In this discussion, we focus on visual perception of space, of forms, and of perceptual constancy.

How do we make sense of what we sense? Perceptual processes help us to recognize and organize in our brains the sensory information we receive from our various sensory receptors by incorporating that information with what we know from previous experiences and what we can figure out.

Finding Your Way   4-2

Before you read the following section, look closely at the engraving by William Hogarth, in Figure 4-14. What kinds of cues did Hogarth use to influence viewers' perceptions of his picture? Which cues are not consistent with some other cues? (For example, notice some oddities about the sign hanging in front of the building.)

Figure 4-14
False Perspective
At first, this engraving by English painter and engraver William Hogarth (1697–1764) seems realistic, but after closer inspection, conflicting perceptual cues become apparent. What are the perceptual cues and miscues the artist has used?

HOW DO WE PERCEIVE WHAT WE SEE?

Space Perception

As you move through space, you constantly look around and visually orient yourself in three-dimensional space. As you look forward into the distance, you look into the third dimension of *depth*. You must make frequent judgments regarding depth, such as whenever you transport your body, reach for or manipulate objects, or otherwise position yourself in your three-dimensional world. Generally, depth cues are either *monocular* (one-eyed) or *binocular* (two-eyed).

Monocular Depth Cues

One way of judging depth is through monocular depth cues. **Monocular depth cues** can be represented in just two dimensions, as in a picture. These depth cues are referred to as "monocular" because you need only one eye to perceive them. In contrast, you need two eyes to perceive binocular depth cues (considered later). Figure 4-15 beautifully shows the following monocular depth cues:

1. *Relative size* is the perception that things that are farther away (such as the rear tiles on the floor in Figure 4-15) appear to be smaller on your retina; the farther away an object is, the smaller is its image on the retina.
2. *Texture gradient* is a change in both the relative sizes of objects and the *densities* in the distribution of objects when viewed at different distances. The distributional density of objects is the distance among particles, parts, or objects, such as distances among various parts of the grating on the window to the right of the corridor in Figure 4-15.
3. *Interposition* is the positioning of objects whereby an object that is perceived to be closer partially blocks the view of an object that is perceived to be farther away. The blocking object (e.g., the peacock in Figure 4-15) is perceived to be in front of the blocked object (e.g., the decorated wall in Figure 4-15).

To see takes time, like to have a friend takes time.

Georgia O'Keefe

monocular depth cue perceived information about depth, which can be gained by using only one eye (*mon-*, one; *ocular*, related to the eyes)

Figure 4-15
Monocular Depth Cues in Art
The Annunciation, *by Venetian artist Carlo Crivelli (1430–1494), illustrates several monocular depth cues: texture gradients, relative size, interposition, linear perspective, and location in the picture plane.*

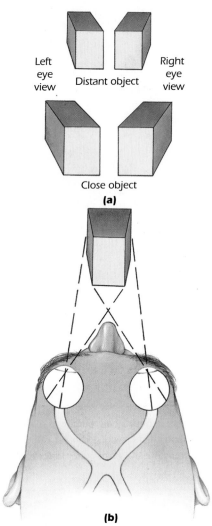

Left eye view   Right eye view

Distant object

Close object

(a)

(b)

Figure 4-16

Binocular Disparity and Binocular Convergence

One of the reasons you are able to see a three-dimensional world is because your two eyes are in slightly different places on your head. (a) Binocular disparity: Each of your eyes sees a slightly different visual field. The disparity in the view from each eye is greater for objects that are closer to you. (b) Binocular convergence: As objects approach you, you adjust the focus of each eye inward, toward your nose. The closer the object is to you, the more your two eyes must turn inward (converge) to focus the image. Your brain uses both convergence and disparity information as depth cues.

---

binocular depth cue perceived information about depth, which can be gained only by using two eyes (*bin-*, both; two)

feature-detector approach an approach to form perception based on observing the activity of the brain; apparently, specific neurons of the visual cortex respond to specific features detected by photoreceptors

4. *Linear perspective* helps us to make judgments about distance on the basis of our perceiving that parallel lines (such as the lines along the sides of the walls in Figure 4-15) seem to be coming together as they move farther into the distance.

5. *Location in the picture plane* indicates depth, in that objects that are farther from the observer are viewed as higher in the picture plane if below the horizon (such as the higher position of the people at the rear of the corridor, as compared with the woman kneeling in the cubicle to the right of the corridor in Figure 4-15) and lower in the picture plane if above the horizon.

6. *Aerial perspective* is perceived by observing the relative distribution of moisture and dust particles in the atmosphere as a means to judge distance. Objects close to us are relatively unaffected by these particles, but as we view objects that are at increasing distances from us, we are looking through increasing numbers of these particles. This greater density of particles makes objects that are farther away appear to be hazier and less distinct.

Another way of perceiving our three-dimensional world involves binocular depth cues.

Binocular Depth Cues

Binocular depth cues depend on the use of two eyes. Each of your eyes views a scene from slightly different angles; the two different viewing angles provide information about depth. The term for three-dimensional perception of the world through the use of binocular (two-eyed) vision is *stereopsis*. With stereo sound, you hear slightly different sounds coming to each ear, and you combine those sounds to form realistic auditory perceptions. With stereopsis, you receive slightly different visual images in each eye, and you *fuse* (fully combine to make a single image) those two images to form realistic visual perceptions. You rely on this fusion to give you a whole visual representation of what you see. Figure 4-16 illustrates two phenomena that lead to stereoscopic vision: *binocular disparity* (slight discrepancy in the viewpoint of each eye) and *binocular convergence* (merging focus of the two eyes).

Another aspect of vision seems to be at least as important as depth perception: form perception—our perception of the shapes of things.

Form Perception

Two of the main attributes of form are size and shape. How, exactly, do we perceive size and shape? One approach to form perception tries to link form perception to the functioning of neurons in the brain. This psychophysiological approach is the **feature-detector approach,** developed by Nobel laureates David Hubel and Torsten Wiesel (1963, 1968, 1979). The research of Hubel and Wiesel focused on specific neurons of the visual cortex. These investigators found that specific cortical neurons respond to varying kinds of visual stimuli. These kinds of stimuli were presented to the specific retinal regions connected to the cortical neurons studied by Hubel and Wiesel. A disproportionately large amount of the visual cortex is devoted to neurons mapped to receptive fields in the central regions of the retina. This overrepresentation of the central fields of vision in the cortex corresponds to the overrepresentation of cones in the center of the retina.

Most of the cells in the cortex respond to "specifically oriented line segments" (Hubel & Wiesel, 1979, p. 9). These specially oriented line segments (e.g., vertical, horizontal, or diagonal lines) are the features for which the feature-detector approach is named. In addition, other cells in the visual cortex respond to other stimuli, which vary in their degree of complexity. These other cells seem to be organized into a hierarchy: In general, as a stimulus proceeds through the visual system to higher levels in the cortex, the size of the receptive field increases, as does the complexity of the stimulus required to prompt a response in the neurons of the cortex.

A different approach to form perception focuses on the integration of various features into a whole configuration. Specifically, the **Gestalt approach** is based on this notion: The whole differs from the sum of its individual parts. Gestalt principles are particularly relevant to understanding how we perceive an assembly of forms—a grouping that fits together various parts or elements into a whole unit.

When you walk into a familiar room, you perceive that some things stand out (e.g., faces in photographs or posters) and that others fade into the background (e.g., undecorated walls and floors). The way in which you perceive each aspect depends on your perception of the whole. A **figure** is any object perceived as being highlighted. Figures are perceived against, or in contrast to, some kind of receding, unhighlighted (back)**ground** (see Figure 4-17a). Table 4-3 summarizes and defines a few of the Gestalt principles of form perception, including *figure–ground, proximity, similarity, continuity, closure,* and *symmetry* (see Figure 4-17).

The Gestalt principles of form perception describe *how* we perceive many aspects of what we see. The feature-detector approach complements the Gestalt approach, explaining *why* we are able to perceive various forms as we do. Other approaches address the perception of forms that fall into various kinds of *patterns* (sets of characteristics that can be detected across various instances, e.g., the set of characteristics of a particular letter or numeral).

Psychologists have had trouble figuring out how people recognize patterns, such as letters, numbers, or faces. Some aspects of pattern recognition are tricky. For example, you might be able to specify in a reasonably complete way the features of a letter. However, how do you specify completely the features that allow you to recognize a familiar face? What you may take for granted—such as the ability to recognize the face of your friend—is not something that everyone can do easily.

Some people have severe problems in perceiving sensory information; these people are said to suffer from **agnosia.** People with visual agnosia have normal sensations of whatever sights are in front of them. However, they cannot recognize

What are some tasks you perform in everyday life that require the use of binocular depth cues?

Imagine that you are magically transported to an alien world, in which you recognize nothing (much as newborns arrive in our strange world). How would you react? How would you learn to orient yourself and to function in this alien world?

 **MINILECTURE**

Depth Perception (Ch 5)

Images are more direct, more immediate than words, and closer to the unconscious. Picture language precedes thinking in words.

Gloria Anzaldua

Figure 4-17

Gestalt Principles of Perception

The Gestalt principles of (a) figure–ground, (b) proximity, (c) similarity, (d) continuity, (e) closure, and (f) symmetry aid in our perception of forms.

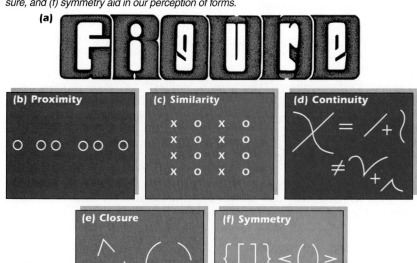

Gestalt approach an approach to form perception, based on the notion that the whole differs from the sum of its parts

figure a highlighted feature of the perceived environment

ground features of the perceived environment that are not highlighted, which serve as a background for highlighted features

agnosia severe problems in recognizing and interpreting information sent to the brain from one or more sense organs (*a-*, lack; *gnosis*, knowledge)

TABLE 4-3
Gestalt Principles of Visual Perception

Gestalt principles	Figure illustrating the principle
Figure–ground—When we perceive a visual field, some objects (figures) seem prominent, and other aspects of the field recede into the background (ground).	In viewing Figure 4-17a, we tend to see the word "figure" as the foreground, against a background of the word "ground." (after Shepard, 1990)
Proximity—When we perceive an assortment of objects, we tend to see objects that are close to each other as forming a group.	In viewing Figure 4-17b, we tend to perceive the circles that are the closest together as belonging together.
Similarity—We tend to group objects on the basis of their similarity.	In viewing Figure 4-17c, the similarity of the items in each column leads us to perceive alternating columns of X's and O's, rather than horizontal rows of unlike items.
Continuity—We tend to perceive smoothly flowing or continuous forms rather than disrupted or discontinuous ones.	In viewing Figure 4-17d, we perceive a line and a curve that intersect, rather than disjointed curves that touch in the middle.
Closure—When tend to perceptually close up, or complete objects that are not, in fact, complete.	In viewing Figure 4-17e, we tend to close up disjointed line segments to perceive a triangle and a circle.
Symmetry—We tend to perceive objects as forming mirror images about their center.	In viewing Figure 4-17f, we perceive an assortment of brackets as forming four sets of brackets rather than eight individual lines because we integrate the symmetrical elements into coherent pairs.

and understand those sights. In many ways, Virgil's difficulties with visual perception appear similar to the difficulties of agnosics. Agnosics see perfectly well, but they cannot organize and interpret what they see.

The perceptual difficulties of agnosics are generally caused by some type of trauma that produces *lesions* (areas damaged by injury or disease) in the agnosics' brains. For example, lesions in particular areas of the visual cortex may be responsible for the inability to identify familiar objects, such as a cat or the face of a loved one. There are many kinds of agnosias, and not all are visual. As we become better able to understand agnosias and other problems in perception, we may be able to understand more fully how normal perception works.

In viewing agnosia, many psychologists are puzzled by the observation that some people cannot recognize patterns. Perhaps even more puzzling, however, is the observation that most of us can do so. How do you know the letter *A* when you see it? What makes it look like an *A* instead of an *H*? Look at Figure 4-18 to see how difficult it is to answer this question. You will probably see the image in Figure 4-18 as the words, "THE CAT," and yet the *H* of *THE* is identical to the *A* of *CAT*. What subjectively feels like a simple process of pattern recognition is almost certainly quite complex.

Some researchers (e.g., Franks & Bransford, 1971; Posner & Keele, 1968) have suggested that we may recognize patterns by using **prototype matching**. The theory is based on the *prototype*, which integrates the most typical features of particular patterns into a best-guess example of the pattern. Prototypes are then used as a basis for finding matches to perceived patterns (see Figure 4-19).

An alternative explanation of pattern perception seems to echo Hubel and Wiesel's findings: According to **feature-matching** theories, we attempt to match features of a pattern to features stored in memory. We do not try to match a whole pattern to a prototype (Biederman, 1987; Selfridge, 1959). One such theory (Selfridge, 1959) suggests that pattern recognition occurs through a hierarchical set of

prototype matching the process of comparing an observed pattern to one or more mental examples, in order to find the typical example that comes closest to fitting the observed pattern

feature matching the process of comparing features of an observed pattern to pattern features stored in memory

Figure 4-18

How Do You Recognize These Letters?

When you read these words, you probably have no difficulty differentiating the "A" from the "H." Look more closely at each of these two letters: Do any features differentiate the two letters? (After Selfridge, 1959)

perceptual mechanisms leading from feature detection through successively more complex integrations of sensory information (see Figure 4-20).

Neither prototype- nor feature-matching theories can account fully for some aspects of pattern perception, such as context effects. **Context effects** are the perceptual effects due to the surrounding information in the environment. For example, because of context effects, we perceived "THE CAT," even though what we perceive as two different letters are actually physically identical. Gestalt psychologists would point out that the whole perception of "THE CAT" differs from the sum of its parts.

Current theories concerning the ways in which we perceive forms and patterns explain some of the observed phenomena of form and pattern perception. However, many phenomena of form and pattern recognition are yet to be explained fully. Another puzzling aspect of perception is perceptual constancy.

MINILECTURE

Gestalt Principles (Ch 5)

Figure 4-19

Prototype Matching—Even Without the Prototype!

(a) These faces are similar to those created in an experiment by Robert Solso and John McCarthy. In this experiment, participants were shown variations of a prototype but not the actual prototype itself. Even so, the participants believed that they had previously seen the prototype. In fact, as (b) shows, when participants were asked to rate their own confidence that they had previously seen each of the faces shown in (a), they gave the highest confidence ratings to the prototype—which they had never seen!

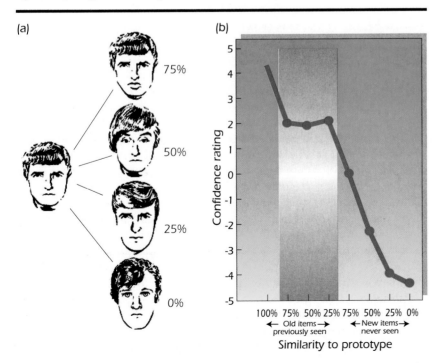

context effects influences on perception that come from information in the surrounding environment

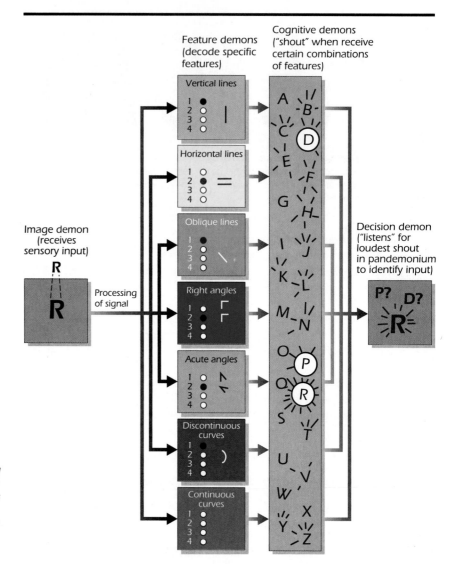

Figure 4-20
Pandemonium
According to Oliver Selfridge's feature-matching model, we begin the process of recognizing patterns by matching observed features to features already stored in memory. These features are then integrated into increasingly complex forms until at last we recognize the patterns for which we have found the greatest number of matches.

Perceptual Constancies

Finding Your Way   4-3

Tilt this book back and forth, so that you observe it from a top view, a side view, and the forward view you normally use for reading. Next, move the book close enough to your face to have it completely block out your view of everything else. Now, move the book away from you, rest it on a surface such as a desk or the floor, and back away from the book, continuing to look at its size and shape. Move back toward the book, pick it up, and hold it at the normal distance for reading.

Reality has changed chameleonlike before my eyes so many times, that I have learned, or am learning, to trust almost anything except what appears to be so.

Maya Angelou

Just now, you watched your book change its shape from a wide rectangle to a very thin one. You also observed it enlarge and shrink in size before your very eyes. Somehow, though, despite this clear sensory evidence that your book was transforming its shape and size, you probably continued to believe that your book retained its distinctive shape and size. Why is that?

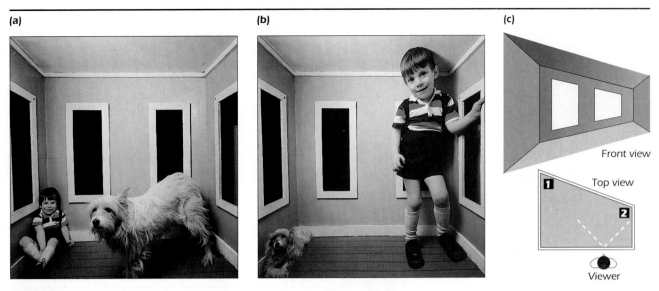

Figure 4-21

Perceptual Constancy

(a,b) The Ames room has been carefully constructed to give us the impression of a normally constructed room in which people take on bizarre sizes. (c) As you can see, however, the room is actually quite distorted, and if you were to view it from an angle other than the one for which it was designed, the room, not the people in it, would seem to be oddly formed. (© Norman Snyder, 1985)

Your perception of this apparent constancy in size is an example of perceptual constancy. **Perceptual constancy** occurs when our perception of an object remains the same even when our immediate sensation of the object changes. Some of the main kinds of perceptual constancies are size, shape, lightness, and color constancies.

Size constancy is the perception that an object maintains the same size despite changes in the size of the stimulus on our retinas. The size of an image on the retina directly depends on the distance of that object from the eye, as well as the size of the object, of course. The same object at two different distances projects different-sized images on the retina. Usually, size constancy helps us to make sense of the changing stimuli we see. Sometimes, however, our perceptual system is fooled by the very same information that usually helps us to achieve size constancy. We often are tricked by various visual illusions. (Compare the three-dimensional illusion shown in Figure 4-21 with the two-dimensional illusions created by painters such as Carlo Crivelli.) An illusion often described in books for engineers, architects, designers, and painters is the *Müller-Lyer illusion* (see Figure 4-22).

This chapter describes several ways in which our expectations affect our perceptions. How do illustrators and other artists make use of your expectations in the artwork that you see around you?

perceptual constancy the perception that stimuli remain the same even when immediate sensations of the stimuli change

Figure 4-22

Size-Constancy Illusion

In the Müller–Lyer illusion, we tend to view two equally long line segments as being of different lengths. In particular, the vertical line segment in panel (a) and the central segment in (c) appear shorter than the line segment in panel (b) and the central segment in (d), even though all the line segments are the same length. We are not yet certain why such a simple illusion occurs.

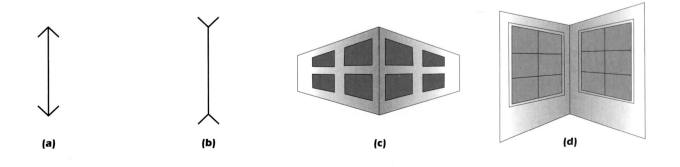

Another form of perceptual constancy is shape constancy. In *shape constancy*, we perceive that the shape of an object remains the same despite changes in our sensations of the object. These sensations may result from changes in our orientation toward the object. Although the changes in orientation cause changes in the shape of its retinal image, we perceive the object as unchanging (see Figure 4-23).

Lightness constancy is our perception that objects have an even appearance of brightness, despite differences in the actual amount of physical light reaching our eyes. Similarly, *color constancy* is the perception that objects remain the same color, even when our senses tell us that a hue (color) is changing. Artists have used lightness and color constancy for centuries.

How do we perceive what we see? We perceive depth by using various monocular and binocular depth cues. We perceive forms by detecting features of objects and by using Gestalt principles of forms. We recognize patterns by matching observed patterns to prototypes or to features we have in our minds, also taking into account the effects of the context of perception. We also perceive various constancies across objects, despite apparent changes in size, shape, lightness, and color.

In concluding our look at sensation and perception, we find that the whole differs from the sum of its parts. As Gestalt psychologists have pointed out, our sensory and perceptual systems accomplish amazing work as an intact whole. As subsequent chapters show, these systems fit into an even larger framework of thoughts, feelings, and actions. Although many aspects of perception occur at an unconscious level, other aspects are subject to conscious manipulation. Just what constitutes consciousness—and what mental processes occur in different states of consciousness—is the subject of the next chapter.

Figure 4-23
Shape Constancy
When you view a door, you perceive it as retaining the same shape, even though your sensations of the shape change as the door shifts in relation to your viewpoint. (After Gibson, 1950)

1. A *sensation* is a message that the brain receives from a sense. A *sense* is a physical system that collects information for the brain and transduces it from one form of energy into electrochemical energy, which the brain can use for making sense of the sensation.

How Do Psychologists Study the Senses? 104

2. *Psychophysics* is the study of the relationship between physical stimulation of a sense organ and its psychological effects.

3. *Detection* refers to the ability to sense a stimulus. The smallest amount of physical energy of a given kind that can be sensed (detected) 50% of the time is operationally defined as the *absolute threshold* for that kind of stimulus.

4. *Signal-detection theory* (SDT) is used for analyzing responses in terms of *hits* (true positive responses), *false alarms* (false positives), *correct rejections* (true negatives), and *misses* (false negatives).

5. *Discrimination* involves distinguishing between one stimulus and another. The *just-noticeable difference* (*jnd*) (also termed the *difference threshold*) is the minimum amount of difference that can be detected between two stimuli at least 50% of the time.

6. As the intensity of a stimulus increases, larger and larger differences between stimuli are needed to generate a jnd.

What Are Some Biological Properties Common to All Senses? 106

7. All of the senses share particular biological properties, such as psychophysical *thresholds, transduction, sensory coding,* and *adaptation.*

8. Each sense has specialized sensory *receptor cells.* These cells take in a particular form of energy and transduce it into an electrochemical form that sensory neurons can transmit to the brain.

9. Through sensory coding, sensory receptors convey a range of information, such as the *intensity (amplitude)* and the *quality* (e.g., *wavelength*) of a stimulus.

10. When our senses detect changes in energy, receptor cells send an alert to the brain. *Adaptation* is the temporary physiological response to a change in the environment; it varies according to the intensity of the change stimulus.

How Do We See? 108

11. We can see because the receptors of our eyes receive and transduce energy from a portion of the electromagnetic spectrum of light.

12. The cornea and the *lens* of the eye bend light and focus it on the retina. *Accommodation* is the process by which the focusing of the lens enables us to see objects clearly at varying distances from us.

13. The *retina* is the structure in which photoreceptors transduce the electromagnetic energy in light into the electrochemical energy of neural impulses.

14. There are two separate visual systems of photoreceptors. The *rod* system is used primarily for vision in dim light, and the *cone* system is used primarily for vision in bright light.

15. Three properties of color are *hue*, which matches the psychological sensation of color; *saturation*, which is the psychological sensation of the richness of a color; and *brightness*, which is our psychological impression of physical light intensity. Color, saturation, and brightness are psychological, rather than physical, phenomena.

16. The *trichromatic theory* of color vision posits that we see color through the actions and interactions of cone receptors for three primary colors—red, green, and blue.

17. The *opponent-process theory* of color vision states that we see color through the opposing actions of paired cone receptors for red versus green and blue versus yellow, as well as black versus white.

How Do We Hear? 112

18. In the inner ear is a *basilar membrane.* On the surface of this membrane are *hair cells*, which transduce the mechanical energy of sound waves into electrochemical energy that can be processed by the brain.

19. According to *place theory*, we hear differing pitches based on the differing locations of the hair cells that are stimulated on the basilar membrane.

20. According to *frequency theory*, the vibrations of the basilar membrane reproduce the vibrations of the sounds that enter the ear.

21. The two methods for locating the source of a sound both depend on the different locations of each ear on the head: The *time-difference method* works best for low-frequency sounds, and the *intensity-difference method* works best for high-frequency sounds.

How Do We Sense Taste, Smell, Touch, Movement, and Other Sensations? 116

22. We are able to taste because of interactions between chemical substances and *taste buds*, which are sensory receptors on the bumps on our tongues. According to a widely accepted theory of taste, the various sensory receptors in the tongue are particularly sensitive to various combinations of the four primary tastes: *sweet, sour, bitter,* and *salty.*

23. We are able to smell because of interactions between chemical substances and sensory receptors in our nasal cavities. According to *lock-and-key theory*, we smell something when there is a special fit between the shape of a molecule that enters our noses and the olfactory receptors there. According to *vibration theory*, we smell something when a molecule which has entered our nasal cavity creates a unique vibratory pattern that is picked up by receptor cells.

24. Skin-sense nerves respond to pressure, pain, and temperature information.
25. Through *kinesthesis*, we can sense whether we are moving or stationary, where our various body parts are, and how (if at all) the parts are moving.
26. Receptors of the *vestibular system*, located in the inner ear, allow us to maintain our sense of balance.

How Do We Make Sense of What We Sense?   121

27. From the moment we emerge from the womb, we begin trying to make sense of our sensations, organizing our sensory experiences into specific objects and settings. These sensory experiences form the basis for perception.

How Do We Perceive What We See?   123

28. Two kinds of depth cues enable us to perceive three-dimensional space. *Monocular depth cues*, which can be noted by just a single eye, include relative size, texture gradients, interposition, linear perspective, location in the picture plane, and aerial perspective.
29. *Binocular depth cues* depend on using both eyes at the same time. Binocular-disparity cues capitalize on the fact that each of the two eyes receives a slightly different image of the same object being viewed. Binocular-convergence cues depend on the degree to which our two eyes must turn inward toward each other as objects get closer to us.
30. Two main approaches to form perception are the feature-detector approach and the Gestalt approach. According to the *feature-detector approach* to form perception, various neurons in the visual cortex can be mapped to specific receptive fields on the retina. Differing cortical neurons respond to different kinds of forms, such as line segments in various spatial orientations. Visual perception seems to depend on increasing levels of complexity in the cortical neurons. Complexity seems to increase as it is farther removed from the incoming information from the sensory receptors.
31. According to the *Gestalt approach*, the whole of form perception differs from the sum of its parts. *Gestalt principles of form perception* include figure–ground, proximity, similarity, closure, continuity, and symmetry.
32. *Agnosia* is an inability to recognize and understand what the senses are receiving. Visual agnosics cannot recognize objects that their visual senses transmit to their brains.
33. Two of the main theoretical approaches to pattern perception are prototype matching and feature matching. In *prototype matching*, we recognize a pattern by matching it to a typical example in our minds. In *feature matching*, we recognize a pattern by comparing the features or aspects of the pattern to features in our minds. Neither of these two models of pattern perception can fully account for *context effects*, which are influences of the overall situation in which perception occurs.
34. *Perceptual constancies* result when our perceptions of objects remain constant despite changes in the stimuli being sensed. Examples of perceptual constancies are size, shape, lightness, and color constancies. A size-constancy illusion is the Müller-Lyer illusion, which may be affected by cultural experiences.

PATHWAYS TO KNOWLEDGE

Choose the best answer to complete each sentence.

1. Psychophysics is the study of
   (a) how physics and psychology combine to allow understanding of the movement of particles.
   (b) why particle movements may be psychologically undetectable.
   (c) the measurement of the relationship between a form of physical stimulation and the psychological sensations it produces.
   (d) how psychological functions can be broken down into discrete components.

2. Signal-detection theory attempts to
   (a) assess the intensity of a given stimulus.
   (b) eliminate possible errors in psychological measurement.
   (c) control measurement error in detection experiments.
   (d) explain how a person's expectations influence his or her perception of a stimulus.

3. The minimum amount of difference that can be detected between two stimuli is called the
   (a) detection threshold.
   (b) just noticeable difference.
   (c) discriminatory level.
   (d) perceivable difference.

4. The theory of smell that posits that different-shaped olfactory receptors are receptive to different-shaped molecules is the
   (a) lock-and-key theory.
   (b) place theory.
   (c) vibration theory.
   (d) specificity theory.

5. The electromagnetic spectrum refers to
   (a) a range of varying wavelengths of electomagnetic energy.
   (b) wavelengths of light visible to the naked eye.
   (c) a range of all the colors visible to the naked eye.
   (d) the spectrum of energy variations that result from exposure to light.

6. Rods and cones are two types of photoreceptors that are
   (a) responsible for the transduction of neural energy into a form that can be received in the sensory receptors.
   (b) more activated in bright sunlight (rods) or in dim light (cones).

(c) both highly sensitive to the color and the brightness of visible light.

(d) responsible for transducing electromagnetic energy into electrochemical energy.

7. The psychological experience of hue relates closely to

(a) a physical property of wavelengths of light.

(b) the actual brightness of what we observe.

(c) a physical property of intensity of light.

(d) the actual saturation of what we observe.

8. The feature-detection approach to perception is intended to explain

(a) why some people are unable to perceive forms that they can see.

(b) how our brains use various processes and kinds of cells in the perception of forms.

(c) why some features of objects (e.g., color or size) are more noticeable than are others.

(d) why our perception of an object remains the same even when our immediate sensation of the object changes.

9. Perceptual constancy refers to our

(a) perception of an object as remaining the same even when our immediate sensation of the object changes.

(b) tendency to perceive objects as being grouped together, based on their similarity.

(c) perception of an object as changing even when our immediate sensation of the object remains the same.

(d) tendency to perceive a constant closed-up shape of an object even when our perception of it is incomplete.

Answer each of the following questions by filling in the blank with an appropriate word or phrase.

10. _____ is the process whereby energy is converted from a form that enters the sensory receptors to a form that the brain can process.

11. According to the _____-_____ theory

of color vision, we have specialized photoreceptors for each of the two opposing pairs of colors—red–green and yellow–blue—as well as for the opposing pair of white–black.

12. The _____, a thin layer on the rear surface of the eye, contains the photoreceptors responsible for transducing electromagnetic energy into electrochemical energy.

13. The four primary psychological qualities of taste are _____, saltiness, _____, and bitterness.

Match the following depth cues to their descriptions:

14. linear perspective

15. interposition

16. relative size

17. aerial perspective

18. location in the picture plane

19. binocular convergence

20. binocular disparity

(a) objects farther away from the observer appear higher in the picture plane (as long as the objects are below the horizon)

(b) objects that are farther away are viewed through a greater density of dust and moisture particles

(c) objects that are closer present more noticeably different images to each of the two eyes

(d) as parallel lines move farther into the distance, they appear to come together at the horizon

(e) objects that are farther away appear to be smaller

(f) objects that are closer may block the view of objects that are farther away

(g) objects that are closer require the eye muscles to pull more strongly inward toward the nose

Answers

1. c, 2. d, 3. b, 4. a, 5. a, 6. d, 7. a, 8. b, 9. a, 10. Transduction, 11. opponent-process, 12. retina, 13. sweetness, sourness, 14. d, 15. f, 16. e, 17. b, 18. a, 19. g, 20. c

PATHWAYS TO UNDERSTANDING

1. Many people earn their living based on perfecting at least one of their senses. Describe at least two examples of professionals who depend on each of the senses discussed in this chapter.

2. Suppose that you conduct research for a manufacturer of food, perfume, or car-seat covers. How would you design an experiment to study human perception of taste, smell, or skin senses?

3. If you had to memorize a long list of terms and definitions, would you be better off trying to remember them by seeing them (e.g., reading printed flashcards) or by hearing them (e.g., by having someone drill you by saying the words aloud)? Do you seem to be able to remember material better if it is presented visually (e.g., in a book) or auditorily (e.g., in a lecture)? How do you tailor your studying to your sensory preferences?

CHAPTER OUTLINE

How Does Attention Work?

What Levels of Consciousness
Do We Experience?
    The Preconscious Level
    The Subconscious Level

What Happens During Altered
States of Consciousness?

What Happens When We Sleep
and Dream?
    Stages of Sleep
    Sleep Deprivation
    Circadian Rhythms
    Sleep Disorders
    How to Get a Good Night's Sleep
    Dreams

Is Hypnosis an Altered State?
    The Phenomenon of Hypnosis: Real
      or Fake?
    Theories of Hypnosis

What Happens When We
Meditate?

How Do Drugs Induce Alterations
in Consciousness?
    Pattern of Drug Use
    Narcotics
    Central Nervous System
      Depressants
    Is Someone You Know an Alcoholic?
    Central Nervous System Stimulants
    Hallucinogenics
    Treatment of Drug Abuse

Consciousness

It was a warm dreamy sleep all about flying, sailing high over the earth . . . . floating, cruising, in the relaxed position of a man flying on a couch reading a newspaper. Part of his flight was over the dark sea, but it didn't frighten him because he knew he could not fall. . . .

When he awoke the next morning . . . , he couldn't shake the dream, and didn't really want to . . . . he still felt the sense of lightness and power that flying had given him.

Toni Morrison

Nobel Prize winner Toni Morrison frequently explores consciousness from a literary perspective. In the preceding excerpt, the lead character illustrates how an altered state of consciousness, such as dreaming, can affect waking experiences. Psychologists, too, observe that our conscious awareness of the world and even of ourselves often changes from moment to moment. Both our sensations of the outer world around us and our inner thoughts and feelings about ourselves and the inner world within our minds influence our consciousness. **Consciousness** is the complex process of evaluating our environment and then filtering that information through our minds.

Consciousness seems to serve various essential and interrelated purposes. For one thing, consciousness aids in survival by allowing us to obtain, manipulate, and apply information for adapting to the environment. Through consciousness, we can make sense of the world and can act accordingly in order to avoid danger, to find mates, to plan for future successes, and to fulfill countless other purposes we determine for ourselves.

Consciousness provides both monitoring and controlling functions (Kihlstrom, 1984). We can *monitor* (keep track of) our sensations from the external environment, as well as our own internally generated thoughts, feelings, and desires. Through consciousness, we can *control* (direct and shape) our lives.

Consciousness actively processes and integrates ever-changing information from various sources: from our senses (e.g., visual or auditory stimuli in the environment), from memory (e.g., stored information gained from previous experiences), and from mental processing itself (e.g., beliefs, dreams, strategies, plans). Although the information is constantly changing, consciousness provides us with a sense of continuity—of a unique self that continues to exist throughout these processes.

Through consciousness, we can control the flow of perceived, remembered, and mentally produced information. It is impossible to process actively all of the information available to us, so consciousness restricts the flow of information being processed at one time. It screens out some information and selectively allows in the most noticeable and relevant information for processing. While you are dreaming about waterfalls, you are probably not dreaming about desert wastelands. Although you have a wealth of memories on which you can draw at will, you are not remembering simultaneously everything you know, all at once. Nor are you actively processing all of the sensory stimuli—or all of the thoughts, beliefs, hopes, or plans—that may be available for use by your conscious mind.

A phenomenon related to consciousness is **attention,** which serves as the link between the enormous amount of information that reaches our consciousness and the limited amount of information that we actually are aware of processing. If you are having a hard time figuring out the difference between attention and consciousness, you are not alone. At one time, psychologists also believed that consciousness was the same thing as attention. To get an idea of how they came to believe that the two phenomena are different, try the following activity.

To be conscious that we are perceiving or thinking is to be conscious of our own existence.

Aristotle

consciousness the complex phenomenon of actively processing perceptions, thoughts, feelings, wishes, and memories, to create a mental reality for adapting to the world

attention the process by which we focus our awareness on some of the information available in consciousness and screen out other information

Finding Your Way　5-1

Repeatedly write your name on a piece of paper while you picture everything you can remember about the room in which you slept when you were 10 years old. While continuing to write your name and picturing your old bedroom, now take a mental journey through your bodily sensations. Start by noticing the sensations in one of your big toes, and continue by proceeding up your leg, across your torso, to the opposite shoulder, and down your arm. What sensations do you feel—pressure from the ground, your shoes, your clothing; or even pain anywhere? Are you still managing to write your name while retrieving remembered images from memory and continuing to pay attention to your current sensations?

You may have found the preceding activity awkward but not impossible. Why is it difficult, yet possible? It is difficult because it places a heavy workload on your active mental processing (i.e., your consciousness). It is possible because you do not have to pay attention to all of the mental processes involved. When you started to write your name, you paid attention to doing so. However, at this time in your life, writing your own name requires no active awareness and very little attention. Hence, you may write it while focusing your attention on other activities. Similarly, once you got started picturing your old bedroom, you could continue to cruise mentally around the room while shifting some of your attention to the next task.

In this particular activity, each time you started a new task, you had to focus your attention on the new task. Once the task was started, however, the task did not require your full attention, so you had some attentional resources available for other mental processing. Note that when you were paying attention, you were not only processing information actively, but also were aware of doing so. What allowed you to continue the other tasks? Your consciousness, in which the active processing of sensory information, remembered information, and cognitive information may proceed with or without our awareness of doing so. You do not have to pay attention to information in order for conscious processes to act on the information.

It is while trying to get everything straight in my head that I get confused.

Mary Virginia Micka

HOW DOES ATTENTION WORK?

As you read these words, you are paying attention to the words on the text page, and you are probably disregarding all the other visual sensations reaching your eyes. If you paid attention to all the sensory information available to you at any one time, you would never be able to concentrate on the important and ignore the unimportant.

In **selective attention,** we attempt to track one message and to ignore another. Psychologist Colin Cherry (1953) was interested in how we follow one conversation even when we are distracted by other conversations. Cherry referred to this phenomenon as the *cocktail party problem*, based on his observation that cocktail parties provide an excellent setting for observing selective attention.

Cherry did not actually study conversations by hanging out at cocktail parties. Rather, he studied selected messages spoken in a more carefully controlled experimental setting. He used *shadowing*, in which each of your ears listens to a different message, and you are required to repeat back the message from only one of the ears as soon as possible after you hear it. In other words, you are to follow one message (think of a detective "shadowing" a suspect) but to ignore the other. This form of presentation is often referred to as dichotic presentation. In **dichotic presentation,** each ear receives a different message. When the two ears receive the same message (or messages), it is referred to as *binaural presentation* (see Figure 5-1).

Cherry's research prompted additional work in this area. For example, Anne Treisman (1960) noted that participants shadowing the message presented to one ear heard almost nothing of the message presented to the other ear. Participants were not, however, totally ignorant of what they heard in the other ear. For instance, they could hear whether the voice in the unattended ear was replaced by a tone, or they could hear whether a man's voice was replaced by a woman's.

When you have a particular goal you want to achieve (such as studying psychology), how do you monitor your attention? What do you do to keep your attention focused on your goal instead of being distracted?

selective attention the conscious attempt to perceive some stimuli (e.g., the voice and gestures of a speaker) and to ignore others (e.g., background noises and sights)

dichotic presentation perceptual experience in which each ear receives a different message (*dich-*, in two parts [Greek]; *-otic*, related to the ears [Greek])

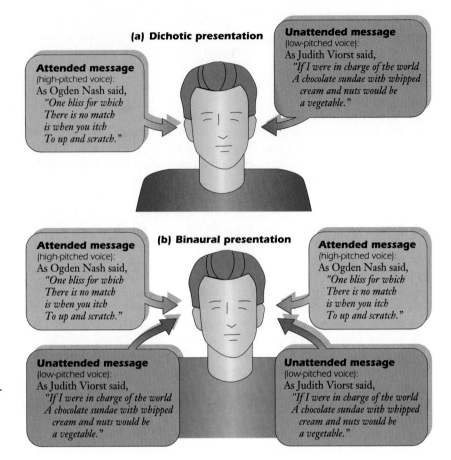

Figure 5-1
Selective Attention
Colin Cherry studied both (a) dichotic presentation, in which a different message is presented to each ear, and (b) binaural presentation, in which the same message is presented to both ears.

It seemed rather incongruous that in a society of supersophisticated communication, we often suffer from a shortage of listeners.

Erma Bombeck

What do you think explains why you attend to some things and not to others? Why do you think that you sometimes find it hard to choose how to focus your attention?

Stroop effect interference experienced in selectively attending to one sensory stimulus (e.g., the color of the ink) while trying to ignore another sensory stimulus (e.g., the word that is printed with the ink of a different color)

Moreover, if the unattended message was identical to the attended one, all participants noticed it, even if one of the messages was not matched perfectly in timing with the other.

Much of the research on selective attention has focused on auditory processing. However, researchers have also studied selective attention through visual processing. One of the most common tasks used for studying selective visual attention was first formulated by John Ridley Stroop (1935). Stroop's task highlights the difficulty of selectively attending to some visual stimuli and not to others. Compare the ease of performing the first of the following two tasks with the second of the tasks.

Finding Your Way   **5-2**

*First, quickly identify aloud the ink colors of the printed color names in Figure 5-2 (a), in which the color of the ink matches the name of the color word. Easy, isn't it? Now, look at Figure 5-2 (b), in which the colors of the inks differ from the color names that are printed with those inks. Quickly identify aloud the colors of the inks in that figure. You will probably find the second task very difficult: Each of the written words interferes with your naming the color of the ink. This interference is the **Stroop effect.***

(a) Name as quickly as possible the color of ink in which each word is printed. Name from left to right across each line.

Red	Yellow	Blue	Green
Blue	Red	Green	Yellow
Yellow	Green	Red	Blue

(b) Name as quickly as possible the color of ink in which each word is printed. Name from left to right across each line.

Red	Blue	Green	Yellow
Yellow	Red	Blue	Green
Blue	Yellow	Green	Red

Figure 5-2
The Stroop Effect
Quickly identify aloud the names of the colors of the inks *in each set of words,* disregarding the words *showing the various colors of ink.*

How does attention work? A key aspect of attention is selective attention, in which we choose to pay attention to some stimuli and not to others.

MINILECTURE
Attention (Ch 5)

WHAT LEVELS OF CONSCIOUSNESS DO WE EXPERIENCE?

Generally, when we are paying attention to stimuli, we see ourselves as being at a fully conscious level of awareness. In addition to full conscious awareness, there are lower levels of consciousness, two of which are described here: the preconscious and the subconscious.

The Preconscious Level

The **preconscious level** of consciousness includes information that can become conscious readily, but that is not continuously available at the conscious level. This information includes stored memories that we are not using at a given time, but that we can call to mind when needed. For example, if prompted, you can remember what your bedroom looks like. Obviously, however, you are not always thinking about your bedroom. Also stored at the preconscious level are automatic behaviors. **Automatic behaviors** require no conscious decisions regarding which muscles to move or which actions to take. For instance, automatic behaviors include signing your name, dialing a familiar telephone number, or driving a car to a familiar place by way of empty roads.

Perhaps our most common experience of preconsciousness is the **tip-of-the-tongue phenomenon.** This phenomenon occurs when we are trying to remember something we already know but cannot quite pull from memory. Psychologists have tried to come up with experiments that measure this phenomenon. For example, they have tried to find out how much people can draw from information that seems to be stuck at the preconscious level. In one study (Brown & McNeill, 1966), participants were read a large number of dictionary definitions of uncommon words. For each definition, the participants were then asked to supply the corresponding words having these meanings (similar to the game on the television

Most people live . . . in a very restricted circle of their potential being. They make use of a very small portion of their possible consciousness.

William James

What are a few automatic behaviors that you have learned? What are the advantages of having these behaviors be automatic? When might it be a disadvantage that these behaviors are automatic?

preconscious level a level of consciousness comprising information that is accessible to, but not continuously available in, awareness

automatic behavior conduct that requires no conscious decisions regarding which muscles to move or which actions to take

tip-of-the-tongue phenomenon an experience of preconsciousness, in which a person cannot successfully retrieve information known to be stored in memory

When do you experience the tip-of-the-tongue phenomenon? What seems to help you to grasp the word or idea you want to pull into conscious awareness? What seems to make it harder for you to do so?

Words . . . are clumsy tools with which we grope in the dark towards truths more inaccessible but no less significant.

Helen Merrell Lynd

A retentive memory may be a good thing, but the ability to forget is the true token of greatness.

Elbert Hubbard

subliminal perception a form of preconscious processing in which people may have the ability to detect information without being fully aware that they are doing so

show *Jeopardy*). For instance, they might have been given this clue: "an instrument used by navigators to measure the angle between a heavenly body and a horizon."

In the study, some participants could not come up with the word but thought they knew it. These participants were then asked to perform various tasks related to the word. For instance, they were asked to identify the first letter, indicate the number of syllables, or make a guess about the word's sounds. The participants often answered these questions correctly. In this example (of the navigation instrument), the participants might have been able to say that the appropriate word for the instrument begins with an *s*, has two syllables, and sounds like "sextet." Eventually, some participants realized that the proper word was *sextant*. These results indicate that particular preconscious information may be hard to recall but still available to consciousness.

Other researchers have shown evidence of preconscious processing (Greenwald, Klinger, & Schuh, 1995; Marcel, 1983). In one of a series of experiments (Marcel, 1983), participants were shown words very briefly (20–110 *milliseconds*—thousandths of a second). After each word was presented, it was replaced by a visual mask. A *visual mask* blocks an image from staying on the retina at the back of the eye. The rate at which the words were shown was so fast that observers could not guess whether they had even seen a word at better than chance levels—that is, they made correct guesses only as often as would be expected if they were basing their guesses on the toss of a coin.

Next, the participants were shown a series of letters, and they were asked to indicate whether the letters did or did not form a word. For example, participants might be expected to indicate that "MARD" is not a word, but that "HARD" is a word. It turned out that the participants could classify this second string of letters more quickly when it related to the first word than when it did not. For example, "BUTTER is typically classified as a word faster if it follows BREAD than if it follows NURSE" (Marcel, 1983, p. 219).

How could the presentation of associated words enhance people's speed of response when they were not even aware that they had seen these words? Clearly, some kind of preconscious recognition of the rapidly presented word must have taken place. In this kind of preconscious processing, people can detect information without being aware that they are doing so. This preconscious processing is termed **subliminal perception** (*sub-*, below; *liminal*, threshold; below the threshold of consciousness).

Subliminal perception came into public awareness in the 1950s. During this decade, some advertisers inserted subliminal messages into sequences of movie frames. The frames flashed by too quickly for the conscious mind to perceive them, but the frames still might have been noticed by the preconscious. Advertisers tried to use these messages to influence buying behavior by flashing subliminal commands to consumers. For example, "Buy Popcorn" could be shown along with a tempting photo of a bag of popcorn. The effectiveness of this technique has never been proved (Cherry, 1953; Vokey & Read, 1985). Even so, advertisers were forced to abandon such methods when people protested against being subjected to influences outside of their conscious control.

More recently, various companies have produced an assortment of self-help audiotapes conveying subliminal messages designed to improve almost any aspect of your life, from your love life to your work life. The idea is that when you play these tapes, while you consciously listen to soothing music or nature sounds, the subliminal messages will miraculously change how you think, feel, or act, thereby changing your life. You will become more assertive or more self-disciplined; you will improve your memory, or you will lose weight.

Anthony Greenwald, Anthony Pratkanis, and their colleagues (Greenwald et al., 1991; Pratkanis, Eskenazi, & Greenwald, 1994) have tested the effectiveness of these tapes. They recruited volunteers interested in memory enhancement or in improving their self-esteem. All of the participants were given tests of self-esteem and of memory.

The researchers then divided the participants into four groups: (1) participants who were told that they were being given a memory-enhancement tape and who were indeed given such a tape; (2) participants who were told that they were being given a memory-enhancement tape but who were given a self-esteem-enhancing tape instead; (3) participants who were told that they were being given a self-esteem-enhancing tape and who were indeed given such a tape; and (4) participants who were told that they were being given a self-esteem-enhancing tape but who were given a memory-enhancement tape instead. The experiment was administered using a **double-blind procedure,** so that both the participants and the experimenters who gave the instructions to the participants were kept in the dark as to which participants actually received which tapes. (Of course, the researchers used a coding technique so that they could later figure out which participant received which tape, and the researchers could analyze the results at the end of the study.) All participants were instructed to use the tapes at home for 5 weeks.

When the participants returned, they were again tested for memory and for self-esteem. How did participants feel about the effectiveness of the tapes? The participants reported experiencing the improvements they expected (memory or self-esteem enhancement), regardless of which tape they received (the memory tape or the self-esteem tape). However, their actual scores on the tests of memory and of self-esteem showed no such improvements. What can we conclude? The tapes do not work. The tapes will, however, produce a **placebo effect**—they will make people feel as though the treatment worked, as long as they strongly expect it to do so.

To summarize, automatic behaviors, tip-of-the-tongue phenomena, subliminal perception, and other preconscious knowledge are outside our conscious awareness. Nevertheless, the preconscious information is available for use by our conscious minds under many circumstances. At the same time, tapes based on subliminal perception appear to be ineffective in influencing people to change their behavior, their mental abilities, or their personal characteristics.

The Subconscious Level

Unlike knowledge stored at the preconscious level, information stored at the **subconscious** (unconscious) level is not easily pulled into the conscious mind. In this chapter, the terms *subconscious* and *unconscious* are used interchangeably. However, the term *unconscious* is usually preferred by followers of Sigmund Freud. Freud believed that many of our most important memories and impulses are unconscious, but that they nonetheless deeply and powerfully affect our behavior. For example, Freud believed that our early relationships with our parents affect our views of ourselves, and thus our lifelong behavior. Despite their importance, we cannot easily remember every aspect and interaction of those relationships.

According to Freud, the reason we remember so little about these crucial early experiences is because we often find some memories too difficult to handle at a conscious level. We therefore **repress** this information—that is, we never let it enter consciousness. In Freud's view, although these difficult experiences, feelings, and desires are not conscious, their effects can be seen through careful observation. For instance, according to Freud, our dreams and slips of the tongue actually indicate unconscious processing. As an example, suppose that you are introduced to someone against whom you are competing for something you want. You say, "I'm glad to beat you," when you intended to say, "I'm glad to meet you." Freud would interpret the slip as being psychologically significant. This sort of verbal error is still sometimes called a "Freudian slip."

Classical Freudian theory can be neither proved nor disproved: It focuses on concepts of the unconscious mind that are affected by variables that psychologists cannot control in experiments. Without control of the varibles, psychologists cannot test these concepts; thus, there is little experimental evidence for Freud's theories of the mind. Nonetheless, Freud's theories of the levels of consciousness were

double-blind procedure an experimental technique whereby neither the experimenters nor the participants know which participants will have received which kind of treatment, or even any treatment at all (e.g., in a control condition)

placebo effect a perceived improvement that occurs simply because people believe that they have received a given treatment, even when they did not actually receive the treatment

subconscious (noun) a level of consciousness that involves less awareness than full conscious awareness and from which information is not easily pulled into the conscious mind

repression a Freudian defense mechanism, by which a person keeps troublesome internally generated thoughts and feelings from entering consciousness and thereby causing internal conflicts or other psychological discomfort

ground-breaking when first proposed. Even now, his theories continue to influence many people. Another innovative idea of Freud's that continues to be influential is the probing of the unconscious through psychological treatments involving altered states of consciousness, such as hypnosis and dreams.

What levels of consciousness do we experience? At the preconscious level, we experience automatic behaviors, tip-of-the-tongue phenomena, and subliminal perception. The subconscious level contains knowledge we cannot easily pull into conscious awareness or even use for conscious purposes.

WHAT HAPPENS DURING ALTERED STATES OF CONSCIOUSNESS?

In an altered state of consciousness, awareness is somehow changed from our normal, waking state. In this chapter, we discuss several forms of altered consciousness: sleep and dreams, hypnosis, meditation, and drug-induced altered states of consciousness. There are some *quantitative* (involving increases or decreases in amounts) changes associated with states of consciousness, such as increases or decreases in alertness and awareness. However, the key features of the various states of consciousness are *qualitative* changes, which involve changes in the characteristics (qualities) that are present in a given state. That is, some qualities that are very important in one state of consciousness are either absent altogether or just not important in another state.

Altered states of consciousness have several common characteristics related to changes in thinking, in perception, and in behavioral self-control (Martindale, 1981). First, during altered states, you may not think as deeply or as carefully as usual. For example, during sleep, you accept unrealistic dream events as being real, although you would never accept those events as realistic while you are awake. Second, your perceptions of yourself and of the world may change from what they are during wakefulness. Under the influence of particular kinds of drugs, for example, you may perceive illusions or hallucinations. **Illusions** are distorted perceptions of objects (e.g., surfaces of objects may appear to quiver or to take on bizarre forms). **Hallucinations** are perceptions of objects that do not exist (e.g., the floor may appear to be covered with nonexistent spider webs). Third, your normal inhibitions and level of control over your own behavior may weaken. People under the influence of alcohol, for example, may do things they normally would not do when sober.

The most common altered state of consciousness is sleep, to which we now turn.

What happens during altered states of consciousness? We experience qualitative (and to a lesser degree, quantitative) changes in how we think, in what we perceive, and in how we control our own behavior.

It's far harder to kill a phantom than a reality.

Virginia Woolf

Some of my best friends are illusions. Been sustaining me for years.

Sheila Ballantyne

Should people be held legally accountable for the behavior they show when under the influence of drugs that they took voluntarily (such as alcohol)?

---

illusion distorted perception of physical stimuli, sometimes due to altered states of consciousness, to psychological disorder, or to misleading cues in the objects themselves

hallucination perception of sensory stimulation (usually sounds, but sometimes sights, smells, or tactile sensations) in the absence of any actual corresponding sensory input from the physical world

WHAT HAPPENS WHEN WE SLEEP AND DREAM?

Scientists do not know why we sleep. One way to study sleep is to study carefully the physiology of animals before, during, and after sleeping, as well as when the animals are unable to sleep for various reasons. These studies have led some psychologists to conclude that there are chemical causes of sleep. Not all psychologists agree with this conclusion, however. To find out more about human sleep, most sleep researchers study people.

Stages of Sleep

How do psychologists study sleep in people? For one thing, psychologists often test people's thought processes and their moods during various degrees of sleepiness and wakefulness. Psychologists also observe people's natural sleeping and waking behavior. Another common method of studying sleep is to examine people's brain-wave patterns, as recorded on electroencephalograms. **Electroencephalograms (EEGs)** are recordings that show the electrical activity of the brain as

electroencephalogram (EEG) a recording (*-gram*) of the electrical activity of the living brain, as detected by various electrodes (*en-*, in, *cephalo-*, head [Greek])

Sleep researchers monitor the patterns of brain-wave activity throughout the sleep cycle of their participants.

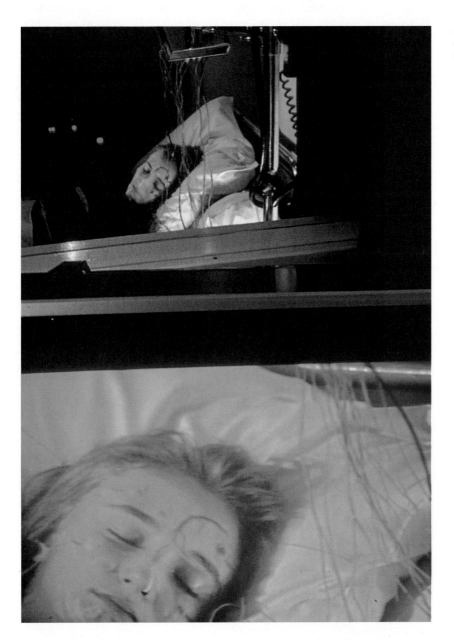

Awake

Alpha activity

Stage 1 sleep

Stage 2 sleep

Seconds
0 1 2 3 4 5

Stage 3 sleep

Stage 4 sleep

REM sleep

Figure 5-3
EEG Patterns Showing the
Stages of Sleep
These EEG patterns show changes in brain
waves. The brain-wave changes reflect
changes in consciousness during REM sleep
and during the four stages of N-REM sleep. (a)
Alpha waves typify relaxed wakefulness. (b)
More rapid, irregular brain waves typify Stage 1
of N-REM sleep. (c) During Stage 2, large, slow
waves are interrupted by bursts of rapid brain
waves. (d) During Stages 3 and 4, extremely
large, slow brain waves are the most common.
(e) During REM sleep, the brain waves look
very much like those of the waking brain.

MINILECTURE
Stages of Sleep (Ch 6)

No day is so bad it can't be fixed with a nap.

Carrie Snow

N-REM sleep the four stages of sleep that
are not characterized by rapid eye movements and that are less frequently associated
with dreaming

REM sleep the distinctive kind of sleep
that is characterized by rapid eye movements (REMs) and that is frequently associated with dreaming

patterns of waves (see Figure 5-3). The EEGs of sleeping people have shown that
sleep occurs in stages common to almost everyone (see Figure 5-3). The first four
stages of sleep make up **N-REM sleep** (non-rapid eye movement sleep). During
these four stages, as the name "N-REM" implies, people's eyes do not move much.

During a fifth stage of sleep, however, our eyes roll around in their sockets
(Kleitman, 1963). When sleep researchers rouse sleepers during this eye-rolling
stage of sleep, the sleepers usually report being wakened in the middle of a dream
(Dement & Kleitman, 1957). The distinctive kind of sleep that occurs during this
stage has become known as **REM sleep,** for "rapid eye movement" sleep. REM
sleep is the stage of sleep most often associated with dreaming. (Dreaming is discussed later in this chapter.)

EEG patterns become extremely active during REM sleep. The EEG of
REM sleep somewhat resembles the EEG of the awake brain (see Figure 5-3), although REM sleep is so deep that it is usually difficult to waken a person from it.
Because this sleep stage is both the deepest in terms of how difficult it is to waken
people and the most like wakefulness in terms of people's EEG patterns, REM
sleep is sometimes called "paradoxical sleep." Here, as always, the paradox seems
self-contradictory, but is nevertheless true.

The paradox of REM sleep points out an important aspect of psychophysiological measurements. In this case, a measurement (EEG) recorded very similar
physiological data from two different states of consciousness (REM sleep and waking). What would have happened if psychologists had relied only on EEGs for assessing the two states? They might have concluded that REM sleep is very similar
to the waking state. Fortunately, psychologists and other scientists also searched for
supporting evidence based on observations of behavior. In this way, they discovered the paradoxical nature of REM sleep. Neither psychophysiological nor behavioral measurement tells the full story. However, each method of measurement
provides a kind of information that adds to the other kind of information.

Using both EEG studies and behavioral measurements, psychologists have
found out more about sleep stages: The stages of N-REM and REM sleep alter-
nate throughout the night, roughly in 90-minute cycles. As the night progresses,
the length and sequence of the sleep stages may vary.

Sleep Deprivation

In addition to studying how people sleep, scientists study what happens when people are deprived of sleep. In *sleep deprivation,* participants are not allowed to sleep
for fixed amounts of time. The scientists then measure the resulting changes in
mood, motor activity, thought patterns, task performance, and brain-wave patterns
(e.g., Borbely, 1986; Dement, 1976). Participants usually have few problems after
the first sleepless night, and they appear to be relaxed and cheerful. They have
more difficulty staying awake during the second night. Usually, they are severely
tired by 3 A.M. of the second day. If they are given long test problems to solve,
they may fall asleep but will deny having done so.

By the third day, the participants appear tense. Increasingly, they are irritable
when disturbed. They may follow the instructions of the experimenter, but they do
very little that they are not specifically told to do. Their moods can swing wildly.
By the third night, they cannot stay awake unless special steps are taken to keep
them awake.

Starting with this third night, periods of *microsleep* are observed: Participants
stop what they are doing for periods of several seconds and stare into space. During these periods, their EEGs show brain-wave patterns similar to the patterns typical of sleep. Participants may start to experience illusions and hallucinations. For
instance, they may perceive auditory hallucinations, such as hearing voices in the
sound of running water.

Things really start to fall apart after 4 days. Beyond 4 days, participants typically become *paranoid,* sometimes believing that the experimenters or other people

are planning to harm them in some way. It is possible to keep sleep-deprived participants awake for longer than 4 days. Clearly, however, prolonged sleep deprivation is serious. Nonetheless, no one is known to have died or even to have become seriously ill for a long time just because of lack of sleep.

Circadian Rhythms

People go through periods of sleeping and waking even before birth. Usually, newborn humans switch back and forth often between sleep and wakefulness, for a total of about 17 hours of sleep per day. Within the first 6 months, however, their sleep patterns change. Most infants have about two short naps and one long stretch of sleep at night, for a total of about 13 hours per day. By about 5 to 7 years of age, most people follow about the same pattern of sleep as adults (Berger, 1980). Adults sleep about 8 hours each night and remain awake about 16 hours each day.

Regardless of the average, the actual range of sleep needed varies widely across individuals. Some people need as little as an hour of sleep each day, and others need 10 to 12 hours of sleep per day. *Long sleepers* regularly sleep more than 9.5 hours per day. *Short sleepers* regularly sleep less than 4.4 hours per day. Studies of long sleepers and short sleepers show no differences in their average relative health (Kolb & Whishaw, 1990).

Despite individual differences, the typical pattern roughly corresponds to our planet's cycle of darkness and light. Humans go through physiological changes that can be measured according to this daily rhythm. For example, our body temperature generally lowers at night. The term for these cyclical daily changes is **circadian rhythm** (*circa*, about, around; *dies*, day [Latin]).

Several investigators have studied circadian rhythms (see Hobson, 1989; Wever, 1979). Participants in one study were placed in a specially built underground living environment. In this environment, the participants were deprived of all the cues people normally use for telling the time of day—the rising and setting of the sun, clocks, scheduled activities, and so on (Wever, 1979). For 1 month, participants were told that they could create their own schedules. They could sleep whenever they wished to, but they were asked not to nap.

The results were striking and have since been shown many times. As participants became used to having no time cues, their internally determined days became longer, averaging about 25 hours. Participants showed stable individual

What good does sleep do for you? What changes do you notice in yourself when you do not get enough sleep?

What are some practical benefits that may result from the study of sleep deprivation?

circadian rhythm the usual sleeping–waking pattern of physiological changes corresponding roughly to the cycle of darkness and light associated with a single day (*circa*, around [Latin]; *dies*, day [Latin])

French geologist Michel Siffre (left) was shielded from all time cues for 6 months in this underground cavern (right). When people have no external time cues, their natural circadian rhythms gradually shift from a 24-hour day to a 25-hour day. When they return to a normal environment, their circadian rhythms return to a 24-hour day, cued by clocks and by the daily cycle of our planet.

circadian rhythms, although the rhythms differed somewhat from person to person. When returned to the normal, time-cued environment, the participants reestablished a 24-hour cycle.

Anything that changes our circadian rhythm can interfere with sleep. Many of us have experienced jet lag. *Jet lag* is a disturbance in circadian rhythm caused by changing the light–dark cycle when we travel through time zones. Even if you have never flown out of your own time zone, however, you may have experienced a mild case of jet lag: Recall what happens when you change to and from daylight savings time. Think about how you feel that first Monday morning after setting your clocks forward an hour. You may have trouble adjusting to waking up and going to sleep an hour earlier than usual.

Sleep Disorders

Sleep disorders can be very troublesome: Lack of sleep (caused by insomnia) can wreak havoc on a person's life. Likewise, sudden uncontrollable sleep (caused by narcolepsy), sleepwalking (somnambulism), and breathing difficulties during sleep (caused by sleep apnea) can cause serious problems.

Insomnia is a sleep disorder that may involve difficulty in falling asleep, waking up during the night and being unable to go back to sleep, or waking up too early in the morning (without feeling well rested). Insomnia is often upsetting to the millions of people who are affected by it. Almost everybody has trouble falling asleep occasionally, but about 6% of adults surveyed have tried to get medical help because of sleeplessness (Borbely, 1986). Insomnia is more common among women than among men and is also more common among persons who are past middle age than among younger people (Borbely, 1986).

BRANCHING OUT: How to Get a Good Night's Sleep

Physicians often recommend the following steps to sleep well and to avoid **medication** (Borbely, 1986):

Establish a regular bedtime, and try to keep to it. If you occasionally go to bed late, still try to get up at the same time the following morning.

■ Avoid taking occasional naps. Either take naps regularly, or do not nap at all.

■ Establish a regular bedtime routine. Include in your routine some restful, relaxing activities (e.g., reading, taking a warm bath, or listening to soothing music).

■ Avoid engaging in strenuous mental or physical activities in the evening. Although a regular program of exercise will help you to sleep well in general, if you are highly active just before you go to bed, you may have trouble getting to sleep.

■ Avoid eating too much before going to bed. If you eat at all, eat only a light snack. Also, there is some support for the old wives' tale that a glass of warm milk may help you to get to sleep.

■ Avoid alcohol, caffeine, and nicotine (e.g., in cigarettes). Alcohol probably will not prevent you from getting to sleep, but it may keep you from staying asleep throughout the night. Caffeine and nicotine may make it difficult for you to get to sleep in the first place.

■ Avoid taking sleeping pills. They provide some short-term help for some people, but over the long term, they can actually cause insomnia. Also, the effects of sleeping pills often carry over through at least part of the day after their use.

■ Try to sleep in a quiet, dark room with adequate circulation and a comfortable temperature.

A good cure for insomnia is to get plenty of sleep.
W. C. Fields

insomnia any of various disturbances of sleep, such as difficulty in falling asleep or in staying asleep

■ If you wake up during the night, and you do not go back to sleep quickly and easily, try getting out of bed and doing something restful. Do not stay in bed, tossing and turning, worrying about not sleeping. (The frustration will increase your anxiety level, which can in turn make your insomnia worse.)

What appears to be the opposite problem to insomnia is **narcolepsy,** which is a disorder causing an uncontrollable urge to fall asleep periodically during the day. Narcolepsy affects about 1 or 2 people in 1,000 (Borbely, 1986). The loss of consciousness can occur at any time. It may even occur when the person is driving or otherwise is doing something in which sudden sleep can be dangerous. Fortunately, medication can usually control the symptoms of this disease.

Another sleep disorder is **sleep apnea,** a breathing disturbance in which the *apneic* (person who has apnea) repeatedly stops breathing during sleep. These attacks can occur hundreds of times per night. The episodes usually last only a few seconds, but they may last as long as 2 minutes in severe cases.

Somnambulism (sleepwalking) combines aspects of waking and sleeping. Sleepwalkers can see, walk, and perhaps even talk, but they usually cannot remember the sleepwalking episodes after they waken. For many years, scientists believed that sleepwalkers were merely acting out their dreams. In fact, however, sleepwalking usually begins during N-REM sleep, when dreaming is rare. If the sleepwalking episode is short, sleepwalkers may stay in deep sleep. If the episode is long, the EEG patterns begin to look like those of light sleep or even those of the waking state.

Scientists have not found a cause or a cure for sleepwalking. Sleepwalking puzzles us because it occurs completely outside our conscious control. Similarly, dreams come in the night, when we are asleep and have no conscious control over our thoughts.

Dreams

All of us have dreams every night, whether or not we remember them (Ornstein, 1986). Dreams fill our heads with fantastic ideas—sometimes pleasant, sometimes frightening, and frequently creative. Many of the fantastic events of our dreams are implausible to our waking minds, but they may seem reasonable to us as we sleep.

Why do we dream? Consider several theories. Perhaps the best known theory of dreaming was proposed by Sigmund Freud (1900/1954). According to Freud, dreams are the "royal road to the unconscious": They are one of the few ways in which we allow the hidden contents of the unconscious (e.g., sexual desires) to be expressed. These contents are expressed in a disguised form, however. Apparently, our unconscious wishes would be so threatening if expressed directly and clearly that we might awaken every time we dreamed. Freud applied his psychodynamic theory to the interpretation of the disguised meanings expressed in dreams. Freudians spend a lot of time trying to detect the hidden meanings in the contents of dreams.

Other theorists, however, have suggested that many of the events and symbols of dreams are not mysteriously disguised longings. In fact, sometimes the meaning underlying dream content is easily interpreted (Dement, 1976). For example, William Dement (1976) studied the dreams of participants who were prevented from drinking liquids before they fell asleep. Unsurprisingly, many of their dreams involved wanting to drink liquids (Dement, 1976, p. 69): "Just as the bell went off, somebody raised a glass and said something about a toast. I don't think I had a glass."

An alternative view of dreams is the **activation–synthesis hypothesis** (McCarley & Hobson, 1981). According to this hypothesis, dreaming represents our attempts to interpret the neural activity of our brains during sleep. Just as our brains organize sensory information during wakefulness, our brains also organize sensory information during sleep. For example, while we dream, our ability to

"Wait! Don't! It can be dangerous to wake them!"

© 1994 Joe Dator/The Cartoon Bank, Inc.

This cartoon makes light of the potentially disastrous consequences of sleepwalking. Realistically, however, sleepwalkers are sometimes endangered by their somnambulism.

I've dreamt in my life dreams that have stayed with me ever after, and changed my ideas: they've gone through and through me, like wine through water, and altered the color of my mind.

Emily Brontë

Many creative persons have experienced breakthrough insights or other creative ideas while dreaming or in a dreamlike state of mind. What is it about dreaming that may facilitate such breakthroughs?

narcolepsy a disturbance of the pattern of wakefulness and sleep, in which the narcoleptic periodically experiences an uncontrollable urge to fall asleep and then briefly loses consciousness

sleep apnea a breathing disturbance that occurs during sleep, in which the sleeper repeatedly stops breathing during sleep; a sleep disorder

somnambulism disorder characterized by sleepwalking

activation–synthesis hypothesis a belief that dreams result from subjective organization and interpretation (synthesis) of neural activity (activation) that takes place during sleep

MINILECTURE
Why We Dream (Ch 6)

Behold! at once the little people [who create dreams] begin to bestir themselves in the same quest, and labour all night long, . . . and at last a jubilant leap to wakefulness, with the cry, "I have it, that'll do!" upon [the dreamer's] lips.

Robert Louis Stevenson

command the movements of our skeletal muscles is blocked. According to the activation–synthesis hypothesis, our brains may interpret this inability to move as a dream of being unable to escape from some danger.

Yet another theory of dreaming is nearly the opposite of Freud's. According to this theory (Crick & Mitchison, 1983), dreaming is the mind's attempt to get rid of mental garbage. Thus, whereas Freud suggested that we should examine our dreams closely, Francis Crick and G. Mitchison suggested that we should ignore the mental garbage being tossed out by our brains.

Scientists may never be able to come up with a theory of dream interpretation that applies to all people in all situations. Dreams are highly personal, so many people can and do freely interpret their own dreams as they choose to do so. Within the context of their current lives and past memories, they draw whatever conclusions seem appropriate to them.

Finding Your Way   5-3

This is probably the first time you have seen this instruction in a textbook: Stop reading your textbook, and take a few minutes to daydream. When you return to studying, think about both the content and the process of your daydreaming. How does daydreaming seem to differ from what you know about the content and the process of dreams that come to you during your sleep?

What happens when we sleep and dream? The normal circadian rhythms of adults include about 8 (give or take 4) hours of sleep, but sleep disorders can disturb this normal pattern. Sleep occurs in a series of four N-REM stages, as well as in a REM stage during which we dream. Various theories of dreaming have been suggested, but none has yet been confirmed by research.

IS HYPNOSIS AN ALTERED STATE?

The Phenomenon of Hypnosis: Real or Fake?

An altered state of consciousness that somewhat resembles sleep is **hypnosis.** A person undergoing hypnosis is usually deeply relaxed and extremely sensitive to suggestion. For example, hypnotized people may imagine that they see or hear things when they are prompted to do so (Bowers, 1976). Hypnotized people may also receive a posthypnotic suggestion. In a **posthypnotic suggestion,** participants are given instructions during hypnosis to carry out after they wake from the hypnotic state. Participants often do not remember receiving the instructions, and many do not even recall having been hypnotized (Ruch, 1975).

Hypnotized research participants also may not sense things that they otherwise would sense. For example, a hypnotized person may not feel pain when dipping an arm into icy cold water. Hypnosis has been particularly effective in

hypnosis an altered state of consciousness that usually involves deep relaxation and extreme sensitivity to suggestion and appears to bear some resemblance to sleep

posthypnotic suggestion an instruction received during hypnosis, which the individual is to implement after having wakened, often despite having no recollection of having received the instruction

Franz Anton Mesmer (1734–1815) was one of the first to discover hypnosis. Here, he is shown supposedly helping his patients to recover from any number of mysterious illnesses, through his healing powers of hypnosis. Mesmer was apparently sincere in believing that he could cure the illnesses of his patients. However, most physicians and scientists doubted his abilities. Eventually, he was prevented from practicing his mesmerizing treatments.

relieving pain for which physical causes have not yet been found (e.g., Siegel, 1979).

Hypnotized persons may also be induced to remember things that they have forgotten. On the other hand, hypnotized people may be induced just as easily to create apparent *pseudomemories*—false recollections of details they never observed (Spanos, 1992; Whitehouse et al., 1988). Some scientists have even argued that the very phenomenon of hypnosis is phony (Meeker & Barber, 1971; also described in Barber, 1964a, 1964b). According to this view, hypnotized research participants actually only pretend to be hypnotized. Some people may participate in the hoax even without realizing that they are doing so. These people may believe so strongly in the powers of the hypnotist that they believe that they are hypnotized, even when they are not.

How can psychologists tell whether hypnotism is genuinely affecting people who appear to be hypnotized? One way is to use the simulating paradigm (Orne, 1959). In the **simulating paradigm,** one group of participants is hypnotized, and another group (a control group) is not. The participants in the unhypnotized group are then asked to *simulate* being hypnotized—that is, to behave as though they were hypnotized. Experimenters must then try to distinguish the behavior of the hypnotized group from the behavior of the control group. As it turns out, simulators can imitate some, but not all, of the behavior of hypnotized participants (Gray, Bowers, & Fenz, 1970).

How would you design an experiment to differentiate simulators from truly hypnotized participants?

simulating paradigm a research technique for determining the true effects of a psychological treatment (e.g., hypnosis); one group of participants is subjected to the treatment and another group (a control group) does not receive the treatment but is asked to simulate the behavior of persons who do; observers try to distinguish the behavior of the treatment group from that of the control group trying to simulate the treatment group's behavior

Theories of Hypnosis

Suppose that we accept hypnosis as potentially a genuine psychological phenomenon. We still need to determine exactly what goes on during hypnosis. One theory holds that hypnosis is a form of deep relaxation (Edmonston, 1981). Although EEG patterns obtained during hypnosis are different from those for sleep, there may be a close connection between hypnosis and deep relaxation, which sometimes precedes or resembles sleep.

Psychoanalysts have suggested that during hypnosis, we partially return to a way of thinking that is like that of infants or young children. According to this view, hypnotized persons act in ways that adults would normally avoid because their mature thought processes would rule out those actions (Gill, 1972). Empirical studies have shown, however, that hypnotized participants who show what appear to be childlike ways of speaking or acting still retain adult modes of thinking and speaking, as well as adult capabilities (Nash, 1987).

A widely accepted view of hypnosis is neodissociative theory. According to the **neodissociative theory,** some people can *dissociate* (separate) one part of their minds from another. In effect, when hypnotizable participants are hypnotized, their consciousness splits. One part of the conscious mind responds to the hypnotist's commands, while another part becomes a hidden observer. This hidden observer monitors everything that is going on. In the responding part of the hypnotized participant's mind, some of the events taking place may not be observed consciously (Hilgard, 1977).

For example, studies of pain relief through hypnosis have found an interesting paradox: Some participants respond to a hypnotist's suggestion and agree that they feel no pain (as reported by the responding part of the mind). At the same time, if they are asked to describe how the pain feels, they can do so (as reported by the observing part of the mind). In other experiments, participants can be made to do one task consciously and another without realizing they are doing it. For example, while they are consciously engaged in a task, they can write down messages that they do not consciously realize they are writing (see Kihlstrom, 1985; Knox, Crutchfield, & Hilgard, 1975; Zamansky & Bartis, 1985). Thus, it seems that part of the participant's consciousness is un-self-consciously involved in the hypnosis. Meanwhile, another part of the person's consciousness observes and thereby knows, at some level, what is going on.

To conclude this discussion, the results are inconclusive. Psychologists do not agree about what hypnosis is, or even whether it is a genuine phenomenon. There is persuasive evidence that hypnosis is more than fakery. Some people easily become deeply hypnotized, others are less likely to be hypnotized, and still others appear incapable of being hypnotized (Hilgard, 1965).

Today, hypnosis is used in clinical settings (e.g., hospitals and physicians' offices) to control smoking and to treat various health-related problems, such as asthma, high blood pressure, and migraine headaches. Unsurprisingly, hypnosis is more successful as a clinical treatment with highly hypnotizable participants. The effects of hypnosis appear to be temporary, however. For this reason, hypnotism generally is used along with other kinds of therapy.

Is hypnosis an altered state? It appears that for some people, hypnosis is an altered state of consciousness, characterized by distinctive EEG patterns associated with deep relaxation but distinct from sleep. Various theories have been proposed to explain hypnosis, but these theories remain controversial. At present, the most widely accepted theory is neodissociative theory.

neodissociative theory a view of hypnosis asserting that some individuals can separate one part of their conscious minds (which responds to the hypnotist's instructions) from another part (which observes and monitors the events and actions taking place)

WHAT HAPPENS WHEN WE MEDITATE?

Meditation, another means of achieving an altered state of consciousness, may also offer possible therapeutic benefits. During **meditation,** people shift away from focusing their thoughts on actions and events in the external world. Instead, they shift toward allowing their thoughts and sensations to float and drift through their minds, including sensations and impressions from the internal world of their bodies and minds. Meditation can be soothing and calming, allowing a person to stop thinking about past actions and future plans, as well as present events taking place in the world outside the person's body.

What happens during meditation? In general, breathing rate, heart rate, blood pressure, and muscle tension decrease (Shapiro & Giber, 1978; Wallace & Benson, 1972). Meditation also seems to help patients with bronchial asthma (Honsberger & Wilson, 1973), with high blood pressure (Benson, 1977), with insomnia (Woolfolk et al., 1976), and with some symptoms of psychiatric problems (Glueck & Stroebel, 1975). EEG studies suggest that meditation tends to produce a concentration of brain waves associated with relaxation and the beginning stages of sleep (Ornstein, 1977). Many drug-induced alterations in consciousness also are related to sleep and relaxation.

Acquire inner peace and a multitude will find their salvation near you.

Catherine de Hueck Doherty

Why might certain productive ideas come to a person who is meditating that do not occur to the person when he or she is not in a meditative state?

What happens when we meditate? During meditation, we relax deeply, decreasing our tension, our blood pressure, our pulse, and our breathing rate.

In your opinion, why are so many people drawn to using consciousness-altering drugs, such as alcohol and tobacco?

HOW DO DRUGS INDUCE ALTERATIONS IN CONSCIOUSNESS?

Various drugs introduced into the body may destroy bacteria, ease pain, or alter consciousness. In this chapter, we are concerned only with psychoactive drugs. **Psychoactive drugs** achieve a **psychopharmacological** effect whereby they affect behavior, mood, and consciousness. Psychoactive drugs can be classified into four basic categories (Seymour & Smith, 1987): narcotics, central nervous system depressants, central nervous system stimulants, and hallucinogenics. Table 5-1, at the close of this chapter, summarizes the drugs in each category.

In addition to these four categories of psychoactive drugs, two other kinds of drugs produce psychoactive effects: antipsychotic drugs (discussed in Chapter 14) and mild **analgesics** (painkillers). Mild analgesics include acetaminophen (the active ingredient in Tylenol®), ibuprofen (the active ingredient in Advil®), and salicylic acid (the active ingredient in aspirin). (Pain relief is discussed more fully in Chapter 15.) Before we discuss each of the four main categories of psychoactive drugs, we consider the general pattern of the body's reactions to a psychoactive drug.

Pattern of Drug Use

The use of psychoactive drugs typically follows a particular pattern: When the person starts using the drug, the person has an initial psychoactive reaction to the drug. The particular psychoactive reaction depends on the particular drug being used. For some drugs, the person may appear to be **intoxicated.** *Toxic* means poisonous, and psychoactive drugs act as poisons when taken into the body at high

meditation a set of techniques, used for altering consciousness, to become more contemplative

psychoactive drug drug (e.g., depressants, stimulants, narcotics, or hallucinogenics) that produces a psychopharmacological effect, thereby affecting behavior, mood, and consciousness

psychopharmacological a drug-induced influence on behavior, mood, and consciousness

analgesics pain-relieving drugs (e.g., acetaminophen, ibuprofen, and salicylic acid [aspirin])

intoxicated characterized by grogginess, insensibility, or temporary trouble thinking clearly and making reasoned judgments due to the effects of toxins such as alcohol or sedative–hypnotic drugs

What is likely to be the effect of trying to drive or to do mentally challenging work (such as studying) while under the influence of narcotics?

tolerance a consequence of prolonged use of psychoactive drugs, in which the drug user feels decreasing psychopharmacological effects of a given drug at one level of dosage and must take increasing amounts of drugs in order to achieve the same effects, eventually reaching such a high level that further increases will cause overdose

overdose ingestion of a life-threatening or lethal dose of drugs, often associated with the use of psychoactive drugs

addiction a persistent, habitual, or compulsive physiological or at least psychological dependency on one or more psychoactive drugs

withdrawal the temporary discomfort (which may be extremely unpleasant and sometimes even life-threatening) associated with a reduction or discontinuation of the use of a psychoactive drug, during which the drug user's physiology and mental processes must adjust to an absence of the drug

acute toxicity the negative health consequences of a single instance of ingesting a poisonous substance, such as a single overdose of a psychoactive drug

chronic toxicity the negative health consequences of repeated ingestion of one or more poisonous substances, such as narcotics

levels. At low levels, intoxication produces trouble in thinking clearly and in making reasoned judgments.

If a person repeatedly and regularly uses a given drug, the person develops a tolerance for the drug. When **tolerance** occurs, increasingly high doses of the drug are required to produce the same psychoactive effect. Eventually, the person's tolerance reaches a very high level. At this level, the dose that would be required to produce a psychoactive effect would also produce an overdose. An **overdose** occurs when a person takes a life-threatening or lethal dose of a drug.

Once tolerance reaches this high level, the person clearly is **addicted** to the drug. How many uses of a drug are required for developing an addiction? That number depends on the characteristics of the particular drug and of the drug user. Some drugs are rapidly addictive, and others are less so. The rate of forming an addiction also varies from person to person. In any case, as the level of tolerance increases, the level of psychoactive effect from using the drug decreases.

When an addict stops using a drug, the addict experiences symptoms of **withdrawal.** During withdrawal, the body must adjust to being without the addictive drug. The particular symptoms of withdrawal vary for different persons and different drugs.

Treatment of drug dependence is based on whether the patient suffers from medical problems that are acute or chronic. **Acute toxicity** is the injury to health resulting from a particular overdose. **Chronic toxicity** is the damage caused by long-term drug addiction.

Most forms of treatment address the problems of acute toxicity first. Once the acute toxicity is managed, the treatment of chronic toxicity begins. This treatment generally involves some form of withdrawal from the drug, which is supervised by a doctor or other therapist. For many psychoactive drugs, medical supervision is needed because of the potentially deadly consequences of drug withdrawal. In general, substance abusers need to do the following:

- Become drug free.
- Develop a lifestyle that will enable them to stay drug free.
- Understand what got them addicted in the first place.
- Take proactive steps to stay off drugs and to avoid situations that may lead to drug use.

What happens in the brain to cause the actions of psychoactive drugs? How do neuroscientists explain the initial effects, the prolonged effects, and the withdrawal symptoms of psychoactive drugs? Many psychoactive drugs behave like the body's natural *neurochemicals* (neurotransmitters and related substances that are naturally produced in the brain) (see Chapter 2; see also Figure 5-4). Some neurochemicals are relaxing, others are stimulating, and some neurochemicals (known as "endorphins") are even associated with pain relief and potentially with feelings of *euphoria* (intense happiness and sense of well-being).

Initially, the use of psychoactive drugs tricks the body into behaving in ways that exaggerate normal, natural processes of the brain. As Figure 5-4 shows, these drugs manage to trick the brain because their molecular shape is very similar to the molecular shape of naturally occurring neurochemicals. For example, drugs that have a molecular shape similar to that of endorphins may provide pain relief and feelings of euphoria. If psychoactive drugs have a molecular shape similar to that of a neurochemical with a calming effect, those drugs may produce a calming effect. Drugs with a molecular shape similar to that of a stimulating neurochemical may produce stimulating effects. Psychoactive drugs produce intense levels of psychoactive symptoms that the brain may produce naturally, and usually less intensely, from time to time.

Unfortunately, the brain seems to react to prolonged use of these drugs by slowing down the body's natural production of these neurochemicals. Hence, over time, the brain becomes less able to produce its own calming, stimulating, pain-

If users of illicit drugs share needles for inject-ing drugs into the bloodstream, they risk devel-oping AIDS (acquired immune deficiency syndrome), hepatitis, and various other infec-tions. Infections acquired through the blood-stream have much more serious consequences because they bypass many of our body's pro-tective responses.

relieving, or euphoria-inducing effects. This slowing down of production leads to tolerance. Gradually, the body stops producing much of the natural substances at all. It also stops reacting as strongly to the psychoactive drugs. At this point, the person is addicted to the drug. If the person withdraws from the drug, the brain gradually begins again to produce more of the natural substances. Usually, the brain eventually returns to its normal neurochemical balance: It produces and re-acts normally to the endorphins, neurotransmitters, and related substances in the brain.

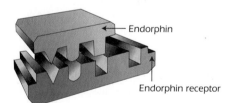

Figure 5-4
Chemical Twins
The molecules of some psychoactive drugs (e.g., heroin) and some natural brain sub-stances (e.g., endorphins) have very similar shapes. Because the molecules have similar structural shapes, these drugs easily fit into the places ("receptor sites") in the brain where the natural substances usually belong.

Narcotics

The term **narcotic** (Greek for "numbness") originally was used to describe only opium and drugs derived from opium, such as codeine, morphine, and heroin. More recently, chemists have been able to produce narcotics either naturally from opium or synthetically from combinations of chemicals. Narcotics made from the opium poppy bulb are termed *opiates.* Narcotics produced synthetically are termed *opioids.* Both opiates and opioids may be injected intravenously (using needles to get the drug into the bloodstream), smoked, inhaled nasally ("snorted"), or in-gested orally (eaten as pills or syrups). Narcotic drugs generally produce some degree of numbness or stupor and lead to addiction. The psychopharmaco-logical effects are like the effects produced by endorphins, such as euphoria or analgesia.

Because narcotics are highly addictive and potentially harmful, they are usu-ally either regulated by prescription or banned outright. Narcotics primarily affect the functioning of the brain and of the bowel (the intestines). With respect to the former, they bring about pain relief, relaxation, and sleepiness. With respect to the

narcotic any drug in a class of drugs de-rived from opium or synthetically produced to create the numbing, stuporous effects of opium and that lead to addiction

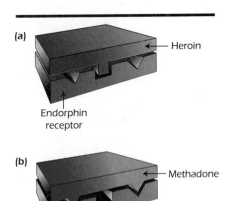

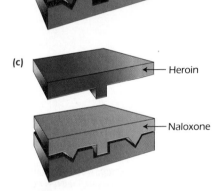

Figure 5-5
Chemical Mate
(a and b) Opiate (heroin) and opioid (methadone) drugs, which have similar molecular shapes to endorphins, can trick the brain into intense levels of response, based on the brain's natural responses to endorphins. (c) The molecular shape of naloxone fits the receptor site so well that it effectively blocks the ability of opiates, opioids, and endorphins, but it does not trigger the pain-relieving and euphoric effects that these substances produce. Hence, naloxone can provide life-saving blockage of the effects of narcotic overdose.

central nervous system (CNS) depressant drug that slows the operation of the CNS and is often prescribed in low doses to reduce anxiety and in relatively higher doses to combat insomnia

sedative–hypnotics one of the two primary types of CNS depressants, used for calming anxiety and relieving insomnia

barbiturates the most widely used type of sedative–hypnotic drug; prescribed to reduce anxiety but may lead to grogginess that can impair functioning in situations requiring alertness

tranquilizer one of the sedative–hypnotic drugs used for combating anxiety; considered to be safer than barbiturates, although the potential for addiction remains problematic

latter, they produce constipation. They also slow down other physiological processes, such as breathing. Narcotics are usually prescribed for acute pain, and very low doses are sometimes prescribed for severe diarrhea. Because of the dangers of addiction, narcotics are not usually prescribed for chronic pain or mild diarrhea. Typically, narcotics users have trouble concentrating and feel mentally clouded and fuzzy. Typical narcotic withdrawal symptoms are chills, sweating, intense stomach cramps, diarrhea, headache, and repeated vomiting—symptoms similar to those of a really horrible case of intestinal flu.

For narcotics, acute toxicity is usually treated with *naloxone*, which blocks the effects of the narcotics (see Figure 5-5). For chronic toxicity, the addict is given one of two treatments: (1) The addict is weaned from the drug. (2) The addict is allowed to switch to using a legal substitute for the drug, from which the addict is, in theory, eventually weaned. The eventual weaning may or may not occur in practice. For example, many addicts are treated with methadone, which can be taken orally (not intravenously) and which has more long-lasting effects than heroin, so that the user can wait longer between doses without experiencing withdrawal.

Central Nervous System Depressants

General Drug Actions

Relatively few people regularly use narcotics; many people, however, regularly use **central nervous system (CNS) depressants** such as alcohol and the sedative–hypnotics (which are usually sleeping pills or pills that produce a calming effect). Depressants, like narcotics, slow the operation of the CNS. In general, CNS depressants reduce *anxiety* (general feelings of uneasiness or even fear) and guilt, and they relax normal inhibitions. However, intoxicated persons may also show sudden shifts in mood and experience *increased* anxiety and irritability. High doses of depressants can cause slow reflexes, unsteady walking and other movements, slurred speech, and impaired judgment. Overdoses can slow physiological responses to the point of causing death.

Alcohol

Alcohol is the most well known and widely used CNS depressant. Alcoholism, now widely regarded as a disease, is one of the most common afflictions in the United States. Many factors influence the effects of alcohol: the amount a person drinks, the rate at which the person drinks, the amount and kind of food the person has consumed before starting to drink or while drinking, and the person's body weight, tolerance, and metabolism (use and storage of energy and other resources). Most dosages of alcohol cause the expected depressant effects of slowed reflexes, slurred speech, and so on, as well as difficulty with attention. About 10% of people who use alcohol have problems in their lives related to alcohol use. About 90% of all assaults, 50% to 60% of all murders, and more than 50% of the rapes and sexual attacks on children are alcohol related. Alcohol also impairs health, and alcoholics generally have their life expectancy cut short by an average of 10 to 12 years (Block, 1970; Ciompi & Eisert, 1969). To help detect signs of alcoholism, see Practical Psychology 5-1.

Sedative–Hypnotics

Sedative–hypnotics are depressant drugs used in order to calm anxiety and to relieve insomnia. The two most widely used sedative–hypnotics are barbiturates and tranquilizers. When used properly, **barbiturates** are effective sedative–hypnotics. However, barbiturates are also highly addictive and dangerous. **Tranquilizers** are generally safer than barbiturates: They do not cause sleepiness, they are effective at low dosages, and they cause fewer risks to normal breathing. Still, tranquilizers can also be addictive.

PRACTICAL PSYCHOLOGY 5-1

Is Someone You Know an Alcoholic?

The National Institute on Alcohol Abuse and Alcoholism has developed the following seven questions for you to use to check whether you or someone you know may be having problems due to alcoholism. If you answer "yes" to even one question, alcohol may be a problem in your life (or in the life of someone you know). If you answer "yes" to several questions, you (or someone you know) may be an alcoholic. Most of these questions boil down to a central issue: Is the use of alcohol creating problems in one or more areas of your life?

1. Has someone close to you expressed concern about your drinking?
2. When faced with a problem, do you often turn to alcohol for relief?
3. Are you sometimes unable to meet home or work responsibilities because of drinking?
4. Have you ever required medical attention as a result of drinking?
5. Have you ever experienced a blackout—a total loss of memory while still awake—when drinking?
6. Have you ever come in conflict with the law in connection with your drinking?
7. Have you often failed to keep the promises you have made to yourself about controlling or cutting out your drinking?

What kinds of treatment for addiction would you like to have our society provide to drug addicts? If you would not like to see any treatment made available, why not?

Wine mocks, strong drink bawls. No one under the influence is wise.

Proverbs 20:1

Should alcohol or other psychoactive drugs be banned? What drugs should or should not be banned, and why?

Treatment for addiction or overdose varies according to the sedative–hypnotic drug. In any case, both a psychological and a physiological dependence must be addressed. Recall that withdrawal from narcotic drugs is extremely uncomfortable but usually not life-threatening. In contrast, withdrawal from sedative–hypnotic drugs can be both painful and life-threatening. Therefore, medical professionals should supervise withdrawal, carefully watching for symptoms of acute and chronic toxicity. Withdrawal symptoms can include anxiety, *tremors* (uncontrollable shaking), nightmares, insomnia, *anorexia* (unwillingness to eat despite the need for food), nausea, vomiting, fever, *seizures* (attacks that may affect both

Many criminal prosecutions are related to the use and sale of illicit drugs, but the psychoactive drug that is most often linked to assaults, homicides, and suicides is alcohol.

consciousness and muscular control), and *delirium* (mental disturbance involving distortions of thinking and of perception) (Seymour & Smith, 1987).

Central Nervous System Stimulants

In contrast to CNS depressants, **central nervous system stimulants** excite the CNS. They do so either by stimulating the heart (making it work harder) or by reducing the activity of natural compounds that slow down brain activity. One way to picture how stimulants work in the brain is to think of stimulants as substances that limit the effectiveness of chemical "brakes" in the brain. When these natural chemical brakes do not work properly, brain activity races ahead, sometimes out of control. Common CNS stimulants include caffeine, nicotine (found in tobacco), amphetamines, and cocaine. Short-term use of mild CNS stimulants can increase the user's alertness, increase the user's ability to continue activity despite being physically tired, help the user to stave off hunger pains, and create a sense of euphoria in the user. In stronger doses, the drugs can cause anxiety and irritability.

Overdoses of stimulants may produce intoxication, *paranoia* (false perceptions that other people are trying to harm the drug user), confusion, hallucinations, and death due to breathing failure or wild and rapid changes in body temperature. Withdrawal symptoms may include extreme tiredness and depression. Occasional off-again, on-again use of amphetamines also seems to produce the paradoxical effect of sensitization. In **sensitization,** the rare or occasional user of stimulants actually becomes *more* sensitive to low doses of the drug.

Nicotine is the psychoactive ingredient in tobacco. At present, nicotine is believed to be among the most addictive substances known: Nine out of 10 people who start smoking become addicted. Compare that number to 1 in 6 people who become addicted after trying crack cocaine and 1 in 10 people who become alcoholics after experimenting with alcohol (Kornblum & Julian, 1992). In pregnant women, smoking has been linked both to preterm birth and to unusually low birth weight. Both problems can pose serious risks for newborns. In addition, tobacco users often produce direct effects on other persons in the environment through secondary smoke.

The most common treatment for addiction to stimulants is psychotherapy. Acute toxicity from stimulants must be treated medically. The exact treatment depends on the particular stimulant. Drug-substitution therapy is generally not used except in the case of nicotine. However, for acute nicotine withdrawal, nicotine gum and epidermal (skin) patches appear to be effective, when used in combination with some other form of therapy.

Hallucinogenics

Hallucinogenic drugs (also known as "psychedelics") alter consciousness by inducing hallucinations and affecting the way the users perceive both their inner worlds and their external environments. To some clinicians, these drugs seem to mimic the effects produced naturally in *psychosis* (very serious psychological disturbances). Other clinicians, however, suggest that these drug-induced hallucinations have different qualities than do the hallucinations produced by psychosis. Mescaline, LSD, and marijuana (the most commonly used) are a few of the hallucinogenic drugs. Hallucinogenic drugs seem to produce different effects, depending on the type of situation in which they are used.

Acute overdoses of hallucinogenics are normally treated by having a therapist use talk therapy. Typically, the therapist attempts to talk to the user in order to reduce any anxiety and to make the user feel as comfortable as possible ("talking the user down"). Tranquilizers are also sometimes used, and a final alternative is *antipsychotic drugs* (drugs used for treating psychosis; see Chapter 14). Chronic use of hallucinogenics can lead to prolonged psychotic reactions; severe and sometimes life-threatening depression; a worsening of psychiatric problems that existed before

---

Cocaine is God's way of saying you're making too much money.

Robin Williams

---

central nervous system (CNS) stimulant drug that arouses and excites the CNS, either by stimulating the heart or by inhibiting the actions of natural compounds that depress brain activity (thereby acting as a "double-negative" on brain stimulation)

sensitization paradoxical phenomenon in which an intermittent user of a drug actually demonstrates heightened sensitivity to low doses of the drug

hallucinogenic a type of psychoactive drug that alters consciousness by inducing hallucinations and by affecting the way the drug users perceive both their inner worlds and their external environments

the drug was taken; and *flashbacks*, in which the drug user re-experiences hallucinations or distortions associated with past drug use, without actually taking the drug again (Seymour & Smith, 1987). Scientists do not yet understand how flashbacks occur because no physiological mechanism has been found that can account for them.

Treatment of Drug Abuse

Table 5-1 briefly summarizes the four categories of drugs and lists some of the common drugs in each category. It does not, however, address the central question of interest to psychologists: Why do people use psychoactive drugs at all? The reasons are various and are not yet well understood. Many behaviorally oriented psychologists have suggested that these drugs are linked to rewarding feelings or mental states. Drug users learn to use drugs because they receive this reward. Other psychologists disagree. They point out that the strength of the reward lessens (as a result of increasing tolerance), but the drug use continues anyway.

Given our ignorance about what causes people to engage in the abuse of psychoactive drugs, does it do any good to try to treat persons addicted to these drugs? Yes. According to a study by the Institute of Medicine of the National Academy of Science (Gerstein & Harwood, 1990), the cost of drug-treatment programs is more than offset by their success in reducing the much higher costs related to drug abuse, including drug-related crime, health care, and lost productivity.

Each of the preceding sections on psychoactive drugs has included a brief mention of treatment for acute or chronic toxicity related to specific drugs. What, if anything, is likely to increase the probability that drug treatment of any kind will be successful? The single most important factor that seems to enhance the likeli-

TABLE 5-1

Four Basic Categories of Psychoactive Drugs

Category and its effects	Drugs in this category
Narcotics—Produce numbness or stupor, relieve pain	Opium and its natural derivatives: morphine, codeine, heroin ("junk," "smack," "boy," "stuff") Opioids (synthetic narcotics): meperidine (Demerol®), propoxyphene (Darvon®), oxycodone (Percodan®), methadone

CNS depressants ("downers")—Slow (depress) the operation of the central nervous system	Alcohol ("booze," "hair of the dog")
	 Sedative–hypnotics
	     Barbiturates ("barbs," "downers"): secobarbital (Seconal®), phenobarbital (Dilantin®),
	     Tranquilizers (benzodiazepines): chlorpromazine (Thorazine®), chlordiazepoxide (Librium®), diazepam (Valium®), alprazolam (Xanax®)
	     Methaqualone (Quaalude®), "ludes")
	     Chloral hydrate ("knockout drops")

CNS stimulants ("uppers")—Excite (stimulate) the central nervous system	Caffeine (found in nondecaffeinated coffee, teas, cola drinks) Amphetamines ("speed," "uppers"): amphetamine (Benzedrine®, "bennies"), dextroamphetamine (Dexedrine®), methamphetamine (Methedrine®) Cocaine ("coke," "crack," "blow," "snow," "flake," "rocks," "freebase," "she") Nicotine (in tobacco) ("coffin nails," "cancer sticks," "butts")
Hallucinogenics (psychedelics, psychotomimetics)—Induce alterations of consciousness	LSD ("acid," "space caps") Mescaline ("mescal," "buttons," "cactus") Marijuana ("pot," "dope," "reefer," "Mary Jane," "ganja") Hashish ("hash") Phencyclidine ("PCP," "angel dust")

hood of treatment success is to increase the length of time in treatment (Gerstein & Harwood, 1990). About one third of recovering addicts who remain in treatment for 3 months or more continue to resist drugs a year later, and about two thirds of recovering addicts who remain in treatment for a year or more manage to stay drug free long afterward (Falco, 1992). Also, even when individuals do not fully succeed in remaining drug free following initial treatment, there may still be gains from treatment, such as reduced use, reduced criminal activity, and increased likelihood of returning to treatment, thereby leading to future possibilities for success (Falco, 1992).

Other factors that improve the likelihood of treatment success include having a stable family, being employed, and having access to other rewarding activities. Having adequate financial resources may also be helpful. For example, a 70% success rate was achieved with affluent cocaine addicts in a Beverly Hills treatment program. However, when the same program was implemented with impoverished crack addicts, the success rate plummeted to 30% (Falco, 1992). The approach used in this particular program is to help addicts to understand both the physiological and the psychological processes of addiction and recovery. The program encourages addicts to focus on the drug-using behavior and on the many environmental stimuli that contribute to whether the person will be able to resist using drugs. The behavioral view of addictions and other learned behavior is described more fully in the following chapter.

How do drugs induce alterations in consciousness? In general, psychoactive drugs produce psychopharmacological effects by fitting into the brain's receptor sites for natural neurochemicals that produce pain-relieving, calming, stimulating, euphoria-inducing, or even hallucinogenic (psychosis-like) effects.

SUMMARY

1. *Consciousness* is a stream of active mental processing. It is the state of mind through which we obtain, manipulate, and apply information available from our senses, from memory, and from our ongoing mental processes.
2. *Attention* is the process by which we focus mental awareness on particular information available in consciousness, allowing other information to remain outside of our awareness.

How Does Attention Work?   137

3. People use *selective attention* to track one message while ignoring other messages.
4. In *dichotic presentation*, each of the ears receives a *different* auditory message. In contrast, during *binaural presentation*, both ears receive the *same* message.

5. The *Stroop effect* occurs when a person is asked to identify the ink color of color words when the ink color of the words differs from what the printed word means (e.g., the word "red," printed in blue ink).

What Levels of Consciousness Do We Experience?   139

6. Consciousness occurs on *multiple levels*.
7. Information in the *preconscious* level is just outside of consciousness and is usually available for conscious retrieval or use. *Subliminal perception* occurs at the preconscious level.
8. Information in the *subconscious* level is normally not available to consciousness, except with great difficulty or perhaps through dreams.

What Happens During Altered States of Consciousness?   142

9. Altered states of consciousness can involve illusions, which are distorted perceptions of objects, or hallucinations, which are perceptions of objects that do not exist.

What Happens When We Sleep and Dream?   143

10. There are two basic kinds of sleep—*REM sleep* and *non-REM* (N-REM) sleep. In REM sleep, the eyes move rapidly, and the sleeper is usually dreaming. N-REM sleep is usually divided into four stages of successively deeper sleep, which seldom involve dreaming. The stages of N-REM and REM sleep cycle repeatedly through the night.

11. If people are subjected to *sleep deprivation* for several days, they show increasingly serious symptoms of being mentally disturbed.

12. People seem to show a *circadian* (daily) rhythm that corresponds to the night–day pattern of our planet.

13. In *insomnia*, individuals have trouble falling asleep, wake up during the night, or wake up too early in the morning. Persons with *narcolepsy* feel sudden, overwhelming impulses to sleep when they do not really want to. In *sleep apnea*, breathing is temporarily interrupted during sleep. *Somnambulists* (sleepwalkers) typically do not dream while they are acting out wakeful-seeming behaviors in their sleep.

14. Several different theories of dreaming have been proposed. According to Freud, dreams express the hidden wishes of the unconscious. According to McCarley and Hobson's *activation–synthesis theory*, dreams represent our own interpretations of our brain activity during sleep. According to Crick and Mitchison, dreams are the brain's way of clearing itself during the night—essentially, for disposing of "mental garbage."

Is Hypnosis an Altered State?   148

15. During *hypnosis*, some people become extremely responsive to whatever the hypnotist tells them, and they are often quite willing (within limits) to obey the hypnotist's instructions to do things or even to feel things they would not normally do or feel. A *posthypnotic suggestion* is a means by which hypnotized participants can be asked to do something after the hypnotic trance is removed.

16. Various theories of hypnosis have been proposed. One theory views it as a form of deep relaxation. Another views it as a return to childlike ways of thinking. Still another theory views hypnosis as a set of play-acted roles, and the actors may be sincere or insincere in acting out their roles. Research has not supported the return-to-childhood view, and findings from research on the play-acting view are mixed. A fourth theory, which is now widely accepted, views hypnosis as a form of split consciousness: There is a hidden observer in the person who observes what is going on, as though from the outside, at the same time that the person responds to hypnotic suggestions.

What Happens When We Meditate?   151

17. *Meditation* is a set of techniques used to alter state of consciousness; the person becomes more relaxed, inner directed, and calm, as well as less tense, goal oriented, and outer directed.

How Do Drugs Induce Alterations in Consciousness?   151

18. The state of consciousness can be altered by four kinds of *psychoactive drugs: narcotics, CNS depressants, CNS stimulants,* and *hallucinogenics.* The *psychopharmacological* effects of these drugs are related to similar effects produced by naturally occurring neurochemicals in the brain.

19. A typical pattern of drug use involves *intoxication, tolerance,* and *addiction,* as well as the possibilities for *withdrawal* and even for *overdose.* Drug treatment must address either *acute toxicity* and *chronic toxicity.*

20. *Narcotics* include natural opiates and synthetic opioids. Narcotics produce some degree of numbness or stupor and often a feeling of euphoria or pain relief.

21. *Depressants,* including alcohol and sedative–hypnotic drugs, slow the operation of the CNS. In contrast, *stimulants*—including caffeine, nicotine, cocaine, and amphetamines—speed up the operation of the CNS.

22. *Hallucinogenics*—including LSD, mescaline, and marijuana—produce distorted perceptions of reality.

PATHWAYS TO KNOWLEDGE

Choose the best answer to complete each sentence.

1. Tolerance to a psychoactive drug occurs when
   (a) drug users no longer care whether they receive the drug.
   (b) drug users need successively greater doses of a drug to achieve the same effect.
   (c) drug users stop having withdrawal symptoms.
   (d) people get used to the idea that an addict is not likely to stop taking drugs.

2. The purpose of the simulating paradigm in studies of hypnosis is to determine whether
   (a) hypnotized people can act as though they are not hypnotized.

(b) nonhypnotized people can act as though they are hypnotized.

(c) hypnotized people know that they are hypnotized.

(d) hypnotized people can act as though they received a posthypnotic suggestion.

3. Which of the following is typically a symptom of severe sleep deprivation?

(a) illusions or hallucinations

(b) apnea

(c) irritability

(d) all of the above

(e) a and c, but not b

4. Subliminal perception occurs

(a) only at night.

(b) in persons who are successfully hypnotized.

(c) without conscious awareness.

(d) during dreams.

Answer each of the following questions by filling in the blank with an appropriate word or phrase.

5. The stage of sleep during which most dreaming occurs is called "_____ _____."

6. A syndrome in which the sleeper has difficulty in breathing is called sleep "_____."

7. The hypothesis that dreaming represents a person's subjective awareness and interpretation of neural activity during sleep is called the "_____–_____ hypothesis."

8. According to Freud, people _____ information that they find too threatening to permit to enter conscious awareness, but this information may be revealed through slips of the tongue or through _____.

Match the following drugs to their descriptions:

9.	nicotine	(a)	a type of sedative–hypnotic drug
10.	barbiturates	(b)	an opiate
11.	cocaine	(c)	the most commonly used CNS depressant
12.	CNS depressants	(d)	a category of drugs associated with symptoms that may appear similar to those of psychosis
13.	CNS stimulants	(e)	a category of drugs that produces psychopharmacological effects related to the effects of endorphins
14.	narcotics	(f)	an opioid
15.	heroin	(g)	a highly addictive substance found in tobacco
16.	methadone	(h)	a category of CNS depressants, including tranquilizers
17.	alcohol	(i)	a category of drugs that slows down the activity of the central nervous system
18.	naloxone	(j)	a strong CNS stimulant
19.	LSD	(k)	a category of drugs that speeds up the activity of the central nervous system
20.	hallucinogenics	(l)	a drug that effectively blocks the psychopharmacological effects of opiates and opioids
21.	sedative–hypnotic drugs	(m)	a hallucinogenic

Answers

1. b, 2. b, 3. e, 4. c, 5. REM sleep, 6. apnea, 7. activation–synthesis, 8. repress, dreams, 9. g, 10. a, 11. j, 12. i, 13. k, 14. e, 15. b, 16. f, 17. c, 18. l, 19. m, 20. d, 21. h

PATHWAYS TO UNDERSTANDING

 1. Freud suggested that particular imagery in dreams has particular symbolic meanings. Think of a recent dream you have had—or make up a fanciful dream. Try to analyze the symbolic meanings for the objects and events in your dream. What would you say that your dream meant? What are some more ordinary interpretations of your dream?

 2. What are your normal sleep patterns? How do you react when your normal patterns are interrupted? How do your experiences compare with the experiences of participants in sleep-deprivation research?

 3. What are some of the factors that you believe can lead people to abuse psychoactive drugs? In your opinion, how can we help people to avoid becoming involved in the abuse of these drugs?

CHAPTER OUTLINE

What Are Some Preprogrammed Responses?

What Is Classical Conditioning?
Pavlov's Discovery of Classical Conditioning
The Basics of Classical Conditioning
Why Does Classical Conditioning Occur?
Phases and Features of Classical Conditioning
Surprising Relationships Between the Stimulus and the Response
Classical Conditioning and Emotional Responses

What Is Operant Conditioning?
Thorndike's Law of Effect
Reinforcement
Punishment
Enhancing the Effectiveness of Punishment
How Is Operant Conditioning Implemented?
Skinner and the Experimental Analysis of Behavior
Putting Operant Conditioning Into Practice

What Is Social Learning?

CHAPTER
6

Learning

Stop for a moment, and think about all the simple things you have learned in order to get through a single day: What do you do when you feel hunger pangs? What foods do you like to eat, and what foods do you dislike eating? Why do you like some foods and not others? What other simple things have you learned about adapting to your environment?

Psychologists generally define **learning** as any relatively permanent change in the behavior, thoughts, or feelings of an individual, which results from experience. This chapter considers relatively simple forms of learning. More complex forms of learning (e.g., the learning that enables you to understand and remember the concepts in this chapter) are considered in other chapters. Through learning, we may more effectively adapt to our environment.

WHAT ARE SOME PREPROGRAMMED RESPONSES?

Although we must learn a great deal in order to adapt effectively to our environments, we seem to know some things even at the moment we are born, without having to learn them. These things are biologically preprogrammed into us. One kind of preprogrammed response is **habituation,** in which we tune out relatively familiar stimuli about which we are not trying to learn more information. That is, based on prior experience, particular stimuli become familiar to us, and we generally tune out those familiar stimuli. As I am typing these words, countless stimuli are available to my senses—the steady drone of my old air conditioner; the sights of photos, books, and office supplies surrounding my desk; the feel of my hands on the keyboard; the changing tensions of the muscles in my arms; and so on. One paragraph ago, I was habituated to these familiar stimuli, so I paid no attention to any of them.

With a little conscious effort, however, any of these stimuli are available to my awareness. That is, simply by deciding to pay attention to these stimuli, I can notice them again. A complement to habituation is *dishabituation,* in which we tune in to relatively unusual stimuli or to changing stimuli about which we are trying to learn more: If one of my books falls onto the floor, I will become dishabituated and will pay attention to the book.

To see how habituation and dishabituation work together, think about this example: Suppose that a radio was playing instrumental music while you were studying your psychology textbook. At first, the sound might have distracted you, but after a while, you might have become habituated to the familiar sound and scarcely noticed it. However, if the style of music changed dramatically (e.g., from classical to hard rock), you might have dishabituated to the sound, at least temporarily. In this case, the pattern of sound that had been familiar would have entered your awareness as an unusual sound. Similarly, if someone were to ask you a question about the music, you might dishabituate to the music in order to answer the question.

Habituation and dishabituation may seem somewhat similar to sensory adaptation (see Chapter 4), but sensory adaptation differs from habituation in several key ways (see Table 6-1). The chief difference is that habituation and dishabituation depend on prior experiences with stimuli (and thereby relate closely to learning), whereas sensory adaptation does not depend on prior experiences. Instead, the degree to which sensory adaptation occurs depends on the intensity of the stimulus, and there is essentially no difference in sensory adaptation between the first exposure to a given stimulus and the millionth exposure to the stimulus.

Habituation and dishabituation also serve a helpful purpose for learning: By using these two processes, we turn our attention to novel stimuli about which we can learn a great deal, and we ignore relatively familiar stimuli about which we can learn very little. (Actually, some psychologists consider habituation to be a simple form of learning, rather than a preprogrammed response, because it involves change that results from experience; in this chapter, however, because habituation does not involve "relatively *permanent* change," we do not consider habituation to be a form of learning.)

Although habituation can pave the way for complex learning, it involves a relatively simple form of preprogrammed response. In many species of animals, how-

---

learning any relatively permanent change in the behavior, thoughts, and feelings of an individual, which results from experience

habituation a phenomenon in which a person gradually becomes more familiar with a stimulus and notices it less and less; in *dishabituation,* a once familiar stimulus changes to become unfamiliar, so the person notices the stimulus once again

TABLE 6-1

Differences Between Adaptation and Habituation

Responses involving physiological adaptation take place mostly in our sense organs, whereas responses involving cognitive habituation take place mostly in our brains (and relate to learning).

Adaptation	Habituation
Not accessible to conscious control *Example:* You cannot decide how quickly to adapt to a partic-ular smell or a particular change in light intensity.	Accessible to conscious control *Example:* You can decide to become aware of background music to which you have become habituated (dishabituation).
Tied closely to stimulus intensity *Example:* The more the intensity of a bright light increases, the more strongly your senses will adapt to the light.	Not tied very closely to stimulus intensity *Example:* Your level of habituation will not differ much in your response to the sound of a loud fan and to that of a quieter air conditioner.
Unrelated to the number, length, and recency of prior exposures *Example:* The sense receptors in your skin will respond to changes in temperature in basically the same way, no matter how many times you have been exposed to such changes, and no matter how recently you have experienced these changes.	Tied very closely to the number, length, and recency of prior exposures *Example:* You will become more quickly habituated to the sound of a chiming clock when you have been exposed to the sound more often, for longer times, and on more recent occasions.

ever, even fairly complex responses may be preprogrammed. These more complex forms of preprogrammed responses are **instincts.** For example, if a male stickle-back fish swims too close to the nest of another male, the second male stickleback will warn and possibly attack the first male. The preprogrammed defensive pattern of the second stickleback is automatic, and it is triggered by a red area on the belly of the first (or any other) male stickleback (Tinbergen, 1951).

Some instinctive behaviors also involve a degree of learning. In particular, during **imprinting,** a newborn animal seeks out a particular kind of stimulus and then responds with a preprogrammed behavior when it senses the right kind of stimulus. Although both the particular response and the general kind of stimulus are preprogrammed, the animal learns from experience the specific stimulus to which it will respond. For example, Konrad Lorenz (1937, 1950) watched newly hatched goslings form an immediate attachment to the first moving object near them.

Usually, the mother is the first moving object the goslings see, so they become attached to her and follow her. That is, when the goslings observe their mother

instinct an inherited, species-specific, stereotyped, and often relatively complex pattern of behavior

imprinting a preprogrammed response in which a newborn animal looks for a particu-lar kind of stimulus and then carries out the response; the specific stimulus that prompts the response is learned

Ethologist Konrad Lorenz had young goslings imprint to him, waddling behind him on the ground and swimming behind him in the water. Canadian ethologist Bill Lishman was able to go beyond Lorenz, leading his imprinted goslings into the air, as he flew in his ultralight plane.

move, they focus on her as the object of imprinting, and they carry out their pre-programmed instinctive behavior in response to her. In rare cases, however, the mother is not available, so the newborns imprint on other moving objects—including even walking, flying, or swimming human researchers.

There are many variations of imprinting. The stimulus for imprinting may be seen (e.g., the movement of a mother duck), smelled (e.g., the odor of a salmon's native stream), or otherwise sensed (e.g., hearing a mother's call or tasting a mother's milk). Although the imprinted behaviors can vary widely, they usually are associated with survival either for the individual (e.g., following a parent who will provide food and will help in avoiding or defending against predators) or for the species (e.g., finding a mate—such as becoming imprinted on the sight or the smell of opposite-sex members of the same species). Although there is generally a critical period for imprinting, imprinted behavior occasionally may be modified somewhat later on. For example, it has happened that a gosling that is not offered a moving object to follow during the critical period for imprinting has imprinted on a moving mother duck at a somewhat later time.

Are preprogrammed responses a help or a hindrance? On the one hand, pre-programmed responses can be adaptive—such as when you habituate to minor distractions while studying. On the other hand, preprogrammed responses do not allow for much flexibility. If the environment changes, and the old preprogrammed responses are no longer adaptive in the newly changed environment, the individual has no way to adapt effectively to the changes.

For instance, newly hatched salmon imprint to the odor of their native stream as they swim downstream to the ocean. As long as their natural environment remains essentially the same, the adult salmon, ready to mate, masterfully follow the imprinted odor upstream through complex waterways to their spawning grounds. However, when a salmon's native stream is altered by loggers, hikers, or adventurers, the salmon's imprinting does little to help the salmon find its way to its native spawning ground. A more flexible alternative to preprogrammed behavior is learned behavior. If individuals can learn new responses to a changing environment, they have a much better chance of adapting to and surviving in a changing world.

What are preprogrammed responses? Preprogrammed responses include habituation and dishabituation, as well as instincts such as imprinting. None of these behaviors are learned, although some, such as dishabituation, may pave the way for learning to occur.

WHAT IS CLASSICAL CONDITIONING?

Do the smells of particular foods turn your stomach? Does the sound of barking or growling dogs make your heart pound? Do you feel delight at the mere mention of a particular person you know? These common responses result from classical conditioning. In **classical conditioning,** an individual learns to associate a stimulus that causes a particular physiological or emotional response with a second stimulus, which produces no particular response before the two stimuli are linked. After the individual learns to associate the two stimuli, however, the second stimulus alone starts to produce the same physiological or emotional response as the first stimulus.

classical conditioning the learning process whereby an originally neutral stimulus becomes associated with a particular physiological or emotional response that the stimulus did not originally produce

For instance, if the smell of a particular food sickens you, you probably learned to associate the smell of that food with feeling ill or at least uncomfortable after eating it. If the mention of a particular person delights you, you probably associate that person with a very pleasant experience (or set of experiences). In each of these examples, you were classically conditioned to learn an association between stimuli.

Pavlov's Discovery of Classical Conditioning

How was classical conditioning discovered? Did a group of psychologists go to a smelly restaurant, eat some sickening bad-smelling food, and jointly discover the mechanisms of classical conditioning as a form of learning? No, but food did play an important role in this discovery. Ivan Pavlov (1849–1936), a Nobel Prize–winning physiologist, accidentally noticed this form of learning while he was studying how saliva influenced the digestion of food in dogs.

In one set of studies, Pavlov was measuring the saliva dogs produced when the dogs were given food (meat powder). After running a few experiments, however, Pavlov noticed that the dogs started to produce saliva even before they were given the meat powder. In fact, the dogs would start salivating in response to the sight of one of his lab technicians or even to the sound of the lab technician's footsteps. What a nuisance! If Pavlov could not keep the dogs from salivating *before* they smelled the meat powder, he would not be able to measure accurately how much saliva they produced *after* smelling it. He would end up with ambiguous results that would be of no use to him or to anyone else. For a while, Pavlov tried to invent ways to keep this annoying problem from interfering with his important research on digestion.

Chance favors only the prepared mind.

Louis Pasteur

After using a buzzer in his first experiments, Ivan Pavlov went on to investigate whether other sound cues and even cues to other sensory modalities—such as sight and touch—could be manipulated systematically to prompt the associative learning. His creative exploration of alternative stimuli well illustrates the scientific method at work. For example, to study the effects of touch stimulation, he rigged a device for touching various parts of the dog's body so that each part could be touched without introducing other sensory stimuli, such as the sight or sounds of an experimenter.

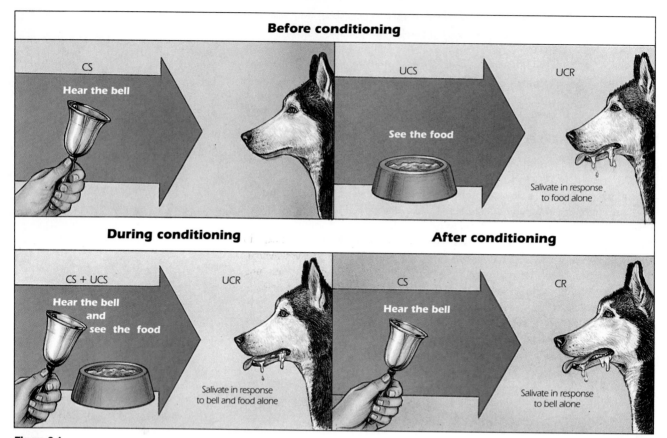

Figure 6-1

Pavlov's Classic Experiment

The first classical-conditioning experiment began as an accidental discovery, developed through a simple procedure, and started an entirely new way of looking at learning. Before the experiment, the sound yielded no response from the dog, whereas the food (UCS) made the dog salivate (UCR). During the experiment, Ivan Pavlov paired the sound (CS) with the food (UCS) to prompt the dog to salivate (UCR). After many repetitions, the sound (CS alone) prompted the dog to salivate (CR).

Happily for psychology, however, Pavlov was open to new discoveries. Soon, he saw a startling implication of the dogs' behavior. Some kind of associative learning must have taken place. Originally, only the food led to the physiological response (salivation). After repeated experience, however, other stimuli came to be associated with the food, and these other stimuli also led to the salivation response. Psychologists refer to this form of learning as *classical conditioning* (or sometimes "Pavlovian conditioning," in honor of Pavlov).

After making his discovery, Pavlov set out to study classical conditioning systematically. First, he showed that a dog naturally salivated only when it tasted food, not when it sensed a nonfood stimulus, such as a buzzer. Second, Pavlov rigged his equipment so that a buzzer would sound, and then soon after, meat powder would be placed on the dog's tongue. After this procedure was repeated many times, the buzzer was sounded, but no meat powder was placed on the dog's tongue. The dog still salivated. By pairing the buzzer with the food, Pavlov had classically conditioned the dog to salivate in response to the buzzer alone (see Figure 6-1).

MINILECTURE

Pavlov's Study (Ch 7)

The Basics of Classical Conditioning

The particular stimuli and responses used in classical conditioning can vary, but the basic structure of classical conditioning does not change. If you were to create a classical-conditioning experiment like the ones Pavlov conducted, you would do (more or less) as follows:

1. Start with an **unconditioned stimulus (UCS)** (e.g., the meat powder), which elicits a physiological or emotional response.
2. Note your participant's **unconditioned response (UCR)**—the automatic physiological response (e.g., salivation) to this stimulus.
3. Choose a stimulus (e.g., a buzzer) that originally produces no particular response. This **conditioned stimulus (CS)** is originally neutral but will later elicit the physiological response.
4. Pair your CS and your UCS, so that the CS and the UCS become associated. Eventually, you may obtain from this CS a **conditioned response (CR)** (e.g., salivation). The CR is essentially identical to the UCR, except that it is elicited by the CS rather than by the UCS.

Why Does Classical Conditioning Occur?

Since classical conditioning was first discovered, psychologists have tried to explain why it occurs. An obvious explanation for classical conditioning is *temporal contiguity:* Simply because the CS and the UCS occur close together in time, conditioning occurs. At one time, many researchers believed that temporal contiguity was the basis for classical conditioning, and a few researchers (e.g., Papini & Bitterman, 1990) continue to hold this view. Indeed, research has shown that temporal contiguity does facilitate learning; if too long a time period passes between the end of the CS and the start of the UCS, classical conditioning will not take place.

Finding Your Way   6-1

Think about the last time you felt frightened. What are all the sights and sounds you now associate with that experience? How many of those sensations occurred during or close to the time when you felt frightened? (If you are like most people, those sensations occurred at about the same time as when you were frightened.)

Although temporal contiguity clearly plays a role in conditioning, most psychologists now believe that temporal contiguity alone does not lead to learning. Think again about a frightening experience you have had. Do you associate absolutely everything you were doing, wearing, and saying with the experience? Do you associate all aspects of where you were living, working, or attending school with the experience? If the frightening experience lasted only a short time, you probably associate some things, but not others, with the experience.

If temporal contiguity does not explain how classical conditioning works, what does explain it? A classic study by Robert Rescorla (1967) suggests that the key to conditioning is contingency, not just temporal contiguity. In **contingency,** one or more actions or events *depend on* either the occurrence of an event or the presence of a stimulus. For example, suppose that you eat a rotten tuna sandwich, and you feel sick afterward. In this case, feeling sick is contingent on—it depends on—having eaten a rotten tuna sandwich. Feeling sick is not contingent, however, on what you were wearing at the time you ate the sandwich. Although your having felt sick was temporally contiguous with both your wearing of particular clothes and your eating of the rotten sandwich, your sick feelings were contingent only on your eating of the sandwich. You can wear those clothes again safely without worrying about becoming ill (as long as you steer clear of other things that make you sick).

Of course, Rescorla did *not* study contingency by recruiting human volunteers who were eager to eat rotten tuna sandwiches and to feel ill afterward. Instead,

unconditioned stimulus (UCS) stimulus that elicits a physiological or emotional response

unconditioned response (UCR) automatic physiological or emotional response to a UCS

conditioned stimulus (CS) originally neutral stimulus that will later elicit a physiological or emotional response

conditioned response (CR) response that is like the UCR, but that is elicited from the CS rather than from the UCS

contingency phenomenon in which one or more stimuli depend on the presence of another stimulus

Rescorla followed Pavlov's example and tested his notion of contingency by studying dogs. Rescorla designed an experiment with dogs to test the notion that contingency is the basis for classical conditioning. In the experiment, the CS was a tone, and the UCS was a painful shock. He predicted that the physiological and emotional UCRs to the pain would be fear. The results of Rescorla's experiment confirmed the contingency point of view: Fear conditioning took place when the shock was contingent (i.e., dependent) on the occurrence of the tone. That is, when the tone provided information helpful in predicting the appearance of the shock, conditioning occurred. However, conditioning did *not* occur if the shock and the tone were associated in time (were temporally contiguous) but the occurrence of the tone did not predict the occurrence of the shock.

In his experiment, Rescorla showed that classical conditioning is based on contingency rather than on contiguity. He also suggested that the basis for classical conditioning involves phenomena of a kind different from what most behaviorists had believed previously. According to Rescorla, individuals try to make sense of the stimuli in their environments that affect them. When the UCS first appears, it is unexpected and is therefore surprising. This element of surprise sets the stage for learning.

In Rescorla's view, when individuals are surprised by the appearance of the UCS, they try to figure out how to predict when the UCS may appear again. If they succeed in predicting the UCS, it will not surprise them in the future. Being able to predict the appearance of the UCS makes it easier to understand the environment.

For example, suppose that Irena is strongly attracted to Tom, who is in her chemistry class. One afternoon, while she is in the library, she hears someone clearing his throat and looks up to see Tom glancing at her. The next afternoon, she shows up at the library again, she hears someone clear his throat, and she looks up and finds Tom looking her way again. When a CS contingently predicts the occurrence of the UCS, learning occurs easily and rapidly. For Irena, hearing someone clear his throat in the library seems accurately to predict the appearance of Tom. (Irena soon becomes a regular afternoon visitor to the library. When Irena and Tom finally start dating each other, they both confess to having rarely visited the library prior to that first accidental meeting.) To summarize, individuals learn to associate a CS (e.g., hearing someone clear his throat in the library) with a UCS (e.g., feeling excited by seeing an attractive person) because the first stimulus accurately predicts the occurrence of the second one.

Phases and Features of Classical Conditioning

Phases of Classical Conditioning

Given a contingent relationship between the CS and the UCS, the likelihood that learning will occur increases over learning trials. The time when the probability of learning increases is the acquisition phase of learning. During this phase, the individual acquires the CR to the CS. Eventually, at the peak of the **acquisition** phase, the CR reaches its most stable probability of occurrence (see Figure 6-2).

After the individual acquires the CR to the CS, what happens if the CS and the UCS become unlinked? That is, what would happen if the CS were to continue to be presented, but in the absence of the UCS? For example, suppose that a buzzer (CS) that previously had gone off before a shock (UCS) no longer was followed by a shock. What would happen at this time? Gradually, the probability of the CR occurring would go down until it almost completely vanished. This phase of learning is the **extinction** phase: The probability of the CR decreases over time, eventually approaching zero. A curve showing the CR during extinction would start out at high levels, then it would go down gradually until the CR seemed to disappear altogether (see Figure 6-2).

The term *extinction* may be somewhat misleading. It might seem that an extinguished CR would completely disappear forever, as if the CR had never existed at

MINILECTURE
Bedwetting (Ch 7)

acquisition phase of learning during which the probability of learning increases

extinction phase of learning when the probability of the CR decreases over time, eventually approaching zero

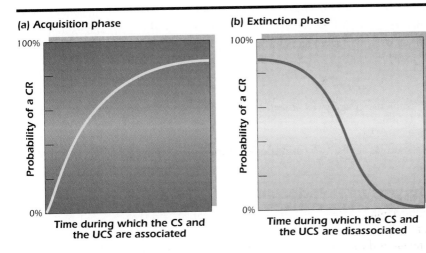

(a) Acquisition phase

Probability of a CR

100%

0%

Time during which the CS and
the UCS are associated

(b) Extinction phase

Probability of a CR

100%

0%

Time during which the CS and
the UCS are disassociated

Figure 6-2
Phases of Classical Conditioning
Once a learner acquires a CR (during the acquisition phase), if the CS and the UCS are uncoupled, the CR may be extinguished (during the extinction phase).

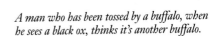

MINILECTURE
Phases of Classical Conditioning (Ch 7)

all. That is not quite the case. The CR may be extinguished, but the memory of the learning has not been erased completely, and an individual still can be stimulated to show the behavior again.

Features of Classical Conditioning

Sometimes, when an individual acquires a CR to one particular CS, stimuli that are similar to the original CS also lead to the CR. When stimuli similar to the CS also lead to the CR, **stimulus generalization** has occurred. For example, suppose that particular ice cream–loving participants are classically conditioned to learn that a particular bell always rings before the appearance of ice cream. Even if the pitch of the bell is changed very slightly, the ice cream–loving participants probably will be about as likely to show the CR as if they had heard the original CS bell.

However, as the bell's sound is changed more and more so that the sound is less and less like the sound of the original bell, the participants are less and less likely to show the CR to the sound of the new bell. The process by which an individual increasingly is able to distinguish the new stimulus from the original CS is **stimulus discrimination.** The more the new stimulus differs from the original CS, the less likely it is that the new stimulus will lead to the CR.

As stimuli become less similar to the CS, stimulus discrimination becomes more likely, stimulus generalization becomes less likely, and the likelihood of a CR decreases. Conversely, as stimuli become more similar to the CS, stimulus generalization becomes more likely, stimulus discrimination becomes less likely, and the

A man who has been tossed by a buffalo, when he sees a black ox, thinks it's another buffalo.

Kenyan proverb

stimulus generalization response to the observed similarity of a stimulus to the CS, thereby increasing the likelihood that the CR will occur following presentation of the stimulus

stimulus discrimination response to the observed difference between a new stimulus and the original CS, which makes it less likely that the new stimulus will lead to the CR

Diane Berry and Leslie McArthur (1986; McArthur & Berry, 1987) have found an interesting illustration of stimulus generalization. It appears that both Korean and American adults expect that adults with childlike facial qualities (i.e., baby-faced adults) will show childlike psychological qualities. That is, we generalize from one stimulus (infants' and young children's faces) to similar stimuli (i.e., adult faces with features similar to those of infants and young children).

likelihood of a CR increases. To summarize, increased stimulus similarity leads to increased stimulus generalization, which leads to an increased likelihood of a CR; in contrast, decreased stimulus similarity leads to increased stimulus discrimination, which leads to a decreased likelihood that a CR will occur:

more   **more**   higher

stimulus similarity → **stimulus generalization** → likelihood of CR

less   **more**   lower

stimulus similarity → **stimulus discrimination** → likelihood of CR

Surprising Relationships Between the Stimulus and the Response

MINILECTURE
*Generalization and Discrimination
(Cb 7)*

Up to this point, we have described conditioned and unconditioned stimuli that have had only an arbitrary relationship to each other. In these instances, prior to classical conditioning, there is no meaningful connection between the conditioned and the unconditioned stimuli. For example, there is no particular reason to link a tone with an electric shock, except when the presence of one appears to be contingent on the presence of the other. Does it make any difference if the CS and the UCS also seem to have some natural or meaningful relationship to each other, in addition to their contingently conditioned relationship? Yes.

John Garcia and Robert Koelling (1966) surprised other behaviorists when they showed that some CS–UCS pairs seem to have a natural relationship that makes it easier to link the two through classical conditioning. At first, Garcia and Koelling rigged their equipment so that whenever a group of experimental rats licked a drinking spout, the rats sensed two types of conditioned stimuli: The rats tasted some flavored liquid, and they also heard a clicking noise accompanied by a flash of light. After licking the spout, some of the rats were mildly poisoned (UCS) (causing them to vomit), whereas other rats were shocked (an alternative UCS). After a number of learning trials for both the poisoned rats and the shocked rats, a new procedure was introduced: The CS of the flavoring was separated from the combined CS using the clicking noise and the flash of light. For each group of rats, on one day, when the rats licked the spout, the rats tasted the flavored liquid without the light and noise. On another day, when the rats licked the spout, they experienced the light and the noise, but the rats tasted only regular tap water instead of the flavored liquid.

The critical finding was that when poison was the UCS, taste was a more effective CS than was the combination of light and noise. In contrast, when electric shock was the UCS, the "bright, noisy water" was a more effective CS than was the flavored liquid. In other words, there was a natural association between taste and poison. Similarly, there was a natural link between electric shock and the combination of the light and sound. Subsequent research (e.g., Holder, Bermudez-Rattoni, & Garcia, 1988; Holder et al., 1989) has confirmed that taste and illness are easily linked, as are noise and shock, but noise and illness generally fail to produce learned associations.

When Garcia and Koelling found that a natural association between the CS and the UCS could affect classical conditioning, they surprised the scientific community. Garcia had yet another surprise for fellow psychologists: Conditioning could occur after only a single learning trial. Garcia found that rats showed a CR to the flavored liquid after just one experience in which they were poisoned after drinking the liquid. Garcia's finding was so unexpected that many people did not want to believe—and did not believe—his results (Garcia, 1981). As someone outside the field of behaviorism, how surprising do you consider Garcia's findings to be? Think about your own reactions to foods that have made you ill. Have you ever experienced the *Garcia effect*, in which you have learned to avoid a particular food because of a past, single unpleasant association?

What everyday stimulus–response pairs do you believe would effectively lead to strong associations? Describe an everyday situation in which one of these stimulus–response pairs might actually lead to a conditioned association.

Although John Garcia and Robert Koelling's findings may not have been welcomed with open arms by their fellow behaviorists, sheep ranchers soon learned to appreciate their findings (Gustavson & Garcia, 1974; Gustavson & Nicolaus, 1987). Coyotes such as the one shown here normally love to prey on sheep. On the other hand, the coyotes also prey on the rabbits that gobble up the sheep's grass, so it is counterproductive to wipe out the coyote population altogether. Instead, ranchers can taint the lamb meat with lithium chloride, which sickens but does not kill the coyotes. After a sickening feast of tainted lamb, the coyotes turn their attention away from the sheep and toward the grass-munching rabbits. Similar strategies have been used to deter mongooses from eating the eggs of endangered species (Nicolaus & Nellis, 1987), crows from eating chicken eggs (Nicolaus et al.,1983), and even rats from eating food grains (Nicolaus et al.,1989).

The Garcia effect illustrates how classical conditioning may have served an adaptive purpose for animals across the span of evolutionary history: Suppose that Bobo and Bibi get sick after eating rotten fruit; Bibi learns to stop eating rotten fruit, but Bobo does not. Bobo probably will not end up mating and producing as many offspring as Bibi does. Classical conditioning also seems to serve some other adaptive purposes, such as helping some animals to perform more effectively some behaviors related to survival. For example, Karen Hollis and her colleagues (Hollis, 1990; Hollis, Cadieux, & Colbert, 1989; Hollis et al., 1984; Hollis, ten Cate, & Bateson, 1991) have observed that through classical conditioning, animals may become more alert to cues signaling the presence of territorial intruders or of potential reproductive partners.

Psychologists have found that in addition to classical conditioning, an entirely different type of conditioning further lends itself to a wide assortment of practical uses. This other type of associative learning, when understood and applied appropriately, further expands the possibilities for improving people's lives.

What is classical conditioning? In classical conditioning, individuals learn to associate a stimulus that causes a physiological or emotional response with a second stimulus, which is originally neutral. At first, the second stimulus produces no particular response, but when the second stimulus contingently predicts the occurrence of the original stimulus, the individual is conditioned such that the second stimulus alone prompts the physiological or emotional response. In classical conditioning, responses may be acquired or extinguished. Particular stimuli may lead to generalization or to discrimination. Some stimuli and responses show a natural relationship and are readily associated, whereas others are less readily linked. Classical conditioning has broad applications.

PRACTICAL PSYCHOLOGY   6-1

Classical Conditioning and Emotional Responses

Although the principles of classical conditioning have been studied mostly in the laboratory, using animal subjects, these principles also apply to humans in everyday situations outside of the laboratory. Psychologists have explained many psychological phenomena—such as emotional responses—in terms of classical conditioning. For instance, we can become conditioned to feel both *fear* (a specific frightened feeling about a particular object, such as an injection needle) and *anxiety* (a more generalized feeling of unease about a situation or an experience, such as feeling anxious in the dark). When a conditioned stimulus (e.g., the sight or sound of a dog) is linked to a fearsome unconditioned stimulus (e.g., a dog's bite), we begin to feel fearful of the conditioned stimulus, too. Classical conditioning may account for many of our other emotional responses, as well, such as disgust, anger, or joy.

Most *conditioned emotional responses* (sometimes called "CERs") are linked to distinctive physiological (bodily) feelings. For example, most of us have experienced something akin to the Garcia effect. We are especially likely to consider a particular food distasteful if we feel nauseous after eating it, although other responses (e.g., breathing difficulties, diarrhea, or rashes) may also motivate us to avoid eating the particular food (Pelchat & Rozin, 1982). The mere sight or smell or even mention of the offending food disgusts us (an emotional reaction), making our stomachs queasy (a physiological reaction).

CERs need not be negative. For example, as you see your loved one approach, you may feel joyful, tingling from head to toe, due to previous pleasurable experiences with that person. Positive emotions are also frequently prompted by catchy television advertisements, which use classical-conditioning techniques for associating positive emotions with particular products or services. TV advertisers know how to use classical conditioning to appeal to our appetites for food and for sexual gratification, leading us to associate satisfaction with new cars, perfumes, cosmetics, and foods of every shape, smell, texture, and color. What do advertisers expect you to learn about a product by watching a sexy driver steering a flashy convertible on a narrow road winding around a cliff?

WHAT IS OPERANT CONDITIONING?

Imagine a hungry cat in the puzzle box shown in Figure 6-3. The cat inside the puzzle box can see and smell a piece of fish just outside the box. The cat tries to reach the fish through the openings in the box, but its paws cannot reach the fish. At first, the cat starts scratching, bumping, and jumping around the box, with no luck. Eventually, however, it happens to release the latch, simply through trial-and-error. When the latch gives way, the door to the puzzle box opens, and the cat runs to get the fish. Later, the cat is placed again in the box, and the whole process is repeated. This time, the scratching and jumping around do not last very long before the cat manages to open the box. "After many trials, the cat will, when put in the box, immediately claw the button or loop in a definite way" (Thorndike, 1898, p. 13) to release the latch, thereby opening the puzzle box, to get the fish.

Now imagine another situation. Joe wants to go to an action-adventure movie with his friend, Suzi, but Suzi wants to go dancing. Their voices get louder and angrier as they argue more and more heatedly. They are getting nowhere. Finally, Suzi gives in, saying that their friendship is worth a lot more to her than going

Figure 6-3
Thorndike's Puzzle Box
Imagine being a hungry cat, trapped inside one of Edward Lee Thorndike's various puzzle boxes. Outside your puzzle box, just out of reach, is some delicious fish. Unfortunately, the door is held tightly shut by a simple latch. After many attempts to get the puzzle box to burst open, you accidentally release the triggering device (a button, a loop, a string, or whatever else Thorndike thought to use), and the door to your puzzle box opens easily, allowing you to leap to the fish. The next time you are trapped in the puzzle box, what will you do?

dancing. Much to Suzi's surprise, Joe looks her straight in the eye and suggests that they go dancing after all. The next time the two disagree about what to do, they argue again, but for a shorter time. Suzi again gives in for the sake of the friendship, and again Joe goes along with her preference. The next time, there is no argument. Suzi immediately asserts the value of the friendship after stating her preference, and Joe immediately agrees with her. Suzi has learned how to avoid conflict and at the same time to get what she wants.

Thorndike's Law of Effect

Both of the preceding situations—with the hungry cat and with Joe and Suzi's friendship—involve operant conditioning. The study of operant conditioning is usually viewed as starting with Edward Lee Thorndike (1874–1949). Through the experiments such as the one with the cat in the puzzle box, Thorndike (1898, 1911) discovered the basic phenomenon of operant conditioning. **Operant conditioning** (also termed *instrumental conditioning*) is learning that occurs when an individual produces an active behavioral response (an *operant*), which is followed by an environmental stimulus, which influences the likelihood that the response will be repeated again in the future. In operant conditioning, some environmental outcomes tend to strengthen active behavior (making it more likely to occur again in the future), and other outcomes tend to weaken it (making it less likely to occur again in the future). For the hungry cat, getting to reach the fish strengthened the cat's operant behavior—namely, opening the puzzle-box latch. For Suzi, getting to go dancing strengthened her operant behavior—namely, making conflict-avoiding statements to Joe.

Thorndike proposed a mechanism to account for operant conditioning, which he termed the *law of effect*. According to Thorndike, much of our behavior constitutes random, trial-and-error exploration of the environment. Occasionally, our actions result in a reward—an outcome with pleasurable consequences. At other times, our actions result in a punishment—an outcome with unpleasant and unwanted consequences. According to Thorndike's law of effect, the outcomes of particular actions will influence the likelihood that the actions will be repeated again in the future. Actions that are rewarded will tend to be strengthened and thereby will become more likely to occur in the future; in contrast, actions that are punished will tend to be weakened and thus will be less likely to occur in the future.

How might you apply the law of effect to your own experiences? If you reward your friend for doing you a favor, your friend is more likely to do you a favor again in the future. For example, if your friend helps you move into a new apartment, you might reward your friend by treating her or him to a meal or to a fun

operant conditioning process of increasing or decreasing the likelihood that an individual will produce an active behavior (an operant) as a result of interacting with the environment

activity as soon as you finish moving in. For behavior you wish to reinforce, you may use reinforcers, and for behavior you wish to eliminate or at least reduce, you may use punishment. For instance, if you punish your roommate for leaving dirty dishes on the floor (e.g., by placing a stack of dirty dishes by your roommate's bed), your roommate is less likely to leave dirty dishes on the floor again in the future. (Using punishment is a little more tricky than using rewards, however. For example, if your roommate's personality resembles that of Freddy Krueger, you may find that your roommate will respond to punishment in ways that you will not like.)

The main difference between classical and operant conditioning is in the role of the individual:

■ In classical conditioning, the individual is largely *passive:* The experimenter or the environment controls the reinforcement schedule—for example, by repeatedly pairing a CS with a UCS.

■ In operant conditioning, the individual is largely *active:* The individual operates on the environment in order to create reinforcement.

In addition, each of the two kinds of conditioning (also known as "associative learning") centers around a different key association:

■ In classical conditioning, the crucial association for conditioning is between the *conditioned stimulus* (something you sense, e.g., the smell of coffee) and the *unconditioned stimulus* (something that prompts a physiological or emotional response, e.g., the caffeine in coffee).

■ In operant conditioning, the fundamental association is between a *behavioral response* (something you do, e.g., calling a pizza-delivery service) and an *environmental stimulus* (something that influences whether the behavioral response will be repeated, e.g., receiving a pizza to eat) affecting the probability of the response.

Operant conditioning is of great importance in our lives, literally from the day we are born: Parents reward some actions and punish others in order to get their children to behave in ways that the parents prefer. Parents hope that rewards will strengthen the behavior they like and that punishments will weaken the behavior they do not like. The same basic procedures are used in school: Some kinds of behavior are rewarded by nods, good grades, and so on, whereas other kinds of behavior result in being kept away from other students, being sent to the principal's office, and so on.

Reinforcement

In the study of operant conditioning, an **operant** is a *response* that has some effect on the world. Asking for help, drinking a glass of water, threatening to hurt someone, kissing your lover—all of these are operants. Operant conditioning leads to either an increase or a decrease in the probability that these operant behaviors will be performed again.

A **reinforcer** is a *stimulus* that increases the probability that the operant associated with the stimulus will happen again. (Usually, the response has occurred immediately or almost immediately before the reinforcing stimulus.) Reinforcers can be either positive or negative. A **positive reinforcer** is a reward (or any pleasing stimulus) that follows an operant and strengthens the associated behavioral response. Examples of positive reinforcers are a smile or compliment following something we say or do, or a candy bar released by a vending machine after we put in the required change. When a positive reinforcer (stimulus) occurs soon after an operant (response), the pairing of the two is termed **positive reinforcement.**

Negative reinforcement is the removal or the stopping of an unpleasant stimulus, such as physical or psychological pain or discomfort. Examples of negative reinforcements are having someone stop hurting you or being allowed to

The cattle [are] as good as the pasture in which [they graze].

Ethiopian proverb

operant a *response* that has some effect on the world

reinforcer a *stimulus* that increases the probability that the operant associated with it will be repeated

positive reinforcer a reward (pleasant stimulus) that follows an operant and strengthens the associated behavioral response

positive reinforcement presentation of a positive reinforcer (stimulus) soon after an operant (response)

negative reinforcement removal or cessation (stopping) of an unpleasant stimulus, such as physical or psychological pain or discomfort

TABLE 6-2

Examples of Negative Reinforcement

Negative reinforcer	Operant behavior	Negative reinforcement
An intensely noisy environment	Put in ear plugs	Relief from noise
A mildly annoying noisy environment	Put on headphones that play soothing music	
A loudly wailing ambulance passes by	Cover your ears with your hands	
Physical pain	Take analgesics; use biofeedback techniques; get acupuncture treatments	Relief from pain or discomfort
Traumatic injury, discomfort, or disease	Seek a physician's aid	
Mildly burned skin	Run cold water over burned area of skin	
Bright sunlight	Wear sunglasses	Relief from overly intense light

escape from an uncomfortable or unpleasant situation. The **negative reinforcer** is the unpleasant stimulus that is removed, thereby leading to an increased probability that an operant response will be repeated. Whether it is negative or positive, reinforcement always strengthens a response. Just as steel reinforcers may be used to strengthen concrete, operant reinforcers may be used to strengthen the likelihood of operant behavior. Table 6-2 shows several examples of negative reinforcement.

Punishment

Punishment is the delivery of a stimulus that *decreases* the probability of an associated response; punishment involves either presenting an unpleasant stimulus or removing a pleasant one. (In contrast, negative reinforcement *increases* the likelihood of a response by removing or at least reducing the impact of an unpleasant stimulus.) Examples of punishment include being hit, scolded, humiliated, or laughed *at* (not *with*); being restricted from an enjoyable activity such as viewing television or visiting with friends; or receiving a failing grade in a course or a negative evaluation from a work supervisor. The aversive stimulus is called a *punisher*.

Frequently, punishment is used for **aversive conditioning,** a means of encouraging an individual to try to escape from or to avoid a situation. The goal of aversive conditioning is **avoidance learning,** whereby an individual learns to stay away from something. Individuals can learn to avoid a particular behavior by being aversively conditioned to avoid that behavior. For example, rats can learn to avoid scratching at a door latch if they are shocked every time they scratch the latch. Sometimes, the aversive conditioning that leads to avoidance learning also may lead to classical conditioning. Specifically, the object or situation that the individual is being conditioned to avoid may serve as a conditioned stimulus for a fear response. For example, in the case of rats that learn to avoid scratching at a latch, the rats also may learn to feel fearful of the latch or even of the area near the latch. Operant conditioning through the use of punishment leads to the *behavioral outcome of avoidance,* and the classical conditioning that may accompany it leads to an *emotional and physiological response of fear.* Thus, the two forms of learning may interact cooperatively to strengthen the outcome.

Consequences of Punishment: Intended and Unintended

In general, punishment is less effective in achieving behavioral change than is positive reinforcement (Sulzer-Azaroff & Mayer, 1991). In addition, punishment may lead to several unintended consequences (Bongiovanni, 1977), such as the following ones:

Do not call to a dog with a whip in your hand.

Zululand proverb

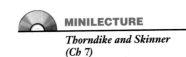

MINILECTURE

Thorndike and Skinner
(Ch 7)

negative reinforcer an unpleasant stimulus that is removed following an operant response, thereby leading to an increased probability that the operant will be repeated

punishment delivery of a stimulus that *decreases* the probability of an associated response; involves either presenting an unpleasant stimulus or removing a pleasant one

aversive conditioning use of punishment as a means of encouraging an individual to try to escape from or to avoid a situation

avoidance learning the goal of aversive conditioning: an individual learns to stay away from something

Describe a situation in which a child might try to avoid punishment, but the child might do so despite continuing to engage in the behavior that led to the punishment. How could you modify the child's behavior, perhaps by using positive reinforcement?

What are some undesirable outcomes of punishment that you have observed in your own experience?

1. Although punishment does lead a person to try to avoid punishment, the person may find some way to avoid the punishment or to reduce its effects, without necessarily avoiding the undesired behavior.

2. Punishment can increase the likelihood that the person being punished will show an increase in aggressive behavior. That is, the person being punished may imitate the punishing behavior in other interactions, such as through physical aggression (Vissing et al., 1991). An example of this pattern might be as follows: Kim's boss yells at Kim, Kim goes home and screams at her child, her child howls at the family dog, and the dog growls at the family cat.

3. The punished person may be injured. Punishment becomes child abuse when the child is damaged, physically or psychologically—an unfortunately common occurrence (Gelles & Straus, 1988).

4. Punishment may lead to extreme fear of the punishing person and context. This fear may in turn lead to problems in the relationship between the punished person and the punishing person or situation. Sometimes, the fear even worsens the unwanted behavior. For example, screaming at a child who scores poorly on a test may increase the child's feelings of test anxiety, which may cause further lowering of the child's test scores.

Despite the potential problems of using punishment, punishment can be made more effective by using it carefully (Park & Walters, 1967; Walters & Grusec, 1977).

BRANCHING OUT: Enhancing the Effectiveness of Punishment

Although there are many potential problems of using punishment, punishment can be made more effective by taking the following steps.

■ Make it easy for the punished individual to choose other responses to replace the responses that are being punished. A Kenyan proverb suggests the intuitive wisdom of this strategy: "When you take a knife away from a child, give him a piece of wood instead."

■ In addition to using punishment, use positive reinforcement to encourage the punished individual to choose to repeat a more desirable operant behavior.

■ Make sure that the individual being punished knows exactly what behavior is being punished and why.

■ Carry out the punishment *immediately* after the undesirable operant behavior.

■ Choose a punishment that is strong enough and that lasts long enough to stop the undesirable behavior, but that is no stronger and lasts no longer than is necessary.

■ Try to ensure that it is impossible to escape punishment at any time that the individual shows the operant behavior.

■ Prefer the use of *penalties*—removal of pleasant stimuli—to the use of physical or emotional pain as punishments.

■ Take advantage of the natural tendency to try to escape from and to avoid punishment: Use punishment when you want the punished person to try to escape from or to avoid a particular situation (e.g., teaching a child to seek escape from dangerous places or to avoid dangerous objects).

Learned Helplessness

An additional possible consequence of punishment deserves special attention because of its far-reaching implications. This consequence is the phenomenon of

learned helplessness, in which an individual is operantly conditioned to act (and perhaps to feel) helpless to do anything to avoid an unpleasant situation. Martin Seligman and Steven Maier (Seligman, 1975; Seligman & Maier, 1967) discovered learned helplessness when studying two groups of dogs. The dogs were placed in an electrified chamber where the dogs received painful (but not harmful) electric shocks. In the first group, the dogs were unable to escape the shock, despite their efforts to do so. Later, the chamber was divided into two parts, with a barrier separating the two parts. In this divided chamber, only one part was electrified to deliver shocks, so that the dogs could have escaped the shocks simply by jumping over the barrier into the nonelectrified part of the chamber. However, because these dogs had previously learned that they could not escape, they did not even try to escape. They just whined helplessly. They appeared to believe that escape from pain was impossible.

In contrast, a second group of dogs was not forced to stay in an undivided chamber in which the dogs were unable to escape shocks. Rather, these other dogs were placed only in the divided chamber, and the shock was turned on in only one part of the chamber. As soon as the dogs in this second group saw the barrier, they jumped over it, escaping the shocks. Whenever the shock was turned on, these dogs quickly jumped the barrier, thereby spending as little time as possible feeling any pain.

Apparently, the first group of dogs had learned to feel helpless to do anything about their situation. For these dogs, their learned feelings of helplessness were caused by their previous inability to escape the pain. In contrast, the second group of dogs, which had not learned to feel helpless, quickly learned how to escape the painful shocks. Observers of just this second group of dogs might leap to the conclusion that virtually all animals would try to escape from pain, without considering their previous experiences. The observers would be wrong.

Humans are also subject to the effects of learned helplessness. We try something; we fail. Maybe we try again and fail again. Soon we have learned that we cannot perform that task or master that skill; as a result, we never try again. The child who fails in school and the adult who fails on the job may learn to feel helpless. Our past conditioning may tell us that we cannot succeed. Some people stop accepting new challenges because they have learned to feel helpless to avoid any unwanted consequences of challenging situations.

Both Maier and Seligman have extended their work in learned helplessness, exploring how learned helplessness may influence other psychological phenomena. Maier and his colleagues (Maier, Watkins, & Fleshner, 1994) have studied how learned helplessness may influence the immune system, suppressing its defensive responses against disease. Seligman (1989) has suggested that learned helplessness may play a key role in depression, and other researchers have expanded Seligman's notion by proposing a specific type of depression known as "hopelessness depression" (Abramson, Metalsky, & Alloy, 1989).

It is beyond a doubt that all our knowledge begins with experience.

Immanuel Kant

How Is Operant Conditioning Implemented?

Discriminating Between Reinforcement and Punishment

To summarize what we know about reinforcement and punishment, reinforcement *increases* the probability of some future response; punishment *decreases* it. Reinforcement can involve presenting a rewarding stimulus (positive reinforcement, e.g., smiles or candy) or removing an unpleasant stimulus (negative reinforcement, e.g., relief from pain or discomfort). Similarly, punishment can involve the presentation of an unpleasant and unwanted stimulus (e.g., a scolding) or the removal of a rewarding one (i.e., a penalty, e.g., the revoking of driving privileges). In other words, both forms of reinforcement (positive or negative) teach the person what to do, whereas punishment teaches the learner what *not* to do. Table 6-3 summarizes these differences.

learned helplessness a learned behavior in which an individual gives up trying to escape a painful situation after repeatedly failing to escape

TABLE 6-3
Summary of Operant Conditioning

Operant conditioning technique	Stimulus introduced in the environment as an outcome of operant behavior	Effect of stimulus on operant response
Positive reinforcement	*Positive reinforcer*—pleasant stimulus	Strengthens and increases the likelihood of the operant behavior
Negative reinforcement	*Negative reinforcer*—unpleasant stimulus (that is removed)	Strengthens and increases the likelihood of the operant behavior
Punishment	*Punisher*—unpleasant stimulus	Weakens and decreases the likelihood of the operant behavior

"Remember, every time he gives you a pellet reinforce that behavior by pulling the lever."

© 1994 Joe Dator/The Cartoon Bank, Inc.

How could adults who are trying to influence the behavior of adolescents benefit from knowing about gradients of reinforcement? How could they use such knowledge to help adolescents avoid the dangers of illegal drugs or unsafe sexual practices? Give specific suggestions.

gradient of reinforcement phenomenon in which increases in the length of time between an operant and a reinforcer directly decrease the effect of the reinforcement

The Gradient of Reinforcement: Effects of Delays

When implementing either reinforcement or punishment, an important consideration is the **gradient of reinforcement:** The longer we wait to reinforce (or to punish) a given operant, the weaker the effect of the reinforcement (or punishment) will be. This principle is important both for establishing behavior and for suppressing it. For example, if parents want to change their children's behavior (e.g., to get a child to put away toys), the parents should reinforce the desired behavior immediately after it occurs. If, instead, the parents reward the children for the desired behavior long after it occurs, the parents will be ineffective in changing it. Hence, a father who tells a child that she will be rewarded for her excellent behavior when her mother comes home is reducing the effectiveness of the reinforcement by having the child wait for hours before receiving it.

The effectiveness of reinforcement generally *decreases* rapidly as the time between the response and the reinforcement *increases*. This decreased effectiveness may be because the passage of time quickly weakens the link between the reinforcement and the behavior it reinforces. As time passes, many other stimuli may appear between the response and the reinforcing stimulus.

The gradient of reinforcement seems to play a key role in the sexual behavior and contraceptive practices of adolescent girls (Loewenstein & Furstenberg, 1991). Specifically, when adolescent girls are making decisions regarding their own behavior, they may find the reinforcing benefits of unprotected sexual activity to be immediate and certain (e.g., getting and perhaps keeping the attention of an attractive member of the opposite sex). On the other hand, the reinforcing benefits of contraception and of abstinence are delayed and uncertain (e.g., avoiding unwanted pregnancy or sexually transmitted disease).

For persons of all ages, *increases* in the delay time between an operant behavior and an environmental reinforcer lead to *decreases* in the strength of the conditioning. Children have particular difficulty with tolerating delays between the operant behavior and the presentation of the reinforcement. When offered access to immediate reinforcers, such as food or toys, children often find it particularly difficult to *delay gratification;* that is, they do not easily postpone their enjoyment of immediate reinforcers in order to receive some other (usually greater) reward at a future time. Even when a future reward is much more appealing than a present one, children often have difficulty delaying gratification (Rodriguez, Mischel, & Shoda, 1989). Children who can divert their attention away from attractive items seem better able to delay gratification. Similarly, children are better able to delay gratification when they know that it is easier to delay gratification if they avoid thinking about the desirable characteristics of the coveted items.

Until children develop their own strategies for delaying gratification, adults may need to help them to divert their attention away from appealing immediate reinforcers and toward other activities or objects. An additional means of enhancing self-control in delaying gratification is to increase the perceived difference between the delayed reinforcer and the immediate reinforcer. Even adults will be more likely to delay gratification when they perceive that a delay will lead to a much greater reward (King & Logue, 1987; Logue et al., 1990).

Primary and Secondary Reinforcers

In the laboratory, researchers can provide **primary reinforcers,** which are immediately satisfying or enjoyable rewards, such as food, water, or comfort. In most situations outside the laboratory, however, it is not practical to provide primary reinforcers for every operant behavior we want to encourage. At the very least, primary reinforcement must often be delayed. How do we use operant conditioning when we cannot provide immediate primary reinforcers? We offer **secondary reinforcers,** which have reinforcing value only through their association with primary reinforcers. Secondary reinforcers may include money, good grades, high-status objects, praise, and other rewards that have become attached to primary reinforcers.

A secondary reinforcer that works well for people of all ages is sincere praise. In a study of elementary and junior high students, researchers were able to reduce school vandalism by an average of more than 75% and to obtain significant improvements in classroom behavior simply by increasing the reinforcing properties of the school, such as the rates at which teachers praised their students at treatment schools, as compared with control schools where extra praise was not given (Mayer, et al.,1983). In contrast, the use of *destructive criticism* (which is inconsiderate and nonspecific, and which attributes poor performance to intrinsic characteristics of the individual) leads to anger, tension, resistance, and avoidance in college students and other adults (Baron, 1988).

Successive Approximations: The Shaping of Behavior

Sometimes, it is easy to see how to encourage an individual to behave in a particular way: Just wait for the desired behavior to occur, and then reinforce it immediately and powerfully. However, not all desirable behavior is likely to occur by chance. For example, how do you get someone to start washing the dishes when the person never goes near the kitchen? When the behavior is complex or is very different from the normal behavior of the individual, can we realistically expect the behavior to occur by chance? We cannot. Instead, we can **shape** behavior through the method of **successive approximations,** in which we gradually reinforce a series of actions that increasingly approach the behavior we want to obtain. This method is used for training animals, such as in circuses and other shows.

To implement this method, you first reward a very rough beginning step for performing the behavior of interest (e.g., praising a reluctant dish-washer for going near the kitchen). After a while, that first rough step toward the behavior is established. Next, you begin to look for some changes so that the observed behavior comes a little closer to the desired behavior, and you reward only those closer steps toward the desired behavior (e.g., moving toward the kitchen sink). You continue with this procedure, getting closer and closer to the desired behavior until you finally condition the individual to show the desired behavior (e.g., actually washing a few grimy dishes).

Sometimes people try to shape their own behavior through **autoshaping.** If so, they may set up a system of reinforcements that results in gradual behavioral change. For example, if you want to increase how much you exercise, you might create a system of rewards in which at first you would reward yourself for small amounts of exercise each week. Then you would gradually increase the amount of exercise you required of yourself in order to get the reward.

American corporate investors are often accused of seeking short-term boosts in profits each quarter, rather than trying to increase their profits over the long term, particularly if the long-term increases would mean lower short-term profits. How would behavioral psychologists explain this tendency?

She who does not yet know how to walk cannot climb a ladder.

Ethiopian proverb

primary reinforcer stimulus that provides an immediate reward that satisfies the senses

secondary reinforcer stimulus that gains reinforcing value through association with a primary reinforcer

shape bring behavior under control by providing a program of reinforcement

successive approximations a method for shaping behavior by gradually reinforcing operants that are increasingly more similar to the desired behavior

autoshaping a system of reinforcements that individuals design for themselves, to lead to gradual behavioral change

Schedules of Reinforcement

Up to now, we have discussed **continuous reinforcement,** whereby a reinforcement always follows a particular operant behavior. A continuous **schedule of reinforcement** (timing of reinforcers in relation to operants) is fairly easy to establish in a laboratory, but it is actually quite rare in everyday life. People who behave in desirable ways are not always rewarded, and people who misbehave are not always punished. In normal everyday life, we are much more likely to face a **partial-reinforcement schedule** (also termed an *intermittent-reinforcement schedule*), in which an operant is reinforced only part of the time. Luckily, operant responses that are strengthened by partial-reinforcement schedules are less easily extinguished than operant responses that rely on continuous schedules of reinforcement.

Partial reinforcement may be given either after a particular number of operant responses (e.g., treating yourself to a rest break after you read 20 pages of your chemistry textbook) or after a particular amount of time has passed during which an operant response has been shown (e.g., treating yourself to a rest break after you read your physics textbook for 30 minutes). In general, a higher rate of responding occurs when the reinforcement is tied to the number of responses, rather than to an interval of time. In addition, the strength of an operant response will be at a more consistently high rate if the reinforcement is given after a variable number of responses (e.g., winning a bet after placing between 1 and 50 bets), rather than after a fixed number of responses (e.g., receiving 1 free item for buying 25 items).

Skinner and the Experimental Analysis of Behavior

The psychologist who may have done the most to promote the study and application of operant conditioning was B. F. Skinner (1904–1990), who developed the theory and methods for the experimental analysis of behavior. Skinner (e.g., 1988) believed that all behavior should be studied and analyzed in terms of reinforcement contingencies. He particularly valued the observation of animal behavior, which can be experimentally analyzed more easily than can human behavior.

To Skinner (e.g., 1986), what mattered were the contingent reinforcements that produce various patterns of behavior, regardless of what might go on inside the head of the individual producing the behavior. When Skinner defined the problem of understanding human behavior only in terms of reinforcement contingencies, he more narrowly limited the field of psychology than most psychologists typically do now. In fact, even many contemporary behaviorists find Skinner's radical behaviorism to be too extreme (e.g., Amsel, 1992).

On the other hand, many present-day psychologists still agree with Skinner's belief that behaviorism can be applied to many of society's problems. For instance, operant conditioning continues to offer many practical uses in managing the behavior of persons in institutional settings (e.g., prisons, mental hospitals, and custodial or residential facilities for persons who cannot care for themselves for various reasons). For example, caregivers have successfully used operant conditioning to decrease the frequency with which some individuals engage in self-injurious behavior (e.g., head-hitting) (Linscheid, Hartel, & Cooley, 1993). Surprisingly, when mildly aversive shocks are administered after an individual attempts to engage in self-injurious behavior, the likelihood of further attempts seems to decrease, at least for some persons.

Behavioral psychologists have also addressed a broad range of psychological problems among persons outside of institutional settings. Behavioral treatments have been devised for such diverse disorders as depression, anxiety disorders, schizophrenia (a serious psychological disorder associated with a drastic break from

---

MINILECTURE
Recording Reinforcement Schedules (Ch 7)

Whether behavior analysis will be called psychology is a matter for the future to decide.

B. F. Skinner

continuous reinforcement a learning program in which reinforcement always follows a particular operant behavior

schedules of reinforcement patterns by which reinforcements follow operants

partial-reinforcement schedule an operant-conditioning program in which a given operant is reinforced at some times, but not at other times

B. F. Skinner practiced what he preached. Shown here are his wife and his daughter, Debby, who herself was partially raised in a modified "Skinner box" when she was young.

reality), obesity, anorexia nervosa (an eating disorder), sexual dysfunction, abuse of children or spouses, and substance abuse (Bellack, Hersen, & Kazdin, 1990). In each case, the behavioral psychologist analyzes the behavior of the patient, and then determines appropriate ways to reduce the reinforcement of (or even to punish) unwanted behavior and to use reinforcement to increase the frequency of desirable behavior.

PRACTICAL PSYCHOLOGY 6-2

Putting Operant Conditioning Into Practice

What do we know about how to use operant conditioning? Briefly, to get the greatest benefit from operant conditioning, do the following:

1. To get someone to do something, use reinforcement; to get someone not to do something, use punishment, but be aware that punishment may also lead to some unwanted additional outcomes.
2. To reinforce behavior effectively, offer reinforcers as soon as possible after the desired behavior.
3. When you cannot avoid delay of gratification, try to divert attention away from the desired object, and try to avoid thinking about the object's desirable features.
4. Use successive approximations to shape complex or highly unusual behaviors.
5. Provide reinforcement after particular numbers of operant responses, rather than after particular intervals of time, in order to produce high rates of response. Use variable rather than fixed schedules of reinforcement to obtain more constant rates of response and to encourage greater self-control. Avoid using continuous reinforcement schedules, which are easily subject to extinction.

TABLE 6-4

Comparison of Classical and Operant Conditioning

Characteristics	Classical (or Pavlovian)	Operant (or instrumental)
Key relationship	Conditioned stimulus **and** unconditioned stimulus	Organism's response **and** Environment's stimulus (reinforcement or punishment)
Organism's role	Passively (emotionally or physiologically) responds to stimuli (CS or UCS)	Actively operates on environment
Sequence of events	Initiation of conditioning: CS → UCS → UCR	Operant response → Reinforcement → Increases response probability
	Peak of acquisition phase: CS → CR	Operant response → Punishment → Decreases response probability
Extinction techniques	Uncouple the CS from the UCS, repeatedly presenting the CS in the absence of the UCS	Uncouple the operant response from the stimulus reinforcer or punisher; repeatedly fail to reinforce or to punish the operant behavior

To reinforce what you have learned about operant and classical conditioning before we proceed to considering social influences on learning, it may be helpful to review Table 6-4, which briefly summarizes the features of each type of conditioning.

What is operant conditioning? *Operant conditioning* is learning produced by the active behavior of an individual. Operant actions that are positively or negatively reinforced will tend to be strengthened and thus to be more likely to occur in the future, whereas operants that are punished will tend to be weakened and thus to be less likely to occur in the future. Schedules of reinforcement may be fixed or variable, and they may be tied either to intervals of time or to numbers of operant responses.

Personally, I'm always ready to learn, although I do not always like being taught.

> Winston Churchill

WHAT IS SOCIAL LEARNING?

Suppose that you wanted to teach someone how to do something—to type, to tie her or his shoes, to write a term paper, or whatever. What is the first thing you would do? If you are like most of us, neither classical nor operant conditioning techniques would leap to mind. Instead, you would probably *show* the person what to do, using your own actions as a model for what you wanted the other person to do.

In our everyday lives, we often learn by observing what other people are doing. Through **social learning,** we do not learn directly, but rather by observing others. Is there really any empirical evidence that supports the concept of social learning (also termed *vicarious learning* or *observational learning*)?

Wise [persons] learn by others' mistakes, fools by their own.

> Henry George Bohn

Albert Bandura (1965, 1969, 1986) and his colleagues have performed numerous experiments showing that social learning is an effective way of learning. In a typical experiment, preschool children were shown a film featuring an adult who punched, kicked, hit, and threw things at a large, inflatable *Bobo doll* (see Figure 6-4). The given film ended in one of three different ways, depending on the group

social learning learning that occurs by observing the behavior of others, as well as by observing any environmental outcomes of the behavior

Figure 6-4
Social Learning
In numerous experiments, Albert Bandura has shown that children learn to imitate the behavior of adult models. By observing a video of a woman behaving aggressively toward a Bobo doll, this girl and boy have learned to kick and punch the doll. The doll has a weighted bottom that causes it to bounce back to an upright position after being tipped off balance.

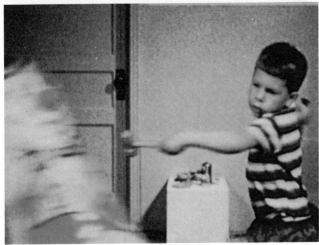

to which a particular child viewer was assigned. In one group, the adult model was rewarded for the aggressive behavior. In a second group, the adult model was punished. In a third (control) group, the adult model was neither rewarded nor punished. After seeing the film, the children were allowed to play with a Bobo doll. Those children who had seen the adult model rewarded for aggressive behavior were more likely than the controls to behave aggressively with the doll, whereas those who had observed the adult model being punished were less likely than the controls to behave aggressively with the doll. Clearly, social learning had taken place.

Other studies show that behavioral reinforcement is not needed for social learning to take place. In another experiment (Bandura, Ross, & Ross, 1963), preschool children watched an adult model either sit quietly next to the Bobo doll or attack it. The adults were neither rewarded nor punished for their behavior. Later, these children were left alone with the doll. As expected, those children who had observed aggressive behavior were more likely to behave aggressively than were the children who saw no aggressive behavior.

What conditions are necessary for social learning to occur? There appear to be four (Bandura, 1977b):

1. *Attention* to the behavior on which the learning might be based
2. *Retention* (memory) of the observed scene when the chance arises later to apply the learning
3. *Motivation* to imitate the observed behavior
4. *Potential reproduction* of the behavior—in other words, the observer must be able to do whatever he or she observed being done

When you follow in the path of your father, you learn to walk like him.

Ashanti proverb

Sometimes, social learning seems to guide us to limit ourselves in terms of the options we feel are available to us. What are some specific ways in which parents can help their children to broaden their horizons through social learning?

In addition, four factors can increase the likelihood that observers will imitate the behavior of a given model: (1) The model stands out in contrast to other competing models; (2) the model is liked and respected by the observer (or by others in the environment); (3) the model is perceived to be similar to the observer, in the eyes of the observer; and (4) the model's behavior is reinforced. Although each of these factors increases the likelihood of social learning, such learning can occur even when these factors are absent.

Social learning is not limited to scenes with Bobo dolls, of course. Many people of all ages spend countless hours in front of televisions watching violent behavior. Considerable evidence suggests that exposure to violent activity on television is linked to aggressive behavior in real life (e.g., Friedrich-Cofer & Huston, 1986; Huesmann, Lagerspetz, & Eron, 1984; Parke et al., 1977). In addition, social learning extends to the development of many other behaviors, such as gender-role behavior, gender expectations, and even gender identity (described in Basow, 1986; Gilly, 1988). Such learning is based on both media images and the behavior of same-sex parents and peers.

Social learning may also lead to behavior that is highly *prosocial* (favorable to society). For instance, during the Nazi Holocaust, many German rescuers showed altruism, risking their own lives and well-being to protect and aid Jews and members of other persecuted groups. In a study of more than 100 such rescuers (Oliner & Oliner, 1993), a common theme emerged, in which the rescuers' early family experiences served as models for their subsequent altruism.

Social learning also seems to influence much more mundane, ordinary behavior, and it occurs in children as young as 9 to 24 months of age. In a pair of studies, children watched adult models demonstrate how to pull apart and put back together a toy designed specifically for these experiments. After observing the adult either in person (9-month-olds) or on television (14- and 24-month-olds), the children imitated the behavior they observed. Even when the children did not have an opportunity to imitate the observed behavior until the next day, they correctly imitated the behavior they had observed (Meltzoff, 1988a, 1988b).

What is social learning? Social learning occurs through observing the behavior of others, assuming that we attend to and remember the observed behavior, and that we are both motivated and able to reproduce the observed behavior. Social learning occurs in people of all ages, and it may apply to a broad range of prosocial, antisocial, and nonsocial behavior, whether observed in person or via a medium such as television or film.

Humans are born with a variety of preprogrammed responses (e.g., habituation and instincts such as in imprinting), but much of what we know we learn as a result of experience, through classical conditioning, operant conditioning, and social learning. In order to learn from experience, we must have some means of remembering our experiences. The many factors that influence our ability to remember what we have learned from experience are the subject of the next chapter.

SUMMARY

What Are Some Preprogrammed Responses?   164

1. *Learning* is a relatively permanent change in behavior, thoughts, or feelings as a result of past experience.

2. *Habituation* and *instincts* such as *imprinting* are preprogrammed responses that are mainly determined by biology (nature), although learning (nurture) may also play a role, particularly in imprinting.

What Is Classical Conditioning?   166

3. Pavlov identified *classical conditioning* when he observed that dogs produced saliva when they sensed stimuli that came before the arrival of meat powder. For example, Pavlov realized that he could condition dogs to produce saliva in response to a sound, a response that would not occur naturally.

4. In classical conditioning, an individual pairs a neutral stimulus with a stimulus that produces an unconditioned physiological or emotional response.

5. In Pavlov's experiment, the dog's salivating for the meat powder was the *unconditioned response* (UCR), the meat powder was the *unconditioned stimulus* (UCS), the buzzer (an originally neutral stimulus) became the *conditioned stimulus* (CS), and the salivation (originally the UCR) in response to the buzzer became the *conditioned response* (CR).

6. In the standard classical conditioning experiment, the start of the CS comes soon before the start of the UCS.

7. *Temporal contiguity* alone does not lead to classical conditioning; in addition, a *contingency* must be established between the stimulus and the response if conditioning is to occur.

8. The phase during which the probability of a CR increases is the *acquisition* phase of learning. If the UCS is not presented with the CS over many learning trials, eventually, the learned response, the CR, is *extinguished*.

9. When individuals respond to stimuli that are similar to the CS, they show *stimulus generalization*. When individuals do not respond to stimuli that differ from the CS, they show *stimulus discrimination*.

10. Individuals seem to be predisposed toward making some associations and not others. For example, for rats who were exposed to poison as the UCS, taste was a more effective CS than was the combination of light and noise.

11. Classical conditioning applies to everyday human experiences. Many of our conditioned emotional responses—such as fear, anxiety, or even joy—are linked to distinctive physiological feelings (e.g., increased heart rate).

What Is Operant Conditioning?   174

12. *Operant conditioning* is learning produced by the active behavior (i.e., an *operant*) of an individual. According to the *law of effect*, operant actions that are rewarded will tend to be strengthened and thus to be more likely to occur in the future, whereas operant actions that are punished will tend to be weakened and thus to be less likely to occur in the future.

13. A *reinforcer* is a stimulus that increases the probability that the operant associated with it will happen again.

14. A *positive reinforcer* is a reward that strengthens an associated response. A *negative reinforcer* is an unpleasant stimulus whose removal strengthens an associated response. *Positive reinforcement* refers to the pairing of a positive reinforcer with an operant. *Negative reinforcement* refers to the pairing of the removal of a negative reinforcer with an operant. Both types of reinforcement are welcomed by the individual and strengthen the associated operant response.

15. *Punishment* is the administration of a stimulus that decreases the probability of a response. Punishment should be administered carefully because it can lead to unwanted consequences.

16. *Avoidance learning* occurs when an individual learns to stay away from something. Under some circumstances, avoidance learning can occur after just a single trial of *aversive conditioning*.

17. Individuals show *learned helplessness* when they feel helpless to escape a painful or otherwise unpleasant stimulus. Individuals learn to feel helpless after they repeatedly fail to escape unpleasant stimuli.

18. The *gradient of reinforcement* is a feature of operant conditioning: the longer the time between the operant behavior and the reinforcement, the weaker the reinforcement.

19. Often, it is not easy to provide *primary reinforcers* (e.g., food and other immediately satisfying or enjoyable rewards). *Secondary reinforcers* (e.g., money, sincere praise, good grades, high-status objects) can provide reinforcement after being associated with primary reinforcers.

20. When *shaping* behavior, the method of *successive approximations* reinforces operant behaviors that are successively closer to the desired behavior. Sometimes a person can change to the desired behavior through *autoshaping*, without help from anyone else.

21. In operant conditioning, *partial reinforcement* may occur after a particular number of operant responses or after a particular interval of time during which operant responses have occurred.

What Is Social Learning?   184

22. When we watch the behaviors of others, as well as the outcomes of those behaviors, we engage in *social learning*. A classic example of social learning is Bandura's experiment with children who watched and mimicked aggressive behavior toward a Bobo doll.

23. Learning by observation seems to take place when the potentially learnable behavior is attended, retained, and reproducible by the observer, and when the individual is motivated to reproduce that behavior.

PATHWAYS TO KNOWLEDGE

Choose the best answer to complete each sentence.

1. Instincts
   (a) are preprogrammed responses.
   (b) are patterns of behavior that bypass normal neuronal-brain pathways.
   (c) can be learned.
   (d) are actions that are performed without conscious awareness.

2. Classical conditioning is a process whereby
   (a) certain physiological or emotional responses accurately predict the appearance of particular stimuli.
   (b) actions that are desirable are strengthened, and actions that are undesirable are weakened.
   (c) actions that are rewarded tend to be strengthened.
   (d) learning occurs when one stimulus accurately predicts the appearance of another stimulus, which prompts a physiological or emotional response.

3. A mechanism whereby a new stimulus is distinguished from a similar, older one so that conditioning does not take place is termed stimulus
   (a) selectivity.
   (b) degeneralization.
   (c) discrimination.
   (d) extinction.

4. In order to be most effective, punishment should **not** be
   (a) delivered immediately after the undesirable response.
   (b) used as the only means for eliciting behavioral change.
   (c) inescapable when the operant is demonstrated.
   (d) delivered with sufficient intensity to stop the undesirable behavior.

5. Albert Bandura's social-learning theory holds that
   (a) learning is greatest in group settings.
   (b) learning can be achieved by observing and modeling another person's behavior.
   (c) exposure to an aggressive scene for a fraction of a second can later elicit aggressive behavior.
   (d) social learning takes place at an unconscious level.

Answer each of the following questions by filling in the blank with an appropriate word or phrase.

6. In Pavlov's historic experiment on classical conditioning, the unconditioned response was _____.

7. An unpleasant stimulus that is presented immediately after a response, in the hope of decreasing the probability of that response, is called a _____.

8. In order to shape a complex behavior, a behaviorist may use _____ _____, which involve continually reinforcing behavior that comes closer and closer to the desired behavior.

9. _____ and _____, such as _____, are preprogrammed responses that are mainly determined by biology (nature), rather than as a result of learning.

10. In classical conditioning, the conditioned response is _____ upon the occurrence of the conditioned stimulus.

11. When a person who is afraid of rats also shows fear of any small furry animals, this person is showing _____ _____.

12. When a mother smiles back at her laughing baby, she is providing a positive _____ for the infant's laughter.

13. A battered wife decides to stay with her husband, although he continually beats her. At one time, when she tried to leave him, she was repeatedly prevented from doing so. She now no longer even tries to leave. This wife is showing _____ _____.

14. When a student drops out of school after being humiliated in front of the whole class, this student is showing _____ learning.

15. In operant conditioning, the _____ of _____ refers to the observation that the strength of a reinforcer *decreases* as the length of time between the operant and the reinforcement *increases*.

Match the following forms of learning to the examples of each kind.

16. imprinting

17. habituation

18. classical conditioning

19. operant conditioning

20. social learning

(a) Shareen once got sick after eating raw fish, and now the smell of fish makes her feel nauseous.

(b) After a while, Jaime got used to the country-western music playing in the background and did not even notice it was there.

(c) Goslings followed Lorenz wherever he went because he was the first moving object they saw.

(d) Sarah's mother participated in civil rights, ban-the-bomb, and other protest marches ever since Sarah was a little girl; when the Gulf War started, Sarah was on the front lines to protest against the war.

(e) Buffy gets paid for every part she solders together, and she now solders many parts per hour.

Answers

1. a, 2. d, 3. c, 4. b, 5. b, 6. salivation, 7. punisher, 8. successive approximations, 9. Habituation, instincts, imprinting, 10. contingent, 11. stimulus generalization, 12. reinforcer, 13. learned helplessness, 14. avoidance, 15. gradient, reinforcement, 16. c, 17. b, 18. a, 19. e, 20. d

PATHWAYS TO UNDERSTANDING

1. Suppose that you were a storyteller or a movie maker. How might you use classical conditioning to influence your audience's emotions? (Use a real story or movie plot for your example.)

2. What is something (a skill, a task, or an achievement) that you think is worthwhile, but that you feel a sense of learned helplessness about successfully accomplishing? How could you design a conditioning program for yourself to overcome your learned helplessness?

3. Given the powerful effects of social learning, how might the medium of television be used as a medium for *lowering* the rate of violent crimes in our society?

CHAPTER OUTLINE

How Do Psychologists Study Memory?

Case Studies of Memory
Deficiencies: Amnesia
Case Studies of Outstanding
Memory: Mnemonists
Experimental Study of Memory

How Have Psychologists Traditionally Viewed Memory?

Sensory Memory
Short-Term Memory
Long-Term Memory

What Are Some Alternative Ways to View Memory?

Alternative Views of
Memory Processes
A Neuropsychological View
of Memory

How Is Information Encoded, Stored, and Retrieved?

Encoding of Information
Storage and Forgetting
Retrieval

How Do We Construct Our Own Memory?

Eyewitness Testimony—What's
Your Judgment?
A Baker's Dozen Tips for Improving
Your Memory

Memory

Carefully read over the following passage, and think about how you can help your-self to remember as much as possible of this passage. Near the end of this chap-ter, you will be asked to recall it.

War of the Ghosts

One night two young men from Egulac went down to the river to hunt seals, and while they were there it became foggy and calm. Then they heard war-cries, and they thought, "Maybe this is a war-party." They escaped to the shore, and hid be-hind a log. Now canoes came up, and they heard the noise of paddles, and saw one canoe coming up to them. There were five men in the canoe, and they said:

"What do you think? We wish to take you along. We are going up the river to make war on the people."

One of the young men said, "I have no arrows."

"Arrows are in the canoe," they said.

"I will not go along. I might be killed. My relatives do not know where I have gone. But you," he said, turning to the other, "may go with them."

So one of the young men went, but the other returned home.

And the warriors went on up the river to a town on the other side of Kalama. The people came down to the water, and they began to fight, and many were killed. But presently the young man heard one of the warriors say: "Quick, let us go home; that Indian has been hit." Now he thought: "Oh, they are ghosts." He did not feel sick, but they said he had been shot.

So the canoes went back to Egulac, and the young man went ashore to his house, and made a fire. And he told everybody and said: "Behold I accompanied the ghosts, and we went to fight. Many of our fellows were killed, and many of those who attacked us were killed. They said I was hit, and I did not feel sick."

He told it all, and then he became quiet. When the sun rose he fell down. Something black came out of his mouth. His face became contorted. The people jumped up and cried.

He was dead.

(Bartlett, 1932, p. 65)

Your attempt to memorize the preceding story illustrates some of the difficult questions psychologists have faced when trying to understand human memory: What do we do when we decide to try to remember something? In fact, just what is memory, anyway? How does memory work? Are there different kinds of memory, and if so, what are they? How is memory organized? How are different kinds of memories related? How can we measure memory, and how can we improve it? We start to answer these questions by investigating how psychologists study memory.

HOW DO PSYCHOLOGISTS STUDY MEMORY?

Memory is the means by which we use information that we gained in the past. Through memory, we store and retrieve information about past experience (Crowder, 1976). One of the ways that psychologists study memory is by examining case studies of persons with exceptional memory, such as persons who lack the normal ability to store and retrieve information.

Case Studies of Memory Deficiencies: Amnesia

One of the most famous cases of **amnesia** (severe loss of memory function) is the case of Henry M., reported by Brenda Milner, Suzanne Corkin, and Hans-Lukas Teuber (1968). Following an experimental surgery performed by neurosurgeon William Scoville (Scoville & Milner, 1957), Henry suffered severe **anterograde amnesia:** He had difficulty deliberately forming new memories of factual information (e.g., the names and faces of people who cared for him following his surgery), and he was unable to store memories of events that took place after the surgery (e.g., what he had done even minutes earlier if he was distracted from an activity). Nonetheless, he remembered whatever he had known before his operation.

After his surgery, Henry's intelligence test score was somewhat above average. However, his score on the memory portion of the test was far below average. Moreover, shortly after taking one of the tests, he could no longer remember that he had even taken the test. Henry once remarked on his situation: "Every day is alone in itself, whatever enjoyment I've had, and whatever sorrow I've had" (Scoville & Milner, 1957, p. 217).

Another type of memory loss is **retrograde amnesia,** in which individuals lose their ability purposefully to recall events that occurred before the event that

memory the means by which existing knowledge, based on past experience and learning, can be used in the present

amnesia damage to memory processes or severe loss of information from memory

anterograde amnesia difficulty in deliberately forming new memories after an injury to memory function, without any effect on the ability to retrieve old memories from before the injury; one meaning of *antero-* is "before"; people with anterograde amnesia forget new information about facts and events *before* they have a chance to store it in memory

retrograde amnesia memory loss affecting deliberate retrieval of events that occurred before injury causing memory loss, without any effect on the ability to form new memories; one meaning of *retro-* is "backward"; people with retrograde amnesia forget *old* information about events, going *backward* from the time the amnesia began

"I apologise for the non-arrival of the guest speaker – – who I'am almost sure I invited"
Reproduced with the permission of the SOUTH WALES ECHO, U.K.

led to the memory loss. W. Ritchie Russell and P. W. Nathan (1946) reported a case of retrograde amnesia following a motorcycle accident: A 22-year-old man suffered severe memory loss due to *trauma* (an event that causes injury). By 10 weeks after the accident, however, he had recovered most of his memory. His recovery of memory started with the events in the most distant past and gradually progressed up to more recent events. Eventually, he was able to recall everything that had happened up to a few minutes before the accident. As is often the case, the events that occurred immediately before the accident were never recalled.

Case Studies of Outstanding Memory: Mnemonists

In contrast to amnesia is **mnemonism,** the use of special techniques for enhancing memory skill. Perhaps the most well-known mnemonist was a man whom Alexander Luria (1902–1977) called "S." Luria (1968) reported that S., a newspaper reporter, showed up in his laboratory and asked to have his memory tested. Luria tested him and discovered that the man's memory appeared to have no limits. S. could recall series of words of any length whatsoever, regardless of how long before the words had been presented to him. Luria studied S. over a period of 30 years. Luria found that even when he tested S.'s memory for a list of words 15 or 16 years after S. had learned the list, S. could still recall the list. S. eventually became a professional entertainer, amazing audiences with his ability to recall whatever was asked of him.

What was S.'s trick? How did he remember so much? Apparently, he seemed automatically to convert words and other information that he needed to remember into visual images. For example, he reported that for remembering numbers, "1 is a proud, well-built man, 2 is a high-spirited woman," and so on (Luria, 1968, p. 31). S. often used his "graphic thinking" (p. 112) to solve problems (visually manipulating various concrete objects in his mind), or to recall what he read (visualizing the words and phrases in a text). Sometimes, however, his automatic construction of images would interfere with his ability to grasp lengthy passages: "A point is . . . reached at which images begin to guide one's thinking, rather than thought itself being the dominant element" (p. 116). In addition, when S. tried to understand abstract concepts that are not easily visualized, such as *infinity* or *nothing*, S. observed, "I can only understand what I can visualize" (p. 130).

In contrast to Luria's S., S. F. (a mnemonist studied by Ericsson, Chase, & Faloon, 1980) started out with relatively ordinary memory abilities when he was first tested. He developed his mnemonic abilities during 200 memory-testing sessions in a 2-year period. S. F. learned to use information with which he was already familiar (running times for various races) as a tool for remembering new and unfamiliar information (long strings of numbers). He did so by breaking down the long numbers into groups of three or four digits each, and then memorizing the number groups as running times for different races. His memory skill was severely limited, however, when the experimenters purposely gave him sequences of digits that could not be translated into running times.

The work with S. F. suggests that people with ordinary memory abilities can greatly increase their abilities if they put considerable effort into doing so. Similarly, Luria observed that people with ordinary memory abilities can intentionally find ways to use visual imagery as a means for remembering information. On the other hand, the work with both S. and S. F. indicates that mnemonic techniques that are successful in certain situations do not necessarily work under all circumstances.

Experimental Study of Memory

Clearly, psychologists learn a great deal by examining case studies of exceptional individuals such as Scoville and Milner's Henry M. and Luria's S. By carefully observing and describing how exceptional memory works, we may gain insight into

Frequently, amnesia occurs as a result of some kind of traumatic injury to the head (and brain).

It's a poor sort of memory that only works backwards.

Lewis Carroll (Charles Luttwidge Dodson)

How would anterograde or retrograde amnesia affect your own life if you were to fall victim to either one? How does memory affect the way we think and feel about ourselves and about our surrounding environment?

[At age 29, S.] couldn't conceive of the idea that his memory differed in some way from other people's.

A. R. Luria

How would it help you to do well in college if you had S.'s memory abilities? How would S.'s abilities be a drawback—or at least of no help—to you?

To remember well is not necessarily a sign of wisdom.

Samuel Luzatto

mnemonism the use of special techniques for improving memory skill

how normal memory works. Another obvious way in which to probe the depths of normal memory functions is to study normal memory directly. One of the first psychologists to study normal memory functions was Hermann Ebbinghaus (1850–1909). Although Ebbinghaus had no support from a university and no formal laboratory in which to conduct his research, his research continues to be cited and discussed a century later. Astonishingly, this pioneer in memory research studied the memory performance of a single individual, whom he could observe 24 hours a day, 7 days a week: himself.

One of the most difficult problems Ebbinghaus faced is one that continues to plague researchers today. How do you study a phenomenon that cannot be photographed, measured, or otherwise observed directly? Like other psychological phenomena, memory is a **hypothetical construct.** Its functions and processes can be observed and measured only indirectly. Its very existence can only be inferred by observing the outcomes it produces. One way to observe the outcomes of memory is to find situations where people use memory, and then to record what happens. Another way is to design controlled experiments, using specialized memory tasks, and to record the outcomes in a relatively controlled manner.

Ebbinghaus pioneered the use of various kinds of tasks for studying memory. He carefully recorded his own responses to each task, noting such outcomes as number of errors, the time it took to make each response, and so on. From these careful self-observations, he could infer conclusions about what factors impeded memory and what factors enhanced memory. For one thing, he found that the number of items he could recall decreased over time (see Figure 7-1a). On the other hand, he noted that the more frequently he rehearsed (repeated) a particular set of items, the more easily he could recall the items (see Figure 7-1b).

Since Ebbinghaus's day, we have learned a great deal about memory—as well as about effective techniques for psychological experimentation. Most psychologists now would question research findings based solely on self-observation. In addition, psychologists now view memory as comprising multiple aspects, not just one. Hence, to study memory, psychologists observe people performing tasks that call on different aspects of memory (e.g., recall vs. recognition memory, implicit vs. explicit memory, and declarative vs. procedural memory). By studying how people

Figure 7-1

Ebbinghaus: Pioneer in Memory Research

Hermann Ebbinghaus's investigation of his own memory processes blazed a trail followed by countless other researchers. (a) Memory researchers have confirmed Ebbinghaus's observation of the "forgetting curve," which shows that the number of items that can be recalled decreases over time. (b) One of the many techniques Ebbinghaus developed involved "relearning," in which he memorized some material in one learning session, and then in a subsequent session, he observed how quickly he could relearn the material from the first session. As this graph shows, the more frequently he had repeated (rehearsed) a particular list of items on the first day, the less time it took him to relearn the list of items on the second day.

hypothetical construct a phenomenon that is believed to exist but that cannot be measured or perceived directly; a hypothetical construct (e.g., memory or intelligence) is *constructed* (built) from *hypotheses* (beliefs); although we cannot directly touch, see, hear, taste, or smell these constructs, we still believe they exist

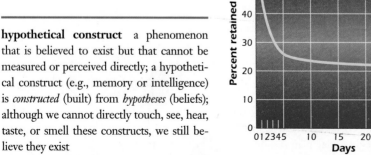

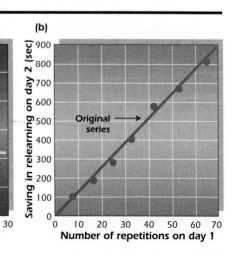

use memory to perform various tasks, psychologists learn new information about how memory works.

If you were to be given a task that requires **recall** from memory, you would be asked to produce a fact, a word, or another item from memory. On the other hand, if you were given a task that required **recognition,** you would have to select or otherwise to identify an item as being one that you had learned previously. Three types of recall tasks used in experiments are *serial recall, free recall,* and *cued recall.* (To try each kind of task for yourself, see Table 7-1.) By using both recognition tasks and recall tasks, psychologists have found that recognition memory is usually much better than recall memory. For example, one study found that research participants could recognize close to 2,000 pictures in a recognition-memory task (Standing, Conezio, & Haber, 1970). Can you imagine anyone recalling 2,000 pictures they were just asked to memorize?

Ebbinghaus and other researchers focused on memory tasks involving lists of individual items (e.g., the tasks described at the top of Table 7-1). More recently,

As you read about tasks that measure memory, think about how these tasks might have real-world applications. What have you done that has required some of the same memory skills as the skills measured in these tasks?

recall production of an item from memory

recognition identification as to whether a particular item is one that was previously stored in memory

TABLE 7-1

Tasks Used for Measuring Memory

Measuring explicit memory about declarative knowledge	Examples: Try the following tasks for yourself
Explicit memory tasks—You must consciously recall information. Declarative-knowledge tasks—You must recall facts.	
Recall tasks Produce a fact, a word, or other item from memory.	What is the kind of amnesia in which a person is unable deliberately to recall information, going backward from the time of the trauma that causes the amnesia?
Serial-recall task Repeat the items in a list in the exact order in which you heard or read them.	Look at the following digits, and then look away and write down the digits in the exact order in which you see them: 2-8-7-1-6-4-3
Free-recall task Repeat the items in a list in any order in which you can recall them.	Look at the following list of words, and then look away and write down the words in any order at all: *dog, pencil, time, hair, monkey, restaurant*
Cued-recall task Memorize a list of paired items, then when you are given a cue of one item in the pair, you must recall the mate for that cued item.	Memorize the following list of word pairs: "time–city, mist–home, switch–paper, credit–day, fist–cloud, number–branch." On a sheet of paper, write the following words, one word per line: time, mist, switch, credit, fist, number. Next, recall the word pairs, and write the corresponding words for each pair.
Recognition tasks Select or otherwise identify an item as being one that you learned previously.	Which is the kind of amnesia in which a person is unable deliberately to form new memories of events?(a) reactive amnesia; (b) anterograde amnesia; (c) traumatic amnesia; or (d) retrograde amnesia
Measuring implicit memory and procedural knowledge	**Examples: Try the following tasks for yourself**
Implicit memory tasks Draw on information in memory, without consciously realizing that you are doing so.	Fill in the blanks for the following words: imp _ _ _ _ _, am _ _ _ _ _ You are more likely to fill in these blanks with words you have read recently than with other words that you know.
Tasks involving procedural knowledge Remember learned skills and automatic behaviors, rather than facts.	Practice "mirror writing," by writing words that you see only as they are reflected in a mirror. Over time, you will improve your ability to use mirror writing; even if you could not recall ever having practiced this skill (e.g., as in persons who suffer from amnesia), your performance would improve.

many psychologists have become increasingly interested in studying how people recall or recognize integrated, context-rich information, such as information from lengthy text passages, lectures, experiences and events, and so on. Usually, when people are performing recall or recognition tasks, they are expected to use **explicit memory,** in which they consciously try to recall or to recognize information. For example, if you were asked to recall the text passage at the outset of this chapter, you would make a conscious effort to retrieve the information from memory.

In addition to studying explicit memory, many psychologists seek to understand **implicit memory** (Graf & Schacter, 1985), in which our performance is enhanced by the use of remembered information, even when we are not consciously aware of recalling the information. Every day, you do many things that involve your implicit memory. As you read this book, you unconsciously remember the meanings of words, as well as how to read in the first place. Surprisingly, the use of implicit memory improves your performance even when you have not been instructed to use implicit recollections and when you are not aware of doing so. In fact, persons who suffer from amnesia seem to benefit from using implicit memory (Baddeley, 1989).

Amnesia victims also show puzzling abilities in regard to tasks that involve **procedural knowledge** (e.g., how to ride a bicycle or how to sign their names). Even when amnesia sufferers have great difficulty in remembering **declarative knowledge** (e.g., the terms in a psychology textbook), they still remember procedural knowledge. For example, amnesia victims usually perform very poorly on traditional memory tasks requiring recall or recognition memory of declarative knowledge. On the other hand, they seem to be able to learn from previous experience in performing skill-based tasks that depend on procedural knowledge. Their remembered practice helps them to improve their performance, even when they do not remember having seen the task before (Baddeley, 1993). For instance, Henry M. showed improvement in his skill in doing *mirror writing* (tracing words seen only in a mirror), but he had no recollection of ever having performed the task relatively soon after completing it (described in Hilts, 1995).

When psychologists study persons who have amnesia, the psychologists learn more than just how memory works in cases of amnesia. They also get ideas about how memory works in general. For one thing, by studying amnesia victims, psychologists have found that the ability consciously to retrieve information from memory about prior experience seems to differ from the ability to use remembered information without being aware of doing so (Baddeley, 1989). Thus, persons with

explicit memory remembering that requires individuals to make a conscious effort at recollection of information

implicit memory remembering in which an individual retrieves information from prior experience to enhance performance, but without being conscious of retrieving the infomation

procedural knowledge "knowing how"—skills that require a person to follow a set of steps for carrying out a procedure

declarative knowledge "knowing that"—factual information that a person can state in words

Persons with amnesia may be unable to learn to remember the names of new musical works (which requires explicit memory), even if they are repeatedly told those names. Nonetheless, their ability to play new pieces shows improvement as a result of repeated experience in playing those pieces (which shows their use of implicit memory).

amnesia may show relatively normal use of implicit memory and procedural knowledge, even when they show very poor use of explicit memory and declarative knowledge.

What is the value of having implicit memory? Wouldn't it be better if we could remember everything explicitly? Tell why you believe that implicit memory is or is not distinctly helpful.

How do psychologists study memory? Psychologists study cases of persons with exceptional memory (e.g., amnesics, mnemonists), and also do experiments involving persons with normal memories, performing various kinds of memory tasks (e.g., recall vs. recognition, implicit vs. explicit, and procedural vs. declarative memory tasks).

HOW HAVE PSYCHOLOGISTS TRADITIONALLY VIEWED MEMORY?

What have psychologists learned about memory by conducting case-study and experimental research? Just what is memory, and how does it work? The answers to these questions depend on whom you ask. For years, the most common way to view memory has been one that was originally proposed by Richard Atkinson and Richard Shiffrin (1968). Although other models have since been proposed and are gaining acceptance, the Atkinson–Shiffrin model is still widely accepted, so it is the primary model discussed in this chapter. Later in this chapter, however, some other views are described.

Atkinson and Shiffrin thought of memory in terms of three different memory *stores* (containers for holding what we remember): sensory memory (the sensory store), short-term memory (the short-term store), and long-term memory (the long-term store). (1) **Sensory memory** can very briefly (for less than 1 second) store very limited amounts of information. (2) **Short-term memory** can store information for somewhat longer periods of time (up to a couple minutes under most circumstances), but it also has a relatively limited capacity. (3) **Long-term memory** has a very large capacity (perhaps limitless) and can store information for very long periods of time (perhaps indefinitely).

Psychologists do not believe that these three stores are distinct physiological structures. Rather, the stores are metaphors for hypothetical constructs of memory processes. Figure 7-2 shows a simple model of these stores (e.g., Atkinson & Shiffrin, 1968).

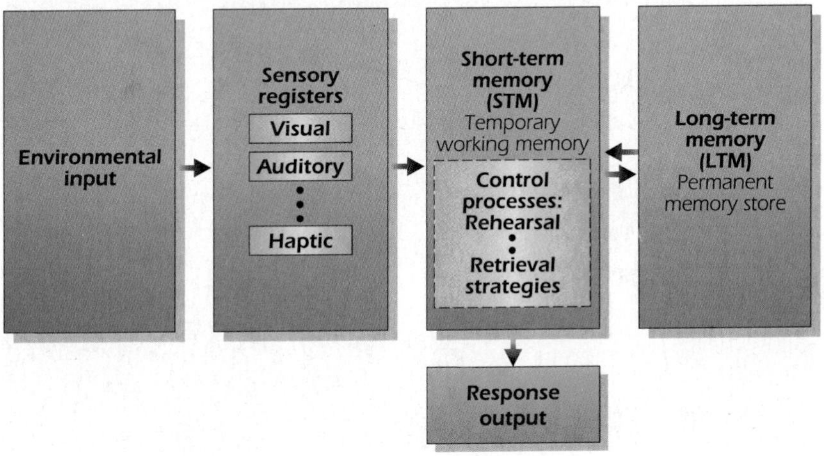

sensory memory storage of very limited amounts of information for a fraction of a second or slightly more

short-term memory relatively brief memory storage of about seven items, give or take a couple of items

long-term memory storage of a practically limitless amount of information for such long periods of time that its limits are not known

Figure 7-2
The Three-Stores View
In Richard Atkinson and Richard Shiffrin's model of memory, information flows from sensory to short-term to long-term memory stores. Atkinson and Shiffrin's metaphor for memory has long served as a basis for research on memory processes. (Adapted from "The control of short-term memory" by R. C. Atkinson and R. M. Shiffrin (1971). In Scientific American, *225, 82–90.)*

Environmental input → **Sensory registers** [Visual, Auditory, Haptic] → **Short-term memory (STM)** Temporary working memory / **Control processes: Rehearsal · Retrieval strategies** ⇄ **Long-term memory (LTM)** Permanent memory store

Response output

In the three-stores model, all three memory stores process information by using three mental operations: encoding, storage, and retrieval. First is **encoding,** in which you transform sensory information into an understandable mental representation that can be used in memory. For example, when you meet someone new, you encode the person's name and face into a form of mental representation. Next is **storage,** in which you keep the encoded information in memory. For example, if you expect to have future dealings with a person you have just met, you will probably try to store the person's name and face in memory. Last is **retrieval,** in which you pull the information from a memory store into active use or awareness. For instance, if you meet someone again whom you have met previously, you will probably try to retrieve the person's name to go with the face—which may not always be easy to do! Although encoding, storage, and retrieval are usually viewed as sequential stages, the processes interact with and depend on each other. Next, we investigate each memory store, starting with the sensory store.

Sensory Memory

The sensory store is considered the first mental storage area for much of the information that eventually enters the other two stores. Excellent evidence has shown the existence of a separate visual sensory store, termed an **iconic store.** It is called an "iconic store" because information may be stored there in the form of *icons* (visual images that look somewhat like the things that they represent). The notion of the iconic store came from the PhD dissertation of George Sperling (1960), a graduate student at Harvard who revealed the existence of this sensory store.

Sperling found that the iconic store can hold about nine items, but that these items fade very rapidly (see Figure 7-3). We are not normally aware of any fading at all, however. What we see in iconic memory we believe to be in the environment.

Visual information appears to enter our memory system through the iconic store, which holds the visual information for fractions of a second. In the normal course of events, this information may be either transferred to another store or erased. The sensory information is erased if other information replaces it before the information can be transferred to another memory store.

Short-Term Memory

Although most of us have little or no ability to control our sensory memory, we all have some control over our short-term memory. In short-term memory, we can

What is an aspect of your own memory that you find puzzling? How would the study of this phenomenon fit into the Atkinson–Shiffrin model?

MINILECTURE

Sperling's Experiments (Ch 8)

encode transform sensory information into an understandable mental representation that can be stored in memory

store keep encoded information in memory

retrieve pull information from memory into active use or awareness

iconic store sensory memory for very brief storage of visual images

Have you ever "written" anything with a bright light in the dark? If so, you have experienced the persistence of a visual memory in the iconic store. That is, you briefly "saw" your name, even though the light left no physical trace of its path.

hold information for matters of seconds and, occasionally, up to a minute or two. Whenever we look up a phone number in the phone book and remember it long enough to make our call, we are using our short-term memory.

You may also have had this experience: After you entered a number, the phone line was busy, and then you had to look up the number again in order to enter it again. Why do we forget such simple information so easily? It appears that our ability to hold information in short-term memory is quite limited.

George Miller (1956) noted that our short-term memory capacity for a wide range of items appears to be about 7 items, plus or minus 2. An item can be something simple, such as a digit, or something more complex, such as a word. If we were to **chunk** a string of 20 items (e.g., letters or numbers) into 7 meaningful items, we could remember them. If we did not chunk the items, we could not remember 20 items and repeat them immediately. For example, most of us could not easily hold in short-term memory this string of 20 letters: *t, s, x, r, q, n, m, n, a, f, s, y, w, e, i, u, e, o, e, u.* However, if we chunked this series into larger units, such as *foxes, yams, quiet, new,* and *run,* we would easily be able to reproduce the 20 letters as 5 items. Once we have formed mental chunks of new information, we can store the information in memory. With a little effort, we can then move the information into long-term memory.

Long-Term Memory

According to the Atkinson–Shiffrin model, the long-term store is where we keep memories that stay with us over long periods of time, perhaps indefinitely.

Organization of Information in Long-Term Memory

It appears that we organize declarative knowledge stored in memory differently, depending on whether it is tied to our own particular experiences. Information in **semantic memory** is general world knowledge—our memory for facts that are not unique to us and that are not recalled in any particular time-bound situation (Tulving, 1972). Information in **episodic memory** is tied to personally experienced events or episodes. We use episodic memory when we learn meaningless lists of words, or when we need to recall something that occurred to us at a particular time or in a particular situation. For example, if I need to remember that I saw Hector Hinklemeyer in the lunchroom yesterday, I must draw on episodic memory. However, if I need to remember the name of the person I now see in the lunchroom again today ("Hector Hinklemeyer"), I must draw on semantic memory. There is no particular time tag associated with the fact that this individual is named Hector, but there is a time tag associated with my having seen him at lunch yesterday. Semantic and episodic memory may not be two distinct systems, but they do appear to function, at times, in different ways. Some physiological evidence also suggests that episodic memories are stored separately from semantic memories (described in Schacter, 1989a).

Semantic memory operates on **concepts,** which are ideas about things; our concepts may be about concrete things, such as cars or apples, or about abstract things, such as truth or justice. People mentally organize concepts in various ways, such as in categories (e.g., types of fruits), in ranked orderings (e.g., degrees of truthfulness), or in sets of features (e.g., the attributes of cars). We can better understand memory by understanding how information is organized in memory.

Psychologists often use the term **schema** to describe how people pull together and organize an assortment of information in memory. For example, a schema for having lunch might associate all the things you have personally experienced regarding lunch, as well as what you have learned about lunch from other information sources. When you think about all that you know about one simple meal, and then you consider all of the schemas for information you have stored

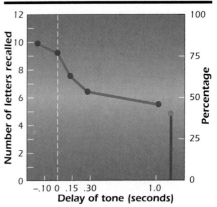

Figure 7-3

Effects of Delay on Visual Recall

The line graph shows the average number of letters available (left axis; percentage equivalents indicated on right axis) to a participant using a partial-report procedure, as a function of the delay between the presentation of the letters and the tone signaling when to show recall. As the delay interval approaches 1 second, recall ability falls sharply. At the far right is shown a bar graph for recall from a whole-report procedure. (From "The information available in brief visual presentations," by G. Sperling (1960). In Psychological Monographs, 74 *(Whole No. 11).)*

What is the value of having a short-term memory store? Wouldn't it be better just to store everything in long-term memory? What useful purpose does short-term memory serve?

chunk grouping by which a collection of items is organized into a coherent whole

semantic memory memory for general knowledge of facts that are not tied to any particular personal experiences

episodic memory a person's memory for particular events that the individual has experienced, as well as any information that is tied to those experiences

concept idea to which a person may attach various characteristics and with which the person may connect various other ideas

schema a cognitive framework for organizing information about a particular concept

What is 119 divided by 7? To figure out the answer to this question, you must use your short-term memory to remember the problem, retrieve what you know about division from long-term memory, apply what you know to this problem, and then come up with an answer.

MINILECTURE

Short-Term Memory Capacity (Ch 8)

MINILECTURE

Mental Images (Ch 8)

A retentive memory may be a good thing, but the ability to forget is the true token of greatness.

                      Elbert Hubbard

Most of us have stored a lot of information in semantic memory which relates to cars (e.g., various makes and models of cars, automotive parts and systems, traffic laws to be obeyed). In addition, most of us have episodic memories of particular experiences related to cars, such as when learning to drive or when taking car trips.

in memory, you may begin to realize the enormity of your long-term memory capacity.

The Capacity of Long-Term Memory

How much information can we hold in long-term memory, and just how long does the information stay in memory? Unfortunately, we do not now know how much information can be stored in long-term memory. In fact, we do not even know how we would find out its capacity. Some theorists have suggested that there is no practical limit to long-term memory capacity (Hintzman, 1978).

At present, it is also hard to know how long information can be stored because we have no proof that there is any absolute outer limit to the time that information stays in long-term memory. Some researchers have found evidence in support of the durability of long-term memories. An interesting study on memory for names and faces was conducted by Phyllis Bahrick, Harry Bahrick, and Roy Wittlinger (1975). They tested how well people remember names and photographs of their

high school classmates. Even after 25 years, people showed pretty good memory for recognizing names and faces. They tended to recognize names as belonging to classmates rather than to outsiders, and they could match the names of many classmates to the classmates' graduation photos. As you might expect, recall of names showed a higher rate of forgetting than did recognition of names. According to Harry Bahrick, we keep some information in *permastore*, which offers permanent or at least very long-term storage of memories.

Research such as Bahrick's can give some idea of how much information we remember. However, it cannot really show how much information we have forgotten. After all, how do we know that we are no longer storing information that we cannot retrieve? Instead of losing information from storage, perhaps we just do not know how to find and retrieve the stored information. For the present, it seems impossible to ascertain any limits to long-term memory.

Thus far, we have discussed memory within the context of the three-stores model of memory. Next, we consider whether there are reasonable alternative ways to view what we know about memory.

What is the name of the person in this photo? You might not recognize the face of this person from her high school photo, but her high school classmates probably would. Most of us show surprisingly good memory for the faces of persons we knew many years before now. Chances are, though, you did not know Tina Turner, pictured here, when she was in high school.

How have psychologists traditionally viewed memory? Psychologists have traditionally viewed memory in terms of three memory stores: sensory, short-term, and long-term memory. For each memory store, we encode, store, and retrieve information.

WHAT ARE SOME ALTERNATIVE WAYS TO VIEW MEMORY?

The Atkinson–Shiffrin model is only one of several ways of viewing memory. Because memory is a hypothetical construct (and therefore cannot be observed directly), different psychologists can look at the same data about memory and can interpret those data in different ways, depending on their point of view. The main differences among these various points of view center on the metaphor they use for thinking about memory (Roediger, 1980).

Why do psychologists use metaphors for thinking about memory and other hypothetical constructs? Metaphors often make it easier to form a mental picture of ideas that are highly abstract and difficult to think about. Metaphors provide a way to organize ideas about hypothetical constructs. Once psychologists have organized their ideas, they can more easily figure out how to study the construct. As the research progresses, they may need to change the metaphor to fit the new data, or other researchers may propose new metaphors that seem better to fit the new information. Next, we consider some alternatives to the Atkinson–Shiffrin metaphor for thinking about memory.

Alternative Views of Memory Processes

Some psychologists (e.g., Baddeley, 1990a, 1990b; Cantor & Engle, 1993; Daneman & Carpenter, 1980; Daneman & Tardif, 1987; Engle, 1994; Engle, Cantor, & Carullo, 1992) view short-term and long-term memory from a different perspective than that of the three-stores model. Table 7-2 contrasts the Atkinson–Shiffrin model with this alternative perspective. Note the differences in the terminology (choice of words), in the choice of metaphors, and in the emphasis of each view.

TABLE 7-2

Traditional Versus Nontraditional Views of Memory

Different kinds of choices	Traditional three-stores view	Alternative view of memory[a]
Terminology	*Working memory* is another name for short-term memory (STM), which is distinct from long-term memory (LTM).	*Working memory* (active memory) is the part of LTM that includes all the knowledge (both facts and procedures) that has been recently activated in memory, including the brief, fleeting STM and its contents.
Relationships of stores	STM is viewed as being distinct from LTM, perhaps either alongside it or hierarchically linked to it.	STM, working memory, and LTM may be viewed as nested concentric spheres, in which working memory encompasses only the most recently activated portion of LTM, and STM encompasses only a very small portion of working memory.
Movement of information	Information moves directly from STM to LTM, or vice versa, and is never in both locations at once.	Information remains within LTM; when activated, information moves into working memory, a specialized portion of LTM. The working memory actively moves information into and out of STM.
Emphasis	This view distinguishes between LTM and STM.	This view emphasizes the role of activation in moving information into working memory and the role of working memory in memory processes.

[a] View of working memory suggested by Cantor & Engle, 1993; Engle, 1994; Engle, Cantor, & Carullo, 1992.

working memory recently activated portion of long-term memory, as well as a means for moving activated elements into and out of short-term memory

parallel processing information processing in which multiple operations are occurring all at once

levels-of-processing framework a view of memory in which memory storage varies continuously in terms of the depth at which information is encoded

The key feature of the alternative view is the emphasis on working memory. **Working memory** may be viewed as a specialized, highly active part of long-term memory. Within working memory is short-term memory, which is the small pool of information in conscious awareness at any given moment. From this perspective, working memory holds only the portion of long-term memory that has become active recently, and it moves both the active elements and any new information into and out of brief, temporary memory storage.

Whereas the three-stores view emphasizes the structural containers for stored information, the working-memory view focuses on the functions and processes of memory. One way of picturing the two views of memory is to suppose that a metaphor for the three-stores view is a warehouse, in which information is passively stored. Sensory memory is the loading dock, and short-term memory is the area surrounding the loading dock, where information may be stored temporarily until it is moved into a permanent location in the body of the warehouse—the long-term memory store.

In contrast, a metaphor for the working-memory model may be a multimedia production house, which continually generates and manipulates images and sounds, integrating them into meaningful arrangements for storage and use. These stored images and sounds are frequently reformatted and rearranged, as new demands and new information become available to working memory.

In the working-memory model, memory activity involves **parallel processing,** in which multiple operations are all occurring at once. For example, when you draw from memory information about your best friend, you simultaneously activate many things you know about your friend (e.g., appearance, voice, facial expressions, pet peeves, favorite activities). The working-memory model has gained support from the use of computer models (artificial intelligence) of memory processes, as well as from experiments with people and from neuropsychological research.

A more radical departure from the three-stores view of memory is the **levels-of-processing framework,** originally proposed by Fergus Craik and Robert

Lockhart (1972). In their framework, memory is not made of any specific number of separate stores. Rather, memory storage varies continuously in terms of the depth at which information is encoded.

Different levels of encoding are based on different kinds of encoding. For example, the authors noted the following three different levels of processing: *physical* (based on physical appearance, e.g., the letters of the word "fizz"), *acoustic* (based on sounds, e.g., the sounds of the word "fizz"), and *semantic* (based on word meanings, e.g., the meaning of the word "fizz"). At first, it seemed that some levels (e.g., semantic) were better than others (e.g., physical or acoustic) for remembering information. It turns out that the key to remembering is a match between the level of encoding and the form of the recall. In addition, when information is encoded at more than one level, it appears to be more easily retrieved later on.

This framework has immediate practical applications: In studying, the more ways in which you encode material, the more readily you are likely to recall it later. Just looking at material again and again in the same way is less likely to be productive for learning the material. Instead, find more than one way in which to learn the material. On the other hand, you may want to give particular emphasis to encoding information at a level that closely matches the level at which you will want to retrieve it. If you will be given a test on rhyming words, for instance, you should focus on acoustic encoding. If you will be tested on meanings (more likely in most college classes), you should give extra time to semantic encoding.

A Neuropsychological View of Memory

Another way of viewing memory is to observe the cerebral processes and structures involved in memory. Some structures of the brain, such as the hippocampus and other nearby structures (see Chapter 2), clearly play a vital role in memory (Squire, 1987). Damage to these areas causes severe memory problems. Studies of brain-injured patients such as Henry M. (mentioned earlier in this chapter) offer distinctive insights into memory not available by observing normal research participants. It appears that different structures of the brain may be involved in different kinds of memory (Squire, 1987). For example, the importance of the hippocampus for forming new memories of declarative knowledge largely started with studies of amnesic Henry M., as the portion of Henry's brain that was removed by Scoville included chiefly the hippocampus. Once psychologists noticed that the removal of the hippocampus tragically destroyed some of Henry's memory abilities, they were able to infer the role of the hippocampus in memory formation. In addition to the hippocampus, the cortex is also involved in the memory for declarative knowledge (Zola-Morgan & Squire, 1990), and the basal ganglia are primarily involved in memory for procedural knowledge (Mishkin & Petri, 1984).

When trying to figure out which brain structures and regions are involved in which functions, neuropsychologists often look for dissociations. In *dissociations*, people with lesions in particular areas of the brain show particular deficits of brain function, but people without lesions in those areas do not show those deficits of function. Whenever possible, neuropsychologists try to find *double dissociations*, in which people with lesions in different areas of the brain show opposite patterns of deficits. For example, people with lesions in the left parietal lobe show impairments of short-term memory, but not of long-term memory (Warrington & Shallice, 1972). People with lesions in the temporal lobe, however, show impairments of long-term memory but not of short-term memory (Warrington, 1982). Both single and double dissociations help psychologists to confirm or to disconfirm their present hypotheses regarding how memory works; in addition, dissociations lead psychologists to discover new insights about memory.

Larry Squire, using his own research and that of fellow psychologists and neuropsychologists, has proposed a *taxonomy* (classification scheme) for memory (see Figure 7-4). His taxonomy distinguishes declarative from nondeclarative memory.

MINILECTURE

Biology of Memory (Ch 8)

Figure 7-4

Squire's Types of Memory

Based on extensive neuropsychological research, Larry Squire has proposed that memory includes two fundamental types: declarative memory and various forms of nondeclarative memory. Each type of memory may be associated with distinct cerebral structures and processes.

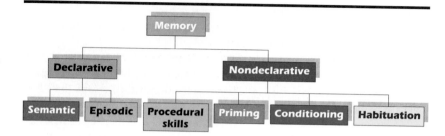

Nondeclarative memory includes procedural memory, as well as simple learning (operant and classical conditioning; see Chapter 6), habituation (see Chapter 6), some memory phenomena related to perception (see Chapter 4), and priming. In **priming**, information stored in memory becomes activated by stimuli that are identical to or related to the primed information. For example, hearing the word "palm" may prime the word *palm* itself, stored in memory, and it may prime information related to parts of the hand or to various kinds of trees. If you have recently visited a palm-studded beach, your memories of the trip may also be primed.

In addition to learning about the macroscopic structures involved in memory (e.g., the hippocampus or areas of the cortex), we are starting to understand how memory works at the microscopic level. The synapses between neurons seem to be particularly important for forming, keeping, and strengthening memories (e.g., Kandel & Schwartz, 1982). For one thing, chemical neurotransmitters powerfully affect how and how well memory works. Both serotonin and acetylcholine seem to be important to normal memory processes. If these processes are disrupted by drugs (e.g., alcohol—Shimamura & Squire, 1986) or by disease (e.g., Alzheimer's disease—Squire, 1987), memory does not function properly. Even hormones have been found to affect memory under some circumstances, either enhancing or inhibiting memory function.

priming enhanced access to a particular stimulus or item of information, as a result of recent activation of or exposure to the same stimulus or a related one

The hippocampus is crucial for moving new declarative information into long-term memory. Both this elderly woman and this young toddler do not readily move declarative information into long-term memory. Whereas the hippocampus of the woman is deteriorating (possibly due to repeated strokes) and is decreasingly able to aid in storage of declarative information, the hippocampus of the toddler is maturing and is increasingly able to do so.

What are some alternative ways to view memory? Some alternative ways of viewing memory include the working-memory model, the levels-of-processing framework, and the neuropsychological approach, which considers the memory functions of both the major macroscopic structures of the brain and the microscopic actions of key neurotransmitters in the brain.

HOW IS INFORMATION ENCODED, STORED, AND RETRIEVED?

Neurotransmitters, hormones, and other substances influence memory by affecting the three main memory processes: *encoding* (in which we move information into memory), *storage* (in which we keep information in memory), and *retrieval* (in which we gain access to stored information). In this section, we discuss each of these processes.

Encoding of Information

Encoding for Temporary Storage of Information

When you encode information to move it into temporary memory storage, what kind of code do you use? That is, in what form is the mental representation that is used for moving information into short-term (or working) memory? R. Conrad (1964) found the answer to this question: The mental representation in temporary memory storage is based on sounds, rather than on icons or some other form.

Conrad found the answer through a serial-recall task. He quickly showed participants various lists of six letters each. Immediately after each list was shown, participants had to write down the correct sequence of items in the list. Conrad was particularly interested in the kinds of recall errors participants made. The pattern of errors was clear. Even though the letters were presented *visually*, errors tended to be based on how easily the sounds of the letters could be confused. Sometimes, instead of recalling the letters they were supposed to recall, participants substituted letters that sounded like the correct letters. Thus, the participants were likely to confuse F for S, B for V, P for B, and so on. These confusions are the same ones shown when people simply listen to single letters in a noisy setting. Alan Baddeley (1966) expanded on Conrad's work by using words instead of letters to study encoding in short-term memory. His work confirmed that such encoding relies primarily on an *acoustic code* (based on sounds) rather than on a *semantic code* (based on word meanings).

Encoding for Long-Term Storage

Information in short-term memory is encoded primarily based on sounds, so encoding errors are often based on confusions of sounds. In contrast, information in long-term memory seems to be primarily encoded *semantically*, based on the meanings of words, and errors are based on confusions of word meanings. In addition, however, we can also hold visual (sight) and acoustic (sound) information in long-term memory. Some researchers (e.g., Anderson & Bower, 1973; Clark & Chase, 1972) have proposed that we store all information in terms of underlying meanings of the information, rather than in terms of word meanings or any other form of

MINILECTURE

Encoding, Storage, and Retrieval (Ch 8)

How we remember, what we remember, and why we remember form the most personal map of our individuality.

Christina Baldwin

MINILECTURE

Mnemonic Devices (Ch 8)

mnemonic devices methods for improving memory by translating unrelated random bits of information into meaningful verbal information or into visual images

mental representation. Other researchers (e.g., Kosslyn, 1975, 1988; Paivio, 1971) have suggested that we store some information in terms of mental images. There is some evidence for mental storage of both underlying meanings and mental images.

Using Techniques for Encoding Information

So far, we know that we encode information in the form of underlying meanings and mental images. How can we apply what we know to develop our own memory skills? A clear application is that when we wish to remember information, we should find ways to encode information by enriching or deepening its meaning or by forming mental images of the information.

Mnemonists often take advantage of the normal processes of encoding and translate unrelated, random, or abstract bits of information into either more meaningfully connected information or more concrete visual images. You do not have to be a mnemonist to use these methods for improving your own memory abilities. For example, anyone can use **mnemonic devices** (see Table 7-3). These devices are techniques for translating abstract lists of unrelated items into specific meanings or images. Because these devices add meaning or imagery to an otherwise random listing, they make it much easier to memorize the lists.

Mnemonic devices such as the ones described in Table 7-3 (*categorical clustering, acronyms, acrostics, interactive images* among words in a list, a *pegword system*, and the *method of loci*) help in handling many memory tasks, particularly when the tasks

TABLE 7-3
Mnemonic Devices

Technique	Example
Categorical clustering Organize a list of items into a set of categories	If you needed to remember to buy apples, milk, bagels, grapes, yogurt, rolls, Swiss cheese, and grapefruit, you would be better able to do so if you tried to memorize the items by categories: *fruits*—apples, grapes, grapefruit; *dairy products*—milk, yogurt, Swiss cheese; *breads*—bagels, rolls.
Acronym Form a word or expression in which each of its letters stands for a certain other word or concept	USA, IQ, and laser are all acronyms.
Acrostic Form a sentence rather than a single word to help you remember the new words	Music students trying to memorize the names of the notes found on lines of the treble clef (the higher notes; specifically E, G, B, D, and F above middle C) learn that "*Every Good Boy Does Fine.*"
Interactive images Create interactive images that link the isolated words in a list	Suppose that you need to remember a list of unrelated words: *aardvark, table, pencil, book, radio*. You might better remember these words by generating *interactive images*. For example, you might imagine an *aardvark* sitting on a *table* holding a *pencil* in its claws and writing in a *book*, while listening to a *radio*.
Pegword system Associate each new word with a word on a previously memorized list to form an interactive image between the new word and the previously memorized word	One such list is from a nursery rhyme: One is a bun, two is a shoe, three is a tree, four is a door, five is a hive, six is a stick, seven is heaven, eight is a gate, nine is a dime, ten is a hen. You might visualize an *aardvark* eating a delicious *bun*. Next, you might imagine a *shoe* atop a tall *table*. Then you would form interactive images for each of the words in the list.
Method of loci Visualize walking around an area with distinctive landmarks that you know well, and then link the various landmarks to specific items to be remembered	Envision an *aardvark* nibbling at the roots of a familiar tree, a *table* sitting on the sidewalk, a *pencil*-shaped statue in the center of a fountain, and so on.

Suppose that you were familiar with the key landmarks of Washington, D.C., as shown in this aerial photo. To use the *method of loci*, you would take a mental walk from one landmark to another, placing or retrieving one item you wished to remember at each of the key landmarks on your mental walk. How could you put this method to work for you in remembering important information?

involve lists of items (e.g., shopping lists or lists of key terms, important names, steps in a procedure, or topics in a speech or a debate). Often, however, what we want to remember does not easily lend itself to the use of mnemonic devices.

Finding Your Way 7-1

Consider, for example, the following passage from an experiment by John Bransford and Marcia Johnson (1972, p. 722). As you read the following passage, try to memorize the information so that you can recall it effectively.

> The procedure is actually quite simple. First you arrange items into different groups. Of course one pile may be sufficient depending on how much there is to do. If you have to go somewhere else due to lack of facilities that is the next step; otherwise, you are pretty well set. It is important not to overdo things. That is, it is better to do too few things at once than too many. In the short run this may not seem important but complications can easily arise. A mistake can be expensive as well. At first, the whole procedure will seem complicated. Soon, however, it will become just another facet of life. It is difficult to foresee any end to the necessity for this task in the immediate future, but then, one can never tell. After the procedure is completed one arranges the materials into different groups again. Then they can be put into their appropriate places. Eventually they will be used once more and the whole cycle will then have to be repeated. However, that is part of life.

Cover the preceding passage with your hand, and try to recall as much as possible of the information. If you are like the people studied by Bransford and Johnson, you will have found it hard to understand and will have had trouble recalling the steps involved. The information seems meaningless, and you have no way to organize the information into a mental representation. You (and Bransford and Johnson's research participants) therefore may have found it hard to encode the information and then to store and retrieve it. However, a simple verbal label can make it easier to encode, store, and retrieve this information. Research participants did much better with the passage when given its title, "Washing Clothes." Once they had the verbal label, they could easily encode, and therefore remember, a passage that otherwise seemed to make no sense. Similarly, once you have encoded information into a form that can be represented in memory, you can store the information.

Storage and Forgetting

How We Keep Information in Storage

Psychologists largely agree about how information is kept in short-term memory. The key technique people use for keeping information in short-term memory is **rehearsal.** An obvious method of rehearsal is simply to repeat the information over and over again, in order to remember it. Effective rehearsal leads to **practice effects,** in which recall is enhanced as a result of repeating the information. Although simple repetition helps to keep information in short-term memory, it does not help in moving the information from short-term memory to long-term memory or in keeping it in long-term memory.

To transfer information into long-term memory, an individual must use elaborative rehearsal. In *elaborative rehearsal,* the person somehow elaborates the information to be remembered in a way that makes the information either more meaningfully integrated into what the person already knows or more meaningfully connected as a whole and therefore more memorable. For example, once you had the label for the "Washing Clothes" passage, you could integrate it into a whole and more easily remember it. Recall, too, the effects of chunking, in which people can chunk many smaller units of information into larger units of integrated information, to remember the information more easily. You could also easily integrate the new information into what you already know about washing clothes, further enhancing your ability to remember the information.

Although most adults and older children seem to use rehearsal naturally for keeping information in memory, young children do not. That is, unlike older children and adults, younger children do not understand that to keep information in memory, they need to rehearse the information. In fact, the major difference between the memory abilities of younger children and the abilities of older children and adults may lie in the use of learned memory strategies, such as rehearsal (Flavell & Wellman, 1977). Young children have not yet developed *metamemory* skills—that is, knowledge and understanding of their own memory abilities.

Metamemory is one aspect of **metacognition,** in which you think about and try to understand your own thought processes. For example, if you were given a

I can understand that memory must be selective, else it would choke on the glut of experience. What I cannot understand is why it selects what it does.

Virgilia Peterson

rehearsal the repeated reciting of information or the repetition of a procedure

practice effects the outcomes of rehearsal, which usually involve an improvement in recall or skill

metacognition the process of thinking about how we use strategies and skills to enhance our thought processes; thinking about how we think

This storyteller elaboratively rehearses each story in her repertoire during each retelling of a narrative. At each retelling, the storyteller reconstructs the story from a known set of characters and events, using rhythm and perhaps rhyme as cues for retelling the same sequence of events in about the same way.

list of items to remember (perhaps you wanted to recall key concepts from a psychology lecture), you might think about your own thinking and decide to use a mnemonic device to help you form mental images or meaningful relationships among the items. If you were given a passage of text to learn (e.g., a psychology chapter you were asked to read), you might try to find ways to relate the information to what you already know and to your own experiences.

The way in which you rehearse new information clearly affects how well you will remember it. In addition, the amount of time you spend on rehearsal will affect your ability to remember the rehearsed information. According to the widely accepted *total-time hypothesis*, the amount of information you will remember depends mainly on the total amount of time you spend studying the material in each study session, regardless of how you budget your time within a given session.

On the other hand, although it makes little difference how you divide up your time in any one session, it makes a lot of difference how you divide up your time across study sessions. More than a century ago, Hermann Ebbinghaus (1885/1964, cited in Schacter, 1989a) noticed that the distribution of study (memory rehearsal) sessions over time affects how well you will recall the information later on. Much more recently, Harry Bahrick and Elizabeth Phelps (1987), while studying people's long-term recall of information, have offered support for Ebbinghaus's observation: **Distributed learning** (which is spaced over time) is more effective than **massed learning** (i.e., learning that is crammed together all at once). The more widely the learning trials are distributed over time, the more ably people remember the information. The enhancement of recall due to distributed learning has been termed the *spacing effect* (Glenberg, 1977, 1979).

What might explain the spacing effect? Arthur Glenberg (1977, 1979) has studied this effect extensively, and he and others (e.g., Leicht & Overton, 1987) have linked the spacing effect to the process by which memories are consolidated in long-term memory. In memory **consolidation,** we integrate new information into stored information. This process of consolidation can continue for many years (Squire, 1986).

Hence, the spacing effect may occur because at each learning session, you have new opportunities for consolidating the information in long-term memory. The principle of the spacing effect is important to remember in studying: You will recall more information for a longer time, on average, if you space out your learning of subject matter, rather than trying to cram your learning into a short period of time. In addition, if you use various strategies for integrating the new information into what you already know, you will help yourself to consolidate the information in long-term memory.

How We Forget Information

What we have learned about consolidation in long-term memory suggests the way in which we forget information. Before information is consolidated, it is unstable and is easily forgotten. If the information is not used or reinforced during consolidation, the somewhat shaky information may simply be lost. In addition, during consolidation of information, new information may distort the consolidation of information that is not yet established. Of course, if something happens to disrupt the consolidation process (e.g., a trauma such as a blow to the head), the information may very well be forgotten altogether.

We have yet to discuss how we forget information from short-term memory, but the experience of forgetting is familiar to all of us. If we do not use rehearsal or other strategies to keep information in short-term memory, the information seems to disappear. Why do we forget information—such as a phone number—after a brief period of time?

Several theories of forgetting have been proposed. The two most well-known theories are *interference theory* and *decay theory*. In **interference,** competing information causes us to forget something. For example, suppose that you are in a

Use metacognition to think about your own thinking. How can you use rehearsal and other methods to keep from forgetting the meanings of the various kinds of memory described in this chapter?

What might cause a student to use massed learning, rather than distributed learning? How could you make it more likely for a student to use distributed rather than massed learning?

If you wish to forget anything on the spot, make a note that this thing is to be remembered.

Edgar Allan Poe

Nothing fixes a thing so intensely in the memory as the wish to forget it.

Michel de Montaigne

distributed learning storage of information in memory that occurs over a long period of time, rather than all at once

massed learning storage of information in memory that occurs over a very brief period of time

consolidation process by which people integrate new information into their existing information stored in long-term memory

interference process by which competing information causes people to forget stored information

MINILECTURE

Interference Theory (Cb 8)

Memories are like stones, time and distance erode them like acid.

Ugo Betti

decay forgetting of stored information due to the passage of time

serial processing information processing in which operations occur sequentially, one after another

The U.S. Library of Congress contains more than 88 million items, including more than 14 million books (Grolier, 1992). Clearly, a great deal of information is available in this national library. For the information to be accessible, as well, it must be extremely well organized.

phone booth, dialing a phone number you have just looked up. Someone taps you on the shoulder and asks you for the correct time. It takes you just a few seconds to answer, but when you turn back to the phone dial, you no longer remember the number you were dialing. This example illustrates *retroactive interference*, which occurs *after* the memorable information is stored.

In addition to our being affected by retroactive interference, we may be affected by *proactive interference*, which occurs *before* the memorable information is stored. For example, if you were trying to remember a list of details to tell a mechanic whom you were calling from the phone booth, the list of details might proactively interfere with your ability to remember the mechanic's phone number. The evidence for interference is rather strong (Brown, 1958; Peterson & Peterson, 1959), but at present, it is unclear as to the extent to which the interference is retroactive, proactive, or both (Keppel & Underwood, 1962).

An alternative means for forgetting is **decay,** in which simply the passage of time causes us to forget. The evidence for decay is not airtight, but it is certainly suggestive (Reitman, 1974). Hence, it appears that both interference and decay affect short-term memory.

Retrieval

Retrieval From Temporary Storage

Once information is encoded and stored in short-term memory, how do people retrieve that information? Saul Sternberg carried out a classic series of experiments on the issue of retrieval from short-term memory. The phenomenon he studied is short-term memory scanning. In *memory scanning*, a retrieval task, you check the items contained in your short-term memory, to see whether any of the items accomplishes a particular goal. For example, suppose that you were asked to remember these digits: 1, 7, 8, 5, 2, 6, 9. You might then be asked to scan your memory to determine whether the digit 6 was in the list of digits you were asked to remember.

Saul Sternberg and other psychologists wondered whether we retrieve items all at once, using *parallel processing*, or one by one, using **serial processing.** If we retrieve the items serially (one by one), the question then arises, do we use *exhaustive serial processing*, always retrieving all of the items? Or instead, do we use *self-terminating serial processing*, stopping retrieval of items as soon as an item seems to

accomplish our goal? If we use exhaustive serial processing, we retrieve the wanted item only after checking all of the items in short-term memory. If we use self-terminating serial processing, we stop retrieval as soon as we find a suitable item that accomplishes our goal. As a result of his research, Sternberg (1966, 1969) concluded that exhaustive serial processing is probably the method used for retrieval from short-term memory. To return to the example, if you were given the digits 1, 7, 8, 5, 2, 6, 9, you would scan your memory of all the digits, one by one. After you had scanned all seven digits, you would determine that one of the digits was indeed 6. Although there have been other interpretations of Sternberg's data (see, e.g. Townsend, 1971), Sternberg's interpretation is still probably the most widely accepted.

Retrieval From Long-Term Memory

If we cannot retrieve particular information from short-term memory, we can infer that the information is no longer present in short-term memory. We cannot reach similar inferences regarding long-term memory. That is, information may still be stored in long-term memory even if we find it difficult—or even impossible—to retrieve the information. Psychologists distinguish between *availability* of information (whether information is permanently stored in long-term memory) and *accessibility* of information (the degree to which we can gain access to stored information). What helps us, and what hinders us as we try to gain access to information stored in long-term memory?

What we can retrieve from memory depends on what we know and how we organize what we know. Our existing knowledge and schemas provide an internal context that affects memory retrieval. Because adults have greater knowledge and more elaborate schemas than children do, adults have more diverse internal contexts for retrieving information than children have. Diversity and richness of context may offer one reason why adults generally perform better on memory tests than children do. On the other hand, when a memory task involves a subject about which children have more knowledge and more elaborate schemas than adults do (namely, the subject of dinosaurs), children outperform adults (Chi & Koeske, 1983).

Even our moods and our states of consciousness may provide an internal context for encoding and retrieving information. That is, we may more readily retrieve information that we encode during a particular mood or state of consciousness when we are in the same state again (Baddeley, 1993; Bower, 1983). For example, some (e.g., Baddeley, 1989) have suggested that memory processes may play a role in maintaining depression: Persons who feel depressed may more readily retrieve memories of previous sad experiences, which may further prolong the depression. If this vicious cycle can somehow be stopped from continuing, the person may begin to feel happier. This happier mood will then lead to retrieval of happier memories, thus leading to further relief from the depression, and so on. Perhaps the folk wisdom to "think happy thoughts" is not entirely unfounded.

Other aspects of consciousness and mood also affect memory. For example, when people encode information while under the influence of alcohol or other drugs, they can often more readily retrieve that information when in the same state again. Thus, a person who feels anxious as a result of the psychoactive effects of stimulants may more easily retrieve anxiety-related memories, which may lead to further feelings of anxiety.

External contexts may also affect our ability to recall information. We appear to be better able to recall information when we are in the same context as the one in which we learned the material. In one experiment, 16 underwater divers were asked to learn a list of 40 unrelated words, either while they were on shore or while they were 20 feet beneath the sea (Godden & Baddeley, 1975). Later, the divers were asked to recall the words either when in the same environment as where they

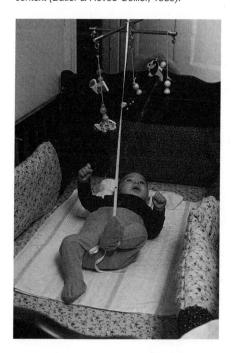

Even infants show the effects of context on memory: When given an opportunity to kick a mobile in the same context in which they first learned to kick it (e.g., the patterned crib bumper shown here) or in a different context (e.g., a crib bumper with a different pattern), the infants kicked more strongly when in the same context (Butler & Rovee-Collier, 1989).

According to Endel Tulving and Donald Thomson (1973), we can retrieve information from memory more readily when the context for encoding closely matches the context for retrieval. Given the notion of encoding specificity, which of these students will more readily retrieve the information they are now encoding, when the need arises: (a) the student in a simulated air traffic control center, who is responding to realistic situations; or (b) the student in this language laboratory, who is parroting back phrases from a predetermined dialogue?

had learned them, or in the other environment. Recall was better when it occurred in the same place as did the learning.

To summarize, internal contexts (such as schemas and moods) and external contexts (such as locations and situations) affect recall. Each of the preceding context effects involves a match between what is encoded and what is recalled. Many other experiments confirm that the way in which items are encoded powerfully influences how and how well the items are retrieved. Endel Tulving and Donald Thomson (1973) have termed the relationship between encoding and retrieval, **encoding specificity:** What is recalled depends on what is encoded.

Another influence on recall of information is the degree to which the information is organized into mental categories. In general, better organization leads to easier recall. Some tasks requiring recall do not lend themselves to the use of categories, however. In such situations, people often make up their own memory cues for recalling information. These self-generated cues can be quite effective. For example, Timo Mantyla (1986) found that when people made up their own retrieval cues, they were able to remember, almost without errors, lists of 500 and even 600 words.

How should you study for a test if you want to recall the information well at the time of testing? What are some strategies that you can use that will help you?

How is information encoded, stored, and retrieved? Information is encoded for temporary storage in the form of an acoustic code. Information may be encoded for long-term storage in a semantic code, in mental images, or in terms of underlying meanings. There is some evidence for each form of encoding. We may use mnemonic devices to facilitate our encoding of information. We keep information in memory by using rehearsal and by using other metacognitive strategies. Over time, we consolidate information into long-term memory. We probably forget information as a result of both interference and decay. The way in which we encode information relates directly to our ability later to retrieve the information.

encoding specificity phenomenon in which the retrieval of information depends on the organizational representation of the information during encoding

HOW DO WE CONSTRUCT OUR OWN MEMORY?

We more readily recall meaningful than meaningless information, and sometimes we even create the meaning that we later recall. During consolidation, we integrate

When Simon Rodia built the Watts Towers in East Los Angeles (c. 1921–1954), he assembled it from fragments of realistic objects (such as the broken plates and cups shown here), according to his own preexisting ideas. Similarly, we construct our memories from fragments of realistic events, according to our own preexisting schemas.

new information into what we already know, and new information sometimes even changes existing information that is still being consolidated. Hence, memory is not just **reconstructive** (based only on actual events and experiences); it is also **constructive** (based also on expectations, existing schemas, and even information gained after memory consolidation begins). The influence of existing schemas was shown in the Bransford and Johnson (1972) study mentioned earlier: Participants could remember a passage quite well once they realized that the passage fit their existing schemas about washing clothes. Before then, however, they had trouble remembering or understanding the passage.

Some cross-cultural work (Tripathi, 1979) shows how schemas may serve as a mental framework for constructive memory. For example, Indian children were asked to read several stories from *The Panchatantra*, a collection of ancient Hindi fables and folktales. The stories contain unusual names and settings that seem strange to contemporary Indian schoolchildren. After hearing these stories, the children were asked to recall the stories. Over time, the children added words and sentences not originally presented in the stories. In general, their reconstructions changed the stories from unfamiliar to more familiar forms, as well as from complex to more simple forms.

Decades before the Indian study, Frederic Bartlett (1932) had found similar results when he studied the effects of schemas on recall in British students who read a passage of text from a native North American legend, the full text of which you read at the outset of this chapter.

Sometimes what we call "memory" and what we call "imagination" are not so easily distinguished.

Leslie Marmon Silko

I can never remember things I didn't understand in the first place.

Amy Tan

reconstructive memory phenomenon by which people accurately encode, store, and retrieve only the sensations and events they have actually experienced

constructive memory phenomenon by which people build stored memories, based on existing schemas, expectations, and additional stored information, as well as on previous sensations and events; some distortions in encoding, storage, and retrieval may occur as a result

Drawing by W. Miller; © 1987 The New Yorker Magazine, Inc.

In memory each of us is an artist: each of us creates.

Patricia Hampl

Finding Your Way 7-2

Stop for a moment, and jot down everything you remember about Bartlett's "War of the Ghosts." Now, flip back to the beginning of this chapter, and compare what you recalled with what the legend actually described. Bartlett found that British readers had trouble recalling this traditional North American legend. They frequently distorted their recall in ways that fit with their own existing schemas. How easily were you able to recall the information in Bartlett's passage? How did your existing schemas affect your recall?

Some of the strongest evidence for the constructive nature of memory recall has come from studies on eyewitness testimony. In one such study, Elizabeth Loftus, David Miller, and Helen Burns (1978) showed participants a series of 30 slides, in which a red Datsun appeared to go down a street, stop at a stop sign, turn right, and then knock down a pedestrian who was crossing at a crosswalk. As soon as the participants finished seeing the slides, they had to answer 20 questions about the accident. One of the questions contained information that was either consistent or inconsistent with what they had been shown. Half of the participants were asked: "Did another car pass the red Datsun while it was stopped at the stop sign?" This question was consistent with what they saw. The other half of the participants received the same question, except that the word *yield* replaced the word *stop*. For the second group of participants, the information in the question was inconsistent with what they had seen.

Figure 7-5
Droodles

Droodles *are nonsense pictures that can be given funny interpretations. (a) Quickly glance at the droodles at the left: The top droodle depicts "a [very short person] playing a trombone in a telephone booth," and the bottom droodle depicts "uncooked spaghetti, then cooked spaghetti and meatballs." Now, look away and draw the droodles. (b) Quickly glance at the unlabeled droodles on the right, then look away and draw the sets of droodles. If you are like the research participants studied by Gordon Bower, Martin Karlin, and Alvin Dueck (1975), you will have found it easier to recall the droodles that were labeled (giving you a schema for the droodles) than the droodles that were not labeled. (In this demonstration, order of looking may affect recall. By the way, the labels for the droodles on the right are printed upside-down here.)*

The top droodle depicts "an early bird who caught a very strong worm," and the bottom droodle depicts the "rear end of a pig disappearing into a fog bank, and his nose coming out the other side of the fog."

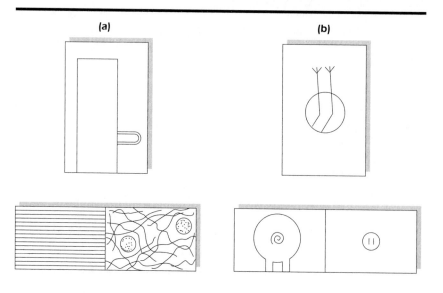

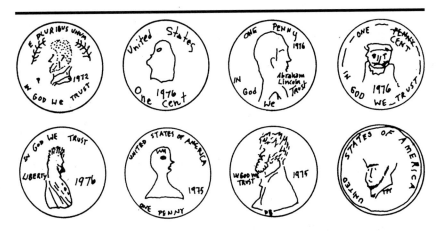

Figure 7-6
What's Wrong With This Picture?
*Eight different American adults drew these
eight depictions of the U.S. penny (Nickerson &
Adams, 1979). Can you tell what is right or
wrong about each one? Clearly, many people
have trouble recollecting the appearance of an
object as common as the penny. Given this difficulty, how easily can people recall the appearance of a person whom they see only briefly,
during a time of great psychological stress,
such as during the eyewitness observation of a
crime?*

*By the way, in case you're penny-less but curi-
ous, the drawing with the most correct features
is the far left one on the bottom row.*

Later, after a different activity, all participants were shown two slides and were asked which they had seen. One slide showed a stop sign, the other a yield sign. Accuracy on this task was 34% better for participants who had received the consistent (stop-sign) question than for participants who had received the inconsistent (yield-sign) question. This experiment and many others (e.g., Loftus, 1975, 1977; described in Loftus & Doyle, 1992) have shown how easily eyewitness accounts can become distorted. We can easily be led to construct a memory that differs from what we really observed.

Loftus (e.g., Loftus & Ketcham, 1991; Loftus, Miller, & Burns, 1987) has been instrumental in pointing to the potential problems of wrongful conviction when eyewitness testimony is used as the sole or even the primary basis for convicting persons accused of crimes. Further, she has noted that eyewitness testimony is often a strong determinant of whether a jury will convict an accused person. The effect is particularly pronounced if eyewitnesses appear to be highly confident of their testimony, even if the eyewitnesses can provide few perceptual details or offer apparently conflicting responses. John Brigham, Roy Malpass, and others (e.g., Bothwell, Brigham, & Malpass, 1989; Brigham & Malpass, 1985; Shapiro & Penrod, 1986) have pointed out that eyewitness identification is particularly suspect when witnesses identify persons of a race other than their own. Astonishingly, even infants seem to be influenced by postevent information when recalling an experience, as shown through their behavior in operant-conditioning experiments (Rovee-Collier et al., 1993).

Not everyone views eyewitness testimony with such skepticism, however (e.g., see Zaragoza, McCloskey, & Jamis, 1987). Judith McKenna, Molly Treadway, and Michael McCloskey (1992) have argued that psychologists need to know a great deal more about the circumstances that impair eyewitness testimony before opposing such testimony before a jury. At present, the verdict on eyewitness testimony is still not in.

Recall a situation in which you and at least one other person were in the same place, at the same time, thus sharing the same experience, yet you both remember the experience differently. That is, each of you recalls different sights or sounds, different sequences of events, or different statements as having been said. How do you account for these differences?

MINILECTURE

*Eyewitness Testimony
(Ch 8)*

How do we construct our own memory? During consolidation of information in long-term memory, we construct our memories based on what we already know, what we expect, and what we learn after we have gained new information but before it has been consolidated into memory.

PRACTICAL PSYCHOLOGY 7-1

Eyewitness Testimony—What's Your Judgment?

In 1986, Timothy was convicted of brutally murdering a mother and her two young daughters (Dolan, 1995). For committing this gruesome crime, he was sentenced to die, and for 2 years and 4 months, Timothy lived on death row. Although the physical evidence did not point to Timothy, eyewitness testimony placed him near the scene of the crime at the time of the murder. Subsequently, it was discovered that a man who looked like Timothy was a frequent visitor to the neighborhood of the murder victims, and Timothy was given a second trial. After Timothy's family spent more than $100,000 on legal fees, Timothy was acquitted. Although Timothy is now deeply in debt, he was lucky to be able to return to his wife and child and to his job in the U.S. Army.

A survey of U.S. prosecutors estimated that about 77,000 suspects are arrested each year, based primarily on eyewitness identification (Dolan, 1995). Studies of more than 1,000 known wrongful convictions have pointed to errors in eyewitness identification as being "the single largest factor leading to these false convictions" (Wells, 1993, p. 554). What proportion of eyewitness identifications are mistaken? The answer to that question varies widely ("from as low as a few percent to greater than 90%"; Wells, 1993, p. 554), but even the most conservative estimates of this proportion suggest frightening possibilities. Clearly, there are tragic consequences for the falsely convicted, but another outcome of wrongful conviction is that the police stop searching for the true criminal, who is then free to continue committing further crimes.

Steps can be taken to enhance eyewitness identification (e.g., using methods to reduce potential biases, to reduce the pressure to choose a suspect from a limited set of options, and to ensure that each member of an array of suspects fits the description given by the eyewitness, yet offers diversity in other ways; described in Wells, 1993). In addition, some psychologists (e.g., Loftus, 1993a, 1993b) and many defense attorneys feel that jurors should be advised that the degree to which the eyewitness feels confident of her or his identification does not necessarily correspond to the degree to which the eyewitness is actually accurate in her or his identification of the defendant as being the culprit. On the other hand, some psychologists (e.g., Egeth, 1993; Yuille, 1993) and many prosecutors feel that the existing evidence, based largely on simulated eyewitness studies rather than on actual eyewitness accounts, is not strong enough to risk attacking the credibility of eyewitness testimony when such testimony might send a true criminal to prison, thereby preventing the person from committing further crimes. Still others (e.g., Bekerian, 1993; described also in LaFraniere, 1992) suggest that there are no typical eyewitnesses, and conclusions based on an average case should not necessarily be applied to all other cases.

Suppose that you were a juror in a case of murder, for which the defendant would be sentenced to death or to life in prison if convicted. How would you weigh eyewitness testimony in such a case? How would your views change if you were not a juror, but rather the family member or close friend of the defendant? What about if you were a close friend of the victim of the crime?

Given the workings of constructive memory, how might you now explain the differing experiences you and your friend had previously "shared"? (See previous margin question)

Memory is the thing you forget with.

Alexander Chase

(a) Witnesses to accidents often forget crucial details, or misremember what they saw. (b) Although the accuracy of eyewitness identification may be questionable in various cases, prosecutors note that jurors find eyewitness testimony very convincing: "Everybody in the jury box looks at the witness, looks at the finger and follows the line right to the defendant, and just about every defendant squirms," said former federal prosecutor John Shepard Wiley Jr. (cited in Dolan, 1995, p. A1).

Future studies of memory will help us to understand memory better than we do now. Although we still have much to learn, we have already learned a great deal, as may be seen in the following memory tips, gleaned from the information in this chapter.

BRANCHING OUT: A Baker's Dozen Tips for Improving Your Memory

1. Be aware of constructive memory processes. If others remember information differently than you do, their memories may be vividly recalled but still inaccurate—just as yours may be.

2. Use external memory aids, such as shopping lists, calendars (for noting key appointments and dates), and alarms and timers. Make lists of things you need to do; designate specific customary locations for things you tend to misplace often (e.g., keys or sunglasses); and place important items and reminders where you cannot miss noticing them.

3. Use either of two basic strategies often used by mnemonists such as S. and S. F.: When you are asked to remember many isolated items of information, you should either (a) translate the items into visual images or (b) try to find ways to connect the items to one another so that you can recall them more easily. You also may want to use particular mnemonic devices (e.g., categorical clustering, interactive images, pegwords, method of loci, acronyms, and acrostics) that take advantage of these strategies.

4. Along the same lines, use chunking to group a large number of unconnected items into a smaller number of interconnected items.

5. Rehearse (practice learning) information that you want to remember. For instance, suppose that you have trouble remembering the names of people you meet. Pay close attention to people's names when they first say their names, and then address them by name several times during your initial meeting.

6. Recall that the more time you spend trying to learn information, the better you will learn it. Make use of your spare moments (e.g., while waiting in line or while waiting for an event to begin) as opportunities for learning whatever information you wish to remember.

7. Try to avoid cramming your study sessions all together. Spread them out as much as possible.

8. When trying to remember information (e.g., when studying), try to find more than one way in which to encode the information, so that you may recall it better later. On the other hand, give particular emphasis to encoding

information at the same level (e.g., physical, acoustic, semantic) at which you will be asked to recall it.

9. As much as possible, try to encode information in a context that matches as closely as possible the context in which you expect to need to retrieve it. Along the same lines, if you are having trouble retrieving information (e.g., where you put your keys), try to put yourself in about the same context in which you encoded the information. (If you cannot put yourself physically in the same context, use your imagination to re-create the same context as much as possible.)

10. Use metamemory to think about your own memory processes. Monitor your own experiences with memory, to find for yourself the circumstances that enhance—as well as those that hinder—your own memory abilities.

11. Look for ways to find meaning in the information you want to remember. If the meaning of the information does not seem obvious, find ways to relate it to your own experiences as much as possible.

12. Organize information you want to remember, and make up your own cues for retrieving the information.

13. Be wary of using drugs (e.g., alcohol or marijuana) that may impair your memory.

Many of the suggestions for enhancing your memory involve the use of language and thought. We depend on language and thought in order meaningfully to encode, store, and retrieve information. On the other hand, we cannot think or use language without depending on our memory. Now that we have probed the workings of memory, we are ready to examine the processes of language and thought, discussed in the next chapter.

SUMMARY

How Do Psychologists Study Memory? 192

1. *Memory* (a *hypothetical construct*) is the means by which we use our knowledge gained from past experiences in handling our present experiences.

2. Severe loss of memory is referred to as *amnesia*. *Anterograde amnesia* refers to difficulty in remembering facts about events that occurred after the loss of memory function (i.e., in anterograde amnesia, people seem to forget facts *before* they have a chance to store the facts), whereas *retrograde amnesia* refers to severe difficulty in remembering facts about events that occurred before the loss of memory function (i.e., in retrograde amnesia, people seem to forget information, going *backward* from the time of the trauma).

3. *Mnemonists* rely on special techniques, such as imagery, for greatly improving their memory; anyone can use these techniques.

4. Two of the main kinds of tasks used for studying memory are *recall*, in which a person is asked to produce items from memory, and *recognition*, in which a person must indicate whether presented items have been observed previously.

5. In addition to recall and recognition tasks, which involve *explicit memory* (participants are asked to recall information intentionally), memory researchers study *implicit memory* (participants show that they are using information stored in memory without necessarily trying to do so or even realiz-

ing that they are doing so). Psychologists also study *procedural knowledge* ("knowing how"—skills, such as how to ride a bicycle) and *declarative knowledge* ("knowing that"—factual information, such as the meanings of terms in a psychology textbook).

How Have Psychologists Traditionally Viewed Memory? 197

6. Memory is often viewed as involving three stores: (1) *sensory memory*, capable of holding up to about nine images in memory for fractions of a second; (2) *short-term memory*, capable of holding about five to nine items of information for a minute or two; and (3) *long-term memory*, capable of storing large amounts of information almost indefinitely.

7. Three operations that occur in all three kinds of memory are (1) *encoding*, by which information is placed into memory storage; (2) *storage*, by which information is kept in storage; and (3) *retrieval*, by which information is pulled from memory into consciousness.

8. The *iconic store* refers to visual sensory memory.

9. We often organize lengthy or complex information into smaller and simpler *chunks*, which we can remember more easily.

10. Some theorists distinguish between (a) *semantic memory*, our memory for facts that are not tied to any particular pre-

vious experiences, and (b) *episodic memory*, our memory for events that are tied to particular previous experiences. Semantic memory operates on *concepts*, organized in the form of *schemas*.

What Are Some Alternative Ways to View Memory? 201

11. From one perspective, *working memory* usually is defined as being part of long-term memory, and it also includes short-term memory. Working memory holds only the most recently activated portions of long-term memory, and it moves these activated elements, via *parallel processing*, into and out of short-term memory.

12. The *levels-of-processing framework* suggests that memory involves a continuum of successively deeper levels at which information can be processed.

13. According to Squire's taxonomy, there are several kinds of memory: declarative (including semantic and episodic memory) and nondeclarative (including procedural memory, conditioning, habituation and some other simple forms of memory, and *priming*, in which information in memory becomes activated by stimuli).

14. Although researchers have yet to identify particular locations for particular memories, they have been able to learn a great deal about the specific structures of the brain that are involved in memory (e.g., the hippocampus, the cortex, and the basal ganglia). In addition, researchers are studying microscopic physiological processes involved in memory, such as the role of some specific neurotransmitters (e.g., serotonin and acetylcholine) and hormones.

How Is Information Encoded, Stored, and Retrieved? 205

15. Encoding of information in short-term memory appears to be largely based on sounds.

16. Information in long-term memory is encoded primarily in a *semantic* form, based on the meanings of words.

17. Theorists disagree as to whether all information in long-term memory is encoded in terms of underlying meanings or whether some information is also encoded in terms of *images* (mental pictures).

18. *Mnemonic devices* (e.g., categorical clustering, interactive imagery, acronyms, and acrostics) are used to improve memory recall.

19. How we *rehearse* information influences how well we keep it in memory. When we use elaborative rehearsal, connecting new information to what we already know, we are better able to remember the new information.

20. Using *metacognition*, we think about our thinking and how to use strategies to improve it. Through metamemory, we use strategies to influence our memory processes.

21. People tend to remember better when they use *distributed learning* (learning that is spaced over time), rather than *massed learning* (learning that occurs within a short period of time). This spacing effect may occur as a result of the process of *consolidation*, by which we gradually integrate new information into long-term memory.

22. Two of the main theories of forgetting are (1) *interference theory*, in which information is forgotten when new information replaces the information that was to be remembered; and (2) *decay theory*, in which information is lost over time.

23. Information retrieval from short-term memory appears to be handled through *serial processing* (each item in short-term memory is processed one at a time) that is exhaustive (all items in short-term memory are checked before the desired item is retrieved).

24. According to *encoding specificity*, how information is encoded at the time of learning will greatly affect how it is later recalled. The context of encoding and the organization of information also influence encoding and later retrieval of information.

How Do We Construct Our Own Memory? 212

25. Memory appears to be not only *reconstructive* (a reproduction of what was learned), but also *constructive* (influenced by existing expectations and schemas).

PATHWAYS TO KNOWLEDGE

Choose the best answer to complete each sentence.

1. Ellen was in a car crash and subsequently had difficulty recalling events that occurred prior to the crash. She is showing signs of
   (a) retrograde amnesia.
   (b) anterograde amnesia.
   (c) automotive amnesia.
   (d) concussive amnesia.

2. Implicit memory differs from explicit memory, in that
   (a) implicit memory involves conscious awareness of memory retrieval, whereas explicit memory does not.
   (b) explicit memory involves conscious awareness of memory retrieval, whereas implicit memory does not.
   (c) explicit memory is primarily procedural, whereas implicit memory is primarily declarative.
   (d) explicit memory involves a deeper level of processing.

3. The short-term store
   (a) encodes primarily visual information.
   (b) holds information for just a few days at a time.

(c) holds information for about 2 minutes or less.

(d) registers discrete visual images for fractions of a second.

4. Metamemory refers to

(a) the ability to increase your long-term memory capacity through extensive training.

(b) memories of experiences that occurred prior to the age of 4 years.

(c) individuals' understanding of and control over their own memories.

(d) a reserve source for memory enhancement.

5. Which of the following is **not** one of the ways in which interference affects short-term memory?

(a) New information makes it more difficult to remember previously learned information.

(b) Old information makes it more difficult to remember new information.

(c) What you have already memorized makes it more difficult to memorize new information.

(d) Information decays through time and subsequent learning.

6. Researchers studying long-term memory have suggested that information is encoded in three of the following ways. Which of the following is **not** one of the ways in which information is encoded in long-term memory?

(a) in underlying meanings.

(b) in words.

(c) in images.

(d) in completely accurate reconstructions of events.

7. Memories for personally experienced events with associated time tags are referred to as

(a) episodic.

(b) semantic.

(c) reconstructive.

(d) schematic.

8. Which of the following does **not** influence the ease of recall of information from long-term memory?

(a) what a person already knows

(b) the person's mood or state of consciousness (e.g., influence of drugs)

(c) the environmental context in which the person is recalling the information

(d) the use of retroactive-interference strategies

9. Studies of eyewitness testimony by Elizabeth Loftus have shown that

(a) the accuracy of participants' recall of events is, on average, about 95%.

(b) participants' memories are influenced by prior experiences, which shape their recall of events.

(c) if research participants are given certain retrieval cues, particularly while under the influence of hypnosis, they will reproduce events with extraordinary detail.

(d) visual memories have high permanence and are not easily manipulated by external probing.

10. Which of the following is **not** a primary reason that adults perform better on memory tasks than do 6-year-old children?

(a) Adults know to use specialized strategies for remembering information.

(b) Adults have much bigger brains than children do.

(c) Adults simply know more and can therefore more easily integrate new information into what they already know.

(d) Adults generally have much more elaborate schemas for organizing what they know than children do.

11. If you want to remember the contents of this chapter, you should probably

(a) spread out your studying over many study sessions, across an extended period of time.

(b) study as much as possible at one study session, instead of scattering your attention by spreading out your study sessions.

(c) repeat the important information over and over as many times as possible, being careful to use exactly the same words, sequences, and methods for repeating the information each time.

(d) avoid getting side-tracked by seeing how the information in the chapter relates to your own experiences and to what you already know.

Answer each of the following questions by filling in the blank with an appropriate word or phrase.

12. _____ _____ are used to aid in memory retrieval.

13. _____ is an effective way of maintaining information in short-term memory, perhaps even for eventual transfer to long-term memory.

14. _____ _____ is the term used by Tulving to describe the effects of a close match between the context of encoding and the context of retrieval.

15. An alternative to the three-stores view of memory suggests that there is not any particular number of memory stores, but rather that memory occurs at multiple _____ of _____.

Match the following descriptions to the type of memory being described:

16. primarily involves acoustic encoding

17. very briefly holds iconic images

18. primarily involves semantic encoding

19. holds an almost limitless number of items virtually indefinitely

20. involves consolidation of memories

21. generally holds information for up to 2 minutes

(a) long-term memory

(b) short-term memory

(c) sensory memory

Answers

1. a, 2. b, 3. c, 4. c, 5. d, 6. d, 7. a, 8. d, 9. b, 10. b, 11. a, 12. Mnemonic devices, 13. Rehearsal, 14. Encoding specificity, 15. levels, processing, 16. b, 17. c, 18. a, 19. a, 20. a, 21. b

PATHWAYS TO UNDERSTANDING

1. How might constructive memory processes help to support a person's prejudices? How might prejudices lead to greater distortions in constructive memory?

2. Suggest an experiment to show that memory is not just reconstructive, but also very much *constructive*.

3. How might you increase the likelihood that you would remember the meanings for the key terms in this or any other chapter?

CHAPTER OUTLINE

What Is Problem Solving?
Well-Structured Problems:
    Heuristics and Algorithms
Ill-Structured Problems: Insight
Hindrances to Problem Solving
Aids to Problem Solving
Expertise: Knowledge and Problem
    Solving
Problem Solving on the Job

What Are Judgment and Decision Making?
Decision-Making Strategies
Heuristics and Biases of Judgment
Decision Making and Risk
    Assessment

What Is Reasoning?
Deductive Reasoning
Inductive Reasoning

What Is Language?

How Do We Acquire Language?

How Do We Understand and Arrange Words?
Semantics: The Study of Meaning
Syntax: The Study of Structure
Take My Disk, Make Me a Hard
    Copy, and Xerox It for Me!

How Do We Use Language in a Social Context?
Linguistic Relativity and Linguistic
    Universals
Bilingualism

Thought and Language

Prior to the final signing of the North American Free-Trade Agreement (NAFTA), a Canadian plane crashed on the border between the United States and Canada. The plane was carrying 32 Canadian citizens, 44 U.S. citizens, and 6 other travelers. The plane started out in Montreal, was headed to New York, and was to proceed on to Mexico City. On which side of the border should the survivors be buried?

Thoughts have power. . . . you can make your world or break your world by your thinking.

Susan L. Taylor

Which would help you more in solving the preceding problem: a calculator or a law book? Perhaps you would do better to restate the question: If you had survived the crash, on which side of the border would you want to be buried? To figure out the answer to the preceding problem, you very likely had to stop and think.

When we **think,** we process information in our minds. Thinking involves *representation* (creating and organizing mental images, statements, or underlying meanings of information). Generally, our mental representations involve **language,** the use of an organized way of combining words in order to communicate. Nonetheless, it is entirely possible to think without using language. For example, if you were putting together a jigsaw puzzle, you might use some language as you thought about solving the puzzle (e.g., "Is this blue piece part of the sky or part of the water?"), but you could probably put a puzzle together perfectly well without using language. Recall from Chapter 7 that memories and thoughts may be represented in visual or other sensory images, or they may be represented in the form of language or underlying meanings. Later in this chapter, we focus specifically on how we think in terms of language, and we consider some of the ways in which language and thought interact. First, however, we focus our thoughts on thinking.

Usually, when psychologists talk about thinking, they are talking about critical thinking. In **critical thinking,** we consciously direct our mental processes to reach particular goals, such as solving problems, making judgments or decisions, and reasoning. In everyday thinking, these three kinds of goals overlap somewhat. Nonetheless, the goal of thinking differs for each one. The goal of **problem solving** is to overcome obstacles (e.g., not having enough money to buy a car) in order to reach a solution. The goal of **judgment and decision making** is to evaluate various possibilities and to choose one or more of them (e.g., choosing the car that would please you the most for the amount of money you have to spend). The goal of **reasoning** is to draw conclusions from evidence (e.g., infer the relative safety of a given model after reviewing the safety records of various cars). First, we address problem solving.

thinking a psychological function that involves the representation and processing of information in the mind

language the use of an organized means of combining words in order to communicate

critical thinking the conscious direction of mental processes toward representing and processing information, usually in order to find thoughtful solutions to problems

problem solving a set of processes for which the goal is to overcome obstacles obstructing the path to a solution

judgment and decision making cognitive processes by which an individual may evaluate various options and select the most suitable option from among various alternatives

reasoning a set of cognitive processes by which an individual may infer a conclusion from an assortment of evidence or from statements of principles

When trying to find a suitable place to live, you may use three kinds of critical thinking: (1) problem solving (e.g., finding a way to get enough money together for moving expenses and for deposits and rent on an apartment); (2) reasoning (e.g., gathering information about various neighborhoods and apartment features, to determine the likely amount you'll have to pay to get the features you want in an area you like); and (3) decision making (choosing an apartment that best suits your needs for the amount you have available to spend).

WHAT IS PROBLEM SOLVING?

Psychologists have noticed that the way in which we solve problems depends on whether we face **well-structured problems,** for which there is a clear path for finding a solution, or **ill-structured problems,** for which there is no obvious path to solution. When we face well-structured problems (sometimes called "routine problems"), we can usually reach a solution by following an orderly series of steps.

You probably have extensive experience in solving countless well-structured problems. In school, you have tried to solve numerous problems in specific content areas (e.g., math, history, geography). These problems had clear paths—if not necessarily easy paths—to their solutions. For example, you can probably see a clear path for solving each of the following problems: "What is 98,453,179,305 divided by 413,253,763?" "How did scientific, medical, and technological advances influence the outcome of the Civil War?" "How does the climate and topography of India influence Indian agriculture?" Although the path may not be easy, at least it is relatively clear.

When solving ill-structured problems (sometimes called "insight problems"), on the other hand, we may have no idea of how to find a solution. We may struggle with the problem for a long time, feeling that we are getting no closer to a solution, when all of a sudden, the solution becomes clear to us. Once we see a solution, we may consider it so simple and so obvious that we cannot believe that we did not see it before. To get an idea of how difficult it is to see a path for solving an ill-structured problem, find an answer to the following one (after Gardner, 1978, cited in Weisberg, 1995):

How do you work to solve the most difficult problems you face?

Finding Your Way 8-1

The Schneeville Wolverines won the championship basketball game 72–49, yet not one man on the team scored as much as a single point. How is that possible?

It isn't that they can't see the solution. It's that they can't see the problem.

G. K. Chesterton

Well-Structured Problems: Heuristics and Algorithms

In solving the preceding ill-structured problem, you will either suddenly realize the correct answer, or you will find it very difficult to see a path for solving the problem. In contrast, the paths toward solving well-structured problems are generally clear, if not easy. In fact, most well-structured problems can generally be solved using one of two kinds of strategies: heuristics or algorithms. **Heuristics** are informal strategies, often described as "rules of thumb," for solving problems. They can be seen as mental shortcuts, which sometimes work and sometimes do not. In fact, one heuristic strategy is simply trial and error—try whatever solution comes to mind, and see whether it works; if it does not work, try something else. For example, in solving the history problem mentioned previously, you could look up various scientific, medical, and technical advances that occurred before the end of the Civil War; then you could check to see which ones may have influenced the outcome of the war.

In solving the long-division problem, you probably could try to find a more formal way of finding an answer, rather than just guessing at solutions and then checking to see whether they are correct. For this problem and many others, you might prefer to use **algorithms,** which are much more formal strategies than are heuristics. To use algorithms, you repeatedly follow a particular series of steps until you reach the correct solution. For example, to figure out a long-division problem, you repeatedly divide the digits of one number (the dividend) by another number

well-structured problem problem with a well-defined path to solution

ill-structured problem problem with no clear, obvious, readily available path to solution

heuristics informal, speculative, shortcut strategies for solving problems, which sometimes work and sometimes do not

algorithm formal path for reaching a solution, which involves one or more successive processes that usually lead to an accurate answer to a question

(the divisor). Algorithms work quite well for solving some kinds of problems. In fact, if you can find an algorithm that applies to your problem, and you accurately carry out all the steps of the algorithm, you are virtually guaranteed to reach an accurate solution to the problem.

What are the pros and cons of using algorithms versus heuristics? If you can find the right algorithm and then follow it correctly, you will feel much more confident of reaching an accurate solution than you will if you use heuristics. On the other hand, heuristics generally apply to a wider variety of problems. Many problems that can be solved by using a heuristic have no obvious algorithm for reaching a solution. Can you think of an algorithm for figuring out how the climate and topography of India influence Indian agriculture? Probably not. Even if you could think of an algorithm for figuring out how the climate and topography of India influence Indian agriculture, the algorithm would probably be so complicated and take so long to apply that you might give up before finding an answer. Some algorithms may be so complex and may take so long to carry out that it is just not practical to use them. For instance, an algorithm for cracking a safe would be to try all possible combinations of numbers—not a practical strategy for the safe-cracker in a hurry.

Before we move from well-structured problems to ill-structured ones, we should consider two complementary processes that greatly enhance our ability to see a path to the solution of a problem: **analysis,** in which we break down wholes into various parts, and **synthesis,** in which we put parts together into wholes. For example, to find a solution for a mechanical problem with a car, you would use analysis. Suppose that your car will not start. You would analyze (break down) the whole car-starting process into its various parts, then you would look for the origin of the problem in each of those parts. On the other hand, you would probably use synthesis to create a new type of sauce for pasta. You would take various ingredients (your parts) and combine them to make a delicious sauce (the whole).

Analysis and synthesis can also work together to serve various purposes. As any good mechanic knows, once you have broken down the problem, you must still put the car back together. As any good cook knows, if the sauce does not taste good, you must analyze the problem to figure out which ingredients or which steps in cooking led to the unpleasant taste.

Computer programs used as an aid to medical diagnosis make frequent use of algorithms *for carrying out routine operations during problem solving. On the other hand, physicians and* pathologists *often use* heuristics *when trying to diagnose the source of a medical problem.*

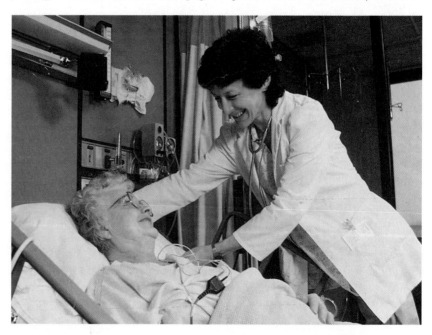

analysis the process of breaking down a complex whole into smaller elements

synthesis the process of integrating various elements into a more complex whole

Wild Campus
9:00 Center
2nd Floor

Ill-Structured Problems: Insight

Some problems just do not lend themselves to either analysis or synthesis. Recall the earlier example, in which the Schneeville Wolverines won the game 72–49, but not one single man scored a single point. Were you able to figure out how that was possible? If you were, you probably did not follow a clear path to find the answer; instead, you realized the answer all of a sudden: The Schneeville Wolverines are all women. This problem is a good example of an ill-structured problem. Now that you have an idea of how puzzling ill-structured problems can be, stop for a minute and try to solve another ill-structured problem, shown in Figure 8-1 (after Sternberg, 1986b).

Like other ill-structured problems, the nine-dot problem requires **insight:** In order to solve it, you need to see the problem in a new way—different from the way you would probably see the problem at first, and different from the way you would probably solve problems in general. You will not find a clever algorithm or even a handy heuristic for solving insight problems. When you have an insight, you form a new idea about a problem, which helps you to understand either the problem or a strategy for solving the problem. Frequently, insight leads you to see how to put together old and new information to come up with a solution. You are more likely to have an insight when solving ill-structured problems than when solving well-structured ones. Insights usually seem to be sudden. However, they often appear following a lot of thought and hard work, without which the insight would never have occurred.

Insight problems have interested many psychologists, particularly Gestalt psychologists, for decades. According to Gestalt psychologists, insight problems require problem solvers to perceive the problems as wholes. Gestalt psychologist Max Wertheimer (1945/1959) observed that to solve insight problems, you have to break away from the associations and information you already know, and you have to see the problems from a new outlook. For example, to solve the Wolverines problem, you had to break away from your expectations regarding arithmetic word problems to see the problem in a different way.

To Gestalt psychologist Wolfgang Köhler (1927), insight involves suddenly becoming aware of a whole strategy for solving a problem. To study the emergence of insight, Köhler observed how apes reacted to ill-structured problems. As you can see in Figure 8-2, Köhler's ape showed sudden insight in figuring out to stack a

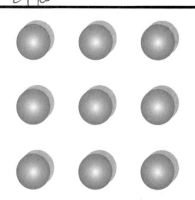

Figure 8-1

The Nine-Dot Problem

Pictured here are nine dots. Try to connect all nine dots with no more than four line segments. Do not lift your pencil off the page, do not go through a dot more than once, and do not use more than four straight line segments. Can you connect the nine dots without ever taking your pencil off the page? (After Sternberg, 1986b)

 **MINILECTURE**

Well-Formed and Ill-Formed Problems (Ch 10)

insight a seemingly sudden understanding of the nature of something, often as a result of taking a novel approach to the object of the insight

Figure 8-2

Insightful Problem Solving

Wolfgang Köhler, a Gestalt psychologist, studied insight by observing problem solving in apes. In the study depicted here, he placed an ape in a cage with a few boxes. At the top of the cage, just out of reach, was a bunch of bananas. After trying to grab the bananas, the ape showed sudden insight: The ape realized that the boxes could be stacked on top of one another, to make a structure tall enough to reach the bunch of bananas.

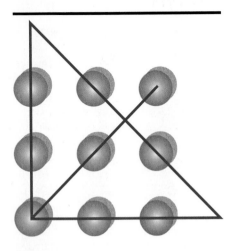

Figure 8-3

A Solution to the Nine-Dot Problem

Most people assume that the line segments must stay within the square that seems to be formed by the nine dots. Therefore, they do not allow their solution to go beyond the boundaries of the dots. The problem does not state this limitation. In fact, the problem cannot be solved if the four line segments must stay inside the dotted figure.

Real progress in understanding nature is rarely incremental. All important advances are sudden intuitions, new principles, new ways of seeing.

Marilyn Ferguson

mental set a cognitive phenomenon in which an individual is predisposed to use an existing model for representing information, even when the existing model inadequately represents the information in a new situation

negative transfer the hindrance of problem solving as a result of prior experience in solving apparently related or similar problems

set of boxes to reach a luscious bunch of bananas. In other studies, Köhler's ape figured out how to connect two short sticks to make one long stick to reach bananas lying just outside the cage. In each case, the ape appeared to grapple with the problem for a while and then suddenly, in a flash of insight, to see a path to the solution.

More recently, Janet Metcalfe (1986; Metcalfe & Wiebe, 1987) has studied insight in humans and has found that people, too, show a distinctive pattern of insight during problem solving. In her experiments, she asked people to rate their own progress in solving routine (well-structured) and insight (ill-structured) problems. When solving routine problems, people perceive steady progress toward solving the problems. In contrast, when solving insight problems, they do not feel that they are making progress at all until moments before they solve the problems.

Finding Your Way   8-2

Try your own hand at solving one of the insight problems Metcalfe used (Metcalfe & Wiebe, 1987): "A prisoner was attempting to escape from a tower. He found in his cell a rope which was half long enough to permit him to reach the ground safely. He divided the rope in half and tied the two parts together and escaped. How could he have done this?" Record your own progress toward reaching the answer.

Now that you have an idea of how insight works in solving ill-structured problems, we return to the nine-dot problem. Did you have an insight when trying to solve that problem? Most people find the problem extremely hard to solve, and many very bright persons never solve it. One common difficulty is a mistaken assumption. Figure 8-3 shows the solution to the nine-dot problem. Before you read the figure caption, can you guess the mistaken assumption that many people make?

As the solution to the nine-dot problem shows, many people make mistakes when defining the problems they face. Speaking of solutions and problem definitions, the solution to Metcalfe's rope problem is that the man divided the rope lengthwise, separating the strands into two parts, then using the two sets of strands to make the rope long enough. You may not have considered this solution because you defined "divided" as meaning that the rope had to be cut across its diameter. Such a cut would divide the rope into two segments, but not change the length of the rope. You might not have considered that the lengthwise strands of the rope could also be divided. Sometimes a misdefined problem can be hard—if not impossible—to solve. When solving problems, it helps to try to free ourselves of assumptions that can get in the way of solving the problems.

Hindrances to Problem Solving

Many insight problems are hard to solve because problem solvers tend to bring old mental sets to new problems. **Mental sets** are frames of mind in which we carry old ways of thinking to new situations, and in which the old ways do not fit the new situations. The old ways of thinking often involve methods for solving problems that may have worked for solving many problems in the past, but that do not work for solving the present problem. For example, in the nine-dot problem, many people use an old way of seeing the problem ("Stay within the dots"). They carry the old information from a situation where the information helped (e.g., when solving dot-to-dot problems) to a situation where it actually makes problem solving more difficult. The carryover of information that makes problem solving more difficult is termed **negative transfer.** (A related process, *positive transfer,* is discussed later.)

One type of mental set that leads to negative transfer involves fixation on a particular use (function) for an object: Specifically, **functional fixedness** is the inability to realize that something known to have a particular use may also be used for performing other functions. Functional fixedness prevents us from using old tools in novel ways to solve new problems. Becoming free of functional fixedness is what first allowed people to use a reshaped coat hanger to get into a locked car, and it is what first allowed thieves to pick simple spring door locks with a credit card. It is also what might allow you to think of an introductory psychology textbook as a resource for criminal ideas.

In what kinds of situations has negative transfer made problem solving more difficult for you? What else seems to hinder your ability to solve problems?

Aids to Problem Solving

If mental sets and negative transfer make problem solving harder, what might make problem solving easier? Among other things, cognitive psychologists have noticed two positive influences on problem solving: positive transfer and incubation.

Positive Transfer

As you may have guessed, based on the meaning of negative transfer, **positive transfer** occurs when what you know about solving an old problem helps you to solve a new problem. Mary Gick and Keith Holyoak (1980, 1983) have studied positive transfer involving *analogies,* in which some similarities are observed between things that appear dissimilar in other ways. To do their work, they used the "radiation problem," a problem first studied by Karl Duncker (1945):

Finding Your Way 8-3

Imagine that you are a doctor treating a patient with a cancerous stomach tumor. You can not operate on the patient, but unless you destroy the tumor somehow, the patient will die. You could use X rays to destroy the tumor. If the X rays are strong enough, they will destroy the tumor. Unfortunately, the X rays that are strong enough to destroy the tumor will also destroy healthy cells of the body, and the X rays must pass through healthy cells to get to the tumor. X rays that are not strong enough, however, will not destroy the tumor. Your problem is to figure out how to destroy the tumor without also destroying the healthy cells surrounding the tumor.

What solutions would you suggest for solving this problem? Duncker had an insightful solution for this problem. This solution involves dispersion: Direct many weak X rays toward the tumor from different points outside the body (see Figure 8-4). No single X ray will be strong enough to destroy either the healthy tissue or the tumor. However, the rays will be aimed so that they will all converge (come together) on the tumor. This idea is used today in some X-ray treatments.

Before Gick and Holyoak showed Duncker's radiation problem to research participants, they presented another problem, called the "military problem" (after Holyoak, 1984, p. 205). This problem involved a somewhat similar convergence solution, applied to the capture of a fortress by way of various roads. The correspondence between the radiation and the military problems was quite close, although not perfect. The question is this: When participants were shown a convergence solution to the military problem, were they helped in solving the radiation problem? If research participants received the military problem with the

functional fixedness a mental set in which an individual fails to see an alternative use for something that has been known previously to have a particular use

positive transfer the facilitation of problem solving as a result of prior experience in solving related or similar problems

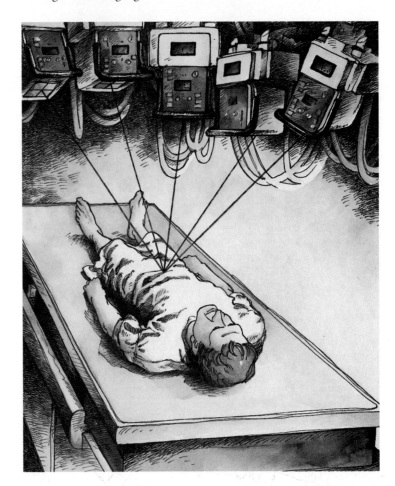

Figure 8-4
The X-ray Problem
Karl Duncker's X-ray problem requires an insightful solution: Issue several weak X rays from different directions, which converge on a single point—in this case, the tumor. Duncker and other psychologists have studied whether insight into one problem involving convergence paves the way for positive transfer to other problems involving convergence. (After Duncker, 1945)

convergence solution and then were given a hint to apply it in some way to the radiation problem, about 75% of the participants reached the correct solution to the radiation problem. In comparison, fewer than 10% of the research participants who did not first receive the military story reached the correct solution to the X-ray problem.

Incubation

Another aid to problem solving is incubation. In **incubation,** you simply put the problem aside for a while. For example, suppose that you find yourself unable to solve a problem, and none of the strategies you can think of seem to work. Try just setting the problem aside for a while to incubate. During incubation, you do not consciously think about the problem. Still, you may be processing the solution to the problem subconsciously. Some cognitive psychologists even say that incubation is an essential stage of problem solving (e.g., Cattell, 1971; Helmholtz, 1896; Poincaré, 1913).

Craig Kaplan and Janet Davidson (1989) have reviewed the literature on incubation and have found that the benefits of incubation can be enhanced in two ways: (1) Invest enough time in the problem initially; perhaps explore all aspects of the problem, and investigate several possible avenues of solving it. (2) Allow sufficient time for incubation to permit your old associations due to negative transfer to weaken somewhat. A drawback of incubation is that it takes time. If you have a deadline for the problem solution, you must begin solving the problem early enough to meet the deadline, including the time you need for incubation.

[Cuando en duda, consúltalo con tu almohada.]
When in doubt about what is right, consult your pillow overnight.

Mexican proverb

incubation a period of rest, following a period of intensive effort in problem solving, during which the problem solver puts aside the problem for a while

Expertise: Knowledge and Problem Solving

Experts solve problems in their areas of expertise more readily than novices solve such problems. What can explain the benefits of expertise for problem solving? The research that launched the study of expertise was a study of chess experts and novices, conducted by William Chase and Herbert Simon (1973). Chase and Simon found that chess experts were better able to recall positions of chess pieces on a chess board, but only if the chess pieces were arranged in a way that they might be in an actual chess game. Chase and Simon therefore suggested that experts differed from novices in their amount and organization of knowledge—in the Chase and Simon study, the experts' knowledge of positions of pieces in chess games helped during the recall of positions from actual games.

Many psychologists, such as Michelene Chi and her colleagues, have studied large numbers of experts in various fields (e.g., see Chi, Glaser, & Farr, 1988). What most clearly separates experts from novices is that experts know more, and they can better organize what they know. For example, Jill Larkin and her colleagues compared experts with novices in physics. Because the experts knew more than did the novices, the experts could more effectively represent physics problems in their minds (Larkin et al., 1980).

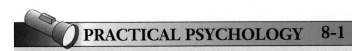

PRACTICAL PSYCHOLOGY 8-1

Problem Solving on the Job

A problem almost all of us face at one time or another is the need to find a job we enjoy, at which we feel both competent and useful. According to career consultants (described in Cooper, 1994), a good way for you to get a job is to think in terms of finding out the problems faced by potential employers and then to show how you can help them to solve their problems. If you have good organizational skills, search for potential employers who need help with organizing large quantities of things or facts (e.g., parts distributors or libraries). If you know how to make strangers feel at ease, think about potential employers who need help in getting strangers to feel relaxed and comfortable (e.g., hospitals and lawyers' offices). Whatever your skills may be, the key to solving your problem of needing to find a job is to shift your perspective to think of yourself as a problem solver who can put your talents to work in solving the problems faced by your potential employers.

If you enjoy solving problems of all kinds, you may even enjoy being an independent consultant or a corporate troubleshooter, helping companies to solve a variety of problems, from product development to manufacturing to marketing (described in Corcoran, 1993). Some companies even use problem solving as a strategy for fostering team spirit and company morale and for enhancing the collaboration and productivity among team members (described in Johnson, 1994). For example, in 1994, ITT Hartford Insurance Group tackled a communitywide problem—homelessness—by assigning 60 of its white-collar employees the task of painting 20 rooms in a homeless shelter within 7 hours (Johnson, 1994). Various participants in the project gave mixed reviews regarding how well this particular effort would affect their performance on the job, but most seemed to support the general idea of addressing community problems as a means of enhancing productivity and cooperation at work.

What kinds of problems do you find interesting and challenging? What skills and knowledge do you find useful in solving these problems, and how do these resources help in solving the problems?

Psychologists are not the only people interested in problem solving. In fact, one of the rare points about which almost all psychologists can agree is that all people face problems to be solved.

To summarize this section, problem solving involves inventing or discovering strategies in order to overcome obstacles (see Practical Psychology 8-1). Another kind of thinking involves evaluating various possibilities and then choosing one (or some). The next section deals with how we make judgments and decisions.

What is problem solving? People generally solve well-structured problems by using heuristics or algorithms. Well-structured problems also often lend themselves to analysis and to synthesis. In contrast, ill-structured problems often require insight. Hindrances to problem solving include negative transfer of mental sets, as in functional fixedness. Positive transfer, incubation, and expertise may help in problem solving.

WHAT ARE JUDGMENT AND DECISION MAKING?

What career should you choose? In what subject area should you major in college? What courses should you take? Whom should you choose as friends, as dates, as lifetime partners? Many of the decisions and judgments we make have long-term consequences. More often, in the course of our everyday lives, we make less crucial judgments (e.g., "Which of my friends is the most reliable and supportive if I need help?") and decisions (e.g., "Which menu item do I want to eat now?").

Decision-Making Strategies

Just how do people make judgments and decisions? Early theorists, many of whom were economists rather than psychologists, assumed that decision makers operate in ideal circumstances and make ideal decisions. Since then, theorists have recognized that we humans may not make ideal decisions, although we often try to do so. More often than not, we make decisions based on personal preferences, biases, and mental shortcuts.

Leading the way in this realization was Herbert Simon (1957), who went on to win the Nobel Memorial Prize in Economic Science. Simon noted that we often show **bounded rationality:** We are rational, but within limits. Simon then described one of the most common decision-making strategies: satisficing. In **satisficing,** we do *not* first consider all possibilities and then carefully compute which one will give us the most gains, with the fewest losses. Instead, we consider various possibilities one by one, and we choose the first one that is satisfactory—just good enough. In this way, we satisfy our minimum requirements, but we do so by considering as few choices as we can. For example, you may use satisficing when considering research topics for a term project or paper. Of the countless possible topics, you probably consider quite a few, but then you may settle on the first satisfactory or even fairly good topic you think of, without continuing your search endlessly.

In the 1970s, Amos Tversky (1972a, 1972b) built on Simon's notion of bounded rationality and observed that we sometimes use a different strategy when we are faced with far more alternatives than we feel that we can reasonably consider in the time we have available. In such situations, we do not try to manipulate mentally all the important attributes of all the options available to us. Rather, we use a process of **elimination by aspects:** We focus on one aspect (attribute) of the various options, and we form a minimum criterion for that aspect. We then eliminate all options that do not meet that criterion. Then, for the remaining options, we select a second aspect for which we set a minimum criterion by which to eliminate additional options. We continue using a sequential process of elimination of

bounded rationality the recognition that although humans are rational, there are limits to the degree to which they demonstrate rational cognitive processes across situations

satisficing a decision-making strategy in which an individual chooses the first acceptable alternative that becomes available, without considering all possible alternative options

elimination by aspects a decision-making strategy in which an individual focuses on one attribute of an overabundance of options, forms a minimum criterion for that attribute, and then eliminates all options that do not meet that criterion; the process is repeated until either a single option remains or few enough remain that a more careful selection process may be used

Whatever your age and experience, making a decision can be difficult. As much as possible, we may try to make ideal choices, but we frequently settle for using shortcut methods that make the selection process easier and less time consuming.

options by considering a series of aspects, until eventually only a single option remains.

For example, in choosing a car to buy, we may focus on total price as an aspect, dismissing factors such as maintenance costs, insurance costs, or other factors that might realistically affect the money we will have to spend on the car in addition to the sale price. Once we have weeded out the alternatives that do not meet our criterion, we choose another aspect, set a criterion value, and weed out additional alternatives. We continue in this way, weeding out more alternatives, one aspect at a time, until we are left with a single option. In practice, it appears that we may use some elements of elimination by aspects or satisficing to narrow the range of options to just a few; then we use more thorough and careful strategies for selecting among the few remaining options (Payne, 1976).

Heuristics and Biases of Judgment

Amos Tversky was not content just to observe that we often make decisions based on less than optimal strategies. Adding insult to injury, Tversky and his associate Daniel Kahneman observed that we often use mental shortcuts and even biases that limit and sometimes distort our ability to make rational decisions. Tversky and Kahneman have studied several heuristics (mental shortcuts) and biases of decision making and other judgments.

Availability

One of the heuristics studied by Tversky and Kahneman is the availability heuristic. According to the **availability heuristic** (Tversky & Kahneman, 1973), people make judgments on the basis of how easily they can call to mind what they perceive as relevant instances of a phenomenon. In one study of this heuristic, Tversky and Kahneman (1973) asked people the following question: "Are there more words in the English language that begin with the letter *R*, or are there more words that have *R* as their third letter?" Most people could more easily think of words beginning with R than they could of words having R as the third letter (Tversky & Kahneman, 1973), but there are actually more English words with R as the third letter.

Note that heuristics (such as availability) do not always lead to wrong judgments. Indeed, we use heuristics because they are so often right. For instance, one of the factors that makes particular events more available in our minds is that these events may occur more frequently. However, availability may also be influenced by how recently we observed the event, as well as how unusual, distinctive, or salient the particular event is for us. Because we generally make decisions in which the most common instances are the most relevant and valuable ones, the availability heuristic is often a convenient shortcut with few costs. However, when particular instances are better recalled because of biases (e.g., the media has sensationalized a particular event), the availability heuristic may lead to less than optimal decisions.

For example, suppose that someone were to ask you, "What is the likelihood that a former football star and likable actor would be accused of murdering his ex-wife?" You might well give a higher estimate now than you would have in 1990. In many situations, however, the answer that first comes to mind is correct because common answers are often more likely to be correct than are uncommon ones.

A conclusion is the place where you get tired thinking.

Martin H. Fischer

---

availability heuristic a cognitive shortcut in which an individual makes judgments on the basis of how easily he or she can call to mind what are perceived as relevant instances of a given phenomenon

Representativeness

Another heuristic studied by Tversky and Kahneman is essentially a mental shortcut most of us use when trying to guess about the likelihoods of particular occurrences. For instance, suppose that you had been talking to someone while standing in line at a supermarket. This stranger said to you, "Did you see that big burly guy that just left? I know that he has rough hands and that he likes to watch sports on TV. One of the clerks told me that he's a lawyer, and someone else told me that he's a bus mechanic. Which one do you think he is?" In your opinion, which occupation is this person more likely to have? Why do you think this occupation is more likely to fit the description?

The stranger's description seems better to *represent* bus mechanics than to represent lawyers, so most people would answer that the burly man is a bus mechanic. That may seem like a pretty good first guess, but it leaves out important information that should be considered: In general, there are more lawyers than there are bus mechanics. This information suggests that this person is more likely to be a lawyer than to be a bus mechanic, so "lawyer" might be a better guess. Of course, if you really wanted to make a superb guess, you would figure out the statistical likelihood that any given person is a lawyer versus a bus mechanic, and then you would figure out the likelihood that a person with this description fits into either of these occupational categories. I feel certain that the likelihood that most people would go to that trouble approaches zero, but I may be overly confident about my guess. What do you think?

Overconfidence

Most of us occasionally fall prey to **overconfidence**—being overly trustful of personal skills, knowledge, or judgment. In one study (Fischhoff, Slovic, & Lichtenstein, 1977), people were given 200 two-choice statements. For example, choose the correct answer to complete this statement: "Absinthe is (a) a liqueur, (b) a precious stone." People were asked to choose the correct answer and to give the probability that their answer was correct. People were strangely overconfident. For example, when people were 100% confident of their answers, they were right only 80% of the time! (*Absinthe* is a liqueur.)

That would be a good thing for them to cut on my tombstone: Wherever she went, including here, it was against her better judgment.

Dorothy Parker

✺ BRANCHING OUT: Decision Making and Risk Assessment

The consequences of decision making extend through all aspects of our lives, at every age, but the decisions we make early in life often have more long-term consequences than the decisions we make later on. "Adolescents are the only age group in which mortality has risen since 1960. Three-quarters of adolescent deaths are caused by accidents, homicide and suicide, all of which indicate a lethal propensity for risk-taking" (Goleman, 1987, p. C1). One reason that many adolescents seem to engage in risky behavior is that they do not understand how to evaluate the probabilities associated with a given risk. For example, if a particular teen couple engages in unprotected sexual behavior, and pregnancy or sexually transmitted diseases do not result from a first encounter, they may actually believe that because they beat the odds the first time, the cumulative probability of these outcomes goes *down*, rather than *up* for each subsequent unprotected sexual encounter.

Some psychologists (e.g., Elkind, 1967) have suggested that many adolescents irrationally believe that they (the teenagers) are *invincible:* The dangerous situations that bother, injure, or even kill other persons will not harm them. Perhaps the invincibility fallacy is one reason for adolescents' false belief that when they take more chances, their risks go down, rather than up: Each time they beat the odds, their belief in their own invincibility is strengthened.

Another reason for risk-taking among adolescents may be their tendency grossly to under- or overestimate the number of their peers who engage in particular behaviors. For instance, although only 15% of 10- to 14-year-olds reported occasionally smoking, adolescents guessed that almost 80% of 10- to 14-year-olds occasionally smoke (described in Goleman, 1987). Yet another consideration may be simply that adolescents give differing emphasis to particular risks than adults would give to these risks. For example, most adults would give far more weight to a

overconfidence a bias affecting decision making, in which individuals overestimate the probability that their own responses are accurate or even more broadly overvaluate their own skills, knowledge, or judgment

"More than 30% of regular smokers will die from some diseases connected to their habit, losing an average of 8.3 years from normal life expectancy" (Specter, 1989, p. A20). Surprisingly, however, many smokers have a greater fear of dying in a plane crash, dying of AIDS, or dying from some other cause that is much less likely because these less probably outcomes are nonetheless more readily available in their minds.

Can your reasoning be accurate but your conclusion incorrect? If so, how? If not, why not?

deductive reasoning a set of processes by which an individual tries to draw a logically certain and specific conclusion from a set of general propositions

inductive reasoning a set of processes by which an individual attempts to reach a probable general conclusion, based on a set of specific facts or observations

risk of death, disease, or unwanted pregnancy than to a risk of social rejection; many adolescents, however, would not do so.

On the other hand, adults are not entirely rational in their assessment of risk, either. For example, the risk of contracting AIDS from a dentist who has the disease is between 1 in 263,000 and 1 in 2,600,000 (Scott, 1991). Nonetheless, many adults who think nothing of driving a car to work each day (thereby facing much greater odds of confronting death) will shun an AIDS-infected dentist, even if the dentist wears protective gear and rigorously follows sterile techniques. Similarly, many adults grossly overestimate the health risks associated with artificial sweeteners, traces of pesticides remaining on fruits and vegetables, occasional medical or dental X rays (Specter, 1989), and immunizations.

Much of the work on judgment and decision making has focused on the mistakes people make. As Jonathan Cohen (1981) has pointed out, however, people do act rationally much of the time, even though they do not act rationally all of the time.

What are judgment and decision making? Psychologists have come to recognize that people often show bounded rationality when making decisions, frequently using strategies such as satisficing and elimination by aspects. People are also subject to various heuristics of judgment, such as availability and overconfidence.

WHAT IS REASONING?

As this chapter has shown, people often make decisions and other judgments based on very informal methods. Reasoning involves a more formal process, in which we draw conclusions based on evidence (Wason & Johnson-Laird, 1972). Reasoning is often classified as either deductive or inductive. **Deductive reasoning** is the process of drawing conclusions based on one or more general statements regarding what is known; through deductive reasoning, we can reach a logically certain conclusion, which usually involves a specific application of the general statements. In contrast, **inductive reasoning** proceeds from specific facts or observations in order to reach a probable general conclusion that may explain the facts. Inductive reasoning cannot lead to a logically certain conclusion—only to a particularly well-founded or likely conclusion. Thus, inductive reasoning proceeds from specifics to an uncertain but probable general conclusion, but deductive reasoning proceeds from a set of general premises to a specific and logically certain conclusion.

For example, given these known statements— "If Joan is a college student, then Joan can read; Joan is a college student"—we can deduce with certainty, "Therefore, Joan can read." Of course, the truthfulness of these statements influences the accuracy of the deductive inference. Nonetheless, this conclusion is unequivocally certain, given that we accept the initial statements as being true. In contrast, when given a set of observations, such as, "Every person we've seen carrying books is able to read; Jim is carrying books," we can induce a probable conclusion, such as, "Jim can probably read." An inductive conclusion is probable, but it is not certain. (For instance, Jim might be illiterate and carrying the books for someone else.)

Deductive Reasoning

Deductive reasoning is based on *logical propositions*, which are assertions that may be either true or false. For example, you can judge for yourself whether the following propositions are true or false: "All politicians are dishonest." "Some students like peanut butter." "No students are illiterate." Each isolated proposition states what is already believed to be true. What intrigues psychologists (and other people) is that when you relate two or more propositions through deductive reasoning, you can infer new information that was not stated in the propositions. For example, "If all politicians are dishonest, and John is a politician, then John is dishonest." "If some students like peanut butter, and no students are illiterate, and Joaquim is a student, then Joaquim is not illiterate." (We cannot infer that Joaquim likes peanut butter because only some students like it.) Thus, by making inferences from a set of general premises stating what is known, deductive reasoners can reach a specific new conclusion.

Logic, n., the art of thinking and reasoning in strict accordance with the limitations and incapacities of human misunderstanding.

Ambrose Bierce

Inductive Reasoning

Suppose that you are not given a neat set of logical propositions from which you can draw a conclusion. Instead, you are given a set of observations. For example, suppose that you notice that all the cars you have observed run on gasoline fuel. From these observations, you might inductively reason that all cars run on gasoline fuel. However, unless you can observe all the cars that ever have existed or ever will exist, you will be unable to prove your conclusion. Even one car that runs on fuel other than gasoline would disprove your conclusion. Still, after you made many observations, you might conclude that you could draw a reasonable inductive inference.

Everybody gets so much information all day long that they lose their common sense.

Gertrude Stein

In the preceding situation and in many other situations requiring reasoning, we are not given clear premises from which to deduce a surefire conclusion. In these types of situations, we simply cannot deduce logically valid conclusions. An alternative kind of reasoning is needed. Inductive reasoning involves gathering specific facts or observations to infer a general conclusion that may explain the facts. For example, when Jessica Fletcher (of the TV show *Murder, She Wrote*) uses inductive reasoning to solve crimes, she gathers clues (many specific observations) and develops a general idea about what probably happened at the scene of a crime.

Scientific research is based on inductive reasoning. A key feature of this method is that we cannot reasonably leap from saying, "All observed instances of X are Y," to saying, "Therefore, all X are Y." For example, suppose that a child has seen many different kinds of birds flying in the sky. She may reasonably conclude, "All birds fly." However, when she visits the zoo and meets penguins and ostriches for the first time, she sees that her inductive conclusion is false. She finds that her inductive conclusion, based on many observations, can be disproved by just one observation that differs from her conclusion.

Furthermore, inductively based conclusions can never be proved, regardless of how many observations are made or how well reasoned the conclusions are. Such conclusions can only be supported, to a greater or lesser degree, by what is known at the time. Thus, inductive reasoners must state any conclusions about a hypothesis in terms of likelihoods, such as "There is a good chance of rain tomorrow," or "There is a 99% probability that these findings are not a result of random events."

Thus far in this chapter, we have focused on various kinds of thinking. Throughout this discussion, we have alluded to processes that involve our use of language, but we have not addressed the ways in which language and thought interact. It is as if we were discussing various aspects of how fish swim without mentioning the watery environment in which fish do so. Because language and thought are so thoroughly intertwined, it is difficult to separate them, even in a chapter dedicated to understanding language and thought as distinct phenomena. The

Weather prediction is based on gathering a large quantity of data and then inductively inferring the likelihood of particular weather patterns, given the current conditions. As the people on the right have discovered, inductive reasoning does not lead to 100% certain conclusions.

language we hear and read shapes our thoughts, and our thoughts shape what we say and write. Hence, if we are to understand thinking, we must know more about language.

Think about how you reason, make judgments and decisions, solve problems, and do other kinds of thinking. If you could not use language to think, how would you think?

What is reasoning? Deductive reasoning involves reaching logically certain conclusions based on one or more general statements about what is believed to be true. Inductive reasoning involves reaching probable general conclusions based on various specific facts or observations.

WHAT IS LANGUAGE?

It is difficult to imagine how we might be able to think without using *language*, an organized way of combining words in order to communicate. It is not impossible to think without using language, however. As was mentioned in Chapter 7, we may be able to represent information in the forms of images and of abstract underlying codes that may be viewed as a sort of "mentalese" for representing the meanings underlying our thoughts (Pinker, 1994).

Essentially, there are two fundamental aspects of using language to communicate: (1) understanding the language we hear (or see signed) and read, and (2) speaking (or signing) and writing. Psycholinguists often describe these two aspects as (1) **verbal comprehension,** the ability to understand written and spoken language, such as words, sentences, and paragraphs; and (2) **verbal fluency,** the ability to produce language.

The great diversity of languages around the world all serve these fundamental communicative functions. Surprisingly, however, many people believe that their own language is somehow better than other languages. Although this belief is quite popular, no evidence supports the notion that any language is meaningfully better than any other language. Based on observations of countless languages, psychologists, *psycholinguists* (who study the interaction of language and thought), *linguists* (who study language), and anthropologists have observed that all languages seem to have the following six general properties (e.g., Brown, 1965; Clark & Clark, 1977; Glucksberg & Danks, 1975): Language is

Effective speech is stronger than all fighting.

Husia proverb

verbal comprehension the ability to comprehend written and spoken linguistic input, such as words, sentences, and paragraphs

verbal fluency the ability to produce written and spoken linguistic output, such as words, sentences, and paragraphs

1. *Communicative*—Language lets us communicate with one or more persons who share our language.
2. *Arbitrary*—Language creates an arbitrary (not based on any meaningful pattern) relationship between a symbol (such as a word) and whatever the symbol represents—an idea, a thing, a process, a relationship, a characteristic, or a description.
3. *Productive*—Although language users must stick to the general patterns of a given language, they can produce their own original and new combinations of words; in fact, the possibilities for creating new combinations are virtually limitless.
4. *Dynamic*—Languages constantly change.
5. *Meaningfully structured*—Language has a structure; only particular patterns of symbols have meaning. Different arrangements lead to different meanings.
6. *Multiply structured*—Language can be analyzed at more than one level (e.g., sounds, words, and sentences).

Sounds and gestures can be used to communicate without language. However, both spoken and signed languages involve far more complexity than simple communication. For instance, both spoken English and American Sign Language (ASL) have all the properties of any other languages: They involve arbitrary symbols; they are communicative, productive, dynamic, and meaningfully structured; and they can be analyzed at more than one level.

The ability to analyze language at more than one level has made the science of **linguistics,** the study of language, quite complex. For starters, language may be analyzed in terms of sounds, words, phrases, sentences, and even larger units of language such as conversations, stories, or discussions in textbooks. At the level of sounds, the smallest distinguishable unit of all possible human speech sounds is the *phone,* of which there are more than 100. No known language uses all of the possible phones, however. Each language uses only some of these possibilities; the particular speech sounds that the users of a particular language can identify are *phonemes.* In English, phonemes are generally identifiable as vowel or consonant sounds.

For example, in English, the difference between the /p/ and the /b/ sound is an important phonemic distinction. We hear a difference between "they bit the buns from the bin" and "they pit the puns from the pin" (a meaningless sentence). On the other hand, we ignore the differences between some phones. (Figure 8-5, a diagram of a human vocal tract, shows where and how some phones—human speech sounds—are produced.)

Finding Your Way   8-4

Put your open hand about 1 inch (about 2½ cm) from your lips. Now, use your normal speech, without trying to add any sounds you do not normally pronounce, and say aloud, "Put the paper cup to your lip." If you are like most English speakers, you felt a tiny puff of air when you pronounced the /pʰ/ in Put and paper and no puffs of air when you pronounced the /p/ in cup or lip.

One or more phonemes can become a **morpheme,** the smallest unit of individual or combined phonemes that gives meaning within a particular language. You may already know two forms of morphemes: (1) *root words,* to which we add (2) *affixes*—both *suffixes,* which follow the root word, and *prefixes,* which come before the root word. The word *affixes* itself comprises (a) the root word *fix;* (b) the prefix *af-,* which is a variant of the prefix *ad-,* meaning "toward," "to," or "near"; and (c) the suffix *-es,* which indicates the plural form of a noun.

Linguists use the term **lexicon** to describe the entire set of morphemes in a given language or in a given person's vocabulary. The average English-speaking high school graduate has a lexicon of about 60,000 root morphemes, and most college students have lexicons about twice that large (Miller, 1990).

linguistics the study of language structure and change

morpheme the smallest unit of single or combined sounds denoting meaning within a given language

lexicon the entire set of morphemes in a given language or in a given person's linguistic repertoire

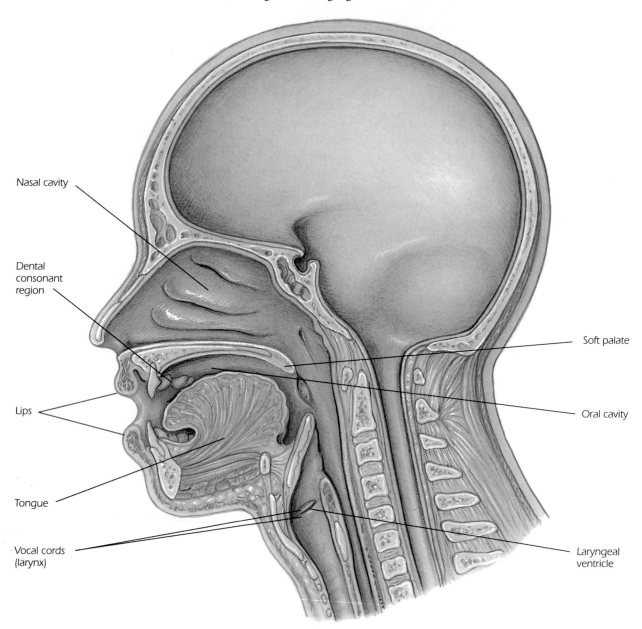

Figure 8-5
The Human Vocal Tract
The human vocal tract enables us to produce the various phonemes (speech sounds), many of which other animals cannot produce.

syntax a level of linguistic analysis, which centers on the patterns by which users of a particular language put words together at the level of the sentence

discourse the most comprehensive level of linguistic analysis, which encompasses language use at the level beyond the sentence, such as in conversation, in paragraphs, and so on

The next level of analysis is **syntax,** which refers to the way in which users of a particular language put words together into sentences. A sentence has at least two parts: (1) a *noun phrase,* which contains at least one noun (usually the subject of the sentence) and (2) a *verb phrase,* which contains at least one verb and whatever the verb acts on. The verb phrase states something about the subject, usually an action or a characteristic of the subject. Linguists consider the study of syntax to be basic to understanding the structure of language.

The final level of linguistic analysis is **discourse,** which encompasses language use at the level beyond the sentence, such as in conversation, in paragraphs, in stories, and in textbooks. When linguists analyze discourse, they consider many features of the social context in which language occurs. Table 8-1 summarizes these aspects of language. Next, we discuss how people learn to use language.

TABLE 8-1
Summary of a Description of Language

Language input			Language output
D e c o d i n g	Phonemes (distinctive subset of all possible phones)	. . . /t/ + /ā/ + /k/ + /s/ . . .	E n c o d i n g
	Morphemes (from the distinctive lexicon of morphemes)	. . . take (content morpheme) + s (plural function morpheme) . . .	
	Words (from the distinctive vocabulary of words)	It + takes + a + heap + of + sense + to + write + good + nonsense.	
	Phrases: Noun phrases (NP: a noun and its descriptors) Verb phrases (VP: a verb and whatever it acts on)	NP = It + VP = takes a heap of sense to write good nonsense.	
	Sentences (based on the language's syntax—syntactical structure)	It takes a heap of sense to write good nonsense.	
	Discourse	"It takes a heap of sense to write good nonsense," was first written by Mark Twain (Lederer, 1991, p. 131).	
Comprehend language			**Produce language**

Finding Your Way 8-5

Write a paragraph (or choose one in this book) containing at least three sentences. For each level of linguistic analysis shown in Table 8-1, find an example, using the paragraph you wrote or chose.

What is language? Language is an organized way of combining words in order to communicate; it is communicative, arbitrary, productive, dynamic, meaningfully structured, and multiply structured. It can be analyzed in terms of phones, phonemes, and morphemes, as well as in terms of lexicon, syntax, and discourse.

Language grows out of life, out of its needs and experiences. . . . Language and knowledge are indissolubly connected; they are interdependent.

Annie Sullivan

HOW DO WE ACQUIRE LANGUAGE?

Around the world, people seem to *acquire* their first language in just about the same way. As revolutionary linguist Noam Chomsky (1959) hypothesized, and

*"No, Jimmy, it's not 'I sawed a chair' -- it's
'I have seen a chair' or 'I saw a chair'."*

© Glenn Bernhardt

numerous cross-cultural and naturalistic studies have suggested, humans may have an innate *language-acquisition device (LAD)*, which helps people to acquire language. Within the first years of life, we start out listening and responding to language, and then we become able to produce it ourselves.

Before birth, fetuses may be sensitive to the sounds spoken by their mothers, as shown by their responses to her voice immediately after birth (DeCasper & Fifer, 1980; DeCasper & Spence, 1986). After birth, newborns seem to move rhythmically in response to the speech of their caregivers (Field, 1978; Martin, 1981; Schaffer, 1977; Snow, 1977; Stern, 1977). The emotional expressions of infants also respond to and match those of their caregivers (Fogel, 1992). Although crying may be the most obvious sound produced by infants, linguists are more interested in their cooing. When infants **coo,** they try making all the possible phones that humans can make. The cooing of infants around the world, including that of deaf infants, is about the same for all babies and all languages.

As infants progress to the babbling stage, they gradually become unable to tell the differences among all phones, and deaf infants generally stop making playful sounds. When infants are **babbling,** they start producing and perceiving only the phonemes of their own language. Thus, although the cooing of infants around the world is pretty much the same, infant babbling is different for different languages.

Eventually, the child's first wondrous word is spoken (or signed)—followed shortly by 1 or 2 more, and so on, until by age 18 months, children typically have vocabularies of 3 to 100 words (Siegler, 1991), most of which are nouns that identify familiar objects. Because young children's vocabulary cannot yet communicate all they wish to say, children often overextend the meanings of the words they know to cover things and ideas for which they do not yet have distinct words. This overly broad use of a few words to cover many concepts is an **overextension error.** For example, the general term for any man may be "Dada"—which can be quite upsetting to a new father in a public place.

Gradually, by about 2½ years of age, children begin to combine single words to produce two-word phrases. At this time, they begin to understand syntax. These early phrases seem more like telegrams than like conversations: The articles, prepositions, and so on, are usually left out. Hence, linguists refer to these early phrases as **telegraphic speech.** In fact, telegraphic speech can be used to describe three-word phrases and even slightly longer ones if the phrases include only nouns or verbs, leaving out prepositions, articles, conjunctions, and so on. Vocabulary grows rapidly, more than tripling from about 300 words at about 2 years of age to about 1,000 words at about 3 years of age. Almost incredibly, by age 4 years, children learn the basics of adult syntax and language structure. By age 5 years, most children can also understand and produce quite complex and uncommon sentence constructions, and by age 10 years, children's language is basically the same as that of adults.

cooing oral expression that explores the production of all the phones that humans can possibly produce

babbling a prelinguistic preferential production of only those distinct phonemes characteristic of the language being acquired

overextension error overapplication of the meaning of a given word to more things, ideas, and situations than is appropriate for the word; usually made by children or other persons acquiring a language

telegraphic speech rudimentary syntactical communications of two words or more, which are characteristic of very early language acquisition, and which seem more like telegrams than like conversation because function morphemes are usually omitted

How do we acquire language? When acquiring language, we progress from cooing to babbling to one-word utterances, in which we may commit overextension errors. When we begin to use telegraphic speech, we begin using syntax, and from that point on, both vocabulary and syntax become increasingly sophisticated.

HOW DO WE UNDERSTAND AND ARRANGE WORDS?

Semantics: The Study of Meaning

One way to analyze the structure of language is through **semantics,** the study of the meanings of words. Linguistic meanings can take two forms: (1) The strict, dictionary definition of a word is its **denotation;** (2) the emotional overtones and other less well-defined meanings of a word are its **connotations.** For example, when you look up "good" in the dictionary, you see many meanings for the word. In addition, when you use "good" in conversation, you may suggest many shades of meaning that are not listed in the dictionary.

In addition to understanding words based on dictionary meanings of words, we may also come to understand the meanings of words based on typical examples that represent these words. For instance, when we hear the word *bird*, we base our understanding of the word on typical examples of birds, such as robins or sparrows, rather than on unusual instances, such as vultures, penguins, or ostriches.

Psychologists learn a lot about how we figure out the meanings of words through the study of semantics. Language involves more than just word meanings, however. We also need to understand another aspect of language in order to understand what we hear and read. For example, the word *read* may be used to describe present or past actions. (I *read* now, and I *read* yesterday.) The word *run* can be used as a noun (e.g., home *run*) or as a verb (e.g., *run* home). To figure out the meanings of some words, we must understand syntax.

Syntax: The Study of Structure

Syntax is the systematic way in which words can be put together in a particular order to make meaningful phrases and sentences (Carroll, 1986). The meaning of a sentence depends not only on the meanings of the words in it, but also on how those words are put together. Syntax begins with the study of the grammar of phrases and sentences.

Language is very difficult to put into words.

Voltaire

What are a few ways in which you find or figure out the meanings of words? What are some of the ways in which you can *shade* the meanings of words when you speak?

PRACTICAL PSYCHOLOGY   8-2

Take My Disk, Make Me a Hard Copy, and Xerox It for Me!

Many people find it impossible to graciously welcome changes in a language's syntax, and many people consider such changes hard to put up with. For example, most contemporary grammar books now say that it is okay to split an infinitive (e.g., "to graciously welcome") or to end a sentence with a preposition (e.g., "to put up with"). However, many people still find these usages distressing.

The same people who resist syntactical changes in language, however, often welcome new words into the lexicon. For example, who among us does not recognize the verb "to xerox" (first entered the lexicon in 1965), the noun "hard copy" (first entered in 1954), and the use of the noun "disk" as meaning a flat magnetic medium for storing computer data (first entered in 1972)? What new words have entered your lexicon recently? (Many additional examples are described in Levine, 1993, and Roark, 1992; also, *Merriam-Webster's Collegiate Dictionary* [10th edition] lists the years when many words entered the American English lexicon.)

---

semantics the study of meanings of words in language

denotation the strict dictionary definition of a word

connotation an emotional overtone, presupposition, or other nonexplicit meaning of a word

Most English teachers use the word *grammar* to refer to how people *ought* to structure their sentences. In contrast, psycholinguists use **grammar** to mean the study of the regular patterns of language. Although these patterns relate to the uses and relationships of words in a sentence, they also extend to larger and smaller units of language (such as whole conversations and the pronunciation of individual words). Your English teachers may have taught you *prescriptive grammar*, which prescribes the "correct" ways in which to pattern your use of language. Psycholinguists study *descriptive grammar*, which describes the existing patterns in the language that you use. In particular, linguists are interested in syntax.

To assure yourself that you are, indeed, highly proficient in using English syntax, try the following activity:

Finding Your Way   **8-6**

Using the following 10 words, create (a) five strings of words that make grammatical sentences and (b) five sequences of words that violate the syntax rules of English grammar: ball, hoop, rolled, into, put, round, bounced, big, the, girl.

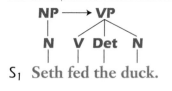

S_1 Seth fed the duck.

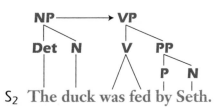

S_2 The duck was fed by Seth.

Figure 8-6
Phrase-Structure Grammar
The phrase structure of S_1 differs from that of S_2, even though the two sentences clearly have very similar meanings. Noam Chomsky's transformational grammar highlights the relationships among various phrase structures, such as the relationship between S_1 and S_2.

MINILECTURE
Structure of Language (Ch 9)

grammar the study of language in terms of regular patterns that relate to the functions and relationships of words in a sentence—extending as broadly as the level of discourse and as narrowly as the pronunciation and meaning of individual words

Linguists have found that every known language in the world has a grammatical syntax. No one has ever discovered a human language that has no grammatical structure. Similarly, variations of some languages may have differing grammatical structures. For example, some variations of English have a grammar that differs from the grammar of standard English. These various grammars fulfill the purposes of grammar about equally well; they just do so in different ways.

Phrase-structure grammars analyze sentences according to the order in which each word appears. The specific sequence of words in a given sentence is the *surface structure* of the sentence. Phrase-structure grammars are also termed *surface-structure grammars* because they focus on surface structures of individual sentences. Basically, any sentence in a given language can be broken down according to the phrase-structure grammar for the given language.

Phrase-structure grammars are commonly used, but they may not be of great value for understanding the relationships between sentences. Noam Chomsky (1957) changed the way linguists study syntax by demonstrating that phrase-structure grammars cannot show how the structures of different sentences are related. Consider the following two sentences (see Figure 8-6).

S_1: Seth fed the duck.
S_2: The duck was fed by Seth.

Oddly enough, as Figure 8-6 shows, phrase-structure grammar indicates no particular relationship between sentences S_1 and S_2. Phrase-structure analyses of each sentence look very different. In contrast, according to Chomsky's *transformational grammar*, the two sentences are clearly related, in that one sentence is simply a transformation of the other. The structural difference between the two sentences shows a difference in attitude. The *attitude* is how the speaker looks at the events or items being described. In the first sentence, the speaker's attitude emphasizes the actions being taken by Seth. In the second sentence, the speaker's attitude highlights what is happening to the duck.

Chomsky proposed that sentences can be analyzed both at a surface-structure level (as in phrase-structure grammars) and at a deep-structure level. A *deep-*

structure level takes into account the underlying relationships among sentences that have related meanings. Chomsky proposed a way to change deep structures into one or more surface structures. The processes for transforming (changing) deep structures into surface structures are referred to as *transformations.*

Finding Your Way **8-7**

Look over the following sentences, and figure out how the surface structure of each one can be transformed into the others.

1. *The book was bought by the student.*
2. *By whom was the book bought?*
3. *The student was bought by the book.*
4. *Who bought the book?*
5. *The book bought the student.*

Many psycholinguists believe that even the combined study of syntax and semantics does not fully explain our use of language. According to these psycholinguists, to understand language, we must also study language in a social context.

How do we understand and arrange words? Linguists study semantics, the analysis of word meanings. Linguists are also interested in the descriptive grammar of syntax. Whereas phrase-structure grammars describe the surface structures of individual phrases, transformational grammar highlights the meaningful relationships among sentences, as shown in transformations among surface structures.

The basic agreement between human beings, indeed what makes them human and makes them social, is language.

Monique Wittig

HOW DO WE USE LANGUAGE IN A SOCIAL CONTEXT?

In recent decades, linguists have become increasingly interested in pragmatics and sociolinguistics. **Pragmatics** is the study of how people use language. More specifically, *sociolinguistics* is the study of how people use language in the context of social interaction. Some sociolinguists even study how people use nonverbal (wordless) communication in conversational contexts. For example, when you use language in conversations, you use gestures and *vocal inflections* (the natural rise and fall in the pitch of your voice).

During job interviews and perhaps first dates, you may be painfully aware of how you use nonverbal and verbal communication in context. Under most circumstances, however, you change how you use language to fit your context without giving these changes much thought. For example, imagine yourself in the following situations:

How do you change the ways in which you use language (e.g., in conversations) to suit the context for using the language (e.g., at work with your supervisor vs. at home with friends)?

pragmatics the study of how people use language, emphasizing the contexts in which language is used

Finding Your Way   8-8

Suppose that you and your friend are going to meet right after work. Suppose also that something comes up, so you must call your friend to change the time or place for your meeting. When you call your friend at work, your friend's supervisor answers and offers to take a message. Exactly what will you say to your friend's supervisor, to ensure that your friend will know about the change in time or location? Suppose, instead, that the 4-year-old son of your friend's supervisor answered. Exactly what would you say in this situation? Finally, suppose that your friend answered directly. How would you have changed your language to suit each context? Note that you would have made these changes even though your purpose in all three contexts was the same.

Linguistic Relativity and Linguistic Universals

Different languages use different lexicons and different patterns of syntax. These differences often relate to differences in the environments in which the languages developed. For example, in terms of lexicon, the Garo of Burma distinguish among many different kinds of rice, which is understandable, because they are a rice-growing culture. Clearly, the Garo have more words for rice than do most other people. The question is this: As a result of these linguistic differences, do the Garo think about rice differently than other people do?

Although some linguists say that language differences do not relate to differences in thinking, others disagree. Many linguists believe in the hypothesis of **linguistic relativity,** which states that the speakers of different languages have differing cognitive systems (systems for thinking). In turn, these different cognitive systems influence how people think. According to the linguistic-relativity view, the Garo think about rice differently than do other people. For example, when the Garo think about rice, they may think about it in more complex ways than may persons who have only a few words for rice. Thus, language shapes thought. The linguistic-relativity hypothesis is sometimes referred to as the *Sapir–Whorf hypothesis,* named after the two people (Edward Sapir and Benjamin Lee Whorf) who first defended it. The Sapir–Whorf hypothesis has been one of the most widely mentioned ideas in all of the social and behavioral sciences (Lonner, 1989).

linguistic relativity a proposition regarding the relationship between thought and language, which asserts that the speakers of different languages have differing cognitive systems, based on the languages they use, and that these different cognitive systems influence the ways in which people speaking the various languages think about the world

Does the bedouin think about sand differently than other people do? If so, do these cognitive differences influence language, or do linguistic differences lead to differences in thinking?

Perhaps because of its widespread acceptance, however, some people have distorted the interpretation of this hypothesis. Even some of the facts that are believed to support the hypothesis have been found false. For example, many social scientists have said that Eskimos have a huge number of words for the single English word *snow*. These social scientists have been wrong. Anthropologist Laura Martin (1986) has firmly stated that Eskimos do *not* have numerous words for snow. Martin understands why her colleagues might think the snow-word myth charming, but she has been quite "disappointed in the reaction of her colleagues when she pointed out the fallacy; most, she says, took the position that true or not 'it's still a great example'" (Adler, 1991, p. 63; described also in Pullum, 1991).

Based on Martin's findings, we can see that it is very hard to find accurate, unbiased information about cultures other than our own. Therefore, we should be careful when drawing conclusions based on cross-cultural studies of language. Sometimes, cross-cultural research distorts both the data and the conclusions, overemphasizing cultural differences.

One way to offset an overemphasis of cultural differences is to study cultural similarities. Some cross-cultural research has focused on **linguistic universals**—characteristic patterns that seem to be true of all languages. One area of research has examined the use of color names. At first glance, color words seem to be an ideal focus of research because people in every culture can be expected to be exposed to pretty much the same range of colors.

Although the color ranges people see are about the same, different languages name colors quite differently. Does this finding mean that there are no linguistic universals? No. It appears that there is a systematic pattern for naming colors across languages, even though the system is used somewhat differently in different languages. Two anthropologists (Berlin & Kay, 1969; Kay, 1975) found what seem to be two linguistic universals about color naming across languages. First, all of the languages surveyed took their basic color terms from a set of just 11 color names: black, white, red, yellow, green, blue, brown, purple, pink, orange, and gray. Languages ranged from using all 11 color names, as in English, to using just 2 of the names, as in New Guinean Dani. Second, when only some of the color names are used, the naming of colors falls into a hierarchy of five levels, as shown in Figure 8-7.

Bilingualism

Cross-cultural research offers one way to study the interactions among language, thought, and social context. Another way is to study **bilinguals**—people who can speak two languages. If a person can speak and think in two languages, does the person think differently in each language? In fact, do bilinguals think differently from *monolinguals*—people who can speak only one language? What differences, if any, arise from being able to speak two languages instead of just one?

Some bilinguals seem to benefit from knowing two languages well, but other bilinguals suffer when they try to master a second language before they have a firm grasp of their first language. In particular, persons who are highly skilled in each language profit from having more than one language (Hakuta, 1986). However, bilinguals suffer ill effects if they are less skilled in their first language, and the second language partially replaces the first.

James Cummins (1976) has suggested that we note a difference between additive and subtractive bilingualism. In *additive bilingualism*, a second language is taught in addition to a relatively well-developed first language. In *subtractive bilingualism*, parts of a second language replace parts of the first language. Cummins believes that the additive form improves people's ability to think. However, the subtractive form harms people's ability to think. In particular, individuals may need to have reached a relatively high level of skill in both languages for bilingualism to improve people's thinking.

Language exerts hidden power, like the moon on the tides.

Rita Mae Brown

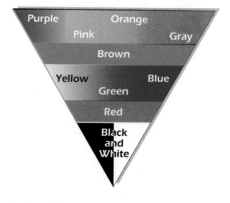

Figure 8-7
A Color Hierarchy
Brent Berlin and Paul Kay found some linguistic universals regarding color naming. Many languages use a set of 11 color names: black, white, red, yellow, green, blue, brown, purple, pink, orange, and gray. When only some of the color names are used, the naming of colors falls into a hierarchy of five levels, as shown here: (1) black, white; (2) red; (3) yellow, green, blue; (4) brown; and (5) purple, pink, orange, gray. Thus, if a language names only two colors, they will be black and white. If it names three colors, they will be black, white, and red. A fourth color will be taken from the set of yellow, green, and blue, and so on until all 11 colors have been labeled.

bilingual person who can speak two languages

linguistic universals characteristic patterns of language that apply across all of the languages of various cultures

In a 1992 poll of U.S. citizens of Hispanic descent (Mexican, Puerto Rican, and Cuban), 90% asserted that all residents and citizens of the United States should learn to speak English (Duke, 1992). This task is often more readily accomplished by children of immigrants than by adult immigrants. Frequently, children born of adult immigrants are fully bilingual, acquiring native fluency in their parents' language, as well as native (or nativelike) fluency in the language of their new country. Sadly, subsequent generations of immigrants all too often fail to become fluent in languages other than English.

Many people enter school in the United States speaking a language other than English. What kinds of programs should be developed to avoid problems of subtractive bilingualism? What kinds of programs should be developed to increase the benefits of additive bilingualism?

Ellen Bialystok and Kenji Hakuta (1994) have found that there probably is no one best way for acquiring a second language. Rather, the kinds of learning experiences that facilitate second-language acquisition should match the context and uses for the second language once it is acquired. For example, the language-acquisition experiences needed by an 8-year-old immigrant who wants to play with nonimmigrant school- and playmates differ from those of a 38-year-old American businesswoman who wants to conduct business in Japan.

How do we use language in a social context? Cross-linguistic studies of language have revealed many linguistic universals. It seems, however, that the distinct language we use may also influence the way we think, but evidence of these differences is not clear-cut. Whereas additive bilingualism may enhance thinking, subtractive bilingualism may hinder it.

This chapter has briefly skimmed the surface of the many issues involved in how we think and how we use language. Many of our most remarkable thoughts and our most appealing uses of language reflect both intelligence and creativity, the subjects of the next chapter.

SUMMARY

What Is Problem Solving?   225

1. *Problem solving* involves working to overcome obstacles.
2. It is easy to see how to find a solution to *well-structured* problems, although it may not be easy actually to solve them. For *ill-structured problems*, such as insight problems, it is hard to see how to find a solution.

3. *Heuristics* are informal strategies for solving problems, which sometimes work and sometimes do not. Heuristics are often contrasted with *algorithms*, which are more formal strategies that generally can guarantee an accurate solution to the problem if they are applied and implemented correctly.

4. *Mental set* refers to the use of a strategy that has worked in the past but that may not work for a particular problem to be solved in the present.

5. *Transfer,* which may be either positive or negative, refers to the carryover of knowledge or skills from one problem or kind of problem to another.

6. *Incubation,* which follows a period of working hard to solve a problem, involves putting aside the problem for a while. During incubation, you may subconsciously work on the problem while you consciously ignore it.

7. Experts differ from novices in both the amount and the organization of knowledge that they can use for solving problems.

What Are Judgment and Decision Making? 232

8. *Satisficing* involves choosing the first acceptable possibility that comes to mind. *Elimination by aspects* involves gradually eliminating various options, based on a ranked set of criteria. Both methods involve *bounded rationality.*

9. People using the *availability heuristic* make judgments based on how easily they can think of relevant instances of a phenomenon.

10. People often show *overconfidence,* appearing overly trusting of their own abilities or judgments.

What Is Reasoning? 236

11. *Reasoning* is the process of drawing conclusions from evidence.

12. In *deductive reasoning,* a person tries to figure out whether one or more logically certain conclusions can be drawn from a set of logical propositions.

13. *Inductive reasoning* involves reasoning from specific facts or observations to reach a general conclusion that may explain the specific facts. Such reasoning is used when it is not possible to draw a logically certain conclusion from a set of premises.

What Is Language? 238

14. *Language* is the use of an organized way of combining words in order to communicate. *Communication* is the exchange of thoughts and feelings, which may or may not include language. Language and thought constantly interact.

15. Language involves (a) *verbal comprehension*—the ability to comprehend written and spoken language, such as words, sentences, and paragraphs; and (b) *verbal fluency*—the ability to produce language.

16. Psycholinguistics is the psychology of language use, and *linguistics* is the study of language.

17. There are at least six properties of language: (1) Language lets us communicate with one or more persons who share our language. (2) Language creates an arbitrary relationship between a symbol and its referent—an idea, a thing, a process, a relationship, or a description. (3) Language has a structure; only particularly patterned arrangements of symbols have meaning, and different arrangements lead to different meanings. (4) The structure of language can be analyzed at more than one level (e.g., phonemes and morphemes). (5) Language users can produce new combinations of words, and the possibilities for new combinations are almost limitless. (6) Languages constantly change.

18. The smallest distinguishable unit of all possible human speech sounds is the phone. The particular set of distinctive speech sounds in a particular language are phonemes. The smallest semantically meaningful unit in a language is a *morpheme.* The entire set of morphemes in a given language is the *lexicon* of the language. *Discourse* encompasses language at a level beyond that of the sentence.

How Do We Acquire Language? 241

19. Humans seem to progress through the following stages in acquiring language: (a) prenatal responsivity to human voices; (b) *cooing,* which includes all possible phones; (c) *babbling,* which includes only the distinct phonemes that characterize the primary language of the infant; (d) one-word expressions; (e) two-word expressions; (f) *telegraphic* speech; (g) basic adult sentence structure (present by about age 4 years).

20. During language acquisition, children make *overextension errors,* in which they extend the meaning of a word to cover more concepts than the word is intended to cover.

21. Children seem to have an innate language-acquisition device (LAD), which makes it easier to acquire language.

How Do We Understand and Arrange Words? 243

22. *Semantics* is the study of meanings of words.

23. *Syntax* is the study of the structure of language in sentences.

24. Two common approaches to grammar are (a) phrase-structure grammars, which analyze sentences according to the order in which words appear in phrases and sentences; and (b) transformational grammars, which analyze sentences in terms of transformational relationships among phrase structures.

How Do We Use Language in a Social Context? 245

25. *Pragmatics* is the study of how language is used. Sociolinguistics is the study of the relationship between social interaction and language.

26. The *linguistic-relativity* hypothesis states that differences in thinking arise from different languages, and that these differences cause people who speak the various languages to perceive the world differently.

27. *Bilinguals* can speak two languages. Additive bilingualism occurs when a second language is taught in addition to a relatively well-developed first language; in contrast, subtractive bilingualism occurs when a second language partially replaces a first language.

PATHWAYS TO KNOWLEDGE

Choose the best answer to complete each sentence.

1. Ill-structured problems
   (a) have no solutions.
   (b) are commonly found in textbooks.
   (c) are formulated so that efforts to answer them are futile.
   (d) have no obvious path to solution.

2. Negative transfer in problem solving refers to
   (a) the transfer of knowledge that was useful in solving a previous problem to a new problem for which the knowledge interferes with the solution.
   (b) the transfer of negative information from one problem to another.
   (c) the transfer of nonconstructive problem-solving strategies that were useless in solving an earlier problem.
   (d) the habitual use of a poor problem-solving strategy.

3. Researchers have found that expert problem-solvers differ from novice problem-solvers primarily in that
   (a) experts can solve problems more quickly, as a result of greater motivation to solve the problems rapidly.
   (b) experts have always been good problem solvers, even at a young age.
   (c) experts have a wider and better organized knowledge base.
   (d) novices' problem solving has become more automatized, so that the novices can avoid the unnecessary, methodical steps in problem solving.

4. If all the news stations repeatedly report the appearance of a horrendous case of leprosy, and viewers conclude that leprosy has become rampant, which type of cognitive strategy are viewers using?
   (a) the availability heuristic.
   (b) the overconfidence algorithm.
   (c) bounded rationality.
   (d) the top-of-the mind heuristic.

5. The smallest meaningful unit in a language is called a(n)
   (a) morpheme.
   (b) phoneme.
   (c) root word.
   (d) affix.

6. The analysis of language, proceeding from the most elementary to the most complex level of sophistication, is
   (a) phoneme, morpheme, syntax, discourse.
   (b) phoneme, morpheme, lexicon, vocabulary.
   (c) morpheme, phoneme, syntax, discourse.
   (d) morpheme, phoneme, vocabulary, discourse.

7. Semantics is the study of
   (a) culture and its effects on language.
   (b) the origins of words.
   (c) how words are organized into meaningful sentences.
   (d) the meanings of words.

Answer each of the following questions by filling in the blank with an appropriate word or phrase.

8. A person shows _____ _____ when she or he views a wine bottle exclusively as a container to hold wine.

9. A _____ is composed of an individual's repertoire of morphemes.

10. The period of time during which a problem solver temporarily stops consciously working on a problem, in order to work on it subconsciously, is called _____.

11. _____ is a level of linguistic analysis, focused on the organized arrangement of words into meaningful sentences.

12. _____ is a seemingly sudden understanding of the nature of something, often as a result of taking a novel approach to a problem.

13. _____ _____ involves the recognition that although humans are rational, there are limits to the degree to which humans demonstrate rational cognitive processes across situations.

Match the following linguistic terms to their descriptions:

14.	phoneme	(a) the study of the interaction of language and thought
15.	pragmatics	(b) a unit of speech sound in a given language
16.	morpheme	(c) the study of how words have meaning in a language
17.	semantics	(d) the level of linguistic analysis that encompasses linguistic units beyond the level of the sentence
18.	lexicon	(e) the smallest semantically meaningful unit in a language
19.	psycholinguistics	(f) the entire repertoire of morphemes in a given language (or a given person's repertoire of morphemes)
20.	discourse	(g) the study of how people use language, such as in social interactions

Answers

1. d, 2. a, 3. c, 4. a, 5. a, 6. a, 7. d, 8. functional fixedness, 9. lexicon, 10. incubation, 11. Syntax, 12. Insight, 13. Bounded rationality, 14. b, 15. g, 16. e, 17. c, 18. f, 19. a, 20. d

PATHWAYS TO UNDERSTANDING

 1. If you were the head of a problem-solving team, and your team members seemed to be running into a block in their approach to the problem being addressed, what would you have the team members do to get around the block?

 2. How do advertisers use invalid reasoning to influence people? Give some specific examples of ads, and compare and contrast their means of persuasion.

 3. What are some heuristics you use for figuring out what things to study for an upcoming examination?

CHAPTER OUTLINE

What Are Two Traditional Approaches to Studying Intelligence?

How Do Psychologists Assess Intelligence?
Mental Age and the Intelligence Quotient
Deviation IQ Scores
The Stanford–Binet Intelligence Scales
The Wechsler Scales
Additional Tests Related to Intelligence Testing
Characteristics of Intelligence Tests

How Should We Try to Understand the Nature of Intelligence?
Structures and Processes of Intelligence
Context and Intelligence
Is Jane Intelligent?
Intelligence Testing and Immigration Policies
Intelligence as a System

What Have We Learned About Extremes of Intelligence?
Intellectual Giftedness
Mental Retardation

Is Intelligence Inherited?

Can We Improve Intelligence?

What Is Creativity, and How Does It Emerge?
How Can You Become More Creative?

Intelligence and Creativity

What do you mean when you say that someone is "smart" or "intelligent" or "bright" or "quick"? Try completing the following tasks, and think about whether you believe that your performance on these tasks gives a good indication of your intelligence.

1. Geriatrics is to old age as pediatrics is to (a) cardiology, (b) childhood, (c) senior citizens, or (d) doctors.
2. If you were to classify a stream with a pair of items, with which of the following pairs would you categorize it? (a) ocean, sea; (b) lake, pond; (c) river, brook; (d) puddle, pool
3. Complete this series—¼, one half, 0.75; (a) three fourths, (b) 0.25, (c) ½, (d) 100%
4. Choose an answer to complete this figural analogy.

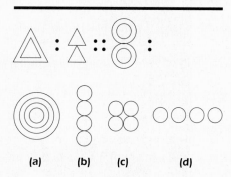

(a)   (b)   (c)   (d)

5. Fifteen percent of the people in Los Diablos have unlisted telephone numbers. You select 200 names at random from the local telephone directory. How many of these people can be expected to have unlisted phone numbers?
6. Do you think that your responses to the preceding tasks accurately reflect your intelligence? What aspects of your intelligence do these tasks fail to address? What is intelligence, anyway?

The answers to the questions in Tasks 1 through 5 appear in the next section of this chapter. Regarding the questions in Task 6, there are few short answers, but I hope that you will find some help in answering these questions by the time you finish reading this chapter. Many psychologists (myself included) spend a lifetime trying to answer questions such as these, in order to gain a clear understanding of intelligence. I define **intelligence** as comprising the abilities needed to engage in goal-directed adaptive behavior, but other psychologists who study intelligence may define it somewhat differently.

WHAT ARE TWO TRADITIONAL APPROACHES TO STUDYING INTELLIGENCE?

intelligence comprises the abilities needed to engage in goal-directed adaptive behavior

Almost a century ago, two highly intelligent men came up with two completely different answers to the question, What is intelligence? According to Francis Galton (1822–1911), *intelligence* comprises two general qualities: energy (the capacity for labor) and sensitivity to physical stimuli (Galton, 1883). That is, Galton held

On Francis Galton's psychophysical tests of intelligence, boxer George Foreman (top, left) would probably have fared far better than scientist Albert Einstein (top, right), and Olympic athlete Bonnie Blair (bottom left) would probably have surpassed writer Toni Morrison (bottom right). Do you agree with Galton that these tests would accurately indicate the differences in intelligence among these individuals? Why or why not?

that intelligence is based on physical strength (e.g., muscular strength, speed, and accuracy) and psychophysical abilities. Recall from Chapter 4 that psychophysical ability involves *sensory acuity* (e.g., keen ability to see, hear, smell, taste, touch). Galton actually set up a laboratory to test the psychophysical abilities of people who visited his lab.

Think about how various people might have scored on Galton's tests: heavyweight champion George Foreman versus scientist Albert Einstein, Olympic speed skater Bonnie Blair versus Nobel Prize–winning author Toni Morrison. It is pretty likely that Forman would be considered a genius, in comparison with Einstein. Similarly, although I am sure that Toni Morrison has perfectly good psychophysical abilities, I suspect that Bonnie Blair would have outshined her on Galton's tests.

Although Galton's tests might still be considered useful by Olympic committees, athletic teams, and a few others who value physical prowess, few (if any) colleges or other educational institutions would consider his tests highly useful in assessing a person's intelligence. An alternative to Galton's approach to intelligence emerged from a need to use measures of intelligence as a guide for predicting success in school. In the early 1900s, the Minister of Public Instruction in Paris, France, asked Alfred Binet (1857–1911) and his collaborator, Théodore Simon (1873–1961), to come up with tests that could distinguish children who were truly mentally retarded from children who were not succeeding in school for other reasons. Based on this practical concern for educating children who were likely to succeed in school, Binet and Simon launched the **psychometric** (psychological measurement) tradition of intelligence theory and research.

For Binet and Simon (1916), the core of intelligence is "judgment, otherwise called good sense, practical sense, initiative, the faculty of adapting one's self to circumstances" (pp. 42–43). The test they devised was intended to tap intellectual abilities as expressed through judgment and adaptation. The questions posed at the outset of this chapter are also based on the view that intelligence involves judgment and adaptability. The answers to the questions posed at the beginning of this chapter are as follows:

1. (b) Geriatrics is the branch of medicine that focuses on the health of older persons, just as pediatrics is the branch that focuses on the health of children.
2. (c) A stream is a flowing body of water, as are a river and a brook.
3. (d) ¼, one half, 0.75, and 100% are increasing amounts (obtained by adding one fourth each time).
4. (b) Just as the pair of concentric triangles were rearranged to form two like-sized vertically aligned triangles, the two pairs of concentric circles may be rearranged to form four like-sized vertically aligned circles.
5. Zero; none of the 200 people listed in the local phone directory have unlisted phone numbers.
6. It depends: Some people believe that Questions 1 through 5 are of a kind that can accurately indicate your intelligence, but other people disagree. Those who agree generally give at least some credence to the psychometric approach to intelligence.

Intelligence means a person who can see implications and arrive at conclusions.

Talmud

MINILECTURE
Measuring Intelligence (Ch 11)

What are two traditional approaches to studying intelligence? According to Galton's approach, we should test intelligence by measuring people's psychophysical abilities, such as sensory acuity, physical strength, and other sensory and physical abilities. According to Binet's more academically oriented approach, we should test intelligence by measuring people's

psychometric characterized by psychological measurement (*psycho-*, pertaining to the mind or mental processes; *-metric*, measurement)

judgments and adaptations to their environment, particularly in regard to tasks pertaining to performance in school. Over the years, Binet's approach has gained greater favor than has Galton's.

HOW DO PSYCHOLOGISTS ASSESS INTELLIGENCE?

Mental Age and the Intelligence Quotient

Schools have usually classified children according to their chronological age (i.e., the amount of time they have lived since birth), with this criterion serving as a basis for separating children into 12 or 13 (counting kindergarten) school grades. One rationale for using this criterion is the assumption that most children of the same chronological age have about the same general mental abilities. The schools then may compare children of the same general age and may assign different evaluations (grades such as "A," "B," "C," etc.) to children who show different levels of academic performance.

Binet suggested an alternative to comparing and classifying children based on their chronological age. Instead, according to Binet, a better way to compare children's intelligence (and to sort them into appropriate school classes) is based on their **mental age,** their level of intelligence based on the mentally "average" person of a given chronological age. Suppose, for example, that a person performs on a test at about the same level as an average 12-year-old. In this case, the person's mental age will be 12, regardless of the person's chronological age. For example, suppose that José's chronological age is 10 years. However, his performance on a test of intelligence equals that of the average 12-year-old. His mental age will be 12.

William Stern (1912) noted that mental age is less useful when comparing children of differing chronological ages. A mental age of 12, for example, is more impressive in a 10-year-old than in a 14-year-old. Stern suggested that instead of measuring intelligence in terms of mental age, we should measure intelligence by using an **intelligence quotient** *(IQ):* a ratio of mental age (MA) to chronological age (CA), multiplied by 100. This ratio can be expressed mathematically as follows: $IQ = (MA \div CA) \times 100$. For example, José's mental age is 12, and his chronological age is 10. Therefore, his ratio IQ is 120, because $(12 \div 10) \times 100 = 120$. A **ratio IQ** expresses intelligence as the ratio of mental age to chronological age, times 100.

Unfortunately, ratio IQs have their problems, too. It turns out that calculations based on mental age just do not work very well for people over 16 or so years of age. Up to about age 16, children's measured intelligence goes up each year. After that time, however, measured intelligence does not go up as much, and some measurements of intelligence actually go down as people approach the end of the life span. To get an idea of the problem, think about the likely differences in intellectual ability among a 4-year-old, a 10-year-old, and a 16-year-old, and compare those differences with the likely intellectual differences among a 40-year-old, a 46-year-old, and a 52-year-old. You probably would notice big differences between ages 4 and 16, but few differences between ages 40 and 52.

Deviation IQ Scores

Once psychologists gave up on comparing people based on mental age, they needed some other way of comparing people's scores on intelligence tests. The solution that occurred to them was to give each test to a huge number of people of various ages and then to compare a given person's test scores with the scores of people of about the same chronological age as that individual. When tests are given to thousands of people, the scores obtained generally approximate a *normal distribution,* in which most people score somewhere near the middle, and fewer

No person is too old to learn.

French Jewish saying

mental age a means of indicating a person's level of intelligence (generally in reference to a child), based on the individual's performance on tests of intelligence, by indicating the average chronological age of persons who typically perform at the same level of intelligence as the test-taker

intelligence quotient broadly, a normative score on an intelligence test, with a mean of 100 and a standard deviation of 15 or 16

ratio IQ a means of indicating performance on intelligence tests; expressed as a quotient of mental age divided by chronological age, times 100

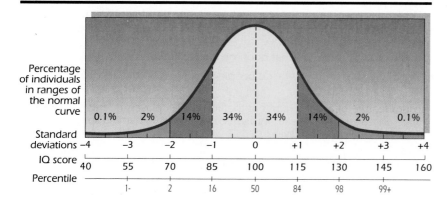

Figure 9-1
**Normal Distribution
of Deviation IQs**
This figure shows a normal distribution as it ap-plies to IQ, including percentile equivalents for various levels of IQ.

people score on either side of the middle. Only a very few people have extremely high or extremely low scores. A normal distribution is generally based on measuring the characteristics (e.g., test scores) of a large number of individuals.

The actual number of items that a person answers correctly is the person's *raw score* for the test. To make it easy to compare a particular person's score with the scores of other people, the raw scores for many psychological tests are converted into **normative scores,** scores based on a normal distribution of many individual scores, which show how various test-takers scored in relation to one another. For most IQ tests, the normative scores are calculated so that the middle score is 100. (For example, if the average person scored 19 out of 55 on a given test, a raw score of 19 would be converted to a score of 100, and the other scores on each test would be converted in a similar way.)

In a normal distribution of IQ scores for a large population, roughly two thirds of the normative scores fall between 85 and 115, and about 95% of the scores fall between 70 and 130. From this distribution of normative scores, psychologists can calculate **deviation IQs,** based on degree of difference from the average score. The deviation IQ scores lend themselves to comparisons among individual test-takers, based on how the individual's scores deviate from the average scores. Figue 9-1 shows an example of how a normal distribution of scores can be plotted on a graph.

The Stanford–Binet Intelligence Scales

Scores on Binet and Simon's original intelligence test were calculated based on mental age alone. Next, Lewis Terman (a Stanford University professor), together with Maud Merrill, modified Binet and Simon's test, using ratio IQs for comparing intelligence across different individuals. Terman and Merrill thereby developed the earliest versions of the *Stanford–Binet Intelligence Scales* (Terman & Merrill, 1937, 1973; see Figure 9-2). In psychological assessment, a *scale* is a test or subtest that includes a graded series of questions or problems that measure an ability or another psychological construct (e.g., a personality trait). The idea is that a greater amount of skill, ability, or some other characteristic is required to reach each of the graded levels of the scale. Most modern intelligence tests include a set of scaled subtests.

For years, the Stanford–Binet test was the most widely used intelligence test, and it is still widely used. In recent years, however, another test, authored by psychologist David Wechsler, has become even more widely used than the Stanford–Binet.

The Wechsler Scales

The Wechsler intelligence scales include the *Wechsler Adult Intelligence Scale—Revised (WAIS-R),* the third edition of the *Wechsler Intelligence Scale for Children (WISC-III),* and the *Wechsler Preschool and Primary Scale of Intelligence (WPPSI).*

normative scores the set of normative equivalents for a range of raw test scores that represent the normal distribution of scores obtained by giving a test to a huge number of individuals

deviation IQs a means of determining intelligence-test scores, based on deviations from an average score, calculated such that the normative equivalent for the median score is 100; not IQs, strictly speaking, because no quotient is involved

Content area	Explanation of tasks/questions	Example of a possible task/question
Verbal reasoning		
Vocabulary	Define the meaning of a word	What does the word **diligent** mean?
Comprehension	Show an understanding of why the world works as it does	Why do people sometimes borrow money?
Absurdities	Identify the odd or absurd feature of a picture	(Point out that ice hockey players do not ice-skate on lakes into which swimmers in bathing suits are diving.)
Verbal relations	Tell how three of four items are similar to one another yet different from the fourth item	(Note that an apple, a banana, and an orange can be eaten, but a cup or mug cannot be.)
Quantitative reasoning		
Number series	Complete a series of numbers	Given the numbers 1, 3, 5, 7, 9, what number would you expect to come next?
Quantitative	Solve simple arithmetical-word problems	If María has six apples, and she wants to divide them evenly among herself and her two best friends, how many apples will she give to each friend?
Figural/abstract reasoning		
Pattern analysis	Figure out a puzzle in which the test-taker must combine pieces representing parts of geometric shapes, fitting them together to form a particular geometric shape	Fit together these pieces to form a rectangle. 
Short-term memory		
Memory for sentences	Listen to a sentence; then repeat it back exactly as the examiner said it	Repeat this sentence back to me: "Harrison went to sleep late and awoke early the next morning."
Memory for digits	Listen to a series of digits (numbers); then repeat the numbers either forward or backward	Repeat these numbers backward: "9, 1, 3, 6."
Memory for objects	Watch the examiner point to a series of objects in a picture; then point to the same objects in exactly the same sequence as the examiner	(Point to the carrot, then the hoe, then the flower, then the scarecrow, then the baseball.) 

Figure 9-2

Stanford–Binet Intelligence Scales

The above sample questions illustrate each of the subtests in the Stanford–Binet; each subtest measures abilities Lewis Terman, one of the authors of the first edition of the test, included in his overall view of intelligence. The sample questions used throughout this chapter are not actual questions from any of the scales; they are intended only to illustrate the types of questions that might appear in each of the main content areas of the tests. How would you respond to these questions? What do your responses indicate about your intelligence?

Each of the Wechsler tests yields three scores, all of which are based on deviation IQs: a verbal score, a performance score, and an overall score. The *verbal score* is based on subtests that tap the ability to understand and to use words, such as vocabulary tests. The *performance score* is based on subtests that, for the most part, require test-takers to perform physical manipulations of materials, rather than to supply verbal responses. For example, one of the performance subtests involves *picture completion*, in which test-takers are asked to find a missing part in a picture of an object. The overall score is a combination of the verbal and the performance scores. Figure 9-3 shows various types of items from each of the Wechsler adult-scale subtests. You may wish to compare sample items from the Wechsler with sample items from the Stanford–Binet.

Content area	Explanation of tasks/questions	Example of a possible task/question
Verbal scale		
Comprehension	Answer questions of social knowledge	What does it mean when people say, "A stitch in time saves nine"? Why are convicted criminals put into prison?
Vocabulary	Define the meaning of a word	What does **persistent** mean? What does **archaeology** mean?
Information	Supply generally known information	Who is Chelsea Clinton? What are six New England states?
Similarities	Explain how two things or concepts are similar	In what ways are an ostrich and a penguin alike? In what ways are a lamp and a heater alike?
Arithmetic	Solve simple arithmetical-word problems	If Paul has $14.43, and he buys two sandwiches, which cost $5.23 each, how much change will he receive?
Digit span	Listen to a series of digits (numbers), then repeat the numbers either forward or backward or both	Repeat these numbers backward: "9, 1, 8, 3, 6."
Performance scale		
Object assembly	Put together a puzzle by combining pieces to form a particular common object	Put together these pieces to make something. 
Block design	Use patterned blocks to form a design that looks identical to a design shown by the examiner	Assemble these blocks to make this design. 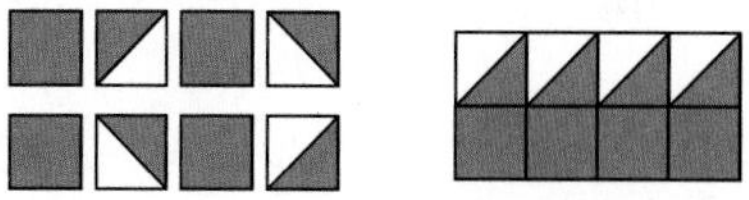
Picture completion	Tell what is missing from each picture	What is missing from this picture? 
Picture arrangement	Put a set of cartoonlike pictures into a chronological order, so they tell a coherent story	Arrange these pictures in an order that tells a story, and then tell what is happening in the story. 
Digit symbol	When given a key matching particular symbols to particular numerals, copy a sequence of symbols, transcribing from symbols to numerals, using the key	Look carefully at the key. In the blanks, write the correct numeral for the symbol above each blank.

Figure 9-3

Wechsler Adult Intelligence Scale—Revised (WAIS-R)

The Wechsler scales are based on deviation IQs. Given the content areas and the kinds of questions shown here, how does the Wechsler differ from the Stanford–Binet?

Wechsler did not limit his thinking about intelligence to test scores. Although Wechsler (1974) clearly considered test scores important, he believed that intelligence involves more than just what is measured on tests. Intelligence affects our everyday life, as when we take tests and do homework, or relate to people and do our jobs effectively. In Wechsler's view, a person's intelligence is that person's ability to adapt to the environment in all aspects of her or his life.

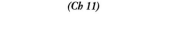

MINILECTURE

Wechsler Scales: The WAIS-R (Ch 11)

Additional Tests Related to Intelligence Testing

In the United States today, hundreds of intelligence tests are in everyday use. Some of these tests are given to just one person at a time by a highly trained psychologist; other tests are group tests, which can be given to large numbers of people at once.

Tests of intelligence are not the only tests of abilities being used today; many tests are designed to measure abilities not normally assessed on intelligence tests, such as musical or athletic abilities. Most of these tests are intended to measure **aptitudes,** a person's potentials for learning new information or for mastering skills in a specific area of knowledge (e.g., language, mathematics, athletics, or music).

Finding Your Way   9-1

What is a skill or an area of knowledge that you have mastered pretty well by now? Stop for a moment to think about how you could assess another person's aptitude for learning what you have learned or for mastering the skill you have mastered. What are some of the questions or tasks you would include on an aptitude test for this area of knowledge? Jot down a few ideas for the kinds of test items you would include.

We start as fools and become wise through experience.

Tanzanian proverb

How would you go about creating your own test of intelligence? How would you choose the questions to ask or the tasks to include in your test?

aptitude a capability for accomplishing something, for attaining a level of expertise on performance of a task or a set of tasks, or for acquiring knowledge in a given domain or set of domains

achievement an accomplishment; an attained level of expertise on performance of a task, or an acquired base of knowledge in a domain or a set of domains

validity the extent to which a given form of measurement assesses what it is supposed to measure

reliability the dependability of a measurement instrument (e.g., a test), indicating that the instrument consistently measures the outcome being measured

standardization the administration of a test in a way that ensures that the conditions for taking the test are the same for all test-takers

As you have probably discovered, it is difficult to come up with legitimate ways in which to assess a person's aptitude for learning new information or for mastering a skill. In contrast, it is much easier to find ways to assess a person's **achievement,** what the individual has already accomplished or learned in a given area of knowledge, by the time of the test.

Characteristics of Intelligence Tests

Once test developers know what it is they want to assess, they must develop questions and tasks that effectively measure what they want to assess. Test developers evaluate their tests to see whether the tests show three key properties:

1. **Validity** is the extent to which a test measures what it is supposed to measure. For example, do people who score high on a test of intelligence actually show greater intelligence, as measured by other tests or other kinds of outcomes such as school grades?
2. **Reliability** is the extent to which a test consistently measures whatever it actually measures in just the same way every time. For example, will people who had relatively high (or low) scores on April 27 be the same ones who have relatively high (or low) scores on November 13?
3. **Standardization** is the extent to which the conditions for taking a test are the same for all test-takers. For example, do all people taking the test have the same amount of time to answer the questions, and will they answer these questions under the same conditions (e.g., temperature in the room, freedom from distractions, etc.)?

How do psychologists assess intelligence? Intelligence has been measured in terms of mental age, ratio IQs, and deviation IQs. Various tests of intelligence have been devised, such as the Wechsler scales and the Stanford–Binet scales; in addition, tests of aptitude and achievement are widely used. Responsible developers of such tests generally seek to ensure validity and reliability of their tests, as well as standardization of the implementation of the tests.

HOW SHOULD WE TRY TO UNDERSTAND THE NATURE OF INTELLIGENCE?

In designing tests of intelligence, test designers spend more time deciding how they will measure intelligence than they do studying just what is the nature of intelligence. Some researchers, however, spend much of their time trying to understand the nature of intelligence. One way to try to understand the nature of intelligence is to *start* with tests of intelligence.

Structures and Processes of Intelligence

Factor Analysis: Exploring the Structure of the Mind

During the first half of the twentieth century, psychologists studied intelligence by trying to map out the abilities that make up intelligence. These psychologists tried to chart the innermost regions of the mind. To chart the territory of intelligence, they needed tools. The tool they found the most valuable for this work was *factor analysis*, which is a statistical method for separating an overall concept or phenomenon (e.g., intelligence) into a number of distinct aspects (abilities, in the case of intelligence).

Both the overall phenomenon and the numerous distinct abilities are hypothetical constructs. Recall from Chapter 7 that a hypothetical construct is a phenomenon that is believed to exist even though the phenomenon (e.g., intelligence) cannot be observed directly. Because the hypothetical construct of intelligence cannot be observed directly, researchers must devise other means to find out about it.

One way to find out about the hypothetical construct of intelligence is to give tests to people that require them to use the abilities believed to constitute intelligence. Researchers who use the tool of factor analysis believe that these hypothetical abilities form the bases of individual differences in test performance. Of course, the particular factors that are separated statistically still depend on what is being measured and how it is being measured. Factor analysis identifies test performances that are highly related to each other as deriving from the same factor. For example, vocabulary and reading comprehension might be grouped together as testing an ability of verbal comprehension.

Charles Spearman (1863–1945) is generally considered to have invented factor analysis (1927). Using this technique, Spearman concluded that intelligence could be understood in terms of both a single general factor (which he believed to be "mental energy") and a set of specific factors. Later, Louis Thurstone (1887–1955) and others suggested that intelligence comprises various separate factors (e.g., Thurstone, 1938), such as verbal comprehension (measured by vocabulary), number skills (measured by simple arithmetic problems), and memory (measured by recall of words).

In 1993, John Carroll proposed a hierarchical model of intelligence, based on his extensive analysis of data obtained between 1927 and 1987. Carroll's model involves a hierarchy comprising three levels: At the top of the hierarchy is general ability; at the bottom of the hierarchy are many narrow, specific abilities (e.g., spelling ability, speed of reasoning); and in the middle are various broad abilities (e.g., learning and memory processes, effortless production of many ideas, and the ability to cope with novel tasks and situations).

In general, the factor-analytic model does a pretty good job of describing the mental abilities that make up intelligence. Although it describes *what* structures characterize intelligence, it does not say much about *how* intelligence works in the mind of an individual. That is, factor-analytic models say little about the mental processes underlying intelligence.

Don't look where you fell, but where you slipped.

Liberian proverb

Intelligence and Information Processing

Information processing is the set of mental actions by which people manage and use knowledge. Information-processing investigators study intelligence in various

information processing operations by which people mentally manipulate what they learn and know about the world

We often say that a highly intelligent person is "mentally quick." How important is speed to intelligence in everyday life?

What do you think will be some practical uses for physiological measurements of intelligence? Do you think that these uses will be beneficial or harmful, or do you think that such measurements will lead to both benefits and risks? Explain your answer.

contextualist psychologist who theorizes about a psychological phenomenon (e.g., intelligence) strictly in terms of the context in which an individual is observed, and who suggests that the phenomenon cannot be understood—let alone measured—outside the real-world context of the individual

ways. Most of these differences relate to the processes being studied. Some of these processes are extremely simple, and others are quite complicated. Among the main information-processing theorists are Earl Hunt (1978), who believes that an important aspect of intelligence is the ability quickly to retrieve information about words from memory, and Herbert Simon (1976), who believes that complex problem solving is central to intelligence. Each has studied both the speed and the accuracy with which people process information.

Although the information-processing approach offers more understanding of the processes of intelligence than does the psychometric approach, it often does not link the processing of information directly to specific biological aspects of brain function. Some investigators who study intelligence try to understand just how our brains work while engaging in activities that require intelligence.

The Biology of Intelligence

Biological psychologists try to understand intelligence by studying the brain directly (see Chapter 2). Through such studies, researchers have found that intelligence correlates with complex patterns of electrical activity (Barrett & Eysenck, 1992), with speed of neuronal conduction (e.g., McGarry-Roberts, Stelmack, & Campbell, 1992; Reed & Jensen, 1992; Vernon & Mori, 1992), and with particular ways of using a simple sugar, glucose, during mental activities (e.g., Haier et al., 1992). As an example, it appears that the brains of more intelligent people use up less glucose (and spend less energy) than do the brains of less intelligent persons performing the same task. The reason for this difference in energy use may be that the brains of more intelligent people may find the tasks easier than do the brains of less intelligent people. Further, Richard Haier and his colleagues have found that the efficient use of glucose increases as a result of learning. Perhaps persons who are more intelligent have learned how to use their brains more efficiently than have persons who are less intelligent. Some psychologists (e.g., Matarazzo, 1992) believe that we will be able to find practical uses for the information from this research in the near future.

The biological approach certainly offers promising insights into intelligence, but many psychologists question whether we can fully understand intelligence by studying the human brain in isolation. They believe that we also must consider the entire human being and the entire environment within which the person engages in intelligent actions. Such researchers and theorists would urge us to take a more anthropological (culture-based) view of intelligence.

Context and Intelligence

Up to now, we have discussed models of intelligence with an internal orientation: The psychologists we have discussed view intelligence as something occurring inside the head. In contrast, **contextualist** theorists of intelligence prefer an externally oriented approach to intelligence. The idea is that intelligence cannot be understood outside its real-world context. Take, for example, the following hypothetical dialogue (from Chieh Li, personal communication, September 28, 1995):

BRANCHING OUT: Is Jane Intelligent?

Jane is a student in the classes of Professor Blaine, a European American educated in Western schools influenced by Judeo-Christian religious traditions, and of Professor Chang, an Asian-American educated in traditional Chinese schools influenced by Buddhism, Confucianism, and Taoism. By chance, Jane passed by and greeted the two professors as they were discussing what constitutes intelligence.

"There," said Dr. Blaine, "Jane is an excellent example of an intelligent student. She always responds quickly and accurately to questions I ask, and I hear that she is an excellent chess player. Is she an 'A' student in your class, too?"

"Yes," responded Dr. Chang.

"Well, wouldn't you say that Jane is intelligent?"

"I don't know yet. She seems to be a quick learner, but she has not shown me her wisdom yet."

"What do you mean when you say 'her wisdom'?"

"A quick learner may not be wise. A wise person does not always show her smartness but rather her modesty. A wise student listens, observes, and tries to learn from others. When solving a problem, a wise person considers all factors involved and considers the immediate, short-term, and long-term outcomes of various possible solutions."

The preceding dialogue illustrates the importance of cultural context in what people value as reflecting intelligence. Contextualists believe that each culture creates its own conception of intelligence in order to serve two purposes: (1) to define the nature of adaptive behavior; and (2) to explain why some people perform better than others on the tasks that the culture values (e.g., in U.S. society, getting good grades in school). Contextualist psychologists study how intelligence relates to the context in which intelligence is being studied.

As an example, Michael Cole and his colleagues (Cole et al., 1971) conducted an interesting cross-cultural study of intelligence. These investigators asked adult members of the Kpelle tribe in Africa to sort various *terms* (such as names of fruits or vegetables). In Western culture, when adults are asked to sort terms, more intelligent people typically sort the terms *hierarchically* (i.e., to sort the terms into various categories, with various levels being more specific or less so). Less intelligent people sort the terms *functionally* (in terms of the uses of the terms). In *hierarchical sorting*, for example, people may sort names of different kinds of fruit together. Then they may place the word "fruit" over the names of the particular kinds of fruit, and so on. In *functional sorting*, people may sort "fruit" with "eat," for example, because we eat fruit. The Kpelle sorted functionally—even after investigators unsuccessfully tried to get the Kpelle to sort hierarchically.

Finally, in desperation, one of the experimenters (Joseph Glick) asked a Kpelle person to sort the way a foolish person would. When asked to sort in this way, the Kpelle had no trouble at all sorting hierarchically. This individual and others had been able to sort this way all along. They just had not done so because they believed that hierarchical sorting is not intelligent. They may also have considered the questioners rather unintelligent for asking what may have seemed like stupid questions. Why would the Kpelle view functional sorting as intelligent? Simple. In ordinary life, we normally think functionally. When we think of a fruit, we think of eating it. However, in Western schooling, we learn what is expected of us on tests. The Kpelle did not have Western schooling and had not been exposed to Western testing. As a result, they solved the problems the way Western adults might solve them in their everyday lives, but not on a test of cognitive abilities.

The Kpelle people are not the only ones who might question Western understandings of intelligence. In the Puluwat culture of the Pacific, for example, sailors figure out how to travel incredibly long distances to precise locations. They do so without using any of the special equipment that sailors from technologically advanced countries need in order to get from one place to another (Gladwin, 1970). If Puluwat sailors were to design intelligence tests for us, we might not seem very intelligent. Similarly, the highly skilled Puluwat sailors might not do well on Western tests of intelligence. Because of these and other observations, several theorists have suggested the importance of considering cultural context when measuring intelligence.

The preceding examples make it clear that it is very difficult—if not actually impossible—to come up with a test that everyone would consider culture fair. A **culture-fair** test is equally appropriate and fair for members of all cultures. Finding test items for such a test is almost impossible if members of different cultures have different ideas of what it means to be smart. That is, the very behaviors that

MINILECTURE

Culture-Fair Intelligence Tests (Ch 11)

Design a task that a 12-year-old who lived far from cities (such as in the Amazon forest) and who had never seen a book, a radio, or a bicycle might do easily, but that an intelligent American adult probably would find pretty hard to do.

culture-fair describes assessment that is equally appropriate for members of all cultures and that comprises items that are equally fair to members of all cultures; probably impossible to attain

When Michael Cole and other researchers asked Kpelle adults to sort items intelligently, the Kpelle sorted the items according to the functional uses of the items. When asked to sort items as a foolish person would sort them, Kpelle adults sorted the items hierarchically, according to attribute categories. In contrast, the majority of Western researchers generally consider hierarchical sorting to reflect greater intelligence than does functional sorting. What conclusions would Kpelle researchers have drawn regarding the intelligence of Westerners if they had administered intelligence tests to Cole and his colleagues? What should we infer regarding cultural definitions of intelligence?

may be considered intelligent in one culture may be viewed as unintelligent in another. For example, Americans often put a premium on mental quickness, but other cultures may put a higher value on careful and deliberate decision making, considering hasty decisions to be unwise (Sternberg, 1985a, 1990). Because various cultures conceive of intelligence differently, it is probably unrealistic to expect that a truly culture-fair test of intelligence will be developed.

Early in the twentieth century, some experts on intelligence attempted to bar many European immigrants from entering the United States because these immigrants scored poorly on group intelligence tests. Subsequent generations of Americans descended from these immigrants have IQs slightly above the national average. If IQ scores are not used as immigration criteria, what criteria should be used to determine who should be allowed to enter and remain legally in this country?

BRANCHING OUT: Intelligence Testing and Immigration Policies

Even though it may not be possible to provide culture-fair tests of intelligence, a study by Seymour Sarason and John Doris (1979) illustrates the importance of looking for ways to allow for cultural differences in the design and use of intelligence tests. Sarason and Doris tracked the IQs of an immigrant population: Italian Americans. Less than a century ago, first-generation Italian-American children showed a median IQ of 87 (low average; range 76–100), even when nonverbal measures were used and when so-called mainstream American attitudes were considered. Some social commentators and intelligence researchers of the day pointed to heredity and other nonenvironmental factors as the basis for the low IQs—much as they do today for other minority groups.

For example, a leading researcher of the day, Henry Goddard, pronounced that 79% of immigrant Italians were "feeble-minded." He also asserted that about 80% of immigrant Jews, Hungarians, and Russians were similarly dull-witted (Eysenck & Kamin, 1981). Goddard (1917) also said that moral decadence accompanied this deficit in intelligence. He recommended that the intelligence tests he used be administered to all immigrants and that the U.S. authorities prevent the entry of any persons found to be below a reasonable minimum level of intelligence, as measured by these tests.

Stephen Ceci (1991) has noted that the present generation of Italian-American students who take IQ tests show slightly above-average IQs. Other immigrant groups that Goddard had wanted to bar from admission to the United States have shown similar "amazing" increases. The kinds of genes possessed by Italian Americans have probably not changed much in just a few generations. Instead, it seems much more likely that the dramatic gains in IQ scores can be explained by cultural assimilation and education.

The observations of Ceci and others suggest a specific question of public policy: Should intelligence tests be used as a means of determining who should or should not be permitted to immigrate to the United States? What do you think?

A broader question posed by these findings is this one: Should researchers try to influence public policy? Was Goddard correct to try to use his findings to influence who should or should not be allowed to immigrate to the United States? Should Ceci speak up regarding his observations to influence public policy regarding immigration?

Many psychologists believe that research findings should be used when determining issues of public policy, such as decisions regarding immigration or regarding the use of intelligence tests. To these psychologists, people who shape public policy should be provided with research findings, so that policy issues can be based on the best available data. Other psychologists, however, warn that researchers should not concern themselves with issues of public policy and should leave policy matters outside the laboratory door. To these other psychologists, as soon as researchers begin to think about public policy, they become less concerned with objective observation of what does exist and more concerned with subjective evaluation of what should exist.

What do you think? Should researchers always avoid concerning themselves with issues of public policy? Should researchers always speak up about issues of public policy? What considerations should influence a researcher's decision regarding whether to speak up about issues of public policy?

Although we probably cannot design culture-fair tests of intelligence, we may be able to design culture-relevant tests. **Culture-relevant** tests tap skills and knowledge that *relate* to the cultural experiences of the test-takers. For example, memory abilities are one aspect of intelligence, as Western culture defines it. Daniel Wagner (1978) studied memory abilities in Western culture versus in Moroccan culture. Wagner found that the level of recall depended on the content that was being remembered. Culture-relevant content was remembered more

"YOU CAN'T BUILD A HUT, YOU DON'T KNOW HOW TO FIND EDIBLE ROOTS AND YOU KNOW NOTHING ABOUT PREDICTING THE WEATHER. IN OTHER WORDS, YOU DO TERRIBLY ON OUR I.Q. TEST."

© 1996 Sidney Harris

---

culture-relevant describes assessment of skills and knowledge that relate to the cultural experiences of the test-takers, by using content and procedures that are appropriate to the cultural context of the test-takers

Intricate patterns on Moroccan rugs were more easily remembered by Moroccan rug merchants than by Westerners. In contrast, Westerners more easily remembered information unfamiliar to Moroccan rug merchants.

Knowledge is like a garden: If it is not cultivated, it cannot be harvested.

Guinean proverb

effectively than was nonrelevant content. For instance, Moroccan rug merchants were better able to recall complex visual patterns on black-and-white photos of Oriental rugs than were Westerners.

Stephen Ceci (Ceci & Roazzi, 1994) has found similar context effects in performance on various tasks. For example, Ceci and his associates (Ceci, Bronfenbrenner, & Baker, 1988) compared children's ability to learn to predict where an image would end up on a video screen. Children learned more easily if they believed the images were butterflies to be captured than if they believed the images were abstract geometric figures. Brazilian women had no difficulty with *proportional reasoning* (figuring out how various amounts relate to each other) when they were asked to pretend they were buying food, but they had great difficulty with such reasoning when they were asked to pretend they were buying medicinal herbs (Schliemann & Magalhües, 1990). Brazilian children who had become street vendors showed no difficulty in doing complicated arithmetic computations when selling things, but they had great difficulty doing similar calculations in a classroom (Carraher, Carraher, & Schliemann, 1985). In these studies, the context in which people act clearly affects how intelligently they perform.

Some psychologists have criticized the contextual approach because it fails to define exactly what a context is, and it fails to specify exactly how context affects intelligence. In addition, whereas the internal approaches to intelligence perhaps place too much emphasis on what goes on in a single person's head, the contextual (external) approach may say too little about what goes on in an individual's mind. Some theorists have sought a more comprehensive approach to try to understand intelligence in terms of its relationship to both the internal and the external worlds of the individual.

Intelligence as a System

Some theorists view intelligence as a complex system. They try to combine the best aspects of the various theories of intelligence, such as by specifying both the structure and the function of intelligence, rather than just one or the other.

Multiple Intelligences

theory of multiple intelligences a theory suggesting that there are seven distinct intelligences that function somewhat independently: bodily–kinesthetic, interpersonal, intrapersonal, linguistic, logical–mathematical, musical, and spatial intelligence

Howard Gardner (1983, 1993b) has proposed a **theory of multiple intelligences,** which comprises seven distinct intelligences (linguistic, logical–mathematical, spatial, musical, bodily–kinesthetic, interpersonal, and intrapersonal),

TABLE 9-1

Gardner's Seven Intelligences

On which of Howard Gardner's seven intelligences do you show the greatest ability? In what contexts can you use your intelligences most effectively? (After Gardner, 1983, 1993b)

Type of intelligence	Tasks reflecting this type of intelligence
Linguistic intelligence	Reading a book; writing a paper, a novel, or a poem; and understanding spoken words
Logical–mathematical intelligence	Solving math problems, balancing a checkbook, doing a mathematical proof, and logical reasoning
Spatial intelligence	Getting from one place to another, reading a map, and packing suitcases in the trunk of a car so that they all fit into a compact space
Musical intelligence	Singing a song, composing a sonata, playing a trumpet, or even appreciating the structure of a piece of music
Bodily–kinesthetic intelligence	Dancing, playing basketball, running a mile, or throwing a javelin
Interpersonal intelligence	Relating to other people, such as when we try to understand another person's behavior, motives, or emotions
Intrapersonal intelligence	Understanding ourselves—the basis for understanding who we are, what makes us tick, and how we can change ourselves, given the existing constraints on our abilities and our interests

each of which is relatively independent of the others (see Table 9-1). Each intelligence is a separate system of functioning, although the systems can interact to produce what we see as intelligent performance.

Gardner (1983; 1993b) based his theory on evidence that goes well beyond factor analysis. He put together various sources and types of data. Among the diverse kinds of support Gardner used were evidence from studies of brain damage, from observed patterns by which a given ability develops, from the behavior of exceptional individuals (at both ends of the spectrum), and from evolutionary history (in which increases in intelligence are associated with enhanced adaptation to the environment). In addition, Gardner has gathered supporting evidence from psychometric and experimental research.

The Triarchic Theory

Gardner's theory emphasizes the separateness of the various aspects of intelligence. In my **triarchic theory of human intelligence** (Sternberg, 1985a, 1988b), I tend to emphasize the extent to which the aspects of intelligence work together. According to the triarchic (*tri-*, three; *-archic*, governed) theory, there are three main aspects of intelligence: analytical, creative, and practical. You use the *analytical aspect* of intelligence when you compare and contrast ideas, or when you evaluate them. You use the *creative aspect* of intelligence when you think in new ways and when you cope with new kinds of situations. You use the *practical aspect* of intelligence when you adapt to the various demands of your everyday environment. For example, comparing two theories of visual perception would involve analysis, coming up with your own theory would involve creativity, and applying the theory to helping people see better in dark places would involve practical intelligence. Figure 9-4 illustrates the parts of the theory and their interrelationships.

According to the triarchic theory, people may differ in how well they apply their intelligence to different kinds of problems. For example, some people may be more intelligent when they face problems in their studies in school, whereas others may be more intelligent when they face practical problems. The theory does not define an intelligent person as someone who necessarily is excellent in all aspects of

When you say one thing, the clever person understands three.

Chinese proverb

triarchic theory of human intelligence a theory of intelligence, which asserts that intelligence comprises three aspects (analytical, creative, and practical)

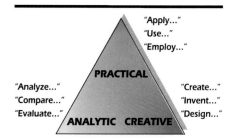

Figure 9-4

Triarchic Theory of Intelligence

According to Robert Sternberg, intelligence comprises analytical, creative, and practical abilities. In analytical thinking, we try to solve familiar problems by using strategies that manipulate the elements of a problem or the relationships among the elements; in creative thinking, we try to solve new kinds of problems that require us to think about the problem and its elements in a new way; in practical thinking, we try to solve problems that apply what we know to everyday contexts.

According to Howard Gardner's theory of intelligence, gifted musicians such as Itzhak Perlman show high levels of musical intelligence.

What is one of your key intellectual strengths? What is one of your key intellectual weaknesses? Might you be able to use your strength to compensate for your weakness? If so, how?

intelligence. Rather, intelligent people know their own strengths and weaknesses. They then find ways to make the most of their strengths, and they either try to fix or to make up for their weaknesses. For example, suppose that a person is strong in psychology but weak in physics. This person might choose a physics project that uses psychology, such as creating a physics aptitude test (which I did when I took physics!). In whatever you do, you should make the most of your strengths, and find ways to improve upon or at least to make up for your weaknesses.

The systems theories of intelligence are broader and more comprehensive than the theories of intelligence considered earlier. Some psychologists (e.g., Eysenck, 1984; Jackson, 1984; Yussen, 1984) say that the systems theories are too broad and that these theories are therefore difficult to test. Nonetheless, the trend in the coming years seems to be toward broader theories of intelligence, which encompass abilities that earlier theorists downplayed or even neglected.

How should we try to understand the nature of intelligence? One approach to trying to understand intelligence is to analyze the various mental structures that constitute intelligence. It is important as well to try to study the mental processes that underlie intelligent behavior. Many biological psychologists investigate the structures and processes of the brain that underlie intelligence. Psychologists also may try to understand intelligence within its cultural context, rather than in isolation. A comprehensive approach considers intelligence as a complex system, in which greater understanding can be achieved by considering multiple perspectives and methods of investigation.

WHAT HAVE WE LEARNED ABOUT EXTREMES OF INTELLIGENCE?

Every theory of intelligence must somehow address the extremes of intelligence. Although most people fall within the broad middle of the range of intelligence, some people fall at the upper and lower extremes. People at the upper extreme are often labeled as *intellectually gifted*, whereas those at the lower extreme are often labeled as *mentally retarded*.

Intellectual Giftedness

Psychologists disagree regarding how to define intellectual giftedness. For example, some school programs for the gifted choose candidates largely on the basis of several tests of intelligence. Such programs may take children in the top 1% (IQ roughly equal to 135 or above) or 2% (IQ roughly equal to 132 or above) of IQ scores. Other programs also use other measures for determining giftedness, such as school achievement or motivation.

Lewis Terman, developer of the *Stanford–Binet Intelligence Scales*, conducted a longitudinal study of gifted individuals. A *longitudinal study* is research that follows a particular group of individuals across many years. Terman and his collaborators followed particular gifted individuals over the course of their life span (Terman, 1925; Terman & Oden, 1959). The longitudinal study has continued, even after Terman's death. The core of Terman's sample was 621 children from California under age 11 years with IQs over 140. The average IQ of the entire sample of participants was 151.

The later accomplishments of the children were extraordinary. By 1959, 70 were listed in *American Men of Science*, 3 were members of the prestigious National Academy of Sciences, 31 were listed in *Who's Who in America*, and 10 appeared in the *Directory of American Scholars*. Numerous others were highly successful in businesses or professions. One of the people studied by Terman, Robert Sears, became a professor at Stanford and even took over the Terman study for some time. During the time of Terman's study, most of the women in Terman's study became housewives. Thus, it is impossible to compare meaningfully the accomplishments of the men and the women in Terman's sample.

Many factors other than IQ also could have contributed to the success of Terman's sample. Among the most important of these factors are familial

To want to be the cleverest of all is the biggest folly.

Shalom Aleichem

How can we identify intellectual giftedness? Stephen Hawking is widely regarded as extremely gifted because of his creative insights regarding time and space, as well as for his depth of knowledge of physics. How are we able to identify Hawking as being intellectually gifted?

How do you account for the differing achievements of men and of women in Terman's sample? Be specific.

socioeconomic status (SES; income, education, etc.) and the final educational status of these individuals. As with all correlational data, we cannot infer what caused what.

Today, many psychologists believe that intellectual giftedness involves more than a high IQ (Sternberg & Davidson, 1986). For example, Joseph Renzulli (1986) believes that high commitment to tasks (motivation) and high creativity are important to giftedness, in addition to above-average (although not necessarily outstanding) intelligence, as measured by IQ tests.

I believe that there are many ways to be gifted, and scores on standard intelligence tests represent only one of these ways. Indeed, some highly gifted persons, such as Albert Einstein or Thomas Edison, were not outstanding students or test-takers during their early years. Moreover, Einstein did not even speak until he was 3 years old. Einstein was near the top of the scale of intellectual performance; many individuals are closer to the opposite extreme.

Mental Retardation

Mental retardation refers to very low levels of intelligence—simple enough. Much less simple is determining whom to label as mentally retarded. Different viewpoints lead to different conclusions. The American Association on Mental Retardation includes two main parts in its definition of mental retardation: low IQ and low adaptive competence. *Adaptive competence* refers to how a person gets along in the world. In other words, to be labeled as retarded, an individual would have to meet two criteria: (1) poor performance on an intelligence test, and (2) problems in

mental retardation very low level of intelligence, usually reflected by both poor performance on tests of intelligence and poor *adaptive competence* (the degree to which a person functions effectively within a normal situational context)

TABLE 9-2
Levels of Mental Retardation

Degree of retardation	Adaptive life skills
Mild (IQ score 50–70; ≈85% of retarded persons; about 2% of general population)	May acquire and demonstrate mastery of academic skills at or below the sixth-grade level, particularly if given special education. Likely to acquire various social and vocation-related skills, given adequate training and appropriate environment. Given appropriate environmental support and assistance (especially during times of stress), may achieve independent living and occupational success.
Moderate (IQ score 35–55; ≈10% of retarded persons; 0.1% of the general population)	Have considerable difficulty in school, but may acquire and demonstrate mastery of academic skills at or below the fourth-grade level if given special education. Given appropriate, very structured environmental support and supervision, may be able to engage in unskilled or possibly highly routinized semiskilled vocational activities that contribute to self-support. Able to engage in many personal self-maintenance activities. A sheltered home and work environment, in which supervision and guidance are readily available, often works well.
Severe (IQ score 20–40; ≈4% of retarded persons; <0.003% of the general population)	May learn to talk or at least to communicate in some manner. Unlikely to profit from vocational training, but given adequate full supervision and highly structured environmental support, may be able to perform simple tasks required for personal self-maintenance (including toileting) and possibly even some limited vocational activity. Some custodial services may be required, in addition to a carefully controlled environment.
Profound (IQ score below 25; <2% of retarded persons)	Limited motor development and little or no speech. Generally unresponsive to training, but may be trained to participate in some self-maintenance activities (not including toileting). Constant supervision and assistance in performing fundamental self-maintenance within a custodial setting are required.

adapting to the environment. By this definition, a child with a low IQ would not be classified as mentally retarded if the child performed normally in all or most other ways. Table 9-2 illustrates some of the ways in which particular IQ scores have been related to particular adaptive life skills.

It is not always easy to measure adaptive competence, however, as the following example (Edgerton, 1967) shows. A retarded man (who had scored low on tests of intelligence) was unable to tell time—an indication of some kind of thinking problem. However, the man figured out a clever way to find out the time: He wore a nonfunctional watch, so that whenever he wanted to know the time, he could stop, look at his watch, pretend to notice that his watch did not work, and then ask a nearby stranger (who would have observed his behavior) to tell him the correct time. How should we measure this man's adaptive competence—in terms of his strategy for determining the time or in terms of his inability to tell time by looking at a watch?

There is often wisdom under a shabby coat.

Latin proverb

What have we learned about extremes of intelligence? Intellectual giftedness involves more than just high IQ; for example, high commitment to task performance and high creativity may also contribute to giftedness. Similarly, mental retardation involves more than low IQ; in particular, it involves low adaptive competence.

"Acually, Lou, I think it was more than just being in the right place at the right time. I think it was my being the right race, the right religion, the right sex, the right socioeconomic group, having the right accent, the right clothes, going to the right schools..."

Drawing by W. Miller; © 1992 The New Yorker Magazine, Inc.

IS INTELLIGENCE INHERITED?

Psychologists believe that both heredity and environment can contribute to mental retardation. For example, environmental contributions to low intelligence may involve limited opportunities for learning. Even the prenatal environment may cause permanent retardation. For instance, retardation may result if a pregnant mother is poorly nourished or if she consumes poisonous substances, such as alcohol, during the child's prenatal development. Even a brief trauma (e.g., an injury caused by a car accident or a fall) can damage the functioning of the brain, leading to mental retardation.

We do not yet have a clear understanding of how heredity influences intelligence. Even so, we do know of several genetic syndromes that cause mental retardation. One of the more common ones is *Down syndrome*.

Sometimes, heredity interacts with the environment to produce mental retardation. Although we cannot prevent the inheritance of genetic disorders or diseases once a child is conceived, we can try to keep the environment from contributing to the retardation. For example, we now know how to prevent serious mental retardation resulting from *phenylketonuria (PKU)*. PKU is a rare hereditary disease that results in mental retardation if nothing is done to prevent retardation from occurring. With a special diet, however, damage to the brain can be avoided or at least limited, and serious retardation can be avoided altogether. In PKU, the interaction of nature and nurture is clear. For most of us, however, the distinctive influences of nature and nurture are less clear.

How do psychologists try to determine the relative influences of nature and nurture? Several methods have been used for determining the *heritability of intelligence*—the degree to which variation in levels of intelligence is due to heredity, assuming that environmental factors are held constant. The main methods involve studies of separated identical twins, studies of identical versus fraternal twins, and studies of adopted children. These kinds of studies have led to uncertain, mixed results. Many psychologists now believe that heredity and environment each contribute about equally to intelligence. However, many variables can change these estimates. For example, Sandra Scarr (in press) has reported that the heritability of intelligence is greater for white than for black Americans. In other words, environmental factors appear to play a greater role in influencing the observed intelligence of black Americans, as compared with white Americans. Also, the distributions of genes or environments may vary across persons of different ages. There is some

These identical twins were separated at birth and were not reunited until they were 31 years old, when the two firefighters met and discovered striking similarities in their personal habits and interests. Studies of twins reared apart reveal a great deal about how much of our intelligence is due to our nature and how much is due to our nurture.

evidence that the apparent heritability of intelligence increases with age (Plomin, in press), which means that environmental effects become less influential and genetic effects more influential in contributing to differences in observed intelligence as people grow older. Apparently, differential effects of early environment start to moderate with age, leaving more room for genes to express their relative effects as people age.

When we consider intelligence and other characteristics, we must be careful to recognize the role of the environment, as well as of heredity. Even if a characteristic is highly heritable, it can be developed. For example, height is highly heritable, yet heights have been increasing over the past several generations. Clearly, better environments can lead to growth—physical as well as intellectual.

One of the most powerful environmental factors affecting intelligence is societal status. It appears that intelligence may be hindered when individuals are assigned an inferior status within a given society. Across cultures, disadvantaged groups (e.g., native Maoris vs. European New Zealanders) have often shown lower scores on tests of intelligence and aptitude (Steele, 1990; Zeidner, 1990). Such was the case of the Buraku-min tanners in Japan, who, in 1871, were granted emancipation but not full acceptance into Japanese society. Although they generally have low status and show poor academic performance in Japan, those who immigrate to America—and are treated like other Japanese immigrants—perform on IQ tests and in school at a level comparable to that of their fellow Japanese Americans (Ogbu, 1986). Once they are relieved of their lower societal status, their measured intelligence improves.

In the United States, average scores on intelligence tests are about 10 to 15 points higher for whites than for blacks. We cannot say whether the differing societal status of blacks versus whites explains this difference in average test scores. In fact, at present, there are no conclusive explanations for this difference in test scores, although various interpretations have been offered (e.g., Herrnstein & Murray, 1994; Ogbu, 1982). We can say, however, that there is no compelling evidence for a genetic basis underlying apparent racial differences in intelligence-test scores (described in Loehlin, Lindzey, & Spuhler, 1975; Nisbett, 1995).

MINILECTURE

Heritability of Intelligence (Ch 11)

Is intelligence inherited? Intelligence appears to be at least partly heritable, but environmental factors also play an important role in its emergence. That is, both heredity and environment play a role in the development and demonstration of intelligence.

CAN WE IMPROVE INTELLIGENCE?

At one time, it was believed that intelligence is *fixed;* that is, we are stuck forever with whatever level of intelligence we have at birth. Today, many researchers believe that intelligence is *malleable:* It can be shaped and even increased (Detterman & Sternberg, 1982; Ramey, 1994). For one thing, intelligence can be increased simply by using intellectual skills as much as possible in everyday life. Just as musicians may improve their musical abilities through practice, all of us can enrich our intellectual abilities through practice in thinking intelligently in our daily experiences. Another way to increase intelligence is to be involved in an educational

Some people strongly believe that taxpayers would benefit from spending money to educate parents regarding how to provide environments that stimulate the intelligence of their children. Do you agree or disagree with their views? Why?

Wisdom is easy to carry but difficult to gather.

Czech proverb

reaction range the broad limits within which a particular attribute (e.g., intelligence) may be expressed in various possible ways, given the inherited potential for expression of the attribute in the particular individual

setting that fosters the development of intelligence (Ceci, 1990). When teachers emphasize the use of thinking skills in the classroom, the teachers enhance their students' intelligence. In addition, various programs have been designed specifically to help people to increase their intelligence.

For example, the Head Start program was intended to provide preschoolers with an edge on intellectual abilities and accomplishments that would serve the children well when they started school. Studies checking the progress of Head Start children have included matched controls. *Matched controls* are research participants who are in the control condition, but who have been matched to the participants in the treatment condition as closely as possible. For example, the researchers try to ensure that the ages, family backgrounds, income levels, and other characteristics of participants in the control group match those of participants in the treatment group. In the case of the Head Start studies, the treatment group would participate in the Head Start program, and the control group would not.

Long-term follow-ups have indicated that by midadolescence, performance of children who participated in the program was more than a grade ahead of matched controls who did not participate in the program (Lazar & Darlington, 1982; Zigler & Berman, 1983). The children in the program also showed other advantages: They scored higher on various tests of scholastic achievement, were less likely to need remedial attention (involving remedies or treatments for educational problems), and were less likely to show behavioral problems. Although these outcome measures are not direct measures of intelligence, they do show a strong positive correlation with measures such as intelligence tests. Many newer programs in schools or other community settings have also shown some success (see Adams, 1986; Ramey, 1994).

We now know that people's environments (e.g., Ceci, Nightingale, & Baker, 1992; Reed, 1993; Sternberg & Wagner, 1994), their motivation (e.g., Collier, 1994; Sternberg & Ruzgis, 1994), and their training (e.g., Feuerstein, 1980; Sternberg, 1987) can powerfully affect their intellectual skills. Heredity may set some kind of upper limit on how intelligent a person may become. However, for any attribute that is partly genetic, there is a **reaction range.** In a reaction range, the attribute can be expressed in various ways within broad limits of possibilities. Thus, each person's intelligence can be developed further within this broad range of potential intelligence. People have yet to reach their upper limits in developing their intellectual skills. Evidence suggests that we can do quite a bit to help people become more intelligent.

Intelligence is also linked to another ability that appears to be highly malleable: creativity. Surprisingly, perhaps, extremely high intelligence is not necessary for great creativity. Beyond a given level of intelligence, further increases in intelligence do not necessarily correlate with increases in creativity. Thus, to be creative, an individual must be bright but not necessarily brilliant. If extreme brilliance is not necessary for creativity, what characteristics are needed?

Can we improve intelligence? Intelligence is malleable, not fixed; it appears that there is a reaction range within which intelligence can be improved. Programs such as Head Start have shown that intelligent performance in school can be enhanced through environmental influences.

WHAT IS CREATIVITY, AND HOW DOES IT EMERGE?

Although specialists on creativity often disagree about how to define creativity precisely, most psychologists would generally agree that **creativity** is a process of producing something that is both original and worthwhile. The *something* may be a theory, a dance, a chemical, a process or procedure, or almost anything else.

Just what does it mean for that something to be *original?* Almost everything we do is based on the ideas and the work of those who have come before us. Still, we recognize that composers, choreographers, poets, and other artists create original somethings, even if they learn from the techniques, styles, and subjects of other people. Can scientists and other nonartists create anything original?

When Nicolaus Copernicus (1473–1543) proposed his heliocentric (*helio-*, sun; *-centric*, centered) view of our solar system, he based his idea on the work of other people, as well as on his own observations. What makes his work creative? He analyzed and then synthesized (combined) the existing information in an unusual way. Through his creative work, he completely changed the way we see our planet in relation to the universe.

That Copernicus's creation was worthwhile seems doubtless now, but during his lifetime, many people doubted the worth of his idea. Sometimes, people do not appreciate the value of the creative work until long after the creator dies. This fact is not as odd as it might seem: By definition, creative work moves away from what has already been done by others. It may take a while for other people to see that the unusual can have great value. Even after quite some time, a creative product may not be considered valuable by everyone. For example, almost anyone would recognize Giuseppe Verdi's operas as original. However, not everyone considers these works to be worthwhile. What makes something worthwhile is that it is significant, useful, or valuable in some way, to some people.

What does it take to create something original and worthwhile? What are creative people like? Almost everyone would agree that creative individuals show *creative productivity*. Creative people produce inventions, insightful discoveries, artistic products, or other creative products that are both original and worthwhile. Conventional wisdom suggests that highly creative individuals also have creative lifestyles: Their lifestyles are characterized by flexibility, unusual behaviors, and uncommon attitudes.

Many different factors contribute to creativity. Perhaps the most important is a willingness to defy convention—to separate onself from the crowd in terms of one's ideas (Sternberg & Lubart, 1995). Other factors are important as well, including intelligence, knowledge, personality, motivation, and the environment (Sternberg & Lubart, 1991, 1995).

With respect to intelligence, it appears that highly creative people are above average, but not necessarily exceptionally intelligent (Renzulli, 1986). Thus, you do not need sky-high scores on conventional tests of abilities in order to do highly creative work. Knowledge is important, too: To move beyond what is known, you have to be aware of what is known. However, knowledge can be a double-edged sword: Sometimes, knowledge can interfere with thinking flexibly and in new ways about a problem (Frensch & Sternberg, 1989). Several aspects of personality are also important for creativity, such as openness to new ways of seeing things, alertness to opportunities, willingness to take sensible risks, and willingness to overcome obstacles (Barron, 1988; Sternberg & Lubart, 1995). Motivation is important, too. Creative people virtually always love what they do, and they work hard at it for the sheer enjoyment of the work (Hennessey & Amabile, 1988). Finally, the environment matters. Even if you have all the attributes of a creative person, you need a supportive environment that will encourage and recognize your creativity, rather than discourage or even actively suppress it (Csikszentmihalyi, 1988; Gardner, 1993a; Simonton, 1994).

In your lifetime, if you can come up with one original idea you have accomplished a great deal.

Max Roach

The more you know, the more you create.

Julia Child

If you ever have a new idea, and it's really new, you have to expect that it won't be widely accepted immediately. It's a long hard process.

Rosalyn Yarrow

creativity the process of producing something that is both original and valuable

How can we tell a highly creative person from someone who is relatively less creative? Shown here are three highly creative individuals: Salvador Dali, Alice Walker, and Amy Tan.

People who do not break things first will never learn to create anything.

Tagalog (Filipino) proverb

PRACTICAL PSYCHOLOGY   9-1

How Can You Become More Creative?

To increase your own creativity, take the following steps:

1. Become highly motivated to be creative in a particular kind of work. Under most circumstances, however, try to avoid being tempted by extrinsic motivators related to an outcome of your creative work. In general, your primary motivation should be intrinsic, related to the creative work itself.

2. Show some nonconformity, as necessary, to promote your creative work. Boldly question and possibly violate rules or conventions that senselessly inhibit your creative work. Avoid getting side-tracked by the struggle against conventions, however. Remember also that some conventions can be useful. Maintain tough standards of excellence in your performance and your work habits. Demonstrate strong self-discipline as it relates to your creative work.

3. Deeply believe in the value and importance of your creative work; do not let others discourage you from pursuing this work. On the other hand, you should constantly monitor and criticize your own work, seeking always to improve it.

4. Carefully choose the problems or subjects on which to focus your creative attention. Find problems that appeal to you. At first, some creative ideas may be considered distasteful and unappealing by others.

5. Actively seek out information that other people ignore, and seek novel combinations of the pieces of information. Think in terms of many possibilities, rather than in terms of limited options.

6. Choose friends who will encourage you to take sensible intellectual risks, and who do not conform just for the sake of conforming.

7. Gain as much of the available knowledge as possible in your chosen field. In this way, you can avoid reinventing the wheel or producing the same old stuff being produced by others in your field. Find the interesting gaps in the existing information. On the other hand, avoid becoming trapped by mental sets or negative transfer (see Chapter 8). One way in which to get as much knowledge as you need, yet to avoid mental sets, is to study various phenomena that interest you. This variety of interests helps you to avoid getting bogged down in the conventional thinking about one particular phenomenon.

8. Commit yourself deeply to your creative work.

Some researchers believe that only a few rare persons can be creative. However, most psychologists believe that almost anyone can become more creative by working to become so. Quite a few also believe that many more of us could become exceptionally creative if we wished to become so (see Practical Psychology 9-1).

There is some agreement that each of the Practical Psychology suggestions may play a role in creative productivity. Even so, many psychologists and other researchers might disagree about one or more of these suggestions, and many creative individuals do not follow all of these general recommendations. In fact, we might say that, as a group, creative people are defined by their differences. Extraordinary creative productivity may be rare because so many variables must come together, in the right amounts, in a single person. For a highly creative person to express great creativity, that person must find a supportive social context. The influence of the social context is the topic of our next chapter.

What is creativity, and how does it emerge? Creativity is the process of producing something that is both original and valuable. It emerges through a combination of intense intrinsic motivation, keen insight, willingness to go against convention, openness to new ideas, a supportive historical and social context, a preference for generating new ideas rather than for evaluating or carrying out existing ones, and a knack for finding valuable ideas that others have failed to appreciate.

SUMMARY

What Are Two Traditional Approaches to Studying Intelligence? 254

1. Two traditions in the study of intelligence are those of Francis Galton and of Alfred Binet. The tradition of Galton emphasizes *psychophysical* abilities, whereas that of Binet emphasizes *judgmental* abilities.

How Do Psychologists Assess Intelligence? 256

2. *Mental age* refers to a person's level of intelligence, as compared with the average person of a given chronological age. Because of conceptual and statistical problems, mental age is rarely used today as a means of expressing intelligence test scores.

3. The *intelligence quotient (IQ)* originally represented the ratio of mental age to chronological age, multiplied by 100. It was intended to provide a measure of a child's intelligence, relative to his or her agemates.

4. Today, IQs typically are computed to have an average score of 100. IQs that are computed based on deviations from the average are *deviation IQs. Normative scores* represent a translation of raw scores into scaled equivalents; these scaled equivalents reflect the relative performance of individual test-takers, thereby permitting comparison.

5. Two of the most widely used intelligence tests are administered individually. They are the *Stanford–Binet Intelligence Scales* and the *Wechsler Adult Intelligence Scale–Revised*.

6. Test *validity* indicates the degree to which a test measures what it is supposed to measure. Test *reliability* indicates how dependably and consistently a test measures whatever it measures.

7. Test *standardization* refers to the steps taken to ensure that the conditions for taking a test are the same for all test-takers.

How Should We Try to Understand the Nature of Intelligence? 261

8. Intelligence can be understood in terms of its many different aspects. Some investigators focus more on mental structures, others on mental processes. Some investigators seek to understand intelligence in relation to the brain; others study its relation to culture. Systems theories, such

as those of Gardner and Sternberg, integrate a number of these different aspects.

9. In an approach focusing on structure, intelligence is studied via factor analysis, a statistical technique for identifying the underlying sources of individual differences in performance on tests.

10. An alternative approach to intelligence (a computational one) emphasizes *information processing*—the mental manipulation of symbols.

11. Biologically oriented psychologists use sophisticated means of viewing the brain while the brain is engaged in performing tasks that require intelligence.

12. Psychologists taking a *contextual approach* view intelligence as wholly or partly determined by cultural surroundings.

`13. What is considered to be intelligent behavior is, to some extent, culturally relative: The same behavior that is considered to be intelligent in one culture may be considered to be unintelligent in another culture.

14. *Culture-fair* tests, in theory, are equally fair for members of all cultures. It is probably impossible to create a test of intelligence that is truly culture fair. Such tests cannot exist because members of different cultures have different conceptions of what constitutes intelligent behavior. The development of *culture-relevant* tests, however, is both realistic and desirable.

15. A useful approach to understanding intelligence is to understand it as a system. Gardner's *theory of multiple intelligences* specifies that there are seven distinct intelligences, each relatively independent of the others. Sternberg's *triarchic theory of human intelligence* conceives of intelligence as a unified system that integrates information processing with cultural context. Intelligence is seen as having analytical, creative, and practical aspects.

What Have We Learned About Extremes of Intelligence?   269

16. Intellectual giftedness refers to a very high level of intelligence and is often believed to involve more than just high IQ. For example, it may be seen as also involving high creativity and high motivation.

17. The contemporary definition of mental retardation in-

cludes two components: low IQ and low adaptive competence for getting along in the world.

Is Intelligence Inherited?   272

18. Mental retardation can be caused by either hereditary or environmental factors, or by both kinds of factors in interaction.

19. The heritability of intelligence refers to the degree to which variation in levels of intelligence is due to heredity, assuming that environmental factors are held constant. Heritability can differ both across populations and within populations, across different times and places.

Can We Improve Intelligence?   273

20. Intellectual skills can be taught. Thus, intelligence is malleable rather than fixed.

What Is Creativity, and How Does It Emerge?   275

21. *Creativity* involves producing something that is both original and worthwhile. Various researchers have suggested a diverse assortment of views regarding how creativity emerges. For example, one theory suggests that creative individuals produce ideas that are typically undervalued at the time they are produced, but that are eventually considered to be highly valuable.

22. The following factors characterize highly creative individuals: (a) extremely high motivation to be creative in a particular field (e.g., for the sheer enjoyment of the creative process); (b) nonconformity in questioning senseless conventions that inhibit creative work, dedication in maintaining standards of excellence, and self-discipline related to creative work; (c) a deep belief in the value of creative work, as well as a willingness to criticize and improve one's own creative work; (d) careful choice of the problems or subjects on which to focus creative attention; (e) thought processes characterized by both insight and divergent thinking; (f) associates who encourage sensible intellectual risk taking; (g) extensive knowledge of the relevant domain; and (h) profound commitment to the creative endeavor.

PATHWAYS TO KNOWLEDGE

Choose the best answer to complete each sentence or to respond to each question.

1. Alfred Binet devised a battery of tests primarily to
   (a) differentiate average from above average intelligent individuals.
   (b) identify the brightest individuals for future government service.

   (c) test his hypothesis that there is no great range in intellectual ability.
   (d) differentiate students who were mentally retarded from students who merely had behavioral problems.

2. Aptitudes are
   (a) preferences and tendencies to perform certain activities.
   (b) accomplished achievements in an area of endeavor.

(c) individuals' abilities to learn in specific areas of endeavor.

(d) skills that can be focused only on single tasks.

3. In one study, Kpelle individuals had difficulty in performing a classification task until one of the experimenters
(a) showed the chief how to perform the task.
(b) used objects with which the Kpelle were familiar.
(c) asked the Kpelle to perform the task the way the chief would perform it.
(d) asked the Kpelle to perform the task the way a foolish person would perform it.

4. IQ means intelligence quotient,
(a) and psychologists figure out a person's IQ score by dividing the total number of correct answers by the total number of incorrect answers on an intelligence test.
(b) but nowadays, the IQ scores computed from the most widely used intelligence tests are not quotients at all.
(c) which offers an exact indication of a person's intelligence.
(d) which is determined by using tests that are culture-fair when administered by a competent professional.

5. According to Robert Sternberg's triarchic theory, if you were designing a theoretical model explaining how individuals use memory in solving problems, which aspect of intelligence would you be using, for the most part, in designing the model?
(a) creative
(b) practical
(c) memorial
(d) analytic

6. According to Robert Sternberg's triarchic theory, if you were skillfully applying what you learned in school to the problems you face at work, which aspect of intelligence would you be using, for the most part?
(a) creative
(b) practical
(c) memorial
(d) analytic

7. If psychologists were giving an intelligence test to a large group of people, they would probably want to make sure that
(a) the test items included equal numbers of arithmetic problems and vocabulary problems.
(b) if one test-taker had to listen to an annoying cuckoo clock while taking the test, all other test-takers would have to listen to the clock, too.
(c) the test administrators endorsed only the theoretical approach preferred by the test designers.
(d) the test was completely reliable, valid, and culture-fair.

Answer each of the following questions by filling in the blank with an appropriate word or phrase.

8. William Stern originated the concept of the _____ _____, which was later abbreviated as _____, and which is defined as the ratio of mental age over chronological age, multiplied by 100.

9. An individual's _____ _____ is defined as his or her level of intelligence expressed in terms of the performance of an average person of a given age.

10. Two of the more popular adult-level intelligence tests in use today are the _____–_____ Intelligence Scales and the _____ _____ Intelligence Scale.

11. Psychometric theories of intelligence often use the statistical technique of _____ _____ in order to come up with underlying factors that differentiate individuals.

12. _____ is the process of producing something that is both original and valuable.

13. Intelligence is partly inherited, within a _____ _____, which is the expression of intelligence within broad limits and possibilities.

14. According to Howard Gardner, an individual who is very adept at evaluating and analyzing him or herself is high in _____ intelligence.

15. In order for an individual to be classified as mentally retarded, he or she must show low _____ _____, as well as having a low score on a typical intelligence test.

16. The type of IQ we use today is referred to as a _____ _____ because it is calculated on the basis of deviations in the normal distribution of scores.

17. Whereas _____ is the extent to which a given form of measurement assesses what it is supposed to measure, _____ is the consistency of a measurement instrument (e.g., a test).

Match each of the following theories to the appropriate theorist:

18. There are seven distinct intelligences.

19. Intelligence consists of a hierarchy of abilities, varying in their levels of generality.

20. Intelligence involves analytical, creative, and practical aspects.

(a) Charles Spearman
(b) Robert Sternberg
(c) Howard Gardner
(d) John Carroll
(e) Stephen Ceci

Answers

1. d, 2. c, 3. d, 4. b, 5. a, 6. b, 7. b, 8. intelligence quotient, IQ, 9. mental age, 10. Stanford–Binet, Wechsler Adult, 11. factor analysis, 12. Creativity, 13. reaction range, 14. intrapersonal, 15. adaptive competence, 16. deviation IQ, 17. validity, reliability, 18. c, 19. d, 20. b

PATHWAYS TO UNDERSTANDING

1. Suppose that you were to select a job for yourself, solely on the basis of your abilities. What might that job be?

2. How should educators foster the intellectual gifts of their students? Give at least one concrete suggestion.

3. In your view, to what extent are different people born with differing levels of intelligence? To what extent do differences in children's environments affect the development of their intelligence?

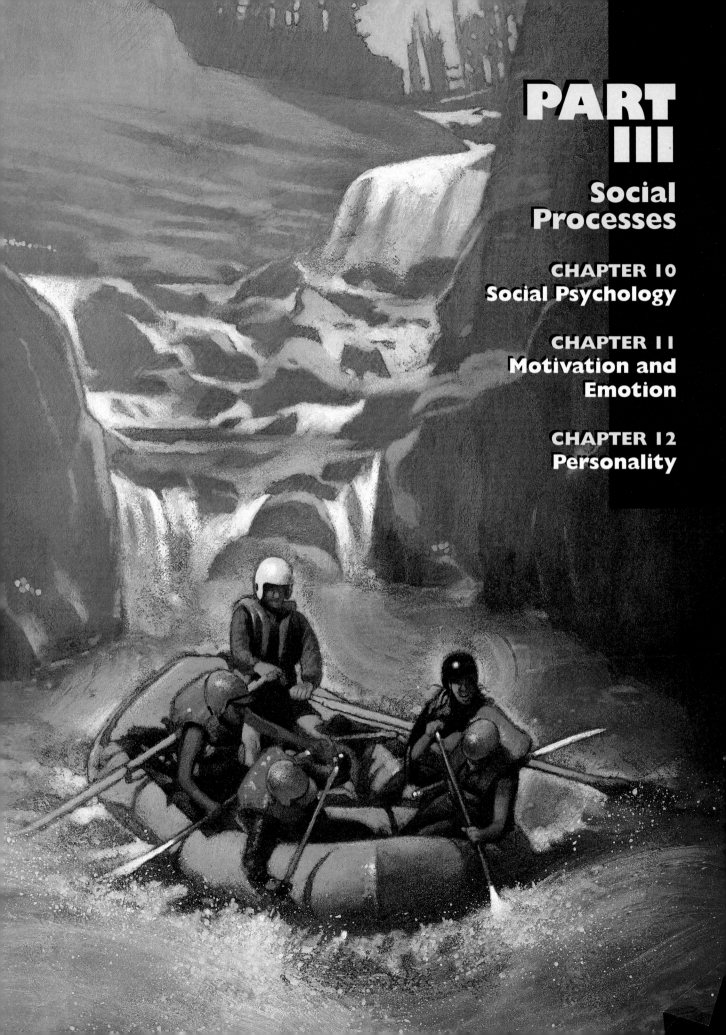

PART III
Social Processes

CHAPTER 10
Social Psychology

CHAPTER 11
Motivation and Emotion

CHAPTER 12
Personality

CHAPTER OUTLINE

What Is Social Cognition?
Cognitive-Consistency Theory
Attribution Theory

How Do We Form and Change Our Attitudes?
Characteristics Affecting
Attitude Change

Why Are We Attracted to the People We Like or Love?
Theories of Liking and
Interpersonal Attraction
Theories of Love
Attraction

How Do We Communicate in Our Personal Relationships?

What Happens When We Interact in Groups?
Social Facilitation and
Social Interference
Social Loafing
Group Polarization
Groupthink

When and How Do We Conform, Comply, and Obey?
Conformity
Compliance
Obedience

What Leads Us to Show Prosocial Behavior?
Latané and Darley's Five-Step
Model of Bystander Intervention

What Leads Us to Show Antisocial Behavior?
Prejudice
Reducing Prejudice
Aggression

CHAPTER
10

Social Psychology

"Miss Gates is a nice lady, ain't she?"

"Why, sure," said Jem. "I liked her when I was in her room."

"She hates Hitler a lot. . . ."

"What's wrong with that?"

"Well, she went on today about how bad it was him treatin' the Jews like that. Jem, it's not right to persecute anybody, is it? I mean have mean thoughts about anybody, even, is it?"

"Gracious no, Scout. What's eatin' you?"

"Well, coming out of the courthouse that night Miss Gates was—she was goin' down the steps in front of us, you musta not seen her—she was talking with Miss Stephanie Crawford. I heard her say it's time somebody taught 'em [African Americans] a lesson, they were gettin' way above themselves, an' the next thing they think they can do is marry us. Jem, how can you hate Hitler so bad an' then turn around and be ugly about folks right at home—"

—*Harper Lee,* To Kill a Mockingbird *(pp. 246–247)*

In this fictional exchange between a young girl and her brother, it appears that although Miss Gates is outraged by Hitler's treatment of Jews in Germany, she supports the mistreatment of African Americans in her own country. What could make an apparently nice person feel justified in wishing harm to an entire group of people? To answer this question requires a study of prejudice, an aspect of social psychology. According to influential social psychologist Gordon Allport (1897–1967), **social psychology** is the attempt "to understand and explain how the thoughts, feelings, and behavior of individuals are influenced by the actual, imagined, or implied presence of others" (1985, p. 3). For instance, it appears that (a) the *actual* presence of other persons may lead people to go along with decisions that they would be less likely to agree with otherwise; (b) the *imagined* presence of other persons may lead people to change how hard they work at a task; and (c) the *implied* presence of other persons may influence whether people will go out of their way to help during an emergency. This chapter briefly elaborates on these and other findings discovered by social psychologists during their search for understanding and explanation.

Most of the studies in this chapter, like the studies cited in similar chapters in other textbooks (Moghaddam, Taylor, & Wright, 1993; Smith & Öngel, 1994; Triandis, 1994), have been conducted in the United States, involving U.S. psychologists and research participants. Many social psychologists question whether findings based on U.S. studies alone can be generalized to other countries and other cultures (Bond, 1988). Different cultures provide a different context for people's thoughts, feelings, and actions, so we must be careful not to overgeneralize findings from one culture to another (Amir & Sharon, 1987). On the other hand, many of the questions we ask about how people think, feel, and act are the same across cultures. First, we consider how we think about ourselves and other people.

Culture is the widening of the mind and of the spirit.

Jawaharlal Nehru

---

social psychology the study of how each person's thoughts, feelings, and behaviors are affected by the presence of others, even if that presence is only implied or imagined

Culture provides a context within which we "are influenced by the actual, imagined, or implied presence of others" (Allport, 1985, p. 3).

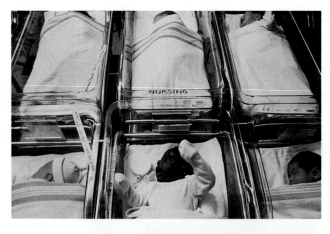

WHAT IS SOCIAL COGNITION?

Social cognition refers to how we perceive and interpret information about ourselves and others, based on our social interactions. In this chapter, we discuss two interrelated theories of social cognition: cognitive-consistency theory and attribution theory.

Cognitive-Consistency Theory

Imagine that you are a research participant in an experiment by Leon Festinger and J. Merrill Carlsmith (1959). The experimenter asks you to perform two mind-numbingly simple tasks of eye–hand coordination. After you have performed these painfully boring tasks for a full hour, the experimenter finally lets you stop. If you are in the control group, you are asked to report how interesting you found the tasks, and that is the end of the experiment.

If you are in one of the experimental groups, however, you are asked to fill in for the research assistant, who has not arrived in time to prepare the next research participant. The experimenter promises to pay you to prepare the next research participant, telling her or him that you thoroughly enjoyed the experimental task. You are told that the experiment is designed to see whether research participants who expect to enjoy the task will perform better.

You agree to fill in, and you work hard to convince the next research participant that the task is great fun. Afterward, you are paid either $1 or $20, depending on the experimental condition to which you are assigned. Finally, a secretary asks you how much you actually enjoyed the task. How will you respond?

The true experiment was designed to measure the relationship between the amount of money the research participants were paid and the amount of enjoyment reported afterward. Surprisingly, research participants paid $1 rated the boring task as much more interesting than did either the participants who were paid $20 or the control participants (see Figure 10-1) (Festinger & Carlsmith, 1959).

Cognitive-Dissonance Theory

Festinger and Carlsmith explained the surprising results by suggesting that research participants' responses could be understood in terms of their efforts to achieve **cognitive consistency** between their beliefs (cognitions) and their behavior. Cognitive consistency is extremely important to our mental well-being. Without it, we feel nervous, irritable, and uncomfortable.

Now, reconsider the experiment: The research participants who were paid $20 performed an extremely boring task and then encouraged someone else to believe that the task was interesting. They were well compensated for doing so, however, so they could achieve cognitive consistency easily by saying to themselves: "I said that the boring task was interesting because I was paid well to do so."

Now consider the research participants who were paid $1. They performed a boring task, and then they tried to convince someone else that it was interesting. These participants experienced **cognitive dissonance** because their beliefs and their behavior did not agree. People need to feel that they have good reasons for behaving as they do. When the participants saw their own behavior in this situation, they needed to find some reason for their behavior. Clearly, money was not the reason in this case. They needed to find a way to bring their behavior and their beliefs more closely into agreement. Therefore, they came to believe that the task must not really have been quite as boring as they had previously thought. That is, they gave themselves reasons for their own behavior by changing their beliefs about the task. Several conditions make cognitive dissonance more likely to occur (see Figure 10-2).

Festinger and Carlsmith (1959) mapped out new territory with their interpretation of their experiment in terms of cognitive-dissonance theory. Since their landmark research and interpretation, other social psychologists have suggested alternative interpretations of their findings. Consider now the rather different

Figure 10-1
When Less Leads to More
The research participants who were paid less money ($1 instead of $20) to convince someone else that the boring task was interesting reported that they actually liked the task more (Festinger & Carlsmith, 1959). Why would research participants who were paid less say that they actually liked the task more?

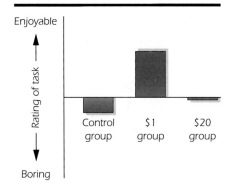

When have you experienced cognitive dissonance? How did the conditions surrounding your own experiences compare with the conditions associated with an increased likelihood of cognitive dissonance?

social cognition the thoughts and beliefs we have regarding ourselves and other people, based on how we perceive and interpret information that we either observe directly or learn from other people

cognitive consistency the reassuring presence of a match between an individual's thoughts (cognition) and that person's behavior

cognitive dissonance the discomforting conflict between an individual's thoughts (cognition) and that person's behavior; often as a result of the person's having acted in a way that does not agree with her or his existing beliefs

Figure 10-2
Conditions for Cognitive Dissonance

Cognitive dissonance seems more likely to occur when (a) you have freely chosen the action that causes the dissonance; (b) you have committed yourself to that behavior and cannot undo your commitment; and (c) your behavior has important consequences for other people.

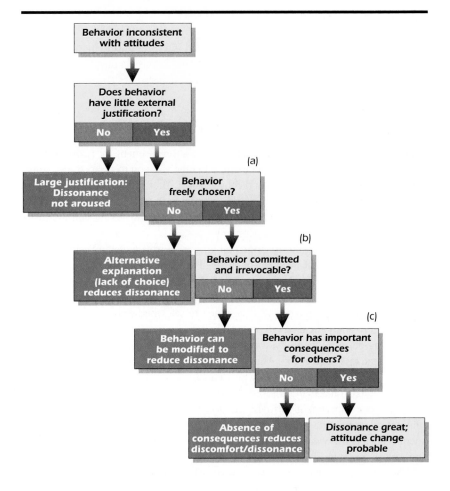

If I have accomplished anything good, then it's mainly because I've been driven by the need to know whether I can accomplish things I'm not sure I have the capacity for.

Václav Havel

When have you tried out something (a new food, a movie, a book, etc.) that you were not sure you would like, but that you ended up liking? What influenced you to change or to form your beliefs in these situations?

self-perception theory the suggestion that when we are not sure of what we believe, we view our behavior much as an outsider might view it, and then infer our beliefs, based on our actions

analysis suggested by self-perception theory, an alternative view of cognitive consistency.

Self-perception Theory

Most of us assume that our behavior is caused by our beliefs. **Self-perception theory** (Bem, 1967, 1972) suggests essentially the opposite: When we are not sure of what we believe, we *infer* our beliefs *from* our behavior. We perceive our actions much as an outside observer would, and then we draw conclusions about ourselves, based on our actions. We form beliefs about ourselves, based on our behavior.

Consider how self-perception theory might interpret the findings of the Festinger and Carlsmith (1959) experiment. As you find yourself explaining to another research participant how much you enjoyed the task, you wonder, "Why in the world am I doing this?" If you are not sure why, then how can you understand your own behavior? If you have been paid $20, an explanation is easy: You are doing it for the money. However, if you have been paid only $1, you cannot be doing it for the money. So, looking at the situation as an outside observer, you conclude that you must have liked the task. Note that according to self-perception theory, you *form* beliefs about yourself, based on your actions. According to cognitive-dissonance theory, you *modify* your beliefs, including your beliefs about yourself and your experiences, when your actions seem to conflict with your existing beliefs.

The results of research on cognitive dissonance and self-perception theory (e.g., Bem, 1967; Cooper, Zanna, & Taves, 1978) are mixed, with some support for each interpretation. Russell Fazio, Mark Zanna, and Joel Cooper (1977) have suggested that dissonance theory seems better to explain *attitude change*, particularly when the change is dramatic and the original beliefs and attitudes are obvious and well defined. Self-perception theory seems better to explain *attitude formation*, when the person's attitudes are still unclear and poorly defined.

Attribution Theory

One of the ways in which we may resolve cognitive dissonance to achieve cognitive consistency is to make **attributions** regarding the causes of our own behavior. Such attributions are not needed in cognitive-dissonance theory, but they are essential to self-perception theory. In self-perception theory, we must make a self-attribution regarding our behavior in order to form our beliefs and attitudes.

Because self-perception theory focuses on making attributions, it is an *attribution theory*, a broad class of social-psychological theories. Attribution theories address how people explain not only their own behavior, but also the behavior of others. People make attributions so that they can understand their social world and can answer questions such as, "Why did I act that way?" "Why did she do that?"

Fritz Heider (1958), an early leader in attribution theory, held that we explain observed behavior by making causal attributions. Then, we often base our own later behavior on the causal attributions we have made. For example, suppose that someone bumps into us. If we attribute the behavior to the person's having been

MINILECTURE
Attribution (Ch 14)

attribution a mental explanation pointing to the cause(s) of a person's behavior, including the behavior of the person making the attribution

TABLE 10-1
Heuristics and Biases of Attribution

Heuristic or bias	Example
Social desirability—We tend to give undeservedly heavy weight to socially undesirable behavior (Jones & Davis, 1965), and we sometimes fail to notice even highly socially desirable behavior.	For example, someone who belches and drools at the dinner table is likely to make a bad impression, despite the person's witty, insightful, thought-provoking conversation.
Common and uncommon effects—We tend to infer attributions based on whether the effects of a behavior are common (in which case, we would infer situational attributions) or uncommon (in which case, we would infer personal attributions) (Jones & Davis, 1965).	For example, if a literature professor asks someone to recite poetry, we tend to infer that situational factors led to the request, but if a physics professor does so, we tend to infer that personal factors led to the request.
Personalism—We tend to make personal, rather than situational, attributions for the behavior of someone who affects us directly, but to be more willing to attribute the cause to situational factors when behavior affects us less directly.	For example, each of us tends to believe that a person who bumps into us is probably a rude jerk by nature, but a person who bumps into somebody else is probably just preoccupied or in a hurry.
Fundamental attribution error—We tend to overemphasize internal causes and personal responsibility and to deemphasize external causes and situational influences when observing the behavior of other people (Ross, 1977).	For example, we are more likely to attribute a person's generous donations to charity to the person's nature, rather than to the person's immediate circumstances.
Actor–observer effects—We tend not only to attribute the actions of others to stable internal personal dispositions, but also to attribute our own actions to external situational variables (Jones & Nisbett, 1971; Nisbett et al., 1973).	For example, if I kick a dog, it is because the dog was about to bite me, but if I see someone else kick a dog, the action shows just how mean and nasty that person really is.
Self-serving biases—We tend to be generous to ourselves when interpreting our own actions.	For example, when students study for examinations and do well, they are likely to take credit for the success. However, when students study and do poorly, they are more likely to attribute the low grade to the examination ("That test was unfair!") or to the professor ("His grading is so strict!") (Whitley & Frieze, 1985).
Self-handicapping—Often, we tend to undermine our own performance so that we will have an excuse in case we fail to perform well (Berglas & Jones, 1978; Sheppard & Arkin, 1989).	For example, a student might not make the time to study for a test. Later, if she does badly on the test, she may then attribute the failure to not being able to study, thereby avoiding the need to attribute her failure to her own inability to do well.

personal attribution a mental explanation pointing to the cause of behavior as lying within the individual who performs the behavior (also termed *dispositional attribution*)

situational attribution a mental explanation pointing to the cause of behavior as lying within the situation in which the individual shows the behavior

social desirability bias the tendency, when trying to infer the dispositions of people, to give undeservedly heavy weight to socially undesirable behavior

common and uncommon effects the tendency to infer attributions based on whether the effects of a behavior are ordinary or are unusual

personalism the tendency to make more personal attributions when the behavior of someone affects us directly, but to make more situational attributions when the behavior affects us less directly

fundamental attribution error the tendency to overemphasize internal causes and personal responsibility and to deemphasize external causes and situational influences when observing the behavior of other people

actor–observer effect the tendency not only to attribute the actions of others to stable internal personal dispositions, but also to attribute our own actions to external situational variables

self–serving bias the tendency to be generous to ourselves when interpreting our own actions, pointing to personal causes when we do well and to situational causes when we do poorly

self-handicapping the tendency to take actions to undermine our own performance in order to have an excuse in case we fail

attitude a learned, stable, and relatively enduring evaluation (e.g., of a person or an idea); such an evaluation can affect an individual's thoughts, feelings, and behavior

preoccupied or in a hurry, we may be gracious about having been bumped. Instead, however, if we attribute the person's behavior to that person's natural disposition as a rude individual, we may behave more rudely toward that person in turn.

Heider pointed out that people make two basic kinds of attributions: personal attributions and situational ones. **Personal attributions** (sometimes called "dispositional attributions") are based on internal factors in a person ("My stubbornness got us into this argument"). **Situational attributions** point to causes in external factors such as settings, events, or other people ("If my roommates hadn't been partying the whole night before my final, I probably wouldn't have flunked my exam").

When people make attributions, they often use mental shortcuts. These shortcuts may save time and energy, but they can lead to distortions and other errors in judgment. Table 10-1 shows some of the common shortcuts and biases that affect how people make causal attributions: **social desirability bias, common and uncommon effects, personalism,** the **fundamental attribution error, actor–observer effects, self-serving biases,** and **self-handicapping.**

What is social cognition? Social cognition is the way in which we understand information about ourselves and other people, based on our social interactions. Two types of theories of social cognition are *cognitive-consistency theories*, which emphasize the importance of reconciling our beliefs with our actions; and *attribution theories*, which highlight the causes to which we attribute our own behavior and that of others.

HOW DO WE FORM AND CHANGE OUR ATTITUDES?

Which is more important: devotion to helping other persons or the accumulation of wealth? How you answer this question depends on your attitudes toward helpfulness and toward wealth. An **attitude** is a learned, stable, and relatively enduring evaluation of a person, object, or idea that can affect an individual's behavior (Allport, 1935; Petty & Cacioppo, 1981). This definition covers several points. First, we are not born with the attitudes we have; we acquire them through experience. Second, attitudes tend to be stable and relatively enduring; they tend not to change easily. Third, attitudes are evaluative; we use them for judging things positively or negatively, and in varying degrees. Some issues may not concern us much one way or the other, whereas other issues may lead to strong opinions. Finally, attitudes can influence behavior, such as when they cause people to act—to vote, protest, work, make friends, and so on. (As you may have guessed from the earlier discussion of cognitive-consistency theories, behavior may also influence attitudes.)

Some psychologists view attitudes as having components that are cognitive (thought-based), behavioral (action-based), *and* affective (emotion-based): Your attitude toward someone or something depends on what you think and feel about the person or thing, as well as on how you act toward the person or thing (Katz & Stotland, 1959). Attitudes are central to the psychology of the individual.

Research has shown that learning influences the formation of our attitudes. For instance, when we are rewarded for expressing particular attitudes, those attitudes are strengthened (Insko, 1965). Similarly, observational learning (also called "social learning"; see Chapter 6) seems to influence both behavior (as shown in

Children learn many of their attitudes about race and gender through observation. Children's TV programs show more than twice as many male roles as female roles. Males are more likely to be shown as the doers who make things happen and who are rewarded for their actions, and females are more likely to be the recipients of actions. The females who do take action are more likely than males to be punished for their activity (Basow, 1986). On prime-time TV, about three fourths of the leading characters are white males. What attitudes are children learning by watching TV?

Figure 6-4) and attitude formation. Do these same processes underlie changes in our attitudes, or do other processes influence such changes? It appears that changes in people's attitudes are influenced by various characteristics of the person who receives the message (e.g., motivated, interested, knowledgeable, and able to use reasoning skills); of the person who sends the message (e.g., likable and credible message giver); and of the message itself (e.g., familiar and strong arguments; one-sided vs. two-sided [balanced] arguments), as shown next.

BRANCHING OUT: Characteristics Affecting Attitude Change

Would you like to know how to influence other people to change their attitudes to resemble more closely the attitudes you favor? Here is how you can increase your effectiveness in persuading other people to change their attitudes:

1. Tailor your persuasive message to the characteristics of the person to whom you are addressing your message. Is your message recipient highly motivated, interested, knowledgeable, and able to *think* about the issues related to the attitude you wish to change? If so, appeal to this person by emphasizing the use of thoughtful, well-reasoned arguments. If not, appeal to this person by emphasizing the use of inviting messages (e.g., colorful photos), attractive and rewarding message senders (e.g., beautiful or sexy models or entertainers), and rewarding message formats (e.g., appealing videos or catchy jingles).

2. Tailor your persuasive message to the situation of the message recipient. Is your message recipient likely to think of—or perhaps to hear about—counterarguments to your persuasive message? If so, use balanced, two-sided arguments when giving your persuasive message (Lumsdaine & Janis, 1953). If not, one-sided arguments will probably do the trick; for message recipients who will neither think of nor face counterarguments, one-sided arguments may even be more effective than two-sided ones, and one-sided arguments will probably take less time and effort on your part.

3. Use strong arguments, rather than weak arguments, and repeat the arguments often, so that they become familiar to the recipients of your message. Sheer repetition of a persuasive message seems to increase its familiarity and its appeal. (Watch commercial television if you wonder whether most advertisers know about this persuasive technique.)

4. Have the attitude-change message delivered by someone who is both believable (Hovland & Weiss, 1951) and appealing (Chaiken & Eagly, 1983; Eagly & Chaiken, 1975).

You may be saying to yourself, "I don't really want to change other people's attitudes very often—if at all. I have a live-and-let-live attitude." Even if you do not wish to know how to persuade other people to change their attitudes, you may still want to be aware of methods for attitude change, however. Why? Because other people—such as politicians and advertisers—are constantly trying to influence you to change your attitudes, and not all of those people will necessarily have your best interests at heart. If you examine some of the variables likely to influence attitude change, you may become more aware of such attempts. Thereby, you may become better able to decide when—or even if—you choose to change your own attitudes.

Finding Your Way   10-1

Recall an effective advertisement that you have recently seen (e.g., on television or in print) or heard (e.g., on the radio). What factors do you believe made this ad effective in leading to attitude change? What is it about this advertisement that would lead you to have a more positive attitude toward the product or service being advertised? Using a scale of 1 (low) to 7 (high), rate the attitude-change characteristics of this advertisement.

- *Characteristics of the message giver (the source of the attitude-change message):*

  Credibility
  1. *Knowledge*   1 2 3 4 5 6 7
  2. *Trustworthiness*   1 2 3 4 5 6 7

  Likability and appeal
  3. *Familiarity*   1 2 3 4 5 6 7
  4. *Attractiveness*   1 2 3 4 5 6 7
  5. *Similarity to you*   1 2 3 4 5 6 7

- *Characteristics of the advertising message:*

  Likability and appeal
  6. *Familiarity*   1 2 3 4 5 6 7
  7. *Attractiveness*   1 2 3 4 5 6 7
  8. *Similarity to your own experiences*   1 2 3 4 5 6 7

  Informativeness
  9. *Balance (one- vs. two-sided arguments)*   1 2 3 4 5 6 7
  10. *Reasoning*   1 2 3 4 5 6 7
  11. *Factual information*   1 2 3 4 5 6 7

  Emotional appeal
  12. *Appeal to emotions (e.g., fear of social rejection due to bad breath)*   1 2 3 4 5 6 7

- *Characteristics of the message receiver (you):*
  13. *Interest*   1 2 3 4 5 6 7
  14. *Knowledge*   1 2 3 4 5 6 7

Overall, which of the preceding characteristics were most important in making the advertisement effective? What other characteristics of this advertisement helped to make it effective?

Once people's attitudes have changed, do their actions always change, as well? Not necessarily. Although attitudes and behaviors are strongly linked, we cannot safely assume that people's behavior always accurately demonstrates their attitudes. Several factors increase the likelihood that people's attitudes will show up in their behavior (described in Baron & Byrne, 1991; Brehm & Kassin, 1990). Attitudes that are more likely to be tied to behavior are stronger, based on more information and more experience, and more highly specific, as compared with attitudes that are less likely to be reflected in people's behavior.

For example, you are more likely to vote to spend tax money on public education if you strongly believe in the value of public education, if you have a great deal of information and experience regarding public education, and if you specifically believe that tax money should be spent for public education, as compared with someone who does not believe strongly in the value of public education, who has very little information and experience regarding public education, and who sees only a vague link between voting to spend tax money on public education and the quality of the public education system.

MINILECTURE

Attitude-Discrepant Behavior
(Ch 14)

What you do speaks so loud that I cannot hear what you say.

Ralph Waldo Emerson

What are some situations in which your behavior did not accurately reflect your attitudes? What factors might have increased the likelihood that your behavior would have reflected your attitudes?

How do we form and change our attitudes? Attitudes are learned, stable, and relatively enduring evaluations of people, things, and ideas; these evaluations can both affect and be affected by our actions, our thoughts, and our feelings. Our attitudes are more likely to affect our actions when our attitudes are strong, based on extensive information and experience, and highly specific.

WHY ARE WE ATTRACTED TO THE PEOPLE WE LIKE OR LOVE?

The preceding section of this chapter described several strategies for persuading people to change their attitudes. One factor that affects the likelihood of being persuaded is the likability of the persuader: We tend to be more easily persuaded by people who are likable. Just what does it *mean* to be "likable"? Why are we more attracted—and more attractive—to one person rather than another?

Each of us needs friendship and love, and each of us feels physical attraction to other persons. In addition, our perceptions of ourselves are partly shaped by our friendships, our loving relationships, and our feelings of attractiveness and attraction to others. Social psychologists have asked, What is going on in the mind of a person who feels attracted to someone?

Theories of Liking and Interpersonal Attraction

Suppose that you are introduced to someone. This person immediately—and quite sincerely—compliments you on your looks, your brains, your physical strength, or something else of which you are proud. Chances are that you will like that person all the more for the compliment. In terms of *learning theory*, you will have been positively reinforced by the complimenter, so you will feel more attracted to him or her. Similarly, you will like a person when you are rewarded in the presence of that person (Clore & Byrne, 1974). For example, if you always see a particular person at a particularly enjoyable type of event, you may feel more attracted to the person by virtue of the person's association with the rewarding event.

An alternative view of attraction combines ideas from learning theory and from cognitive-dissonance theory. According to **equity theory** (Walster, Walster, & Berscheid, 1978), people will be more attracted to those with whom they have an equitable (fair) relationship. We are attracted to people who take from us in proportion to what they give to us. How does equity theory draw on ideas from learning theory and from cognitive-consistency theory? It suggests that we usually expect to receive rewards and punishments in about equal proportion to what we give in relationships, and we try to maintain cognitive consistency by ensuring that what we give is in balance with what we get in relationships.

Other theories of attraction depend more heavily on cognitive-consistency theories. For example, according to **balance theory** (Heider, 1958), we try to maintain a sense of balance (equilibrium) in our personal relationships. One aspect of maintaining balance has to do with *reciprocity*. Similar to the notion of equity, reciprocity refers to the balance of give and take in a relationship. Another aspect of maintaining balance is *similarity*: We expect our friends to have the same positive or negative attitudes that we have, liking the people and ideas that we like, and disliking the people and ideas we dislike.

Theories of Love

Do we like all the people we love and love all the people we like? Are liking and loving the same thing? Most of us distinguish between liking and loving, but we also admit that it is difficult to define precisely all the differences between liking and loving—not to mention the difficulty in trying to define precisely the two terms themselves. To avoid wrestling with this question, we assume here that *love* is a deeper, stronger emotion than is liking. Both feelings are rooted in attraction, but love stems from more powerful—perhaps even instinctual—emotional and physical attractions than does liking. Maybe an even more difficult question is, Why do people feel love? Of the many different answers to that question are the two theories discussed here: attachment theory and the triangular theory of love.

According to an **attachment view of love** (Hazan & Shaver, 1987), how we relate to other people in loving relationships derives from how we related to our parents, and especially our mother, as an infant (Shaver, 1994). *Securely attached* lovers tend to be confident in their relationships and tend not to worry about being abandoned. *Anxious-ambivalent* lovers, on the other hand, do tend to worry about being abandoned, tend to be prone to jealousy, and often feel like their partner is more distant than they would like. *Avoidant* lovers actually seek distance and become uncomfortable when their partner tries to get very close.

An additional view of love is my own **triangular theory of love** (Sternberg, 1986b), according to which love has three basic components: (1) *intimacy*, feelings that promote closeness and connection; (2) *passion*, the intense desire for union with another person (Hatfield & Walster, 1981); and (3) *commitment*, the decision to maintain a relationship over the long term. Different combinations of these three components lead to different kinds of love, as shown in Figure 10-3. The integration of all three components is *consummate love*, in which the loved ones share great intimacy and passion, as well as deep commitment to the relationship.

Attraction

The preceding theories suggest some reasons why we have feelings of attraction, liking, and loving. However, they do not tell exactly why we feel these emotions toward some people, but not toward other people. A recent theory of attraction in love has been proposed (Sternberg, 1994), which attempts to explain why we are attracted to particular individuals and not to others. According to this theory, each of us creates our own personal idealized love stories, in which we formulate particular roles for ourselves and for the partners to whom we are attracted. We are typically unaware, or only vaguely aware, of the stories we create. Each of us is

---

Tell me your friends, and I'll tell you who you are.

Assyrian proverb

*I love thee to the depth and breadth and height /
My soul can reach.*

Elizabeth Barrett Browning

equity theory a theory of attraction suggesting that people feel more strongly attracted to those with whom they have more equitable (fair) relationships of giving and taking

balance theory a cognitive-consistency theory of attraction, suggesting that persons who like each other try to maintain a balance regarding the mutual give and take in the relationship and that they try to maintain similar likes and dislikes

attachment theory of love view that how we relate to loved ones as adults stems from the way in which we attached to our parents, and particularly our mothers, as infants

triangular theory of love a theory suggesting that love has three basic components: intimacy, passion, and commitment

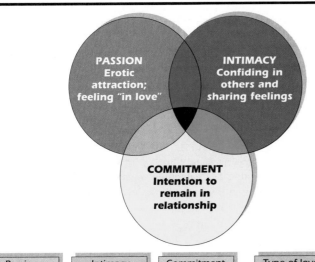

Figure 10-3
Triangular Theory of Love
According to this theory, love has three main components: intimacy, passion, and commitment.

Passion	Intimacy	Commitment		Type of love that results
−	−	−	=	Nonlove
+	−	−	=	● Infatuated Love
−	+	−	=	● Liking (Friendship)
−	−	+	=	○ Empty Love
+	+	−	=	● Romantic Love
−	+	+	=	● Companionate Love
+	−	+	=	● Fatuous Love
+	+	+	=	▼ Consummate Love

attracted to prospective partners who closely match the leading characters in our personal love stories (e.g., the cop and the criminal in a police story, or the prince and the princess in a fairy tale). Further, we continue to find happiness with a given partner as long as we continue to perceive the partner as matching our desired personal love story.

What factors lead people to be attracted to one another? Psychologists have observed that several variables seem to contribute to whether particular people

In a great romance, each basically plays a part that the other really likes.

Elizabeth Ashley

What attracts these people to each other? According to social-psychological research, they probably know each other pretty well, live or work near each other, and have similar attitudes, temperaments, and social and communication skills. They probably also are physically aroused in each other's presence and find each other physically attractive.

will be attracted to one another. The variables underlying attraction include the following:

- *Arousal* (how excited we become about a person)
- *Familiarity* (mentioned as a persuasive feature of a message source)
- *Proximity* (geographical nearness of the person toward whom we are attracted; Festinger, Schachter, & Back, 1950)
- *Physical attractiveness* (e.g., Walster et al., 1966)
- *Similarity* (Murstein, 1986; Sternberg, 1988b; mentioned also in the balance theory of liking)—several aspects of similarity have been found to increase attraction, such as similar attitudes and temperament (Hatfield & Rapson, 1992), social and communication skills (Burleson & Denton, 1992), and even sense of humor (Murstein & Brust, 1985).

Why are we attracted to the people we like or love? We are attracted to people who are similar to ourselves, physically close to us, and familiar to us, as well as to people whom we find arousing and physically attractive. We seem to like people with whom we have an equitable give-and-take relationship. We seem to love people who meet our needs with regard to style of attachment. Deep love for another person may comprise elements of intimacy, passion, and commitment. In addition, it appears that each of us writes our own love story, and we are attracted to persons who closely match the leading romantic characters in our own love stories.

HOW DO WE COMMUNICATE IN OUR PERSONAL RELATIONSHIPS?

In personal relationships of many kinds, communication appears to be an important key to success. Couples in happy marriages truly listen to each other and affirm the value of each other's points of view, whereas couples in unhappy marriages are less likely to do so (Gottman, 1979, 1994). Other factors also contribute to unsuccessful communication in couples (Gottman et al., 1976): One or both partners (a) feel hurt and ignored, (b) feel that the other person does not see her or his point of view, (c) neglect to stay on one problem long enough to resolve the problem, (d) frequently interrupt one another, and (e) drag many irrelevant issues into the discussion.

Talking with one another is loving one another.

Kenyan proverb

Another consideration is that there appear to be gender differences in communication patterns, content, and styles. In general, women seem to disclose more about themselves than do men (Morton, 1978). Based on her extensive research on male–female conversation, Deborah Tannen (1986, 1990) suggests that the conversational differences between men and women largely center on their differing understanding of the goals of conversation. According to Tannen (1990), men see the world as a ranked social order in which the purpose of communication is to negotiate for the upper hand, to preserve independence, and to avoid failure. Each man tries to one-up the other and to "win" the contest. Women, in contrast, try to establish a connection between the two participants, to give support and confirmation to others, and to reach agreement through communication.

Tannen states that when men and women become more aware of their differing styles and traditions, they may be less likely to misinterpret one another's conversational interactions. In this way, they can both work toward achieving their own individual aims, as well as the aims of the relationship. Just as verbal communication is a key aspect of close personal relationships, it is also vital to interactions within larger groups of people, such as in work groups.

How do we communicate in our personal relationships? Communication patterns of mutual affirmation and interested listening tend to indicate happy marriages, whereas patterns of criticism, defensiveness, and avoidance of problem solving tend to indicate unhappy marriages. Women and men seem to have differing styles of communicating.

WHAT HAPPENS WHEN WE INTERACT IN GROUPS?

A **group** is a collection of individuals who interact with each other. What actually happens when members of a group interact? Robert Bales (1950, 1970) suggested that groups serve two basic functions: to get work done and to handle relationships among group members. Different kinds of groups—and different group leaders—give differing emphasis to each of these functions.

How do groups of people reach agreement as to what they will do? What factors influence the route to agreement and the kind of agreement achieved? What makes individuals within a group conform to a group decision, even if they do not believe in it? We consider some of these questions here.

Social Facilitation and Social Interference

Having other people around can affect the quality of the work you do (Triplett, 1898). In **social facilitation,** having other people around improves the performance of an individual. For example, many athletes, actors, and singers find that they perform better when other people are present than when they are alone.

On the other hand, the presence of people can sometimes hurt performance, through the phenomenon of **social interference.** Have you ever had to speak or

group a collection of individuals who interact with each other, usually either to accomplish work or to promote interpersonal relationships (or both)

social facilitation the phenomenon in which the presence of other people positively influences the performance of an individual

social interference the phenomenon in which the presence of other people negatively influences the performance of an individual

Successful entertainers seem to respond particularly to social facilitation, especially if they have rehearsed well enough to be thoroughly familiar with the material they plan to perform.

perform in front of others and found yourself too nervous to perform well? The question then becomes, when do other people facilitate performance, and when do they interfere with it? In general, for familiar, well-learned behavior, the presence of people may lead to facilitation. In contrast, for unfamiliar, poorly learned behavior, the presence of people may lead to interference. The interference may occur because other people are distracting (Baron, 1986) or because the other people cause heightened arousal (Zajonc, 1965, 1980).

Social Loafing

What happens to our performance when we perform not only in front of others but also in cooperation with them? Apparently, as the number of people increases, the average amount of effort put forth by each individual decreases (Ringelmann, 1913). This reduced effort is termed **social loafing** (Latané, Williams, & Harkins, 1979).

Bibb Latané and other social psychologists (1979) studied whether it was the actual presence of others or merely the perceived presence of others that caused social loafing. To assess the influence of social loafing, the experimenters asked research participants either to clap as loudly as they could or to cheer at the top of their voices. They assigned some participants to perform the task alone, others to perform the task in groups, and still others to perform the task in *pseudogroups,* in which the participants believed that they were working with other people, but they were actually working alone. (To create the impression of the pseudogroup, the participants were blindfolded, and they were provided with headphones that produced static, drowning out any other sounds in the surrounding environment.) As Figure 10-4 shows, the research participants put forth more effort when they knew that they were alone, as compared with when they really were working with other people or incorrectly perceived that they were working with other people.

It also appears that social loafing is affected by cultural orientation toward either individualism or collectivism. In **individualism,** we tend to put the interests and well-being of the individual above those of the group, such as the family, the corporation, or the nation. In **collectivism,** we tend to put the welfare of the group ahead of the well-being of the individual. It appears that social loafing may

In what situations have you observed social loafing to occur?

I like work; it fascinates me. I can sit and look at it for hours.

Jerome K. Jerome

social loafing   the phenomenon in which each individual member of a group puts forth less effort as the size of the group increases

individualism   the tendency to emphasize the personal interests and welfare of the individual over those of the group

collectivism   the tendency to emphasize the interests and well-being of the group over those of each individual

Figure 10-4
Social Loafing
When the number of co-workers believed to be in the work group increases, the amount of effort each research participant puts forth decreases (Latané, Williams & Harkins, 1979). How can social loafing be kept to a minimum? Find a way to inform individual participants of how well they are performing as individuals (Harkins, 1987; Harkins & Szymanski, 1987).

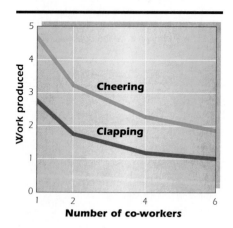

commonly occur in highly individualistic societies, such as in the United States, but it may be less common in societies with a more collectivistic orientation, such as China and Taiwan. For instance, studies involving Chinese research participants have shown that individuals work *harder* when they are in a group than when they are alone (Early, 1989; Gabrenya, Latané, & Wang, 1983; Gabrenya, Wang, & Latané, 1985). Cross-cultural psychologists (e.g., Triandis et al., 1993; Triandis, McCusker, & Hui, 1990) frequently note that many other social-psychological phenomena are also influenced by the degree to which a given culture tends toward individualism or toward collectivism.

Group Polarization

In addition to social facilitation, social interference, and social loafing, in what other ways do people change their behavior when participating in groups rather than acting alone? Are people in groups more or less likely to take risks than individuals? Actually, groups tend to exaggerate the initial views of group members, so that they become more extreme, a phenomenon referred to as **group polarization** (Moscovici & Zavalloni, 1969; Myers & Lamm, 1976). Thus, if the members of a group, on average, initially tend toward taking risks, the group process will tend to move the decision of the group in a direction that exaggerates this risk-taking tendency. However, if the members of a group originally tend toward conservatism, the group discussion will usually lead the group to a more conservative response than that of the individual members. For instance, participants in meetings of a local bungee-jumpers club will be more likely to shift toward making risky decisions, but bank executives at a board meeting will be more likely to shift toward making conservative decisions.

Why does group polarization occur? Two factors appear to be responsible: *new information* and *movement toward the group norm*. When people hear new arguments supporting their point of view, they become even more extreme in their conviction (Burnstein & Vinokur, 1973, 1977). In addition, as people meet other people supporting their point of view, and they receive social approval from these other people, they begin to move in the direction of the group norm. **Norms** are standards of behavior and expressed attitudes, based on the common trends of the majority in a group. When the information and reactions are expressed by people whom the group member identifies as members of his or her respected "in group," the movement toward agreement is even stronger than usual (Turner, 1987). Through the process of group polarization, the group members may become more and more unified as their position becomes more extreme. However, this unification sometimes occurs at the expense of rational decision making.

Groupthink

Irving Janis (1972) has given special attention to **groupthink,** in which the "striving for unanimity [within the group overrides the] motivation to realistically appraise alternative courses of action" (Janis, 1972, p. 9). Janis analyzed a number of foreign-policy decisions that he believed reflected groupthink. For example, Janis noted that the U.S. failure to anticipate the attack on Pearl Harbor during World War II may have resulted partly from groupthink at the top levels of defense and government. During the John Kennedy Administration, the high-level decision making that led to the disastrous Bay of Pigs invasion of Cuba may have been the result of groupthink. In these and other examples cited by Janis, highly intelligent people managed to make appallingly stupid decisions because they fell into the trap of groupthink.

What conditions lead to groupthink? Janis has cited three kinds of conditions: (1) a group with the power to make decisions that is isolated, *cohesive* (sticks together), and *homogeneous* (composed of similar, like-minded individuals); (2) a lack of objective and impartial leadership, either within the group or outside of it; and

group polarization the tendency to exaggerate the initial views of group members, so that the views become more extreme

norm a standard of behavior or an expressed attitude, based on the shared trends of the majority in a group

groupthink a group process in which group members work so hard to achieve unanimous agreement that they fail to consider realistically the various alternative courses of action available to them

Figure 10-5
Janis's Groupthink
This chart summarizes the conditions, symptoms, weak decision making, and results of groupthink (Janis, 1972).

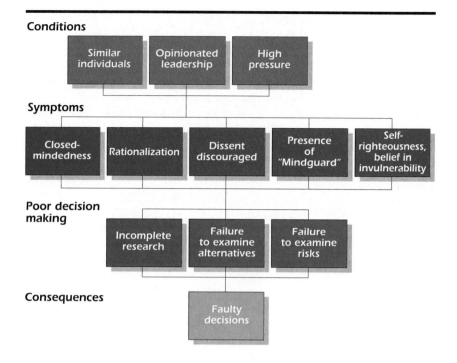

Figure 10-5
Janis's Groupthink
This chart summarizes the conditions, symptoms, weak decision making, and results of groupthink (Janis, 1972).

What are some recent events that you think might have been caused by groupthink?

(3) high levels of stress imposed on the group decision-making process. The groups responsible for making foreign-policy decisions are excellent candidates for groupthink: The group members are often like-minded, and they frequently isolate themselves from what is going on outside of their own group. They are generally trying to meet foreign-policy aims set by the president or the prime minister; hence, they probably believe that they cannot afford to be impartial and objective. Also, of course, they are under very high levels of stress: The consequences of their decisions can be tremendously wide reaching.

Janis has also spelled out six symptoms of groupthink: (1) *closed-mindedness*—the group is not open to a variety of alternative conceptualizations; (2) *rationalization*—the group goes to great lengths to justify both the process and the product of its decision making, distorting reality where necessary in order to accomplish this justification; (3) the *squelching of dissent*—those who do not agree are ignored, criticized, or even rejected; (4) the *formation of a "mindguard"* for the group—a self-appointed keeper of the group norm, who makes sure that people stay in line; (5) the *feeling of invulnerability*—the group believes that it must be right, given both the intelligence of its members and the information available to them; and (6) the *feeling of unanimity*—the group members feel that all members of the group are unanimous in sharing the opinions expressed by the group. Due to groupthink, members fail to examine all reasonable alternatives, to assess fully the risks involved in carrying out the recommended decision, and to search adequately for information about alternatives. The result of groupthink is defective decision making, chiefly due to overeagerness to conform to the thinking of the group (see Figure 10-5).

What happens when we interact in groups? The presence of other people may lead to social facilitation (particularly when we are engaging in well-practiced actions) or to social interference (particularly when we are engaging in unfamiliar actions) or even to social loafing (particularly in individualistic cultures). Members of groups tend to shift toward more extreme views as a result of their participation in like-minded groups. In groupthink, the members of a group may work so hard to maintain unanimity of opinion that they fail to engage in rational decision making.

WHEN AND HOW DO WE CONFORM, COMPLY, AND OBEY?

Based on what we now know, it appears that in 1993, more than 80 members of the Branch Davidian religious sect obeyed their leader by intentionally setting fire to their small fortress and shooting their loved ones, effectively committing group suicide. Unfortunately, numerous other astonishing examples of self-destructive obedience exist, such as the mass suicide of more than 900 followers of a religious sect in Jonestown, Guyana, in 1978. Similar examples can be found in which people showed horrifying obedience in committing genocide, rather than suicide: Nazi soldiers during World War II, and Serbian soldiers in the 1990s.

Conformity, compliance, and obedience all involve changes in one person's behavior, due to the social influence of another individual or group of persons. Through **conformity,** people shape their own behavior to make it consistent with the norms of the group. Through **compliance,** one or more persons shape their behavior in response to a request by one or more other persons. Through **obedience,** people shape their behavior in response to the command of an actual or perceived authority. We consider each of these three kinds of social influence in turn. For each form of social influence, the individual may experience both changes in behavior and changes in perceptions, beliefs, and attitudes.

Conformity

Solomon Asch (1951, 1956) conducted several classic studies on conformity. In Asch's studies, research participants believed that they were participating in an experiment on perceptual judgment. Imagine that you are the sixth of seven participants in one such experiment (see Figure 10-6). The first five members of the group choose an answer that is clearly wrong. What do you say when it is your turn to give your answer?

It is not easy to know what to say, as shown by the look on the face of research participant Number 6 from one of Asch's actual studies (see Figure 10-6). In fact, about three fourths of Asch's research participants went along with the majority,

Why do you sometimes do things that other people ask you to do, even when you do not want to do those things?

conformity the process in which an individual shapes her or his behavior to make it consistent with the norms of a group

compliance the process in which an individual goes along with a request made by one or more other persons

obedience the process in which an individual follows the command of an actual or perceived authority figure

Why are people willing to modify their own behavior in order to conform to the norms of a group, to comply with the request made by a peer, or to obey the command of a person with authority? What are the benefits of doing so? What are the consequences of not doing so?

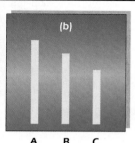

Standard   A   B   C

Figure 10-6

Line Length and the Norm

Asch's research participants were shown a standard line (on the left). Then they were asked to say which of the comparison lines (Lines A, B, or C) matched the standard line. Seem easy? What would you say if all of the other observers who spoke before you chose Line A (or Line C)? Check the facial expression of research participant Number 6. Although he may decide to conform to the group norms in terms of his behavior—agreeing publicly that an incorrect match is correct—his own private beliefs clearly do not conform to the group norm. In fact, if he is given a chance to express his beliefs privately, he is quite likely to disagree with the group norms.

It took me a long time not to judge myself through someone else's eyes.

Sally Field

It is common these days for educators to say that students must "learn to think for themselves." In light of Asch's conformity results, as well as your own experiences, what are the forces at work against people learning to think for themselves?

stating obviously wrong answers about one third of the time, on average. It turns out that all of the other participants were really confederates who were purposely giving wrong answers.

Why did Asch's research participants go along with the majority? Did they really believe that their own perceptions were wrong, or did they bend to the pressure of the social group? In interviews and in a separate set of experiments, Asch's research participants showed that when they went along with the group, they generally did not believe the incorrect responses they announced. Rather, the research participants felt group pressure to conform. Later work (Asch, 1952) showed that Asch's research participants had good reason to want to conform. Participants who deviate from the group norm are indeed put down when in a group of genuine experimental research participants.

Several factors seem to affect the likelihood of conformity (see Table 10-2). These factors are group size, cohesiveness, social status (see Figure 10-7), culture, and the appearance of unanimity. Perhaps the most surprising of these factors is the effect of having even one person disagree with the majority view. Even if the disagreeing person is obviously wrong, the fact of having someone model disagree-

Because this person is deviating from group norms, members of the group are likely to ridicule this person.

TABLE 10-2
Factors Affecting Conformity
Which of the following factors most surprises you? Of which factors were you already intuitively aware?

Factors	Effects on Conformity
Group size	Increases in group size lead to increases in conformity until a group size of 3 or 4 is reached; further increases have little effect under most circumstances (Asch, 1955; Latané, 1981; Tanford & Penrod, 1984).
Cohesiveness	In cohesive groups, group members feel very attracted to the group and feel very much a part of the group; increases in cohesiveness lead to increases in conformity (e.g., Newcomb, 1943).
Social status	Persons who are viewed as being average in social desirability tend to be more likely to conform than persons who are rated as being high, low, or very low in social desirability (Dittes & Kelly, 1956).
Culture	People in individualistic societies tend to conform less than do people in collectivistic societies (Smith & Bond, 1994).
Appearance of unanimity	Conformity is much more likely when the group norm appears to be unanimous. Even a single dissenter can seriously diminish conformity (Asch, 1951). Surprisingly, this effect can occur even if the dissenter offers an answer that is even farther off the mark than the response of the group.

ment strongly reduces the likelihood of conformity based on normative influence. Thus, another consideration in determining your degree of conformity is whether you believe your views to be (a) in the *majority* (most others agree), (b) in the *minority* (one or more others agree, but most disagree with you), or (c) altogether *unique* (one of a kind; everyone else disagrees with you) within the group. In conformity, you shape your behavior to go along with group norms. Another type of social influence is compliance, in which you shape your behavior in response to a request.

Compliance

Do you know somebody who always seems to get his or her way? Do you ever wonder how con artists and cheats manage to trick their *marks* (persons who are the targets of the con artists' compliance-seeking techniques)? Have you ever bought something that you really did not want to buy because you were talked into it by a persuasive salesperson? These questions address the issue of *compliance*—going along with other people's requests. Robert Cialdini (1988) has studied compliance-seeking techniques extensively in the laboratory, but he also did some preliminary fieldwork by studying how professional compliance-seekers operate: He attended countless training seminars for sales personnel. Of the various techniques for eliciting compliance, the following seven are described in Table 10-3: *justification, reciprocity, low-balling, foot-in-the-door, door-in-the-face, that's-not-all,* and *hard-to-get* techniques.

Each of the preceding techniques involves having someone you consider a peer—more or less—ask you to comply with a request. Not all requests come from peers, however. At times, those who make requests of us are in a position of authority. Their superior authority may stem from actual or perceived greater relative power, expertise, or desirability in terms of some criterion we consider important, such as physical attractiveness or social skill. When we go along with the requests of persons who have authority over us, we are being obedient.

Obedience

Consider what you would do if you were a research participant in the following experiment. An experimenter wearing a lab coat and carrying a clipboard meets you

I didn't belong as a kid, and that always bothered me. If only I'd known that one day my differentness would be an asset, then my early life would have been much easier.

Bette Midler

What are some effective ways in which you can guard against various compliance-seeking techniques?

Figure 10-7
Social Status and Conformity
When research participants were told that they had been rated by the group as being high, low, or very low in social desirability, they showed less conformity to the group than when they were told that they had been rated by the group as being average in social desirability (Dittes & Kelley, 1956).

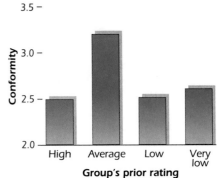

TABLE 10-3

Techniques for Eliciting Compliance

	You are more likely to gain compliance if . . .	Example
Justification	. . . you justify your request (Langer, Blank, & Chanowitz, 1978).	Someone asks to be allowed to go ahead of you in a line at a copying machine, giving you the incredibly weak justification, "because I have to make some copies."
Reciprocity	. . . you appear to be giving your target something, so that the target is thereby obliged to give you something in return (Regan, 1971).	Someone hands you a flower at an exit to a zoo and then asks you to make a contribution to a religious organization.
Low-ball technique	. . . you get the target to commit to a deal under misleadingly favorable circumstances, and then you add the hidden costs or reveal the hidden drawbacks (Cialdini, 1988; Cialdini et al., 1978).	A car salesperson obtains your agreement to a deal, then appears to ask the manager "for approval," only to return with a deal that is less favorable to you.
Foot-in-the-door technique	. . . you ask for compliance with a smaller request, which is designed to "soften up" the target for the big request (De Jong, 1979; Freedman & Fraser, 1966).	Someone asks you if you have time to answer a few questions and then follows that request by asking you to participate in a half-hour interview.
Door-in-the-face technique	. . . you make an outlandishly large request that is almost certain to be rejected, then you make a more reasonable request (Cialdini et al., 1975).	Someone asks you to contribute $100 to a charitable cause and then says that if you can only afford $5, that would be fine.
That's-not-all technique	. . . you offer something at a high price, and then, before the target has a chance to respond, you throw in something else to sweeten the deal (Burger, 1986).	A late-night television advertiser offers you a complete set of golden-oldie CDs for only $29.95 and then says that you will also receive a free CD of Elvis Presley's first hit.
Hard-to-get technique	. . . you convince your target that whatever you are offering is very difficult to obtain (Brehm, 1966; see also Brehm & Brehm, 1981; Hatfield & Walster, 1978).	Another late-night TV advertiser offers you a set of 10 automatic electric slicers and dicers, but you must phone now, while the supplies last.

in the laboratory and tells you that you are about to participate in an experiment on the effects of punishment on learning. You and another research participant, Mr. Wallace (see Figure 10-8), agree to draw lots to determine who will be the "teacher" in the experiment, and who will be the "learner."

You draw the "teacher" lot, so it will be your job to teach the learner a list of words that he must remember. You watch the experimenter strap Mr. Wallace into a chair, roll up Mr. Wallace's sleeves, and swab electrode paste onto his arms, "to avoid blisters and burns" from the shocks (Milgram, 1974, p. 19). The experimenter warns that the shocks may become extremely painful, but he assures Mr. Wallace that they will "cause no permanent tissue damage" (p. 19). You are then shown the machine you will use to deliver shocks, ranging from a mere 15 volts (labeled "slight shock") to a full 450 volts (labeled "XXX," beyond the setting for "danger: severe shock") (see Figure 10-8). Before beginning, the experimenter also gives you a rather painful shock, which he describes as a mild shock, just to give you an idea of what the shocks are like.

The experiment now begins. If Mr. Wallace correctly answers your questions, you move on to the next question. If he answers incorrectly, you tell him the correct answer and administer a shock. Each time Mr. Wallace makes a mistake, you are told to increase the intensity of the shock by 15 volts.

Soon, he makes his first mistake, so you pull the appropriate shock lever. A loud buzzer sounds, and a red light flashes, indicating that the shock has been delivered to Mr. Wallace in the next room. When you reach the level of 75 volts, Mr.

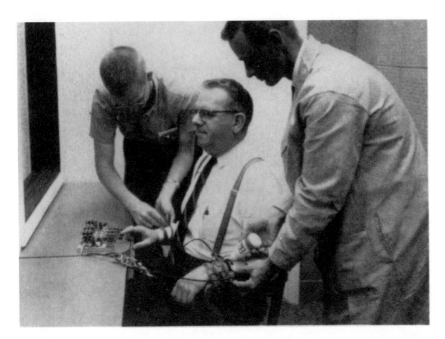

Figure 10-8

**The Shocking Treatment
of Mr. Wallace**

*Mr. Wallace, pictured here as he was being
strapped into the chair where he was expected
to receive the shocks being sent by Milgram's
research participants. It appeared that Mr. Wallace could not possibly escape the shocks that
were given during the experiment.*

Wallace grunts in pain. Grunts are followed by shouting at 120 volts. At 150 volts,
Mr. Wallace screams in agony and protests, "Experimenter! That's all. Get me out
of here. I refuse to go on!" Mr. Wallace refuses to continue at 300 volts, and at 315
volts, following an intense scream, he shouts, "I told you I refuse to answer. I'm no
longer a part of this experiment." At 330 volts, there is an intense, long scream of
agony, and Mr. Wallace shouts, "Let me out of here. Let me out of here. Let me
out, I tell you. . . . You have no right to hold me here. Let me out! . . ." After
330 volts, there is only silence.

Would you continue administering shocks until the end—up to 450 volts?
Perhaps at some point, it would occur to you that something is very wrong
with this experiment, and that you simply do not want to continue. If you tell
the experimenter your concerns, he only responds, "Please continue." If you
protest further, he tells you, "The experiment requires that you continue." If
you continue to argue, he says, "It is absolutely essential that you continue." If you
still protest, he replies, "You have no other choice, you *must* go on." What would
you do? Before you read on, guess how most people would have responded to this
experiment.

Before conducting his experiments, psychologist Stanley Milgram (1974) had
expected that very few research participants would fully obey the commands of the
experimenter and that many might refuse to obey even the early requests of the experimenter. As he was planning the design for the experiment, he consulted with
many other colleagues, all of whose expectations were similar to his. Instead, an
electrifying two thirds of the research participants tested in this procedure continued up to the very end, delivering shocks at the level of 450 volts. Not one participant stopped giving the shocks before 300 volts, the point at which Mr. Wallace let
out an agonizing scream, absolutely refused to answer any more questions, and de-
manded to get out, saying that the experimenter could not hold him. The results
are shown in Figure 10-9(a).

The results so surprised Milgram that he asked members of three different
groups—middle-class adults with various occupations, college students, and psychiatrists—to predict what would happen. Their predictions, like Milgram's, were
that few research participants would demonstrate much obedience in the experiment. On average, the people Milgram surveyed estimated that the "teacher"
would stop at 135 volts. Almost no one surveyed thought anyone would go up to
450 volts. Everyone was wrong (see Figure 10-9b).

The results were more shocking than the machine because the machine was a
fake. So was Mr. Wallace. He was Milgram's confederate and never received any

*I believe in a lively disrespect for most forms of
authority.*

> *Rita Mae Brown*

MINILECTURE

*Conformity, Compliance, &
Obedience (Ch 15)*

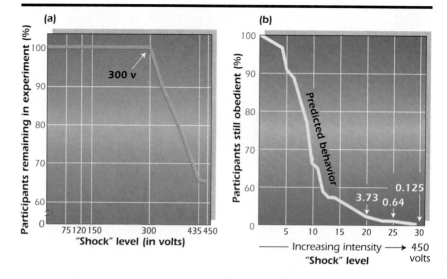

Figure 10-9
Milgram's Actual Results, Com-pared with Predicted Results
(a) To the great surprise of Stanley Milgram, not one research participant stopped administering shocks before the reported level of 300 volts, and an alarming 65% of research participants administered the maximum level of supposed shocks. (b) Compare Milgram's actual results with the predictions made by psychiatrists regarding expected levels of obedience for various reported voltage levels (from Milgram, 1974, p. 30). The psychiatrists estimated that "only a pathological fringe, not exceeding [1 or 2% of the research participants]" would go right up to the end (Milgram, 1974, p. 31).

Although Mr. Wallace was never really hurt by Milgram's experiments, some psychologists have suggested that Milgram psychologically injured the research participants in his experiments. Do you think that Milgram should have conducted his experiments? Why or why not?

shocks at all. Also, both of the lots from which you had drawn said "teacher." No matter which one you drew, you would have ended up being the teacher and Mr. Wallace the learner.

The experiment, as you probably have guessed, had nothing at all to do with the effect of punishment on learning. Rather, it was an experiment on obedience. The motivation for the experiment was Milgram's interest in why German soldiers during World War II had obeyed the outrageous genocidal commands of their leaders. Milgram (1963, 1965, 1974) concluded that people in general, not just German soldiers, are horrifyingly capable of blind, mindless obedience. Later, Milgram and other researchers found similar results in experiments with women research participants, with participants in other parts of the country, and in locations away from college campuses. In fact, Milgram's findings have been repeated both across age groups and across cultures (Shanab & Yahya, 1977, 1978).

The Milgram studies showed us that we may have an appalling ability to tune out the misery of our fellow human beings when responding to the commands of a perceived authority figure. How might we respond to pleas for help from our fellow humans when no authority figure is around?

When and how do we conform, comply, and obey? We tend to conform, molding our own actions to the norms of a group, when we participate in groups that are relatively large and cohesive, and that appear unanimous; our own social status and culture may also influence our tendency to conform. We tend to comply with the requests of other persons when they use various techniques for eliciting our compliance. We tend to show shockingly high levels of obedience to the wishes of authority figures.

WHAT LEADS US TO SHOW PROSOCIAL BEHAVIOR?

prosocial behavior actions that offer some benefit to society in general or to members within society and that are approved by most members of society

Prosocial behavior is any behavior that is approved by society and that benefits individual persons or society as a whole. Of the many kinds of prosocial behavior, this section focuses on how we respond to people who need help. In the Queens section of New York City, in 1964, Kitty Genovese was attacked while returning home from a night job at three o'clock in the morning. Just outside her own apartment building, she was stabbed repeatedly over a period of about a half hour by a maniac who eventually killed her. Thirty-eight people living in her apartment complex heard her cries and screams as she was attacked. How many of these neighbors called the police? How many tried to help her in any way whatsoever? Not one. How could people hear someone be attacked over such a long period of time and do absolutely nothing in response? Bibb Latané and John Darley (1968, 1970) tried to answer this question in a series of studies on helping behavior and *bystander intervention*, in which an observer takes steps to help an unknown person or persons in need.

In one of the Latané and Darley experiments, a research participant arrived and was taken to one of a set of small rooms containing intercoms. The research participant was led to believe that between one and five other people were participating in a confidential discussion over the intercom. During the fairly routine opening of the experiment, one of the research participants admitted that he sometimes had terrifyingly serious seizures. After a while, when it was this person's turn to speak again, it became apparent that he was suffering a seizure. He started stuttering, choking, and sounding as though he were in serious distress (Latané & Darley, 1970, p. 96).

As you may have guessed, the apparent seizure victim was not actually having a seizure. In fact, there was only one true research participant. The voices of the other participants were tape-recorded earlier, and the voices were played back over the intercom for each true research participant. The independent variable was the number of people that were believed to be participating in the experiment. The dependent variables were the percentage of participants who helped the apparent seizure victim and the amount of time it took the participants to respond. The results showed clearly that as the number of perceived bystanders increased, the percentages of participants who responded decreased, and their response times became longer (see Figure 10-10).

Kitty Genovese's neighbors were not alone in being unresponsive. They illustrated what has come to be known as the **bystander effect,** in which the presence of other people inhibits helping behavior. The effect occurs in various situations. Each person involved typically feels a **diffusion of responsibility:** The presence of others leads each person to feel less personally responsible for handling a crisis situation. Many other studies have shown the same results (described in Latané, Nida, & Wilson, 1981). Oddly, the bystander effect appears even when a person's

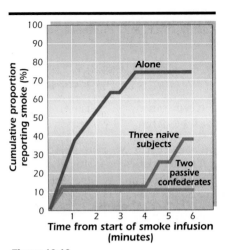

Figure 10-10

Seizing the Opportunity to Help
In every condition of Bibb Latané and John Darley's (1970) experiment, helping behavior increased over time. However, the amount of helping behavior decreased dramatically with increases in the number of other people that the research participant thought were participating. When only the research participant and the seizure victim were involved, all research participants eventually left the room to get help. In the six-person group, about 60% went for assistance. The other roughly 40% of the research participants never left the room, even though the victim seemed to be dying. (Adapted from Latané and Darley, The Unresponsive Bystander, *© 1970. Used with permission of Prentice-Hall, Inc.)*

MINILECTURE
The Case of Kitty Genovese (Ch 15)

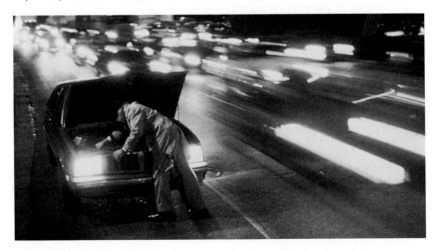

Why isn't anyone stopping to help this motorist? Would a passing motorist be more likely to stop if this person needed help on a lonely country road?

bystander effect the phenomenon in which the presence of increasing numbers of people available to help leads to a decreasing likelihood that any given observer will offer help

diffusion of responsibility the phenomenon in which increases in the number of other persons present leads each person to feel less personal responsibility for the events taking place

TABLE 10-4

Factors That May Influence Helping Behavior

Factor	Effect on likelihood of helping behavior		
	Increase	**Probably increase**	**Decrease**
Characteristics of the victim	Similar to bystander (age, gender, etc.)	Somehow related to bystander (e.g., co-worker, neighbor)	Bleeding or bloody; recognized member of a stigmatized group (e.g., perceived as less attractive)
Characteristics of the situation	Any situation that increases the likelihood of the by-stander being in a good mood	Situation in which the victim and the bystander have an ongoing relationship (e.g., neighbor, co-worker)	Larger number of bystanders; greater time pressures on by-stander (e.g., being in a hurry)
Characteristics of the bystander	Similar to victim (age, gender, etc.); empathetic; knowledgeable about how to help the victim (e.g., knows CPR or has med-ical expertise or other rele-vant knowledge); afraid of appearing unsympathetic by refusing to offer help; in a good mood (having been the recent recipient of the prosocial behavior of others)	Somehow related to victim (e.g., co-worker, neighbor); emotional	Responds negatively to charac-teristics of the victim (e.g., prej-udices, negative reactions to transient characteristics such as clothing, grooming, or bleed-ing); afraid of appearing foolish or incompetent by offering help when unsure of knowing how to help expertly

Note: Preparing to give a speech about the Good Samaritan (a religious figure known for helping strangers) has no effect on helping behavior.

own safety is at stake, such as when the person is in a room being filled with smoke (Latané & Darley, 1968).

Why are people so passive in the face of emergencies, whether the emergen-cies affect others or even themselves? According to Latané and Darley (1970), we are passive because seeking help is actually more complex than it appears to be. Several factors seem to influence whether people will help (see Table 10-4 for a summary of these factors). According to Latané and Darley, there are at least five steps at which a bystander may decide to do nothing—or must decide to do some-thing.

We'd all like a reputation for generosity and we'd all like to buy it cheap.

Mignon McLaughlin

🌿 BRANCHING OUT: Latané and Darley's Five-Step Model of Bystander Intervention

According to Latané and Darley, before you take any action to help another per-son, you must take the following five steps: (1) You need to notice the signs or sig-nals of the emergency. (2) You have to define the situation as an emergency. (3) You have to take responsibility for doing something about the emergency. (4) You have to figure out how to seek or provide help. (5) You must actually carry out your plan for providing or seeking help. If you fail to complete any one of these steps, you will not take any action to provide helpful intervention.

In some situations, people may do more than help themselves and others through a difficult situation. They even may show **altruism**—selfless sacrifice— to help persons in need. Throughout history, there have been many examples of heroism, in which individuals have decided to make great sacrifices and have even risked their own lives, in order to help others. Recall, for example, the heroism of many rescuers who protected Jews and other persecuted persons during the Nazi

altruism generous willingness to help an-other person or persons, even when there is no reward or other observable benefit to the helper; often involves some sacrifice on the part of the helper

Following the 1989 San Francisco earthquake, countless volunteers joined professionals in helping others to survive and to recover from the devastation caused by the temblor. In response to much less dramatic cries for help, people show altruism in hospices, homeless shelters, nursing homes, and other settings.

reign of terror in Germany (Oliner & Oliner, 1993). Altruism is not considered the norm in individualistic societies, but it certainly offers benefits to society.

What leads us to show prosocial behavior? We are more likely to intervene to help other people when we feel individually responsible for helping, when we are similar to or related to the victim, when we are in a good mood, when we are empathetic or emotional, and when we know how to help the victim. We are less likely to do so when others are available to help, when we are in a hurry, or when the victim is bleeding, is a member of a stigmatized group, or is otherwise negatively evaluated by us. Occasionally, however, some of us show altruism, even when we risk self-sacrifice and we gain no apparent rewards for doing so.

WHAT LEADS US TO SHOW ANTISOCIAL BEHAVIOR?

In contrast to prosocial behavior, **antisocial behavior** is condemned by society as a whole and is harmful to society or to its members. Although people may disagree as to which particular behaviors and even which kinds of behaviors are antisocial, there are two classes of behavior that people generally agree are harmful to society: prejudice and aggression.

Prejudice

Prejudice is an unfavorable attitude directed toward other groups of people, based on insufficient or incorrect evidence about those groups. Note that prejudice is an attitude toward a group, not toward an individual. Unfortunately, many of our attitudes toward groups are extended to all of the individual members of the groups as

What makes behavior "antisocial"?

antisocial behavior actions that are harmful to a given society or to its members and that are condemned by the society as a whole

prejudice a negative attitude toward groups of individuals, based on limited or wrong information about those groups

Sometimes [prejudice is] like a hair across your cheek. You can't see it, you can't find it with your fingers, but you keep brushing at it because the feel of it is irritating.

                                        Marian Anderson

MINILECTURE

*Stereotypes, Prejudice, &
Discrimination (Ch 15)*

During my visit at Granny's a sense of the two races had been born in me with a sharp concreteness that would never die until I died.

                                        Richard Wright

social categorization the tendency to sort people into groups, according to various characteristics the observer perceives to be common to members of each group

stereotype perceived typical example that illustrates the main characteristics of a particular social category, usually based on the assumption that the typical example uniformly represents all examples of the social category

well. A negative attitude toward a group, however, is not necessarily a prejudice. For example, if you had ample evidence that a particular group (e.g., a youth gang) was responsible for numerous murders, you would probably not be considered prejudiced for having a negative attitude toward that group. You would be incorrect, however, if you assumed that all members of that group were murderers.

Social Cognition: Social Categorization and Stereotypes

Why do we feel prejudice? Patricia Devine and her colleagues (Devine et al., 1991) have suggested that prejudice may be viewed as a bad habit, which can be overcome. Another way of explaining prejudice is to view it in terms of how people try to understand other people. Often, we use two cognitive strategies for understanding the people around us: social categorization and stereotypes. Through **social categorization,** we tend to sort people into groups, based on perceived common attributes. We readily categorize people according to their gender, occupation, age, ethnicity, perceived attractiveness, and so on (cf. Neto, Williams, & Widner, 1991). These categories generally have particular defining features (e.g., specific sexual or occupational characteristics).

In addition, we tend to think of prototypes for various categories, based on what we perceive as being typical examples of the categories. When these prototypes are applied to people, the prototypes are considered **stereotypes.** We seem to learn many stereotypes during childhood. For example, cross-cultural studies of children show their increasing knowledge about—and use of—gender stereotypes across the childhood years (e.g., Neto, Williams, & Widner, 1991).

Social categorization and stereotyping are useful in many ways. For example, social categories and stereotypes help us to organize our perceptions of people and provide us with speedy access to a wealth of information (e.g., traits and expected behaviors) about new people whom we meet (Sherman, Judd, & Park, 1989; Srull & Wyer, 1989). More broadly, social categories and stereotypes help us know what to expect from people we do not know well. On the other hand, these same processes of social cognition can lead us to misunderstand and misinterpret the words and actions of people we do not know well.

Social psychologist Claude Steele (1990) has warned that the use of stereotypes can also directly influence the members of particular social categories (e.g., women or African Americans), through stereotype vulnerability. In *stereotype vulnerability,* people's awareness of negative stereotypes about social categories to which they belong may actually lead them to perform poorly, as compared with people who are not aware of negative stereotypes that apply to them. (Recall the effects of self-fulfilling prophecies, mentioned previously.) According to Steele, when the context for performance reminds members of any groups regarding the negative stereotypes about their performance, their performance suffers, but when the context provides no such reminders, their performance is enhanced (see Figure 10-11).

Context cues also can affect the likelihood that we will use stereotypes about other persons. For example (see Eagly, Makhijani, & Klonsky, 1992), when research participants evaluated women versus men leaders, they showed greater gender stereotyping and prejudicial responses toward women leaders in particular contexts: (a) contexts in which the leaders used leadership styles considered more stereotypically masculine (e.g., task oriented and directive, rather than interpersonally oriented and collaborative), or (b) contexts in which women were occupying roles that are male dominated in our society (e.g., athletic coaches, manufacturing supervisors, and business managers). In addition, men were more likely to evaluate women negatively than were other women.

Although social cognition plays a role in the formation of stereotypes, other factors may contribute to their use. For example, motivation and the tendency toward conformity to group norms may also influence the use of stereotypes (Rojahn & Pettigrew, 1992), as shown in the following study.

Figure 10-11
What Do You See in This Picture?
Groups of six research participants were asked to describe this picture, but only the first research participant in each group actually saw the picture. The first research participant then described the picture to the second research participant, who described the picture to the third research participant, and so on until the sixth participant described the picture to the experimenter. As you might expect, there were distortions in the research participants' descriptions of the picture. In general, these distortions tended to reinforce racial stereotypes. (After Allport & Postman, 1947)

The Robber's Cave Study

In the summer of 1954, Muzafer Sherif conducted a classic experiment on prejudice at the Robber's Cave State Park in Oklahoma (Sherif et al., 1961/1988). For about a week, two groups of 11-year-old white, middle-class boys participated in typical camp activities (swimming, hiking, etc.). None of the boys had known each other before they went to camp. Each group of boys chose a name for itself, and the boys then printed their groups' names on their caps and on their T-shirts.

After about a week, the boys in each group made a discovery—the existence of the other group of boys. They also discovered that a series of athletic tournaments had been set up that would pit the two groups against each other. During these competitions, conflicts arose and spread well beyond the games. Soon, the members of the two groups had become extremely hostile toward each other. The boys in the opposing groups ransacked each other's cabins, stole from each other, and battled in food fights. Clearly, the investigators had succeeded in creating intergroup prejudice through the competitions.

How could they now reduce or eliminate this prejudice? The investigators created apparent emergencies that had to be resolved through cooperative efforts. In one emergency, the water supply for the camp was lost because of a leak in a pipe. The boys were assigned to intergroup teams to inspect the pipe and to find the leak. In another incident, a truck carrying boys to a campsite got trapped in the mud: Boys from the two teams needed to cooperate in order to get the truck out. By the end of the camping season, the two groups of boys were engaged in a variety of cooperative activities and were playing together peacefully. By forcing people to work together, the prejudices of the members of each group against the other had largely been eliminated.

BRANCHING OUT: Reducing Prejudice

What can be done to reduce prejudice? First, we need to recognize how strongly prejudicial attitudes resist being changed. For example, male police officers and police supervisors commonly have prejudicial attitudes against female members of the force (Balkin, 1988; Ott, 1989), despite clear evidence showing women's effectiveness as field patrol officers (described in Balkin, 1988). Some people have suggested that prejudicial treatment against females (51% of the U.S. population) and minorities will decline when their numbers increase—that is, when the females are in a larger minority. It turns out, however, that negative prejudicial treatment of a minority group is based more on its relatively lower social status than on its number of members (Ott, 1989).

In which of these photos is the aggressor acting impulsively, showing hostile aggression? In which of these photos has the aggressor planned the aggressive act in order to obtain something of value, showing instrumental aggression? What kinds of intervention would be most effective in preventing each kind of aggression?

Design an activity that you believe might help to reduce prejudice against persons who have often been the target of prejudice due to stereotypes.

aggression behavior that is intended to cause harm or injury to another person

hostile aggression behavior that is intended to cause harm, as a result of an emotional, often impulsive, outburst, caused by pain or distress; the consequences usually lead to little gain for the aggressor and may even lead to losses for the aggressor

instrumental aggression behavior that happens to cause harm or injury to another person, as a by-product of trying to get something valued by the aggressor; often is planned, not impulsive

Another suggestion for reducing prejudice has been the *contact hypothesis*, the view that direct contact between groups will decrease intergroup prejudice (Allport, 1954). However, as shown by the conflicts that still exist in many desegregated neighborhoods and school systems, contact alone does not reduce or eliminate prejudice (Miller & Brewer, 1984). The contact must also involve the following four conditions if it is to lessen prejudice: (1) The two interacting groups must be of *equal status;* (2) the contact must involve *personal interactions* between members of the two groups; (3) the groups need to engage in *cooperative activities;* and (4) the surrounding *social norms* must favor reduction of prejudice. An additional way in which to reduce prejudice is to highlight new information that contradicts stereotypes based on limited information (Rojahn & Pettigrew, 1992).

Aggression

Unfortunately, feelings of prejudice sometimes lead to violent actions against persons who are the targets of prejudice. These violent actions (e.g., the many lynchings that took place in the United States from the 1860s through the 1960s) are a form of **aggression,** behavior that is intended to cause harm or injury to another person or persons (Baron, 1977). There are two main kinds of aggression: hostile aggression and instrumental aggression (Baron, 1977; Feshbach, 1970). **Hostile aggression** is emotional and is usually impulsive. It is often provoked by feelings of pain or distress. When we engage in hostile aggression, we intend to cause harm to another, regardless of whether we gain through our aggressive actions. For example, if a woman purposely rams her car into the rear of a car that cut her off on the freeway, she is demonstrating hostile aggression. She gains nothing by her actions, and she probably will suffer various unwanted consequences of her actions (e.g., the damage to her own car and the possible financial and legal outcomes resulting from damage to the other car).

In contrast, the purpose of **instrumental aggression** is to get something we value. Often, it is planned, not impulsive. Paid assassins, bank robbers, con artists, and embezzlers show instrumental aggression. The fact that other people are hurt by their actions is merely a by-product of their actions. Their common goal is to get money or something else the aggressors value, and their aggression is merely a means to that end.

The basic physiology underlying aggression seems to be the same for all humans. Researchers have already identified some brain structures (e.g., the hypothalamus and the amygdala) and some hormones (e.g., testosterone) as being involved in aggressive behavior. In addition to these common physiological aspects of aggression, there are many cross-cultural and individual differences in human aggression. Particular differences include the specific circumstances that prompt aggressive impulses and the specific forms in which aggression is expressed. Environmental factors—such as pain (Berkowitz, Cochran, & Embree, 1981; Ulrich & Azrin, 1962), discomfort (e.g., high heat; Anderson, 1987, 1989), or frustration (e.g., Barker, Dembo, & Lewin, 1941; Dollard et al., 1939)—also contribute to aggression. Another factor that increases the likelihood of aggression is the presence of aggression in the environment.

Violence: Social Learning and Desensitization

Almost all psychologists agree that social learning strongly determines the expression of aggression (Bandura, 1973, 1977b, 1983; Baron & Richardson, 1992). That is, people learn aggressive behavior by watching aggressive models (see Figure 6-4). Therefore, what people learn seems to differ from one context to another because models differ in each context. We know that people show more aggressive behavior in individualistic cultures than in collectivistic cultures (Oatley, 1993). Further, individualistic societies themselves vary in the extent to which they accept and promote aggression (DeAngelis, 1992; Montagu, 1976).

What can we do to prevent aggression, given the importance of social learning in contributing to violent behavior? Clearly, we should pay careful attention to the kinds of role models we provide to one another. For one thing, we should act swiftly to protect children from family violence. In addition, a powerful source of role models is found in almost every American home: television. We know that children play more aggressively immediately after watching violent shows on television (Liebert & Baron, 1972). Similarly, watching violent films seems to increase the aggressiveness of juvenile delinquents, especially among those who are initially the most aggressive (Parke et al., 1977). There are significant correlations between the amount of TV violence watched by children and the children's aggression as rated by their peers (Huesmann, Lagerspetz, & Eron, 1984). Moreover, these correlations appear across four different countries—Australia, Finland, Poland, and the United States.

The viewing of violent images (e.g., on television and in movies) may also do more to promote violence than just to provide models from which people learn aggressive behavior. Watching violent shows also desensitizes us to the tragic consequences of violence. **Desensitization** occurs when we habituate to a particular stimulus. Without any conscious effort or thought, we gradually become less interested in stimuli that we see often. Gradually, we pay less attention to these violent stimuli, and we show less emotional, physiological, and cognitive responses to violence.

Deindividuation

Another possible cause of aggression is that the aggressor dehumanizes (perceives as not human) the victim of the aggression. What enables some of us to dehumanize others? A possible answer may be understood in terms of **deindividuation,** the loss of a sense of individual identity. Once we feel deindividuated, we seem to be less inhibited from engaging in socially unacceptable behavior (Festinger, Pepitone, & Newcomb, 1952) (see Figure 10-12; Zimbardo, 1970). The aggressive behavior of some mobs is often attributed to the fact that the individuals in the mob become deindividuated.

When social psychologist Philip Zimbardo (1972) conducted a study of deindividuation, he ended up surprising himself as much as he did his fellow scientists. Zimbardo converted the basement of the psychology building at Stanford University into a "jail." Volunteer male research participants were randomly assigned to be either "prisoners" or "guards." As Figure 10-13 shows, Zimbardo led both

In violence, we forget who we are.

Mary McCarthy

desensitization the gradual habituation to violent stimuli, in which we gradually become less interested in and less responsive to violent stimuli and their tragic consequences

deindividuation the loss of a sense of individual identity, resulting in fewer controls that prevent the individual from engaging in behavior that violates societal norms and even the individual's personal moral beliefs

Figure 10-12
Deindividuation and Aggression
There is a much greater likelihood that women wearing the mask and nondistinguishing clothing depicted here administered shocks more aggressively than did women who wore their own regular clothing and identifying name tags (Zimbardo, 1970).

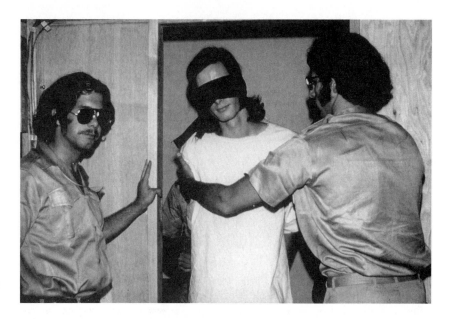

Figure 10-13
Deindividuation: An Arresting Experiment
Philip Zimbardo used a number of techniques to deindividuate both "prisoners" and "guards." The prisoners wore prisonlike uniforms and nylon stocking caps and were referred to by serial numbers instead of by names. Guards also wore uniforms and mirrored sunglasses to hide their facial expressions, and they carried clubs. Members of both groups were encouraged to think of themselves in terms of their roles, rather than in terms of their individual identities. Once people are deindividuated, they may act in ways that they would never have thought possible otherwise, whether on the giving or the receiving end of hostile levels of aggression.

groups of college students to identify with their new roles, not with their individual identities.

Prisoners almost immediately started acting like prisoners, and guards truly acted like guards. The guards harassed and insulted prisoners and even treated prisoners cruelly, apparently with little or no reason. After a prisoner revolt, which was quickly crushed, the prisoners became depressed. Some even started to experience mental breakdowns. At this point, Zimbardo stopped the experiment. Because the assignment of guards and prisoners was random, the astonishing changes could not be attributed to individual differences.

Several specific methods for reducing aggression have also been proposed, some of which seem to be more successful than others. For example, successful strategies include observing nonaggressive models (e.g., Donnerstein & Donnerstein, 1976), generating responses that are incompatible with aggression (e.g., humorous or sympathetic responses; Baron, 1976), and using cognitive strategies (e.g., simply stopping to think about whether the aggressive action is well advised). Several other strategies for reducing aggression have proven to be utter failures. It turns out that people do not become less aggressive, and they may actually become more aggressive, when they are encouraged to vent their aggressive feelings (Berkowitz & Geen, 1966, 1967; Buss, 1976; Geen & Quanty, 1977) or when they receive physical punishment for their aggressive actions (Sears, Maccoby, & Levin, 1957; Stevenson-Hinde, Hinde, & Simpson, 1986). It appears that aggressive actions of any kind tend to increase the likelihood of further aggression.

What leads us to show antisocial behavior? We tend to feel prejudice when we use social categorization and stereotypes based on inadequate or even biased information, when we tend to conform to group norms, and when we perceive our own group as competing with another group. We are less likely to have prejudices against groups that have equal status to our own, when we have personal interactions in cooperative activities with members of other groups, and when the social norms are favorable to reducing prejudice. Aggression may be hostile or instrumental, and it may be more likely to occur as a result of social learning, desensitization, and deindividuation. We may reduce aggression by observing nonaggressive models, generating responses that are incompatible with aggression (e.g., humor or sympathy), and using cognitive strategies, such as simply stopping to think about the consequences of aggressive actions.

This chapter has described various ways in which the actual, imagined, or implied presence of other persons influences the thoughts, feelings, and behavior of individuals. For instance, the presence of other persons often affects the emotions we feel (e.g., love), as well as our motivation to engage in particular actions (e.g., when obeying the commands of persons in authority). In the following chapter, we focus more specifically on the psychology of motivation and emotion.

SUMMARY

1. *Social psychologists* try to understand and to explain how the presence of others (actual, imagined, or implied) affects the thoughts, feelings, and behavior of individuals.

What Is Social Cognition? 285

2. *Social cognition* refers to the ways in which we perceive and interpret information about people, whether the information comes from others or from inside ourselves.

3. An experiment in social psychology established the theory of *cognitive dissonance*, which states that when a person's behavior and cognitions do not go together, discomfort results. To ease this discomfort, the person must justify his or her behavior. The experimental results that led to cognitive-dissonance theory have also been explained in other ways—such as by *self-perception theory*, according to which we form our beliefs about ourselves, based on our actions.

4. Attribution theory deals with how we explain the causes of behavior—why we and other people do what we do. In making *attributions*, we look for the cause of the behavior, which can be *personal* or *situational*.

5. Although biases and heuristics help us to make attributions, these mental shortcuts also sometimes lead to mental distortions.

How Do We Form and Change Our Attitudes? 288

6. *Attitudes* are learned (not inborn), stable, relatively lasting evaluations of people, ideas, and things. Attitudes affect our behavior, but the links between attitudes and behavior are not always predictable.

7. In studying what influences changes in people's attitudes, psychologists consider characteristics of the recipient of the message, of the message itself, and of the source of the message.

Why Are We Attracted to the People We Like or Love? 291

8. Social-psychological research asks why we are attracted to some people and not to others. Learning theory answers that we like (or dislike) a person because of the emotional rewards (or punishments) we get in that person's presence. According to *equity theory*, attraction involves a fair balance of give and take. *Cognitive-consistency* theories such as *balance theory* focus on a balance both of give and take, and of similar likes and dislikes.

9. The *attachment theory of love* suggests there are three main ways in which people relate to those they love: secure, avoidant, and anxious-ambivalent. The *triangular theory of love* posits that love has three components: intimacy, passion, and commitment.

10. According to the love-is-a-story theory of attraction, each of us is drawn to partners who closely match the types of characters in our own personal idealized love stories. Studies show that attraction is based on physical attractiveness, arousal, familiarity, proximity, and similarity.

How Do We Communicate in Our Personal Relationships? 294

11. Successful communication is essential to interpersonal relationships.

12. Men and women appear to communicate differently. Men seem to prefer establishing higher status and preserving their independence; women seem to seek closeness and agreement.

What Happens When We Interact in Groups? 295

13. Some social psychologists try to understand and explain how groups reach agreement and how individuals perform in a group.

14. In *social facilitation*, the presence of other people improves our performance. In *social interference*, the presence of others hurts our performance.

15. In *social loafing*, individuals show less personal effort as the size of the group increases.

16. Groups often become *polarized*, due both to new information and to shifts toward the group's social norms.

17. *Groupthink* occurs when a close-knit group cares more about agreement than about discussing objective, rational opinions regarding suitable actions. Stress, biased leadership, like-minded group members, and isolation from diverse views make the problems of groupthink worse.

When and How Do We Conform, Comply, and Obey? 299

18. People yield to social pressure by *conforming*, *complying*, and *obeying*.

19. A member of a group may conform only publicly or may also conform privately as well. People who deviate from the norm often are rejected by the group, but they may lead the way for others to differ from the group as well.

20. Compliance is encouraged through such techniques as justification, reciprocity, low-balling, foot-in-the-door, door-in-the-face, that's-not-all, and hard-to-get.

21. In Milgram's experiment on obedience to authority figures, most research participants were willing to administer painful shocks to others when following orders to do so. Other research has confirmed Milgram's surprising findings.

What Leads Us to Show Prosocial Behavior? 304

22. *Prosocial behavior* helps society as a whole or helps its individual members. An example of prosocial behavior is *altruism*, selfless sacrifice to help a fellow human being.

23. In the *bystander effect*, the presence of other people leads each bystander to feel less personal responsibility (through *diffusion of responsibility*) and reduces the likelihood that each bystander will help. Particular characteristics of the victim, the bystander, and the situation may also increase or decrease the likelihood that the bystander will help.

What Leads Us to Show Antisocial Behavior? 307

24. *Prejudice* is based on faulty evidence, which is in turn often based on cognitive shortcuts, such as *stereotypes* and *social categorization*. The Robber's Cave study showed how prejudice can be reduced through cooperative activities.

25. *Aggression* is antisocial behavior that harms another person. Aggression may be *hostile* or *instrumental*. People learn aggressive behavior when they see it modeled, such as in the home and in the popular media. The frequent viewing of violence may also lead to *desensitization*. Both physiological and environmental factors also influence aggressive behavior.

26. When *deindividuation* occurs, people lose their sense of individual identity and may behave in ways they would not behave otherwise.

PATHWAYS TO KNOWLEDGE

Choose the best answer to complete each sentence.

1. Jenny is eating cheesecake and feels a sense of discomfort after just declaring to her friend that she is on a diet. The condition invoked by this situation is referred to as
   (a) justification of effort.
   (b) cognitive dissonance.
   (c) cognitive consistency.
   (d) rationalization.

2. If you were to use the fundamental attribution error to explain why a man cut in front of you in the line at the post office, you would assert that the man
   (a) is a mean, self-centered person.
   (b) is in a hurry to catch his train.
   (c) was previously in line, then had to leave the line to pick up something he forgot.
   (d) is a friend of the postmaster.

3. Johnetta loves going out with Samuel because he often compliments her and praises her for her accomplishments. Based on the preceding description, Johnetta's feelings toward Samuel support which theory of interpersonal attraction?

   (a) equity theory
   (b) balance theory
   (c) arousal theory
   (d) learning (reinforcement) theory

4. One variable that is **not** typically cited as a factor underlying interpersonal attraction is
   (a) attitudinal similarity.
   (b) physical attraction.
   (c) proximity.
   (d) prejudice in favor of an individual but against the individual's group.

5. Group polarization is an effect whereby
   (a) extreme opinions in a group become more moderate as a result of increased group interaction.
   (b) disagreements among group members lead to polarization of their views.
   (c) the initial positions of group members become more exaggerated as a result of group interaction.
   (d) the group members' main concern is to avoid polarization of their views.

6. Groupthink is **unlikely** to occur when which of the following factors is present?

(a) There is a high degree of stress in the decision-making process.

(b) There is a strong and impartial leader guiding the decision-making process.

(c) The group comprises mostly like-minded individuals.

(d) The group is ideologically isolated from differing viewpoints.

7. At the request of her husband Billy, Valerie picks up a loaf of bread on her way home from work. Valerie's action shows
   (a) compliance.
   (b) obedience.
   (c) conformity.
   (d) cooperation.

8. The bystander effect occurs when
   (a) the helper is in a good mood.
   (b) the presence of other people inhibits helping behavior.
   (c) the presence of other people facilitates helping behavior.
   (d) helpers feel a close similarity between themselves and the victim.

9. A toddler who forcibly takes away the toy of another toddler is showing
   (a) instrumental aggression.
   (b) hostile aggression.
   (c) displaced aggression.
   (d) secondary aggression.

10. One factor that social psychologists do **not** now consider to be a causal factor in eliciting aggressive behavior is
    (a) exposure to aggressive role models.
    (b) physical discomfort.
    (c) frustration.
    (d) lack of frequent opportunities to show aggression, which would permit the person to "let off steam" and avoid building up aggressive feelings.

Answer each of the following questions by filling in the blank with an appropriate word or phrase.

11. _____ refers to people's efforts to sabotage their own work so as to have an excuse for failure.

12. _____ _____ refers to how we perceive and interpret information about ourselves and other people.

13. Fritz Heider has differentiated _____ and _____ attributions in people's explanatory styles.

14. According to the triangular theory of love, consummate love involves feelings of _____, _____, and _____ .

15. The phenomenon of _____ _____ can account for the fact that Tonya always plays her best tennis when the largest groups are present.

16. The phenomenon of _____ _____ can account for the fact that Joseph usually performs much less ably when other people are present, as compared with when he is alone.

17. _____ is demonstrated by selfless sacrifice.

18. When seeking a person's _____, a salesperson might wait to reveal unexpected costs or drawbacks until after obtaining the person's commitment to the deal.

19. _____ is an unfavorable attitude directed toward a group of people, based on insufficient or incorrect evidence.

20. Some ways of reducing _____ include observing prosocial models, encouraging humor or empathy with another person, and stopping to think about the consequences of any actions that are taken.

Answers

1. b, 2. a, 3. d, 4. d, 5. c, 6. b, 7. a, 8. b, 9. a, 10. d, 11. Self-handicapping, 12. Social cognition, 13. personal, situational, 14. intimacy, passion, commitment, 15. social facilitation, 16. social interference, 17. Altruism, 18. compliance, 19. Prejudice, 20. aggression

PATHWAYS TO UNDERSTANDING

1. Do you believe that human beings are predisposed to feel prejudice, in one form or another? Why or why not?

2. Design an exercise to help prevent a work group from suffering the ill effects of groupthink.

3. Which of the compliance-seeking strategies is the most likely to be effective in gaining your compliance? Which is the least likely? Why?

CHAPTER OUTLINE

How Did Early Psychologists
Explain Motivation?

How Does Human Physiology
Influence Human Motivation?
    Homeostatic-Regulation Theory
    Opponent-Process Theory
    Arousal Theory

How Do Psychological and Other
Needs Influence Motivation?
    Murray's Theory of Needs
    McClelland's Need for Achievement
    Maslow's Need Hierarchy

How Does Cognition Influence
Motivation?
    Intrinsic and Extrinsic Motivators
    How to Internalize Extrinsic
      Motivation
    Curiosity, Self-determination, and
      Self-efficacy
    Goals and Plans

What Emotions Do People Feel?

How Do Psychologists Approach
Trying to Understand Emotions?
    Emotions in an Evolutionary
      Perspective
    Psychophysiological Approaches to
      Emotion
    Cognitive Approaches to Emotion
    Cross-cultural Approaches to
      Emotion
    Polygraphs ("Lie Detectors") and
      the Measurement of Emotion

How Do People Express
Emotions?
    Culture and Emotional Expression
    Social Functions of Emotional
      Expression

Motivation and Emotion

In 1991, Walter Hudson died at 47 years of age. His death was reported in newspapers and magazines throughout the United States, even though he was not a distinguished artist, writer, scientist, executive, or politician. Hudson was one of the heaviest men in the world. He was so big that he was unable to leave his house, and when he died, workers had to make a hole in his bedroom wall so that his body could be removed. At his peak, Hudson weighed 1,400 pounds and had a 119-inch waist. At one point, he actually lost 800 pounds. Later, however, as so many other people do, he regained most of the weight he had lost.

When you feel inclined to do something, under what circumstances are you motivated to take action? Under what circumstances do you lack enough motivation to act on your desires?

What motivates most of us to gain weight or to lose it? What motivates us to explore our environments or to try to achieve success? What emotions do we feel when we accomplish our goals, or when we fail to do so? We address these kinds of questions in this chapter.

Intuitively, the way in which we describe our motivations and our emotions is similar: "I feel like having a hamburger." "I feel nervous." "I feel like dancing." "Dr. Martin Luther King's speeches moved many people to take action." Both motivations and emotions are feelings that cause us to move or to be moved. In fact, the words *motivation* and *emotion* both come from the Latin root *movere*, meaning "to move." Both motivation and emotion seem to come from within us, in response to events or to thoughts. We often feel both as physiological sensations: "I had a gut feeling not to do that." "When I heard his footsteps behind me again, I panicked—I started shaking, my heart pounded, my throat swelled shut, my palms sweated, and I turned to ice."

HOW DID EARLY PSYCHOLOGISTS EXPLAIN MOTIVATION?

Motivation is an impulse, a desire, or a need that causes us to act. Psychologists study why and how we are motivated to act. More specifically, psychologists ask four different questions (Houston, 1985): (1) What motivates us to *start* acting to go after a particular goal? Why do some people take action, whereas others may never act on their wants and needs? (2) In which *direction* do our actions move us? What attracts us, and what repels us? (3) How *intensively* do we take those actions? (4) Why do some people *persist* for longer periods of time in the things that motivate them, whereas other people often change from one pursuit to another?

Why do people do what they do? Early in the twentieth century, psychologists tried to understand motivation in terms of **instinct** (an inherited pattern of behavior, which is typical of a particular species of animal) (Cofer & Appley, 1964). Much of instinctive behavior is vital to survival both for each individual and for each species as a whole. In fact, naturalist Charles Darwin (1859) promoted instinct theory when he proposed his theory of evolution, in which the survival of each species depends on the ability of the species to adapt to the environment.

Psychologist William James (1890) suggested that humans have both physical instincts, such as sucking and locomotion, and mental instincts, such as curiosity, fearfulness, and sociability. Other researchers (e.g., McDougall, 1908) added to James's list of instincts (e.g., adding an instinct to dominate others and an instinctive desire to make things). Because the behavior of human animals is so complex, eventually, instinct theory became too complicated, with literally thousands of instincts having been proposed (Atkinson, 1964; Bernard, 1924). As the appeal of instinct theory waned, drive theory became increasingly attractive.

According to *drive theory* (Hull, 1943, 1952; Woodworth, 1918), people have a number of different basic physiological needs: the needs for food, water, sleep, and so on. Taken together, all of these physiological needs are a source of energy—of **drive,** a compelling urge to expend energy to reduce these physiological needs. Unfortunately, the assumptions underlying drive theory were weak, and evidence piled up against it (White, 1959), so eventually, drive theory also fell out of favor. Other theoretical approaches seemed to be more fruitful in explaining human motivation. For instance, a great deal of research has supported a physiological approach to understanding motivation.

MINILECTURE
Theories of Motivation (Ch 16)

The greatest tranquility is when we desire nothing.

         Middle Eastern proverb

motivation an impulse, a desire, or a need that leads to an action

instinct an inherited, species-specific, stereotyped, and often relatively complex pattern of behavior

drive a hypothesized composite source of energy, which humans and other animals try to reduce

How did early psychologists explain motivation? Early psychologists explained motivation in terms of instincts, which are inherited, species-specific, stereotyped patterns of behavior, and in terms of drives, which are compelling urges to expend energy in order to satisfy needs. Neither theory proved satisfactory for explaining motivation.

HOW DOES HUMAN PHYSIOLOGY INFLUENCE HUMAN MOTIVATION?

The physiological approach to motivation took off almost by accident. Researcher James Olds misplaced an electrode in a portion of a rat's brain. When the rat's brain was stimulated, the rat acted as if it wanted more stimulation. Olds and his associate Peter Milner (1954) then tested whether the rat was trying to get more stimulation. When electrodes were planted in a particular part of the limbic system of the brain, rats spent more than three quarters of their time pressing a bar to repeat the stimulation. Olds had discovered a pleasure center of the brain. Other researchers showed that cats would do whatever they could to avoid electrical stimulation in a different part of the brain (Delgado, Roberts, & Miller, 1954). Apparently, this other part of the brain caused very unpleasant stimulation. Three theories for understanding the relationship between motivation and the physiology of the brain are considered here: homeostatic-regulation theory, opponent-process theory, and arousal theory.

I generally avoid temptation unless I can't resist it.

Mae West

Homeostatic-Regulation Theory

Homeostatic regulation is the tendency of the body to maintain a state of equilibrium. In the course of a day, you are subject to several instances of homeostatic regulation that motivate you to wake up, eat, and drink. When the body lacks some resource (e.g., sleep, food, liquid), the body tries to get more of that resource. When the body has enough of that resource, it sends signals to stop trying to get that resource. We regulate the needs for food and liquid through homeostatic

homeostatic regulation the tendency of the body to maintain a state of equilibrium (balance)

cathy® by Cathy Guisewite

© Cathy Guisewite. Reprinted with permission of Universal Press Syndicate. All rights reserved.

systems. These systems operate by means of a *negative-feedback loop* (see the discussion of hormones in Chapter 2). Most people stop eating when they no longer feel hungry, stop drinking when they no longer feel thirsty, or stop sleeping when they no longer feel tired.

In the body, negative feedback is gradual, not a switch that goes on or off. For example, suppose that you have had a very active day and arrive at dinner feeling very hungry. At first, you are likely to eat and drink rapidly. However, your rate of eating and drinking will slow down as you finish your meal, because you are receiving feedback indicating that your needs are satisfied (Spitzer & Rodin, 1981). Your body signals to you long before you have finished the meal that you are becoming full.

Homeostatic regulation sounds somewhat like drive theory, but the emphases are different. In drive theory, the focus is on avoiding deficits. Instead, homeostatic-regulation theory more broadly emphasizes the need to maintain balance (equilibrium). Both deficits and surpluses are to be avoided. Next, we consider how the body regulates two motivations: hunger and sexual desire.

Hunger

Although most of us perceive feelings of hunger as coming from our stomachs, these feelings actually originate in an organ much higher in our anatomy: our brains. More specifically, the hypothalamus chiefly regulates hunger. Injury to different parts of the hypothalamus can lead to overeating and obesity (Hetherington & Ranson, 1940; Teitelbaum, 1961) or to undereating and self-starvation (Anand & Brobeck, 1951). How does the hypothalamus know when to signal hunger and when to signal fullness? It appears that our bodies monitor the levels of *lipids* (a form of fat) (Hoebel & Teitelbaum, 1966) and of *glucose* (a simple sugar) (Anand, Chhina, & Singh, 1962; Friedman & Stricker, 1976; Mayer, 1953; Oomara, 1976) in the bloodstream. When the levels of lipids or of glucose are too low, the hypothalamus signals us to eat; when the levels are too high, the hypothalamus signals us to stop eating.

Many of us pay a lot of attention to what and how much we eat, in order to control our body weight. Unfortunately, however, statistics on weight loss indicate that more than 90% of weight-losing dieters eventually gain all or almost all of the weight back. There is hope for losing weight, however: The combination of exercise and low-fat, low-calorie dieting may be more effective in achieving weight loss than are dietary restrictions alone (Safer, 1991; Seraganian, 1993).

Dieting often fails because people become more susceptible to binge eating when they are dieting than when they are not dieting (Polivy & Herman, 1983, 1985). When dieters are subjected to anxiety, depression, or stress, or when they are presented with alcohol or with high-calorie foods, many dieters seem to drop the restraints that have kept them from eating and start to binge. Persons who are not dieting do not show comparable behavior.

Other factors seem to contribute to obesity as well. For example, people tend to eat more food when presented with a greater variety of foods (Rolls, 1979; Rolls, Rowe, & Rolls, 1982). People also tend to eat more when other people are present than when they are alone (Berry, Beatty, & Klesges, 1985; deCastro & Brewer, 1992). Further, obese people may be more responsive to these environmental factors than are persons of normal weight (Schachter, 1968, 1971b; Schachter & Gross, 1968; Schachter & Rodin, 1974). Obesity may also be caused by problems in the way the hypothalamus works (Nisbett, 1972).

Unfortunately, fluctuations in weight may be even more damaging to health than is being overweight (Lissner et al., 1991). In other words, you may do yourself more harm by frequently losing and regaining weight than by just leaving your weight alone. To be considered obese, a person must be at least 20% over the normal range for a given height and weight. In the United States, about one in four adults is obese.

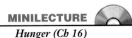

MINILECTURE
Hunger (Ch 16)

Conceptions of physical beauty vary with time and place. For example, what might be considered an ideal weight in one time period, in another might be considered too high or too low.

Some cross-cultural psychologists have suggested that cultural context may explain some differences in weight. Great individual differences can be observed across both cultures and time. For example, in Samoa, Fiji, Tonga, and other Pacific islands, many males and females weigh much more than the cultural norm for weight in Japan, where very heavy people, such as Sumo wrestlers, clearly stand out in a crowd (W. J. Lonner, personal communication, December 1993).

Norms regarding preferred body weight also change across time, as shown by historical collections in art museums. Many time-honored European masterworks, for instance, revere women who have much fuller figures than the slender women who appear in magazines (and other media) in various countries today (Silverstein, Peterson, & Perdue, 1986).

Being overweight is a serious problem for many people, but many others have an opposite problem: being underweight, which may be life-threatening for some. Some people tend to be chronically underweight because they metabolize food very quickly and inefficiently or because they have a kind of hormonal imbalance. In these people, being underweight rarely poses serious health problems.

A minority of underweight people, however, suffer from **anorexia nervosa,** a serious disorder that threatens the health of its sufferers, occasionally ending in death by starvation. People who suffer from anorexia perceive themselves to be fat, so they put themselves on severe weight-loss diets (Heilbrun & Witt, 1990). Up to 30% of anorexics die of causes directly tied to the disorder (Szmukler & Russell, 1986). The vast majority (95%) of anorexics are females between ages 15 and 30 years of age (Gilbert & DeBlassie, 1984). The value that many societies place on slimness seems to help explain why mainly young women suffer from this disorder in the United States and in other countries, such as Denmark and Japan (Nielson, 1990; Suematsu et al., 1985).

anorexia nervosa an eating disorder in which a person undereats to the point of starvation, based on the extremely distorted belief that she (usually) or he is overweight

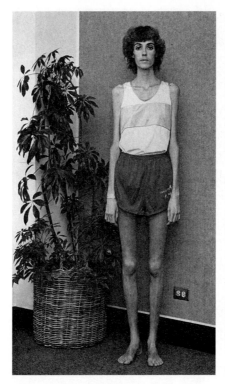

The photo on the right shows that this woman was fortunate to have recovered from the life-threatening disorder of anorexia nervosa. Astonishingly, like other anorexics, at the time the photo on the left was taken, this woman was starving herself to death because she perceived herself to be overweight and flabby.

No one knows exactly what causes anorexia. The roots of anorexia may lie in dysfunctional family relationships (Bruch, 1973), or they may be physiological (Gwirtsman & Germer, 1981). Anorexics may be treated through psychotherapy, drug treatment, and—in severe cases—hospitalization to treat the psychological and physical problems (Martin, 1985).

More common than anorexia is **bulimia,** in which a person goes on eating binges followed either by vomiting or by purging (e.g., through the use of laxatives). This disorder, like anorexia, is far more common in women than in men, and it primarily occurs during adolescence and young adulthood. Like anorexia, it is very difficult to treat.

Sex

None of us can survive without eating, but a lack of sexual gratification is not life-threatening to us as individuals. As a species, however, sexual motivation is as important to survival as is hunger motivation. If no members of the species satisfy their sexual wants, the species will disappear just as certainly as it will from starvation.

The hypothalamus, which plays a role in hunger motivation, also appears to play an important role in sexual motivation. The role is indirect, however. The hypothalamus stimulates the pituitary gland, which in turn releases hormones that influence the production of the sex hormones. There are two main kinds of sexual hormones: androgens and estrogens. Although both males and females have both androgens and estrogens, males usually have more androgens, and females have more estrogens. Without these hormones, sexual desire disappears—usually only gradually among most humans (Money et al., 1976). At any given time, humans may undergo a characteristic pattern of sexual response (see Figure 11-1).

Sexual Scripts and Social Norms. In humans, sexual activity involves at least some degree of cognitive processing. One way to describe the cognitive processes that accompany sexual response is in terms of sexual scripts (Gagnon, 1973; Simon & Gagnon, 1986). **Sexual scripts** are mental representations of how

MINILECTURE
Sexual Response Cycle (Ch 16)

bulimia a disorder characterized by eating binges followed by episodes of getting rid of the food (e.g., by vomiting, taking laxatives)

sexual script mental representation regarding how sexual behavior should be carried out during various episodes of sexual interaction

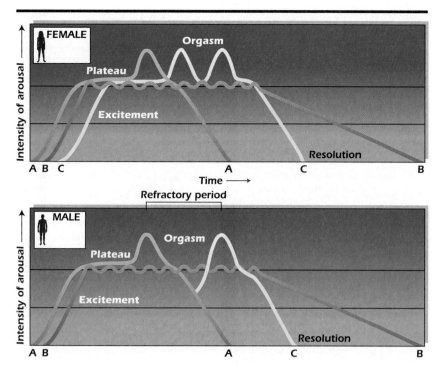

Figure 11-1
Sexual-Response Cycle
William Masters and Virginia Johnson conducted ground-breaking research on the sexual responses of men and women by directly observing human sexual response, rather than by inferring human responses from those of other animals. As line A shows, women and men experience the same phases of excitement, plateau, orgasm, and resolution. However, women are more likely than men not to experience orgasm (Line B), and women, but not men, can experience rapid multiple orgasms before the resolution phase (Line C). (After Masters & Johnson, 1966)

sequences of sexual events should be enacted. Most of us—whether or not we have ever engaged in sexual intercourse—probably could describe some kind of sexual script, particularly if we have read racy novels, seen romantic TV shows, or watched sexy movies.

Most of us have available many possible sexual scripts. We may decide whether or how to use these scripts, depending on the person we are with—or whether we are with another person at all. The desire for sexual consummation is largely a physiological need, but scripts are also socialized through the cultural and societal environment. Some sexual scripts fall outside of societal norms.

Every society attempts to regulate the sexual behavior of its members. For example, all societies impose a taboo against *incest*—sexual contact between particular members of the immediate family. Similarly, most societies attempt to regulate sexual behavior through cultural norms regarding modesty, homosexuality, masturbation, premarital intercourse, marital intercourse, and extramarital intercourse. For example, norms of modesty determine the regions of the male and the female body that should be covered or exposed and that may be decorated or undecorated. Although the specific regions that are to be covered or exposed differ widely from one culture to another, all cultures seem to impose some standards of modesty, at least on one of the sexes, during some times in the life span.

Homosexuality. Most cultural norms and sexual scripts are heterosexual, but homosexual scripts are also common. **Homosexuality** is a tendency to direct sexual desire toward another person of the same sex. In women, this tendency is often referred to as *lesbianism.* Technically, however, the term *homosexual* is gender-neutral, so it refers here to both men and women. Although we often speak of homosexuality and heterosexuality as though the two are separate and never overlap, perhaps it is better to consider them as extreme ends of a continuum. At one end are persons who are exclusively homosexual; at the other end are those who are exclusively heterosexual, and many others fall in-between. People who identify themselves as directing their sexual desire to members of both sexes are sometimes referred to as **bisexual.** Researchers have found that about 4% to 10% of men and a slightly smaller proportion of women identify themselves as having predominantly homosexual orientations (e.g., see Fay et al., 1989; Rogers & Turner, 1991). At one time,

You mustn't force sex to do the work of love or love to do the work of sex.

Mary McCarthy

homosexuality a tendency to direct sexual desire toward another person of the same (*homo-*, same) sex, which probably is based on physiology (nature) but is influenced also by the environment (nurture)

bisexual a person who directs sexual desire toward members of both sexes

many psychiatrists and psychologists believed that homosexuality was a form of mental illness. However, Evelyn Hooker (1993) conducted extensive research and found *no* inherent association between maladjustment or psychopathology and homosexuality.

What causes homosexuality or bisexuality—or heterosexuality, for that matter? Various explanations exist, some more scientific, some less so (Biery, 1990). Some of the less scientific explanations have included (a) *personal choice*—people simply choose their sexual orientations (this explanation begs the question as to why people choose differing orientations); (b) *arrested development*—homosexuals become fixated in a homosexual phase of psychosexual development (this explanation suggests that all heterosexuals pass through a homosexual phase of development); (c) *social-learning theory*—somehow, homosexuals were rewarded for homosexual leanings and punished for heterosexual ones (this explanation seems unlikely, given the prejudice against homosexuals in most contemporary societies); and (d) *weak father, strong mother*—homosexuals must have had weak fathers or overly strong mothers (this explanation has not been supported by research findings). None of these environmental explanations of homosexuality has been supported by research.

If nurture cannot satisfactorily account for sexual orientation, can nature? At present, a biological explanation does seem to have gained the most credible research support. For instance, research (Bailey & Pillard, 1991) has found that if one of a pair of genetically identical male twins is homosexually oriented, then the other is almost three times more likely to have the same orientation as when the twins are fraternal (i.e., not genetically identical). Brain research has also supported a biological basis for homosexuality (LeVay, 1991). Although the biological basis of sexual orientation seems to be well supported by research, other explanations, such as those involving environmental considerations, may also be discovered as a result of further study.

In addition, even if there is a biological basis for homosexuality, other factors may still affect its expression. That is, whether a biological predisposition to homosexuality is actually expressed in homosexual behavior may depend on social learning and other environmental factors. We are unlikely to find a single cause of any given sexual orientation. Rather, it is more likely that a combination of factors leads people one way or another. As Carol Wade and Sarah Cirese (1991) have pointed out, we view homosexuality and sexual orientation according to our culture's prescriptions and prohibitions. To rephrase their thesis, our sexual urges may be inherently biological, but the particular ways in which we are motivated to satisfy those urges seems to be at least partly influenced by our cultural and social environment.

To summarize what we have discussed in this section, homeostatic-regulation theory does a pretty good job of explaining why we seek to satisfy biologically inherited needs such as hunger and thirst. Homeostatic regulation also seems to play a role in our motivation to seek sexual satisfaction. However, this theory alone does not explain why we seek particular expressions of sexual desire (e.g., intercourse with same-sex or opposite-sex consenting adult partners) and not others (e.g., intercourse with other animals or with nonconsenting partners). This theory also fails to address how we *acquire* (get) particular motivations, such as the motivation to use psychoactive drugs such as alcohol or nicotine (the psychoactive drug contained in cigarettes). To explain acquired motivations, a different theory is needed.

Opponent-Process Theory

Richard Solomon (1980; Solomon & Corbit, 1974) developed opponent-process theory to explain his observations of a pattern of emotional experience when people acquire a motivation, such as the motivation to use psychoactive drugs. According to Solomon, originally, people are at a neutral state—a *baseline*—in which they have not acquired a particular motivation to act (e.g., to smoke a cigarette). In this baseline state, the particular stimulus (e.g., cigarettes) is irrelevant to them. Next, they take a dose of a psychoactive drug (e.g., nicotine absorbed from a puff on a cigarette), experience a "high," and feel a positive emotional state. They feel the high because of the positive effect of the chemical on receptors of the brain. They feel good because of the stimulus. Thus, they have an *acquired motivation* to seek out more of the stimulus. As Solomon discovered, the time course of acquiring a motivation (e.g., the motivation to use psychoactive drugs) tends to follow a pattern (see Figure 11-2). Once people have acquired a motivation, if they then try to stop using the substance and to get rid of the motivation, the pattern changes.

According to Solomon's opponent-process theory, human brains sooner or later always seek out emotional neutrality. Therefore, when a motivational source moves us to feel emotions, whether positive or negative, we then come under the influence of an opposing motivational force. This opposing force, an **opponent process,** brings us back to the neutral baseline. As Figure 11-2 (a) shows, our emotional state after smoking a cigarette first rises substantially but then falls. It starts to go down when the opponent process begins to oppose the original process. What was pleasurable at first now starts to become less so. Eventually, the effect of the stimulus wears off, and we reach a *steady state* of response to the stimulus. The original motivating force stops because the stimulus now only keeps us at our baseline level; it no longer elevates us above the baseline.

Thus, after using the substance for a long time, the effect of the substance is quite different than it was originally (see Figure 11-2b). Once we *habituate* to the substance, it no longer boosts us above our baseline level. Unfortunately, the opponent process, which was slower to start, is also slower to stop. When the effect of the substance wears off, the effect of the opponent process remains. Therefore, we fairly quickly go into a state of *withdrawal.* We now feel worse than we did before: irritable, cranky, tired, sad, or upset. We may then seek out more of the stimulus in order to relieve the withdrawal symptoms. Ironically, then, what starts off as a habit to reach a high becomes a habit to avoid a low. Fortunately, however, if we decide to ride out the withdrawal, the withdrawal symptoms that took us below our baseline will eventually end, and we will return to baseline.

Solomon and his colleagues have applied opponent-process theory to many kinds of acquired motivations, such as motivations to take drugs, to be with a particular person, to eat particular kinds of foods, or even to exercise. In each case, the theory has been remarkably effective in accounting for the data. However, the theory does not satisfactorily address why we would be motivated to take psychoactive drugs in the first place. Nor does it suggest why we would seek to feel more stimulated (i.e., more excited) or less stimulated (i.e., more relaxed) in the first place. Yet another theory is needed to explain these motivations.

There was a tiny range within which coffee was effective, short of which it was useless, and beyond which, fatal.

Annie Dillard

opponent process a changing phenomenon that opposes (goes against, in the opposite direction from) an existing force, thereby moving toward a neutral state of balance

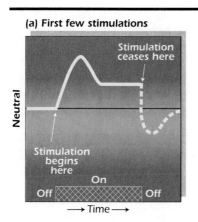

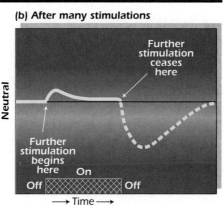

Figure 11-2

Acquired Motivation

In the beginning of the process of physiological addiction (a), the addictive stimulus elevates you above your neutral baseline level of response. At this point, if you stop using the addictive substance, you fairly quickly return to your neutral baseline level. However, once you become addicted (b), your responses to the substance act only to keep you in a steady state, which serves as your current neutral level of response. If you then abstain from the addictive substance, your responses will cause you to fall below your neutral level of response, and you will experience possibly serious withdrawal.

Arousal Theory

Suppose that three students of equal intelligence and subject knowledge are about to take an important test. The first student does not care either about the test or about how well she will do on it. The second student wants to do well, but he is not anxious about doing well. He knows that even if he were to do poorly, his life would not be changed permanently for the worse. The third student is extremely nervous about the test, and she believes that her grade on this test will largely determine her future. Which student do you think is most likely to do best on the test?

These three students vary in their levels of **arousal** (alertness, wakefulness, and activation) (Anderson, 1990). Arousal is caused by the activity of the central nervous system, including the brain. The relationship between arousal and efficiency of performance is expressed by the Yerkes–Dodson law, shown in the inverted U-shaped graph in Figure 11-3.

The *Yerkes–Dodson law* (Yerkes & Dodson, 1908) states that people will perform most efficiently when their level of arousal is moderate. According to this law, the student who is both motivated and relaxed will do the best. People generally also feel the best when their level of arousal is moderate (Berlyne, 1967). At low levels of arousal, people feel bored, listless, and unmotivated. At high levels of arousal, people feel tense or fearful.

The most helpful level of arousal appears also to vary with the task. For relatively simple tasks, the most helpful level of arousal is moderately high. For difficult tasks, the most helpful level of arousal is moderately low (Bexton, Heron, & Scott, 1954; Broadhurst, 1957). If you need to perform a fairly repetitive and boring task, a high level of arousal may help you get through and may motivate you to be efficient. On the other hand, if you have to perform a complex task, a low level of arousal may help you to avoid becoming anxious and thereby may help you to perform better.

The most helpful levels of arousal also vary across individuals. These variations may affect how we choose to work. For example, some of us do our best work when highly aroused, such as when responding to tight deadlines or to extremely high standards. Others of us work best when less aroused, such as when we can proceed at a consistent pace, with less demanding standards. Similarly, different people might seek to raise or lower the level of arousal in their environments—such as by increasing or decreasing the amount of visual and auditory stimulation (bright lights, loud music, etc.). Hence, it appears that arousal theory explains not only why we may seek drugs that raise or lower our level of arousal, but also why we may interact with our environment in particular ways.

Homeostatic-regulation theory, opponent-process theory, and arousal theory explain some of the physiological bases for motivation. In addition, arousal theory

arousal state of alertness, wakefulness, and activation, caused by nervous-system activity

Figure 11-3
The Yerkes–Dodson Law
We feel the strongest motivation when we are moderately aroused—aroused neither too much nor too little. The linear relationship between arousal and performance appears to be a hill-shaped curve, resembling an inverted U. In the hill-shaped curve shown in graph (a), performance is at its peak when arousal is moderate, and performance levels are lower at both the low and the high extremes of arousal. Graph (b) shows that optimally efficient performance is associated with a higher level of arousal for easy than for difficult tasks. (After Yerkes & Dodson, 1908)

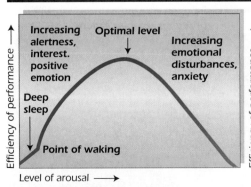

(a) **General relationship between performance and arousal level**

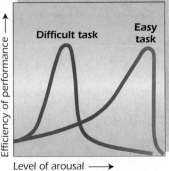

(b) **Relationship between performance and arousal level on difficult vs. easy tasks**

suggests some reasons why different individuals may be motivated to behave differently. Cultural contexts also influence motivation. In earlier chapters (e.g., Chapter 10), we explored how we may be motivated to conform to the social norms of our culture. Can all of motivation be understood in terms of our distinctive physiology and cultural context? What else motivates human behavior?

How does human physiology influence human motivation? The brain plays an important role in motivation. According to homeostatic-regulation theory, we tend to seek to maintain a state of physiological equilibrium. Regions of the hypothalamus in the brain seem to regulate hunger. It also appears that the body monitors levels of lipids or of glucose in the bloodstream, and the body uses these levels as a guide for when to start and to stop eating. Both obesity and eating disorders such as anorexia nervosa and bulimia pose serious health risks. The hypothalamus plays an indirect role in sexual motivation, through the release of pituitary hormones. Although much of sexual motivation is biologically determined, the distinctive expression of sexual behavior is largely culturally and socially determined. Opponent-process theory helps to explain how we acquire physiological motivations such as the motivation to use psychoactive drugs. Arousal theory helps to explain why we seek to feel more stimulated or less stimulated at any given time.

HOW DO PSYCHOLOGICAL AND OTHER NEEDS INFLUENCE MOTIVATION?

Murray's Theory of Needs

Psychologist Henry Murray (1938) believed that needs are based in human physiology, and that they can be understood in terms of the workings of the brain. He saw a particular set of 20 needs as forming the core of a person's personality. In addition to physiological needs, Murray included such needs as a need for *dominance* (power), for *affiliation* (feeling close to other people), and for *achievement*. He believed that people show marked individual differences in the levels of these needs. Thus, his approach emphasized individual differences to a much greater extent than did physiological and other approaches.

Murray believed that the environment creates forces to which people must respond in order to adapt. How a person copes in the world can be understood largely in terms of the interaction between a person's internal needs and the various pressures of the environment. Some of the needs that Murray proposed have prompted a great deal of research interest. For example, much research has been done on Murray's ideas about the need for affiliation and the need for power. Perhaps the most widely researched of Murray's proposed needs, however, is the need for achievement, based on an internal standard of excellent performance.

McClelland's Need for Achievement

David McClelland and his colleagues have been particularly interested in the need for achievement (McClelland, 1961; McClelland et al., 1953; McClelland & Winter, 1969). According to McClelland (1985), people who are high in the need for achievement (e.g., successful entrepreneurs) seek out moderately challenging tasks,

The need for achievement spurs many people to reach academic success.

persist at them, and are especially likely to work to gain success in their occupations. Why would people who are high in this need seek out tasks that are moderately challenging? Because these are the tasks in which they are likely both to succeed and to extend themselves. They do not waste time on tasks so challenging that they have little probability of accomplishing these tasks, nor do they bother with tasks so easy that the tasks pose no challenge at all.

Research has shown that our perception of reality strongly affects our motivation to achieve. That is, perceived competence, rather than actual competence, more powerfully predicts how people—especially children—react to demands for achievement (Phillips, 1984). Particularly as they grow older, girls often perceive their competence to be relatively low. Boys are less likely to show this pattern. The result can be lower expectations for achievement on the part of girls (Phillips & Zimmerman, 1990). The effect seems to start appearing as early as the kindergarten level (Frey & Ruble, 1987).

Mama exhorted her children at every opportunity to "jump at the sun." We might not land on the sun, but at least we would get off the ground.

Zora Neale Hurston

The achievement motive may be present in every culture, and it has been the focus of dozens of crosscultural studies (Maehr & Nicholls, 1980). For example, Chinese parents seem to place great emphasis on their children's achievement, but their focus differs from that of American parents (Ho, 1986). Whereas American children are motivated to achieve primarily for the purpose of being independent, Chinese children are more strongly motivated to achieve to please the family and the community.

Maslow's Need Hierarchy

The needs for affiliation, for power, and for achievement fit well into a hierarchical theory of motivation proposed by Abraham Maslow (1943, 1954, 1970). According to Maslow, our needs form a hierarchy (see Figure 11-4). Once we have satisfied needs at lower levels (e.g., physiological needs and safety needs), we try to satisfy needs at higher levels of the hierarchy (e.g., needs for belongingness and for self-esteem). At the top of the hierarchy is our need for self-actualization, in which we try to obtain greater knowledge, artistic beauty, and personal growth, in order to become the best we can be. The following list shows Maslow's hierarchy, in which the lowest levels (and the lowest numbers) are the more basic needs, and the highest levels are the needs that will be pursued only after the more basic needs are met.

1. At the most basic level are the *physiological needs,* such as the needs for food and water. When these needs are not being met, it is very difficult to concentrate on any needs of a higher order. For example, if you are very hungry or thirsty while you are reading these words, you are probably less able to focus on your

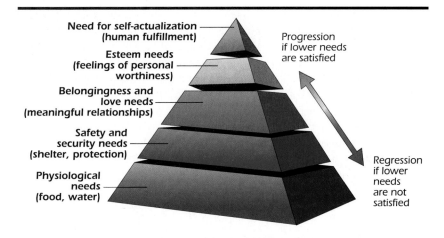

Figure 11-4
Maslow's Hierarchy of Needs
According to Abraham Maslow, we must satisfy our more fundamental needs (nearer the base of the hierarchy) before we try to meet the higher level needs (nearer the top of the hierarchy).

motivation to learn the information in this textbook than to focus on your desire for food or water.

2. At the second level are *safety and security needs*—needs for shelter and for protection. We are able to take care of these needs once our basic physiological needs have been met and before we seek to meet higher-level needs. For example, if you hear a fire alarm go off near you in your building and you smell smoke, you will be more likely to attend to your need for safety and security than to your need to finish reading this chapter.

3. At the third level of the hierarchy are *belongingness needs*—that is, needs to feel as though other people care about you and that you have a meaningful relationship with and belong to a group of people. For example, suppose that your best friend just told you not only that you are not going to go out together this evening, but also that your friend is going with a large group of other people to do something fabulously fun. You are not invited along because you are not welcomed by the group. Chances are that your need for belongingness will now dominate your thoughts and motivations much more than your need to learn this material. (Of course, your best friend would never really treat you this way.)

4. On the next level are *self-esteem needs*—that is, needs to feel worthwhile. For example, suppose that you have consistently received very high grades on tests in your psychology class. Then your teaching assistant gives you what she calls a "Psychology Aptitude Test." You find the test almost incomprehensible; it is so confusing that you cannot even come close to completing the test in the time allowed. At the next class session, your teaching assistant tells you that you scored very low in aptitude for psychology. Your self-esteem plummets, and you feel so upset that you cannot concentrate on reading your psychology textbook. (At your next class meeting, she tells you that the test was bogus, that everyone was told that they had low aptitude, and that she was conducting her own unauthorized experiment on your class. After that, she is not seen or heard from on campus.)

5. At the top level of the hierarchy are *self-actualization needs*, which pertain to the fulfillment of human potential. At last, you may be motivated to learn this material just because you enjoy pursuing knowledge for its own sake.

Why would the more basic needs in Maslow's hierarchical theory of motivation serve a more important evolutionary function than would the higher order needs?

the **BIG** *picture*

How do psychological and other needs influence motivation? According to personality theorists, in addition to having physiological needs, each of us has psychological needs. The levels of these psychological needs differ

Ambition never has its fill.

Mexican proverb

for each individual, according to each person's personality (the relatively permanent and consistent characteristics and moods of a person) and the environment. Murray proposed various psychological needs, three of which are the needs for dominance, for affiliation, and for achievement. McClelland, in investigating the need for achievement, found that high achievers seek tasks that are moderately challenging (i.e., neither too difficult nor too easy). Both culture and perceived competence influence the need for achievement. According to Maslow, our motivational needs are arranged in a hierarchy, in which we must satisfy more basic needs (e.g., physiological needs and safety needs) before striving to satisfy high-level needs (e.g., for belongingness and love, for self-esteem, and eventually for self-actualization).

HOW DOES COGNITION INFLUENCE MOTIVATION?

The pursuit of knowledge has led cognitive theorists to try to discover the cognitive processes underlying why people behave as they do. What makes us feel good? What do we find pleasurable? What kinds of stimuli and situations do we seek?

Intrinsic and Extrinsic Motivators

Psychologists frequently describe motivation as being either intrinsic or extrinsic. **Intrinsic motivators** come from within ourselves: We do something because we enjoy doing it. **Extrinsic motivators** come from outside of us: We do something because someone rewards us or threatens us. (Learning theorists refer to extrinsic motivators as reinforcement and punishment.) We act on the basis of intrinsic reasons, extrinsic reasons, or combinations of the two. For example, you might study hard in a given subject because you are really excited about the material and you want to learn it (intrinsic motivation), or you might study hard because you want to get an "A" in the course (extrinsic motivation). If you are lucky, you are able to gain some extrinsic motivators (e.g., earning a living) for doing things you find intrinsically motivating (e.g., feeling competent and able to make a valuable contribution to society).

Society offers many extrinsic rewards to ensure that people accomplish tasks that benefit society. The emphasis on extrinsic rewards, however, may actually

intrinsic motivation a desire to act, based on reasons that come from within the individual, such as to satisfy curiosity or artistic appeal

extrinsic motivation a desire to act, based on reasons that come from outside the individual, such as offers of rewards or threats of punishment

This music student will probably receive extrinsic rewards (e.g., high grades) for practicing on his musical instrument, but because he has freely chosen to study music, and he has chosen when, where, and how to practice, the undesirable influences of extrinsic motivators will probably be reduced.

create problems in motivation. For one thing, people do their most creative work when they are intrinsically motivated (Amabile, 1983, 1985; described also in Sternberg & Lubart, 1991). For another thing, the use of extrinsic motivators tends to undermine intrinsic motivation (Condry, 1977; Deci, 1971; Greene & Lepper, 1974), even in preschool children (Lepper, Greene, & Nisbett, 1973).

Some extrinsic motivators are less harmful to intrinsic motivation than are others. Edward Deci and his colleagues (Deci et al., 1991) have found that extrinsic motivation has differing effects, depending on how much a person can attribute the control of her or his behavior to internal, rather than to external causes. The harmful effects of extrinsic motivation are greatest when the person attributes the greatest degree of control to external, rather than internal causes. For example, if the person strongly believes that she or he is acting only to obtain rewards or to avoid punishments that are controlled by someone else, the harmful effects of extrinsic motivation will be great.

If you always do what interests you, then at least one person is pleased.

Katharine Hepburn's mother, advice to her daughter

🌿 BRANCHING OUT: How to Internalize Extrinsic Motivation

Almost everyone (e.g., employers, supervisors, parents, and teachers) wishes, at some time, to encourage someone else to be motivated to do something in particular or to act in a particular way. Sometimes, you may need to start out by using some form of extrinsic motivation (e.g., money or praise), and then you can work toward having the person become more intrinsically motivated to do what you want him to. Edward Deci (Deci et al., 1991) and others (e.g., Ross, 1975; Swann & Pittman, 1977) have suggested several ways for you to encourage someone to internalize extrinsic motivation and eventually become intrinsically motivated.

1. Help the individual to feel competent and socially related to other persons. Avoid strategies that reduce the person's feelings of competence and of relatedness.
2. Offer the person as much choice as possible in implementing the desired behavior, including choices of materials, of subtasks, of the organization and scheduling of tasks, and so on.
3. Avoid threats of punishment.
4. When using rewards, avoid tangible (touchable) rewards (e.g., money, prizes) that the person feels a strong desire to obtain. Prefer to use intangible rewards, such as smiles or praise, that have less damaging effects on intrinsic motivation.
5. When using rewards, deemphasize the rewards, perhaps offering them as occasional surprises. In any case, do not focus on the rewards as a means of external control.
6. Avoid strategies that emphasize external control, such as competition and deadlines.
7. Acknowledge how the individual feels about carrying out a given task—even if the person's feelings are negative.
8. Use language that shows your awareness and appreciation of the person's independence and competence, rather than using words such as *should*, *ought*, or *must*.

For what kinds of activities and projects are you intrinsically motivated to work, regardless of extrinsic motivation? How would various extrinsic motivators affect your enjoyment of these projects?

Curiosity, Self-determination, and Self-efficacy

One of the most powerful intrinsic motivators is *curiosity*. What makes people curious about some things and not others? We tend to be curious about things that are moderately new to us and moderately complicated, compared with what we already know and understand (Berlyne, 1960; Heyduk & Bahrick, 1977). This finding seems to make psychological sense. If something is totally familiar to us (e.g., the words to the U.S. "Pledge of Allegiance"), we ignore it; we have nothing to learn from it. At the opposite extreme, if something is wholly new (e.g., technical descriptions of the physics of aircraft-engine designs), we have no basis for understanding it. On the other hand, if we come across something that is new but within our ability to understand it, we become curious about it, and we explore it. For instance, I hope that you find it interesting to investigate (e.g., by reading this psychology textbook) how and why people you know feel, think, and act as they do.

Even in everyday activities, we look for ways to be active, to observe and explore, to manipulate aspects of our environments, and to gain mastery over our surroundings (White, 1959). We also try to see ourselves as making things happen. We try to feel control over ourselves and our environments (deCharms, 1968). That is, we actively try to feel self-determination, and we avoid feeling controlled by outside forces. We are often unhappy when we feel controlled, whether it is by another person or even by a substance (as in an addiction). We generally feel unhappy when we believe that our futures are predetermined, or that others are controlling our actions. Rather, we are motivated to be—and to feel—in charge of our own destiny.

According to **self-determination theory** (Deci et al., 1991), humans need to feel *competent* (capable of performing key tasks), *related* (a sense of belonging and being connected to other people), and *autonomous* (independent). The need for relatedness is similar to Murray's need for affiliation and Maslow's needs for belongingness and love. According to self-determination theory, we are all powerfully motivated to meet these three innate needs.

How do our feelings of competence affect the likelihood that we will reach our goals? Albert Bandura (1977a, 1986) has theorized that our **self-efficacy**—our feelings of being competent enough to achieve our goals—powerfully affects whether we can achieve our goals. Your beliefs in your own self-efficacy can come from many different sources: your own direct experiences, how you interpret the experiences of others, what people tell you that you are able to do, and how you assess your own emotional or motivational state. The important thing is that if you feel greater self-efficacy, you are more likely to create the outcomes you want. Think about how you view your own competence in various areas of your experience. How efficacious (competent) do you feel? How do your feelings of self-efficacy affect both your motivation and your performance?

The impulse to dream had been slowly beaten out of me by experience. Now it surged up again and I hungered for books, new ways of looking and seeing.

Richard Wright

---

self-determination theory a theory suggesting that people need to feel that they can control their own destiny, that they are independent and competent, yet that they are still closely tied to other people

self-efficacy an individual's belief in her or his own competence to master the environment and to reach personal goals

---

Monkeys confined in boxes learn to solve problems even when the only reinforcement they receive is the chance to look outside the box for a few moments (Butler, 1953). The longer the monkeys are confined to the boring boxes, the more they will do to have the chance to look outside. Monkeys will also learn a task (e.g., opening latches) just to have something to do (Harlow, Harlow, & Myer, 1950).

One way to explain the effects of self-efficacy is to say that self-efficacy relates to *self-fulfilling prophecies* (Rosenthal & Jacobson, 1968). When you believe you can do something, you are more likely to try hard enough to succeed. Each success then leads to greater self-efficacy, which leads to further success. In contrast, people who feel a lower level of self-efficacy may believe that they cannot succeed. As a result, they hardly try. The result is likely to be failure, which leads to the expectation of future failure, which then becomes the basis for more failure. One way in which to enhance your ability to reach your goals is simply to set realistic, highly specific goals, and then to make specific plans for meeting your goals.

No one rises to low expectations.

Les Brown

 BRANCHING OUT: Goals and Plans

Years ago, Edward Tolman (1932, 1959) recognized that **goals** can be enormously motivating. Specifically, goals help to motivate high performance in four ways (Locke & Latham, 1985):

1. Focus attention—Goals focus your attention on the tasks you need to complete in order to perform well.
2. Effective use of resources—Goals help you to pull together the resources you need in order to get where you want to be.
3. Persistence—Having goals helps you to continue to try to achieve even when it is hard to do so.
4. Strategy planning—You can use your goals as a basis for developing a plan for achieving success. A **plan** is a specific set of strategies for getting where you want to go from where you are (Miller, Galanter, & Pribram, 1960; Newell & Simon, 1972).

Throughout your life, you must frequently change your goals and your plans, trading off what you ideally want for what you believe you can realistically get. The most effective goals are challenging enough to motivate action while still being reachable.

The day on which one starts out is not the time to start one's preparations.

Nigerian proverb

What is a goal you can set for yourself that will satisfy your need for achievement and will enhance your feelings of competence, autonomy, and self-efficacy? Make a specific plan for reaching your goal, including all the specific steps you will need to finish.

How does cognition influence motivation? Although extrinsic motivators influence people's behavior, when creative or self-initiated behavior is involved, people generally require some source of intrinsic motivation. Although extrinsic motivation can sometimes inhibit intrinsic motivation, steps can be taken to encourage the internalization of motivation. Curiosity, self-determination, and self-efficacy also seem to motivate people in many circumstances. In addition, the simple use of goals and plans helps people to maintain their motivation in performing tasks or in completing projects involving multiple tasks.

Design a plan for increasing the motivation of an underachieving student to work hard in school—to master academic tasks, study information, do homework, and so on. Which of the various theories of motivation is (or are) important to your plan?

Many of the theories of motivation work together, rather than in opposition (see Table 11-1). For example, motivation probably has physiological, personality, and cognitive aspects. Almost certainly, these aspects interact. The physiology of the brain and of the endocrine (hormonal) system affects the personality attributes and cognitions we have, just as these personality attributes and cognitions may in turn affect our physiology. Further research may show how to fit together these various approaches to characterize all of human motivation more fully, yet more simply.

goal a future state that an individual wants to reach

plan a strategy for accomplishing something at some time in the future

TABLE 11-1

Three Approaches to Motivational Theory

Approaches to motivation based on physiology, on personality, and on cognition may be seen as complementary, rather than conflicting, ways of understanding motivation. (Key researchers or theorists are indicated in parentheses following each theory.)

Approaches based on physiology

Homeostatic-regulation theory (e.g., Keesey et al.)	The systems of the body try to maintain a state of equilibrium, using negative-feedback loops. When a needed resource (e.g., food) is lacking, the body signals to get more of the resource. When the levels of the resource are adequate, the body signals to stop trying to get more of the resource.
Opponent-process theory (Solomon)	The human brain tries to achieve a baseline state of emotional neutrality. When stimuli lead to movements above or below the neutral baseline, opposing forces tend to counteract the upward or downward trend, returning us to the neutral baseline.
Arousal theory (e.g., Yerkes & Dodson)	We perform most effectively when we are motivated by moderate levels of arousal. When arousal is too high, we feel overly anxious and tense, and when arousal is too low, we feel bored and uninterested. At either of the extreme levels of arousal, poor performance is more likely than when arousal is moderate.

Approaches based on personality

Theory of needs (Murray)	Physiological and psychological needs form the bases for how we interact with our environment. Among the psychological needs, the most widely studied are the needs for affiliation, for power, and for achievement.
Need for achievement (McClelland)	The need for achievement powerfully influences how we interact. People with a high need for achievement seek out tasks that moderately challenge their abilities.
Hierarchy of needs (Maslow)	We try to satisfy needs at successively higher levels once we satisfy needs at relatively lower levels. The sequence of needs is physiological, safety and security, belonging (social support), self-esteem, and self-actualization (fulfilling personal potential to the greatest extent possible).

Approaches based on cognition

Intrinsic vs. extrinsic motivators (Deci et al.; Lepper)	We can be motivated to take action, based on intrinsic forces, such as personal interest, or on extrinsic forces, such as rewards or punishments controlled by other persons. Unfortunately, the use of extrinsic motivators sometimes undermines the effectiveness of intrinsic motivators.
Curiosity (e.g., Berlyne)	We tend to want to explore whatever is moderately new and moderately complicated, as compared with what we already know and understand.
Self-determination (e.g., deCharms; Deci et al.)	We try to find ways actively to explore and manipulate aspects of our surroundings, particularly so that we can gain a sense of mastery over our environments.
Self-efficacy (e.g., Bandura)	We try to feel competent, and we work harder to achieve what we believe we are competent enough to achieve.
Goals and plans (Tolman)	Goals and plans can improve motivation and increase the likelihood of accomplishing particular tasks.

Finding Your Way   **11-1**

Before you read about what psychologists have to say about emotions, think about what you already know and believe about emotions. Look at the photos of New Guinean adults shown in Figure 11-5. For each photo, guess what

(a)

(b)

(c)

(d)

Figure 11-5
Facial Expression of Emotion
What emotions are these people expressing?

emotion is being expressed. (We return to these photos again later in this chapter.)

Photo	Emotion
(a)	
(b)	
(c)	
(d)	

WHAT EMOTIONS DO PEOPLE FEEL?

Emotions are psychological feelings, usually accompanied by physiological reactions to stimuli. The stimuli that lead to these responses may come from inside our bodies (e.g., the pain of a stubbed toe), from inside our minds (e.g., the thought that a lover is being overly attentive to someone else), or from our environments (e.g., seeing a poisonous snake within striking distance). The various responses include cognitive (experiential), physiological, and behavioral aspects (Carlson & Hatfield, 1992). Particular emotional responses may be either preprogrammed (genetic; e.g., feeling frightened while falling) or learned (e.g., feeling afraid of getting a low grade on a psychology examination).

Emotion and motivation are so closely linked that it is often difficult to distinguish them. For instance, both motivations and emotions are feelings that cause us to move or to be moved; both seem to come from within us, in response to events or to thoughts; and both often involve some accompanying physiological sensations. On the other hand, motivation and emotion differ in some ways, as shown in Table 11-2. Another way to see how motivation and emotion interact is to consider a classic psychological situation: In the **approach–avoidance conflict,** we feel

Feelings are untidy.

Esther Hautzig

emotion a psychological feeling, usually accompanied by a physiological reaction

approach–avoidance conflict the simultaneous presence of two conflicting tendencies: to go toward a stimulus (approach it) and to go away from it (avoid it), based on feeling both positive and negative emotions about the stimulus

TABLE 11-2

Some Differences Between Motivation and Emotion

Although motivation and emotion have many similarities, they also differ in several ways.

Motivation (motives)	Emotion (feelings)
The prompting stimulus (e.g., hunger) is generally not observable	The prompting stimulus is generally observable
Often seems to be cyclical (e.g., hunger occurs in cycles)	Rarely seems to be cyclical
Energizes, directs, and sustains activity (e.g., hunger prompts the pursuit of food)	May interfere with ongoing activity (e.g., sadness may lead to depression) or may lead to a change in activity (e.g., fear may lead to escape-seeking activities)
Responses are directed outward toward interactions with the external environment	Responses are directed inward (e.g., toward physiological and cognitive activities within the individual
Generally prompts action and is seen as active	Generally seen as passive

MINILECTURE

Types of Emotion (Ch 16)

How would you design an experiment to study emotions? What approach or combination of approaches would you use in designing your experiment?

two conflicting tendencies: (1) We feel positive emotions (e.g., joy) about some aspects of a particular stimulus, so we want to go toward it (i.e., approach it); (2) we also feel negative emotions (e.g., fear) about some aspects of the stimulus, so we want to go away from it (i.e., avoid it).

Suppose, for example, you see someone toward whom you feel strongly attracted. You feel happy just to be near the person. He or she appears to be unattached, so you feel even happier. You feel motivated to approach the person and strike up a conversation. You start walking over. As you get closer, however, your feelings of anxiety start to increase. What if you are rejected? What if the person thinks you are a jerk? As you get closer, you chicken out (see Figure 11-6). The tendency toward avoidance becomes stronger as you approach the person. When the tendency for avoidance becomes greater than the tendency for approach, you are motivated to walk away. Your joy of wanting to be near the person loses out to your feelings of fear, and you do nothing. Your motivation to approach the person is intertwined with the emotions you feel as you come closer and closer to making contact.

Before we probe various approaches to emotions, it may help to describe briefly the basic kinds of human emotions. Joy, fear, anger, sadness, and disgust are the emotions most often cited as being fundamental to all humans (see Table 11-3).

Figure 11-6

The Approach–Avoidance Conflict

Motivation and emotion interact in response to a situation that stimulates motivation both to approach something and to avoid it, due to the arousal of both positive and negative emotions toward the object. When the avoidance gradient goes above the approach gradient, the organism pulls away.

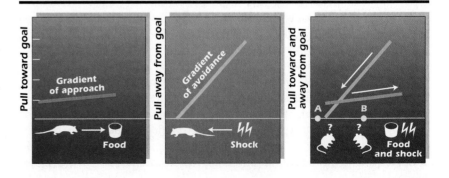

TABLE 11-3

Basic Human Emotions

Although various theorists differ in the emotions they consider to be fundamental, most agree that joy, fear, anger, sadness, and disgust are basic.

Emotion	Findings
Joy A feeling associated with a sense of well-being, inner harmony, and contentment, often associated with smiling	When people rate their own happiness, the mean rating is about 6 on a 10-point scale (Wesman & Ricks, 1966). Ratings for a given person are remarkably constant from one day to the next, but self-reports of happiness differ across cultures (percentages of self-rated happiness ranged from a low of 34% in South Korea to a high of 52% in Italy; Hastings & Hastings, 1982).
Fear An unpleasant emotional arousal in response to perceiving a specific, identified danger or threat, focused on a specific situation or object	Fear serves a protective evolutionary function because it motivates people to avoid harmful objects or situations. In contrast, anxiety—an unpleasant emotional arousal in response to a general perception of an unidentified danger or threat, not focused on any particular situation or object of threat—may lead to serious psychological disorders.
Anger A state of arousal that arises when a person feels frustrated or blocked from reaching a goal, especially if the frustration or injury is believed to have been inflicted intentionally and without justification	About 29% of our overt expression of anger is directed toward people we love, 24% toward people we like, 25% toward acquaintances, and only 8% toward people we actively dislike (Averill, 1980, 1983); only 13% of our expression of anger is directed toward strangers (total = 99%, due to rounding).
Sadness and grief Whereas *sadness* is a relatively mild feeling of unhappiness, *grief* is sharper, deeper, and usually more long-lasting	This emotion results from an unwanted, involuntary, often permanent, separation; the separation may be from a physical object, situation, or person (e.g., a loved one) or from something intangible, such as a personal belief or skill (e.g., being disabled or made to feel incompetent or powerless).
Disgust An emotional reaction to being faced by objects or situations that we find extremely unattractive	Disgust serves an adaptive purpose, motivating us to avoid objects or situations that may be harmful (e.g., spoiled meat). When feeling disgust, we psychologically reject something based on its nature, its origin, or its social history (Rozin & Fallon, 1987). What may seem disgusting in one culture (such as piercing of a woman's ears) may not seem disgusting in another.

To these emotions, some would add surprise (which is much less commonly identified as a fundamental emotion across cultures), guilt (the private sense of being at fault), and shame (public humiliation) (e.g., see Figure 11-7). Refer back to your responses to Finding Your Way 11-1. How do the emotions you observed compare with the basic emotions listed in Table 11-3 and with the emotions depicted in Figure 11-7?

What emotions do people feel? The five basic emotions (tendencies to respond to stimuli in various ways) are joy, fear, anger, sadness, and disgust. Some theorists add to these five the emotions of surprise, guilt, and shame, which are less universally recognized across cultures. The approach–avoidance conflict is an example of how these emotions and motivation may interact.

Figure 11-7

Plutchik's Emotion Wheel

One of the main structural theories of emotion suggests that emotions can be arrayed in a circle (Plutchik, 1980). Emotions closer to each other in the circle are more closely related. Emotions farther away are more distantly related. Emotions opposite each other in the circle are also believed to be emotional opposites.

According to many psychologists, the emotions of joy, fear, anger, sadness, and disgust are fundamental to all humans everywhere, although the particular situations that prompt those emotions, and the particular ways in which they are expressed may differ across cultures.

HOW DO PSYCHOLOGISTS APPROACH TRYING TO UNDERSTAND EMOTIONS?

Just as the approaches to and suggested explanations of motivation are diverse, so, too, are the approaches to understanding human emotions. In reading about evolutionary, psychophysiological, cognitive, and cultural approaches, you may note that many of these approaches offer insights that add to, rather than subtract from, the others.

Emotions in an Evolutionary Perspective

The evolutionary approach to emotions attempts to answer the question, Why have emotions developed within the human species as a whole? Emotions have both a *physiological aspect*, through which we physically react in distinctive ways, and a *cognitive aspect*, through which we interpret how we feel. Both aspects are essential to our survival as a species. From an evolutionary perspective, there are good reasons for emotions (Plutchik, 1983). Obviously, the emotions that help to increase the likelihood of reproduction help our species' survival. As humans have gained increasing control over reproduction, emotions may play an increasingly important role. Brief feelings of lust alone usually do not determine when or with whom we will have children. Rather, much more complex and long-lasting emotions typically govern our reproductive choices.

Consider, too, the love parents feel for their children. Obviously, this love brings happiness to both parents and children. The love that bonds parents and children together also serves a purpose for evolutionary survival: It makes it more likely that the parents will ensure the child's safety, health, and survival while the child still depends on the parents.

We also feel other emotions, such as fear and anger (which we enjoy a lot less than love or lust). How do these other emotions enhance our survival as individuals or as a species? For one thing, these emotions prepare us to behave in particular ways in particular situations. For example, anger can prepare us to fight when we have a pretty good chance of defeating a potential attacker. On the other hand, fear can prepare us to run away from a potential attacker who might harm us. Survival of a species as a whole depends on its members knowing when to fight a beatable enemy and when to run from an unbeatable one. Appropriate emotional reactions to danger may mean the difference between life and death.

Psychophysiological Approaches to Emotion

Today, psychophysiological approaches to emotion involve cutting-edge technologies, state-of-the-art methodologies, and exciting changes in theories. Surprisingly, psychophysiological approaches are also among the most ancient ones. Ancient Greek and Roman physicians believed that emotional states could be understood in terms of the physiology of the body.

Links Between Our Bodies and Our Emotions

The earliest modern theory of emotion was proposed separately by American psychologist William James (1890) and Danish physiologist Carl Lange. Today, the theory that they proposed is termed the *James–Lange theory* of emotion. The James–Lange theory turns common notions about emotion upside-down. The commonsense view of emotion is that first we perceive some event in the environment. That event leads us to feel some kind of emotion. As a result of that emotion, psychophysiological changes occur. For example, sadness might lead to crying, or anger might lead us to clench our fists. James and Lange proposed exactly the reverse (Lange & James, 1922). According to James and Lange, we experience bodily changes in reaction to events in the environment. These psychophysiological changes then lead to the feelings we identify as emotions, rather than the other way around (see Figure 11-8).

Ironically, William James's son-in-law, Walter Cannon, became the leading critic of the James–Lange theory (Cannon, 1929). He noted some reasons why the James–Lange theory could not be right. For example, different emotions are often associated with the same psychophysiological states within the body. In addition, the organs of the body do not provide the kinds of information that people would need to distinguish one emotion from another. Cannon proposed instead that the brain—in particular, the thalamus—controls emotional behavior. Bodily reactions alone do not. Philip Bard (1934) later elaborated Cannon's view, so it is sometimes called the Cannon–Bard theory (see Figure 11-9).

Psychologists now believe that some aspects of both the James–Lange theory and the theory of Cannon are correct. Cannon was correct in recognizing that emotions are largely governed by the brain, especially by several parts of the limbic system (e.g., the hypothalamus and the amygdala; see Chapter 2). James and Lange were also correct, however, in noting that physiological changes contribute to people's perceptions of their emotions.

Figure 11-8
James–Lange Theory of Emotion

Environmental event	→	Physiological reaction	→	Identify emotion
(Slip on a banana, and fall down)	→	(Feel physical pain, flushed skin, rapid pulse, and other physiological signs of increased arousal)	→	(Identify feeling as anger)

Two Systems for Emotional Responses

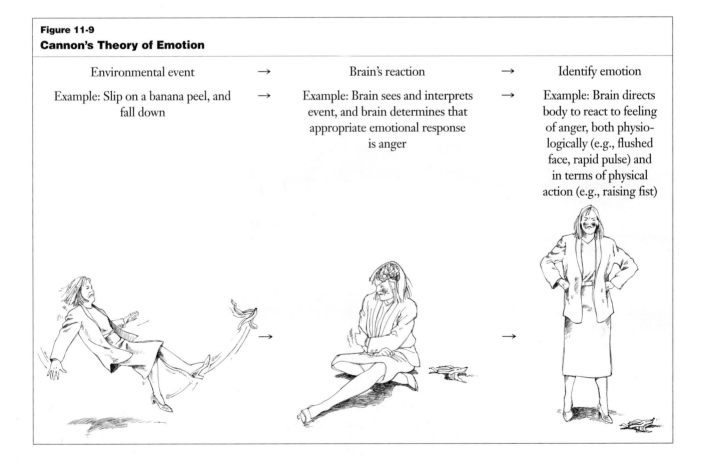

MINILECTURE

Theories of Emotion (Ch 16)

As Cannon suspected, in addition to the brain itself, two physiological systems appear to influence our emotional responses: the autonomic nervous system and the endocrine system (see Chapter 2). According to Joseph LeDoux (1986; LeDoux,

Figure 11-9
Cannon's Theory of Emotion

Environmental event	→	Brain's reaction	→	Identify emotion
Example: Slip on a banana peel, and fall down	→	Example: Brain sees and interprets event, and brain determines that appropriate emotional response is anger	→	Example: Brain directs body to react to feeling of anger, both physiologically (e.g., flushed face, rapid pulse) and in terms of physical action (e.g., raising fist)

Figure 11-10
Contemporary Physiological Theory of Emotion

Environmental event or stimulus	→ Brain senses stimulus event, then brain (limbic system) directs autonomic nervous system and endocrine system to respond appropriately ↕ → Brain thinks about the event (and perhaps also about the physiological reactions), and the brain identifies an emotion	→ The brain determines how to react to the situation
Example: Slip on a banana peel, and fall down	→ Example: Brain senses pain, then it immediately (a) directs the autonomic nervous system to increase pulse and breathing rates, and (b) directs the endocrine system to release noradrenaline ↕ → Example: Brain cognitively interprets the stimulus event (slipping and falling) and perhaps also the physiological reactions (e.g., flushed skin, heavy breathing) as indicating the emotion of anger.	→ The brain figures out how to respond to the situation in terms of taking physical action (e.g., shouting, slapping the floor)

Romanski, & Xagoraris, 1989) and other investigators (Cacioppo & Petty, 1983; Derryberry & Tucker, 1992; Ekman, Levenson, & Friesen, 1983), distinctive patterns of arousal and activity of the autonomic nervous system (see Chapter 2) may correspond to different emotions. For instance, when you feel frightened or angry, your autonomic nervous system directs your heart and lungs to speed up their activity, and it directs your digestive system to slow down its activity.

Other researchers (e.g., Henry & Stephens, 1977) have emphasized the role of the endocrine system in emotion. Thus, different emotions may be linked to different relative concentrations of hormones. For example, anger seems to be

Figure 11-11
Schachter and Singer's Theory of Emotion

Stimulus	→	Physiological component	→	Cognitive component
Environmental event or stimulus	→	We sense feeling aroused.	→	We evaluate the situation and the feeling of arousal, and we label the arousal as a particular emotion.
Exampe: Slip on a banana peel, and fall down	→	Example: We feel both pain and physiological arousal.	→	We evaluate the situation (falling down and feeling pain) and the arousal, and we label the emotion as anger (or perhaps embarrassment).

associated with increased levels of *norepinephrine* (noradrenaline), fear with increased levels of *epinephrine* (adrenaline), and depression with increases in *adrenocorticotropic hormone* (ACTH) (see Chapter 2). In contrast, joy is marked by decreases in ACTH and other hormones. This endocrine-system approach thereby links moods and emotions with concentrations of hormones. Behavior associated with the particular emotions is also subject to hormonal influences. For example, aggression is associated with increased levels of testosterone (Floody, 1983). Strong correlations do not establish causality, however. We cannot tell whether changes in hormone concentrations cause the emotions, the emotions cause the changes in hormone concentrations, or both depend on other kinds of changes (see Figure 11-10).

Cognitive Approaches to Emotion

Schachter and Singer: Arousal, Cognition, and Emotion

Stanley Schachter and Jerome Singer (1962) developed a **two-component theory of emotion,** which includes a physiological component and a cognitive one (see Figure 11-11). The first component is *physiological arousal*, which can be caused by any number of things, such as psychoactive drugs or situational stimuli (e.g., a sudden surprise). The second component, which is cognitive, is how the person *labels* that physiological arousal. According to Schachter and Singer, the label determines the emotion we feel. Thus, people who are aroused and who believe that the appropriate label for the arousal is happiness will feel happy; people who are aroused and who believe that the appropriate emotion label is anger will feel anger. To

two-component theory of emotion a theory asserting that particular emotions have two parts: a feeling of physiological arousal in response to a stimulus, and the cognitive labeling of the physiological arousal as a particular emotion

Figure 11-12
Arnold and Lazarus's Theory of Emotion

Stimulus	→	Primary appraisal	→	Secondary appraisal
Environmental event or stimulus	→	Appraise the situation, and figure out possible outcomes of the situation.	→	Based on the primary appraisal, conduct a secondary appraisal to figure out (a) how to feel emotionally and (b) what to do about the situation.
Exampe: Slip on a banana peel, and fall down	→	Answer questions, such as the following, regarding possible outcomes: Have I been seriously injured so that I'll need to seek medical attention? Are other people watching who will think less of me for having tripped?	→	Based on the primary appraisal (e.g., "I haven't been seriously injured, but other people are watching me"), label the emotion as anger or perhaps embarrassment. In addition, figure out what to do about the situation (e.g., shout angrily about the idiot who left the banana peel on the floor).

Schachter and Singer, the arousal is the same in every case. What distinguishes the various emotions is how we label our arousal.

Follow-up research has shown that Schachter and Singer were partly wrong (see, e.g., Leventhal & Tomarken, 1986; Marshall & Zimbardo, 1979). For one thing, we can feel physiological differences in the kinds of arousal linked with different emotions. Still, the classic work of Schachter and Singer was important in developing an entire area of psychological theory and research.

Lazarus Versus Zajonc: The Relationship Between Emotions and Cognitions

Decades ago, Magda Arnold (1960, 1970) proposed that what and how we think about a situation partly leads us to feel emotions. Richard Lazarus (1977, 1984; Lazarus, Kanner, & Folkman, 1980) has since championed and expanded her point of view. According to Lazarus, we appraise a situation in stages: (1) In *primary appraisal*, we determine the possible outcomes of what is about to happen. For example, is the person approaching us about to beg for money, rob us, or start a conversation? (2) In *secondary appraisal*, we have to decide what to do. Given what

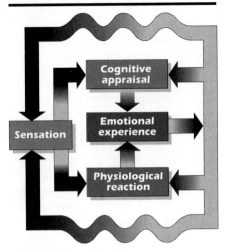

Figure 11-13
Emotional Feedback Loop
Our physiological reactions and our cognitive appraisals constantly and reciprocally interact with our perceived emotional experiences.

Once the emotions have been aroused—a sense of the beautiful, the excitement of the new and the unknown, a feeling of sympathy, pity, admiration or love—then we wish for knowledge about the object of our emotional response.

Rachel Carson

Describe an emotion-arousing event you have experienced. How has your own culture influenced each of the components of emotional experience for you?

we decided about the person coming toward us, how should we act? These appraisals continue as events develop. According to Lazarus, each of our appraisals of a situation determines what emotions we feel. Thus, cognition (thoughts regarding appraisals) precedes emotion (see Figure 11-12).

In contrast to Lazarus, Robert Zajonc (1980, 1984; Zajonc, Pietromonaco, & Bargh, 1982) has argued that cognition and emotion are basically separate. To Zajonc, emotion is basic and does not require any preceding cognitions. Zajonc and others note that emotions preceded thinking in evolutionary history. Therefore, cognitions do not have to precede emotions. Lower animals do not have to think in order to fear predators or to attack prey. For that matter, we humans often know how we feel long before we know what we think about a situation.

A Synthesis View

Many psychologists believe that we should stop trying to figure out one standard sequence for cognitive appraisal, emotional experience, and physiological arousal. Instead, the sequencing may be viewed as a continuous loop of emotional feedback (see Figure 11-13) (Candland, 1977). Although cognitive theories of emotion differ from one another in several ways, all of them agree that emotion and cognition are mutually dependent. Research on *state-dependent memory* supports this mutual dependence. That is, if you learn something while feeling a particular emotion, you are more likely to be able to remember that something when you feel the same emotion again later (Bower, 1981; see also Chapter 7). For example, if you study Chapter 11 in your psychology textbook when feeling happy, then you probably will recall the information from that chapter more easily when you are again happy than when you are feeling other emotions.

Cross-cultural Approaches to Emotion

Physiological and cognitive approaches to emotion narrowly focus on the emotional experiences of each individual. Another approach to the study of emotion takes a broader perspective. Batja Mesquita and Nico Frijda (1992) have conducted an extensive review of the anthropological literature and have a developed a theoretical framework for understanding emotion, based partly on theories by others (such as Lazarus). In their view, when we try to understand emotions, we must consider the following elements: *antecedent events* (events that came before the emotional reaction), *event coding* (interpretation of the event), *appraisal* (evaluation of the event and its possible outcomes), *physiological reaction pattern* (emotion-related changes in the body), *action readiness* (preparedness to respond to the emotion-arousing event), *emotional behavior* (actions following the experience of the emotion), and *regulation* (degree to which the individual tries to make the emotional reaction stronger or weaker). Each of these elements may be influenced by cultural context.

Using an alternative cross-cultural approach, James Russell (1991, 1995) drew two conclusions related to how people categorize emotions: First, not all people sort their emotions according to the basic categories often used by English speakers and other speakers of Indo-European languages. That is, in some cultures, certain ones of the so-called basic emotions may be omitted from the cultural categories for major emotions; in other cultures, additional emotions may be included in the major cultural categories of emotions. Second, despite these cross-cultural differences, there are many similarities across cultures in the emotions people identify, particularly in regard to emotions associated with particular facial expressions (e.g., Ekman, 1971, 1993; Ekman & Oster, 1979) and vocal expressions (e.g., Bezooijen, Otto, & Heenan, 1983). Also, most cultures do have some label for the basic emotions we identify. Although the range of expression for emotions and the boundaries between various emotions may differ, there are many similarities in how distinctive cultures describe human emotions.

PRACTICAL PSYCHOLOGY 11-1

Polygraphs ("Lie Detectors") and the Measurement of Emotion

Various psychophysiological measures have been used to register emotion, including heart rate, respiration rate, blood pressure, and *galvanic skin response (GSR)*, which is affected by sweating. A machine that measures many of these responses at one time is a **polygraph** (*poly-*, many; *-graph*, recording). The polygraph is often called a "lie detector." The idea underlying "lie detection" is to provide an objective measure of whether people are feeling emotional stress. The assumption underlying this idea is that a person who is lying will feel emotional stress and will therefore perspire more, breathe more rapidly, and so on.

Unfortunately, the assumption underlying measurement with a polygraph is not always correct. Polygraphs measure only stress reactions, not the reasons for these reactions. Thus, they will record stress reactions for reasons other than lying, and they will not record as lies statements made by people who feel no stress when telling lies. A common format for polygraph testing is that the polygraph operator asks a series of questions and compares psychophysiological responses to nonthreatening questions ("In what city were you born?") with answers to potentially threatening questions ("Did you cheat on your chemistry exam?"). A more effective format for the use of polygraphs involves questions that assess whether a person possesses information that only a guilty person would know (Bashore & Rapp, 1993).

How accurate are polygraphs? The results of controlled studies are not encouraging. Although professional interpreters of polygraphs have been found to be correct in identifying the guilty parties 76% of the time, these professionals have also labeled as guilty 37% of the innocent subjects they have tested (Kleinmuntz & Szucko, 1984). A review of more than 250 studies of the validity of interpretation of polygraph results shows similar findings (Saxe, Dougherty, & Cross, 1985; see also Ben-Shakhar & Furedy, 1990). Thus, interpreters of results are pretty good at recognizing guilty parties. However, they also identify disturbing numbers of innocent people as being guilty.

In the language of signal-detection theory (see Chapter 4), the hit rate is high, but so is the rate of false alarms. Results such as these indicate that polygraph tests, as they are now interpreted, are far from reliable. Because of the high number of false alarms on polygraph tests, results of these tests are no longer admissible as evidence of guilt in criminal prosecutions. How would you feel about taking a polygraph test if you were accused of doing something you did not do?

Sometimes, even liars tell the truth.

Moses ibn Ezra

The truth often does sound unconvincing.

Agatha Christie

How do psychologists approach trying to understand emotions? From an evolutionary perspective, psychologists observe that many of our emotions aid in the survival of our species. From a physiological perspective, the theories by James and Lange and by Cannon have each proven to be

polygraph equipment that records several (*poly-*, many; *-graph*, recording) different physiological responses (e.g., heart rate, respiration rate, blood pressure) at one time; often used for trying to measure emotional reactions

The idea underlying "lie detection" is to provide an objective measure of whether people are feeling emotional stress. The assumption underlying this idea is that a person who is lying will feel emotional stress and will therefore perspire more, breathe more rapidly, and so on. Unfortunately, not all people who show signs of stress are lying, and not all people who lie show signs of stress. Because of these problems, polygraph results are not generally admissible as evidence during criminal trials.

partly right and partly wrong. It is clear that our brains, our endocrine systems, and our autonomic nervous systems are related to our emotional reactions, but it is not now clear just how these physiological systems and our emotions interact causally. Cognitive theorists have proposed various sequences for cognitive appraisal, emotional experience, and physiological arousal, and each of these sequences may be true in some situations but not in others. Rather than specify one standard sequence for emotional reactions, it seems more accurate to say that our emotions, our thoughts, and our physiology interactively influence one another. Cross-cultural theorists observe that there are some universal categories of emotion, but there are also some culture-specific categories of emotion. Also, many of the ways in which we experience emotions are influenced by the cultural context in which we experience those emotions. Polygraphs are useful in detecting emotional reactions, but they do not accurately indicate whether a person is telling the truth or a lie.

HOW DO PEOPLE EXPRESS EMOTIONS?

Culture and Emotional Expression

Cross-cultural researchers such as Paul Ekman and his colleagues (e.g., Ekman, 1971; Ekman & Oster, 1979) have found great similarity of facial expressions across cultures. Researchers studied the ability of tribal New Guineans to recognize facial expressions in photographs of Westerners (Ekman & Friesen, 1975).

MINILECTURE
Facial Expression of Emotion
(Ch 16)

In the studies by Ekman and his colleagues, both adults and children were quite accurate in recognizing expressions of happiness (Figure 11-5a), sadness (Figure 11-5b), anger (Figure 11-5c), disgust (Figure 11-5d), surprise (not depicted), and fear (not depicted). Americans were also fairly accurate in recognizing New Guinean expressions. The tribe members had had almost no previous contact with Westerners, yet their facial expressions and judgments of facial expressions were very similar to those of people in the United States. In all cases, accuracy was greatest for happiness and lowest for fear. This work was confirmed in Brazil, Chile, Argentina, and Japan (Ekman, 1984). Do your own findings agree with the findings by Ekman and his colleagues? Do you find it easy to identify the emotions of the New Guinean adults? How about the faces of infants?

Social Functions of Emotional Expression

Why do many psychologists believe that the expression of emotion seems to be built into our human physiology? Under most circumstances, we benefit from expressing our emotions. The expression of emotion serves at least four different social functions (Izard, 1989): (1) We can communicate our feelings to other people, even when we cannot communicate our thoughts (e.g., even infants, very young children, and speechless adults can express emotion across language groups). (2) We can influence how other people respond to us; for example, mothers respond in different ways, depending on their babies' facial expressions of emotion (Huebner & Izard, 1988; see also Figure 11-5). (3) We can use emotional expressions to make social interactions easier; for example, a smile can do a lot to "break the ice"—sometimes more than words. (4) We can encourage prosocial behavior. For example, our own emotional expressions (e.g., smiles) can affect other people's emotions. When those other people feel positive emotions, they are more likely to behave prosocially (Isen, 1987). In addition, it appears that our facial expressions of emotion may even influence the intensity of our own emotions (e.g., described in Zuckerman et al., 1981).

Whoever is happy makes others happy too.

Anne Frank

How do people express emotions? Across cultures, people express many of the basic emotions in very similar ways, although cross-cultural differences do exist. There are social benefits to being able to express emotions and to understand the facial expression of emotion.

We all know when we experience emotion, but there is considerable disagreement as to how we experience it. For example, Lazarus (1984) believes that cognition is the primary cause of emotion, whereas Zajonc (1984) does not. Mesquita and Frijda (1992) suggest that emotion is part of a complex that closely involves both cognition and behavior, as influenced by a person's cultural context.

In this chapter, we have considered motivation, emotion, and some of the links between the two. These two constructs are very closely linked to a third one, which in large part determines the kinds of emotions a person experiences. This third construct is personality, which we consider in the next chapter.

SUMMARY

How Did Early Psychologists Explain Motivation? *318*

1. The study of *motivation* considers questions of motivational direction, initiation, intensity, and persistence.
2. Early explanations of motivation focused on *instincts* (inherited, species-specific typical patterns of behavior) and on *drives*, sources of energy that must be reduced. Both explanations proved unsatisfactory.

How Does Human Physiology Influence Human Motivation? *319*

3. Physiological approaches to motivation (homeostatic-regulation, opponent-process, and arousal theories) study how motivation relates to the brain, the autonomic nervous system, and the endocrine system.

4. *Homeostatic regulation* is the tendency of the body to maintain a state of balance. A negative-feedback loop tells us when our physiological needs, such as for food or sex, are satisfied.
5. The hypothalamus (located in the brain) is essential to the experience of hunger. The body monitors the levels of lipids and of glucose in the bloodstream, and then it sends signals to start or to stop eating, based on those levels.
6. Sexual motivation is affected by the hypothalamus, which acts through the pituitary gland to produce and release sexual hormones such as androgens and estrogens.
7. Human sexual behavior is controlled partly by *sexual scripts*. A minority of individuals seem to be biologically predisposed toward homosexuality, although other factors contribute to the expression of sexual orientation.
8. *Opponent-process* theory explains how an addictive drug or

habit, started in order to achieve a "high," becomes a habit to avoid a "low." When we feel the effects of a motivational source, we then experience an opposing force—slower to start, slower to stop—that tends to bring us back to baseline.

9.   According to the Yerkes–Dodson Law, people perform most efficiently and creatively when their level of *arousal* is moderate. The ideal level varies both with the task and with the person. High levels are helpful with simple tasks; lower levels are better for complex tasks.

How Do Psychological and Other Needs Influence Motivation?   327

10.   Personality theorists take a distinctive approach to motivation. For instance, Murray's theory of needs (e.g., the needs for achievement, power, and affiliation) emphasizes the role of personality in motivation. David McClelland has studied in depth the need for achievement. Maslow described a hierarchy of needs starting with physiological needs, proceeding through needs for security, for belongingness and love, for self-esteem, and finally, for self-actualization.

How Does Cognition Influence Motivation?   330

11.   Cognitive approaches to motivation show that people are most creative when *intrinsically motivated; extrinsic motivators* tend to undermine intrinsic ones unless extrinsic motivators can be internalized.

12.   We need to satisfy our curiosity and to feel competent and able to achieve our own goals (*self-determination theory* and *self-efficacy theory*). Moderately new and challenging stimuli are more motivating than are either totally familiar and easy ones or wholly new and overwhelming ones.

13.   *Goals* that are supported by *plans* are effective motivators.

What Emotions Do People Feel?   335

14.   Distinct from but closely linked to motivation is *emotion*, the motivational predisposition to respond experientially, physiologically, and behaviorally to particular internal and external variables. An example of the link between motivation and emotion is the *approach–avoidance conflict*, in which we simultaneously feel conflicting urges both to approach particular stimuli and to avoid them because these stimuli lead to both positive and negative emotions.

15.   Major emotions include joy (happiness), fear and anxiety, anger, sadness and grief, and disgust. These emotions can be charted to show relationships among them.

How Do Psychologists Approach Trying to Understand Emotions?   338

16.   Emotions serve an evolutionary function. For example, emotions may lead us to fight or to run away when facing an attack, depending on how the danger is perceived and which course of action is more likely to lead to survival.

17.   The James–Lange theory claims that bodily changes lead to emotion, rather than the reverse. Cannon and Bard disagreed, claiming that the brain controls emotional reactions.

18.   Cognitive theories differ in some ways, but they agree that emotion and cognition are closely linked. According to the Schachter–Singer *two-component theory*, we distinguish one emotion from another based on how we label our physiological arousal. Emotions and cognitions are linked, but we do not yet know which comes first. Lazarus believes that cognition precedes emotion, whereas Zajonc does not.

19.   Through cross-cultural studies, emotions may be analyzed in terms of antecedent events, event coding, appraisal, physiological response patterns, action readiness, emotional behavior, and regulation. It appears that although not all people categorize emotions in exactly the same way, there are still many similarities across cultures in the way that people express and identify emotions.

20.   We can assess emotional experience through psychophysiological means such as the *polygraph*, although the polygraph is not a reliable way to detect lying.

How Do People Express Emotions?   346

21.   The expression of emotion enables us to communicate feelings, influences how others respond to us, makes social interaction easier, and encourages prosocial behavior.

PATHWAYS TO KNOWLEDGE

Choose the best answer to complete each sentence.

1.   One assumption of the opponent-process theory is that
    (a)   motivations are quick to start and quick to stop.
    (b)   the brain seeks a balance (equilibrium) between positive and negative emotional states.
    (c)   emotions provide an opposing force against thoughts.
    (d)   habituation is inevitable with increased arousal.

2.   Sexual scripts are
    (a)   identical across cultures.
    (b)   the same with each potential sexual partner.
    (c)   mental representations of characteristic sequences of steps in sexual encounters.
    (d)   dependent on the amount of androgen and estrogen in our bodies.

3.   According to Maslow's hierarchy of needs, individuals
    (a)   may bypass no more than two levels in their quest for self-actualization.
    (b)   must satisfy self-esteem needs before achieving belongingness and love needs.
    (c)   always end their lives self-actualized.
    (d)   must satisfy esteem needs before seeking self-actualization.

4.   Edward Deci's research has suggested that extrinsic motivators produce the least hindrance to intrinsic motivation when the extrinsic motivators are
    (a)   stated up front so that the individual knows what he or she will be receiving.

(b) tangible and easily identifiable.

(c) received immediately after the task is accomplished.

(d) intangible, such as verbal praise or a smile.

5. A central tenet of Bandura's self-efficacy theory is that people's performance on a task will be influenced by
   (a) their beliefs about their ability to perform the task.
   (b) the level of intrinsic motivation involved in performing the task.
   (c) their level of extrinsic motivation.
   (d) the complexity of the task.

6. The James–Lange theory of emotion holds that the experience of fear
   (a) occurs when we subjectively attribute our bodily responses as fearful ones.
   (b) is biochemically produced in the hypothalamus.
   (c) is physiologically similar to the experience of rage.
   (d) causes fearful behavior.

7. According to which theory of emotion will the perception and labeling of our physiological arousal lead us to feel a given emotional response?
   (a) Cannon–Bard theory of emotion
   (b) James–Lange theory of emotion
   (c) Schachter and Singer's two-component theory of emotion
   (d) Lazarus's temporal-sequence theory

Answer each of the following questions by filling in the blank with an appropriate word or phrase.

8. The validity of the _____ relies on the assumption of a high correlation between physiological reactions and specific emotional states.

9. Individuals who identify themselves as having sexual interests in both sexes are referred to as _____.

10. A want or need that causes us to act is called a _____.

11. The _____-_____ _____ holds that the efficiency of performance of a task is an inverted U-shaped function of an individual's arousal level.

12. Negative feelings that a person experiences following the elimination or reduction of a substance to which the person is addicted are called "_____ _____."

13. _____ _____ is the tendency of the body to maintain itself in a state of equilibrium.

14. In his theory of motivation, David McClelland has cited the importance of an individual's need for _____.

15. If Ralph continued working even if he were no longer paid, we might assume that his work provided him with a high level of _____ motivation.

Match the following descriptions to the psychological phenomenon (either motivation or emotion) being described:

16. The prompting stimulus is generally observable

17. May interfere with an ongoing activity or even prompt a change in activity; does not energize, direct, or sustain an activity

18. Responses are directed outward toward interactions with the external environment

19. Rarely seems to be cyclical

20. Generally prompts action and is seen as active

    (a) motivation

    (b) emotion

Answers

1. b, 2. c, 3. d, 4. d, 5. a, 6. a, 7. c, 8. polygraph, 9. bisexual, 10. motivation, 11. Yerkes–Dodson law, 12. withdrawal symptoms, 13. Homeostatic regulation, 14. achievement, 15. intrinsic, 16. b, 17. b, 18. a, 19. b, 20. a

PATHWAYS TO UNDERSTANDING

1. Compare and contrast the nature of the need for achievement (theorized by McClelland) with the need for self-efficacy (theorized by Bandura).

2. Design a cross-cultural study of motivation. What are some of the confounding factors that will make the design of this study particularly difficult?

3. When advertisers want to motivate you to buy their products or services, they try to tap into basic human motivations. Describe a recent advertisement you have seen or heard. Tell how the advertiser was trying to manipulate your basic motivations to persuade you to buy the advertised product or service.

CHAPTER OUTLINE

How Do Psychodynamic Psychologists View Personality?

The Nature of Psychodynamic Theories

Psychoanalysis: The Theory of Sigmund Freud

The Neo-Freudians

How Do Humanistic Psychologists View Personality?

How Do Cognitive–Behavioral Psychologists View Personality?

Early Behavioristic Approaches

The Social-Learning Theory of Julian Rotter

The Social-Cognitive Theory of Albert Bandura

How Do Trait Theorists View Personality?

Theories Based on Individual Variations of Universal Personality Traits

Theories Based on Individual Sets of Distinctive Personality Traits

How Do Interactionist Psychologists View Personality?

How Well Does Your Personality Match Your Possible Choice of a Career?

How Do Psychologists Assess Personality?

Assessments Based on Psychodynamic Theories: Projective Personality Tests

Assessments Based on Trait Theories: Objective Tests

Evaluation of Personality Tests

CHAPTER

12

Personality

Two key figures in the psychological study of personality are Gordon Allport and Sigmund Freud. When Allport was 22 years old, he managed to arrange to visit with the celebrated psychoanalytic theorist, Sigmund Freud. Ironically, once Allport finally found himself in Freud's presence, he did not know what to say, so he mentioned that on the train to Vienna, he had observed a young boy with an irrational fear of dirt. The boy had constantly complained to his mother of the dirtiness of the train. Freud then looked at Allport and asked, "Was that little boy you?" Allport considered Freud's response misguided and even silly. For the rest of his life, he followed an approach to personality that was distinctly non-Freudian.

Actually, a psychodynamic theorist might argue as to whether Allport's conclusion was correct. Allport did seem to be greatly concerned with neatness and cleanliness (Faber, 1970). In any case, Allport's reaction to that incident gives us a little insight into Allport's personality.

Personality is an enduring disposition—"all those relatively permanent traits, dispositions, or characteristics within the individual that [give] some measure of consistency to that person's behavior" (Feist, 1990, p. 7). Personality psychologists have come up with several ways to study personality. Some personality psychologists have intensively studied the personalities of individuals over long periods of time. Others have developed and implemented various kinds of tests for measuring the full breadth of personality in many individuals. Still others have studied just a few isolated personality features across individuals.

Finding Your Way   **12-1**

Before reading about how personality theorists have described and explained personality, stop for a moment to consider your own personality. Jot down a list of some of your main personality characteristics. If you are having trouble thinking of your main personality characteristics, think about how people you know might describe your personality. List as many of your main personality characteristics as you can identify.

How do you think you came to have these characteristics? Do some of them seem to "run" in your family? Were you born with them? Did your family and early childhood experiences shape your personality? Did your friends, your schools, your community, and your culture shape you? Does your current environment continue to influence who you are, or do you pretty much have the same personality characteristics now that you had when you were a young adolescent? Do you make your own decisions regarding your own personality (e.g., deciding to become more cheerful, less impulsive, or more easygoing)?

Cherish forever what makes you unique, 'cuz you're really a yawn if it goes!

Bette Midler

Many psychologists have considered the questions you have just asked yourself, and they have come up with a variety of answers to these questions. Some psychologists have developed their own theoretical frameworks for understanding personality and for integrating their observations about personality. These various theories can be classified according to a few major different *paradigms*—approaches to understanding a particular phenomenon. This chapter considers some of the principal alternative paradigms of personality theory: psychodynamic, humanistic, cognitive–behavioral, and trait, as well as interactionist. Within a given paradigm, the various theories share common elements that tie them into a common view of personality. To evaluate the merits of each paradigm, we use the set of criteria shown in Table 12-1. In the conclusion of the discussion for each of the paradigms, we use these criteria to evaluate each paradigm.

HOW DO PSYCHODYNAMIC PSYCHOLOGISTS VIEW PERSONALITY?

The Nature of Psychodynamic Theories

When most of us think about personality, we think about unchanging characteristics of people. To think of personality as a *dynamic* (changing) *process* requires bold thinking. Psychodynamic theories view these changes as occurring within a complex system of diverse sources of *psychic energy* within each person. Of course,

---

personality   the enduring dispositional characteristics of an individual that hold together and explain the person's behavior

TABLE 12-1

Criteria for Evaluating the Various Paradigms of Personality Theory

Although there may be as many ways to evaluate a paradigm as there are psychologists evaluating it, most personality psychologists probably would agree on the importance of the following set of criteria.

1. *Importance to and influence on the field of psychology*—How have the development of theory and research in the field been affected by this paradigm at various times?
2. *Testability*—Has the paradigm given rise to empirically testable propositions, and have these propositions, in fact, been tested?
3. *Comprehensiveness*—To what extent do the theories within the paradigm give a reasonably complete account of the phenomena they set out to describe or explain?
4. *Parsimoniousness*—How well do the theories in the paradigm explain the complexity and richness of the world in terms of a relatively small number of principles?
5. *Usefulness to applications in psychological assessment and psychotherapy techniques*—Can the theory be usefully employed by clinicians and other practitioners?

psychic energy is only a metaphor Freudians used to describe a hypothetical construct for explaining human personality; it is not an actual physical form of energy. According to psychoanalytic theory, each energy source pushes the person in a somewhat different direction. As we observe a person's behavior, we are watching the moment-by-moment workings of these multidirectional sources of psychic energy.

Because these sources of psychic energy push the person in many directions, they lead to *internal conflict*. For example, suppose that Mary feels a strong sexual attraction toward her employee, Joe. She also feels a strong wish not to be punished for expressing her sexual urges, and she may even feel morally outraged at her own urges.

In psychodynamic theories, *biological drives* (especially sexual ones) and other biological forces play a key role. Psychodynamic theories also emphasize *developmental processes* that underlie personality, particularly emphasizing formative processes that occur during early childhood. The biological and developmental characteristics of psychodynamic theories suggest another of the key features of these theories: *determinism*—the idea that our behavior is ruled by forces over which we have little control. Sigmund Freud, who first developed psychodynamic theory, emphasized determinism somewhat more than did **neo-Freudians**, the psychodynamically oriented theorists who followed Freud.

Psychodynamic theorists also emphasize the role of the **unconscious** (an internal structure of the mind that is outside the grasp of our awareness), although they do so in different ways. Freud gave more importance to the unconscious in controlling our behavior than did other psychodynamic theorists. Although each theorist described the unconscious as having some function, the various psychodynamic theorists defined the exact nature and importance of the unconscious differently.

Psychodynamic theorists have chiefly been clinicians. The data on which they have based their theories have tended to come from their *clinical observations* of patients. Clearly, the sample of people observed is not randomly selected: These people are seeking treatment for some kind of psychological problem. If the clinical observer then extrapolates from observations of people in the clinical setting to hypotheses about the rest of the population, the possibility of bias is obvious: The personalities and personality development of people in a clinical setting are not necessarily the same as those of other people. A further problem is that clinical

Conflict begins at the moment of birth.

Jean Baker Miller

neo-Freudian a psychodynamically oriented theorist who has based her or his own views and theories on those of Freud

unconscious the portion of the mind that lies outside of our awareness and that we cannot pull into our awareness

settings typically do not lend themselves readily to controlled observation or to rigorous experimentation.

To summarize, the various psychodynamic approaches share a common focus on dynamic processes, sources of changing psychic energy, conflicts, biological adaptation, developmental changes, deterministic and unconscious forces, and clinical observations. Next, we consider how these commonalities appear in a few of the distinct psychodynamic approaches.

Psychoanalysis: The Theory of Sigmund Freud

Sigmund Freud is considered to be one of the greatest thinkers of the twentieth century. Some psychologists consider his theory to be the most influential in all of psychology.

Organization of the Mind

Freud (1917/1963) believed that the mind exists at two basic levels: conscious and unconscious. In addition to *conscious thought* (of which we are aware) and *unconscious thought* (of which we are unaware), Freud suggested the existence of *preconscious thought* (of which we are not currently aware but which we can bring into awareness more readily than we can bring unconscious thought into awareness). Freud (1933/1964) also believed that the mind can be divided into three basic structures: the id, the ego, and the superego. The id and the superego are largely unconscious, and the ego is largely conscious (with some preconscious and unconscious components).

At the most primitive level, the **id** is the unconscious, instinctual source of our impulses, such as sex and aggression. The id is therefore also the source of the wishes and fantasies that arise from these impulses. The id functions by means of **primary-process thought,** which is irrational, instinct-driven, and out of touch with reality. We engage in primary-process thinking as infants and also later in our dreams and in Freudian slips of the tongue (see Chapter 5). During primary-process thinking, we accept content and forms of thought that we would reject during other thought processes. For example, during our dreams, we accept many illogical sequences of events and impossible situations.

It is our less conscious thoughts and our less conscious actions which mainly mould our lives and the lives of those who spring from us.

Samuel Butler

id a personality structure that is the unconscious, instinctual, and irrational source of primitive impulses

primary-process thought a form of thought that is unrealistic, unreasonable, and driven by instincts

At a time when physicists were exploring the laws of thermodynamics, Sigmund Freud (lower left) was developing his psychodynamic theory of personality, which emphasized the dynamic processes underlying personality. Many other influential psychological thinkers were stimulated by his views.

In his analysis of dreams, Freud also distinguished between the *manifest content* of dreams (the stream of events as we perceive them) and the *latent content* of dreams (the repressed impulses and other unconscious material that give rise to the manifest content). For example, the manifest content of a dream might be to seek refuge from a wild animal. However, the latent content of the dream might be the person's need to seek protection from savage impulses. Freud believed that the primary-process thinking of dreams disguises unacceptable impulses from the id.

Primary-process thinking serves some important functions. It allows for creative ideas that make new and even surprising connections. According to Freudian theory, primary-process thinking offers a way to fulfill some of the wishes that we cannot fulfill in our daily conscious lives. Through our wish fulfillment in dreams, we immediately satisfy the pleasure-seeking impulses of the id. This satisfaction reduces the psychic energy of the id's impulses, thus reducing internal tension and conflict. The psychic energy of the id operates in terms of the **pleasure principle,** focusing on the world as we might like it to be.

The **ego,** in contrast, operates on the basis of the reality principle. Through the **reality principle,** we respond to the real world as we truly perceive it to be. Thus, the ego is the region of the mind that makes direct contact with reality. The ego mediates between the id and the external world, determining how much we can act on our impulses and how much we must suppress our impulses in order to meet the demands of reality. In other words, the ego tries to find realistic ways in which to satisfy the id's impulses.

Each person's ego originally develops from the id during infancy. Throughout life, the ego remains in contact with the id, as well as with the external world. The ego relies on **secondary-process thought,** which is basically rational and based on reality. Through secondary-process thought, we make sense of the world, and we respond to it in a way that will make sense both to us and to others. As you try to make sense of the material in this textbook, you are engaging in secondary-process thought.

Freud's third structure is the **superego,** our internalized representation of the norms and values of our society. The superego emerges later than the id and the ego, largely through our identification with our parents. In fact, to some extent, the superego is an internalized representation of our parents. The superego acts as an internal authority figure, telling us what we can and cannot do. It is based on internalized societal rules.

The superego operates by means of the **idealistic principle,** commanding us to obey our internalized rules for conduct. Whereas the ego is largely rational in its thinking, the superego is not. The superego checks whether we are conforming to our internalized moral authority, not whether we are behaving rationally.

Stages of Psychosexual Development

Recalling that Freud's theory is *psychodynamic* (i.e., involving active processes of the mind), it makes sense that Freud proposed not only a set of personality structures, but also a psychological process through which these structures emerge. Specifically, Freud proposed that each individual's personality develops through a series of psychosexual stages of development. According to Freud, progression through each of these stages is essential to mature personality development.

Unfortunately, however, a person may be unable to progress normally through each of these stages. Occasionally, a person may become *fixated* at one psychosexual stage and unable to progress beyond that stage. In addition, sometimes, a person may face a traumatic or otherwise stressful situation (e.g., the birth of a sibling) and may *regress* (develop backwards—the opposite of *progress*) to an earlier stage of development. Table 12-2 identifies the Freudian psychosexual stages of development and notes some of the personality characteristics associated with difficulty in progressing beyond each given stage of development.

Conscience is the inner voice that warns us that someone may be looking.

H. L. Mencken

Describe a situation in which you felt a moral dilemma about how to act. Describe how you resolved the situation in terms of one or more Freudian personality structures (the id, the ego, or the superego) and its guiding principles.

pleasure principle the principle by which the satisfaction of impulses drives all of the functions of the id

ego a personality structure that is largely conscious and realistic in responding to the events in the world, while trying to satisfy the irrational and unconscious urgings of the id and the prohibitions of the superego

reality principle the principle by which the ego tries to adapt to the real world while still satisfying psychic forces of both the id and the superego

secondary-process thought a form of thought that is reasonable and realistic

superego a personality structure that is unconscious and irrational, based on the rules and prohibitions we have internalized from interactions with our parents

idealistic principle the principle by which the compulsion to obey an internalized set of rules and prohibitions drives all of the functions of the superego

TABLE 12-2

Freud's Stages of Psychosexual Development

Stages and substages	Characteristics associated with difficulty in progressing out of the given stage
Oral (normally occurs during the first two years after birth)	Likely to display many activities centered around the mouth: excessive eating, sometimes followed by dieting and then excessive eating again; excessive drinking; excessive smoking; talking to the point that others wish for ear plugs; and so on.
Oral eroticism	Sucking and eating predominate. Likely to be cheerful, dependent, and needy. Expects to be taken care of by others.
Oral sadism	Biting and chewing predominate. Tends to be cynical and cruel. Always looking to "bite your head off."
Anal (normally occurs during ages 2 to 4 years)	
Anal-retentive	Excessively neat, clean, meticulous, and obsessive.
Anal-expulsive	Tends to be moody, sarcastic, biting, and often aggressive. Also tends to be decidedly untidy in personal habits and is likely to have a room or an office with books and papers strewn all over it.
Phallic (normally occurs during ages 4 years to middle childhood)	Tends to be overly preoccupied with him- or herself. Often vain and arrogant and exudes an unrealistic level of self-confidence as well as of self-absorption.
Latency (middle childhood)	Demonstrates sexual sublimation and repression of sexual desires.
Genital (normal adolescence through adulthood)	Normal adult sexuality, as defined by Freud—i.e., traditional sex roles and heterosexual orientation.

Defense Mechanisms

Failure to progress beyond a given stage of psychosexual development (i.e., fixation) or the return to an earlier stage (i.e., regression) are two of the ways in which the ego attempts to resolve deep conflicts between the id's strong impulses and the superego's strong prohibitions. Sigmund Freud (1933/1964), along with his daughter Anna Freud (1946), suggested that fixation and regression are just two of several ways in which we respond to conflicts between the id and the superego. According to Sigmund and Anna Freud, people use **defense mechanisms** to protect themselves from unacceptable thoughts and impulses. The goal of these defense mechanisms is to protect the ego from having to deal with information that frightens the ego (e.g., the aggressive impulses of the id) or that causes anxiety for the ego (e.g., the irrationally strict prohibitions of the superego). In addition to fixation and regression, there are eight other main defense mechanisms:

- *Denial*—occurs when our minds prevent us from consciously acknowledging or giving attention to our sensations and perceptions about unpleasant, unwanted, or threatening situations or events; for instance, families of alcoholics may deny perceiving all the obvious signs of alcoholism surrounding them.

- *Repression*—occurs when we unknowingly block from consciousness any unacceptable or potentially dangerous impulses emanating from the id; for instance, an adolescent girl may have repressed her memory of having been sexually molested when she was a child.

- *Projection*—occurs when we attribute our own unacceptable and possibly dangerous thoughts or impulses to another person; for instance, people who are attracted to pornography may become very active in local antipornography associations.

defense mechanism the means by which the ego protects itself from unacceptable thoughts (from the superego) and impulses (from the id)

According to Freud's theory of psychosexual development, the most important crisis of early childhood occurs during the phallic stage of development. During this stage, the child experiences the Oedipal conflict, in which the child starts to feel romantic feelings for the parent of the opposite sex. According to Freud, in the Oedipal conflict, a boy feels sexual desire for his mother but fears the fury of his father. The conflict is named for the Greek myth in which Oedipus, who had long been separated from his parents and therefore did not recognize them, killed his father and married his mother. Similarly, Freud presumed that girls would experience an Electra conflict, in which they would desire their fathers but would fear the jealous rage of their mothers. The Electra conflict was named for the myth of Electra, who despised her mother for having cheated on and killed her husband, Electra's father.

■ *Displacement*—occurs when we redirect an impulse away from the person who prompts the impulse and toward another person who is substantially less threatening than the one toward whom the impulse was originally directed; for instance, a young boy who has been harshly punished by his father would like to lash out vengefully against the father, but the boy's ego recognizes that he cannot attack such a threatening figure, so instead, he may become a bully and attack helpless classmates.

■ *Sublimation*—occurs when we transform the psychic energy of unacceptable impulses into acceptable and even admirable behavioral expressions; for instance, an artist may rechannel sexual energy into creative products that are valued by the society as a whole.

■ *Reaction formation*—occurs when we transform an unacceptable impulse or thought into its opposite; for instance, a son might hate and envy his father because his father has sexual access to his mother, but the son cannot consciously admit feeling envious, so the son consciously seems to adore his father.

■ *Rationalization*—occurs when we avoid threatening thoughts and explanations of behavior by replacing them with nonthreatening ones; for instance, a woman who is married to a compulsive gambler may justify (rationalize) her husband's behavior by attributing it to his desire to win a lot of money because of his great concern for the financial well-being of the family.

■ *Identification*—occurs when we feel intense fear of and intense anger toward another person, whom we perceive as powerful; we then seek to identify with the powerful person, fusing our own identity with that of the powerful person; for instance, a young girl whose mother is frequently physically abusive may both fear and hate her mother, but instead of expressing these feelings, she identifies with her mother's power, merging her own identity with her mother's.

Choose two of the Freudian defense mechanisms that you may have observed in your own behavior. Explain how you have used each of them.

Freud's Case Studies

As mentioned earlier, Freud used a clinical case-study approach for developing his theory. His particular approach was *intensive:* Freud would take a single case and study it in great, analytical detail. His analyses were also *qualitative:* Freud did not

In your opinion, why did Freud's psychodynamic theory of personality prompt some theorists to follow him and others to diverge from him?

try to quantify any aspect of the case studies. Other theorists and researchers have used the case-study approach to gain information that is extensive (using many cases) and quantitative (measuring amounts of particular variables).

The Neo-Freudians

Freud's work inspired many people to follow his views and many to react against his ideas. Freud's enormous influence prompted many theorists to create their own theories (see, e.g., Sternberg & Berg, 1992). In general, the neo-Freudians placed more emphasis on the ego and less on the id than did Freud. They also shifted the attention of psychologists more toward conscious processing and away from unconscious processing. The neo-Freudians also deemphasized the role of sexuality and of biology. The shift away from the id, from unconscious processing, and from biological forces also signalled a shift away from extreme Freudian determinism. Instead, the neo-Freudians more strongly emphasized the role of the ego in allowing individuals to control their own lives. The neo-Freudians also highlighted the role of socialization in the development of the individual's personality.

The Individual Psychology of Alfred Adler

Alfred Adler, one of Freud's earliest students, was also one of the first to break with Freud and to disagree with many of Freud's views. For example, Adler did not accept Freud's view that people are victimized by competing forces within themselves. Instead, Adler believed that all psychological phenomena within the individual are unified and consistent among themselves. Adler also believed that people's vision of the future shapes their actions at least as much as do their experiences in the past. You might then wonder why people sometimes seem to behave inconsistently or unpredictably. To Adler, these apparently inconsistent behaviors can be understood when viewed as being consistently directed toward a single goal: *superiority.*

According to Adler, all of us strive for superiority by attempting to become as competent as possible in whatever we do. This striving for superiority gives meaning and coherence to our actions. Unfortunately, however, some of us feel that we cannot achieve superiority. If we dwell on perceived mistakes and feelings of inferiority, we may come to develop an **inferiority complex,** organizing our lives around these feelings of inferiority.

It is easier to fight for one's principles than to live up to them.

Alfred Adler

inferiority complex a maladaptive personality structure in which we organize our lives around feelings of inferiority, based on perceived mistakes and failings

Is the reason for the success of Alec and Billy Baldwin their constant striving for superiority? According to neo-Freudian Alfred Adler (right), each of us constantly tries to become—and to appear—as competent as possible in all of our actions.

The Analytical Psychology of Carl Jung

Like Freud, Carl Jung believed that the mind can be divided into conscious and unconscious parts. However, Jung's view of the unconscious part differed sharply from Freud's view. Jung referred to one layer of the unconscious as the personal unconscious. The **personal unconscious** includes repressed memories and current experiences that are perceived below the level of consciousness. Each person's unique personal unconscious comes solely from his or her own experiences.

Jung referred to a second layer as the **collective unconscious**. This level contains memories and behavioral predispositions that we have inherited from our distant human past. According to Jung, humans have a common collective unconscious because we have the same distant ancestors. Thus, our common ancestral heritage provides each of us with essentially identical shared memories and tendencies.

Across space and time, people tend to interpret experiences in similar ways because of common **archetypes**—inherited tendencies to perceive and act on things in particular ways. Jung found support for the existence of archetypes in the collective unconscious by observing cross-cultural similarities in myths, legends, fairytales, religions, and even cultural customs.

Jung believed that certain archetypes, including the following ones, have evolved in ways that make them particularly important in people's lives: (a) the *persona*—the part of our personality that we show the world, the part that we are willing to share with others; (b) the *shadow*—the part of us that embraces our frightening, hateful, and even evil aspects, which we hide not only from others, but also from ourselves; (c) the *anima*—the feminine side of a man's personality, which shows tenderness, caring, compassion, and warmth toward others, and which is based on emotions; and (d) the *animus*—the masculine side of a woman's personality, the more rational and logical side of the woman. Other archetypes in our collective unconscious include the great mother, the wise old man, the hero, and the villain. What are some traditional stories that you know, which include one or more of these archetypes?

The Ego Psychology of Erik Erikson

Neo-Freudian Erik Erikson differed from Freud and from Jung largely by his turning his attention away from the unconscious mind. Erikson helped shift psychological thinking from emphasizing the role of the unconscious mind (id) to em-

Carl Jung was once considered the intellectual successor to Freud. When Jung increasingly disagreed with Freud's ideas, his relationship with Freud broke off, after which Jung went into a long period of depression. After he recovered, he developed his own views of personality, which were clearly distinguished from those of his former mentor.

personal unconscious the part of the unconscious mind that includes the person's distinctive repressed memories and personal experiences

collective unconscious according to Jungian theory, the part of the unconscious mind that contains memories and behavioral predispositions that all humans share because of our common ancestry

archetype inherited tendency to perceive and act in certain ways, common to all

Fairy tales from around the world include many of the archetypical characters that Jung described. Depicted here is a [non-Western cultural] tale in which the archetypical man and woman are planning a wonderful life together. However, it is a fantasy: The man, Shah Jahan (1629–1658), ordered the building of the Taj Mahal in memory of his beloved deceased wife, Arjumand Banj Bagam, called Muntaz Mahal, or Chosen One of the Palace.

Erik Erikson (top right) was trained as a psychoanalyst and was psycho-analyzed by Anna Freud, Sigmund's daughter (top left). Like Anna Freud, Erikson placed much more importance on the role of the ego than did Sigmund Freud or many other neo-Freudians. According to Erik Erikson, our personality continues to develop across the life span, even into old age as shown in the remaining photos below.

Karen Horney (left) believed that what women really want are the privileges that the culture gives to men but not to women (Horney, 1939). Her own career was delayed until a German university was willing to admit women to study medicine. The young women (right) meet expectations that differ sharply from Western expectations regarding what women are supposed to do.

phasizing the role of the conscious mind (ego). Erikson viewed the ego as doing much more than mediating among the id, the superego, and the real world. In fact, Erikson considered the ego to be the basis for establishing our individual identity. In addition, Erikson's (1963, 1968) view of personality development encompassed the entire life span (see Chapter 3), rather than just childhood. The psychosocial stages proposed by Erikson are trust versus mistrust (early infancy), autonomy versus shame and doubt (about ages 1–3 years), initiative versus guilt (about ages 3–6 years), industry versus inferiority (childhood), identity versus role confusion (adolescence), intimacy versus isolation (early adulthood), generativity versus stagnation (middle adulthood), and integrity versus despair (late adulthood).

We call the unconscious "nothing," and yet . . . The thought we shall think, the deed we shall do, even the fate we shall lament tomorrow, all lie in our unconscious today.

Carl Gustav Jung

The Psychoanalytic Theory of Karen Horney

Although Karen Horney was trained in the psychoanalytic tradition, she later broke with Freud in several key respects. Horney (1937, 1939) believed that Freud's view of personality development was very male oriented, and that his concepts of female development were inadequate. Horney believed that *cultural variables* rather than *biological variables* are the fundamental basis for the development of personality. She argued that the psychological differences between men and women are not the result of biology or anatomy. Rather, they result from cultural expectations for each of the two genders.

The great question . . . which I have not been able to answer, despite my thirty years of research into the feminine soul, is "What does a woman want?"

Sigmund Freud

The essential concept in Horney's theory (1950) is that of basic anxiety in a hostile world. *Basic anxiety* is a feeling of isolation and helplessness in a world conceived as being potentially hostile, due to the competitiveness of modern society. Horney (1937) suggested that we can reduce our basic anxiety by moving toward, against, or away from other people: We move toward other people by showing affection and submissiveness. We move against people by being aggressive, striving for power, prestige, or possessions. We move away from other people by withdrawing from people or simply by avoiding them altogether.

Table 12-3 evaluates psychodynamic research as a whole, using the criteria specified at the outset of this chapter.

TABLE 12-3
Evaluation of the Psychodynamic Paradigm

Criterion	Evaluation
1. Importance to and influence on the field of psychology	This paradigm has spawned, at least indirectly, extensive research to test theories that developed within the paradigm, as a response to it, or even as a reaction against it. Freud, the first major psychodynamic theorist, is often viewed as the seminal thinker in the psychology of personality. No other psychologist's influence has lasted as long as his. Even today, many clinical psychologists (especially psychiatrists) are loyal adherents to Freudian or neo-Freudian perspectives.
2. Testability of its propositions	On this criterion, psychodynamic theories would not rate high, with a relatively small number of experimental investigations. The many case studies tend to be open to various alternative interpretations.
3. Comprehensiveness in accounting for psychological phenomena	The theories are variable regarding the extent to which they give a reasonably complete account of personality phenomena. Freud's theory was comprehensive, as were Adler's and Erikson's, but many other neo-Freudian theories (e.g., Horney) were much less so. All of the psychodynamic theories were generated largely from work with patients who presented adjustment problems, so they may not explain personality in normal persons who have only the usual share of problems.
4. Parsimoniousness of its model of psychological phenomena	In relation to other theories of personality, the psychodynamic ones place in the middle of the range.
5. Usefulness to applications in (a) psychological assessment and (b) psychotherapy techniques	(a) As the text indicates, the *Thematic Apperception Test*, the *Rorschach Inkblot Test*, and other projective tests have arisen from psychodynamic theory. (b) Its extensive influence on psychotherapy is considered in depth in Chapter 14.

How do psychodynamic psychologists view personality? Psychodynamic theories emerged from clinical case studies of individuals. Psychodynamic theorists view personality as a dynamic process, in which a person's early childhood experiences shape the individual's psychosexual development, thereby determining personality in later life. Freud viewed personality as chiefly based on unconscious internal conflicts among the structures of the id, the ego, and the superego. Neo-Freudians put more emphasis on conscious processes involving the ego. Each neo-Freudian theorist devised a distinctive variation of psychodynamic theory, based on Freud's theoretical foundation.

HOW DO HUMANISTIC PSYCHOLOGISTS VIEW PERSONALITY?

Humanists have reacted strongly against the psychodynamic emphasis on determinism and on the importance of the unconscious. Instead, humanists emphasize self-determination and the role of the conscious mind. Humanists share a common view of humans: Unlike other living organisms, we are future oriented and purposeful in our actions. To a large extent, we can create our own lives and shape our own destinies, rather than allowing ourselves to be tossed and turned by inexplicable forces outside our conscious grasp. Although humanists differ widely in their particular beliefs, the core ideas of humanism are well represented in the views of Carl Rogers and of Abraham Maslow (see Chapter 11).

Carl Rogers's *person-centered* approach to personality strongly emphasizes the self and each person's perception of self. In fact, Rogers puts the self at the center of his **self theory** of personality. Reality is what the self defines as reality, not some unknowable objective set of things and events outside the self. Each person's conception of self begins in infancy and continues to develop throughout the life span. This **self-concept** embraces all the aspects of the self that the person perceives, whether or not these perceptions are accurate or are shared by others. In addition, each person has an **ideal self,** those aspects of the self that the person would like to have or to show.

Rogers strongly influenced psychological thinking by suggesting that greater similarity between the self-concept and the ideal self indicates better psychological adjustment (Rogers, 1959, 1980). According to Rogers, a key to self-acceptance (a close match between ideal self and self-concept) is feeling **unconditional positive regard** from one or more loved ones. When positive regard (warm feelings of affection and esteem) is conditional, the person may have more difficulty matching the ideal self (which meets the conditions) with the self-concept (which may not meet those conditions).

Like Abraham Maslow, Rogers (1961a, 1980) believed that all people strive toward self-actualization. To Rogers (1978), people have within them the power to make themselves whatever they want to be, if only they choose to use this self-actualizing power. Self-actualizing persons have at least five characteristics:

1. They constantly grow and evolve.
2. They are open to experience, avoid defensiveness, and accept experiences as opportunities for learning.
3. They trust themselves, although they seek guidance from other people. They make their own decisions rather than strictly following what others suggest.
4. They have achieved unconditional acceptance from at least some others, which allows them to free themselves from the need to be well liked by all. Given this freedom, they still try to achieve harmonious relationships with other people.
5. They live fully in the present, rather than focusing either on past successes or failures or on future possibilities.

To these characteristics, Maslow might have added that self-actualizers value genuineness in themselves and in others, they enjoy their own company, and they form and follow their own system of beliefs and values, while considering both their own needs and the needs of others.

Table 12-4 evaluates the humanistic paradigm in terms of the five basic criteria being used in this chapter.

How do humanistic psychologists view personality? According to humanistic psychologists, each individual is able consciously to shape her or his own personality, without being tossed and turned by unconscious forces, by cruel external forces, or by other controlling influences outside the person's control. Each person strives to be the best person she or he is capable of becoming, and this self-actualization process is enhanced when the individual feels unconditional positive regard from key persons in the life of the individual.

I am not at all the sort of person you and I took me for.

Jane Welsh Carlyle

I change myself, I change the world.

Gloria Anzaldúa

How do humanistic theories differ from psychodynamic theories?

self theory a humanistic theory of personality, in which the person's match between the perceived ideal self and real self is considered central to personality

self-concept all aspects of the self that a person perceives, which may be accurate or inaccurate and may be commonly perceived by other persons as unique

ideal self all aspects of the self that a person ideally would like to perceive as characterizing the self

unconditional positive regard interpersonal feelings of acceptance, affection, appreciation, or esteem, which are not based on any conditions that the object of regard must meet

TABLE 12-4

Evaluation of the Humanistic Paradigm

Criterion	Evaluation
1. Importance to and influence on the field of psychology	The paradigm has generated even less empirical research than has the psychodynamic paradigm. Still, its messages continue to be relevant: Focus on individuals, on personal choices and opportunities to control fate, and on striving toward self-actualization.
2. Testability of its propositions	Because humanists assert the inseparability of experimenter and experimentee, humanistic theories are, by definition, almost untestable. In addition, humanists' predictions have seldom been operationally defined with sufficient precision to generate experimental tests.
3. Comprehensiveness in accounting for psychological phenomena	Although this paradigm deals with some aspects of human nature, such as the need for self-actualization, or the potentials that lie within us, it leaves a lot unsaid. When compared with the more exhaustive taxonomy of human personality shown in Freud's theory or in the trait theories, it lacks comprehensiveness.
4. Parsimoniousness of its model of psychological phenomena	These theories are reasonably parsimonious.
5. Usefulness to applications in assessment and (a) psychological assessment and (b) psychotherapy techniques	(a) Humanists tend to be averse to assessments because tests focus on assigning the client a static set of labels, rather than concentrating on the person's ever-evolving potential for further development. Even the act of giving the test is seen as unduly increasing the apparent distance between therapist and client. (b) Though these theories strongly influenced psychotherapy during the 1960s and early 1970s, they are somewhat less influential today.

What are some of the ideas from behaviorism and from cognitive psychology that may help us to understand personality?

HOW DO COGNITIVE–BEHAVIORAL PSYCHOLOGISTS VIEW PERSONALITY?

Cognitive–behavioral approaches to personality try to answer these questions: (1) How do people behave? (2) How do people think? (3) How do behaving and thinking interact to form an enduring, relatively consistent personality?

Early Behavioristic Approaches

Behaviorists try to understand people in terms of the way people act. Behaviorists either downplay or reject the thought processes that may come between stimulus and response, as the behaviorists believe that such processes are irrelevant to psychological study. Behavioral approaches to personality emphasize the explanation of observable behavior in terms of response to environmental events. These explanations usually embrace environmental contingencies (environmental outcomes that depend on—are contingent on—a person's behavior) that lead to various forms of behavior (Skinner, 1974).

We may be able to see how people develop adaptive personalities in response to patterns of reinforcement contingencies in the environment. How do apparently maladjusted personalities develop, though? According to behaviorist B. F. Skinner (1974), people can become maladjusted in several ways. One way is through reinforcement of antisocial behaviors. For instance, a class clown may be reinforced by receiving attention from the teacher and from fellow classmates; a bully may be reinforced by feeling powerful over others and by getting goods and services from the people being bullied. Another way that people can become maladjusted is through punishment of prosocial behaviors, as when an adult punishes a child for truthfully confessing to accidentally breaking a dish.

Behavioral psychologists have emphasized how environmental contingencies influence the development and maintenance of personality. In reaction against the behavioral approach, cognitive psychologists are very much concerned with processes going on in the mind. Cognitive–behavioral psychologists are concerned with the link between mind and behavior. Two such theorists are Julian Rotter and Albert Bandura.

The Social-Learning Theory of Julian Rotter

To Julian Rotter, behavior does not depend solely on external stimuli and reinforcements. Rather, what is important is the meaning of a given external stimulus or reinforcement for each person. Unlike the behaviorists, Rotter is interested in cognitive aspects of personality, not just behavioral ones. Rotter believes that behavior arises through the interaction between the person and the environment, not just through one or the other (Rotter, 1966, 1990; Rotter & Hochreich, 1975).

By focusing on the individual's perceptions of the environment, Rotter developed a key aspect of his theory: his notion of internal versus external locus of control (Rotter, 1988, 1992). Persons with an **internal locus of control** see a strong causal relationship between what they do and the results of their actions. Internals tend to take personal responsibility for what happens to them. If taken to an extreme, internal persons might even mistakenly blame themselves for events beyond their control. For example, if an extreme internal were laid off during an economic recession in his industry, he would likely feel personally responsible for the layoff and for becoming unemployed.

In contrast, people with an **external locus of control** tend to believe that the environment causes the outcomes that follow their own behavior. If taken to an extreme, externals would tend to blame others for the problems they themselves cause. For example, if an extreme external were fired because of her own lack of effort, she might still feel as though other factors (her boss's prejudice, co-workers' conspiracies, etc.) had caused the termination. Thus, internals believe that they have control over their own fate, whereas externals tend to see fate as controlled by luck, by destiny, or by other persons.

internal locus of control a personality orientation based on people's belief that they are largely able to control both what they do and the probable outcomes of what they do

external locus of control a personality orientation based on people's belief that the environment surrounding them is largely able to control both what they do and the probable outcomes of what they do

Julian Rotter (left) believes that human behavior is directed toward achieving recognition and status, dominance, independence, protection and dependency, love and affection, and physical comfort. If this drug addict (right) has an external locus of control, she believes that the problems in her life are caused by forces outside of her control, not as a result of her own actions, such as by her abuse of drugs.

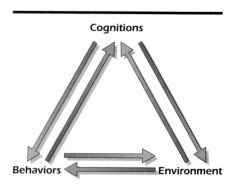

Cognitions

Behaviors   Environment

Figure 12-1

Albert Bandura and Reciprocal Determinism

Albert Bandura views personality and behavior as affected by—but not completely ruled by—external events over which people have no control. Bandura (1986, 1988) probably places more emphasis on the role of chance in people's lives than do some other theorists. He emphasizes the reciprocal nature of behavior and personal and environmental variables.

Thousands of studies have focused on Rotter's (1966) theory, including cross-cultural ones (Dyal, 1984). For example, cross-cultural researchers have studied both the Indian (Hindu) concept of *karma* and the Chinese concept of *yuan.* Both concepts suggest that people have little or no internal control over their own present destiny, although their moral actions in the present are likely to affect them in future incarnations (Kulkarni & Puhan, 1988; Yang, 1986).

Extreme views in either direction typically involve some distortions of the true causes of events, at least some of the time. Even so, having a more internal locus of control is associated with many positive achievement- and adjustment-related outcomes (see, e.g., Lachman, 1986; Phares, 1988, 1991). The tendency toward an internal locus of control leads a person to feel more able to do whatever must be done.

The Social-Cognitive Theory of Albert Bandura

To Albert Bandura, a crucial personal variable in personality is our sense of self-efficacy. **Self-efficacy** is the belief that we are competent to do things. This belief seems actually to lead to our being better able to do those things (Bandura, 1986, 1993; Zimmerman & Bandura, 1994; Zimmerman, Bandura, & Martinez-Pons, 1992). If I tell myself I cannot do something, I often will not try very hard to do it, with the result that I will never really learn how to do it well, if at all. As mentioned in the discussion of self-efficacy in Chapter 11, if I go ahead and try to do the thing, while constantly telling myself that I will not succeed, my negative expectations may get in the way of what I do. This outcome involves a negative, *self-fulfilling prophecy*, in which the very fact of predicting something about someone can make that thing come true (Rosenthal & Jacobson, 1968).

I thought I could change the world. It took me a hundred years to figure I can't change the world. I can only change Bessie. And honey, that ain't easy either.

Bessie Delany

More broadly, Bandura's theory addresses the *interaction* between how we think and how we act. Bandura's model of **reciprocal determinism** (1986) attributes human functioning to a two-way interaction in which personal variables (such as self-efficacy) influence the environment, and the environment, in turn, is influenced by behavior. That is, they both reciprocally determine one another (see Figure 12-1). For example, the decision to go to college will be affected by *personal variables*, such as motivation and the ability to succeed in academic work. This decision will also be affected by *environmental events*, such as parental encouragement and the funds to enroll. The result is *behavior*—going to college—which will in turn affect the opportunities the student has later in life, such as to pursue occupations that will be unavailable to those who choose not to go to college.

self-efficacy an individual's belief in her or his own competence to master the environment and to reach personal goals

reciprocal determinism an interaction in which personal variables and environmental variables both influence and are influenced by the behavior of the individual

Table 12-5 briefly evaluates the cognitive–behavioral paradigm in terms of its influence on theory and research and its testability, comprehensiveness, parsimony, and practical applicability.

TABLE 12-5

Evaluation of the Cognitive–Behavioral Paradigm

Criterion	Evaluation
1. Importance to and influence on the field of psychology	Perhaps because the theories are so testable, they have generated a great deal of research, both by researchers who theorize in this area and by other researchers who choose to test constructs based on these theories.
2. Testability of its propositions	Cognitive–behavioral theories are more testable than psychodynamic or humanistic ones. Theorists have tended to stick closely to their data in their theorizing. Thus, the data base for these theorists tends to be strong.
3. Comprehensiveness in accounting for psychological phenomena	These theories are less comprehensive than some of the competing views of personality. They say a great deal about the aspects of personality and behavior that follow directly from learning, but they do not clearly specify the dimensions on which people differ. By focusing on behavior, they have said somewhat less about the structure of personality than have other theories.
4. Parsimoniousness of its model of psychological phenomena	The theory of Bandura is very parsimonious, primarily because Bandura has adhered so closely to his data, and the theory of Rotter is only slightly less so. In general, these theories rate high on parsimony.
5. Usefulness to applications in (a) psychological assessment and (b) psychotherapy techniques	(a) Regarding assessment, Rotter's locus-of-control scale, as well as his scale for measuring interpersonal trust, have been widely used. However, these scales measure narrow bands of personality, not the whole thing. (b) The cognitive–behavioral approach has been highly generative of different methods of psychotherapy (see Chapter 14) and has been very influential in health psychology (see Chapter 15).

How do cognitive–behavioral psychologists view personality? According to behaviorists, personality is shaped entirely by environmental contingencies that arise as an individual interacts with the environment. Cognitive psychologists recognize that the individual's thoughts also play a role in personality development. According to Rotter, a major aspect of personality is whether a person perceives an internal or an external locus of control. According to Bandura, self-efficacy is instrumental to personality development and expression, and a person's behavior interacts with both personal variables and environmental events.

Describe some of your own personality characteristics in terms of a cognitive–behavioral theory.

HOW DO TRAIT THEORISTS VIEW PERSONALITY?

Whereas the theories discussed so far have emphasized various *processes* of personality, trait theories emphasize various *structures* of personality, known as "traits." **Traits** are stable sources of individual differences that characterize what a person is like. The origins of traits are attributed both to nature (hereditary characteristics or predispositions) and to nurture (environmental influences), but the emphasis on one or the other differs across various trait theories. According to some trait theorists, each of us is born with an individually distinctive set of traits—our nature. We may inherit this distinctive set of inborn traits, or at least a predisposition to develop such traits.

trait stable characteristic that distinguishes each person

TABLE 12-6

Temperament Characteristics

(After Thomas & Chess, 1977; Thomas, Chess, & Birch, 1970)

Characteristic	Question addressed
Activity level	How active are you?
Rhythmicity or regularity of biological cycles	How predictable is your pattern of eating, sleeping, and so on?
Approach/withdrawal	How outgoing are you?
Adaptability	How easily do you adapt your responses to a new situation?
Threshold of reactivity	How high a level of stimulation is needed to prompt a response in you?
Intensity and energy of reaction	How strongly and energetically do you respond to stimuli?
Quality of dominant mood	In what kind of mood are you most of the time?
Distractibility	How easily are you distracted from pursuing an activity in which you were already interested?
Attention span and persistence despite obstacles	How willing are you to continue to attempt an activity or to solve a problem in the face of obstacles?

For instance, Alexander Thomas and Stella Chess have noticed nine distinctive features of *temperament* (characteristic manners of thinking, acting, or reacting) that first appear in infancy and continue at least through adolescence (Thomas & Chess, 1977; Thomas, Chess, & Birch, 1970) (see Table 12-6). Although Thomas and Chess emphasize the importance of nature in the temperament each person shows during infancy, they also recognize the importance of nurture—each individual's interactions with the surrounding environment. In fact, to Thomas and Chess, the key determinant of personality is the match between an individual's temperament and the individual's environment.

For instance, Lupe, an outgoing, energetic, active, and adaptable child, is delighted that her family's home is attached to her parents' veterinary hospital, in which new sights, sounds, and events are constantly appearing and disappearing. Such a stimulating and unpredictable environment is distressing, however, to her older brother Jorge, who is less outgoing, energetic, and adaptable, and who prefers greater predictability and stability. Research indicates that both nature and nurture contribute to the development of our distinctive personality traits (e.g., described in Plomin, 1986, 1989). As adults, however, the effects of our early rearing environments move farther into our past, so that the effects of nature may actually increase with age (Plomin, 1989). That is, as the effects of early rearing environments decrease over time, other factors, such as the influence of heredity, contribute relatively more to individual differences among people.

Finding Your Way   **12-2**

Has your temperament been relatively stable across your life span? Using Table 12-6, report your own observations of your own temperament now. Next, ask someone (e.g., a parent, grandparent, older sibling, aunt, uncle, or family friend) who has known you since your infancy or at least before your adolescence to rate your temperament characteristics, describing your temperament both now and in your early life.

Recall the problems associated with constructive memory of events long past. To reduce the influence of constructive memory, do not tell the person who will answer these questions that you are interested in observing whether personality characteristics are stable across the life span. Emphasize the importance of giving truthful answers. Have the person answer in writing, so that he or she does not tailor his or her answers according to your facial expressions in response. (After the person has answered the questions, you may wish to describe your reason for being interested, but do not do so before the person answers the questions. You may even want this person to review your self-report observations with you after you have both completed these evaluations.)

Some trait theorists hold that personality traits are largely inborn and stable across the life span. Others believe that personality traits develop and change somewhat, although the predisposition to develop particular traits may still be present at birth.

Psychologists often distinguish between two basic kinds of trait theories of personality. According to some theories, all people have essentially the same set of traits, and people differ only in terms of how much they show of each trait. Traits are thus universal. According to other theories, people differ in the set of personality traits they have or at least in the importance of these traits to who they are. Traits thus can be particular to each individual.

Theories Based on Individual Variations of Universal Personality Traits

Some theories emphasizing universal traits try to specify the whole range of personality, suggesting a set of traits that all people possess. This set of traits is believed to characterize fully what people are like. Other theories deal with just a single trait, but in great depth. The following discussion deals with only a few of the many trait theories of personality.

The Factor-Analytic Theory of Raymond Cattell

Raymond Cattell has studied personality by using *factor analysis,* which identifies the essential variables underlying a wide array of individual differences. Cattell basically distinguishes two levels of personality traits: surface traits and source traits. **Surface traits** are what we usually observe as characterizing the differences among people. To Cattell, however, these surface traits are scientifically less interesting and important than are the source traits. **Source traits** are the underlying psychological dimensions that generate the surface traits. Cattell (1979) uncovered 23 source traits (16 main traits, e.g., high vs. low ego strength, submissiveness vs. dominance, social concern vs. unconcern, and naïveté vs. shrewdness; plus 7 questionable traits, e.g., conservatism vs. radicalism and group dependency vs. self-sufficiency) by performing factor analysis on numerous surface traits. This method of analysis uncovers sources of individual differences (the source traits) that underlie the observable scores (surface traits).

The Theory of Hans Eysenck

Hans Eysenck's (1952, 1981) theory of personality is as simple as Cattell's is complex. Eysenck argues that personality embraces just three major traits: extroversion, neuroticism, and psychoticism. These elements vary within each individual, along a continuum. The trait of **extroversion** contrasts people who are sociable, lively, and outgoing—*extroverts*—with people who are quiet, reserved, and generally unsociable—*introverts.* People high in **neuroticism** are moody, ner-

The greater part of our happiness or misery depends on our dispositions and not on our circumstances.

Martha Washington

What are the similarities and differences between trait-based approaches and other approaches?

The psychotic says two and two are five and the neurotic knows two and two are four, and hates it.

Gordon Gammack

surface trait one of many personality features that characterize differences among people

source trait one of a relatively few underlying psychological dimensions of personality that generate the numerous surface traits

extroversion a personality trait characterized by sociability, liveliness, and friendliness

neuroticism a personality trait characterized by sudden and unpredictable mood swings, nervousness, and irritability

vous, irritable, and subject to sudden and seemingly unpredictable mood swings. In contrast, emotionally stable people tend to be less fretful, more uniform in their behavior, and less subject to sudden mood swings. People high in **psychoticism** are solitary, uncaring of others, lacking in feeling and empathy, and insensitive. They are often quite detached from others in their interpersonal relationships.

The "Big Five" Model of Personality

Many personality theorists, including several non–trait theorists, have identified some of the same key personality characteristics in their theories. Arguably, the most widely accepted trait model for the structure of personality is the **Big Five theory of personality,** which recognizes the frequent recurrence of five personality traits across studies (especially factor-analytic studies) and even across theorists. The Big Five traits were proposed early on by Warren Norman (1963) but have since been championed by many other investigators (e.g., Costa & McCrae, 1992a, 1992b; Digman, 1990; McCrae & John, 1992; Peabody & Goldberg, 1989; Watson, 1989).

Although different investigators have given the Big Five different names, they generally have agreed on the following five characteristics as a useful way to organize and describe individual differences in personality. The descriptions following each of the characteristics depict someone rated high in these traits:

1. *Neuroticism* (see Eysenck's theory)—nervous, emotionally unpredictable, tense, and worried
2. *Extroversion* (see Eysenck's theory)—sociable, outgoing, fun-loving, and interested in interacting with other people
3. *Openness*—imaginative, intelligent, curious, artistic, and aesthetically sensitive
4. *Agreeableness*—good-natured, easy to get along with, empathetic toward others, and friendly
5. *Conscientiousness*—reliable, hard-working, punctual, and concerned about doing things right

Finding Your Way   12-3

Review the preceding list of five traits, and describe your own personality in terms of the Big Five traits. Rate yourself on a scale from 1 to 7 on each of the Big Five traits. How would you characterize your strengths and weaknesses, based on these ratings?

Although the Big Five model of personality enjoys widespread acceptance among many personality psychologists, some objections to the model have been raised. Jack Block (1995), for example, has pointed out two major problems with the Big Five model: (1) The methods of statistical analysis used to derive the theory have certain limitations (the nature of which goes beyond the scope of this book), and (2) the data from which the factors are derived often consist of nothing more than people's self-reports about their own personalities. Although Block has criticized some of the bases for trait models of personality, he does not criticize the fundamental notion underlying universal trait theories: He believes there is a particular set of personality traits, which all individuals possess, to a greater or lesser extent. In fact, Block (1981) has found consistency across the life span for two particular personality traits: *ego control* (a person's ability to control his or her impulsive behavior) and *ego resiliency* (a person's flexibility and responsivity to the demands of the environment).

psychoticism   a personality trait characterized by isolation, lack of caring for or about others, lack of feeling and empathy, and insensitivity

Big Five theory of personality   a trait theory suggesting that the five key personality traits are neuroticism, extroversion, openness, agreeableness, and conscientiousness

What aspects of your personality (if any) are not captured by the Big Five traits? How important are these aspects of your personality for influencing what you do?

Theories Based on Individual Sets of Distinctive Personality Traits

According to some theories of personality, there is no common set of traits, shared by all persons. This type of theory dates back at least to Gordon Allport (discussed in the chapter opener and in Chapter 10, regarding prejudice). The critical aspect of Allport's (1937, 1961) theory of personality is that much of personality is characterized by **personal dispositions** (traits that are unique to each individual). Although Allport also mentioned *common traits* (which are the same across individuals), he believed that much of what makes each of us who we are can be found in our personal dispositions rather than in our common traits.

Allport also believed that our various personal dispositions and common traits differ in importance for us. For example, many people possess **cardinal traits;** a cardinal trait is a single trait that dominates an individual's personality and behavior so much that almost everything the person does somehow relates back to this trait (Allport, 1961). For instance, self-effacing compassion may be a cardinal trait of the humanitarian Mother Teresa, a zany sense of humor may be a cardinal trait of the comic Robin Williams, and irreverent defiance of convention may be a cardinal trait of the television comedian and producer Roseanne.

Not everyone has a cardinal trait. However, all people do have **central traits,** which are highly important traits in their dispositions; typically, each person has about 5 to 10 of these traits. At the outset of this chapter, you listed your chief personality traits. These traits may be among your central personality traits. If you listed more than a dozen traits, however, some of these traits may be only **secondary traits,** which influence—but are not central to—your behavior. All people are said to have both central traits and secondary traits.

According to some theories of personality, although there is no universal set of personality traits that can be used to predict the behavior of all persons, each individual does have a distinctive set of personality traits, which can be used to predict the person's behavior across various situations. Daryl Bem and Andrea Allen (1974) have questioned this assumption. Instead, these two researchers have suggested that it may be a mistake to try to predict the behavior of all people all of the time, although it may be quite realistic to try to predict the behavior of some people some of the time. In their approach, Bem and Allen found that some people's behavior is consistent for some traits more than for other traits and that some people show greater consistency than do other people.

Table 12-7 briefly evaluates the success of the trait-based approach to understanding personality, based on the various criteria used for each of the personality paradigms.

How do trait theorists view personality? Trait theorists focus more on studying the structures and contents of personality—personality traits—than on studying the processes by which personality emerges and develops. Nonetheless, most trait theorists believe that both nature and nurture play a

personal disposition a trait that is unique to a given individual, according to Allport's theory of personality

cardinal trait a characteristic that totally dominates the personality and behavior of an individual; many persons do not have a cardinal trait

central trait a characteristic that stands out in its importance for the personality and behavior of an individual

secondary trait a personality characteristic that has some influence on behavior but that is not very important to the personality and behavior of the individual

TABLE 12-7
Evaluation of the Trait-Based Paradigm

Criterion	Evaluation
1. Importance to and influence on the field of psychology	This approach has generated quite a bit of empirical research. Only the cognitive–behavioral approach has equaled the trait-based approach in its ability to generate research. On the other hand, trait theories may be said to rely heavily on factor-analytic studies.
2. Testability of its propositions	This paradigm's testability is high: Most of the theories allow for fairly precise predictions, particularly as compared with psychodynamic or humanistic theories.
3. Comprehensiveness in accounting for psychological phenomena	These theories probably fare at least as well as those of any other paradigm in describing the breadth of personality. However, these theories say relatively less than others about the development of personality—how people come to acquire the traits they have.
4. Parsimoniousness of its model of psychological phenomena	The relative parsimony of these approaches depends on the theory being considered. For example, both Eysenck's theory and the "Big Five" are extremely parsimonious, but Cattell's theory is not.
5. Usefulness to applications in (a) psychological assessment and (b) psychotherapy techniques	(a) With regard to assessment, many of the trait theories have given rise to personality tests, some of which are widely used. (b) On the other hand, these theories have generated far fewer psychotherapeutic techniques than have the other kinds of theories. Perhaps this is because trait theories tend to focus more on static characteristics and less on dynamic processes.

The people who get on in this world are the people who get up and look for the circumstances they want, and, if they can't find them, make them.

George Bernard Shaw

role in personality development. Some theorists believe that all people have pretty much the same set of personality traits, but that people differ in terms of how much of each trait they show. Five of the traits that are widely accepted across theories are neuroticism, extroversion, openness, agreeableness, and conscientiousness. Other theorists believe that different people have altogether different sets of personality traits.

HOW DO INTERACTIONIST PSYCHOLOGISTS VIEW PERSONALITY?

Walter Mischel (1968) has criticized trait theories of personality by pointing out that even when people show particular traits on various tests of personality, they typically show little consistency of behavior across different situations. That is, their traits do not strongly predict their behavior across situations. In fact, the correlations between traits and any meaningful kind of behavior are low, around 0.30 (with 1.0 a perfect positive correlation). Mischel (1968; Mischel & Peake, 1983) has suggested that personality theorists should concentrate on the relations between situations and behavior, rather than on hypothetically stable traits.

Other researchers (Funder & Ozer, 1983) have tested Mischel's claim that situations more strongly influence behavior than do personality traits. Instead of correlating personality traits across situations, they have correlated situations across behaviors. How well could they predict behavior, based on differences in situations rather than on differences in traits? The correlation for predicting behavior based on situations was rarely over 0.30—roughly the same as the correlation Mischel found when predicting behavior based on traits. These researchers have argued, therefore, that situations are no better or worse than traits as a basis for predicting behavior.

Because neither situations nor a person's traits seem fully to explain people's actions, many psychologists have come to embrace an approach that considers both: Specifically, the **interactionist approach** emphasizes the interaction between the person and the situation. Actually, Rotter's theory, Bandura's theory, Thomas and Chess's theory, and some other theorists' approaches can be viewed as broadly interactionist. Even Mischel now views personality from an interactionist perspective.

The basic idea is simple: The correlations among traits or between traits and behaviors depend on the kinds of situations the person encounters. For example, to relate extroversion to happiness, the interactionist might suggest that extroverts will be happy if they are involved in frequent interactions with other people. However, extroverts will be unhappy if left to themselves most of the time.

Thus, the interactionist focuses on the interaction between the person and the situation (Bowers, 1973; Endler & Magnusson, 1976), not just on personality traits

PRACTICAL PSYCHOLOGY   12-1

How Well Does Your Personality Match Your Possible Choice of a Career?

Based on your own personality traits, to which kinds of careers would you be better suited? Here are some questions you might want to ask yourself:

1. Would you prefer a career in which you worked mostly alone (e.g., a laboratory researcher or a painter), or would you prefer to work directly with other people most of the time (e.g., a social worker or a teacher)?

2. Would you prefer to compete with others (e.g., a salesperson or a tennis player), to collaborate with others (e.g., a member of a research-and-development team or a dancing ensemble), or to work independently (e.g., a cabinet-maker or a sculptor)?

3. Would you prefer (a) to be responsible for organizing a project and giving orders to others regarding how they should carry out their work (e.g., a manager or a project leader); (b) to be responsible for carrying out specific instructions given to you by others (e.g., a bookkeeper or a baseball player); or (c) to be responsible for organizing and carrying out your own work, given only a deadline and rough guidelines for how to do your work (e.g., a writer or a teacher)?

4. Would you prefer to set your own standards for your performance, or would you prefer to have other persons give you clear and specific guidelines regarding what is expected of you?

5. Would you prefer to work in a job in which there were many deadlines and time pressures (e.g., a daily newspaper reporter, an entertainer, or a firefighter), a job in which there were few or no deadlines or time pressures (e.g., a store clerk or a construction worker), or a job in which there were occasional deadlines and some time pressures, but in which you had some leeway for meeting the job's demands (e.g., a construction supervisor or a store manager)?

6. What are some of the personality characteristics that you would consider important in your co-workers? What are some of the personality characteristics that you would consider to be intolerable in your co-workers?

7. How important is it to you to feel that your work is making an important contribution to individual people's lives? How important is it to you to feel that your work is making an important contribution to society in general?

Compare your answers to the preceding questions with your evaluation of your own personality. What aspects of your personality seem important for the way in which you answered the preceding questions? What other aspects of your personality, not addressed by the preceding questions, are important to your decisions regarding your choice of a career?

The best career advice given to the young is "Find out what you like doing best and get someone to pay you for doing it."

Katharine Whitehorn

interactionist approach   a view of personality that emphasizes the interaction between the person and the situation

Character cannot be developed in ease and quiet. Only through experience of trial and suffering can the soul be strengthened, vision cleared, ambition inspired, and success achieved.

Helen Keller

considered in isolation or on situations alone. In other words, the interactionist approach combines the trait-based approach with the behavioral approach. Interactionists believe we can predict people's behavior only if we consider both their personalities and the kinds of situations in which their behavior arises.

In evaluating each of the major theories of personality, we have considered how each theory may contribute to the development of personality assessments and to the development of psychotherapy techniques. In the next section of this chapter, we consider some of the personality assessments that have emerged from personality theory. In addition, it may be useful to think about how an interactionist approach to personality may be applied to the choices we make. For instance, in choosing our careers, we may wish to consider a match between our personality characteristics and the situations in which we potentially may find ourselves (see Practical Psychology 12-1).

How do interactionist psychologists view personality? Interactionists believe that personality emerges through the interaction of the characteristics of each individual and the situations in which the individual finds her- or himself.

HOW DO PSYCHOLOGISTS ASSESS PERSONALITY?

Both the psychodynamic approach to personality and the trait-based approach have led researchers to develop tests designed to measure important aspects of personality. Next, we consider some of the tests designed by psychologists using each approach.

Assessments Based on Psychodynamic Theories: Projective Personality Tests

Many assessment techniques based on the psychodynamic paradigm have tried to probe the unconscious. These tests are termed **projective personality tests** because they encourage individuals to express through the test stimuli their unconscious or preconscious personality characteristics and conflicts. Several projective tests based on psychodynamic theory have been used for assessing personality. The most well-known and widely used of these tests are the *Rorschach Inkblot Test* and the *Thematic Apperception Test*. Like most other projective tests, both of these tests are administered in a one-to-one situation, in which a psychologist interviews and observes the responses of one test-taker at a time.

The *Rorschach Inkblot Test*

In 1921, Hermann Rorschach devised the *Rorschach Inkblot Test*, which is still widely used today. Rorschach developed his test as a way of diagnosing psychopathology. Today, however, it is used more commonly for assessing personality across a broad spectrum of individuals. Clinicians who use the test believe that it helps them to explore patients' needs, conflicts, and desires (Exner, 1985; Rapaport, Gill, & Schafer, 1968).

The test consists of 10 symmetrical inkblot designs, each printed on a separate card. Five of the blots are in black, white, and shades of gray, and the other five are in color. (For an example of an inkblot similar to those in the Rorschach test, see

projective personality test a method of personality assessment based on the psychodynamic approach, which attempts to reach people's unconscious or preconscious personality characteristics and conflicts through their imaginative (primary-process) responses to test items

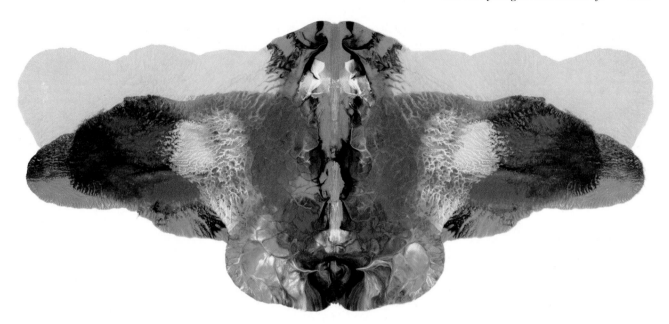

Figure 12-2
Rorschach Inkblot Test
One way of scoring this projective test is to consider the following four factors: location — *the place on the blot where the test-taker sees the image;* determinants — *the examinee's use of three principal characteristics in responding to the blot — form (F), human movement (M), and color (C);* content *of the descriptions — such subject matter as humans, animals, geography, sex objects or acts, and so on; and* popularity — *whether the individual gives responses that are unusual or otherwise outside the mainstream of responses.*

Figure 12-2.) Rorschach intentionally created each of the inkblots so that they would not look like anything in particular. However, when people look at the inkblots, they tend to see things in them, projecting their personalities into the test stimuli. The examiner carefully records how the examinee describes each blot. Typically, each examinee describes several different things in each of the blots. Although many different scoring systems have been devised for the Rorschach, the most widely used at present is John Exner's (1974, 1978, 1985; Viglione & Exner, 1983) "Comprehensive System," which considers the *location*, *determinants*, *content*, and *popularity* of the responses (see Figure 12-2).

The *Thematic Apperception Test*

Another widely used psychodynamic assessment tool is the *Thematic Apperception Test* (TAT) (Morgan & Murray, 1935; Murray, 1943b). In administering the TAT, the examiner presents the test-taker with a series of ambiguous but realistic pictures. (That is, the pictures show realistic drawings of people and objects in ambiguous situations — see Figure 12-3.) Test-takers are expected to project their own personalities into these pictures by describing what has led up to the scene in the picture, what is happening in the picture, and what will happen. *Apperception* refers to this projection of personal information into the stimulus that is perceived.

The TAT may further be scored for different kinds of needs and motivations (see Chapter 11), such as achievement motivation (Atkinson, 1958; McClelland et al., 1953) and power motivation (Veroff, 1957; Winter, 1973). The test has also been used for assessing the use of defense mechanisms. For example, Abigail Stewart (1982; Stewart & Healy, 1985) has used the TAT to find out how different defense mechanisms apply to various psychosexual stages of development. She has classified test-takers as showing characteristics of each of the psychosexual stages,

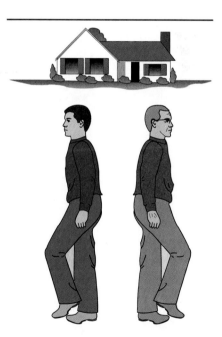

Figure 12-3
Thematic Apperception Test (TAT)
Henry Murray (1943) suggested that the examiner must consider six things when scoring the TAT: (1) the hero of the story; (2) the hero's motives, actions, and feelings; (3) the forces in the hero's environment that act on the hero; (4) the outcomes of the story; (5) the types of environmental stimuli that affect the people in the story; and (6) the interests and sentiments that appear in the story.

based on four aspects of each story: attitude toward authority, relations with other people, feelings, and orientation to action (Stewart et al., 1986).

Assessing Psychodynamic Tests

Some clinicians (e.g., Spangler, 1992; Stewart, 1982; Stewart & Healy 1989) take projective tests, such as the Rorschach and the TAT, very seriously. Others (e.g., Mischel, 1986) believe that these tests may lead clinicians to faulty decisions. Mischel has argued (1977, 1986) that clinicians interpret projective tests based on what the clinicians would like to see in the test data, not on what is actually implied by the test data. Some research has supported his view (see, e.g., Chapman & Chapman, 1969; Dawes, 1994).

Assessments Based on Trait Theories: Objective Tests

The trait-based approach has also led to the development of various personality tests. In order to grasp the wide range of traits expressed in normal and abnormal personalities, psychologists use so-called **objective personality tests,** which are administered to a large number of individuals, using standardized and uniform procedures for scoring. Most objective personality tests are paper-and-pencil tests that psychologists can give to more than one test-taker at one time.

The *Minnesota Multiphasic Personality Inventory*

The most widely used of the objective tests for assessing normal and abnormal personalities is the *Minnesota Multiphasic Personality Inventory* (MMPI) (Hathaway & McKinley, 1943; the more recent version of the scale is MMPI-2; see also Butcher et al., 1989). The MMPI and the MMPI-2 each consist of 550 statements covering a wide range of topics. Subjects respond to each of the statements as either *true* or *false* (Hathaway & McKinley, 1951, p. 28). For instance, a test-taker might be asked to respond to these statements:

I often feel as if things are not real.	T	F
Someone has it in for me.	T	F

Would you answer true or false to statements such as these? On an actual test, your responses would be compared to the answers of many other persons, to come up with a set of scores indicating various characteristics of your personality, as measured at the time of the test.

The MMPI has several strengths: First, the test is objectively scored, which avoids the problems of subjective scoring and interpretation associated with projective tests. Second, the scale has been widely used, so clinicians can use a wealth of data for interpreting and comparing scores. The test can also be used for assessing temporary, situation-related characteristics, as well as for assessing more enduring, stable ones. Third, the test offers several ways for clinicians to assess the believability (validity) of the results. Fourth, the scale covers a wide range of normal and abnormal behaviors and beliefs.

The MMPI also has some drawbacks. The primary drawback is that it is hard to know how to interpret responses to the MMPI. Test-takers may find it hard simply to respond "true" or "false" to items, feeling that such responses are incomplete. People may also try to second-guess the test designers and to answer in ways that will give particular impressions. Also, the MMPI measures only people's impressions of what they are like or of what they do with their time. These responses do not necessarily correspond to what they really are like or to what they actually do. Another criticism has been that both the MMPI and the MMPI-2 (although less so) were standardized using population samples that overrepresented Americans of European ancestry (Butcher & Williams, 1992; Graham, 1990). Hence, the

objective personality test   a method of personality assessment founded on the trait approach, which is standardized and normed based on a large number of individuals, thereby providing scores that allow for easy comparisons across individuals

tests may not adequately indicate the normal range of personality characteristics of individuals outside the United States or even of ethnic minorities within the United States (Greene, 1987; Lonner, 1990). (Further and more detailed criticisms are described in Helmes & Reddon, 1993.)

The *Sixteen Personality-Factor Questionnaire*

MINILECTURE
Trait Theories (Ch 17)

Many of the drawbacks of the MMPI also apply to other objective tests of personality. Raymond Cattell and his colleagues have devised a test that measures 16 of the personality factors Cattell identified: the *Sixteen Personality-Factor Questionnaire* (16PF; Cattell, 1982; Cattell, Eber, & Tatsuoka, 1970). This paper-and-pencil test asks people whether particular attributes characterize them and whether they do particular things. Separate scores are obtained for each of the 16 personality factors. Based on those simple trait scores, individual scores can be combined, using mathematical formulas, in order to obtain measures of what Cattell considers to be more complex traits, such as anxiety and independence. For example, the measure of anxiety is a combination of scores on six factors. According to Cattell, people who are anxious are easily upset, timid (shy), suspicious, apprehensive (worried), low in personal control, and tense.

Like the MMPI, Cattell's 16PF has been used extensively in other cultures. Cattell firmly believes in the universality of his test. Others, however, have found problems with the cross-cultural use of his test. For instance, many of the items may not be appropriate for other societies even if the items are translated carefully (Brislin, 1986; Lonner, 1990). In addition to the difficulty of translating some words specific to Western culture, the difficulty of ensuring cultural relevance seems overwhelming in many cultural contexts.

How would you assess personality if you were to devise your own test?

Evaluation of Personality Tests

The critiques of psychodynamic assessments and of trait-based assessments suggest that the validity of any single test is likely to be limited. When similar results are obtained with multiple kinds of tests, however, we may be more confident in our conclusions. Scientific conclusions must be based on converging sources of information, whether that information is about individuals, groups, or humanity as a whole.

How do psychologists assess personality? The psychodynamic approach to personality has led to the development of various projective tests, such as the *Rorschach Inkblot Test* and the *Thematic Apperception Test (TAT)*. The trait approach to personality has led to the development of various objective tests, such as the *Minnesota Multiphasic Personality Inventory (MMPI)* and the *Sixteen Personality-Factor Questionnaire (16PF)*. Although the validity of any given test may be questioned by many psychologists, the information from various tests, along with other sources of information, may be useful.

Before we conclude this chapter, it may be useful to point to a summary of the major paradigms of personality theory, shown in Table 12-8. This chapter has focused on the many aspects of personality as they apply to the normal range of behavior. The following chapter describes many of the ways that personality may be expressed, which do not fall within the normal range of behavior.

TABLE 12-8

Major Paradigms of Personality Theory

Paradigm	Psychodynamic	Humanistic
Major theorists	Freud; Adler; Jung; Erikson; Horney	Rogers; Maslow
Basis for personality	Conflicting sources of psychic energy	The distinctive human ability to act purposefully and to shape our own destiny by being future oriented
Key features of personality theory	(a) Developmental changes across the life span, with early childhood experiences profoundly influencing adult personality (b) Deterministic view of personality as being largely governed by forces over which the individual has little control (c) Importance of unconscious processes in shaping personality and behavior	*Nondeterministic* view of personality as being subject to the *conscious* control of the individual
Basis for theory development	Case studies of individuals seeking help for psychological problems	Humanistic philosophy, personal experiences, and clinical practice
Key strengths	Importance and influence, comprehensiveness, usefulness to applications	Parsimony
Key weaknesses	Testability	Testability

SUMMARY

1. Personality encompasses those of a person's enduring dispositional characteristics that provide an integrated consistency to the person's behavior.
2. The various approaches to understanding personality can be evaluated in several ways: their importance to and influence on the field of psychology, their testability, their comprehensiveness in accounting for psychological phenomena, their parsimoniousness (simplicity), and their usefulness to applied fields.

How Do Psychodynamic Psychologists View Personality?   352

3. Freud's psychodynamic theory of personality emphasizes dynamic, biologically oriented processes; conflicting sources of psychic energy; and the influence of early development on people's adaptations to their environments.
4. Freud's theory underscored the role of the *unconscious* in the life of the mind. Neo-Freudians were more willing to consider conscious influences, as well.
5. Freud described three components of the mind: the *id* (which is largely instinctual and impulsive, and which seeks

immediate satisfaction of sexual and aggressive wishes), the *ego* (which is rational and seeks to satisfy the id in ways that adapt effectively to the real world), and the *superego* (which is irrational and seeks to avoid the punishment associated with internalized moral rules). The id operates on the basis of the *pleasure principle*, the ego on the basis of the *reality principle*, and the superego on the basis of the *idealistic principle*.
6. Sigmund and Anna Freud described ten main *defense mechanisms*: fixation, regression, denial, repression, projection, displacement, sublimation, reaction formation, rationalization, and identification, which they believed people use to protect themselves from unacceptable thoughts and impulses.
7. Freud's theory was largely based on his case studies of individual patients. Freud used dream analysis extensively with his patients, focusing on the latent content of dreams, rather than on their manifest content.
8. Neo-Freudians—such as Adler, Jung, Erikson, and Horney—originally based their theories on Freud's but later differed from Freud and developed their own psychodynamic theories. Most neo-Freudian theories are less deterministic than is Freud's theory. The theories take into

Cognitive–Behavioral	Trait	Interactionist
Skinner; Rotter; Bandura	Cattell; Eysenck; Allport	Mischel; Bem & Allen
The interactions among thoughts, the environment, and behavior	Stable sources of individual differences that characterize an individual, based on an interaction of nature and nurture	Interaction between the person and the situation
(a) How individuals think about and give meaning to stimuli and events in their environment, as well as to their own behavior (b) People need to feel that they are competent in controlling their environment	(a) *Nomothetic* theorists hold that all people have the same set of traits, but individuals differ in the degree to which they manifest each trait (b) *Idiographic* theorists hold that each individual has a different set of traits that are fundamental to her or his personality	Behavior is determined by interactions between situational factors and personality factors
Experimental findings, as well as the development and use of personality tests	(a) *Nomothetic theories*—factor analysis or comprehensive assessments of individuals (b) *Idiographic theories*—comprehensive assessments of individuals, emphasizing individual differences (e.g., through self-reports and naturalistic observations), bolstered by experimental findings	Combination of behavioral observations and psychometric tests
Importance and influence, testability, usefulness to applications	Importance and influence, testability, applications to assessment techniques	Comprehensiveness, accounting for both person and environment
Comprehensiveness	Applications to psychotherapy techniques	Vagueness

account the ego and the conscious mind more than did Freud's theory. They also give more consideration to continuing development of the personality after childhood, as well as to the broader social context within which the individual's personality operates. In particular, Alfred Adler contributed the notion of the inferiority complex; Carl Jung, the notion of there being both a personal unconscious and a collective unconscious; Erik Erikson, the notion that the conscious workings of the ego, rather than the unconscious impulses of the id, dominate personality development across the life span; and Karen Horney, the importance of cultural, rather than biological, variables in personality, and the idea that basic anxiety leads people to move toward, against, or away from other people.

9. Psychodynamic theories have been criticized because they lack extensive empirical support.

How Do Humanistic Psychologists View Personality? *362*

10. Humanistic theorists emphasize individual responsibility and the distinctive value of human experience.
11. Carl Rogers's person-centered approach to personality may be termed *self theory*. Rogers identified the *self-concept* (the aspects of the self that an individual perceives within her-

or himself) and the *ideal self* (the aspects of the self that the person wishes to embrace) and emphasized the importance of achieving as close a match as possible between the two.

How Do Cognitive–Behavioral Psychologists View Personality? *364*

12. Skinner and other behaviorists tried to explain personality in terms of behavioral responses to environmental contingencies, without considering internal (mental) events.
13. Rotter and Bandura have taken a cognitive–behavioral approach to explaining personality. Rotter has emphasized each person's perceived internal versus external locus of control. Bandura has emphasized the interaction of how we think and how we act in a given situation. To Bandura, perceived self-efficacy is a key aspect of personality.
14. Cognitive–behavioral theories are easy to test, so they have led to a wealth of empirical research and of clinical and assessment applications.

How Do Trait Theorists View Personality? *367*

15. *Traits* are stable sources of individual differences that characterize a person. Both nature and nurture influence these

traits, and different theorists give differing emphasis to one or the other.

16. Some personality theories assert that people have essentially the same set of traits and that they differ only in terms of how much of each trait they have. That is, for each trait in the same set of traits, an individual may have more or less of the trait. Other theories state that people differ in terms of which traits they possess—that is, some people do not possess traits that others do.

17. Theories specifying universal traits include those of Raymond Cattell, who used factor analysis to find 23 *source traits;* of Hans Eysenck, who holds that the key personality traits are *extroversion, neuroticism,* and *psychoticism;* and of the *Big Five theory of personality,* which includes the traits of neuroticism, extroversion, openness, agreeableness, and conscientiousness.

18. Gordon Allport emphasized the role of *personal dispositions* unique to each individual rather than common traits. Some individuals have *cardinal traits,* which explain almost all the behavior of these individuals. In addition, all people have both *central traits* (highly important characteristics) and *secondary traits* (less important characteristics).

19. Walter Mischel has criticized trait theories because they fail to consider situational factors affecting behavior. Others have pointed out that personality factors and situational factors each explain only some of behavioral variation. However, the influence of personality factors on behavior seems higher for some personality character-istics.

How Do Interactionist Psychologists View Personality? 372

20. Many contemporary theorists emphasize an *interactionist approach,* which underscores the interaction between the individual's personality traits and the given situation.

How Do Psychologists Assess Personality? 374

21. *Projective personality tests,* which encourage individuals to project their unconscious characteristics and conflicts in response to open-ended questions, are a product of the psychodynamic tradition.

22. *Objective personality tests* are usually paper-and-pencil tests, which have been standardized and normed, for easy comparison of scores across many individuals. Such tests generally emphasize a trait-based approach to personality.

PATHWAYS TO KNOWLEDGE

Choose the best answer to complete each sentence.

1. Temperament is best described as an individual's
   (a) personality characteristics that begin in adulthood.
   (b) mood, activity level, and disposition, an aspect of personality.
   (c) tendency to get irritable, frustrated, or angry.
   (d) moods that are dependent on situational factors.

2. In which order do Freud's psychosexual stages of development proceed?
   (a) oral, anal, phallic, latency, genital.
   (b) anal, oral, latency, phallic, genital.
   (c) anal, oral, genital, phallic, latency.
   (d) oral, anal, genital, latency, phallic.

3. Psychodynamic determinism refers to
   (a) behavior that is ruled by unconscious forces over which we have no control.
   (b) behavior that is conscious in origin.
   (c) id impulses that will forever remain unfulfilled.
   (d) the delimiting characteristic of the superego.

4. According to Jung, all archetypes are
   (a) held in the collective unconscious.
   (b) dark and forbidden instinctual urges.
   (c) those parts of the unconscious that are unique to each individual.
   (d) the manifest content of dreams.

5. Carl Rogers's self theory assumes that

(a) humans are isolated individuals in an indifferent world.
(b) a person's acceptance of her- or himself leads to a selfish view of the world and to egocentric behavior.
(c) the self is the focal point from which reality is constructed.
(d) most people see problems and difficulties only in terms of themselves, rather than by showing unconditional positive regard for others.

6. According to Julian Rotter's social-learning theory, a primary factor that differentiates individuals is in how they
   (a) devote the majority of their psychic energy.
   (b) cope with the numerous unconscious forces that act on their lives.
   (c) show their sociability.
   (d) view their locus of control.

7. The Big Five theory of personality includes all the following factors **except**
   (a) altruism.
   (b) neuroticism.
   (c) extroversion.
   (d) conscientiousness.

8. Interactionist approaches to personality assume that
   (a) most people tend to show their characteristic traits across various situations, but some people do not.
   (b) neither the situation nor the person's characteristics alone are the sole influence on behavior.
   (c) individuals show consistent behavioral patterns across situations.

(d) situations ultimately determine how a given individual will act.

9. According to Erik Erikson, all of the following are core issues that must be confronted during the course of personality development **except**
   (a) guilt versus initiative.
   (b) trust versus mistrust.
   (c) happiness versus sadness.
   (d) identity versus role confusion.

10. In psychosexual development, according to Freud, latency refers to
    (a) the period during which the child explores both male and female sex roles.
    (b) a period when psychosexual development is very rapid and intense.
    (c) a period of dormant and repressed sexual desires.
    (d) the brief period before which the child's sexual orientation becomes solidified.

Answer each of the following questions by filling in the blank with an appropriate word or phrase.

11. Researchers who endorse a _____–_____ theory of personality are concerned with the relationships among people's thoughts, their actions, and their personality characteristics.

12. That part of a dream that deals with events in the dream as we experience them is referred to as the _____ content.

13. Psychodynamic theorists view the mind as organized at two basic levels—the _____ and the _____.

14. Personality attributes that are consistent in an individual are referred to as _____.

15. According to psychodynamic theory, the _____ mediates among the id, the superego, and the external world.

16. The defense mechanism of _____ is characterized by various forbidden thoughts and impulses being attributed to another person rather than to the self.

17. Alfred Adler believed that a primary motivator in our lives is our striving for _____.

18. Karen Horney has proposed that people experience _____ _____, a condition of isolation and helplessness brought about by a competitive world.

19. Psychodynamic assessment often involves use of _____ _____, which are designed to assess individuals' personality characteristics and conflicts via their responses to ambiguous test questions.

20. According to Eysenck's theory of personality, _____ refers to an individual's tendency to be solitary, lacking in feeling, and insensitive.

21. The _____ _____ _____ _____ is an objective test that is frequently used as a diagnostic tool to assess personality characteristics.

Answers

1. b, 2. a, 3. a, 4. a, 5. c, 6. d, 7. a, 8. b, 9. c, 10. c, 11. cognitive–behavioral, 12. manifest, 13. conscious, unconscious, 14. traits, 15. ego, 16. projection, 17. superiority, 18. basic anxiety, 19. projective tests, 20. psychoticism, 21. Minnesota Multiphasic Personality Inventory

PATHWAYS TO UNDERSTANDING

1. Think about the various theories of personality proposed in this chapter. Which theory seems to you to be most reasonable—that is, which one explains personality most effectively? Describe the strengths and the weaknesses of this theory, as you view them.

2. What steps can you take to ensure that someone you love (hypothetical or real) feels sure of your unconditional positive regard for her or him?

3. What do you consider to be the essential personality characteristics, based on yourself and on the people you know?

PART IV

Clinical and Health Psychology

CHAPTER 13
Abnormal Psychology

CHAPTER 14
Psychotherapy

CHAPTER 15
Health Psychology

CHAPTER OUTLINE

What Is Abnormal Behavior?

How Have People Explained
Abnormal Behavior?
    Demonological Explanations
    Clinical Explanations

How Do Clinicians Diagnose
Abnormal Behavior?

What Are Anxiety Disorders?

What Are Mood Disorders?
    Depressive Disorders
    Bipolar Disorders

What Are Dissociative
Disorders?

What Is Schizophrenia?
    Types of Schizophrenia
    Demographic Issues
        in Schizophrenia

What Are Impulse-Control
Disorders?

What Are Personality Disorders?

What Disorders Are Usually First
Diagnosed in Infancy, Childhood,
or Adolescence?

What Are Some Additional
Psychological Disorders?

How Do Psychologists View
Suicide?
    Myths About Suicide

What Legal Issues Do Clinicians
Face?
    Criminal Law
    Civil Law

CHAPTER 13

Abnormal Psychology

What does it mean to be abnormal? This apparently simple question leads to anything but a simple answer. Consider the following passage from Edgar Allan Poe's "The Tell-Tale Heart":

"True—nervous—very, very dreadfully nervous I had been and am; but why will you say that I am mad? The disease had sharpened my senses—not destroyed—not dulled them. Above all was the sense of hearing acute. I heard all things in the heaven and in the earth. I heard many things in hell. How, then, am I mad? Hearken! and observe how healthily—how calmly I can tell you the whole story.

"It is impossible to say how first the idea entered my brain; but once conceived, it haunted me day and night. . . . I loved the old man. He had never wronged me. He had never given me insult. For his gold I had no desire. I think it was his eye! Yes, it was this! He had the eye of a vulture—a pale blue eye, with a film over it. Whenever it fell upon me, my blood ran cold; and so by degrees—very gradually—I made up my mind to take the life of the old man, and thus rid myself of the eye forever."

WHAT IS ABNORMAL BEHAVIOR?

In deciding to kill a person for such a trivial reason, the narrator in Poe's (1979) story clearly seems to be behaving abnormally, by almost anyone's definition. Psychologists have defined abnormal behavior in many ways. To define abnormal behavior adequately, we need to consider several aspects of this concept. **Abnormal behavior** is sometimes viewed as (a) statistically *unusual* (i.e., it deviates from statistically normal, average behavior), (b) *nonadaptive* (i.e., it hampers the individual's ability to function effectively within her or his given context), (c) *labeled as abnormal* by the surrounding society in which the individual is behaving, and (d) characterized by some degree of *perceptual, emotional, or cognitive distortion*. As you might expect, some kinds of abnormal behavior may not show all four aspects of the definition, but most do. In addition, it is important to emphasize that all normal people engage in certain behavior that may be considered abnormal in some respects. What distinguishes normal deviations from serious psychological disorder is the degree to which the behavior is unusual, nonadaptive, identified as abnormal, and indicative of distortion.

It is hard to fight an enemy who has outposts in your head.

Sally Kempton

Finding Your Way   13-1

Stop for a moment to think about your own behavior. What is something you do that might be considered statistically unusual or perhaps even labeled as abnormal? For example, do you take unusual risks, such as bungee-jumping or skydiving? Do you do any other things that some people may consider unusual? Although you are aware of some unusual things you do, those things are probably not so unusual that others in your environment are alarmed by them. (For example, you probably do not regularly walk the streets, shouting gibberish or warning that the end of the world is near.)

What is something you do that is nonadaptive for you? For instance, do you sometimes postpone starting a term paper or studying for an exam, even though you know that it will be much harder to do a good job because of your procrastination? Do you occasionally eat or drink things that you know are not good for you? In all likelihood, your nonadaptive behavior does not pose a serious threat to your well-being or to the well-being of people around you. Even some seriously nonadaptive behavior (e.g., engaging in unprotected sexual intercourse with an acquaintance) falls well within the range of normal behavior and is not believed to indicate serious psychological disorder. On the other hand, if you regularly abuse alcohol, cocaine, or other psychoactive substances, or you frequently engage in criminal activity, your nonadaptive behavior may seriously threaten your well-being or that of others, and it indicates some degree of psychological disturbance.

What kinds of perceptual, emotional, or cognitive distortions have you experienced? For example, have you ever emotionally overreacted to a situation, becoming overly defensive in response to what someone else does or says? Have you ever shown any cognitive biases (e.g., the availability heuristic described in Chapter 8, or the actor—observer effect described in Chapter 10)? Each of these distortions is shown by psychologically healthy individuals. On the other hand, if you hear voices telling you what to do when you are entirely alone or if you see nonexistent snakes and spiders crawling all over you, you are experiencing distortions that fall outside the range of normal behavior.

Our society allows people to be absolutely neurotic and totally out of touch with their feelings and everyone else's feelings, and yet be very respectable.

Ntozake Shange

abnormal behavior   ways of thinking or acting that are unusual, that impair the ability to function effectively, that are identified as odd within the surrounding social context, or that involve some degree of distortion in thinking, feeling, or perceiving

No one of the four aspects of abnormal behavior (i.e., being statistically unusual, nonadaptive, labeled as abnormal, or characterized by distortion) would in itself adequately define abnormal behavior. For one thing, whether a particular behavior is statistically unusual or maladaptive varies across differing cultural contexts. Behavior that is quite common and adaptive in one cultural context may be considered highly unusual and maladaptive in another. For example, within some subgroups in American culture, it is customary on Monday evenings in autumn for small groups of people to gather around a small box. The box makes sounds and displays moving photos of athletes prancing around a field and bumping into one another. Although the observers do not talk to one another, from time to time, some or all of the observers burst out with cheers or curses directed toward the box. This behavior toward an inanimate object would seem bizarrely abnormal to those unfamiliar with watching Monday Night Football. For some subgroups of American culture, however, such behavior is not only common but also adaptive in promoting social relationships among the observers.

On the other hand, these observers might be tempted to label as "crazy" the rituals of African Yoruba or Alaskan Eskimo *shamans* (religious leaders who use magical rituals to bring about therapeutic effects for individuals or for the cultural group as a whole). The Yorubas and the Eskimos, however, clearly consider the behavior of shamans to be highly adaptive and appropriate. They clearly distinguish between shamans and people whose irrational or bizarre behavior is considered abnormal and neither adaptive nor appropriate (Davison & Neale, 1994; Matsumoto, 1994, 1996).

Differences in context clearly influence which kinds of behavior are labeled as abnormal. For example, political dissidents are often labeled as insane in countries governed by totalitarian rule. In Nazi-occupied lands, many heroic individuals who hid persecuted families were considered abnormal by those who became aware of the heroes' behavior.

Even the labels used by mainstream psychiatrists are sometimes subject to question. Once a person has been labeled as mentally ill, even the person's normal behavior may be viewed as psychologically disturbed. For instance, once persons have been hospitalized for mental illness, their behavior may be perceived as disturbed simply because observers of their behavior expect to see signs of psychological disturbance (Rosenhan, 1973; see Figure 13-1).

How might your own definition of abnormal human behavior be affected by your social context? How might your definition affect how you interact with other people?

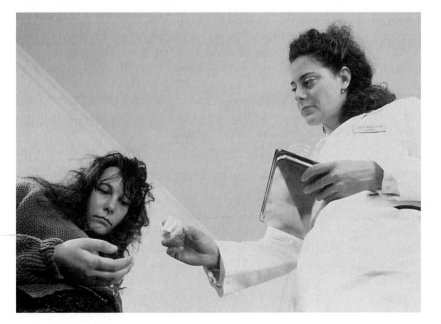

Figure 13-1

What Happens When People Are Labeled as Mentally Ill?

In a highly provocative study, David Rosenhan and seven associates pretended to have symptoms of mental illness in order to be admitted as patients in various mental hospitals (Rosenhan, 1973). Once these impostors were admitted (i.e., identified as mentally ill), they stopped showing any symptoms of mental illness and behaved as they normally would. Surprisingly, even the normal behavior of these impostors was frequently taken as evidence of disturbance by members of the hospital staff. Apparently, once people have been labeled as mentally ill, even their normal behavior may be considered to indicate mental illness.

Even the last of the four characteristics of abnormal behavior—distortion in perception, emotion, and cognition—may be appropriate and even normal under some circumstances. In fact, Shelley Taylor and Jonathon Brown (1988) argue that some degree of perceptual, emotional, and cognitive distortion is good for our mental health. More specifically, assume that you and I are normal, mentally healthy, well-adjusted people. According to Taylor and Brown, one reason for our mental health is that we seem to misperceive reality, using self-serving biases that overinflate our positive evaluations of ourselves. We also tend to exaggerate our own importance and our ability to control our actions and even our environments. We tint our views of reality and of our future prospects to be far more optimistic than the objective reality would seem to justify. These self-serving distortions seem to enhance our sense of self-esteem, boost our ability to feel happy, and increase our ability to be involved in productive, creative work.

A clever person turns great troubles into little ones and little ones into none at all.

Chinese proverb

What is abnormal behavior? Although psychologists have yet to find a perfect definition for all abnormal behavior, psychologists generally agree that most abnormal behavior is statistically unusual, nonadaptive, labeled as abnormal, and characterized by some degree of perceptual, emotional, or cognitive distortion.

HOW HAVE PEOPLE EXPLAINED ABNORMAL BEHAVIOR?

Demonological Explanations

Psychologists seek not only to describe abnormal behavior, but also to explain it. Today we try to understand abnormal behavior through rational and empirical means. It was not always so. In ancient times, people considered abnormal behavior to be an aspect of *demonology.* They believed that people who showed abnormal behavior were possessed by a supernatural force, often in the form of an evil demon such as the devil. For example, during the Middle Ages, many Europeans believed that demons caused abnormal behavior. Both women and men who acted oddly were often considered witches and were tortured cruelly in order to rid them of evil spirits. More often than not, they were killed as a result. By the time of the Renaissance, mentally ill Europeans were hospitalized rather than executed. However, their treatment was still far from humane or therapeutic, and many people continued to consider the mentally ill to be witches.

Often, there appears to be no easy way to refute supernatural explanations for phenomena we cannot yet fully explain by scientific means (e.g., the behavior of persons who are mentally ill). How should a reasonable person respond to supernatural explanations when there are no scientific ones?

Clinical Explanations

Once we rule out demonic explanations of abnormal behavior, other explanations are needed. Modern explanations of abnormal behavior have generally emerged from clinical work. Clinical work involves the treatment of clients (often called "patients" in medical settings such as clinics or hospitals); *clinicians* are people who treat clients. Clinicians who study abnormal behavior are generally either *psychologists,* who have postgraduate training in clinical psychology, a field of psychology; or *psychiatrists,* who have medical degrees, with specialized training in psychiatry, a field of medicine.

Most modern theoretical views of abnormal behavior closely parallel the views of normal behavior suggested by theories of personality. We considered the psychodynamic, humanistic, behavioral, and cognitive approaches to understanding normal behavior and personality in the previous chapter. We briefly review those approaches here, considering how they apply specifically to abnormal behavior and personality. In addition, we consider a psychophysiological approach to understanding abnormal behavior, based on how the physiology of the brain (and the endocrine system) affects the functioning of the mind. We also consider a cultural approach, based on the contextualist notion that a person's culture plays a key role in how the person's abnormal behavior may be interpreted and understood. Finally, we suggest an eclectic perspective, which integrates some of the ideas from other approaches.

Psychodynamic Explanations

According to the *psychodynamic perspective*, abnormal behavior results from intrapsychic conflict. A great deal of this conflict is unconscious, but it nonetheless affects much of what we feel, think, say, and do. For one thing, the ego is constantly battling the id and the superego. The id is governed by the pleasure principle, the ego by the reality principle, and the superego by the idealistic principle, so personality and behavior depend on which psychic force dominates. A person in whom the id dominates will be relatively unrestrained, uninhibited, and perhaps impulsive. A person in whom the ego is stronger will be more restrained, more reality oriented, and more in touch with rational thought. A person dominated by the superego will be almost paralyzed by rules against any behavior that might be considered morally questionable in any way. According to psychodynamic psychologists, powerful intrapsychic conflict among the id, the superego, and the real world may lead to abnormal behavior.

Humanistic Explanations

According to the *humanistic approach* to abnormal behavior, psychological problems arise when people do not accept themselves as they are. People may be overly sensitive to others people's judgments, or they may not accept their own nature. The key problem is low self-regard, in which people are overly critical of themselves. According to humanists, low self-regard is more likely when people have not received sufficient unconditional positive regard from parents or other significant persons.

Behavioral Explanations

According to the *behavioral perspective* on abnormal behavior, people show abnormal behavior as a result of classical or operant conditioning, or perhaps social learning. According to this view, psychological disorders arise when a person acquires a set of responses that is involuntary and maladaptive. For example, through classical conditioning, an exaggerated fear of something that normally would not stimulate fear might result if it were accidentally paired, perhaps repeatedly, with a fear-provoking stimulus (see Chapter 6). Through operant conditioning, individuals may be reinforced for maladaptive behavior, thereby increasing the likelihood that the behavior will be repeated. Similarly, individuals may be punished for adaptive behavior, thereby decreasing the likelihood that such behavior will occur again. Through social learning, persons who observe others (e.g., parents) engaging in abnormal behavior may then engage in such behavior themselves.

Cognitive Explanations

According to the *cognitive perspective*, abnormal behavior is the result of distorted thinking. The distortions may be in the processes of thinking, the contents of thinking, or both. For example, depressed persons may minimize their own accomplishments, or they may believe that no matter what they do, they will fail. People who have an extreme fear of snakes may irrationally believe that all kinds of snakes can seriously harm them. In each case, the person engages in distorted or erroneous thinking. When distorted thoughts are repeated enough to become routine, they may become *automatic thoughts* that lead the individual to feel anxious, depressed, or otherwise disordered much of the time.

Psychophysiological Explanations

According to the *psychophysiological perspective*, abnormal behavior is due to underlying physiological abnormalities in the nervous system, particularly in the brain, or to abnormalities in the endocrine (hormone) system. Often, these physiological problems involve abnormalities in the structure or tissues of the brain or in neuronal transmission (see Chapter 2). For example, brain tumors or injuries may lead to abnormal behavior. Similarly, abnormal behavior may result from too much or too little of a transmitter substance or hormone.

Insanity runs in my family. It practically gallops.
Cary Grant

Cultural Explanations

Whereas physiological psychologists emphasize the importance of biology as a basis for human behavior, cultural psychologists highlight the role of cultural context in explaining human behavior. Cultural psychologists do not claim that all of abnormal behavior arises because of a person's culture. Nonetheless, cultural psychologists do suggest that there are cultural distinctions in what is viewed as abnormal behavior (Matsumoto, 1994, 1996).

What may be viewed as normal behavior within one culture (e.g., Christians who regularly eat beef) may be considered abnormal behavior in another (e.g., Hindus who consider cattle to be sacred). Also, the same basic kind of abnormal behavior may be expressed differently in different cultures. For example, the particular expressions of depression or of anxiety may differ across different cultures. Whereas anxious or depressed persons in one culture may show many bodily symptoms of anxiety or depression, persons in another culture may express these disorders in other ways (e.g., by voicing deep fears or extreme feelings of worthlessness) (Matsumoto, 1996). Some disorders even seem to be distinctive to a particular culture: *Anorexia nervosa* (a life-threatening eating disorder in which a person starves her- or himself because of a distorted perception that she or he is overweight) is distressingly common in the United States, but it is virtually unknown in many African and Asian countries (Swartz, 1985).

Eclectic Explanations

The preceding explanations of abnormal behavior are based on the view that a single approach can explain the entire range of abnormal human behavior. In my view, no single explanation seems best for explaining all abnormal behavior. Instead, different approaches address different aspects of psychological disorders. Each approach may offer insights not available from other perspectives.

Perhaps psychodynamic psychologists are correct in suggesting that many of the reasons for abnormal behavior lie outside the conscious awareness of the disordered individual. As humanists suggest, some people may be depressed, anxious, or otherwise psychologically troubled because they feel little self-regard and they focus on their failures and their weaknesses more than on their successes and their strengths. Behaviorally oriented theorists may be correct in noting that some people show abnormal behavior in response to unfortunate systems of environmental reinforcement or punishment; other people may develop inappropriate or exaggerated emotional and physiological reactions as a result of classical conditioning. In addition, as cognitive psychologists have suggested, distortions in thinking may contribute to abnormal behavior. Particular physiological disorders or malfunctions may also lead to disordered or maladaptive behavior, and this behavior may be interpreted differently, depending on the cultural context of the disordered individual. Although many psychologists might disagree with some of these approaches to understanding abnormal behavior, most psychologists would accept some of the insights offered by more than one of these approaches.

Many psychologists now believe that the most effective way to explain abnormal behavior considers multiple perspectives. One way of integrating these diverse perspectives may be considered an eclectic approach. From an *eclectic approach*, abnormal behavior probably arises as the result of an interaction of an individual's physiological predisposition, particular environmental events and situations within a given cultural context, distorted thought processes, and inappropriate emotional responses.

Insanity is often the logic of an accurate mind overtaxed.

Oliver Wendell Holmes Sr.

How have people explained abnormal behavior? Early demonological explanations focused on supernatural forces thought to inhabit the individual engaging in abnormal behavior. More plausible explanations have been offered by psychodynamic (focusing on unconscious psychic conflict), humanistic (focusing on low self-regard), behavioral (focusing on inappropriate environmental events and reinforcers), cognitive (focusing on distortions of thought), psychophysiological (focusing on abnormalities in the nervous system or the endocrine system), and cultural (focusing on the cultural context of the individual) perspectives. Many psychologists now take an eclectic point of view, seeing multiple kinds of causes of abnormal behavior.

HOW DO CLINICIANS DIAGNOSE ABNORMAL BEHAVIOR?

Although clinicians often disagree about how to *explain* abnormal behavior, by the middle of the twentieth century, clinicians did begin to reach some formal agreement regarding how to *diagnose* psychological disorders. In 1952, the American Psychiatric Association published its *Diagnostic and Statistical Manual* (DSM). The DSM has been revised several times, and the current (1994) version is known as the DSM-IV (fourth edition). The DSM is descriptive and **atheoretical,** not based on any particular theoretical approach to explaining a given disorder. The DSM lists the symptoms necessary for making a diagnosis in each category, without trying to specify the causes of the disorder. Thus, the classification system is based wholly on observable symptoms, making it usable by psychologists and psychiatrists from a wide variety of theoretical orientations.

Any diagnostic system, including DSM-IV, is potentially problematic. First, because the system is atheoretical, it gives us no real insight into the causes of the abnormal behavior. A second problem is that DSM-IV does not adequately consider ethnic and cultural differences among patients (Turner & Hersen, 1985). Third, although DSM-IV allows "clinicians to reach the same diagnosis in a remarkably high proportion of cases" (Sartorius et al., 1993b, p. xvi), agreement

atheoretical having no particular theoretical orientation

What are the advantages of a uniform set of guidelines for making diagnoses of various disorders? Are there any disadvantages?

among clinicians certainly is not perfect. That is, using the DSM-IV, clinicians might not always agree regarding diagnoses. A fourth problem is how to match particular behavior to the descriptive categories. A diagnostician needs to match observed behavior to the symptoms expressed in DSM-IV and then to match those symptoms to a diagnosis.

It is impossible to specify every possible type of behavior, so clinicians must use their own judgment when using any classification system. DSM-IV gives guidelines, but ultimately, the clinician's judgment is key in making the diagnosis. One way that clinicians can improve the effectiveness of their judgment is to use various forms of assessment (see Chapter 12). When various sources of information are used, clinicians can integrate and interpret the information, based on their professional expertise. Next, we discuss some of the kinds of disorders diagnosed by clinicians.

I have a new philosophy. I'm only going to dread one day at a time.

Charles Schulz, Peanuts

How do clinicians diagnose abnormal behavior? In the 1950s, most clinicians agreed to use a standard guide for diagnosing psychological disorders, known as the *Diagnostic and Statistical Manual* (DSM; now in its fourth edition, DSM-IV). The guide provides atheoretical criteria for diagnoses, based on symptom categories.

WHAT ARE ANXIETY DISORDERS?

Anxiety disorders center on the individual's feelings of **anxiety**—tension, nervousness, distress, or uncomfortable arousal. Psychologists often distinguish between *fear*, which is focused on a specific object or event, and *anxiety*, which is vague and is not directed toward any specific object or event. DSM-IV divides anxiety disorders into five main categories: (1) *phobias*, (2) *panic disorder*, (3) *generalized anxiety disorder*, (4) stress disorders (*posttraumatic stress disorder* and *acute stress disorder*), and (5) *obsessive–compulsive disorder* (see Table 13-1). Roughly 15% of the U.S. population suffer from an anxiety disorder at some time during their lives (Robins et al., 1984). All five disorders share several common symptoms that characterize them as anxiety disorders.

In his painting, The Scream, Edvard Munch captured the terror often felt by people with anxiety disorders.

There are four basic kinds of symptoms of anxiety disorders: mood, cognitive, somatic, and motor symptoms. *Mood symptoms* include feelings of tension, apprehension, and sometimes, panic. Often, persons who experience these symptoms do not know exactly why they are feeling this way. For example, they may have a sense of doom but may not know why. Sometimes, anxious persons become depressed, if only because they do not see any way to get rid of the symptoms.

Cognitive symptoms may include spending a lot of time trying to figure out why various mood symptoms are occurring. When unable to identify root causes, the person may then feel frustrated. Often, thinking about the problem actually worsens it, causing the person difficulty in concentrating on other things.

Typical *somatic* (i.e., bodily) *symptoms* include sweating, breathing difficulties, high pulse rate or blood pressure, and muscle tension. These symptoms go along with a high level of arousal of the autonomic nervous system (see Chapter 2). These primary symptoms may lead to secondary ones. For example, intensely rapid breathing may lead to feelings of lightheadedness or breathlessness. Muscular tension can lead to headaches or muscle spasms. High blood pressure can cause strokes or heart problems. People who suffer from anxiety disorders vary widely

anxiety disorder a psychological disorder involving the presence of anxiety that is so intense or so frequently present that it causes difficulty or distress for the individual

anxiety a generalized feeling of dread or apprehension that is not focused on or directed toward any particular object or event

TABLE 13-1
Anxiety Disorder

Phobia	Persistent, irrational, and disruptive fear of a specific object, activity, or type of situation; a substantially greater fear than seems justified, or a fear that has no basis in reality
Simple phobia	Irrational fear of an object in a situation other than one related to agoraphobia or social phobia
Social phobia	Extreme fear of being criticized by others, which leads to the avoidance of groups of people
Agoraphobia	Fear of open spaces or of being in public places from which it might be difficult to escape in the event of an anxiety attack; generally involves a fear of losing control or of some terrible, unspecified thing happening outside of the house
Panic disorder[a]	Brief (usually only a few minutes), sudden, and unprovoked, but recurrent episodes during which a person experiences intense and uncontrollable anxiety and shows psychophysiological symptoms, such as difficulty in breathing, heart palpitations, dizziness, sweating, and trembling; may entail a fear either of losing control of self or of going crazy
Generalized anxiety disorder	General, constant, and often debilitatingly high levels of anxiety that can last any length of time, from a month to years; often described as "free floating" because it cannot be pinned down easily
Stress disorder	An extreme reaction to a highly stressful event or situation
Posttraumatic stress disorder	The psychological reenactment of a traumatic event in the disordered person's past; reexperiencing of the event may take any of several different forms, such as nightmares, powerful memories, or even a perception that the event is occurring again
Acute stress disorder	Acute, brief reactions to stress, which directly follow a traumatic event and last fewer than 4 months
Obsessive–compulsive disorder	A disorder involving obsessions and/or compulsions
Obsession	An unwanted, persistent thought, image, or impulse that an individual is unable to suppress; may include obsessive doubts, thoughts, impulses, fears, or images
Compulsion	An irresistible impulse to perform a relatively meaningless act repeatedly and in a stereotypical fashion

[a] Although agoraphobia and panic disorder are discrete anxiety disorders, the two disorders so commonly occur together that DSM-IV includes a special category for the co-occurrence of the two disorders.

in their somatic symptoms. Some people may express their anxiety more in headaches, others in stomachaches, still others in backaches or other bodily symptoms.

Typical *motor symptoms* include restlessness, fidgeting, and various bodily movements that serve no particular purpose (such as pacing or finger tapping). People are often unaware of their own motor symptoms. For example, they may pace around a room while others are seated, not realizing that their behavior is unusual.

When does anxiety become an anxiety disorder? What distinguishes the normal anxiety that everyone occasionally experiences from serious psychological problems of anxiety? Generally, three factors must be considered:

1. *Level* of anxiety—It is probably normal to have a slight, occasional reluctance to enter elevators, especially overcrowded rickety-looking ones; it is probably abnormal to use the stairs to get to the 110th floor of a building because of feelings of terror that a well-built elevator will fall to the bottom of the elevator shaft.

Everybody knows if you are too careful you are so occupied in being careful that you are sure to stumble over something.

Gertrude Stein

TABLE 13-2

Explanations of Anxiety Disorders

Psychodynamic	In general, anxiety arises because of conflicts between the id and superego. When individuals feel impulses from the id that conflict with the superego, they fear the punishment of the superego. Even if they do not act on those impulses, their fears of potential punishment from the superego may cause anxiety. Regarding phobias in particular, Freud suggested that the object of the phobia (e.g., snakes) represents a symbol of some deeper conflict, often involving sexual impulses of some kind.
Humanistic	When people perceive a big difference between their ideal selves (whom they would like to be) and their perceived selves (whom they perceive themselves to be), they feel anxious about their failure to become closer to their ideal selves.
Behavioral	*Classical conditioning:* When a neutral stimulus (e.g., the sight of a dog) is paired with a fear-producing stimulus (e.g., startlingly loud noises or even a bite), the individual may be classically conditioned to feel fear in the presence of the formerly neutral stimulus. *Operant conditioning:* In obsessive–compulsive anxiety disorder, an individual may temporarily feel less anxiety after engaging in the compulsive behavior and may thus be negatively reinforced (due to reduced anxiety) for the compulsive behavior. *Observational learning:* By observing another person respond fearfully or be seriously harmed in a particular situation, the individual may learn to feel fearful in that situation or in the presence of particular stimuli.
Cognitive	Through *threat-magnifying thoughts*, people may think in ways that exaggerate potential threats and may thereby increase their feelings of anxiety.
Psychophysiological	The levels and activity of neurotransmitters may not be normal, thereby leading to feelings of anxiety. In particular, GABA (gamma-aminobutyric acid), a neurotransmitter substance, acts as a sort of chemical brake on the brain, slowing down the activity of the brain. When the levels of GABA are too low, the activity level of the brain increases, leading to heightened arousal. If people continually feel a heightened level of arousal, they may feel anxious.
Cultural	The cultural context in which people find themselves may influence the development of anxiety disorders. For instance, the anxiety disorder of *koro* (male impotence due to a man's fear that his penis is retracting into his body and that his death is imminent) may be found among some Southeast Asian men, but not among men from other cultures (Matsumoto, 1996).

Briefly describe a situation in which you felt extremely anxious, perhaps justifiably so. What were the mood, cognitive, somatic, and motor symptoms of your anxiety? How did your situation-related anxiety differ from an anxiety disorder?

Our fears always outnumber our dangers.

Latin proverb

2. *Justification* for the anxiety—It is normal to feel somewhat anxious before an important event, such as a final examination, a first date, or an important speech, but it is not normal constantly to feel that same level of anxiety when there are no stressful events on the horizon.

3. *Consequences* of the anxiety—If the anxiety leads to serious negative consequences, such as the loss of a job because of an inability to leave home, the anxiety is more likely to be considered an anxiety disorder.

The particular symptoms diagnosed as disorders vary across cultures. For example, a distinctive anxiety disorder has been observed in Islamic societies, in which the obsessive–compulsive syndrome of *Waswās* has been linked to the Islamic ritual of cleansing and prayer. According to W. Pfeiffer (1982), the syndrome "relates to ritual cleanliness and to the validity of the ritual procedures, which are particularly important in Islam. Thus, the sufferer of *Waswās* finds it hard to terminate the ablutions because he is afraid that he is not yet clean enough to carry out his prayers in a lawful manner" (p. 213). Within culturally diverse countries such as the United States, clinicians often fail to consider variations in symptoms across diverse client populations. For instance, in diagnosing stress-related anxiety disorders, clinicians tend to overemphasize interpersonal sources of stress (e.g., becoming divorced or widowed) and to underemphasize environmental sources of stress (e.g., financial difficulties or low-status and high-pressure jobs) (Turner & Hersen, 1985).

Several explanations of anxiety disorders have been suggested (see Table 13-2). Each explanation offers distinctive insights, and we may better understand particular disorders in particular individuals by using a combination of approaches.

What are anxiety disorders? Anxiety disorders (which include phobias, panic disorder, generalized anxiety disorder, stress disorders, and obsessive–compulsive disorder) are extreme feelings of anxiety that interfere with an individual's enjoyment of life or with the individual's adequate function in daily living.

WHAT ARE MOOD DISORDERS?

There are two major **mood disorders** (extreme disturbances in a person's emotional state) listed in DSM-IV: depressive disorders (also termed *unipolar depression* or *clinical depression*) and bipolar disorders.

Depressive Disorders

Depressive disorders involve serious impairment of function as a result of depression, not just feeling temporarily a little down in the dumps. Depression is relatively common. Roughly 10% of men and 20% of women are clinically depressed at some time in their lives (Weissman & Myers, 1978; Woodruff, Goodwin, & Guze, 1974). A depressed person feels deeply sad and probably feels that life is hopeless. The person probably also experiences a very low level of energy. Even the simplest task, such as getting out of bed or making a meal, may require more effort than the person can call forth. Sometimes, depressed persons show slow body movements and even slow speech. They may lose appetite and therefore lose weight. They may have trouble falling asleep, staying asleep, or waking up; they may sleep most of the time or at least may want to sleep much of the time. Depressed persons are also at greater risk of suicide than are nondepressed persons. (Suicide, which is not actually a specific psychological disorder, but which is clearly abnormal behavior, is discussed later in this chapter.)

The most noticeable symptom of depression relates to mood: Depressed persons feel down, discouraged, and hopeless. It may seem to them that nothing is right with their lives. Typical cognitive symptoms of depression are low self-esteem, low motivation, and pessimism. Depressed people often generalize from a single perceived failure or unfortunate event to an overall view that more failures and worse things are yet to come. Table 13-3 describes the various categories of depression, such as *exogenous depression* (chiefly having environmental origins) versus *endogenous depression* (chiefly due to internal, physiological origins), *primary depression* (in which depression is the principal medical disorder) versus *secondary depression* (depression arising from another medical disorder), *involutional depression* (age-related depression), and *postpartum depression* (serious depression following childbirth).

A large cross-national study involving more than 40,000 subjects in Western and non-Western countries concluded that depressive disorders occur across a broad range of cultures and that more recent generations are at an increased risk of depression, relative to earlier ones (Cross-National Collaborative Group, 1992). The scientists who conducted the study claim that it is the first study to use

The reason I hadn't washed my clothes or my hair was because it seemed so silly. . . . It seemed silly to wash one day when I would only have to wash again the next. It made me tired just to think of it. I wanted to do everything once and for all and be through with it.

Sylvia Plath

mood disorder a psychological disorder involving either periods of extremely sad, low-energy moods, or swings between extremely high and extremely low moods

depressive disorders mood disorders in which the individual feels so sad and has so little energy that the individual cannot function effectively

TABLE 13-3

Categories of Depression

Endogenous versus exogenous depression	
Exogenous depression	Stems primarily from a person's reaction to external, or environmental, factors.
Endogenous depression	Primarily induced by internal, or physiological factors, such as low levels of particular neurotransmitters
Primary versus secondary depression	
Primary depression	Depression is the principal medical problem, not another medical disorder
Secondary depression	Another medical disorder has caused the depression
Involutional depression	Associated with advancing age
Postpartum depression	Occurs after childbirth and can last anywhere from a few weeks to a year (the more common "maternity blues" last only 1 or 2 days)

standard diagnostic criteria across all societies. As other researchers have stated (Kleinman & Good, 1985; Marsella, Hirschfeld, & Katz, 1987), it is very hard to come up with cross-culturally appropriate uniform diagnostic criteria for disorders.

Bipolar Disorders

In addition to depressive disorders, the other main mood disorder is **bipolar disorder,** also termed *manic–depressive disorder,* in which people go through alternating periods of depression (with the same symptoms of depression as just described for depressive disorders) and mania. **Mania** is a mood of boundless joy and highly energetic delight, the opposite polar extreme from depression. The individual is highly excited and often hyperactive. Manic persons may believe that there is no limit to their possible accomplishments and may act accordingly (e.g., trying to climb Mount Everest as an unplanned outing, equipped with a cotton jacket and a pocket knife). (Figure 13-2 illustrates the periodic nature of bipolar disorders.)

bipolar disorder   mood disorder in which the individual alternates between periods of depression and of mania

mania   a mood in which the individual feels highly energetic and extremely joyful

Figure 13-2

Stages of a Manic Episode

Case-study research often provides depth of insight not as easily available through laboratory studies, as shown in this longitudinal analysis of nurses' ratings of manic behavior in a patient hospitalized for mania. (After Carlson and Goodwin, 1973: Carlson, G., and Goodwin, F. K., "The stages of mania: A longitudinal analysis of the manic episode," in Archives of General Psychiatry, February 1973, Vol. 28, No. 2, 221–228. Copyright © 1973 American Medical Association.)

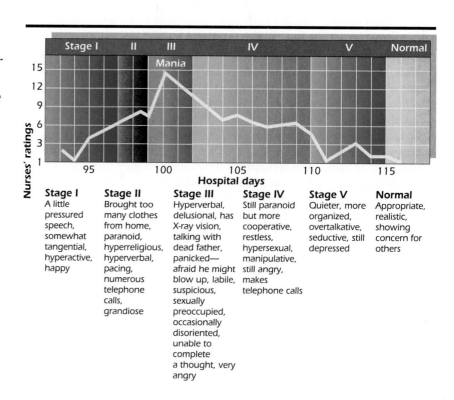

Stage I	Stage II	Stage III	Stage IV	Stage V	Normal
A little pressured speech, somewhat tangential, hyperactive, happy	Brought too many clothes from home, paranoid, hyperreligious, hyperverbal, pacing, numerous telephone calls, grandiose	Hyperverbal, delusional, has X-ray vision, talking with dead father, panicked—afraid he might blow up, labile, suspicious, sexually preoccupied, occasionally disoriented, unable to complete a thought, very angry	Still paranoid but more cooperative, restless, hypersexual, manipulative, still angry, makes telephone calls	Quieter, more organized, overtalkative, seductive, still depressed	Appropriate, realistic, showing concern for others

TABLE 13-4

Explanation of Mood Disorders

Psychodynamic	Depression occurs when we mourn a loss, but usually the loss is symbolic, rather than actual, and the loss usually results from an event that occurred during early childhood. Moreover, people feel depressed when they turn their anger inward, against themselves, rather than outward, against others. Turning anger inward helps not only to avoid the actual punishment of the persons against whom we might turn, but also to minimize punishment from the superego for feeling aggressive impulses.
Humanistic	Victor Frankl (1959) drew largely on his own experience in Nazi concentration camps during World War II. He observed that of those individuals who were not put to death, the greatest difference between those who survived and those who did not seemed to be in the ability to find meaning in their suffering, and to relate the experience to their spiritual life. Generalizing from this experience, Frankl suggested that depression results from a lack of purpose in living. Thus, depressed people may improve if they can be helped to find meaning in their lives.
Behavioral	Depressed persons have received fewer rewards than nondepressed persons, and their lack of activity means that they will continue to receive fewer rewards than will nondepressed persons.
Cognitive	Building on the notion of learned helplessness, cognitivists would add that depressed persons may make cognitive attributions of causality that lead them to believe that they are powerless to make changes in the conditions that are making them unhappy. Depressed persons may also engage in distorted thought processes that exaggerate (a) their sense of hopelessness—their inability to change the situation, (b) the negative characteristics of the situation, and (c) the potential likelihood and harmfulness of future outcomes of their situation. Depressed persons may also minimize existing and potential future positive characteristics of the situation.
Psychophysiological	*Unipolar disorder:* Low levels of either of two neurotransmitters in the brain—norepinephrine or serotinin—may lead to depression. *Bipolar disorder:* As in unipolar disorder, low levels of norepinephrine may lead to the depressive phase, but in bipolar disorder, brain changes may lead to high levels of norepinephrine, associated with the manic phase of the disorder. Also, because drug therapies are highly effective in treating bipolar disorder, it seems that physiological factors play a role in this disorder. Bipolar disorder also appears to run in families, suggesting possible genetic and physiological aspects of the illness.
Cultural	There are large cultural differences in both rate of depression (Marsella, 1980) and symptoms of depression (Matsumoto, 1996). For instance, depressed Chinese persons tend to report somatic symptoms of depression more often than do depressed persons from other cultures (Matsumoto, 1996). On the other hand, depressed Americans and Europeans are more likely to report feeling extremely worthless than are depressed Nigerians (Kleinman, 1988). Some cultural psychologists interpret cultural variations as indicating that culture influences the expression—and perhaps even the experience—of depression.

During the manic phase, an individual shows an overinflated sense of self-esteem. Manic individuals often have trouble focusing their attention and move quickly from one activity to another. Occasionally, the manic person will suffer from **delusions**—false, unfounded beliefs. Manic individuals may spend money wildly, may attempt to start numerous projects they cannot finish, or may engage in a great deal of sexual activity. Consequently, they may end up bankrupt, fired from their jobs, or divorced by their mates. Persons who are experiencing mania have a greatly reduced need for sleep and tend not to feel tired after very strenuous periods of activity that will have exhausted most other people. Bipolar disorder (which occurs in only about 0.75% to 1% of the population) is much less common than is unipolar depression.

Several explanations of mood disorders have been suggested (see Table 13-4). Different explanations may be more plausible for each type of disorder. For example, behavioral explanations offer interesting insights into depression. However, psychophysiological explanations seem better to explain bipolar disorder.

The trouble is not that we are never happy—it is that happiness is so episodical.

Ruth Benedict

delusion a false belief, which contradicts known facts

Describe two situations: (1) a situation in which you felt pretty unhappy, and (2) a situation in which you felt pretty excited. How do your situation-related mood swings compare and contrast with actual mood disorders?

I can't figure out where I leave off and everyone else begins.

George McCabee

Do you believe that there are circumstances under which some degree of dissociation might be adaptive? If so, which? If not, why not?

dissociative disorders psychological disorders in which an individual goes through one or more extreme changes in awareness of past and present experiences, personal history, and even personal identity

What are mood disorders? Mood disorders, which are extreme disturbances in a person's emotional state, include depressive disorders (characterized by extreme sadness and low energy) and bipolar disorder (characterized by alternating periods of depression and mania—extremely high energy and elation).

WHAT ARE DISSOCIATIVE DISORDERS?

Dissociative disorders involve a drastic change in a person's awareness of past experiences, present experiences, and personal identity. For some of the dissociative disorders, environmental traumas have been more strongly implicated than have hereditary factors. There are three main dissociative disorders: *dissociative amnesia, dissociative fugue,* and *dissociative identity disorder* (formerly termed *multiple personality disorder*) (see Table 13-5). All of these disorders involve some kind of change in the normally integrative functions of consciousness and identity. In addition to the three main dissociative disorders, some persons are diagnosed as having *depersonalization disorder,* which involves temporary periods during which such persons experience distortions of their body image, perhaps feeling as if they are detached from their bodies or as if their legs or arms have changed in size.

The most well known of these disorders is dissociative identity disorder. The case of Sybil, which was made into a movie, illustrates interesting aspects of the disorder (Schreiber, 1973). By her adult years, Sybil had developed 15 distinct identities. Some of the identities were of relatively minor importance, others of more importance. One was a baby, and two were male. From her infancy through her late childhood, Sybil had been sexually tortured, brutally maltreated, and almost murdered by her mother, who was schizophrenic. Like Sybil, many of the persons who develop dissociative personality disorders have experienced shockingly horrible abuse during their early years. For these individuals, the ability to dissociate from abusive experiences may actually have had adaptive elements, given the circumstances.

TABLE 13-5
Dissociative Disorders

Dissociative amnesia	An experience of sudden memory loss, usually after a highly stressful life experience; usually, the amnesia affects the recollection of all of the events that have taken place during and immediately after the stressful event (see also *acute stress disorder*); it also causes great difficulty in recalling important personal details (e.g., name, place of residence, and identities of family members).
Dissociative fugue	Persons with this disorder start whole new lives and experience total amnesia about their past; they move away, assume new identities, take new jobs, and behave as though they were completely different persons. Their personalities may even change. As these persons begin their new lives, they do not question the fact that their past is lost.
Dissociative identity disorder (formerly called "multiple personality")	The occurrence of two or more individual identities (personalities) within the same individual, each of which is relatively independent of any others, lives a stable life of its own, and from time to time takes full control of the person's behavior.

People occasionally have tried to fake dissociative identity disorder. For example, Kenneth Bianchi, the infamous "Hillside Strangler," pretended to have multiple identities, hoping to be found not guilty of the murder of numerous women, by reason of insanity. How did the court know that Bianchi was faking? Among the experts on dissociative disorders brought in as expert witnesses was Martin Orne. Orne cited four reasons why he believed that Bianchi's identities were not real. First, the identity of the supposed murderer, "Steve," changed over time: from being passive at first to becoming abusive and aggressive later. In contrast, true dissociative identities tend to be stable, especially if they have existed over a long period of time. Second, when it was mentioned to Bianchi that true dissociative identity cases tend to have more than just two personalities, a new personality quickly appeared. Thus, Bianchi appeared to create the third personality in order better to simulate the disorder. Third, dissociative identities that exist over a period of time tend to be noticed by other people, but no one appeared to have noticed "Steve," the murderer. Finally, when hypnosis was used to reveal the personality of "Steve," Bianchi showed the characteristics of someone simulating deep hypnosis rather than of someone actually under a hypnotic trance.

What are dissociative disorders? People who suffer from dissociative disorders experience a drastic change in their awareness of their past and present experiences or in their personal identity. The most widely known of these is dissociative identity disorder; other dissociative disorders include dissociative amnesia and dissociative fugue, as well as depersonalization disorder.

WHAT IS SCHIZOPHRENIA?

Schizophrenia is actually a set of disorders that encompasses a variety of symptoms, including hallucinations, delusions, disturbed thought processes, disturbed emotional responses—such as *flat affect* (lack of emotional expression) or *inappropriate affect* (inappropriate emotional expression, such as laughing when fear or anger would be appropriate reactions), and odd motor symptoms (see Table 13-6).

The symptoms of schizophrenia are sometimes characterized as either being *negative* (i.e., not showing a behavior that is normal—subtracting it from the behavioral repertoire) or *positive* (i.e., showing a behavior that is abnormal—adding it to the repertoire). **Negative symptoms** include deficits in behavior, such as blunting of emotions (affective flattening), language deficits, apathy, and avoidance of social activity. **Positive symptoms** include delusions, hallucinations, and bizarre behavior, such as the creation of *word salad*, in which a schizophrenic speaker uses strings of words that are only loosely connected, if at all, as in the following passage.

> I want to go to bed. I want to go to bed and be in my head. I want to go to bed and be in my bed and in my head and just wear red. For red is the color that my baby wore and once more, it's true, yes, it is, it's true. Please don't wear red tonight, ohh, ohh, please don't wear red tonight, for red is the color—

(Bloom, 1993, p. 50).

Years ago, I discovered that I could keep the plane I was flying on from crashing by refusing to adjust my watch to the new time zone until we were on the ground, and I have used that method ever since.

Calvin Trillin

schizophrenia a set of psychological disorders involving various perceptual symptoms (e.g., hallucinations), cognitive symptoms (e.g., disturbed thought content or processes), mood symptoms (e.g., lack of appropriate emotional expression), and sometimes even bizarre motor symptoms

negative symptom a characteristic of a disorder, in which the individual lacks a normal behavior (e.g., not speaking, not showing emotional expression, or not interacting socially)

positive symptom a characteristic of a disorder, in which the individual shows an abnormal behavior (e.g., hallucinations or word salad)

TABLE 13-6
Symptoms of Schizophrenia

Cognitive symptoms	
Hallucinations	Perceptual experiences that have no basis in reality—that is, the person experiencing hallucinations will hear, see, feel, or smell things that are not present.
Delusions	Erroneous beliefs that persist despite strong evidence to the contrary; delusions are of various kinds, and they can range from thoughts that are plausible but incorrect to thoughts that are patently ridiculous. A few of the more common delusions follow:
Persecution	The belief that others are spying on the person or are planning to harm the person in some manner. For example, schizophrenics might believe that they are being followed by agents of the CIA. These delusions are the most common ones.
Identity	The deluded person's belief that she or he is somebody else. For example, in *The Three Christs of Ypsilanti*, Milton Rokeach (1964) focused on three patients in a mental hospital in Ypsilanti, Michigan, each of whom believed that he was Jesus Christ.
External causation	The schizophrenics' belief that external forces are making them feel certain things, act in certain ways, or have certain impulses.
Word salad	Rhythmic and rhyming combinations of words are tossed together in ways that make no sense—that is, in addition to having disturbed thought content, the schizophrenic's thought processes are also disturbed.
Cognitive flooding (also termed *stimulus overload*)	The inability to filter out irrelevant internal and external stimuli, and thus being forced to attend to a bewildering array of stimuli; the amount of stimulation may become so great that the schizophrenics become unable to cope with the rate of stimulation.
Affective, emotional symptoms	
Flat affect	The patient may stare lifelessly into space, seeming apathetic to the world. Schizophrenics showing flat affect may not answer questions, but if they do respond, their answers are likely to be given in a toneless voice.
Inappropriate affect	Emotional responses are inappropriate; for example, patients may laugh uncontrollably on hearing that someone close to them is seriously ill or has died, or they may become enraged when asked how they are feeling; somewhat less common than flat affect.
Motor symptoms	
Motor disturbances	Schizophrenics (especially those showing flat affect) often show characteristic motor symptoms. In particular, some types of schizophrenics may appear to be in a daze and may not move for weeks, months, or even years. Other types of schizophrenics may exhibit unusually high levels of activity. Unusual facial expressions, repetitive finger and hand movements, and random and purposeless movements are also characteristic.

MINILECTURE
Defining Schizophrenia
(Ch 18)

In order to be classified as schizophrenic, an individual must show (a) impairment in areas such as work, social relations, and self-care; (b) at least two of the cognitive, affective, or motor characteristics described earlier (see Table 13-6); and (c) persistence of these symptoms for at least 6 months.

The predicted future of persons diagnosed with schizophrenia is not particularly bright. Schizophrenia typically involves a series of *acute* (intense but temporary) episodes with occasional periods of *remission* (relief from symptoms). In many cases, with each successive acute episode of the disorder, the individual becomes less able to function well even during periods of remission. Most clinicians agree that once people have had a full-fledged episode of schizophrenia, they are rarely completely rid of the disorder. That is, the disease process generally appears to be *chronic* (never going away entirely—either constantly present or showing up again and again). Nonetheless, in most cases, a number of the symptoms can be treated through psychotherapy and drugs (Sartorius, Shapiro, & Jablonsky, 1974).

TABLE 13-7

Types of Schizophrenia

Disorganized schizophrenia (formerly termed *hebephrenic schizophrenia*)	Characterized by profound psychological disorganization; hallucinations and delusions are common, but these symptoms do not seem as fully integrated and as coherently organized as in some of the other kinds of schizophrenia, such as paranoid schizophrenia; often involves incoherent speech
Catatonic schizophrenia	Characterized by very long periods of immobility, in which the individuals may stare into space, appearing dazed and completely detached from the rest of the world
Paranoid schizophrenia	Characterized by delusions of persecution or of grandeur
Undifferentiated schizophrenia	A catchall category into which individuals are classified if they do not fit any of the preceding schizophrenic patterns
Residual schizophrenia	A diagnosis applied to individuals who have had at least one schizophrenic episode and who currently show some mild symptoms, but who do not show the profoundly disturbed behavior that characterizes the other schizophrenias

Types of Schizophrenia

DSM-IV recognizes five main types of schizophrenia. Of these types, three were recognized more than a century ago: *disorganized schizophrenia, catatonic schizophrenia*, and *paranoid schizophrenia*. Today, DSM-IV also recognizes *undifferentiated schizophrenia* and *residual schizophrenia* (see Table 13-7). In addition, DSM-IV includes some other psychotic disorders related to schizophrenia (e.g., delusional disorder, shared psychotic disorder, schizophreniform disorder, and schizoaffective disorder), most of which involve less severe symptoms or shorter duration of symptoms.

Demographic Issues in Schizophrenia

Schizophrenia affects 1% to 2% of the U.S. population and is among the most serious of psychological disorders (Robins et al., 1984). Schizophrenia also tends to run in families. Several studies have found that if someone is schizophrenic, chances are good that this person will have other family members who are schizophrenic as well (Gottesman, McGuffin, & Farmer 1987). For example, among

Catatonic schizophrenics show waxy flexibility, assuming odd poses for long periods of time. Although this woman's arm appears to be frozen in place, it can be manipulated into another pose, which she will then continue to hold.

persons with schizophrenia, 44% of identical twins are both schizophrenic, and 12% of fraternal twins are both schizophrenic; moreover, 7% of persons with schizophrenia have schizophrenic siblings, 9% have schizophrenic children, and 3% have schizophrenic grandchildren.

MINILECTURE
Causes of Schizophrenia
(Ch 18)

Schizophrenia is generally diagnosed in early adulthood, usually before the age of 45 years. The incidence of schizophrenia has also been found to vary with socioeconomic status (SES). In particular, persons with lower SES are more likely to be diagnosed as suffering from schizophrenia than are persons with higher SES. The difference is large: Members of the lowest SES group are roughly eight times more likely to be diagnosed with schizophrenia than are members of the middle and upper SES groups (Dohrenwend & Dohrenwend, 1974; Strauss et al., 1978). Many possible explanations (e.g., higher levels of stress associated with lower SES) have been offered regarding this trend (e.g., Hollingshead & Redlich, 1958; Kramer, 1957; Myerson, 1940; Turner & Wagonfeld, 1967). Also, members of

TABLE 13-8

Explanations of Schizophrenia

Psychodynamic	People with schizophrenia return to the earliest (oral) stage of psychological development. In this stage, the ego has not yet adequately differentiated from the id, so the reality principle is not yet operative as a means of checking the id, which operates solely on the pleasure principle.
Humanistic	Humanistic psychologist Thomas Szasz (1961) argued that mental illness is simply a myth—that schizophrenia and other so-called mental illnesses are merely alternative ways of experiencing the world. Humanistic therapist R. D. Laing (1964) has suggested that schizophrenia is not an illness but is merely a label that society applies to behavior it finds problematic. According to Laing, people become schizophrenic when they live in situations that are simply not livable. No matter what they do, nothing seems to work.
Behavioral	People with schizophrenia find their lives and social situations to be so lacking in rewards or even punishments that they begin to ignore the relevant aspects of their environment in favor of irrelevant ones. Their response of paying attention to relevant cues becomes extinguished. Once people are labeled as schizophrenics, their abnormal behavior is more likely to attract the rewarding attention of others and their normal behavior is less likely to do so.
Cognitive	For some reason, people with schizophrenia frequently experience an overload of sensory stimulation or of conflicting thoughts. These bizarre and overwhelming experiences may then cause their other difficulties. For example, when they try to communicate their sensations, perceptions, or thoughts to others, other persons cannot understand them. Some suggest that people with schizophrenia lack an adequate filtering mechanism, so they cannot screen out irrelevant stimuli and thoughts.
Psychophysiological	As in other disorders, levels of neurotransmitters in the brain may be involved in schizophrenia. Specifically, excessively high levels of dopamine have been linked to schizophrenia (Wong et al., 1986). The effectiveness of various antipsychotic drugs (see Chapter 14) also supports the psychophysiological explanation of schizophrenia. Another psychophysiological explanation suggests structural abnormalities in the brain as the cause (Seidman, 1983). In particular, schizophrenia may be linked to deterioration of the brain tissue (Andreasen et al., 1982).
Cultural	Studies by the World Health Organization have found that auditory hallucinations, delusions of reference, and lack of insight are symptoms that characterize schizophrenia across many cultures (e.g., in Asia, Africa, South and North America, and Europe). On the other hand, other researchers have found cross-cultural variations in the rates of schizophrenia and among patterns of symptoms. Similarly, people with schizophrenia seem to show faster recovery in developing countries in which they are able to return to meaningful work and to rely on an extended kin network (described in Matsumoto, 1996). Some of the cultural universals lend support to psychophysiological explanations, but the numerous cultural variations suggest that cultural context influences the expression and interpretation of schizophrenic symptoms.

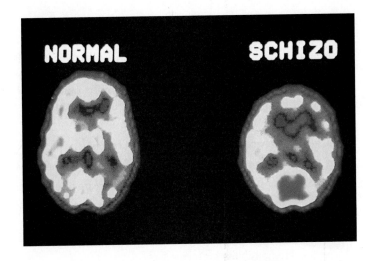

Contemporary brain-imaging techniques offer insights into some of the cerebral processes that underlie psychological disorder. For example, these images show the differences in the patterns of activity in a normal brain, as compared with the brain of a schizophrenic.

groups that experience discrimination and the stress associated with discrimination are more prone to schizophrenia, regardless of SES (Dohrenwend et al., 1992).

Several explanations of schizophrenia have been suggested (see Table 13-8). The great differences across SES suggest that environmental factors play a role. The strong familial trends, particularly among identical twins, suggest that inherited biological factors also contribute to the disorder. Thus, an interaction of various factors probably underlies this disorder.

If a sane dog fights a mad dog, it's the sane dog's ear that is bitten off.

Burmese proverb

What is schizophrenia? Schizophrenia is a set of severe psychological disorders, in which afflicted individuals experience hallucinations, delusions, and disturbed thought processes and emotional responses, as well as odd motor symptoms. In addition to these positive symptoms of schizophrenia, there are some negative symptoms of the disorder, including lack of emotional expression and avoidance of social interaction.

WHAT ARE IMPULSE-CONTROL DISORDERS?

The DSM-IV designates a special category for "impulse-control disorders not elsewhere classified," all of which involve the failure to resist an impulse to engage in a particular behavior. These disorders and their associated impulses follow: (a) *intermittent explosive disorder*—explosive outbursts of emotions; (b) *kleptomania*—stealing; (c) *pyromania*—setting fires; (d) *pathological gambling*—out-of-control betting; and (e) *trichotillomania*—pulling out one's own hair.

What kinds of impulses do you find difficult to control, and why?

What are impulse-control disorders? Impulse disorders include a number of disorders involving a person's apparent inability to resist engaging in impulsive behavior.

WHAT ARE PERSONALITY DISORDERS?

Personality disorders are consistent, long-term, extreme personality characteristics that either seriously impair a person's ability to function well in the person's environment or cause problems for the person or for others when the person is adjusting to normal, everyday situations. The major personality disorders include the following:

- *paranoid* (characteristically suspicious of others)
- *narcissistic* (characteristically have an inflated view of themselves)
- *histrionic* (characteristically act as though they are on stage)
- *avoidant* (characteristically seem reluctant to enter into close personal relationships)
- *dependent* (characteristically lack self-confidence and have difficulty in taking personal responsibility for themselves)
- *obsessive–compulsive* (characteristically show excessive concern with details, rules, and codes of behavior)
- antisocial (characteristically seem superficially charming and apparently sincere, while nevertheless engaging in behavior that harms other individuals)

Although it is possible to detect some features of personality disorders during infancy, childhood, or adolescence, these disorders generally are not diagnosed until at least early adulthood. Several other disorders, however, are usually first diagnosed in infancy, childhood, or adolescence.

Just because you're paranoid doesn't mean they aren't out to get you.

Anonymous

What are personality disorders? Personality disorders are extreme personality characteristics that persist over a long period of time and that seriously impair a person's ability to function well in the environment. Such disorders include paranoid, narcissistic, histrionic, avoidant, dependent, obsessive–compulsive, and antisocial personality disorders.

WHAT DISORDERS ARE USUALLY FIRST DIAGNOSED IN INFANCY, CHILDHOOD, OR ADOLESCENCE?

There are three major **disorders usually first diagnosed in infancy, childhood, or adolescence:** attention-deficit/hyperactivity disorder, conduct disorder, and pervasive developmental disorder (PDD). Children who show *attention-deficit/hyperactivity disorder* have difficulty in focusing attention for reasonable amounts of time; they tend also to be impulsive and disruptive in social settings; they often are unable to sit still and constantly seem to be seeking attention; they are easily distracted by irrelevant stimuli; they have trouble listening to and following instructions; and they often talk excessively and are likely to interrupt others. Children who have *conduct disorder* show habitual misbehavior, such as stealing, being truant from school, destroying property, fighting (occasionally using weapons in these fights), being cruel both to animals and to other people, and frequently telling lies.

Less common than attention-deficit/hyperactivity disorder and conduct disorder is *pervasive developmental disorder* (PDD) (termed *autism* in earlier versions of

personality disorders psychological disorders involving exaggerated and maladaptive personality characteristics that persist over a long period of time and that cause problems in the person's adjustment to everyday situations

disorders usually first diagnosed in infancy, childhood, or adolescence psychological disorders that are first identified before adulthood

DSM, as shown in the movie *Rain Man*). PDD is characterized by three main symptoms: (1) These children show minimal to no responsiveness to others and seem oblivious to the world around them, almost as though they were living in another dimension. (2) They show seriously impaired communication, with only minimal language use, nonsensical verbalizations, and even poor nonverbal communication skills. (3) They show a highly restricted range of interest; for instance, they may sit by themselves staring off into space for hours, without a word or a gesture; or they may rock back and forth or ritualistically repeat gestures with their hands. Until recently, it was believed that PDD might be a form of schizophrenia in childhood. It is now believed, however, that PDD and schizophrenia in childhood are different disorders (American Psychiatric Association, 1994). Whereas children with schizophrenia often show a family history of schizophrenia, children with PDD do not. Also, the drugs that reduce or relieve symptoms of schizophrenia are not effective with PDD (see Chapter 14). In addition, DSM-IV includes various other disorders in this category of disorders usually first diagnosed in infancy, childhood, or adolescence, such as mental retardation (see Chapter 9), learning disorders, motor-skills disorders, feeding and eating disorders, elimination disorders, tic disorders, and communication disorders.

What disorders are usually first diagnosed in infancy, childhood, or adolescence? The main disorders that are usually diagnosed prior to adulthood include attention-deficit/hyperactivity disorder, conduct disorder, and pervasive developmental disorder (PDD).

WHAT ARE SOME ADDITIONAL PSYCHOLOGICAL DISORDERS?

The DSM-IV also discusses somatoform disorders, sexual disorders, and cognitive-impairment disorders. **Somatoform disorders** center on the person's relationship with his or her own body; they are relatively rare bodily symptoms or complaints of bodily symptoms for which no physiological basis can be found. There are five main kinds of somatoform disorders:

1. The most common somatoform disorder is *pain disorder*, in which people experience pain that cannot be attributed to any physical cause (see also Chapter 15).
2. In *conversion disorder*, the sensory or muscular systems are impaired, despite the lack of a known physical cause. The impairment may involve partial or complete paralysis of the arms or legs; seizures; coordination problems; loss or impairment of sensation; insensitivity to pain; inability to see, hear, or speak; or prickly, tingling, or creeping sensations on the skin.
3. In *somatization disorder*, people seek relief from unpleasant chronic physical symptoms for which there is no known physical cause. Of the many symptoms that may arise, some of the most common ones are dizziness, fatigue, nausea, and weakness. Somatization disorder differs from *malingering* (faking symptoms in order to get out of responsibilities) and from *Münchausen syndrome* (in which people fake symptoms in order to keep playing the role of the patient).
4. In *hypochondriasis*, people are preoccupied with the fear that they may have serious illnesses, and they overreact to ordinary physical experiences, such as nausea or pain in the abdomen.

Hypochondria is the only disease I haven't got.
Graffito, New York, 1978

somatoform disorders psychological disorders in which people experience bodily symptoms for which no physiological basis has been found

5. Persons with *body dysmorphic disorder* are preoccupied with a defect in physical appearance. The defect may be either real or imagined; if it is real, however, it is greatly exaggerated.

Another category of disorders with strong physiological associations is that of sexual disorders. In **sexual disorders,** the individual experiences sexual arousal, thoughts, or behaviors that distress the individual or other persons. The disorder may also cause difficulty for the individual in other aspects of her or his life. DSM-IV specifies the following major types of sexual disorders:

1. In *gender-identity disorders,* people feel that their physiological *sex*—either male or female physical identity—differs from their psychological *gender*—either female or male psychological identity with respect to social and societal roles and characteristics.
2. *Paraphilias* are sexual attractions to highly unusual objects. For instance, persons with the following paraphilias are sexually aroused by these unusual objects: *fetishes*—nonhuman objects (e.g., articles of clothing, particularly those of the opposite sex); *pedophilia*—children; *sexual sadism*—the pain of another person; *sexual masochism*—personal experience of pain; *voyeurism*—secret observation of people who are nude or undressing; *exhibitionism*—unwanted public display of areas of the body that are perceived as sexually provocative.
3. *Sexual dysfunctions* are disruptions of people's normal sex lives. People with these disorders have difficulty feeling any sexual urge at all, feeling aroused at appropriate times, or having orgasms at appropriate times. They also may feel pain during intercourse. Each of these disorders can be mild to severe, and of brief to long duration.

The DSM-IV also includes **cognitive-impairment disorders,** such as *delirium*, a confused, disordered state of mind often involving perceptual distortions; *amnesia*, memory loss; and *dementia*, general deterioration in cognitive abilities, especially affecting memory and judgment. Cognitive disorders are generally due to physiological changes in the brain (e.g., Alzheimer's disease, head injury, or *stroke*—sudden changes in the blood supply to the brain). (See Chapters 2, 5, 7, and 8 for discussion of some aspects of cognitive function and its distortions.) In addition, DSM-IV includes eating disorders, sleeping disorders (see Chapter 5), *adjustment disorders* (related to extreme difficulties in adjusting to traumas, stressors, and other difficult situations), and substance-related disorders (see Chapter 5).

What are some additional psychological disorders? Additional psychological disorders include somatoform disorders, sexual disorders, and cognitive-impairment disorders, as well as various other disorders related to eating, sleeping, adjustment to difficult situations, and substance abuse.

sexual disorders psychological disorders involving problems with sexual arousal, thoughts, or behavior that distresses the individual or other persons

cognitive-impairment disorder a psychological disorder in which normal thought processes become impaired or distorted

HOW DO PSYCHOLOGISTS VIEW SUICIDE?

To be, or not to be—that is the question:
Whether 'tis nobler in the mind to suffer
The slings and arrows of outrageous fortune,
Or to take arms against a sea of troubles,
And by opposing end them. (William Shakespeare, *Hamlet*, III, i)

Most of the psychological disorders described in this chapter are rarely life threatening. Depression can be, however, and severe depression often precedes suicide. Although suicide is not a psychological disorder in itself, it is clearly abnormal behavior. In addition, because of its link to depression, it seems appropriate to consider suicide in the context of psychological disorders. Suicide is generally not approved of and is frequently forbidden in society. Even today, several states make it a crime to commit suicide. In this section, we consider first some facts (Douglas, 1967; Gibbs, 1968; Holinger, 1987; National Center for Health Statistics, 1988; Resnik, 1968; Seiden, 1974) and then some myths regarding suicide.

What do we know about suicide? For one thing, suicide occurs in almost all cultures, but it is more common in some cultures than in others. The United States is about average with respect to the other countries of the world. Almost 31,000 suicides are recorded each year in the United States, which makes the U.S. rate of suicide 12.8 per 100,000 people. Many other Western countries have suicide rates of 20 or more per 100,000 people. In fact, Western cultures in general seem to have higher rates of suicide than non-Western cultures (Carson & Butcher, 1992). In contrast, some cultures (e.g., that of the aborigines of Australia) have no known incidence of suicide whatsoever. Western estimates of suicide are probably much too low because many suicides (e.g., questionable accidents) are not counted as such. Thus, although these statistics would lead us to believe that a suicide occurs in the United States once every 20 minutes, the true frequency is undoubtedly higher.

Age is also a factor in suicide. The rate of suicide rises in old age (particularly among white males), reaching a rate of more than 25 per 100,000 for people between the ages of 75 and 84 years. In addition, although suicide ranks only eighth as a cause of death among adults, in general, it ranks third after accidents and homicides as a cause of death among people between the ages of 15 and 24 years. Among young adults, whites are twice as likely as blacks to kill themselves.

BRANCHING OUT: Myths About Suicide

Many of us wrongly believe numerous myths about suicide (Pokorny, 1968; Shneidman, 1973). Perhaps if you are aware of some of these myths, you may be able to prevent a suicide or at least to help the loved ones left behind to cope with someone's suicide.

Myth 1. *People who talk about committing suicide do not actually go ahead and do it.* In fact, close to 8 out of 10 of the people who commit suicide have given some warning beforehand that they were about to take their lives. Often, they have given multiple warnings.

Myth 2. *All people who commit suicide have definitely decided that they want to die.* In fact, many of those who commit suicide are not certain they really want to die. They often take a gamble that someone will save them. Sometimes, for example, persons attempting suicide will take pills and then call someone to tell that person of the suicide attempt. If the person is not there, or if that person does not follow through quickly in response to the call, the suicide attempt may succeed.

Myth 3. *Suicide occurs more often among people who are wealthy.* In fact, suicide is about equally prevalent at all levels of the socioeconomic spectrum.

Myth 4. *People who commit suicide are crazy.* Although suicide is linked to depression, relatively few of the people who commit suicide are truly out of touch with reality.

Myth 5. *People who commit suicide are always depressed beforehand.* Although depression is linked to suicide, some people who take their lives show no signs of depression at all. People with terminal physical illnesses, for example, may commit suicide not because they are depressed, but in order to spare loved ones the suffering of having to support them, or because they have

Contrary to popular belief, threats of suicide should be taken very seriously. Many persons who commit suicide had threatened suicide prior to taking their own lives.

Razors pain you; / Rivers are damp; / Acids stain you; / And drugs cause cramp; / Guns aren't lawful; / Nooses give; / Gas smells awful; / You might as well live.

Dorothy Parker

made peace with the idea of death and have decided that the time has come.

Myth 6. *The risk of suicide ends when a person improves in mood following a major depression or a previous suicidal crisis.* In fact, most suicides occur while an individual is still depressed but after the individual starts to show some recovery. Often, people who are severely depressed are unable even to gather the energy to put together the means to commit suicide. Therefore, the improvement may mean that they will feel better and will have the energy to do something about their wish to die.

Myth 7. *Suicide is influenced by the cosmos—sun spots, phases of the moon, the position of the planets, and so on.* There is no evidence for any of these assertions.

Finding Your Way   13-2

Suppose that you are volunteering to answer telephones on a suicide hotline. What kinds of strategies would you use to convince a person not to commit suicide? How might you at least convince a person to postpone committing suicide until the person has explored other possibilities for solving her or his problems? What might you actually say to try to prevent someone from committing suicide?

Why do people kill themselves? The two main motivations for suicide appear to be *surcease* (the wish to end the present condition) and *manipulation* (the wish to get other persons to feel or act in particular ways). Those who seek surcease have given up on life. They see death as the only solution to their problems, and some take their lives. Slightly more than half of suicides appear to be of this kind. People seeking surcease are usually depressed, hopeless, and relatively certain that they really want their lives to end. The following suicide note, written by author Virginia Woolf to her husband, shows the wish for surcease:

> Dearest, I feel certain that I am going mad again: I feel we can't go through another of those terrible times. And I shan't recover this time. I begin to hear voices, and can't concentrate. So I am doing what seems the best thing to do. . . . If anybody could have saved me it would have been you. Everything has gone from me but the certainty of your goodness. I can't go on spoiling your life any longer.
>
> I don't think two people could have been happier than we have been.

In contrast, those who use suicide as a means of manipulation try to maneuver the world according to their desires. They may view suicide as a way to inflict revenge on a lover who has rejected them, to gain the attention of those who have ignored them, to hurt those who have hurt them, or to have the last word in an ongoing argument. Many of those who attempt suicide in this manner are not fully committed to dying but rather are using suicide as a call for attention and help. Indeed, sometimes these people take precautions so that their suicide attempt will not be successful, but these precautions do not always work. Roughly 13% of suicide attempts are of this kind. Unless they receive help, people who attempt manipulative suicide often try committing suicide again and may continue until they succeed in ending their lives.

Design an advertisement for a suicide hotline or other suicide-prevention measure, applying what you know about the causes and contributing factors underlying suicide.

How do psychologists view suicide? Suicide is disturbingly common across cultures, age groups, and socioeconomic circumstances. Frequently, persons who commit suicide do so to achieve either surcease (an end to their present situation) or manipulation (a means of causing other persons to act or to feel in a particular way).

WHAT LEGAL ISSUES DO CLINICIANS FACE?

Psychologists seek to describe various kinds and aspects of abnormal behavior in order to diagnose the problems of their patients, as well as to understand such behavior. Although these descriptions are imperfect, often permitting ambiguous diagnoses and flawed understandings, they generally serve the purpose for which psychologists intended them. Nonpsychologists, however, may have different requirements, which may lead to different definitions.

How should our legal system handle people with mental disorders who commit crimes?

Criminal Law

In courtrooms and law offices, alternative definitions of abnormal behavior are required, which may differ from the definitions preferred by psychologists. The term *sanity*, for example, is a legal term, not a psychological one, for describing behavior. Some of the most controversial examples of legal descriptions of abnormal behavior have involved criminal behavior. In 1834, a court in Ohio decided that a person could be found not guilty by reason of insanity if the person acted on an "irresistible impulse" that impelled the accused to commit the crime. Thus, the particular category of disorder was not relevant; the ability to resist an impulse was. Two subsequent cases, *Parsons v. the State of Alabama* (in 1887) and *Davis v. The United States* (1897), upheld the legitimacy of the "not-guilty-by-reason-of-insanity" defense.

Perhaps the most well-known construction of the insanity defense is the *M'Naghten Rule*, which came as the result of a murder trial in 1843 by a court in England. This rule holds that "to establish a defense on the ground of insanity, it must be clearly proved that, at the time of committing the act, the party accused was laboring under such a defect of reasoning, from disease of the mind, as not to know the nature and quality of the act he [or she] was doing, or if he [or she] did know it, that he [or she] did not know he [or she] was doing what was wrong" (*Stedman's Medical Dictionary*, 25th edition, 1990, p. 1374).

The American Law Institute provided a set of guidelines in 1962, which were intended to reflect the current state of the insanity defense and its legal and psychological implications. These guidelines state that people cannot be held responsible for criminal conduct if, as a consequence of a mental disease or defect, the accused lack the capacity either to recognize the wrongness of their conduct or to act in conformity with the requirements of the law. The guidelines exclude, however, repeated criminal actions or antisocial conduct. In other words, the intent of the guidelines is to cover extraordinary acts, not habitual criminal behavior.

In 1981, John Hinckley Jr. attempted to assassinate President Ronald Reagan in order to impress actress Jodie Foster. Hinckley was found not guilty by reason of insanity. As a result of this case and the outrage that followed it, a number of states have introduced a new verdict, "guilty but mentally ill." Federal courts have also tightened up guidelines for finding a defendant not guilty by reason of insanity. The Insanity Defense Reform Act, passed by the U.S. Congress in October, 1984, makes it much more difficult for a defendant to escape the punishment of the law, regardless of the defendant's mental state. The topic remains controversial, and some psychiatrists, such as Thomas Szasz (1963; see also Table 13-8), have argued that concepts of mental illness and insanity have no place in the courtroom at all. According to Szasz, acts of violence are as rational and goal directed as any other acts, and perpetrators of such acts should be treated accordingly.

Civil Law

Psychology and the law are also interrelated in noncriminal matters. For example, do the mentally ill have a legal right to treatment? In the case of *Wyatt v. Stickney*, decided in Alabama in 1971, the court ruled that they do. This ruling has generally held up. However, there is always room for various interpretations of who is mentally ill and really needs treatment. Since the 1980s, federal spending on mental institutions has decreased, so many patients who were formerly in psychiatric hospitals have been released into the streets. There, they generally join the ranks of the homeless and can now be seen wandering the streets instead of the halls of mental hospitals.

On the other hand, people suffering from mental illnesses are today also recognized as having a right to refuse treatment unless their behavior is potentially dangerous to themselves or others. In deciding whether to require treatment or confinement, we need to consider not only the rights of the potential patient, but also the rights of persons whom they might harm. We must try to find the right balance between the rights of the prospective patient to be free to refuse treatment or hospitalization and the rights of other persons to be protected from any harm that the prospective patient might cause. It should be noted, however, that mentally ill persons, on average, are no more likely to show aggressive behavior than are persons without mental illness. In fact, many psychological disorders, such as depression and some types of schizophrenia, are characterized by reduced social interaction of any kind.

There was only one catch and that was Catch-22, which specified that a concern for one's own safety in the face of dangers that were real and immediate was the process of a rational mind. . . . Orr would be crazy to fly more missions and sane if he didn't, but if he was sane he had to fly them. If he flew them he was crazy and didn't have to; but if he didn't want to he was sane and had to.

Joseph Heller

Create a list of criteria that you believe should be used in determining a person's (a) right to receive treatment for mental illness and (b) obligation to receive such treatment.

What legal issues do clinicians face? In criminal law, issues regarding abnormal behavior center on how to treat convicted criminals who suffer from psychological disorders. In civil law, issues center on whether an individual has a right either to obtain or to refuse treatment for a psychological disorder.

This chapter described some of the main disorders that constitute much of the subject matter of abnormal psychology. Many psychological disorders have not been discussed here. Some disorders are addressed in other chapters (e.g., Chapter 5 deals with aspects of substance-abuse disorders), and others are simply outside the scope of an introduction to psychology. Whereas clinical psychologists have reached broad agreement regarding the diagnostic categories (as provided by DSM-IV), there is considerable disagreement regarding the causes of the various syndromes. Psychodynamic, humanistic, behavioral, cognitive, psychophysiological, as well as cultural explanations of these causes may be viewed as either competing or complementary. These approaches also lead to competing or complementary ways to treat these disorders. Their implications for psychotherapy are considered in Chapter 14.

SUMMARY

What Is Abnormal Behavior? 386

1. *Abnormal behavior* is statistically unusual, nonadaptive, labeled as abnormal by the surrounding society, and characterized by some degree of perceptual, emotional, or cognitive distortion. Most abnormal behavior can be described in terms of some or all of these characteristics.

How Have People Explained Abnormal Behavior? 388

2. Early explanations of abnormal behavior included witchcraft and spiritual possession by demons.

3. More contemporary explanations of abnormal behavior include psychodynamic, humanistic, behavioral (learning), cognitive, psychophysiological, and cultural perspectives. Eclectic approaches combine aspects of the various explanations.

How Do Clinicians Diagnose Abnormal Behavior? 391

4. Through the development of the *Diagnostic and Statistical Manual*, fourth edition (DSM-IV), clinicians have reached widespread agreement regarding the diagnosis of mental disorders. The DSM-IV classifies psychological disorders according to criteria based on symptoms, rather than in terms of any particular theoretical approach.

What Are Anxiety Disorders? 392

5. *Anxiety disorders* involve the individual's feelings of *anxiety*.

6. DSM-IV divides anxiety disorders into five main categories: (1) phobic disorders, (2) panic disorder, (3) generalized anxiety disorder, (4) stress (posttraumatic or acute) disorders, and (5) obsessive–compulsive disorder.

What Are Mood Disorders? 395

7. DSM-IV lists two major *mood disorders* (extreme disturbances in a person's emotional state): *depressive disorders* (sometimes called "unipolar depression") and *bipolar disorder*. Depression is relatively common and is generally believed to be influenced by situational factors. Bipolar disorder, on the other hand, is much more rare and runs in families, suggesting a possible genetic, biological component. Both disorders, however, probably are influenced by some biological factors and some situational ones.

What Are Dissociative Disorders? 398

8. There are three main *dissociative disorders: dissociative amnesia, dissociative fugue,* and *dissociative identity disorder.* All of these disorders involve some kind of change in the normally integrative functions of consciousness, identity, or motor behavior. This category also includes *depersonalization disorder,* which involves passing episodes during which persons experience distortions of their body image.

9. Environmental traumas have been more strongly implicated for dissociative disorders than have hereditary or biological factors.

What Is Schizophrenia? 399

10. *Schizophrenia* is a set of disorders with a variety of symptoms, including hallucinations, *delusions,* disturbed thought processes, and disturbed emotional responses, as well as some odd motor symptoms.

11. Types of schizophrenia include disorganized schizophrenia, catatonic schizophrenia, paranoid schizophrenia, undifferentiated schizophrenia, and residual schizophrenia.

12. Of the various explanations for schizophrenia, psychophysiological explanations seem particularly interesting because they may explain familial trends in the development of schizophrenia, as well as the positive outcomes associated with antipsychotic drugs. The specific psychophysiological causes remain unknown, however. In addition, environmental stress (e.g., due to low SES or to societal discrimination) seems to increase the likelihood of being diagnosed as schizophrenic.

What Are Impulse-Control Disorders?   403

13. The following impulse-control disorders not elsewhere classified involve the impulse to engage in a particular behavior: intermittent explosive disorder, kleptomania, pyromania, pathological gambling, and trichotillomania.

What Are Personality Disorders?   404

14. *Personality disorders* are consistent, long-term, extreme personality characteristics that cause the person great unhappiness or that seriously impair the person's ability to adjust to the demands of everyday living or to function well in her or his environment.

15. The major personality disorders are paranoid, narcissistic, histrionic, avoidant, dependent, obsessive–compulsive, and antisocial personality disorders.

What Disorders Are Usually First Diagnosed in Infancy, Childhood, or Adolescence?   404

16. Three major *disorders* are *usually first diagnosed in infancy, childhood, or adolescence:* attention-deficit/hyperactivity disorder, conduct disorder, and pervasive developmental disorder (PDD, autism). In addition, DSM-IV includes several other disorders that commonly appear before adulthood.

What Are Some Additional Psychological Disorders?   405

17. *Somatoform disorders* are relatively rare bodily symptoms or complaints of bodily symptoms for which no physiological basis can be found. There are five main kinds of somato-

form disorders: pain disorder, conversion disorder, somatization disorder, hypochondriasis, and body dysmorphic disorder.

18. *Sexual disorders* involve sexual arousal, thoughts, or behaviors that cause the individual or other persons emotional distress or difficulty in other aspects of the person's life. DSM-IV classifies these disorders into gender-identity disorders, paraphilias, sexual dysfunction, and other sexual disorders.

19. DSM-IV also describes various *cognitive-impairment disorders* (e.g., delirium, amnesia, and dementia), eating disorders, sleeping disorders, adjustment disorders, and substance-related disorders.

How Do Psychologists View Suicide?   406

20. On average, every 20 minutes, at least one person in the United States commits suicide.

21. Many myths surround suicide. Perhaps the most important caution is that any person may decide to commit suicide, and that any threats of suicide should be taken seriously.

What Legal Issues Do Clinicians Face?   409

22. The term *sanity* is a legal term, not a psychological one, for describing behavior. At present, a person's sanity is an important factor in determining prosecution and sentencing for the person's criminal behavior. Just how sanity should be determined and how it should be considered in making legal judgments is still being evaluated in the courts.

23. Issues of civil law related to abnormal behavior center on an individual's right to obtain or to refuse treatment.

PATHWAYS TO KNOWLEDGE

Choose the best answer to complete each sentence.

1. According to the various definitions cited, which of the following is **not** a typical characteristic of abnormal behavior?
   (a) labeled abnormal by the society in which the individual lives
   (b) carefully planned
   (c) statistically unusual
   (d) maladaptive to the individual

2. Anxiety disorders may be characterized by both
   (a) psychotic symptoms and somatic symptoms.
   (b) low affect and telegraphic thoughts.
   (c) telegraphic thoughts and somatic symptoms.
   (d) motor symptoms and somatic symptoms.

3. The two main types of mood disorders are
   (a) depressive disorders and generalized anxiety disorders.
   (b) obsessive–compulsive disorders and manic–depressive disorders.
   (c) depressive disorders and bipolar disorders.

   (d) depressive disorders and obsessive–compulsive disorders.

4. An individual cannot remember events during and immediately following a serious airplane crash. The individual probably is suffering from
   (a) dissociative amnesia.
   (b) dissociative fugue.
   (c) dissociative anxiety.
   (d) posttraumatic stress anxiety.

5. A type of schizophrenia characterized by hallucinations, delusions, and disordered thought processes is referred to as
   (a) disorganized.
   (b) residual.
   (c) fragmented.
   (d) dissociative.

6. An individual who is identified as having a histrionic personality disorder shows

(a) persecutory thoughts.
(b) exhibitionistic tendencies.
(c) different personalities for different situations.
(d) exaggerated concern for the well-being of others.

Answer each of the following questions by filling in the blank with an appropriate word or phrase.

7. Depression associated with advanced age is called _____ depression.

8. A(n) _____ is an irresistible desire to perform a certain activity in a specified manner, whereas a(n) _____ refers to the occurrence of unwanted images or impulses one is unable to suppress.

9. A person with _____ _____ is characterized by an extreme fear of being judged or criticized by people, which often leads the individual to become socially isolated.

10. According to DSM-IV, an individual who complains of sudden and inexplicable attacks of fear and anxiety, accompanied by heart palpitations, sweating, and dizziness, will probably be classified as showing _____ _____.

11. Disorders characterized by a drastic change in a person's awareness of past or present experiences and in personal identity are referred to jointly as _____ _____.

12. Some war veterans show _____ _____ _____, which is characterized by recurring, and often painful memories and flashbacks of traumatic experiences.

13. An individual who has alternating periods of depressive and of manic symptoms probably is suffering from _____ _____.

14. A depression that appears to be a reaction to external events is termed _____ depression.

15. The category of schizophrenia known as _____ schizophrenia applies to individuals who have previously had at least one schizophrenic episode, but who currently show only mildly disturbed behavior.

16. A desire for sexual contact with children is called _____.

17. A disorder known as _____-_____ / _____ disorder is usually first diagnosed in childhood, but may extend into adulthood. Children with this disorder have difficulty focusing their attention, and tend to be impulsive and disruptive.

18. _____-_____ disorder occurs when an individual is uncomfortable with the gender roles linked to his or her sex, and the person identifies instead with the gender roles of the opposite sex.

19. A psychodynamic view is that _____ stems from internalized anger we have toward an actual or symbolically lost loved one.

20. According to DSM-IV, obsessive–compulsive disorder is classified as a(n) _____ _____.

Answers

1. b, 2. d, 3. c, 4. a, 5. a, 6. b, 7. involutional, 8. compulsion, obsession, 9. social phobia, 10. panic disorder, 11. dissociative disorders, 12. posttraumatic stress disorder, 13. bipolar disorder, 14. exogenous, 15. residual, 16. pedophilia, 17. attention-deficit/hyperactivity, 18. Gender-identity, 19. depression, 20. anxiety disorder

PATHWAYS TO UNDERSTANDING

1. Choose a psychological perspective that you find well suited to your own beliefs about abnormal behavior. Compare and contrast your preferred perspective with other perspectives, showing why yours makes better sense.

2. Suppose that your English teacher assigns you the task of creating a believable literary character that is schizophrenic. Briefly describe that person as others view the person; then describe how that person sees the world, including other persons.

3. Sometimes, it is tempting to analyze people you know in terms of the disorders they seem to show. What are the risks of assuming this kind of role as an amateur psychologist?

CHAPTER OUTLINE

What Were Some Early Methods of Psychotherapeutic Intervention?

How and Why Do Clinicians Diagnose Abnormal Behavior?

How Do Different Psychologists Approach Psychotherapy?
- Psychodynamic Therapy
- Humanistic Therapies
- Behavior Therapies
- Cognitive Approaches to Therapy
- Biological Therapies
- Multicultural Approaches to Psychotherapy

What Are Some Alternatives to Individual Psychotherapy?
- Group Therapy
- Couples and Family Therapy
- Self-Help

Is There an Optimal Approach to Psychotherapy?

How Effective Is Psychotherapy?
- When and How Should You—or Someone You Care About—Seek Psychotherapy?

What Are Some Key Ethical Issues in Psychotherapy?
- Recovery of Suppressed Memories—What Is Your Judgment?

CHAPTER 14

Psychotherapy

"You had a good time out with your father and mother," I commented.

"Yes," Dibs said. "It was nice. A very nice trip out to the beach and back. And there were no angry words. Not any."

"And no angry words," I commented.

He walked over to the sandbox and sat down on the edge of it. "This is where I made a prison for him and where I locked him in and buried him over with sand. I asked myself why I should let him out of this prison and set him free. And then I told myself just to let him be. Just let him be free?"

"Then you decided he should be set free?"

"Yes. I didn't want to keep him locked up and buried. I just wanted to teach him a lesson."

"I understand. You just wanted to teach him a lesson," I commented.

Dibs smiled. "Today I talked to Papa," he said with a happy, relieved smile.

It is interesting to note that Dibs' expressions of vengeance and hate were expressed more openly and directly and fully only after he felt more secure in his relationship with his father. It was good to hear that he was having more satisfying experiences with his father, who not only poured out information about oceans and rivers and streams but took turns with the shovel and helped build the sand castle with his son.

— *Virginia Axline,* Dibs: In Search of Self *(p. 182)*

In the preceding dialogue between a child psychotherapist and her young patient, we can see that the boy has probably had some trouble in his relationship with his father. However, the boy appears to be aware of his own feelings, quite able to express them, and fully able to cope with them. At the start of therapy, however, Dibs "could not talk at all. Sometimes he sat mute and unmoving all morning or crawled about the schoolroom floor oblivious to the other children or to his teacher. At times he had violent temper tantrums" (Axline, 1964, p. vii). The adults in his world had wondered whether Dibs was brain damaged, mentally retarded, or mentally ill. In her book, Virginia Axline illustrates the use of *play therapy*, in which children freely explore various play materials as a means of coming to understand their experiences and their feelings about those experiences. This passage also illustrates the techniques of *nondirective therapy*, in which the psychotherapist encourages clients to state their feelings, reflects those feelings back to the clients, and helps clients understand and act on their feelings.

Both play therapy and nondirective therapy are forms of **psychotherapy,** an intervention that uses the principles of psychology to try to improve the life of the person who receives the intervention. Axline's work illustrates some of the amazing successes that can be brought about by a compassionate and highly skilled psychotherapist. Unfortunately, we have not always responded to mentally ill persons with competent and humane treatment.

WHAT WERE SOME EARLY METHODS OF PSYCHOTHERAPEUTIC INTERVENTION?

In ancient times, in Europe, abnormal behavior was viewed as being caused by demons (see Chapter 13), so psychotherapeutic "treatment" involved trying to rid the mentally ill person of the supposed demons—often killing or at least torturing the afflicted person in the process. After the end of the Middle Ages, as people became aware that mental illness was not caused by demonic possession, slightly more humane treatments came into being. From about the 1400s through the 1700s, mentally ill persons were housed, and sometimes even treated, in

The present state of insane persons, confined within this commonwealth, in cages, closed cellars, stalls, pens! Chained, naked, beaten with rods, and lashed into obedience.

Dorothea Dix

psychotherapy a means of helping people with their psychological problems by using the principles of psychology

Dorothea Dix was instrumental in encouraging the development of mental hospitals as institutions separate from prisons.

asylums—hospitals for mentally ill patients. Many of these asylums resembled overcrowded prisons more than they did mental hospitals. The inmates were treated more like prisoners than patients, too—often chained to the walls of the cramped quarters, or chained to large iron balls, which they had to drag with them wherever they went.

The pathetic treatment of mentally disturbed persons appalled Parisian physician Phillipe Pinel (1745–1826). In 1793, Pinel removed the inmates' shackles, and as a result, the inmates became much calmer and more manageable. In the United States, mentally ill persons were commonly housed in prisons, along with convicted criminals. Social reformer Dorothea Dix (1802–1887) was instrumental in spurring the development of mental hospitals as separate institutions from prisons, designed for the humane treatment of mentally ill persons.

MINILECTURE

History of Psychotherapy (Ch 19)

How do societal beliefs about mental illness affect society's treatment of persons who engage in abnormal behavior?

What were some early methods of psychotherapeutic intervention? During the Middle Ages in Europe, mentally ill persons were accused of being possessed by demons and were often tortured and then killed. After the Middle Ages, in Europe, mentally ill persons were housed in prisonlike asylums. In the United States, mentally ill persons were actually housed with convicted criminals in prisons. In the eighteenth and nineteenth centuries, social reformers recognized the need for more humane treatment of mentally ill persons.

HOW AND WHY DO CLINICIANS DIAGNOSE ABNORMAL BEHAVIOR?

Before a clinician can treat a mentally ill person, the clinician must diagnose the person's problem. As mentioned in Chapter 13, the *Diagnostic and Statistical Manual* (DSM; now in its fourth edition, DSM-IV) enjoys widespread acceptance as a standard tool for diagnosis (Sartorius et al., 1993a). The DSM-IV is not perfect, however. Also, even if the DSM were flawless, diagnosis and treatment ultimately would depend not on the DSM, but on each individual clinician's judgment, based on his or her clinical experience and professional expertise.

When deciding how to respond to a new client, a clinician must answer three questions: (1) Does the client have a treatable problem? (2) If so, what is the problem? (3) Once the problem is diagnosed, how should the problem be treated? Clinicians use various techniques to answer these questions, some of which were described in Chapter 12 (e.g., projective and objective personality tests). No single technique is perfect, so clinicians often use more than one technique. Clinicians can then integrate and interpret a relatively wide variety of information. Once clinicians have diagnosed particular psychological problems, they can consider how to treat the problems. The particular form of treatment chosen depends on the psychological approach preferred by the individual clinician.

Cross-cultural psychologists have noted that an additional consideration in diagnosis and treatment of psychological disorders should be the cultural context in which the disorders appear (Matsumoto, 1994, 1996). For instance, regarding the diagnosis of schizophrenia, various culture-specific symptoms are observed in the Yoruba of Nigeria, such as "an expanded head and goose flesh" (cited in Matsumoto, 1996, p. 237). In diagnosing depressive disorders among the Hopi in the United States, brief episodes of severe depression are more characteristic than are relatively longer periods of depression (Matsumoto, 1996).

asylum hospital or other institution for housing and possibly treating mentally ill patients

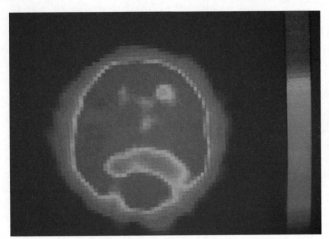
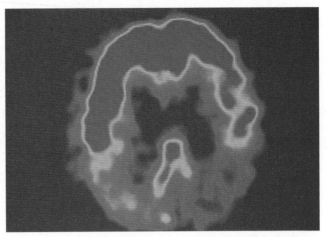

Increasingly, psychologists are able to use various kinds of images of the brain as an aid to diagnosing psychological disorders. Depicted here are PET scans showing a normal brain and the brain of a person diagnosed as having Alzheimer's dementia.

It should also be noted that many people who seek the help of psychotherapists do not suffer from any of the psychological disorders described in Chapter 13. Many people seek psychotherapy because they feel they need help in handling a particular aspect of their lives, because they wish to enhance their enjoyment of their lives, or because they are facing particularly difficult life circumstances. For instance, Joanie has recognized that her use of alcohol is creating problems in her marriage, so she is looking for some form of psychotherapy to help her both to deal with her alcohol use and to address her problems in her marriage. Paulo, a successful middle-aged salesperson, has started to feel that something is missing from his life, although he is not sure just what he lacks. He goes to a psychotherapist to get help in figuring out both what he wants and how to get what he lacks.

Li's husband of 15 years just died, leaving Li with a 6-month-old, a 2-year-old, and a 4-year-old to raise on her own. While her children are awake, Li is so busy that she does not have time to feel miserable and overwhelmed. Once her children are in bed, however, Li feels her life spinning out of her control; every night, she sobs herself to sleep. Li's friend at work keeps telling Li that she should see a psychotherapist to help her through this crisis.

How and why do clinicians diagnose abnormal behavior? Clinicians diagnose their patients' psychological disorders in order to know how to treat their patients. Although clinicians often base their diagnoses on DSM-IV symptom categories, contextual factors such as the culture of the patient should also influence the diagnosis. In addition, many people who do not have serious psychological disorders seek psychotherapy to help them to adjust to difficult situations or to enjoy their lives more fully.

HOW DO DIFFERENT PSYCHOLOGISTS APPROACH PSYCHOTHERAPY?

Each of the many different approaches to psychotherapy has been applied both to serious psychological disorders (such as those described in Chapter 13) and to mild psychological problems that arise because of relatively normal difficulties in adjustment or because of the need to cope with difficult situations. Each approach has accompanying advantages and disadvantages. Many of the therapies overlap, but it is still useful to consider the distinctions among the five main approaches: psychodynamic, humanistic, behavioral, cognitive, and biological. In addition, we consider a multicultural approach to psychotherapy. While reading about the distinctive features of these diverse approaches, bear in mind that many practicing psychotherapists use an *eclectic* approach to treatment, drawing on techniques and ideas from more than one of the main approaches to psychotherapy.

Psychodynamic Therapy

Psychodynamic therapies have in common their emphasis on insight as the key to improvement. The basic assumption is that when patients have *insight* into (understanding of) the sources of their problems, their problems will become manageable, and they will improve. Psychoanalysis is the main type of psychodynamic therapy.

Psychoanalysis

Psychoanalysts assume that psychological disorders result from unconscious conflicts among the id, the superego, and the demands of the environment. In their view, although people are unaware of these underlying conflicts, the conflicts affect their thoughts, feelings, and especially motivations. The key to helping patients to improve is to help them become conscious of ego-threatening material that has been repressed. Thus, treatment focuses on gradually peeling away layers of protective defenses to discover the underlying causes of psychological problems. For example, if a patient enters psychotherapy in order to conquer anxiety, the anxiety is considered a symptom of unconscious repressed conflicts among feelings, thoughts, and motives. To relieve the anxiety, the therapist must uncover and treat the underlying problem.

How does the therapist actually reveal the unconscious conflicts that underlie an observable disorder? Psychoanalysts use several different techniques (e.g., dream analysis; see Chapter 5). The most prominent of these techniques is **free association.** In free association, a person says whatever comes to mind, without stopping to check, think about, or edit his or her statements. At first, the patient may find it hard to report all thoughts through free association. With practice,

MINILECTURE

Approaches to Psychotherapy (Ch 19)

Look into the depths of your own soul and learn first to know yourself, then you will understand why this illness was bound to come upon you and perhaps you will thenceforth avoid falling ill.

Sigmund Freud

All the art of analysis consists in saying a truth only when the other person is ready for it, has been prepared for it by an organic process of gradation and evolution.

Anaïs Nin

free association psychodynamic technique in which patients are encouraged to say whatever comes to mind, without censoring or otherwise editing their statements

Visitors to Vienna can still see Sigmund Freud's treatment room, where his neurological patients served as case studies for Freud's development of his psychodynamic theory. On this world-renowned couch, Freud's patients worked through their unconscious conflicts, in response to Freud's psychoanalytic therapy.

however, the patient usually finds it easier. According to the psychoanalytic view, it is critical not to edit anything out because the most interesting and important details are usually those that the patient does not wish to say aloud. Typically, to enhance free association, the patient is encouraged to relax—for example, by lying down on a couch in a comfortable setting.

If patients could make free associations that immediately led them to repressed material, psychoanalysis would be over quickly. The actual course of therapy rarely works that way. According to psychoanalytic theory, it does not work that way because of resistances. **Resistances** are attempts, usually unconscious, to block progress. Why would patients try to block progress, especially when they are paying for therapy in order to make progress? Resistances protect patients from dealing with the contents of the unconscious, which are often quite painful. For that reason, patients unconsciously try to resist the therapeutic process. Resistances can take various forms, such as remaining silent, making jokes, or even skipping sessions. Trained psychoanalysts identify and deal with resistances when they arise.

Psychoanalytic therapists remain relatively detached from their patients and have little emotional involvement with them. The therapist seems almost like a shadowy parent figure who tries to help the patient without becoming too involved in the patient's problems. The patient, however, often becomes quite involved with the therapist. Indeed, the patient may start treating the therapist as though the therapist were contributing to the patient's problems. The patient's emotional involvement with the therapist is termed **transference.** The basic notion is that patients shift to the therapist the thoughts and feelings they have had toward others in the past, such as toward their parents. By being detached, therapists actually encourage transference because patients can project onto their therapist whatever conflicts or fantasies arise during therapy. The detached therapist is something like a blank screen onto which patients can project their past relationships. According to Sigmund Freud, such transference helps the patient by bringing out into the open any conflicts that have been suppressed in the past.

All psychoanalysts must themselves first be psychoanalyzed in order to understand better their own conflicts and sources of psychological distress. This understanding is particularly important in order to avoid **countertransference,** in which the therapist projects onto the patient the therapist's own feelings. Therapists who project their own problems onto the patient may fail to help their patients and may even cause harm to their patients.

Offshoots of Psychoanalysis

Psychoanalysis has been important to the historical development of psychotherapy. Among its many contributions, it has generated a variety of offshoots. Many of these offshoots developed from the theories of personality offered by Freud's followers, the neo-Freudians, such as Carl Jung, Erik Erikson, and Karen Horney (described in Chapter 12). The various forms of neo-Freudian therapy are sometimes termed *ego analysis* because of their common view that the ego is at least as important as the id. In other words, conscious processing is just as important as—and possibly more important than—unconscious processing. According to ego analysts, to understand their patients fully, therapists need to understand not only their patients' early life history, but also their patients' present experiences and future goals and plans.

Humanistic Therapies

Like psychoanalysis and other psychodynamic therapies, humanistic therapies emphasize insight. Beyond this similarity, however, humanistic therapies differ greatly from psychodynamic therapies. For one thing, humanistic therapists refer to the people they treat as "clients," whereas psychodynamic therapists usually refer to

---

Psychiatry is the art of teaching people to stand on their own feet while reclining on couches.

Shannon Fife

Asking questions in therapy would be so helpful if anyone ever answered them accurately. But no one ever does.

Virginia Mae Axline

It might be said of psychoanalysis that if you give it your little finger it will soon have your whole hand.

Sigmund Freud

A wonderful discovery—psychoanalysis. Makes quite simple people feel they're complex.

Samuel N. Behrman

What is a recent interpersonal problem you have had? What might a psychodynamic therapist tell you regarding your handling of the problem?

Show me a sane man and I will cure him for you.

Carl Gustav Jung

resistance a defensive tactic used by patients, usually unconsciously, to keep from becoming aware of unconscious material that affects the progress of therapy

transference a term used in psychodynamic therapy, describing a patient's emotional involvement with the psychotherapist as an authority figure

countertransference a term used in psychodynamic therapy, describing a situation in which the therapist becomes emotionally involved with the patient, projecting the therapist's own feelings onto the patient

In client-centered therapy, the therapist listens empathically to the client, showing both unconditional positive regard for the client and genuine self-disclosure to the client.

them as "patients." This difference in choice of words reflects a deeper difference between the two approaches. Psychodynamic therapy is based on a model of disorder in which an underlying disease process is considered the source of the patient's troubles. In contrast, the humanistic model views each person as an individual with feelings and thoughts that may come into conflict with each other or with society, thereby causing problems in living.

The role of the therapist also differs across models. Psychodynamic therapists believe that only highly skilled psychoanalysts can understand the complexities of the human mind and behavior. Humanistic therapists, on the other hand, believe that clients can be helped to understand their own minds and behavior. Humanistic therapists do not interpret and then provide insights to their patients. Rather, therapists help clients actively to gain their own insights.

Another key difference is that in the psychodynamic view, we are largely ruled by unconscious forces, whereas in the humanistic view, we have free will and are ruled by our own conscious decisions. Psychodynamic therapists often seem to view people as being tossed about by internal forces that the people can scarcely understand, let alone influence. In contrast, humanistic therapists emphasize free will. When people are mentally well, they are aware of and understand their own behavior. People can thus change their behavior at will. Because people are free to make choices, a goal of therapy is to help each client to *feel* completely free in making choices.

All humanistic therapy is centered on the client. Carl Rogers (1961a, 1961b) developed his particular form of **client-centered therapy** (later called "person-centered therapy") on the assumption that clients can be understood only in terms of their own view of reality, which they build for themselves. To client-centered therapists, the actual events that occur in people's lives are less important than the ways in which people interpret those events. Thus, client-centered therapists do not try to impose a theoretical system (such as Freud's) on the client. Instead, they try to understand how their clients view the world. Client-centered therapy is also *nondirective*—the therapist is not supposed to guide the course of therapy in any particular direction.

Rogers believed that people are basically good and adaptive both in what they do and in the goals they set for themselves. When they act otherwise, they need guidance only to see for themselves how better to adapt to their situations. The goal of client-centered therapy is to help people realize their full potential. Rogers believed that there are three keys to successful therapy:

1. *Genuineness,* as shown in the therapist's openness, honesty, self-disclosure, and expression of genuine feelings with the client, as well as with her- or himself

There can be no proper interpretation of yourself to others if you are confused about yourself. . . . The first job is to get some clarity of understanding about yourself, what you are, and where you are going.

Harry D. Gideonese

When mental [illness] increases until it reaches the danger point, do not exhaust yourself by efforts to trace back to original causes. Better accept them as inevitable and save your strength to fight against the effects.

George Sand

I have come to feel that the only learning which significantly influences behavior is self-discovered, self-appropriated learning.

Carl Rogers

Psychotherapy, unlike castor oil, which will work no matter how you get it down, is useless when forced on an uncooperative patient.

Abigail Van Buren

client-centered therapy a form of humanistic psychotherapy in which the therapeutic interactions center on the client's view of reality

Write a brief fragment of an imaginary dialogue between a humanistic therapist and the therapist's client.

2. *Unconditional positive regard* toward the client, which encourages the client to feel unconditional positive self-regard

3. *Accurate empathic understanding* of the client's view of the world

In client-centered, nondirective therapy, the therapist follows the client's lead; in contrast, in psychodynamic therapy, the therapist has a particular direction in mind regarding how to lead the patient—namely, toward the uncovering of unconscious conflicts. Thus, the course of client-centered therapy is likely to be quite different from that of psychodynamic therapy. Nondirective, client-centered therapists believe that by listening empathically to clients and by helping clients to clarify and explore their own feelings, clients will then feel free to live as they choose.

Behavior Therapies

Behavior therapy refers to a collection of techniques, which is based loosely on principles of classical and operant conditioning, as well as on observational learning from models (see Chapter 6). Several features characterize behavior therapy. First, whereas psychoanalysis shuns the treatment of symptoms, behavior therapy deliberately focuses only on symptoms. To the behavior therapist, the symptom *is* the problem. If a person is experiencing anxiety, then the person needs to reduce that anxiety to function effectively. Behaviorists waste no time looking for underlying causes of the symptoms, rooted in the person's past experiences. In short, behavior therapy concentrates on behavior. Behavior therapists do not try to address psychological insights or changes. They focus only on trying to change the maladaptive behavior.

Second, behavior therapy is extremely directive. Although the behavior therapist works with the client, the therapist alone designs a detailed treatment plan. Next, the patient follows the therapist's treatment plan, and when the plan has been carried out, the therapy ends. Third, behavior therapy is deliberately short term; the goal is to effect behavioral change quickly. Fourth, behavior therapy often involves the institution of changes in the environment. For example, if the environment currently reinforces maladaptive behavior and punishes adaptive behavior, those contingencies must be changed in order to change the behavior. Finally, behavior therapists take an objective approach, both to the therapy and to the evaluation of the outcomes of the therapy.

Behavior therapy consists of a set of explicit techniques. Basically, these techniques can be categorized roughly as involving classical conditioning, operant conditioning, or observational learning (modeling). Table 14-1 summarizes the treatments involving classical or operant conditioning. *Classical conditioning* treatments include various **counterconditioning** techniques (e.g., *aversion therapy* or *systematic desensitization*), which replace an unwanted response (e.g., anxiety) to a particular stimulus (e.g., flying) with an alternative response (e.g., physical relaxation) to that stimulus, as well as **extinction procedures,** which include various techniques (e.g., *flooding* or *implosion therapy*) that weaken maladaptive responses. *Operant conditioning* techniques include the use of a *token economy* or *behavioral contracting*. (Figure 14-1 shows the relative effectiveness of a few behavioral therapies.) In addition, *modeling* may be used as a form of behavioral therapy.

As mentioned in Chapter 6, many of the principles of **modeling** come from the work of Albert Bandura (1969). Bandura's basic idea is that people can change simply by watching other people successfully cope with the problems they face. For example, phobic adults have overcome snake phobias by watching other people confront snakes, either in actual live situations or on film (Bandura, Blanchard, & Ritter, 1969). The clients watched as the models moved closer and closer to the snakes; with time, the clients' phobias decreased. Modeling has also been used in various other kinds of therapy. In fact, the therapeutic effects of many kinds of psychotherapy, including therapy groups, may be at least partly due to modeling (Braswell & Kendall, 1988).

THE FAR SIDE   By GARY LARSON

Professor Gallagher and his controversial technique of simultaneously confronting the fear of heights, snakes and the dark.

The Far Side © 1986 FarWorks, Inc./Distributed by Universal Press Syndicate. Reprinted with permission. All rights reserved.

behavior therapy various psychotherapeutic techniques based mostly on principles of classical and operant conditioning, as well as some techniques based on observational learning from models

counterconditioning behavioral techniques based on classical conditioning, emphasizing the substitution of an adaptive response (e.g., relaxation) in place of a maladaptive one (e.g., anxiety) to a particular stimulus

extinction procedures behavioral techniques based on classical conditioning, in which the goal is to weaken a maladaptive response

modeling a cognitive and behavioral technique in which people are encouraged to change simply by watching other people successfully cope with challenging problems that affect the observer

TABLE 14-1

Behavioral Treatments for Psychological Problems

Procedures based on classical conditioning	
Counterconditioning	A particular response to a particular stimulus is replaced by an alternative response to that stimulus. The alternative substitute response is incompatible with the unwanted initial response, such as replacing an initial positive response with a negative one, or counterconditioning the patient to feel a negative response instead of a positive one.
Aversion therapy	The therapist seeks to teach the client to experience negative feelings in the presence of a stimulus that is considered inappropriately attractive.
Systematic desensitization	The therapist seeks to help the client learn *not* to experience negative feelings (e.g., anxiety) toward a stimulus that currently prompts a negative response (Wolpe, 1958).
Extinction procedures	A particular maladaptive emotional response to a particular stimulus is weakened and eventually extinguished by presenting the particular stimulus in the absence of whatever stimuli may have prompted the learning of the emotional response.
Flooding	Patients are directly exposed to the stimulus that causes them extreme levels of anxiety so that they realize that nothing horrible happens in the presence of the stimulus. They can then learn to cope with the situation when they face it again in the future.
Implosion therapy	Patients are asked to imagine and—to the extent that they can—relive unpleasant experiences with stimuli that are causing them anxiety. As in systematic desensitization, they only imagine a graduated series of steps; anxiety is extinguished by the absence of any harmful or threatening stimuli in association with the stimulus that provokes the anxiety.
Procedures based on operant conditioning	
Token economy	Patients within institutional or other controlled settings receive *tokens* (tangible objects that have no intrinsic worth) as rewards for showing adaptive behavior. The tokens can later be used in exchange for goods or services that the individuals desire. This technique has been used primarily with children who have PDD (pervasive developmental disorder; i.e., autism), although it has been used with other populations as well.
Behavioral contracting	The therapist and the client draw up a contract, and both parties are obliged to live up to it. The contract requires the client to show specific behaviors that are the focus of the therapy, in return for which the therapist will give the client particular things that the client may want, including even permission to terminate the therapy.

Cognitive Approaches to Therapy

Originally, Bandura (1969; Bandura & Walters, 1963) viewed modeling as a behavioral phenomenon. However, as the cognitive revolution proceeded, Bandura started to reformulate the modeling phenomenon in terms of cognitive theory. Indeed, the processes that the observer uses for imitating the model are certainly cognitive ones (Bandura, 1986).

In cognitive approaches to therapy, behavioral change is achieved by changing a person's thinking. If people can be made to think differently about themselves and their experiences, they can feel and act differently as a result. Albert Ellis's rational-emotive therapy and Aaron Beck's cognitive therapy are both cognitive approaches to psychotherapy.

Rational-Emotive Therapy

When Albert Ellis (1962, 1970, 1973, 1989) formulated **rational-emotive therapy (RET),** his basic idea was that psychological problems arise because people mentally recite sentences that express incorrect or maladaptive thoughts. In Ellis's view, cognition precedes emotion (see also Chapter 11). Thus, the emotions we

For which types of disorders do you believe that behavior therapy would be most effective? Why?

Drag your thoughts away from your troubles— by the ears, by the heels, or any other way, so you manage it; it's the healthiest thing a body can do.

Mark Twain

rational-emotive therapy (RET) a form of cognitive therapy, based on the notions that (a) incorrect or maladaptive thoughts lead to emotional and other psychological problems, and (b) changes in these thoughts lead to improvements in psychological well-being

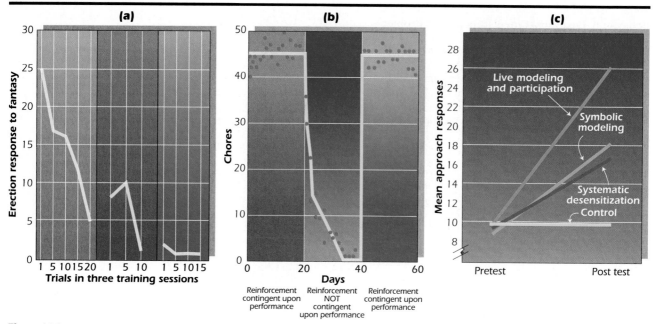

Figure 14-1

Effectiveness of Behavioral Therapies

(a) Aversion therapy, a form of classical conditioning, successfully reduced a patient's response (penile arousal) to an inappropriate stimulus (a fantasy of being tied up). (After Marks & Gelder, 1967) (b) A token economy, a form of operant conditioning, successfully increased the wanted behavior (performance of self-help chores) of individuals in an institutional setting. (c) Comparisons of live modeling, symbolic modeling (in which the patient imagines the anxiety-producing stimulus), and systematic desensitization suggest that although all three techniques lead to some behavioral improvement above that of control patients, live modeling and participation is the most effective of these techniques.

feel are caused by the thoughts we have, and we can change our emotions only by changing our thoughts. The goal of Ellis's psychotherapy, therefore, is to change our incorrect and maladaptive thoughts. Ellis's RET and other forms of cognitive therapy have been particularly effective in treating certain anxious patients (Perris & Herlofson, 1993).

Examples of incorrect beliefs that may lead to maladjustment include the following (Ellis, 1970): "You should be loved by everyone for everything you do." "You need to have perfect self-control at all times." "You should be thoroughly competent in all respects." To Ellis, the best technique for dealing with incorrect and maladaptive beliefs is to confront the client directly and to dispute the client's beliefs. In other words, the therapist tries to show clients that these false beliefs are leading them to be unhappy and dysfunctional in everyday life. Ellis's goals are similar to those of humanistic therapists: to increase a client's sense of self-worth, and to help the client to grow and to make choices by recognizing all of the available options.

Beck's Cognitive Therapy

Like Ellis's RET, the cognitive therapy of Aaron Beck (1976, 1986) celebrates the importance of cognition. However, Beck's approach differs from Ellis's in both the cognitive theorizing and the form of the psychotherapy. In Beck's view, people become maladjusted as a result of cognitive distortion. Beck has concentrated particularly on depression, and some findings suggest that the demonstrated effectiveness for cognitive therapy is higher for depressive disorders than for other disorders (Perris & Herlofson, 1993). In treating depression, Beck particularly targets maladaptive schemas that lead us to believe that we are incompetent or worthless.

Everyone occasionally engages in maladaptive thought patterns. What is a situation you have recently faced in which you could apply some of the ideas from cognitive therapy? How would you apply these ideas?

Behavior therapy may involve classical conditioning, operant conditioning, or observational learning (modeling). (a) Through counterconditioning, phobic flyers can learn to respond to airplane flights by feeling relaxed instead of feeling tense and anxious. (b) Observational learning may be helping these children to avoid developing a fear of snakes, but more than observational learning may be needed to help the woman in the background feel less fearful of snakes.

Biological Therapies

Biological therapies attempt to treat psychological disorders through medical intervention. These therapies differ from all those that we have considered up to this point because in biological therapies, talking (such as in the client–therapist relationship) plays no more of a role than would be the case for any patient–doctor interaction. Biological therapies can be used along with more psychologically oriented ones, of course, and they often are. When used together, however, psychological therapies tend to play a supportive rather than a central role in the therapeutic process.

Brief History of Biological Therapies

Biological therapies date back at least to ancient Rome, where particular psychological disorders were viewed as being caused by poisons or other undesirable substances that had entered the body. To rid the body of these foreign substances, patients were given drugs causing them to vomit or to defecate (Agnew, 1985). Another way of ridding the body of unwanted substances was through selective bleeding. The idea underlying these treatments was to rid the body of whatever substances were causing the mental disturbance. These treatments were used as recently as the eighteenth century. Another early biological treatment was electrical shock, also used in the eighteenth and nineteenth centuries. Apparently, the idea was literally to shock the disorder out of the body, and to shock the client into recovery.

In the early twentieth century, electrical shock therapy took a form known as **electroconvulsive therapy (ECT).** ECT has been used for the treatment of severe, unending depression. This form of therapy, still in occasional use today, causes patients to undergo seizures induced by electrical shock. Use of ECT has always been controversial for at least two reasons: (1) The loss of memory caused by ECT can be long-lasting, and (2) the procedure destroys neurons of the central nervous system. Also, although the treatment seems to be effective for some patients (Abrams, 1988; Scovern & Kilmann, 1980), it does not work for others (Scott, 1989). Thus, it is almost always a treatment of last resort, particularly for

electroconvulsive therapy (ECT) a form of psychophysiological therapy in which patients undergo electrical shocks, which cause convulsive seizures followed by a period of amnesia, and which may relieve severe symptoms of depression

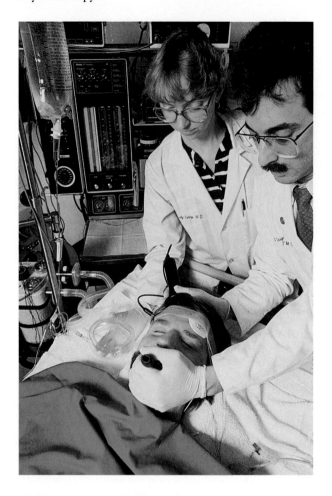

Although electroconvulsive therapy (ECT) is still used by some clinicians, its use is less common and more specific to treatment of severe depression now than it was decades ago. As you can see, even the technical apparatus makes the process seem intimidating. The paddle inserted into the patient's mouth is intended to prevent injury due to the violent contortions associated with the seizures following ECT.

MINILECTURE

Biological Psychotherapies
(Ch 19)

psychosurgery a procedure intended to relieve psychological problems by probing, slicing, dissecting, or removing some part of the brain

prefrontal lobotomy an obsolete procedure in which the frontal lobes of the brain are cut off from contact with the rest of the brain, in order to make patients more compliant

psychotropic drug any of several types of drugs that affect the psychological processes or state of mind of an individual

severely depressed patients (Bolwig, 1993). In most cases, depression can be treated with psychotherapy, sometimes combined with antidepressant drugs, making ECT unnecessary.

Another biological treatment proved to be among the most disastrous of the psychiatric profession's attempts to achieve biological cures: prefrontal lobotomy, a form of psychosurgery. The basic reason to use **psychosurgery** is to relieve or reduce mental disorders through a procedure that probes, slices, dissects, or removes some portion of the brain. **Prefrontal lobotomy** involved severing the frontal lobes from the posterior portions of the brain, thereby cutting off all communication between the frontal lobes and the rest of the brain. The operation left many patients *vegetative*, incapable of functioning independently in any meaningful way. Even those operations that were less disastrously tragic could not be considered successful in terms of restoring mental health and normal cognitive function. Unfortunately, between 1935 (when the operation was first introduced) and 1955 (when antipsychotic drugs became the method of choice for treating many of the symptoms of schizophrenia and other disorders), prefrontal lobotomy is estimated to have victimized tens of thousands of patients, primarily in mental institutions (Freeman, 1959). The inventor of the operation even received the Nobel Prize in medicine for his contributions.

Drug Therapies

Since the mid-1950s, the introduction of drug therapies has unquestionably been the major advance in the biological approach to the treatment of mental disorders. There are four main classes of **psychotropic drugs** (i.e., drugs affecting the individual's psychological processes or state of mind): antipsychotic drugs, antidepressant drugs, antianxiety drugs, and lithium.

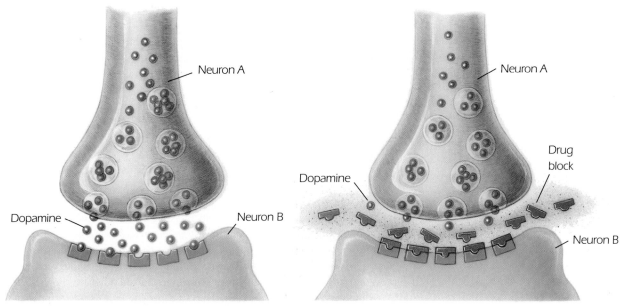

(a) Before drug therapy   (b) After drug therapy

Figure 14-2
Antipsychotic Drugs and Dopamine Receptors
Some types of antipsychotic drugs seem to work because they block the ability of the brain to receive the excessive amounts of the neurotransmitter dopamine that lead to some of the positive symptoms of schizophrenia, such as hallucinations and delusions.

Antipsychotic Drugs.   **Antipsychotic drugs** were a breakthrough in the treatment of psychotic patients. Before the introduction of such drugs, mental hospitals resembled many of our worst stereotypes. They were characterized by wild screaming and even the threat of violence (Carson & Butcher, 1992). Antipsychotic drugs completely changed the atmosphere in many of these wards.

The most commonly used antipsychotic drugs, introduced in the early 1950s, are *phenothiazines*. These antipsychotic drugs relieve the positive symptoms of schizophrenia by blocking receptors for the neurotransmitter dopamine in the schizophrenic brain (see Figure 14-2). Although these drugs successfully treat the positive symptoms of schizophrenia (e.g., hallucinations), they are less successful in treating the negative symptoms (e.g., apathy). The antipsychotic drugs also have serious side effects, such as dryness of the mouth, tremors, and stiffness of the muscles. At present, there is no clear answer as to how to balance the costs and the benefits of antipsychotic medication. We are far from having magic cure-all pills for treating psychoses.

Antidepressant Drugs.   **Antidepressant drugs** have traditionally been of two main kinds: *tricyclics* and *monoamine oxidase (MAO) inhibitors*. Tricyclics are much more frequently used because MAO inhibitors are more toxic, require adherence to a special diet, and generally provide less successful outcomes. However, some people do not respond to tricyclics but do respond to MAO inhibitors, so the MAO inhibitors may be used for these patients.

Both types of antidepressant drugs seem to have roughly the same effect: They increase the concentrations of two neurotransmitters—serotonin and norepinephrine—at particular synapses in the brain (see Chapter 2). Concentrations of these neurotransmitters begin to increase almost immediately after patients start taking the drugs. However, the antidepressant effect does not begin immediately. It can take several weeks, and sometimes longer, before the patient starts to feel the effects.

A third type of antidepressant drug has more recently been introduced: It works by inhibiting the reuptake of serotonin and norepinephrine. This inhibition of reuptake effectively increases the concentrations of the two neurotransmitters,

antipsychotic drug a drug used for treating psychosis (e.g., schizophrenia)

antidepressant drug a drug used for treating depression

but it does so less directly than do the other two types of antidepressant drugs. The most well-known of these new drugs is fluoxetine (Prozac). Depressed patients typically start to show improvement after about 3 weeks of taking the drug. The drug seems to work for a wide variety of patients, but this drug, too, can have side effects, such as nausea and nervousness (Cole & Bodkin, 1990; Papp & Gorman, 1990).

From one point of view, drug treatment of depression has been considerably more successful than drug treatment of schizophrenia. Whereas antipsychotic drugs only suppress the symptoms as long as the patient continues to take the drugs, antidepressant drugs seem to cause more lasting change. Patients who stop taking antipsychotic drugs typically return to their earlier psychotic state, whereas patients who stop taking antidepressant drugs often remain symptom free for quite some time, and possibly indefinitely.

When we consider the difference in the long-term effectiveness of antipsychotic versus antidepressant drugs, however, we must also consider the rates of **spontaneous recovery**. In spontaneous recovery, the person's symptoms seem to disappear, without any treatment whatsoever. The rate of spontaneous recovery for depression is much higher than that for schizophrenia and other psychoses. Therefore, an unknown proportion of the depressed patients who show improvement through the use of drugs or other psychotherapy might have become better even if they had received no treatment at all.

In addition, researchers and clinicians must consider the effects of **placebos:** Patients may improve simply because they believe that they are being helped, even if the treatment they receive actually has no direct effect whatsoever. To rule out both the effects of spontaneous recovery and the effects of placebos, researchers studying the effects of drugs often use both control groups that take placebos and control groups that are simply put on a waiting list for subsequent treatment (e.g., see Figure 14-3). The control group taking placebos may also be studied using a *double-blind technique*, in which both the experimenter administering the treatment and the patient are kept from knowing whether a particular patient is receiving a placebo or an active drug.

Antianxiety Drugs. Clinicians prescribe antianxiety drugs (also called "anxiolytics" or "tranquilizers") to relieve their patients' feelings of tension and anxiety, to increase patients' feelings of well-being, and to combat symptoms of insomnia. The earliest antianxiety drugs, the **barbiturates** (see Chapter 5), are rarely used

Figure 14-3

Effectiveness of Antipsychotic Drugs

The rates of unwanted symptomatic behavior are much higher for patients in the placebo-control group than for patients in the treatment group (who received Mellaril, a brand of phenothiazine). In addition, the rate of symptomatic behavior for the treatment group temporarily rose during a brief trial (Observations 41–45) when a placebo was substituted for the drug, and it declined again following reinstitution of the drug treatment. What do you infer from these findings?

spontaneous recovery the disappearance of a person's symptoms, which occurs without any treatment whatsoever

placebo a pill or other substance that the patient believes to have curative or healing properties, but that actually has no such properties; often used as a means of determining whether drug treatments are truly effective or work only because patients believe that they are being helped

barbiturate a highly addictive and potentially dangerous type of antianxiety drug, used for inducing sleep or a state of calmness

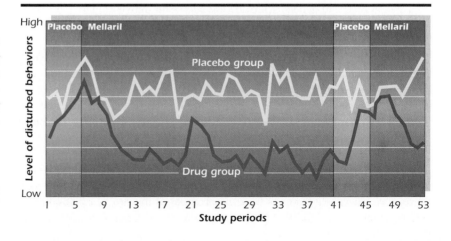

today because they are highly addictive and potentially dangerous. More commonly used are two classes of antianxiety drugs: muscle relaxants and benzodiazepines. The *muscle relaxants* reduce muscular tension and cause feelings of tranquility (calm).

Benzodiazepines also cause muscle relaxation and have an even stronger tranquilizing effect. Two of the most well-known and very widely used drugs are chlordiazepoxide (Librium) and diazepam (Valium). All too often, clinicians have prescribed these drugs without thinking enough about their possible consequences. For example, the use of antianxiety drugs can impair attention and alertness (Schweizer et al., 1990), and tranquilizing effects of these drugs can hinder performance of certain tasks (e.g., listening attentively to a lecture or driving). Thus, the drugs should not be used before or during any activity that requires alertness, intelligent thought, or creativity. The drugs can also be habit forming.

Lithium. In 1949, lithium was found to be effective in treating bipolar (manic–depressive) disorders, and it remains the drug of choice for these disorders. Lithium is very effective, causing almost immediate relief of symptoms in roughly three fourths of cases. However, it does not relieve depressive symptoms in persons who do not have a bipolar disorder. This finding supports the notion that bipolar disorders differ qualitatively from unipolar depression (Baron et al., 1975). We still do not know why lithium has the effect it does (Manji et al., 1991), and the drug must be used with care because overdoses can lead to convulsions and even to death.

Conclusions. The main breakthroughs in pharmacotherapy, represented by the preceding four classes of psychotropic drugs (antipsychotics, antidepressants, antianxiety drugs, and lithium), have revolutionized the psychiatric treatment of mental illness (Sartorius et al., 1993b). Subsequent developments have led to improvements in applying these treatments.

Multicultural Approaches to Psychotherapy

Cross-cultural and multicultural psychologists (e.g., Higginbotham, 1979) have pointed out that many people's responses to treatment depend on the cultural appropriateness of the treatment. For one thing, some psychological disorders more closely match non-Western, culture-specific definitions of abnormal behavior than they match the symptom categories of DSM-IV. The persons suffering from culture-specific disorders may expect that culture-specific healing practices will be more effective in treating those disorders than will the foregoing five main approaches identified in Western cultures. For instance, the culture-specific disorder of *susto* (an anxiety disorder observed in some Latin American cultures) seems to respond more to treatment by native healers (e.g., shamans or *curanderos*) than to Western treatment approaches, such as cognitive–behavioral psychotherapy (Matsumoto, 1996).

Multicultural approaches are also important for treatment of non-culture-specific psychological disorders. In studies in Seattle and in Los Angeles, Asian Americans and Native Americans were less likely to seek mental health services than were European Americans and African Americans (Sue, 1977). Once in treatment, Americans other than European Americans were much more likely to drop out of treatment (Sue, 1977, 1991). According to some research (Atkinson, Ponce, & Martinez, 1984), the key to effective treatment is not necessarily that the therapist and the client share a common (or even similar) culture and gender, but rather that they share similar worldviews and attitudes toward treatment.

It is not always possible for therapist and client to share worldviews, but effective therapists can show sensitivity to the cultural perspectives of their clients (Hedstrom, 1994). Psychotherapists who show cultural sensitivity toward their clients are considered more competent and more believable and trustworthy by clients of diverse cultural backgrounds, including Mexican-American (Atkinson,

There's no medicine for fear.

Scottish proverb

Ideas regarding the optimal form of psycho-threrapy vary widely from one culture to another.

Casa, & Abreu, 1992), African-American (Atkinson, Furlong, & Poston, 1986), and Asian-American clients (Gim, Atkinson, & Kim, 1991). How can psychotherapists gain cultural sensitivity? Psychotherapists become increasingly sensitive by working with culturally diverse clients (Sue, Akutsu, & Higashi, 1985) and by becoming knowledgeable about diverse cultures and lifestyles.

Finally, effective cross-cultural psychotherapists may need to be open to developing their skill in using innovative methods of treating persons from diverse cultures, including in their repertoires various culture-specific treatment approaches and techniques (Aldous, 1994). As an example, a Japanese treatment option is *naikan* therapy, in which the patient spends a week meditating from early morning until late evening, focusing on self-analysis and self-improvement, in order to become more fully reintegrated into her or his social network (Murase & Johnson, 1974; Reynolds, 1989). The *naikan* therapist periodically provides brief instructions to the meditator regarding how to direct meditative self-examination for achieving enhanced social integration.

How do different psychologists approach psychotherapy? Psychodynamic therapists try to help patients gain insight into the unconscious conflicts underlying their psychological difficulties. Humanistic therapists, by providing their clients with acceptance and empathy, enable their clients to gain insight about the psychological obstacles (e.g., low self-regard) that may be preventing the clients from reaching their full potential. Behavioral therapists use techniques based either on classical or operant conditioning or on observational learning, to help people to change their maladaptive behavior. Cognitive therapists help clients to change their maladaptive thought processes or thought contents. Biological therapists use various treatments (e.g., electroconvulsive therapy or psychotropic drugs) to treat the physiological abnormalities that are causing their patients' psychological problems. Multicultural therapists use therapeutic techniques that are appropriate to the cultural expectations, experiences, and outlooks of their clients.

WHAT ARE SOME ALTERNATIVES TO INDIVIDUAL PSYCHOTHERAPY?

The forms of psychotherapy described in the preceding sections of this chapter largely involve one psychotherapist administering some form of treatment to one client at a time. In some situations, however, various alternatives to one-on-one therapy may be useful. These options include group therapy, couples and family therapy, and self-help. These alternatives to individual psychotherapy have also been widely available among many non-Western societies (Langsley, Hodes, & Grimson, 1993).

Group Therapy

Humanistic therapy, behavior therapy, and cognitive therapy can be administered either individually or in groups. Group therapy may offer some distinct advantages over individual psychotherapy: (a) Group therapy is almost always less expensive than is individual therapy. (b) Groups may offer greater support than does individual therapy because groups usually include several individuals with similar problems. (c) Group therapy offers the potential value of social pressure to change; this pressure may add to (or even replace) the authoritative pressure to change that comes from the therapist. (d) The very dynamic of group interaction may lead to therapeutic change, especially in the cases of people who have problems with interpersonal interactions.

Group therapy also has potential disadvantages: (a) The treatment offered by the therapist may be diluted by the presence of other persons requiring the therapist's attention. (b) Group psychotherapy may shift the focus of therapy sessions to other issues, such as group interactions, instead of the presenting problems that prompted the members to seek therapy in the first place.

Couples and Family Therapy

The goal of couples and family therapy is to treat problems from a *systems perspective*. That is, the therapist treats the problems of the couple or the family unit as a

The advantages of receiving psychotherapy in a group setting may include reduced cost, greater social pressure to effect positive changes, and greater diversity of persons who may offer a fresh perspective on a troubling situation. The disadvantages of group therapy include the potential for dilution of the treatment and for group dynamics to take precedence over the presenting problem that stimulated the desire to obtain therapy.

whole system that involves complex internal interactions, instead of treating the separate problems of distinct members of the unit. The identified problem may be centered on the family unit, such as troubled communication among family members. However, the identified problem may also be centered on one member of the unit. The underlying notion in this kind of therapy is that even individual problems often have their roots in the family system. In order to treat the problem, the whole family should be part of the solution. Surprisingly, some apparently individual problems—such as eating disorders—can be treated quite effectively in family therapy, particularly if the disorder is caught early (within 3 years of onset) in a young person (see Langsley et al., 1993).

In cases of marital conflict, couples therapy is more successful than is individual therapy in holding couples together and in bringing them back together (Gurman, Kniskern, & Pinsoff, 1986). Couples therapy tends to be particularly successful for people who have had problems for only a short time before they entered therapy, and when the people have not yet initiated action toward divorce. One reason for the greater success of couples therapy is that the therapist can hear the views of both partners. Hearing both points of view enables the therapist to mediate more effectively than does hearing just a single point of view.

When working with children, perhaps as part of family therapy, it may be useful to engage the child in play activities while helping the child to work through psychological difficulties.

Couples therapy is highly effective in helping couples to resolve interpersonal conflict and to enhance communication, particularly if the presenting problems have been of short duration prior to treatment and the couple has not yet started divorce action.

In couples therapy, communication and mutual empathy are emphasized. Partners are trained to listen carefully and empathically to each other. They learn to restate what the partner is saying, thereby confirming that they accurately understood the partner's point of view. Partners in unsuccessful relationships often fail to hear even the positive things that each one says about the other (Gottman, 1979, 1994). Couples are also taught how to make constructive and direct requests of each other, instead of making indirect requests that can be confusing and easily misinterpreted.

Cognitive therapist Aaron Beck (1988) has emphasized the importance of having each partner understand the perspective of the other. He urges partners to clarify the differences in what each partner seeks for the relationship. Each partner may have secret "shoulds"—things that each of us believes that our partner ought to do. Unfortunately, our partner may not believe these things to be important or worth doing. If one or both partners fail to state their "shoulds" clearly, yet both hold these "shoulds" to be essential, problems arise. Beck believes that many problems in a relationship can be attributed to "shoulds" that become *automatic thoughts*, which can rise into consciousness without any effort or intention on the part of the thinker.

You're either part of the solution or you're part of the problem.

Eldridge Cleaver

Self-Help

The preceding discussion has focused on forms of psychotherapy that involve personal interactions between psychotherapists and the clients they serve. Yet another alternative for people seeking psychotherapeutic assistance is self-help. Sometimes, when people seek to help themselves, they join other persons who need similar kinds of help, and they help one another. Perhaps the best-known self-help group is Alcoholics Anonymous (AA), which was founded in the mid-1930s. Since the founding of AA, many other related 12-step groups have sprung up, including support groups for persons addicted to other substances, the family members of substance abusers, victims of crimes, persons who have terminal or chronic illnesses, and so on. Essentially, for any problem that may be experienced by more than one person in a geographic region, a support group may be formed, which may offer therapeutic benefit. If a person is fortunate, family members and close friends may also offer a form of therapeutic support.

Another form of self-help may come from reading what other people have to say about coping with many of life's obstacles. Your neighborhood bookstore probably offers many self-help books suggesting how to help yourself resolve almost

Frequently, when we face psychological and situational difficulties, we can find a great deal of help from our families and friends, who can offer social support, advice, and perhaps direct help. In addition, however, many of us seek help from people in specialized support groups, who may have had to face similar kinds of problems and can therefore provide both empathy and practical ideas for solutions.

any problem you could imagine: how to treat addiction (including many books based on AA), how to improve your love life, how to become more assertive, and how to overcome various forms of self-defeating behavior.

Do any of these books actually work? No one knows because no one is monitoring the effectiveness of the various programs. Gerald Rosen (1987) has serious concerns about the value of self-help books. In particular, many such books exaggerate how much help they can offer. Many of the authors of these books appear on television and radio talk shows, where their claims may be even more greatly exaggerated. To the extent that these books and talk shows may lead people away from getting professional help when it is needed, such as for the serious disorders discussed in Chapter 13, they may cause more harm than good. On the other hand, these self-help resources can be useful for the relatively common, temporary problems of daily living and for occasional spiritual uplift.

In addition to self-help groups and self-help books, folk wisdom can sometimes provide useful guidance for self-help:

> Change your thoughts and you'll change your moods. (1) *Get up and go.* When you most feel like moping, do something—anything. . . . (2) *Make contact with people you care about.* You may not feel like socializing, but others can help to distract you from your depression, give you hugs, listen to you. (3) . . . *Avoid drugs,* including alcohol, which may depress the nervous system and keep you feeling down. (Linda Tschirart and Mary Ellen Donovan, quoted in Safire & Safir, 1989, p. 92)

Finding Your Way   14-1

Think about what you do to enable yourself to cope more effectively with the psychologically difficult situations you face. What are some self-help strategies you have used when confronting stressful or psychologically troublesome situations? What advice have you offered to your friends or family members when they have faced psychologically difficult situations?

What are some alternatives to individual psychotherapy? For many people, group therapy, couples therapy, and family therapy offer useful alternatives to individual psychotherapy, enabling people both to enhance their interpersonal relationships and to resolve whatever psychological problems led them to seek treatment. In addition, self-help groups and self-help books may sometimes be useful for helping people to solve their own temporary problems of adjustment.

IS THERE AN OPTIMAL APPROACH TO PSYCHOTHERAPY?

Each kind of psychotherapy makes different assumptions about both the nature of psychological disorders and the best ways in which to treat these disorders. In light of this diversity of approaches, it seems obvious that they cannot all be right. However, the various approaches to psychotherapy may be more complementary than they appear to be.

Consider, for example, the issue of what causes mental disorders. Part of the difference in treatment procedures comes from different views about causation. Psychodynamic theories tend to focus on repressed early childhood experiences as the cause of mental disorders. Humanistic theories consider the primary cause of these disorders to be insufficient feelings of self-worth, insufficient unconditional acceptance by others, or lack of acceptance for all parts of the self. Behavior therapies look to faults in conditioning or in modeling, whereas cognitive theories emphasize maladaptive thoughts, beliefs, or schemas. Biological therapies look to psychophysiological causes of distress, such as abnormal levels of neurotransmitters in the brain.

Does support for one approach necessarily mean that alternative approaches are ruled out? No. For one thing, mental disorders may have causes at different levels of analysis. For example, stressful experiences in early childhood may lead to or even be viewed as inappropriate forms of behavioral conditioning. Inappropriate levels of neurotransmitter substances may lead to maladaptive thoughts. Maladaptive thoughts may lead to low self-esteem. Often, what is cause and what is effect is not clear. Perhaps a combined approach most effectively describes causality by allowing for interactions among causes. For instance, psychophysiological vulnerability and environmental stress may interact with low self-esteem and maladaptive thoughts to cause psychological turmoil.

Differing views of causality lead to differing approaches to treatment. Classical psychodynamic approaches tend to focus on treating the fundamental motivations that give rise to psychological problems. Humanistic approaches and some of the ego-psychology approaches tend to focus on coming to terms with who we are and what we want to do with our lives. Behavioral approaches focus on modifying the stimulus–response mechanisms in the environment. Cognitive approaches tend to focus on altering the troubled person's thought patterns. Biological approaches tend to focus on treating the neurochemical and hormonal imbalances underlying a given psychological disturbance. To understand the nature of psychological processes, we need to combine the various explanations. Similarly, to treat a mental disorder at multiple levels most effectively, we may combine several different

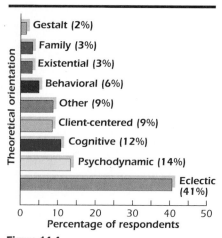

Figure 14-4

Psychotherapeutic Approaches of Clinical Psychologists

Out of 415 clinical psychologists surveyed, almost half indicated that they followed an eclectic approach. (After Smith 1982)

therapies into an *eclectic* therapy, a strategy that integrates several approaches (see Figure 14-4).

Ideally, before a clinician chooses an approach to psychotherapy, the clinician should have information regarding the relative effectiveness of each approach. In addition to personal clinical experience, the clinician should have access to information based on empirical research. Ideally, this empirical research would analyze each of the major diagnoses (as shown in Chapter 13, based on DSM-IV) in terms of each of the major types of therapies (psychodynamic, humanistic, behavioral, cognitive, and biological). In addition, each investigation would include both placebo control groups and waiting-list control groups. For each type of treatment of each type of diagnosed disorder, the analysis would evaluate each diagnosis in terms of which type of therapy was most effective. In addition, researchers would conduct *meta-analyses*, in which psychologists evaluate and analyze the findings from many studies at a time.

Truly ideal research would also consider other factors that may affect treatment outcomes. For example, the length of treatment dramatically affects outcomes. In one meta-analytic study (Howard et al., 1986), the rate of improvement ranged from 29–38% of psychotherapy clients attending between 1 and 3 sessions to 85% of clients attending between 1 and 104 sessions. Clearly, the length of treatment can make a big difference in the observed rate of success. (The average number of psychotherapy sessions for Americans receiving treatment is 14 in a given year [Goleman, 1993].) In addition, an ideal research program might consider the social context of therapy (e.g., individual, family, couple, or group therapy); the type of setting (e.g., inpatient or outpatient); and so on. Although the call for this kind of research first went out decades ago (e.g., Kiesler, 1966; Paul, 1967), this highly complex research has yet to be conducted.

What do we know about the relative benefits of the various approaches to therapy, based on existing studies? When the researchers' preferences for a particular therapy are ruled out, each type of psychotherapy seems to be just about as effective as the next. However, when the researchers' loyalties are not ruled out, whatever therapy program the researcher prefers seems to fare better in the comparisons across therapy programs. Perhaps, then, the best suggestion to clinicians and their clients is that they should choose the approach—or synthesis of approaches—that seems to work best for them. In addition, a match between the particular therapist and client may be important to successful treatment. For example, some cross-cultural researchers suggest that psychotherapists must consider cultural and other differences when tailoring psychotherapy to individual clients (see, e.g., Axelson, 1993; Ivey, Ivey, & Simek-Morgan, 1993; Pedersen et al., in press; Sue & Sue, 1990).

How should an optimal approach to psychotherapy be chosen? At present, research has not adequately shown that any one approach is consistently better than any other for the treatment of psychological disorders. The various approaches to psychotherapy may be viewed as complementary, rather than competing, alternatives for helping people to overcome or to manage serious psychological disorders, as well as temporary psychological difficulties. Many practicing psychotherapists use an eclectic approach, selecting and applying the most effective psychotherapy techniques for a given client in a particular situation.

HOW EFFECTIVE IS PSYCHOTHERAPY?

No one has yet conducted the ideal research that would allow clinicians to choose an optimal approach to psychotherapy, let alone to tailor psychotherapy perfectly to particular client diagnoses. Even so, meta-analytic and other research clearly shows that psychotherapy produces significant improvement in clients, above and beyond any spontaneous recovery that might have occurred (e.g., Andrews, 1993; Smith & Glass, 1977; Stiles, Shapiro, & Elliott, 1986). In particular, clients who received psychotherapy were, on average, better off than 75% or more of research control subjects who did not receive any psychotherapy. Clients who received psychotherapy showed significant improvements in self-esteem and significant reduction in anxiety (greater improvement than about 82% of untreated controls). For persons institutionalized for psychotic, alcoholic, or criminal behaviors, those who received psychotherapy showed increases in their level of adjustment greater than only 71% of untreated controls (Smith & Glass, 1977). However, if you cared deeply about one of the 7 in 10 who responded well to treatment, you would probably be quite pleased with the outcome.

In addition, length of treatment may be confounding the interpretation of results. For example, see Table 14-2 and Figure 14-5, which show the results of a meta-analytic study by Kenneth Howard and his colleagues (1986). If researchers were to determine the effectiveness of therapy for borderline-psychotic patients in terms of therapist ratings at the conclusion of 8 sessions, the results would be very discouraging, yet if the researchers were to assess therapist ratings for these same patients at the conclusion of 104 sessions, the studies would be highly encouraging. On the other hand, for depressed and anxious clients, therapy results would be much more positive after much shorter durations of therapy.

Why are many different kinds of psychotherapy about equally effective for many different people? For one thing, as mentioned previously, research has not yet been conducted that effectively analyzes each type of approach in relation to each type of diagnosis. Also, different therapists may implement each approach in distinctive ways, so that not all psychoanalysts are alike, just as not all behaviorists are alike. This lack of uniformity also makes it difficult to distinguish among the differential effects of the various types of psychotherapy.

Another alternative has been suggested (e.g., Torrey, 1986; Stiles et al., 1986): The various approaches to psychotherapy may have underlying commonalities that

TABLE 14-2

Meta-analysis of the Course of Psychotherapy

In a meta-analytic study of psychotherapy, the number of patients who rated themselves as improved generally increased in relation to the number of therapy sessions, as did the therapists' ratings of patient improvement (Howard et al., 1986). The specific ratings at each measurement period differed, however, depending on the clinical diagnosis and the source of the rating (patient or therapist).

Total number of sessions	Depressed patients (% rated as improved)		Anxious patients (% rated as improved)		Borderline psychotic patients (% rated as improved)	
	Self-ratings	Therapists' ratings	Self-ratings	Therapists' ratings	Self-ratings	Therapists' ratings
1–4	44%	31%	36%	5%	21%	0%
5–8	53	46	46	25	33	3
9–13	60	57	54	53	42	11
14–26	69	73	64	87	60	38
27–52	77	86	74	99	75	74
53–104	84	94	82	99	87	95

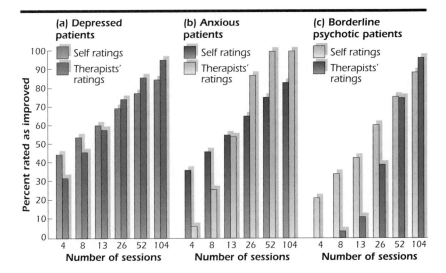

Figure 14-5
Ratings of Psychotherapy
Although self-ratings and therapist ratings differed, and the degree of improvement differed across different diagnoses, on the whole, the data seem to show that psychotherapy is highly effective for helping persons with psychological problems.

go deeper than the superficial differences across therapeutic approaches. For example, cross-cultural research shows that across such diverse psychotherapists as U.S. and European psychiatrists, Native American *shamans*, Latin American *curanderos* (or *curanderas*, in Mexico and elsewhere), and Yoruban *babalawo* (in Nigeria), psychotherapy appears to have five basic components (Torrey, 1986): (1) an emphasis on a shared world view between client and therapist, including a common language and similar conceptions of causes and effects; (2) distinctive therapist characteristics such as warmth, genuineness, and empathy; (3) client expectations that reflect the culturally relevant beliefs of the client and the therapist; (4) a set of specific techniques used by the therapist (e.g., talking, performing rituals such as systematic desensitization or ceremonial dances, or using biological techniques such as herbs, drugs, or shock therapy); and (5) a process by which the therapist enables or empowers the client to gain increased knowledge, awareness, and mastery, thereby gaining hope. According to E. Torrey, psychotherapists across various cultures "perform essentially the same function in their respective cultures. [Both Western and non-Western] therapists . . . treat patients using similar techniques; and both get similar results."

William Stiles and his colleagues (Stiles et al., 1986) would add to Torrey's list the importance of establishing mutual trust between therapist and client, the therapist's "communication of a new perspective of the [client and the client's] situation" (p. 172), the client's willingness to engage in open and self-disclosing communication, the client's desire to improve, and the client's belief in the effectiveness of the particular psychotherapy being offered. Although we have yet to understand fully the processes by which psychotherapy produces desirable outcomes, it is reassuring to know that such outcomes occur.

BRANCHING OUT: When and How Should You—or Someone You Care About—Seek Psychotherapy?

Few of us have serious psychological disorders that require psychological treatment. Serious disorders, by their nature, interfere with the person's ability to carry out normal work and normal interpersonal relationships. All of us occasionally feel anxious, but few of us feel so anxious that we are unable to leave the house for weeks at a time. All of us experience occasional distortions of our thoughts, our emotions, and our perceptions, but few of us experience such serious distortions that the people around us notice that we cannot stay in touch with reality much of the time. Many of us seem to be a little excessive in our tidiness or our cleanliness, but few of us wash our hands hundreds of times each day.

On the other hand, from time to time, each of us faces difficult situations—the loss of a job or of a loved one; conflicts in our interpersonal relationships; serious accidents, injuries, disease, or other health problems; and so on. Sometimes, our family and friends are able to provide us with all the support we need to cope with the difficulties we face. At other times, however, the extent of our need goes beyond the ability of our loved ones to help us. It is at these times that many of us seek professional help from psychotherapists.

Once you make the decision to seek psychotherapy, what kind of psychotherapist should you look for? Following are a few tips:

1. Try to find the particular treatment approach that best suits the problem that leads you to seek psychotherapy. For instance, if you believe that you suffer from bipolar disorder, biological therapies may be one of your best choices. If you seek to get rid of your phobia of flying, behavior therapy may be your best bet. If you are having trouble adapting to a difficult situation, and you want guidance in figuring out your own solution to your problem, you may prefer a talk-oriented therapy such as humanistic or cognitive therapy.
2. Make sure that you have faith in the competence and trustworthiness of the therapist and the therapist's approach to treatment.
3. Find a therapist who seems to understand your view of the world, given your distinctive cultural and social experiences.
4. Choose a therapist who seems warm and empathetic toward you.
5. After sessions with the psychotherapist, assess whether you feel a greater sense of being able to cope with the difficulties you face. Does the psychotherapist seem to have confidence that you will be able to handle the problems you face?
6. Consider your finances—does your choice of psychotherapist fit within your budget? In most communities, there are quite a few mental-health agencies that offer various kinds of psychotherapy for modest fees. In addition to publicly funded agencies (e.g., community mental-health agencies), many religious and charitable organizations offer lowcost mental-health services (e.g., Jewish Family Service, Lutheran Social Services), communities with medical schools often offer low-cost (sliding financial scale) psychotherapy, and many communities offer free or low-cost specialized mental-health services (e.g., for veterans and for children). Also, many health insurance plans pay for at least some mental-health services. Do not let finances be your main concern, however. If you get inappropriate free advice at a time when

Many communities provide free telephone counseling to people who are facing crises, such as following a rape, spousal abuse, or other violent crime; following sexual molestation; or when contemplating suicide.

It has been suggested that effective psychotherapists essentially provide the same function as a good friend. In your own experience, what therapeutic benefits do you provide to and receive from your good friends? What therapeutic benefits might a professional psychotherapist provide that a good friend might not provide?

Design a checklist offering specific recommendations to guide clinicians in their decisions regarding when they should consider breaching confidentiality. (For example, at what point does a therapist have sufficient reason to suspect child abuse?)

you need help, it could cost you a great deal. Most psychotherapists are willing to work with you regarding payment for services. If you find that a particular psychotherapist is right for you or for someone you love, ask the therapist to help you work out a financial arrangement that is satisfactory.

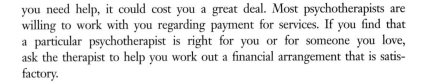

How effective is psychotherapy? Meta-analytic research shows that psychotherapy is effective; more than three in four clients show greater improvement following therapy than they would have shown as a result of spontaneous recovery. The effectiveness of the treatment depends, however, on the length of the treatment and on the nature of the psychological problem. It appears that the effectiveness of the treatment depends less on the psychotherapist's choice of treatment approach than on the therapist's warmth, genuineness, empathy, and encouragement, and the client's confidence in the therapist and his or her approach.

WHAT ARE SOME KEY ETHICAL ISSUES IN PSYCHOTHERAPY?

In the fall of 1992, Ann Landers, an advice columnist, devoted her entire column to exposing the unethical behavior of a psychiatrist who had held various prestigious positions in psychiatric associations. The disgraced psychiatrist was forced to resign from the American Psychiatric Association after losing a lawsuit brought by former patients of his, who claimed that he had abused them sexually and in other ways. His type of case is not unique, although it is, fortunately, rare. Because psychotherapists are trusted with deeply personal information, when they violate that trust, they can cause enormous harm to their patients. Unfortunately, a few of them do so. Through their unethical behavior, they hurt not only their clients and themselves, but also the entire profession. Of course, unethical behavior is not limited to psychotherapists: It occurs in every profession. (See Practical Psychology 14-1 regarding an ethical problem arising from a questionable therapeutic technique.)

Perhaps even more than many other professionals, psychotherapists are expected to behave ethically toward clients. For example, psychotherapists are expected to refrain from becoming sexually involved with clients. Moreover, psychotherapists are expected to maintain the *confidentiality* (privacy) of communications between themselves and their clients. Only in rare cases may they divulge the contents of these communications. Such cases arise primarily when the therapist determines that clients may be dangerous to themselves or to others. In addition, in some states, psychotherapists must breach confidentiality in a few other situations in which it is believed that greater harm will result if confidentiality is not breached.

Another ethical protection for clients involves *informed consent:* Before clients participate in what are viewed as experimental treatments (e.g., the alleged recovery of repressed childhood memories), they must fully understand what the treatments will involve, including both the experimental nature of the treatments and the likelihood of harmful side effects or consequences. Also, during the experimental treatment, the psychotherapist is expected to preserve the well-being of the participant to the fullest extent possible.

PRACTICAL PSYCHOLOGY   14-1

Recovery of Suppressed Memories— What Is Your Judgment?

In May of 1994, a civil court awarded half a million dollars to a man whose adult daughter had accused him of sexually abusing her during her childhood (Berkman, 1994; La Ganga, 1994; Shuit, 1994). The award followed a verdict asserting that the daughter's therapists had negligently reinforced false memories of sexual abuse. The man's 23-year-old daughter had accused him of sexually abusing her after she underwent treatment that her psychotherapists asserted was designed to "recover suppressed memories." When the daughter made those accusations, her father lost his $400,000-a-year job as a vice president of marketing for a major company, and her mother divorced him.

In this case, the therapist used questionable therapeutic techniques to elicit the daughter's horrifying recollections. The daughter remains entirely sure of her memories, but many other people—including the jurors in her father's civil case—question their accuracy. Whatever the verdict in cases such as this one, it is clear that both the parent and the child will have suffered greatly. One source (described in Geyelin, 1994) estimates that thousands of parents and their adult children are confronting the heart-wrenching problems posed by trying to determine whether disturbing memories have arisen from accurate recollection, elicited by techniques that facilitate their recovery, or from inaccurate distortions, introduced by techniques that lead to their creation. Professional organizations of clinical therapists are grappling with the need to guide therapists in the treatment of persons who appear to be suffering ill effects from suppressed or repressed memories of painful events.

Perhaps the foremost psychologist in questioning the use of recovered memory in legal proceedings is Elizabeth Loftus (e.g., 1993b). Loftus is particularly concerned about recovered memory in cases of repressed memories of murder (which are very rare) and in cases of childhood sexual abuse (which are less unusual). Childhood sexual abuse appears to be distressingly common (estimates of the proportion of women who have been victimized range from 10% to 50%), and the consequences of allegations of abuse are devastating for both the victim and the accused, as well as their family members and friends. Therefore, determinations regarding the accuracy of recovered memories profoundly affect the lives of many people.

Although many therapists continue to believe in the validity of recovered memories, the evidence available at present suggests that we do not yet have the ability to distinguish true repressed memories from false ones. Until we are better able to be sure of the accuracy of such memories, therapists should continue to help clients to clarify their own feelings and beliefs, to show compassion and empathy for clients who are clearly suffering from some source of inner turmoil, and to help clients to heal and to recover from the pain they are experiencing, whatever its origin.

When you next hear the media discuss a case of recovered memory, how will you judge the accuracy of the memory?

What are some key ethical issues in psychotherapy? Because the persons who seek psychotherapy are particularly vulnerable, psychotherapists are in a distinctive position of trust, which obliges them to show extraordinary concern for the welfare of their patients. Two key ethical issues faced by psychotherapists are confidentiality and informed consent. In addition, as innovative methods of treatment become available, psychotherapists must develop guidelines for the use of such methods, in order to avoid unwanted outcomes.

When psychotherapy is implemented appropriately, another benefit of psychotherapy appears to be a reduction in overall health-care costs. Thus, when companies provide mental-health counseling for their employees, they obtain not only increases in productivity and decreases in employee absenteeism and turnover, but also savings in the overall cost of health care (Docherty, 1993). Health psychology is the topic of the next—and final—chapter.

SUMMARY

What Were Some Early Methods of Psychotherapeutic Intervention? 416

1. Because early views of mental illness relied on demonological explanations, early treatments centered on trying to expel the demons that caused the illness. Later treatment in *asylums* involved keeping mentally ill persons off the streets, out of sight, with little thought given to humane treatment, let alone possible *psychotherapy*.

How and Why Do Clinicians Diagnose Abnormal Behavior? 417

2. The DSM system of diagnostic classification has helped clinicians to make appropriate and widely understood diagnoses as a basis for treatment.

How Do Different Psychologists Approach Psychotherapy?   418

3. There are five main approaches to psychotherapy: psychodynamic, humanistic, behavioral, cognitive, and biological approaches. A cultural approach to psychotherapy is an additional important option. Also, many psychologists use an eclectic approach, which employs aspects of more than one of the main approaches.

4. Psychodynamic therapies emphasize insight into underlying unconscious processes as the key to the therapeutic process. Psychodynamic therapies may be based on Freudian psychoanalysis or on neo-Freudian ego psychology.

5. Humanistic therapies emphasize the therapeutic effects of the therapist's unconditional positive regard for the client, as exemplified by Rogers's *client-centered therapy*.

6. *Behavior therapies* emphasize techniques based on principles of operant and classical conditioning, as well as observational learning. Classical techniques include *counterconditioning*, such as aversion therapy and systematic desensitization, as well as *extinction procedures*, such as flooding and implosion therapy. Operant techniques include the use of token economies and behavioral contracting. The use of *modeling* may be viewed as a kind of behavioral treatment with an allowance for cognitive processes.

7. Cognitive therapies encourage clients to change their thought contents and processes in order to achieve therapeutic changes in behavior and other desired outcomes. Ellis's *rational-emotive therapy (RET)* and Beck's cognitive therapy are two of the main types of cognitive therapy.

8. Historically, biological treatments of mental illness have included a wide array of treatments, such as *electroconvulsive therapy (ECT)* and *psychosurgery*.

9. The development of effective *psychotropic drugs* has revolutionized biological treatments. Today, the four key classes of psychotropic drugs are *antipsychotics*, *antidepressants*, antianxiety drugs, and lithium. Although these drugs are certainly not cure-alls, they help many patients to function more effectively and to feel better about how well they function.

What Are Some Alternatives to Individual Psychotherapy? 431

10. Alternatives to individual psychotherapy include group therapy, couples and family therapy, and self-help. Group therapy, couples therapy, and family therapy often address problems specific to interpersonal relationships. They address these problems through the dynamic interplay that occurs during group, couple, or family interactions. In self-help therapies, individuals try to manage their own stressful situations or minor psychological difficulties, with the guidance of books, mutual support groups, and other sources of information.

Is There an Optimal Approach to Psychotherapy? 435

11. There is no one single approach to psychotherapy that is ideal for all persons, in all situations. Rather, the various approaches to psychotherapy may be viewed as complementary alternatives.

12. Each approach to psychotherapy has distinctive advantages and disadvantages, and it may be best to view the approaches as complementary rather than competing. Unfortunately, we have not yet reached the point at which we can prescribe a particular form of therapy for a particular type of psychological problem.

13. The length of treatment and other factors not specific to a particular approach may also play a role in the relative effectiveness of psychotherapy.

How Effective Is Psychotherapy? 437

14. Psychotherapies of various forms have proven to be about equally effective. It may be that commonalities across types of therapy explain most of the positive outcomes of psychotherapy. These commonalities include the therapist's trustworthiness, warmth, sincerity, empathy, and communication of a new perspective on the client's situation.

What Are Some Key Ethical Issues in Psychotherapy? 440

15. Because psychotherapists have the potential to influence clients profoundly, psychotherapists must be especially mindful of ethical considerations, such as the need for confidentiality and for obtaining informed consent for participation in any experimental therapeutic procedures.

PATHWAYS TO KNOWLEDGE

Choose the best answer to complete each sentence.

1. In psychodynamic terminology, *countertransference* refers to the process whereby
   (a) thoughts and feelings the patient has toward other individuals are projected onto the therapist.
   (b) the therapist projects her or his own intrapsychic conflicts onto the patient.
   (c) the patient avoids confronting uncomfortable thoughts and feelings by thwarting the progress of therapy.
   (d) the patient's ambivalent feelings toward his or her therapist are projected onto other individuals.

2. Client-centered therapy suggests that all the following factors are keys for successful therapy **except**
   (a) the client's willingness to take constructive criticism from the therapist.
   (b) genuineness on the part of the therapist.
   (c) unconditional positive regard for the client.
   (d) empathetic understanding of the client.

3. Two explicitly directive psychotherapeutic approaches are
   (a) behavior therapy and biological therapy.
   (b) psychodynamic therapy and humanistic therapy.
   (c) humanistic therapy and cross-cultural therapy.
   (d) cross-cultural therapy and biological therapy.

4. A behavioral technique whereby a therapist conditions the client to experience negative feelings in response to a certain undesirable response is termed
   (a) flooding.
   (b) implosion therapy.
   (c) aversion therapy.
   (d) systematic desensitization.

5. If a behavior therapist directly places a patient into an anxiety-provoking situation, in the hope that the anxiety will eventually cease, the therapist is using the technique of
   (a) flooding.
   (b) aversion therapy.
   (c) systematic desensitization.
   (d) maximum sensitization.

6. Biological treatments include all of the following **except**
   (a) antidepressant medication.
   (b) electroconvulsive shock therapy.

    (c) systematic desensitization.

    (d) antipsychotic medication.

Answer each of the following questions by filling in the blank with an appropriate word or phrase.

7. During the fifteenth and sixteenth centuries, persons classified as mentally ill were kept in _____, which generally provided harsh treatment in poorly maintained facilities.

8. Cognitive therapy focuses on altering a client's _____ contents and processes, which are viewed as causing the client's psychological distress.

9. In psychoanalysis, the unconscious attempts by the client to sabotage the course of therapy are referred to as _____.

10. MAO inhibitors and tricyclics are examples of _____ drugs.

11. One behavior-therapy technique used to reduce anxiety, _____ _____, teaches the client relaxation techniques and then instructs the client to use those techniques through successively more intense anxiety-provoking situations.

12. In the behavior-therapy technique of _____, an unwanted response to a stimulus is replaced with another, more desirable response.

13. _____ and _____ are examples of extinction procedures whereby unwanted responses are weakened.

14. In _____ therapy, therapists may encourage clients to alter their thought patterns by changing the maladaptive statements they make to themselves in response to stressful situations.

15. Therapists must obtain _____ _____ from clients—that is, an assurance that the clients understand the conditions under which therapy will be conducted.

16. Psychotherapists assure their clients of _____, which means that whatever the client says to the therapist will be kept private.

17. In addition to antidepressant, antianxiety, and antipsychotic drugs, biological psychologists use _____ as a psychotropic drug for treating _____.

Match the following psychotherapeutic approaches to their descriptions of how therapists address the psychological problems of their clients:

18. behavior therapy

19. psychodynamic therapy

20. cultural therapy

21. humanistic therapy

22. biological therapy

(a) treating clients in ways that are appropriate to the clients' worldviews, expectations, and experiences

(b) resolving unconscious conflicts among the id, the superego, and the events that take place in the real world

(c) changing what the client does in response to whatever is happening in the environment

(d) treating the underlying physiological bases for psychological disorders

(e) nondirectively showing the client unconditional positive regard so that the client can fulfill her or his potential

Answers

1. b, 2. a, 3. a, 4. c, 5. a, 6. c, 7. asylums, 8. thought, 9. resistance, 10. antidepressant, 11. systematic desensitization, 12. counterconditioning, 13. Flooding, implosion, 14. cognitive, 15. informed consent, 16. confidentiality, 17. lithium, bipolar disorders, 18. c, 19. b, 20. a, 21. e, 22. d

PATHWAYS TO UNDERSTANDING

1. Suppose that you are the editor for psychological self-help books in a large publishing house. Describe the manuscript for a self-help book that you hope to receive or that you plan to have written by one of the authors you know. What psychological problems does the book tackle, and how does it handle them?

2. If you were to have a need for psychotherapy, which method of therapy would you choose? What if you were to decide to become a psychotherapist? Would your choice be the same? Analyze the benefits and drawbacks of the method you would prefer in each role.

3. How could you use the ideas expressed in this chapter to improve your own life?

CHAPTER OUTLINE

What Do Health Psychologists Study?
— Safe Sexual Practices

How Can People Enhance Their Health Through Lifestyle Choices?

How Do Personality and Stress Influence Health?
Stressors
— Stressors at Work
Stress Responses
Personality and Perceived Stress

How Do Personality Patterns Relate to Illness?
Type-A Versus Type-B Behavior Patterns
Hardiness and Stress Resistance

How Do Our Minds Experience Pain?
Kinds of Pain
Personality and Pain
— Control of Pain

How Do People Live with Serious, Chronic Health Problems?
AIDS: Incidence and Prevention
Psychological Models for Coping with Chronic Illness

CHAPTER

15

Health Psychology

Before she retired, Jan had been looking forward to enjoying an active social life, including many volunteer activities, vigorous recreational pursuits, and extensive travel. A year after she retired, she was diagnosed as having asthma (a breathing disorder) and polymyocitis (a muscle disorder), which combined to limit her energy level and to lower her resistance to infectious diseases. "I think of [my life with the disorders] as a bridge over a deep chasm. As I cross the bridge, I move away from a broad, open past into a much more restricted and narrow lifestyle. While on the bridge, if I don't carefully balance what I do, I can fall off on either side. On the other hand, I still have a way to move forward, and I keep the hope that by some miracle, I'll reach another open area some time in the future. . . . Staying healthy is a continuous balancing act: I try to do as much as I can, but I have to avoid doing too much or it takes me days—or weeks—to recover. . . . I'm basically a very cheerful, energetic person, and I've always had a knack for enjoying whatever I have now. That really helps. . . . I think that the trick is to move forward with a positive attitude as much as possible, but to accept that I sometimes feel sad because I can't travel as I'd love to, I can't do many of the activities I enjoy, and I can't see my friends as much as I'd like to."

Jan's experiences with her illness illustrate aspects of the field of **health psychology**, the study of the two-way interaction between the mind and the physical health of the body. For Jan—and for all of us—the interaction of psychological and physiological processes works both ways. The physiological processes of Jan's illness affect how Jan thinks and feels about her life and her lifestyle. In addition, Jan believes that her mental state influences her illness. For Jan, the trick to feeling—and being—as healthy as possible is a mental and physical balancing act: (a) She has to accept many of the limitations of her illness (e.g., avoiding fatigue or exposure to infectious diseases); but (b) she continually fights against letting the restrictions confine her any more than is necessary (e.g., seeking the company of friends, walking and exercising as much as she can).

WHAT DO HEALTH PSYCHOLOGISTS STUDY?

Health psychologists are interested in the psychological aspects of how people stay healthy, prevent illness, become ill, and respond to illness. Specifically, health psychologists often ask the following kinds of questions:

1. *Staying well*—How can people enhance their sense of health and well-being through health-enhancing behavior and lifestyle choices? For example, why do many people have difficulty sticking to an exercise or diet program? What situations might make it easier for people to stick to exercise or diet programs?
2. *Preventing illness or becoming ill*—How do people become vulnerable to illness or injury? How do people prevent illness or injury? How do psychological processes affect people's vulnerability to illness or injury? How do people respond to physical changes that may be symptoms of illness? (*Symptoms* are unusual feelings in the body—e.g., a queasy stomach—or observable features of the body—e.g., an itchy rash on the neck—which may indicate some kind of illness or injury.) For example, why do many couples still choose not to use condoms during sexual encounters, despite the risk to both partners of contracting acquired immune deficiency syndrome (AIDS) or other diseases, and the risk of an unplanned pregnancy for the female? Why do people smoke, drink heavily, or overeat, when they know that these behaviors harm them and make them vulnerable to illness?
3. *Responding to illness*—How do people respond to becoming ill? How do they respond to long-term illness? How do people with terminal illnesses cope with their situation? For example, why do some patients with tuberculosis sometimes stop taking their medicine and thereby make their tuberculosis untreatable? Why do some patients with terminal illnesses seem to cope so well with the situations they face?

Health psychologists have observed that people's reactions to illness are usually different when they face an illness that they believe to be **chronic**—occurring repeatedly or constantly present (e.g., migraine headaches or diabetes)—versus one they believe to be **acute**—perhaps intense, but only of short duration on one occasion (e.g., a cold or pneumonia). People suffering from chronic illnesses face a variety of psychological challenges, such as depression and anxiety, which are usually unrelated to the actual physical cause of the illness. Therefore, a part of the mission of health psychology is to help people deal with their psychological reactions to serious illness, particularly if the illness has long-term effects.

The field of health psychology is wide-reaching. Some topics covered within health psychology have already been discussed elsewhere in this book. For example, we discussed sleep and sleep disorders in Chapter 5; drug use and drug treatment in Chapters 5 and 11; normal, healthy development and functioning of the nervous system in Chapters 2 and 3; and hunger and sexual motivation in Chapter 11. Other aspects of health psychology have been considered in other chapters as

Medicine left in the container can't help.

Yoruban (West African) proverb

Diseases have no eyes. They pick with a dizzy finger anyone, just anyone.

Sandra Cisneros

health psychology the study of how the mind and the physical health of the body interact

chronic always present or repeatedly occurring again and again

acute characteristic of symptoms or illness occurring only for a short time, although probably intense

PRACTICAL PSYCHOLOGY 15-1

Safe Sexual Practices

Why do many adolescents—and even many adults—fail to use measures to avoid sexually transmitted diseases (e.g., AIDS) and unwanted pregnancies? Several reasons have been suggested.

1. *Sheer ignorance*—Many sexually active persons simply underestimate the risk of pregnancy or of sexually transmitted disease.
2. *Moral beliefs that lead to anxiety or guilt about engaging in sexual activity*—For some people, planning for the possibility of sexual intercourse makes them feel too anxious or guilty for comfort.
3. *Reluctance to talk about sexual activity or contraception*—Some people feel reluctant to discuss the use of condoms and other forms of protection. It may help for them to bear in mind that it would be far more difficult to discuss various unfortunate outcomes of unprotected sexual intercourse, such as sexually transmitted disease or unwanted pregnancy.
4. *Poor impulse control*—Some people may actually have condoms available, but when the need arises, they may fail to use one because they believe that the condom may inhibit their pleasure or the spontaneity of their sexual activity. Poor impulse control can be made worse as a result of using alcohol or other drugs.
5. *Media images*—Most of the love-making that appears on television shows or in the movies does not include scenes in which the lovers use condoms as a part of their lovemaking. Hence, these models for romantic and sexual love do not promote the use of safe sexual practices.
6. *Gradient of reinforcement*—The potential undesirable outcomes of using condoms or other protection (e.g., embarrassment) are immediate, whereas the potential unwanted outcomes of failing to use such protection (e.g., disease or unwanted pregnancy) are not immediate.
7. *Feeling of invulnerability*—Surprisingly, many adolescents and even some adults believe that they are somehow protected from contracting sexually transmitted diseases because of their general health, their careful selection of partners, or through some magical protection that they believe will lower their risk of pregnancy or disease.

Which of these reasons seems to you to be the most influential in causing people's failure to protect themselves against unwanted pregnancy or disease? How may health psychologists encourage people to engage in safe sexual practices?

well (e.g., what makes [health-related] messages persuasive was discussed in Chapter 10). The present chapter includes only those topics of health psychology that have not been discussed elsewhere.

What do health psychologists study? Health psychologists study how people stay well, prevent illness, become ill, and respond to illness, including both chronic and acute illnesses.

Would it be a good idea for more movie-makers and TV-show producers to show sexy couples using condoms as they prepare to make love?

HOW CAN PEOPLE ENHANCE THEIR HEALTH THROUGH LIFESTYLE CHOICES?

One of the primary goals of health psychology is to promote health through the influence of the mind on the body, such as by choosing to engage in health-enhancing behavior. Of course, health psychologists recognize that engaging in health-enhancing behavior does not ensure perfect health. Serious psychological and physiological disorders (e.g., schizophrenia or cancer) can arise despite excellent health practices. Nonetheless, health psychologists assume that people can influence their health through the psychological regulation of their behavior. Research supports this assumption, particularly for health-related behavior that is subject to our conscious control.

    For example, people can significantly reduce their risk of dying at any given age by following seven health-related practices (Belloc & Breslow, 1972; Breslow, 1983). In fact, the risk of death at a given age has been found to decrease almost linearly with the number of the following seven health-related practices that have been implemented: (1) sleeping 7 to 8 hours a day, (2) eating breakfast almost every day, (3) rarely eating between meals, (4) being at a roughly appropriate weight in relation to height, (5) not smoking (see Figure 15-1), (6) drinking alcohol only in moderation or not at all, and (7) exercising or otherwise engaging in rigorous physical activity regularly.

    Of the various types of exercise, by far the most important for overall health and well-being is aerobic exercise. **Aerobic exercise** involves intense activities that last more than 20 or 30 minutes and that increase both heart rate and oxygen consumption. These activities enhance *cardiovascular* (heart and blood vessels) and *respiratory* (breathing) fitness (Alpert et al., 1990). Cardiovascular fitness and

It is better to prevent than to cure.

        Peruvian proverb

---

aerobic exercise activities that are sufficiently intense and long lasting to stimulate increased heart rate and respiration (breathing)

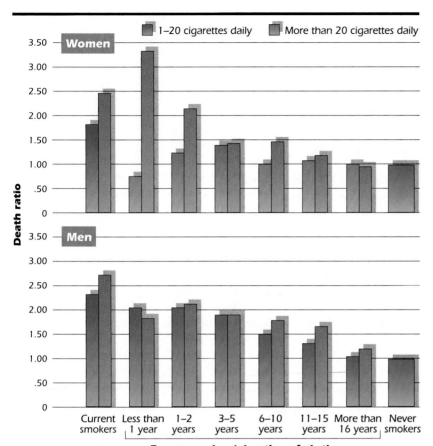

Figure 15-1

Death Rates and Smoking
The death rates for former smokers eventually (after about 15 years of not smoking) reach about the same levels as the rates for people who have never smoked.

For persons of all ages, exercise is one of the key ways to promote health and well-being. How should you evaluate your exercise program? Focus on how consistently you implement the program, not on how intensely you exercise at a given session or on how formal your program is (e.g., in a scheduled class vs. in a less formal setting).

respiratory fitness particularly help psychological well-being because they increase the amount of oxygen reaching the brain, thereby enhancing cognitive and neurological functions. Aerobic exercises include jogging, speed-walking, running, bicycling, rowing, and swimming.

Many people report that they feel more alert and more generally satisfied with their lives when they exercise aerobically. Immediately during and after exercise, this reaction may be a physiological response to the exercise. In part, the increased *oxygenation* (presence of more oxygen) of the brain may enhance alertness. Also, it has been suggested that aerobic exercise triggers the production or release of endorphins. *Endorphins* (a word based on the combination, "*endo*genous *morphine*s") are pain-relieving biochemicals that the body produces naturally (e.g., during sexual orgasm). The presence of endorphins may partly account for the sense of well-being that accompanies aerobic exercise.

A number of studies have suggested specific psychological benefits of exercise programs, in addition to enhanced health and well-being. For example, regular programs of exercise have been tied to improvements in self-esteem, as well as to reduction of depression (Hayes & Ross, 1986; Rodin & Plante, 1989; see Taylor, 1991, for a review). Employee fitness programs, which have become increasingly common, have even resulted in reduced absenteeism, increased job satisfaction, and reduction in health-care costs (Rodin & Plante, 1989).

I like long walks, especially when they are taken by people who annoy me.

Fred Allen

Why do some people seem to go all out to enhance their health, whereas others seem to choose lifestyles that compromise their health?

Finding Your Way 15-1

In the past week, how many of the seven health-related practices have you followed? In what aerobic-exercise activities have you participated? How well are you currently promoting your wellness through your lifestyle? What are five steps you can take to improve your health, starting this week?

How can people enhance their health through lifestyle choices? Healthful lifestyle choices include getting regular aerobic exercise, sleeping 7–8 hours/day, eating nourishing meals regularly and in moderation, and refraining from smoking and from drinking to excess.

HOW DO PERSONALITY AND STRESS INFLUENCE HEALTH?

The preceding section described some of the ways in which people can influence their own health by engaging in health-promoting behavior and by avoiding behavior that compromises their health. Certainly, people's personalities and life circumstances influence their health-related choices. In what other ways do personality and personal circumstances influence health? For one thing, both factors interact to affect the likelihood that people will fall prey to illness or will experience other problems related to health. The interactions of distinctive individual personalities and specific factors in the environment influence many aspects of health. The word describing these interactions is stress. What is stress, and how does it affect our health?

Usually, when we think of stress, we think of feeling mentally and perhaps even physically distressed because of some forms of external pressures, such as time pressure, work pressure, or family pressure. That view of stress is only part of the picture. When researchers investigate stress, they define the term more broadly. **Stress** is the response of a person to a situation in which an event or an aspect of the environment causes a person to feel challenged in some way. The causes of stress are termed **stressors.** That is, stressors are changes in the environment that challenge people to cope with the situations they face. Their adaptations to these perceived challenges are **stress responses.** Frequently, the response to stress leads to an increased likelihood of becoming ill (Totman, 1990; Totman et al., 1980), although occasional exposure to stressful situations for brief periods of time may actually enhance the ability to tolerate further stress at a later time (Dienstbier, 1989).

If there is no struggle, there is no progress.

Frederick Douglas

Stressors

Stressors may include *major life events* (e.g., starting or graduating from college, marrying or divorcing) or *everyday hassles* (e.g., getting stuck in traffic, trying to please a difficult boss).

Stressful Life Events

Surprisingly, stressors do not necessarily have to be things we perceive as negative. For example, having a new baby, getting married, and moving to a new home are all stressors because they require the new parent, spouse, or home-dweller to adapt in many ways. Table 15-1 shows the *Social Readjustment Rating Scale* (SRRS), which lists 43 stressors that have been found to affect our health and well-being (Holmes & Rahe, 1967). Most of us would welcome many of these stressors, such as outstanding personal achievement or marriage. Many other stressors are measured only in terms of change, not indicating whether the change was considered positive or negative: change in financial status, living conditions, residence, school, recreation, social activities, the health status of a family member, and so on.

Not all stressors are alike. In the SRRS, Thomas Holmes and Richard Rahe ranked the 43 stressors and assigned different weights to them (described in Holmes & David, 1989). For example, getting married was rated as more stressful—more challenging—than having trouble with a boss. These researchers then correlated the stressors with the likelihood of becoming ill. This likelihood was positively correlated with the totals for the weighted values of these stressors. (Recall, however, that correlations suggest only a connection between the two. We cannot determine causality based on correlations alone.)

Each of us has the right and the responsibility to assess the roads which lie ahead and . . . if the future road looms ominous or unpromising . . . then we need to gather our resolve and . . . step off . . . into another direction.

Maya Angelou

---

stress a person's response to the presence of something in the environment that causes the person to feel challenged in some way

stressor an event or situation that causes stress

stress response an adaptation to challenging changes in the environment

According to Thomas Holmes and Richard Rahe, the most stressful life event is the death of a spouse. Do you agree?

TABLE 15-1

Social Readjustment Rating Scale (SRRS)

Thomas Holmes and Richard Rahe (1967) developed a scale for measuring a person's level of stress, based on weightings of life events to which the person has had to adapt. For your own information, in the far right column, enter the weightings for life events you have experienced within the past year.

Rank (most to least stressful)	Life event	Weighting assigned by Holmes & Rahe	Weighting for events in your life in the past year
1	Death of a spouse	100	
2	Divorce	73	
3	Marital separation	65	
4	Jail term	63	
5	Death of close family member (other than spouse)	63	
6	Personal injury or illness	53	
7	Marriage	50	
8	Fired at work	47	
9	Marital reconciliation	45	
10	Retirement	45	
11	Change in health of family member	44	
12	Pregnancy	40	
13	Sex difficulties	39	
14	Gain of new family member	39	
15	Business readjustment	39	
16	Change in financial state	38	
17	Death of close friend	37	
18	Change to different line of work	36	
19	Change in number of arguments with spouse	35	
20	Mortgage over $10,000 [based on 1967 dollars; would be a higher number today]	31	
21	Foreclosure of mortgage or loan	30	
22	Change in responsibilities at work	29	
23	Son or daughter leaving home	29	
24	Trouble with in-laws	29	
25	Outstanding personal achievement	28	
26	Spouse begins or stops work	26	
27	Begin or end school	26	
28	Change in living condition	25	
29	Revision of personal habits	24	
30	Trouble with boss	23	
31	Change in work hours or conditions	20	

Rank (most to least stressful)	Life event	Weighting assigned by Holmes & Rahe	Weighting for events in your life in the past year
32	Change in residence	20	
33	Change in schools	20	
34	Change in recreation	19	
35	Change in church activities	19	
36	Change in social activities	18	
37	Mortgage or loan less than $10,000 [based on 1967 dollars; would be a higher number today]	17	
38	Change in sleeping habits	16	
39	Change in number of family get-togethers	15	
40	Change in eating habits	15	
41	Vacation	13	
42	Christmas	12	
43	Minor violations of the law	11	
	Total		

Since the SRRS was introduced in 1967, the scale has been introduced to other countries, either in its original form or in an adapted form (e.g., Woon et al., 1971; Yahiro, Inoue, & Nozawa, 1993). Research on the cross-cultural implementation of the SRRS suggests that the scale does have wide cross-cultural applicability (Lin, Masuda, & Tazuma, 1984), particularly if it is modified appropriately (Woon et al., 1971). Some of the items, some descriptions of the items, and some of the weightings and rankings given to the items may need to be adapted to suit different cultural contexts or different ethnic contexts within a richly diverse country such as the United States (Hwang, 1981; Komaroff, Masuda, & Holmes, 1968).

In some occupations, workers are prone to experiencing highly stressful events (see Figure 15-2). Stressful life events can also be relatively minor or temporary changes, such as being on vacation from work, going away for a weekend, or having a treasured friend or family member visit for a few days. These pleasant changes are stressors because they cause you to adapt in some way: In the middle of the night, in your hotel, or at your campsite, you must find your way to the bathroom; while your best friend is visiting, you must cope with new demands on your time and on your physical space.

Everyday Hassles

Not all sources of stress involve major or even minor events in your life. Some stressors are simply *daily hassles*—those routine annoyances or challenges to your ability to cope, such as traffic hassles, disagreements with an acquaintance, getting accustomed to new equipment or appliances, or finding things after you rearrange the items in a cabinet (see, e.g., Figure 15-3). Although no single hassle may be a major source of stress, an accumulation of hassles may very well be (e.g., Pearlstone, Russell, & Wells, 1994).

Daily hassles have been associated with reduced immune-system resistance to infection (Brosschot et al., 1994; Farne et al., 1994); with minor physical ailments

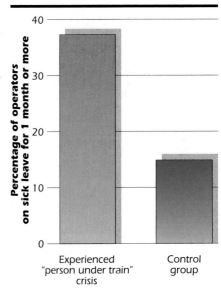

Figure 15-2

Stressful Life Events

Tragically, on occasion, people fall under moving subway trains and are seriously hurt or killed. The subway train operators who actually learn that the train they were operating accidentally killed or maimed someone are much more likely to be on sick leave for a month or more during the year following such a tragic accident. In what other kinds of occupations might you expect workers occasionally to experience highly stressful events?

Hassles		Uplifts	
Item	Percentage of times checked	Item	Percentage of times checked
1. Concerns about weight	52.4%	1. Relating well with your spouse or lover	76.3%
2. Health of a family member	48.1	2. Relating well with friends	74.4
3. Rising prices of common goods	43.7	3. Completing a task	73.3
4. Home maintenance	42.8	4. Feeling healthy	72.7
5. Too many things to do	38.6	5. Getting enough sleep	69.7
6. Misplacing or losing things	38.1	6. Eating out	68.4
7. Yard work or outside home maintenance	38.1	7. Meeting your responsibilities	68.1
8. Property, investment, or taxes	37.6	8. Visiting, phoning, or writing someone	67.7
9. Crime	37.1	9. Spending time with family	66.7
10. Physical appearance	35.9	10. Home (inside) pleasing to you	65.5

Figure 15-3
Hassles and Uplifts
This figure shows the ten most frequently cited daily hassles and the ten most frequently cited daily uplifts.

Everything has two handles, one by which it may be borne, another by which it cannot.

Epictetus

(Kohn et al., 1994); with negative mood, even lasting through the next day (Caspi, Bolger, & Eckenrode, 1987); and with work-related injuries (Savery & Wooden, 1994). On the other hand, the negative outcomes of daily hassles can be reduced by trying not to think about the hassles (Farne et al., 1994) and by seeking and getting social support (e.g., conversations and fun activities with friends) (Flett et al., 1995).

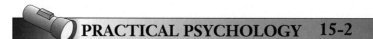

PRACTICAL PSYCHOLOGY   15-2

Stressors at Work

For many people, a major source of stress (particularly in terms of everyday hassles) is their work. Several characteristics of a particular job can make the work particularly stressful:

■ *Job overload*—Time pressures, such as assembly-line work (where the machine, not the worker, determines the pace) and long workdays (e.g., required overtime or after-hours meetings) (Argyle, 1992). For instance, Malía, a tax accountant, feels pressured to work nonstop from early in the morning until late at night every day during the tax season.

■ *Repetitive work*—When the same worker performs the same task again and again, the worker may experience increased levels of stress (Argyle, 1992).

■ *Lack of control*—Workers who feel that they have no control over most aspects of their work feel high levels of stress, as well as being subject to increased risk of high blood pressure and heart disease (Steptoe & Appels, 1989); for instance, assembly-line workers have very little to say about when and how to carry out the work they do, so they may feel high levels of stress.

■ *Danger*—Police officers, firefighters, undersea divers, and coal miners have relatively high levels of stress associated with danger; for instance, each time that Angie, a police officer, rushes to a scene of potential danger, her heart rate and blood pressure increase, and if she is frequently in such situations, she may have greater health risks, as well as the risk of death by homicide, accident, or injury.

■ *Job insecurity*—When workers feel unsure of whether they will continue to be employed (e.g., due to economic turmoil or hardships in a given industry), they experience greater levels of stress (Heaney, Israel, & House, 1994).

■ *Environmental stress*—Some kinds of workers (e.g., coal miners, steel manufacturers, and rock-concert technicians) suffer from increased stress as a direct result of the environment in which they work (Argyle, 1992). For instance, high levels of dust, industrial pollutants, extreme temperatures, and noise can directly cause illness or injury, as well as increased stress. Other sources of stress include the need to work at odd hours (e.g., firefighters and shift nurses in hospitals) or to commute frequently or for long periods of time (e.g., suburban dwellers who work in cities).

■ *Role conflict*—Most people experience some degree of stressful role conflict at work (e.g., trying to please a client while trying to carry out company policies that the client hates); managers (who must please both their superiors and their subordinates) are often particularly likely to suffer stress as a result of role conflicts (Argyle, 1992).

■ *Responsibility for others*—Another reason that managers and supervisors experience high levels of stress is that they must take responsibility for the well-being and the actions of other people (Argyle, 1992); perhaps even more than managers, caregivers (e.g., nurses, social workers, teachers of children with special needs, persons who take care of needy adults) suffer from tremendous stress as a result of continually feeling responsible for other people (Maslach & Jackson, 1984; Wilber & Specht, 1994).

On the other hand, employers can take steps to reduce the amount of stress at work, as well as the impact of work-related stress: (a) Enhance job safety (thereby reducing the danger of the work), (b) reduce the level of noise, dust, and other environmental stressors, (c) enrich the diversity of each worker's job, such as by using automated equipment to reduce the amount of repetitive work and by rotating workers across various tasks, (d) give workers as much autonomy and decision-making authority as is realistic for them to perform their work satisfactorily, (e) provide as much role clarity as possible, so that managers and other workers better understand which of their conflicting roles takes priority in a given situation, and (f) increase the amount of social support provided to caregivers, managers, and workers at all levels, such as by creating opportunities for collaboration and for social interactions—help executives and supervisors to be more supportive of their subordinates. Note, however, that whereas voluntary social interactions seem to reduce stress, obligatory social contacts do not (Bolger & Eckenrode, 1991). The final step is to (g) encourage employees to suggest various ways to minimize stress in the workplace.

MINILECTURE

Stress and Stressors (Ch 20)

What are some examples of stressors (both life events and daily hassles) in your own life?

Stress Responses

The discussion thus far has focused on the environment outside the individual. Environmental events alone do not create stress; the individual must perceive the stressor and must respond to the stressor in some way. Often—at least at first—the primary response of the individual is physiological. When we feel challenged (e.g., by the need to adapt), our bodies physiologically prepare us to confront ("fight") or to escape from ("flight") the challenge. This physiological fight-or-flight response may have adaptive evolutionary origins.

MINILECTURE

Selye: General Adaptation Syndrome (Ch 20)

A ship in port is safe, but that's not what ships are built for.

Grace Murray Hopper

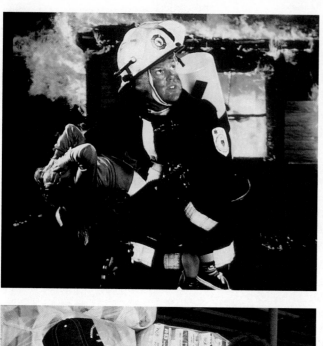

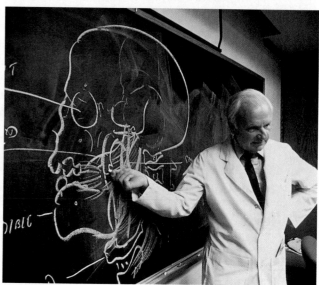

Which of these workers is under the greatest amount of stress? Factors such as overload, repetitive operations, lack of control, physical danger, job insecurity, environmental discomfort, role conflict, and responsibility for other persons all contribute to the stress level of a job.

How do you react to the potentially stressful situations you confront? How do your reactions affect your health and well-being?

The physiological fight-or-flight response was discovered by accident. Hans Selye was looking for a new sex hormone when he accidentally happened across a surprising phenomenon: When the body is attacked or is somehow damaged, it seems to respond in the same general way, regardless of the nature of the assault (e.g., shock, extreme temperatures, or fatigue) or the target of the damage (e.g., the whole body or only a particular body part or organ). Selye soon saw the possible implications of this discovery. He then shifted his research to focus on this puzzling physiological response. Selye and other researchers have noted some patterns in our physiological response, which Selye (e.g., 1976) termed the **general adaptation syndrome (GAS).** There appear to be three phases of response to stress: alarm, resistance, and exhaustion (see Figure 15-4).

Alarm

general adaptation syndrome (GAS) a general pattern of physiological response to stress, involving three phases: alarm, resistance, and exhaustion

In the alarm phase, the body immediately is aroused, and the hypothalamus activates the pituitary gland to release a hormone (adrenocorticotropic hormone—ACTH) that triggers the release of hormones from the adrenal glands: corticosteroids, epinephrine (adrenaline), and norepinephrine. These adrenal hormones stimulate the sympathetic nervous system to prompt the heart and lungs to work harder (increasing heart and respiration rate); slow down or stop the activity of the digestive tract, making more blood available to other organs; increase tension in the muscles; increase the production and use of energy (which produces heat); increase perspiration (which helps cool the body); and increase the release of clotting factors into the bloodstream, to minimize blood loss in case of injury (see Figure 15-5). All of these highly adaptive physiological responses go on without our ever having to think about them.

Resistance

The alarm state cannot continue indefinitely. After a short while, the brain and the endocrine (hormonal) system activate the parasympathetic nervous system, thereby applying chemical brakes to slow down how quickly the sympathetic nervous system uses up the body's energy stores. For example, the demands on the heart and lungs decline. Overall, the physiological stress responses decrease in intensity, although they do not return to normal if the perceived stress continues.

Exhaustion

Eventually, even at the reduced rates of use associated with the resistance phase, the body's reserves are exhausted. The body is less able to restore damaged or worn-out tissues, and it is less able to resist *opportunistic infections* (infections that take advantage of weakened resistance to disease) (Borysenko & Borysenko, 1982). Normally, when our bodies detect the presence of a threat (e.g., a foreign disease-causing microorganism), we immediately use two lines of natural defense: (1) a specific reaction to a known threat that the body has fought off on previous occasions, and (2) a generalized defensive reaction (e.g., the reaction associated with stress) (Maier, Watkins, & Fleshner, 1994).

As an example of your first line of defense, once you have fought off a particular kind of cold or flu virus, your body can immediately recognize and quickly fight off that particular virus if it attacks again. That is, you have been *immunized* (provided with an immune-system defense against a specific disease). Vaccinations can also immunize you against particular diseases by tricking your body into recognizing particular disease-causing microorganisms, so that the body can quickly attack the microorganisms before they have a chance to make you sick.

Your second line of defense is a more general reaction of your immune system to fight off unknown causes of disease. It appears that high levels of stress can weaken your immune system's ability to resist unknown attackers, particularly if the stress continues for an extended period of time (see Figure 15-6). The link between stress and illness has been clearly documented. For instance, stress has been linked to a large number of infectious diseases, including various types of herpes virus infections (such as cold sores, chicken pox, mononucleosis, and genital lesions) (Jemmott & Locke, 1984; Kiecolt-Glaser & Glaser, 1987; VanderPlate, Aral, & Magder, 1988). Even the anticipation of stress can result in suppressed functioning of the immune system (Kemeny et al., 1989).

Researchers in the dynamic, cross-disciplinary field of **psychoneuroimmunology** study how our psychological processes, our neural physiology (especially our brains), and our immune systems interact in ways we never imagined—let alone understood—previously (e.g., Ader, Felten, & Cohen, 1990, 1991; Cohen et al., 1991). For instance, accumulating evidence suggests that our bodies may be classically conditioned to strengthen or to weaken our natural immune-system defenses against disease (Ader & Cohen, 1991, 1993).

Personality and Perceived Stress

How does personality interact with a person's level of stress? In order for a stressor to lead to a stress response, an individual must perceive the stressor (Cohen,

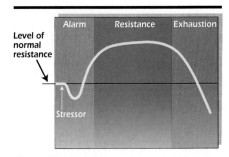

Figure 15-4

General Adaptation Syndrome (GAS)

According to Hans Selye, we undergo three phases in responding to stressors: an alarm phase, *in which we shift into high gear, using up our bodily resources at a rapid rate; a* resistance phase, *in which we somewhat shift down from using our resources in such a spendthrift manner; and an* exhaustion phase, *in which our bodily resources are depleted. (After Selye, H. (1974).* Stress without distress. *New York: HarperCollins. Figure 3, page 39. Copyright © 1974 by M.D.)*

Figure 15-5

The Body's Response to a Stressful Event

As soon as we face a challenge from the environment, our bodies undergo physiological challenges that alarm and prepare us to react to a potential threat to our well-being.

psychoneuroimmunology a cross-disciplinary field that blends psychology, neurology (the study of the brain and nervous system), and immunology (the study of the immune system), as well as physiology (e.g., the study of the endocrine system and other biological systems of the body)

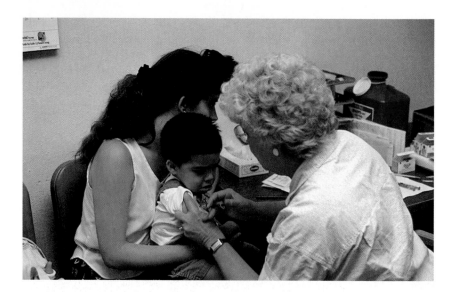

Although the injection of vaccines can be stressful for all concerned, the widespread use of vaccines has provided immunization to millions of people around the world.

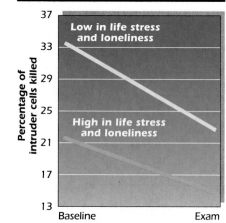

Figure 15-6

Stress, Social Isolation, and Immune Defenses

For students who score comparatively high in life stress and in loneliness, the stress of approaching final examination time leads to a notably weakened immune response to attacking intruder cells that may cause infectious disease (adapted from Kiecolt-Glaser et al., 1984).

Kamarck, & Mermelstein, 1983). That is, it is not the set of events, per se, that results in stress responses such as compromise of the immune system. Rather, stress responses arise from the stress that a person perceives as resulting from these events. For example, if you truly do not notice any need to make any adaptations to having a new roommate or a new job, you may not experience these events as being stressful.

Also, each of us perceives some stressors as more distressing than others. For example, suppose that you hate conflict or confrontation of any kind, and you experience situations of conflict or confrontation as being extremely stressful. Someone else might feel little distress in confrontational situations or might even enjoy conflict. If you and this conflict-loving person argue, both of you may experience the physiological alarm phase of the stress response and even the resistance phase. However, because you fret about the confrontation for a while afterward, you may reach the stage of exhaustion. In contrast, the other person may forget all about the conflict moments after it ends, thereby avoiding the exhaustion phase. The notion that perception affects physiology is not new, as shown in the adage regarding mind over matter, "If you don't mind, it doesn't matter."

Each of us also experiences different degrees of internal conflict in response to clashing external demands (work vs. family, spouse vs. friend, etc.). In addition, the very same environment can be experienced as quite different, depending on personality variables. An extrovert who works in a library serving a remote community of illiterates might be about as distressed as an introvert who leads the recreational activities for a large cruise ship. Each, however, might consider the other's job idyllic.

Finding Your Way **15-2**

Think about your own pet peeves or the situations you love to hate. What situations might literally make you sick? Now think about who might consider these peevish situations pleasant. What is it in your personality that makes some situations sickeningly stressful and others quite tolerable?

Appraisal and Coping

Susan Folkman and Richard Lazarus (1988; Folkman et al., 1986) have proposed a model for the way in which personality factors, stressful circumstances, and health

Some health problems attack more than one person at a single blow. For instance, the health of loved ones who care for patients with dementia (e.g., as the result of Alzheimer's disease or multiple strokes) may suffer after providing 24-hour care, 7 days/week to patients who may not even recognize them at all any more.

interact. According to Folkman and Lazarus, when we are confronted with a potentially stressful situation, we go through a two-step appraisal process and then a two-dimensional coping process. Both processes interact with our distinctive personalities and with the situation at hand. In **primary appraisal,** we analyze just how much of a stake we have in the outcome of the particular situation. If we have no stake in the outcome, the entire process stops right there.

For example, suppose that I were to tell you of an alarming situation at your college: Some professors have been observed wearing dirty socks! You cannot let this situation continue! Right this instant, you must write a letter to the faculty senate of your college, urging the senate to pass a policy insisting that professors wear clean socks at all times! You must get the letter into the mail immediately!

Did you feel your stress level go up? Probably not. You probably have very little stake in persuading professors to wear clean socks. You may even decide to ignore my urgent plea altogether. Now, compare that level of stress with the level of stress you feel when you think about the final examinations in all of your courses. Unless you are an extraordinarily relaxed student, you probably appraise final exams as being something in which you have a lot at stake. In considering final exams, you would proceed to the next step in the appraisal process: secondary appraisal.

In **secondary appraisal,** we assess what we can do to maximize the likelihood of potentially beneficial outcomes and to minimize the likelihood of potentially harmful outcomes of a given situation. In thinking about final exams, you would try to assess how you could increase the probability that you would score well and decrease the possibility that you would score poorly on any of your exams. The decision to read textbooks and study lecture notes might figure prominently in your secondary appraisal.

Note that both primary and secondary appraisal occur at a cognitive level. At this level, you have not yet cracked a book or jotted a note. Once your primary and secondary appraisals are complete, you are ready to begin **coping** with the situation—that is, actually trying to manage the internal and external challenges posed by the situation. According to Folkman and Lazarus, two dimensions of coping serve two different functions: **Problem-focused coping** tackles the

Please know that I am aware of the hazards. I want to do it because I want to do it. Women must try to do things as men have tried. When they fail, their failure must be but a challenge to others.

Amelia Earhart

primary appraisal the first step in coping with a situation that may be stressful, involving analysis of how much the person will be affected by outcomes of the particular situation

secondary appraisal the process of assessing what can be done about a challenging situation to make it more likely that positive outcomes will result and less likely that harmful outcomes will result

coping the processes of managing the internal and external changes presented by a challenging situation

problem-focused coping adapting to a challenging situation by using strategies to fix the situation and to make it less challenging

problem itself and involves behavioral strategies to resolve the situation. For example, your problem-focused coping strategies might include studying the textbook, attending study sessions, and reviewing your lecture notes. **Emotion-focused coping** involves handling your own emotions in regard to the situation. For example, while studying for the exams, you might try to suppress your anxiety about the exams. Just before taking the exams, you might try some relaxation techniques to reduce your anxiety during the exam.

In situations over which we have more control (e.g., exam grades), problem-focused coping strategies are more likely to lead to more satisfactory outcomes. In situations over which we have less control (e.g., determining what questions your instructor will ask on the exam), emotion-focused coping is more likely to lead to more satisfactory outcomes. The net interaction of primary and secondary appraisal and of problem-focused and emotion-focused coping strategies determines the degree of stress that the individual experiences. According to Folkman and Lazarus, when people feel that their options for coping are inadequate for the situation at hand, they experience greater stress. Low self-esteem can also diminish people's sense of being able to cope with challenging situations (DeLongis, Folkman, & Lazarus, 1988). This perceived inadequacy increases perceived stress, thereby increasing the threat to health and well-being.

Social Contacts and Social Support

Social isolation is another factor that seems to threaten people's health and well-being (House, Landis, & Umberson, 1988) (see Figure 15-6, shown previously). Although obligatory social contacts (e.g., meetings at work or social obligations) do not seem to offer benefits to mental or physical health, voluntary social contacts do (Bolger & Eckenrode, 1991). One reason for the benefits of social contacts may be the opportunities for receiving social support. Social support from various other persons is believed to *buffer* against (i.e., reduce the potentially damaging impact of) harmful levels of stress (Schwarzer & Leppin, 1989, 1991a, 1991b). Adequate social support can help people to cope with stressors, particularly if such support suits the personality and situational needs of the recipient of the support (Sarason, Pierce, & Sarason, 1994). The need for social support may even have direct effects on health and well-being: People who have high needs for affiliation, relative to their needs for power and achievement, seem to have stronger immune systems (McClelland, 1987).

Certain kinds of social support also lead to particular health benefits. For instance, friends offer an important source of enjoyable social contacts. Families can also be a resource for pleasant leisure and recreational activities. In addition, friends and families seem to offer distinctive health benefits: People who are married or who have children are also more likely to avoid risky behavior, to take fewer drugs (e.g., alcohol or nicotine [in cigarettes]), and to take other measures to enhance their health (Umberson, 1987). Spouses tend to monitor one another's health and to encourage one another's health-enhancing behavior (Umberson, 1992). On the other hand, for dealing with stress on the job, people seem to be helped more by receiving support from their colleagues and supervisors than by receiving support from family members (Argyle, 1992).

What are some realistic things that you can do to minimize your experience of stress in your life?

Finding Your Way **15-3**

---

emotion-focused coping adapting to a challenging situation by handling one's own emotions that arise in regard to the situation

Think about how your social world can help you cope with the aspects of your life that are stressful to you. How can you increase the enjoyable social contacts in your life? Are you experiencing a lot of stress at work or at school? Who are some of the people to whom you can reach out, who can offer you social support for handling the stressful aspects of your life? If you are not close to members of your family, how else might you find encouragement to practice health-enhancing behavior?

How do personality and stress influence health? Stress is associated with increased likelihood of becoming ill. Stressors may include major or minor life events, as well as everyday hassles. Stress responses involve the general adaptation syndrome, which has three phases: alarm, resistance, and exhaustion. The field of psychoneuroimmunology studies the interaction of the brain and nervous system, the immune system, and psychological processes, such as in the complex dynamics of stress responses. In responding to stressful situations, people seem to appraise their stake in the situation and then to appraise the potential harms and benefits of the situation. Once they have appraised the situation, people cope with it through emotion-focused and problem-focused coping. Social contacts and social support may help to buffer us against the harmful effects of stress and otherwise to enhance health, such as by encouraging healthful behavior.

HOW DO PERSONALITY PATTERNS RELATE TO ILLNESS?

Type-A Versus Type-B Behavior Patterns

As this chapter has shown, our psychological makeup affects our choices in health-related behaviors and our responses to potentially stressful situations. How else may our personal psychological characteristics affect our health? In 1974, Meyer Friedman and Ray Rosenman noticed that men who suffered from heart disease seemed to have a particular set of personality characteristics, known as the **Type-A behavior pattern,** which comprises (1) a competitive orientation

Type-A behavior pattern a personality characterized by *high* levels of hostility, as well as by the *pursuit* of competition and time pressure

Two personality patterns seem to influence the likelihood of coronary heart disease: Persons with a Type-A personality pattern (such as the woman on the left) feel a sense of urgency to complete tasks and to achieve success, and they are easily angered when things do not go well. Persons with a Type-B personality pattern (such as the men on the right) seem to be able to respond to work pressures without feeling undue urgency, compulsion to achieve success, or high levels of hostility in response to minor frustrations.

toward achievement, (2) a sense of urgency about time, and (3) high levels of feelings of anger and hostility. Thus, Type-A's tend to work very hard and competitively toward achieving goals, often without feeling much enjoyment in the process; they constantly tend to be racing against the clock; and they tend to feel anger and hostility easily toward other people and other sources of frustration. In contrast to the Type-A behavior pattern is the **Type-B behavior pattern,** characterized by relatively low levels of competitiveness, urgency about time, and hostility. Type-B people tend to be more easygoing, relaxed, and willing to enjoy the process of life as they live it.

Finding Your Way   **15-4**

Before you read on, stop for a moment to reflect on which pattern describes your own behavior. (Clue: If you felt angry at the suggestion to take the time to stop working toward your goal of finishing this chapter as quickly as possible, perhaps you do not need to think too long about which pattern best describes you.) If you are unsure of how you would describe yourself, think about how a family member or a close friend might describe your behavior.

When the habitually even-tempered suddenly fly into a passion, that explosion is apt to be more impressive than the outburst of the most violent amongst us.

Margery Allingham

MINILECTURE
Personality and Health (Ch 20)

Design a program for a Type-A individual to help that person to be more resistant to the ill effects of Type-A behavior. Include some stress-reduction techniques, as well as some appropriate cognitive techniques for handling stressful situations (e.g., saying aloud, "Even if this guy cuts me off on the highway, I will still make it to work on time").

A number of studies have found a link between Type-A behavior and coronary heart disease (Booth-Kewley & Friedman, 1987; Friedman et al., 1994; Haynes, Feinleib, & Kannel, 1980). However, some studies have not confirmed the link (e.g., Shekelle et al., 1985). It appears that the three components of Type-A behavior may not contribute equally to heart attack. Redford Williams (1986) has argued that the component of anger and hostility is the most deadly one (also described in Taylor, 1990). Other studies have supported this position (e.g., Barefoot, Dahlstrom, & Williams, 1983). Anger and hostility directed against one's self may be quite damaging to health (Dembroski et al., 1985; Williams, 1986). Also, hostility characterized by suspiciousness, resentment, frequent anger, and antagonism toward others seems to be quite harmful to health (Barefoot et al., 1989; Dembroski & Costa, 1988; Williams & Barefoot, 1988). A further refinement of this body of research suggests that the expression of anger and hostility may have more serious health consequences for men than for women (e.g., Burns, Hutt, & Weidner, 1993; Spicer, Jackson, & Scragg, 1993; Wright et al., 1994).

Type-A behavior appears to be somewhat modifiable (Friedman et al., 1994; Levenkron & Moore, 1988). A variety of techniques have been used, including relaxation (Roskies et al., 1978), aerobic exercise, cognitive–behavioral stress management (Blumenthal et al., 1988; Roskies et al., 1986), or some combinations of these techniques (Bruning & Frew, 1987). To a certain extent, you can influence your perceptions by changing your thinking. Some health psychologists focus on changing people's reactions to events so that they feel less distressed in the face of life's challenges. In addition, lifestyle changes might be appropriate interventions. Type-A individuals tend to have very different lifestyles from those of Type-B individuals, and it may be as much the lifestyle as the personality itself that leads to coronary heart disease. For example, the Type-A individuals are more likely to place themselves in competitive situations, and in situations with great demands on their time.

Hardiness and Stress Resistance

The discovery of heart-attack-prone personalities occurred because many health researchers wanted to know how personality attributes may increase people's vulnerability to illness. In contrast, Suzanne Kobasa (1982, 1990; Kobasa et al., 1994) has focused on studying a personality trait she calls "hardiness," an aspect of

Type-B behavior pattern a personality characterized by *low* levels of hostility, as well as by the *avoidance* of competition and time pressure

personality that seems to help people resist the health-weakening effects of stress. **Hardiness** includes high internal locus of control, strong commitment to work and to other activities, and an outlook that views change as a challenge and an opportunity for growth. Compared with other people, people with hardy personalities also tend to find out more information about health in general and about the prevention of illnesses to which they may be vulnerable in particular (Lau, 1988). They also show more health-enhancing behavior, and they believe that they can control their own health (Lau, 1988).

How do personality patterns relate to illness? In the 1970s, the Type-A behavior pattern was observed to be related to coronary heart disease. Subsequent research has shown that the component of the Type-A pattern most strongly related to heart attacks is the expression of anger and hostility. On a more positive note, hardiness seems to be associated with resistance to becoming ill.

HOW DO OUR MINDS EXPERIENCE PAIN?

Among the most troubling symptoms of illness is pain. **Pain** is the sensory and emotional discomfort associated with actual, imagined, or threatened damage to or irritation of the body (Sanders, 1985). Chapter 4 described the sensory aspects of pain, including the importance of pain as a warning system to alert us that our body tissues are being injured or are recovering from injury. Pain stimuli warn us to avoid further injury or to seek safety and rest to aid in recovery and healing. Here, we discuss the cognitive and emotional aspects of pain, as well as different kinds of pain and various methods for relieving pain.

Many psychologists conceptualize pain in a way very similar to the popular conception of pain: It has both a sensory component (the sensations at the site where the pain starts, e.g., throbbing, aching, or stinging pain) and an affective component (the emotions that go along with the pain, e.g., fear, anger, or sadness). Each of these two components strongly affects the other. Nonetheless, it is possible, at least at some level, to distinguish the contribution of each (Fernandez & Turk, 1992).

Our perceptions of pain also interact with our cognitions regarding pain. Based on our own experiences with and observations of pain, we form our own schemas regarding pain, as well as beliefs regarding our own ability to control pain. The interaction goes both ways: Just as our cognitions are affected by our experiences with pain, our cognitions also affect our perception of pain. For example, if we believe that we will be able to overcome pain, we may be more effective in doing so than if we believe that we will be defeated by our sensations of pain (described as "catastrophizing," sometimes as a result of learned helplessness). In fact, self-efficacy beliefs may play an important role in pain control (described in Turk & Rudy, 1992).

One mechanism by which cognition, emotion, and sensation may interact to affect pain perception has been proposed by Ronald Melzack and Patrick Wall (1965, 1982). According to Melzack and Wall's **gate-control theory** of pain, the central nervous system (CNS) serves as a physiological gating mechanism (see Figure 15-7). This gating mechanism can increase or decrease the degree to which pain is perceived, by widening or narrowing the opening of the gate. Through the gating mechanism, cognitions and emotions in the brain can cause the spinal cord to intensify or to inhibit the transmission of pain sensations.

There was never yet philosopher / That could endure the toothache patiently.

William Shakespeare

hardiness a personality attribute characterized by high internal locus of control, strong commitment to work and other activities, and an outlook that favors challenge and opportunities for personal growth

pain sensory and emotional discomfort associated with actual, imagined, or threatened damage to or irritation of tissues of the body

gate-control theory a possible explanation of pain, suggesting that the central nervous system acts as a physiological barrier through which pain may be allowed to pass under particular circumstances

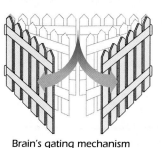

If more fearful, bored, depressed, or focused on the self, **widen** the gate (allowing *more* pain to pass through).

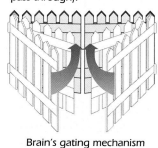

If more calm and relaxed, distracted, happy, or focused on external events, **narrow** the gate (allowing *less* pain to pass through).

Pain sensations

Brain's gating mechanism

Brain's gating mechanism

PAIN THRESHOLD

Awareness/perception of pain

Figure 15-7

Gate-Control Theory of Pain
According to Ronald Melzack and Patrick Wall, the central nervous system (particularly the brain) acts as a kind of physiological gate, which widens or narrows to allow some pain sensations to enter awareness, but not others.

According to this theory, some cognitions and emotions may widen the opening of the gate, lowering our *pain threshold* (the amount of stimulus required to cross the threshold and trigger the awareness of pain), and permitting greater transmission of pain sensations that reach our awareness. Other cognitions and emotions may narrow the passage through the gate, raising our pain threshold and permitting less transmission of pain sensations that reach our awareness. For example, fearful attention to the possibility of pain may widen the gate and lower our pain threshold. However, relaxed attention to other sensations may narrow the gate and raise our pain threshold. Naturally, as the pain reaches the brain, the brain's perception of pain also may affect emotions and cognitions that follow. The distinct patterns of emotion, cognition, and sensation affect the quality—as well as the intensity—of the pain the individual experiences at a given time.

Kinds of Pain

Psychologists (and other clinicians) often distinguish between organic pain and psychogenic pain. **Organic pain** is caused by damage to bodily tissue, such as bruises, cuts, and internal injuries. **Psychogenic pain** is the discomfort that occurs when there appears to be no physical cause of the pain. We need to be careful in labeling pain as "psychogenic" because it is impossible to prove the null hypothesis: Just because the medical profession has been unable to find an organic source of pain does not mean therefore that such pain does not exist or even that there is no organic cause of the pain. Our current tools for diagnosis of the sources of pain are still imprecise (see Turk & Rudy, 1992). A cause may exist, which simply has not been found.

In most cases, the experience of pain represents an interaction between physiological and psychological factors. The link between the perception of pain and the presence of a known pathology or injury is not always clear. For instance, in many situations, the experience of pain is delayed for a while after injury or is altogether absent despite serious pathology of the body tissues (Melzack, Wall, & Ty, 1982; see also Fernandez & Turk, 1992).

Whether pain is organic or psychogenic, it can be classified as either acute or chronic. *Acute pain* is the discomfort that a person experiences over a relatively short period of time. Some researchers (e.g., Turk, Meichenbaum, & Genest, 1983) have used a time period of 6 months as a cutoff. In other words, the patient who experiences pain for less than 6 months is classified as experiencing acute pain. Pain lasting more than 6 months is referred to as *chronic pain.*

organic pain discomfort caused by observed physical damage to bodily tissue

psychogenic pain discomfort for which an observed source of physical damage to bodily tissues has not been found

Personality and Pain

Several investigators have tried to discover whether there is a relationship between personality attributes and the experiencing of pain. Such research might sound relatively easy to do. First, you think of a few traits that you believe might be associated with pain perceptions (e.g., irritability or impatience). Next, you test to see whether those traits match up to measurements of people's perceptions of pain.

The problem with this research is the same problem that arises with most correlational studies: Suppose that you find a strong correlation between particular traits and the likelihood of experiencing pain. Which came first—the personality attribute or the experiencing of pain? The existence of a relationship does not indicate the direction or the cause of the relationship. For instance, suppose that high degrees of irritability or impatience are associated with pain. Perhaps a person may be susceptible to experiencing pain because of these particular personality attributes. However, an equally plausible relationship is that the person acquired these personality attributes (e.g., irritability or impatience) as a result of having experienced the pain.

As an example, suppose that we were to find a correlation between scores on tests of anxiety or depression and scores on a scale measuring chronic pain. We would scarcely be surprised if we were to learn that the anxiety or depression was caused by the pain, rather than vice versa. It is also possible that both the personality attribute and the experiencing of pain may depend on a third factor, such as having a painful and life-threatening disease.

Some research has shown that responses to the *Minnesota Multiphasic Personality Inventory* (MMPI) (see Chapter 12) can help to identify patients who are particularly susceptible to experiencing pain. Michael Bond (1979) has found that patients who experience either acute or chronic pain tend to score especially high on the hypochondriasis and hysteria scales of the MMPI. People high in *hysteria* tend to show extreme emotional behavior and also tend to exaggerate the level and seriousness of the symptoms they experience. Chronic-pain patients also tend to score high on depression.

The fact that greater indications of depression are seen in chronic- but not in acute-pain patients suggests that the depression is a result, rather than a cause, of the pain. However, Thomas Rudy, Robert Kerns, and Dennis Turk (1988) have found that the development of depression may be related not just to the experience of pain itself, but also to the conditions associated with pain, such as the reduction in level of activity, a general sense of inability to master the environment, and a diminished sense of personal control. (For some ideas regarding how to control pain, see Practical Psychology 15-3.)

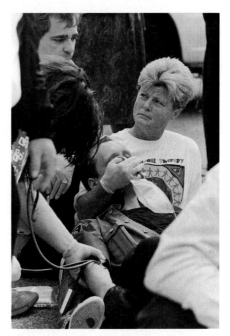

The pain that this wounded police officer experiences will be a product of the physical injury he has sustained, as well as of his personality.

How do our minds experience pain? Our experience of pain has an affective (emotional) component, a cognitive (thinking) component, and a sensory component. According to the gate-control theory of pain, the CNS may increase or decrease the amount of pain we feel before we recognize a stimulus as being painful. Pain may be psychogenic or organic. Various personality characteristics have been associated with higher reporting of pain, but it is not clear whether the pain leads to the personality characteristics or vice versa. The search for pain relief prompts many people to seek medical attention, and the various treatments for pain have varying degrees of effectiveness.

PRACTICAL PSYCHOLOGY 15-3

Control of Pain

How can pain be controlled? A wide variety of techniques have been used for controlling pain (Taylor, 1991), many of which are successful, at least for some people some of the time. Following are some of the major methods of pain control:

1. *Pharmacological control*—The administration of drugs (e.g., aspirin, acetaminophen, or ibuprofen, or, for more severe pain, morphine) to reduce pain
2. *Surgical control*—Surgical cuts in the fibers that carry the sensation of pain, intended to prevent or at least to diminish the transmission of pain sensations along the offending nerve fibers; used in treating localized pain, particularly in the limbs
3. *Biofeedback*—Machine-translated feedback given to patients regarding their physiological responses; the feedback translates the body's responses into a form that the patient can easily observe and therefore bring under conscious control; biofeedback methods have been helpful for pain symptoms related to muscle tension (e.g., tension headaches) or to vascular (blood-vessel) disorders (e.g., migraine headaches)
4. *Acupuncture*—A technique originating in Asia, which involves the use of needles on particular points on the body; a related Western adaptation of acupuncture is transcutaneous electrical nerve stimulation (TENS)
5. *Hypnosis*—An induced state of deep relaxation, during which patients are given the suggestion that they are not feeling pain (Weisenberg, 1977)
6. *Relaxation techniques*—Techniques for relaxing muscles, controlling breathing, and entering a state of low arousal (Davidson & Schwartz, 1976)
7. *Guided imagery*—Used with relaxation techniques, as a means to aid relaxation; also may be used as a means of mentally combating the pain or the underlying disease causing the pain
8. *Sensory control through counterirritation*—Involves stimulating or mildly irritating a part of the body that differs from the one experiencing pain; may work as a means of distracting patients from their primary source of pain
9. *Distraction*—Using any means to shift patients' attention away from the pain, to focus on something else

Because so many people experience chronic pain, many pain-treatment centers have arisen around the world. Of those patients who seek treatment in pain clinics, the average amount of time they have endured chronic pain is about 7 years (Turk & Rudy, 1992). Most of these centers use a variety of techniques from among those listed here, in helping their patients to cope with pain. Finding the most successful technique becomes particularly important in cases of chronic pain related to serious illness.

Why do we feel pain, and what can we do to minimize our feelings of pain?

HOW DO PEOPLE LIVE WITH SERIOUS, CHRONIC HEALTH PROBLEMS?

We often do not truly value our health until we no longer have it. When we recover from acute illnesses, we sometimes briefly return to cherishing our health, only to forget about it after a little while. People with chronic illnesses do not have

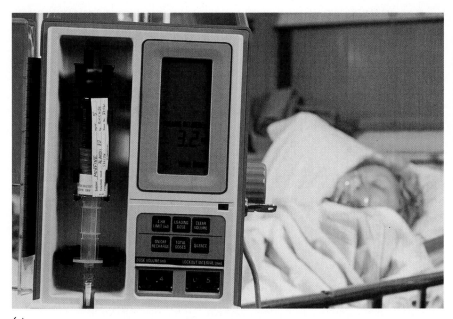
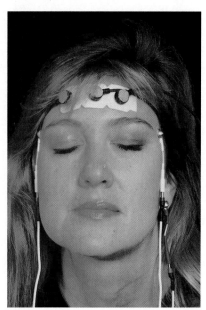

(a)   (b)

Two of the techniques used for treating severe pain are (a) self-regulated morphine drip, and (b) biofeedback.

this luxury. A widely feared serious chronic illness of our time is acquired immune deficiency syndrome, better known as AIDS.

AIDS: Incidence and Prevention

AIDS is caused by a *retrovirus*, which is a slow-acting virus. The retrovirus, human immunodeficiency virus (HIV), attacks the immune system and especially the helper *T-cells* (specialized, relatively long-living cells that protect the body at the cellular level) (Solomon & Temoshok, 1987). The virus is transmitted by the exchange of bodily fluids that contain the virus, most notably blood and semen.

Tests are now available that can detect whether HIV antibodies are in the body. The presence of these antibodies, which fight the virus as much as possible, indicate whether a person has been infected with HIV. When the antibodies are present, the person is said to be *HIV-positive* (i.e., the HIV retrovirus is in the person's blood).

Being HIV-positive does not mean that the person already has developed AIDS. Individuals differ widely in the time it takes them to develop AIDS from the time they first contract the virus; the latency period can even be as long as 8 to 10 years. Even with full-blown AIDS, it is not the AIDS virus itself that kills people. Rather, death strikes through opportunistic infections that are deadly because the immune system is impaired and cannot fight these infections. Some of the illnesses that eventually kill AIDS patients include rare forms of pneumonia and cancer that do not normally kill people with strong immune systems. Both the rate of diagnosis and the rate of AIDS-related deaths are increasing (see Figure 15-8).

Despite its rapid spread, AIDS can be controlled and, in principle, entirely eliminated through behavioral interventions. Men who engage in sexual relations should always use condoms during sexual intercourse, and both men and women should restrict their number of sexual partners. People who inject themselves with drugs by using needles (whether intravenous drugs, steroids, or other drugs administered via needles) should not share needles with other drug users. Prevention is especially important because there is no known cure for AIDS. Moreover, as far as we know, virtually everyone who contracts HIV eventually will develop AIDS.

I plan on going on living for a long time. You don't have to run from me. You can give me hugs, my high fives, my kisses.

Magic Johnson

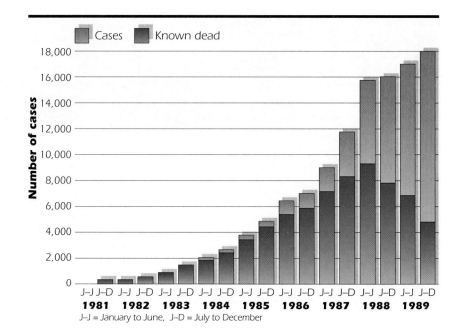

Figure 15-8

Rates of AIDS Cases and Deaths

Since 1981, the number of people diagnosed with AIDS has sharply increased, as has the number of people who have died of the disease.

In your opinion, what are the pros and the cons of requiring extensive, lengthy testing of drugs and other treatments for life-threatening ailments such as AIDS? Do you believe that special exceptions to drug restrictions should be made in the case of drugs for treating people with terminal illnesses? Why or why not?

Particular drugs seem to postpone the development of the disease but do not head it off entirely.

Tests are now available that can detect HIV antibodies in the body, thereby indicating whether a person has been infected. Many people choose to have testing done anonymously via the use of numbered reports (without names) because of the discrimination that has been encountered by people who are HIV-positive—even those who have not shown symptoms of the virus. For example, virtually all life insurance companies now require HIV testing for the issuance of insurance policies, and policies are almost never issued to those who test positive. Moreover, people have lost jobs when they have been identified as HIV-positive. Of course, the most difficult psychological phenomenon associated with HIV infection is the knowledge of the virtual certainty that it will become AIDS, a disease that is still considered to be fatal for all persons who contract it.

Psychological Models for Coping with Chronic Illness

Franklin Shontz (1975) has proposed a stage model of how people react when they realize that they have a serious, chronic, and probably life-threatening disease. The first stage is one of *shock*. People are stunned, bewildered, and often feel detached from the situation: How can this illness be happening to me? The second stage is *encounter*. The person gives way to feelings of despair, loss, grief, and hopelessness. During this stage, people are often unable to function effectively: They do not think well, they have difficulty in planning, and they are ineffective in solving problems. During *retreat*, the third stage, individuals often try to deny the existence of the problem. At the least, they deny the implications of what the illness means for them. Eventually, however, people reach a fourth stage, *adjustment*. During the adjustment stage, they make whatever changes are necessary in order to cope effectively with the reality of the disease.

Shontz's model focuses on the emotional and behavioral aspects of coping. In contrast, Shelley Taylor (e.g., 1983; Taylor & Aspinwall, 1990) has proposed a model highlighting the ways in which people adapt cognitively to serious chronic illness. According to Taylor, patients first try to *find meaning* in the experience of the illness. They may try to figure out what they were doing wrong that led to the illness. Then they start doing right whatever they were doing wrong, or they may simply rethink their own attitudes and priorities, in light of their new perspective. Next, patients try to *gain a sense of control* over the illness and over the rest of their lives. They may seek as much information as possible regarding their illness and its treatment. They also may undertake activities that they believe will help either to restore function and well-being or at least to slow down the destructive progress of their illness. Third, patients try to *restore their self-esteem* despite the offense of being struck by such an illness. They may compare their situations with those of others, in ways that shed favorable light on their own situations.

Shontz and Taylor focused on processes commonly experienced by people who have chronic illnesses. Other researchers, however, have focused on individual differences in how people cope with chronic illness. Rudolf Moos (1982, 1988; Moos & Schaefer, 1986) has described a *crisis theory* of coping with chronic illness (shown in Figure 15-9). In his theory, Moos attempts to characterize individual differences in people's abilities to cope with serious health problems. According to this model, how well a person copes depends on three sets of factors:

1. *Background and personal factors* (such things as emotional maturity, self-esteem, religious beliefs, and age)—For example, men are more likely to respond negatively to diseases that compromise their ability to work; older people will have to live fewer years with a chronic illness than will younger ones, so they may be better able to cope with the prospects.
2. *Illness-related factors* (such things as how disabling, painful, or life-threatening the disease is)—Unsurprisingly, the greater the disability, pain, and threat, the more difficulty people have in coping with the illness.
3. *Environmental factors* (such things as social supports, the ability of the person to remain financially sound, and the kinds of conditions in which the person lives)—Some factors (e.g., financial difficulties) may diminish the ability to cope, whereas others (e.g., social support) may increase it.

In addition to identifying these three sources of individual differences in coping, Moos has indicated three main components of the coping process: cognitive appraisal, the decision to adapt, and the development of coping skills. *Cognitive appraisal* identifies the meaning and significance of the health problem for the person's life. This cognitive appraisal is similar to the appraisal processes described by Folkman and Lazarus in the perception of stress. Next, as a result of this cognitive appraisal, the person decides how to perform tasks in ways that adapt to the limitations posed by the illness. Once the person has made *decisions regarding how to adapt* to the illness, the person *develops coping skills* for living with the illness. The outcome of the coping process will in turn affect the outcome of the crisis in general—how well the person is able to live with the disabling illness.

Ultimately, the key to coping with serious chronic illness is *adaptation:* The individual will need to make changes and adjustments in order to live happily and effectively. Persons with serious chronic illnesses often must make extraordinary efforts in order to adapt to the environment.

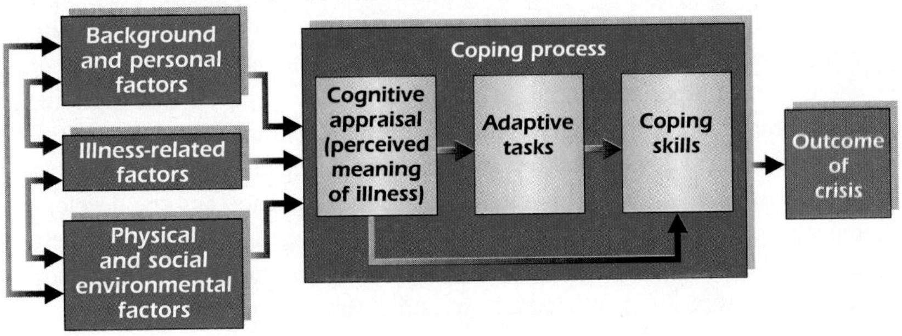

If I can stop one heart from breaking, / I shall not live in vain; / If I can ease one life the aching, / Or cool one pain, . . . / I shall not live in vain.

Emily Dickinson

If the rich could hire others to die for them, the poor could make a nice living.

Yiddish proverb

If a close friend of yours had to confront chronic health problems, what advice would you suggest to your friend?

Figure 15-9

Three Sets of Factors in Coping

In Rudolf Moos's crisis theory, there are three sets of factors involved in the patient's early phases of adjusting to serious illness. It is the interaction of individual differences and the coping process itself that influences the outcome of the crisis.

Background and personal factors

Illness-related factors

Physical and social environmental factors

Coping process

Cognitive appraisal (perceived meaning of illness)

Adaptive tasks

Coping skills

Outcome of crisis

This young diabetic seems to be making the adjustment to his disease. With the help of caring adults, he will probably also manage to find meaning, gain a sense of control, and restore his sense of self-esteem after learning about his illness.

How do people live with serious, chronic health problems? AIDS is perhaps the most widely feared serious chronic health problem of our time. Although a cure for AIDS is not yet available, for most people, it is not difficult to prevent AIDS. When coping emotionally and behaviorally with chronic illness, people may experience the stages of shock, encounter, and retreat before reaching emotional and behavioral adjustment. One view of the cognitive aspects of coping with chronic illness suggests that cognitive coping may involve the stages of finding meaning, gaining a sense of control, and restoring self-esteem. Yet another model suggests that the coping process involves cognitive appraisal, the decision to adapt, and the development of coping skills. Each of these views of coping may be at least partly correct. Factors that affect individual responses to chronic illness include personal factors, illness-related factors, and environmental factors.

Although most of us do not experience pain or ill health very often, we do confront situations requiring us to adapt in varying ways and to varying degrees. We constantly need to adjust ourselves in order to fit ourselves to our environment. In addition, whether we are healthy or ill, young or old, lucky or not, we can shape our environment. Just as we need to adapt ourselves to fit the environment, we can modify the environment in order to suit ourselves. If there is a key to psychological adjustment, perhaps it is in the balance between adaptation to and shaping of the environment, with the added option of selection. When we find that a particular environment simply cannot be shaped to fit us, and we cannot adapt ourselves to fit it, we can try to find another more suitable environment. It is my hope that you can adapt to, shape, and select your environments, to find what you want in life, reach for it, and ultimately attain it.

Be careful in choosing what you want in life because you may very well get it.

Anonymous

SUMMARY

What Do Health Psychologists Study? 448

1. *Health psychology* is the study of the reciprocal interaction between psychological processes and physiological health.
2. We classify illnesses according to their duration: *acute* illnesses are relatively brief; *chronic* illnesses last for a long time, often across the entire life span.

How Can People Enhance Their Health Through Lifestyle Choices? 450

3. People may enhance their health by making positive lifestyle choices, such as by regularly engaging in *aerobic exercise*, proper diet, and adequate rest, as well as by avoiding harmful drugs.

How Do Personality and Stress Influence Health? 452

4. *Stress* is the situation in which environmental factors cause a person to feel challenged in some way. *Stressors* are situations or events that cause the person to have to adapt to or cope with changes in the situation. These adaptations are *stress responses*.
5. The initial stress response is adaptive in helping the person to prepare to flee from or to fight in the threatening situation. After the initial alarm phase of stress, if the perceived stressor continues to confront the individual, the body shifts down to a resistance phase and finally to an exhaustion phase.
6. Stress has been linked to many diseases, and its direct effects on the immune system are now being explored in the cross-disciplinary field of *psychoneuroimmunology*.
7. Personality influences the perception of stress through the processes of primary and secondary appraisal. In *primary appraisal*, we analyze our stake in the outcome of handling a particular situation. In *secondary appraisal*, we assess what we can do to maximize the probability that helpful outcomes will occur and to minimize the probability that harmful outcomes will occur.

8. In *coping* with stressful situations, we may use *problem-focused coping*, which is directed at solving a problem, and *emotion-focused coping*, which is directed at handling the emotions experienced as a result of the problem.
9. Social contacts and social support play important roles in promoting health and in recovering from illness.

How Do Personality Patterns Relate to Illness? 463

10. Several personality factors influence health, particularly the personality characteristics related to competitiveness, sense of urgency, and anger and hostility. Persons who rate high on these three characteristics have a *Type-A behavior pattern*; persons with a *Type-B behavior pattern* rate low on these characteristics. Of the three characteristics, feelings of anger and hostility seem most clearly threatening to health, particularly in terms of coronary heart disease. Lifestyle differences may also contribute to these effects.
11. The personality trait known as *hardiness* (characterized by internal locus of control, strong commitment to work, and a view of change as being a challenging opportunity for growth) appears to be linked to increased resistance to illness.

How Do Our Minds Experience Pain? 465

12. *Pain* has a sensory component, an affective component, and perhaps also a cognitive component. According to the *gate-control theory* of pain, the CNS acts as a gate that can either raise or lower our threshold for pain.
13. *Organic pain* is caused by damage to bodily tissue. *Psychogenic pain* is the discomfort felt when there appears to be no physical cause of the pain. What may appear to be psychogenic pain, however, may be caused by unidentified organic pathology.
14. Pain may be *acute* (lasting less than 6 months) or *chronic* (lasting 6 months or more).
15. Although several personality traits have been associated with pain, it has proven difficult to determine the direction of causality for these correlations.

16. Methods for controlling pain include pharmacological control (via drugs), surgical control, biofeedback, acupuncture, hypnosis, relaxation techniques, guided imagery, sensory control (e.g., counterirritation), and distraction.

How Do People Live with Serious, Chronic Health Problems? 468

17. AIDS (acquired immune deficiency syndrome) is a fatal illness caused by human immunodeficiency virus (HIV). AIDS is contracted largely through contact with the semen or blood of someone who carries HIV.

18. When people recognize that they have a serious, chronic health problem, they may experience shock (stunned detachment), encounter (grief and despair), and retreat (withdrawal from the problem) before they finally make the needed adjustment. An alternative model describes cognitive adaptations to chronic illness as the needs to find meaning, to gain control, and to restore self-esteem. Factors influencing these reactions include characteristics of the individual (including experiences and background), of the illness, and of the environment. In addition, how well people cope depends on their cognitive appraisal of the illness, their decision to adapt, and their development of coping skills.

19. Three adaptive ways in which to respond to challenging situations are to change the individual (and her or his lifestyle), to change the environment (making it adapt to the individual's different needs and abilities), or to select a different environment.

PATHWAYS TO KNOWLEDGE

Choose the best answer to complete each sentence.

1. *Health psychology* is the study of
   (a) the mental processes of health professionals.
   (b) mental illness.
   (c) the reciprocal interaction between psychological processes and physiological health.
   (d) mental wellness.

2. *Stress* is
   (a) a reaction to environmental events and stimuli that cause a person to feel challenged in some way.
   (b) a source of physical pain.
   (c) known to be a leading cause of cancer.
   (d) made worse by having too many friends.

3. After the initial *alarm phase* of stress, if the perceived stressor continues to confront the individual, the body shifts down to a *resistance phase* and finally to a(n)
   (a) *breakdown phase.*
   (b) *exhaustion phase.*
   (c) *overworked phase.*
   (d) *physical wipe-out phase.*

4. Persons who show a Type-A pattern of behavior rate high on the following characteristics:
   (a) competitiveness, sense of urgency, and particularly, anger and hostility.
   (b) bossiness, greed, and particularly, anger and hostility.
   (c) competitiveness, sense of urgency, and particularly, bossiness.
   (d) competitiveness, greed, and particularly, anger and hostility.

5. *Psychogenic pain*
   (a) appears not to have a physical cause.
   (b) is known not to have a physical cause.
   (c) is caused by damage to bodily tissue.
   (d) is caused by a known organic pathology.

6. Several personality traits have been associated with pain,
   (a) and it is generally easy to determine the direction of causality for these associations.
   (b) most of which have to do with hypochondria and malingering.
   (c) and these traits are generally recognized as being the result of living with pain.
   (d) but it has proven difficult to determine the direction of causality for these associations.

7. Existing methods for controlling pain
   (a) are almost always fully effective for all persons.
   (b) include pharmacological control (via drugs), surgical control, biofeedback, aversion therapy, relaxation techniques, guided imagery, hypnosis, and acupuncture.
   (c) vitually never work for persons who have chronic pain.
   (d) include pharmacological control (via drugs), surgical control, biofeedback, relaxation techniques, distraction, guided imagery, and acupuncture.

8. AIDS is contracted largely
   (a) through sexual relations between monogamous partners who use a condom.
   (b) through contact with the semen or blood of someone who carries HIV.
   (c) through contact with the saliva or nasal fluids of someone who has AIDS.
   (d) by touching, hugging, kissing, or shaking the hand of someone who has AIDS.

Answer each of the following questions by filling in the blank with an appropriate word or phrase.

9. We classify illnesses according to their duration:
   _____ illnesses are relatively brief;
   _____ illnesses last for a long time, often across the entire life span.

10. _____ are situations or events that cause a person to have to adapt to or cope with changes in the situation. These adaptations are _____.

11. The effect of stress on the immune system is now being explored in the cross-disciplinary field of _____.

12. In _____ _____ we analyze our stake in the outcome of handling a particular situation.

13. In _____ _____, we assess what we can do to maximize the probability that helpful outcomes will occur and to minimize the probability that harmful outcomes will occur.

14. _____-_____ coping is directed at solving a difficulty with which a person is coping.

15. _____-_____ coping is directed at handling the feelings a person experiences as a result of a problem.

16. When people recognize that they have serious, chronic health problems, they may experience _____ (stunned detachment), _____ (grief and despair),

and _____ (withdrawal from the problem) before they finally make the needed _____.

17. AIDS (acquired immune deficiency syndrome) is a fatal illness caused by _____ _____ _____ (HIV).

18. A theoretical model regarding how people cope with chronic illness describes cognitive adaptations to chronic illness in terms of the needs to find _____, to gain _____, and to restore _____.

19. How well people cope depends on their cognitive _____ of their illness, their _____ to adapt, and their development of _____ _____.

20. Three adaptive ways in which to respond to challenging situations are to modify the individual, to modify the environment, or to choose a different _____.

Answers

1. c, 2. a, 3. b, 4. a, 5. a, 6. d, 7. d, 8. b, 9. Acute, chronic, 10. Stressors, stress responses, 11. psychoneuroimmunology, 12. primary appraisal, 13. secondary appraisal, 14. Problem-focused, 15. Emotion-focused, 16. shock, encounter, retreat, adjustment, 17. human immunodeficiency virus, 18. meaning, control, self-esteem, 19. appraisal, decision, coping skills, 20. environment

PATHWAYS TO UNDERSTANDING

1. Choose the three pain-control methods you consider to be the most generally effective. Describe three situations in which pain control would be needed and in which one (or two) of the three techniques might be preferable to the other ones. Tell why the chosen method (or methods) would be best.

2. What advice would you give doctors, based on your knowledge of psychology, to help them communicate to patients that the patients have a life-threatening illness?

3. Design a program for enhancing the healthful quality of your lifestyle. Build on successive small steps, rather than to trying to make sweeping changes all at once. What are five small steps you can take this week?

Statistical Appendix

Do you ever wonder whether some groups of people are smarter or more honest than others? Or do you wonder whether students who earn better grades work more, on the average, than do students who do not earn such high grades? Or do you wonder whether, in close relationships, women feel more intimacy toward men, or men toward women? All of these questions can be addressed by using statistics.

Although statistics can help us answer questions, they cannot themselves provide definitive answers. The interpretation of statistics and not the statistics themselves determine how questions are answered. Statistics provide people with tools—with information to explore issues, to answer questions, to solve problems, and to make decisions. Statistics do not actually explore, answer questions, solve problems, or make decisions. People do.

Statistics are useful in psychology, and they can be useful to you in your life. To introduce you to statistics, I would like for you to consider this example. Suppose you are interested in aspects of love, and how they relate to satisfaction in close relationships. In particular, you decide to explore the three aspects of love in the triangular theory of love (Sternberg, 1986b, 1988a): intimacy (feelings of warmth, closeness, communication, and support), passion (feelings of intense longing and desire), and commitment (desire to remain in the relationship) (see Chapter 10). You might be interested in the relation of these aspects to each other; or of each of the aspects to overall satisfaction in a close relationship; or of the relative levels of each of these aspects of love people experience in different close relationships, for example, with lovers, friends, or parents. Statistics can help you explore these interests.

In order to use statistics to evaluate these aspects of love, you first need a scale to measure them. The *Triangular Love Scale*, a version of which is shown in Table A-1, is such a scale (Sternberg, 1988). If you wish, take it yourself to compare your data with those from a sample of 84 adults whose summary data will be presented later.

Note that this version of the scale has a total of 36 items: 12 items measure intimacy, 12 measure passion, and 12 measure commitment. Each item consists of a statement rated on a 1 to 9 scale, where 1 means that the statement does not characterize the person at all, 5 means that it is moderately characteristic of the person, and 9 means that it is extremely characteristic. Intermediate points represent intermediate levels of feelings. The final score on each of the three subscales is the average of the numbers assigned to each of the statements in that subscale (i.e., the sum of the numbers divided by 12, the number of items).

DESCRIPTIVE STATISTICS

Descriptive statistics are numbers that summarize quantitative information. They reduce a larger mass of information down to a smaller and more useful base of information.

descriptive statistics numbers that summarize quantitative information, reducing a larger mass of information to a smaller, more useful base of information

TABLE A-1

Triangular Love Scale

The blanks represent a person with whom you are in a close relationship. Rate on a 1-to-9 scale the extent to which each statement characterizes your feelings, where 1 = "not at all"; 5 = "moderately"; and 9 = "extremely." Use intermediate points on the scale to indicate intermediate levels of feelings.

Intimacy
1. I have a warm and comfortable relationship with ___ .
2. I experience intimate communication with ___ .
3. I strongly desire to promote the well-being of ___ .
4. I have a relationship of mutual understanding with ___ .
5. I receive considerable emotional support from ___ .
6. I am able to count on ___ in times of need.
7. ___ is able to count on me in times of need.
8. I value ___ greatly in my life.
9. I am willing to share myself and my possessions with ___ .
10. I experience great happiness with ___ .
11. I feel emotionally close to ___ .
12. I give considerable emotional support to ___ .

Passion
1. I cannot imagine another person making me as happy as ___ does.
2. There is nothing more important to me than my relationship with ___ .
3. My relationship with ___ is very romantic.
4. I cannot imagine life without ___ .
5. I adore ___ .
6. I find myself thinking about ___ frequently during the day.
7. Just seeing ___ is exciting for me.
8. I find ___ very attractive physically.
9. I idealize ___ .
10. There is something almost "magical" about my relationship with ___ .
11. My relationship with ___ is very "alive."
12. I especially like giving presents to ___ .

Commitment
1. I will always feel a strong responsibility for ___ .
2. I expect my love for ___ to last for the rest of my life.
3. I cannot imagine ending my relationship with ___ .
4. I view my relationship with ___ as permanent.
5. I would stay with ___ through the most difficult times.
6. I view my commitment to ___ as a matter of principle.
7. I am certain of my love for ___ .
8. I have decided that I love ___ .
9. I am committed to maintaining my relationship with ___ .
10. I view my relationship with ___ as, in part, a thought-out decision.
11. I could not let anything get in the way of my commitment to ___ .
12. I have confidence in the stability of my relationship with ___ .

Scores are obtained by adding scale values for each item in each subscale, and then dividing by 12 (the number of items per subscale), yielding a score for each subscale of between 1 and 9.

Measures of Central Tendency

In studying love, you might be interested in typical levels of intimacy, passion, and commitment for different relationships—say, for a lover and a sibling. There are three ways in which you might find the typical value, or **central tendency,** of a set of data.

central tendency the typical value

The **mean** is the arithmetical average of a series of numbers. To compute the mean, you add up all of the values, and divide by the number of values you added.

Another measure of central tendency is the **median,** which is the middle of a set of values. With an odd number of values, the median is the number right in the middle. For example, if you have seven values ranked from lowest to highest, the median will be the fourth (middle) value. With an even number of values, there is no one middle value. For example, if you have eight values ranked from lowest to highest, the median will be the number halfway between (the average of) the fourth and fifth values—again, the middle.

A third measure of central tendency is the **mode,** or most frequent value. Obviously, the mode is useful only when there are at least some repeated values.

Consider, for example, scores of eight people on the intimacy subscale, rounded to the nearest whole number and ranked from lowest to highest: 3, 4, 4, 4, 5, 5, 6, 7. In this set of numbers, the mean is 4.75, or $(3 + 4 + 4 + 4 + 5 + 5 + 6 + 7) / 8$; the median is 4.5, or the average of the fourth and fifth values (4 and 5); and the mode is 4, the value that occurs most frequently.

Because the mean fully takes into account the information in each data point, it is generally the preferred measure of central tendency. However, the mean is also sensitive to extremes. If just a few numbers in a set are extreme, the mean will be greatly affected by them. For example, if five people took the passion subscale to indicate their feelings toward their pet gerbils, and their scores were 1, 1, 1, 1, and 8, the mean of 3 would reflect a number that is higher than the rating given by four of the five people surveyed.

The median is less sensitive to extremes. In the distribution of passion scores for pet gerbils, the median is 1, better reflecting the distribution than does the mean. However, the median does not take into account all of the information given. For example, the median would have been the same if the fifth score were 2 rather than 8.

The advantage of the mode is that it provides a quick index of central tendency. It is rough, though. Sometimes no number in a set appears more than once, and hence there is no mode. Other times, several numbers appear more than once, so that the distribution is **multimodal** (having more than one mode). The mode takes into account the least amount of information in the set. For these reasons, the mode is the least used of the three measures of central tendency.

Sometimes, it is useful to show obtained values by a **frequency distribution,** which shows numerically the number or proportion of cases at each score level (or interval). In the two cases mentioned in connection with the *Triangular Love Scale,* the frequency distributions would be as follows:

Intimacy Subscale		Passion Subscale	
Value	*Frequency*	*Value*	*Frequency*
3	1	1	4
4	3	8	1
5	2		
6	1		
7	1		

mean the arithmetical average of a series of numbers

median the middle of a set of values

mode the most frequent value of a set of values

multimodal having more than one mode

frequency distribution the number or proportion of cases at each score level or interval

Frequency distributions can also be represented graphically in various ways. People use graphs to help readers visualize the relations among numbers and to help the readers clarify just what these relations are, as shown in the various line and bar graphs in this textbook.

Measures of Variability

You now know three ways to see the central tendency of a distribution of numbers. Another question you might have concerns the spread of the distribution. How much do scores vary? There are different ways in which you might assess spread, or variability.

A first measure of variability is the **range,** which is the difference between the lowest and the highest values in a distribution. For example, the range of intimacy scores represented earlier is 4 (i.e., 7−3). However, the range is a rough measure. For example, consider two distributions of intimacy scores: 3, 4, 5, 6, 7, and 3, 3, 3, 3, 7. Although the range is the same, the variability of scores seems different. Other measures take more information into account.

A second measure of variability is the **standard deviation,** which is, roughly speaking, a measure of the average variation of values around the mean. The advantage of the standard deviation over the range is that the standard deviation takes into account the full information in the distribution of scores. Researchers care about the standard deviation because it indicates how much scores clump together, on the one hand, or are more widely spread, on the other.

To compute the standard deviation, you must

1. compute the difference between each value and the mean;
2. square the difference between each value and the mean (to get rid of negative signs);
3. sum the squared differences;
4. take the average of the sum of squared differences; and
5. take the square root of this average, in order to bring the final value back to the original scale.

Take the two distributions above to see whether their standard deviations are indeed different. The mean of 3, 4, 5, 6, 7 is 5, so the squared differences of each value from the mean are 4, 1, 0, 1, and 4. The sum of the squared differences is 10, and the average is 2. The square root of 2 is about 1.41, which is the standard deviation. In contrast, the mean of 3, 3, 3, 3, 7 is 3.80. So the squared differences of each value from the mean are .64, .64, .64, .64, and 10.24. The sum of the squared differences is 12.80, and the average, 2.56. The square root of 2.56 is 1.60. Thus, the second distribution has a higher standard deviation, 1.60, than the first distribution, for which the standard deviation is 1.41.

What does a standard deviation tell us? As a measure of variability, it tells us how much scores depart from the mean. At the extreme, if all values were equal to the mean, the standard deviation would be 0. At the opposite extreme, the maximum value of the standard deviation is the value of the range (for numerical values that are very spread apart).

For typical (but not all) distributions of values, about 68% of the values fall between the mean and plus or minus one standard deviation from that mean; about 95% of the values fall between the mean and plus or minus two standard deviations from that mean. Well over 99% of the values fall between the mean and plus or minus three standard deviations. For example, the mean of the scale for intelligence quotients (IQs) is 100, and the standard deviation is typically 15 (see Chapter 11). Thus, roughly two thirds of IQs fall between 85 and 115 (plus or minus one standard deviation from the mean), and about nineteen out of twenty IQs fall between 70 and 130 (plus or minus two standard deviations from the mean).

Now that you have read about measures of central tendency and variability, you can appreciate the use of two of these measures—the mean and standard deviation—for the *Triangular Love Scale.* Table A-2 shows means and standard deviations of intimacy, passion, and commitment scores for various relationships computed from a sample of 84 adults. If you took the scale yourself, you can compare your own scores to those of our normative sample.

range the difference between the lowest and highest values in a distribution

standard deviation a measure related to the average variation of values around the mean

TABLE A-2

Basic Statistics for the *Triangular Love Scale*

	Intimacy		Passion		Commitment	
	Mean	*SD*	*Mean*	*SD*	*Mean*	*SD*
Mother	6.49	1.74	4.98	1.90	6.83	1.57
Father	5.17	2.10	3.99	1.84	5.82	2.22
Sibling	5.92	1.67	4.51	1.71	6.60	1.67
Lover	7.55	1.49	6.91	1.65	7.06	1.49
Friend	6.78	1.67	4.90	1.71	6.06	1.63

Note: "Friend" refers to best friend of the same sex. "SD" refers to standard deviation. Statistics are based on a sample of 84 adults from southern Connecticut.

The Normal Distribution

In the above discussion of the percentages of values between the mean and various numbers of standard deviations from the mean, we have been making an assumption without making that assumption explicit. The assumption is that the distribution of values is a **normal distribution,** that is, a particular distribution in which the preponderance of values is near the center of the distribution, with values falling off rather rapidly as they depart from the center. The shape of the normal distribution is shown in Figure A-1. Notice that the distribution of scores is symmetrical, and that indeed, the large majority of scores fall close to the center of the distribution.

Nature seems to favor normal distributions, because the distributions of an amazing variety of attributes prove to be roughly normal. For example, heights are roughly distributed around the average, as are intelligence quotients. In a completely normal distribution, the mean, the median, and the mode are all exactly equal.

Types of Scores

Tests and other measures can be scored in different kinds of ways. What are the main kinds of scores that are used in psychological testing and in research, in general?

A standard score is a score that can be used for any distribution at all in order to equate the scores for that distribution to scores for other distributions. *Standard scores*, also called *z-scores*, are arbitrarily defined to have a mean of 0 and a standard deviation of 1. If the distribution of scores is normal, therefore, roughly 68% of the scores will be between -1 and 1, and roughly 95% of scores will be between -2 and 2.

Why bother to have standard scores? The advantage of standard scores is that they render comparable scores that are initially on different scales. For example, suppose two professors who teach the same course to two comparable classes of students differ in the difficulty of the tests they give. Professor A tends to give relatively difficult tests, and the mean score on his tests is 65%. Professor B, on the other hand, tends to give relatively less difficult tests, and the mean score on his tests is 80%. Yet, the difference in these two means reflects not a difference in achievement, but a difference in the difficulty of the tests the professors give. If we convert scores separately in each class to standard scores, the mean and standard deviation will be the same in the two classes (that is, a mean of 0 and a standard deviation of 1), so that it will be possible to compare achievement in the two classes in a way that corrects for the differential difficulty of the professors' tests.

Standard scores can also be applied to the distributions of love-scale scores described earlier. People who feel more intimacy, passion, or commitment toward a

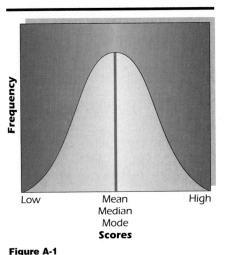

Figure A-1
Normal Distribution
As this figure shows, in a normal distribution, the mean, median, and mode are the same.

normal distribution a particular distribution in which the preponderance of values is near the center of distribution, with values falling off rather rapidly as they depart from the center

partner will have a higher standard score relative to the mean, and people who feel less intimacy, passion, or commitment will have a lower standard score.

The computation of standard scores is simple. In this computation, you start with a **raw score,** which is simply the score on a given test in whatever units the test is originally scored. The steps for converting a raw score to a standard score are these:

1. Subtract the mean raw score from the raw score of interest;
2. Divide the difference by the standard deviation of the distribution of raw scores.

You can now see why standard scores always have a mean of 0 and a standard deviation of 1. Suppose that a given raw score equals the mean. If the raw score equals the mean, when you subtract the mean from that score, you will have the number minus itself, yielding a difference in the numerator (see Step 1 above) of 0. As you know, 0 divided by anything equals 0. Suppose now that you have a score one standard deviation above the mean. When you subtract the mean from that score, the difference will be the value of the standard deviation. When you divide this value (the standard deviation) by the standard deviation (in Step 2 above), you will get a value of 1, because as you know, any value divided by itself equals 1.

Thus, if we take our distribution of intimacy scores of 3, 4, 5, 6, 7, with a mean of 5 and a standard deviation of 1.41, the standard score for a raw score of 6 will be $(6 - 5) / 1.41$, or .71. The standard score for a raw score of 5, which is the mean, will be $(5 - 5) / 1.41$, or 0. The standard score for a raw score of 4 will be $(4 - 5) / 1.41$, or $-.71$.

Many kinds of scores are variants of standard scores. For example, an IQ of 115, which is one standard deviation above the mean, corresponds to a z-score (standard score) of 1. An IQ of 85 corresponds to a z-score of -1, and so on. The *Scholastic Assessment Test* (SAT) has a mean of 500 and a standard deviation of 100. Therefore, a score of 600 represents a score of one standard deviation above the mean (i.e., a z-score of 1), whereas a score of 400 represents a score of one standard deviation below the mean (i.e., a z-score of -1).

Another convenient kind of score is called the **percentile.** This score refers to the percentage of other individuals in a given distribution whose scores fall below a given individual's score. Thus, on a test, if your score is higher than that of half (50%) of the students who have taken the test (and lower than that of the other half), your percentile will be 50. If your score is higher than everyone else's (and lower than no one else's), your percentile will be 100. In the distribution 3, 4, 5, 6, 7, the score corresponding to the 50th percentile is 5 (the median), because it is higher than half the other scores and lower than half the other scores. The 100th percentile is 7, because it is higher than all the other scores, and lower than none of them.

Correlation and Regression

So now you know something about central tendency and variability, as well as about the kinds of scores that can contribute to central tendency and variability. You may also be interested in a different question: How are scores on one kind of measure related to scores on another kind of measure? For example, how do people's scores on the intimacy subscale relate to their scores on the passion subscale, or to their scores on the commitment subscale? The question here would be whether people who feel more intimacy toward someone also tend to feel more passion or commitment toward that person.

The statistical measure called the **correlation coefficient** addresses the question of the degree of relation between two arrays of values. Basically, correlation expresses the degree of relation between two variables. A correlation of 0 indicates no relation at all between two variables; a correlation of 1 indicates a perfect (positive) relation between the two variables; a correlation of -1 indicates a perfect in-

raw score   the score on a given test in whatever units the test is originally scored

percentile   the percentage of other individuals in a given distribution whose scores fall below a given individual's scores

correlation coefficient   a statistical measure that addresses the question of the degree of relation between two arrays of values

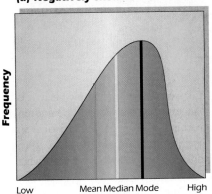

(a) Negatively skewed distribution

Frequency

Low   Mean Median Mode   High
Scores

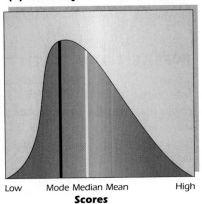

(b) Positively skewed distribution

Low   Mode Median Mean   High
Scores

Figure A-2
Skewed Distribution
In a skewed distribution, the mean, median, and mode differ. When it is negatively skewed (a), the values of the median and mode are greater than the value of the mean. When a distribution is positively skewed (b), the value of the mean is greater than the other values.

verse relation between the two variables. Figure A-2 shows distributions with correlations of 0, 1, and −1.

Well, what are the correlations among the various subscales of the *Triangular Love Scale?* For love of a lover, the correlations are very high: .88 between intimacy and passion, .84 between intimacy and commitment, and .85 between passion and commitment. These data suggest that if you feel high (or low) levels of one of these aspects of love toward a lover, you are likely also to feel high (or low) levels of the other two of the aspects toward your lover. However, the correlations vary somewhat with the relationship. For example, the comparable correlations for a sibling are .79, .77, and .76. Incidentally, in close relationships with a lover, the correlations between satisfaction and each of the subscales are .86 for intimacy, .77 for passion, and .75 for commitment.

So now you know that there is a strong relation between intimacy, passion, and commitment in feelings toward a lover, as well as between each of these aspects of love and satisfaction in the relationship with the lover. Can you infer anything about the causal relations from these correlations? For example might you be able to conclude that intimacy leads to commitment? Unfortunately, you cannot infer anything for sure. Consider three alternative interpretations of the correlation between intimacy and commitment.

One possibility is that intimacy produces commitment. This interpretation makes sense. As you develop more trust, communication, and support in a relationship, you are likely to feel more committed to that relationship. However, there is a second possibility, namely, that commitment leads to intimacy. This interpretation also makes sense. You may feel that until you really commit yourself to a relationship, you do not want to trust your partner with the more intimate secrets of your life, or to communicate some of your deepest feelings about things. A third possibility exists as well, namely, that both intimacy and commitment depend on some third factor. In this view, neither causes the other, but rather, both are dependent on some third variable. For example, it may be that intimacy and commitment both depend on a shared sense of values. Without such shared values, it may be difficult to build a relationship based on either intimacy or commitment.

The point is simple: As is often said in statistics, correlation does not imply causation. You cannot infer the direction of causality without further information. Correlation indicates only that there is a relation, not how the relation came to be. You can make a guess about the direction of causal relationship, but to be certain, you would need additional data.

In the example of the correlation between intimacy and commitment, you have a problem in addition to direction of causality. How much of a correlation do you need in order to characterize a relationship between two variables as statistically meaningful? In other words, at what level is a correlation strong enough to take it as indicating a true relationship between two variables, rather than a relationship that might have occurred by chance—by a fluke? Fortunately, there are statistics that can tell us when correlations, and other indices, are statistically meaningful. These statistics are called inferential statistics.

INFERENTIAL STATISTICS

Inferential statistics are statistics that are used to determine how likely it is that results that are obtained are *not* due to chance. When we speak of the meaningfulness of statistical results, we often use something called a **test of statistical significance.** Such a test tells us the probability that a given result is *not* due to chance fluctuations in the data. A result, therefore, is **statistically significant** when the result is ascribed to systematic rather than to chance factors. It is important for you to realize that a statistical test can only show the probability that one group differs from another in some respect. For example, you can compute the probability that a mean or a correlation is *different* from zero, or the probability that one mean *differs* meaningfully from another. You cannot use statistics to estimate the probability that two samples are the *same* in any respect.

The distinction is an important one. Suppose you have two hypothetical individuals who are identical twins and who have always scored exactly the same on every test they have ever been given. There is no statistical way of estimating the probability that they truly are the same on every test. There might always be some future test that would distinguish them.

Your chances of finding a statistically significant result generally increase as you test more subjects, because with greater numbers of subjects, random errors tend to average out. Thus, if you tested only one male subject and one female subject for their feelings of intimacy toward their partners, you would probably hesitate to draw any conclusions from this sample about whether there is difference between men and women in general in their experiencing of intimacy toward their partners. However, if you tested 10,000 men and 10,000 women, you would probably have considerable confidence in your results, so long as your sample was representative of the population of interest.

It is important to distinguish between statistical significance and **practical significance,** which refers to whether a result is of any practical, or everyday import. Suppose, for example, that I find that the difference between the men and the women in intimacy feelings is .07 on a 1 to 9 scale. With a large enough sample, the result may reach statistical significance. Is this result of practical significance? Perhaps not. Remember, an inferential statistical test can only tell you the probability that any difference at all exists. It does not tell you how large the difference is, nor whether the difference is great enough really to matter for whatever practical purposes you might wish to use the information. In research, investigators often pay primary attention to statistical significance. However, as a consumer of research, you need to pay attention to practical significance as well, whether the researchers do or not. Ultimately, in psychology, we need to concentrate on results that make a difference to us as we go about living our lives.

inferential statistics statistics that are used to determine how likely it is that results that are obtained are not due to chance

test of statistical significance a test that tells us the probability that a given result is not due to chance fluctuations in the data

statistically significant characterization of a result as most likely due to systematic rather than chance factors

practical significance characterization of a result as having practical or everyday import

Abnormal behavior ways of thinking or acting that are unusual, that impair the ability to function effectively, that are identified as odd within the surrounding social context, or that involve some degree of distortion in thinking, feeling, or perceiving

Absolute threshold a hypothetical minimum amount of physical energy that an individual can detect for each kind of sensory stimulation; operationally defined as the level at which a stimulus is first detected 50% of the time during many attempts to detect the stimulus

Accommodation (as an aspect of vision) the process by which the lens of the eye changes its curvature to focus on objects at different distances

Accommodation (as an aspect of cognitive development) the process of trying to restore cognitive equilibrium by modifying existing **schemas** or even creating new schemas to fit new information (see also **assimilation**)

Achievement an accomplishment; an attained level of expertise on performance of a task, or an acquired base of knowledge in a domain or a set of domains (see also **aptitude**)

Acquisition phase of **learning** during which the probability of learning increases

Action potential a change in the electrochemical balance inside and outside a neuron; occurs when electrochemical stimulation of the neuron reaches or exceeds the neuron's **threshold of excitation**

Activation–synthesis hypothesis a belief that dreams result from subjective organization and interpretation (synthesis) of neural activity (activation) that takes place during sleep

Actor–observer effect the tendency not only to attribute the actions of others to stable internal **personal dispositions,** but also to attribute our own actions to external situational variables

Acute characteristic of symptoms or illness occurring only for a short time, although is probably intense

Acute toxicity the negative health consequences of a single instance of ingesting a poisonous substance, such as a single overdose of a **psychoactive drug**

Adaptation (sensory) a temporary physiological response to a sensed change in the environment, which is neither learned nor consciously controlled; the degree of adaptation depends directly on the degree of change in the stimulus, with greater changes producing greater adaptation (see also **habituation**)

Addiction a persistent, habitual, or compulsive physiological or at least psychological dependency on one or more **psychoactive drugs**

Additive mixture a combination of light waves of varying wavelengths, in which each wavelength of light adds to the other wavelengths (see also **subtractive mixture**)

Adolescence stage of psychological development between the start of puberty and the time the individual accepts the full responsibilities of being an adult in a given society

Aerobic exercise activities that are sufficiently intense and long lasting to stimulate increased heart rate and respiration (breathing)

Aggression behavior that is intended to cause harm or injury to another person

Agnosia severe problems in recognizing and interpreting information sent to the brain from one or more sense organs (*a-*, lack; *gnosis*, knowledge)

Algorithm formal path for reaching a solution, which involves one or more successive processes that usually lead to an accurate answer to a question

Altruism generous willingness to help another person or persons, even when there is no reward or other observable benefit to the helper; often involves some sacrifice on the part of the helper

Amnesia damage to memory processes or severe loss of information from memory

Analgesics pain-relieving drugs (e.g., acetaminophen, ibuprofen, and salicylic acid [aspirin])

Analysis the process of breaking down a complex whole into smaller elements (see also **synthesis**)

Anorexia nervosa an eating disorder in which a person undereats to the point of starvation, based on the extremely distorted belief that she (usually) or he is overweight

Anterograde amnesia difficulty in purposefully forming new memories after an injury to memory function, without any effect on the ability to retrieve old memories from before the injury; one meaning of *antero-* is "before"; people with anterograde amnesia forget *new* information about facts and events *before* they have a chance to store it in memory

Antidepressant drug a drug used for treating depression

Antipsychotic drug a drug used for treating psychosis (e.g., schizophrenia)

Antisocial behavior actions that are harmful to a given society or to its members and that are condemned by the society as a whole (see also **prosocial behavior**)

Anxiety a generalized feeling of dread or apprehension that is not focused on or directed toward any particular object or event

Anxiety disorder a psychological disorder involving the presence of **anxiety** that is so intense or so frequently present that it causes difficulty or distress for the individual

Applied research investigations that are intended to lead to clear, immediate, obvious, and practical uses, which may not lead to fundamental understandings of the human mind and behavior

Approach–avoidance conflict the simultaneous presence of two conflicting tendencies: to go toward a stimulus (approach it) and to go away from it (avoid it), based on feeling both positive and negative emotions about the stimulus

Aptitude a capability for accomplishing something, for attaining a level of expertise on performance of a task or a set of tasks, or for acquiring knowledge in a given domain or set of domains (see also **achievement**)

Archetype inherited tendency to perceive and act in certain ways, common to all

Arousal state of alertness, wakefulness, and activation, caused by nervous-system activity

Assimilation the process of trying to restore cognitive equilibrium by incorporating new information into existing **schemas** (see also **accommodation**)

Association areas regions of the cerebral lobes that are not part of the sensory or motor cortices but that are believed to connect (associate) the activity of the sensory and motor cortices

Associationism a school of psychology that examines how events or ideas can become associated with one another in the mind

Asylum hospital or other institution for housing and possibly treating mentally ill patients

Atheoretical having no particular theoretical orientation

Attachment a strong and relatively long-lasting emotional tie between people

Attachment theory of love view that how we relate to loved ones as adults stems from the way in which we attached to our parents, and particularly our mothers, as infants

Attention the process by which we focus our awareness on some of the information available in **consciousness** and screen out other information

Attitude a learned, stable, and relatively enduring evaluation (e.g., of a person or an idea), which can affect an individual's thoughts, feelings, and behavior

Attribution a mental explanation pointing to the cause(s) of a person's behavior, including the behavior of the person making the attribution (see also **personal attribution, situational attribution**)

Automatic behavior conduct that requires no conscious decisions regarding which muscles to move or which actions to take

Autoshaping a system of reinforcements that individuals design for themselves, to lead to gradual behavioral change

Availability heuristic a cognitive shortcut in which an individual makes judgments on the basis of how easily he or she can call to mind what are perceived as relevant instances of a given phenomenon

Aversive conditioning use of punishment as a means of encouraging an individual to try to escape from or to avoid a situation

Avoidance learning the goal of aversive conditioning: an individual learns to stay away from something

Axon the long, thin, tubular part of the **neuron,** which responds to information received by the **dendrites** and **soma** of the neuron by either ignoring or transmitting the information through the neuron to the axon's terminal buttons

Babbling a prelinguistic preferential production of only those distinct phonemes characteristic of the language being acquired

Balance theory a **cognitive-consistency** theory of attraction, suggesting that persons who like each other try to maintain a balance regarding the mutual give and take in the relationship and that they try to maintain similar likes and dislikes

Barbiturates the most widely used type of **sedative–hypnotic drug;** prescribed to reduce **anxiety** but may lead to grogginess that can impair functioning in situations requiring alertness; a highly addictive and potentially dangerous type of antianxiety drug, used for inducing sleep or a state of calmness

Basic research investigations devoted to the study of fundamental underlying relationships and principles, which may not offer any immediate, obvious, or practical value

Basilar membrane one of the membranes separating two of the fluid-filled canals of the inner ear; on this membrane are the hair cells that transduce sound waves

Behavior therapy various psychotherapeutic techniques based mostly on principles of classical and operant conditioning, as well as some techniques based on observational learning

Behaviorism a school of psychology that focuses entirely on the association between the environment and emitted behavior

Big Five theory of personality a trait theory suggesting that the five key personality traits are neuroticism, extroversion, openness, agreeableness, and conscientiousness

Bilingual person who can speak two languages

Binocular depth cue perceived information about depth, which can be gained only by using two eyes (*bin-,* both; two) (see also **monocular depth cue**)

Bipolar disorder **mood disorder** in which the individual alternates between periods of depression and of mania

Bisexual a person who directs sexual desire toward members of both sexes

Bounded rationality the recognition that although humans are rational, there are limits to the degree to which they demonstrate rational cognitive processes across situations

Brain the organ of the body that most directly controls thoughts, emotions, motivations, and actions, and that responds to information received from elsewhere in the body, such as through sensory receptors

Bulimia a disorder characterized by eating binges followed by episodes of getting rid of the food (e.g., by vomiting or taking laxatives)

Bystander effect the phenomenon in which the presence of increasing numbers of people available to help leads to a decreasing likelihood that any given observer will offer help

Cardinal trait a characteristic that totally dominates the personality and behavior of an individual; many persons do not have a cardinal trait (see also **central trait, secondary trait**)

Case study intensive investigation of a single individual or set of individuals

Central nervous system the part of the nervous system comprising the **brain** and the **spinal cord** (see also **peripheral nervous system, endocrine system**)

Central nervous system (CNS) depressant drug that slows the operation of the CNS and is often prescribed in low doses to reduce **anxiety** and in relatively higher doses to combat **insomnia**

Central nervous system (CNS) stimulant drug that arouses and excites the CNS, either by stimulating the heart or by inhibiting the actions of natural compounds that depress brain activity (thereby acting as a "double negative" on brain stimulation)

Central tendency the typical value

Central trait a characteristic that stands out in its importance for the personality and behavior of an individual (see also **cardinal trait, secondary trait**)

Cerebellum a brain structure that controls bodily coordination, balance, and muscle tone

Cerebral cortex a thin layer of tissue on the surface of the brain; it is responsible for most high-level cognitive processes

Chromosomes rod-shaped bodies that occur in pairs and contain countless **genes**

Chronic always present or repeatedly occurring again and again

Chronic toxicity the negative health consequences of repeated ingestion of one or more poisonous substances, such as **narcotics**

Chunk grouping by which a collection of items is organized into a coherent whole

Circadian rhythm the usual sleeping–waking pattern of physiological changes corresponding roughly to the cycle of darkness and light associated with a single day (*circa,* around [Latin]; *dies,* day [Latin])

Classical conditioning the learning process whereby an originally neutral stimulus becomes associated with a particular physiological or emotional response that the stimulus did not originally produce

Client-centered therapy a form of humanistic **psychotherapy** in which the therapeutic interactions center on the client's view of reality

Cognitive consistency the reassuring presence of a match between an individual's thoughts (cognition) and that person's behavior

Cognitive development the process by which people's thinking changes across the life span

Cognitive dissonance the discomforting conflict between an individual's thoughts (cognition) and that person's behavior; often a result of the person's having acted in a way that does not agree with her or his existing beliefs

Cognitive-impairment disorder a psychological disorder in which normal thought processes become impaired or distorted

Cognitivism a school of psychology that underscores the importance of perception, learning, and thought as bases for understanding much of human behavior

Collective unconscious according to Jungian theory, the part of the unconscious mind that contains memories and behavioral predispositions that all humans share because of our common ancestry (see also **personal unconscious**)

Collectivism the tendency to emphasize the interests and well-being of the group over those of each individual (see also **individualism**)

Common and uncommon effects the tendency to infer attributions based on whether the effects of a behavior are ordinary or are unusual

Compliance the process in which an individual goes along with a request made by one or more other persons

Concept idea to which a person may attach various characteristics and with which the person may connect various other ideas

Concrete-operational stage Piaget's third stage of development (about the period of elementary school), during which the child can mentally manipulate images of concrete objects (see also **formal-operational stage, preoperational stage, sensorimotor stage**)

Conditioned response (CR) response that is like the **UCR**, but that is elicited from the **CS** rather than from the **UCS**

Conditioned stimulus (CS) originally neutral stimulus that will only elicit a physiological or emotional response after **classical conditioning** takes place

Cone relatively short and thick type of **photoreceptor**, responsible mostly for very clear color vision in bright lighting; less numerous than **rods**

Confidentiality an ethical practice in which researchers ensure the privacy of personal information regarding individual research participants

Conformity the process in which an individual shapes her or his behavior to make it consistent with the norms of a group

Connotation an emotional overtone, presupposition, or other nonexplicit meaning of a word (see also **denotation**)

Consciousness the complex phenomenon of actively processing perceptions, thoughts, feelings, wishes, and memories, to create a mental reality for adapting to the world

Conservation of quantity the principle that the quantity of something remains the same as long as nothing is removed or added, even if the appearance of the substance changes in form

Consolidation process by which people integrate new information into their existing information stored in long-term memory

Constructive memory phenomenon by which people build stored memories, based on existing schemas, expectations, and additional stored information, as well as on previous sensations and events; some distortions in encoding, storage, and retrieval may occur as a result

Context effects influences on perception that come from information in the surrounding environment

Contextualist psychologist who theorizes about a psychological phenomenon (e.g., intelligence) strictly in terms of the context in which an individual is observed, and who suggests that the phenomenon cannot be understood—let alone measured—outside the real-world context of the individual

Contingency phenomenon in which one or more stimuli depend on the presence of another stimulus

Continuous reinforcement a learning program in which reinforcement always follows a particular operant behavior

Control condition a situation in which some experimental participants are subjected to a carefully prescribed set of circumstances, which are like those of the **experimental condition** but do not involve the introduction of the **independent variable**

Controlled experimental design a plan for conducting research in which the experimenter carefully manipulates or controls **independent variables** in order to see their effects on **dependent variables**

Cooing oral expression that explores the production of all the phones (cf. phonemes) that humans can possibly produce (see also **babbling**)

Coping the process of managing the internal and external changes presented by a challenging situation (see also **emotion-focused coping, problem-focused coping**)

Cornea the clear dome-shaped window through which light passes and which serves primarily as curved exterior surface of the eye that gathers and focuses the entering light

Corpus callosum a dense body of nerve fibers that connect the two cerebral hemispheres

Correlation the statistical relationship between two attributes, expressed as a number ranging from −1 (a negative correlation) to 0 (no correlation) to +1 (a positive correlation)

Correlation coefficient a statistical measure that addresses the question of the degree of relation between two arrays of values

Correlational design a plan for conducting research by assessing the degree of association between two (or more) attributes (characteristics of research participants or of a setting or situation)

Counterconditioning behavioral techniques based on classical conditioning, emphasizing the substitution of an adaptive response (e.g., relaxation) in place of a maladaptive one (e.g., anxiety) to a particular stimulus

Countertransference a term used in psychodynamic therapy, describing a situation in which the therapist becomes emotionally involved with the patient, projecting the therapist's own feelings onto the patient

Creativity the process of producing something that is both original and valuable

Critical period a time of rapid growth and development, during which particular changes typically occur if they are ever to occur; that is, such changes typically do not occur after the critical period

Critical thinking the conscious direction of mental processes toward representing and processing information, usually in order to find thoughtful solutions to problems

Cultural psychology a school of psychology that emphasizes the importance of cultural context in the study of the human mind and behavior

Culture-fair describes assessment that is equally appropriate for members of all cultures and that comprises items that are equally fair to members of all cultures; probably impossible to attain (see also **culture-relevant**)

Culture-relevant describes assessment of skills and knowledge that relate to the cultural experiences of the test-takers, by using content and procedures that are appropriate to the cultural context of the test-takers (see also **culture-fair**)

Dark adaptation the physiological adjustment to decreases in light intensity, during which the rods become more active

Data facts, numbers, and other information

Decay forgetting of stored information due to the passage of time (see also **interference**)

Declarative knowledge "knowing that"—factual information that a person can state in words

Deductive reasoning a set of processes by which an individual tries to draw a logically certain and specific conclusion from a set of propositions (see also **inductive reasoning**)

Defense mechanism the means by which the **ego** protects itself from unacceptable thoughts (from the **superego**) and impulses (from the **id**)

Deindividuation the loss of a sense of individual identity, resulting in fewer controls that prevent the individual from engaging in behavior that violates societal **norms** and even the individual's personal moral beliefs

Delusion a false belief, which contradicts known facts

Dendrites the primary parts of the **neuron** involved in receiving communications from other cells via distinctive receptors on their external membranes

Denotation the strict dictionary definition of a word (see also **connotation**)

Dependent variable an outcome characteristic that varies as a consequence of variation in one or more **independent variables**

Depressive disorders **mood disorders** in which the individual feels so sad and has so little energy that the individual cannot function effectively

Descriptive statistics numbers that summarize quantitative information, reducing a larger mass of information to a smaller, more useful base of information

Desensitization in social psychology, a gradual habituation to violent stimuli, in which we gradually become less interested in and less responsive to violent stimuli and their tragic consequences

Detect notice the presence of a sensory stimulus

Development changes that are associated with increasing physiological maturity, experience, or an interaction of physiological changes and experiences with the environment

Deviation IQs a means of determining intelligence-test scores, based on deviations from an average score, calculated such that the normative equivalent for the median score is 100; not IQs, strictly speaking, because no quotient is involved (see also **intelligence quotient, mental age, ratio IQ**)

Dichotic presentation perceptual experience in which each ear receives a different message (*dich-*, in two parts [Greek]; *-otic*, related to the ears [Greek])

Difference threshold a hypothetical minimum amount of difference that can be detected between two stimuli (see also **just noticeable difference [jnd]**)

Differentiate become more highly specialized into distinct parts or types

Diffusion of responsibility the phenomenon in which increases in the number of other persons present leads each person to feel less personal responsibility for the events taking place

Discourse the most comprehensive level of linguistic analysis, which encompasses language use at the level beyond the sentence, such as in conversation, in paragraphs, and so on

Disorders usually first diagnosed in infancy, childhood, or adolescence psychological disorders that are first identified before adulthood

Dissociative disorders psychological disorders in which an individual goes through one or more extreme changes in awareness of past and present experiences, personal history, and even personal identity

Distributed learning storage of information in memory that occurs over a long period of time, rather than all at once (see also **massed learning**)

Dominant trait the stronger expression of a genetic trait, which appears in the **phenotype** of an organism when the **genotype** comprises two dominant expressions of a trait or a dominant and a recessive expression of a trait (see also **recessive trait**)

Double-blind procedure an experimental technique whereby neither the experimenters nor the participants know which participants will have received which kind of treatment, or even any treatment at all (e.g., in a **control condition**)

Drive a hypothesized composite source of energy, which humans and other animals try to reduce

Effectors the **neurons** and **nerves** that transmit motor information from the brain through the spinal cord (voluntary movements) or directly from the spinal cord (reflexes), thus controlling bodily responses (see also **receptors, motor neuron**)

Ego a personality structure that is largely conscious and realistic in responding to the events in the world, while trying to satisfy the irrational and unconscious urgings of the **id** and the prohibitions of the **superego**

Egocentric focused on one's own views, without being able to see how others may view a situation

Electroconvulsive therapy (ECT) a form of psychophysiological treatment in which patients undergo electrical shocks, which cause convulsive seizures followed by a period of **amnesia,** and which may relieve severe symptoms of depression

Electroencephalogram (EEG) a recording (*-gram*) of the electrical activity of the living brain, as detected by various electrodes (*en-*, in; *cephalo-*, head [Greek])

Elimination by aspects a decision-making strategy in which an individual focuses on one attribute of an overabundance of options, forms a minimum criterion for that attribute, and then eliminates all options that do not meet that criterion; the process is repeated until either a single option remains or few enough remain that a more careful selection process may be used

Embryo an individual in the second of the three stages of prenatal development (from about 2 weeks after conception until about the end of the 8th week) (see also **fetus, zygote**); the individual undergoes tremendous differentiation and rapid growth and is easily influenced by the maternal environment

Emotion a psychological feeling, usually accompanied by a physiological reaction

Emotion-focused coping adapting to a challenging situation by handling one's own emotions that arise in regard to the situation (see also **problem-focused coping**)

Empiricism approach asserting that knowledge is most effectively acquired through observation

Encode transform sensory information into an understandable mental representation that can be stored in memory

Encoding specificity phenomenon in which the retrieval of information depends on the organizational representation of the information during encoding

Endocrine system a physiological communication network that operates via glands that secrete hormones directly into the bloodstream (see also **central nervous system**)

Episodic memory a person's memory for particular events that the individual has experienced, as well as any information that is tied to those experiences (see also **semantic memory**)

Equity theory a theory of attraction suggesting that people feel more strongly attracted to those with whom they have more equitable (fair) relationships of giving and taking

Experiment an investigation of cause–effect relationships done by controlling or carefully manipulating particular variables to note their effects on other variables

Experimental condition a situation in which some experimental participants are exposed to a specific set of circumstances, involving a treatment linked to an **independent variable** (see also **control condition**)

Explicit memory remembering that requires individuals to make a conscious effort at recollection of information (see also **implicit memory**)

External locus of control a personality orientation based on people's belief that the environment surrounding them is largely able to control both what they do and the probable outcomes of what they do (see also **internal locus of control**)

Extinction phase of learning when the probability of the **CR** decreases over time, eventually approaching zero

Extinction procedures behavioral treatment techniques based on **classical conditioning,** in which the goal is to weaken a maladaptive response

Extrinsic motivation a desire to act, based on reasons that come from outside the individual, such as offers of rewards or threats of punishment (see also **intrinsic motivation**)

Extroversion a personality trait characterized by sociability, liveliness, and friendliness

Feature-detector approach an approach to form perception based on observing the activity of the brain; apparently, specific neurons of the visual cortex respond to specific features detected by **photoreceptors**

Feature matching the process of comparing features of an observed pattern to pattern features stored in memory

Fetus an individual in the third of the three stages of prenatal development (from about the 9th week until birth) (see also **embryo, zygote**); a time during which the individual develops enough sophistication to be able to survive outside the mother's uterus

Figure a highlighted feature of the perceived environment

Formal-operational stage Piaget's fourth stage of development (about the time of adolescence), during which the child becomes able to manipulate abstract ideas and formal relationships (see also **concrete-operational stage, preoperational stage, sensorimotor stage**)

Free association psychodynamic technique in which patients are encouraged to say whatever comes to mind, without censoring or otherwise editing their statements

Frequency distribution the number or proportion of cases at each score level or interval

Frequency theory a theory that sensed variations in pitch arise from variations in the frequencies of the sound waves, which cause the **hair cells** to transmit neural impulses at the same rate as the frequency of the original sound wave (see also **place theory**)

Functional fixedness a **mental set** in which an individual fails to see an alternative use for something that has been known previously to have a particular use

Functionalism a school of psychology that focuses on active psychological processes, rather than on passive psychological structures or elements

Fundamental attribution error the tendency to overemphasize internal causes and personal responsibility and to deemphasize external causes and situational influences when observing the behavior of other people

Gate-control theory a possible explanation of **pain,** suggesting that the **central nervous system** acts as a physiological barrier through which pain may be allowed to pass under particular circumstances

Gender typing process of acquiring gender-related roles for a given society

Gene a basic physiological building block for the hereditary transmission of genetic traits in all life forms

General adaptation syndrome (GAS) a general pattern of physiological response to **stress,** involving three phases: alarm, resistance, and exhaustion

Genotype the genetic makeup for inherited traits, which is *not* subject to environmental influence (except in cases of genetic mutation) (see also **phenotype**)

Gestalt approach an approach to form perception, based on the notion that the whole differs from the sum of its parts (pronounced "gess-TAHLT")

Gestalt psychology a school of psychology holding that psychological phenomena are best understood when viewed as organized, structured wholes, rather than when analyzed into numerous components

Gland group of cells that secretes **hormones** (see also **endocrine system**)

Goal a future state that an individual wants to reach

Gradient of reinforcement phenomenon in which increases in the length of time between an **operant** and a **reinforcer** directly decrease the effect of the reinforcement

Grammar the study of **language** in terms of regular patterns that relate to the functions and relationships of words in a sentence—extending as broadly as the level of **discourse** and as narrowly as the pronunciation and meaning of individual words

Ground features of the perceived environment that are not highlighted, which serve as a background for highlighted features

Group a collection of individuals who interact with each other, usually either to accomplish work or to promote interpersonal relationships (or both)

Group polarization the tendency to exaggerate the initial views of group members, so that the views become more extreme

Groupthink a group process in which group members work so hard to achieve unanimous agreement that they fail realistically to consider the various alternative courses of action available to them

Habituation a phenomenon in which a person gradually becomes more familiar with a stimulus and notices it less and less; in *dishabituation,* a once familiar stimulus changes to become unfamiliar, so the person notices the stimulus once again (see also **adaptation**)

Hair cell auditory receptor that **transduces** sound waves into electrochemical energy

Hallucination perception of sensory stimulation (usually sounds, but sometimes sights, smells, or tactile sensations) in the absence of any actual corresponding sensory input from the physical world

Hallucinogenic a type of **psychoactive drug** that alters consciousness by inducing **hallucinations** and by affecting the way the drug users perceive both their inner worlds and their external environments

Hardiness a personality attribute characterized by high **internal locus of control,** strong commitment to work and other activities, and an outlook that favors challenge and opportunities for personal growth

Health psychology the study of how the mind and the physical health of the body interact

Heuristics informal, speculative, shortcut strategies for solving problems, which sometimes work and sometimes do not

Hippocampus a portion of the **limbic system;** plays an essential role in the formation of new memories (*hippocampus,* seahorse, its approximate shape [Greek])

Homeostatic regulation the tendency of the body to maintain a state of equilibrium (balance)

Homosexuality a tendency to direct sexual desire toward another person of the same (*homo-,* same) sex, which probably is based on physiology (nature) but is influenced also by the environment (nurture)

Hormone chemical substance secreted by one or more **glands;** hormones regulate many physiological processes through specific actions on cells and may affect the way a receptive cell goes about its activities

Hostile aggression behavior that is intended to cause harm, as a result of an emotional, often impulsive, outburst, caused by pain or distress; the consequences usually lead to little gain for the aggressor and may even lead to losses for the aggressor (see also **instrumental aggression**)

Humanistic psychology a school of psychology that emphasizes human potential, as guided by holistic approaches to conscious experiences, rather than by analytic approaches to unconscious experience

Hypnosis an altered state of **consciousness** that usually involves deep relaxation and extreme sensitivity to suggestion and appears to bear some resemblance to sleep

Hypothalamus a brain structure that plays a key role in regulating behavior related to species survival (fighting, feeding, fleeing, and mating)

Hypothesis tentative statement of belief regarding expected outcomes

Hypothetical construct a phenomenon that is believed to exist but that cannot be measured or perceived directly; a *hypothetical construct* (e.g., memory or intelligence) is *constructed* (built) from *hypotheses* (beliefs); although we cannot directly touch, see, hear, taste, or smell these constructs, we still believe they exist

Iconic store sensory memory for very brief storage of visual images

Id a personality structure that is the unconscious, instinctual, and irrational source of primitive impulses (see also **ego, superego**)

Ideal self all aspects of the self that a person ideally would like to perceive as characterizing the self

Idealistic principle the principle by which the compulsion to obey an internalized set of rules and prohibitions drives all of the functions of the **superego**

Ill-structured problem problem with no clear, obvious, readily available path to solution (see also **well-structured problem**)

Illusion distorted perception of physical stimuli, sometimes due to altered states of **consciousness,** to psychological disorder, or to misleading cues in the objects themselves

Imaginary audience an adolescent's unfounded belief that other persons are constantly observing, paying attention to, and judging the adolescent

Implicit memory remembering in which an individual retrieves information from prior experience to enhance performance, but without being conscious of retrieving the information (see also **explicit memory**)

Imprinting a preprogrammed response in which a newborn animal looks for a particular kind of stimulus and then carries out the response; the specific stimulus that prompts the response is learned

Incubation a period of rest, following a period of intensive effort in problem solving, during which the problem solver puts aside the problem for a while

Independent variable an attribute that is manipulated by the experimenter, while other attributes are held constant (not varied) (see also **dependent variable**)

Individualism the tendency to emphasize the personal interests and welfare of the individual over those of the group (see also **collectivism)**

Inductive reasoning a set of processes by which an individual attempts to reach a probable general conclusion, based on a set of specific facts or observations (see also **deductive reasoning**)

Inferential statistics statistics that are used to determine how likely it is that results that are obtained are not due to chance

Inferiority complex a maladaptive personality structure in which we organize our lives around feelings of inferiority, based on perceived mistakes and failings

Information processing operations by which people mentally manipulate what they learn and know about the world

Informed consent an experimental procedure in which prospective participants are fully informed regarding the general nature of the anticipated treatment procedure and any possible harmful consequences of the treatment

Insight a seemingly sudden understanding of the nature of something, often as a result of taking a novel approach to the object of the insight

Insomnia any of various disturbances of sleep, such as difficulty in falling asleep or in staying asleep

Instinct an inherited, species-specific, stereotyped, and often relatively complex pattern of behavior

Instrumental aggression behavior that happens to cause harm or injury to another person, as a by-product of trying to get something valued by the aggressor; often is planned, not impulsive (see also **hostile aggression**)

Intelligence comprises the abilities needed to engage in goal-directed adaptive behavior

Intelligence quotient broadly, a test score based on a **normative score** on an intelligence test, with a mean of 100 and a standard deviation of 15 or 16; see **ratio IQ** (see also **deviation IQs, mental age**)

Interactionist approach a view of personality that emphasizes the interaction between the person and the situation

Interference process by which competing information causes people to forget stored information (see also **decay**)

Internal locus of control a personality orientation based on people's belief that they are largely able to control both what they do and the probable outcomes of what they do (see also **external locus of control**)

Internalization the process of absorbing knowledge from a given social environmental context

Interneuron a type of nerve cell that transmits information between **sensory neurons** and **motor neurons**

Interpersonal development process by which people change across the life span in the way they relate to other people

Intoxicated characterized by grogginess, insensibility, or temporary trouble thinking clearly and making reasoned judgments due to the effects of toxins such as alcohol or **sedative–hypnotic drugs**

Intrinsic motivation a desire to act, based on reasons that come from within the individual, such as to satisfy curiosity or artistic appeal (see also **extrinsic motivation**)

Introspection self-examination of inner ideas and experiences

Iris a circular membrane that reflects light beams outward and away from the eye; surrounds the pupil, which is essentially a hole in the center of the iris

Judgment and decision making cognitive processes by which an individual may evaluate various options and select the most suitable option from among various alternatives

Just noticeable difference (jnd) a term operationally defined as the point at which an individual can detect the difference between two stimuli at least 50% of the time, over a series of attempts to detect the difference

Kinesthesis the sense through which receptors within our muscles and connective tissues inform us about the positions and movements of our skeletal muscles

Language the use of an organized means of combining words in order to communicate

Learned helplessness a learned behavior in which an individual gives up trying to escape a painful situation after repeatedly failing to escape

Learning any relatively permanent change in the behavior, thoughts, and feelings of an individual, which occurs as a result of experiences

Lens a curved interior structure of the eye, which bends light slightly to focus the light on the center of the rear surface of the eye

Levels-of-processing framework a view of memory in which memory storage varies continuously in terms of the depth at which information is encoded

Lexicon the entire set of **morphemes** in a given language or in a given person's linguistic repertoire

Life-span development the changes that occur within a person over the life span

Light adaptation the physiological adjustment to increases in light intensity, during which the **cones** become more active

Limbic system a system of brain structures involved in emotion, motivation, and learning

Linguistic relativity a proposition regarding the relationship between thought and language, which asserts that the speakers of different languages have differing cognitive systems, based on the languages they use, and that these different cognitive systems influence the ways in which people speaking the various languages think about the world

Linguistic universals characteristic patterns of language that apply across all of the languages of various cultures

Linguistics the study of language structure and change

Lobes each of the four major regions of the **cerebral cortex,** comprising the frontal lobe (motor, planning), occipital lobe (visual), parietal lobe (somatosensory), and temporal lobe (auditory)

Lock-and-key theory a theory of how we smell, based on the matching of particular odorous molecules and particular smell receptors (see also **vibration theory**)

Long-term memory storage of a practically limitless amount of information for such long periods of time that its limits are not known

Mania a mood in which the individual feels highly energetic and extremely joyful

Massed learning storage of information in memory that occurs over a very brief period of time (see also **distributed learning**)

Maturation any relatively permanent change in an individual that occurs strictly as a result of biological processes of getting older

Mean the arithmetical average of a series of numbers (see also **median, mode**)

Median the middle of a set of values (see also **mean, mode**)

Meditation a set of techniques, used for altering **consciousness,** to become more contemplative

Memory the means by which existing knowledge, based on past experience and learning, can be used in the present

Mental age a means of indicating a person's level of intelligence (generally in reference to a child), based on the individual's performance on tests of intelligence, by indicating the average chronological age of persons who typically perform at the same level of intelligence as the test-taker (see also **deviation IQs, intelligence quotient, ratio IQ**)

Mental retardation very low level of intelligence, usually reflected by both poor performance on tests of intelligence and poor *adaptive competence* (the degree to which a person functions effectively within a normal situational context)

Mental set a cognitive phenomenon in which an individual is predisposed to use an existing model for representing information, even when the existing model inadequately represents the information in a new situation

Metacognition the process of thinking about how we use strategies and skills to enhance our thought processes; thinking about how we think

Mnemonic devices methods for improving memory by translating unrelated random bits of information into meaningful verbal information or into visual images

Mnemonism the use of special techniques for improving memory skill

Mode the most frequent value of a set of values (see also **mean, median**)

Modeling a cognitive and behavioral technique in which people are encouraged to change simply by watching other people successfully cope with challenging problems that affect the observer

Monocular depth cue perceived information about depth, which can be gained by using only one eye (*mon-*, one; *ocular*, related to the eyes) (see also **binocular depth cue**)

Mood disorder a psychological disorder involving either periods of extremely sad, low-energy moods, or swings between extremely high and extremely low moods

Morpheme the smallest unit of single or combined sounds denoting meaning within a given language

Motivation an impulse, a desire, or a need that leads to an action

Motor related to moving the muscles

Motor neuron nerve cell that carries information *away from* the **spinal cord** and the brain and toward the body parts that are supposed to respond to the information in some way (see also **interneuron, sensory neuron**)

Multimodal having more than one **mode**

Myelin sheath a protective, insulating layer of myelin, which coats the axons of some **neurons**

N-REM sleep the four stages of sleep that are not characterized by rapid eye movements and that are less frequently associated with dreaming (see also **REM sleep**)

Narcolepsy a disturbance of the pattern of wakefulness and sleep, in which the narcoleptic periodically experiences an uncontrollable urge to fall asleep and then briefly loses **consciousness**

Narcotic any drug in a class of drugs derived from opium or synthetically produced to create the numbing, stuporous effects of opium and that lead to **addiction**

Natural selection evolutionary mechanism by which organisms have developed and changed, based on what is commonly called the "survival of the fittest"

Naturalistic observation a research method in which the researcher observes people engaged in the normal activities of their daily lives

Nature–nurture controversy a debate regarding whether our psychological makeup arises from our inherited characteristics (our *nature*) or from our interactions with the environment (our *nurture*)

Negative reinforcement removal or cessation (stopping) of an unpleasant stimulus, such as physical or psychological pain or discomfort (see also **positive reinforcement**)

Negative reinforcer an unpleasant stimulus that is removed following an operant response, thereby leading to an increased probability that the operant will be repeated (see also **positive reinforcer**)

Negative symptom a characteristic of a disorder, in which the individual lacks a normal behavior (e.g., not speaking, not showing emotional expression, or not interacting socially) (see also **positive symptom**)

Negative transfer hindrance of problem solving as a result of prior experience in solving apparently related or similar problems (see also **positive transfer**)

Neodissociative theory a view of **hypnosis** asserting that some individuals can separate one part of their conscious minds (which responds to the hypnotist's instructions) from another part (which observes and monitors the events and actions taking place)

Neo-Freudian a psychodynamically oriented theorist who has based her or his own views and theories on those of Freud

Neonate newborn (*neo-*, new; *-nate*, born)

Nerve bundle of **neurons** that can be observed as a fiber extending from the **central nervous system** out to various parts of the body

Neuron nerve cell, involved in neural communication within the nervous system

Neuroticism a personality trait characterized by sudden and unpredictable mood swings, nervousness, and irritability

Neurotransmitter chemical messenger released by the terminal buttons on the **axon** of a presynaptic **neuron;** it carries the chemical messages across the **synapse** to receptor sites on the receiving **dendrites** or **soma** of the postsynaptic neuron

Norm a standard of behavior or an expressed attitude, based on the shared trends of the majority in a group (see also **normative scores**)

Normal distribution a particular distribution in which the preponderance of values is near the center of distribution, with values falling off rather rapidly as they depart from the center

Normative scores set of normative equivalents for a range of raw test scores that represent the normal distribution of scores obtained by giving a test to a huge number of individuals

Null hypothesis a proposed expectation of *no* difference or relation

Obedience the process in which an individual follows the command of an actual or perceived authority figure

Object permanence the cognitive realization that objects may continue to exist even when they are not currently being sensed

Objective personality test a method of personality assessment founded on the trait approach, which is standardized and normed based on a large number of individuals, thereby providing scores that allow for easy comparisons across individuals (see also **projective personality test**)

Olfaction the sense of smell

Operant a response that has some effect on the world

Operant conditioning process of increasing or decreasing the likelihood that an individual will produce an active behavior (an **operant**) as a result of interacting with the environment

Operational definition a means for researchers to specify exactly how to test or to measure particular phenomena being studied

Opponent process (in motivation) a changing phenomenon that opposes (goes against, in the opposite direction from) an existing force, thereby moving toward a neutral state of balance

Opponent-process theory (of color vision) a theory of color vision based on opposing pairs (red–green, yellow–blue, and black–white) of receptors, in which the activity of the pairs either increases or decreases, depending on which member of the pair is being stimulated by a given sensation (see also **trichromatic theory of color vision**)

Organic pain discomfort caused by observed physical damage to bodily tissue (see also **psychogenic pain**)

Overconfidence a bias affecting decision making, in which individuals overestimate the probability that their own responses are accurate or even more broadly overvaluate their own skills, knowledge, or judgment

Overdose ingestion of a life-threatening or lethal dose of drugs, often associated with the use of **psychoactive drugs**

Overextension error overapplication of the meaning of a given word to more things, ideas, and situations than is appropriate for the word; usually made by children or other persons acquiring a language

Pain sensory and emotional discomfort associated with actual, imagined, or threatened damage to or irritation of tissues of the body (see also **organic pain, psychogenic pain**)

Parallel processing information processing in which multiple operations occur at one time

Partial-reinforcement schedule an **operant-conditioning** program in which a given **operant** is reinforced at some times, but not at other times

Percentile the percentage of other individuals in a given distribution whose scores fall below a given individual's scores

Perception the mental processes that organize and interpret sensory information that has been transmitted to the brain

Perceptual constancy the perception that stimuli remain the same even when immediate sensations of the stimuli change

Peripheral nervous system one of the two main parts of the nervous system (the other is the **central nervous system**), comprising the nerve cells that lie outside of the brain and the spinal cord, including the nerves of the face and head (see also **endocrine system**)

Person–environment interaction the distinctive fit between a given person and his or her environment

Personal attribution a mental explanation pointing to the cause of behavior as lying within the individual who performs the behavior (also termed *dispositional attribution*) (see also **situational attribution**)

Personal disposition a trait that is unique to a given individual, according to Allport's theory of personality

Personal unconscious the part of the unconscious mind that includes the person's distinctive repressed memories and personal experiences (see also **collective unconscious**)

Personalism the tendency to make more **personal attribu-**

tions when the behavior of someone affects us directly, but to make more **situational attributions** when the behavior affects us less directly

Personality the enduring dispositional characteristics of an individual that hold together and explain the person's behavior

Personality disorders psychological disorders involving exaggerated and maladaptive personality characteristics that persist over a long period of time and that cause problems in the person's adjustment to everyday situations

Phenotype expression of an inherited trait, based on the dominant expression of the trait in the **genotype** and also subject to environmental influence

Photoreceptor receptor cell that receives and transduces light (*photo-*, light) energy into electrochemical energy

Place theory a theory that sensed variations in pitch arise from variations in the locations of the hair cells that are stimulated by particular sounds (see also **frequency theory**)

Placebo a treatment (e.g., a pill or other substance) that the patient believes to have curative or healing properties, but that actually has no such properties, often used as a means of determining whether drug treatments are truly effective or work only because patients believe that they are being helped

Placebo effect a perceived improvement that occurs simply because people believe that they have received a given treatment, even when they did not actually receive the treatment

Placenta a protective membrane containing a dense network of blood vessels through which a mother's body supplies needed resources (e.g., oxygen, sources of energy, and material resources such as protein and minerals) and removes waste products for the infant she carries

Plan a strategy for accomplishing something at some time in the future

Pleasure principle the principle by which the satisfaction of impulses drives all of the functions of the **id**

Polygraph equipment that records several (*poly-*, many; *-graph*, recording) different physiological responses (e.g., heart rate, respiration rate, blood pressure) at one time; often used for trying to measure emotional reactions

Pons a brain structure containing nerve cells that pass signals from one part of the brain to another, thereby serving as a kind of bridge

Positive reinforcement presentation of a **positive reinforcer** (stimulus) soon after an **operant** (response) (see also **negative reinforcement**)

Positive reinforcer a reward (pleasant stimulus) that follows an **operant** and strengthens the associated behavioral response (see also **negative reinforcer**)

Positive symptom a characteristic of a disorder, in which the individual shows an abnormal behavior (e.g., hallucinations or word salad) (see also **negative symptom**)

Positive transfer the facilitation of problem solving as a result of prior experience in solving related or similar problems (see also **negative transfer**)

Posthypnotic suggestion an instruction received during **hypnosis,** which the individual is to implement after having wakened, often despite having no recollection of having received the instruction

Practical significance characterization of a result as having practical or everyday import

Practice effects the outcomes of **rehearsal,** which usually involve an improvement in recall or skill

Pragmatics the study of how people use language, emphasizing the contexts in which language is used

Pragmatism a school of psychology that focuses on the usefulness of knowledge

Preconscious level a level of **consciousness** comprising information that is accessible to, but not continuously available in, awareness

Prefrontal lobotomy an obsolete procedure in which the frontal lobes of the brain are cut off from contact with the rest of the brain, in order to make patients more compliant

Prejudice a negative attitude toward groups of individuals, based on limited or wrong information about those groups

Preoperational stage Piaget's second stage of development (about age 2 years until the age of starting elementary school), during which the child develops language and concepts about physical objects (see also **concrete-operational stage, formal-operational stage, sensorimotor stage**)

Primary appraisal the first step in coping with a situation that may be stressful, involving analysis of how much the person will be affected by outcomes of the particular situation (see also **secondary appraisal**)

Primary-process thought a form of thought that is unrealistic, unreasonable, and driven by instincts (see also **secondary-process thought**)

Primary reinforcer stimulus that provides an immediate reward that satisfies the senses (see also **secondary reinforcer**)

Priming effect enhanced access to a particular stimulus or item of information, as a result of recent activation of or exposure to the same stimulus or a related one

Problem-focused coping adapting to a challenging situation by using strategies to fix the situation and to make it less challenging (see also **emotion-focused coping**)

Problem solving a set of processes for which the goal is to overcome obstacles obstructing the path to a solution

Procedural knowledge "knowing how"—skills that require a person to follow a set of steps for carrying out a procedure

Projective personality test a method of personality assessment based on the psychodynamic approach, which attempts to reach people's unconscious or preconscious personality characteristics and conflicts through their imaginative (primary-process) responses to test items (see also **objective personality test**)

Prosocial behavior actions that offer some benefit to society in general or to members within society and that are approved by most members of society (see also **antisocial behavior**)

Prototype matching the process of comparing an observed pattern to one or more mental examples, in order to find the typical example that comes closest to fitting the observed pattern

Psychoactive drug drug (e.g., **CNS depressant, CNS stimulant, narcotic,** or **hallucinogenic**) that produces a **psychopharmacological** effect, thereby affecting behavior, mood, and consciousness

Psychobiology a branch of psychology that seeks to understand behavior through studying anatomy and physiology, especially of the brain

Psychodynamic psychology a school of psychology that emphasizes the importance of (a) conflicting unconscious mental processes and (b) early childhood experiences

Psychogenic pain discomfort for which an observed source of physical damage to bodily tissues has not been found (see also **organic pain**)

Psychology the study of the mind and of the behavior of people and other organisms

Psychometric characterized by psychological measurement (*psycho-*, pertaining to the mind or mental processes, *-metric*, measurement)

Psychoneuroimmunology a cross-disciplinary field that blends psychology, *neurology* (the study of the brain and nervous system), and *immunology* (the study of the immune system), as well as *physiology* (e.g., the study of the **endocrine system** and other biological systems of the body)

Psychopharmacological a drug-induced influence on behavior, mood, and **consciousness**

Psychophysics the systematic study of the relationship between the physical stimulation of a sense organ and the psychological sensations produced by that stimulation

Psychosurgery a procedure intended to relieve psychological problems by probing, slicing, dissecting, or removing some part of the brain (see also **prefrontal lobotomy**)

Psychotherapy a means of helping people with their psychological problems by using the principles of psychology

Psychoticism a personality trait characterized by isolation, lack of caring for or about others, lack of feeling and empathy, and insensitivity

Psychotropic drug any of several types of drugs that affect the psychological processes or state of mind of an individual

Puberty the period of physiological development during which males and females develop primary sex characteristics (i.e., functioning sex organs) and secondary sex characteristics (e.g., body hair and distinctive shape), thereby reaching sexual maturity

Punishment delivery of a stimulus that *decreases* the probability of an associated response; involves either presenting an unpleasant stimulus or removing a pleasant one

Pupil the hole in the iris (roughly in its center) through which light gains access to the interior of the eye, particularly the retina

Quasi-experimental design a plan for conducting research that resembles a controlled experimental design but that does not ensure the random assignment of subjects to the treatment and the control groups

Questionnaire a set of questions used for conducting a **survey**

Range the difference between the lowest and highest values in a distribution

Ratio IQ a means of indicating performance on intelligence tests; expressed as a quotient of **mental age** divided by chronological age, times 100 (see also **intelligence quotient, deviation IQs**)

Rational-emotive therapy (RET) a form of cognitive therapy, based on the notions that (a) incorrect or maladaptive thoughts lead to emotional and other psychological problems, and (b) changes in these thoughts lead to improvements in psychological well-being

Rationalist person who believes that knowledge is most effectively acquired through **reasoning**

Raw score the score on a given test in whatever units the test is originally scored

Reaction range the broad limits within which a particular attribute (e.g., intelligence) may be expressed in various possible ways, given the inherited potential for expression of the attribute in the particular individual

Reality principle the principle by which the **ego** tries to adapt to the real world while still satisfying psychic forces of both the **id** and the **superego**

Reasoning a set of cognitive processes by which an individual may infer a conclusion from an assortment of evidence or from statements of principles

Recall production of an item from memory (see also **recognition**)

Receptor a physiological structure designed to receive something (e.g., a given substance or a particular kind of information), such as sensory information from the sense organs

Receptor cell body cell that is especially suited to detecting and transforming a particlar kind of energy that reaches the cell (see also **photoreceptor**)

Recessive trait the weaker expression of a genetic trait in a pair of traits, which appears in the **phenotype** when the **genotype** comprises two recessive expressions of that trait (see also **dominant trait**)

Reciprocal determinism an interaction in which personal variables and environmental variables both influence and are influenced by the behavior of the individual

Recognition identification as to whether a particular item is one that was previously stored in memory (see also **recall**)

Reconstructive memory phenomenon by which people accurately encode, store, and retrieve only the sensations and events they have actually experienced (see also **constructive memory**)

Reflex an automatic physiological response to an external stimulus, which occurs directly through the **spinal cord**

Rehearsal the repeated reciting of information or the repetition of a procedure

Reinforcer a stimulus that increases the probability that the **operant** associated with it will be repeated

Reliability the dependability of a measurement instrument (e.g., a test), indicating that the instrument consistently measures the outcome being measured (see also **validity**)

REM sleep the distinctive kind of sleep that is characterized by rapid eye movements (REMs) and that is frequently associated with dreaming (see also **N-REM sleep**)

Representational thought thinking involving mental images, such as images of tangible objects

Representative sample a subset of a population, carefully chosen to represent the proportionate diversity of the population

Repression a Freudian **defense mechanism,** by which a person keeps troublesome internally generated thoughts and feelings from entering consciousness and thereby causing internal conflicts or other psychological discomfort

Research design a way of choosing and interrelating a set of experimental variables, and of selecting and assigning subjects to experimental and control conditions

Resistance a defensive tactic used by patients, usually unconsciously, to keep from becoming aware of unconscious material that affects the progress of therapy

Reticular activating system a complex network of neurons essential to the regulation of consciousness and to such vital functions as heartbeat and breathing

Retina a network of neurons covering most of the rear surface inside the eye; contains the **photoreceptors** that **transduce** light energy into electrochemical energy

Retrieve pull information from memory into active use or awareness

Retrograde amnesia memory loss affecting purposeful retrieval of events that occurred before whatever injury caused the memory loss, without any effect on the ability to form new memories; one meaning of *retro-* is "backward"; people with retrograde amnesia forget *old* information about events, going *backward* from the time the amnesia began

Rod long, thin, and abundant type of **photoreceptor,** responsible mostly for vision in dim lighting (see also **cone**)

Satisficing a decision-making strategy in which an individual chooses the first acceptable alternative that becomes available, without considering all possible alternative options

Schedules of reinforcement patterns by which reinforcements follow **operants**

Schema a cognitive framework for organizing what is known about a particular **concept**

Schizophrenia a set of psychological disorders involving various perceptual symptoms (e.g., **hallucinations**), cognitive symptoms (e.g., disturbed thought content or processes), mood symptoms (e.g., lack of appropriate emotional expression), and sometimes even bizarre motor symptoms

Secondary appraisal the process of assessing what can be done about a challenging situation to make it more likely that positive outcomes will result and less likely that harmful outcomes will result (see also **primary appraisal**)

Secondary-process thought a form of thought that is reasonable and realistic (see also **primary-process thought**)

Secondary reinforcer stimulus that gains reinforcing value through association with a **primary reinforcer**

Secondary trait a personality characteristic that has some influence on behavior but that is not very important to the personality and behavior of the individual (see also **cardinal trait, central trait**)

Sedative–hypnotic drugs one of the two primary types of **CNS depressants,** used for calming **anxiety** and relieving **insomnia**

Selective attention the conscious attempt to perceive some stimuli (e.g., the voice and gestures of a speaker) and to ignore others (e.g., background noises and sights)

Self theory a humanistic theory of personality, in which the person's match between the perceived ideal self and real self is considered central to personality

Self-concept all aspects of the self that a person perceives, which may be accurate or inaccurate and may be commonly perceived by other persons as unique; an individual's beliefs, understandings, and judgments about her- or himself

Self-determination theory a theory suggesting that people need to feel that they can control their own destiny, that they are independent and competent, yet that they are still closely tied to other people

Self-efficacy an individual's belief in her or his own competence to master the environment and to reach personal goals

Self-handicapping the tendency to take actions to undermine our own performance in order to have an excuse in case we fail

Self-perception theory the suggestion that when we are not sure of what we believe, we view our behavior much as an outsider might view it, and then infer our beliefs, based on our actions

Self-serving bias the tendency to be generous to ourselves when interpreting our own actions, pointing to personal causes when we do well and to situational causes when we do poorly

Semantic memory memory for general knowledge of facts that are not tied to any particular personal experiences (see also **episodic memory**)

Semantics the study of meanings of words

Sensation a message regarding physical stimulation of a sensory receptor

Sense a physical system for receiving a particular kind of physical stimulation and translating that stimulation into an electrochemical message

Sensitization paradoxical phenomenon in which an intermittent user of a drug actually demonstrates heightened sensitivity to low doses of the drug

Sensorimotor stage Piaget's first stage of development (about the first 2 years after birth), during which the child builds on reflexes and develops the first mental representations of things that are not being sensed at the moment (see also **concrete-operational stage, formal-operational stage, preoperational stage**)

Sensory coding the physiological form of communication through which sensory receptors convey a range of information about stimuli within the nervous system

Sensory memory storage of very limited amounts of information for a fraction of a second or slightly more

Sensory neuron nerve cell that receives information from the environment through sensory receptors and then carries that information toward the **central nervous system** (see also **interneuron, motor neuron**)

Separation anxiety fear of being separated from a primary caregiver, such as a parent

Serial processing information processing in which operations occur sequentially, one after another

Sexual disorders psychological disorders involving problems with sexual arousal, thoughts, or behavior that distresses the individual or other persons

Sexual script mental representation regarding how sexual behavior should be carried out during various episodes of sexual interaction

Shape bring behavior under control by providing a program of reinforcement

Short-term memory relatively brief memory storage of about seven items, give or take a couple of items

Signal-detection theory (SDT) a method of measuring the detection of a sensation, which takes into account the influence of expectations and decision making on detection

Simulating paradigm a research technique for determining the true effects of a psychological treatment (e.g., **hypnosis**); one group of participants is subjected to the treatment and another group (a control group) does not receive the treatment but is asked to simulate the behavior of persons who do; observers try to distinguish the behavior of the treatment group from that of the control group trying to simulate the treatment group's behavior

Situational attribution a mental explanation pointing to the cause of behavior as lying within the situation in which the individual shows the behavior (see also **personal attribution**)

Skin senses the means by which we become sensitive to pressure, temperature, and pain stimulation directly on the skin

Sleep apnea a breathing disturbance that occurs during sleep, in which the sleeper repeatedly stops breathing during sleep; a sleep disorder

Social categorization the tendency to sort people into groups, according to various characteristics the observer perceives to be common to members of each group

Social cognition the thoughts and beliefs we have regarding ourselves and other people, based on how we perceive and interpret information that we either observe directly or learn from other people

Social desirability bias the tendency, when trying to infer the dispositions of people, to give undeservedly heavy weight to socially undesirable behavior

Social facilitation the phenomenon in which the presence of other people positively influences the performance of an individual

Social interference the phenomenon in which the presence of other people negatively influences the performance of an individual

Social learning learning that occurs by observing the behavior of others, as well as by observing any environmental outcomes of the behavior

Social loafing the phenomenon in which each individual member of a group puts forth less effort as the size of the group increases

Social psychology the study of how each person's thoughts, feelings, and behaviors are affected by the presence of others, even if that presence is only implied or imagined

Socioemotional development the process by which people learn about themselves as human beings, as well as by which they learn to interact with each other, across the life span; may be viewed as including emotional, personality, interpersonal, and moral development

Soma the part of the **neuron** that performs vital functions for the life of the cell

Somatoform disorders psychological disorders in which people experience bodily symptoms for which no physiological basis has been found

Somnambulism disorder characterized by sleepwalking

Source trait one of a relatively few underlying psychological dimensions of personality that generate numerous **surface traits**

Spinal cord a slender, roughly cylindrical bundle of interconnected neural fibers, which is enclosed within the spinal column and which extends through the center of the back, starting at the brain and ending at the base of the spine

Spontaneous recovery the disappearance of a person's symptoms, which occurs without any treatment whatsoever

Standard deviation a measure related to the average variation of values around the mean

Standardization the administration of a test in a way that ensures that the conditions for taking the test are the same for all test-takers

Statistically significant characterization of a result as most likely due to systematic rather than chance factors

Stereotype perceived typical example that illustrates the main characteristics of a particular social category, usually based on the assumption that the typical example uniformly represents all examples of the social category

Stimulus discrimination response to the observed difference between a new stimulus and the original **conditioned stimulus (CS),** which makes it less likely that the new stimulus will lead to the **conditioned response (CR)**

Stimulus generalization response to the observed similarity of a stimulus to the **conditioned stimulus (CS),** thereby increasing the likelihood that the **conditioned response (CR)** will occur following presentation of the stimulus

Store keep encoded information in memory

Stress a person's response to the presence of something in the environment that causes the person to feel challenged in some way

Stress response an adaptation to challenging changes in the environment

Stressor an event or situation that causes **stress**

Stroop effect interference experienced in selectively attending to one sensory stimulus (e.g., the color of the ink) while trying to ignore another sensory stimulus (e.g., the word that is printed with the ink of that color)

Structuralism the first major school of thought in psychology which focuses on analyzing the components of the mind, such as particular sensations

Subconscious (noun) a level of **consciousness** that involves less awareness than full conscious awareness and from which information is not easily pulled into the conscious mind

Subliminal perception a form of preconscious processing in which people may have the ability to detect information without being fully aware that they are doing so

Subtractive mixture the remaining combined **wavelengths** of light that are reflected from an object after other wavelengths of light have been absorbed (*subtracted* from the reflected light)

Successive approximations a method for shaping behavior by gradually reinforcing **operants** that are increasingly more similar to the desired behavior

Superego a personality structure that is unconscious and irrational, based on the rules and prohibitions we have internalized from interactions with our parents (see also **id, ego**)

Surface trait one of many personality features that characterize differences among people (see also **source trait**)

Survey a method of observing various people's responses to questions regarding their beliefs and opinions

Synapse the area comprising the interneuronal gap, the terminal buttons of one neuron's **axon,** and the **dendrites** (or sometimes the **soma**) of the next **neuron**

Syntax a level of linguistic analysis, which centers on the patterns by which users of a particular language put words together at the level of the sentence

Synthesis the process of integrating various elements into a more complex whole (see also **analysis**)

Taste buds clusters of taste **receptor cells** located on the tongue

Telegraphic speech rudimentary syntactical communications of two words or more, which are characteristic of very early language acquisition, and which seem more like telegrams than like conversation because function **morphemes** are usually omitted

Temperament a person's distinctive tendency to show a particular mood and a particular intensity and duration of emotions

Test a method for measuring a given ability or attribute in particular individuals at a particular time and in a particular place

Test of statistical significance a test that tells us the probability that a given result is not due to chance fluctuations in the data

Thalamus a brain structure that primarily serves as a relay station for sensory information

Theory a statement of general principles explaining one or more phenomena (events or processes)

Theory of multiple intelligences a theory suggesting that there are seven distinct intelligences that function somewhat independently: bodily–kinesthetic, interpersonal, intrapersonal, linguistic, logical–mathematical, musical, and spatial intelligence

Thinking a psychological function that involves the representation and processing of information in the mind

Threshold of excitation the level of electrochemical stimulation, at or above which an **action potential** may be generated, but below which an **action potential** cannot be generated

Tip-of-the-tongue phenomenon an experience of preconsciousness, in which a person cannot successfully retrieve information known to be stored in memory

Tolerance a consequence of prolonged use of **psychoactive drugs,** in which the drug user feels decreasing **psychopharmacological** effects of a given drug at one level of dosage and must take increasing amounts of drugs in order to achieve the same effects, eventually reaching such a high level that further increases will cause **overdose**

Trait (of personality) stable characteristic that distinguishes each person

Tranquilizer one of the **sedative–hypnotic drugs** used for combating **anxiety;** considered to be safer than **barbiturates,** although the potential for **addiction** remains problematic

Transduce convert incoming energy from one form (e.g., mechanical, chemical, electromagnetic) into an electrochemical form of energy for use within the nervous system

Transference a term used in psychodynamic therapy, describing a patient's emotional involvement with the psychotherapist as an authority figure

Triangular theory of love a theory suggesting that love has three basic components: intimacy, passion, and commitment

Triarchic theory of human intelligence a theory of intelligence, which asserts that intelligence comprises three aspects (analytical, creative, and practical)

Trichromatic theory of color vision a theory that color vision depends on the responses of three different types of cones

(for detecting red, green, and blue), in which the combined responses of these cones permit sensation of **additive mixtures** of the primary colors (see also **opponent-process theory** [of color vision])

Two-component theory of emotion a theory asserting that particular emotions have two parts: a feeling of physiological **arousal** in response to a stimulus, and the cognitive labeling of the physiological arousal as a particular emotion

Type-A behavior pattern a personality characterized by *high* levels of hostility, as well as by the *pursuit* of competition and time pressure

Type-B behavior pattern a personality characterized by *low* levels of hostility, as well as by the *avoidance* of competition and time pressure

Unconditional positive regard interpersonal feelings of acceptance, affection, appreciation, or esteem, which are not based on any conditions that the object of regard must meet

Unconditioned response (UCR) automatic physiological or emotional response to an unconditioned stimulus **(UCS)**

Unconditioned stimulus (UCS) stimulus that elicits a physiological or emotional response

Unconscious the portion of the mind that lies outside of our awareness and that we cannot pull into our awareness

Validity the extent to which a given form of measurement assesses what it is supposed to measure (see also **reliability**)

Verbal comprehension the ability to comprehend written and spoken linguistic input, such as words, sentences, and paragraphs

Verbal fluency the ability to produce written and spoken linguistic output, such as words, sentences, and paragraphs

Vestibular system sense of balance, governed by receptors in the inner ear, which detect the position and movement of the head, relative to a source of gravity

Vibration theory a theory that we smell because particular molecules generate particular frequencies of vibrations, which smell receptors transduce into electrochemical messages about particular smells (see also **lock-and-key theory**)

Well-structured problem problem with a well-defined path to solution (see also **ill-structured problem**)

Withdrawal the temporary discomfort (which may be extremely unpleasant and sometimes even life-threatening) associated with a reduction or discontinuation of the use of a **psychoactive drug,** during which the drug user's physiology and mental processes must adjust to an absence of the drug

Working memory recently activated portion of **long-term memory,** as well as a means for moving activated elements into and out of **short-term memory**

Zone of proximal development (ZPD) a range between the developed abilities that a child clearly shows and the latent capacities that the child might be able to show, given the appropriate environment in which to do so

Zygote an individual in the first of three stages of prenatal development (from the time of conception to implantation and cell differentiation) (see also **embryo, fetus**)

References

Abel, E. L. (1984). *Fetal alcohol syndrome and fetal alcohol effects.* New York: Plenum.

Abrams, R. (1988). *Electroconvulsive treatment: It apparently works, but how and at what risks are not yet clear.* New York: Oxford University Press.

Abramson, L. Y., Metalsky, G. I., & Alloy, L. B. (1989). Hopelessness depression: A theory-based subtype of depression. *Psychological Review, 96*(2), 358–372.

Adams, M. J. (Ed.) (1986). *Odyssey: A curriculum for thinking* (Vols. 1–6). Watertown, MA: Charlesbridge.

Ader, R., & Cohen, N. (1991). The influence of conditioning on immune responses. In R. Ader, D. L. Felten, & N. Cohen (Eds.), *Psychoneuroimmunology* (2nd ed., pp. 611–646). San Diego, CA: Academic Press.

Ader, R., & Cohen, N. (1993). Psychoneuroimmunology: Conditioning and stress. *Annual Review of Psychology, 44,* 53–85.

Ader, R., Felten, D., & Cohen, N. (1990). Interactions between the brain and the immune system. *Annual Review of Pharmacology & Toxicology, 30,* 561–602.

Ader, R., Felten, D. L., & Cohen, N. (Eds.) (1991). *Psychoneuroimmunology* (2nd ed.). San Diego, CA: Academic Press.

Adler, J. (1991, July 22). The melting of a mighty myth. *Newsweek,* p. 63.

Adler, T. (1989). Cocaine babies face behavior deficits. *APA Monitor, 20,* 14.

Agnew, J. (1985). Man's purgative passion. *American Journal of Psychotherapy, 39*(2), 236–246.

Aldous, J. L. (1994). Cross-cultural counselling and cross-cultural meanings: An exploration of Morita psychotherapy. *Canadian Journal of Counselling, 28*(3), 238–249.

Allport, G. W. (1935). Attitudes. In C. M. Murchison (Ed.), *Handbook of social psychology.* Worcester, MA: Clark University Press.

Allport, G. W. (1937). *Personality: A psychological interpretation.* New York: Holt, Rinehart and Winston.

Allport, G. W. (1954). *The nature of prejudice.* Reading, MA: Addison-Wesley.

Allport, G. W. (1961). *Pattern and growth in personality.* New York: Holt, Rinehart and Winston.

Allport, G. W. (1985). The historical background of social psychology. In G. Lindzey & E. Aronson (Eds.), *Handbook of social psychology* (Vol. 1, 3rd ed., pp. 1–46). New York: Random House.

Allport, G. W., & Postman, L. J. (1947). *The psychology of rumor.* New York: Henry Holt.

Alpert, B., Field, T., Goldstein, S., & Perry, S. (1990). Aerobics enhances cardiovascular fitness and agility in preschoolers. *Health Psychology, 9,* 48–56.

Amabile, T. M. (1983). *The social psychology of creativity.* New York: Springer-Verlag.

Amabile, T. M. (1985). Motivation and creativity: Effects of motivational orientation on creative writers. *Journal of Personality and Social Psychology, 48,* 393–399.

American Association of University Women Educational Foundation and the Wellesley College Center for Research on Women. (1992). *The AAUW Report: How schools shortchange girls—A study of major findings on girls and education.* Washington, DC: Author.

American Psychiatric Association. (1994). *Diagnostic and statistical manual of mental disorders* (4th ed.). Washington, DC: Author.

Amir, Y., & Sharon, I. (1987). Are social-psychological laws cross-culturally valid? *Journal of Cross-Cultural Psychology, 18,* 383–470.

Amoore, J. E. (1970). *Molecular basis of odor.* Springfield, IL: Thomas.

Amsel, A. (1992). B. F. Skinner and the cognitive revolution. *Journal of Behavior Therapy & Experimental Psychiatry, 23*(2), 67–70.

Anand, B. K., & Brobeck, J. R. (1951). Hypothalamic control of food intake in rats and cats. *Yale Journal of Biology and Medicine, 24,* 123–140.

Anand, B. K., Chhina, G. S., & Singh, B. (1962). Effect of glucose on the activity of hypothalamic "feeding centers." *Science, 138,* 597–598.

Anderson, C. A. (1987). Temperature and aggression: Effects on quarterly, yearly, and city rates of violent and nonviolent crime. *Journal of Personality and Social Psychology, 52,* 1161–1173.

Anderson, C. A. (1989). Temperature and aggression: Ubiquitous effects of heat on occurrence of human violence. *Psychological Bulletin, 106*(1), 74–96.

Anderson, J. R., & Bower, G. H. (1973). *Human associative memory.* New York: Wiley.

Anderson, K. L. (1990). Arousal and the inverted-U hypothesis: A critique of Neiss's "Reconceptualizing arousal." *Psychological Bulletin, 107,* 96–100.

Andersson, B. E. (1989). Effects of public daycare: A longitudinal study. *Child Development, 60,* 857–866.

Andreasen, N. C., Olsen, S. A., Dennert, J. W., & Smith, M. R. (1982). Ventricular enlargement in schizophrenia: Definition and prevalence. *American Journal of Psychiatry, 139,* 292–296.

Andrews, G. (1993). The benefits of psychotherapy. In N. Sartorius, G. de Girolano, G. Andrews, G. A. German, & L. Eisenberg (Eds.), *Treatment of mental disorders: A review of effectiveness.* Geneva, Switzerland, and Washington, DC: World Health Organization and American Psychiatric Press.

Andrich, D., & Styles, I. (1994). Psychometric evidence of intellectual growth spurts in early adolescence. *Journal of Early Adolescence, 14,* 328–344.

Argyle, M. (1992). *The social psychology of everyday life.* New York: Routledge.

Aristotle. (1987). *The works of Aristotle* (Vol. 1). Chicago, IL: Encyclopaedia Britannica. (Original work ca. 335 B.C.)

Arnold, M. B. (1960). *Emotion and personality* (Vols. 1, 2). New York: Columbia University Press.

Arnold, M. B. (1970). Perennial problems in the field of emotion. In M. B. Arnold (Ed.), *Feelings and emotions* (pp. 169–185). New York: Academic Press.

Asch, S. E. (1951). Effects of group pressure upon the modification and distortion of judgments. In H. Guetzkow (Ed.), *Groups, leadership, and men.* Pittsburgh: Carnegie.

Asch, S. E. (1952). *Social psychology.* New York: Prentice-Hall.

Asch, S. E. (1955). Opinions and social pressure. *Scientific American, 193,* 31–35.

Asch, S. E. (1956). Studies of independence and conformity: A minority of one against a unanimous majority. *Psychological Monographs, 70,* 416.

Atkinson, D. R., Casa, A., & Abreu, J. (1992). Mexican American acculturation, counselor ethnicity and cultural sensitivity, and perceived counselor competence. *American Psychologist, 39,* 515–520.

Atkinson, D. R., Furlong, M. J., & Poston, W. C. (1986). Afro-American preferences for counselor characteristics. *Journal of Counseling Psychology, 33,* 326–330.

Atkinson, D. R., Ponce, F. Q., & Martinez, F. M. (1984). Effects of ethnic, sex, and attitude similarity on counselor credibility. *Journal of Counseling Psychology, 31,* 588–590.

Atkinson, J. W. (Ed.) (1958). *Motives in fantasy, action, and society.* Princeton, NJ: Van Nostrand.

Atkinson, J. W. (1964). *Introduction to motivation.* New York: Van Nostrand.

Atkinson, R. C., & Shiffrin, R. M. (1968). Human memory: A proposed system and its control processes. In K. W. Spence & J. T. Spence (Eds.), *The psychology of learning and motivation: Advances in research and theory* (Vol. 2). New York: Academic Press.

Atkinson, R. C., & Shiffrin, R. M. (1971). The control of short-term memory. *Scientific American, 225,* 82–90.

Averill, J. R. (1980). A constructivist view of emotion. In R. Plutchik & H. Kellerman (Eds.), *Emotion: Theory, research, and experience (Vol. 1) Theories of emotion* (pp. 305–339). New York: Academic Press.

Averill, J. R. (1983). Studies on anger and aggression: Implications for theories of emotions. *American Psychologist, 38,* 1145–1160.

Axelson, J. A. (1993). *Counseling and development in a multicultural society* (2nd ed.). Pacific Grove, CA: Brooks/Cole.

Axline, V. (1964). *Dibs: In search of self.* New York: Ballantine.

Baddeley, A. D. (1966). Short-term memory for word sequences as function of acoustic, semantic, and formal similarity. *Quarterly Journal of Experimental Psychology, 18,* 362–365.

Baddeley, A. (1989). The psychology of remembering and forgetting. In T. Butler (Ed.), *Memory: History, culture and the mind.* London: Basil Blackwell.

Baddeley, A. (1990a). *Human memory.* Hove, England: Erlbaum.

Baddeley, A. (1990b). *Human memory: Theory and practice.* Needham Heights, MA: Allyn & Bacon.

Baddeley, A. (1993). *Your memory: A user's guide.* London: Prion, Multimedia Books.

Bahrick, H. P., Bahrick, P. O., & Wittlinger, R. P. (1975). Fifty years of memory for names and faces: A cross-sectional approach. *Journal of Experimental Psychology:* General, *104,* 54–75.

Bahrick, H. P., & Phelps, E. (1987). Retention of Spanish vocabulary over eight years. *Journal of Experimental Psychology: Learning Memory and Cognition, 13,* 344–349.

Bailey, J. M., & Pillard, R. C. (1991). A genetic study of male sexual orientation. *Archives of General Psychiatry, 48*(12), 1089–1096.

Bales, R. F. (1950). *Interaction process analysis: A method for the study of small groups.* Reading, MA: Addison-Wesley.

Bales, R. F. (1970). *Personality and interpersonal behavior.* New York: Holt, Rinehart and Winston.

Balkin, J. (1988). Why policemen don't like policewomen. *Journal of Police Science and Administration, 16*(1), 29–38.

Bandura, A. (1965). Influence of models' reinforcement contingencies on the acquisition of imitative responses. *Journal of Personality and Social Psychology, 1,* 589–595.

Bandura, A. (1969). *Principles of behavior modification.* New York: Holt, Rinehart and Winston.

Bandura, A. (1973). *Aggression: A social learning analysis.* Englewood Cliffs, NJ: Prentice-Hall.

Bandura, A. (1977a). Self-efficacy: Toward a unifying theory of behavioral change. *Psychological Review, 84,* 181–215.

Bandura, A. (1977b). *Social learning theory.* Englewood Cliffs, NJ: Prentice-Hall.

Bandura, A. (1983). Psychological mechanisms of aggression. In R. G. Geen & E. I. Donnerstein (Eds.), *Aggression: Theoretical and empirical reviews: Vol. I. Theoretical and methodological issues* (pp. 1–40). New York: Academic Press.

Bandura, A. (1986). *Social foundations of thought and action: A social cognitive theory.* Englewood Cliffs, NJ: Prentice-Hall.

Bandura, A. (1988). Self-efficacy conception of anxiety. *Anxiety Research, 1*(2), 77–98.

Bandura, A. (1993). Perceived self-efficacy in cognitive development and functioning. Annual meeting of the American Educational Research Association, San Francisco, California. *Educational Psychologist, 28*(2), 117–148.

Bandura, A., Blanchard, E. B., & Ritter, B. (1969). Relative efficacy of desensitization and modelling approaches for inducing behavioral, affective, and attitudinal changes. *Journal of Personality and Social Psychology, 13,* 173–199.

Bandura, A., Ross, D., & Ross, S. A. (1963). Imitation of film-mediated aggressive models. *Journal of Abnormal and Social Psychology, 66,* 3–11.

Bandura, A., & Walters, R. H. (1963). *Social learning and personality development.* New York: Ronald Press.

Banks, M. S., & Salapatek, P. (1983). Infant visual perception. In M. M. Haith & J. J. Campos (Eds.), *Handbook of child psychology: Infancy and developmental psychobiology* (Vol. 2, 4th ed.). New York: Wiley.

Barber, T. X. (1964a). Hypnotic "colorblindness," "blindness," and "deafness." *Diseases of the Nervous System, 25,* 529–537.

Barber, T. X. (1964b). Toward a theory of "hypnotic" behavior: Positive visual and auditory hallucinations. *Psychological Record, 14,* 197–210.

Bard, P. (1934). On emotional experience after decortication with some remarks on theoretical views. *Psychological Review, 41,* 309–329.

Barefoot, J. C., Dahlstrom, W. G., & Williams, R. B. (1983). Hostility, CHD incidence and total mortality: A 25-year follow-up study of 255 physicians. *Psychosomatic Medicine, 45,* 559–563.

Barefoot, J. C., Dodge, K. A., Peterson, B. L., Dahlstrom, W. G., & Williams, R. B. (1989). The Cook-Medley hostility scale: Item content and ability to predict survival. *Psychosomatic Medicine, 51,* 46–57.

Barker, R. G., Dembo, T., & Lewin, K. (1941). Frustration and regression: An experiment with young children. *University of Iowa Studies in Child Welfare, 18*(1).

Baron, J. (1988). *Thinking and deciding.* New York: Cambridge University Press.

Baron, M., Gershon, E. S., Rudy, V., Jonas, W. Z., & Buchsbaum, M. (1975). Lithium carbonate response in depression. *Archives of General Psychiatry, 32,* 1107–1111.

Baron, R. A. (1976). The reduction of human aggression: A field study of the influence of incompatible reactions. *Journal of Applied Social Psychology, 6,* 260–274.

Baron, R. A. (1977). *Human aggression.* New York: Plenum.

Baron, R. A., & Byrne, D. (1991). *Social psychology: Understanding human interaction* (6th ed.). Boston: Allyn & Bacon.

Baron, R. A., & Richardson, D. R. (1992). *Human aggression* (2nd ed.). New York: Plenum.

Baron, R. S. (1986). Distraction-conflict theory: Progress and problems. In L. Berkowitz (Ed.), *Advances in experimental social psychology.* Orlando, FL: Academic Press.

Barr, H. M., Streissguth, A. P., Darby, B. L., & Sampson, P. D. (1990). Prenatal exposure to alcohol, caffeine, tobacco, and aspirin: Effects on fine and gross motor performance in 4-year-old children. *Developmental Psychology, 26,* 339–348.

Barrett, P. T., & Eysenck, H. J. (1992). Brain evoked potentials and intelligence: The Hendrickson paradigm. *Intelligence, 16*(3, 4), 361–381.

Barron, F. (1988). Putting creativity to work. In R. J. Sternberg (Ed.), *The nature of creativity* (pp. 76–98). New York: Cambridge University Press.

Bartlett, F. C. (1932). *Remembering: A study in experimental and social psychology.* Cambridge, England: Cambridge University Press.

Bartoshuk, L. M. (1991). Sensory factors in eating behavior. 31st annual meeting of the Psychonomic Society: Symposium on experimental approaches to eating and its disorders (1990, New Orleans, Louisiana). *Bulletin of the Psychonomic Society, 29*(3), 250–255.

Bartoshuk, L. M., Duffy, V. B., & Miller, I. J. (1994). PTC/PROP taste: Anatomy, psychophysics, and sex effects. Kirin International Symposium: On bitter taste (1993, Tokyo, Japan), *Physiology & Behavior, 56*(6), 1165–1171.

Bashore, T. R., Osman, A., & Hefley, E. F. (1989). Mental slowing in elderly persons: A cognitive psychophysiological analysis. *Psychology and Aging, 4,* 235–244.

Bashore, T. R., & Rapp, P. E. (1993). Are there alternatives to traditional polygraph procedures? *Psychological Bulletin, 113*(1), 3–22.

Basow, S. A. (1986). *Gender stereotypes: Traditions and alternatives* (2nd ed.). Belmont, CA: Brooks/Cole.

Baumrind, D. (1986). Sex differences in moral reasoning: Response to Walker's (1984) conclusion that there are none. *Child Development, 57,* 511–521.

Bayley, N. (1968). Behavioral correlates of mental growth: Birth to thirty-six years. *American Psychologist, 23,* 1–17.

Beall, A., & Sternberg, R. J. (Eds.) (1993). *Perspectives on the psychology of gender.* New York: The Guilford Press.

Beck, A. T. (1976). *Cognitive therapy and the emotional disorders.* New York: International Universities Press.

Beck, A. T. (1986). Cognitive therapy: A sign of retrogression of progress. *The Behavior Therapist, 9,* 2–3.

Beck, A. (1988). Cognitive approaches to panic disorder: Theory and therapy. In S. Rachman & J. D. Maser (Eds.), *Panic: Psychological perspectives.* Hillsdale, NJ: Erlbaum.

Bekerian, D. A. (1993). In search of the typical eyewitness. *American Psychologist, 48*(5), 574–576.

Bellack, A. S., Hersen, M., & Kazdin, A. E. (Eds.) (1990). *International handbook of behavior modification and therapy* (2nd ed.). New York: Plenum.

Belloc, N. D., & Breslow, L. (1972). Relationship of physical health status and family practices. *Preventive Medicine, 1,* 409–421.

Bellugi, U., Poizner, H., & Klima, E. S. (1989). Language, modality and the brain. *Trends in Neuroscience, 12*(10), 380–388.

Belsky, J. (1990). Parental and nonparental child care and children's socioemotional development: A decade in review. *Journal of Marriage and the Family, 52,* 885–903.

Bem, D. J. (1967). Self-perception: An alternative interpretation of cognitive dissonance phenomena. *Psychological Review, 74,* 183–200.

Bem, D. J. (1972). Self perception theory. In L. Berkowitz (Ed.), *Advances in experimental social psychology* (Vol. 6). New York: Academic Press.

Bem, D. J., & Allen, A. (1974). On predicting some of the people some of the time: The search for cross-situational consistencies in behavior. *Psychological Review, 81,* 506–520.

Bem, S. L. (1981). Gender schema theory: A cognitive account of sex typing. *Psychological Review, 88,* 354–364.

Benbow, C. P., & Stanley, J. C. (1980). Sex differences in mathematical ability: Fact or artifact? *Science, 210,* 1262–1264.

Ben-Shakhar, G., & Furedy, J. J. (1990). *Theories and applications in the detection of deception: A psychophysiological and international perspective.* New York: Springer-Verlag.

Benson, H. (1977). Systemic hypertension and the relaxation response. *New England Journal of Medicine, 296,* 1152–1156.

Berger, K. S. (1980). *The developing person.* New York: Worth.

Berglas, S., & Jones, E. E. (1978). Drug choice as a self-handicapping strategy in response to noncontingent success. *Journal of Personality and Social Psychology, 36,* 405–417.

Berkman, L. (1994, May 22). "I really was hurt by the verdict." (Holly Ramona says jury's decision will undermine her attempt to recover damages from her father, Gary Ramona, who she alleges molested her). *Los Angeles Times,* p. A3.

Berkowitz, L., Cochran, S., & Embree, M. (1981). Physical pain and the goal of aversively stimulated aggression. *Journal of Personality and Social Psychology, 40,* 687–700.

Berkowitz, L., & Geen, R. G. (1966). Film violence and the cue properties of variable targets. *Journal of Personality and Social Psychology, 3,* 525–530.

Berkowitz, L., & Geen, R. G. (1967). Stimulus qualities of the target of aggression: A further study. *Journal of Personality and Social Psychology, 5,* 364–368.

Berlin, B., & Kay, P. (1969). *Basic color terms: Their universality and evolution.* Los Angeles: University of California Press.

Berlyne, D. E. (1960). *Conflict, arousal, and curiosity.* New York: McGraw-Hill.

Berlyne, D. E. (1967). Arousal reinforcement. In D. Levine (Ed.), *Nebraska Symposium on Motivation* (pp. 1–110). Lincoln, NE: University of Nebraska Press.

Bernard, L. L. (1924). *Instinct.* New York: Holt, Rinehart and Winston.

Berry, D. S., & McArthur, L. Z. (1986). Perceiving character in faces: The impact of age-related craniofacial changes on social perception. *Psychological Bulletin, 100*(1), 3–18.

Berry, J. W., Poortinga, Y. H., Segall, M. H., & Dasen, P. R. (1992). *Cross-cultural psychology.* New York: Cambridge University Press.

Berry, S. L., Beatty, W. W., & Klesges, R. C. (1985). Sensory and social influences on ice cream consumption by males and females in a laboratory setting. *Appetite, 6,* 41–45.

Bexton, W. H., Heron, W., & Scott, T. H. (1954). Effects of decreased variation in the sensory environment. *Canadian Journal of Psychology, 8,* 70–76.

Bezooijen, R. V., Otto, S. A., & Heenan, T. A. (1983). Recognition of vocal expressions of emotion: A three nation study to identify universal characteristics. *Journal of Cross-Cultural Psychology, 14,* 387–406.

Bialystok, E., & Hakuta, K. (1994). *In other words: The science and psychology of second-language acquisition.* New York: Basic Books.

Biederman, I. (1987). Recognition-by-components: A theory of human image understanding. *Psychological Review, 94,* 115–147.

Biery, R. E. (1990). *Understanding homosexuality: The pride and the prejudice.* Austin, TX: Edward-William.

Binet, A., & Simon, T. (1916). *The development of intelligence in children* (E. S. Kite, Trans.). Baltimore: Williams & Wilkins.

Block, J. (1981). Some enduring and consequential structures of personality. In A. I. Rabin, J. Arnoff, A. M. Barclay, & R. A. Zucker (Eds.), *Further explorations in personality.* New York: Wiley.

Block, J. (1995). A contrarian view of the five-factor approach to personality description. *Psychological Bulletin, 117*(2), 187–215.

Block, M. A. (1970). Alcohol: Man and science. *New York State Journal of Medicine, 70*(21), 2732–2740.

Bloom, A. (1993). Silver water. In A. Bloom, *Come to me* (pp. 87–98), New York: HarperCollins.

Bloom, B. S. (1964). *Stability and change in human characteristics.* New York: Wiley.

Blumenthal, J. A., Emery, C. F., Walsh, M. A., Cox, D. R., Kuhn, C. M., Williams, R. B., & Williams, R. S. (1988). Exercise training in healthy Type A middle-aged men: Effects to behavioral and cardiovascular responses. *Psychosomatic Medicine, 50,* 418–433.

Bolger, N., & Eckenrode, J. (1991). Social relationships, personality, and anxiety during a major stressful event. *Journal of Personality & Social Psychology, 61*(3), 440–449.

Bolwig, T. G. (1993). Biological treatments other than drugs (electroconvulsive therapy, brain surgery, insulin therapy, and photo therapy). In N. Sartorius, G. de Girolano, G. Andrews, G. A. German, & L. Eisenberg (Eds.), *Treatment of mental disorders: A review of effectiveness.* Geneva, Switzerland, and Washington, DC: World Health Organization and American Psychiatric Press.

Bond, M. H. (Ed.) (1988). *The cross-cultural challenge to social psychology.* Newbury Park, CA: Sage.

Bond, M. R. (1979). *Pain: Its nature, analysis and treatment.* New York: Longman.

Bongiovanni, A. (1977). *A review of research on the effects of punishment in the schools.* Paper presented at the Conference on Child Abuse, Children's Hospital National Medical Center, Washington, DC.

Booth-Kewley, S., & Friedman, H. S. (1987). Psychological predictors of heart disease: A quantitative review. *Psychological Bulletin, 101,* 343–362.

Borbely, A. (1986). *Secrets of sleep.* New York: Basic Books.

Bornstein, M. H., & Bruner, J. S. (Eds.) (1989). *Interaction on human development: Crosscurrents in contemporary psychology services.* Hillsdale, NJ: Erlbaum.

Bornstein, M. H., & Krasgenor, N. A. (Eds.) (1989). *Stability and continuity in mental development: Behavioral and biological perspectives.* Hillsdale, NJ: Erlbaum.

Borysenko, M., & Borysenko, J. (1982). Stress, behavior, and immunity: Animal models and mediating mechanisms. *General Hospital Psychiatry, 4,* 59–67.

Bothwell, R. K., Brigham, J. C., & Malpass, R. S. (1989). Cross-racial identification. *Personality & Social Psychology Bulletin, 15*(1), 19–25.

Bower, G. H. (1981, February). Mood and memory. *American Psychologist, 36*(2), 129–148.

Bower, G. H. (1983). Affect and cognition. *Philosophical Transaction: Royal Society of London* (Series B), *302,* 387–402.

Bower, G. H., Karlin, M. B., & Dueck, A. (1975). Comprehension and memory for pictures. *Memory and Cognition, 3,* 216–220.

Bowers, K. S. (1973). Situationism in psychology: An analysis and critique. *Psychological Review, 80,* 307–336.

Bowers, K. S. (1976). *Hypnosis for the seriously curious.* New York: Norton.

Bransford, J. D., & Johnson, M. K. (1972). Contextual prerequisites for understanding: Some investigations of comprehension and recall. *Journal of Verbal Learning and Verbal Behavior, 11,* 717–726.

Braswell, L., & Kendall, P. C. (1988). Cognitive-behavioral methods with children. In K. S. Dobson (Ed.), *Handbook of cognitive-behavioral therapies.* New York: The Guilford Press.

Brazelton, T. B. (1983). Precursors for the development of emotions in early infancy. In R. Plutchik & H. Kellerman (Eds.), *Emotion: Theory, research, and experience* (Vol. 2). New York: Academic Press.

Brehm, J. (1966). *A theory of psychological reactance.* New York: Academic Press.

Brehm, S. S., & Brehm, J. W. (1981). *Psychological reactance: A theory of freedom and control.* New York: Academic Press.

Brehm, S. S., & Kassin, S. M. (1990). *Social psychology.* Boston: Houghton Mifflin.

Breslow, L. (1983). The potential of health promotion. In D. Mechanic (Ed.), *Handbook of health, health care, and the health professions.* New York: The Free Press.

Brigham, J. C., & Malpass, R. S. (1985). The role of experience and contact in the recognition of faces of own- and other-race persons. *Journal of Social Issues, 41*(3), 139–155.

Brislin, R. W. (1986). The wording and translation of research instruments. In W. J. Lonner & J. W. Berry (Eds.), *Field methods in cross-cultural research.* Newbury Park, CA: Sage.

Broadhurst, P. L. (1957). Emotionality and the Yerkes–Dodson law. *Journal of Experimental Psychology, 54,* 345–352.

Brosschot, J. F., Benschop, R. J., Godaert, G. L. R., Olff, M., et al. (1994). Influence of life stress on immunological reactivity to mild psychological stress. *Psychosomatic Medicine, 56*(3), 216–224.

Brown, J. A. (1958). Some tests of the decay theory of immediate memory. *Quarterly Journal of Experimental Psychology, 10,* 12–21.

Brown, R. (1965). *Social psychology.* New York: The Free Press.

Brown, R., & McNeill, D. (1966). The "tip of the tongue" phenomenon. *Journal of Verbal Learning and Verbal Behavior, 5,* 325–337.

Bruch, H. (1973). *Eating disorders: Obesity, anorexia nervosa, and the person within.* New York: Basic Books.

Bruning, N. S., & Frew, D. R. (1987). Effects of exercise, relaxation, and management skills training on physiological stress indicators: A field experiment. *Journal of Applied Psychology, 72*(4), 515–521.

Burger, J. M. (1986). Increasing compliance by improving the deal: The that's-not-all technique. *Journal of Personality and Social Psychology, 51,* 277–283.

Burleson, B. R., & Denton, W. H. (1992). A new look at similarity and attraction in marriage: Similarities in social-cognitive and communication skills as predictors of attraction and satisfaction. *Communication Monographs, 59*(3), 268–287.

Burns, J. W., Hutt, J., & Weidner, G. (1993). Effects of demand and decision latitude on cardiovascular reactivity among coronary-prone women and men. *Behavioral Medicine, 19*(3), 122–128.

Burnstein, E., & Vinokur, A. (1973). Testing two classes of theories about group-induced shifts in individual choice. *Journal of Experimental Social Psychology, 9,* 123–137.

Burnstein, E., & Vinokur, A. (1977). Persuasive arguments and social comparison as determinates of attitude polarization. *Journal of Experimental Social Psychology, 13,* 315–332.

Buss, A. H. (1976). Aggression pays. In J. L. Singer (Ed.), *The control of aggression and violence: Cognitive and physiological factors.* New York: Academic Press.

Butcher, J. N., Dahlstrom, W. G., Graham, J. R., Tellegen, A., & Kaemmer, B. (1989). *Minnesota Multiphasic Personality Inventory: MMPI-2: Manual for administration and scoring.* Minneapolis, MN: University of Minnesota Press.

Butcher, J. N., & Williams, C. L. (1992). *Essentials of MMPI-2 and MMPI-A interpretation.* Minneapolis, MN: University of Minnesota Press.

Butler, J., & Rovee-Collier, C. (1989). Contextual gating of memory retrieval. *Developmental Psychobiology, 22,* 533–552.

Butler, R. A. (1953). Discrimination learning by rhesus monkeys to visual exploration motivation. *Journal of Comparative and Physiological Psychology, 46,* 95–98.

Byrnes, J. P. (1988). Formal operations: A systematic reformulation. *Developmental Review, 8,* 66–87.

Cacioppo, J. T., & Petty, R. E. (1983). *Social psychophysiology: A sourcebook.* New York: The Guilford Press.

Candland, D. K. (1977). The persistent problems of emotion. In D. K. Candland, J. P. Fell, E. Keen, A. I. Leshner, R. Plutchik, & R. M. Tarpy (Eds.), *Emotion* (pp. 1–84). Monterey, CA: Brooks/Cole.

Cannon, W. B. (1929). *Bodily changes in pain, hunger, fear, and rage, on account of recent researches into the function of emotional excitement* (2nd ed.). New York: Appleton.

Cantor, J., & Engle, R. W. (1993). Working memory capacity as long-term memory activation: An individual differences approach. *Journal of Experimental Psychology: Learning, Memory, and Cognition, 19*(5), 1101–1114.

Carlson, G., & Goodwin, F. K. (1973). The stages of mania: A longitudinal analysis of the manic episode. *Archives of General Psychiatry, 28*(2), 221–228.

Carlson, J. G., & Hatfield, E. (1992). *Psychology of emotion.* New York: Harcourt Brace Jovanovich.

Carraher, T. N., Carraher, D., & Schliemann, A. D. (1985). Mathematics in the streets and in the schools. *British Journal of Developmental Psychology, 3,* 21–29.

Carroll, D. W. (1986). *Psychology of language.* Monterey, CA: Brooks/Cole.

Carroll, J. B. (1993). *Human cognitive abilities: A survey of factor-analytic studies.* New York: Cambridge University Press.

Carson, R. C., & Butcher, J. N. (1992). *Abnormal psychology and modern life* (9th ed.). New York: HarperCollins.

Caspi, A., Bolger, N., & Eckenrode, J. (1987). Linking person and context in the daily stress process. *Journal of Personality & Social Psychology, 52*(1), 184–195.

Cattell, R. B. (1971). *Abilities and their structure, growth and action.* Boston: Houghton Mifflin.

Cattell, R. B. (1979). *Personality and learning theory.* New York: Springer.

Cattell, R. B. (1982). *The inheritance of personality and ability: Research methods and findings.* New York: Academic Press.

Cattell, R. B., Eber, H. W., & Tatsuoka, M. M. (1970). *Handbook for the Sixteen Personality Factor Questionnaire.* Champaign, IL: Institute for Personality and Ability Testing.

Ceci, S. J. (1990). *On intelligence . . . more or less.* Englewood Cliffs, NJ: Prentice-Hall.

Ceci, S. J. (1991). How much does schooling influence general intelligence and its cognitive components? A reassessment of the evidence. *Developmental Psychology, 27*(5), 703–722.

Ceci, S. J., Bronfenbrenner, U., & Baker, J. G. (1988). Prospective remembering, temporal calibration, and context. In M. M. Grunberg, P. Morris, & U. R. Sykes (Eds.), *Practical aspects of memory: Current research and issues.* New York: Wiley.

Ceci, S. J., Nightingale, N. N., & Baker, J. G. (1992). In D. K. Detterman (Ed.), *Current topics in human intelligence: Vol. 2. Is mind modular or unitary?* (pp. 61–82). Norwood, NJ: Ablex.

Ceci, S. J., & Roazzi, A. (1994). The effects of context on cognition: Postcards from Brazil. In R. J. Sternberg & R. K. Wagner (Eds.), *Minds in context: Interactionist perspectives on human intelligence.* New York: Cambridge University Press.

Cerella, J. (1985). Information processing rates in the elderly. *Psychological Bulletin, 98,* 67–83.

Chaiken, S., & Eagly, A. (1983). Communication modality as a determinant of persuasion: The role of communicator salience. *Journal of Personality and Social Psychology, 45,* 241–256.

Chapman, L. J., & Chapman, J. P. (1969). Illusory correlation as an obstacle to the use of valid psychodiagnostic signs. *Journal of Abnormal Psychology, 74,* 271–280.

Chase, W. G., & Simon, H. A. (1973). The mind's eye in chess. In W. G. Chase (Ed.), *Visual information processing* (pp. 215–281). New York: Academic Press.

Chasnoff, I. J., Griffith, D. R., MacGregor, S., Dirkes, K., & Burns, K. (1989). Temporal patterns of cocaine use in pregnancy. *Journal of the American Medical Association, 261,* 1741–1744.

Cherry, E. C. (1953). Some experiments on the recognition of speech with one and two ears. *Journal of the Acoustical Society of America, 25,* 975–979.

Chi, M. T. H., Glaser, R., & Farr, M. (Eds.) (1988). *The nature of expertise.* Hillsdale, NJ: Erlbaum.

Chi, M. T. H., & Koeske, R. D. (1983). Network representations of a child's dinosaur knowledge. *Developmental Psychology, 19,* 29–39.

Chomsky, N. (1957). *Synactic structures.* The Hague, The Netherlands: Mouton.

Chomsky, N. (1959). [Review of *Verbal behavior,* by B. F. Skinner]. *Language, 35,* 26–58.

Cialdini, R. B. (1988). *Influence: Science and practice* (2nd ed.). Glenview, IL: Scott, Foresman/Little, Brown.

Cialdini, R. B., Cacioppo, J. R., Bassett, R., & Miller, J. A. (1978). Lowball procedure for producing compliance: Commitment and cost. *Journal of Personality and Social Psychology, 36,* 463–476.

Cialdini, R. B., Vincent, J. E., Lewis, S. K., Catalan, J., Wheeler, D., & Darby, B. L. (1975). Reciprocal concessions procedure for inducing compliance: The door-in-the-face technique. *Journal of Personality and Social Psychology, 31,* 206–215.

Ciompi, L., & Eisert, M. (1969). Mortality and causes of death in alcoholics. *Social Psychiatry, 4*(4), 159–168.

Clark, H. H., & Chase, W. G. (1972). On the process of comparing sentences against pictures. *Cognitive Psychology, 3,* 472–517.

Clark, H. H., & Clark, E. V. (1977). *Psychology and language: An introduction to psycholinguistics.* New York: Harcourt Brace Jovanovich.

Clarke-Stewart, K. A. (1989). Infant day care: Maligned or malignant? *American Psychologist, 44,* 266–273.

Clore, G. L., & Byrne, D. (1974). A reinforcement–affect model of attraction. In T. L. Huston (Ed.), *Foundations of interpersonal attraction* (pp. 143–170). New York: Academic Press.

Cofer, C. N., & Appley, M. H. (1964). *Motivation: Theory and research.* New York: Wiley.

Cohen, J. (1981). Can human irrationality be experimentally demonstrated? *Behavioral and Brain Sciences, 4,* 317–331.

Cohen, N., Moynihan, J. A., Grota, L. J., & Ader, R. (1991). Behavioral and immunological evidence of reciprocal signaling between the immune system and the central nervous system. In R. C. A. Frederickson, J. L. McGaugh, & D. L. Felten (Eds.), *Peripheral signaling of the brain: Role in neural–immune interactions and learning and memory: Vol. 6. Neuronal control of bodily function: Basic and clinical aspects* (pp. 37–54). Lewiston, NY: Hogrefe & Huber.

Cohen, S., Kamarck, T., & Mermelstein, R. (1983). A global measure of perceived stress. *Journal of Health & Social Behavior, 24*(4), 385–396.

Cole, J. O., & Bodkin, J. A. (1990). Antidepressant drug side effects. *Journal of Clinical Psychiatry, 51,* 21–26.

Cole, M., Gay, J., Glick, J., & Sharp, D. W. (1971). *The cultural context of learning and thinking.* New York: Basic Books.

Collier, G. (1994). *Social origins of mental ability.* New York: Wiley.

Condry, J. (1977). Enemies of exploration: Self-initiated versus other-initiated learning. *Journal of Personality and Social Psychology, 18,* 105–115.

Conrad, R. (1964). Acoustic confusions in immediate memory. *British Journal of Psychology, 55,* 75–84.

Cooper, J., Zanna, M. P., & Taves, P. A. (1978). Arousal as a necessary condition for attitude change following induced compliance. *Journal of Personality and Social Psychology, 36,* 1101–1106.

Cooper, V. M. (1994, May 3). Need a job? Find a problem you can solve. *Christian Science Monitor, 76,* p. 36.

Corcoran, E. (1993, February 21). Computers, cultures and solving problems. *The Washington Post, 116,* p. H6.

Corina, D. P., Poizner, H., Bellugi, U., Feinberg, T., et al. (1992a). Dissociation between linguistic and nonlinguistic gestural systems: A case for compositionality. *Brain & Language, 43*(3), 414–447.

Corina, D. P., Vaid, J., Bellugi, U. (1992b). The linguistic basis of left hemisphere specialization. *Science 255*(5049), 1258–1260.

Costa, P. T., & McCrae, R. R. (1992a). Four ways five factors are basic. *Personality & Individual Differences, 13*(6), 653–665.

Costa, P. T., & McCrae, R. R. (1992b). "Four ways five factors are not basic": Reply. *Personality & Individual Differences, 13*(8), 861–865.

Craik, F. I. M., & Lockhart, R. S. (1972). Levels of processing: A framework for memory research. *Journal of Verbal Learning and Verbal Behavior, 11,* 671–684.

Crick, F., & Mitchison, G. (1983). The function of dream sleep. *Nature, 304,* 111–114.

Cross-National Collaborative Group. (1992). The changing rate of major depression. *Journal of the American Medical Association, 268*(21), 3098–3105.

Crowder, R. G. (1976). *Principles of learning and memory.* Hillsdale, NJ: Erlbaum.

Csikszentmihalyi, M. (1988). Society, culture, and person: A systems view of creativity. In R. J. Sternberg (Ed.), *The nature of creativity* (pp. 325–339). New York: Cambridge University Press.

Cummins, J. (1976). The influence of bilingualism on cognitive growth: A synthesis of research findings and explanatory hypothesis. *Working Papers on Bilingualism, 9,* 1–43.

Damon, W., & Hart, D. (1982). The development of self-understanding from childhood to adolescence. *Child Development, 53,* 841–864.

Daneman, M., & Carpenter, P. A. (1980). Individual differences in working memory and reading. *Journal of Verbal Learning and Verbal Behavior, 19,* 450–466.

Daneman, M., & Tardif, T. (1987). Working memory and reading skill reexamined. In M. Coltheart (Ed.), *Attention and performance: Vol. 12. The psychology of reading* (pp. 491–508). Hove, England: Erlbaum.

Darwin, C. (1859). *Origin of species.* London: John Murray.

Davidson, G. C., & Neale, J. M. (1994). *Abnormal psychology* (6th ed.). New York: Wiley.

Davidson, R. J., & Schwartz, G. E. (1976). Psychobiology of relaxation and related states: A multiprocess theory. In D. Mostofsky (Ed.), *Behavior modification and control of physiologic activity.* Englewood Cliffs, NJ: Prentice-Hall.

Dawes, R. M. (1994). *House of cards.* New York: The Free Press.

DeAngelis, T. (1992, May). Senate seeks answers to rising tide of violence. *APA Monitor,* p. 11.

DeCasper, A. J., & Fifer, W. P. (1980). Of human bonding: Newborns prefer their mothers' voices. *Science, 208,* 1174–1176.

DeCasper, A. J., & Spence, M. J. (1986). Prenatal maternal speech influences newborns' perception of speech sounds. *Infant Behavior and Development, 9,* 133–150.

deCastro, J. M., & Brewer, E. M. (1992). The amount eaten in meals by humans is a power function of the number of people present. *Physiology and Behavior, 51,* 121–125.

deCharms, R. (1968). *Personal causation: The internal affective determinants of behavior.* New York: Academic Press.

Deci, E. L. (1971). Effects of externally mediated rewards on intrinsic motivation. *Journal of Personality and Social Psychology, 18,* 105–115.

Deci, E. L., Vallerand, R. J., Pelletier, L. G., & Ryan, R. M. (1991). Motivation and education: The self-determination perspective. *Educational Psychologist, 26*(3, 4), 325–346.

De Jong, W. (1979). An examination of self-perception mediation of the foot-in-the-door effect. *Journal of Personality and Social Psychology, 37,* 2221–2239.

Delgado, J. M. R., Roberts, W. W., & Miller, N. E. (1954). Learning motivated by electrical stimulation of the brain. *American Journal of Physiology, 179,* 587–593.

DeLongis, A., Folkman, S., & Lazarus, R. S. (1988). The impact of daily stress on health and mood: Psychological and social resources as mediators. *Journal of Personality and Social Psychology, 54*(3), 486–495.

Dembroski, T. M, & Costa, P. T. (1988). Assessment of coronary-prone behavior: A current overview. *Annals of Behavioral Medicine, 10,* 60–63.

Dembroski, T. M., MacDougall, J. M., Williams, R. B., Haney, T. L., & Blumenthal, J. A. (1985). Components of Type A, hostility, and anger in relationship to angiographic findings. *Psychosomatic Medicine, 47,* 219–233.

Dement, W. C. (1976). *Some must watch while some must sleep.* New York: Norton.

Dement, W. C., & Kleitman, N. (1957). The relation of eye movements during sleep to dream activity: An objective method for the study of dreaming. *Journal of Experimental Psychology, 55,* 543–553.

Denny, N. W. (1980). Task demands and problem-solving strategies in middle-aged and older adults. *Journal of Gerontology, 35,* 559–564.

Derryberry, D., & Tucker, D. M. (1992). Neural mechanisms of emotion. *Journal of Consulting and Clinical Psychology, 60,* 329–338.

Detterman, D. K., & Sternberg, R. J. (Eds.) (1982). *How and how much can intelligence be increased?* Norwood, NJ: Ablex.

Devine, P. G., Monteith, M. J., Zuwerink, J. R., & Elliot, A. J. (1991). Prejudice with and without compunction. *Journal of Personality and Social Psychology, 60*(6), 817–830.

Dienstbier, R. A. (1989). Arousal and physiological toughness: Implications for mental and physical health. *Psychological Review, 96*(1), 84–100.

Digman, J. M. (1990). Personality structure: Emergence of the five-factor model. *Annual Review of Psychology, 41,* 417–440.

Dittes, J. E., & Kelley, H. H. (1956). Effects of different conditions of acceptance upon conformity to group norms. *Journal of Abnormal and Social Psychology, 53*, 100–107.

Docherty, J. (1993, May 23). Pay for mental health care—and save. *The New York Times*, Sect. 3, p. 13.

Dohrenwend, B. P., Levav, I., Schwartz, S., Naveh, G., Link, B. G., Skodol, A. G., & Stueve, A. (1992). Socioeconomic status and psychiatric disorders: The causation-selection issue. *Science, 255*, 946–952.

Dohrenwend, B. S., & Dohrenwend, B. P. (1974). *Stressful life events.* New York: Wiley.

Dolan, M. (1995, February 11). When the mind's eye blinks. *Los Angeles Times, 114*, pp. A1, A24, A25.

Dollard, J, Miller, N., Doob, L., Mowrer, O. H., & Sears, R. R. (1939). *Frustration and aggression.* New Haven, CT: Institute of Human Relations, Yale University Press.

Donnerstein, E., & Donnerstein, M. (1976). Research in the control of interracial aggression. In R. G. Geen & E. C. O'Neal (Eds.), *Perspectives on aggression* (pp. 133–168). New York: Academic Press.

Douglas, J. D. (1967). *The social meanings of suicide.* Princeton, NJ: Princeton University Press.

Duke, L. (1992, December 16). Poll of Latinos counters perceptions on language, immigration. *The Washington Post, 116*, p. A4.

Duncker, K. (1945). On problem-solving. *Psychological Monographs, 58*(5, Whole No. 270).

Durlach, N. I., & Colburn, H. S. (1978). Binaural phenomenon. In E. C. Carterette & M. P. Friedman (Eds.), *Handbook of perception* (Vol. 4). New York: Academic Press.

Dyal, J. A. (1984). Cross-cultural research with the locus of control concept. In H. Lefcourt (Ed.), *Research with the locus of control construct: Vol. 3. Extensions and limitations.* San Diego, CA: Academic Press.

Eagly, A. H., & Chaiken, S. (1975). An attribution analysis of communicator attractiveness. *Journal of Personality and Social Psychology, 32*, 136–144.

Eagly, A. H., Makhijani, M. G., & Klonsky, B. G. (1992). Gender and the evaluation of leaders: A meta-analysis. *Psychological Bulletin, 111*(1), 3–22.

Early, P. C. (1989). Social loafing and collectivism: A comparison of the United States and the People's Republic of China. *Administrative Science Quarterly, 34*, 565–581.

Ebbinghaus, H. E. (1964). *Memory: A contribution to experimental psychology.* New York: Dover. (Original work published 1885)

Edgerton, R. (1967). *The cloak of competence.* Berkeley, CA: University of California Press.

Edmonston, W. E., Jr. (1981). *Hypnosis and relaxation.* New York: Wiley.

Egeth, H. E. (1993). What do we *not* know about eyewitness identification? *American Psychologist, 48*(5), 577–580.

Ekman, P. (1971). Universals and cultural differences in the facial expression of emotion. In J. Cole (Ed.), *Nebraska Symposium on Motivation* (Vol. 19, pp. 207–284). Lincoln, NE: University of Nebraska Press.

Ekman, P. (1984). Expression and the nature of emotion. In P. Ekman & K. Scherer (Eds.), *Approaches to emotion* (pp. 319–343). Hillsdale, NJ: Erlbaum.

Ekman, P. (1993). Facial expression and emotion. *American Psychologist, 48*, 384–392.

Ekman, P., & Friesen, W. V. (1975). *Unmasking the face.* Englewood Cliffs, NJ: Prentice-Hall.

Ekman, P., Levenson, R. W., & Friesen, W. V. (1983). Autonomic nervous system activity distinguishes among emotions. *Science, 221*, 1208–1210.

Ekman, P., & Oster, H. (1979). Facial expression of emotion. *Annual Review of Psychology, 30*, 527–554.

Elkind, D. (1967). Egocentrism in adolescence. *Child Development, 38*, 1025–1034.

Elkind, D. (1981). Recent research in cognitive and language development. In L. T. Benjamin, Jr. (Ed.), *The G. Stanley Hall lecture series* (Vol. 1). Washington, DC: American Psychological Association.

Elkind, D. (1985). Egocentrism redux. *Developmental Review, 5*, 218–226.

Ellis, A. (1962). *Reason and emotion in psychotherapy.* Secaucus, NJ: Lyle Stuart.

Ellis, A. (1970). *Reason and emotion in psychotherapy.* New York: Lyle Stuart.

Ellis, A. (1973). Rational-emotive therapy. In R. J. Corsini (Ed.), *Current psychotherapies.* Itasca, IL: Peacock.

Ellis, A. (1989). The history of cognition in psychotherapy. In A. Freeman, K. M. Simon, L. E. Beutler, & H. Arkowitz (Eds.), *Comprehensive handbook of cognitive therapy* (pp. 5–19). New York: Plenum.

Endler, N. S., & Magnusson, D. (1976). Toward an interactional psychology of personality. *Psychological Bulletin, 83*, 956–974.

Engle, R. W. (1994). Individual differences in memory and their implications for learning. In R. J. Sternberg (Ed.), *Encyclopedia of intelligence.* New York: Macmillan.

Engle, R. W., Cantor, J., & Carullo, J. J. (1992). Individual differences in working memory and comprehension: A test of four hypotheses. *Journal of Experimental Psychology: Learning, Memory, and Cognition, 18*(5), 972–992.

Engle, R. W., Carullo, J. J., & Collins, K. W. (1992). Individual differences in working memory for comprehension and following directions. *Journal of Educational Research, 84*(5), 253–262.

Ericsson, K. A., Chase, W. G., & Faloon, S. (1980). Acquisition of a memory skill. *Science, 208*, 1181–1182.

Erikson, E. H. (1963). *Childhood and society* (2nd ed.). New York: Norton.

Erikson, E. H. (1968). *Identity, youth, and crisis.* New York: Norton.

Exner, J. E. (1974). *The Rorschach: A comprehensive system* (Vol. 1). New York: Wiley.

Exner, J. E. (1978). *The Rorschach: A comprehensive system (Vol. 2). Current research and advanced interpretation.* New York: Wiley.

Exner, J. E. (1985). *The Rorschach: A comprehensive system* (Vol. 1, 2nd ed.). New York: Wiley.

Eysenck, H. J. (1952). *The scientific study of personality.* London: Routledge & Kegan Paul.

Eysenck, H. J. (Ed.) (1981). *A model for personality.* New York: Springer.

Eysenck, H. J. (1984). Intelligence versus behaviour. *The Behavioral and Brain Sciences, 7*(12), 290–291.

Eysenck, H. J., & Kamin, L. (1981). *The intelligence controversy: H. J. Eysenck vs. Leon Kamin.* New York: Wiley.

Faber, M. D. (1970). Allport's visit with Freud. *The Psychoanalytic Review, 57*, 60–64.

Falco, M. (1992). *The making of a drug-free America: Programs that work.* New York: Times Books.

Fantz, R. L. (1958). Pattern vision in young infants. *Psychological Record, 8*, 43–47.

Fantz, R. L. (1961). The origin of form perception. *Scientific American, 204*, 66–72.

Farah, M. J. (1988). The neuropsychology of mental imagery: Converging evidence from brain-damaged and normal subjects. In J. Stiles-Davis, M. Kritchevsky, & U. Bellugi (Eds.), *Spatial cognition: Brain bases and development* (pp. 33–56). Hillsdale, NJ: Erlbaum.

Farne, M. A., Boni, P., Corallo, A., Gnugnoli, D., et al. (1994). Personality variables as moderators between hassles and objective indications of distress (S-IgA). *Stress Medicine, 10*(1), 15–20.

Fay, R. E., Turner, C. F., Klassen, A. D., & Gagnon, J. H. (1989). Prevalence and patterns of same-gender sexual contact among men. *Science, 1989, 243*, 338–348.

Fazio, R. H., Zanna, M. P., & Cooper, J. (1977). Dissonance and self-perception: An integrative view of each theory's proper domain of application. *Journal of Experimental Social Psychology, 13*, 464–479.

Feist, J. (1990). *Theories of personality* (3rd ed.). Fort Worth, TX: Holt, Rinehart and Winston.

Fernandez, E., & Turk, D. C. (1992). Sensory and affective components of pain: Separation and synthesis. *Psychological Bulletin, 112*(2), 205–217.

Feshbach, S. (1970). Aggression. In P. H. Mussen (Ed.), *Carmichael's manual of child psychology.* New York: Wiley.

Festinger, L., & Carlsmith, J. M. (1959). Cognitive consequences of forced compliance. *Journal of Abnormal and Social Psychology, 58*, 203–210.

Festinger, L., Pepitone, A., & Newcomb, T. (1952). Some consequences of de-individuation in a group. *Journal of Abnormal and Social Psychology, 47,* 382–389.

Festinger, L., Schachter, S., & Back, K. (1950). *Social pressures in informal groups: A study of human factors in housing.* New York: Harper & Brothers.

Feuerstein, R. (1980). *Instrumental enrichment: An intervention program for cognitive modifiability.* Baltimore: University Park Press.

Field, T. (1978). Interaction behaviors of primary versus secondary caregiver fathers. *Developmental Psychology, 14,* 183–184.

Field, T. (1990). *Infant daycare has positive effects on grade school behavior and performance.* Unpublished manuscript, University of Miami, Coral Gables, Florida.

Finnegan, L. P. (1982). Outcome of children born to women dependent upon narcotics. In B. Stimmel (Ed.), *The effects of maternal alcohol and drug abuse on the newborn.* New York: Haworth Press.

Fischhoff, B., Slovic, P., & Lichtenstein, S. (1977). Knowing with certainty: The appropriateness of extreme confidence. *Journal of Experimental Psychology: Human Perception and Performance, 3,* 552–564.

Flavell, J. H., & Wellman, H. M. (1977). Metamemory. In R. V. Kail, Jr., & J. W. Hagen (Eds.), *Perspectives on the development of memory and cognition* (pp. 3–33). Hillsdale, NJ: Erlbaum.

Flett, G. L., Blankstein, K. R., Hicken, D. J., & Watson, M. S. (1995). Social support and help-seeking in daily hassles versus major life events stress. *Journal of Applied Social Psychology, 25*(1), 49–58.

Floody, O. R. (1983). Hormones and aggression in female mammals. In B. B. Svare (Ed.), *Hormones and aggressive behavior* (pp. 39–89). New York: Plenum.

Fogel, A. (1992). Movement and communication in human infancy: The social dynamics of development. *Human Movement Science, 11*(4), 387–423.

Folkman, S., & Lazarus, R. S. (1988). *Manual for the ways of coping questionnaire.* Palo Alto, CA: Consulting Psychologists Press.

Folkman, S., Lazarus, R. S., Gruen, R. J., & DeLongis, A. (1986). Appraisal, coping, health status, and psychological symptoms. *Journal of Personality and Social Psychology, 50*(3), 571–579.

Frankl, V. (1959). *From death camp to existentialism.* Boston: Beacon.

Franks, J. J., & Bransford, J. D. (1971). Abstraction of visual patterns. *Journal of Experimental Psychology, 90*(1), 65–74.

Frazier, T. M., David, G. H., Goldstein, H., & Goldberg, I. D. (1961). Cigarette smoking and prematurity. *American Journal of Obstetrics and Gynecology, 81,* 988–996.

Freedman, J. L., & Fraser, S. C. (1966). Compliance without pressure. *Journal of Personality and Social Psychology, 4,* 195–202.

Freeman, W. (1959). Psychosurgery. In S. Arieti (Ed.), *American handbook of psychiatry* (Vol. 2, pp. 1521–1540). New York: Basic Books.

Frensch, P. A., & Sternberg, R. J. (1989). Expertise and intelligent thinking: When is it worse to know better? In R. J. Sternberg (Ed.), *Advances in the psychology of human intelligence.* Hillsdale, NJ: Erlbaum.

Freud, A. (1946). *The ego and the mechanisms of defense.* New York: International Universities Press.

Freud, S. (1954). *Interpretation of dreams.* London: Allen & Unwin. (Original work published 1900)

Freud, S. (1963). Introductory lectures on psychoanalysis. In *Standard edition of the complete psychological works of Sigmund Freud* (Vols. 15 & 16). London: Hogarth. (Original work published 1917)

Freud, S. (1964). *New introductory lectures.* In *Standard edition of the complete psychological works of Sigmund Freud* (Vol. 21). London: Hogarth. (Original work published 1933)

Frey, K. S., & Ruble, D. N. (1987). What children say about classroom performance: Sex and grade differences in perceived competence. *Child Development, 58,* 1066–1078.

Friedman, M., & Rosenman, R. H. (1974). *Type A behavior and your heart.* New York: Knopf.

Friedman, M. I., & Stricker, E. M. (1976). The physiological psychology of hunger: A physiological perspective. *Psychological Review, 83,* 409–431.

Friedman, M., Thoresen, C. E., Gill, J. J., Ulmer, D., et al. (1994). Alteration of Type A behavior and its effect on cardiac recurrences in post myocardial infarction patients: Summary results of the recurrent coronary prevention project. In A. Steptoe & J. Wardle (Eds.), *Psychosocial processes and health: A reader* (pp. 478–506). Cambridge, England: Cambridge University Press.

Friedrich-Cofer, L., & Huston, A. C. (1986). Television violence and aggression: The debate continues. *Psychological Bulletin, 100*(3), 364–371.

Funder, D. C., & Ozer, D. J. (1983). Behavior as a function of the situation. *Journal of Personality & Social Psychology, 44*(1), 107–112.

Gabrenya, W. K., Latané, B., & Wang, Y. E. (1983). Social loafing in cross-cultural perspective: Chinese in Taiwan. *Journal of Cross-Cultural Psychology, 14,* 368–384.

Gabrenya, W. K., Wang, Y. E., & Latané, B. (1985). Social loafing on an optimizing task: Cross-cultural differences among Chinese and Americans. *Journal of Cross-Cultural Psychology, 16,* 223–242.

Gagnon, J. H. (1973). Scripts and the coordination of sexual conduct. In J. K. Cole & R. Riensteiber (Eds.), *Nebraska Symposium on Motivation* (Vol. 21, pp. 27–59). Lincoln, NE: University of Nebraska Press.

Galton, F. (1883). *Inquiry into human faculty and its development.* London: Macmillan.

Garcia, J. (1981). Tilting at the paper mills of academe. *American Psychologist, 36*(2), 149–158.

Garcia, J., & Koelling, R. A. (1966). The relation of cue to consequence in avoidance learning. *Psychonomic Science, 4,* 123–124.

Gardner, H. (1983). *Frames of mind: The theory of multiple intelligences.* New York: Basic Books.

Gardner, H. (1993a). *Creating minds: An anatomy of creativity seen through the lives of Freud, Einstein, Picasso, Stravinsky, Eliot, Graham, and Gandhi.* New York: HarperCollins.

Gardner, H. (1993b). *Multiple intelligences: The theory in practice.* New York: Basic Books.

Gardner, M. (1978). *Aha! Insight.* New York: Freeman.

Gazzaniga, M. S. (1985). *The social brain: Discovering the networks of the mind.* New York: Basic Books.

Geen, R. G., & Quanty, M. B. (1977). The catharsis of aggression: An evaluation of a hypothesis. In L. Berkowitz (Ed.), *Advances in experimental social psychology* (Vol. 10). New York: Academic Press.

Gelles, R. J., & Straus, M. A. (1988). *Intimate violence.* New York: Simon & Schuster.

Gelman, S., Bullock, M., & Meck, E. (1980). Preschoolers' understanding of simple object transformations. *Child Development, 51,* 691–699.

Gerstein, D. R., & Harwood, H. J. (Eds.) (1990). *Treating drug problems: A study of the evolution, effectiveness, and financing of public and private drug treatment systems.* Washington, DC: National Academy of Science Institute of Medicine, National Academy Press.

Geyelin, M. (1994, May 15). Lawsuits over false memories face hurdles. *Wall Street Journal,* p. 10(N).

Gibbs, J. (Ed.) (1968). *Suicide.* New York: Harper & Row.

Gibbs, J. C., Arnold, K. D., Ahlborn, H. H., & Cheesman, F. L. (1984). Facilitation of sociomoral reasoning in delinquents. *Journal of Consulting and Clinical Psychology, 52,* 37–45.

Gibson, J. J. (1950). *The perception of the visual world.* Boston: Houghton-Mifflin.

Gick, M. L., & Holyoak, K. J. (1980). Analogical problem solving. *Cognitive Psychology, 12,* 306–355.

Gick, M. L., & Holyoak, K. J. (1983). Schema induction and analogical transfer. *Cognitive Psychology, 15,* 1–38.

Gilbert, E., & DeBlassie, R. (1984). Anorexia nervosa: Adolescent starvation by choice. *Adolescence, 19,* 840–846.

Gill, M. M. (1972). Hypnosis as an altered and regressed state. *International Journal of Clinical and Experimental Hypnosis, 20,* 224–337.

Gilligan, C. (1982). *In a different voice: Psychological theory and women's development.* Cambridge, MA: Harvard University Press.

Gilligan, C., & Attanucci, J. (1988). Two moral orientations: Gender differences and similarities. *Merrill-Palmer Quarterly, 34,* 223–237.

Gilly, M. C. (1988). Sex roles in advertising: A comparison of television advertisements in Australia, Mexico, and the United States. *Journal of Marketing, 52*(2), 75–85.

Gim, R. H., Atkinson, D. R., & Kim, S. J. (1991). Asian-American acculturation, counselor ethnicity and cultural sensitivity, and ratings of counselors. *Journal of Counseling Psychology, 38,* 57–62.

Gladwin, T. (1970). *East is a big bird.* Cambridge, MA: Belknap.

Glenberg, A. M. (1977). Influences of retrieval processes on the spacing effect in free recall. *Journal of Experimental Psychology: Human Learning & Memory, 3*(3), 282–294.

Glenberg, A. M. (1979). Component-levels theory of the effects of spacing of repetitions on recall and recognition. *Memory & Cognition, 7*(2), 95–112.

Glucksberg, S., & Danks, J. H. (1975). *Experimental psycholinguistics.* Hillsdale, NJ: Erlbaum.

Glueck, B. C., & Stroebel, C. F. (1975). Biofeedback and meditation in the treatment of psychiatric illness. *Comprehensive Psychiatry, 16,* 302–321.

Goddard, H. H. (1917). Mental tests and immigrants. *Journal of Delinquency, 2,* 243–277.

Godden, D. R., & Baddeley, A. D. (1975). Context-dependent memory in two natural environments: On land and underwater. *British Journal of Psychology, 66,* 325–331.

Golbus, M. S. (1980). Teratology for the obstetrician: Current status. *American Journal of Obstetrics and Gynecology, 55,* 269.

Goleman, D. (1987, November 24). Teen-age risk-taking: Rise in deaths prompts new research effort: Experts seek ways to head off the peril. *The New York Times,* p. 13(N).

Goleman, D. (1993, April 18). When a long therapy goes a little way. *The New York Times,* Sect. 4, p. 6.

Gottesman, I. I., McGuffin, P., & Farmer, A. E. (1987). Clinical genetics as clues to the "real" genetics of schizophrenia. *Schizophrenia Bulletin, 13,* 23–47.

Gottfried, A. E., & Gottfried, A. W. (Eds.) (1988). *Maternal employment and children's development.* New York: Plenum.

Gottman, J. M. (1979). *Marital interaction.* New York: Academic Press.

Gottman, J. M. (1994). *Why marriages succeed or fail.* New York: Simon & Schuster.

Gottman, J. M., Notarius, C., Gonso, J., & Markman, H. J. (1976). *A couple's guide to communication.* Champaign, IL: Research Press.

Graf, P., & Schacter, D. L. (1985). Implicit and explicit memory for new associations in normal and amnesic subjects. *Journal of Experimental Psychology: Learning, Memory, and Cognition, 11,* 501–518.

Graham, J. R. (1990). *MMPI-2: Assessing personality and psychopathology.* New York: Oxford University Press.

Gray, A. L., Bowers, K. S., & Fenz, W. D. (1970). Heart rate in anticipation of and during a negative visual hallucination. *International Journal of Clinical and Experimental Hypnosis, 18,* 41–51.

Green, D. M., & Swets, J. A. (1966). *Signal detection theory and psychophysics* (Reprint). New York: Krieger.

Greene, D., & Lepper, M. R. (1974). Effects of extrinsic rewards on children's subsequent intrinsic interest. *Child Development, 45,* 1141–1145.

Greene, R. L. (1987). Ethnicity and MMPI performance: A review. *Journal of Consulting and Clinical Psychology, 55,* 497–512.

Greenfield, P. M. (1994). Independence and interdependence as developmental scripts: Implications for theory, research, and practice. In P. M. Greenfield & R. R. Cocking (Eds.), *Cross-cultural roots of minority child development* (pp. 1–37). Hillsdale, NJ: Erlbaum.

Greenfield, P. M., & Cocking, R. R. (Eds.) (1994). *Cross-cultural roots of minority child development.* Hillsdale, NJ: Erlbaum.

Greenwald, A. G., Klinger, M. R., & Schuh, E. S. (1995). Activation by marginally perceptible ("subliminal") stimuli: Dissociation of unconscious from conscious cognition. *Journal of Experimental Psychology: General, 125*(1), 22–42.

Greenwald, A. G., Spangenberg, E. R., Pratkanis, A. R., & Eskenazi, J. (1991). Double-blind tests of subliminal self-help audiotapes. *Psychological Science, 2*(2), 119–122.

Gregory, R. L. (1987). Recovery from blindness. In R. L. Gregory, *The Oxford companion to the mind* (pp. 94–96). New York: Oxford University Press.

Grolier's international encyclopedia. (1992). Danbury, CT: Grolier.

Gruber, H. E. (1981). *Darwin on man: A psychological study of scientific creativity* (2nd ed.). Chicago: University of Chicago Press. (Original work published 1974)

Gruber, H. E. (1995). Insight and affect in the history of science. In R. J. Sternberg & J. E. Davidson (Eds.), *The nature of insight* (pp. 398–431). Cambridge, MA: MIT Press.

Gurman, A. S., Kniskern, D. P., & Pinsoff, W. M. (1986). Research on the process and outcome of marital and family therapy. In S. L. Garfield & A. E. Bergin (Eds.), *Handbook of psychotherapy and behavior change* (3rd ed.). New York: Wiley.

Gustavson, C. R., & Garcia, J. (1974). Aversive conditioning: Pulling a gag on the wily coyote. *Psychology Today, 8*(3), 68–72.

Gustavson, C R., & Nicolaus, L K. (1987). Taste aversion conditioning in wolves, coyotes, and other canids: Retrospect and prospect. In H. Frank (Ed.), *Man and wolf: Advances, issues, and problems in captive wolf research: Vol. 4. Perspectives in vertebrate science* (pp. 169–203). Dordrecht, Netherlands: Junk, Publishers.

Gwirtsman, H. E., & Germer, R. H. (1981). Abnormalities of dexamethasone suppression test and urinary MHPG in anorexia nervosa. *American Journal of Psychiatry, 138,* 650–653.

Haglund, M. M., Ojemann, G. A., Lettich, E., Bellugi, U., et al. (1993). Dissociation of cortical and single unit activity in spoken and signed languages. *Brain & Language, 44*(1), 19–27.

Haier, R. J., Siegel, B., Tang, C., Abel, L., & Buchsbaum, M. S. (1992). Intelligence and changes in regional cerebral glucose metabolic rate following learning. *Intelligence, 16*(3, 4), 415–426.

Haith, M. M. (1979). Visual cognition in early infancy. In R. B. Kearsley & I. E. Sigel (Eds.), *Infants at risk: Assessment of cognitive functioning.* Hillsdale, NJ: Erlbaum.

Hakuta, K. (1986). *Mirror of language.* New York: Basic Books.

Harkins, S. G. (1987). Social loafing and social facilitation. *Journal of Experimental Social Psychology, 23,* 1–18.

Harkins, S. G., & Szymanski, K. (1987). Social loafing and social facilitation: New wine in old bottles. In C. Hendrick (Ed.), *Review of personality and social psychology: Group processes and intergroup relations* (Vol. 9, pp. 167–188). Beverly Hills, CA: Sage.

Harlow, H. F. (1949). The formation of learning sets. *Psychological Review, 56,* 51–65.

Harlow, H. F., Harlow, M. K., & Meyer, D. R. (1950). Learning motivated by a manipulation drive. *Journal of Experimental Psychology, 40,* 228–234.

Harter, S. (1990). Causes, correlates, and the functional role of global self-worth: A life-span perspective. In R. J. Sternberg & J. Kolligian, Jr., (Eds.), *Competence considered* (pp. 67–97). New Haven, CT: Yale University Press.

Hastings, E. H., & Hastings, P. K. (Eds.) (1982). *Index on international public opinion, 1980–81.* Westport, CT: Greenwood Press.

Hatfield, E., & Rapson, R. L. (1992). Similarity and attraction in close relationships. *Communication Monographs, 59*(2), 209–212.

Hatfield, E., & Walster, G. W. (1978). *A new look at love.* Reading, MA: Addison-Wesley.

Hathaway, S. R., & McKinley, J. C. (1943). *Manual for the Minnesota Multiphasic Personality Inventory.* New York: Psychological Corporation.

Hathaway, S. R., & McKinley, J. C. (1951). *The Minnesota multiphasic personality inventory* (rev. ed.). New York: Psychological Corporation.

Havighurst, R. J. (1967). *Development tasks and education.* New York: David McKay.

Hayes, D., & Ross, C. E. (1986). Body and mind: The effect of exercise, overweight, and physical health on psychological well-being. *Journal of Health and Social Behavior, 27,* 387–400.

Haynes, S. G., Feinleib, M., & Kannel, W. B. (1980). The relationship of psychosocial factors to coronary heart disease in the Framingham Study: III. Eight-year incidence of coronary heart disease. *American Journal of Epidemiology, 111,* 37–58.

Hazan, C., & Shaver, P. R. (1987). Romantic love conceptualized as an attachment process. *Journal of Personality and Social Psychology, 52,* 511–524.

Heaney, C. A., Israel, B. A., & House, J. S. (1994). Chronic job insecurity among automobile workers: Effects on job satisfaction and health. *Social Science & Medicine, 38*(10), 1431–1437.

Heath, S. B. (1983). *Ways with words*. New York: Cambridge University Press.

Hedstrom, L. J. (1994). Morita and Naikan therapies: American applications. *Psychotherapy, 31*(1), 154–160.

Heider, F. (1958). *The psychology of interpersonal relations*. New York: Wiley.

Heilbrun, A. B., & Witt, N. (1990). Distorted body image as a risk factor in anorexia nervosa: Replication and clarification. *Psychological Reports, 66,* 407–416.

Helmes, E., & Reddon, J. R. (1993). A perspective on developments in assessing psychopathology: A critical review of the MMPI and MMPI-2. *Psychological Bulletin, 113*(3), 453–471.

Helmholtz, H. von. (1896). *Vorträge und Reden*. Braunschweig: Vieweg und Sohn.

Helmholtz, H. E. L. von. (1930). *The sensations of tone* (A. J. Ellis, Trans.). New York: Longmans, Green. (Original work published 1863)

Helmholtz, H. E. L. von. (1962). *Treatise on physiological optics* (3rd ed., J. P. C. Southall, Ed. and Trans.). New York: Dover. (Original work published 1909)

Hennessey, B. A., & Amabile, T. M. (1988). The conditions of creativity. In R. J. Sternberg (Ed.), *The nature of creativity* (pp. 11–38). New York: Cambridge University Press.

Henry, J. P., & Stephens, P. M. (1977). *Stress, health, and the social environment: A sociobiologic approach to medicine*. New York: Springer-Verlag.

Hering, E. (1964). *Outlines of a theory of the light sense* (L. M. Hurvich & D. Jameson, Trans.). Cambridge, MA: Harvard University Press. (Original work published 1878)

Herrnstein, R., & Murray, C. (1994). *The bell curve*. New York: The Free Press.

Hetherington, A. W., & Ranson, S. W. (1940). Hypothalamic lesions and adiposity in the rat. *Anatomical Record, 78,* 149–172.

Heyduk, R. G., & Bahrick, L. E. (1977). Complexity, response competition, and preference implications for affective consequences of repeated exposure. *Motivation and Emotion, 1,* 249–259.

Higginbotham, H. N. (1979). Culture and mental health services. In A. J. Marsella, G. De Vos, & F. L. K. Hsu (Eds.), *Perspectives on cross-cultural psychology* (pp. 307–332). New York: Academic Press.

Hilgard, E. R. (1965). *Hypnotic susceptibility*. New York: Harcourt, Brace & World.

Hilgard, E. R. (1977). *Divided consciousness: Multiple controls in human thought and action*. New York: Wiley.

Hilts, P. J. (1995). *Memory's ghost: The strange tale of Mr. M and the nature of memory*. New York: Simon & Schuster.

Hintzman, D. L. (1978). *The psychology of learning and memory*. San Francisco: Freeman.

Ho, D. Y. F. (1986). Chinese patterns of socialization. In M. H. Bond (Ed.), *The psychology of the Chinese people*. Hong Kong: Oxford University Press.

Hobson, J. A. (1989). *Sleep*. New York: Scientific American Library.

Hoebel, B. G., & Teitelbaum, G. (1966). Weight regulation in normal and hypothalamic hyperphagic rats. *Journal of Comparative and Physiological Psychology, 61,* 189–193.

Hoffman, L. W. (1989). Effects of maternal employment in the two-parent family. *American Psychologist, 44,* 283–292.

Holder, M. D., Bermudez-Rattoni, F., & Garcia, J. (1988). Taste-potentiated noise–illness associations. *Behavioral Neuroscience, 102*(3), 363–370.

Holder, M. D., Yirmiya, R., Garcia, J., & Raizer, J. (1989). Conditioned taste aversions are not readily disrupted by external excitation. *Behavioral Neuroscience, 103*(3), 605–611.

Holinger, P. C. (1987). *Violent deaths in the United States*. New York: The Guilford Press.

Hollingshead, A. B., & Redlich, F. C. (1958). *Social class and mental illness*. New York: Wiley.

Hollis, K. L. (1990). The role of Pavlovian conditioning in territorial aggression and reproduction. In D. A. Dewsbury (Ed.), *Contemporary issues in comparative psychology* (pp. 197–219). Sunderland, MA: Sinauer Associates.

Hollis, K. L., Cadieux, E. L., & Colbert, M. M. (1989). The biological function of Pavlovian conditioning: A mechanism for mating success

in the blue gourami (*Trichogaster trichopterus*). *Journal of Comparative Psychology, 103*(2), 115–121.

Hollis, K. L., Martin, K. A., Cadieux, E. L., & Colbert, M. M. (1984). The biological function of Pavlovian conditioning: Learned inhibition of aggressive behavior in territorial fish. [Special issue: Ecological and developmental contexts in the study of learning.] *Learning & Motivation, 15*(4), 459–478.

Hollis, K. L., ten Cate, C., & Bateson, P. (1991). Stimulus representation: A subprocess of imprinting and conditioning. *Journal of Comparative Psychology, 105*(4), 307–317.

Holmes, T. H., & David, E. M. (Eds.) (1989). *Life change, life events, and illness: Selected papers*. New York: Praeger.

Holmes, T., & Rahe, R. (1967). The social readjustment rating scale. *Journal of Psychosomatic Research, 11,* 213–218.

Holyoak, K. J. (1984). Analogical thinking and human intelligence. In R. J. Sternberg (Ed.), *Advances in the psychology of human intelligence* (Vol. 2, pp. 199–230). Hillsdale, NJ: Erlbaum.

Honsberger, R. W., & Wilson, A. F. (1973). Transcendental meditation in treating asthma. *Respiratory Therapy: The Journal of Inhalation Technology, 3,* 79–80.

Hooker, E. (1993). Reflections of a 40-year exploration: A scientific view on homosexuality. *American Psychologist, 48*(4), 450–453.

Horney, K. (1937). *The neurotic personality of our time*. New York: Norton.

Horney, K. (1939). *New ways in psychoanalysis*. New York: Norton.

Horney, K. (1950). *Neurosis and human growth: The struggle toward self-realization*. New York: Norton.

House, J. S., Landis, K. R., & Umberson, D. (1988). Social relationships and health. *Science, 241*(4865), 540–545.

Houston, J. P. (1985). *Motivation*. New York: Macmillan.

Hovland, C. I., & Weiss, W. (1951). The influences of source credibility on communication effectiveness. *Public Opinion Quarterly, 15,* 635–650.

Howard, K. I., Kopta, S. M., Krause, M. S., & Orlinsky, D. E. (1986). The dose–effect relationship in psychotherapy. *American Psychologist, 41*(2), 159–164.

Hubel, D., & Wiesel, T. (1963). Receptive fields of cells in the striate cortex of very young, visually inexperienced kittens. *Journal of Neurophysiology, 26,* 994–1002.

Hubel, D., & Wiesel, T. (1968). Receptive fields and functional architecture of the monkey striate cortex. *Journal of Physiology, 195,* 215–243.

Hubel, D. H., & Wiesel, T. N. (1979). Brain mechanisms of vision. *Scientific American, 241,* 150–162.

Huebner, R. R., & Izard, C. E. (1988). Mothers' responses to infants' facial expressions of sadness, anger, and physical distress. *Motivation and Emotion, 12,* 185–196.

Huesmann, L. R., Lagerspetz, K., & Eron, L. D. (1984). Intervening variable in the TV violence–aggression relation: Evidence from two countries. *Developmental Psychology, 20,* 746–775.

Hull, C. L. (1943). *Principles of behavior*. New York: Appleton-Century-Crofts.

Hull, C. L. (1952). *A behavior system: An introduction to behavior theory concerning the individual organism*. New Haven, CT: Yale University Press.

Hunt, E. B. (1978). Mechanics of verbal ability. *Psychological Review, 85,* 109–130.

Hunt, M. M. (1959). *A natural history of love*. New York: Knopf.

Hurvich, L., & Jameson, D. (1957). An opponent-process theory of color vision. *Psychological Review, 64,* 384–404.

Huston, A. C. (1983). Sex-typing. In E. M. Hetherington (Ed.) & P. H. Mussen (Series Ed.), *Handbook of child psychology* (4th ed., Vol. 4, pp. 387–467). New York: Wiley.

Huston, A. C. (1985). The development of sex-typing: Themes from recent research. *Developmental Review, 5,* 1–17.

Hwang, K. K. (1981). Perception of life events: The application of nonmetric multidimensional scaling. *Acta Psychologica Taiwanica, 22,* 22–32.

Inhelder, B., & Piaget, J. (1958). *The growth of logical thinking from childhood to adolescence*. New York: Basic Books.

Insko, C. A. (1965). Verbal reinforcement of attitude. *Journal of Personality and Social Psychology, 21*, 621–623.

Intelligence and its measurement: A symposium. (1921). *Journal of Educational Psychology, 12*, 123–147, 195–216, 271–275.

Isen, A. M. (1987). Passive affect, cognitive processes, and social behavior. In L. Berkowitz (Ed.), *Advances in experimental social psychology* (Vol. 20, pp. 203–253). New York: Academic Press.

Ivey, A. E., Ivey, M. B., & Simek-Morgan, L. (1993). *Counseling and psychotherapy: A multicultural perspective.* Boston: Allyn & Bacon.

Izard, C. E. (1989). The structure and functions of emotions: Implications for cognition, motivation, and personality. In I. S. Cohen (Ed.), *The G. Stanley Hall lecture series* (Vol. 9, pp. 39–73). Washington, DC: American Psychological Association.

Izard, C. E., Kagan, J., & Zajonc, R. B. (1984). *Emotions, cognition, and behavior.* New York: Cambridge University Press.

Jackson, N. E. (1984). Intellectual giftedness: A theory worth doing well. *The Behavioral and Brain Sciences, 7*(12), 294–295.

James, W. (1890). *Psychology.* New York: Holt.

Janis, I. L. (1972). *Victims of groupthink.* Boston: Houghton Mifflin.

Jemmott, J. B., III, & Locke, S. E. (1984). Psychosocial factors, immunologic mediation, and human susceptibility to infectious diseases: How much do we know? *Psychological Bulletin, 95*, 78–108.

Johnson, K. (1994, July 2). Corporate conscience: Insurer gives retreat a social mission. *The New York Times, 143*, pp. 21, 24.

Jones, E. E., & Davis, K. E. (1965). From acts to dispositions: The attribution process in person perception. In L. Berkowitz (Ed.), *Advances in experimental social psychology* (Vol. 2). New York: Academic Press.

Jones, E. E., & Nisbett, R. (1971). *The actor and the observer: Divergent perceptions of the causes of behavior.* Morristown, NJ: General Learning Press.

Kandel, E. R., & Schwartz, J. H. (1982). Molecular biology of learning: Modulation of transmitter release. *Science, 218*(4571), 433–442.

Kaplan, C. A., & Davidson, J. E. (1989). *Incubation effects in problem solving.* Manuscript submitted for publication.

Katz, D., & Stotland, E. (1959). A preliminary statement to a theory of attitude structure and change. In S. Koch (Ed.), *Psychology: A study of a science* (Vol. 3, pp. 423–475). New York: McGraw-Hill.

Kay, P. (1975). Synchronic variability and diachronic changes in basic color terms. *Language in Society, 4*, 257–270.

Keller, H. (1902/1988). *The story of my life.* New York: Penguin.

Keller, M., Eckensberger, L. H., & von Rosen, K. (1989). A critical note on the conception of preconventional morality: The case of stage 2 in Kohlberg's theory. *International Journal of Behavioral Development, 12*(1), 57–69.

Kemeny, M. E., Cohen, R., Zegans, L. S., & Conant, M. A. (1989). Psychological and immunological predictors of genital herpes recurrence. *Psychosomatic Medicine, 51*, 195–208.

Kenrick, D. T., & Trost, M. R. (1993). The evolutionary perspective. In A. Beall & R. J. Sternberg (Eds.), *Perspectives on the psychology of gender.* New York: The Guilford Press.

Keppel, G., & Underwood, B. J. (1962). Proactive inhibition in short-term retention of single items. *Journal of Verbal Learning and Verbal Behavior, 1*, 153–161.

Kiecolt-Glaser, J. K., et al. (1984). Psychosocial modifiers of immunocompetence in medical students. *Psychosomatic Medicine, 46*(1), 7–14.

Kiecolt-Glaser, J. K., & Glaser, R. (1987). Psychosocial influences on herpes virus latency. In E. Kurstak, Z. J. Lipowski, & P. V. Morozov (Eds.), *Viruses, immunity, and mental disorders* (pp. 403–412). New York: Plenum.

Kiesler, D. J. (1966). Some myths of psychotherapy research and the search for a paradigm. *Psychological Bulletin, 65*, 110–136.

Kihlstrom, J. F. (1984). Conscious, subconscious, unconscious: A cognitive view. In K. S. Bowers & D. Meichenbaum (Eds.), *The unconscious: Reconsidered.* New York: Wiley.

Kihlstrom, J. F. (1985). Hypnosis. *Annual Review of Psychology, 36*, 385–418.

King, G. R., & Logue, A. W. (1987). Choice in a self-control paradigm with human subjects: Effects of changeover delay duration. *Learning & Motivation, 18*(4), 421–438.

Kitchener, K. S., & Brenner, H. G. (1990). *Wisdom and reflective judgment: Knowing in the face of uncertainty.* In R. J. Sternberg (Ed.), *Wisdom* (pp. 212–229). New York: Cambridge University Press.

Kleinman, A. (1988). *Rethinking psychiatry: From cultural category to personal experience.* New York: The Free Press.

Kleinman, A., & Good, B. (1985). *Culture and depression.* Berkeley, CA: University of California Press.

Kleinmuntz, B., & Szucko, J. J. (1984). A field study of the fallibility of polygraphic lie detection. *Nature, 308*, 449–450.

Kleitman, N. (1963). *Sleep and wakefulness* (2nd ed.). Chicago: University of Chicago Press.

Knox, V. J., Crutchfield, L., & Hilgard, E. R. (1975). The nature of task interference in hypnotic dissociation: An investigation of hypnotic behavior. *International Journal of Clinical and Experimental Hypnosis, 23*, 305–323.

Kobasa, S. C. (1982). The hardy personality: Toward a social psychology of stress and health. In G. S. Sanders & J. Suls (Eds.), *Social psychology of health and illness.* Hillsdale, NJ: Erlbaum.

Kobasa, S. C. O. (1990). Stress-resistant personality. In R. E. Ornstein & C. Swencionis (Eds.), *The healing brain: A scientific reader* (pp. 219–230). New York: The Guilford Press.

Kobasa, S. C. O., Maddi, S. R., Puccetti, M. C., & Zola, M. A. (1994). Effectiveness of hardiness, exercise, and social support as resources against illness. In A. Steptoe & J. Wardle (Eds.), *Psychosocial processes and health: A reader* (pp. 247–260). Cambridge, England: Cambridge University Press.

Kohlberg, L. (1963). The development of children's orientations toward a moral order: Pt. 1. Sequence in the development of moral thought. *Vita Humana, 6*, 11–33.

Kohlberg, L. (1983). *The psychology of moral development.* New York: Harper & Row.

Kohlberg, L. (1984). The psychology of moral development: The nature and validity of moral stages. *In Essays on moral development* (Vol. 2). New York: Harper & Row.

Köhler, W. (1927). *The mentality of apes.* New York: Harcourt Brace.

Kohn, P. M., Gurevich, M., Pickering, D. I., & MacDonald, J. E. (1994). Alexithymia, reactivity, and the adverse impact of hassles-based stress. *Personality & Individual Differences, 16*(6), 805–812.

Kolb, B., & Whishaw, I. Q. (1990). *Fundamentals of human neuropsychology* (3rd ed.). New York: Freeman.

Komaroff, A. L., Masuda, M., & Holmes, T. H. (1968). *The Social Readjustment Rating Scale:* A comparative study of Negro, Mexican and white Americans. *Journal of Psychosomatic Research, 12*(2), 121–128.

Kosslyn, S. (1975). Information representation in visual images. *Cognitive Psychology, 7*(3), 341–370.

Kosslyn, S. M. (1988). Aspects of a cognitive neuroscience of mental imagery. *Science, 240*, 1621–1626.

Kramer, M. A. (1957). A discussion of the concepts of incidence and prevalence as related to epidemiologic studies of mental disorders. *American Journal of Public Health, 47*, 826–840.

Kulkarni, S. S., & Puhan, B. N. (1988). Psychological assessment: Its present and future trends. In J. Pandey (Ed.), *Psychology in India: The state of the art: Vol. 1. Personality and mental processes.* New Delhi: Sage.

Lachman, M. E. (1986). Locus of control in aging research: A case for multi-dimensional and domain-specific assessment. *Psychology and Aging, 1*, 34–40.

LaFraniere, S. (1992, August 27). Identifying "Ivan": Does memory mislead? *The Washington Post, 115*, p. A29.

La Ganga, M. L. (1994, May 14). Father wins in "false memory" case. *Los Angeles Times*, p. A1.

Laing, R. D. (1964). Is schizophrenia a disease? *International Journal of Social Psychiatry, 10*, 184–193.

Lange, R. D., & James, W. (1922). *The emotions.* Baltimore: Williams & Wilkins.

Langer, E. J., Blank, A., & Chanowitz, B. (1978). The mindlessness of ostensibly thoughtful action. *Journal of Personality and Social Psychology, 36*, 635–642.

Langsley, D. G., Hodes, M., & Grimson, W. R. (1993). In N. Sartorius,

G. de Girolano, G. Andrews, G. A. German, & L. Eisenberg (Eds.), *Treatment of mental disorders: A review of effectiveness.* Geneva, Switzerland, and Washington, DC: World Health Organization and American Psychiatric Press.

Larkin, J. H., McDermott, J., Simon, D. P., & Simon, H. A. (1980). Expert and novice performance in solving physics problems. *Science, 208,* 1335–1342.

Latané, B. (1981). The psychology of social impact. *American Psychologist, 36,* 343–356.

Latané, B., & Darley, J. M. (1968). Group inhibition of bystander intervention. *Journal of Personality and Social Psychology, 10,* 215–221.

Latané, B., & Darley, J. M. (1970). *The unresponsive bystander: Why doesn't he help?* New York: Appleton-Century-Crofts.

Latané, B., Nida, S. A., & Wilson, D. W. (1981). The effects of a group size on helping behavior. In J. P. Rushton & R. M. Sorrentino (Eds.), *Altruism and helping behavior: Social, personality, and developmental perspectives.* Hillsdale, NJ: Erlbaum.

Latané, B., Williams, K., & Harkins, S. (1979). Many hands make light the work: The causes and consequences of social loafing. *Journal of Personality and Social Psychology, 37,* 822–832.

Lau, R. R. (1988). Beliefs about control and health behavior. In D. S. Gochman (Ed.), *Health behavior* (pp. 43–63). New York: Plenum.

Lazar, I., & Darlington, R. (1982). Lasting effects of early education: A report from the consortium for longitudinal studies. *Monographs of the Society for Research in Child Development, 47*(2–3, Serial No. 195).

Lazarus, R. S. (1977). A cognitive analysis of biofeedback control. In G. E. Schwartz & J. Beatty (Eds.), *Biofeedback: Theory and research* (pp. 69–71). New York: Academic Press.

Lazarus, R. S. (1984). On the primacy of cognition. *American Psychologist, 39,* 124–129.

Lazarus, R. S., Kanner, A., & Folkman, F. (1980). Emotions: A cognitive-phenomenological analysis. In R. Plutchik & H. Kellerman (Eds.), *Emotion: Theory, research and experience: Vol. 1. Theories of emotion.* New York: Academic Press.

Lederer, R. (1991). *The miracle of language.* New York: Pocket Books.

LeDoux, J. E. (1986). The neurobiology of emotion. In J. E. LeDoux & W. Hirst (Eds.), *Mind and brain: Dialogues in cognitive neuroscience* (pp. 301–354). Cambridge, England: Cambridge University Press.

LeDoux, J. E., Romanski, L., & Xagoraris, A. (1989). Indelibility of subcortical emotional memories. *Journal of Cognitive Neuroscience, 1,* 238–243.

Leicht, K. L., & Overton, R. (1987). Encoding variability and spacing repetitions. *American Journal of Psychology, 100*(1), 61–68.

Lepper, M. R., Greene, D., & Nisbett, R. E. (1973). Undermining children's intrinsic interest with extrinsic rewards: A test of the "overjustification" hypothesis. *Journal of Personality and Social Psychology, 28,* 129–137.

LeVay, S. (1991). A difference in hypothalamic structure between heterosexual and homosexual men. *Science, 253,* 1034–1037.

Levenkron, J. C., & Moore, L. G. (1988). The Type A behavior pattern: Issues for intervention research. *Annals of Behavioral Medicine, 10,* 78–83.

Leventhal, H., & Tomarken, A. J. (1986). Emotion: Today's problems. *Annual Review of Psychology, 37,* 565–610.

Levine, B. (1993, January 20). How to tell a "woopie" from a "fizzbo." *Los Angeles Times, 112,* pp. E1, E6.

Liebert, R. M., & Baron, R. A. (1972). Some immediate effects of televised violence on children's behavior. *Developmental Psychology, 6,* 469–475.

Lin, K-M., Masuda, M., & Tazuma, L. (1984). Problems of eastern refugees and immigrants: IV. Adaptational problems of Vietnamese refugees. *Psychiatric Journal of the University of Ottawa, 9*(2), 79–84.

Linscheid, T. R., Hartel, F., & Cooley, N. (1993). Are aversive procedures durable? A five-year follow-up of three individuals treated with contingent electric shock. (Special issue: Aversives: II.) *Child and Adolescent Mental Health Care, 3*(2), 67–76.

Lissner, L., Odell, P. M., D'Agostino, R. B., Stokes, J., Kreger, B. E., Belanger, A. J., & Brownell, K. D. (1991). Variability of body weight and health outcomes in the Framingham population. *New England Journal of Medicine, 324,* 1839–1844.

Locke, E. A., & Latham, G. P. (1985). The application of goal setting to sports. *Journal of Sport Psychology, 7,* 205–222.

Loehlin, J. C., Lindzey, G., & Spuhler, J. N. (1975). *Race differences in intelligence.* New York: Freeman.

Loehlin, J. D., Vandenberg, S. G., & Osborne, R. T. (1973). Blood-group genes and Negro–white ability difference. *Behavioral Genetics, 3,* 267–270.

Loewenstein, G., & Furstenberg, F. F. (1991). Is teenage sexual behavior rational? *Journal of Applied Social Psychology, 21*(12), 957–986.

Loftus, E. F. (1975). Leading questions and the eyewitness report. *Cognitive Psychology, 7,* 560–572.

Loftus, E. F. (1977). Shifting human color memory. *Memory and Cognition, 5,* 696–699.

Loftus, E. F. (1993a). Psychologists in the eyewitness world. *American Psychologist, 48*(5), 550–552.

Loftus, E. (1993b). The reality of repressed memories. *American Psychologist, 48*(5), 518–537.

Loftus, E. F., & Doyle, J. M. (1992). *Eyewitness testimony: Civil and criminal* (2nd ed.). Charlottesville, VA: Michie Co.

Loftus, E., & Ketcham, K. (1991). *Witness for the defense: The accused, the eyewitness, and the expert who puts memory on trial.* New York: St. Martin's Press.

Loftus, E. F., Miller, D. G., & Burns, H. J. (1978). Semantic integration of verbal information into a visual memory. *Journal of Experimental Psychology: Human Learning and Memory, 4,* 19–31.

Loftus, E. F., Miller, D. G., & Burns, H. J. (1987). Semantic integration of verbal information into a visual memory. In L. W. Wrightsman, C. E. Willis, & S. M. Kassin (Eds.), *On the witness stand: Vol. W. Controversies in the courtroom.* Newbury Park, CA: Sage.

Logue, A. W., King, G. R., Chavarro, A., & Volpe, J. S. (1990). Matching and maximizing in a self-control paradigm using human subjects. *Learning & Motivation, 21*(3), 340–368.

Lonner, W. J. (1989). The introductory psychology text: Beyond Ekman, Whorf, and biased IQ tests. In D. M. Keats, D. Munro, & L. Mann (Eds.), *Heterogeneity in cross-cultural psychology.* Amsterdam: Swets & Zeitlinger.

Lonner, W. J. (1990). An overview of cross-cultural testing and assessment. In R. W. Brislin (Ed.), *Applied cross-cultural psychology.* Newbury Park, CA: Sage.

Lonner, W. J., & Berry, J. W. (1986). Sampling and surveying. In W. J. Lonner & J. W. Berry (Eds.), *Field methods in cross-cultural research: Vol. 8. Cross-cultural research and methodology series.* Beverly Hills, CA: Sage.

Lorenz, K. (1937). The companion in the bird's world. *Auk, 54,* 245–273.

Lorenz, K. (1950). The comparative method in studying innate behavior patterns. *Symposium for the Society for Experimental Biology, 4,* 221–268.

Lumsdaine, A. A., & Janis, I. L. (1953). Resistance to "counterpropaganda" produced by one-sided and two-sided "propaganda" presentation. *Public Opinion Quarterly, 17,* 311–318.

Luria, A. R. (1968). *The mind of a mnemonist.* New York: Basic Books.

Ma, H. K. (1988). The Chinese perspectives on moral judgment development. *International Journal of Psychology, 23*(2), 201–227.

MacFarlane, A. (1975). Olfaction in the development of social preferences in the human neonate. *Ciba Foundation Symposium, 33,* 103–117.

Maehr, M., & Nicholls, J. (1980). Culture and achievement motivation: A second look. In N. Warren (Ed.), *Studies in cross-cultural psychology* (Vol. 2). London: Academic Press.

Maier, S. F., Watkins, L. R., & Fleshner, M. (1994). Psychoneuroimmunology: The interface between behavior, brain, and immunity. *American Psychologist, 49*(12), 1004–1017.

Mandler, J. M. (1990). A new perspective on cognitive development in infancy. *American Scientist, 78,* 236–243.

Manji, H. K., Hsiao, J. K., Risby, E. D., et al. (1991). The mechanisms of action of lithium: I. Effects on serotonergic and noradrenergic systems in normal subjects. *Archives of General Psychiatry, 48,* 505–512.

Mantyla, T. (1986). Optimizing cue effectiveness: Recall of 500 and 600 incidentally learned words. *Journal of Experimental Psychology: Learning, Memory, and Cognition, 12,* 66–71.

Maqsud, M., & Rouhani, S. (1990). Self-concept and moral reasoning among Batswana adolescents. *Journal of Social Psychology, 130*(6), 829–830.

Marcel, A. J. (1983). Conscious and unconscious perception: An approach to the relations between phenomenal experience and perceptual processes. *Cognitive Psychology, 15,* 238–300.

Marcia, J. E. (1966). Development and validation of ego identity status. *Journal of Personality and Social Psychology, 3*(5), 551–558.

Marcia, J. E. (1980). Identity in adolescence. In J. Adelson (Ed.), *Handbook of adolescent psychology* (pp. 159–187). New York: Wiley.

Marks, I. M., & Gelder, M. G. (1967). Transvestism and fetishism: Clinical and psychological changes during faradic aversion. *British Journal of Psychiatry, 113,* 711–729.

Markus, H. R., & Kitayama, S. (1991). Culture and the self: Implications for cognition, emotion, and motivation. *Psychological Review, 98*(2), 224–253.

Marsella, A. J. (1980). Depressive experience and disorder across cultures. In H. C. Triandis & J. Draguns (Eds.), *Handbook of cross-cultural psychology: Vol. 6. Psychopathology* (pp. 237–289). Boston: Allyn & Bacon.

Marsella, A. J., Hirschfeld, R. M. A., & Katz, M. M. (1987). *The measurement of depression.* New York: The Guilford Press.

Marshall, G. D., & Zimbardo, P. G. (1979). Affective consequences of inadequately explained arousal. *Journal of Personality and Social Psychology, 37,* 970–985.

Martin, F. E. (1985). The treatment and outcome of anorexia nervosa in adolescents: A prospective study and five-year follow-up. *Journal of Psychiatric Research, 19,* 509–514.

Martin, J. A. (1981). A longitudinal study of the consequences of early mother–infant interaction: A microanalytic approach. *Monographs of the Society for Research in Child Development, 46*(203, Serial No. 190).

Martin, L. (1986). Eskimo words for snow: A case study in the genesis and decay of an anthropological example. *American Psychologist, 88,* 418–423.

Martindale, C. (1981). *Cognition and consciousness.* Homewood, IL: Dorsey Press.

Maslach, C., & Jackson, S. E. (1984). Burnout in organizational settings. *Applied Social Psychology Annual, 5,* 133–153.

Maslow, A. H. (1943). A theory of human motivation. *Psychological Review, 50,* 370–396.

Maslow, A. H. (1954). *Motivation and personality.* New York: Harper & Row.

Maslow, A. H. (1970). *Motivation and personality* (2nd ed.). New York: Harper.

Masters, W. H., & Johnson, V. E. (1966). *Human sexual response.* Boston: Little, Brown.

Matarazzo, J. D. (1992). Biological and physiological correlates of intelligence. *Intelligence, 16*(3, 4), 257–258.

Matsumoto, D. (1994). *People: Psychology from a cross-cultural perspective.* Belmont, CA: Brooks/Cole.

Matsumoto, D. (1996). *Culture and psychology.* Belmont, CA: Brooks/Cole.

Mayer, D. J. (1953). Glucostatic mechanism of regulation of food intake. *New England Journal of Medicine, 249,* 13–16.

Mayer, G. R., Butterworth, T., Nafpaktitis, M., & Sulzer-Azaroff, B. (1983). Preventing school vandalism and improving discipline: A three-year study. *Journal of Applied Behavior Analysis, 16*(4), 355–369.

McArthur, L. Z., & Berry, D. S. (1987). Cross-cultural agreement in perceptions of babyfaced adults. *Journal of Cross-Cultural Psychology, 18*(2), 165–192.

McCarley, R. W., & Hobson, J. A. (1981). REM sleep dreams and the activation–synthesis hypothesis. *American Journal of Psychiatry, 138,* 904–912.

McClelland, D. C. (1961). *The achieving society.* Princeton, NJ: Van Nostrand.

McClelland, D. C. (1985). *Human motivation.* New York: Scott, Foresman.

McClelland, D. (1987). *Human motivation.* Cambridge, England: Cambridge University Press.

McClelland, D. C., Atkinson, J. W., Clark, R. A., & Lowell, E. L. (1953). *The achievement motive.* New York: Appleton-Century-Crofts.

McClelland, D. C., & Winter, D. G. (1969). *Motivating economic achievement.* New York: The Free Press.

McCrae, R., & John, O. (1992). An introduction to the five-factor model and its applications. *Journal of Personality, 60,* 175–215.

McDougall, W. (1908). *An introduction to social psychology.* London: Methuen.

McGarry-Roberts, P. A., Stelmack, R. M., & Campbell, K. B. (1992). Intelligence, reaction time, and event-related potentials. *Intelligence, 16*(3, 4), 289–313.

McKenna, J., Treadway, M., & McCloskey, M. E. (1992). Expert psychological testimony on eyewitness reliability: Selling psychology before its time. In P. Suedfeld & P. E. Tetlock (Eds.), *Psychology and social policy* (pp. 283–293). New York: Hemisphere.

Meeker, W. B., & Barber, T. X. (1971). Toward an explanation of stage hypnosis. *Journal of Abnormal Psychology, 77,* 61–70.

Meltzoff, A. N. (1988a). Imitation of televised models by infants. *Child Development, 59*(5), 1221–1229.

Meltzoff, A. N. (1988b). Infant imitation and memory: Nine-month-olds in immediate and deferred tests. *Child Development, 59*(1), 217–225.

Melzack, R., & Wall, P. D. (1965). Pain mechanisms: A new theory. *Science, 150,* 971–979.

Melzack, R., & Wall, P. D. (1982). *The challenge of pain.* New York: Basic Books.

Melzack, R., Wall, P. D., & Ty, T. C. (1982). Acute pain in an emergency clinic: Latency of onset and descriptor patterns related to different injuries. *Pain, 14*(1), 33–43.

Merriam-Webster's collegiate dictionary (10th ed.) (1993). Springfield, MA: Merriam-Webster.

Mesquita, B., & Frijda, N. H. (1992). Cultural variations in emotions: A review. *Psychological Bulletin, 112*(3), 179–204.

Metcalfe, J. (1986). Feeling of knowing in memory and problem solving. *Journal of Experimental Psychology: Learning, Memory, and Cognition, 12*(2), 288–294.

Metcalfe, J., & Wiebe, D. (1987). Intuition in insight and noninsight problem solving. *Memory & Cognition, 15*(3), 238–246.

Milgram, S. (1963). Behavioral study of obedience. *Journal of Abnormal and Social Psychology, 67,* 371–378.

Milgram, S. (1965). Some conditions of obedience and disobedience to authority. *Human Relations, 18,* 57–76.

Milgram, S. (1974). *Obedience to authority: An experimental view.* New York: Harper & Row.

Miller, G. A. (1956). The magical number seven, plus or minus two: Some limits on our capacity for processing information. *Psychological Review, 63,* 81–97.

Miller, G. A. (1990). *The science of words.* New York: Scientific American Library.

Miller, G. A., Galanter, E. H., & Pribram, K. H. (1960). *Plans and the structure of behavior.* New York: Holt, Rinehart and Winston.

Miller, N., & Brewer, M. B. (Eds.) (1984). *Groups in contact: The psychology of desegregation.* New York: Academic Press.

Milner, B., Corkin, S., & Teuber, H. L. (1968). Further analysis of the hippocampal amnesic syndrome: 14-year follow-up study of H. M. *Neuropsychologia, 6,* 215–234.

Mischel, W. (1968). *Personality and assessment.* New York: Wiley.

Mischel, W. (1977). On the future of personality measurement. *American Psychologist, 32,* 246–254.

Mischel, W. (1986). *Introduction to personality* (4th ed.). New York: Holt, Rinehart and Winston.

Mischel, W., & Peake, P. K. (1983). Some facets of consistency: Replies to Epstein, Funder, and Bem. *Psychological Review, 90,* 394–402.

Mishkin, M., & Petri, H. L. (1984). Memories and habits: Some implications for the analysis of learning and retention. In L. R. Squire & N. Butters (Eds.), *Neurophysiology of memory* (pp. 287–296). New York: The Guilford Press.

Moghaddam, F. M., Taylor, D. M., & Wright, S. C. (1993). *Social psychology in cross-cultural perspective.* New York: Freeman.

Money, J., Wiedeking, C., Walker, P. A., & Gain, D. (1976). Combined antiandrogenic and counseling program for treatment of 46 XY and 47 XYY sex offenders. *Hormones, Behavior, and Psychopathology, 66,* 105–109.

Montagu, A. (1976). *The nature of human aggression.* New York: Oxford University Press.

Moos, R. H. (1982). Coping with acute health crises. In T. Millon, C. Green, & R. Meagher (Eds.), *Handbook of clinical health psychology.* New York: Plenum.

Moos, R. H. (1988). Life stressors and coping resources influence health and well-being. *Psychological Assessment, 4,* 133–158.

Moos, R. H., & Schaefer, J. A. (1986). Life transitions and crises: A conceptual overview. In R. H. Moos (Ed.), *Coping with life crises: An integrated approach.* New York: Plenum.

Morgan, C. D., & Murray, H. A. (1935). A method for investigating fantasy: The Thematic Apperception Test. *Archives of Neurology and Psychiatry, 34,* 289–306.

Morton, T. U. (1978). Intimacy and reciprocity of exchange: A comparison of spouses and strangers. *Journal of Personality and Social Psychology, 36,* 72–81.

Moscovici, S., & Zavolloni, M. (1969). The group as a polarizer of attitudes. *Journal of Personality and Social Psychology, 12,* 125–135.

Murase, T., & Johnson, F. (1974). Naikan, Morita, and Western psychotherapy: A comparison. *Archives of General Psychiatry, 31*(1), 121–128.

Murray, H. A. (1938). *Explorations in personality.* New York: Oxford University Press.

Murray, H. A. (1943a). *Explorations in personality.* New York: Oxford University Press. (Original work published 1938)

Murray, H. A. (1943b). *Thematic Apperception Test.* Cambridge, MA: Harvard University Press.

Murray, H. A. (1943c). *The Thematic Apperception Test: Manual.* Cambridge, MA: Harvard University Press.

Murstein, B. I. (1986). *Paths to marriage.* Beverly Hills, CA: Sage.

Murstein, B. I., & Brust, R. G. (1985). Humor and interpersonal attraction. *Journal of Personality Assessment, 49*(6), 637–640.

Myers, D. G., & Lamm, H. (1976). The group polarization phenomenon. *Psychological Bulletin, 83,* 602–627.

Myerson, A. (1940). [Review of *Mental disorders in urban areas: An ecological study of schizophrenia and other psychoses.*] *American Journal of Psychiatry, 96,* 995–997.

Nash, M. (1987). What, if anything, is regressed about hypnotic age regression? A review of the empirical literature. *Psychological Bulletin, 102*(1), 42–52.

National Center for Health Statistics. (1988). Advance report of final mortality statistics, 1986. *NCHS Monthly Vital Statistics Report, 37*(Suppl. 6).

Neisser, U. (1982). Snapshots or benchmarks? In U. Neisser (Ed.), *Memory observed: Remembering in natural contexts.* San Francisco: Freeman.

Nelson, C. (1990). *Gender and the social studies: Training preservice secondary social studies teachers.* Doctoral dissertation, University of Minnesota.

Neto, F., Williams, J. E., & Widner, S. C. (1991). Portuguese children's knowledge of sex stereotypes: Effects of age, gender, and socioeconomic status. *Journal of Cross-Cultural Psychology, 22*(3), 376–388.

Newcomb, T. M. (1943). *Personality and social change.* New York: Dryden.

Newell, A., & Simon, H. A. (1972). *Human problem solving.* Englewood Cliffs, NJ: Prentice-Hall.

Nickerson, R. S., & Adams, M. J. (1979). Long-term memory for a common object. *Cognitive Psychology, 11,* 287–307.

Nicolaus, L. K., Cassell, J. F., Carlson, R. B., & Gustavson, C. R. (1983). Taste-aversion conditioning of crows to control predation on eggs. *Science, 220*(4593).

Nicolaus, L. K., Farmer, P. V., Gustavson, C. R., & Gustavson, J. C. (1989). The potential of estrogen-based conditioned aversion in controlling depredation: A step closer to the "magic bullet." *Applied Animal Behaviour Science, 23*(1, 2), 1–14.

Nicolaus, L. K., & Nellis, D. W. (1987). The first evaluation of the use of conditioned taste aversion to control predation by mongooses upon eggs. *Applied Animal Behaviour Science, 17*(3, 4), 329–346.

Nielson, S. (1990). Epidemiology of anorexia nervosa in Denmark from 1983–1987: A nationwide register study of psychiatric admission. *Acta Psychiatrica Scandinavica, 81,* 507–514.

Niemczynski, A., Czyzowska, D., Pourkos, M., & Mirski, A. (1988). The Cracow study with Kohlberg's moral judgment interview: Data pertaining to the assumption of cross-cultural validity. *Polish Psychological Bulletin, 19*(1), 43–53.

Nisan, M., & Kohlberg, L. (1982). Universality and variation in moral judgment: A longitudinal and cross-sectional study in Turkey. *Child Development, 53,* 865–876.

Nisbett, R. E. (1972). Hunger, obesity, and the ventromedial hypothalamus. *Psychological Review, 79,* 433–453.

Nisbett, R. (1995). Race, IQ, and scientism. In S. Fraser (Ed.), *The bell curve wars: Race, intelligence and the future of America* (pp. 36–57). New York: Basic Books.

Nisbett, R. E., Caputo, C., Legant, P., & Maracek, J. (1973). Behavior as seen by the actor and as seen by the observer. *Journal of Personality and Social Psychology, 27,* 154–164.

Noel, J. G., Forsyth, D. R., & Kelley, K. N. (1987). Improving the performance of failing students by overcoming their self-serving attributional biases. *Basic & Applied Social Psychology, 8*(1, 2), 151–162.

Norman, W. T. (1963). Toward an adequate taxonomy of personality attributes: Replicated factor structure in peer nomination personality ratings. *Journal of Abnormal and Social Psychology, 66,* 574–583.

Notarius, C., & Markman, H. (1993). *We can work it out.* New York: Putnam.

Oatley, K. (1993). Those to whom evil is done. In R. S. Wyer & T. K Srull (Eds.), *Perspectives on anger and emotion: Advances in social cognition* (Vol. 6, pp. 159–165). Hillsdale, NJ: Erlbaum.

Ogbu, J. U. (1982). Origins of human competence: A cultural–ecological perspective. *Annual Progress in Child Psychiatry & Child Development,* 113–140.

Ogbu, J. U. (1986). The consequences of the American caste system. In U. Neisser (Ed.), *The school achievement of minority children.* Hillsdale, NJ: Erlbaum.

Ogbu, J. U. (1988). Cultural diversity and human development in black children and poverty: A developmental perspective. In D. T. Slaughter (Ed.), *New directions in child development* (Vol. 42). San Francisco: Jossey-Bass.

Olds, J., & Milner, P. (1954). Positive reinforcement produced by electrical stimulation of septal area and other regions of the rat brain. *Journal of Comparative and Physiological Psychology, 47,* 419–427.

Oliner, S., & Oliner, P. (1993). The roots of human attachments. In Arthur Dobrin (Ed.), *Being good and doing right: Readings in moral development* (pp. 121–139). Lanham, MD: University Press of America.

Oomara, Y. (1976). Significance of glucose insulin and free fatty acid on the hypothalamic feeding and satiety neurons. In D. Novin, W. Wyrwicka, & G. Bray (Eds.), *Hunger: Basic mechanisms and clinical implications.* New York: Raven Press.

Orne, M. T. (1959). Hypnosis: Artifact and essence. *Journal of Abnormal Psychology, 58,* 277–299.

Ornstein, R. (1977). *The psychology of consciousness* (2nd ed.). New York: Harcourt Brace Jovanovich.

Ornstein, R. (1986). *The psychology of consciousness* (2nd Rev. ed.). New York: Pelican Books.

Ott, E. M. (1989). Effects of male–female ratio at work: Policewomen and male nurses. *Psychology of Women Quarterly, 13*(1), 41–57.

Overton, W. F. (1990). *Reasoning, necessity, and logic: Developmental perspectives.* Hillsdale, NJ: Erlbaum.

Paivio, A. (1971). *Imagery and verbal processes.* New York: Holt, Rinehart and Winston.

Papini, M. R., & Bitterman, M. E. (1990). The role of contingency in classical conditioning. *Psychological Review, 97*(3), 396–403.

Papp, L., & Gorman, J. M. (1990). Suicidal preoccupation during fluoxetine treatment. *American Journal of Psychiatry, 147,* 1380.

Park, R. D., & Walters, R. H. (1967). Some factors influencing the efficacy of punishment training for inducing response inhibition. *Monographs of the Society for Research in Child Development, 32*(1, Whole No. 109).

Parke, R. D., Berkowitz, L., Leyens, J. P., West, S. G., & Sebastian, R. J. (1977). Some effects of violent and nonviolent movies on the behavior of juvenile delinquents. In L. Berkowitz (Ed.), *Advances in experimental social psychology* (Vol. 10). New York: Academic Press.

Paul, G. L. (1967). Strategy of outcome research in psychotherapy. *Journal of Consulting Psychology, 31*, 109–118.

Pavlov, I. P. (1928). *Lectures on conditioned reflexes: The higher nervous activity of animals* (Vol. 1, H. Gantt, Trans.). London: Lawrence & Wishart.

Pavlov, I. P. (1955). *Selected works.* Moscow: Foreign Languages Publishing House.

Payne, J. (1976). Task complexity and contingent processing in decision making: An information search and protocol analysis. *Organizational Behavior and Human Performance, 16*, 366–387.

Peabody, D., & Goldberg, L. R. (1989). Some determinants of factor structures from personality-trait descriptors. *Journal of Personality and Social Psychology, 57*(3), 552–567.

Pearlstone, A., Russell, R. J. H., & Wells, P. A. (1994). A re-examination of the stress/illness relationship: How useful is the concept of stress? *Personality & Individual Differences, 17*(4), 577–580.

Pedersen, P. B., Draguns, J. G., Lonner, W. J., & Trimble, J. E. (Eds.) (in press). *Counseling across cultures* (4th ed.). Newbury Park, CA: Sage.

Pelchat, M. L., & Rozin, P. (1982). The special role of nausea in the acquisition of food dislikes by humans. *Appetite, 3*(4), 341–351.

Perris, C., & Herlofson, J. (1993). Cognitive therapy. In N. Sartorius, G. de Girolano, G. Andrews, G. A. German, & L. Eisenberg (Eds.), *Treatment of mental disorders: A review of effectiveness.* Geneva, Switzerland, and Washington, DC: World Health Organization and American Psychiatric Press.

Peterson, L. R., & Peterson, M. J. (1959). Short-term retention of individual verbal items. *Journal of Experimental Psychology, 58*, 193–198.

Petty, R. E., & Cacioppo, J. T. (1981). *Attitudes and persuasion: Classic and contemporary approaches.* Dubuque, IA: William C. Brown.

Pfaffman, C. (1974). Specificity of the sweet receptors of the squirrel monkey. *Chemical Senses and Flavor, 1*, 61–67.

Pfeiffer, W. M. (1982). Culture-bound syndromes. In I. Al-Issa (Ed.), *Culture and psychopathology.* Baltimore: University Park Press.

Phares, E. J. (1988). *Introduction to personality* (2nd ed.). Glenview, IL: Scott, Foresman.

Phares, E. J. (1991). *Introduction to personality* (3rd ed.). New York: Harper-Collins.

Phillips, D. A. (1984). The illusion of incompetence among academically competent children. *Child Development, 55*, 2000–2016.

Phillips, D. A., & Zimmerman, M. (1990). The developmental course of perceived competence and incompetence among competent children. In R. J. Sternberg & J. Kolligian, Jr. (Eds.), *Competence considered* (pp. 41–77). New Haven, CT: Yale University Press.

Piaget, J. (1969). *The child's conception of physical causality.* Totowa, NJ: Littlefield, Adams.

Piaget, J. (1972). *The psychology of intelligence.* Totowa, NJ: Littlefield, Adams.

Pinker, S. (1994). *The language instinct.* New York: William Morrow.

Plomin, R. (1986). *Development, genetics, and psychology.* Hillsdale, NJ: Erlbaum.

Plomin, R. C. (1989). Environment and games: Determinants of behavior. *American Psychologist, 44*, 105–111.

Plomin, R. (in press). Identifying genes for cognitive abilities and disabilities. In R. J. Sternberg & E. Grigorenko (Eds.), *Intelligence, heredity, and environment.* New York: Cambridge University Press.

Plutchik, R. (1980). *Emotion: A psychoevolutionary analysis.* New York: Harper & Row.

Plutchik, R. (1983). Emotions in early development: A psychoevolutionary approach. In R. Plutchik & H. Kellerman (Eds.), *Emotion: Theory, research, and experience* (Vol. 2). New York: Academic Press.

Poe, E. A. (1979). The tell-tale heart. In *Tales of Edgar Allan Poe* (p. 179). Franklin Center, PA: Franklin Library. (Original work published 1843)

Poincaré, H. (1913). *The foundations of science.* New York: Science Press.

Poizner, H., Bellugi, U., & Klima, E. S. (1990). Biological foundations of language: Clues from sign language. *Annual Review of Neuroscience, 13*, 282–307.

Poizner, H., Kaplan, E., Bellugi, U., & Padden, C. A. (1984). Visual–spatial processing in deaf brain-damaged signers. *Brain & Cognition, 3*(3), 281–306.

Pokorny, A. D. (1968). Myths about suicide. In H. Resnik (Ed.), *Suicidal behaviors.* Boston: Little, Brown.

Polivy, J., & Herman, C. P. (1983). *Breaking the diet habit.* New York: Basic Books.

Polivy, J., & Herman, C. P. (1985). Dieting and binging. *American Psychologist, 40*, 193–201.

Poon, L. W. (1987). *Myths and truisms: Beyond extant analyses of speed of behavior and age.* Address to the Eastern Psychological Association Convention.

Posner, M., & Keele, S. W. (1968). On the genesis of abstract ideas. *Journal of Experimental Psychology, 77*(3, Pt. 1), 353–363.

Pratkanis, A. R., Eskenazi, J., & Greenwald, A. G. (1994). What you expect is what you believe (but not necessarily what you get): A test of the effectiveness of subliminal self-help audiotapes. *Basic & Applied Social Psychology, 15*(3), 251–276.

Pullum, G. K. (1991). *The Great Eskimo vocabulary hoax and other irreverent essays on the study of language.* Chicago: University of Chicago Press.

Ramey, C. T. (1994). Abecedarian project. In R. J. Sternberg (Ed.), *Encyclopedia of human intelligence* (Vol. 1, pp. 1–3). New York: Macmillan.

Rapaport, D., Gill, M. M., & Schafer, R. (1968). *Diagnostic psychological testing.* New York: International Universities Press.

Reed, T. E. (1993). Effect of enriched (complex) environment on nerve conduction velocity: New data and review of implications for the speed of information processing. *Intelligence, 17*(4), 533–540.

Reed, T. E., & Jensen, A. R. (1992). Conduction velocity in a brain nerve pathway of normal adults correlates with intelligence level. *Intelligence, 16*(3, 4), 259–272.

Regan, D. T. (1971). Effects of a favor and liking on compliance. *Journal of Experimental Social Psychology, 7*, 627–639.

Reitman, J. S. (1974). Without surreptitious rehearsal, information in short-term memory decays. *Journal of Verbal Learning and Verbal Behavior, 13*, 365–377.

Renzulli, J. S. (1986). The three ring conception of giftedness: A developmental model for creative productivity. In R. J. Sternberg & J. E. Davidson (Eds.), *Conceptions of giftedness* (pp. 53–92). New York: Cambridge University Press.

Rescorla, R. A. (1967). Pavlovian conditioning and its proper control procedures. *Psychological Review, 74*, 71–80.

Resnik, H. L. P. (Ed.) (1968). *Suicidal behaviors.* Boston: Little, Brown.

Rest, J. R. (1983). Moral development. In P. H. Mussen (Ed.), *Handbook of child psychology* (4th ed., Vol. 3, pp. 556–629). New York: Wiley.

Restak, R. (1984). *The brain.* New York: Bantam.

Reynolds, D. K. (1989). On being natural: Two Japanese approaches to healing. In A. A. Sheikh & K. S. Sheikh (Eds.), *Eastern and Western approaches to healing: Ancient wisdom and modern knowledge (Wiley series on health psychology/behavioral medicine)* (pp. 180–194). New York: Wiley.

Ringelmann, M. (1913). Recherches sur les moteurs animés: Travail de l'homme. *Annales de l'Institur National Agronomique, 2s série, tom XII*, 1–40.

Roark, A. C. (1992, August 18). It's dope, so chill; for the young, slang's "mad" new words are straight off the streets of Los Angeles. *Los Angeles Times, 111*, pp. E1, E7.

Robins, L. N., Helzer, J. E., Weissman, M. M., Orvaschel, H., Gruenberg, E., Burke, J. D., & Regier, D. (1984). Lifetime prevalence of specific psychiatric disorders in three sites. *Archives of General Psychiatry, 41*, 949–958.

Rodin, J., & Plante, T. (1989). The psychological effects of exercise. In R. S. Williams & A. Wellece (Eds.), *Biological effects of physical activity* (pp. 127–137). Champaign, IL: Human * Kinetics.

Rodriguez, M., Mischel, W., & Shoda, Y. (1989). Cognitive person variables in the delay of gratification of older children at risk. *Journal of Personality & Social Psychology, 57*(2), 358–367.

Roediger, H. L., III. (1980). Memory metaphors in cognitive psychology. *Memory and Cognition, 8*(3), 231–246.

Rogers, C. R. (1959). A theory of therapy, personality, and interpersonal relationships, as developed in the client-centered framework. In S. Koch (Ed.), *Psychology: A study of a science* (Vol. 3). New York: McGraw-Hill.

Rogers, C. R. (1961a). *On becoming a person: A client's view of psychotherapy.* Boston: Houghton Mifflin.

Rogers, C. R. (1961b). *On becoming a person: A therapist's view of psychotherapy.* Boston: Houghton Mifflin.

Rogers, C. R. (1978). The formative tendency. *Journal of Humanistic Psychology, 18*(1), 23–26.

Rogers, C. R. (1980). *A way of being.* Boston: Houghton Mifflin.

Rogers, S. M., & Turner, C. F. (1991). Male–male sexual contact in the U.S.A.: Findings from five sample surveys, 1970–1990. *Journal of Sex Research, 28*(4), 491–519.

Rojahn, K., & Pettigrew, T. F. (1992). Memory for schema-relevant information: A meta-analytic resolution. *British Journal of Social Psychology, 31*(2), 81–109.

Rokeach, M. (1964). *The three Christs of Ypsilanti.* New York: Columbia University Press.

Rolls, B. J. (1979). How variety and palatability can stimulate appetite. *Nutrition Bulletin, 5*, 78–86.

Rolls, B. J., Rowe, E. T., & Rolls, E. T. (1982). How sensory properties of food affect human feeding behavior. *Physiology and Behavior, 29*, 409–417.

Rosch, E. (1973). On the internal structure of perceptual and semantic categories. In T. E. Moore (Ed.), *Cognitive development and the acquisition of language.* New York: Academic Press.

Rosen, G. M. (1987). Self-help treatment books and the commercialization of psychotherapy. *American Psychologist, 42*(1), 46–51.

Rosenhan, D. L. (1973). On being sane in insane places. *Science, 179*, 250–258.

Rosenthal, R., & Jacobson, L. (1968). *Pygmalion in the classroom: Teacher expectation and pupils' intellectual development.* New York: Holt, Rinehart and Winston.

Roskies, E., Seraganian, R., Hanley, J. A., Collu, R., Martin, N., & Smilga, C. (1986). The Montreal Type A intervention project: Major findings. *Health Psychology, 5*, 45–69.

Roskies, E., Spevack, M., Surkis, A., Cohen, C., & Gilman, S. (1978). Changing the coronary-prone (Type A) behavior pattern in a nonclinical population. *Journal of Behavioral Medicine, 1*, 201–216.

Ross, L. (1977). The intuitive psychologist and his shortcomings: Distortions in the attribution process. In L. Berkowitz (Ed.), *Advances in experimental social psychology* (Vol. 10). New York: Academic Press.

Ross, R. (1975). Salience of reward and intrinsic motivation. *Journal of Personality and Social Psychology, 32*, 245–254.

Rotter, J. B. (1966). Generalized expectancies for internal versus external control of reinforcement. *Psychological Monographs, 80*(1, Whole No. 609).

Rotter, J. B. (1988). Internal versus external control of reinforcement: A case history of a variable. American Psychological Association: Distinguished Scientific Contributions Award Address (1988, Atlanta, Georgia). *American Psychologist, 45*(4), 489–493.

Rotter, J. B. (1990). Internal versus external control of reinforcement: A case history of a variable. *American Psychologist, 45*, 489–493.

Rotter, J. B. (1992). "Cognates of personal control: Locus of control, self-efficacy, and explanatory style": Comment. *Applied & Preventive Psychology, 1*(2), 127–129.

Rotter, J. B., & Hochreich, D. J. (1975). *Personality.* Glenview, IL: Scott, Foresman.

Rovee-Collier, C., Borza, M. A., Adler, S. A., & Boller, K. (1993). Infants' eyewitness testimony: Effects of postevent information on a prior memory representation. *Memory & Cognition, 21*(2), 267–279.

Rozin, P., & Fallon, A. (1987). A perspective on disgust. *Psychological Review, 94*, 23–41.

Ruch, J. C. (1975). Self-hypnosis: The result of heterohypnosis or vice versa? *International Journal of Clinical and Experimental Hypnosis, 23*, 282–304.

Rudy, T. E., Kerns, R. D., & Turk, D. C. (1988). Chronic pain and depression: Toward a cognitive-behavioral mediation model. *Pain, 35*, 129–140.

Russell, J. A. (1991). Culture and categorization of emotions. *Psychological Bulletin, 110*(3), 426–450.

Russell, J. A. (1995). Is there universal recognition of emotion from facial expression? A review of the cross-cultural studies. *Psychological Bulletin, 115*(1), 102–141.

Russell, M. J. (1976). Human olfactory communication. *Nature, 260*, 520–522.

Russell, W. R., & Nathan, P. W. (1946). Traumatic amnesia. *Brain, 69*, 280–300.

Sacks, O. (1990). *Seeing voices: A journey into the world of the deaf.* New York: HarperPerennial.

Sacks, O. (1995). *An anthropologist on Mars: Seven paradoxical tales.* New York: Knopf.

Sadker, M., & Sadker, D. (1984). *Year three: Final report, promoting effectiveness in classroom instruction.* Washington, DC: National Institute of Education.

Safer, D. J. (1991). Diet, behavior modification, and exercise: A review of obesity treatments from a long-term perspective. *Southern Medical Journal, 84*, 1470–1474.

Safire, W., & Safir, L. (Eds.) (1989). *Words of wisdom: More good advice.* New York: Fireside, Simon & Schuster.

Sanders, S. H. (1985). Chronic pain: Conceptualization and epidemiology. *Annals of Behavioral Medicine, 7*(3), 3–5.

Sarason, S. B., & Doris, J. (1979). *Educational handicap, public policy, and social history.* New York: The Free Press.

Sarason, I. G., Pierce, G. R., & Sarason, B. R. (1994). General and specific perceptions of social support. In W. R. Avison & I. H. Gotlib (Eds.), *Stress and mental health: Contemporary issues and prospects for the future (Plenum series on stress and coping)* (pp. 151–177). New York: Plenum.

Sartorius, N., de Girolano, G., Andrews, G., German, G. A., & Eisenberg, L. (Eds.) (1993a). *Treatment of mental disorders: A review of effectiveness.* Geneva, Switzerland, and Washington, DC: World Health Organization and American Psychiatric Press.

Sartorius, N., Kaelber, C., Cooper, J. E., Roper, M. T., et al. (1993b). Progress toward achieving a common language in psychiatry: Results from the field trial of the clinical guidelines accompanying the WHO classification of mental and behavioral disorders in ICD-10. *Archives of General Psychiatry, 50*(2), 115–124.

Sartorius, N., Shapiro, R., & Jablonsky, A. (1974). The international pilot study of schizophrenia. *Schizophrenia Bulletin, 2*, 21–35.

Savery, L. K., & Wooden, M. (1994). The relative influence of life events and hassles on work-related injuries: Some Australian evidence. *Human Relations, 47*(3), 283–305.

Saxe, L., Dougherty, D., & Cross, T. (1985). The validity of polygraph testing: Scientific analysis and public controversy. *American Psychologist, 40*, 355–366.

Scarr, S. (in press). Behavior genetic and socialization theories of intelligence: Truce and reconciliation. In R. J. Sternberg & E. L. Grigorenko (Eds.), *Intelligence, heredity, and environment.* New York: Cambridge University Press.

Schachter, S. (1968). Obesity and eating. *Science, 161*, 751–756.

Schachter, S. (1971a). *Emotion, obesity, and crime.* New York: Academic Press.

Schachter, S. (1971b). Some extraordinary facts about obese humans and rats. *American Psychologist, 26*, 129–144.

Schachter, S., & Gross, L. (1968). Manipulated time and eating behavior. *Journal of Personality and Social Psychology, 10*, 98–106.

Schachter, S., & Rodin, J. (1974). *Obese humans and rats.* Hillsdale, NJ: Erlbaum.

Schachter, S., & Singer, J. (1962). Cognitive, social, and physiological determinants of emotional state. *Psychological Review, 69*, 379–399.

Schacter, D. L. (1989a). Memory. In M. I. Posner (Ed.), *Foundations of cognitive science* (pp. 683–725). Cambridge, MA: MIT Press.

Schacter, D. L. (1989b). On the relation between memory and consciousness: Dissociable interactions and conscious experience. In H. L.

Roediger & F. I. M. Craik (Eds.), *Varieties of memory and consciousness: Essays in honor of Endel Tulving*. Hillsdale, NJ: Erlbaum.

Schaffer, H. R. (1977). *Mothering*. Cambridge, MA: Harvard University Press.

Schaie, K. W. (1989). Perceptual speed in adulthood: Cross-sectional and longitudinal studies. *Psychology and Aging, 4*, 443–453.

Schliemann, A. D., & Magalhües, V. P. (1990). *Proportional reasoning: From shops, to kitchens, laboratories, and, hopefully, schools*. Proceedings of the Fourteenth International Conference for the Psychology of Mathematics Education, Oaxtepec, Mexico.

Schreiber, F. R. (1973). *Sybil*. New York: Warner Paperback.

Schwarzer, R., & Leppin, A. (1989). Social support and health: A meta-analysis. *Psychology & Health, 3*(1), 1–15.

Schwarzer, R., & Leppin, A. (1991). Social support and health: A theoretical and empirical overview. *Journal of Social & Personal Relationships, 8*(1), 99–127.

Schweizer, E., Rickels, K., Case, G., & Greenblatt, D. J. (1990). Long-term therapeutic use of benzodiazepines: II. Effects of gradual taper. *Archives of General Psychiatry, 47*(10), 908–915.

Scott, A. I. F. (1989). Which depressed patients will respond to electro-convulsive therapy? The search for biological predictors of recovery. *British Journal of Psychiatry, 154*, 8–17.

Scott, J. (1991, August 26). Judging the risk of infection: The AIDS epidemic is making patients fearful of being infected by health-care workers. But some say the odds are far less that one will be hit by lightning. *Los Angeles Times*, p. A1.

Scovern, A. W., & Kilmann, P. R. (1980). Status of electroconvulsive therapy: Review of the outcome literature. *Psychological Bulletin, 87*, 260–303.

Scoville, W. B., & Milner, B. (1957). Loss of recent memory after bilateral hippocampal lesions. *Journal of Neurology, Neurosurgery, and Psychiatry, 20*, 11–19.

Sears, R. R., Maccoby, E., & Levin, H. (1957). *Patterns of child rearing*. Evanston, IL: Row, Peterson.

Segall, M. H., Campbell, D. T., & Herskovits, M. J. (1966). *The influence of culture on visual perception*. New York: Bobbs-Merrill.

Seiden, R. H. (1974). Suicide: Preventable death. *Public Affairs Report, 15*(4), 1–5.

Seidman, L. J. (1983). Schizophrenia and brain dysfunction: An integration of recent neurodiagnostic findings. *Psychological Bulletin, 94*, 195–238.

Selfridge, O. G. (1959). Pandemonium: A paradigm for learning. In D. V. Blake & A. M. Uttley (Eds.), *Proceedings of the Symposium on the Mechanization of Thought Processes* (pp. 511–529). London: Her Majesty's Stationery Office.

Seligman, M. E. P. (1975). *Helplessness*. San Francisco: Freeman.

Seligman, M. E. P. (1989). Research in clinical psychology: Why is there so much depression today? In Ira S. Cohen (Ed.), *The G. Stanley Hall lecture series* (Vol. 9, pp. 79–96). Washington, DC: American Psychological Association.

Seligman, M. E. P., & Maier, S. F. (1967). Failure to escape traumatic shock. *Journal of Experimental Psychology, 74*, 1–9.

Selman, R. (1981). The child as friendship philosopher. In J. M. Gottman (Ed.), *The development of children's friendships*. Cambridge, England: Cambridge University Press.

Selye, H. (1974). *Stress without distress*. Philadelphia: Lippincott.

Selye, H. (1976). *The stress of life* (Rev. ed.). New York: McGraw-Hill.

Seraganian, P. (Ed.) (1993). *Exercise psychology: The influence of physical exercise on psychological processes*. New York: Wiley.

Seymour, R. B., & Smith, D. E. (1987). *Guide to psychoactive drugs: An up-to-the-minute reference to mind-altering substances*. New York: Harrington Park Press.

Shanab, M. E., & Yahya, K. A. (1977). A behavioral study of obedience in children. *Journal of Personality and Social Psychology, 35*, 530–536.

Shanab, M. E., & Yahya, K. A. (1978). A cross-cultural study of obedience. *Bulletin of the Psychonomic Society, 11*, 267–269.

Shapiro, D. H., & Giber, D. (1978). Meditation and psychotherapeutic effects: Self-regulation strategy and altered states of consciousness. *Archives of General Psychiatry, 35*, 294–302.

Shapiro, P., & Penrod, S. (1986). Meta-analysis of facial identification studies. *Psychological Bulletin, 100*(2), 139–156.

Shaver, P. R. (1994, August). *Attachment and care giving in adult romantic relationships*. Paper presented at the annual meeting of the American Psychological Association, Los Angeles.

Shekelle, R. B., Hulley, S. B., Neaton, J. D., Billings, J. H., Borhani, N. O., Gerace, T. A., Jacobs, D. R., Lasser, N. L., Mittelmark, M. B., & Stamler, J. (1985). The MRFIT behavior pattern study: II. Type A behavior and incidence of coronary heart disease. *American Journal of Epidemiology, 122*, 559–570.

Shepard, R. N. (1990). *Mindsights*. New York: W. H. Freeman.

Sheppard, J. A., & Arkin, R. M. (1989). Self-handicapping: The moderating role of public self-consciousness and task importance. *Personality and Social Psychology Bulletin, 15*, 252–265.

Sherif, M., Harvey, L. J., White, B. J., Hood, W. R., & Sherif, C. W. (1988). *The Robber's Cave experiment: Intergroup conflict and cooperation*. Middletown, CT: Wesleyan University Press. (Original work published 1961)

Sherman, S. J., Judd, C. M., & Park, B. (1989). Social cognition. *Annual Review of Psychology, 40*, 281–326.

Shimamura, A. P., & Squire, L. R. (1986). Korsakoff's syndrome: A study of the relation between anterograde amnesia and remote memory impairment. *Behavioral Neuroscience, 100*(2), 165–170.

Shneidman, E. S. (1973). Suicide. In *Encyclopedia Britannica*. Chicago: Encyclopedia Britannica.

Shontz, F. C. (1975). *The psychological aspects of physical illness and disability*. New York: Macmillan.

Shuit, D. P. (1994, May 22). Verdict heats up memory debate. *Los Angeles Times*, p. A3.

Siegel, E. F. (1979). Control of phantom limb pain by hypnosis. *American Journal of Clinical Hypnosis, 21*(4), 285–286.

Siegler, R. S. (1986). *Children's thinking*. Englewood Cliffs, NJ: Prentice-Hall.

Siegler, R. (1991). *Children's thinking* (2nd ed.). Englewood Cliffs, NJ: Prentice-Hall.

Silverstein, B., Peterson, B., & Perdue, L. (1986). Some correlates of the thin standard of bodily attractiveness in women. *International Journal of Eating Disorders, 5*, 145–155.

Simon, H. A. (1957). *Administrative behavior* (2nd ed.). Totowa, NJ: Littlefield, Adams.

Simon, H. A. (1976). Identifying basic abilities underlying intelligent performance of complex tasks. In L. B. Resnick (Ed.), *The nature of intelligence* (pp. 65–98). Hillsdale, NJ: Erlbaum.

Simon, W. H., & Gagnon, J. H. (1986). Sexual scripts: Permanence and change. *Archives of Sexual Behavior, 15*(2), 97–120.

Simonton, D. (1994). *Greatness: Who makes history and why*. New York: The Guilford Press.

Siskin, B., Staller, J., & Rorvik, D. (1989). *What are the chances? Risks, odds, and likelihood in everyday life*. New York: Penguin.

Skinner, B. F. (1974). *About behaviorism*. New York: Knopf.

Skinner, B. F. (1986). Why I am not a cognitive psychologist. In T. J. Knapp & L. C. Robertson (Eds.), *Approaches to cognition: Contrasts and controversies* (pp. 79–90). Hillsdale, NJ: Erlbaum.

Skinner, B. F. (1988). The phylogeny and ontogeny of behavior. In A. C. Catania & S. Harnad (Eds.), *The selection of behavior: The operant behaviorism of B. F. Skinner: Comments and consequences* (pp. 382–461). New York: Cambridge University Press.

Smith, D. (1982). Trends in counseling and psychotherapy. *American Psychologist, 37*, 802–809.

Smith, M. L., & Glass, G. V. (1977). Meta-analysis of psychotherapy outcome studies. *American Psychologist* (November), 752–760.

Smith, P. B., & Bond, M. H. (1994). *Social psychology across cultures: Analysis and perspectives*. Boston: Allyn & Bacon.

Smith, P. B., & Öngel, Ö. (1994). Who are we and where are we going? JCCP approaches its hundredth issue. *Journal of Cross-Cultural Psychology, 25*(1), 25–54.

Snarey, J. R., Reimer, J., & Kohlberg, L. (1985a). Development of social–moral reasoning among kibbutz adolescents: A longitudinal cross-cultural study. *Developmental Psychology, 21*, 3–17.

Snarey, J. R., Reimer, J., & Kohlberg, L. (1985b). The kibbutz as a model for moral education: A longitudinal cross-cultural study. *Journal of Applied Developmental Psychology, 6,* 151–172.

Snow, C. E. (1977). The development of conversation between mothers and babies. *Journal of Child Language, 4,* 1–22.

Solomon, G. F., & Temoshok, L. (1987). A psychoneuroimmunologic perspective on AIDS research: Questions, preliminary findings, and suggestions. *Journal of Applied Social Psychology, 17,* 286–308.

Solomon, R. L. (1980). The opponent-process theory of motivation: The costs of pleasure and the benefits of pain. *American Psychologist, 35,* 681–712.

Solomon, R. L., & Corbit, J. D. (1974). An opponent-process theory of motivation: I. Temporal dynamics of affect. *Psychological Review, 81,* 119–145.

Spangler, W. (1992). Validity of questionnaire and TAT measures of need for achievement: Two meta-analyses. *Psychological Bulletin, 112,* 140–154.

Spanos, N. P. (1992). Compliance and reinterpretation in hypnotic responding. *Contemporary Hypnosis, 9*(1), 7–15.

Spearman, C. (1927). *The abilities of man.* New York: Macmillan.

Specter, M. (1989, May 7). Seeing risk everywhere: In epidemic of fear, major threats ignored. *The Washington Post,* pp. A1, A20.

Sperling, G. (1960). The information available in brief visual presentations. *Psychological Monographs: General and Applied, 74,* 1–28.

Sperry, R. W. (1964). The great cerebral commissure. *Scientific American, 210*(1), 42–52.

Spicer, J., Jackson, R., & Scragg, R. (1993). The effects of anger management and social contact on risk of myocardial infarction in Type As and Type Bs. *Psychology and Health, 8*(4), 243–255.

Spitzer, L., & Rodin, J. (1981). Human eating behavior: A critical review of studies in normal weight and overweight individuals. *Appetite, 2,* 293–329.

Springer, S. P., & Deutsch, G. (1985). *Left brain, right brain.* New York: Freeman.

Squire, L. R. (1986). Mechanisms of memory. *Science, 232,* 1612–1619.

Squire, L. R. (1987). *Memory and the brain.* New York: Oxford University Press.

Sroufe, L. A. (1979). Socioemotional development. In J. D. Osofsky (Ed.), *Handbook of infant development.* New York: Wiley.

Srull, T. K., & Wyer, R. S., Jr. (1989). Person memory and judgment. *Psychology Review, 96*(1), 58–83.

Standing, L., Conezio, J., & Haber, R. N. (1970). Perception and memory for pictures: Single-trial learning of 2500 visual stimuli. *Psychonomic Science, 19,* 73–74.

Stedman's medical dictionary (25th ed.) (1990). Baltimore: Williams & Wilkins.

Steele, C. (1990, May). A conversation with Claude Steele. *APS Observer,* pp. 11–17.

Steptoe, A., & Appels, A. (Eds.) (1989). *Stress, personal control and health.* Chichester, England: Wiley.

Stern, D. (1977). *The first relationship: Mother and infant.* Cambridge, MA: Harvard University Press.

Stern, W. (1912). *Psychologische Methoden der Intelligenz-Prüfung.* Leipzig, Germany: Barth.

Sternberg, R. J. (1985a). *Beyond IQ: A triarchic theory of human intelligence.* New York: Cambridge University Press.

Sternberg, R. J. (1985b). Implicit theories of intelligence, creativity, and wisdom. *Journal of Personality and Social Psychology, 49,* 607–627.

Sternberg, R. J. (1986a). *Intelligence applied: Understanding and increasing your intellectual skills.* San Diego, CA: Harcourt Brace Jovanovich.

Sternberg, R. J. (1986b). A triangular theory of love. *Psychology Review, 93,* 119–135.

Sternberg, R. J. (1987). Teaching intelligence: The application of cognitive psychology to the improvement of intellectual skills. In J. B. Baron & R. J. Sternberg (Eds.), *Teaching thinking skills: Theory and practice* (pp. 182–218). New York: W. H. Freeman.

Sternberg, R. J. (1988a). Triangulating love. In R. J. Sternberg & M. L. Barnes (Eds.), *The psychology of love* (pp. 119–138). New Haven, CT: Yale University Press.

Sternberg, R. J. (1988b). *The triarchic mind.* New York: Viking.

Sternberg, R. J. (Ed.) (1990). *Wisdom: Its nature, origins, and development.* New York: Cambridge University Press.

Sternberg, R. J. (1994). Love is a story. *The General Psychologist, 30*(1), 1–11.

Sternberg, R. J., & Berg, C. A. (1992). Adults' conceptions of intelligence across the adult life span. *Psychology and Aging, 7*(2), 221–231.

Sternberg, R. J., & Davidson, J. E. (Eds.) (1986). *Conceptions of giftedness.* New York: Cambridge University Press.

Sternberg, R. J., & Lubart, T. I. (1991). An investment theory of creativity and its development. *Human Development, 34,* 1–31.

Sternberg, R. J., & Lubart, T. (1995). *Defying the crowd.* New York: The Free Press.

Sternberg, R. J., & Ruzgis, P. (Eds.) (1994). *Personality and intelligence.* New York: Cambridge University Press.

Sternberg, R. J., & Wagner, R. K. (Eds.) (1994). *Mind in context: Interactionist perspectives on human intelligence.* New York: Cambridge University Press.

Sternberg, S. (1966). High-speed memory scanning in human memory. *Science, 153,* 652–654.

Sternberg, S. (1969). Memory-scanning: Mental processes revealed by reaction-time experiments. *American Scientist, 4,* 421–457.

Stevenson-Hinde, J., Hinde, R. A., & Simpson, A. E. (1986). Behavior at home and friendly or hostile behavior in preschool. In D. Olweus, J. Block, & M. Radke-Yarrow (Eds.), *Development of antisocial and prosocial behavior: Research, theorism and issues.* Orlando, FL: Academic Press.

Stewart, A. J. (1982). The course of individual adaptation to life changes. *Journal of Personality and Social Psychology, 42,* 1100–1113.

Stewart, A. J., & Healy, J. M., Jr. (1985). Personality and adaptation to change. In R. Hogan & W. H. Jones (Eds.), *Perspectives in personality* (Vol. 1, pp. 117–144). Greenwich, CT: JAI Press.

Stewart, A. J., & Healy, J. M. (1989). Linking individual development and social changes. *American Psychologist, 44*(1), 30–42.

Stewart, A. J., Sokol, M., Healy, J. M., & Chester, N. L. (1986). Longitudinal studies of psychological consequences of life changes in children and adults. *Journal of Personality and Social Psychology, 50,* 143–151.

Stiles, W. B., Shapiro, D. A., & Elliott, R. (1986). Are all psychotherapies equivalent? *American Psychologist, 41*(2), 165–180.

Strauss, J. S., Kokes, F. R., Ritzler, B. A., Harder, D. W., & Van Ord, A. (1978). Patterns of disorder in first admission psychiatric patients. *Journal of Nervous and Mental Disease, 166,* 611–623.

Stroop, J. (1935). Studies of interference in serial verbal reactions. *Journal of Experimental Psychology, 18,* 624–643.

Sue, D., & Sue, D. (1990). *Counseling the culturally different* (2nd ed.). New York: Wiley.

Sue, S. (1977). Community mental health services to minority groups: Some optimism, some pessimism. *American Psychologist, 32,* 616–624.

Sue, S. (1991, August). *Ethnicity and mental health: Research and policy issues.* Invited address presented at the annual meeting of the American Psychological Association, San Francisco.

Sue, S., Akutsu, P. D., & Higashi, C. (1985). Training issues in conducting therapy with ethnic-minority-group clients. In P. Pedersen (Ed.), *Handbook of cross-cultural counseling and therapy.* New York: Greenwood Press.

Suematsu, H., Ishikawa, H., Kuboki, T., & Ito, T. (1985). Statistical studies on anorexia nervosa in Japan: Detailed clinical data on 1,011 patients. *Psychotherapy and Psychosomatics, 43,* 96–103.

Sulzer-Azaroff, B., & Mayer, G. R. (1991). *Behavior analysis for lasting change.* Fort Worth, TX: Holt, Rinehart and Winston.

Swann, W. B., Jr., & Pittman, T. S. (1977). Initiating play activity in children: The moderating influence of verbal cue on intrinsic motivation. *Child Development, 48,* 1125–1132.

Swartz, L. (1985). Anorexia nervosa as a culture-bound syndrome. *Social Science and Medicine, 20,* 725–730.

Swets, J. A., Tanner, W. P., Jr., & Birdsall, T. G. (1961). Decision processes in perception. *Psychological Review, 68,* 301–340.

Szasz, T. S. (1961). *The myth of mental illness.* New York: Harper & Row.

Szasz, T. S. (1963). *Law, liberty, and psychiatry.* New York: Macmillan.

Szmukler, G. I., & Russell, G. F. M. (1986). Outcome and prognosis of anorexia nervosa. In K. D. Brownell & J. P. Foreyt (Eds.), *Handbook of eating disorders.* New York: Basic Books.

Tanford, S., & Penrod, S. (1984). Social influence model: A formal integration of research on majority and minority influence processes. *Psychological Bulletin, 95,* 189–225.

Tannen, D. (1986). *That's not what I meant! How conversational style makes or breaks relationships.* New York: Ballantine.

Tannen, D. (1990). *You just don't understand: Women and men in conversation.* New York: Ballantine.

Taylor, S. E. (1983). Adjustment to threatening events: A theory of cognitive adaptation. *American Psychologist, 38,* 1161–1173.

Taylor, S. E. (1990). Health psychology: The science and the field. *American Psychologist, 45*(1), 40–50.

Taylor, S. E. (1991). *Health psychology* (2nd ed.). New York: McGraw-Hill.

Taylor, S. E., & Aspinwall, L. G. (1990). Psychological aspects of chronic illness. In G. R. Van den Bos & P. T. Costa, Jr. (Eds.), *Psychological aspects of serious illness.* Washington, DC: American Psychological Association.

Taylor, S. E., & Brown, J. D. (1988). Illusion and well-being: A social psychological perspective on mental health. *Psychological Bulletin, 103*(2), 193–210.

Teitelbaum, P. (1961). Disturbances in feeding and drinking behavior after hypothalamic lesions. In M. R. Jones (Ed.), *Nebraska Symposium on Motivation.* Lincoln, NE: University of Nebraska Press.

Terman, L. M. (1925). *Genetic studies of genius: Mental and physical traits of a thousand gifted children* (Vol. 1). Stanford, CA: Stanford University Press.

Terman, L. M., & Merrill, M. A. (1937). *Measuring intelligence.* Boston: Houghton Mifflin.

Terman, L. M., & Merrill, M. A. (1973). *Stanford–Binet Intelligence Scale: Manual for the third revision.* Boston: Houghton Mifflin.

Terman, L. M., & Oden, M. H. (1959). *Genetic studies of genius: The gifted group at midlife* (Vol. 4). Stanford, CA: Stanford University Press.

Thomas, A., & Chess, S. (1977). *Temperament and development.* New York: Brunner/Mazel.

Thomas, A., Chess, S., & Birch, H. G. (1970). The origin of personality. *Scientific American, 223*(2).

Thompson, S. K. (1975). Gender labels and early sex role development. *Child Development, 46,* 339–347.

Thorndike, E. L. (1898). Animal intelligence: An experimental study of the associative processes in animals. *Psychological Monographs, 2* (Whole No. 8).

Thorndike, E. L. (1911). *Animal intelligence: Experimental studies.* New York: Macmillan.

Thurstone, L. L. (1938). *Primary mental abilities.* Chicago: University of Chicago Press.

Tinbergen, N. (1951). *The study of instinct.* Oxford, England: Clarendon.

Tolman, E. C. (1932). *Purposive behavior in animals and men.* New York: Appleton-Century-Crofts.

Tolman, E. C. (1959). Principles of purposive behavior. In S. Koch (Ed.), *Psychology: A study of science* (Vol. 2, pp. 92–157). New York: McGraw-Hill.

Torrey, E. F. (1986). *Witchdoctors and psychiatrists: The common roots of psychotherapy and its future.* New York: Harper & Row.

Totman, R. (1990). *Mind, stress, and health.* London: Souvenir Press.

Totman, R., Kiff, J., Reed, S. E., Craig, J. W. (1980). Predicting experimental colds in volunteers from different measures of recent life stress. *Journal of Psychosomatic Research, 24*(3, 4), 155–163.

Townsend, J. T. (1971). A note on the identifiability of parallel and serial processes. *Perception and Psychophysics, 10,* 161–163.

Treisman, A. (1960). Contextual cues in selective listening. *Quarterly Journal of Experimental Psychology, 12,* 242–248.

Triandis, H. C. (1994). Culture and social behavior. In W. J. Lonner & R. S. Malpass (Eds.), *Psychology and culture.* Boston: Allyn & Bacon.

Triandis, H. C., McCusker, C., Betancourt, H., Iwao, S., et al. (1993). An etic–emic analysis of individualism and collectivism. *Journal of Cross-Cultural Psychology, 24*(3), 366–383.

Triandis, H. C., McCusker, C., & Hui, C. H. (1990). Multimethod probes of individualism and collectivism. *Journal of Personality and Social Psychology, 59,* 1006–1020.

Tripathi, A. N. (1979). Memory for meaning and grammatical structure: An experiment on retention of a story. *Psychological Studies, 24*(2), 136–145.

Triplett, N. (1898). The dynamogenic factors in pacemaking and competition. *American Journal of Psychology, 9,* 507–533.

Tulving, E. (1972). Episodic and semantic memory. In E. Tulving & W. Donaldson (Eds.), *Organization of memory.* New York: Academic Press.

Tulving, E., & Thomson, D. M. (1973). Encoding specificity and retrieval processes in episodic memory. *Psychological Review, 80,* 352–373.

Turk, D. C., Meichenbaum, D., & Genest, M. (1983). *Pain and behavioral medicine: A cognitive behavioral perspective.* New York: The Guilford Press.

Turk, D. C., & Rudy, T. E. (1992). Cognitive factors and persistent pain: A glimpse into Pandora's box. *Cognitive Therapy and Research, 16*(2), 99–122.

Turner, J. C. (1987). *Rediscovering the social group: A self-categorization theory.* Oxford, England: Basil Blackwell.

Turner, R. J., & Wagonfeld, M. O. (1967). Occupational mobility and schizophrenia: An assessment of the social causation and the social selection hypothesis. *American Sociological Review, 32,* 104–113.

Turner, S. M., & Hersen, M. (1985). The interviewing process. In M. Hersen & S. M. Turner (Eds.), *Diagnostic interviewing* (pp. 12–13). New York: Plenum.

Tversky, A. (1972a). Choice by elimination. *Journal of Mathematical Psychology, 9*(4), 341–367.

Tversky, A. (1972b). Elimination by aspects: A theory of choice. *Psychological Review, 79,* 281–299.

Tversky, A., & Kahneman, D. (1973). Availability: A heuristic for judging frequency and probability. *Cognitive Psychology, 5,* 207–232.

Ulrich, R., & Azrin, N. H. (1962). Reflexive fighting in response to aversive stimulation. *Journal of the Experimental Analysis of Behavior, 5,* 511–520.

Umberson, D. (1987). Family status and health behaviors: Social control as a dimension of social integration. *Journal of Health and Social Behavior, 28,* 306–319.

Umberson, D. (1992). Gender, marital status, and the social control of health behavior. *Social Science & Medicine, 34*(8), 907–917.

United States Department of Labor, Bureau of Labor Statistics (1992). *Statistical Abstract of the United States* (112th ed.). Washington, DC: U.S. Department of Commerce.

United States Department of Labor, Bureau of Labor Statistics (1994). *Statistical Abstract of the United States* (114th ed.). Washington, DC: U.S. Department of Commerce.

VanderPlate, C., Aral, S. O., & Magder, L. (1988). The relationship among genital herpes simplex virus, stress, and social support. *Health Psychology, 7,* 159–168.

Vernon, P. A., & Mori, M. (1992). Intelligence, reaction times, and peripheral nerve conduction velocity. *Intelligence, 16*(3, 4), 273–288.

Veroff, J. (1957). Development and validation of a projective measure of power motivation. *Journal of Abnormal and Social Psychology, 54,* 1–8.

Viglione, D. J., & Exner, J. E. (1983). Current research in the comprehensive Rorschach system. In J. N. Butcher & C. D. Spielberger (Eds.), *Advances in personality assessment* (Vol. 2, pp. 13–40). Hillsdale, NJ: Erlbaum.

Vissing, Y. M., Straus, M. A., Gelles, R. J., & Harrop, J. W. (1991). Verbal aggression by parents and psychosocial problems of children. *Child Abuse & Neglect, 15*(3), 223–238.

Vokey, J. R., & Read, J. D. (1985). Subliminal messages: Between the devil and the media. *American Psychologist, 40,* 1231–1239.

Vygotsky, L. S. (1962). *Thought and language.* Cambridge, MA: MIT Press. (Original work published 1934)

Vygotsky, L. S. (1978). *Mind in society: The development of higher psychological processes.* Cambridge, MA: Harvard University Press.

Wade, C., & Cirese, S. (1991). *Human sexuality* (2nd ed.). New York: Harcourt Brace Jovanovich.

Wagner, D. A. (1978). Memories of Morocco: The influence of age, schooling, and environment on memory. *Cognitive Psychology, 10,* 1–28.

Walker, L. J. (1989). A longitudinal study of moral reasoning. *Child Development, 60,* 157–166.

Wallace, R. K., & Benson, H. (1972). The physiology of meditation. *Scientific American,* 84–90.

Walster, E., Aronson, E., Abrahams, D., & Rottman, L. (1966). The importance of physical attractiveness in dating behavior. *Journal of Personality and Social Psychology, 4,* 508–516.

Walster, E., & Berscheid, E. (1974). A little bit about love: A minor essay on a major topic. In T. L. Huston (Ed.), *Foundations of interpersonal attraction.* New York: Academic Press.

Walster, E., Walster, G. W., & Berscheid, E. (1978). *Equity: Theory and research.* Boston: Allyn & Bacon.

Walters, G. C., & Grusec, J. F. (1977). *Punishment.* San Francisco: Freeman.

Warrington, E. (1982). The double dissociation of short- and long-term memory deficits. In L. S. Cermak (Ed.), *Human memory and amnesia.* Hillsdale, NJ: Erlbaum.

Warrington, E., & Shallice, T. (1972). Neuropsychological evidence of visual storage in short-term memory tasks. *Quarterly Journal of Experimental Psychology, 24*(1), 30–40.

Wason, P. C., & Johnson-Laird, P. N. (1972). *Psychology of reasoning: Structure and content.* London: B. T. Batsford.

Watson, D. (1989). Strangers' ratings of the five robust personality factors: Evidence of a surprising convergence with self-report. *Journal of Personality & Social Psychology, 57*(1), 120–128.

Wechsler, D. (1974). *The measurement and appraisal of adult intelligence.* Baltimore: Williams & Wilkins.

Weisberg, R. W. (1995). Prolegomena to theories of insight in problem solving: A taxonomy of problems. In R. J. Sternberg & J. E. Davidson (Eds.), *The nature of insight* (pp. 157–196). Cambridge, MA: MIT Press.

Weisenberg, M. (1977). Pain and pain control. *Psychological Bulletin, 84,* 1008–1044.

Weiss, R. S. (1975). *Marital separation.* New York: Basic Books.

Weissman, M. M., & Myers, J. K. (1978). Affective disorders in a United States urban community: The use of research diagnostic criteria in an epidemiologic survey. *Archives of General Psychiatry, 35,* 1304–1311.

Wells, G. L. (1993). What do we know about eyewitness identification? *American Psychologist, 48*(5), 553–571.

Wertheimer, M. (1959). *Productive thinking* (Rev. ed.). New York: Harper & Row. (Original work published 1945)

Wesman, A. E., & Ricks, D. F. (1966). *Mood and personality.* New York: Holt, Rinehart and Winston.

Wever, R. A. (1979). *The circadian system of man.* Heidelberg, West Germany: Springer-Verlag.

White, R. W. (1959). Motivation reconsidered: The concept of competence. *Psychological Review, 66,* 297–33.

Whitehouse, W. G., Dinges, D. F., Orne, E. C., & Orne, M. T. (1988). Hypnotic hypermnesia: Enhanced memory accessibility or report bias? *Journal of Abnormal Psychology, 97*(3), 289–295.

Whitley, B. E., Jr., & Frieze, I. H. (1985). Children's causal attributions for success and failure in achievement settings: A meta-analysis. *Journal of Educational Psychology, 77,* 608–616.

Wilber, K. H., & Specht, C. V. (1994). Prevalence and predictors of burnout among adult day care providers. *Journal of Applied Gerontology, 13*(3), 282–298.

Williams, R. (1986). An untrusting heart. In M. G. Walraven & H. E. Fitzgerald (Eds.), *Annuals editions: Human development 86/87.* Guilford, CT: Dushkin.

Williams, R. B., Jr., & Barefoot, J. C. (1988). Coronary-prone behavior: The emerging role of the hostility complex. In B. K. Houston & C. R. Snyder (Eds.), *Type A behavior pattern: Current trends and future directions* (pp. 189–211). New York: Wiley.

Winter, D. G. (1973). *The power motive.* New York: The Free Press.

Wolpe, J. (1958). *Psychotherapy by reciprocal inhibition.* Stanford, CA: Stanford University Press.

Wong, D. F., Wagner, H. N., Tune, L. E., Dannals, R. F., Pearlson, G. D., Links, J. M., Tamminga, C. A., Broussolle, E. P., Ravert, H. T., Wilson, A. A., Toury, J. K. T., Malat, J., Williams, J. A., O'Tuma, L. A., Snyder, S. H., Kuhar, M. J., & Gjedde, A. (1986). Positron emission tomography reveals elevated Dz dopamine receptors in drug-naive schizophrenics. *Science, 234,* 1558–1563.

Woodruff, R. A., Goodwin, D. W., & Guze, S. B. (1974). *Psychiatric diagnosis.* New York: Oxford University Press.

Woodworth, R. S. (1918). *Dynamic psychology.* New York: Columbia University Press.

Woolfolk, R. L., Carr-Kaffashan, K., McNulty, T. F., & Lehrer, P. M. (1976). Meditation training as a treatment for insomnia. *Behavior Therapy, 7,* 359–365.

Woon, T., Masuda, M., Wagner, N. N., & Holmes, T. H. (1971). The *Social Readjustment Rating Scale:* A cross-cultural study of Malaysians and Americans. *Journal of Cross-Cultural Psychology, 2,* 373–386.

Wright, L., Abbanato, K. R., Lancaster, C., Bourke, M. L., et al. (1994). Gender-related subcomponent differences in high Type A subjects. *Journal of Clinical Psychology, 50*(5), 677–680.

Wright, R. H. (1977). Odor and molecular vibration: Neural coding of olfactory information. *Journal of Theoretical Biology, 64,* 473–502.

Wright, R. H. (1982). *The sense of smell.* Boca Raton, FL: CRC Press.

Yahiro, K., Inoue, M., & Nozawa, Y. (1993). An examination on the *Social Readjustment Rating Scale* (Holmes et al.) by Japanese subjects. *Japanese Journal of Health Psychology, 6*(1), 18–32.

Yang, K. (1986). Chinese personality and its change. In M. H. Bond (Ed.), *The psychology of the Chinese people.* Hong Kong: Oxford University Press.

Yerkes, R. M., & Dodson, J. B. (1908). The relation of strength of stimulus to rapidity of habit formation. *Journal of Comparative Neurology and Psychology, 18,* 459–482.

Yuille, J. C. (1993). We must study forensic eyewitnesses to know about them. *American Psychologist, 48*(5), 572–573.

Yussen, S. R. (1984). A triarchic reaction to a triarchic theory of intelligence. *The Behavioral and Brain Sciences, 7*(12), 303.

Zaidel, E. (1983). A response to Gazzaniga: Language in the right hemisphere, convergent perspectives. *American Psychologist, 38*(5), 542–546.

Zajonc, R. B. (1965). Social facilitation. *Science, 149,* 269–274.

Zajonc, R. B. (1980). Compliance. In P. B. Paulus (Ed.), *Psychology of group influence* (pp. 35–60). Hillsdale, NJ: Erlbaum.

Zajonc, R. B. (1984). On the primacy affect. *American Psychologist, 39,* 117–129.

Zajonc, R. B., Pietromonaco, P., & Bargh, J. (1982). Independence and interaction of affect and cognition. In M. S. Clark & S. T. Fiske (Eds.), *Affect and cognition* (pp. 211–227). Hillsdale, NJ: LEA.

Zamansky, H. S., & Bartis, S. P. (1985). The dissociation of an experience: The hidden observer observed. *Journal of Abnormal Psychology, 94,* 243–248.

Zaragoza, M. S., McCloskey, M., & Jamis, M. (1987). Misleading postevent information and recall of the original event: Further evidence against the memory impairment hypothesis. *Journal of Experimental Psychology: Learning, Memory, and Cognition, 13*(1), 36–44.

Zeidner, M. (1990). Perceptions of ethnic group modal intelligence scores: Reflections of cultural stereotypes or intelligence test scores? *Journal of Cross-Cultural Psychology, 21,* 214–231.

Zigler, E., & Berman, W. (1983). Discerning the future of early childhood intervention. *American Psychologist, 38,* 894–906.

Zimbardo, P. G. (1970). The human choice: Individuation, reason, and order versus deindividuation, impulse, and chaos. In W. J. Arnold &

D. Levine (Eds.), *Nebraska symposium on motivation, 1969*. Lincoln, NE: University of Nebraska Press.

Zimbardo, P. G. (1972, April). Psychology of imprisonment. *Transition/Society*, 4–8.

Zimmerman, B. J., & Bandura, A. (1994). Impact on self-regulatory influences on writing course attainment. *American Educational Research Journal, 31*(4), 845–862.

Zimmerman, B. J., Bandura, A., & Martinez-Pons, M. (1992). Self-motivation for academic attainment: The role of self-efficacy beliefs and personal goal setting. *American Educational Research Journal, 29*(3), 663–676.

Zola-Morgan, S. M., & Squire, L. R. (1990). The primate hippocampal formation: Evidence for a time-limited role in memory storage. *Science, 250*, 228–290.

Zuckerman, M., Klorman, R., Larrance, D. T., & Speigel, N. H. (1981). Facial, autonomic, and subjective components of emotion: The facial feedback hypothesis versus the externalizer–internalizer distinction. *Journal of Personality and Social Psychology, 41*, 929–944.

Acknowledgments

Figure 3–1 "Familiar Versus Unfamiliar" from Mandler, "A New Perspective on Cognitive Development in Infancy" in *American Scientist*, Vol. 78, pp. 236–243.

Table 3–3 "Kohlberg's Theory of the Development of Moral Reasoning." Adapted from L. Kohlberg, *The Psychology of Moral Development*. Copyright © 1983 Harper & Row.

Figure 4–1 "Snellen Vision Chart." Copyright © The Optical Society of America.

Figure 4–17 "Gestalt Principles of Perception" from Roger Shepard, *Mind Sights*, 1990. Copyright © 1990 by W. H. Freeman & Co. All rights reserved.

Figure 4–19 "Prototype Matching—Even Without the Prototype." Adapted from Robert Solso and Judith McCarthy, "Prototype Formation of Faces: A Case of Pseudomemory" in *British Journal of Psychology*, November 1981, Vol. 72, No. 4, pp. 499–503. British Psychological Society.

Figure 4–23 "Shape Constancy." Based on J. J. Gibson, *The Perception of the Visual World*, 1950.

CO 7 "War of the Ghosts" from Bartlett, *Remembering: A Study in Experimental and Social Psychology*, 1932. Published by Cambridge University Press. All rights reserved by the publisher.

Figure 7–2 "The Three-Stores View." Adapted from Atkinson & Shiffrin, "The Control of Short-term Memory" in *Scientific American*, Vol. 225, 1971, pp. 82–90. Copyright © 1971 by Scientific American, Inc. All rights reserved.

Figure 7–6 "What Is Wrong with This Picture?" Drawings of US Cent from R. S. Nickerson and M. J. Adams, "Long-term Memory for a Common Object" in *Cognitive Psychology*, Vol. 11, pp. 287–307.

Table 9–1 "Gardner's Seven Intelligences" from Howard Gardner, "Seven Intelligences" in *Multiple Intelligences*, 1993. Published by Basic Books, Inc. All rights reserved.

Figure 10–6 "Line Length and the Norm" from Solomon Asch, "Line Length and Group Influence," 1956. All rights reserved by the author.

Figure 10–7 "Social Status and Conformity" from R. A. Lippa, *Introduction to Social Psychology*, p. 536. Wadsworth Publishing.

Figure 10–9 "Milgram's Results on Voltage Levels" based on Stanley Milgram, *Obedience to Authority*, 1974. Published by HarperCollins. All rights reserved by the publisher.

Figure 10–11 "What Do You See In This Picture?" Adapted from Brehm & Kassin, *Social Psychology*, 1990, p. 180. Published by Houghton Mifflin Co. All rights reserved by the publisher.

Figure 11–1 "Human Sexual Response Cycle" from Masters & Johnson, *Human Sexual Response*, 1966. Published by Little, Brown & Company. No portion of this text may be reproduced without permission of the authors.

Figure 11–2 "Acquired Motivation," based on Solomon & Corbit, "An Opponent-Process Theory of Motivation: I. Termporal Dynamics of Affect" in *Psychological Review*, Vol. 81, 1974, pp. 119–145. Copyright © 1974 Psychological Review. No portion of this text may be reproduced without permission of American Psychological Association.

Table 11–4 "Some Differences Between Motivation and Emotion." Adapted from J. G. Carlson and E. Hatfield, *Psychology of Emotion*, 1992, p. 30. Copyright © 1992 Harcourt Brace Jovanovich.

Figure 11–7 "Plutchik's Emotion Wheel." Based on Plutchik, "A Language for the Emotions" in *Psychology Today* magazine. Copyright © 1980 Sussex Publishers, Inc. All rights reserved.

Table 12–9 "Examples of Cattell's Source Traits," from R. B. Cattell, *Personality and Learning Theory*, Vol. 1. Copyright ©1979 Springer Publishing Company, Inc. (NY). All rights reserved.

Chapter 14 "ELIZA—A Computer Program for the Study of Natural Language Communication Between Man & Machine" from Weizenbaum, *Communications of the Association for Computing Machinery*, Vol. 9, pp. 36–45. All rights reserved by Association for Computing Machinery (NY, NY).

Figure 14–1c "Effectiveness of Various Therapies," from *Journal of Personality and Social Psychology*, Vol. 13, pp. 173–199. Copyright © 1969 by the American Psychological Association. No portion of this text may be reprinted without permission of the American Psychological Association.

Table 14–2 *The Twelve Steps and Twelve Traditions* of Alcoholics Anonymous. Copyright © 1952 by Alcoholics Anonymous World Services, Inc. Permission to reprint this material does not mean AA has reviewed or approved the contents of this publication, nor that AA agrees with the views expressed herein.

Figure 15–2 "Stressful Life Events" from Kagan & Segal, 1995, 8th Edition, p. 440. Copyright © 1995 by Harcourt Brace & Company, Inc.

Table 15–2 "Proportion of Cancer Deaths Attributed to Various Risk Factors." Adapted from *The Causes of Cancer: Quantitative Estimates of Avoidable Risks of Cancer in the United States Today* (p. 1256) by R. Doll and R. Peto, 1981, Oxford, England: Oxford University Press. Copyright © 1981 by Oxford University Press.

Figure 15–4 "General Adaptation Syndrome (GAS)." From H. Selye, *Stress Without Distress*, 1974, p. 39. Copyright © 1974 HarperCollins Publishers, Inc. All rights reserved.

End paper photos © 1996 DUOMO William R. Sallaz; p. 5, top left, © Larry Mulvehill/ Rainbow; p. 5, top right, © Elena Rooraid/ PhotoEdit; p. 5, bottom left, © Bob Daemmrich/ Stock Boston; p. 5, bottom right, © H. Gans/ The Image Works; p. 6, top left, © Kathleen Olson; p. 6, top right, © Matthew McVay/ Tony Stone Images; p. 6, bottom left, © Bob Strong/ The Image Works; p. 6, bottom right, © Bill Bachmann/ The Image Works; p. 7, © David Hiser/ Tony Stone Images; p. 9, © Robert E. Daemmrich/ Tony Stone Images; p. 10, © Jonathan Selig/ Photo 20-20; p. 13, © Jeff Greenberg / PhotoEdit; p. 18, © 1987 Lawrence Migdale; p. 19, © Tom McCarthy/ PhotoEdit; p. 24, © Nubar Alexanian/ Stock Boston; p. 26, Vatican Museum & Galleries/ Scala/ Superstock; p. 37, left, © Michael Tweedie/ Photo Researchers; p. 37, right, © Michael W. F. Tweedie/ Bruce Coleman, Inc.; p. 38, © CNRI/ SPL/ Photo Researchers; p. 47, © H. Christoph/ Black Star; p. 51, © Biophoto Associates/ Science Source/ Photo Researchers; p. 52, © John Coletti/ Stock Boston; p. 55, © D. W. Fawcett/ Komuro/ Science Source/ Photo Researchers; p. 70, top left, © Network Pro/ The Image Works; top right, © Greg Gawlowski/ Photo 20-20; bottom left, © Robert Brenner/ PhotoEdit; bottom right, © Tony Freeman/ PhotoEdit; p. 72, © Robert Daemmrich/ Tony Stone Images; p. 73, left, © Bill Anderson/ Monkmeyer; right, © G. L. Vygodskaya; p. 75, top left and right, bottom left, © Lennart Nilsson, A CHILD IS BORN, Dell Publishing Company, bottom right, © Bob Daemmrich/ The Image Works; p. 76, © Bob Daemmrich/ The Image Works; p. 78, © Myrleen Ferguson Cate/ PhotoEdit; p. 79, top left, © Michael Newman/ PhotoEdit; top right, © Tom McCarthy/ PhotoEdit; bottom left and right, © Goodman/ Monkmeyer; p. 80, © Rhoda Sidney/ Stock Boston; p. 85, © Tony Freeman/ PhotoEdit; p. 87, John F. Kennedy Library; p. 94, Harvard University News Office; p. 111, © Fritz Goro, Life Magazine © Time Warner; p. 122, The Granger Collection; p. 123, National Gallery, London/ E. T. Archive, London/ Superstock; p. 129, © Norm Snyder 1995; p. 143, © Phillipe Plailly/ SPL/ Photo Researchers; p. 145, Michel Siffre, © National Geographic Society; p. 149, The Granger Collection, New York; p. 153, © Esbin-Anderson/ The Image Works; p. 155, © Bill Bachmann/ Photri Inc.; p. 165, left, © Nina Leen/ Life Magazine; p. 165, right, William Lishman and Associates; p. 167, Bettmann Archive; p. 171, © Jonathon Nourok/ PhotoEdit; p. 173, © Stuart R. Ellins, PhD; p. 183, UPI/ Bettmann; p. 185, Dr. Albert Bandura; p. 193, © 1988 Joseph Nettis/ Stock Boston; p. 196, © Michael Newman/ PhotoEdit; p. 198, © 1988 Peter Menzel/ Stock Boston; p. 200, top, © 1988 Lawrence Migdale; p. 200, bottom, © Phyllis Picardi/ Stock Boston; p. 201, © Visual/ Gamma Liaison; p. 204, left, © Jerry Berndt/ Stock Boston; right, © Peter Southwick/ Stock Boston; p. 207, © Stacy Pick/ Stock Boston; p. 208, © 1993 Lawrence Migdale; p. 210, © Rob Crandall/ The Image Works; p. 211, © Dr. Carolyn Rovee-Collier; p. 212, left, © Charles Feil/ Stock Boston; p. 212, right, © Bonnie Kamin; p. 213, © Michael Newman/ PhotoEdit; p. 217, left, © Bob Daemmrich/ The Image Works; p. 217, right, © Dennis MacDonald/ PhotoEdit; p. 224, © Daniel Bosler/ Tony Stone Images; p. 226, © Bill Stanton/ Rainbow; p. 227, © Superstock; p. 232, © Russell Schleipman/ Offshoot; p. 233, © Michael Newman/ PhotoEdit; p. 236, © Dorothy Littell Greco/ Stock Boston; p. 238, left, © Photri; p. 238, right, © Tony Savino/ The Image

Works; p. 239, © Bob Daemmrich/ Stock Boston; p. 246, © Sylvain Grandadam/ Tony Stone Images; p. 248, © Tony Freeman/ PhotoEdit; p. 254, top left, UPI/ Bettmann; p. 254, top right, The Bettmann Archive; p. 254 , bottom left, UPI/ Corbis - Bettmann; p. 254, bottom right, © Ulf Anaerson/ Gamma Liaison; p. 264, top, Dr. Michael Cole; p. 264, bottom, © Superstock; p. 266, © George Holton/ Photo Researchers; p. 268, © Topham/ The Image Works; p. 270, © Rob Crandall/ Stock Boston; p. 272, bottom, © T. K. Wanstal/ The Image Works; p. 284, top left, © Herb Snitzer/ Stock Boston; p. 284, top right, © Hazel Hankin/ Stock Boston; p. 284, bottom left, © Dan McCoy/ Rainbow; p. 284, bottom right, © Cary Wolinsky/ Stock Boston; p. 289, © Tom McCarthy/ Rainbow; p. 293, left, © Bill Bachmann/ The Image Works; p. 293, right, © Michael Newman/ PhotoEdit; p. 295, © J. Berndt/ Stock Boston; p. 296, © Sue Klemens/ Stock Boston; p. 299, left, © Terry Vinel/ Tony Stone Images; p. 299, middle, © Kathleen Olson; p. 299, right, © John Chiasson/ Gamma Liaison; p. 300, top, Dr. Solomon Asch; p. 300, bottom, © Owen Franken/ Stock Boston; p. 303, Copyright 1965 by Stanley Milgram. From the film OBEDIENCE, distributed by the Pennsylvania State University, Audio Visuals Service; p. 305, © Charlie Westerman/ Gamma Liaison; p. 307, © Bob Daemmrich/ Stock Boston; p. 310, top, © Frank Siteman/ Stock Boston; p. 310, bottom, © Cathlyn Melloan/ Tony Stone Images; p. 311, P. G. Zimbardo, Inc.; p. 312, P. G. Zimbardo, Inc.; p. 321, Scala/ Art Resource, NY; p. 322, © William Thompson/ The Picture Cube; p. 328, © Myrleen Ferguson/ PhotoEdit; p. 330, © 1990 Lawrence Migdale; p. 332, Harlow Primate Laboratory, University of Wisconsin; p. 335, Copyright Paul Ekman, 1972; p. 338, top right, © Superstock; p. 338, bottom left, © Mark Greenlar/ The Image Works; p. 338, bottom right, © Lawrence Migdale/ Stock Boston; p. 346, © M. Siluk/ The Image Works; p. 354, The Bettmann Archive; p. 357, Erich Lessing/ Art Resource, NY; p. 358, right, UPI/ Bettmann Newsphotos; p. 358, left, © D. Alfano/ Gamma Liaison; p. 359, top, The Bettmann Archive; p. 359, bottom, © Christina Dameyer/ Photo 20-20; p. 360, left, The Bettmann Archive (right) UPI/ Bettmann; p. 360, bottom five, Courtesy of Arnold Michlin/ PhotoEdit; p. 361, left, The Bettmann Archive; p. 361, right, © Daniel Putlerman/ Stock Boston; p. 362, left, © Dan McCoy/ Rainbow; middle, AP/ Wide World Photos; right, © A. Berliner/ Gamma Liaison; p. 365, left, Courtesy of Dr. Julian B. Rotter; p. 365, right, © Dan McCoy/ Rainbow; p. 366, Dr. Albert Bandura; p. 387, © Michael Newman/ PhotoEdit; p. 392, National Gallery, Oslo, Norway/ Bridgeman Art Library/ London/ Superstock; p. 401, © Grunnitus/ Monkmeyer; p. 403, © NIH/ Science Source/ Photo Researchers; p. 408, © Michael Newman/ PhotoEdit; p. 416, © Stock Montage; p. 418, © Dan McCoy/ Rainbow; p. 419, AP/Wide World Photos; p. 421, © Michael Newman/ PhotoEdit; p. 425, left, © Richard Howard/ Offshoot Stock; p. 425, right, © Lionel Delevingne/ Stock Boston; p. 426, © Will and Deni McIntyre/ Photo Researchers; p. 430, © Martin Rogers/ Stock Boston; p. 432, top, © Michael Newman/ PhotoEdit; p. 432, bottom, © David Young-Wolff/ PhotoEdit; p. 433, © David Young-Wolff/ PhotoEdit; p. 434, © Bob Daemmrich/ The Image Works; p. 439, © Mary Kate Denny/ PhotoEdit; p. 450, © Esbin-Anderson/ The Image Works; p. 451, Reuters/ Bettmann; p. 453, © David Young-Wolff/ PhotoEdit; p. 458, top left, ©

Dan and Will McCoy/ Rainbow;   p. 458, top right, © Andre Abecassis/ Photo 20-20;   p. 458, bottom left, © Bob Daemmrich/ Stock Boston;   p. 458, bottom right, © Richard Pasley/ Stock Boston;   p. 460, © Tony Freeman/ PhotoEdit; p. 461, © Glen Korengold/ Stock Boston;   p. 463, right, © Dana White/ PhotoEdit;   p. 463, left, © Jim Pickerell/ The Image Works;   p. 467, © J. Pat Carter/ Gamma Liaison;   p. 469, left, © Michael English/ Medical Images, Inc.;   p. 469, right, © William McCoy/ Rainbow;   p. 472, © Jean Claude Lejeune/ Stock Boston

Abel, E. L., 74
Abrams, R., 425
Abramson, L. Y., 179
Abreu, J., 430
Ackerman, D., 105, 107
Adams, M. J., 215, 274
Adamson, J., 24
Ader, R., 459
Adler, A., 358, 362, 378
Adler, J., 247
Adler, T., 74
Agnew, J., 425
Akutsu, P. D., 430
Aldous, J. L., 430
Aleichem, S., 269
Allen, A., 371, 379
Allen, F., 452
Allingham, M., 464
Alloy, L. B., 179
Allport, G. W., 284, 288, 309, 310, 351, 352, 371, 379
Alpert, B., 450
Amabile, T. M., 275, 331
Amir, Y., 284
Amoore, J. E., 119
Amsel, A., 182
Anand, B. K., 320
Anderson, C. A., 310
Anderson, J. R., 205
Anderson, K. L., 326
Anderson, M., 308
Andersson, B. E., 88
Andreasen, N. C., 402
Andrews, G., 437
Andrich, D., 90
Angelou, M., 128, 453
Anzaldua, G., 125, 363
Appels, A., 456
Appley, M. H., 318
Aral, S. O., 459
Argyle, M., 456, 457, 462
Aristotle, 25, 136
Arkin, R. M., 287
Arnold, M., 343
Asch, S., 299–300, 301
Ashley, E., 293
Aspinwall, L. G., 470
Atkinson, D. R., 429
Atkinson, J. W., 318, 375
Atkinson, R. C., 197
Attanucci, J., 94
Averill, J. R., 337
Axelson, J. A., 436
Axline, V., 415, 416, 420
Azrin, N. H., 310

Back, K., 294
Baddeley, A., 196, 201, 205, 211
Bahrick, H., 200–201, 209
Bahrick, L. E., 331
Bahrick, P., 200–201
Bailey, J. M., 324

Baker, J. G., 266, 274
Baldwin, C., 206
Bales, R., 295
Balkin, J., 309
Ballantyne, S., 142
Bandura, A., 22, 87, 184–185, 310, 332, 334, 365, 366, 367, 373, 379, 422, 423
Banks, J., 17
Banks, M. S., 76
Barber, T. X., 149
Bard, P., 339
Barefoot, J. C., 464
Bargh, J., 344
Barker, J., 17
Barker, R. G., 310
Baron, J., 181
Baron, M., 429
Baron, R. A., 291, 296, 310, 311, 312
Barr, H. M., 74
Barrett, P. T., 262
Barron, F., 275
Bartis, S. P., 150
Bartlett, F. C., 191, 213
Bartoshuk, L. M., 116, 119
Bashore, T. R., 95, 345
Basow, S. A., 289
Bateson, P., 173
Baumrind, D., 94
Bayley, J., 77, 78
Beall, A., 87
Beatty, W. W., 320
Beck, A., 423, 424, 433
Behrman, S. N., 420
Bekerian, D. A., 216
Bellack, A. S., 183
Belloc, N.D., 450
Bellugi, U., 52
Belsky, J., 88
Bem, D. J., 286, 371, 379
Bem, S. L., 87
Benbow, C. P., 87
Benedict, R., 397
Ben-Shakhar, G., 345
Benson, H., 151
Berg, C. A., 358
Berger, K. S., 145
Berglas, S., 287
Berkman, L., 441
Berkowitz, L., 310, 312
Berlin, B., 247
Berlyne, D. E., 326, 331, 334
Berman, W., 274
Bermudez-Rattoni, F., 172
Bernard, L. L., 318
Berry, D., 171
Berry, J. W., 18, 90
Berry, S. L., 320
Berscheid, E., 292
Betti, U., 210
Bexton, W. H., 326
Bezooijen, R. V., 344
Bialystok, E., 248

Bianchi, K., 399
Biederman, I., 126
Bierce, A., 237
Biery, R. E., 324
Binet, A., 255–256
Birch, H. G., 81, 368
Birdsall, T. G., 105
Bitterman, M. E., 169
Blair, B., 254
Blanchard, E. B., 422
Blank, A., 302
Block, J., 370
Block, M. A., 154
Bloom, A., 399
Bloom, B. S., 77
Blumenthal, J. A., 464
Bodkin, J. A., 428
Bohn, H. G., 184
Bolger, N., 456, 457, 462
Bolwig, T. G., 426
Bombeck, E., 138
Bond, M. H., 284, 301
Bond, M. R., 467
Bongiovanni, A., 177
Booth-Kewley, S., 464
Borbely, A., 144, 146, 147
Bornstein, M. H., 75
Borysenko, J., 459
Borysenko, M., 459
Bothwell, R. K., 215
Bower, G. H., 205, 211, 314, 344
Bowers, K. S., 148, 149, 273
Bransford, J. D., 126, 213, 207
Braswell, L., 422
Brazelton, T. B., 79
Brehm, J. W., 302
Brehm, S. S., 291, 302
Brenner, H. G., 90
Breslow, L., 450
Brewer, E. M., 320
Brewer, I., 18
Brewer, M. B., 310
Brigham, J. C., 215
Brislin, R. W., 377
Broadhurst, P. L., 326
Brobeck, J. R., 320
Broca, P., 50
Bronfenbrenner, U., 266
Bronte, E., 147
Brosschot, J. F., 455
Brown, J. A., 210, 388
Brown, L., 333
Brown, R., 139, 238
Brown, R. M., 303
Browning, E. B., 292
Bruch, H., 322
Bruner, J. S., 75
Bruning, N. S., 464
Brust, R. G., 294
Bullock, M., 83
Burger, J. M., 302
Burleson, B. R., 294

Burns, H., 214, 215
Burns, J. W., 464
Burnstein, E., 297
Buss, A. H., 312
Butcher, J. N., 376, 377, 407, 427
Butler, J., 211
Butler, S., 354
Byrne, D., 291
Byrnes, J. P., 90

Cacioppo, J. T., 288, 341
Cadieux, E. L., 173
Campbell, K. B., 262
Candland, D. K., 344
Cannon, W., 339, 345
Cantor, J., 201, 202n
Carlsmith, J. M., 285, 286
Carlson, G., 396
Carlson, J. G., 335
Carlyle, J. W., 363
Carpenter, P. A., 201
Carraher, D., 266
Carraher, T. N., 266
Carroll, D. W., 243
Carroll, J., 261
Carroll, L., 193
Carson, R., 118, 344
Carson, R. C., 407, 427
Carullo, J. J., 201, 202n
Casa, A., 430
Caspi, A., 456
Cattell, R. B., 230, 369, 372, 377, 379
Ceci, S. J., 265, 266, 274
Cerella, J., 95
Chaiken, S., 290
Chanowitz, B., 302
Chapman, J. P., 376
Chapman, L. J., 376
Chase, A., 216
Chase, W. G., 193, 205, 231
Chasnoff, I. J., 74
Cherry, E. C., 137, 138, 140
Chess, S., 80–82, 368, 373
Chesterton, G. K., 225
Chhina, G. S., 320
Chi, M. T. H., 211, 231
Chieh Li, 262
Child, J., 275
Chomsky, N., 241–242, 244–245
Christie, A., 345
Churchill, W., 184
Cialdini, R. B., 301, 302
Ciompi, L., 154
Cirese, S., 324
Cisneros, S., 448
Clark, E. V., 238
Clark, H. H., 205, 238
Clarke, A. C., 47
Clarke-Stewart, K. A., 88
Cleaver, E., 433
Clore, G. L., 291
Cochran, S., 310
Cocking, R. R., 86
Cofer, C. N., 318
Cohen, J., 236
Cohen, N., 459
Cohen, S., 459
Colbert, M. M., 173
Colburn, H. S., 114

Cole, J. O., 428
Cole, M., 30, 263, 264
Collaso, J. W., 78
Collier, G., 274
Condry, J., 331
Conezio, J., 195
Conrad, R., 205
Cooley, N., 182
Cooper, J., 286
Cooper, V. M., 231
Copernicus, N., 275
Corbit, J. D., 324
Corcoran, E., 231
Corina, D. P., 52
Corkin, S., 192
Costa, P. T., 370, 464
Craik, F. I. M., 202–203
Crick, F., 148
Crivelli, C., 123, 129
Cross, T., 345
Crowder, R. G., 192
Crutchfield, L., 150
Csikszentmihalyi, M., 275
Cummins, J., 247

Dahlstrom, W. G., 464
Dali, S., 276
Damon, W., 87
Daneman, M., 201
Danks, J. H., 238
Darley, J., 7
Darlington, R., 274
Darwin, C., 12, 36, 318
Davidson, J. E., 230, 270
Davidson, R. J., 468
Davis, K. E., 287
Davison, G. C., 387
Dawes, R. M., 376
DeAngelis, T., 310
DeBlassie, R., 321
DeCasper, A. J., 242
DeCastro, J. M., 320
DeCharms, R., 332, 334
Deci, E. L., 331, 332, 334
De Jong, W., 302
Delany, B., 366
Delgado, J. M. R., 319
DeLongis, A., 462
Dembo, T., 310
Dembroski, T. M., 464
Dement, W. C., 144, 147
Denny, N. W., 95
Denton, W. H., 294
Derryberry, D., 341
Desor, J., 36
De Trevino, E. B., 111
Detterman, D. K., 273
Deutsch, G., 52
Devine, P., 308
Dewey, J., 27
Dickinson, E., 471
Dienstbier, R. A., 453
Digman, J. M., 370
Dillard, A., 325
Dittes, J. E., 301
Dix, D., 416, 417
Docherty, J., 442
Dodson, J. B., 326, 334
Doherty, C. de H., 151

Dohrenwend, B. P., 402, 403
Dohrenwend, B. S., 402
Dolan, M., 216, 217
Dollard, J., 310
Donnerstein, E., 312
Donnerstein, M., 312
Donovan, M. E., 434
Doris, J., 265
Dougherty, D., 345
Douglas, F., 453
Douglas, J. D., 407
Doyle, J. M., 215
Dueck, A., 214
Duffy, V. B., 116
Duncker, K., 229, 230
Durlach, N. I., 114
Dyal, J. A., 366

Eagly, A. H., 290, 308
Earhart, A., 461
Early, P. C., 297
Ebbinghaus, H., 26, 27, 194, 195, 209
Eber, H. W., 377
Eckenrode, J., 456, 457, 462
Eckensberger, L. H., 94
Edgerton, R., 271
Edmonston, W. E., Jr., 150
Egeth, H. E. 216
Einstein, A., 254, 270
Eisert, M., 154
Ekman, P., 341, 344, 346
Eliot, G., 23
Elkind, D., 91, 235
Elliott, R., 437
Ellis, A., 423–424
Ellison, R., 86
Embree, M., 310
Emerson, R. W., 291
Endler, N. S., 273
Engle, R. W., 201, 202n
Epictetus, 456
Ericsson, K. A., 193
Erikson, E., 30, 82, 86, 91, 95, 96,
   359–361, 362, 378, 420
Eron, L. D., 186, 311
Eskenazi, J., 140
Exner, J., 374, 375
Eysenck, H. J., 262, 265, 268, 369–370,
   372, 379

Faber, M. D., 352
Falco, M., 158
Fallon, A., 337
Faloon, S., 193
Fantz, R. L., 76
Farah, M. J., 51
Farmer, A. E., 401
Farne, M. A., 455
Farr, M., 231
Fay, R. E., 323
Fazio, R., 286
Feinleib, M., 464
Feist, J., 352
Felten, D. L., 459
Fenz, W. D., 149
Ferguson, M., 228
Fernandez, E., 465, 466
Feshbach, S., 310
Festinger, L., 285, 286, 294, 311

Feuerstein, R., 274
Field, S., 300
Field, T., 88, 242
Fife, S., 420
Fifer, W. P., 242
Finnegan, L. P., 74
Fischer, M. H., 234
Fischhoff, B., 235
Flavell, J. H., 208
Fleshner, M., 179, 459
Flett, G. L., 456
Floody, O. R., 342
Fogel, A., 242
Folkman, F., 343
Folkman, S., 460–462
Foreman, G., 254
Forsyth, D. R., 43
Foster, J., 410
Frank, A., 347
Frankl, V., 397
Franks, J. J., 126
Fraser, S. C., 302
Frazier, T. M., 74
Freedman, J. L., 302
Freeman, W., 426
Frensch, P. A., 275
Freud, A., 356, 360
Freud, S., 29, 30, 141–142, 147, 351,
    353, 354–358, 359, 360, 361, 362,
    378, 394, 419, 420
Frew, D. R., 464
Frey, K. S., 328
Friedman, H. S., 464
Friedman, M., 463–464
Friedman, M. I., 320
Friedrich-Cofer, L., 186
Friesen, W. V., 341
Frieze, I. H., 287
Frijda, N., 344, 347
Funder, D. C., 372
Furedy, J., 345
Furlong, M. J., 430
Furstenberg, F. F., 180

Gabrenya, W. K., 297
Gagnon, J. H., 322
Galanter, E. H., 333
Galton, F., 104, 254–255
Gammack, G., 369
Garcia, J., 172–173
Gardner, H., 52, 266–267, 268, 275
Gardner, M., 225
Gazzaniga, M. S., 55
Geen, R. G., 312
Gelder, M. G., 424
Gelles, R. J., 178
Gelman, S., 83
Genest, M., 466
Genovese, K., 305
Germer, R. H., 322
Gerstein, D. R., 157, 158
Geyelin, M., 441
Gibbs, J., 407
Gibbs, J. C., 94
Giber, D., 151
Gibson, J. J., 130
Gick, M., 229
Gideonese, H. D., 421
Gilbert, E., 321

Gill, M. M., 150, 374
Gilligan, C., 94
Gilman, C. P., 40
Gim, R. H., 430
Ginzburg, N., 90
Gladwin, T., 263
Glaser, R., 231, 459
Glass, G. V., 437
Glenberg, A., 209
Glick, J., 263
Glucksberg, S., 238
Glueck, B. C., 151
Goddard, H., 265
Godden, D. R., 211
Golbus, M. S., 74
Goldberg, L. R., 370
Goleman, D., 235, 436
Good, B., 396
Goodwin, D. W., 395
Goodwin, F. K., 396
Gorman, J. M., 428
Gottesman, I. I., 401
Gottfried, A. E., 88
Gottfried, A. W., 88
Gottman, J. M., 9, 294, 433
Graf, P., 196
Graham, J. R., 377
Grant, C., 390
Gray, A. L., 149
Green, C., 20
Green, D. M., 105
Greene, D., 331
Greene, R. L., 377
Greenfield, P., 30, 86–87
Greenwald, A. G., 140
Gregory, R. L., 117
Grimson, W. R., 431
Gross, L., 320
Gruber, H., 12, 16
Grusec, J. F., 178
Guisewite, C., 319
Gurman, A. S., 432
Gustavson, C. R., 173
Guze, S. B., 395
Gwirtsman, H. E., 322

Haber, R. N., 195
Haglund, M. M., 52
Haier, R., 262
Haith, M. M., 76
Hakuta, K., 247, 248
Hampl, P., 214
Harkins, S., 296
Harlow, H. F., 332
Harlow, M. K., 332
Hart, D., 87
Hartel, F., 182
Harter, S., 87
Harvel, V., 286
Harwood, H. J., 157, 158
Hastings, E. H., 337
Hastings, P. K., 337
Hatfield, E., 292, 294, 302, 335
Hathaway, S. R., 376
Hawking, S., 270
Hayes, D., 452
Haynes, S. G., 464
Hazan, C., 292

Healy, J. M., 376
Heaney, C. A., 457
Heath, S., 12
Hedstrom, L. J., 429
Heenan, T. A., 344
Hefley, E. F., 95
Heider, F., 287–288, 292
Heilbrun, A. B., 321
Heller, J., 49, 410
Helmes, E., 377
Helmholtz, H. L. F. von, 111, 114, 230
Hennessey, B. A., 275
Henry, J. P., 341
Hering, E., 112
Herlofson, J., 424
Herman, C. P., 320
Heron, W., 326
Herrnstein, R., 273
Hersen, M., 183, 391, 394
Hetherington, A. W., 320
Heyduk, R. G., 331
Higashi, C., 430
Higginbotham, H. N., 429
Hilgard, E. R., 150
Hilts, P. J., 196
Hinckley, J., Jr., 410
Hinde, R. A., 312
Hintzman, D. L., 200
Hirschfeld, R. M. A., 396
Ho, D. Y. F., 328
Hobson, J. A., 145, 147
Hochreich, D. J., 365
Hodes, M., 431
Hoebel, B. G., 320
Hoffman, L. W., 88
Hogarth, W., 122
Holder, M. D., 172
Holinger, P. C., 407
Hollingshead, A. B., 402
Hollis, K. L., 173
Holmes, O. W., Sr., 391
Holmes, T., 453, 454, 455
Holyoak, K., 229
Honsberger, R. W., 151
Hooker, E., 324
Hoover, H., 38
Hopper, G. M., 457
Horney, K., 361, 362, 378, 420
House, J. S., 457, 462
Houston, J. P., 318
Hovland, C. I., 290
Howard, K. I., 436, 437
Hubbard, E., 140, 200
Hubel, D., 50, 124
Hudson, W., 317
Huebner, R. R., 347
Huesmann, L. R., 186, 311
Hui, C. H., 297
Hull, C. L., 318
Hunt, E., 262
Hunt, M. M., 6
Hurston, Z. N., 11, 327
Hurvich, L., 112
Huston, A. C., 87, 186
Hutt, J., 464
Hwang, K. K., 455

Inhelder, B., 90
Inoue, M., 455

Insko, C. A., 288
Isen, A. M., 347
Israel, B. A., 457
Ivey, A. E., 436
Ivey, M. B., 436
Izard, C. E., 79, 347

Jablonsky, A., 400
Jackson, J., 80
Jackson, N. E., 268
Jackson, R., 464
Jackson, S. E., 457
Jacobson, L., 333, 366
James, W., 27, 139, 318, 339, 345
Jameson, D., 112
Jamis, M., 215
Janis, I. L., 289, 297-298
Jemmott, J. B., III, 459
Jensen, A. R., 262
Jerome, J. K., 296
John, O., 370
Johnson, F., 430
Johnson, K., 231
Johnson, M., 469
Johnson, M. K., 207, 213
Johnson, V., 323
Johnson-Laird, P. N., 236
Jones, E. E., 287
Judd, C. M., 308
Julian, 156
Jung, C. G., 30, 359, 361, 378, 420

Kagan, J., 79
Kahneman, D., 234
Kamarck, T., 460
Kamin, L., 265
Kandel, E. R., 204
Kannel, W. B., 464
Kanner, A., 343
Kant, I., 179
Kaplan, C., 230
Karlin, M., 214
Kassin, S. M., 291
Katz, D., 288
Katz, M. M., 396
Kay, P., 247
Kazdin, A. E., 183
Keele, S. W., 126
Keesey, R., 334
Keller, H., 103, 116, 117, 374
Keller, M., 94
Kelley, K. N., 43
Kelly, H. H., 301
Kempton, S., 386
Kendall, P. C., 422
Kenrick, D. T., 87
Keppel, G., 210
Kerns, R., 467
Ketcham, K., 215
Kiecolt-Glaser, J. K., 459, 460
Kiesler, D. J., 436
Kihlstrom, J. F., 136, 150
Kilmann, P. R., 425
Kim, S. J., 430
Kimbro, D., 104
King, G. R., 181
Kitayama, S., 86
Kitchener, K. S., 90
Kleinman, A., 396, 397

Kleinmuntz, B., 345
Kleitman, N., 144
Klesges, R. C., 320
Klima, E. S., 52
Klinger, M. R., 140
Klonsky, B. G., 308
Kniskern, D. P., 432
Knox, V. J., 150
Kobasa, S., 464–465
Koelling, R., 172, 173
Koeske, R. D., 211
Koffka, K., 30
Kohlberg, L., 92–94, 96
Köhler, W., 30, 227–228
Kohn, P. M., 456
Kolb, B., 49, 145
Komaroff, A. L., 455
Kornblum, 156
Kosslyn, S. M., 52, 206
Kramer, M. A., 402
Krasgenor, N. A., 75
Kulkarni, S. S., 366

Lachman, M. E., 366
LaFraniere, S., 216
La Ganga, M. L., 441
Lagerspetz, K., 186, 311
Laing, R. D., 402
Lamm, H., 297
Landers, A., 440
Landis, K. R., 462
Lange, C., 339, 345
Langer, E. J., 302
Langsley, D. G., 431, 432
Larkin, J., 231
Latané, B., 7, 296, 297, 301, 305, 306
Latham, G. P., 333
Lau, R. R., 465
Lazar, I., 274
Lazarus, R., 343–344, 347, 460–462
Lederer, R., 241
LeDoux, J., 340–341
Lee, H., 283
Leicht, K. L., 209
Lepper, M. R., 331, 334
Leppin, A., 462
LeVay, S., 324
Levenkron, J. C., 464
Levenson, R. W., 341
Leventhal, H., 343
Levin, H., 312
Levine, B., 243
Lewin, K., 310
Lichtenstein, S., 235
Liebert, R. M., 311
Lin, K-M., 455
Lindzey, G., 273
Linscheid, T. R., 182
Lishman, B., 165
Lissner, L., 320
Locke, E. A., 333
Locke, S. E., 459
Lockhart, R., 202–203
Loehlin, J. D., 273
Loewenstein, G., 180
Loftus, E., 214, 215, 216, 441
Logue, A. W., 181
Lonner, W. J., 18, 246, 321, 377
Lorenz, K., 156

Lubart, T. I., 275, 331
Lumsdaine, A. A., 289
Luria, A. R., 193
Luzatto, S., 193
Lynd, H. M., 140

Ma, H. K., 94
Maccoby, E., 312
MacFarlane, A., 77
Maehr, M., 328
Magalhües, V. P., 266
Magder, L., 459
Magnusson, D., 273
Maier, S. F., 179, 459
Maimonides, 72
Makhijani, M. G., 308
Malpass, R. S., 215
Mandler, J., 77, 83
Manji, H. K., 429
Mantyla, T., 212
Maqsud, M., 94
Marcel, A. J., 140
Marcia, J., 91, 92
Markman, H., 9
Marks, I. M., 424
Markus, H. R., 86
Marley, J., 305, 306
Marsella, A. J., 396, 397
Marshall, G. D., 343
Martin, F. E., 322
Martin, J., 91
Martin, J. A., 242
Martin, L., 247
Martindale, C., 142
Martineau, H., 15
Martinez, F. M., 429
Martinez-Pons, M., 366
Maslach, C., 457
Maslow, A., 30, 328–330, 332, 334, 363, 378
Masters, W., 323
Masuda, M., 455
Matarazzo, J. D., 262
Matsumoto, D., 387, 390, 394, 397, 402, 417, 429
Mayer, D. J., 320
Mayer, G. R., 177, 181
McArthur, L., 171
McCabe, G., 398
McCarley, R. W., 147
McCarthy, J., 127
McCarthy, M., 311, 323
McClelland, D. C., 327–328, 330, 333, 375, 462
McCloskey, M., 215
McCrae, R. R., 370
McCusker, C., 297
McDougall, W., 318
McGarry-Roberts, P. A., 262
McGuffin, P., 401
McKenna, J., 215
McKinley, J. C., 376
McNeill, D., 139
Mead, M., 90
Meck, E., 83
Meeker, W. B., 149
Meichenbaum, D., 466
Meltzoff, A. N., 186
Melzack, R., 465–466

Mencken, H. L., 354
Mermelstein, R., 460
Merrill, M., 257
Mesmer, F. A., 149
Mesquita, B., 344, 347
Metalsky, G. I., 179
Metcalfe, J., 228
Micka, M. V., 137
Midler, B., 301, 352
Milgram, S., 24, 302, 303–304
Miller, D., 214, 215
Miller, G. A., 199, 239, 333
Miller, I. J., 116
Miller, J. B., 353
Miller, N., 310
Miller, N. E., 319
Milner, B., 192
Milner, P., 319
Mischel, W., 180, 372–373, 376, 379
Mishkin, M., 203
Mitchison, G., 148
Moghaddam, F. M., 284
Money, J., 322
Montagu, A., 310
Montaigne, M. de, 209
Moore, L. G., 464
Moos, R., 471
Morgan, C. D., 375
Mori, M., 262
Morrison, T., 135, 136, 254
Morton, T. U., 294
Moscovici, S., 297
Moyes, P., 16
Munch, E., 392
Murase, T., 430
Murray, C., 273
Murray, H., 327, 330, 334, 375
Murstein, B. I., 294
Myer, D. R., 332
Myers, D. G., 297
Myers, J. K., 395
Myerson, A., 402

Nash, M., 150
Nash, O., 138
Nathan, P. W., 193
Neale, J. M., 387
Nehru, J., 284
Neisser, U., 30
Nellis, D. W., 173
Nelson, C., 87
Neto, F., 308
Newcomb, T. M., 301, 311
Newell, A., 333
Nicholls, J., 328
Nickerson, R. S., 215
Nicolaus, L. K., 173
Nida, S. A., 305
Nielson, S., 321
Niemczynski, A., 94
Nightingale, N. N., 274
Nin, A., 419
Nisan, M., 94
Nisbett, R. E., 273, 287, 320, 331
Noel, J. G., 43
Norman, W., 370
Notarius, C., 9
Nozawa, Y., 455

Oatley, K., 310
Oden, M. H., 269
Ogbu, J. U., 273
O'Keefe, G., 123
Olds, J., 319
Oliner, P., 186, 307
Oliner, S., 186, 307
Öngel, Ö., 284
Oomara, Y., 320
Orne, M. T., 149, 399
Ornstein, R., 151
Osman, A., 95
Oster, H., 344, 346
Ott, E. M., 309
Otto, S. A., 344
Overton, R., 209
Overton, W. F., 90
Ozer, D. J., 372

Paivio, A., 206
Papini, M. R., 169
Papp, L., 428
Park, B., 308
Park, R. D., 178
Parke, R. D., 186, 311
Parker, D., 235, 408
Pasteur, L., 167
Paul, G. L., 436
Pavlov, I., 27, 167–168
Payne, J., 234
Peabody, D., 370
Peake, P. K., 372
Pearlstone, A., 455
Pedersen, P. B., 436
Péguy, C., 46
Pelchat, M. L., 174
Penrod, S., 215, 301
Pepitone, A., 311
Perdue, L., 321
Perez, J., 13–14
Perris, C., 424
Peterson, B., 321
Peterson, L. R., 210
Peterson, M. J., 210
Peterson, V., 208
Petri, H. L., 203
Pettigrew, T. F., 308, 310
Petty, R. E., 288, 341
Pfaffman, C., 116
Pfeiffer, W., 394
Phares, E. J., 366
Phelps, E., 209
Phillips, D. A., 328
Piaget, J., 72–73, 74, 77, 82–83, 85, 90, 92, 96
Pierce, G. R., 462
Pietromonaco, P., 344
Pillard, R. C., 324
Pinel, P., 417
Pinker, S., 238
Pinsoff, W. M., 432
Pittman, T. S., 331
Plante, T., 452
Plath, S., 395
Plato, 25, 26
Plomin, R. C., 273, 368
Plutchik, R., 337
Poe, E. A., 209, 385, 386
Poincaré, H., 230

Poizner, H., 52
Pokorny, A. D., 407
Polivy, J., 320
Ponce, F. Q., 429
Poole, M. P., 18
Poon, L. W., 95
Popper, K., 9
Posner, M., 126
Postman, L. J., 309
Poston, W. C., 430
Pratkanis, A. R., 140
Pribram, K. H., 333
Puhan, B. N., 366
Pullum, G. K., 247

Quanty, M. B., 312

Rahe, R., 453, 454
Ramey, C. T., 273, 274
Ranson, S. W., 320
Rapaport, D., 374
Rapp, P. E., 345
Rapson, R. L., 294
Read, J. D., 140
Reddon, J. R., 377
Redlich, F. C., 402
Reed, T. E., 262, 274
Regan, D. T., 302
Reimer, J., 94
Reitman, J. S., 210
Renzulli, J. S., 270, 275
Rescorla, R., 169–170
Resnik, H. L. P., 407
Rest, J. R., 94
Restak, R., 60
Reynolds, D. K., 430
Richardson, D. R., 310
Ricks, D. F., 337
Ritter, B., 422
Roach, M., 275
Roark, A. C., 243
Roazzi, A., 266
Roberts, W. W., 319
Robins, L. N., 392, 401
Rodia, S., 213
Rodin, J., 320, 452
Rodriguez, M., 180
Roediger, H. L., III, 201
Rogers, C., 30, 363, 378, 421–422
Rogers, S. M., 323
Rojahn, K., 308, 310
Rokeach, M., 400
Rolls, B. J., 320
Rolls, E. T., 320
Romanski, L., 341
Rorschach, H., 374–375
Rorvik, D., 18
Rosen, G., 434
Rosenhan, D., 387
Rosenman, R., 463–464
Rosenthal, R., 333, 366
Roskies, E., 464
Ross, C. E., 452
Ross, D., 185
Ross, L., 287
Ross, R., 331
Ross, S. A., 185
Rotter, J., 365–366, 367, 373, 379
Rouhani, S., 94

Rovee-Collier, C., 211, 215
Rowe, E. T., 320
Rozin, P., 174, 337
Ruble, D. N., 328
Ruch, J. C., 148
Rudy, T. E., 465, 466, 467, 468
Russell, B., 27
Russell, G. F. M., 321
Russell, J., 344
Russell, M. J., 77
Russell, R. J. H., 455
Russell, W. R., 193
Ruzgis, P., 274

Sacks, O., 117, 121
Sadker, D., 87
Sadker, M., 87
Safer, D. J., 320
Safir, L., 434
Safire, W., 434
Salanter, I., 108
Salapatek, P., 76
Sand, G., 421
Sanders, S. H., 465
Santayana, G., 24
Sapif, E., 246
Sarason, B. R., 462
Sarason, I. G., 462
Sarason, S., 265
Sartorius, N., 391, 400, 429
Savery, L. K., 456
Saxe, L., 345
Scarr, S., 272
Schachter, S., 294, 320, 342–343
Schacter, D. L., 196, 199, 209
Schaefer, J. A., 471
Schafer, R., 374
Schaffer, H. R., 242
Schaie, K. W., 95
Schliemann, A. D., 266
Schreiber, F. R., 398
Schuh, E. S., 140
Schultze, M., 109
Schulz, C., 392
Schwartz, G. E., 468
Schwartz, J. H., 204
Schwarzer, R., 462
Schweizer, E., 429
Scott, A. I. F., 425
Scott, J., 236
Scott, T. H., 326
Scovern, A. W., 425
Scoville, W., 192
Scragg, R., 464
Sears, R. R., 269, 312
Segun, M., 91
Seiden, R. H., 407
Seidman, L. J., 402
Selfridge, O. G., 126, 127, 128
Seligman, M., 179
Selman, R., 88, 96
Selye, H., 458, 459
Seraganian, P., 320
Seymour, R. B., 151, 156, 157
Shakespeare, W., 406, 465
Shallice, T., 203
Shanab, M. E., 304
Shange, N., 386

Shapiro, D. A., 437
Shapiro, D. H., 151
Shapiro, P., 215
Shapiro, R., 400
Sharon, I., 284
Shaver, P. R., 292
Shaw, G. B., 372
Shekelle, R. B., 464
Shepherd, R. N., 126
Sheppard, J. A., 287
Sherif, M., 309
Sherman, S. J., 308
Shiffrin, R. M., 197
Shimamura, A. P., 204
Shneidman, E. S., 407
Shoda, Y., 180
Shontz, F., 470, 471
Shuit, D. P., 441
Siegel, E. F., 149
Siegler, R., 90, 242
Siffre, M., 145
Silko, L. M., 213
Silverstein, B., 321
Simek-Morgan, L., 436
Simon, H. A., 30, 231, 233, 262, 333
Simon, T., 255
Simon, W. H., 322
Simonton, D., 275
Simpson, A. E., 312
Singer, J., 342–343
Singh, B., 320
Siskin, B., 18
Skinner, B. F., 9, 30, 182–183, 364–365, 379
Slovic, P., 235
Smith, D., 436
Smith, D. E., 151, 156, 157
Smith, M. L., 437
Smith, P. B., 284, 301
Snarey, J. R., 94
Snow, C., 144
Snow, C. E., 242
Solomon, G. F., 469
Solomon, R. L., 324–325, 334
Solso, R., 127
Spangler, W., 376
Spanos, N. P., 149
Spearman, C., 261
Specht, C. V., 457
Specter, M., 236
Spence, M. J., 242
Sperling, G., 198, 199
Sperry, R. W., 30, 50
Spicer, J., 464
Spitzer, L., 320
Springer, S. P., 52
Spuhler, J. N., 273
Squire, L. R., 203–204, 209
Sroufe, L. A., 79
Srull, T. K., 308
Staller, J., 18
Standing, L., 195
Stanley, J. C., 87
Steele, C., 273, 308
Stein, G., 237, 393
Stelmack, R. M., 262
Stephens, P. M., 341
Steptoe, A., 456

Stern, D., 242
Stern, W., 256
Sternberg, R. J., 87, 227, 264, 267, 268, 270, 273, 274, 275, 292, 294, 331, 358, A1
Sternberg, S., 210–211
Stevenson, R. L., 148
Stevenson-Hinde, J., 312
Stewart, A., 376
Stiles, W. B., 437, 438
Stotland, E., 288
Straus, M. A., 178
Strauss, J. S., 402
Stricker, E. M., 320
Stroebel, C. F., 151
Stroop, J. R., 138
Stuart, J. E., 91
Styles, I., 90
Sue, D., 436
Sue, S., 429, 430
Suematsu, H., 321
Sullivan, A., 117, 241
Sulzer-Azaroff, B., 177
Swann, W. B., Jr., 331
Swartz, L., 390
Swets, J. A., 105
Szasz, T., 402, 410
Szmukler, G. I., 321
Szucko, J. J., 345
Szymanski, K., 296

Tan, A., 214, 276
Tanford, S., 301
Tannen, D., 294–295
Tanner, W. P., Jr., 105
Tardif, T., 201
Tatsuoka, M. M., 377
Taves, P. A., 286
Taylor, D. M., 284
Taylor, S. E., 19–20, 388, 464, 468, 470–471
Taylor, S. L., 224
Tazuma, L., 455
Teitelbaum, G., 320
Teitelbaum, P., 320
Temoshok, L., 469
Ten Cate, C., 173
Terman, L., 257, 269–270
Teuber, H. L., 192
Thomas, A., 80–82, 368, 373
Thompson, S. K., 87
Thomson, D., 212
Thorndike, E. L., 27, 174, 175–176
Thurstone, L., 261
Tinbergen, N., 165
Titchener, E., 27
Tolman, E., 333, 334
Tolstoy, L., 42
Tomarken, A. J., 343
Torrey, E. F., 437, 438
Totman, R., 453
Townsend, J. T., 211
Treadway, M., 215
Treisman, A., 137
Triandis, H. C., 284, 297
Trillin, C., 399
Tripathi, A. N., 213
Triplett, N., 295

Trost, M. R., 87
Tschirart, L., 434
Tucker, D. M., 341
Tulving, E., 199, 212
Turk, D. C., 465, 466, 467, 468
Turner, C. F., 323
Turner, J. C., 297
Turner, R. J., 402
Turner, S. M., 391, 394
Tversky, A., 233, 234
Twain, M., 69, 423
Ty, T. C., 466

Ulrich, R., 310
Umberson, D., 462
Underwood, B. J., 210

Vaid, J., 52
Valéry, P., 7
Van Burn, A., 421
VanderPlate, C., 459
Verdi, G., 275
Vernon, P. A., 262
Veroff, J., 375
Viglione, D. J., 375
Vinokur, A., 297
Viorst, J., 138
Vissing, Y. M., 178
Vokey, J. R., 140
Voltaire, 243
Von Rosen, K., 94
Vygotsky, L., 72, 73–74

Wade, C., 324
Wagner, D., 265
Wagner, R. K., 274
Wagonfeld, M. O., 402
Walker, A., 276
Walker, L., 94
Wall, P. D., 465–466
Wallace, R. K., 151
Walster, E., 292, 294
Walster, G. W., 292, 302
Walters, G. C., 178

Walters, R. H., 178, 423
Wang, Y. E., 297
Warrington, E., 203
Washington, M., 369
Wason, P. C., 236
Watkins, L. R., 179, 459
Watson, D., 370
Watson, J., 30, 45
Weber, E., 106
Wechsler, D., 257–259
Weidner, G., 464
Weisberg, R. W., 225
Weisenberg, M., 468
Weiss, R. S., 9, 12
Weiss, W., 290
Weissman, M. M., 395
Wellman, H. M., 208
Wells, G. L., 216
Wells, H. G., 36
Wells, P. A., 455
Wernicke, C., 50
Wertheimer, M., 30, 227
Wesman, A. E., 337
West, M., 319
Wever, R. A., 145
Wheelwright, J. H., 113
Whishaw, I. Q., 49, 145
White, R. W., 318, 332
Whitehorn, K., 273
Whitehouse, W. G., 149
Whitley, B. E., Jr., 287
Widner, S. C., 308
Wiebe, J., 228
Wiesel, T. N., 50, 124
Wilber, K. H., 457
Wiley, J. S., Jr., 217
Williams, C. L., 377
Williams, J. E., 308
Williams, K., 296
Williams, R., 156
Williams, R. B., 464
Wilson, A. F., 151
Wilson, D. W., 305

Winter, D. G., 327, 375
Witt, N., 321
Wittig, M., 245
Wittlinger, R., 200–201
Wolpe, J., 423
Wong, D. F., 402
Wooden, M., 456
Woodruff, R. A., 395
Woodworth, R. S., 318
Woolf, V., 408
Woolfolk, R. L., 151
Woon, T., 455
Wright, L., 464
Wright, R., 308, 332
Wright, R. H., 119
Wright, S. C., 284
Wundt, W., 27
Wyer, R. S., Jr., 308

Xagoraris, A., 341

Yahiro, K., 455
Yahya, K. A., 304
Yang, K., 366
Yarrow, R., 275
Yee, K., 8
Yerkes, R. M., 326, 334
Young, T., 111
Yuille, J. C., 216
Yussen, S. R., 268

Zaidel, E., 55
Zajonc, R. B., 79, 296, 343–344, 347
Zamansky, H. S., 150
Zanna, M., 286
Zaragoza, M. S., 215
Zavalloni, M., 297
Zeidner, M., 273
Zigler, E., 274
Zimbardo, P. G., 24, 311–312, 343
Zimmerman, B. J., 366
Zimmerman, M., 328
Zola-Morgan, S. M., 203
Zuckerman, M., 347

Subject Index

AA. *See* Alcoholics Anonymous (AA)
Abnormal behavior, 386–388
  anxiety disorders and, 392–395
  clinical diagnoses of, 391–392
  clinical explanations of, 388–391
  demonological explanations of, 388
  diagnosis in infancy, childhood, or
    adolescence, 404–405
  dissociative disorders and, 398–399
  impulse-control disorders and, 403
  legal issues of clinicians, 409–411
  mood disorders and, 395–398
  personality disorders defined, 404
  schizophrenia and, 399–403
  somatoform disorders and, 405–406
  suicide and, 406–409
Absolute threshold, 105
Absorption of light, 111
Accessibility, of information, 211
Accommodation, 73
  by eye, **109**
Acetylcholine (ACh), 61
  and memory, 204
ACh. *See* Acetylcholine (ACh)
Achievement, 260
  needs for, 327–328, 334
Acoustic code, 205
Acoustic processing, 203
Acquired motivation, 325, *325*
Acquisition phase of learning, **170**
Acronym, for encoding, 206
Acrostic, for encoding, 206
ACTH. *See* Adrenocorticotropic
    hormone (ACTH)
Action potential, 58–59, *59*
Action readiness, and emotion, 344
**Activation–synthesis hypothesis,
    147**–148
Actor–observer effect, 187, 288
Acupuncture, pain control and, 468
Acute, 448
Acute episodes, of schizophrenia, 400
Acute pain, 466
Acute stress disorder, 392, 393
Acute toxicity, 152
Adaptation
  behaviorism and, 364
  classical conditioning and, 173
  habituation and, 165
  to light and dark, 109, 110
  sensory, **108**
  to sightless or soundless environment,
    117
Adaptive competence, 270
Addiction, 152
  self-help for, 433–434
  treatment of, 154
Additive bilingualism, 247
Additive mixture, 111
Adjustment disorders, 406
Adjustment stage, illness and, 470
Adlerian psychology, 358

Adolescence, 90
  cognitive development in, 90–91
  physical development in, 90
  socioemotional development in,
    91–95
Adrenal glands, *63*
  adrenal cortex and, *63*
  adrenal medulla and, *63*
Adrenocorticotropoic hormone
    (ACTH), and emotion, 342
Adulthood, development in, 95–96
Aerial perspective, 124
Aerobic exercise, 450–452
Affective component, of attitudes, 188
Affective symptoms, of schizophrenia,
    400
Affiliation needs, 327
Affixes, 139
African Americans, 429, 430
  intelligence scores of, 273
Age, heritability of intelligence and,
    273
Aggression, 310–312
  deindividuation and, 311–312
  desensitization and, 310–311
  television and, 186
Agnosia, 125–126
Agoraphobia, 393
Agreeableness, 370
AIDS (acquired immune deficiency
    syndrome), *153*
  cases and deaths from, *470*
  living with, 469–470
Alarm response, to stress, 458–459
Alcohol and alcoholism, 154
  impact on embryo, 74, 75
Alcoholics Anonymous (AA), 433
Algorithms, 225–226
Altered states of consciousness, 142
  drug-induced, 151–158
  hypnosis as, 148–150
  meditation as, 151
  sleep as, 143–148
Altruism, 306–307
Alzheimer's disease, 35, 47, 204
American Association on Mental
    Retardation, 270
American Law Institute, insanity defense
    and, 410
American Psychiatric Association, DSM
    of, 391–392
American Sign Language, *52*
Ames room, *129*
Amino-acid transmitters, 61
Amnesia, 192, *196*, 406
  retrograde, 192–193
Amplitude, of stimulus, 107
Amygdala, 47
Anal-expulsive personality, 356
Analgesics, 151
Analogies, in problem solving, 229
Anal-retentive personality, 356

Anal stage, of psychosexual development,
    356
Analysis
  of behavior, 182–183
  and problem solving, **226**
Analytical psychology, of Jung, 359
Anatomy, 36. *See also* Ear; Eye
Androgyny, 87–88
Anger, 337
Angiograms, 46
Anima, 359
Animals
  association areas of, 53
  as subjects, 23–24
Animus, 359
Anorexia nervosa, 155, **321**–322, 390
Antecedent events, and emotion, 344
Anterograde amnesia, 192
Antianxiety drugs, 428–429
Antidepressant drugs, 427–428
Antipsychotic drugs, 427, *428*
  dopamine receptors and, *427*
Antisocial behavior, 307–313, 404
  aggression, 310–312
  prejudice as, 307–308
Anxiety, 361, 392
  as disorder, 393–394
  separation, 80
  stranger, 80
Anxiety disorders, 392–395
  behavioral explanation of, 394
  cognitive explanation of, 394
  cultural explanation of, 394
  humanistic explanation of, 394
  psychodynamic explanation of, 394
  psychophysiological explanation of,
    394
Anxious–ambivalent lovers, 292
Apes, insightful thinking of, *227*,
    227–228
Aphasia, 50
Applied research, 16
Appraisal
  coping with stress and, 460–462
  and emotion, 344
**Approach–avoidance conflict,
    335**–336, *336*
Aptitude, measurement of, **260**
Archetypes, 359
Arousal
  love and, 294
  motivation and, **326**–327
Arousal theory, 334
Arrested development, homosexuality
    and, 324
Art, monocular depth cues in, *123*
Asian Americans, 429, 430
Assessment, of personality, 374–377
Assimilation, 72
Association areas, 53
Associationism, 27
Atheoretical, DSM as, **391**

Atkinson-Shiffrin model, 197, *197*
Attachment, 80
Attachment view of love, 292
Attention, 136–137
    functioning of, 137–138
    selective, 137
Attention-deficit/hyperactivity disorder,
    404
Attitude, 288
    changing, 289–291
    formation of, 286, 288–291
    language and, 244
Attraction, 292–294, *293*
    interpersonal, 291–292
Attribution, 287–288
Audience, imaginary, 91
Auditory processing, brain and, 52
Auditory system, 107
Autism, 404–405
Automatic behavior, 139
Autonomic nervous system, *44*, 45
Autonomy, 86
Autoshaping, 181
Availability, of information, 211
Availability heuristic, 234
Aversion therapy, 422, 423
Aversive conditioning, 177
Avoidance. *See* Approach–avoidance
    conflict
Avoidance learning, 177
Avoidant lovers, 292
Avoidant personality disorder, 404
Axon, *57*, **57**–58

Babalawo, *438*
Babbling, 242
Backbone, 40
Background. *See* Ground
Balance, 107, 120
Balance theory, 292
Barbiturates, 154, 428–429
Basal ganglia, 47
Baseline, opponent-process theory and,
    324–325
Basic anxiety, 361
Basic research, 16
Basilar membrane, 113
Bayley Scales of Infant Development, 77, 78
Beauty, weight and, 321
Behavior. *See also* Consciousness;
    Learning; Personality
    abnormal, 386–388
    antisocial, 307–313
    attitude change and, 291
    attitude formation and, 288
    automatic, 139
    helping, 305–306
    prosocial, 304–307
    shaping of, 181
    Skinner and experimental analysis of,
        182–183
Behavioral contracting, 422, 423
Behavioral explanations
    of abnormal behavior, 389
    of anxiety disorders, 394
    of mood disorders, 397
    of schizophrenia, 402
Behavioral therapy, effectiveness of, *424*

Behavior therapy, 422, 423
Behaviorism, 28, 30
    early approaches of, 364–365
Belongingness needs, 329
Benzodiazepines, 429
Biases
    of attribution, 287
    confirmation, 8–9
    of judgment, 234–236
Big Five theory of personality, 370
Bilingual, 247–248
Binaural presentation, 137, *138*
Binocular convergence, 124
Binocular depth cues, 124
Binocular disparity, 124
Biofeedback, pain control and, 468
Biological drives, 353
Biological properties, common to all
    senses, 106–108
Biological psychology, 28–29, 35–67
    evolutionary theory and, 36
    genetics and, 37–39
Biological therapies, 425–429
    drug therapies, 426–429
    history of, 425–426
Biological variables, 361
Biology. *See also* Brain
    homosexuality and, 324
    of intelligence, 262
Bipolar disorders, 396–398
    lithium and, 429
Bisexual, 323–324
Black Americans. *See* African Americans
Blindness, 117. *See also* Vision
Blood–brain barrier, 450
Bobo doll, 184–185, *185*
Body dysmorphic disorder, 406
Body senses, 120–121
Bounded rationality, 233
Brain, 40. *See also* Depressants;
    Hemispheres; Nervous system
    agnosia and, 126
    antidepressant drugs and, *427, 427*
    cerebral hemispheres and cerebral
        cortex in, 49–55
    form perception and, 124–125
    intelligence and, 262
    memory and, 203–204
    narcotics and, 153
    normal vs. schizophrenic, *403*
    prenatal development of, 75
    psychoactive drugs and, 152–153
    sensation and, 104
    sleep deprivation and, 144
    sleep stages and, 143–144
    stimulants and, 156
    structures and functions of, 47–49, *49*
    taste and, 116
    viewing techniques, 45–47
Brightness, 111
Broca's area, 50, 53
Buffers, against stress, 462
Bulimia, 322
Bystander effect, model of intervention,
    305

Cardinal trait, 371
Careers, personality and, 373

Case studies, 11–12
    of Freud, 357–358
Catatonic schizophrenia, 401, *401*
Categorical clustering, 206
Categorization, social, 308
CAT (computerized axial tomography)
    scans, 46
Causal attributions, 288
Causal inferences, 16–22
    controlled experimental design and,
        16–20
    correlational design and, 20–22
    quasi-experimental design, 17, 18
    representative sample and, 18
Causality, conclusions about, 14
Causal relationships, understanding in
    preoperational stage, 83
Cell differentiation, 74
Cells. *See also* Neurons
    hair, 113
    receptor, 106–107
Central nervous system, 40–44
**Central nervous system (CNS)
    depressants, 154**–156, 157
**Central nervous system (CNS)
    stimulants, 156,** 157
Central tendency, 478–479
Central trait, 371
Centration, 83
Cerebellum, 49
Cerebral cortex, 49
    cerebral hemispheres and, 49–55
    lobes of, *51, 52*–54
Cerebral hemispheres, 50
    lobes of, 52–54
Cerebrospinal fluid (CSF), 40
CERs. *See* Conditioned emotional
    responses
Child care, effects of, 88, 89
Childhood. *See also* Acquisition phase of
    learning
    Freud on crises in, *357*
    personality emergence in, 86–88
Children, interpersonal relationships
    and, 88. *See also* Infants and infancy
Chlordiazepoxide. *See* Librium
Chromosomes, 37, 38, *38*
Chronic, 448
Chronic health problems
    living with, 468–473
    psychological models for coping with,
        470–473
Chronic pain, 466
Chronic symptoms, and schizophrenia,
    400
Chronic toxicity, 152
Chunk, 199
Circadian rhythms, *145,* **145**–146
Civil law, clinicians and, 410
Classical conditioning, 166–174, 422,
    423, *425*
    basics of, 168–169
    and emotional responses, 174
    features of, 171–172
    operant conditioning compared with,
        184
    Pavlov and, *167,* 167–168, *168*
    phases of, 170–*171*
    punishment and, 177

Client-centered therapy, 421
Clients, 388
    concept of, 420–421
Clinical explanations, of abnormal
        behavior, 388–391
Clinical observations, 353–354
Clinical psychology, 4
Clinical work, 11
Clinicians, 11–12, 388
Closure, form perception and, 125, 126
Clustering, 206
CNS. *See* Central nervous system entries
Cocktail party problem, 137
Cognition. *See also* Thinking
    attitude formation and, 288
    and emotions, 338–339
    sexual scripts and, 322–323
    social, 285–288
Cognitive approaches to emotion,
        342–344
Cognitive approaches to motivation,
        330–334
Cognitive approaches to therapy,
        423–424
    Beck's cognitive therapy, 424
    rational-emotive therapy, 423–424
Cognitive–behavioral paradigm,
        evaluation of, 367
Cognitive–behavioral theory of
        personality, 364–367
    Bandura's social-cognitive theory and,
        366
    Rotter's social-learning theory and,
        365, 365–366
    social-learning theory and, 365–366
Cognitive consistency, 285
Cognitive development, 70, 96
    in adolescence, 90–91
    in adulthood, 95
    in infancy, 77
    Piaget and Vygotsky on, 72–74
    preoperational stage of, 82
Cognitive dissonance, 285–286, *286*
Cognitive explanations
    of abnormal behavior, 390
    of anxiety disorders, 394
    of mood disorders, 397
    of schizophrenia, 402
Cognitive flooding, and schizophrenia,
        400
Cognitive-impairment disorder, 406
Cognitive psychology, 4
Cognitive symptoms
    of anxiety, 392
    of schizophrenia, 400
Cognitive therapy, of Beck, 424
Cognitivism, 28, 30
Cohesiveness, and group conformity,
        301
Collective unconscious, 359
Collectivism, 296–297
Color
    characteristics of color vision,
        109–111
    mixtures of, 111, *111*
Color constancy, 130
Color vision
    opponent-process theory of, 112
    trichromatic theory of, 111–112

Common and uncommon effects,
        287, **288**
Common traits, 371
Communication. *See also* Language
    in personal relationships, 294–295
Competence, 70
Compliance, 299, 301
    techniques for eliciting, 302
Comprehension, verbal, 238
Compulsion, 393
Computerized axial tomography. *See*
    CAT (computerized axial
    tomography) scans
Concept, 199
Concrete-operational stage, 85–86
Conditioned emotional responses
        (CERs), 174
Conditioned response (CR), 169
    and stimulus generalization and
        discrimination, 171–172
Conditioned stimulus (CS), 169
    and response, 172–173
Conditioning
    aversive, 177
    classical, 166–174
    instrumental, 174–184
Conduct disorder, 404
Conduction, intraneuronal, 58
Cones, 109
Confidentiality, 23
    of psychotherapy, 440
Confirmation bias, 8–9, *9*
Conflict
    approach-avoidance, 335–336
    internal, 353
Conformity, 299–301. *See also*
        Obedience
    Asch's studies of, 299–300
    factors affecting, 301
Confounding variables, 14
Connotation, 243
Conscientiousness, 370
Consciousness, 136–137
    altered states of, 142
    attention and, 136, 137–138
    drug-induced changes in, 151–158
    hypnosis and, 148–150
    levels of, 139–142
    meditation and, 151
    and memory, 211
    preconscious level of, 139–141
    sleep, dreams, and, 143–148
Conservation of quantity, 83, *84, 85*
    concrete-operational stage and, 85–86
Consolidation, 209
Constructive memory, 213–215
Consummate love, 292
Contact hypothesis, prejudice and, 310
Context
    abnormal behavior and, 387
    for creativity, 275, 277
    culture as, 284, *284*
    and memory, 211–212, *212*
Context effects, 127
Contextualist, 262
Contiguity, temporal, 169
Contingency phenomenon, **169**–170
Continuity, form perception and, 125,
        126

Continuous reinforcement, 182
Contraceptive practices, gradient of
        reinforcement and, 180
Contralateral transmission, 50
Control, 8
    over illness, 471
    locus of, 365–366
    psychotherapy as, 9–10
Control condition, 14
Control function, of consciousness, 136
Controlled experimental design,
        16–20
Conventional morality, 93
Conversion disorder, 405
Cooing, 242
Coping, 461
    with stress, 460–462
Coping skills
    for chronic illness, 471
    factors in, *471*
Cornea, 108, *110*
Corpus callosum, 50
Correlation, 20
    graphic representation of, *122*
    positive vs. none vs. negative, 21
    and regression, 482–484
Correlation coefficient, 482–483
Correlational design, 17, 20–22
Cortex, 47
    cerebral, 49–50
Counterconditioning, 422, 423, *425*
Countertransference, 420
Couples therapy, 431–433, *433*
CR. *See* Conditioned response (CR)
Creativity, 275–277
Crime and criminality, addiction and, *155*
Criminal law, clinicians and, 409–410
Crises, in childhood, *357*
Crisis theory, of coping with chronic
        illness, 471
Critical period, 74
Critical thinking, 224, *224*
Criticism, as reinforcer, 181
Cross-cultural approaches, to emotion,
        344–346
Cross-cultural developmental
        psychology, self-concept and,
        86–87
Cross-cultural studies
    of emotional expression, 346
    of intelligence, 263
    and memory, 213
CS. *See* Conditioned stimulus (CS)
CSF. *See* Cerebrospinal fluid
Cultural explanations
    of abnormal behavior, 390
    of anxiety disorders, 394
    of mood disorders, 397
    of schizophrenia, 402
Cultural psychology, 29, 30
Cultural variable, 361
Culture
    as context, 284, *284*
    and emotion, 344–346
    emotional expression and, 346
    and group conformity, 301
    and intelligence, 262–266
    intelligence of disadvantaged and, 273
    weight and, 321

Culture-fair, 263–265
Culture-relevant tests, **265**–266
Cumulative nature, of science, 8–9
Curanderos, 429, 438
Curiosity, 331–333, 334

Daily hassles, 455–456
Dark adaptation, 109, 110
Data, 7
Davis v. The United States, 409
Deafness, 117. *See also* Hearing
Death rates, and smoking, *451*
Debriefing, 23
Decay, 209, **210**
Deception. *See* Ethical issues
Decibel (dB), 113
Decision making, *233*
    judgment and, **224,** 232–236
    and risk assessment, 235–236
    strategies for, 232–234
Declarative knowledge, 196
Deductive reasoning, 83, 90, **236,** 237
Deep-structure level, 244–245
Defense mechanisms, 356–357
    Freudian theory and, 141
Deindividuation, 311–312
    Zimbardo's research on, 311–312, *312*
Delay
    effects of, 180–181
    and visual recall, *199*
Delayed gratification, 180–181
Delirium, 156, 406
Delusions, 397
    and schizophrenia, 400
Dementia, 406
Demographics, of schizophrenia,
    401–403
Demonological explanations, of
    abnormal behavior, 388
Dendrites, 57, *57*
Denial, 356
Denotation, 243
Dependent personality disorder, 404
Dependent variable, 13
Depressants, 154–156
Depression
    categories of, 396
    pain and, 467
    spontaneous recovery from, 428
Depressive disorders, 395–396
Depth. *See* Space perception
Description, 7–8
Descriptive statistics, 477–484
Desensitization, violence and,
    310–**311**
Destructive criticism, as reinforcer, 181
Detection, 105
    absolute threshold and, 105
    signal-detection theory and, 105
    of stimulus, 105
Determinism, 353
    reciprocal, 366
Development, 70–71
    in adulthood, 95–96
    concrete-operational stage of, 85–86
    in infancy, 76–82
    interpersonal, 88
    life-span, 95
    prenatal, 74–75

during puberty and adolescence,
    90–95
socioemotional, 86–88
trends in, 71
Developmental processes, 353
Developmental psychology, 4
Developmental stages, formal-
    operational, 90
Developmental theories, of Piaget and
    Vygotsky, 72–74
Deviation, 480
Deviation IQs, 256–257
Diagnosis
    DSM and, 391–392
    of personality disorders, 404–405
Diagnostic and Statistical Manual. See
    DSM; DSM-IV
Diazepam. *See* Valium
Dichotic presentation, 137, *138*
Dieting, 320
Difference threshold, 106
Differentiation, 71. *See also* Personality
Diffusion of responsibility, 305–306
Discourse, 240
Discrimination
    justnoticeable difference and, 106
    stimulus, 171–172
Disease, personality and, 463–464
Disgust, 337
Dishabituation, 164
Disorders usually first diagnosed in
    infancy, childhood, or
    adolescence, 404–405
Disorganized schizophrenia, 401
Displacement, 357
Dissection, 45, 46
Dissent, groupthink and, 298
Dissociating, 150, 203
Dissociative disorders, 398–399
    dissociative amnesia, 398
    dissociative fugue, 398
    dissociative identity disorder, 398
Distraction, for pain control, 468
Distributed learning, 209
Distribution
    frequency, 479
    normal, 481
    skewed, *483*
Dominance needs, 327
Dominant trait, 37
Dopamine, 61
Dopamine receptors, antipsychotic drugs
    and, *427*
Double-blind procedure, 141, 428
Double dissociations, 203
Doubt, 86
Down's syndrome, 272
Dreams, 147–148
    activation-synthesis hypothesis of,
    147–148
    Freudian analysis of, 354–355
    Freudian theory of, 147
Drive, 318
Drive theory, 318
Droodles, memory and, *214*
Drug abuse, treatment of, 157–158
Drugs
    altered states of consciousness and,
    151–158

analgesics, 151
central nervous system depressants,
    154–156
depressants, 154–156
hallucinogenics, 156–157
impact on embryo, 74
narcotics, 153–154
overdose of, 152
psychoactive, 151
stimulants, 156
treatment of dependence on, 152
Drug-substitution therapy, 156
Drug therapies, 426–429
    antianxiety drugs, 428–429
    antidepressant drugs, 427–428
    antipsychotic drugs, 427, *427, 428*
DSM, 391
DSM-IV, 391–392
    on cognitive-impairment disorders,
    406
    on impulse control disorders, 403
    on schizophrenia, 401
    on sexual disorders, 406
    on somatoform disorders, 405–406
Dynamic processes, preoperational stage
    and, 83

Ear
    anatomy of, *115*
    locating sound with, 114–116, *116*
Earnings
    by educational level, 19
    by gender, 19
Eating. *See* Hunger
Eating disorders, 406
    anorexia nervosa, 321–322
    bulimia, 322
Eclectic approach, 436
Eclectic explanations, of abnormal
    behavior, 390–391
ECT. *See* Electroconvulsive therapy
    (ECT)
EEGs. *See* Electroencephalograms
    (EEGs)
Effectors, 41
Egg. *See* Ovum
Ego, 354, **355**
Ego analysis, 420
Egocentric, 73
Egocentrism, adolescence and, 91
Ego control, 370
Ego psychology, of Erikson, 359–361
Ego resiliency, 370
Elaborative rehearsal, 208
Electra conflict, *357*
Electrochemical activity, 57
Electrochemical information,
    transmission of, 58–60
Electroconvulsive therapy (ECT),
    425–426, *426*
Electroencephalograms (EEGs),
    46
    sleep stages and, 143–144
Electromagnetic spectrum, 108, *109*
Elimination by aspects, 233
Embryo, 74
Emotion, 335–347
    basic, 337
    brain and, 47

cognitive approaches to, 342–344
cognitive aspect of, 338–339
cross-cultural approaches to, 344–346
evolutionary perspective on, 338–339
expressing, 346–347
Lazarus vs. Zajonc and, 343–344
motivation and, 336
physiological aspect of, 338–339
psychological understanding of, 338–345
psychophysiological approaches to, 339–342
Schachter and Singer's two-component theory of, 342–344
Emotional development, in infancy, 79–80
Emotional feedback loop, *344*
Emotional responses, classical conditioning and, 174
Emotion-focused coping, 462
Empiricism, 25–26
Encoding, 198
of information, 205–208
levels of, 203
for long-term storage, 205–206
techniques for, 206–208
Encoding specificity, 212
Encounter stage, illness and, 470
Endocrine system, 47, 62–64
and emotion, 341–342
major glands of the body, *63*
Endogenous depression, 395, 396
Endorphins, 452
drugs and, 152–153, *153*
Engineering psychology, 104–105
English language, bilingualism and, *248*
Environment. *See also* Nature-nurture controversy
adapting to sightless or soundless, 117
behaviorism and, 364, 365
evolutionary theory and, 36
heredity and, 38
homosexuality and, 324
infant stimulation by, 77
intelligence and, 272
Environmental events, 366
Epilepsy, split-brain patients and, 51
Epinephrine (adrenaline), 61
and emotion, 342
Episodic memory, 199, *200*
Equity theory, 292
Erikson's ego psychology, 359–361, *360*
Establishment phase, in adulthood, 95
Ethical issues, 22–24
in psychotherapy, 440–442
European Americans, 429
Event coding, and emotion, 344
Event-related potentials (ERPs), 46
Evolution, of emotions, 338–339
Evolutionary theory, 36
Exercise, aerobic, 450–452
Exhaustion response, to stress, 459
Exhaustive serial processing, 210
Exhibitionism, 406
Exogenous depression, 395, 396
Experiment, 12, **13**–14
ethical issues in, 23–24
hypothetical, 21

Experimental analysis of behavior, 182–183
Experimental condition, 14
Experimental method, terminology in, 14
Experimental treatments, ethics of, 440
Expertise, knowledge, problem solving, and, 231
Explanation, 8
Explicit memory, 196
Exploration phase, in adulthood, 95
Expression. *See* Emotion
External causation delusions, 400
External locus of control, 365
Extinction phase, of learning, **170**–171
Extinction procedures, 422, 423
Extrinsic motivation, 330–331
Extroversion, 369, 370
Eye, anatomy of, 108–109, *110. See also* Vision
Eye color, inheritance of, 39, *39*
Eyewitness testimony, 216
memory and, 214–215

Factor analysis, 261
Factor-analytic model, of intelligence, 261
Factor-analytic theory, 369
Facts. *See* Data
Failure. *See* Learned helplessness
Familiarity, love and, 294
Family, schizophrenia in, 401–402
Family therapy, 431–433, *432*
Fathers, homosexuality and, 324
Fear, 337
Feature-detector approach, 124
Feature matching, 126–127
Feedback. *See* Emotional feedback loop
Fetus, 75
Field study, 12
Fight-or-flight response, to stress, 457–458
Figure, 125
Figure-ground form perception, 125, 126
Firing, of neurons, 59, 60–62
Fitness, 450–452
Fixation, 355
Flashbacks, 157
Flat affect, and schizophrenia, 400
Flooding, 422, 423
Fluency, verbal, 238
Fluoxetine (Prozac), 428
Forebrain, 47
structures of, *49*
Foreclosure, 91
Forgetting. *See also* Amnesia; Memory
processes of, 209–210
storage and, 208–210
Forgetting curve, of Ebbinghaus, *194*
Formal-operational stage, 90
Form perception, 124–130
feature-detector approach to, 124–125
Gestalt approach to, 125
Fossils, evolution and, 36
Free association, 419–420
Frequency distribution, 479
Frequency theory, 114

Freudian slips of the tongue, 141, 354
Freudian theory
on dreaming, 147
subconscious level and, 141–142
Friendship, stage of, 88
Frontal lobe, 52
Functional fixedness, 229
Functionalism, 27
Functional sorting, 263
Functions, 36
Fundamental attribution error, 287, 288

Garcia effect, 172–173, *173*
GAS. *See* General adaptation syndrome (GAS)
Gate-control theory, 465–466, *466*
Gender. *See also* Sex and sexuality
communication patterns by, 294
moral reasoning and, 94–95
Gender-identity disorders, 406
Gender typing, *87,* **87**–88
Gene, 37
General adaptation syndrome (GAS), 458, *459*
Generalized anxiety disorder, 392, 393
Generativity vs. stagnation, 95
Genetics, 37–39
Genetic traits, 37
Genital stage, of psychosexual development, 356
Genotype, 37–38
Germany, World War II obedience and, 304
Gestalt approach, 125, *125*
principles of, 126
Gestalt psychology, 28, 30
and insightful thinking, 227–228
Gestures, language and, *239*
Giftedness, 269–270
Glands, 62
major, *63*
Glucose, 40, 320
Goals, 333, 334
Gradient of reinforcement, 180–181
Grammar, 244
Graphic thinking, as memory, 193
Gratification, delaying, 180–181
Gray matter, 50
Grief, 337
Ground, 125
Group, 295
experimental and control, 14
interaction in, 295–299
size of, and conformity, 301
Group polarization, 297
Group therapy, 431, *432*
Groupthink, 297–298
Guided imagery, pain control and, 468
Guilt, 86
Guilty plea, insanity defense and, 410. *See also* Legal issues
Gustatory system, 107

Habituation, 164, 325
adaptation and, 165
Hair cell, 113
Hallucinations, 142
and schizophrenia, 400

Hallucinogenic drugs, **156**–157
Hardiness, and stress resistance, 464–**465**
Head Start program, 274
Healers, 429
Health psychology, 4, 447, **448**
content of, 448–449
lifestyle choices and, 450–452
personality, stress, and, 452–463
Hearing, 107
brain and, 52
frequency theory of, 114
place theory of, 114
process of, 113–114
sound and, 112–116
Heart disease, personality and, 464
Helplessness, learned, 178–179
Hemispheres. *See also* Brain
cerebral, 50
specialization of, 50–52
Hepatitis, *153*
Heredity
and environment, 38
intelligence and, 272
Hertz (Hz), 113
Heterosexuality, homosexuality and, 323
Heuristics, 225–226
of attribution, 287
availability heuristic, 234
and biases of judgment, 234–236
Hierarchic sorting, 263
Hierarchy of needs, 328–329, *329*, 334.
See also Humanistic explanations
"Hillside Strangler," 399
Hindbrain, 47
structures of, *49*
Hippocampus, 47
Hispanics, bilingualism and, *248*
History
of psychology as science, 25–28
20th-century perspectives, 28–30
Histrionic personality disorder, 404
HIV. *See* Human immunodeficiency virus (HIV)
HIV-positive person, 469
Homeostatic regulation, 319–324, 334
Homosexuality, 323–324
biological basis for, 324
environmental explanations of, 324
Homunculus
of motor cortex, *53*
of sematosensory cortex, *54*
Hormones, 62–63
and emotion, 341–342
and neurotransmitters, 63, 64
Hostile aggression, 310
Hue, 111
Human behavior, reasons for studying, 6–7
Human immunodeficiency virus (HIV), 469
Humanistic explanations
of abnormal behavior, 389, 394
of mood disorders, 397
of schizophrenia, 402
Humanistic psychologists
Maslow as, 363
Rogers as, 363

Humanistic psychology, 29, 30, 362–363, 364
Humanistic therapies, 420–421
Hunger, motivation and, 320–322
Hypnosis, 148–150
pain control and, 468
theories of, 150
uses of, 150
Hypochondriasis, 405
Hypothalamus, 47
hunger and, 320
sex and, 322
Hypotheses, 8
Hypothetical construct, memory as, **194**

Iconic store, 198
Id, 354, 355
Ideal self, 363
Idealistic principle, 355
Identical twins, intelligence of, *272*
Identification, 357
Identity
emergence in childhood, 86–88
gender, 87–88
personal, 91
and role confusion, 91
Identity achievement, 91
Identity delusions, 400
Identity development, Erikson's theory of, 86, 91
Identity diffusion, 91
Illness. *See also* Chronic illness
health psychology and, 448–449
personality and, 464–465
Ill-structured problem, 225
insight and, 227–228
Illusion, 142
Imagery, pain control and, 468
Imaginary audience, 91
Imitation, as social learning, *185*, 186
Immigration, intelligence testing and, *264*, 265
Immune defenses, stress and, *460*
Implicit memory, 196
Implosion therapy, 422, 423
Imprinting, *165*, **165**–166
Impulse-control disorders, 403
Inappropriate affect, and schizophrenia, 400
Incest, 323
Incubation, 230
Independence vs. interdependence, self-concept and, 86
Independent variable, 13
Individualism, 296
Individual psychology, of Adler, 358
Induction, 25
Inductive reasoning, 83, 90, **236**, 237–238
Industry vs. inferiority, 86
Infants and infancy. *See also* Neonate
cognitive development in, 77–78
development during, 76–82
language acquisition by, 242
language development and, 83
physical development in, 77
socioemotional development in, 78–82

Inferences, causal, 16
Inferential statistics, 19–20, **484**
Inferiority complex, 358
Inflections. *See* Vocal inflections
Information. *See also* Knowledge; Memory
conduction within neurons, 58–60
encoding of, 205–208
parallel processing of, 202
storage of, 208–209
Information processing, 261–262. *See also* Information
in nervous system, 55–62
Informed consent, 23
and psychotherapy, 440
Inheritance
of eye color, *39*
of intelligence, 272–273
Initiative, 86
Inkblot Test. *See* Rorschach Inkblot Test
Insanity defense, 409–410
Insanity Defense Reform Act, 410
Insight, 227, 227–228
Insomnia, 146
Instinct, 165, 318
Instrumental aggression, 310
Instrumental conditioning. *See* Operant conditioning
Insurance, for mental health services, 439–440
Integrity vs. despair, 95
Intelligence, 253–256, **254**. *See also* Creativity; Intelligence tests; Tests and testing
biology of, 262
cultural context of, 262–266
extremes of, 269–270
Galton's studies of, 254–255
Gardner's seven intelligences, 266–267
giftedness and, 269–270
improvement of, 273–275
inheritance of, 272–273
measurement of, 256–260
psychometric approach to, 255
psychophysical tests of, *254*
structures and processes of, 261–262
as system, 266–269
theories of, 266–268
traditions in study of, 254–256
triarchic theory of, 267–268, *268*
Intelligence quotient (IQ), 256
deviation IQs, 256–257
Intelligence tests
aptitude tests and, 260
culture-fair, 263–265
culture-relevant, 265–266
deviation IQ scores, 256–257
mental age and IQ, 256
Stanford–Binet Intelligence Scales, 257, 258
Wechsler scales, 257–258
Intensity
of light, 111
of sound, 113
of stimulus, 107
Intensity–difference method, of locating sound, 116, *116*
Intensive approach, to case studies, 357

Interaction
  in groups, 295–299
  reciprocal determinism and, 366
Interactionist approach, 372–374
Interactive images, for encoding, 206
Interdependence, self-concept and, 86
Interference, 209–210
Intermittent explosive disorder, 403
Intermittent-reinforcement schedule,
  182
Internal conflict, 353
Internal locus of control, 365
Internalization, 73
Interneuron, 56
Interneuronal transmission, 58
Interpersonal attraction, 291–292
Interpersonal development, 88
Interpersonal relations. *See*
  Communication; Personal relations;
  Social psychology
Interposition, 123
Interventions, therapeutic, 9–10
Intimacy, 292
Intimacy scores. *See* Statistics
Intimacy vs. isolation, 95
Intoxicated, 151
Intraneuronal conduction, 58
Intrinsic and extrinsic motivators, 334
Intrinsic motivation, 330–331
Introspection, 25
Invincibility fallacy, of adolescents, 91
In vivo techniques, for studying brain,
  46–47
Involutional depression, 395, 396
Invulnerability, groupthink and, 298
Ions, 58
Ipsilateral transmission, 50
IQ. *See* Intelligence quotient
Iris, 108
Irreversibility of thought, 83
ITT Hartford Insurance Group,
  problem solving at, 231

James–Lange theory, of emotion, 339,
  340–342
Japan, *Naikan* therapy in, 430
jnd. *See* Just noticeable difference (jnd)
Joy, 337
Judgment and decision making, 224
  biases of, 234–236
  and decision making, 232–236
Jungian psychology, 359
Just noticeable difference (jnd), 106

Karma, 366
Kinesthesis, 120
Kinesthetic system, 107
Kleptomania, 403
Knowledge. *See also* Language; Learning;
  Memory; Problem solving
  creativity and, 275
  expertise, problem solving, and, 231
  procedural and declarative, 196
Kpelle tribe, intelligence studies and,
  263, *264*

Labels, for physiological arousal,
  342–343
LAD. *See* Language-acquisition device

Language, 224, 238–241. *See also*
  Thinking
  acquisition of, 241–242
  and brain, *52*
  description of, 241
  end of infancy and, 83
  fluency and, 238
  pragmatics and, 245
  semantics and, 243
  social context of, 245–248
  syntax and, 243–245
  understanding and arranging words,
    243–245
Language-acquisition device (LAD), 242
Late-career phase, in adulthood, 95
Latency stage, of psychosexual
  development, 356
Latent content of dreams, 355
Latin America, 438
  treatments in, 429
Law. *See* Legal issues
Law of effect, 175–176
Learned helplessness, 178–179
Learning, 72, 164. *See also* Intelligence;
  Memory
  avoidance, 177
  brain and, 47
  classical conditioning and, 166–174
  distributed, 209
  massed, 209
  operant conditioning and, 174–184
  preprogrammed responses and,
    164–166
  roles of, 71–74
  social, 184–186
Learning theories
  extrinsic motivators and, 330
  interpersonal attraction and, 291
  of Piaget, 72–74
  of Vygotsky, 72–74
Legal issues
  civil law and, 410–411
  criminal law and, 409–410
  facing clinicians, 409–411
Lens, 108–109, *110*
Lesbianism, 323
Lesions
  agnosia and, 126
  in brain, 45–46
  memory and, 203
**Levels-of-processing framework,
  202**–203
Lexicon, 239
Library of Congress, information
  accessibility in, *210*
Librium, 429
Lie detector. *See* Polygraph (lie detector)
Life events, stressful, 453–457, *455*
Life-span development, 95, *360*, 361
  changes during, 96
Light, nature of, 108
Light adaptation, 109, 110
Lightness constancy, 130
Light waves, 107
Liking and interpersonal attraction,
  291–292
Limbic system, 47
Linear perspective, 124
Linguistic relativity, 246–247

Linguistic universals, 247
Linguistics, 239. *See also* Language
Lipids, 320
Lithium, 429
Lobes, 52
  of cerebral hemispheres and cerebral
    cortex, *51*, *52*–54
Lobotomy, 426
Location in the picture plane, 124
Lock-and-key theory, 119
Longitudinal study, 269
Long-term memory, 197, *200*
  capacity of, 200–203
  retrieval from, 211–212
Long-term storage, encoding for,
  205–206
Love, theories of, 292

Magnetic resonance imaging. *See* MRI
  (magnetic resonance imaging)
Maladjustment, behaviorism and, 364
Malingering, 405
Mania, 396
Manic–depressive disorder, 396–398
Manifest content of dreams, 355
Manipulation, suicide and, 408, 409
MAO inhibitors. *See* Monoamine
  oxidase (MAO) inhibitors
Marital conflict, therapy and, 432–433,
  433
Maslow's needs hierarchy, 328–329, *329*,
  334
Masochism, 406
Massed learning, 209
Matched controls, 274
Matching
  feature, 126–127
  prototype, 126, *127*
Maturation, 72
  roles of, 71–74
McClelland's needs theory, 327–328, 334
Mean 1, 479
Meaning
  in illness, 470–471
  semantics as, 243
Measurement
  of detection, 105
  of intelligence (*See* Intelligence tests;
    Tests and testing)
  of memory, 195
Median, 479
Meditation, 151
  as psychotherapy, 430
Medulla oblongata, 47–49
Memory, 191–192. *See also* Learning
  alternative views of, 201–204, 205
  amnesia, 192–193
  brain and, 47
  constructing, 212–215, *213*
  construction of personal, 212–218
  droodles and, *214*
  encoding for, 205–208
  episodic, 199
  explicit vs. implicit, 196
  in infancy, 77–78
  information encoding, storage, and
    retrieval, 205–212
  long-term, 197
  metaphors for, 201

mnemonists and, 193
neuropsychological view of, 203–204
priming of, 204
processing in, 202–203
psychological view of, 197–201
retrieval and, 198
retrieval from long-term, 211–212
semantic, 199
sensory, 197, 198
short- vs. long-term, 197, 198–199
Squire's types of, *204*
state-dependent, 344
study of, 192–197
suppressed, 441
tasks used for measuring, 195
three-stores model of, 197–198
tips for improving, 217–218
traditional vs. nontraditional views of, 202
working, 202
Memory scanning, 210
Memory stores, 197–198
Men, moral reasoning and, 94–95
Mental age, 256
Mental-health services, 439–440. *See also* Psychotherapy
Mental hospitals, development of, *416*
Mental illness
civil law and, 410
labeling and, 387, *387*
Mental retardation, 270–271
inheritance and, 272
levels of, 271
Mental set, 228–229
Mesmerizing, *149*
Meta-analyses, 436
of course of psychotherapy, 436, 437
Metabolism, 45
Metacognition, 86, 208–209
Metamemory skills, 208
Metaphors, memory and, 201
Methadone, 154
Method of loci, for encoding, 206
Mexican Americans, 429–430
Microsleep, 144
Midbrain, 47
structures of, *49*
Midcareer phase, in adulthood, 95
Military problem, 229–230
Mind
and behavior, 365–367
brain and, 50
organization of, 354–355
structure of, 261
"Mindguard," groupthink and, 298
Minnesota Multiphasic Personality Inventory, 376
determining pain-susceptible personalities with, 467
MMPI-2, 376
Minority position, and conformity, 301
Mirror writing, 196
Mixed genotype, 37–38
MMPI and MMPI-2. *See Minnesota Multiphasic Personality Inventory*
M'Naghten Rule, 409
Mnemonic devices, 206. *See also* Memory
Mnemonism, 193

Mode, 479
Modeling, 422, *425*
Monitoring function, of consciousness, 136
Monoamine oxidase (MAO) inhibitors, 427
Monocular depth cue, 123, *123*
Monolinguals, 247
Mood, and memory, 211
Mood disorders, 395–398
bipolar disorders as, 396–398
depressive disorders, 395–396
Mood symptoms, of anxiety, 392
Moral reasoning
Gilligan's model of, 94–95
Kohlberg's model of, *92*, 92–94
Moratorium, 91
Morpheme, 239
Motherese, 77
Mothers, homosexuality and, 324
Motion, 107
Motivation, 318
approaches to, 334
arousal theory and, 326–327
brain and, 47
cognition and, 330–334
curiosity, self-determination, self-efficacy, and, 331–333, 334
emotion and, 336
historical explanations of, 318
homeostatic regulation theory and, 319–324
hunger and, 320–322
intrinsic and extrinsic, 330–331
James on, 318
needs theories and, 327–330
opponent-process theory and, 324–325
physiological approach to, 319–327
sex and, 322–324
Motor cortex, homunculus of, *53*
Motor neurons, 56
Motor symptoms
of anxiety, 393
and schizophrenia, 400
Motor tasks, 77
MRI (magnetic resonance imaging), 46
Müller–Lyer illusion, 129, *129*
Multicultural approaches
effectiveness of, 438
to psychotherapy, 429–430
Multimodal, 479
Multiple intelligences theory, 266–267
Multiple personality. *See* Dissociative disorders, dissociative identity disorder
Münchausen syndrome, 405
Murray's theory of needs, 327, 334
Muscle relaxants, 429
Muscles, nonskeletal, 45. *See also* Motor tasks
Mutation, 37
Myelin, 57–58
Myelin sheath, 57, *57*

N-REM sleep, 144
Naikan therapy, 430
Naloxone, 154
Narcissistic personality disorder, 404

Narcolepsy, 147
Narcotics, 153–154, 157
Nasal cavity, *119*
National Association for the Education of Young Children, child care recommendations of, 89
National Institute on Alcohol Abuse and Alcoholism, 155
Native Americans, 429, 438
Natural selection, 36, *37*
genetics and, 37
Naturalistic observation, 12–13, *13*
Nature. *See* Nature–nurture controversy; Prenatal development
Nature–nurture controversy, 71–72
Piaget, Vygotsky, and, 72–74
Needs theory, 334
Maslow's hierarchy and, 328–329, *329*
of McClelland, 327–328
of Murray, 327
Negative correlation, *21*, 22, *22*
Negative-feedback loop, 64, *64*, 320
Negative reinforcement, 176–177
Negative reinforcer, 177
Negative symptom, 399
Negative transfer, 228
Neodissociative theory, 150
Neo-Freudians, 353, 358–362
Adler as, 358
Jung as, 359
Neo-Freudian therapy, 420
Neonate, 76, 76–77
Nerve, 40
Nerve cells. *See* Neurons
Nervous system. *See also* Depressants
autonomic, *44*
divisions of, *41*
information processing in, 55–62
organization of, 40–45
parasympathetic, 45
Neural transmission, 58
Neurochemicals, psychoactive drugs and, 152–153
Neurological disorders, 47
Neurologist, 29
Neuromodulators, 60
listing of, 61
Neurons, 40, 55–58
communication between, 60–62
conduction of information within, 58–60
firing of, 59
interneurons, 56
motor, 56
parts of, 57, *57*
sensory, 55–56
Neuropeptides, 61
Neuropsychological view, of memory, 203–204
Neuroscientists, 60
Neuroticism, 369–370
Neurotransmitters, 60
drugs and, 427–428
hormones and, 63, 64
listing of, 61
Newborn. *See* Neonate
Nicotine, 156
Nine-dot problem, 227, *227*, 228, *228*
Nodes of Ranvier, 58

Nondeclarative memory, 204
Nondirective therapy, 416
Nonskeletal muscles, 45
Norepinephrine (noradrenaline), 61,
  427–428
  and emotion, 342
Normal distribution, 481, *(481)*
Normative scores, 257
Norms, 297
  body weight and, 321
Noun phrase, 240
Null hypothesis, 20
Nurture. *See* Nature-nurture
  controversy

Obedience, 299, 301–304
  Milgram's experiments on, 301–304,
  303
Obesity, 320. *See also* Hunger
Object permanence, 78, *79*
Objective personality tests, 376–377
  *Minnesota Multiphasic Personality
  Inventory* (MMPI), 376–377
  Sixteen Personality-Factor Questionnaire,
  377
Observation
  in inductive reasoning, 237
  naturalistic, 12–13
Observational learning. *See* Modeling;
  Social learning
Obsession, 393
Obsessive-compulsive disorder, 392, 393,
  404
Occipital lobe, 52–53
Odor, theories of, 119–120
Oedipal conflict, *357*
Olfaction, 118
Olfactory bulb, 119, *119*
Olfactory epithelium, 119, *119*
Olfactory nerve, 119, *119*
Olfactory system, 107
Openness, 370
Operant, 175, 176
Operant behavior, gradient of
  reinforcement and, 180–181
Operant conditioning, 174–184, **175,**
  422, 423, *425*
  application of, 183
  classical conditioning compared with,
  184
  implementation of, 179–182
  punishment and, 177
  techniques of, 180
Operational definitions, 105
Opiates, 153, *153*
Opioids, 153, *153*
Opponent process, 324–**325**
Opponent-process theory, 112, *112,*
  334
Opportunistic infections, 459
Oral eroticism, and psychosexual
  development, 356
Oral sadism, and psychosexual
  development, 356
Oral stage, of psychosexual development,
  356
Organic pain, 466
Organ systems, in prenatal development,
  75

Originality. *See* Creativity
Ovaries, *63*
Overconfidence, 234
Overdose, 152
Overextension error, 242
Ovum, 74
Oxygen, 40
Oxygenation, 452

Pain, 120, 465
  analgesics and, 151
  in conditioning experiments, 170
  control of, 468
  experiencing of, 467
  kinds of, 466
  perceptions of, 465–466
  personality and, 467
Pain disorder, 405
Pain threshold, 466
Pancreas, *63*
Pandemonium, *128*
Panic disorder, 392, 393
Papillae, 116
Paradigms of personality theory, 352. *See
  also* Psychodynamic theories
  cognitive–behavioral, 364–367
  evaluating, 353
  humanistic, 362–363, 364
  interactionist psychology, 372–374
  listing of, 378
  psychodynamic, 352–362
  trait theory as, 367–372
Parallel processing, 202, 210
Paranoid behavior, sleep deprivation and,
  144–145
Paranoid personality disorder, 404
Paranoid schizophrenia, 401
Paraphilias, 406
Parasympathetic nervous system, 45
Parietal lobe, 52
Parsons v. the State of Alabama, 409
Partial-reinforcement schedule, 182
Passion, 292
Pathological gambling, 403
Patients, 388
  concept of, 421
Pattern recognition, 125
  by feature matching, 126–127
  by prototype matching, 126, *127*
Pavlovian conditioning. *See* Classical
  conditioning
PDD. *See* Pervasive developmental
  disorder (PDD)
Pedophilia, 406
Peer relationships, development of,
  91–92
Pegword system, for encoding, 206
Percentile, 482
Perception, 104, 121
  context effects and, 127
  feature matching and, 126–127
  Gestalt approach to, 125–126
  of pain, 465–466
  prototype matching and, 126, *127*
  space, 123–124
  subliminal, 140–141
Perceptual constancies, 128–130, **129,**
  129
Performance, 70

Performance score, on Wechsler tests,
  258
**Peripheral nervous system (PNS),
  44**–45
Permastore, 201
Persecution delusions, 400
Person-centered therapy, 421
  of Rogers, 363
Person-environment interaction, 82
Persona, 359
Personal attribution, 288
Personal choice, homosexuality and, 324
Personal disposition, 371
Personal fable, of adolescents, 91
Personal identity, 91
Personal relationships, communication
  in, 294–295
Personal unconscious, 359
Personal variables, 366
Personalism, 287, 288
Personality, 351, 352. *See also* Type-A
  behavior pattern; Type-B behavior
  pattern; other Personality entries
  assessment of, 374–377
  career choices and, 373
  cognitive–behavioral theory of,
  364–367
  creativity and, 275
  dynamic nature of, 352–353
  emergence in childhood, 86–88
  Erikson's theory of, 82, 86
  gender identity and, 87–88
  health and, 452–463
  humanistic psychologists on,
  362–363, 364
  illness and, 463–465
  interactionist psychologists on,
  372–374
  life-span development of, 95, 96, *360,
  361*
  neo-Freudian views of, 358–362
  and pain, 467
  paradigms of, 352
  and perceived stress, 459–463
  psychodynamic theories of, 352–362
  psychologists' assessments of,
  374–377
  self-concept and, 86–87
  temperament and, 80–82
  trait theory of, 367–372
Personality approaches, to motivation,
  327–330, 334
Personality disorders, 404
  diagnosed in infancy, childhood, or
  adolescence, 404–405
Personality psychology, 4
Personality tests, evaluation of, 377
Personality traits. *See* Trait
Personality types. *See* Stress
Perspective
  false, *122*
  perception of, 124
Pervasive developmental disorder
  (PDD), 404
PET (positron emission tomography)
  scan, 46
Phallic stage, of psychosexual
  development, 356
Pharmacological control, of pain, 468

Phenotype, 37
Phenylketonuria (PKU), 272
Philosophy, 25
Phobias, 392, 393
Photoreceptors, 109
Phrase-structure grammar, 244, *244*
Physical development
in adolescence, 90
in infancy, 77
Physical processing, 203
Physical stimulation, 104
Physiological approach, to motivation,
319–327, 334
Physiological arousal, emotion and, 342
Physiological psychology, 28
Physiological reaction pattern, and
emotion, 344
Physiology, 25, 36. *See also* Ear; Eye
and emotions, 338–339
Pitch, 113
frequency theory and, 114
place theory and, 114
Pituitary gland, *63*
PKU. *See* Phenylketonuria (PKU)
Place theory, 144
Placebo effect, 141
Placebos, 428
Placenta, 74
Plans, 333, 334
Play therapy, 416
Pleasure principle, 355
Plutchik's emotion wheel, *337*
PNS. *See* Peripheral nervous system
Polygraph (lie detector), **345,** *346*
Pons, 49
Positive correlation, 20, *21, 22*
Positive reinforcement, 176
Positive reinforcer, 176
Positive symptom, 399
Positive transfer, 229–230
Positron emission tomography scan. *See*
PET scan
Postconventional morality, 93
Posthypnotic suggestion, 148
Postpartum depression, 395, 396
Posttraumatic stress disorder, 392, 393
Practical significance, 484
Practice effects, 208
Pragmatics, 245
Pragmatism, 27
Preconscious level, 139–141
Preconscious thought, 354
Preconventional morality, 93
Predictions, 8, 9
Prefrontal lobotomy, 426
Pregnancy, smoking and, 156
Prejudice, 307–308
Robber's Cave study and, 309
Prenatal development, 74–75
brain and, 47
Preoperational stage, 82–83
Preprogrammed responses, 164–166
Primary appraisal, 343, 461
Primary colors, 111–112
Primary depression, 395, 396
Primary-process thought, 354–355
Primary reinforcers, 181
Primary sex characteristics, 90
Priming, 204

Proactive interference, 210
Problem-focused coping, 461–462
Problems
ill-structured, 227–228
well-structured, 225–226
Problem solving, 224, 225–232
aids to, 229–230
analysis and, 226
expertise and, 231
hindrances to, 228–229
incubation in, 230
insightful, *227,* 227–228
job-related, 231
synthesis and, 226
Procedural knowledge, 196
Processing. *See* Information; Memory
Productivity, creative, 275
Progress, in psychosexual development,
355
Projection, 356
Projection areas, 53
Projective personality tests, 374–376
assessing, 376
Rorschach Inkblot Test, 374–375, *375*
Thematic Apperception Test (TAT),
375, 375–376
Proportional reasoning, 266
Prosocial behavior, 304–307
Latané-Darley experiments on, 305
opportunity for, *305*
Prototype matching, 126, 127
Proximity
form perception and, 125, 126
love and, 294
Prozac, 428
Pschyoanalytic theories, of Horney, 361
Pseudomemories, hypnosis and, 149
Psyche, myth of, 25
Psychiatrists, 388
Psychic energy, 352
Psychoactive drugs, 151
categories of, 157
and endorphins, 152–153
Psychoanalysis, *419,* 419–420
Freud and, 354–358
Psychobiology, 4, 28–29, 30. *See also*
Biological psychology
Psychodynamic explanations
of abnormal behavior, 389, 394
of mood disorders, 397
of schizophrenia, 402
Psychodynamic personality tests. *See*
Projective personality tests
Psychodynamic psychology, 29, 30
Psychodynamic theories, 352
evaluation of, 362
of Horney, 361
nature of, 352–354
neo-Freudians and, 358–362
psychoanalysis and, 354–358
Psychodynamic therapy, 419–420
offshoots of psychoanalysis, 420
psychoanalysis as, 419–420
Psychogenic pain, 466
Psychological models, for coping with
chronic illness, 470–473
Psychological needs, 328–329
Psychological research, goals of, 7–8. *See
also* Research

Psychological sensations, 104
Psychologists, 388
approaches to psychotherapy by,
418–431
ethical issues and, 22–24
functions of, 4, 7–11
research of, 11–16
study of memory by, 192–197
traditional views of memory, 197–201
Psychology, 4–7
biological, 35–67
emergence as science, 24–28
fields of, 4
20th-century perspectives on, 28–30
Psychometric approach, to intelligence,
255
Psychoneuroimmunology, 459
Psychopharmacological effect, 151
Psychophysics, 104–105
Snellen Vision Chart and, *105*
Psychophysiological explanations
of abnormal behavior, 390
of anxiety disorders, 394
of mood disorders, 397
of schizophrenia, 402
Psychophysiology, of emotions,
339–342
Psychosexual development, stages of,
355, 356
Psychosocial theory, of personality
development, 82
Psychosurgery, 426
Psychotherapeutic intervention, early
methods of, 416–417
Psychotherapy, 9–10, 415–416
alternatives to individual, 431–435
approaches to, 418–431
behavior therapies, 422
biological therapies, 425–426
choosing, 438–440
diagnosing abnormal behavior and,
417–418
effectiveness of, 437–440
ethical issues in, 440–442
humanistic therapies, 420–421
hypnosis in, 150
multicultural approaches to, 429–430
optimal approach to, 435–436
psychodynamic therapy, 419–420
ratings of, *438*
for stimulant addiction, 156
Psychoticism, 370
Psychotropic drug, 426
Puberty, 90. *See also* Adolescence
Puluwat culture, intelligence studies and,
263
Punishment, 177–179
conformity and, 302–303
consequences of, 177–178
enhancing effectiveness of, 178
response and, 179
Pupil, 108
Purity, of color, 111
Puzzle box, of Thorndike, *175*
Pyromania, 403

Qualitative analyses, of Freud, 357–358
Qualitative changes, in thinking, 90
Quality, of stimulus, 107

Quantitative changes, in thinking, 90
Quantity, conservation of, 83, *84*
Quasi-experimental design, 17, **18**
Questionnaires, 11

Race, intelligence scores and, 273
Range, 480
Ratio IQ, 256
Rational-emotive therapy (RET),
    423–424
Rationalist approach, **25**–26
Rationality. *See* Bounded rationality
Rationalization, 357
Raw score, 482
Reaction formation, 357
Reaction range, 274
Reality principle, 355
Reasoning, 224. *See also* Moral
    reasoning
  in adolescence, 90
  brain and, 52
  deductive, 236, 237
  inductive, 236, 237–238
  in preoperational stage, 83
Recall, 195. *See also* Memory
  visual, *199*
Receptive field, 107
Receptor, 40–41, 60
Receptor cell, 106–107
Receptor nerves, 53
Recessive trait, 37
Reciprocal determinism, 366, *366*
Recognition, 195
Reconstructive memory, 213
Reflex, 41
  spinal, 41–44
Regression, 355
  correlation and, 482–484
Regulation, and emotion, 344
Rehearsal, 208
Reinforcement. *See also* Conditioning
  behaviorism and, 364
  gradient of, 180–181
  instrumental conditioning and,
    176–177
  response and, 179
  schedules of, 182
Reinforcer, 176
  primary and secondary, 181
Relationships, personal, 294–295
Relative size, 123
Relativity, linguistic, 246–247
Relaxation techniques, pain control and,
  468
Reliability, 260
Remission, and schizophrenia, 400
REM sleep, 144
Replication, of findings, 9
Representational thought, 83
Representations, 82
Representativeness, 234–235
Representative sample, 18, *18*
Repression, 141, 356
Research
  applied, 16
  basic, 16
  case studies as, 11–12
  ethical issues in, 22–24
  on hypnosis, 149

methods of, 12
  statistics and, 19
  surveys as, 11, 12
  tests as, 11, 12
Research design, 16. *See also*
    Controlled experimental design
Residual schizophrenia, 401
Resistance response, to stress, 459
Resistances, 420
Response. *See also* Sensation; Stimulus
  conditioned, 169
  operant as, 176
  relationship with stimulus, 172–173
  to stress, 457–463
  unconditioned, 169
Responsibility, diffusion of, 305–306
RET. *See* Rational-emotive therapy
  (RET)
Retardation. *See* Mental retardation
Retina, 109, *110*
Retreat stage, illness and, 470
Retrieval, 198, 210–212
  context and, 211–212, *212*
  encoding and, 212
  from long-term memory, 211–212
  from temporary storage, 210–211
Retroactive interference, 210
Retrograde amnesia, 192–193. *See also*
    Amnesia
Retrovirus, AIDS and, 469
Reuptake inhibitors, 427–428
Risk assessment, 235–236
Robber's Cave study, 309
Rods, 109
Role confusion, identity and, 91
Roles, gender typing and, 87–88
Root words, 239
Rorschach Inkblot Test, 374–375, *375*
Rubella, impact on embryo, 75
"Rules of thumb," heuristics as, 225–226

Sadness and grief, 337
Safe sexual practices, 449, *450*
Safety and security needs, 329
Saliva, 116
Samples
  of convenience, 18
  representative, 18
Sapir-Whorf hypothesis, 246
Satisficing, 233
Saturation, 111
Scale, in psychological assessment, 257
Scanning, memory, 210
Scatterplots, *122*
Schedules of reinforcement, 182
Schema (schemata), **72,** 199
Schizophrenia, 399–403
  demographics and, 401–403
  drug treatment of, 428
  symptoms of, 400
  types of, 401
School, entry during concrete-
    operational stage, 86
Science, psychology as, 24–28
Scientists, types of, 5
Scores, types of, 481–482
Scripts, sexual, 322–323
SDT. *See* Signal-detection theory (SDT)
Secondary appraisal, 343–344, **461**

Secondary depression, 395, 396
Secondary-process thought, 355
Secondary reinforcers, 181
Secondary sex characteristics, 90
Secondary trait, 371
Secure lovers, 292
Sedative-hypnotics, 154
Seeing, brain and, 52. *See also* Vision
Seizures, 155–156
Selective attention, 137–138, *138*
Self, ideal, 363
Self-acceptance, 363
Self-actualization
  Maslow on, 363
  needs, 329
Self-concept, 86–87, 363
Self-determination theory, 331–332,
    334
Self-disclosure, in client-centered
    therapy, *421*
Self-efficacy, 22, 331, 332–333, 334,
    366
Self-esteem, 87
  and illness, 471
  needs, 329
Self-fulfilling prophecies, 333
Self-handicapping, 287, 288
Self-help, 433–434
Self-perception theory, 286
Self-serving bias, 287, 288
Self-terminating serial processing,
    210–211
Self theory, 363
Self-understanding, 87
Semantic code, 205
Semantic encoding, 205
Semantic memory, 199
Semantic processing, 203
Semantics, 243
Sensation, 104
  biological properties of, 106–108
  body senses (kinesthesis), 120–121
  brain and, 52
  consciousness and, 136
  hearing and, 112–116
  making sense of, 121–122
  perception and, 121–130
  seeing and, 108–112
  skin senses, 120–123
  smell and, 118–120
  study of, 104–106
  taste and, 116, 118
Sense, 104. *See also* Sensation
  infants and, 77, *77*
Sensitization, 156
Sensorimotor stage, 77
Sensory acuity, 255
Sensory adaptation, 108, 164
  habituation and, 165
Sensory coding, 107
Sensory control, of pain, 468
Sensory development, 77
Sensory information, 41
Sensory memory, 197, 198
Sensory neurons, 55–56
Sentences, 240
Separation anxiety, 80, *80*
Septum, in brain, 47
Serial processing, 210

Serotonin, 61, 427–428
and memory, 204
Sex and sexuality, 322–324
bisexuality, 323–324
homosexuality, 323–324
Sex characteristics, 90
Sexual behavior, gradient of
reinforcement and, 180
Sexual disorders, 406
Sexual drives, 353
Sexual dysfunctions, 406
Sexual masochism, 406
Sexual practices, safe, 449, *450*
Sexual-response cycle, of Masters and
Johnson, *323*
Sexual script, 322–323
Shadow, 359
Shadowing, 137
Shamans, 387, 429, 438
Shame, 86
Shape, 181
perception of, 124–130
Shape constancy, 130, *130*
Shocks, in conditioning experiments, 170
Shock stage, illness and, 470
Short-term memory, 197, 198–199,
200
Sightedness, 117
Signal-detection theory (SDT), 105
Signs, 82
Similarity
form perception and, 125, 126
love and, 294
Simulating paradigm, 149
Situational attribution, 288
Sixteen Personality-Factor
Questionnaire, 377
Size constancy, 129, *129*
Skewed distribution, *483*
Skinner box, *183*
Skin senses, 120
Sleep
as altered state of consciousness,
143–148
circadian rhythms and, 145–146
N-REM, 144
REM, 144
steps for getting a good night's sleep,
146–147
Sleep apnea, 147
Sleep deprivation, 144–145
Sleep disorders, 146–147, 406
Slips of the tongue, 354
Smell, 118–120
lock-and-key theory of, 119
taste and, *118*
vibration theory of, 119–120
Smoking. *See also* Tobacco
death rates and, *451*
impact on embryo, 74
Snellen Vision Chart, *105*
Social categorization, 308
Social cognition, 285–288
categorization, stereotypes, and, 308
Social contacts, stress and, 462
Social context, language in, 245–248
Social desirability, 287
Social desirability bias, 288
Social facilitation, 295

Social functions, of emotional
expression, 347
Social interference, 295–296
Social isolation, stress and, *460*
Social learning, 184–186, *185*
attitude formation and, 288–289
violence and, 310–311
Social-learning theory, 365, 365–366
homosexuality and, 324
Social loafing, *296*, 296–297
Social phobia, 393
Social psychology, 4, 283–284
antisocial behavior and, 307–313
attitude and attitude change, 288–291
conformity, compliance, obedience,
and, 299–304
interpersonal and group perspectives
on, 294–299
liking, loving, and interpersonal
attraction, 291–294
prosocial behavior and, 304–307
social cognition and, 285–288
Social Readjustment Rating Scale (SRRS),
453, 454
Social scientists, types of, 5
Social status
and group conformity, 301, *301*
intelligence and, 273
prejudice and, 309, 310
Social support, stress and, 462
Socioeconomic status (SES),
schizophrenia and, 402–403
Socioemotional development, 70–71,
86–88, 96
in adolescence, 91–95
Sociolinguistics, 245
Soma, 57, *57*
Somatic nervous system, 45
Somatic symptoms, of anxiety, 392–393
Somatization disorder, 405
Somatoform disorders, 405–406
Somatosensory cortex, *53*
homunculus of, *54*
Somatosensory processing, 52
Somnambulism, 147
Sound
hearing and, 112–116
language and, *239*
locating, 114–116
vocal tract and, *240*
Sound amplitude, 113
Sound waves, 107
properties of, 113, *113*
Source trait, 369
Space perception, 123–124
Spacing effect, 209
Specialization, hemispheric, 50–52
Specially ordered line segments, 124
Speech. *See also* Language
brain and, 50
newborn and, 77
telegraphic, 242
Spinal column, 40
Spinal cord, 40
reflex response and, 42
Spinal reflex, 41–44, *42*
neurons and, *56*
Split-brain patients, 51
Spontaneous recovery, 428

Spouse, death of, *453*
SRRS. *See Social Readjustment Rating
Scale* (SRRS)
Stages
of adulthood, 95–96
formal-operational, 90
of friendship, 88
Stages of development
concrete-operational, 85–86
preoperational, 82–83
Standard deviation, 480
Standardization, 260
Standard score, 481–482
Stanford–Binet Intelligence Scales, 257, 258
State-dependent memory, 344
States, development and, 83
States of consciousness. *See* Altered states
of consciousness; Consciousness
Static conditions, preoperational stage
and, 83
Statistical significance, 19, 484
Statistics
causal inferences and, 18–19
central tendency, 478–479
correlation and, 20–22
descriptive, 19, 477–484
inferential, 19–20, 484
Status. *See* Societal status
Stereopsis, 124
Stereotypes, 308, *309*. *See also* Gender
typing
Stereotype vulnerability, 308
Stimulants, 156
Stimulation, detection of, 105. *See also*
Psychophysics
Stimulus
classical conditioning and, *167*–168
conditioned, 169
detecting changes in, 107–108
hormones and, 63
infant responses to, 77
relationship with response, 172–173
unconditioned, 169
Stimulus discrimination, 171–172
Stimulus generalization, *171,*
171–172
Stimulus overload, 400
Stimulus-response, opponent process
theory of motivation and, 324–325
Storage, 198. *See also* Memory
and forgetting, 208–210
retrieval and, 210–211
Storytelling, memory and, *208*
Stranger anxiety, 80
Stress, 453
hardiness and, 464–465
personality, health, and, 452–463
responses to, 457–463
Stress disorders, 392, 393
Stress response, 453
Stressors, 453–457
Stroke, 406
Stroop effect, 138, 139
Structuralism, 27
Structures, 36
Subconscious, 141
Subjects, informed consent of, 23
Sublimation, 357
Subliminal perception, 140–141

Substance-related disorders, 406
Subtractive bilingualism, 247
Subtractive mixture, 111
Successive approximations, 181
Suffixes, 239
Suicide, *408*
 myths about, 407–408
 psychologists' views of, 406–409
Superego, 354, **355**
Superiority, Adler on, 358
Support groups, *434. See also*
 Psychotherapy; Self-help
Suppressed memories, recovery of, 441
Surcease, suicide and, 408–409
Surface-structure grammar, 244
Surface trait, 369
Surgical control, of pain, 468
Surveys, 11, 12
Survival of the fittest, 36
Susto, 429
Symbols, 82
Symmetry, form perception and, 125,
 126
Symptoms
 of anxiety disorders, 392
 negative and positive, 399
 of schizophrenia, 400
Synapse, 58, *59*
 communication between neurons and,
 60–61
Syntax, 240
Synthesis, 226
 perception and, 104
Synthesis view, of emotion, 344
Systematic desensitization, 422, 423
Systems. *See* systems by name
Systems perspective, couples and family
 therapy as, 431–432, *433*

Tactile system, 107
Taste, 116
 smell and, *118*
Taste bud, 116, *118*
TAT. *See* Thematic Apperception Test
 (TAT)
Taxonomy, 203–204
T-cells, 469
Telegraphic speech, 242
Television
 attitude formation and, *289*
 social learning and, 186
"Tell-Tale Heart, The" (Poe), 385
Temperament, 80–82
 characteristics of, 81, 368
Temporal contiguity, 169
Temporal lobe, 52
Temporary storage, retrieval from,
 210–211
Terminal buttons, 57, *57,* 58
Terminology, in experimental method,
 14
Testes, *63*
Test of statistical significance, 484
Tests and testing, **11,** 12. *See also*
 Statistics
 of intelligence, 256–260
 of personality, 374–376
 psychophysical measurements and,
 104

Texture gradient, 123
Thalamus, 47, 53
Thematic Apperception Test (TAT),
 374, *375,* 375–376
Theory, 9
**Theory of multiple intelligences,
 266**–267
Therapeutic interventions, 9–10
Therapy. *See* Psychotherapy
Thinking, 224. *See also* Language
 judgment, decision making, and, 224,
 232–236
 primary-process thought, 354
 problem solving and, 225–232
 reasoning and, 236–238
Thorndike's puzzle box, *175*
Thought. *See* Thinking
Three-stores model
 alternative perspectives to, 201–205
 of memory, 197–198
Threshold of excitation, 59
Thresholds
 absolute, 105
 sample ideal compared with real
 absolute, *106*
Thyroid gland, *63*
Timbre, 113
Time-difference method, of locating
 sound, 116, *116*
**Tip-of-the-tongue phenomenon,
 139**–140
Tobacco, 156
Toddlers. *See also* Infants and infancy
Token economy, 422, 423
Tolerance, for drugs, **152**
Tongue, 116
Total-time hypothesis, 209
Touch, 107
 skin senses and, 120
Trait, 372
 dominant, 37
 recessive, 37
Trait theory, 367–372
 "big five" model of personality and,
 370
 Cattell's factor-analytic theory, 369
 characteristics of temperament, 368
 evaluation of, 372
 Eysenck's theory, 369–370
 individual sets of traits, 371–372
 personality assessments based on,
 376–377
Tranquilizers, 154
Transduce, 107
Transductive reasoning, 83
Transfer
 negative, 228
 positive, 229–230
Transference, 420
Transformational grammar, 244
Transformations, in language, 245
Transmission
 interneuronal, 58
 neural, 58
Trauma, memory and, 193
Treatment
 of drug abuse, 157–158
 effectiveness of psychotherapy,
 437–440

outcomes of psychotherapy, 436
 for stimulant addiction, 156
Treatment condition, 14
Tremors, 155
Trends, developmental, 71
Triangular Love Scale, 478, 479. *See also*
 Statistics
 basic statistics for, 481
 correlation among subscales of, 483
 mean and standard deviation for, 480
Triangular theory of love, 292, *293.*
 See also Triangular Love Scale
**Triarchic theory of human
 intelligence, 267**–268, *268*
Trichotillomania, 403
**Trichromatic theory of color vision,
 111**–112
Tricyclic drugs, 427
12-step groups, 433
Twins
 heredity of, 38
 studies of, *272*
**Two-component theory of emotion,
 342**–344
Type-A behavior pattern, *463,*
 463–464
Type-B behavior pattern, 463, **464**

UCR. *See* Unconditioned response
 (UCR)
UCS. *See* Unconditioned stimulus
 (UCS)
Unanimity
 and group conformity, 301
 groupthink and, 298
Unconditional positive regard, 363
Unconditioned response (UCR), 169
Unconditioned stimulus (UCS), 169
 and response, 172–173
Unconscious, 141, **353**
 personal, 359
Unconscious thought, 354
Undifferentiated schizophrenia, 401
Universal personality traits, individual
 variations of, 369–370
Universals, linguistic, 247

Validity, 260
Valium, 429
Variability, measures of, 480
Variables
 confounding, 14
 cultural and biological, 361
 dependent, 13
 independent, 13
Verbal comprehension, 238
Verbal fluency, 238
Verbal score, on Wechsler tests, 258
Verb phrase, 240
Vertebrae, 40
Vestibular system, 107, **120**
Vibration theory, 119–120
Vicarious learning. *See* Social learning
Violence
 aggression and, 310
 social learning, desensitization, and,
 310–311
 television and, 186
Vision

anatomy of eye, 108–109, *110*
color and, 109–112
nature of light, 108, *109*
process of seeing, 108–112
Visual mask, 140
Visual processing, brain and, 52
Visual recall, delay and, *199*
Visual systems, 109
Vocal inflections, 245
Vocal tract, *240*
Voyeurism, 406
Vulnerability, stereotype, 308

Waswäs, 394
Wavelength
hue and, 111
seeing, hearing, and, 107

Wechsler intelligence scales, 257–258
*Wechsler Adult Intelligence Scale–Revised
(WAIS-R)*, 257, 259
*Wechsler Intelligence Scale for Children
(WISC III)*, 257
*Wechsler Preschool and Primary Scale of
Intelligence (WPPSI)*, 257
Weight. *See* Hunger
Well-structured problems, 225
heuristics, algorithms, and, 225–226
Wernicke's area, 50, 53
White Americans, intelligence scores of,
273
White matter, 50
Wish fulfillment, in dreams, 355
Withdrawal, 152, 155–156, 325
Women, moral reasoning and, 94–95

Words. *See* Language
Word salad, and schizophrenia, 400
Work, stressors and, 456–457
Working memory, 202
World War II, obedience in, 304
Wyatt v. Stickney, 410

X-ray photos, 46
X-ray problem, 229, *230*

Yerkes–Dodson law, 326, *326*
Yorubans, 438
Yuan, 366

**Zone of proximal development
(ZPD), 73**
z-score, 482
Zygote, 74